Religious Liberty in a Pluralistic Society

Religious Liberty in a Pluralistic Society

Second Edition

Michael S. Ariens

Robert A. Destro

Carolina Academic Press

Durham, North Carolina

ISBN 0-89089-660-7
LCCN 2002110020

Carolina Academic Press
700 Kent Street
Durham, North Carolina 27701
Telephone (919) 489-7486
Fax (919) 493-5668
www.cap-press.com

Printed in the United States of America

To Renée
whom I love more each day
MSA

To Brenda
whose love and support made this possible
RAD

Contents

Table of Cases

Table of Statutes

Constitutions

United States Constitution: *passim*

State Constitutions

Foreign Constitutions

Statutes

United States Federal

11 U.S.C. §548, 612
2 U.S.C. §1302, 708
26 U.S.C. §102, 788
26 U.S.C. §107, 772
26 U.S.C. §1402, 227, 230
26 U.S.C. §170, 612
26 U.S.C. §212, 360, 361
26 U.S.C. §501(c)(3), 757
26 U.S.C. §6096(a) , 719,
26 U.S.C. §7421, 729, 772
26 U.S.C. §7611, 625, 787
28 U.S.C. §1341, 772
28 U.S.C. §2201, 772
42 U.S.C. § 604a (2001), 381, 396
42 U.S.C. §1981, 375, 403, 430
42 U.S.C. §1982, 375, 403, 430
42 U.S.C. §1983, 403, 632
42 U.S.C. §1985(3), 632
42 U.S.C. §2000, 642
42 U.S.C. §2000e(k), See Pregnancy Discrimination Act
42 U.S.C. §300a-7, 667, 705–706,
5 U.S.C. §2105, 711
50 U.S.C. §456, 991, 1001
Americans with Disabilities Act ("ADA"), 42 U.S.C. §12101 *et seq.* , 629, 675, 701
Child Abuse Prevention and Treatment Act of 1974, 893
Church Audit Procedures Act, 26 U.S.C. §7611 (1995), 787–788
Civil Rights Act of 1991, 631
Disabilities Education Act ("IDEA"), 20 U.S.C. §§ 1400-1487 (2002), 489
Equal Access Act 20 U.S.C. §§4071 et seq. (1984), 372, 379, 388, 468
Fair Labor Standard Act, 660
Family and Medical Leave Act, 29 U.S.C. §2611 *et seq.* , 629
Internal Revenue Code of 1954, *passim*
Nation's Capital Religious Liberty and Academic Freedom Act, 847
National Labor Relations Act, 646, 647, 659, 704
National Prohibition Act, 41 Stat. 308, 243
Northwest Ordinance of 1787, 92, 497
Payne-Aldrich Tariff Act of 1909, 741
Pledge of Allegiance, 68 Stats. 249, 45, 806, 868
Pregnancy Discrimination Act, 42 U.S.C. §2000e(k), 629, 706
Religious Freedom Restoration Act, 42 U.S.C. §§2000bb-2000bb-4 (2001), 391
Religious Land Use and Institutionalized Persons Act of 2000, 42 U.S.C.A. §§2000cc-2000cc-5, 396
Religious Liberty and Charitable Donation Protection Act, 11 U.S.C. §544(b), 612
Revenue Act of 1870, 16 Stat. 256, 741
Revenue Act of 1894, 28 Stat. 556, 779
Revenue Act of 1913, 38 Stat. 114, 741
Title IX of the Education Amendments of 1972, 20 U.S.C. §§ 1681 *et seq.* (2002), 403, 705
Civil Rights Act of 1964, Title VI, 42 U.S.C. §2000d, , 403, 704, 711

Treaties

State Statutes

Foreign Statutes

Other Statutes and Regulations

Preface

Americans have been described aptly as an "incorrigibly religious" people. Survey research conducted over much of the last half of the twentieth century confirms that observation. *Religious Liberty in a Pluralistic Society*, we believe, is the most complete overview of the ongoing legal struggle of those incorrigibly religious people to protect their "First Freedom."

Religious Liberty in a Pluralistic Society is designed for use in a variety of two- or three-credit course offerings, including Church-State Relations and Law and Religion; as a basic text in an advanced course or seminar in First Amendment law; or as the text in a survey course which focuses on churches and religious institutions as a "regulated industry." As indicated by the table of contents, our book develops the material on the contours of religious liberty as its primary subject, rather than as an adjunct to a collection of cases whose primary focus is the Speech and Press Clause.

The introductory chapter focuses on constitutional theory and interpretation, and asks the students to reflect upon the judiciary's perception of the place (or "role") of religious liberty in the American democratic experiment. Chapters two through four provide an historical survey of the ways in which America's ever-increasing ethnic and religious diversity has contributed to our current understanding of the combined commands of the First and Fourteenth Amendments. Chapter five offers a comprehensive overview of the contours of the jurisprudence of the Religious Liberty Guarantee, and Chapter thirteen is an examination of the meaning of the term "religion." Chapters six through twelve consider the ways in which the courts have attempted to balance religious liberty against other important individual and social interests in a wide variety of physical and regulatory environments.

Writing the second edition of this book has taken us more time than we planned, and we thank those whose criticisms and suggestions have allowed us to better adapt these materials for use in law schools.

Michael Ariens
San Antonio, Texas

Robert A. Destro
Washington, D.C.

May 2002

Religious Liberty in a Pluralistic Society

Chapter 1

Introduction

A. The Role of Characterization and "Levels of Generality" in Constitutional Interpretation

1. Introduction

Quidquid recipitur ad modum recipientis recipitur ("What is received is received according to the mode of the receiver") is an important axiom. For professionals whose work centers on the ideas and concepts conveyed by the written or spoken word, it suggests caution. Even when those who craft the language of the law seek clarity, words and phrases can be ambiguous: "A word is but the skin of a living thought." *Towne v. Eisner*, 245 U.S. 418, 425 (1918) (Holmes, J.). Context, perspective, and phrasing are crucial, and what is written is "received according to the mode of the receiver." Were the "meaning" of legal rhetoric easily ascertained, there would be no need to limit the selection of judges to the "few men in the society who will have sufficient skill in the laws [, and]...who unite the requisite integrity with the requisite knowledge." *The Federalist* No. 78 (Alexander Hamilton).

The task of interpretation is rendered more difficult by nature of the legislative process in a representative democracy. A major function of legislative or constitutional language is to capture and record as "law" a faithful rendition of the bargains struck between and among the factions that participated in the drafting process. The interests of the factions participating in the process will be affected by the terms of the bargain, and, often, so too will those of factions not represented. As a result, the choice of mutually agreeable words or phrases to describe the agreed-upon policy position(s) is *the* critical factor in the legislative or constitution-drafting process. (Hence, the phrase "The devil is in the details.")

Once the law goes into effect, the received meaning of the words remains an important concern. A law must be understood before compliance or enforcement can be undertaken, and both responses require interpretation. Article II of the Constitution of the United States requires that the laws "be faithfully executed," a process that presupposes enforcement interpretation by the Executive Branch. Private parties and their attorneys must also interpret the law to determine how to comply. And because interpretations vary "according to the mode of the receiver," cases or controversies "arising under the Constitution and laws of the United States" and of the several states are one obvious outcome of differences in perception.

The power to decide "cases or controversies" affecting individuals is the heart of Article III and analogous provisions of state constitutions. Article III makes it clear that the judicial function is twofold. Whether the trial is by jury or before the judge alone, the judge must ascertain the meaning of the words, phrases, and concepts embodied in the *specific* laws alleged to apply to the case. When the parties urge alternative constructions of the same statutory or constitutional language, "it is emphatically the province and duty of the judicial department to say what the law is," *Marbury v. Madison*, 5 U.S. (1 Cranch) 137, 177 (1803).

The legislative branch, by contrast, makes general policies that seek to balance the interests of individuals and the requirements of the common good. Its bias is majoritarian, and thus particularly unsuited to the task of deciding individual cases or controversies. *Cf.* U.S. Const. art. I, §9, cl. 2 (Writ of Habeas Corpus), cl. 3 (prohibiting Bills of Attainder and ex post facto laws). Its task is to make general policies which take into account both the interests of the individual and the requirements of the common good. The role of the executive branch is to see that the law is "faithfully" and impartially executed. Though accommodation of individual claims is possible, the Constitution makes it clear that unless it is authorized by statute, the scope of executive discretion to grant individualized exemptions from laws of general applicability is limited. *See* U.S. Const. art. II, §2 (power to grant pardons). Thus, although all branches share the power to interpret the law, the power to do so in the context of a specific dispute over the application of particular laws to specific facts is a structural attribute of the judicial branch of government.

The process of ascertaining the meaning of the words, phrases and concepts contained in constitutions and laws, however, is neither easy nor apolitical. In 1985, for example, now-retired Justice William J. Brennan, Jr., remarked that "Like every text worth reading, [the Constitution] is not crystalline. The phrasing is broad and the limitations of its provisions are not clearly marked. Its majestic generalities and ennobling pronouncements are both luminous and obscure." William J. Brennan, Jr., *The Constitution of the United States: A Contemporary Ratification*, 27 So. Tex. L. Rev. 433 (1986). His comments provoked a political firestorm over the legitimacy of using extra-constitutional sources as a means of ascertaining the "meaning" of the constitutional text.

Because resolving individual disputes is particularly within its competence, the Judicial Branch enjoys the final word on the application of the law to any specific case or controversy. The holdings of the Supreme Court carry the weight of precedent, and they are often treated as "infallible"[1] statements of constitutional law until they are modified or overruled. *See generally* Charles J. Cooper, *Stare Decisis: Precedent and Principle in Constitutional Adjudication*, 73 Cornell L. Rev. 401 (1988); William O. Douglas, *Stare Decisis*, 49 Colum. L. Rev. 735 (1949). In Federalist 78, Alexander Hamilton sought to reassure those who feared the interpretive power of the federal judiciary: "[T]he courts", wrote Hamilton, "were designed to be an intermediate body between the people and the legislature in order, among other things, to keep the latter within the limits assigned to their authority." *The Federalist* No. 78, at 467. He argued that the President should not nominate, nor should the Senate confirm, anyone who did not possess the requisite level of wisdom, experience, and learning to resolve "cases or controversies" involving the meaning of the Constitution or laws of the United States. As if

---

1. Justice Robert Jackson coined the now-famous phrase: "We are not final because we are infallible, but we are infallible only because we are final." Brown v. Allen, 344 U.S. 443, 540 (1953) (opinion concurring in result). The use of such imagery to describe the Court's work leads to quite a few misunderstandings concerning the nature of the Court's power in the federal system.

to underscore the delicacy of the task, Hamilton added a caveat: The intermediate role of the judiciary was to be governed by a clear understanding on the part of the judges that "[a] constitution is, in fact, and must be regarded by [them] as, a fundamental law." *Id.*

Determining whether the judiciary has regulated its decisions by that "fundamental law" raises a number of questions about the power of judicial review. What are the component parts of that power? Is the process of interpretation a rational one, governed by clearly articulated rules, or does the development of the case law proceed on an *ad hoc* basis? Are analogous provisions analyzed in a consistent manner, or does the body of decisional law contain fundamental and irreconcilable inconsistencies? Is it possible, or even desirable, to attempt to identify "neutral principles" against which the decisions of the judiciary can be measured? And perhaps most importantly, what remedies, or, in political terms, "checks and balances," are available if the rule announced in a specific case, or developed in a line of cases, is challenged as politically unacceptable?

It is fairly easy to determine whether one agrees or disagrees with the outcome in a particular case, or with the interpretation of a specific word or phrase. Because of the nature of judicial review, however, it is much harder to make the case that an outcome or interpretation is "unconstitutional" as beyond the *power* of the Court. Although the Court will occasionally describe one of its decisions in those terms, *see Erie Railroad Co. v. Tompkins*, 304 U.S. 64 (1938), *overruling Swift v. Tyson*, 41 U.S. (16 Pet.) 1 (1842), the more common interpretation is that the judicial process inevitably involves striking balances between and among constitutional values that are sometimes in tension. Viewed from this perspective, criticism of a particular outcome tends to focus on the specific balance struck, rather than the process by which it is accomplished.

One way to draw attention to judicial review *as a rational process* is to examine some of the critical, but often unstated, steps in the interpretive process. One of the most important of these steps is the manner in which competing interests are described, "characterized," or "classified" *before* the balances are struck. Because characterization can mask the process of "rule-selection," characterization of the interests involved can exert a powerful, yet unstated, influence on the outcome of any given case or controversy. Careful attention to the process by which the Constitution is given "meaning" thus becomes another method by which to measure or review the Court's holdings.

2. Characterization as a Process

The most extensive literature on the process of characterization is found in the field of conflict of laws (private international law). P.M. North & J.J. Fawcett, CHESHIRE & NORTH'S PRIVATE INTERNATIONAL LAW 43–52 (12th ed. 1992). *See generally* Roger Cramton, David Currie, Herma Hill Kay & Larry Kramer, CONFLICT OF LAWS: CASES-COMMENTS-QUESTIONS (6th ed. 2001).

Given the importance of characterization in the pleading, practice and decision of constitutional claims and defenses, it may be helpful to examine first the meaning of the concept in a non-constitutional context. British scholars Peter North and J.J. Fawcett describe the process in the choice-of-law context as follows:

> What is meant by the "classification of the cause of action" is the allocation of the question raised by the factual situation before the court to its correct legal category, and its object is to reveal the relevant rule for the choice of [the applicable] law. The rules of any given system of law are arranged under different categories, some being concerned with status, others with succession, procedure, tort and so on, and until a judge, faced with a case involving a foreign element, has determined the particular category into which the question before him falls, he can make no progress, for he will not know what... rule to apply. He must discover the true basis of the... claim.
>
> Occasionally, however, the matter is far from simple. In the first place, it may be a case near the line in which it is difficult to determine whether the question falls naturally within this or that judicial category. Secondly, it may be a case where [different jurists or systems] hold diametrically opposed views on the correct classification. There may, in other words, be a conflict of classification,.... The crucial question, therefore, is—on what principles do... judges classify the cause of action?

North & Fawcett, *Private International Law*, at 42–43.

In American constitutional law, the question raised by Professors North and Fawcett—on what principles do judges classify causes of action?—generally has been subsumed within the much larger topic of judicial review. Consider, for example, Professor Kathleen Sullivan's discussion of "categorical" and "balancing" approaches to constitutional interpretation:

> Categorization and balancing each employ quite different rhetoric. Categorization is the taxonomist's style—a job of classification and labeling. When categorical formulas operate, all the important work in litigation is done at the outset. Once the relevant right and mode of infringement have been described, the outcome follows, without any explicit judicial balancing of the claimed right against the government's justification for the infringement. Balancing is more like grocer's work (or Justice's)—the judge's job is to place competing rights and interests on a scale and weigh them against each other. Here the outcome is not determined at the outset, but depends on the relative strength of a multitude of factors. These two styles have competed endlessly in contemporary constitutional law; neither has ever entirely eclipsed the other.

Kathleen M. Sullivan, *Post-Liberal Judging: The Roles of Categorization and Balancing*, 63 U. Colo. L. Rev. 293, 293–294 (1992).

Professor Sullivan's analysis explicitly assumes that characterization and balancing are competing styles of interpretation. Do you agree with that assumption? Is it also appropriate to describe them as *devices* that can be employed at different stages in the analysis?

Professor Steven Gottlieb, among others, takes the position that much of the "balancing" v. "categorical analysis" debate to which Professor Sullivan is referring is actually about a different question: the role that the value-orientation of the judge (the "*receiver*" of the message embodied in the law being interpreted) plays in the process of interpretation:

> The pro and con positions [concerning categorical and balancing approaches] themselves are largely categorical—one is preferable, the other lamentable. The foundations of the argument are philosophical. They deal with the role of judges in a democratic system.

> The dispute over categorization and balancing is miscast for three reasons. First, the methods are not often determinative. Second, the methods can often be translated into one another. Third, . . . , the dispute is miscast because the decision between balancing and not balancing is illusory. The only 'real' decisions are when intuitive judgments, whether described as balancing or otherwise, should be allowed to enter the analysis, which assumptions should be articulated, and which should be left inchoate.
>
> Categorization is often balancing; it requires deciding which category to put things in, and that is often done by noticing the consequences and deciding (often subconsciously) if they are tolerable, better, or worse than certain alternatives.

Stephen E. Gottlieb, *The Paradox of Balancing Significant Interests*, 45 Hastings L.J. 825, 837, 846 (1994).

Do you agree with Professor Gottlieb that the "only 'real' decisions are when intuitive judgments, whether described as balancing or otherwise, should be allowed to enter the analysis, which assumptions should be articulated, and which should be left inchoate"? Is this the same process described by Professors North and Fawcett in the conflict of laws/private international law context? If not, how does it differ?

a) A Note on Fact-Finding in Constitutional Adjudication

Before we examine the practical application of these theories in constitutional litigation, it may be helpful to consider the preliminary steps that must be taken when an individual wants to go to court to claim or defend a constitutional right.

Pleading is the process by which an individual or attorney characterizes the facts in order to fashion a claim for relief. Thus, the individual or attorney requesting constitutional relief must understand that the process of characterizing the facts will affect both the possible legal claims he or she can make, and the kinds of proof that will be permitted at a trial or hearing. The trial court's understanding of the facts will thus inevitably affect the way that it will eventually characterize the case. At the appellate level, courts ordinarily accept the facts as found by the trial court, and spend the bulk of their time evaluating the trial (or intermediate appellate) court's characterization of the claim and the correctness of lower court's understanding of how the legal doctrines applicable to the case should be applied in a particular factual setting.

A **standard of review** announces the process and rules under which a court evaluates a legal claim. Standards of review are thus the "directions" that tell the parties and the court what facts are relevant, and which of the parties to the case is responsible for proving them. *See* Henry P. Monaghan, *Constitutional Fact Review*, 85 Colum. L. Rev. 229 (1985). As a practical matter, the characterization of the case will often determine the standard of review.

Generally speaking, it is very difficult to challenge laws that regulate life in the economic and social communities. This is so because the courts assume they are constitutional, and place the burden of proving their invalidity on the individual or organization challenging the statute. The law will be upheld if there is "*any rational basis*" for the legislature's decision.

When those challenging a law allege that it violates an express or implied limitation on government authority, the standard of review shifts accordingly. More than "a rational basis" is required to defend the law. If the court finds that the law imposes a burden on a right characterized as "fundamental," the standard of review is "*strict scrutiny*," and the government must prove that the law is necessary to accomplish a "compelling state interest." Justice Kennedy's analysis of the exemptions written into the ban on animal sacrifice challenged in *Church of the Lukumi Babalue Aye, Inc. v. City of Hialeah*, 494 U.S. 872 (1990), noted in Chapter Five § D(7), illustrates how the strict scrutiny-compelling state interest standard of review works in practice. Though it is possible for government action to survive a "strict scrutiny" review, it is very difficult to do so. (Hence, the adage "strict in theory, but fatal in fact."[2])

b) Putting Theory into Practice: Characterizing a Constitutional Case

In light of the foregoing discussion, consider the following statement of facts taken verbatim from the Supreme Court's opinion in *Capitol Square Review and Advisory Board v. Pinette*, 515 U.S. 753, 757–758 (1995):

> Capitol Square is a 10-acre, state-owned plaza surrounding the Statehouse in Columbus, Ohio. For over a century the square has been used for public speeches, gatherings, and festivals advocating and celebrating a variety of causes, both secular and religious. Ohio Admin. Code Ann. § 128-4-02(A) (1994) makes the square available "for use by the public... for free discussion of public questions, or for activities of a broad public purpose," and Ohio Rev. Code Ann. § 105.41 (1994) gives the Capitol Square Review and Advisory Board responsibility for regulating public access. To use the square, a group must simply fill out an official application form and meet several criteria, which concern primarily safety, sanitation, and non-interference with other uses of the square, and which are neutral as to the speech content of the proposed event. [citations omitted] It has been the Board's policy "to allow a broad range of speakers and other gatherings of people to conduct events on the Capitol Square." Such diverse groups as homosexual rights organizations, the Ku Klux Klan and the United Way have held rallies. The Board has also permitted a variety of unattended displays on Capitol Square: a State-sponsored lighted tree during the Christmas season, a privately-sponsored menorah during Chanukah, a display showing the progress of a United Way fundraising campaign, and booths and exhibits during an arts festival. Although there was some dispute in this litigation regarding the frequency of unattended displays, the District Court found, with ample justification, that there was no policy against them.
>
> In November 1993, after reversing an initial decision to ban unattended holiday displays from the square during December 1993, the Board authorized the State to put up its annual Christmas tree. On November 29, 1993, the Board

2. The phrase had its origin in Gerald Gunther, *Foreword: In Search of Evolving Doctrine on a Changing Court: A Model for a Newer Equal Protection*, 86 Harv. L. Rev. 1, 8 (1970). Justice Thurgood Marshall used the phrase in *Fullilove v. Klutznick*, 448 U.S. 448, 519 (1980) (Marshall, J., concurring in the judgment), *overruled by Adarand Constructors, Inc. v. Peña*, 515 U.S. 200, 237 (1995) to criticize the Court's approach to fact-finding. In *Adarand*, the Court replied to Justice Marshall, and underscored the fact-finding purpose of the "strict scrutiny standard":

> [W]e wish to dispel the notion that strict scrutiny is "strict in theory, but fatal in fact."... When race-based action is necessary to further a compelling state interest, such an action is within constitutional constraints if it satisfied the "narrow tailoring" test this Court has set out in previous cases.

> granted a rabbi's application to erect a menorah. That same day, the Board received an application from respondent Donnie Carr, an officer of the Ohio Ku Klux Klan, to place a cross on the square from December 8, 1993, to December 24, 1993. The Board denied that application on December 3, informing the Klan by letter that the decision to deny "was made upon the advice of counsel, in a good faith attempt to comply with the Ohio and United States Constitutions, as they have been interpreted in relevant decisions by the Federal and State Courts."

What provisions of the United States Constitution are potentially "controlling" with respect to this set of facts?

The First Amendment itself presents several options: non-establishment, free exercise, speech and press, peaceable assembly, and petition for redress of grievances. The Fourteenth Amendment forbids states from depriving "any person of life, liberty or property, without due process of law" and from denying to any person "the equal protection of the laws." If the factual setting described in *Pinette* were to be "characterized," in turn, as a case arising under *each* of the provisions you have identified, how, if at all, might the differences in standard of review associated with each of these provisions affect the outcome?

Is it either necessary or appropriate to select *one* of the available options as *the* "controlling" provision? Attorneys often plead or defend their cases "in the alternative" because they want to present the facts in a way that takes advantage of all of the potentially applicable standards of review. Taking a categorical approach at the outset of a case thus limits both creativity and flexibility.

When a court utilizes a characterization process to select the rule of decision, the crucial decision is the category into which the judge places the facts and law involved. Thus, if *Pinette* were characterized as a case involving "speech" alone, only the rules and standards of review applicable to "speech cases" would apply. Adding "religion" because the facts involve a cross, or "equal protection" because the Ku Klux Klan was the "speaker," will change both the nature of the arguments, and the facts that are relevant to the selection of the rule to be applied.

Balancing, by contrast, is a multi-stage process. First the court analyzes the facts to determine what legal issues are presented. (**characterization**) The court then uses the law applicable to such a case to "weigh" the importance of the interests involved. When interests are alleged to be in conflict, the court will examine a specific interest and compare it with the others affected. In the *Pinette* example set out above, a balancing approach might examine, in turn: 1) the Klan's interest in free speech, including its right of access to a public forum; 2) its religiously based interests in placing the cross; and 3) its right to be governed by the same rules that govern other organizations that wish to place displays on the Capitol Square. "Balanced" against these interests are the State and public interests affected by, among other things: 1) the Klan's purpose in placing the cross; 2) its history and reputation as a group that fosters division along racial and religious lines; 3) the State's interest in assuring the public that neither the symbolic message of the cross, nor the permit given to the Klan constitute an official endorsement of the message or the group, and 4) the State's interest in the preservation of public order.

Since the constitutional revolution of 1937, the Supreme Court has often preferred a "balancing" to a "categorical" approach. Several members of the Court have argued that modern constitutional decision-making almost always involves striking a balance between or among two or more important interests. Thus, it is important to be aware that the initial characterization of the case, or the specific interests involved, can be used as a means of striking a *preliminary* balance in favor of, or against, one of the interests involved. That categorization is then used in the formal balancing of interests that is used to decide the case. Consider two examples.

The first is *Pinette*. After reciting the facts, the very first question decided by the majority in *Pinette* is the characterization of the case: "First, a preliminary matter: Respondents contend that we should treat this as a case in which freedom of speech (the Klan's right to present the message of the cross display) was denied because of the State's disagreement with that message's political content, rather than because of the State's desire to distance itself from sectarian religion." 515 U.S. at 759. The Court refused to consider the argument that the case should be recharacterized on appeal as a "political speech" case because the parties themselves chose to focus on the "religious speech" aspects of the case.

Why do you suppose the Klan wanted to change the characterization? Was it a more difficult case for them if the question is whether the Establishment Clause permits Ohio to ban a cross on the Capitol Square? Would characterizing the case as one involving a ban on "symbolic political speech" make it any easier? *See id.* at 770 (Thomas, J. concurring) ("The erection of such a cross is a political act, not a Christian one.")

The second example is the doctrine of "selective incorporation." When the United States Supreme Court decides to incorporate a selected provision of the Bill of Rights into the Fourteenth Amendment, the result is the application of that right to state as well as federal action.[4] How does the Court decide which portions of the Bill of Rights "incorporate" and which do not?

The process begins with characterization: Does this particular provision of the Bill of Rights protect a "fundamental right" that is "implicit in the concept of ordered liberty"? If so, the provision is characterized as "fundamental," it "incorporates," and the courts "apply" it to action taken by the States. If not, the right applies only to federal action.

Notes

1. The process of incorporating specific provisions of the Bill of Rights into the Due Process Clause began in the 1920s, and continued after many fits and starts through the 1960s, but the Court has never really answered the question: "How do we know that a specific right is 'fundamental'?" Justice John Paul Stevens observed in *Wallace v. Jaffree*, 472 U.S. 38 (1985) that the incorporation of the First Amendment into the Fourteenth is an "elementary proposition of law." *Id.* at 49. Does this mean that the characterization process that is utilized to *decide* whether a right is "fundamental" is also "elementary"?

In *Structural Free Exercise*, Professor Mary Ann Glendon and Raul Yanes suggest that:

> [T]he [Supreme] Court offered no systematic account of [the development of the Incorporation Doctrine] until 1937 when, in *Palko v. Connecticut*, Justice Cardozo undertook to explain why it had made sense to take a piecemeal approach, rather than to incorporate the entire Bill of Rights.
>
> The teaching of *Palko* is that the Bill of Rights contains an implied hierarchy of constitutional values. According to Cardozo, certain rights so "implicit in the concept of ordered liberty" and "'so rooted in the traditions and con-

4. The Incorporation Doctrine is described in greater detail in Chapter 5 § B(3).

> science of our people as to be ranked as fundamental.'" These especially important "fundamental" rights are to be distinguished from various other rights (such as the double jeopardy provision involved in *Palko*) in the absence of which "[j]ustice... would not perish." The concept of due process, Cardozo explained, required that the former, but not the latter, be made binding on the states. Cardozo did not suggest any more sophisticated ranking than "in" and "out," nor did he offer an exhaustive catalog of the rights that ought to be "in." But he made it plain that freedom of speech, thought, and religion were among them. Of these, Cardozo's rhetoric implied, speech was the most essential. The freedom of thought and speech, he wrote, was the "matrix, the indispensable condition, of nearly every other form of freedom."

Mary Ann Glendon & Raul F. Yanes, *Structural Free Exercise*, 90 Mich. L. Rev. 477, 479–480, 482 (1991).

Do you agree that what has become known as "fundamental rights analysis" is no "more sophisticated [a] ranking than 'in' and 'out'"? If so, the "fundamental rights" approach is a good example of "balancing through characterization" because the concept of an "implied hierarchy of constitutional values" depends on how important the right appears to a specific group of Justices. If, by contrast, the hierarchy is embedded in the text and structure of the Constitution itself, those who wrote and ratified the Constitution struck the balance, not the Justices.

2. The Framers of the Bill of Rights viewed the twin structures of federalism and separation of powers as important components of "ordered liberty." To what extent, if at all, should the federalism concerns be taken into account when characterizing First Amendment rights and interests? *See* Robert A. Destro, *The Structure of the Religious Liberty Guarantee*, 11 J. Law & Rel. 355 (1995). What about separation of powers? *See, e.g.*, Mark P. Denbeaux, *The First Word of the First Amendment*, 80 Nw. L. Rev. 1156 (1986); Robert A. Destro, *By What Right? The Sources and Limits of Federal Jurisdiction Over Matters "Touching Religion,"* 29 Ind. L. Rev. 1 (1996). What of the separation of powers concerns that motivated the adoption of Section Five of the Fourteenth Amendment? *See generally* Louis A. Fisher, *The Curious Belief in Judicial Supremacy*, 25 Suffolk L. Rev. 85 (1991).

3. What are the federalism and separation of powers implications of choosing a "due process" over a "privileges and immunities" mechanism for incorporating the Bill of Rights (selectively or *en masse*)? Would a right to free speech incorporated under the Privileges and Immunities Clause of the Fourteenth Amendment apply to all persons, or only to "citizens of the United States"? *See The Slaughter-House Cases*, 83 U.S. (16 Wall.) 36 (1873). *See, e.g.*, Robert A. Destro, *Federal Jurisdiction "Touching" Religion*; Akhil Reed Amar, *The Bill of Rights and the Fourteenth Amendment*, 101 Yale L.J. 1193 (1992); Akhil Reed Amar, *The Bill of Rights as a Constitution*, 100 Yale L.J. 1131 (1991); Steven L. Carter, *The Independent Counsel Mess*, 102 Harv. L. Rev. 105 (1988); Steven G. Calabresi & Kevin H. Rhodes, *The Structural Constitution: Unitary Executive, Plural Judiciary*, 105 Harv. L. Rev. 1153 (1992); E. Donald Elliot, *Why Our Separation of Powers Jurisprudence Is So Abysmal*, 57 Geo. Wash. L. Rev. 506 (1989); Clifton McClesky, *Judicial Review in a Democracy: A Dissenting Opinion*, 3 Hous. L. Rev. 354, 360–61 (1966); Martin Shapiro, FREEDOM OF SPEECH: THE SUPREME COURT AND JUDICIAL REVIEW 29–30 (1966).

4. To what extent should the values protected by the Equal Protection Clause be taken into account when characterizing, or balancing, the interests of individuals under

the First Amendment? *See generally* Timothy L. Hall, *Religion, Equality, and Difference*, 65 Temp. L. Rev. 1 (1992); Michael S. Paulsen, *Religion, Equality, and the Constitution: An Equal Protection Approach to Establishment Clause Adjudication*, 61 Notre Dame L. Rev. 311 (1986). Should the values protected by the Equal Protection Clause be taken into account explicitly, or should they be subsumed within a broader "First Amendment" analysis?

5. Consider, once again, Glendon and Yanes' point concerning the "implied hierarchy of constitutional values" that seemingly undergirds the Court's decision that incorporation should be "selective." On what basis should such a hierarchy proceed? Is it obvious, for example, that the right to freedom of speech is more important than the right to a trial by a jury of twelve members? The Court has suggested a number of different formulations for addressing this issue. *See Planned Parenthood of Southeastern Pennsylvania v. Casey*, 505 U.S. 8331 (1992); *Posadas de Puerto Rico. Associates v. Tourism Co. of Puerto Rico*, 478 U.S. 328 (1986); *Virginia State Board of Pharmacy v. Virginia Citizens Consumer Council*, 425 U.S. 738 (1976); *Poe v. Ullman*, 367 U.S. 497 (1961) (Harlan J., dissenting); *United States v. Carolene Prods. Co.*, 304 U.S. 144, 152 n.4 (1938) (Stone, C.J.); *Palko v. Connecticut*, 302 U.S. 319 (1937).

3. Characterization and the Constitutional Norm: Ascertaining the Appropriate Level of Generality

We are now prepared to look at the actual taxonomy of the First Amendment. There is a considerable body of literature concerning the appropriate definitions of both "religion" and "speech," and it bears noting that most of the literature argues in favor of "broad" definitions of both concepts. The reasons are varied and need not be repeated here. For present purposes, the focus will remain on the manner in which the constitutional norm, which can be either a grant or a limit, is characterized.

Consider, for example, the definition of the term "religion." At its most specific levels of generality, it can refer to belief in a Supreme Being, or actions which reflect that belief, such as worship. At its most abstract or "high" level of generality, it can refer to virtually any belief system which deals with transcendent questions concerning the nature of good and evil. When described at this "high" level of generality, the focus is necessarily upon the holder of the belief and the influence that belief has on the life of that person. To the extent the level of generality is "low," the question is more concrete. In this formulation, "religion" becomes an attachment to a specific theological perspective or mode of worship which exists independently of the person subscribing to the belief. Other provisions of the Constitution, including the first amendment, can be analyzed in similar fashion.

Determining the appropriate level of generality can influence one's understanding of the meaning of a key concept. Consider for example, the terms of the Religion Clause. Several of the bracketed terms have been incorporated into Chart 1-1 on page 14.

> "[Congress] shall make [no law] [respecting] [an establishment] [of religion] or [prohibiting] the [free exercise] [thereof]..."

Does the chart present a reasonably accurate set of possibilities for characterizing First Amendment rights and interests? At what levels of generality are each of the norms ordinarily described? Are the levels of generality which are used to describe the non-establishment, free exercise, speech and press, petition for redress of grievances, and peaceable assembly norms uniform, or do the levels of generality vary in accordance with the nature of the specific provision in question?

The point of these questions is to prompt you to "strictly scrutinize" the case law developed under the First Amendment, and to reflect upon the role characterization plays in the development of an interpretation of the specific liberties being considered. When reading the cases excerpted in this book, consider whether the writers of the various opinions clearly articulate and define the appropriate level of generality. Consider also whether the effort at characterization currently utilized by the Supreme Court represents an implicit balancing of interests, and if so, what interests are balanced.

When evaluating these decisions, consider the following:

1. The textual source of the constitutional power or limit in question;
2. The sources, in addition to the text, upon which the Court relies for guidance in interpreting the relevant constitutional terms, including constitutional structure, history, the common law, other precedent, the experience of the people of the United States, and present-day American attitudes;
3. How the Justices choose to characterize the individual right or interest before them;
4. How the Justices choose to characterize or describe the state's interests;
5. The value or weight assigned to either the individual interest (Is it a "fundamental" right?), or the interest of the state (Is the state's interest "compelling," "important," "rational," or "arbitrary"?);
6. The appropriate standard of judicial review given the suggested characterization (Is the Court evaluating the case by determining whether the law is minimally rational or presumptively unconstitutional?);
7. The choices reasonably available to the Court which might accommodate the allegedly conflicting interests (Should the Court subordinate one interest to the other, or attempt to strike a reasonable balance between them?); and
8. The forum in which such a balance should ultimately be struck, whether in one of the three federal branches, in the states, or in the constitution-making process set forth in Article V.

4. Characterization and the Search for Neutral Principles

Because the process of characterization is, or should be, a rational process constrained by the same principles that govern the decisions of other constitutional issues, it is necessary to assess the manner in which judicial discretion is to be confined in such matters. Is it possible, or even desirable, to formulate "neutral principles" of law that will confine the discretion of the decision-maker?

Professor Steven Winter has observed that the problem of constitutional interpretation poses several dilemmas for those who "would like [constitutional] theory to work as a check on, or counterbalance to, or replacement for the current practices of... constitutional decisionmaking." Steven Winter, *Indeterminacy and Incommensurability in Constitutional Law*, 78 Cal. L. Rev. 1441, 1446–1449 (1991). Though Winter was speak-

CHART 1-1
CHARACTERIZING "SUBSTANTIVE" FIRST AMENDMENT CLAIMS

	Non-establishment	Religious Liberty Free Exercise	The Concept of "Religion"	Speech & Press	Peaceable Assembly	Petition for a Redress of Grievances
abstract	No official recognition of religion by the state that offends a citizen	Personal autonomy	Personal autonomy in the formation of individual beliefs	Personal autonomy	Personal autonomy	Personal autonomy regarding grievances, public or private
formulation	No collaboration by the state for any purpose with religious individuals or associations	Freedom to act in a manner consistent with public order	Maintenance of doctrinal integrity through non-association with contrary beliefs	Non-association with disagreeable messages	Non-association with disagreeable individuals or groups	Non-association with disagreeable advocacy
(high)	No state participation in religious affairs, or participation by religious individuals and groups in politics	Freedom of conscience	Personal belief systems	Freedom to learn about religious ideas	Intimate Association	Collective support of political campaigns
↓	No aid to any activity characterized as "religious" or "sectarian"	Religious autonomy	Any beliefs concerning "the good" and other moral or ethical questions	Access to religious information and ideas	Collective action for any otherwise legitimate purpose	Personal support of political campaigns
Level	No public assistance for religious organizations	No state-compelled association with repugnant beliefs or practices	Philosophical views concerning "the good" and other metaphysical questions	Freedom of inquiry, information, and media	Association or membership in an organization for any legitimate purpose	Lobbying by hired proxy
of Generality	No tax support for churches	Freedom to act in a manner consistent with religious beliefs or practices	Moral and ethical beliefs	Freedom to communicate religious ideas	Association or membership in an organization for expressive purposes	Collective, issue-oriented political action or activity

↑	No preference among churches or religions	Freedom to practice in accordance with one's beliefs, religion, or traditions	Beliefs and practices animated by moral or ethical beliefs functionally equivalent to traditional religions	Freedom of religious expression and ritual	Association or membership in political organizations	Collective, issue-oriented litigation
specific	No compelled association of individuals with any organized religion, sect, or activity	Freedom to worship	Nontheistic beliefs, practices or rituals	Communication of religious ideas or perspectives through symbolic representations	Peaceable assembly for any purpose	Personal communication with any legislator on any issue
formulation	No compulsion or punishment in matters of religious belief or exercise	Freedom to hold religious beliefs	Communal worship or rituals of "traditional" or theistic believers	Personal speech or publication of religious perspectives on any legitimate subject	Peaceable assembly for political purposes	Personal communication with one's own representatives
(low)	No "official" church, churches, or religions	Toleration	Personal and private prayer, ritual, or relationship with God	Personal speech or publication about religion, including prayer and prosyletization	Peaceable assembly at the seat of government for political purposes	Communication with administrators or the courts regarding personal interests

ing to those most often described as "liberals" who would use constitutional theory to constrain "conservative" jurists, the same dilemmas exist for those who wish to wield constitutional theory as a check on the practices of courts dominated by those whose views are described as "liberal."

In Winter's view, "[m]uch of the rhetoric of legal decisionmaking [since 1937] seems to promise a neutrality and objectivity that it does not deliver." 78 Cal. L. Rev. at 1449. Balances are routinely struck between opposing or conflicting interests in ways which make sense to some, and which are anathema to others. The process is clearly value-laden, and there seems little doubt that parties arguing implausible constructions of the Constitution would rarely get a chance to have them considered—and rejected—by the Supreme Court. *Cf.* F.R. Civ. P. 11.

When liberals or conservatives are dissatisfied with the Court's jurisprudence, they can adopt one of two possible approaches: law or politics. A "legal" approach involves an attempt to synthesize earlier precedents "into coherent theories that could bind or persuade a Court of radically different mind." 78 Cal. L. Rev. at 1445. The problem with such an approach is that even if a judge or Justice can be persuaded to pay attention to legal arguments which rely for their validity on a body of precedent the judge finds of doubtful current validity, the substantive argument itself is likely to be rejected on its merits.

A current example of this phenomenon can be seen in the jurisprudence of the Establishment Clause of the First Amendment. One faction of the Justices takes the position that such analyses are governed by the "three-pronged test" announced in *Lemon v. Kurtzman,* 403 U.S. 602 (1971). Another has taken the position that *Lemon* is best viewed through the lens of an "endorsement analysis" championed by Justice Sandra Day O'Connor in *Lynch v. Donnelly*, 465 U.S. 668, 687–688 (1984) (O'Connor, J. concurring). A third faction, led by Justice Scalia, openly ridicules arguments, and decisions, which are based on the *Lemon* test. *See Lamb's Chapel v. Center Moriches Union Free Sch. Dist.*, 508 U.S. 384, 398 (1993) (Scalia & Thomas, JJ., concurring) (comparing the Court's periodic use of the *Lemon* test to "some ghoul in a late-night horror movie that repeatedly sits up in its grave and shuffles abroad, after being repeatedly killed and buried"). An attorney who is called upon to argue such a case must take care to craft an argument that takes all of these positions into account.

A more overtly political tactic might involve what Professor Winter's article describes as the "reactive task of desynthesizing…[the Court's] precedents in an effort to undermine its program and to persuade others (presumably political actors) that it lacks legitimacy." In this context, the purpose of legal analysis is to lay the groundwork for a political "checking" maneuver.

But taking the "political" rather than the "legal" tack has risks. By undertaking an overtly political campaign to delegitimize and supplant the policy announced by the Court with a more congenial one obtained through the political process, those who undertake it confront head-on what has been called "the myth of neutrality." In Winter's view, that myth is exploded by a political response "because the question is not *whether* there is meaning [in the constitutional text], but rather *how* there is meaning and what that meaning is." Winter, *supra* at 1449. More importantly, it raises an important separation of powers issue: to what extent does the Constitution authorize the political branches to give "meaning" to the operative provisions of the First Amendment through the passage of legislation or the adoption of administrative regulations?

And therein lies the critical point about constitutional interpretation. "The question is not *whether* there is meaning" in the constitutional text. Everyone assumes that there is. The *interpretive* questions are "*how* there is meaning," "what that meaning is," and who supplies it in cases where there is a dispute. *See id.*; *See also* Robert A. Destro, *By What Right?* (discussing the power of Congress, the President, and the States to supply such "meaning" when the Court fails to do so).

For present purposes, however, it makes no difference whether the "interpreting" is done by the Court in the course of deciding a case or controversy properly within its jurisdiction, by the Congress in the exercise of its enumerated powers, or by the President in the day-to-day execution of the law or the conduct of foreign affairs. It is the process by which the "meaning" of words and phrases are ascertained which we are attempting to pin down. Defending the meaning chosen, or the manner in which the meaning of a specific word or phrase is integrated into the interpretation of a particular constitutional provision or statutory framework, is another matter entirely.

The Court has been deeply divided about the appropriate level of generality in cases in which an individual has claimed a constitutional right not enumerated in the Bill of Rights. In *Bowers v. Hardwick*, 478 U.S. 186 (1986), a bare majority, in an opinion by Justice White, characterized the constitutional issue before it as "whether the Federal Constitution confers a fundamental right upon homosexuals to engage in sodomy...." *Id.* at 190. Justice Blackmun's dissenting opinion, quoting the late Justice Louis D. Brandeis, claimed "this case is about 'the most comprehensive of rights and the right most valued by civilized men,' namely, 'the right to be let alone.'" *Id.* at 199. Several years later, in *Michael H. v. Gerald D.*, 491 U.S. 110 (1989), the Court upheld California's then-existing irrebuttable presumption that a child born to a married woman is the child of the husband. Blood taken from Michael H. showed he was the biological father to a probability of 98.07%, and he sued for visitation rights to the child, and claimed the conclusive presumption was unconstitutional. The California courts upheld the law, and the Supreme Court affirmed. Only a plurality joined Justice Scalia's opinion upholding the law, and only Chief Justice Rehnquist joined Justice Scalia's footnote six, which stated that resort to "tradition" must be based on the most "specific" level of generality at which the tradition could be perceived. Justice O'Connor, along with Justice Kennedy, joined all of Justice Scalia's opinion except footnote six, and refused to limit herself to the most specific level of generality available. Justice Brennan's dissent rejected Justice Scalia's interpretive methodology as not providing "the objective boundary that it seeks," and for ignoring "the Constitution's deliberately capacious language." *Id.* at 137, 140.

Note

Justice Brennan states:

> Successive generations of Americans have continued to respect the... fundamental choices [made in the constitution and to] adopt them as their own guide to evaluating quite different historical practices. Each generation has the choice to overrule or add to the fundamental principles enunciated by the Framers; the Constitution can be amended or it can be ignored.... We current Justices read the Constitution in the only way that we can: as Twentieth Century Americans. We look to the history of the time of framing and to the intervening history of interpretation. *But the ultimate question must be, what do the words of the text mean in our time.*

Remarks of Justice William J. Brennan, Jr. To the Text and Teaching Symposium, in William J. Brennan, *The Constitution of the United States: Contemporary Ratification,* 27 S. Tex. L. Rev. 433, 438 (1986) (emphasis added).

What is Justice Brennan's point? Would it be legitimate, for example, for the Court to ignore the word "exercise" in the Free Exercise Clause? Can the Court subsume "prayer" under the rubric of "speech"? *See Good News Club v. Milford Central School,* 533 U.S. 98 (2001); *Widmar v. Vincent,* 454 U.S. 263 (1981). Is it possible to collapse the entire First Amendment into one or two operative norms via such a process? If viewed broadly, isn't religious ritual a form of "expressive conduct," and thus speech?

Chart 1-2
Would a Different Organizing Principle Affect the Meaning of the Religious Liberty Guarantee? Consider the Options.

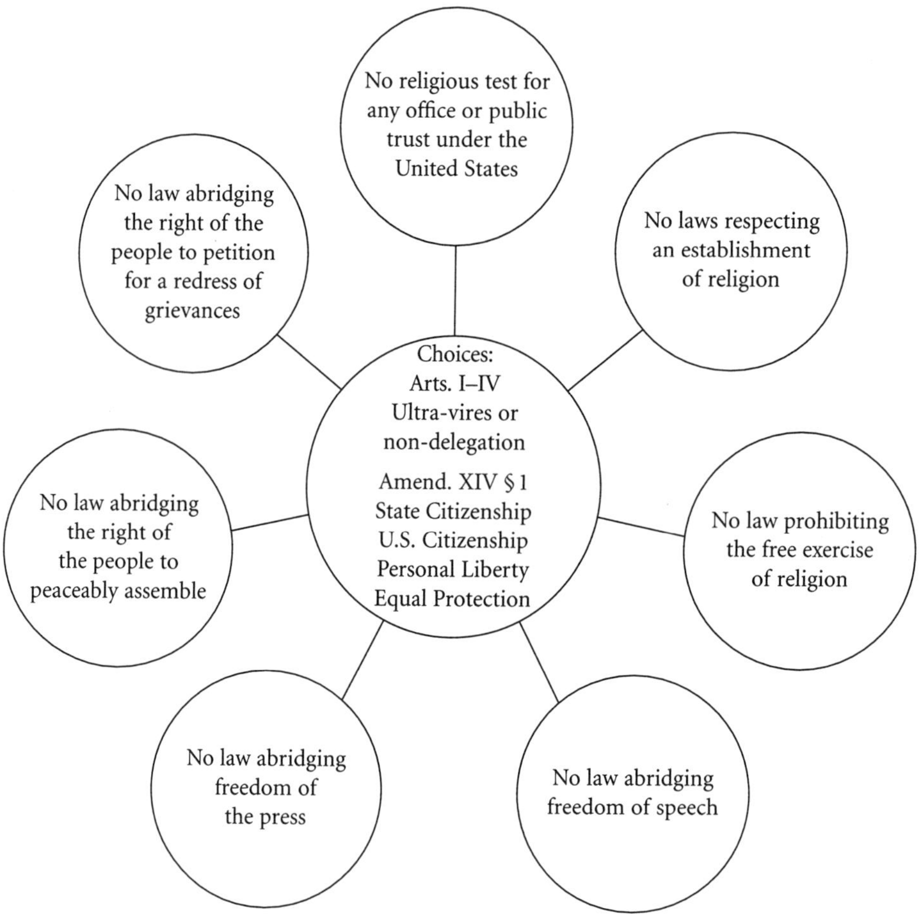

5. Characterization and the Incorporated First Amendment

Chart 1-2 is a representation of the components of the Religious Liberty Guarantee embodied in the No Religious Test Clause of Article VI, and the First and Fourteenth Amendments. How does the choice of an "organizing principle" affect the meaning of each of these provisions?

Recall, for example, the Federalists' argument that a Bill of Rights was not necessary because Articles I–VI granted Congress no regulatory authority over topics such as religious liberty or freedom of the press. In this conception of religious liberty and freedom of the press, the organizing principle is the "ultra-vires" concept of non-delegation: "Congress shall make no law" respecting or abridging the interests protected because it lacks the authority regulate in the first instance.

The United States Supreme Court understands the Religious Liberty Guarantee as part of a more generalized conception of personal liberty embodied in the Due Process Clause of the Fourteenth Amendment. *See* Chapter Five. What impact would the choice of alternative organizing principles—such as State citizenship or equal protection have—on our understanding of these rights?

Notes

1. What characterizations are possible, or desirable, as the organizing principles change? How, for example, does one's understanding of the Establishment Clause norm change if its "central meaning" is equal protection of the laws?

2. States are free to apply more "stringent" standards under their own constitutions and laws, provided that the outcome is otherwise consistent with the Supreme Court's interpretation of the Federal Constitution. What is the source of this claim of federalism? The structure of the Constitution itself? The Privileges and Immunities Clause of Article IV? The Ninth Amendment? The Tenth? The Citizenship Clause of the Fourteenth? See Chapter Five § K.

3. These are not "abstract" questions. Consider *Texas Monthly v. Bullock*, 489 U.S. 1 (1989), excerpted in Chapter Nine. *Texas Monthly* was a challenge by a non-religious magazine to a sales tax-exemption granted to all periodicals "published or distributed by a religious faith and that consist wholly of writings promulgating the teaching of the faith and books that consist wholly of writings sacred to a religious faith." Tex. Tax Code Ann. § 151.312 (1982). Although six Justices agreed that the law was unconstitutional, the 6–3 decision divides as follows. Three (3) Justices in the plurality (William Brennan, Thurgood Marshall, and John Paul Stevens) voted to strike the law on Establishment Clause grounds, but included an extensive discussion on how the free exercise and non-establishment norms relate to one another. One, Justice Byron White, voted to strike the law under the Free Press Clause alone. He and did not address any other issue. Two (2) Justices, Sandra Day O'Connor and Harry Blackmun, saw the potential for conflict between these norms, but sought to avoid it on the facts of the case. The three dissenters (Justices Scalia, Kennedy, and Chief Justice Rehnquist) took the Justices in the plurality to task for making no attempt to reconcile the inconsistencies in their opinions. How does one determine the "rule of decision" in such a case? *See* Chapter Five § E(4).

B. The Problem of Religious Liberty: The "Role" of Religion and the Democratic Experiment

What is, or should be, the "function" or "role" of religious liberty in a democratic society? *See* Suzanna Sherry, *Lee v. Weisman: Paradox Redux,* 1992 Sup.Ct. Rev. 123, 149 (asking "What purposes does religion serve in a modern democracy, and how should we best foster those goals?"). Must one determine what the particular substantive value of religious liberty *is* in order to decide its "function"? Is "religion" protected in the First Amendment in order to "serve" democracy? Can democracy "serve" religion?

There have been divergent opinions concerning the relationship among law, religion and government since the settlement of America by Europeans in the seventeenth century. These paired cases from the early nineteenth and mid-twentieth centuries exemplify the differing views of courts in constructing a legal vision of church/state interaction. The first two cases, one decided by the Virginia Court of Appeals and the other decided by the Supreme Court of the United States, concern the impact of the American Revolution on the ownership of land used exclusively by and for the Church of England before the Revolution. The differing opinions tell us something about both the meaning of the Revolution, and about the role of religion (or, more particularly, the Church of England) in Virginia during the late eighteenth and early nineteenth centuries. As we shall see, the Virginia legislature desired both the disestablishment of the Church of England, and some continued public role for religion in the maintenance of the state. The Virginia Court of Appeals held by an equally divided court that the legislature's disestablishment of the Church of England caused ownership of the land to revert to the state. A decade later, the Supreme Court, in an opinion written by Joseph Story, held that the Revolution, and the consequent disestablishment of the church, did not affect the ownership of the property.

The two cases from the mid-twentieth century determined whether states were constitutionally permitted to expel public school students for refusing, for religious reasons, to salute the American flag. In the first case, *Minersville Sch. Dist. v. Gobitis,* 310 U.S. 586 (1940), the Court held that the Fourteenth Amendment's Due Process Clause, which incorporated the First Amendment to the Constitution, did not forbid the public school authorities in Pennsylvania from expelling students for refusing to salute the flag for religious reasons. Three years later, in 1943, the Court reversed itself, declaring that such laws violated the First Amendment. *West Virginia State Bd. of Educ. v. Barnette,* 319 U.S. 624 (1943).

One purpose of these cases is to show that a picture of the "right" relationship between church and state (or among law, religion, and government) historically has been a Sisyphean task. A second purpose of these cases is to offer an introduction to the different ways in which courts have expressed their views of the "role" of religion in American public life. A final purpose of these cases is their value as symbols of the continuing difficulty of American courts in evaluating this area of law.

Turpin v. Locket

6 Call 113 (Va. 1804)

[Before 1776, the established religion of the colony of Virginia was the Church of England, formed when King Henry VIII broke from the Roman Catholic Church after the church refused to annul his first marriage. The Church of England in Virginia was the beneficiary of grants of land in the colony, called glebes, which were used by the Church to build houses of worship. On June 12, 1776, the Virginia Constitutional Convention passed Article 16 of the Virginia Declaration of Rights, which stated in part that "all men are equally entitled to the free exercise of religion." Later that year, the Virginia General Assembly passed an act disestablishing the Church of England. In the same act, however, it "saved and reserved to the use of the church by law established the several tracts of glebe land already purchased...." In 1784, the Protestant episcopal church, the "successor" to the Church of England, was incorporated pursuant to a legislative act. Two years later, the act incorporating the Protestant episcopal church was repealed, "Saving to all religious societies the property to them respectively belonging...." That same year, the Virginia legislature passed Thomas Jefferson's Bill Establishing Religious Freedom (excerpted in Chapter Two). In 1788, the Virginia General Assembly passed an act giving to successors of the vestries of the Church of England the power to manage the property of the Protestant episcopal church. In 1798, all of these acts were legislatively repealed. In so doing, the General Assembly stated that only the 1786 Act for Establishing Religious Freedom remained in effect. Relying on this 1798 Act, the Virginia legislature passed an act in January 1802 permitting overseers of the poor to sell any vacant glebe lands. Shortly after the passage of this final act, Locket and other overseers of the poor offered for sale a vacant glebe claimed by the Manchester Protestant episcopal church. Turpin was a vestryman of the Manchester Protestant episcopal church. Turpin filed a bill to enjoin the sale of the glebe. Turpin's argument to the chancery court was that, except for its name, the Protestant episcopal church was the same as the Church of England, and that a right to own property, once vested in the Protestant episcopal church, could not be divested by subsequent legislation. Locket argued that the Protestant episcopal church and the Church of England were different religious bodies, because the former was a voluntary body and the latter was established by law. Locket argued that because the glebes were purchased for the benefit of an established church, the end of that establishment caused the ownership of that property to revert back to the community. The court of chancery dismissed the bill, and Turpin and the other plaintiffs appealed to the Virginia Court of Appeals, the highest court of the Commonwealth.]

TUCKER, Judge. On the present occasion, we are solemnly called on...to decide, whether [the 1802 Act impermissibly deprives the Protestant episcopal church of land purchased for it while Virginia was a colony.]

We must therefore enquire,

1. [Judge Tucker initially concluded that, from 1696 until the time of the Revolution, titles to the glebe lands were held by church vestries, an entity acknowledged in law as capable of holding title.]

2. I shall now proceed to enquire, Whether the legal title to the glebes, thus supposed to be vested in the vestries of the several parishes respectively, still subsists and remains in those bodies?

[Judge Tucker discusses the various acts noted above.]

The act of 1798, ch. 9, expressly repeals all those acts.

The act of 1784, ch. 88, for incorporating the Protestant episcopal church, in the preamble sets forth, "That the clergy of the Protestant episcopal church, by their petition presented, have requested that their church may be incorporated." This petition may, therefore, be considered as a surrender on the part of the clergy (if not the vestries) of their former rights and privileges: Which, says judge Blackstone, is a kind of suicide, and one of the modes by which a corporation may be dissolved. And the act made in consequence of that petition, seems to amount to an acceptance of that surrender, by the general assembly, on the one hand, and the declaration that the former vestries should be dissolved on the Easter Monday following, and that all former laws concerning vestries, glebes and churches, should be repealed, seems to be a kind of parliamentary sanction given to that transaction, and amounts, I presume, to an absolute dissolution of those bodies, by a legislative act, which is another mode by which the ancient books agree that a corporation may be dissolved.

To this it may be objected, that a body politic may be incorporated by one name, and after by another name, and then they shall use their name according to their second incorporation; and, yet shall continue their possessions, and all other franchises and privileges, which they had before by the other name. So that in this case there was no dissolution of the body politic, in whom the legal estate in the glebes vested; but a mere alteration in the style and name of the body politic, with alteration as to some of its privileges, but none of those which relate to its capacity to hold lands for the use of the minister of the parish for the time being.

To this it may be answered, that under the former laws and constitution of the colony of Virginia, the parson, and the vestry were considered as part of the general body politic, or state; and not as a mere private incorporation, with capacity to hold lands, to a certain amount, for a special purpose: The former being a branch of the hierarchy of the monarchical constitution, and engrafted upon the government itself; whereas, the latter were, at most, an eleemosinary body, for private, although in some measure, spiritual purposes: and that the acceptance of such a private foundation, in lieu of their former privileges, immediately connected with the government itself, must be construed as a total surrender of their former state; and an acceptance of an entire new, and essentially different, constitution of incorporation.

And if this should be the true light in which the act for incorporating the Protestant episcopal church ought to be viewed, it will probably lead us to get clear of some of those embarrassments in which this complicated and intricate question is involved.

Cogent as this moral principle is in my mind, and fortified as it is by many instances which occur in the acts of the legislature, which I have just referred to, since I cannot discover any principle of law to support it, I am driven to seek for the law of the case elsewhere; and consequently to say, that, if the property in them could not, upon the dissolution of the body politic in whom the legal title was vested, revert to the parish, that is to say, to the parishioners, at large, it must have vested in the commonwealth: for no other owner can I find for it, under the existing laws of the land.

Taking it, therefore, that the mere act of rejecting the king and the ancient constitution of the colony, and adopting one totally different therefrom, did operate an immediate dissolution of every part of the body politic connected with, and dependent upon, the ancient constitution, or form of government; or taking it, that these subordinate parts of the body politic might continue to enjoy such parts of their ancient rights (not incompatible with the new constitution) as the legislature, in their wisdom, should permit, I am constrained to say, 1. That the ancient vestries were dissolved, either by the change of government, or by the act for incorporating the Protestant episcopal church: and that the new bodies corporate, consisting of the minister and vestry (or in case of a vacancy in the ministry), in the vestry alone, were private incorporations, essentially differing from the former, and owing their existence and their rights, solely to that act of the legislature: And, 2. That the property in those glebes, which were either in fact, or in contemplation of law, given to the ancient parishes by the crown; or which were purchased by the ancient vestries for the use of their respective churches did, in fact, (but whether constitutionally, or not, will be examined hereafter,) pass and vest in the new incorporations, authorized by the act for incorporating the Protestant episcopal church, wherever the inhabitants of the parishes did proceed to elect, and did elect vestries, pursuant to that act. 3. That upon the repeal of that act, in 1786, the property in the glebes was not thereby taken away, from those new incorporations, but that they might continue to hold the property as trustees, under the saving clause, until other trustees should be elected....

3. Our next enquiry, therefore, must be, Whether the property thus vested in the ministers and vestries, or the trustees thereafter authorized by the act of 1788, ch. 47, to be appointed, for the use of the Protestant episcopal church, still remains in them? or, in other words, Whether these newly incorporated bodies are still of capacity to hold the glebes for the use of that church, or have been, and are dissolved?

Now, the act of 1798, ch. 9, expressly repeals [all of these acts] and declares the same to be void, and of none effect.

Consequently, unless that act be contrary to the constitution of this commonwealth, these newly incorporated bodies are likewise dissolved.

This is an unpleasant, and in some respects an arduous, task; for surely no task can be more arduous than that of reconciling the conflicting, and even opposite, acts of the legislative body. If they cannot be reconciled to each other, it will be our duty to pronounce those to be valid, which are most easily reconcilable to the dictates of moral justice, and the principles of the constitution of this commonwealth.

Two principles, neither of which can, or ought to be, shaken by this court, or by any authority in that state, are to be found in our bill of rights. art. 1 and 16.

First, that the right of private property; and,

Secondly, that the right of conscience in matters of religion, shall be held sacred and inviolate.

A third principle, scarcely inferior in point of importance, and not inferior in point of obligation is, That no man, or set of men, are entitled to exclusive or separate emoluments or privileges from this community, but in consideration of public services. Art. 4.

What are public services?

Such, in which the community have, or may be presumed to have, a common interest.

Can the dissenters from the Protestant episcopal church (infinitely more numerous than the adherents to that church) be presumed to have a common interest, with them, in the promulgation or religious tenets, of which they disapprove, and from which they avowedly dissent?

If this be the fact, of which I believe no doubt is entertained, are the members of the Protestant episcopal church entitled to receive from the community at large, exclusive, or separate emoluments, for teaching doctrines, from which a majority of the community dissent, as the rents and profits of the glebes must be considered as an annual stipend paid by the commonwealth to the ministers of the Protestant episcopal church?

If the legislature had thought proper to appropriate the glebes and churches purchased and built, at the expense of all the parishioners, in each parish, for the use of such minister, or teacher of religion as a majority of the parish could choose, without regard to sects or denominations of religion, whether Christian, jew, mahometan or other whatsoever, this article, I apprehend, would not have stood in the way of such a general appropriation. But where one religious society (inferior in numbers to several others, and perhaps to any other) receive exclusively a bounty from the state, such exclusive bounty, so long as it remains exclusive, must, I conceive, appear to be granted in opposition both to the letter and spirit of the article. And if it be, the grant is void.

This interpretation does not, I apprehend, in the least, interfere with, or violate the fundamental principle of our constitution, that private property shall be sacred and inviolable.

The glebes, as such, were never private property. They were purchased at the common expense of the whole parish, and (according to the prevailing maxim of the government at that time) for the common benefit of all the parishioners, without distinction.

The revolution put an entire period to the maxim, that "mankind may be benefited by the promulgation of religious doctrines, from which they wholly dissent."

From that moment, the promulgation of the religious doctrines of any religious sect ceased to be a common benefit to the community.

But the incumbents of the respective parishes had acquired legal rights, under the existing laws, which the legislature were too just to violate. A life, or lives in being, would not long retard the operation of any plan, which might be recommended by the change of constitution, and of principle, which had taken place. Besides, those incumbents, who, upon the faith of the existing constitution and laws, had qualified themselves for the function to which they were elected, and renounced all other pursuits on that account, had acquired a moral right to be continued in the enjoyment of their legal estates, thus acquired.

So far as any act of the legislature has operated for that purpose, it may be considered as pursuing the injunctions of moral justice, and of the first article of our bill of rights. Beyond that point, I conceive every such act to have been void.

If one act of the legislature be void, as repugnant to the constitution, a subsequent act, declaring such repugnant act to be void, and repealing it accordingly, cannot be contrary to the constitution in that respect.

The act of 1798, ch. 9, repealing the act for incorporating the Protestant episcopal church, and several others relating to the glebes, therefore, is not itself unconstitutional.

The consequence is, that the newly incorporated bodies, incorporated, authorized and continued by those acts respectively, have no longer any legal existence, being entirely dissolved.

It follows that the plaintiffs, as vestrymen, have not any legal title to the glebe.

I am therefore of opinion that the bill was properly dismissed, and that the decree ought to be affirmed.

ROANE, Judge.

I will consider the effect of the revolution, and the principles of the constitution, upon the subject in question: when I speak of the effect of the revolution, I know I stand upon an important ground. I know, also, the danger of different inferences being drawn, from this source, owing to the different media through which they pass. I know that some men have more fervor than others; more sensibility in the cause of equal rights. I know that, from this cause, the inferences to be drawn from this source, will, unavoidably, be tinged and diversified. But there are certain cardinal points, upon which all men must agree. It must, I presume, be admitted by all, that, that memorable event, established, in America, the reign of equal justice, delivered our dissenting brethren, from the tyranny exercised over them, and exempted the rights of conscience, from the power of the civil magistrate. If in aid of these great principles of the revolution, the expressions, or the clear principles of the constitution, are to be found, then indeed we have attained to the acme of human sanction. This desideratum appears to me to exist in the present case. Our bill of rights, on a large and liberal view, comes full up to the point of liberating dissenters from future contributions: and when we reflect, that an instrument of this kind, exists not in detail, and only declares, in general, the great principles of free government, it is supposed, that the 4th and 16th articles thereof are almost expressly in point: at least they give us great principles which are decisive of the present question. There is not a human being who can read those articles, and justify, as constitutional, future exactions from dissenters. This has been universally admitted, from the beginning, in relation to the salaries; but a difference is set up, in relation to the glebes. I confess, as I have already said, that I cannot see a difference. They stand upon the same reason, if not precisely upon the same ground; and it must be readily conceded, that the reason of an instrument of this kind, must emphatically apply. The claim of post revolutionary salary, by even a contemporary incumbent, is justly abandoned by the appellants' counsel: but the case embraced by the act of 1802, of a vacant glebe, is infinitely less strong. It does not invade the interest of an existing incumbent. It only intercepts the contingent and possible title, which might have accrued to some future minister as successor to the last incumbent. In this view, his remote, contingent, and possible claim, stands reprobated, as a source of title, by the uniform decisions of this court.

Much has been said, in this cause, of the identity of the Protestant episcopal church, in relation to our ante-revolutionary church. I am not disposed to cavil about names, or about trifles. I admit this identity in its fullest extent, in respect to the component members of the church, and its doctrines and discipline. But there is no identity of character between the two. That church, formerly paramount and triumphant, has now taken its just and equal station with other religious societies. Its quality, as a national church, in consideration of which, the grant of the glebes was made, no longer exists. That clergy then stood only in the character of an established clergy. As a national church, some semblance of justification may be found, for its endowment with public property. But even the enormities of those times, do not justify an appropriation of the property of the people, to the use of particular individuals or societies. There is no conceivable ground, which can justify such a conduct, in the government; and the want of such irresistibly determines the character of the grant. In opposition to such principles, it is at least incumbent on the appellants, to show the endowment to have been made to the clergy, in their particular character. But this cannot be done: the words and complexion of the grant itself, confronts that idea, and supports the general principle.

The only crime of these men, was, their worshiping God according to the dictates of their own consciences! There is not a gentleman old enough to know the fact, who has not seen ministers of the gospel of Christ, teaching their doctrines through the grated windows of prison! I mention these things, but to shew the character and tendencies of the hierarchical government; the utter annihilation which then existed, of every semblance of religious liberty!

The revolution, however, has brought down this powerful hierarchy to the standard of free and equal government: the cause of the grant has ceased; and it has become unlawful for the church or corporation to act up to the end for which it was established. In this view, of a reversion of the glebe lands, to the government, for the benefit of the people, any after disposition or continuation of them, by law, or by construction, to the use of a particular society, is, in fact, equally with the levies of salaries, a coercive contribution from the dissenters: it stands precisely on a common ground with such levy: it is, equally with it, in the teeth of the bill of rights.

We were exhorted by one of the appellants' counsel, at the former argument and the substance is repeated in the last, "to put deism to flight, and restore the altars of our forefathers." If there is a league, of deists or others, in the legislature or elsewhere, to overturn religion, or impair morality, it is to me a subject of the deepest regret. I can never cease to believe, that these are the firmest pillars of civil society, the surest basis of human happiness. For myself, I am now called to discharge a painful duty. That duty must not be obstructed, by any sympathies, or partialities of mine. While sitting in this seat, the stern maxims of judicial independence, scarcely permits me to recognize in the respectable society now before us, the revered patron of my early youth, the depository of my best wishes.

CARLINGTON, Judge, and LYONS, President.

We have no doubt as to the jurisdiction.

We are equally clear upon the merits. For it has been frequently decided by the court, that unconstitutional laws are void; and we think the statute, now under consideration, is of that class.

It is a mistake to suppose, that the church, here, was identified with that of the mother country, and had no capacity to hold lands.

For although the church of England was the prototype, it certainly was not the actual church of Virginia; which was founded by the local legislature; and its structure and capacities are to be sought for in the laws of the colony only.

The question then is, what effect the revolution had upon the property of the church?

It was contended by the counsel for the appellees, That, if the church had capacity to hold lands before the date of independence, that event destroyed it; and that, upon the dissolution, the glebes devolved upon the commonwealth. But revolutions are intended to preserve, not to take away rights: Nor was it ever pretended, that an alternation, in the form of a government, affected private property. Such a consequence would prevent all revolutions, as no set of men would ever unite in a measure productive of such fatal effects; and therefore we unhesitatingly pronounce, that the revolution did not produce that result.

2. That incorporated religious societies are contrary to the sixteenth article of the bill of rights.

Not that with respect to the sixteenth article of the bill of rights:

Because there is nothing in that article, which forbids the continuation of the establishment, or the incorporation of religious societies. For the whole relates to the rights of conscience, and the mutual charities which men owe each other.

Upon no sound construction, therefore, of the bill of rights, compared with the laws antecedent to the revolution, can the church be considered as dissolved by that event, or divested of its property, in consequence of it: and the uniform interpretation and practice of the country have been agreeable to this opinion.

[Judge Carlington then cites to actions in 1776 supporting the view that the glebes remained the property of the church.]

Upon the whole, we think, that the church had a right to the glebes, at the date of the revolution; that, that event had no effect upon the title; that nothing has happened since to divest it; that the act of 1802 is unconstitutional; and that the injunction ought to have been awarded. But, as the other judges are of a different opinion, the decree of the chancellor stands, and it is to be affirmed, as upon a division of the court.

Memorandum.—The above case had been argued at a former term; and, during the succeeding vacation, Mr. Pendleton, then president of the court, and who sat in the cause, prepared his opinion in writing, (which the reporter has seen,) that the glebes belonged to the Protestant episcopal church; and that the act of 1802, was unconstitutional. But the opinion was not delivered, as he died the night before it was to have been pronounced.

Notes

1. The opinions of Judges St. George Tucker and Spencer Roane, although quite different in tone, are premised on a strongly "voluntarist" notion of religious practice critical of the established church's suppression of religious liberty, as exemplified by Roane's statement, "The only crime of these men [religious dissenters], was, their worshiping God according to the dictates of their own consciences!" Is Roane's passionate opinion better explained as his effort to dismantle the last vestiges of the established church or of traces of English rule or as an interpretation of the law of property? Is Tucker's more "legalistic" argument more convincing? Tucker and Roane dismiss the argument that religion must be protected for the betterment of society. Tucker states, "The revolution put an entire period to the maxim, that 'mankind may be benefited by the promulgation of religious doctrines, from which they wholly dissent.'" This dismissal of the role of Christian religious practice (no matter the sect or doctrine taught) as benefitting society by inculcating general morality is challenged by Justice Joseph Story in *Terrett v. Taylor*, below.

2. The opinions in *Turpin* mention Article 16 of the Virginia Declaration of Rights, adopted by the Commonwealth in June 1776. Article 16 declares in part that "all men are equally entitled to the free exercise of religion, according to the dictates of conscience; and that it is the mutual duty of all to practice Christian forbearance, love and charity towards each other." Is Article 16 applicable to this case? A survey of the Virginia experience regarding liberty of conscience is found in Chapter Two.

3. The reporter Call's memorandum notes the death of Edmund Pendleton the night before he was to read his opinion holding the 1802 Act unconstitutional. Tucker took Pendleton's seat, although not the Presidency of the Court, after Pendleton's death. On the personal rivalry and sharp professional differences between Tucker and Roane in the Virginia Court of Appeals, see F. Thornton Miller, Juries and Judges Versus the Law: Virginia's Provincial Legal Perspective, 1783–1828 69–73 (1994).

4. *Selden v. Overseers of the Poor*, 11 Leigh 127 (Va. 1840), reaffirmed the decision of *Turpin v. Locket*. The case was decided below by Chancellor Henry St. George Tucker, son of St. George Tucker, in an opinion that discussed nearly all of the issues discussed in *Turpin*. 2 Henry St. George Tucker, Commentaries on the Laws of Virginia Appendix (2 vols. 1837) (Chancellor Tucker's decision was handed down in 1830).

5. What explanation is there for the mass of conflicting legislation pouring out of the Virginia legislature during the last two decades of the eighteenth century? Do its roots lie in religious differences? Class differences? Political differences? In 1800 and 1801, camp meetings in Kentucky, formerly a part of Virginia, resulted in a Protestant religious revival that has become known as the Second Great Awakening. This revival

was not a product of Episcopalian efforts, but was fostered by Presbyterian, Baptist, and Methodist evangelists, who roamed the rural "western" frontier in search of converts. Roane's "dissenters" included many Baptists, Methodists, and Presbyterians. In the late eighteeenth and early nineteenth centuries, religious differences among Protestants implicated class differences, which may suggest a reason why the legislature kept revisiting this issue.

6. Virginia's 1830 constitution, Art. III, § 11, barred its legislature from "pass[ing] any law requiring or authorizing any religious society." Francis Newton Thorpe, VII The Federal and State Constitutions 3824 (7 vols. 1909). That prohibition remains, which means that no religious organization may incorporate in Virginia.

Terrett v. Taylor

9 Cranch 43 (1815)

[In 1770, a tract of land was purchased in Fairfax County, Virginia, for the use of the Church of England in Virginia. After the American Revolution, when the district of Columbia was created from Maryland and Virginia, this land became part of the district of Columbia. Before the land was made part of the district of Columbia, both the 1784 Act incorporating the Protestant episcopal church and the 1786 Act repealing the 1784 Act were passed. Taylor and other vestrymen for the Episcopal Church of Alexandria wanted to sell the land and use the proceeds for the Protestant episcopal church. They sued Terrett, an overseer for the poor in Virginia, in equity, to enjoin Terrett from utilizing the Act of 1802 to sell the glebe and use the proceeds for the poor in Fairfax County, Virginia. The district of Columbia was separated from the state of Virginia before the passage of the 1802 Act. The lower court held for Taylor and the other vestrymen.]

February 17th. Absent.... JOHNSON, *J. and* TODD, *J.*

STORY, J. delivered the opinion of the Court as follows:

If the Plaintiffs have shown a sufficient title to the trust property in the present bill, we have no difficulty in holding that they are entitled to the equitable relief prayed for. And in our judgment it would make no difference whether the Episcopal church were a voluntary society, or clothed with corporate powers; for in equity, as to objects which the laws cannot but recognize as useful and meritorious, the same reason would exist for relief in the one case as in the other. Other considerations arising in this case, material to the title on which relief must be founded, render an enquiry into the character and powers of the Episcopal church, indispensable.

At a very early period the religious establishment of England seems to have been adopted in the colony of Virginia. [A]mong other things, the church was capable of receiving endowments of land, and that the minister of the parish was, during his incumbency, seized of the free-hold of its inheritable property, as emphatically *persona ecclesiae*, and capable as a sole corporation, of transmitting that inheritance to his successors.

[T]he property so acquired by the church remained unimpaired, notwithstanding the revolution; for the statute of 1776, *ch.* 2, completely confirmed and established the rights of the church to all of its lands and other property.

The stat. 1784, *ch.* 88, proceeded yet further. It expressly made the minister and vestry, and, in case of a vacancy, the vestry of each parish respectively, and their successors forever, a corporation by the name of the Protestant Episcopal church in the parish where they respectively resided, to have, hold, use and enjoy all the glebes, churches and chapels, burying grounds, books, plate and ornaments appropriated to the use of, and every other thing the property of the late Episcopal church, to the sole use and benefit of the corporation. The same statute also provided for the choice of new vestries, and repealed all former laws relating to vestries and church wardens, and to the support of the clergy, &c. and dissolved all former vestries; and gave the corporation extensive powers as to the purchasing, holding, aliening, repairing and regulating the church property. This statute was repealed by the statute of 1786, *ch.* 12, with a proviso saving to all religious societies the property to them respectively belonging, and authorizing them to appoint, from time to time, according to the rules of their sect, trustees who should be capable of managing and applying such property to the religious use of such societies; and the statute of 1788, *ch.* 47, declared that the trustees appointed in the several parishes to take care of and manage the property of the Protestant Episcopal church, and their successors, should, to all intents and purposes, be considered as the successors to the former vestries, with the same powers of holding and managing all the property formerly vested in them. All these statutes, from that of 1776, *ch.* 2, to that of 1788, *ch.* 47, and several others, were repealed by the statute of 1798, *ch.* 9, as inconsistent with the principles of the constitution and of religious freedom; and by the statute of 1801 [sic], *ch.* 5, (which was passed after the district of Columbia was finally separated from the states of Maryland and Virginia) the legislature asserted their right to all the property of the Episcopal churches in the respective parishes of the state; and, among other things, directed and authorized the overseers of the poor, and their successors in each parish wherein any glebe land was vacant or should become so, to sell the same and appropriate the proceeds to the use of the poor of the parish.

It is under this last statute that the bill charges the Defendants (who are overseers of the poor of the parish of Fairfax) with claiming a title to dispose of the land in controversy.

This summary view of so much of the Virginia statutes as bears directly on the subject in controversy, presents not only a most extraordinary diversity of opinion in the legislature as to the nature and propriety of aid in the temporal concerns of religion, but the more embarrassing considerations of the constitutional character and efficacy of those laws touching the rights and property of the Episcopal church.

It is conceded on all sides that, at the revolution, the Episcopal church no longer retained its character as an exclusive religious establishment. And there can be no doubt that it was competent to the people and to the legislature to deprive it of its superiority over other religious sects, and to withhold from it any support by public taxation. But, although it may be true that "religion can be directed only by reason and conviction, not by force or violence," and that "all men are equally entitled to the free exercise of religion according to the dictates of conscience," as the bill of rights of Virginia declares, yet it is difficult to perceive how it follows as a consequence that the legislature may not enact laws more effectually to enable all sects to accomplish the great objects of religion by giving them corporate rights for the management of their property, and the regulation of their temporal as well as spiritual concerns. Consistent with the constitution of Virginia the legislature could not create or continue a religious establishment which should have exclusive rights and prerogatives, or compel the citizens to worship under a stipulated form or discipline, or to pay taxes to those whose creed they could not conscientiously believe. But the free exercise of religion cannot be justly deemed to be restrained by aiding with equal attention the votaries of every sect to perform their own religious duties, or by establishing funds for the support of ministers, for public charities, for the endowment of churches, or for the sepulture of the dead. And that these purposes could be better secured and cherished by corporate powers, cannot be doubted by any person who has attended to the difficulties which surround all voluntary association. While, therefore, the legislature might exempt the citizens from a compulsive attendance and payment of taxes in support of any particular sect, it is not perceived that either public or constitutional principles required the abolition of all religious corporations.

Be, however, the general authority of the legislature as to the subject of religion, as it may, it will require other arguments to establish the position that, at the revolution, all the public property acquired by the Episcopal churches, under the sanction of the laws, became the property of the state. Had the property thus acquired been originally granted by the state or the king, there might have been some color (and it would have been but a color) for such an extraordinary pretension. But the property was, in fact and in law, generally purchased by the parishioners, or acquired by the benefactions of pious donors. The title thereto was indefeasibly vested in the churches, or rather in their legal agents. It was not in the power of the crown to seize or assume it; nor of the parliament itself to destroy the grants, unless by the exercise of a power the most arbitrary, oppressive and unjust, and endured only because it could not be resisted. It was not forfeited; for the churches had committed no offence. The dissolution of the regal government no more destroyed the right to possess or enjoy this property than it did the right of any other corporation or individual to him or its own property. The dissolution of the form of government did not involve in it a dissolution of civil rights, or an abolition of the common law under which the inheritances of every man in the state were held. The state itself succeeded only to the rights of the crown; and, we may add, with many a flower of prerogative struck from its hands. It has been asserted as a principle of the common law that the division of an empire creates no forfeiture of previously vested rights of property. And this principle is equally consonant with the common sense of mankind and the maxims of eternal justice. Nor are we able to perceive any sound reason why the church lands escheated or devolved upon the state by the revolution any more than the property of any other corporation created by the royal bounty or established by the legislature. The revolution might justly take away the public patronage, the exclusive cure of souls, and the compulsive taxation for the support of the church. Beyond these we are not prepared to admit the justice or the authority of the exercise of legislation.

It is not, however, necessary to rest this cause upon the general doctrines already asserted; for, admitting that, by the revolution, the church lands devolved on the state, the statute of 1776, *ch.* 2, operated as a new grant and confirmation thereof to the use of the church.

If the legislature possessed the authority to make such a grant and confirmation, it is very clear to our minds that it vested an indefeasible and irrevocable title.

[W]e think ourselves standing upon the principles of natural justice, upon the fundamental laws of every free government, upon the spirit and the letter of the constitution of the United States, and upon the decisions of most respectable judicial tribunals, in resisting [the state's claim to take the property of a private corporation]. The statutes of 1798 *ch.* 9, and of 1801 [sic], *ch.* 5, are not, therefore in our judgment, operative so far as to divest the Episcopal church of the property acquired, previous to the revolution, by purchase or by donation.

On the whole the majority of the Court are of opinion that the land in controversy belongs to the Episcopal church of Alexandria, and has not been divested by the revolution, or any act of the legislature passed since that period.

The decree of the Circuit Court is to be reformed so as to conform to this opinion.

Notes

1. The Court's opinion in *Terrett* was rendered at a time when relations between the Supreme Court and the Virginia Court of Appeals were, to say the least, strained. Justice Story's *Terrett* opinion was given two years after his opinion in *Fairfax's Devisee v. Hunter's Lessee*, 7 Cranch 603 (1813), in which the Court held constitutionally impermissible the effort by the Commonwealth of Virginia to confiscate land from English subjects after the Revolution. The Court remanded the case to the Virginia Court of Appeals and ordered it to enter judgment for the English subjects, whose successors in interest included Chief Justice John Marshall. The Virginia Court of Appeals refused to do so, claiming that §25 of the Judiciary Act of 1789, which provided the Supreme Court with the jurisdiction to decide cases appealed from state courts, was unconstitutional. Virginia Court of Appeals Judge Spencer Roane, one of the two judges who held the 1802 Act allowing overseers of the poor to sell vacant glebes constitutional in *Turpin*, led the effort to claim the equality of the sovereign courts of Virginia and the United States. In 1816, in *Martin v. Hunter's Lessee*, 14 U.S. (1 Wheat.) 304 (1816), Justice Story held §25 constitutional. Marshall did not participate in either case because of his interest in the litigation. However, Marshall joined Story's opinion in *Terrett v. Taylor*. Although there was no dissenting opinion in *Terrett v. Taylor*, Story makes the unusual statement at the conclusion of his opinion that a majority of the Court agrees with his conclusion. Because two Justices were absent and presumably did not vote, this suggests that Story may have had just a bare majority supporting his opinion.

2. As is discussed in Chapter Three, Justice Story was a devout Unitarian from Massachusetts, who believed strongly in the necessity of religion to maintain a civilized public order. At the time he wrote the opinion in *Terrett*, Massachusetts was one of only three remaining states to maintain some form of an established church. Connecticut and New Hampshire continued their religious assessments until 1818 and 1819, respectively. *See* Chapter Two.

Minersville School District v. Gobitis

310 U.S. 586 (1940)

[In this 8–1 opinion, Justice McReynolds concurring in the result, the Court upheld the dismissal of Lillian and William Gobitis from public school for refusing, on religious grounds, to recite the pledge of allegiance to the American flag. Justice Harlan Fiske Stone dissented, insisting that "by this law the state seeks to coerce these children to express a sentiment which violates their deepest religious convictions."]

Mr. Justice FRANKFURTER delivered the opinion of the court.

A grave responsibility confronts this Court whenever in course of litigation it must reconcile the conflicting claims of liberty and authority. But when the liberty invoked is liberty of conscience, and the authority is authority to safeguard the nation's fellowship, judicial conscience is put to its severest test. Of such nature is the present controversy.

Lillian Gobitis, aged, twelve, and her brother William, aged ten, were expelled from the public schools of Minersville, Pennsylvania, for refusing to salute the national flag as part of a daily school exercise. The local Board of Education required both teachers and pupils to participate in this ceremony. The ceremony is a familiar one. The right hand is placed on the breast and the following pledge recited in unison: "I pledge allegiance to my flag, and to the Republic for which it stands; one nation indivisible, with liberty and justice for all." While the words are spoken, teachers and pupils extend their right hands in salute to the flag. The Gobitis family are affiliated with "Jehovah's Witnesses," for whom the Bible as the Word of God is the supreme authority. The children had been brought up conscientiously to believe that such a gesture of respect for the flag was forbidden by command of Scripture.

The Gobitis children were of an age for which Pennsylvania makes school attendance compulsory. Thus they were denied a free education, and their parents had to put them into private schools. To be relieved of the financial burden thereby entailed, their father, on behalf of the children and in his own behalf, brought this suit. He sought to enjoin the authorities from continuing to exact participation in the flag-statute ceremony as a condition of his children's attendance at the Minersville school. After trial of the issues, Judge Maris gave relief... [and]... his decree was affirmed by the Circuit Court of Appeals. Since this decision ran counter to several *per curiam* dispositions of this Court, we granted certiorari to give the matter full reconsideration.

We must decide whether the requirement of participation in such a ceremony, exacted from a child who refuses upon sincere religious grounds, infringes without the process of law the liberty granted by the Fourteenth Amendment.

Centuries of strife over the erection of particular dogmas as exclusive or all-comprehending faiths led to the inclusion of a guarantee for religious freedom in the Bill of Rights. The First Amendment, and the Fourteenth through its absorption of the First, sought to guard against repetition of those bitter religious struggles by prohibiting the establishment of a state religion and by securing to every sect the free exercise of its faith. So pervasive is the acceptance of this precious right that its scope is brought into question, as here, only when the conscience of individuals collides with the felt necessities of society.

Certainly the affirmative pursuit of one's convictions about the ultimate mystery of the universe and man's relation to it is placed beyond the reach of law. Government may not interfere with organized or individual expression of belief or disbelief. Propagation of belief—or even of disbelief—in the supernatural is protected, whether in church or chapel, mosque or synagogue, tabernacle or meeting-house. Likewise the Constitution assures generous immunity to the individual from imposition of penalties for offending, in the course of his own religious activities, the religious views of others, be they a minority or those who are dominant in government.

But the manifold character of man's relations may bring his conception of religious duty into conflict with the secular interests of his fellow-men. When does the constitutional guarantee control exemption from doing what society thinks necessary for the promotion of some great common end, or from a penalty for conduct which appears dangerous to the general good? To state the problem is to recall the truth that no single principle can answer all of life's complexities. The right to freedom of religious belief, however dissident and however obnoxious to the cherished beliefs of others—even a majority—is itself the denial of an absolute. But to affirm that the freedom to follow conscience has itself no limits in the life of a society would deny that very plurality of principles which, as a matter of history, underlies protection of religious toleration.

Our present task, then, as so often the case with courts, is to reconcile two rights in order to prevent either from destroying the other. But, because in safe-guarding conscience we are dealing with interests so subtle and so dear, every possible leeway should be given to the claims of religious faith.

In the judicial enforcement of religious freedom we are concerned with a historic concept. The religious liberty which the Constitution protects has never excluded legislation of general scope not directed against doctrinal loyalties of particular sects. Judicial nullification of legislation cannot be justified by attributing to the framers of the Bill of Rights views for which there is no historic warrant. Conscientious scruples have not, in the course of the long struggle for religious toleration, relieved the individual from obedience to a general law not aimed at the promotion or restriction of religious beliefs. The mere possession of religious convictions which contradict the relevant concerns of a political society does not relieve the citizen from the discharge of political responsibilities. The necessity for this adjustment has again and again been recognized. In a number of situations the exertion of political authority has been sustained, while basic considerations of religious freedom have been left inviolate. *Reynolds v. United States*, 98 U.S. 145 (1879) [criminally punishing bigamy]; *Davis v. Beason*, 133 U.S. 333 (1890) [same]; *Selective Draft Law Cases*, 245 U.S. 366 (1918) [conscientious objector cases]; *Hamilton v. Regents*, 293 U.S. 245 (1934) [pacifist refused to perform military duty and was denied diploma]. In all these cases the general laws in question, upheld in their application to those who refused obedience from religious conviction, were manifestations of specific powers of government deemed by the legislature essential to secure and maintain the orderly, tranquil, and free society without which religious toleration itself is unattainable. Nor does the freedom of speech assured by Due Process move in a more absolute circle of immunity than that enjoyed by religious freedom. Even if it were assumed that freedom of speech goes beyond the historic concept of full opportunity to utter and to disseminate views, however heretical or offensive to dominant opinion, and includes freedom from conveying what may be deemed an implied but rejected affirmation, the question remains whether school children, like the Gobitis children, must be excused from conduct required of all the other children in the promotion of national cohesion. We are dealing with an interest inferior to none in the hierarchy of legal values. National unity is the basis of national security. To deny the legislature the right to select appropriate means for its attainment presents a totally different order of problem from that of the property of subordinating the possible ugliness of littered streets to the free expression of opinion through distribution of handbills.

Situations like the present are phases of profoundest problem confronting a democracy—the problem which Lincoln cast in memorable dilemma. "Must a government of necessity be too *strong* for the liberties of its people, or too *weak* to maintain its own existence?" No mere textual reading or logical talisman can solve the dilemma. And when the issue demands judicial determination, it is not the personal notion of judges of what wise adjustment requires which must prevail.

Unlike the instances we have cited, the case before us is not concerned with an exertion of legislative power for the promotion of some specific need or interest of secular society—the protection of the family, the promotion of health, the common defense, the raising of public revenues to defray the cost of government. But all these specific activities of government presuppose the existence of an organized political society. The ultimate foundation of a free society is the binding tie of cohesive sentiment. Such sentiment is fostered by all those agencies of the mind and spirit which may serve to gather up the traditions of a people, transmit them from generation to generation, and thereby create that continuity of a treasured common life which constitutes a civilization. "We live by symbols." The flag is the symbol of our national unity, transcending all internal differences, however large, within the framework of the Constitution.

The case before us must be viewed as though the legislature of Pennsylvania had itself formally directed to the flag-salute for the children of Minersville; had made no exemption for children whose parents were possessed of conscientious scruples like those of the Gobitis family; and had indicated its belief in the desirable ends to be secured by having its public school children share a common experience at those periods of development when their minds are supposedly receptive to its assimilation, by an exercise appropriate in time and place and setting and one designed to evoke in them appreciation of the nation's hopes and dreams, its sufferings and sacrifices. The precise issue, then, for us to decide is whether the legislatures of the various states and the authorities in a thousand counties and school districts of this country are barred from determining the appropriateness of various means to evoke that unifying sentiment without which there can ultimately be no liberties, civil or religious. To stigmatize legislative judgment in providing for this universal gesture of respect for the symbol of our national life in the setting of the common school as a lawless inroad on that freedom of conscience which the Constitution protects, would amount to no less than the pronouncement of pedagogical and psychological dogma in a field where courts possess no marked and certainly no controlling competence. The influences which help toward a common feeling for the common country are manifold. Some may seem harsh and others no doubt are foolish. Surely, however, the end is legitimate. And the effective means for its attainment are still so uncertain and unauthenticated by science as to preclude us from putting the widely prevalent belief in flag-saluting beyond the pale of legislative power. It mocks reason and denies our whole history to find in the allowance of a requirement to salute our flag on fitting occasions the seeds of sanction for obeisance to a leader.

The wisdom of training children in patriotic impulses by those compulsions which necessarily pervade so much of the educational process is not for our independent judgment. Even were we convinced of the folly of such a measure, such belief would be no proof of its unconstitutionality. For ourselves, we might be tempted to say that the deepest patriotism is best engendered by giving unfettered scope to the most crotchety beliefs. Perhaps it is best, even from the standpoint of those interests which ordinances like the one under review seek to promote, to give to the least popular sect leave from conformities like those here in issue. But the courtroom is not the arena for debating issues of educational policy. It is not our province to choose among competing considerations in the subtle process of securing effective loyalty to the traditional ideals of democracy, while respecting at the same time individual idiosyncracies among a people so diversified in racial origins and religious allegiances. So to hold would in effect make us the school board for the country. That authority has not been given to this Court, nor should we assume it.

We are dealing here with the formative period in the development of citizenship. Great diversity of psychological and ethical opinion exists among us concerning the best way to train children for their place in society. Because of these differences and because of reluctance to permit a single, iron-cast system of education to be imposed upon a nation compounded of so many strains, we have held that, even though public education is one of our most cherished democratic institutions, the Bill of Rights bars a state from compelling all children to attend the public schools. But it is a very different thing for this Court to exercise censorship over the conviction of legislatures that a particular program or exercise will best promote in the minds of children who attend the common schools an attachment to the institutions of their country.

What the school authorities are really asserting is the right to awaken in the child's mind considerations as to the significance of the flag contrary to those implanted by the parent. In such an attempt the state is normally at a disadvantage in competing with the parent's authority, so long—and this is the vital aspect of religious toleration—as parents are unmolested of their right to counteract by their own persuasiveness the wisdom and rightness of those loyalties which the state's educational system is seeking to promote. Except where the transgression of constitutional liberty is too plain for argument, personal freedom is best maintained—so long as the remedial channels of the democratic process remain open and unobstructed—when it is ingrained in a people's habits and not enforced against popular policy by the coercion of adjudicated law. That the flag-salute is an allowable portion of a school program for those who do not invoke conscientious scruples is surely not debatable. But for us to insist that, though the ceremony may be required, exceptional immunity must be given to dissidents, is to maintain that there is no basis for a legislative judgment that such an exemption might introduce elements of difficulty into the school discipline, might cast doubts in the minds of the other children which would themselves weaken the effect of the exercise.

The preciousness of the family relation, the authority and independence which give dignity to parenthood, indeed the enjoyment of all freedom, presuppose the kind of ordered society which is summarized by our flag. A society which is dedicated to the preservation of these ultimate values of civilization may in self-protection utilize the educational process of inculcating those almost unconscious feelings which bind men together in a comprehending loyalty, whatever may be their lesser differences and difficulties. That is to say, the process may be utilized so long as men's right to believe as they please, to win others to their way of belief, and their right to assemble in their chosen places of worship for the devotional ceremonies of their faith, are fully respected.

Judicial review, itself is a limitation on popular government, is a fundamental part of our constitutional scheme. But to the legislature no less than to courts is committed the guardianship of deeply-cherished liberties. Where all the effective means of inducing political changes are left free from interference, education in the abandonment of foolish legislation is itself a training in liberty. To fight out the wise use of legislative authority in the forum of public opinion and before legislative assemblies rather than to transfer such a contest to the judicial arena, serves to vindicate the self-confidence of a free people.

Reversed.

Notes

1. The Court decided *Gobitis* on June 3, 1940. War was raging in Europe and Asia, but the United States had not yet entered World War II. At the Court Frankfurter's opinion in *Gobitis* was referred to as "'Felix's Fall-of-France Opinion.'" John P. Frank, *Book Review*, 32 J. Legal Educ. 432, 442 (1982). Justice Frankfurter was born in Vienna, and emigrated with his parents to New York in 1896, when he was twelve. For the remainder of his life, Justice Frankfurter would, in an extraordinary number of ways, including his support of civil liberties, prove his undivided loyalty to his adopted homeland. Justice Frankfurter was also the third Jewish Justice on the Supreme Court, an appellation with which he likely would have disagreed. (In his reminiscences Frankfurter stated that "I was not a Jewish professor at the Harvard Law School, but I was a

Harvard Law School professor who happened to be a Jew." Harlan Phillips, FELIX FRANKFURTER REMINISCES 37 (1960).) He was nominated to replace the late Justice Benjamin N. Cardozo. Shortly after Frankfurter took his seat on the Court, his mentor and the first Jewish Justice, Louis D. Brandeis, retired, leaving Frankfurter as the only Jewish Justice for the remainder of his years on the Court. (Frankfurter retired in 1962.) A fascinating study tying Frankfurter's personality and beliefs with his opinions in these paired cases is Richard J. Danzig, *Justice Frankfurter's Opinions in the Flag Salute Cases: Blending Logic and Psychologic in Constitutional Decisionmaking*, 36 Stan. L. Rev. 675 (1984). Frankfurter had been a member of the Court for just under seventeen months when the *Gobitis* decision was published, and it was his first major opinion on civil liberties. A number of Frankfurter's old friends, including Harvard Law School Professor Zechariah Chafee, Jr. and lawyers Grenville Clark and Monte Lemann, joined an *amicus curiae* brief urging the Court affirm the Court of Appeals and hold the law unconstitutional.

2. Frankfurter's opinion begins with a cherished defense of the primacy of religious liberty: "[w]e are dealing with interests so subtle and so dear, every possible leeway should be given to the claims of religious faith." But this feint is quickly uncovered: "Conscientious scruples have not, in the course of the long struggle for religious toleration, relieved the individual from obedience to a general law not aimed at the promotion or restriction of religious beliefs." When Gobitis was decided, the Court's religion Clause jurisprudence was in its infancy. Since 1940, members of the Court have regularly disagreed about the type of judicial scrutiny that should be given general laws "not aimed at" restricting religious beliefs. Since 1990, a majority of the Court has agreed with Frankfurter, declaring that neutral and generally applicable laws are subject to rational basis scrutiny and not strict scrutiny. *Employment Div. v. Smith*, 494 U.S. 972 (1990), excerpted in Chapter Five. Frankfurter also states, "Propagation of belief—or even of disbelief—in the supernatural is protected, whether in church or chapel, mosque or synagogue, tabernacle or meeting-house." As you have already seen in § A of this Chapter, the decision to equate religious belief with disbelief raises the level of generality of the free exercise of religion to something like liberty of (religious or non-religious) conscience. When you read the historical materials in the next several chapters, assess whether Frankfurter's decision to raise the level of generality is true to the intent of the framers of the First Amendment. Additionally, Justice Frankfurter repeatedly speaks of "religious toleration" rather than religious liberty. Does this suggest that the Government merely "tolerates" religion, rather than respects it as a "fundamental right" enjoyed by Americans? You will see in Chapter Two that the initial proposal to protect liberty of religious conscience in the 1776 Virginia constitution was phrased by Gorge Mason as declaring "that all men should enjoy the fullest toleration in the exercise of religion." James Madison objected to the language of toleration. For Madison, toleration speaks of condescension, of some institution in a superior position permitting an inferior to engage in a misguided practice or activity. On his second attempt, Madison obtained consent to edit Article 16 of the Virginia Declaration of Rights to declare that "all men are equally entitled to the free exercise of religion." To be "equally entitled" admits of no superior concerning religion. Why would Frankfurter, who was extremely well versed in American history, use the language of "toleration" in this case? Finally, Justice Frankfurter also notes that, "What the school authorities are really asserting is the right to awaken in the child's mind considerations as to the significance of the flag contrary to those implanted by the parent." Shouldn't this acknowledgment that the state is attempting to create conflict between children and parents lead Justice Frankfurter to a

different conclusion? Justice Frankfurter was a proud product of public schools, and a devout believer in the "democratic faith" inculcated in students at those schools. An important purpose of the public school at this time was to assimilate children of different faiths and cultures into the American melting pot, a purpose of which Frankfurter approved. Does that explain his apparent lack of concern about the asserted "right" of the school authorities to espouse values contradictory to those values embraced by the parents of the school children? Based on his reading of history, his legal education and his experience as a lawyer and professor, Justice Frankfurter was also passionate believer in judicial restraint. Does that passion for judicial restraint make *Gobitis* one of those hard cases that cannot otherwise be decided in a principled fashion?

3. Justice James McReynolds concurred in the result without writing an opinion. One of the notorious Four Horsemen whose opposition to the New Deal eventually led to the constitutional revolution of 1937, McReynolds had fifteen years earlier written the opinion of the Court forbidding the state of Oregon from requiring all children under the age of sixteen to attend public schools. This case, *Pierce v. Society of Sisters*, 268 U.S. 510 (1925), excerpted in Chapter Six, recognized a parental right to educate their children in religious schools. Shortly after *Pierce* was decided, Frankfurter wrote an unsigned editorial in the *New Republic* criticizing the Court for using its power to decide the case. *Can the Supreme Court Guarantee Toleration?*, New Republic, June 17, 1925, at 85. He also incisively noted the decision assumed the state enjoyed the power to require some studies "essential to good government." *Id.* at 87. Frankfurter's opinion in *Gobitis* distinguished *Pierce*, and this may be the reason McReynolds merely concurred in the result. McReynolds was also, however, a notorious anti-Semite, and his unwillingness to join the opinion may rest on this aspect of his character.

West Virginia State Board of Education v. Barnette

319 U.S. 624 (1943)

Mr. Justice JACKSON delivered the opinion of the court.

Following the [*Gobitis*] decision, the West Virginia legislature amended its statutes to require all schools therein to conduct courses of instruction in history, civics, and in the Constitution of the United States and of the State "for the purpose of teaching, fostering and perpetuating the ideals, principles and spirit of Amercanism, and increasing the knowledge of the organization and machinery of the government."

The Board of Education on January 9, 1942, adopted a resolution containing recitals taken largely from the Court's *Gobitis* opinion and ordering that the salute of the Flag become "a regular part of the program of activities in the public schools," that all teachers and pupils "shall be required to participate in the salute honoring the Nation represented by the Flag; provided, however, that refusal to salute the Flag be regarded as an Act of insubordination, and shall be dealt with accordingly."

The resolution originally required the "commonly accepted salute to the Flag" which it defined. Objections to the salute as "being too much like Hitler's" were raised by the Parent and Teacher's Association, the Boy and Girl Scouts, the Red Cross, and the federation of Women's Clubs. Some modification appears to have been made in deference to these objections, but no concession was made to Jehovah's Witnesses. What is now required is the "stiff-arm" salute, the saluter to keep the right hand raised with palm turned up while the following is repeated: "I pledge allegiance to the Flag of the United States of America and to the Republic for which it stands; one Nation, indivisible, with liberty and justice for all."

Failure to conform is "insubordination" dealt with by expulsion. Readmission is denied by statute until compliance. Meanwhile, the expelled child is "unlawfully absent" and may be proceeded against as a delinquent. His parents or guardians are liable to prosecution and if convicted are subject to fine not exceeding $50 and jail term not exceeding thirty days.

[The Barnettes] brought suit in the United States District Court for themselves and others similarly situated asking its injunction to restrain enforcement of these laws and regulations against Jehovah's Witnesses. The Witnesses are an unincorporated body teaching that the obligation imposed by law of God is superior to that of laws enacted by temporal government. Their religious beliefs include a literal version of Exodus, Chapter 20, verses 4 and 5, which says: "Thou shalt not make unto thee any graven image, or any likeness of anything that is in heaven above, or that is in the earth beneath, or that is in the water under the earth; thou shalt not bow down thyself to them nor serve them." They consider that the flag is an "image" within this command. For this reason they refuse to salute it.

Children of this faith have been expelled from school and are threatened with exclusion for no other cause. Officials threaten to send them to reformatories maintained for criminally inclined juveniles. Parents of such children have been prosecuted and are threatened with prosecutions for causing delinquency.

The Board of Education moved to dismiss the complaint. The cause was submitted on the pleadings to a District Court of three judges. It restrained enforcement as to the plaintiffs and those of that class. The Board of Education brought the case here by direct appeal.

This case calls upon us to consider a precedent decision, as the Court throughout its history often has been required to do. Before turning to the *Gobitis* case, however, it is desirable to notice certain characteristics by which this controversy is distinguished.

The freedom asserted by these appellees does not bring them into collision with rights asserted by any other individuals. It is such conflicts which most frequently require intervention of the State to determine where the rights of one end and those of another begin. But the refusal of these persons to participate in the ceremony does not interfere with or deny rights of others to do so. Nor is there any question in this case that their behavior is peaceable and orderly. The sole conflict is between authority and rights of the individual. The State asserts power to condition access to public education on making a prescribed sign and profession and at the same time to coerce attendance by punishing both parent and child. The latter stand on a right of self-determination in matters that touch individual opinion and personal attitude.

As the present Chief Justice [Stone] said in dissent in the *Gobitis* case, the State may "require teaching by instruction and study of all in our history and in the structure and organization of our government, including the guaranties of civil liberty which tend to inspire patriotism and love of country." Here, however, we are dealing with a compulsion of students to declare a belief. They are not merely made acquainted with the flag salute so that they may be informed as to what it is or even what it means. The issue here is whether this slow and easily neglected route to aroused loyalties constitutionally may be short-cut by substituting a compulsory salute and slogan. This issue is not prejudiced by the Court's previous holding that where a State, without compelling attendance, extends college facilities to pupils who voluntarily enroll, it may prescribe military training as part of the course without offense to the Constitution. It was held that those who take advantage of its opportunities may not on ground of conscience refuse compliance with such conditions. In the present case attendance is not optional. That case is also to be distinguished from the present one because, independently of college privileges or requirements, the State has power to raise militia and impose the duties of service therein upon its citizens.

There is no doubt that, in connection with the pledges, the flag salute is a form of utterance. Symbolism is a primitive but effective way of communicating ideas. The use of an emblem or flag to symbolize some system, idea, institution, or personality, is a short cut from mind to mind. Causes and nations, political parties, lodges and ecclesiastical groups seek to knit the loyalty of their followings to a flag or banner, a color or design. The State announces rank, function, and authority through crowns and maces, uniforms and black robes; the church speaks through the Cross, the Crucifix, the altar and shrine, and clerical raiment. Symbols of State often convey political ideas just as religious symbols come to convey theological ones. Associated with many of these symbols are appropriate gestures of acceptances or respect: a salute, a bowed or bared head, a bended knee. A person gets from a symbol the meaning he puts into it, and what is one man's comfort and inspiration is another's jest and scorn.

Over a decade ago Chief Justice Hughes led this Court in holding that the display of a red flag as a symbol of opposition by peaceful and legal means to organized government was protected by the free speech guaranties of the Constitution. Here it is the State that employs a flag as a symbol of adherence to government as presently organized. It requires the individual to communicate by word and sign his acceptance of the political ideas it thus bespeaks. Objection to this form of communication when coerced is an old one, well known to the framers of the Bill of Rights.

It is also to be noted that the compulsory flag statute and pledge requires affirmation of a belief and an attitude of mind. It is not clear whether the regulation contemplates that pupils forego any contrary convictions of their own and become unwilling converts to the prescribed ceremony or whether it will be acceptable if they simulate assent by words without belief and by a gesture barren of meaning. It is now a commonplace that censorship or suppression of expression of opinion is tolerated by our Constitution only when the expression presents a clear and present danger of action of a kind the State is empowered to prevent and punish. It would seem that involuntary affirmation could be commanded only on even more immediate and urgent grounds than silence. But here the power of compulsion is invoked without any allegation that remaining passive during a flag salute ritual creates a clear and present danger that would justify an effort even to muffle expression. To sustain the compulsory flag salute we are required to say that a Bill of Rights which guard the individual's right to speak his own mind, left it open to public authorities to compel him to utter what is not in his mind.

Whether the First Amendment to the Constitution will permit officials to order observance of ritual of this nature does not depend upon whether as a voluntary exercise we would think it to be good, bad or merely innocuous. Any credo of nationalism is likely to include what some disapprove or to omit what others think essential, and to give off different overtones as it takes on different accents or interpretations. If official power exists to coerce acceptance of any patriotic creed, what it shall contain cannot be decided by courts, but must be largely discretionary with the ordaining authority, whose power to prescribe would no doubt include power to amend. Hence validity of the asserted power to force an American citizen publicly to profess any statement of belief or to engage in any ceremony of assent to one presents questions of power that must be considered independently of any idea we may have as to the utility of the ceremony in question.

Nor does the issue as we see it turn on one's possession of particular religious views or the sincerity with which they are held. While religion supplies appellees' motive for enduring the discomforts of making the issue in this case, many citizens who do not share these religious views hold such a compulsory rite to infringe constitutional liberty of the individual. It is not necessary to inquire whether nonconformist beliefs will exempt from the duty to salute unless we first find power to make the salute a legal duty.

The *Gobitis* decision, however, *assumed*, as did the argument in that case and in this, that power exists in the State to impose the flag salute discipline upon school children in general. The Court only examined and rejected a claim based on religious beliefs of immunity from an unquestioned general rule. The question which underlies the flag salute controversy is whether such a ceremony so touching matters of opinion and political attitude may be imposed upon the individual by official authority under powers committed to any political organization under our Constitution. We examine rather than assume existence of this power and against this broader definition of issues in this case, reexamine specific grounds assigned for the *Gobitis* decision.

1. It was said that the flag-salute controversy confronted the Court with "the problem which Lincoln cast in memorable dilemma: 'Must a government of necessity be too *strong* for the liberties of its people, or too *weak* to maintain its own existence?'" and that the answer must be in favor of strength.

We think these issues may be examined free of pressure or restraint growing out of such considerations.

It may be doubted whether Mr. Lincoln would have thought that the strength of government to maintain itself would be impressively vindicated by our confirming power of the state to expel a handful of children from school. Such oversimplification, so handy in political debate, often lacks the precision necessary to postulates of judicial reasoning. If validly applied to this problem, the utterance cited would resolve every issue of power in favor of those in authority and would require us to override every liberty thought to weaken or delay execution of their policies.

Government of limited power need not be anemic government. Assurance that rights are secure tends to diminish fear and jealousy of strong government, and by making us feel safe to live under it makes for its better support. Without promise of a limiting Bill of Rights it is doubtful if our Constitution could have mustered enough strength to enable its ratification. To enforce those rights today is not to choose weak government over strong government. It is only to adhere as a means of strength to individual freedom of mind in preference to officially disciplined uniformity for which history indicates a disappointing and disastrous end.

The subject now before us exemplifies this principle. Free public education, if faithful to the ideal of secular instruction and political neutrality, will not be partisan or enemy of any class, creed, party, or faction. If it is to impose any ideological discipline, however, each party or denomination must seek to control, or failing that, to weaken the influence of the educational system. Observance of the limitations of the Constitution will not weaken government in the field appropriate for its exercise.

2. It was also considered in the *Gobitis* case that functions of educational officers in states, counties and school districts were such that to interfere with their authority "would in effect make us the school board for the country."

The Fourteenth Amendment, as now applied to the States, protects the citizen against the State itself and all of its creatures—Boards of Education not excepted. These have, of course, important, delicate, and highly discretionary functions, but none that they may not perform within the limits of the Bill of Rights. That they are educating the young for citizenship is reason for scrupulous protection of Constitutional freedoms of the individual, if we are not to strangle the free mind at its source and teach youth to discount important principles of our government as mere platitudes.

Such Boards are numerous and their territorial jurisdiction often small. But small and local authority may feel less sense of responsibility to the Constitution, and agencies of publicity may be less vigilant in calling it to account. The action of Congress in making flag observance voluntary and respecting the conscience of the objector in a matter so vital as raising the Army contrasts sharply with these local regulations in matters relatively trivial to the welfare of the nation. There are village tyrants as well as village Hampdens, but none who acts under color of law is beyond reach of the Constitution.

3. The *Gobitis* opinion reasoned that this is a field "where courts possess no marked and certainly no controlling competence," that it is committed to the legislatures as well as the courts to guard cherished liberties and that it is constitutionally appropriate to "fight out the wise use of legislative authority in the form of public opinion and before legislative assemblies rather than to transfer such a contest to the judicial arena," since all the "effective means of inducing political changes are left free."

The very purpose of a Bill of Rights was to withdraw certain subjects from the vicissitudes of political controversy, to place them beyond the reach of majorities and officials and to establish them as legal principles to be applied by the courts. One's right to life, liberty, and property, to free speech, a free press, freedom of worship and assembly, and other fundamental rights may not be submitted to vote: they depend on the outcome of no elections.

In weighing arguments of the parties it is important to distinguish between the due process clause of the Fourteenth Amendment as an instrument for transmitting the principles of the First Amendment and those cases in which it is applied for its own sake. The test of legislation which collides with the Fourteenth Amendment, because it also collides with the principles of the First, is much more definite than the test when only the Fourteenth is involved. Much of the vagueness of the due process clause disappears when the specific prohibitions of the First become its standard. The right of a State to regulate, for example, a public utility may well include, so far as the due process test is concerned, power to impose all of the restrictions which a legislature may have a "rational basis" for adopting. But freedom of speech and of press, of assembly, and of worship may not be infringed on such slender grounds. They are susceptible of restriction only to prevent grave and immediate danger to interests which the state may lawfully protect. It is important to note that while it is the Fourteenth Amendment which bears directly upon the State it is more specific limiting principles of the First Amendment that finally govern this case.

Nor does our duty to apply the Bill of Rights to assertions of official authority depend upon our possession of marked competence in the field where the invasion of rights occurs. True, the task of translating the majestic generalities of the Bill of Rights, conceived as part of the pattern of liberal government in the eighteenth century, into concrete restraints on officials dealing with the problems of the twentieth century, is one to disturb self-confidence. These principles grew in soil which also produced a philosophy that the individual was the center of society, that his liberty was attainable through mere absence of governmental restraints, and that the government should be entrusted with few controls and only the mildest supervision over men's affairs. We must transplant these rights to a soil in which the *laissez-faire* concept or principle of non-interference has withered at least as to economic affairs, and social advancements are increasingly sought through closer integration of society and through expanded and strengthened governmental controls. These changed conditions often deprive precedents of reliability and cast us more than we would choose upon our own judgment. But we act in these matters not by authority of our competence but by force of our commissions. We cannot, because of modest estimates of our competence in such specialties as public education, withhold the judgment that history authenticates as the function of this Court when liberty is infringed.

4. Lastly, and this is the very heart of the *Gobitis* opinion, it reasons that "National unity is the basis of national security," that the authorities have "the right to select appropriate means for its attainment," and hence reaches the conclusion that such compulsory measures toward "national unity" are constitutional. Upon the verity of this assumption depends our answer in this case.

National unity as an end which officials may foster by persuasion and example is not in question. The problem is whether under our Constitution compulsion as here employed is a permissible means for its achievement.

Struggles to coerce uniformity of sentiment in support of some end thought essential to their time and country have been waged by many good as well as by evil men. Nationalism is a relatively recent phenomenon but at other times and places the ends have been racial or territorial security, support of a dynasty or regime, and particular plans for saving souls. As first and moderate methods to attain unity have failed, those bent on its accomplishment must resort to an ever increasing severity. As governmental pressure toward unity becomes greater, so strife becomes more bitter as to whose unity it shall be. Probably no deeper division of our people could proceed from any provocation than from finding it necessary to choose what doctrine and whose program public educational officials shall compel youth to unite in embracing. Ultimate futility of such attempts to compel coherence is the lesson of every such effort from the Roman drive to stamp out Christianity as a disturber of its pagan unity, the Inquisition, as a means to religious and dynastic unity, the Siberian exiles as a means to Russian unity, down to the last failing efforts of our present totalitarian enemies. Those who begin coercive elimination of dissent soon find themselves exterminating dissenters. Compulsory unification of opinion achieves only the unanimity of the graveyard.

It seems trite but necessary to say that the First Amendment to our Constitution was designed to avoid these ends by avoiding these beginnings. There is no mysticism in the American concept of the State or of the nature or origin of its authority. We set up a government by consent of the governed, and the Bill of Rights denies those in power any legal opportunity to coerce that consent. Authority here is to be controlled by public opinion, not public opinion by authority.

The case is made difficult not because the principles of its decision are obscure but because the flag involved is our own. Nevertheless, we apply the limitations of the Constitution with no fear that freedom to be intellectually and spiritually diverse or even contrary will disintegrate the social organization. To believe that patriotism will not flourish if patriotic ceremonies are voluntary and spontaneous instead of a compulsory routine is to make an unflattering estimate of the appeal of our institutions to free minds. We can have intellectual individualism and the rich cultural diversities that we owe to exceptional minds only at the price of occasional eccentricity and abnormal attitudes. When they are so harmless to others or to the State as those we deal with here, the price is not too great. But freedom to differ is not limited to things that do not matter much. That would be a mere shadow of freedom. The test of its substance is the right to differ as to things that touch the heart of the existing order.

If there is any fixed star in our constitutional constellation, it is that no official, high or petty, can prescribe what shall be orthodox in politics, nationalism, religion, or other matters of opinion or force citizens to confess by word or act their faith therein. If there are any circumstances which permit an exception, they do not now occur to us.

We think the action of the local authorities in compelling the flag salute and pledge transcends constitutional limitations on their power and invades the sphere of intellect and spirit which it is the purpose of the First Amendment to our Constitution to reserve from all official control.

The decision of this Court in *Minersville School District v. Gobitis* and the holdings of those few per curiam decisions which preceded and foreshadowed it are overruled, and the judgment enjoining enforcement of the West Virginia Regulation is

Affirmed.

Mr. JUSTICE ROBERTS and Mr. JUSTICE REED adhere to the views expressed by the Court in *Minersville School District v. Gobitis* and are of the opinion that the judgment below should be reversed.

[The concurring opinion of Justices Black and Douglas, and the concurring opinion of Justice Murphy are omitted.]

Mr. Justice FRANKFURTER, dissenting.

One who belongs to the most vilified and persecuted minority in history is not likely to be insensible to the freedoms guaranteed by our Constitution. Were my purely personal attitude relevant I should whole-heartedly associate myself with the general libertarian views in the Court's opinion, representing as they do the thought and action of a lifetime. But as judges we are neither Jew nor Gentile, neither Catholic nor agnostic. We owe equal attachment to the Constitution and are equally bound by our judicial obligations whether we derive our citizenship from the earliest or the latest immigrants to these shores. In the light of all the circumstances, including the history of this question in this Court, it would require more daring than I possess to deny that reasonable legislators could have taken the action which is before us for review. Most unwillingly, therefore, I must differ from my brethren with regard to legislation like this. I cannot bring my mind to believe that the "liberty" secured by the Due Process Clause gives this Court authority to deny to the State of West Virginia the attainment of that which we all recognize as a legitimate legislative end, namely, the promotion of good citizenship, by employment of the means here chosen.

Notes

1. The most remarkable feature of this decision is its timing. In the midst of World War II, the Court supported the religious and intellectual freedom of school children who were members of an often-despised religious minority and whose refusal to salute the flag was viewed by many as unpatriotic.

In the three years between the *Gobitis* and *Barnette* decisions, two new members of the Court were appointed. They were Robert H. Jackson, the author of the *Barnette* decision, who assumed the seat of Harlan Fiske Stone (Stone was named Chief Justice after the retirement of Charles Evans Hughes), and Wiley Rutledge, who replaced James Byrnes, who in turn replaced the retired McReynolds. Consequently, the change in the Court's composition cannot alone explain *Barnette*. Overruling *Gobitis* was a result of a change of mind by Justices Hugo Black, William O. Douglas and Frank Murphy, all of whom wrote short concurrences to explain their decision.

Shortly after the decision in *Gobitis*, and apparently in part because of the decision, a "wave of anti-Witness hysteria" "swept the country." David R. Manwaring, Render Unto Caesar: The Flag-Salute Cases 163 (1962). When the members of the Court returned to Washington after their summer recess, Frankfurter and Justice William O. Douglas had the following conversation, recorded by Frankfurter in his scrapbook: "Hugo [Black] tells me that now he wouldn't go with you in the *Gobitis* case." Frankfurter replied, "Has Hugo been re-reading the Constitution during the summer?" "No—he has been reading the papers." H.N. Hirsch, The Enigma of Felix Frankfurter 152 (1981). The public shift in the stance of Black, Douglas and Murphy became clear two years later in *Jones v. City of Opelika*, 316 U.S 584 (1942). Although the Court upheld the convictions of Jehovah's Witnesses for distributing religious literature without a license, the decision was by a bare majority, with Justices Black, Douglas and Murphy joining Chief Justice Stone in dissent. The first three justices used their dissent in *Jones v. Opelika* to make the remarkable statement that, "Since we joined in the opinion in the *Gobitis* Case, we think that this is an appropriate occasion to state that we now believe that it was also wrongly decided." *Id.* at 623–24.

In concurring in *Barnette*, Black and Douglas claimed that the law was "a form of test oath, and the test oath has always been abhorrent in the United States." *Barnette*, 319 U.S. at 644. Although "[r]eligious faiths, honestly held, do not free individuals from responsibility to conduct themselves obediently to laws which... [are] imperatively necessary to protect society as a whole from grave and pressingly imminent dangers," the "[d]ecision as to the constitutionality of particular laws which strike at the substance of religious tenets and practices must be made by this Court," and in this case, the refusal to salute the flag did not "create[ ] a grave danger to the nations." *Id.* For Justice Murphy, a Roman Catholic and strong civil libertarian derisively called "the Saint" by Frankfurter, "[r]eflection has convinced me that as a judge I have no loftier duty or responsibility than to uphold that spiritual freedom to it farthest reaches." *Id.* at 645. The standard history of these cases is Manwaring, Render Unto Caesar. Does the Test Clause of Art. VI apply to these cases?

2. Justice Jackson's opinion in *Barnette* is best remembered today for its ringing endorsement of individual liberty. His statement, "If there is any fixed star in our constitutional constellation, it is that no official, high or petty, can prescribe what shall be orthodox in politics, nationalism, religion, or other matters of opinion or force citizens to confess by word or act their faith therein," remains a landmark in constitutional law. Is he convincing? Does Justice Frankfurter's opinion in *Gobitis* unfairly raise the stakes by asserting the necessity of national unity? Does Justice Jackson unfairly raise the stakes himself by suggesting that the law coerces orthodoxy? The standard view of the cases is that Jackson has the better of the argument. What, if anything, does Jackson's argument suggest concerning Free Exercise claims? Does his decision to ignore the specifically religious reason for refusing to salute the flag in favor of the more abstract freedom from orthodoxy mean that this is really a free speech or free thought case? Is Justice Jackson persuasive when he asserts that the "validity of the asserted power to force an American citizen publicly to profess *any* statement of belief or to engage in *any* ceremony of assent to one presents questions of power that must be considered independently of any idea we may have as to the utility of the ceremony in question"? Do the emphasized words indicate that the government may *never* require an affirmation of belief, no matter what its reasons? *See* Chapter Eleven, § A.

3. The words "under God" were not added to the Pledge of Allegiance until 1954, when Congress decided to add them to the Pledge. Act of June 14, 1954, 68 Stats. 249.

4. Can these two sets of paired cases be neatly divided into "Establishment" and "Free Exercise" cases? Are they as much about notions of property and speech rights as religion? Or about the nature and form of the American democratic experiment, or the relation between cultural and religious majorities and minorities in a pluralistic society? Keep these cases in mind when reading about the history of the Religion Clauses and about the present interpretation of the language of the First Amendment.

Chapter 2

History of the Religion Clauses

A. Background to the Passage of the First Amendment: A Short Study of Religious Liberty in the Colonies

The first sixteen words of the First Amendment state: "Congress shall make no law respecting an establishment of religion, or prohibiting the free exercise thereof." The meaning of those words is the subject of continuing dispute. Many of the efforts to resolve the meaning of the prohibition against any "law respecting an establishment of religion, or prohibiting the free exercise thereof" have turned upon the history of the relation of law, government and religion in the colonies, and later, states before, during and after the passage of the Bill of Rights. The best source for a full account of the relationship between religion and government in the colonial era is Thomas J. Curry, THE FIRST FREEDOMS: CHURCH AND STATE IN AMERICA TO THE PASSAGE OF THE FIRST AMENDMENT (1986). In addition, there are a number of works which discuss in detail the history of this relationship from colonial to modern times. The most comprehensive is Anson Phelps Stokes, CHURCH AND STATE IN AMERICA (3 vols. 1950). Other works include Sanford H. Cobb, THE RISE OF RELIGIOUS LIBERTY IN AMERICA (1902 reissued 1968); Leo Pfeffer, CHURCH, STATE AND FREEDOM (rev. ed. 1967); Mark DeWolfe Howe, THE GARDEN AND THE WILDERNESS (1965); and Chester J. Antieau, Arthur T. Downey and Edward C. Roberts, FREEDOM FROM FEDERAL ESTABLISHMENT (1964). Two broad surveys of the history of religion in America are Martin E. Marty, PILGRIMS IN THEIR OWN LAND: 500 YEARS OF RELIGION IN AMERICA (1984), and Sydney E. Ahlstrom, A RELIGIOUS HISTORY OF THE AMERICAN PEOPLE (1972). A number of studies of the history and theory of the First Amendment were written in the 1980s, from several different perspectives. They include Gerard V. Bradley, CHURCH-STATE RELATIONSHIPS IN AMERICA (1987); John T. Noonan, Jr., THE BELIEVER AND THE POWERS THAT ARE (1987); Daniel L. Dreisbach, REAL THREAT AND MERE LIBERTY: RELIGIOUS LIBERTY AND THE FIRST AMENDMENT (1987); John M. Swomley, RELIGIOUS LIBERTY AND THE SECULAR STATE (1987); Leonard W. Levy, THE ESTABLISHMENT CLAUSE: RELIGION AND THE FIRST AMENDMENT (1986 rev. ed. 1994); William Lee Miller, THE FIRST LIBERTY: RELIGION AND THE AMERICAN REPUBLIC (1985); A. James Reichley, RELIGION IN AMERICAN PUBLIC LIFE (1985). Robert L. Cord, SEPARATION OF CHURCH AND STATE (1982); and CHURCH AND STATE IN AMERICAN HISTORY (2d ed. John F. Wilson & Donald L. Drakeman eds., 1987). An important bibliography of the history of the interaction of law and religion in America is CHURCH AND STATE IN AMERICA: A BIBLIO-

GRAPHIC GUIDE (2 vols. John F. Wilson ed. 1987). Recent works include Steven D. Smith, FOREORDAINED FAILURE: THE CONSTITUTIONAL QUEST FOR A CONSTITUTIONAL PRINCIPLE OF RELIGIOUS FREEDOM (1995); John H. Garvey, WHAT ARE FREEDOMS FOR? (1996); John T. Noonan, Jr., THE LUSTRE OF OUR COUNTRY: THE AMERICAN EXPERIENCE OF RELIGIOUS FREEDOM (1998); and John Witte, RELIGION AND THE AMERICAN CONSTITUTIONAL EXPERIMENT: ESSENTIAL RIGHTS AND LIBERTIES (2000).

The relationship between religion and government in the thirteen colonies is best viewed geographically: The New England colonies (Massachusetts, Connecticut, Rhode Island and New Hampshire) have a different history than the Middle Colonies (New York, New Jersey, Pennsylvania, Delaware and Maryland), which have a different history than the Southern Colonies (Virginia, North Carolina, South Carolina and Georgia). The history in New England, and particularly Massachusetts, is a history of the Puritan (later Congregational) establishment of religion despite the protests of Protestant "dissenters." Rhode Island, founded by the religious seeker Roger Williams, provides a notable counterpoint to the rest of New England, for that colony freely respected the religious liberty of all Protestants, and, to a limited extent, the religious liberty of Roman Catholics and Jews. The liberty of conscience enjoyed by residents of the middle colonies diverged depending on time and place, with much greater fluctuation in tone and temper than in New England. They are grouped largely because of those differences. In the southern colonies, the Church of England was the established religion, although its power to influence law and society was quite weak. As the colonies became states and wrote constitutions, this relationship in the middle and southern colonies greatly changed. Of these thirteen colonies, the historical relationship of law and religion in Massachusetts and Virginia have been the most influential to later judicial thinking about the legal parameters of religious liberty.

1. New England

Massachusetts

New England was founded by two sets of dissenters from the Church of England. In 1620, a group of dissenters from the Church of England called Pilgrims (or Separates or Calvinists) landed at Plymouth Rock in present day Massachusetts. These Pilgrims were given a charter by King James I of England to settle in present day Virginia. Their boat sailed off course, however, and they landed hundreds of miles north of their intended destination. Pilgrims were persecuted for their religious beliefs in England, and were killed or forced to move to the Netherlands before coming to America. The Pilgrims believed that the Church of England was infected with the disease of "Papacy", because it kept intact much of the liturgy, bishops (including a hierarchical church structure), mode of worship and other rituals of the degenerate Roman Catholic Church. After formally separating from the established Church of England, the Pilgrims were persecuted in England. These Pilgrims were a small group, and because they possessed no charter to create a new colony at Plymouth Rock, their influence in colonial Massachusetts was slight.

The other, more influential group colonizing what is now Massachusetts were the Puritans. In 1630, the Puritans, also dissenters from aspects of the Church of England, sailed with a royal charter to form the Massachusetts Bay Colony. In their view, they were to create a new, perfect union of church and state. It is highly unlikely that King

Charles I wanted the Puritans to create a government different than that found in the mother country. These Puritans began building a society which fostered the perfection of their religion. Although Puritans disagreed with the direction of the Church of England, they did not formally separate from the Mother Church. They were called Independents, for they remained formally within the church for some time, but were interested in forming independent churches free from bishops and other indicia of Papish hierarchy. Each church was a congregation unto itself, and the Puritans eventually became, in America, Congregationalists.

The Puritans created a society based on their views of the proper relationship among men (women had limited, particular roles in this society), society (which encompassed church) and God. One result was that the rules of governance were based on particular religious beliefs. Public worship (and rest) on Sundays was required, swearing was a serious criminal offense and the Ten Commandments formed the basic laws of the society. In the mid-1630s, two dissenters from Puritan faith, Roger Williams and Anne Hutchinson, were banished from Massachusetts. In January 1636, before he could be sent back to England, Williams left Massachusetts for Narragansett Bay, where he eventually founded the colony of Rhode Island and Providence Plantations. Shortly after Williams's departure, Governor John Winthrop and the General Court summoned Anne Hutchinson to answer for her seditious actions. Hutchinson believed that anyone saved by God was led by the Holy Ghost, and that whether one was saved could not be determined by one's actions in a "sanctified" manner. These two views made Hutchinson a heretic, an Antinomian, for refusing to recognize that sanctified actions led to one's religious justification, and believing that the Holy Ghost resides in a saved person, might be perceived as beliefs in immediate personal revelation, both of which appeared contrary to the heart of Puritan theology. Puritans believed "that God's will could be discovered only through the Bible." Edmund S. Morgan, The Puritan Dilemma: The Story of John Winthrop 139 (1958). Near the close of her trial before the General Court, apparently just as she had bested her accusers, Anne Hutchinson spoke of divine revelations personally heard by her. For this heresy, she was banished to what became the colony of Rhode Island.

Quakers arriving in New England were dealt with harshly. Between 1658–1661, four Quakers were hung in the Boston common for returning to the colony after being expelled for proclaiming the truth of Quaker beliefs. The Puritans also attempted to rid the Bay Colony of Baptists, although by the late 1660s, prominent members of the colony requested toleration of Baptists because of their upstanding ways. Curry, First Freedoms, at 21–25.

The Puritans always found it difficult to keep safe their "Bible Commonwealth." In the aftermath of the Glorious Revolution of 1688–89, when William and Mary were enthroned King and Queen of England, the Puritans in America lost their colonial charter. William and Mary were required to grant official religious toleration in England to non-Anglicans such as Presbyterians (the official religion in Scotland) and other Protestants by the English Act of Toleration of 1689. In 1692, William and Mary granted a second charter to the Massachusetts Bay Colony, with the proviso that the colony grant religious toleration to Protestants. From that time to the Great Awakening in the late 1730s and early 1740s, there was officially a policy of toleration, at least for the Protestant dissenters. In 1728, the General Court first passed laws exempting Anabaptists, Quakers and Churchmen (Anglicans) from paying taxes in support of the Standing church as long as they "usually attend the meeting of their respective societys assembling upon the Lord's day for the worship of God, and that they live within five miles of the place of the meeting." I William G. McLoughlin, New England Dissent 1630–1883: The Baptists and the Separation of Church and State 225 (2 vols. 1971), *quoting* II Acts and Resolves, Public and Private, of the Province of Massachusetts 494–95 (1869–1922). Although this exemption was "an important turning point in the whole relationship of dissenters to the establishment," McLoughlin, at 227–28, the standing order remained the Puritans or Congregationalists. In addition to McLouglin's work on this era in Massachusetts, see generally Susan M. Reed, Church and State in Massachusetts, 1691–1740 (1914).

Before the War of Independence, two groups challenged the hegemony of the Congregationalists in Massachusetts. The first group consisted of Separate or New Light Baptists, and was led by a minister named Isaac Backus. In 1773, Backus wrote a pamphlet complaining about the infringement of the religious conscience of Baptists by the Commonwealth titled *An Appeal to the Public for Religious Liberty against the Oppressors of the Present Day*. On Backus's views of church and state, see William G. McLoughlin, *Isaac Backus and the Separation of Church and State in America*, 73 Am. Hist. Rev. 1392 (1967). The next year, Backus petitioned the First Continental Congress in 1774, complaining of the treatment of Baptists by Congregationalists in Massachusetts. The complaints were that Baptists were forced to pay taxes to support Congregationalist ministers, as New Light or Separate Baptists were often unable to obtain certificates to avoid paying such taxes. In addition, Baptists objected to the requirement that they obtain certificates exempting them from taxation in support of ministers. In their view, such a requirement proved that the Congregationalist church was the established church in Massachusetts. The complaints of the Baptists were greeted with bewilderment by many Massachusetts public officials, including John Adams, for the certificate of exemption did not create an "establishment" of the Congregational church as he and others understood that word. The complaints were also greeted with criticism, for the Baptists had allied themselves with Quakers in pressing this issue. Because Quakers enjoyed many influential friends in London and were viewed as Tories (loyalists to Britain), the Baptists were accused of disloyalty to colonial interests.

The second group challenging Congregationalists in Massachusetts were Anglicans. Anglicans argued that the Congregationalists had established their religion in Massachusetts contrary to the official (Anglican) religion in England, and they wanted the government, including the Privy Council (a governing body of the colonies located in London) to rectify this error. One suggestion was that the Church of England send an Anglican bishop to the United States, an idea met with great hostility. The differing Protestant denominations in the colonies, with the exception of some Anglicans, were strongly opposed to a bishop being sent to the United States. One reason for this opposition was the fear of "Popery." In 1763, the French & Indian War ended, and England took control of Canada. However, there were many French Catholic settlers in the province of Quebec whose right to practice their faith with the aid of priests was guaranteed by the Quebec Act of 1773. Another fear was that the installation of a bishop in America was an effort to create uniformity of Protestant religious belief and worship. Finally, as a political matter, an Anglican bishop symbolized English governance of the colonies. No bishop was sent. On bishops, see Bernard Bailyn, The Ideological Origins of the American Revolution 254–257 (1967); Curry, First Freedoms at 126–129.

Four years after the colonies declared their independence from Great Britain, the Massachusetts Constitution was adopted. Articles II and III offer the official views of the relationship between church and state:

Article II

> It is the right as well as the duty of all men in Society, publicly, and at stated seasons, to worship the SUPREME BEING, the great creator and preserver of the universe. And no subject shall be hurt, molested, or restrained, in his person, liberty, or estate, for worshipping GOD in the manner and season most agreeable to the dictates of his own conscience; or for his religious profession or sentiments; provided he doth not disturb the public peace, or obstruct others in their religious worship.

Article III

> As the happiness of a people, and the good order and preservation of a civil government, essentially depend upon piety, religion and morality; and as these cannot be generally diffused through a community, but by the institution of the public worship of GOD, and of public instructions in piety, religion and morality: Therefore, to promote their happiness and to secure the good order and preservation of their government, the people of this Commonwealth have a right to invest their legislature with power to authorize and require, and the legislature shall, from time to time, authorize and require, the several towns, parishes, precincts, and other bodies-politic, or religious societies, to make suitable provision, at their own expense, for the institution of the public worship of GOD, and for the support and maintenance of public protestant teachers of piety, religion and morality, in all cases where such provision shall not be made voluntarily...
>
> And every denomination of christian, demeaning themselves peaceably, and as good subjects of the Commonwealth, shall be equally under the protection of the law: And no subordination of any one sect or denomination to another shall be established by law.

In effect, this granted to local towns (the vast majority of which were Congregational) the option of choosing the established religion, and allowed the towns to tax its residents "for the support and maintenance of public protestant teachers of piety, religion and morality." Six years later, Massachusetts passed a law which appeared to allow townspeople to set up a church other than the standing church (Congregational or otherwise). Jacob C. Meyer, Church and State in Massachusetts from 1740 to 1833 113 (1930). This act, however, was denounced by "all those who demanded the extension of individual liberty," *id.*, and increased the opposition of dissenters to the Standing Order.

Congregationalists were closely aligned with Federalist politics, and Republicans were aligned with the cause of the dissenters. In 1811, while in control of the Massachusetts legislature, the Republicans passed the Religious Freedom Act. The Act permitted a citizen taxed for the support of a "public teacher of religion" to apply the amount "to the support of the public teacher or teachers of his own religious sect or denomination..." and allowed any person who "shall become a member of any religious society" to be "exempted from taxation for the support of public worship and public teachers of religion in every other religious corporation whatsoever, so long as he shall continue such membership." 1811 Mass. Acts and Resolves, Ch. 6, §§ 1,2. In *Adams v. Howe*, 14 Mass. 340 (1817), Chief Justice Isaac Parker held the act constitutional, permitting a tax exemption for a Baptist.

The end of the Massachusetts system of establishment was caused in large part by a split in Congregationalism. Unitarians, so called because they did not believe Jesus of

Nazareth was more divine than any other human being, managed to wrest control of a number of parish churches (a parish was a geographical area) from the Trinitarian Congregationalists, with the help of townspeople who were not members of the church, but who were members of the parish. In 1812, the Supreme Judicial Court permitted the parish to dismiss its minister, even though the vast majority of the members of the church supported the minister. *Burr v. The Inhabitants of the First Parish in Sandwich*, 9 Mass. 276 (1812). *Baker v. Fales*, 16 Mass. 488 (1820), was a bitter dispute between the members of the church and the members of the parish over the selection of a new minister for the parish church. Although a majority of the members of the church opposed the appointment by the Dedham parish of the Unitarian Alvan Lamson, the parish ordained Lamson. This led to secession by the Trinitarians. The secessionists elected new Deacons, including Fales, who sued the old deacons for the church property.

Despite the efforts of Daniel Webster and Deacon Fales (who reportedly spent $3,000 of his own money on the suit, Meyer, at 177 n.40), the Court, in a decision written by Chief Justice Parker, a Unitarian, held that the members of the church held the property in trust for the parish, which consisted of "the assembly of Christians in Dedham." Even before *Baker v. Fales,* Unitarians were gradually taking over parish churches in eastern Massachusetts, which, Meyer records, Trinitarians called a "plundering" of over $600,000 of "their" property. *Id.* at 177. As Meyer notes, "Religion suffered no less than respect for law and judicial decisions when a decision rendered by Unitarian judges seemed to go to the limit in favoring the Unitarian churches." *Id.* at 178.

A few months after *Baker v. Fales* was decided, a convention was called to revise the Massachusetts constitution. Three amendments concerning religion were proposed: 1) admitting the ministers of every denomination of Christians to the Harvard board of overseers; 2) eliminating the test oath for public office; and 3) amending Article III of the 1780 Constitution. The first amendment failed of adoption. The second proposed amendment, eliminating the test oath for public office, see 3 Francis Newton Thorpe, III The Federal and State Constitutions 1912–13 (7 vols. 1909), was narrowly (13,782–12,480, Meyer, at 200) approved by the voters. The major amendment concerning religion, however, was the proposal to amend Article III. This amendment consisted of seven parts. Meyer, at 197–98. Among other things, the amendment continued a taxing system, although the money was to be apportioned to the church at which the taxpayer worshiped, eliminated the language in Article III which restricted tax support to "Protestant teachers," recognized unincorporated religious societies, and ended mandatory public worship. In addition, provisions concerning the requirement of indictments for major crimes and allowing a criminal defendant to be heard by himself and counsel were part of the proposal to amend Article III. This amendment failed by nearly a 2–1 margin, 19,547–11,065. Meyer, at 198. Jacob Meyer suggests that the proposed amendment to Article III failed because "it pleased neither the dissenters nor those who favored an established church." *Id.* at 199. Merrill Peterson agrees. *See* Democracy, Liberty, and Property: The State Constitutional Conventions of the 1820's 16 (Merrill D. Peterson ed. 1966) ("In all probability the convention's revision pleased neither side, or any side, in the religious disputes of the commonwealth").

Democratic-Republican legislation in 1824 permitted any group of ten persons to form a religious society and thus avoid paying the tax to support the parish church. Meyer, at 213. By 1830, Trinitarian Congregationalists, no longer the beneficiaries of the established church in Massachusetts, began working with others to end the system fostered by Article III of the 1780 Constitution. The next year, the Massachusetts House of Representatives voted to amend Article III to disestablish the church, and in 1833, Article XI was added to the Massachusetts Constitution with a favorable vote of over 90% of the voters. Meyer, at 220. Replacing Article III, it gave to members of religious societies the sole authority to "elect their pastors or religious teachers" and provided equal protection of the laws to "all religious sects and denominations," rather than solely to "every denomination of christians." The next year, the Massachusetts legislature repealed the 1811 Act, ended the system of taxation and granted religious liberty to all churches and religious societies. 1834 Mass. Acts and Resolves, ch. 183 (1834). The Massachusetts system of local established churches lasted longer than any other state establishment. After the disestablishment of the parish church, the Trinitarians and Unitarians kept the property in their possession, despite *Baker v. Fales*. Meyer, at 183.

Connecticut

The land that became Connecticut was originally colonized based on the Massachusetts charter. In 1631 a patent was received from the Crown, and in 1636 Connecticut became a colony separate from Massachusetts. Congregationalism was the "established" religion in Connecticut from at least 1662 until 1818, although Leonard Levy states that despite its formal lack of recognition, the Church of England enjoyed a kind of parity with the Congregational church for "[b]oth had the seal of approval backed by coercive taxation and laws compelling church attendance." Levy, Establishment Clause, at 22. Connecticut first recognized Separates in 1777, and in 1784, a certificate system was adopted allowing all persons who were members of a "Christian" denomination to exempt themselves from taxation for support of the Congregationalist minister of the gospel. II McLoughlin, Dissent, at 922. That same year, after 76 years, Connecticut abandoned the Saybrook Platform, which effectively established Congregationalism by law (although not in name). Even so, Connecticut retained Congregationalism as the established religion of the state, while tolerating the practice of religion by other Protestants. In its Organic Act of 1784, public worship was required and Protestant teachers were maintained by a state tax assessment.

The most famous proponent of religious liberty in late 18th and early 19th century Connecticut was John Leland, an itinerant preacher. Although Leland lived for only two months in 1791 in New London before settling in the western Massachusetts town of Cheshire, Leland's influence in Connecticut's history was considerable. Leland was a strict "separationist," opposed to the use of tax money for the support of Congressional and army chaplains, as well as to proclamations of days of thanksgiving. Before returning to his native New England in 1791, Leland had lived for fifteen years in Virginia, and while there, "had been one of the most influential among the Baptist ministers and a great power in politics." M. Louise Greene, The Development of Religious Liberty in Connecticut 374 (1905 repr. 1970). According to William McLouglin, Leland's "radical doctrine of separation of church and state" was much broader than that of Isaac Backus and other Baptists at the time. II McLoughlin, Dissent, at 931. In May 1791, Leland attacked the recently passed Connecticut certificate system:

> This certificate law is founded on this principle, "that it is the duty of all persons to support the gospel and the worship of God." Is this principle founded in justice? Is it the duty of a deist to support that which he believes to be a cheat and imposition? Is it the duty of a Jew to support the religion of Jesus Christ, when he really believes that he was an impostor? Must the Papists be forced to pay men for preaching down the supremacy of the pope, who they

> are sure is the head of the church? Must a Turk maintain a religion, opposed to the Alkoran, which he holds as the sacred oracle of heaven? These things want better confirmation.

II McLouglin, DISSENT, at 933, *quoting* John Leland, THE WRITINGS OF JOHN LELAND 187 (L.F. Greene ed. 1845) (The title of Leland's polemic was *The Rights of Conscience Inalienable, and Therefore Religious Opinions Not Cognizable by Law or, The High-Flying Churchman Stripped of His Legal Robes Appears a Yaho.*). Shortly after Leland's polemic, the Connecticut legislature repealed its restrictive certificate system, and allowed dissenters simply to file a certificate exempting them from taxation for the established church.

Unlike almost all Christians in New England, Leland acknowledged "that even non-Christians had rights of conscience which must be respected: the right to support non-Christian religions or to give no support whatever to religion." II McLouglin, DISSENT, at 933. For Leland, unlike Isaac Backus and most other Baptists, as well as most Congregationalists and other Protestants, the United States was not a Christian commonwealth, and never could become so.

Just as in Massachusetts, the standing order was closely tied to Federalist politics, and in 1800 the Federalists were united in their opposition to the Republican Presidential candidate (and eventual winner) Thomas Jefferson. It was to the (dissenting) Danbury Baptist Association of western Connecticut that Jefferson, as President, wrote explaining his view that there should exist a "wall of separation" between church and state, a metaphor that has guided establishment clause jurisprudence for over 100 years.

Although the Connecticut general assessment and thus, the Congregational establishment, was abolished with the adoption of a new Constitution in 1818, Article 7th of which guaranteed religious liberty, see I Thorpe, FEDERAL AND STATE CONSTITUTIONS at 544–45, civil rights were guaranteed only to "each and every society or denomination of Christians." An exceptional study of the relatively minor impact of the Connecticut Constitution of 1818 on liberty of religious conscience for non-Christians, as well as its lack of impact on the crime of blasphemy, is Carol Weisbrod, *On Evidences, and Intentions: "The More Proof, The More Doubt"*, 18 Conn. L. Rev. 803 (1986). Professor Weisbrod concludes her history of religious freedom in Connecticut by noting that discussing "contemporary issues as though they were historical... seems inadequate as the sole basis for current decision making." *Id.* at 825.

NEW HAMPSHIRE

New Hampshire was settled as part of the Massachusetts Bay Colony in 1641, and in 1679 became a separate colony (there was a second union with Massachusetts from 1690–92, when William and Mary were contemplating the restructuring of the American colonies). As expected, colonial New Hampshire established Congregationalism by law. However, its history shows much more lenience toward "dissenters" than Massachusetts or Connecticut. Because it was more sparsely settled than Massachusetts, settlement in New Hampshire by Baptists and Anglicans was not as greatly feared. In 1693, as a result of the ascension to the throne of William and Mary, all Protestants dissenters were permitted to pay taxes only to their own ministers.

The New Hampshire Constitution was adopted in 1784. Article V granted liberty of conscience and Article VI, copied from Article III of the Massachusetts Constitution, created a general assessment for support of ministers of the gospel. IV Thorpe, FEDERAL

AND STATE CONSTITUTIONS at 2454. The lenience toward dissenters is exemplified by the 1784 Constitution, which recognized in two places the religious scruples of Quakers. First, Article XIII declared, "No person who is conscientiously scrupulous about the lawfulness of bearing arms, shall be compelled thereto, provided he will pay an equivalent." *Id.* at 2455. Second, the Constitution permitted any public official, including members of "the denomination called quakers," "scrupulous of swearing," to affirm rather than swear an oath. *Id.* at 2468. However, this lenience was limited to Protestant dissenters, for the Constitution also required that all state legislative representatives "shall be of the protestant religion, and shall cease to represent such town, parish, or place immediately on ceasing to be qualified as aforesaid." *Id.* at 2461–62.

Like Massachusetts, church-state relations in New Hampshire were organized around local establishments, a system that largely protected Congregationalism, although other Protestant sects might be established in towns in which a majority of residents chose that sect. Article VI was amended in 1791 to read, "No person of any particular religious sect or denomination shall ever be compelled to pay towards the support of the teacher or teachers of another persuasion, sect, or denomination." For refusing to pay a tax of seventy-five cents to support the Congregationalist minister in Amherst, John Muzzy, who claimed he was a Presbyterian, was put in jail. II McLoughlin, DISSENT, at 863. He later sued the parish church assessors in trespass. In *Muzzy v. Wilkins*, 1 Smith (N.H.) Rep. 1 (1803), Chief Justice Jeremiah Smith concluded that there was no established religion in New Hampshire, for "A religious establishment is where the State prescribes a formulary of faith and worship for the rule and government of all the subjects." *Id.* at 12–13. However, because Presbyterians and Congregationalists were of "different sects, because they differ in church government and discipline, though they agree in doctrines," *id.* at 36, Muzzy was granted judgment in his favor by the court. In dicta, Smith interpreted the Constitution to permit towns to tax "atheists, deists, revilers and contemners of religion, and persons of no religion at all, and who consequently belong to no particular denomination of Christians." *Id.* at 30.

According to Levy, the end of this establishment in 1819 was the result of "state politics, not [] the drive to separate church and state because of the principle of voluntarism." Levy, ESTABLISHMENT CLAUSE, at 40. As in Massachusetts, the Congregationalists were aligned with Federalists, and dissenters with Republicans. The Toleration Act of 1819 stated, "No person shall be compelled to join or support nor be classed with nor associated to any congregation, church or religious society without his express consent first had and obtained." II McLoughlin, DISSENT, at 894. *See also* Charles B. Kinney, CHURCH AND STATE: THE STRUGGLE FOR SEPARATION IN NEW HAMPSHIRE (1955).

McLoughlin notes that the Toleration Act did not "draw a clear line between church and state in New Hampshire." II McLoughlin, DISSENT, at 910. He concludes that the Act implicitly assumed New Hampshire remained a Protestant state, for "the Protestant religion was so essential to the welfare of the civil state that in certain respects the state should encourage and support it." *Id.* One example of this support is the requirement that all public officials be members "of the protestant religion," a requirement that lasted until 1867.

RHODE ISLAND

Rhode Island was founded by Roger Williams, who is today the most famous pre-Revolutionary speaker on the relation of law and religion in America. Williams was a Puritan minister who left Massachusetts for speaking against the Puritan elect then governing Massachusetts. Williams spent a howling winter in the wilds of Narragansett Bay and during that time continued his religious transformation. He was a Baptist for some time, but his refusal to join in communion with any unregenerate person eventually left him communing only with his wife. The metaphor of the garden and the wilderness was coined by Williams in a response to the Puritan preacher Cotton Mather. Discussing the Christian church on earth, Williams wrote of the "hedge or wall of separation between the garden of the church and the wilderness of the world," Perry Miller, ROGER WILLIAMS: HIS CONTRIBUTION TO THE AMERICAN TRADITION 98 (1953), *quoting* Roger Williams, *Mr. Cotton's Letter Lately Printed, Examined and Answered* (1644). When that hedge or wall was demolished by the church, God made "His garden a wilderness as at this day." *Id.*

After sailing back to England during the middle of the English Civil War, Williams was able to obtain a royal patent to the Colony of Rhode Island and Providence Plantations. With a royal patent, Williams was a nearly omnipotent ruler. In order to create a place where persons could seek God, he enjoined the state from interfering in any way with a person's right of religious conscience. The colony's original articles of incorporation, apparently written by Williams, extend the power of the state only to civil matters, a radically different approach from the Bible Commonwealth then existing in Massachusetts. Its 1663 charter (in part due to the restoration of the Crown in England, Rhode Island no longer enjoyed a kind of sovereignty from English rule) stated,

> that noe person within the sayd colonye, at any tyme hereafter, shall bee any wise molested, punished, disquieted, or called in question, for any differences in opinione in matters of religion, and doe not actually disturb the civil peace of our sayd colony; but that all and everye person and persons may, from tyme to tyme, and at all tymes hereafter, freelye and fullye have and enjoye his and theire owne judgments and consciences, in matters of religious concernments....

VI Thorpe, FEDERAL AND STATE CONSTITUTIONS at 3213.

This charter remained the guiding constitution of Rhode Island until 1842. Rhode Island, throughout its history as a colony, permitted Baptists, Antinomians, Quakers, and other "dissenting" Protestants to worship freely. By 1719, however, Protestant Christianity "enjoyed an exalted status" in Rhode Island. Jacob R. Marcus, THE COLONIAL AMERICAN JEW, 1492–1776 435 (3 vols. 1970). Despite this preference, Rhode Island was unlike most other colonies, for no tax for the public support of religion was ever imposed, and the colony also permitted Roman Catholics and Jews to live freely in the colony, although by a law of 1730 they were not permitted to become citizens of the colony. *Id.* Thus, Catholics and Jews were neither permitted to vote nor hold public office in Rhode Island during the colonial period.

Although Roger Williams first gave us the ruling metaphor of the "wall of separation," it is difficult to ascertain both his influence on the history of disestablishment in late 18th and early 19th century America and the meaning of his metaphor. In THE FIRST LIBERTY: RELIGION AND THE AMERICAN REPUBLIC (1986), William Lee Miller assesses Williams's historical reputation. Portrayed in the late 19th and early 20th century as a quintessential liberal democrat, a political progressive, Williams's deeply religious nature was not resurrected until the publication in 1953 of Perry Miller's ROGER WILLIAMS. Perry Miller's revisionist view concluded that Williams "exerted little or no direct influence on theorists of the Revolution and the Constitution, who drew upon quite different intellectual sources." Perry Miller, ROGER WILLIAMS, at 245. William McLoughlin believes that Williams was the least influential thinker in the group including Jefferson, Madison and Isaac Backus. McLoughlin, *Isaac Backus*, 73 Am. Hist. Rev. at 1413, and the American Catholic social thinker John Courtney Murray concluded that Williams must be "ruled out as the original theologian of the First Amendment." John Courtney Murray, WE HOLD THESE TRUTHS 65 (1964). *See also* Timothy L. Hall, SEPARATING CHURCH AND STATE: ROGER WILLIAMS AND RELIGIOUS LIBERTY 116–18 (1998) (arguing that Roger Williams has an important role in constitutional discourse, but not claiming any direct link between Williams and Madison, Jefferson or the text of the First Amendment). Professor David Little believes these views are "seriously misleading," and traces Williams's influence on 18th century thinking about religion and government through John Locke and Isaac Backus. David Little, *Roger Williams and the Separation of Church and State*, in RELIGION AND THE STATE: ESSAYS IN HONOR OF LEO PFEFFER 3, 6 (James E. Wood, Jr., ed. 1985). William Lee Miller suggests that the best portrayal of Williams is found in Edmund S. Morgan, ROGER WILLIAMS: THE CHURCH AND THE STATE (1967). Perry Miller disabused readers of the progressive historian's tendency to deemphasize Roger Williams's religious faith to promote Williams as modernist defender of freedom of conscience. He emphasized Williams's role as a theologian. Morgan did not contest Perry Miller's thesis, he simply redirected it. Morgan noted that Roger Williams's interest was less in theology than in the proper relationship of the institutions of church and state. Edmund Morgan concluded that Williams was concerned not only with what a church should be, but what the state should do, and how one should treat the conscience of individual human beings. William Lee Miller, FIRST LIBERTY, at 166–171.

Concerning Williams's metaphor, Professor Mark DeWolfe Howe wrote that Williams should be understood as a religious seeker who feared the impurity of the state upon religion, not as one who feared religion would harm the state. *See* Mark DeWolfe Howe, THE GARDEN AND THE WILDERNESS 6 (1965). Little argues that Howe's interpretation is inaccurate, for Williams believed, "A wall of separation was needed to protect the state from the church, every bit as much as the other way around." Little, *Roger Williams*, at 15. Professor William Lee Miller suggests that because Williams believed that no church in existence represented the "true" church, the metaphor of the wall of separation did not protect the existing church from the state. Instead, the garden in which the "true" church was located was separated both from the state and most and maybe all Christian institutions on earth. Both the state and the church on earth were in the wilderness. Miller, FIRST LIBERTY, at 222.

Finally, did Williams have a position on exemptions from general laws for religious reasons, and, if so, what was it? In his writings, Williams opposed excusing religious pacifists from military service, and believed Quakers could be punished for addressing civil officials as "thou," language the Quakers took from the Christian Bible, and which Williams considered disrespectful. The difficulty with ascertaining Williams's view is that the religious exemption question, as currently put, was not an issue with which Williams was concerned. *See* Steven D. Smith, *Separation and the Fanatic*, 85 Va. L. Rev. 213, 229–34 (1999) (reviewing Hall, SEPARATING CHURCH AND STATE, and discussing whether Williams supported religious exemptions).

VERMONT

Vermont was the fourteenth state of the Union, entering on March 4, 1791, and was one of the 11 (out of 14) states to ratify the Bill of Rights. Vermont was settled by the French in 1666, by the Dutch and English in 1724 and became English territory after the French & Indian War in 1763. New Hampshire and New York both claimed it as its territory, and in 1777 Vermont declared itself an independent republic. In 1783, the Vermont legislature adopted a law creating a system of local taxation for support of Protestant ministers of the gospel. As McLoughlin notes, however, "[u]nlike the systems in Massachusetts and Connecticut—which, without specifically saying so, clearly favored the Congregationalists—the Vermont ecclesiastical system set forth in this law was an honest attempt to accommodate the religious diversity of the new state while retaining the principle of a general assessment for the support of the Protestant religion." II McLoughlin, Dissent, at 798. This law exempted religious dissenters from the general assessment, although the dissenter was required to file a certificate signed by a "Minister of the Gospel, Deacon" or other church official of the church in which the dissenter was a member. The general assessment was abolished by statute in 1807. *Id.* at 810–11.

The state gradually broadened its view of the "rights of conscience" in its constitutional declarations during the late 18th century, amending provisions on religious liberty in 1786 and 1793. Chapter I, article III of the 1777 Constitution, largely copied from the Pennsylvania constitution, granted the "natural and unalienable right to worship ALMIGHTY GOD, according to the dictates of their own consciences and understanding, regulated by the word of GOD," but limited the protection of civil rights and public office to "any man who professes the protestant religion." However, unlike Pennsylvania, Vermont added "nevertheless, every sect or denomination of christians ought to observe the Sabbath, or the lord's day, and keep up, and support some sort of religious worship, which to them shall seem most agreeable to the revealed will of God." VI Thorpe, at 3740. The 1786 Constitution omitted the phrase "who professes the protestant religion," thus extending civil rights to deists, Catholics and Jews. In the same constitution, however, the substitution of the word "people" for "christians" appeared to require all citizens to observe the Sabbath and support some sort of religious worship. *Id.* at 3752. The 1777 Constitution also followed the Pennsylvania Constitution by permitting those conscientiously scrupulous of bearing arms from being forced to do so, as long as they paid an equivalent. VI Thorpe, at 3741. This provision was continued in the 1786 and 1793 Constitutions. *Id.* at 3573, 3763.

The 1777 Constitution also required all state officers to swear they "believe in one God, the Creator and Governor of the universe, and rewarder of the good and punisher of the wicked. And I do acknowledge the scriptures of the Old and New Testament to be given by divine inspiration, and own and profess the protestant religion." IV Thorpe, at 3743. The religious oath of office was omitted in its 1793 Constitution.

2. The Middle Colonies

Pennsylvania

Pennsylvania received its name from William Penn, the son of a man who was one of Oliver Cromwell's trusted aides during the Puritan Revolution in England in the 1640s. Penn was taunted and jeered after his conversion to the Quaker faith while a student at Oxford. Penn received a colonial charter in 1681. The area had been settled by the French and Dutch in the 1640s and by the English in 1664. In the 1682 "Frame of Government," Penn extended the right of conscience and civil liberties to any person who believed in one God. This extended freedom of religious conscience to both Jews and

Roman Catholics. The 1776 Pennsylvania Constitution granted liberty of conscience to all citizens, although, like Vermont, it also required all legislators to acknowledge their belief in "God, the creator, and the governor of the universe" and the divine inspiration of the Old and New Testaments. 2 FEDERAL AND STATE CONSTITUTIONS OF THE UNITED STATES at 1541, 1543 (Ben Perly Poore comp. 2d ed. 1924). In 1783, several prominent Pennsylvanian Jews, including Jonas Phillips, publicly complained about this oath, which effectively barred Jews from public office, Curry, FIRST FREEDOMS, at 161. Four years later, Phillips wrote to the members of the Constitutional Convention requesting they bar all religious tests for public office. Max Farrand, III RECORDS OF THE FEDERAL CONVENTION 78–79 (3 vols. rev. ed. 1937). Article IX, §4 of the 1790 Pennsylvania Constitution eliminated this bar to office, stating "no person, who acknowledges the being of a God and a future state of rewards and punishments, shall, on account of his religious sentiments, be disqualified to hold any office or place of trust or profit under this commonwealth." V Thorpe, FEDERAL AND STATE CONSTITUTIONS at 3100.

Delaware

Delaware was originally part of Pennsylvania. In 1702, the counties located upon the Delaware River were given some legislative autonomy, but remained under the executive authority of Pennsylvania during the entire colonial period. In its 1776 constitution, it granted all men a right of conscience to worship God in their own manner and it prohibited the subordination of any religious sect in preference to any other sect. On the other hand, it limited civil rights and officeholding to Trinitarian Christians (by an Act of 1777 Roman Catholics were permitted to hold office). The religious test for office was eliminated in Article I, §2 of Delaware's 1792 Constitution. I Thorpe, FEDERAL AND STATE CONSTITUTIONS at 582.

New York

New York was settled by the Dutch in 1624. In 1669, the English began exercising civil authority in the colony. Due in part to the different groups of Europeans settled in New York, at the time of the American Revolution, the Church of England was established (a claim disputed by non-Anglicans) only in four counties in and around New York City, as part of English colonial administration of the colony. Because the Church of England was the religion of the English monarchy, this establishment was abolished by New York's 1777 Constitution. The Constitution provided for "Free exercise and enjoyment of religious profession and worship, without discrimination or preference." 2 FEDERAL AND STATE CONSTITUTIONS OF THE UNITED STATES at 1338 (Ben Perly Poore comp. 2d ed. 1924). Although several of the original states barred ministers from holding some or all political offices, New York was the only northern state to do so. This officeholding ban was complete. Article 39 of the 1777 Constitution barred "ministers of the gospel" from "holding any civil or military office or place, within this State." The New York constitution also contained a provision, offered by John Jay, requiring all foreigners settling in New York to "abjure and renounce all allegiance and subjection to all and every foreign Kin, Prince, Potentate and State, in all matters ecclesiastical as well as civil." John Webb Pratt, RELIGION, POLITICS, AND DIVERSITY: THE CHURCH-STATE THEME IN NEW YORK HISTORY 95 (1967) (*quoting* 1777 N.Y. Const. Art. 42). As Pratt notes, this oath was designed "to prevent foreign Catholics from settling in New York." *Id.* In 1788, the New York legislature passed a test oath for all public officials effectively banning Catholics from holding public office for the remainder of the 18th century. *See* Pratt, at 107; Curry, FIRST FREEDOMS, at 161–162. Pratt estimates that in 1790 there were approximately 1,000 Catholics in New York, when the state's population was in excess of 300,000. Pratt, at 107. In 1806, after the first Catholic legislator was elected, and refused to take the required oath, the New York legislature amended the oath, excluding the last clause, which permitted conscientious Catholics to hold office. Pratt, at 124–25.

NEW JERSEY

New Jersey was first settled by the Dutch in 1609 and by the English in 1664. From 1664 until 1702 complete religious liberty was given to all by its Quaker proprietors. From 1702–1738, New Jersey became a royal colony and shared a colonial governor with New York, but at all times as a colony retained religious liberty. Its 1776 constitution again proclaimed liberty of conscience, and provided, "There shall be no establishment of any religious sect in the Province in preference to another." 2 FEDERAL AND STATE CONSTITUTIONS OF THE UNITED STATES at 1313 (Ben Perly Poore comp. 2d ed. 1924). Its constitution also forbade the imposition of "tithes, taxes, or any other rates, for the purpose of building or repairing any other church or churches, place or places of worship, or for the maintenance of any minister or ministry, contrary to what he believes is right, or has deliberately or voluntarily engaged himself to perform." V Thorpe, FEDERAL AND STATE CONSTITUTIONS at 2597. However, public office was limited to persons "professing a belief in the faith of any Protestant sect." *Id.* This limitation of public office to Protestants remained until passage of the New Jersey Constitution of 1844, which forbade religious tests for public office. *Id.* at 2599.

MARYLAND

Maryland was founded in 1632 by the Calverts (the first and second Lords Baltimore), who converted to Roman Catholicism from Anglicanism. The Calverts received a charter from the King giving them complete control of the colony. The ship taking the colonists to Maryland was not supposed to carry any Catholics, but somehow approximately 200 Catholics were transported to Maryland. The colony was never a great success for Catholics, due in part to religious upheavals in England (the Revolution in 1642 placed the Puritans in power under Oliver Cromwell, and the Glorious Revolution of 1688 ended the brief three year reign of Catholic King James II), and in part to the hostility of the other colonies (particularly Virginia) to this outpost of Catholicism. Because Maryland Catholics were a minority, the Calverts, through the Maryland Assembly in 1649, passed "An Act of Religious Toleration" for all except blasphemers and Jews. In 1691, the Calvert charter was annulled and in 1702 the Church of England was officially established. Catholics were not granted religious toleration under this new regime.

The Maryland constitution of 1776 guaranteed to "all persons professing the Christian religion, are equally entitled to protection in their religious liberty." III Thorpe, FEDERAL AND STATE CONSTITUTIONS at 1690, and permitted the legislature to tax the citizens "for the support of the Christian religion." *Id.* at 1689. The legislature refused to levy a general assessment to support the Christian religion at that time. In 1784, a general assessment was proposed. It was defeated not simply because this was believed to violate religious conscience or some older understanding of the separation of church and state, but also because the proposed general assessment limited the tax to certain Protestant sects and because Marylanders believed themselves to be overtaxed. This provision of the Maryland constitution permitting a general assessment was repealed in 1810.

Article XXXVI of the 1776 Constitution permitted public office holders to affirm rather than swear, III Thorpe, at 1690, and the Constitution was specifically amended in 1795 to permit Quakers to affirm to hold public office. *Id.* at 1702. (Three years later, the Constitution was amended to permit Quakers called to testify at witnesses to affirm, as long as the court found the prospective witness was "conscientiously scrupulous of taking an oath." *Id.* at 1702.) In 1795, the Constitution was amended requiring all public office holders to "subscribe a declaration of his belief in the Christian religion," *id.* at 1700, a provision which, although later amended to require a belief in God, remained until the Supreme Court held the test unconstitutional in the mid-20th century.

3. The Southern Colonies

North Carolina

North Carolina was settled in the 1650s and was chartered as a colony in 1663. North Carolina nominally established the Church of England in 1711. However, a large percentage of Protestant dissenters settled in North Carolina after being driven from Virginia, and the Church of England was never firmly established during the colonial era.

Article XIX of the Declaration of Rights of North Carolina's 1776 constitution guaranteed "the natural and unalienable right to worship Almighty God according to the dictates of their own conscience." III Thorpe, Federal and State Constitutions at 2788. The Forms of Government abolished the "establishment of any one religious church or denomination in this State, in preference to any other," and prohibited taxing a person for the support of a church in which he did not worship. *Id.* at 2793. It also barred from public office anyone "who shall deny the being of God or the truth of the Protestant religion." *Id.* Although the legislature passed a number of laws between 1776 and 1791 aiding religion, it never enacted a general assessment tax to support religion.

In 1835, the Constitution was amended to bar from office anyone who denied the truth of the "Christian" religion, thus allowing Catholics but not Jews to hold public office. *Id.* at 2798–99. This limitation of office ended with the adoption of the Constitution of 1868. On the relationship of church and state in colonial North Carolina, see Paul Conkin, *The Church Establishment in North Carolina, 1765–1776*, 32 N.C. Hist. Rev. 1 (1955), and see generally Stephen B. Weeks, Church and State in North Carolina (1893).

South Carolina

South Carolina was part of the original Carolina grant of 1663 and was first settled in 1670. It became a separate colony in 1735, and at that time formally established the Church of England.

Article XXXVIII of the 1778 Constitution of South Carolina declared: "The Christian Protestant religion shall be deemed, and is hereby constituted and declared to be, the established religion of the State." VI Thorpe, Federal and State Constitutions at 3255. This provision is the only official proclamation by a state after independence was declared of a religious establishment. *See* Curry, First Freedoms, at 191. This declaration lasted only two years, and appears to have been introduced in order to provide a method for incorporating churches. *Id.* The Constitution also limited public office to Protestants and provided that "All persons and religious societies who acknowledge that there is one God and a future state of rewards and punishments...shall be freely tolerated." 2 Federal and State Constitutions of the United States at 1626–27 (Ben Perly Poore comp. 2d ed. 1924). The Roman Catholic church was not permitted to incorporate, because the law of incorporation was structured to pertain only to Protestant societies, and a 1778 law of the state required the Governor to take an oath to "maintain and defend the laws of God, the protestant religion and the liberties of America." The Public Laws of South Carolina 297 (John D. Cushing comp. 1981)(No. 1211, 1778). The 1790 Constitution eliminated the religious test of office, as well as the establishment of the "Christian Protestant religion," and granted "free exercise and enjoyment of religious profession and worship of faith, without discrimination or preference." VI Thorpe, Federal and State Constitutions at 3264.

Georgia

In 1732, Georgia became the last of the original thirteen states to be chartered. It was settled shortly thereafter, for four disparate reasons: "imperialistic, mercantile, humanitarian, and evangelical." Reba Carolyn Strickland, Religion and the State in Georgia in the Eighteenth Century 14 (1939 repr. 1967). Although a large part of the colony's population consisted of Protestant dissenters, *id.* at 102, the Church of England was established as the state religion from 1758 until 1777. This meant little, as there "were rarely more than two" Anglican ministers in Georgia at the same time during the colonial era. *Id.* at 108.

The 1777 Constitution which disestablished the Church of England permitted the legislature to require towns to reserve two lots in the center of town for "houses of public worship," The First Laws of the State of Georgia 234 (John D. Cushing comp. 1981), and limited public office to Protestants. II Thorpe, Federal and State Constitutions at 779. Although there were apparently no more than four Catholics in the colony of Georgia, there was a substantial Jewish settlement in Savannah, which had dated back to the colonization of the colony. Strickland, at 42–43. This limitation of office was deleted from the 1789 Constitution, as was the phrase "so help me God" deleted from the oath of office. Article IV, § 5 of that Constitution also contains the following halfway position of religious liberty: "All persons shall have the free exercise of religion, without being obliged to contribute to the support of any religious profession but their own." II Thorpe, at 789. In 1785, after the end of the Revolutionary War, the legislature enacted a law taxing citizens for the support of their own religion, although it apparently never went into effect. Strickland, at 164–67. The 1798 Constitution guaranteed free exercise of religion and deleted any reference concerning a duty to support. II Thorpe, at 800–01. The religious freedom clause concluded: "No one religious society shall ever be established in this State, in preference to another; nor shall any person be denied the enjoyment of any civil right merely on account of his religious principles." *Id.* at 801. By the turn of the century, slaves were permitted to worship freely, and "[b]y 1800, the African Baptist Church was an accepted part of the religious scene in Savannah." Strickland, at 182.

Virginia

Virginia was permanently settled by the English in 1607, in Jamestown. Two years later, the Church of England was formally established in Virginia. Anglican ministers did not find Virginia hospitable to them. Ministers were kept on a short leash by the wealthy landowners, who paid the ministers salary in tobacco. The Two-Penny Act, enacted in 1759, "ignited the colonists' smoldering anticlericalism." Bailyn, IDEOLOGICAL ORIGINS, at 252. The act permitted Virginians to pay ministers in pence rather than, as customary and previously required by law, in tobacco. Due to a crop shortage in 1758, the market price of tobacco was six cents a pound, and the act permitted payment of the salary at the rate of two cents a pound. I Stokes, CHURCH AND STATE, at 367. Anglican ministers claimed (with some justification) that this act reduced their already meager incomes, and it was nullified in England. A minister named James Mauzy filed suit to recover the back salary. Called the *Parson's Cause,* the vestry was defended by Patrick Henry, who claimed English interference with colonial action was tyranny. Henry's eloquence led the jury to award Mauzy one cent in damages. *Id. See also* Rhys Isaac, THE TRANSFORMATION OF VIRGINIA, 1740–1790 144–57 (1982).

In *Everson v. Bd. of Educ.*, 330 U.S. 1 (1947), excerpted in Chapter Five, the Supreme Court relied on the history of the disestablishment of the Church of England in Virginia to interpret the First Amendment. Although much criticized, the history of religious freedom in Virginia has formed the basis for the Court's understanding of the meaning of the First Amendment. Much of this is due to the roles played by Thomas Jefferson and James Madison in securing religious freedom in Virginia and in the United States. Jefferson, of course, was the primary author of the Declaration of Independence, and Madison was a member of the Constitutional Convention and a key participant in the framing of the First Amendment. In addition to the public offices held by both men in Virginia, as well as the other important offices held by them in the federal government, Jefferson and Madison were the third and fourth Presidents of the United States, respectively.

The history of Virginia from colony to independent state to member of the United States is well told in Isaac, TRANSFORMATION OF VIRGINIA. The effort to disestablish the Church of England is well detailed in Thomas E. Buckley, CHURCH AND STATE IN REVOLUTIONARY VIRGINIA, 1776–1787 (1977). A more general but thorough discussion is found in William Lee Miller, THE FIRST LIBERTY, at 1–150. The following is a survey of the disestablishment of the Church of England and the protection of liberty of conscience from 1776–1790.

Although the Church of England was the established church in 1776, and remained the most influential religious group in Virginia, "Presbyterians claimed the religious allegiance of a large majority of the settlers beyond the Blue Ridge Mountains." Buckley, at 13. In addition, Baptists were quickly growing in number and political power. *Id.* In May 1776, the colonial government instructed its representatives in the Continental Congress to propose independence from Great Britain. The government then proposed adopting a Declaration of Rights and a Constitution. The last provision of the Declaration of Rights, Article 16, was a proposal concerning liberty of conscience.

ARTICLE 16 OF THE VIRGINIA DECLARATION OF RIGHTS

On June 12, 1776, the Virginia Declaration of Rights was adopted. Largely written by George Mason (and adapted by Thomas Jefferson when he shortly thereafter wrote the Declaration of Independence), the original draft of Article 16 of the Declaration of Rights perceives religious belief in terms of toleration rather than right. As originally drafted by Mason, Article 16 provided:

> That *as* religion or the duty which we owe to our *divine and omnipotent* Creator, and the manner of discharging it, can be governed only by reason and

> conviction, not by force or violence; and therefore that all men should enjoy the fullest toleration in the exercise of religion, according to the dictates of conscience, unpunished and unrestrained by the magistrate, unless, under color of religion, any man disturb the peace, the happiness, or safety of society, *or of individuals*. And that it is the mutual duty of all, to practice Christian forbearance, love and charity towards each other. (italics added.)

A special committee amended Mason's draft by eliminating the words italicized above and by replacing "governed" with "directed." Madison first attempted to substitute the idea that "all men are equally entitled to the full and free exercise of [religion] according to the dictates of conscience" for Mason's grant of toleration. His effort failed. His second effort, more eloquent but with the same idea and essentially the same language, was more successful. As finally adopted, Article 16 read:

> That Religion, or the duty which we owe to our Creator, and the manner of discharging it can be directed only by reason and conviction, not by force or violence, and therefore all men are equally entitled to the free exercise of religion, according to the dictates of conscience; and that it is the mutual duty of all to practice Christian forbearance, love and charity towards each other.

Although the Virginia Declaration of Rights assured liberty of conscience, it did not resolve a number of issues concerning the relationship of the Church of England and the commonwealth of Virginia. In Thomas Buckley's view, one consequence of Thomas Jefferson's anticlericalism was that "although advocating freedom of conscience and the voluntary system of church support, Jefferson did not envision a truly free church, separated from state control." Buckley, at 21. In late 1776, after calls to disestablish the Church of England, to exempt dissenters from contributing to the established church, and to reserve title in the parish glebes in the state, as well as responses to those calls, the Assembly deferred devising a system concerning the relationship of religion and government, including any general assessment. It did, however, invalidate all British laws limiting religious opinions. *Id.* at 30–36. The legislature's actions "left religion in Virginia and particularly the established church in an ambiguous situation." *Id.* at 36. Dissenters were not required to support the established church, nor their own churches, but the public officials retained the discretion whether to license dissenting meeting houses, and the established church remained under the state's regulatory control.

In late 1779, Virginia repealed the law providing salaries for the established clergy, and a bill to establish the "Christian religion" as "the true Religion" failed. *Id.* at 60–61, 57. Efforts to enact Jefferson's Bill 82 "for Establishing Religious Freedom" and to provide a general assessment also failed.

In the 1784–85 session of the Virginia General Assembly, a proposed bill taxing citizens of Virginia to pay for teachers of Christian religion was introduced. Included among the supporters of the general assessment were Patrick Henry, George Washington, John Marshall, Governor Benjamin Harrison and Edmund Randolph. Opposed were Thomas Jefferson (then in Paris), George Mason, and James Madison, the authors of Article 16 of the Virginia Declaration of Rights. After a third reading of the bill in the General Assembly was postponed in late December 1784, the bill was distributed to Virginia counties by the House of Delegates:

A Bill Establishing a Provision for Teachers of the Christian Religion

> Whereas the general diffusion of Christian knowledge hath a natural tendency to correct the morals of men, restrain their vices, and preserve the peace

of society; which cannot be effected without a competent provision for learned teachers, who may be thereby enabled to devote their time and attention to the duty of instructing such citizens, as from their circumstances and want of education, cannot otherwise attain such knowledge; and it is judged that such provision may be made by the Legislature, without counteracting the liberal principle heretofore adopted and intended to be preserved by abolishing all distinctions of pre-eminence amongst the different societies or communities of Christians;

Be it therefore enacted by the General Assembly, That for the support of Christian teachers, per centum on the amount, or in the pound on the sum payable for tax on the property within this Commonwealth, is hereby assessed, and shall be paid by every person chargeable with the said tax at the time the same shall become due; and the Sheriffs of the several Counties shall have power to levy and collect the same in the same manner and under the like restrictions and limitations, as are or may be prescribed by the laws for raising the Revenues of this State.

And be it enacted, That for every sum so paid, the Sheriff or Collector shall give a receipt, expressing therein to what society of Christians the person from whom it may receive the same shall direct the money to be paid, keeping a distinct account thereof in his books. The Sheriff of every County, shall, on or before the day of in every year, return to the Court, upon oath, two alphabetical lists of the payments to him made, distinguishing in columns opposite to the names of the persons who shall have paid the same, the society to which the money so paid was by them appropriated; and one column for the names where no appropriation shall be made. One of which lists, after being recorded in a book to be kept for that purpose, shall be filed by the Clerk in his office; the other shall by the Sheriff be fixed up in the Court-house, there to remain for the inspection of all concerned. And the Sheriff, after deducting five per centum for the collection, shall forthwith pay to such person or persons as shall be appointed to receive the same by the Vestry, Elders, or Directors, however denominated of each such society, the sum so stated to be due to that society; or in default thereof, upon the motion of such person or persons to the next or any succeeding Court, execution shall be awarded for the same against the Sheriff and his security, his and their executors or administrators; provided that ten days previous notice be given of such motion. An upon every such execution, the Officer serving the same shall proceed to immediate sale of the estate taken, and shall not accept of security for payment at the end of three months, nor to have the goods forthcoming at the day of sale; for his better direction wherein, the Clerk shall endorse upon every such execution that no security of any kind shall be taken.

And be it further enacted, That the money to be raised by virtue of this Act, shall be by the Vestries, Elders, or Directors of each religious society, appropriated to a provision for a Minister or Teacher of the Gospel of their denomination, or the providing places of divine worship, and to none other use whatsoever; except in the denominations of Quakers and Menonists, who may receive what is collected from their members, and place it in their general fund, to be disposed of in a manner which they shall think best calculated to promote their particular mode of worship.

And be it enacted, That all sums which at the time of payment to the Sheriff or Collector may not be appropriated by the person paying the same, shall be accounted for with the Court in manner as by this Act is directed; and after deducting for his collection, the Sheriff shall pay the amount thereof (upon account certified by the Court to the Auditors of Public Accounts, and by them to the treasurer) into the public Treasury, to be disposed of under the direction of the General Assembly, for the encouragement of seminaries of learning within the Counties whence such sums shall arise, and to no other use or purpose whatsoever.

THIS Act shall commence, and be in force from and after the ____ day of ____ in the year ____.

After distribution of the bill, Madison anonymously wrote his *Memorial and Remonstrance* against the proposed general assessment. This bill was never passed, in part due to the effectiveness of the *Memorial and Remonstrance* in generating unified opposition to the bill from Baptists, Methodists, Presbyterians and Enlightenment thinkers. The *Memorial and Remonstrance*, however, became one of the most important documents in the history of law and religion, embraced by the Supreme Court as defining the meaning of the First Amendment.

To the Honorable the General Assembly of the Commonwealth of Virginia: A Memorial and Remonstrance

[James Madison]

We the subscribers, citizens of the said Commonwealth, having taken into serious consideration, a Bill printed by order of the last Session of General Assembly, entitled "A Bill establishing a provision for Teachers of the Christian Religion," and conceiving that the same if finally armed with the sanctions of a law, will be a dangerous abuse of power, are bound as faithful members of a free State to remonstrate against it, and to declare the reasons by which we are determined. We remonstrate against the said Bill,

1. Because we hold it for a fundamental and undeniable truth, "that Religion or the duty which we owe to our Creator and the manner of discharging it, can be directed only by reason and conviction, not by force or violence." The Religion then of every man must be left to the conviction and conscience of every man; and it is the right of every man to exercise it as these may dictate. This right is in its nature an unalienable right. It is unalienable, because the opinions of men, depending only on the evidence contemplated by their own minds cannot follow the dictates of other men: It is unalienable also, because what is here a right towards men, is a duty towards the Creator. It is the duty of every man to render to the Creator such homage and such only as he believes to be acceptable to him. This duty is precedent, both in order of time and in degree of obligation, to the claims of Civil Society. Before any man can be considered as a member of Civil Society, he must be considered as a subject of the Governour of the Universe: And if a member of Civil Society, who enters into any subordinate Association, must always do it with a reservation of his duty to the General Authority; much more must every man who becomes a member of any particular Civil Society, do it with a saving of his allegiance to the Universal Sovereign. We maintain therefore that in matters of Religion, no mans right is abridged by the institution of Civil Society and that Religion is wholly ex-

empt from its cognizance. True it is, that no other rule exists, by which any question which may divide a Society, can be ultimately determined, but the will of the majority; but it is also true that the majority may trespass on the rights of the minority.

2. Because if Religion be exempt from the authority of the Society at large, still less can it be subject to that of the Legislative Body. The latter are but the creatures and viceregents of the former. Their jurisdiction is both derivative and limited: it is limited with regard to the co-ordinate departments, more necessarily is it limited with regard to the constituents. The preservation of a free Government requires not merely, that the metes and bounds which separate each department of power be invariably maintained; but more especially that neither of them be suffered to overleap the great Barrier which defends the rights of the people. The Rulers who are guilty of such an encroachment, exceed the commission from which they derive their authority, and are Tyrants. The People who submit to it are governed by laws made neither by themselves nor by an authority derived from them, and are slaves.

3. Because it is proper to take alarm at the first experiment on our liberties. We hold this prudent jealously to be the first duty of Citizens, and one of the noblest characteristics of the late Revolution. The free men of America did not wait till usurped power had strengthened itself by exercise, and entangled the question in precedents. They saw all the consequences in the principle, and they avoided the consequences by denying the principle. We revere this lesson too much soon to forget it. Who does not see that the same authority which can establish Christianity, in exclusion of all other Religions, may establish with the same ease any particular sect of Christians, in exclusion of all other Sects? That the same authority which can force a citizen to contribute three pence only of his property for the support of any one establishment, may force him to conform to any other establishment in all cases whatsoever?

4. Because the Bill violates that equality which ought to be the basis of every law, and which is more indispensable, in proportion as the validity or expediency of any law is more liable to be impeached. If "all men are by nature equally free and independent," all men are to be considered as entering into Society on equal conditions; as relinquishing no more, and therefore retaining no less, one than another, of their natural rights. Above all are they to be considered as retaining an "*equal* title to the free exercise of Religion according to the dictates of Conscience." Whilst we assert for ourselves a freedom to embrace, to profess and to observe the Religion which we believe to be of divine origin, we cannot deny an equal freedom to those whose minds have not yet yielded to the evidence which has convinced us. If this freedom be abused, it is an offence against God, not against man: To God, therefore, not to man, must an account of it be rendered. As the Bill violates equality by subjecting some peculiar burdens, so it violates the same principle, by granting to others peculiar burdens, so it violates the same principle, by granting to others peculiar exemptions. Are the Quakers and Menonists the only sects who think a compulsive support of their Religions unnecessary and unwarrantable? Can their piety alone be entrusted with the care of public worship? Ought their Religions to be endowed above all others with extraordinary privileges by which proselytes may be enticed from all others? We think too favorably of the justice and good sense of these denominations to believe that they either covet pre-eminences over their

fellow citizens or that they will be seduced by them from the common opposition to the measure.

5. Because the Bill implies either that the Civil Magistrate is a competent Judge of Religious Truth; or that he may employ Religion as an engine of Civil policy. The first is an arrogant pretension falsified by the contradictory opinions of Rulers in all ages, and throughout the world: the second an unhallowed perversion of the means of salvation.

6. Because the establishment proposed by the Bill is not requisite for the support of the Christian Religion. To say that it is, is a contradiction of the Christian Religion itself, for every page of it disavows a dependence on the powers of this world: it is a contradiction to fact; for it is known that this Religion both existed and flourished, not only without the support of human laws, but in spite of every opposition from them, and not only during the period of miraculous aid, but long after it had been left to its own evidence and the ordinary care of Providence. Nay, it is a contradiction in terms; for a Religion not invented by human policy, must have pre-existed and been supported, before it was established by human policy. It is moreover to weaken in those who profess this Religion a pious confidence in its innate excellence and the patronage of its Author; and to foster in those who still reject it, a suspicion that its friends are too conscious of its fallacies to trust its own merits.

7. Because experience witnesseth that ecclesiastical establishments, instead of maintaining the purity and efficacy of Religion, have had a contrary operation. During almost fifteen centuries has the legal establishment of Christianity been on trial. What have been its fruits? More or less in all places, pride and indolence in the Clergy, ignorance and servility in the laity, in both, superstition, bigotry and persecution. Enquire of the Teachers of Christianity for the ages in which it appeared in its greatest lustre; those of every sect, point to the ages prior to its incorporation with Civil policy. Propose a restoration of this primitive State in which its Teachers depended on the voluntary rewards of their flocks, many of them predict its downfall. On which Side ought their testimony to have greatest weight, when for or when against their interest?

8. Because the establishment in question is not necessary for the support of Civil Government. If it be urged as necessary for the support of Civil Government only as it is a means of supporting Religion, and it be not necessary for the latter purpose, it cannot be necessary for the former. If Religion be not within the cognizance of Civil Government how can its legal establishment be necessary to Civil Government? What influence in fact have ecclesiastical establishments had on Civil Society? In some instances they have been seen to erect a spiritual tyranny on the ruins of the Civil Authority; in many instances they have been seen upholding the thrones of political tyranny; in no instance have they been seen the guardians of the liberties of the people. Rulers who wished to subvert the public liberty, may have found an established Clergy convenient auxiliaries. A just Government instituted to secure & perpetuate it needs them not. Such a Government will be best supported by protecting every Citizen in the enjoyment of his Religion with the same equal hand which protects his person and his property; by neither invading the equal rights of any Sect, nor suffering any Sect to invade those of another.

9. Because the proposed establishment is a departure from that generous policy, which, offering an Asylum to the persecuted and oppressed of every

Nation and Religion, promised a lustre to our country, and an accession to the number of its citizens. What a melancholy mark is the Bill of sudden degeneracy? Instead of holding forth an Asylum to the persecuted, it is itself a signal of persecution. It degrades from the equal rank of Citizen all those whose opinions in Religion do not bend to those of the Legislative authority. Distant as it may be in its present form from the Inquisition, it differs from it only in degree. The one is the first step, the other the last in the career of intolerance. The magnanimous sufferer under this cruel scourge in foreign Regions, must view the Bill as a Beacon on our Coast, warning him to seek some other haven, where liberty and philanthropy in their due extent, may offer a more certain repose from his Troubles.

10. Because it will have a like tendency to banish our Citizens. The allurements presented by other situations are every day thinning their number. To superadd a fresh motive to emigration by revoking the liberty which they now enjoy, would be the same species of folly which has dishonoured and depopulated flourishing kingdoms.

11. Because it will destroy that moderation and harmony which the forbearance of our laws to intermeddle with Religion has produced among its several sects. Torrents of blood have been spilt in the old world, by vain attempts of the secular arm, to extinguish Religious discord, by proscribing all difference in Religious opinion. Time has at length revealed the true remedy. Every relaxation of narrow and rigorous policy, wherever it has been tried, has been found to assuage the disease. The American Theatre has exhibited proofs that equal and compleat liberty, if it does not wholly eradicate it, sufficiently destroys its malignant influence on the health and prosperity of the State. If with the salutary effects of this system under our own eyes, we begin to contract the bounds of Religious freedom, we know no name that will too severely reproach our folly. At least let warning be taken at the first fruits of the threatened innovation. The very appearance of the Bill has transformed "that Christian forbearance, love and charity," which of late mutually prevailed, into animosities and jealousies, which may not soon be appeased. What mischiefs may not be dreaded, should this enemy to the public quiet be armed with the force of a law?

12. Because the policy of the Bill is adverse to the diffusion of the light of Christianity. The first wish of those who enjoy this precious gift ought to be that it may be imparted to the whole race of mankind. Compare the number of those who have as yet received it with the number still remaining under the dominion of false Religions; and how small is the former! Does the policy of the Bill tend to lessen the disproportion? No; it at once discourages those who are strangers to the light of revelation from coming into the Region of it; and countenances by example the nations who continue in darkness, in shutting out those who might convey it to them. Instead of Levelling as far as possible, every obstacle to the victorious progress of Truth, the Bill with an ignoble and unchristian timidity would circumscribe it with a wall of defense against the encroachments of error.

13. Because attempts to enforce by legal sanctions, acts obnoxious to so great a proportion of Citizens, tend to enervate the laws in general, and to slacken the bands of Society. If it be difficult to execute any law which is not generally deemed necessary or salutary, what must be the case, where it is

deemed invalid and dangerous? And what may be the effect of so striking an example of impotency in the Government, on its general authority?

14. Because a measure of such singular magnitude and delicacy ought not to be imposed, without the clearest evidence that it is called for by a majority of citizens, and no satisfactory method is yet proposed by which the voice of the majority in this case may be determined, or its influence secured. "The people of the respective counties are indeed requested to signify their opinion respecting the adoption of the Bill to the next Session of Assembly." But the representation must be made equal, before the voice of either of the Representatives or of the Counties will be that of the people. Our hope is that neither of the former will, after due consideration, espouse the dangerous principle of the Bill. Should the event disappoint us, it will still leave us in full confidence, that a fair appeal to the latter will reverse the sentence against our liberties.

15. Because finally, "the equal right of every citizen to the free exercise of his Religion according to the dictates of conscience" is held by the same tenure with all our other rights. If we recur to its origin, it is equally the gift of nature; if we weigh its importance, it cannot be less dear to us; if we consult the "Declaration of those rights which pertain to the good people of Virginia, as the basis and foundation of Government," it is enumerated with equal solemnity, or rather studied emphasis. Either then, we must say, that the Will of the Legislature is the only measure of their authority; and that in the plenitude of this authority, they may sweep away all our fundamental rights; or, that they are bound to leave this particular right untouched and sacred: Either we must say, that they may controul the freedom of the press, may abolish the Trial by Jury, may swallow up the Executive and Judiciary Powers of the State; nay that they may despoil us of our very right of suffrage, and erect themselves into an independent and hereditary Assembly or, we must say, that they have no authority to enact into law the Bill under consideration. We the Subscribers say, that the General Assembly of this Commonwealth have no such authority: And that no effort may be omitted on our part against so dangerous an usurpation, we oppose to it, this remonstrance; earnestly praying, as we are in duty bound, that the Supreme Lawgiver of the Universe, by illuminating those to whom it is addressed, may on the one hand, turn their Councils from the very act which would affront his holy prerogative, or violate the trust committed to them: and on the other, guide them into every measure which may be worthy of his [blessing, may re]dound to their own praise, and may establish more firmly the liberties, the prosperity and the happiness of the Commonwealth.

Well before the general assessment controversy, Thomas Jefferson introduced and urged the General Assembly in 1779 to pass a bill establishing religious freedom based on Article 16 of the Virginia Declaration of Rights, which granted the free exercise of religion to all citizens in Virginia. William Lee Miller suggests that the bill was first drafted in 1777, and based on ideas spoken by Jefferson in the Virginia House of Delegates in 1776. It was introduced as Bill 82, along with 125 other laws revising the code of Virginia. In 1779, Jefferson had recently been named governor, and consequently was no longer a member of the House of Delegates. After the defeat of the general assessment bill in 1785, Madison reintroduced Bill 82. With Jefferson "looking on" in Paris as the American ambassador to France, on January 16, 1786, a Bill establishing Religious Freedom was passed by the Virginia Assembly.

A Bill for Establishing Religious Freedom

Well aware that the opinions and belief of men depend not on their own will, but follow involuntarily the evidence proposed in their minds; that Almighty God hath created the mind free, *and manifested his supreme will that free it shall remain by making it altogether insusceptible of restraint;* that all attempts to influence it by temporal punishments, or burthens, or by civil incapacitations, tend only to beget habits of hypocrisy and meanness, and are a departure from the plan of the holy author of our religion, who being lord both of body and mind, yet chose not to propagate it by coercions on either, as was in his Almighty power to do, *but to extend it by its influence on reason alone;* that the impious presumption of legislators and rulers, civil as well as ecclesiastical, who, being themselves but fallible and uninspired men, have assumed dominion over the faith of others, setting up their own opinions and modes of thinking as the only true and infallible, and as such endeavoring to impose them on others, hath established and maintained false religions over the greatest part of the world and through all time: That to compel a man to furnish contributions of money for the propagation of opinions which he disbelieves *and abhors*, is sinful and tyrannical: that even the forcing him to support this or that teacher of his own religious persuasion, is depriving him of the comfortable liberty of giving his contributions to the particular pastor whose morals he would make his pattern, and whose powers he feels most persuasive to righteousness; and is withdrawing from the ministry those temporary rewards, which proceeding from an approbation of their personal conduct, are an additional incitement to earnest and unremitting labours for the instruction of mankind; that our civil rights have no dependence on our religious opinions, any more than our opinions in physics or geometry; that therefore the proscribing any citizen as unworthy the public confidence by laying upon him an incapacity of being called to offices of trust and emolument, unless he profess or renounce this or that religious opinion, is depriving him injuriously of those privileges and advantage to which, in common with his fellow citizens, he has a natural right; that it tends also to corrupt the principles of that *very* religion it is meant to encourage, by bribing with a monopoly of worldly honours and emoluments, those who will externally profess and conform to it; that though indeed these are criminal who do not withstand such temptation, yet neither are those innocent who lay the bait in their way; *that the opinions of men are not the object of civil government, nor under its jurisdiction*; that to suffer the civil magistrate to intrude his powers into the field of opinion and to restrain the profession or propagation of principles on supposition of their ill tendency is a dangerous fallacy, which at once destroys all religious liberty, because he being of course judge of that tendency will make his opinions the rule of judgment, and approve or condemn the sentiments of others only as they shall square with or differ from his own; that it is time enough for the rightful purpose of civil government for its officers to interfere when principles break out into overt acts against peace and good order; and finally, that truth is great and will prevail if left to herself; that she is the proper and sufficient antagonist to error, and has nothing to fear from the conflict unless by human interposition disarmed of her natural weapons, free argument and debate; errors ceasing to be dangerous when it is permitted freely to contradict them.

We the General Assembly of Virginia do enact that no man shall be compelled to frequent or support any religious worship, place, or ministry whatsoever, nor shall be enforced, restrained, molested, or burthened in his body or goods,

> nor shall otherwise suffer, on account of his religious opinions or belief; but that all men shall be free to profess, and by argument to maintain, their opinions in matters of religion, and that the same shall in no wise diminish, enlarge, or affect their civil capacities.
>
> And though we well know that this assembly, elected by the people for the ordinary purposes of legislation only, have no power to restrain the acts of succeeding Assemblies, constituted with powers equal to our own, and that therefore to declare this act irrevocable would be of no effect in law; yet we are free to declare, and do declare, that the rights hereby asserted are of the natural rights of mankind, and that if any act shall be hereafter passed to repeal the present or to narrow its operation, such act will be in infringement of natural right. (italics added.)

After amending the Bill by deleting the phrases italicized above, Bill 82 passed, and liberty of religious conscience was secured in Virginia. A little more than a year later, Madison was a Virginia representative at the Constitutional Convention in Philadelphia.

Notes

1. Several ideas recur in the efforts of the states to determine how religion "fit" in a republic. One strand of thought is exemplified by Article III of the Massachusetts Constitution, which both creates a general assessment system for the support of ministers of the Gospel and which guarantees that all "Christians" are "equally under the protection of the laws" and that "no sect" shall be "subordinated" to another. A similar approach to Article 16 of the Virginia Declaration of Rights was exemplified by George Washington, Patrick Henry and others as a bar to the authority of the state to tax its citizens to support a minister of the gospel. Was this because Protestant Christianity was believed necessary to inculcate virtue in the people, and the virtue of the people was necessary to the survival of the United States, and thus the proper subject of public support? Article III of the 1780 Massachusetts Constitution answered this question in the affirmative: "As the happiness of a people, and the good order and preservation of a civil government, essentially depend upon piety, religion and morality; and as these cannot be generally diffused through a community, but by the institution of the public worship of GOD, and of public instructions in piety, religion and morality...." As stated by Virginian Richard Henry Lee, "Refiners may weave as fine a web of reason as they please, but the experience of all times shews Religion to be the guardian of morals—And he must be a very inattentive oberver in our Country, who does not see that avarice is accomplishing the destruction of religion, for want of a legal obligation to contribute something to its support." Gerard V. Bradley, Church-State Relationships in America 38 (1987), *quoting* James Curtis Ballagh, 2 The Letters of Richard Henry Lee 304–05 (1911). The historian Gordon Wood notes that religion was considered a mainstay for promoting virtue. Gordon S. Wood, The Creation of the American Republic, 1776–1787 427 (1969). Madison's *Memorial and Remonstrance* exemplifies another influential point of view: that of the dissenter, who rejects the idea that public support of religion is necessary to the maintenance of the moral virtue of the people, and asserts that public support of religion was actually harmful to both Christianity and the state. In ¶ 8 of the *Memorial and Remonstrance*, Madison writes, "the establishment in question is not necessary for the support of Civil Government. If it be urged as necessary for the support of Civil Government only as it is a means of supporting Religion, and it be not necessary for the latter purpose, it cannot be necessary for the former." The general

assessment, Madison argues, harms Christianity, for it "discourages those who are strangers to the light of revelation from coming into the Region of it." It harms society because "attempts to enforce by legal sanctions, acts obnoxious to so great a proportion of Citizens, tend to enervate the laws in general, and to slacken the bands of Society." Gordon Wood concludes that "so pronounced was the encouragement of religion in the critical period that Virginia's 1786 act for the establishment of religious freedom...became something of an anomaly." Wood, at 427. Madison's liberal rather than republican understanding of religious liberty took root in Virginia, and slowly spread to the other states, eventually reaching even New England.

2. Another influential factor in the struggle for religious liberty was demographic. Although the sects varied in size from state to state, members of one Protestant sect or another formed a majority of the population in each of the states. Although the views on religious liberty held by the various sects differed, it was nevertheless a Protestant Christian sect's view that predominated in each of the states. In 1776, there were approximately 20,000 Roman Catholics in the United States (out of a population of about 2.5 million people), the majority of whom resided in Maryland. John Tracy Ellis, CATHOLICS IN COLONIAL AMERICA 395–96 (1965) (*citing* Charles H. Metzger, CATHOLICS AND THE AMERICAN REVOLUTION: A STUDY IN RELIGIOUS CLIMATE 96 (1962)). By the end of 1790, that number had grown, Ellis estimates, to about 35,000. *Id.* at 459. The number of Jews in colonial America numbered approximately 2,500 at the time of the Revolution, and never more than 500 families at any point in the 18th century. Marcus, *Colonial Jew in America,* at 1210, xxvii. Because of the limitation of public office to "Protestants," Catholics were barred from holding office in several states, although not in Maryland and Pennsylvania, where most Catholics lived. Because of that limitation, and the later limitation of office to "Christians," or to those who swore an oath declaring as true the divine inspiration of the Old and New Testaments of the Christian Bible, Jews were barred more thoroughly and longer than Catholics from public office. Four states abolished religious tests for office in the 1790s. Does that suggest a dramatic change in the idea of liberty of conscience? Pennsylvania was the state with the largest number of Catholics next to Maryland, and its 1776 oath barred only Jews. There was a substantial population of Jews in Philadelphia during the last third of the 18th century, and Pennsylvania rephrased its religious test for office in Article IX, § 4 of its 1790 Constitution, which allowed all those who believed in God and a future state of rewards and punishments to serve. Delaware forbade religious tests for office in 1792, reversing its 1776 position. Two southern states, Georgia and South Carolina, reversed their positions in 1789 and 1790, respectively. None of these states had a substantial population of Jews or Catholics, and the last two were quite hostile to the settlement of both Jews and Catholics. Are these concessions to non-Protestants consistent with a more liberalized view of religious liberty? Marcus writes that the colony of Rhode Island denied the application to citizenship of two Jews in the early 1760s. Marcus, at 436–38. What does it mean that Jews in Rhode Island, the colony founded by Roger Williams and where liberty of conscience was always protected, were not permitted to hold public office until the adoption of Rhode Island's Constitution in 1842? Does the absence of a liberalization of the oath of office until well into the nineteenth century in other states, like Massachusetts, New Jersey and North Carolina, lessen a claim of greater toleration or respect for non-Protestants or non-Christians? How should the differing decisions by the various states affect any interpretation of the meaning of religious liberty in late eighteenth century America?

3. Several state constitutions of the late eighteenth century permitted those conscientiously scrupulous of bearing arms to choose to pay an equivalent. As might be expected, Pennsylvania included such a provision in its 1776 Constitution, V Thorpe, FEDERAL AND STATE CONSTITUTIONS at 3083, a provision copied the next year by Vermont. *Id.* at 3741. New York and New Hampshire also constitutionally permitted "Quakers" (New York) or the conscientiously scrupulous (New Hampshire) to pay an equivalent instead of bearing arms. In addition, North Carolina, Rhode Island and Virginia all enacted statutory exemptions. Chester James Antieau, *et al.*, RELIGION UNDER THE STATE CONSTITUTIONS 116 (1965). Further, Maryland, Delaware and New Hampshire all permitted Quakers to affirm rather than swear an oath. Are these constitutional provisions proof that the varying dictates of religious conscience required the state to acknowledge and respect those differences in law? Is the absence such provisions in other state constitutions proof otherwise? In light of the earlier control exercised by Congregationalists in New England, should the decisions of the New England states in the late eighteenth and early nineteenth centuries to permit dissenters to pay taxes to their own churches rather than to the Standing Order be viewed as another example of a religious liberty exemption?

4. Although there was a great deal of ferment during the late eighteenth century, the Congregational establishment in New England lasted until the nineteenth century (Vermont, in 1807, ended its establishment first, and Massachusetts, in 1833, ended its establishment last). What importance should we attach to these events in discerning the meaning of the First Amendment? Is this a consequence of the ties between politics and religion? Is it important that the "establishment" might be the Congregational church in one town, and the Episcopalian church in another? The five southern colonies, as well as Maryland and New York, all disestablished the Church of England during the Revolutionary War. Does this suggest that the reasons for disestablishment had less to do with a philosophical turn concerning the proper relationship of church and state than with a political turn regarding institutions affiliated with England? Does Article XXXIII of Maryland's 1776 Constitution, which both guaranteed liberty of conscience and which permitted the legislature to "lay a general and equal tax, for the support of the Christian religion," suggest a different understanding of the relationship of liberty of conscience and disestablishment than in either Virginia in 1786 or in the Supreme Court today? Is Virginia's experience qualitatively different from the other southern colonies because Madison and Jefferson and other important figures were involved in the events from 1776 to 1785? Because the reasons for the debate were crystallized at a philosophical level? Because of Virginia's relatively large population? Because of its variety of Protestant groups? Justice Wiley Rutledge, dissenting in the 1947 decision in *Everson v. Bd. of Educ.*, 330 U.S. 1 (1947), concluded that the effort to ensure religious liberty in Virginia became the "warp and woof of our constitutional tradition" "by the common unifying force of Madison's life, thought and sponsorship." *Id.* at 39. Do you agree?

5. The fundamental law of the middle colonies of Pennsylvania, Delaware and New Jersey, along with Rhode Island, both guaranteed liberty of religious conscience and barred the establishment of any religion. Should we look to those colonies for clues about the proper relationship of religious faith and government, rather than to New England or the south? What clues should we look for? The absence of persecution, the ability to worship freely, or formal grants or denials of civil rights and liberties in law? Should grants of rights of conscience be assessed in light of the relationship or power of differing Protestant sects? Should the legal or cultural position of Roman Catholics and Jews be ignored because of their small numbers? To what extent should the lack of concern in almost all colonies, including the middle colonies, for the rights of the non-reli-

gious (atheists and agnostics) affect our understanding? Are the middle colonies representative of the tenor of revolutionary times? If so, which one(s)?

6. As mentioned earlier, a number of the original states, including New York and border and southern states, including Virginia, constitutionally prohibited "ministers of the gospel" from holding public office. *See* I Stokes, CHURCH AND STATE, at 622–26. To what extent is this evidence of a policy of divorcing church and state? To what extent is it helpful to interpret the meaning of liberty of conscience or the free exercise of religion in the eighteenth century?

7. Professor John Witte suggests that one cannot understand the development of the ideas of religious liberty in the 18th century without being aware of two theological and two political views prominent at that time. The theological views were Puritan and Evangelical, and the political views were Enlightenment and Civic Republican. The Puritan view was exemplified by the Massachusetts experience, and the Evangelical by the Baptist Isaac Backus and other religious dissenters. The Enlightenment view is exemplified by Madison and Jefferson, and the Civic Republican view by George Washington, John Adams and others. The Puritan view was linked with Civic Republicanism, and Evangelicals were tied to Enlightenment thinkers. The competing views, then, are found in the Massachusetts (Puritan-Civic Republican) and Virginia (Evangelical-Enlightenment) constitutions. Although there was both movement by the founders among those views, and a pairing of the theological and political views, they remained distinct approaches to the idea of religious liberty. Understanding the views of the founders on religion and government, then, "must be sought in the tensions among [those views] and in the general principles that emerged from their interaction." John Witte, Jr., RELIGION AND THE AMERICAN CONSTITUTIONAL EXPERIMENT: ESSENTIAL RIGHTS AND LIBERTIES 24–25 (2000). Does this support the view that attention to Madison at the cost of neglecting the views of others distorts the history of religious liberty in the late 18th century? Those four views, Witte states, led to six "first principles": (1) liberty of conscience, (2) free exercise of religion, (3) religious pluralism, (4) religious equality, (5) separation of church and state, and (6) disestablishment of religion. *Id.* at 37. Can all of those principles be reconciled given the various approaches states took with regard to religion and government?

B. Framing and Debating the Constitution

The proposed Constitution composed in Philadelphia contained several references to religion. On August 20, 1787, Charles Pinckney proposed, among other things, the following: "No religious test or qualification shall ever be annexed to any oath of office under the authority of the U.S." Max Farrand, II RECORDS OF THE FEDERAL CONVENTION 342 (3 vols. rev. ed. 1937) (*quoting* the Journal of James Madison). Pinckney's proposal was referred to the Committee of five on the same day. *Id.* at 335. Ten days later, the Convention agreed to add the words "or affirmation" after "oath" in Article VI, § 3, cl. 1 by a vote of 8 states in favor, 1 against, and 2 divided. *Id.* at 461. Consequently, Quakers and others opposed to swearing an oath to uphold the Constitution for religious reasons were permitted instead to affirm. Immediately after this vote, the Convention unanimously agreed to the following: "But no religious test shall ever be required as a qualification to any office or public trust under the authority of the United States."

Id. The Report of the Committee of Style eliminated the words "the authority of," and, as edited, Article VI, §3, cl. 2 was adopted.

On November 29, 1787, Maryland delegate Luther Martin, who had left the Constitutional Convention early and who opposed the Constitution, delivered to the Maryland state legislature his "Genuine Information" concerning the proposed Constitution. In this report, he stated that the religious test provision "was adopted by a great majority and without much debate; however, there were some members *so unfashionable* as to think, that a *belief of the existence of a Deity*, and of a *state of future rewards and punishments* would be some security for the good conduct of our rulers, and that, in a Christian country, it would be *at least decent* to hold out some distinction between the professors of Christianity and downright infidelity or paganism." III Farrand, at 227. Martin's sarcasm was designed to heighten opposition to the Constitution. His statement touched upon the fear that the ban on religious tests for public office would have deleterious consequences for the United States. *See Letter by David*, Massachusetts Gazette, March 7, 1788, in 4 THE COMPLETE ANTI-FEDERALIST §4.24 (Herbert Storing ed. 1981) ("Never did any people possess a more ardent love of liberty than the people of this state; yet that very love of liberty has induced them to adopt a religious test, which requires all publick officers to be of some Christian, protestant persuasion, and to abjure all foreign authority. Thus religion secures our independence as a nation, and attaches the citizens to our own government."); *The Reverend Daniel Shute and Colonel William Jones on Religious Tests and Christian Belief* in 1 THE DEBATE ON THE CONSTITUTION 919–20 (Bernard Bailyn ed. 1993) (recording, in Massachusetts convention, debate between Shute, who favored the ban on religious tests, and Jones, who "thought, that the rulers ought to believe in God or Christ...."). Luther Martin was a well known and quite able lawyer, and his reference to the phrase "state of future rewards and punishments" was to the requirement that any prospective witness swear or affirm his belief in a state of future rewards and punishments before being allowed to testify. Any person who did not believe in a state of future rewards and punishments was not a competent witness. *See* Chapter Three. The state of Maryland retained a religious test for state and local public offices until the Supreme Court held it unconstitutional in 1961 in *Torcaso v. Watkins*, 367 U.S. 488.

In an April 10, 1788 letter to Edmund Randolph, to quash fears that the prohibition on religious tests would allow the federal government the power to regulate matters of religion, James Madison wrote the following: "As to the religious test, I should conceive that it can imply at most nothing more than that without that exception, a power would have been given to impose an oath involving a religious test as a qualification for office. The constitution of necessary offices being given to the Congress, the proper qualifications seem to be evidently involved." III Farrand, at 297. Finally, included in Farrand's RECORDS OF THE FEDERAL CONVENTION is a letter from Jonas Phillips, "being one of the people called Jews of the City of Philadelphia," complaining that the religious test in Pennsylvania barred all Jews from holding "publick office or place of Government," and requesting that

> if the honourable Convention shall in ther Wisdom think fit and alter the said oath and leave out the words to viz—and I do acknoweledge the scripture of the new testement to be given by devine inspiration then the Israeletes will think them self happy to live under a goverment where all Relegious societys are on an Eaquel footing—I solecet this favour for my self my Childreen and posterity and for the benefit of all the Isrealetes through the 13 united States of america."

III Farrand, at 79.

Phillips's letter is dated September 7, 1787, just over a week after the passage of Pinckney's motion barring religious tests. (Jonas Phillips joined the Whig militia in 1778, was a "fighter for civil rights" and arrived in the colonies "possibly even an indentured servant, and became a successful merchant." Marcus, Colonial American Jew, at 1297, 1423, 835.) Phillips is the same Jonas Phillips who refused six years later to testify in Pennsylvania court as a witness because the session was taking place on Saturday, his Sabbath. *See Stansbury v. Marks*, 2 Dall. 213 (Pa. 1793), excerpted in Chapter Three.

On September 14, Madison and Pinkney moved to add to Congress's powers the power "to establish an University, in which no preference or distinctions should be allowed on account of religion." New York delegate Gouverneur Morris opposed the motion, arguing that it was "not necessary. The exclusive power at the Seat of Government, will reach the object." II Farrand, at 616. This proposal was defeated by a vote of 4 in favor, 6 opposed and 1 divided. (Voting in favor of the proposal were Pennsylvania, Virginia, North Carolina and South Carolina. Connecticut's vote was divided.)

The issue of religious liberty was much discussed during the ratification period by both Federalists and Antifederalists. The last five original states to ratify the Constitution, New Hampshire, Virginia, New York, North Carolina, and Rhode Island, requested an amendment to the Constitution protecting religious liberty. Among the twelve amendments proposed by the New Hampshire convention was "XI. Congress shall make no laws touching religion, or to infringe the rights of conscience." 1 The Debates, Resolutions, and Other Proceedings, in Convention, on the Adoption of the Federal Constitution on the Adoption of the Federal Constitution 326 (Jonathan Elliot ed. 2d ed. 1888) (Elliot's Debates). Five days after New Hampshire's ratification of the Constitution, Virginia ratified the Constitution by a vote of 89–79. During its debate, Edmund Randolph, who had refused to sign the Constitution as a delegate, voiced his change of opinion. One of the reasons he gave in support of ratifying the Constitution was that he no longer feared religious freedom was in danger. Some opposed to the Constitution believed that the ban on religious tests was an exception to a grant of power to Congress concerning religion. Randolph responded to them: "I inform those who are of this opinion, that no power is given expressly to congress over religion." III Farrand, at 310, *quoting* Edmund Randolph to the Virginia Convention on June 10, 1788. This followed Madison's interpretation, given to Randolph in Madison's letter of April 10, 1788. In its ratification statement, the Virginia Convention stated that it understood the United States government had no power to limit religious liberty: "[A]mong other essential rights, the liberty of conscience, and of the press, cannot be cancelled, abridged, restrained, or modified, by any authority of the United States." 1 Elliot's Debates at 327. Virginia also suggested adding a bill of rights to the Constitution. The last two provisions of this bill of rights were:

> 19th. That any person religiously scrupulous of bearing arms ought to be exempted, upon payment of an equivalent to employ another to bear arms in his stead.
>
> 20th. That religion, or the duty which we owe to our Creator, and the manner of discharging it, can be directed only by reason and conviction, not by force or violence; and therefore all men have an equal, natural, and unalienable right to the free exercise of religion, according to the dictates of conscience, and that no particular religious sect or society ought to be favored or established, by law, in preference to others.

3 Elliot's Debates at 659.

The 20th proposed amendment, of course, was identical to Article 16 of the Virginia Constitution.

New York, the eleventh and next state to ratify the Constitution, also recommended the passage of a bill of rights:

> That the people have an equal, natural, and unalienable right freely and peaceably to exercise their religion, according to the dictates of conscience; and that no religious sect or society ought to be favored or established by law in preference to others.
>
> That the people have a right to keep and bear arms; that a well-regulated militia, including the body of the people *capable of bearing arms*, is the proper, natural, and safe defence of a free state.

1 ELLIOTT'S DEBATES at 328.

North Carolina rejected the Constitution in August 1788 because it lacked a Bill of Rights. A little more than a month after the Bill of Rights was sent to the states for ratification, North Carolina ratified the Constitution with amendments. During its second debate on the Constitution, North Carolina delegate Henry Abbott stated that

> Some are afraid, Mr. Chairman, that should the Constitution be received, they would be deprived of the privilege of worshipping God according to their consciences, which would be taking from them a benefit they enjoy under the present Constitution. They wish to know if their religious and civil liberties be secured under this system, or whether the general government may not make laws infringing their religious liberties.

2 THE DEBATE ON THE CONSTITUTION 902 (Bernard Bailyn ed. 1993). Specifically, Abbott was concerned that Congress "might make a treaty engaging with foreign powers to adopt the Roman catholic religion in the United States." *Id.* Convention delegate James Iredell responded:

> [Congress] certainly ha[s] no authority to interfere in the establishment of any religion whatsoever, and I am astonished that any gentleman should conceive they have. Is there any power given to Congress in matters of religion? Can they pass a single act to impair our religious liberties? If they could, Sir, no man would have more horror against it than myself. Happily no sect here is superior to another. As long as this is the case, we shall be free from those persecutions and distractions with which other countries have been torn. If any future Congress should pass an act concerning the religion of the country, it would be an act which they are not authorised to pass by the Constitution, and which the people would not obey.

Id. at 904.

Iredell then noted that "The power to make treaties can never be supposed to include a right to establish a foreign religion among ourselves, though it might authorise a toleration of others." *Id.* at 904–05. He also stated, "Had Congress undertaken to guarantee religious freedom, or any particular species of it, they would then have had a pretence to interfere in a subject they have nothing to do with." *Id.* at 906. In ratifying the Constitution, the North Carolina convention resolved: "That a declaration of rights, asserting and securing from encroachments the great principles of civil and religious liberty, and the unalienable rights of the people,... ought to be laid before Congress...." 1 ELLIOT'S DEBATES at 331–32. The convention then adopted the 20 amendments proposed by the Virginia Convention. 4 ELLIOT'S DEBATES at 243–44. A month later, North Carolina ratified the Bill of Rights.

Rhode Island, which had refused to send a delegation to the Constitutional Convention in Philadelphia, belatedly ratified the Constitution in May 1790, and it largely adopted the amendments proposed by the Virginia Convention. The two amendments concerning religion were worded exactly as worded by the Virginia Convention. 1 ELLIOT'S DEBATES at 334–35. Ten days after ratifying the Constitution, Rhode Island ratified the Bill of Rights.

In Pennsylvania, where the Constitution was earlier ratified by a vote of 46–23, the minority proposed, among other amendments, one concerning religious liberty: "1. The right of conscience shall be held inviolable; and neither the legislative, executive nor judicial powers of the United States shall have authority to alter, abrogate, or infringe any part of the Constitution of the several states, which provide for the preservation of liberty in matters of religion." 1 THE DEBATE ON THE CONSTITUTION 532. The minority also believed that the Constitution was defective because in providing for the possibility of a disciplined militia and permanent standing army, "The rights of conscience may be violated, as there is no exemption of those persons who are conscientiously scrupulous of bearing arms." *Id.* at 550. A minority of delegates in Maryland proposed 15 amendments. Among the proposed amendments were:

> 10. that no person, conscientiously scrupulous of bearing arms in any case, shall be compelled personally to serve as a soldier.
>
> 12. that there be no national religion established by law, but that all persons be equally entitled to protection in their religious liberty.

Address of a Minority of the Maryland Ratifying Convention, (Baltimore) Maryland Gazette, May 6, 1788, in 5 THE COMPLETE ANTI-FEDERALIST §5.4.7 (Herbert Storing ed. 1981).

As indicated by the statements of the minorities in Pennsylvania and Maryland, Anti-Federalists strongly believed the failure of the Constitution to protect liberty of conscience from possible Congressional regulation was a defect of the document. *See* 1 COMPLETE ANTI-FEDERALIST at 64 (essay by Herbert Storing); 3 *id.* at §3.3.29 (Essays of An Old Whig, (Philadelphia) Independent Gazetter, October 1787–February 1788) ("[I]f a majority of the continental legislature should at any time think fit to establish a form of religion, for the good people of this continent, with all the pains and penalties which in other countries are annexed to the establishment of a national church, what is there in the proposed constitution to hinder their doing so? Nothing; for we have no bill of rights, and every thing therefore is in their power and at their discretion."); 6 *id.* at §6.1.19 (Essays by Cincinnatus, New York Journal, November–December 1787) ("In equal insecurity, or rather equally at mercy, are we left as to—liberty of conscience. We find nothing that regards it, except the following;—[quoting religious test provision]. This exception implies, and necessarily implies, that in all other cases whatever liberty of conscience may be regulated."). *See also* 2 *id.* at §2.7.55 (Letters of Centinel); *id.* at §2.8.53, 2.8.86 (Letters from The Federal Farmer). Storing also notes, however, that "an important concern of many Anti-Federalists" was "the dependence of civil institutions of religious sanction." 5 *id.* at 125. For example, Charles Turner wrote, "But I hope it will be considered by persons of all orders, ranks and ages, that without the prevalence of *Christian piety, and morals,* the best republican Constitution can never save us from slavery and ruin." 4 *id.* at §4.18.2. *See also id.* at §4.18.2 n.2 (citing similar writings of Anti-Federalists). As he had in his Memorial and Remonstrance, Madison rejected this intertwining of religious exhortation and republican government. In Federalist Nos. 10 and 51, Madison concluded that a variety of religious sects best secured the country from religious factions and tyranny. *See also* 4 *id.* at §4.24 n.1 (citing Federalist opposition to suggestion that Constitution contain preamble declaring a belief in God).

By the time the First Congress was convened, the drafting of a Bill of Rights, including a provision regarding liberty of conscience, was to become part of Congress's work.

C. The Adoption of the First Amendment

Beginning in mid-1789, the Congress of the United States began working on a Bill of Rights. On June 8, 1789, Virginia Representative James Madison, filling a campaign promise and responding to the demands of the ratifying body of Virginia and other states, proposed approval by the House of amendments to the Constitution. Accompanying Madison's proposal was a list of amendments. Three proposals concerned religion. To prevent infringement of religious freedom by the federal government, Madison proposed: "The civil rights of none shall be abridged on account of religious belief or worship, nor shall any national religion be established, nor shall the full and equal rights of conscience be in any manner, or on any pretext, infringed," 1 ANNALS OF CONGRESS 434 (1834). In late July, this proposal was amended by a House Committee consisting of one representative from each of the eleven states, including Madison. The Committee reported its results to the House on July 28, and when introduced for debate on August 15, the proposal read: "no religion shall be established by law, nor shall the equal rights of conscience be infringed." *Id.* at 729. Madison's second proposed amendment was: "A well regulated militia, composed of the body of the people, being the best security of a free state, the right of the people to keep and bear arms shall not be infringed; but no person religiously scrupulous shall be compelled to bear arms." *Id.* at 434. Madison's final proposal concerning religion and government was: "No state shall violate the equal rights of conscience." *Id.* at 435. Because of the press of other issues, as well as a lack of enthusiasm about a Bill of Rights, the House delayed its discussion of amending the Constitution to August.

There is little record concerning the ratification by the states of the Bill of Rights. *See* Daniel A. Farber & Suzanna Sherry, A HISTORY OF THE AMERICAN CONSTITUTION 243 (1990). Ten of the thirteen original states, as well as Vermont, ratified the First Amendment, which was the third proposed amendment to the Constitution. (The first two amendments were rejected by the states.) The Bill of Rights became effective on December 15, 1791, after Virginia ratified the amendments. Only Georgia and Connecticut refused to adopt the Bill of Rights. Massachusetts is not included as one of the states ratifying the bill of rights because, although its legislature voted in favor of Bill of Rights, it apparently never enacted a bill signifying assent, *id.* at 244 (Table 8.1 n.**). Massachusetts did not formally adopt the Bill of Rights until 1939.

The record of the Congressional debate on the First Amendment is marred by the lack of official records. In the House, reporters were permitted to take notes for purposes of publication. This process, however, appears to have resulted in a number of omissions, emendations, and errors. Reports of the first House debates were published in the ANNALS OF CONGRESS in 1834, based largely on Lloyd's *Congressional Register.* But a comparison of Lloyd's shorthand notes with what was printed in the Register suggests that "[i]n many respects what Lloyd published bears only slight resemblance to the literal transcript of his own notes." Marion Tinling, *Thomas Lloyd's Reports of the First*

Federal Congress, 18 Wm. & Mary Q. 519, 530 (3d ser. 1961). In addition to his "wandering mind," it also appears that "[f]ar from improving by 1789, Lloyd's technical skills had become dulled by excessive drinking." James H. Hutson, *The Creation of the Constitution: The Integrity of the Documentary Record*, 65 Tex. L. Rev. 1, 36 (1986). The Senate conducted its debates in private, so we lack even an unofficial record of Senatorial debate about the wording of the First Amendment. The following is the debate of the House of Representatives concerning all three of Madison's proposals as published in the ANNALS OF CONGRESS.

House of Representatives

SATURDAY, August 15.

AMENDMENTS TO THE CONSTITUTION.

The House again went into a Committee of the Whole on the proposed amendments to the Constitution, Mr. BOUDINOT in the Chair.

The fourth proposition being under consideration, as follows:

Article 1. Section 9. Between paragraphs two and three insert "no religion shall be established by law, nor shall the equal rights of conscience be infringed."

Mr. SYLVESTER had some doubts of the propriety of the mode of expression used in this paragraph. He apprehended that it was liable to a construction different from what had been made by the committee. He feared it might be thought to have a tendency to abolish religion altogether.

Mr. VINING suggested the propriety of transposing the two members of the sentence.

Mr. GERRY said it would read better if it was, that no religious doctrine shall be established by law.

Mr. SHERMAN thought the amendment altogether unnecessary, inasmuch as Congress had no authority whatever delegated to them by the Constitution to make religious establishments; he would, therefore, move to have it struck out.

Mr. CARROLL.—As the rights of conscience are, in their nature, of peculiar delicacy, and will little bear the gentlest touch of governmental hand; and as many sects have concurred in opinion that they are not well secured under the present Constitution, he said he was much in favor of adopting the words. He thought it would tend more towards conciliating the minds of the people to the Government than almost any other amendment he had heard proposed. He would not contend with gentlemen about the phraseology, his object was to secure the substance in such a manner as to satisfy the wishes of the honest part of the community.

Mr. MADISON said, he apprehended the meaning of the words to be, that Congress should not establish a religion, and enforce the legal observation of it by law, nor compel men to worship God in any manner contrary to their conscience. Whether the words are necessary or not, he did not mean to say, but they had been required by some of the State Conventions, who seemed to entertain an opinion that under the clause of the Constitution, which gave power to Congress to make all laws necessary and proper to carry into execution the Constitution, and the laws made under it, enabled them to make laws of such a nature as might infringe the rights of conscience, and establish a national religion; to prevent these effects he presumed the amendment was intended, and he thought it as well expressed as the nature of the language would admit.

Mr. HUNTINGTON said that he feared, with the gentleman first up on this subject, that the words might be taken in such latitude as to be extremely hurtful to the cause of religion. He understood the amendment to mean what had been expressed by the gentleman from Virginia [Madison]; but others might find it convenient to put another construction upon it. The ministers of their congregations to the Eastward were maintained by the contributions of those who belonged to their society; the expense of building meeting-houses was contributed in the same manner. These things were regulated by by-laws. If an action was brought before a Federal Court on any of these cases, the person who had neglected to perform his engagements could not be compelled to do it; for a support of ministers or building of places of worship might be construed into a religious establishment.

By the charter of Rhode Island, no religion could be established by law; he could give a history of the effects of such a regulation; indeed the people were now enjoying the blessed fruits of it. He hoped, therefore, the amendment would be made in such a way as to secure the rights of conscience, and a free exercise of the rights of religion, but not to patronise those who professed no religion at all.

Mr. MADISON thought, if the word "national" was inserted before religion, it would satisfy the minds of honorable gentlemen. He believed that the people feared one sect might obtain a pre-eminence, or two combine together, and establish a religion to which they would compel others to conform. He thought if the word "national" was introduced, it would point the amendment directly to the object it was intended to prevent.

Mr. LIVERMORE was not satisfied with that amendment; but he did not wish them to dwell long on the subject. He thought it would be better if it were altered, and made to read in this manner, that Congress shall make no laws touching religion, or infringing the rights of conscience.

Mr. GERRY did not like the term national, proposed by the gentleman from Virginia, and he hoped it would not be adopted by the House. It brought to his mind some observations that had taken place in the conventions at the time they were considering the present Constitution. It had been insisted upon by those who were called anti-federalists, that this form of Government consolidated the Union; the honorable gentleman's motion shows that he considers it in the same light. Those who were called anti-federalists at that time, complained that they had injustice done them by the title, because they were in favor of a Federal Government, and the others were in favor of a national one; the federalists were for ratifying the Constitution as it stood, and the others not until amendments were made. Their names then ought not to have been distinguished by federalists and anti-federalists, but rats and anti-rats.

Mr. MADISON withdrew his motion, but observed that the words "no national religion shall be established by law," did not imply that the Government was a national one; the question was then taken on Mr. LIVERMORE'S motion, and passed in the affirmative, thirty-one for, and twenty against it.

[1 ANNALS OF CONGRESS at 729–31.]

MONDAY, August 17.

AMENDMENTS TO THE CONSTITUTION.

The House again, resolved itself into a committee, Mr. BOUDINOT in the Chair, on the proposed amendments to the Constitution. The third clause of the fourth proposition in the report was taken into consideration, being as follows: "A well regulated militia, composed of the body of the people, being the best security of a free state, the right of the people to keep and bear arms shall not be infringed; but no person religiously scrupulous shall be compelled to bear arms."

Mr. GERRY.—This declaration of rights, I take it, is intended to secure the people against the mal-administration of the Government; if we could suppose that, in all cases, the rights of the people would be attended to, the occasion for guards of this kind would be removed. Now, I am apprehensive, sir, that this clause would give an opportunity to the people in power to destroy the Constitution itself. They can declare who are those religiously scrupulous, and prevent them from bearing arms.

What, sir, is the use of a militia? It is to prevent the establishment of a standing army, the bane of liberty. Now, it must be evident, that, under this provision, together with their other powers, Congress could take such measures with respect to a militia, as to make a standing army necessary. Whenever Governments mean to invade the rights and liberties of the people, they always attempt to destroy the militia, in order to raise an army upon their ruins. This was actually done by Great Britain at the commencement of the late Revolution. They used every means of their power to prevent the establishment of an effective militia to the Eastward. The Assembly of Massachusetts, seeing the rapid progress that administration were making to divest them of their inherent privileges, endeavored to counteract them by the organization of the militia; but they were always defeated by the influence of the Crown.

Mr. SENEY wished to know what question there was before the committee, in order to ascertain the point upon which the gentleman was speaking.

Mr. GERRY replied that he meant to make a motion, as he disapproved of the words as they stood. He then proceeded. No attempts that they made were successful, until they engaged in the struggle which emancipated them at once from their thraldom. Now, if we give a discretionary power to exclude those from militia duty who have religious scruples, we may as well make no provision on this head. For this reason, he wished the words to be altered so as to be confined to persons belonging to a religious sect scrupulous of bearing arms.

Mr. JACKSON did not expect that all the people of the United States would turn Quakers or Moravians; consequently one part would have to defend the other in case of invasion. Now, this, in his opinion, was unjust, unless the Constitution secured an equivalent: for this reason, he moved to amend the clause, by inserting at the end of it, "upon paying an equivalent, to be established by law."

Mr. SMITH, of South Carolina, inquired what were the words used by the conventions respecting this amendment. If the gentleman would conform to what was proposed by Virginia and Carolina, he would second him. He thought they were to be excused provided they found a substitute.

Mr. JACKSON was willing to accommodate. He thought the expression was, "No one, religiously scrupulous of bearing arms, shall be compelled to render military service, in person, upon paying an equivalent."

Mr. SHERMAN conceived it difficult to modify the clause and make it better. It is well known that those who are religiously scrupulous of bearing arms, are equally scrupulous of getting substitutes or paying an equivalent. Many of them would rather die than do either one or the other; but he did not see an absolute necessity for a clause of this kind: We do not live under an arbitrary Government, said he, and the States, respectively, will have the government of the militia, unless when called into actual service; besides, it would not do to alter it so as to exclude the whole of any sect, because there are men amongst the Quakers who will turn out, notwithstanding the religious principles of the society, and defend the cause of their country. Certainly it will be improper to prevent the exercise of such favorable dispositions, at least whilst it is the practice of nations to determine their contests by the slaughter of their citizens and subjects.

Mr. VINING hoped the clause would be suffered to remain as it stood, because he saw no use in it if it was amended so as to compel a man to find a substitute, which, with respect to the Government, was the same as if the person himself turned out to fight.

Mr. STONE inquired what the words "religiously scrupulous" had reference to: was it of bearing arms? If it was, it ought so to be expressed.

Mr. BENSON moved to have the words "but no person religiously scrupulous shall be compelled to bear arms," struck out. He would always leave it to the benevolence of the Legislature, for, modify it as you please, it will be impossible to express it in such a manner as to clear it from ambiguity. No man can claim this indulgence of right. It may be a religious persuasion, but it is no natural right, and therefore ought to be left to the discretion of the Government. If this stands part of the Constitution, it will be a question before the Judiciary on every regulation you make with respect to the organization of the militia, whether it comports with this declaration or not. It is extremely injudicious to intermix matters of doubt with fundamentals.

I have no reason to believe but the Legislature will always possess humanity enough to indulge this class of citizens in a matter they are so desirous of; but they ought to be left to their discretion.

The motion for striking out the whole clause being seconded, was put, and decided in the negative—22 members voting for it, and 24 against it.

[*Id.* at 749–51.]

[After debating several other provisions of what would become the Bill of Rights, the debate continued:]

Article I. section 10. between the first and second paragraph, insert, "no State shall infringe the equal rights of conscience, nor the freedom of speech or of the press, nor of the right of trial by jury in criminal cases."

Mr. TUCKER.—This is offered, I presume, as an amendment to the constitution of the United States, but it goes only to the alteration of the constitutions of particular States. It will be much better, I apprehend, to leave the State Governments to themselves, and not to interfere with them more than we already do; and that is thought by many to be rather too much. I therefore move, sir, to strike out these words.

Mr. Madison conceived this to be the most valuable amendment in the whole list. If there was any reason to restrain the Government of the United States from infringing upon these essential rights, it was equally necessary that they should be secured against the State Governments. He thought that if they provided against the one, it was as necessary to provide against the other, and was satisfied that it would be equally grateful to the people.

Mr. LIVERMORE had no great objection to the sentiment, but he thought it not well expressed. He wished to make it an affirmative proposition; "the equal rights of conscience, the freedom of speech or of the press, and the right of trial by jury in criminal cases, shall not be infringed by any State."

This transposition being agreed to, and Mr. TUCKER'S motion being rejected, the clause was adopted.

[*Id.* at 755.]

THURSDAY, August 20.

AMENDMENTS TO THE CONSTITUTION.

The House resumed the consideration of the report of the Committee of the Whole on the subject of amendment to the Constitution.

Mr. AMES'S proposition was taken up. Five or six other members introduced propositions on the same point, and the whole were, by mutual consent, laid on the table. After which, the House proceeded to the third amendment, and agreed to the same.

On motion of Mr. AMES, the fourth amendment was altered so as to read "Congress shall make no law establishing religion, or to prevent the free exercise thereof, or to infringe the rights of conscience." This being adopted.

The first proposition was agreed to.

Mr. SCOTT objected to the clause in the sixth amendment, "No person religiously scrupulous shall be compelled to bear arms." He observed that if this becomes part of the Constitution, such persons can neither be called upon for their services, nor can an equivalent be demanded: It is also attended with still further difficulties, for a militia can never be depended upon. This would lead to the violation of another article in the Constitution, which secures to the people the right of keeping arms, and in this case recourse must be had to a standing army. I conceived it, said he, to be a Legislative right altogether. There are many sects I know, who are religiously scrupulous in this respect; I do not mean to deprive them of any indulgence the law affords; my design is to guard against those who are of no religion. It has been urged that religion is on the decline; if so, the argument is more strong in my favor, for when the time comes that religion shall be discarded, the generality of persons will have recourse to these pretexts to get excused from bearing arms.

Mr. BOUDINOT thought the provision in the clause, or something similar to it, was necessary. Can any dependence, said he, be placed in men who are conscientious in this respect? Or what justice can there be in compelling them to bear arms, when, according to their religious principles, they would rather die than use them? He adverted to several instances of oppression on this point, that occurred during the war. In forming a militia, an effectual defence ought to be calculated, and no characters of this religious description ought to be compelled to take up arms. I hope that in establishing this Government, we may show the world that proper care is taken that the Government may not interfere with the religious sentiments of any person. Now, by striking out the clause, people may be led to believe that there is an intention in the General Government to compel all its citizens to bear arms.

Some further desultory conversation arose, and it was agreed to insert the words "in person," to the end of the clause; after which, it was adopted, as was the fourth, fifth, sixth, seventh, and eighth clauses of the fourth proposition; then the fifth, sixth, and seventh propositions were agreed to, and the House adjourned.

[*Id.* at 766–67.]

SATURDAY, August 22.

Mr. TUCKER proposed the following amendment to the Constitution:

In the third section of the sixth article insert the word "other" between the word "no" and the word "religious."

And on the question that the House do agree to the said amendment, it passed in the negative.

Mr. BENSON introduced a resolution to the following purport:

Resolved by the House of Representatives of the United States in Congress assembled, That the following amendments to the Constitution of the United States having been agreed to by two-thirds of both Houses, be submitted to the Legislatures of the several States; which, when ratified, in whole or in part, by three-fourths of the said Legislatures, shall be valid to all intents and purposes as parts of the said Constitution.

This resolution was referred to a committee consisting of Messrs. BENSON, SHERMAN, and SEDGWICK, who were directed to arrange the said amendments and make report thereof.

On Monday, August 24, 1789, House sent its proposed amendments to the Constitution to the Senate. The three provisions concerning religion follow:

Article the Third

Congress shall make no law establishing religion or prohibiting the free exercise thereof, nor shall the rights of conscience be infringed.

Article the Fifth

A well regulated militia, composed of the body of the People, being the best security of a free State, the right of the people to keep and bear arms, shall not be infringed, but no one religiously scrupulous shall be compelled to render military service in person.

Article the Fourteenth

No state shall infringe the right of trial by Jury in criminal cases, nor the rights of conscience, nor the freedom of speech, or of the press.

Notes

1. The language concerning religious liberty took shape as follows in the House of Representatives. Madison's original proposal stated: "The civil rights of none shall be abridged on account of religious belief or worship, nor shall any national religion be established, nor shall the full and equal rights of conscience be in any manner, or on any pretext, infringed." The proposal offered to the House on August 15 stated: "[N]o religion shall be established by law, nor shall the equal rights of conscience be infringed." At the end of debate that day, the House adopted, 31–20, the following: "Congress shall make no laws touching religion, or infringing the rights of conscience." On August 20, after a motion to amend by Fisher Ames of Massachusetts, the House accepted the following: "Congress shall make no law establishing religion, or to prevent the free exercise thereof, or to infringe the rights of conscience." A House committee rephrased the August 20 version to read: "Congress shall make no law establishing religion, or prohibiting the free exercise thereof, nor shall the rights of conscience be infringed." This version was adopted and then sent to the Senate. Is there a substantive difference among these various proposals, and, if so, what is that difference? Are the grammatical changes indicative of a difference in meaning?

2. In addition to the amendment noted above, the House also adopted as Article the Fifth: "A well regulated militia, composed of the body of the People to keep and bear arms, shall not be infringed, but no one religiously scrupulous of bearing arms, shall be compelled to render military service in person." Creating the Bill of Rights: The Documentary Record from the First Federal Congress 38 (Helen E. Veit, et al., eds. 1991). Does this proposal assist our understanding of the drafters' views of liberty of conscience? Should it assist courts in determining whether to provide a constitutional exemption from a generally applicable law? *See* Ellis M. West, *The Right to Religion-Based Exemptions in Early America: The Case of Conscientious Objectors to Conscription*, 10 J. L. & Rel. 367 (1993–94) (concluding "the historical record warrants the stronger conclusion that early Americans clearly and explicitly rejected... a right to be exempt from obeying conscription laws.").

3. Finally, the House adopted on August 17 an amendment stating, "the equal rights of conscience, the freedom of speech or of the press, and the right of trial by jury in criminal cases, shall not be infringed by any State." This was reframed in Article the Fourteenth as "No State shall infringe the right of trial by Jury in criminal cases, nor the rights of conscience, nor the freedom of speech, or of the press." Creating the Bill of Rights, at 41. No vote of the House membership is given in the Annals of Congress, and the record of the "debate" is sparse and unrevealing, except for Madison's comment that this was the most "valuable" amendment of all. Can this proposal suggest something about the meaning of the First Amendment, or only about its applicability to the states? If merely the latter, need judges and lawyers consult the record of the debate concerning the Fourteenth Amendment to determine whether the First Amendment was "incorporated" into the Fourteenth Amendment?

4. One of the issues underlying the debate is the extent of the authority of Congress concerning liberty of conscience. During the August 15 debate on liberty of conscience, Madison agreed with Roger Sherman's assessment that the amendment was "altogether unnecessary, inasmuch as Congress had no authority whatever delegated to them by the constitution to make religious establishments." According to Thomas Curry, "Americans in 1789 largely believed that issues of Church and State had been sat-

isfactorily settled by the individual states. They agreed that the federal government had no power in such matters, but some individuals and groups wanted that fact stated explicitly." Curry, First Freedoms, at 194. Does this debate suggest that the amendment was designed simply to prevent the federal government from intervening in a subject properly the authority of the states? That is, was this an issue of federalism? Even if the House was concerned with limiting Congressional authority concerning religion, should this affect the interpretation of the First Amendment, given the massive changes in federal-state relations in the intervening 200 years? Is the debate over the Test Clause of Article VI relevant to this issue?

5. Another issue, also related to Congress's authority, concerns the implications of the language used in these early proposals. Madison's original proposal barred the establishment of any national religion. The word "national" was eliminated from the committee draft given to the House on August 15, a committee whose members included Madison. However, after Connecticut Representative Benjamin Huntington suggested that the proposed language "no religion shall be established by law, nor shall the equal rights of conscience be infringed," "could be harmful to the cause of religion," Madison proposed inserting the word "national" (before the word "religion") to allay Huntington's fears. Madison explained that adding the word "national" would put to rest the fear that one or two sects might combine to "establish a religion to which they would compel others to conform." The response of Anti-Federalist Elbridge Gerry of Massachusetts was to pounce on the word "national" as proof that the Constitution created a national rather than a federal government. As a result, Madison withdrew his amendment, all the while disclaiming Gerry's accusations. Is this evidence of Madison's specific intentions concerning the meaning of the First Amendment? If so, what are the implications for the historical understanding of the First Amendment? Should the search for the historical record include a deeper understanding of the proper relationship of law and religion envisioned by other members of the House, like Huntington and others?

Senate

On September 3, 1789, the Senate began consideration of several different forms of the amendments concerning liberty of conscience. That day, three motions to amend the House's language were defeated. The first would have amended the religious liberty proposal to read: "Congress shall make no law establishing One Religious Sect or Society in preference of others, nor shall the rights of conscience be infringed." The second stated: "Congress shall not make any law, infringing the rights of conscience, or establishing any Religious Sect or Society." The third: "Congress shall make no law establishing any particular denomination of religion in preference to another, or prohibiting the free exercise thereof, nor shall the rights of conscience be infringed." *See* Antieau, et al., Freedom From Federal Establishment at 130, *quoting* Senate Journal 70 (1820). The Senate finally agreed to amend the House proposal to read, "Congress shall make no law establishing religion, or prohibiting the free exercise thereof." On September 9, however, after a motion by Connecticut Senator Oliver Ellsworth, two-thirds of the Senate adopted the following language: "Congress shall make no law establishing articles of faith or a mode of worship, or prohibiting the free exercise of Religion." Ellsworth's motion also appended the phrase "or abridging the freedom of speech, or of the press" after this clause. *Id.* The Senate deleted the phrase "but no one religiously scrupulous of bearing arms, shall be compelled to render military service," from what would become the Second Amendment, and eliminated the House's proposed Fourteenth Article barring the states from infringing the equal right of conscience. CREATING THE BILL OF RIGHTS, at 48–49.

THE CONFERENCE COMMITTEE

The House refused to agree to the Senate's proposal concerning the Third Article, and on September 21 requested a Conference to reach some decision concerning this language. A Committee of Conference consisting of Senators (and chairman) Oliver Ellsworth of Connecticut, Charles Carroll of Maryland and William Paterson of New Jersey and Representatives (and chairman) James Madison of Virginia, Roger Sherman of Connecticut and John Vining of Delaware was appointed. Three days later, the House agreed to the first sixteen words of the First Amendment: "Congress shall make no law respecting an establishment of religion, nor prohibiting the free exercise thereof." The next day, the Senate concurred in the House's action, and as written was given to President George Washington to send to the states.

Notes

1. The final language of the First Amendment is similar to the proposal made by Fisher Ames and adopted (as edited) by the House, with two differences: first, the language of the last clause "nor shall the rights of conscience be infringed" was eliminated; and second, the active verb "establishing" was replaced with the more passive phrase "respecting an establishment of." Historians do not know which of the six conference members drafted the final language regarding religious liberty, how the passive phrase "respecting an establishment of" replaced the more active verb "establishing", whether that change was significant to some (or all) of the members of Congress, whether the phrase "nor shall the rights of conscience be infringed," was deleted because it was deemed surplusage, or because the rights of conscience might be infringed, nor finally, whether the language was intended to create two separate clauses, two interdependent clauses, or one clause. It is generally agreed that the House version was written more broadly than the Senate version, and that the final language is much closer to the House version.

2. Those evaluating the phrase "respecting an establishment of religion" have largely interpreted the language in two conflicting ways. The first approach is called the "separationist" or "no aid" interpretation. In this interpretation, the phrase as historically understood prohibits Congress from aiding any or all religions, even if such aid was allocated without discriminating among religious sects. The important facts in the separationist interpretation include: 1) the grammar of the phrase. The word "respecting" means "related to," and thus the phrase prohibits more than a law that attempts to establish "a" religion, Douglas Laycock, *Nonpreferential Aid to Religion: A False Claim About Original Intent*, 27 Wm. & Mary L. Rev. 875, 881 (1986), and additionally means that "Congress shall make no law on that subject." Levy, *Establishment Clause*, at 111. Further, the use of the word "an" represents a decision to bar more than "the establishment of religion", Laycock, at 881–82; 2) rejection by the House of the Senate's narrow proposal, as well as the Senate's successive rejection of three narrow proposals offered in its own deliberations, indicate a broad prohibition of aid to religion, Laycock, at 882–83; and 3) because the Constitution gave the Congress no authority to regulate religion, and because the Bill of Rights, including the First Amendment, was explicitly designed to limit Congress's exercise of power, the phrase was designed to prohibit Congress from any legislation "on matters concerning reli-

gion." Any interpretation of the phrase granting power to Congress concerning religion is therefore untenable. Should this reasoning be applied to the other federal branches as well?

The other approach is called the "nonpreferentialist" or "accommodationist" interpretation of the historical evidence of the First Amendment, and disputes the separationist conclusion that the federal government was absolutely prohibited from granting nondiscriminatory aid to religion. Several important facts noted by nonpreferentialists include: 1) the grammar of the phrase. The use of "an" rather than "the" indicates that the drafters of the First Amendment were concerned with prohibiting official favoritism toward one sect, and were not concerned with official favoritism toward religion rather than irreligion. Michael Malbin, RELIGION AND POLITICS: THE INTENTIONS OF THE AUTHORS OF THE FIRST AMENDMENT 14 (1978); 2) the issue of federalism. Madison's original proposal prohibited the establishment of a "national" religion, and the debate was largely couched in terms of what "Congress" could not do. Therefore, the meaning of the language ultimately adopted must be read in light of the fear that the federal government might otherwise interfere with actions properly within the authority of the states. *See* Bradley, at 92–94. Additionally, the phrase "respecting an" does not just prohibit Congressional actions "tending toward" an establishment, but also respects the division of power between the federal and state governments by barring Congress from interfering with state establishments. Malbin, at 14–16; Dreisbach, REAL THREAT, at 65; and 3) contemporary actions by the first Congress, from appointing chaplains to requesting Washington issue a thanksgiving proclamation to reenacting the Northwest Ordinance all militate against a separationist interpretation of the language "Congress shall make no law respecting an establishment of religion."

After reading the materials in this Chapter, which interpretation appears most persuasive to you? Are there problems with both interpretations? If so, what are those problems and how should they be solved? If one problem is a lack of proof, who should bear the burden of providing that proof?

3. To what extent is James Madison's state of mind important to evaluating the First Amendment? As noted earlier, Justice Wiley Rutledge's dissenting opinion in *Everson* noted that "the common unifying force of Madison's life, thought and sponsorship" was essential to understanding the First Amendment. "He epitomized the whole of that tradition in the Amendment's compact, but nonetheless comprehensive, phrasing." *Id.* at 39. This has spawned, as one critical commentator has noted, "a scholarly cottage industry" concerning Madison's thought. Bradley, at 86.

In part because the federal government was one of enumerated powers only, Madison did not favor a bill of rights, and changed his mind only for political reasons. *See* Donald L. Drakeman, *Religion and the Republic: James Madison and the First Amendment*, 25 J. Church & State 427, 428–29 (1983). Gerard Bradley suggests that Madison introduced the amendments to "ensure his political survival." Bradley, at 88. Leonard Levy concludes that Madison introduced the bill of rights only "to satisfy the popular clamor for a bill of rights and deflate Anti-Federalist charges that the new national government imperiled liberty." Levy, *Establishment Clause*, at 79 (1st ed.). Should Madison's reluctance or the reason for his change of mind affect a subsequent interpretation of the Bill of Rights?

Madison was involved in framing Article 16 of the Virginia Declaration of Rights, and in 1784 led the efforts against the general assessment by authoring the *Memorial and Remonstrance* and worked in favor of Jefferson's bill for Establishing Religious

Freedom. As a Representative in 1789, he introduced a proposed bill of rights, was a member of the Committee of eleven that drafted the proposed amendments for House consideration, and was a member of the Conference Committee whose draft of the First Amendment was eventually adopted. In 1811, while President, he twice vetoed bills to aid churches after concluding those bills violated the dictates of the establishment clause. *See* JAMES MADISON ON RELIGIOUS LIBERTY 79–80 (Robert S. Alley ed. 1985), *quoting* veto messages. In his retirement, Madison wrote letters opposing the "indefinite accumulation of property [and] the capacity of holding it in perpetuity" by ecclesiastical corporations, the existence of Congressional and military chaplains and presidential proclamations of days of thanksgiving and prayer. *Id.* at 91. (These *Detached Memoranda* were discovered in 1946 in the papers of Madison's biographer William Cabell Rives, and were published that year in the William & Mary Quarterly. *See* Elizabeth Fleet ed., *Madison's Detached Memoranda*, 3 Wm. & Mary Qt. 532 (3rd ser. Oct. 1946)).

On the other hand, as a delegate in the Virginia House of Burgesses, Madison introduced Thomas Jefferson's "Bill for Appointing Days of Public Fasting and Thanksgiving," and shortly after passage of the "Bill Establishing Religious Freedom," introduced "A Bill to Punish... Sabbath Breakers," which was duly enacted into law. In Congress, Madison was a member of the Congressional committee that approved the creation of the office of chaplain in the House, Pfeffer, CHURCH, STATE, AND FREEDOM at 247, and as President, Madison issued four thanksgiving proclamations. Dreisbach, at 177–81, *quoting* proclamations. In 1829, as a delegate to the Virginia Constitutional Convention, a motion asking the clergy of Richmond "to open the session of the Convention each morning by prayer" was adopted. PROCEEDINGS AND DEBATES OF THE VIRGINIA STATE CONVENTION OF 1829–30 7 (1830). Although delegate Alfred Powell requested a tally of the vote, the request was ruled too late, so Madison's vote on this motion was not recorded. He did not, however, make any statement concerning this issue. *Id.*

Do these varying actions by Madison provide any insight into his thought? Donald Drakeman concludes that Madison's views of religious liberty must be understood in light of "the virtually ubiquitous perception of the divine destiny of the new American nation." Drakeman, at 442. Madison's support of the chaplaincy as a representative and his decisions to issue presidential proclamations of thanksgiving were efforts of civil religion. To understand Madison's actions, one must understand that "[t]he Protestant Christian myth and theology shared by so many of the citizens of the new Republic provided a cultural framework in which the events of the world were viewed." *Id.* Does this create a consistency in Madison's thought? Does it suggest that the First Amendment must be read in light of "the Protestant Christian myth and theology," and if so, how should that be undertaken in a society much more religious diverse (and much more secular) than eighteenth century America? Does it mean that the First Amendment was anchored by a religious commitment to religious liberty, rather than a secular commitment to individual liberty?

4. Should "framers" or "Founding Fathers" other than Madison and Jefferson be studied? In assessing the views of other members of the first Congress, Professor Bradley has concluded that "they were, virtually to a man, quite hostile to [Madison's] personal viewpoint." Bradley, at 89. *See generally* Bradley, at 88–95.

5. Because the Senate debated in secret until the mid-1790s, there is scant evidence about the Senate's reasons for eliminating the "conscientious objector" proposal

and the proposal barring the states from interfering with the equal rights of conscience. How should lawyers and judges interpret these silences?

6. On September 25, 1789, the day after the House adopted the First Amendment, Representative Boudinot offered a resolution to request the President "recommend to the people of the United States a day of public thanksgiving and prayer, to be observed by acknowledging, with grateful hearts, the many signal favors of Almighty God...." 1 ANNALS OF CONGRESS at 914. Although Representative Burke believed this a "mimicking of European customs," which could result in a "mockery of thanksgivings," and Congressman Tucker believed this resolution of no concern to the House, Boudinot was supported by Roger Sherman as "worthy of Christian imitation" and the resolution carried the House. *Id.* at 915. The House was informed on September 28 of the Senate's assent to the resolution, *id.* at 923, and on October 3, 1789, Washington proclaimed November 16 as a day of prayer and thanksgiving. Washington's Proclamation began, "Whereas it is the duty of all nations to acknowledge the providence of Almighty God, to obey His will, to be grateful for His benefits, and humbly to implore His protection and favor." Does Congress's request provide evidence of its intentions concerning the First Amendment? Does Washington's assent to Congress's request provide any evidence of the meaning of the First Amendment? Both Aedenas Tucker and Thomas Burke, each of South Carolina, voted against the language of the First Amendment agreed to by the Conference Committee, and Elias Boudinot and Sherman both voted for the First Amendment on September 24. CREATING THE BILL OF RIGHTS at 53. Are their respective positions on the proposed day of public thanksgiving and prayer indicative of the meaning of the First Amendment?

In April, 1789, the Congress agreed to the creation of the offices of House and Senate Chaplain, with the proviso that the chaplains be of two different denominations. 1 ANNALS OF CONGRESS 19. Later that year, Congress agreed to pay chaplains $500 per annum. Cord, SEPARATION OF CHURCH AND STATE, at 24, *citing* II *Reports of Committees of the House of Representatives*, Document 124, at 4 (3 vols. 1854).

On August 7, 1789, shortly before the debate on the protection of religious liberty began, Congress reenacted the Continental Congress's Northwest Ordinance of 1787. 1 Stats. 50 (2d ed. Richard Peters ed. 1861). The Northwest Ordinance was "originally drafted by Jefferson," I Stokes, CHURCH AND STATE, at 480, and included the following:

> Article I. No person, demeaning himself in a peaceable and orderly manner, shall ever be molested on account of his mode of worship, or religious sentiments, in the said territory.
>
> Article III. Religion, morality and knowledge, being necessary to good government and the happiness of mankind, schools and the means of education shall forever be encouraged.

Id. What effect, if any, does this action suggest about Congress's intent concerning religious liberty?

7. In addition to Washington and Madison, other Presidents, including John Adams, James Madison and James Monroe, proclaimed days of thanksgiving, prayer, fasting and humility. Thomas Jefferson, while President, refused to issue a proclamation of a day of thanksgiving, insisting that this violated the First Amendment. However, the institution continues to the present day. Is this practice evidence of the meaning of the First Amendment, or evidence of politics, or both?

D. Jefferson's Letter to the Danbury Baptist Association

The most famous statement concerning the proper relationship of religion and government is Jefferson's metaphor of the "wall of separation between Church and State." When the Constitution was written in Philadelphia in the summer of 1787, Jefferson was in Paris as the American Ambassador to France. He was disappointed that the Constitution did not contain a Bill of Rights, including a provision on liberty of conscience. In the election of 1800, Jefferson stood as the presidential candidate of the Republican party. His opponent was the incumbent President and candidate of the Federalist party, John Adams of Massachusetts. As noted above, the Federalists were closely tied to the Congregationalist establishments in New England. During the campaign, New England Federalists encouraged opposition to Jefferson by claiming he was an atheist. Because the electoral commission did not separately vote for president and vice-president, both Jefferson and his running mate, Aaron Burr, received 73 electoral votes. The election was then sent to the House of Representatives, where Jefferson finally was elected President.

In late 1801, a committee of the Danbury [Connecticut] Baptist Association wrote to Jefferson. At this time, the Congregational church was the established church of the state of Connecticut, a fact that rankled not just Baptists, but other Protestant "dissenters."

> **The address of the Danbury Baptist Association in the State of Connecticut, assembled October 7th 1801, To Thomas Jefferson Esq. President of the United States of America.**
>
> Sir,
>
> Among the many millions in America and Europe who rejoice in your Election to office, we embrace the first opportunity which we have enjoyed in our collective capacity, since your Inauguration, to express our great satisfaction, in your appointment to the chief Majestracy in the United States: And though our mode of expression may be less courtly and pompous than what many others clothe their addresses with, we beg you, Sir to believe, that none are more sincere.
>
> Our Sentiments are uniformly on the side of Religious Liberty—That Religion is at all times and places a matter between God and individuals—That no man ought to suffer in name, person, or effects on account of his religious Opinions—That the legitimate Power of civil government extends no further than to punish the man who works ill to his neighbors: But Sir our constitution of government is not specific. Our antient charter together with the Laws made coincident therewith, were adopted as the Basis of our government, at the time of our revolution and such had been our Laws and usages, and such still are; that Religion is considered as the first object of Legislation; and therefore what religious privileges we enjoy (as a minor part of the State) we enjoy as favors granted, and not as inalienable rights: and these favors we receive at the expense of such degrading acknowledgments, as are inconsistent with the rights of freemen. It is not to be wondered at therefore, if those, who seek after power & gain under the pretense of government & Religion should reproach their fellow men—should reproach their chief Magistrate, as an enemy of reli-

gion Law & good order because he will not, dare not assume the prerogatives of Jehovah and make Laws to govern the Kingdom of Christ.

Sir, we are sensible that the President of the United States, is not the national legislator, and also sensible that the national government cannot destroy the Laws of each State; but our hopes are strong that the sentiments of our beloved President, which have had such genial affect already, like the radiant beams of the Sun, will shine and prevail through all these States and all the world till Hierarchy and Tyranny be destroyed from the Earth. Sir, when we reflect on your past services, and see a glow of philanthropy and good will shining forth in a course of more than thirty years we have reason to believe that America's God has raised you up to fill the chair of State out of that good will which he bears to the Millions which you preside over. May God strengthen you for the arduous task which providence and the voice of the people have cald you to sustain and support you in your Administration against all the predetermined opposition of those who wish to rise to wealth & importance on the poverty and subjection of the people.

And may the Lord preserve you safe from every evil and bring you at last to his Heavenly Kingdom through Jesus Christ our Glorious Mediator.

Signed in behalf of the association

Nehh Dodge

Ephram Robbins

The Committee

Stephen S. Nelson

On January 1, 1802, in office less than a year, Jefferson wrote a reply to the Association:

Messrs. Nehemiah Dodge, Ephraim Robbins, and Stephen S. Nelson, a committee of the Danbury Baptist Association, in the state of Connecticut

Washington, January 1, 1802

GENTLEMEN,—The affectionate sentiments of esteem and approbation which you are so good as to express towards me, on behalf of the Danbury Baptist Association, give me the highest satisfaction. My duties dictate a faithful and zealous pursuit of the interest of my constituents, and in proportion as they are persuaded of my fidelity to those duties, the discharge of them becomes more and more pleasing.

Believing with you that religion is a matter which lies solely between man and his God, that he owes account to none other for his faith or his worship, that the legislative powers of government reach actions only, and not opinions, I contemplate with sovereign reverence that act of the whole American people which declared that their legislature should "make no law respecting an establishment of religion, or prohibiting the free exercise thereof," thus building a wall of separation between Church and State. Adhering to this expression of the supreme will of the nation in behalf of the rights of conscience, I shall see with sincere satisfaction the progress of those sentiments which tend to restore to man all his natural rights, convinced he has no natural right in opposition to his social duties.

I reciprocate your kind prayers for the protection and blessing of the common Father and Creator of man, and tender you for yourselves and your religious association, assurances of my high respect and esteem.

Notes

1. Jefferson's letter makes several points about the relationship between law and religion. He first distinguishes between religious action and religious opinions, so that "the legislative powers of government reach actions only." After citing Jefferson's letter, the Supreme Court in 1879 adopted this distinction in *Reynolds v. United States*, 98 U.S. 145, 164, excerpted in Chapter Four. Does this interpretation square with the language of the First Amendment, which bars Congress from interfering with the free exercise of religion? Professor David Little suggests that "[t]he sharp distinction between belief and action is mistaken" because Jefferson's theory "minimizes the importance and relevance of the reasons behind our actions." David Little, *Thomas Jefferson's Religious Views and Their Influence on the Supreme Court's Interpretation of the First Amendment*, 26 Cath. U. L. Rev. 57, 72 (1976). Do you agree? After quoting the language of the First Amendment, Jefferson then suggests his famous "wall" metaphor. He does not cite Roger Williams, the seventeenth century religious seeker and founder of Rhode Island, who used a similar metaphor. Was this because New England Baptists would have understood that Jefferson was adopting a metaphor originated by Williams, at one time a Baptist? Was it because Williams was a largely forgotten figure? Is Jefferson interested in protecting the church from the state, the state from the church, the religious individual from either the church or the state, or some combination of these interests?

2. The letter to the Danbury Baptist Association, particularly the metaphor of the "wall of separation between Church and State," has animated the Supreme Court's interpretation of both the Free Exercise Clause, *Reynolds v. United States*, 98 U.S. 145 (1879), and the Court's interpretation of the Establishment Clause, *Everson v. Bd. of Educ.*, 330 U.S. 1 (1947). After you read those cases, assess whether the weight the Court has accorded the letter by the Court is appropriate in interpreting the religious liberty guarantee.

3. Because of the weight the Supreme Court has given to Jefferson's letter, the letter's importance has been much discussed among academic commentators. Some have viewed Jefferson's letter to the Danbury Baptist Association as simply an offhand reply to political supporters, meaning little in terms of constitutional jurisprudence. *See, e.g.*, Edward S. Corwin, *The Supreme Court as National School Board*, 14 Law and Contemp. Probs. 1, 14 (1949) (concluding, while disagreeing with Court's 1948 *McCollum* decision, that the letter was not a "deliberate" or "carefully considered" statement of his views). Others have read the letter as a clear statement of Jefferson's views. *See* Levy, Establishment Clause at 182–83 (1st ed.1986) (noting that before he sent his reply, Jefferson wrote to his Attorney General for approval indicating his desire to "sow[] useful truths and principles among the people, which might germinate and become rooted among their political tenets.").

Levy notes that Jefferson also wrote his Attorney General Levi Lincoln on the same day, enclosing his response to the Danbury Baptists, and asking Lincoln's advice. Jefferson's note to Lincoln states, in part:

> The Baptist address, now enclosed, admits of a condemnation of the alliance between Church and State, under the authority of the Constitution. It furnishes an occasion, too, which I have long wished to find, of saying why I do not proclaim fastings and thanksgivings, as my predecessors did.... I know it will give great offence to the New England clergy; but the advocate of religious freedom is to expect neither peace nor forgiveness from them.

I Stokes, at 490.

The first version of Jefferson's letter included the following sentence, in the second paragraph, immediately after the "building a wall of separation between Church and State" language:

> Congress thus inhibited from acts respecting religion, and the Executive authorised only to execute their acts, I have refrained from prescribing even occasional performances of devotion, prescribed indeed legally where an Executive is the legal head of a national church, but subject here, as religious exercises only to the voluntary regulations and discipline of each respective sect.

Daniel L. Dreisbach & John D. Whaley, *What the Wall Separates: A Debate on Thomas Jefferson's "Wall of Separation" Metaphor*, 16 Const. Comm. 627, 645 (1999). This sentence was omitted, according to Jefferson's notes in the margin, because it might "give uneasiness to some of our republican friends in the eastern States" who were accustomed to those proclamations. *Id.* Whaley concludes that this sentence suggests that Jefferson believed that "religious exercises [are] the *sole* responsibility of the sects themselves, not of *any* government authority, neither *state* nor federal." *Id.* at 647. Driesbach concludes that the letter, including the omitted language above, is better understood as confirming that the First Amendment was jurisdictional only. It prevented the federal government from any involvement with religion, but said nothing about the interaction of state governments and religion. *Id.* at 661.

Two days after writing his letter to the Danbury Baptist Association, Jefferson attended a Sabbath (Sunday) religious service in the House of Representatives, at which the "separationist" and Baptist John Leland preached. Leland was a resident of western Massachusetts, and involved in the cause of religious freedom in both that state and in Connecticut. He had preached in Virginia for 15 years (1776–91) before returning to his native Massachusetts, and was a friend of Jefferson. I Stokes, at 499–500. To understand the meaning of the guarantee of religious liberty, is it more important to focus on the fact that Jefferson attended a service at which a famous Baptist minister, involved in the disestablishment effort in New England, preached, or is it more important to note the fact that religious services were conducted in the House of Representatives? Is this event consistent with the present understanding of the requirements of the First Amendment? If not, why not? Are these facts mere curiosities? Can answers to these questions be crucial in understanding the Court's interpretation of the First Amendment, or in understanding the original meaning of the First Amendment?

4. Among the first four Presidents, Jefferson refused to issue religious proclamations, which he believed violated the Constitution. He publicly stated his reasons for so acting in his Second Inaugural address:

> In matters of religion, I have considered that its free exercise is placed by the Constitution independent of the powers of the General Government. I have therefore undertaken, on no occasion, to prescribe the religious exercises suited to it, but have left them as the Constitution found them, under the direction and discipline of State and Church authorities acknowledged by the several religious societies.

10 THE WORKS OF THOMAS JEFFERSON 127, 131 (12 vols. Paul L. Ford ed. 1905).

Does this statement suggest that the language of the first Amendment was understood by Jefferson to bar any assertion of Congressional and/or Executive power on matters of religion? Can it be understood more broadly? Dreisbach notes that when Jefferson was a member of Virginia's colonial House of Burgesses, he participated in drafting and enacting a resolution for a "Day of Fasting, Humiliation, and Prayer." He also issued a proclamation of "publick and solemn THANKSGIVING and prayer to Almighty God" as Governor of Virginia in 1779. Dreisbach & Whaley, at 657.

In concluding his Second Inaugural address, Jefferson acknowledged the Deity:

> I shall need, too, the favor of that Being in whose hands we are, who led our fathers, as Israel of old, from their native land, and planted them in a country flowing with all the necessaries and comforts of life; who has covered our infancy with His providence and our riper years with His wisdom and power; and to whose goodness I ask you to join in supplications, that He will so enlighten the minds of your servants, guide their councils, and prosper their measures, that whatsoever they do shall result in your good, and shall secure to you the peace, friendship, and approbation of all nations.

Id. at 136.

How should this conclusion be understood?

5. While President, Jefferson sent a proposed treaty between the United States government and the Kaskaskia and other native tribes to the Senate for confirmation. The treaty included a provision which stated, "the United States will give, annually, for seven years, one hundred dollars towards the support of a priest of that [Roman Catholic] religion, who will engage to perform for said tribe the duties of his office, and also to instruct as many of their children as possible, in the rudiments of literature. And the United States will further give the sum of three hundred dollars, to assist the said tribe in the erection of a church." Does an agreement to expend funds to meet the obligations of a treaty explain Jefferson's state of mind, or decode the First Amendment?

E. On History and the First Amendment

In no other area of constitutional law has the search for the meaning of the text been as driven by the study of the historical record as the phrase "Congress shall make no law respecting an establishment of religion, or prohibiting the free exercise thereof." As stated by the authors of a well-known treatise on constitutional law, "There is a seemingly irresistible impulse to appeal to history when analyzing issues under the religion clauses." John E. Nowak & Ronald D. Rotunda, Constitutional Law 1310 (6th ed. 2000).

Much of this impulse is a consequence of the Supreme Court's appeal to history to justify its decisions detailing the contours of the religious liberty guarantee. In *Everson v. Bd. of Educ.*, 330 U.S. 1 (1947), both Justice Hugo Black, for the five-person majority, and Justice Wiley Rutledge, for the four-person dissent, relied extensively on history, particularly the history of Virginia, in determining the constitutionality of government-funded bus transportation for children attending religious schools. Relying in part on the nineteenth century decisions of *Reynolds v. United States*, 98 U.S. 145 (1879), and *Davis v. Beason*, 133 U.S. 333 (1890), Black stated, "This Court has previously recognized that the provisions of the First Amendment, in the drafting and adoption of which Madison and Jefferson played such leading roles, had the same objective and were intended to provide the same protection against government intrusion on religious liberty as the Virginia statute." *Everson*, at 13. Justice Rutledge asserted, "No provision of the Constitution is more closely tied to or given content by its generating history than the religious clause of the First Amendment." *Id.* at 33. That history, in Rutledge's view, was largely based on the struggle for religious liberty in Virginia in the 1780s:

> All the great instruments of the Virginia struggle for religious liberty thus became warp and woof of our constitutional tradition, not simply by the course of history, but by the common unifying force of Madison's life, thought and sponsorship. He epitomized the whole of that tradition in the Amendment's compact, but nonetheless comprehensive, phrasing.

Id. at 39.

Although Justice William Brennan wrote in 1963 that "[a] too literal quest for the advice of the Founding Fathers upon the issues of these cases seems to me futile and misdirected," *Abington Sch. Dist. v. Schempp*, 374 U.S. 203, 237 (1963) (Brennan, J., concurring), he too relied on history to support his conclusions. In *Walz v. Tax Comm'n*, 396 U.S. 367 (1970), a case concerning the constitutionality of property tax exemptions for religious organizations, Justice Brennan concluded that while history was not determinative of a statute's constitutionality, it remained an important aid for the Court's decision, and in this case, the history of property tax exemptions for religious organizations strongly suggested its constitutionality. *Id.* at 693–94.

In 1983, the Court upheld Nebraska's practice of opening each legislative day with a prayer by a chaplain, based solely on the history of the practice, which went back to the appointment of chaplains by the first Congress. *Marsh v. Chambers*, 463 U.S. 783 (1983). Two years later, Justice William Rehnquist attacked the *Everson* Court's understanding of the history of the First Amendment, and concluded, "[t]here is simply no historical foundation for the proposition that the Framers intended to build the 'wall of separation' that was constitutionalized in *Everson*." *Wallace v. Jaffree*, 472 U.S. 38, 106 (1985) (Rehnquist, J., dissenting).

In a thoughtful article concerning the history of the religion clauses, Professor Rodney K. Smith wrote:

> Examining history rarely, if ever, yields clear-cut answers. Rather, an examination of history provides one with parameters within which legitimate judicial decision-making should take place.
>
> A study of the Framers' intent in using the language that they did in the religion clauses reveals that there are confines or parameters within which decisions should properly fall. It also reveals that there is substantial room for discretion within those parameters, thereby providing the Court with both the flexibility and the legitimacy it needs to resolve contemporary cases.

Rodney K. Smith, *Getting Off on the Wrong Foot and Back on Again: A Reexamination of the History of the Framing of the Religion Clauses of the First Amendment and a Critique of the* Reynolds *and* Everson *Decisions*, 20 Wake Forest L. Rev. 569, 573–74 (1984).

One important difficulty in understanding the original meaning of the religious liberty provision is that an understanding of the Framers takes place only through an understanding of those who have offered interpretations of those Framers. As stated by William Lee Miller:

> The meaning of these ancient, important, instructive people—James Madison, Roger Williams—is much altered by the intermediary interpreters, now

> this way, now that. One is interpreting American culture not only by looking at Roger Williams, but by looking at Vernon Parrington and Perry Miller and Edmund Morgan looking at Roger Williams.

William Lee Miller, First Liberty at 170. Not only are we condemned to attempting to understand any Framer through the prism of interpretation, we are limited in understanding the language used by the Framers in light of our present definition of those words. The historian Thomas Curry notes:

> One will look in vain for the analytical distinctions scholars presume the generation that enacted the First Amendment made between government establishment of a particular sect and government establishment or favor to may sects. When they condemned an establishment, they had in their minds an image of tyranny, not a definition of a system...
>
> Moreover, during the revolutionary period, when Americans, irrespective of their stance on Church and State, spoke of banning the establishment of a particular sect or church in preference to others, they were not advocating a particular party viewpoint on establishment but employing an inherited terminology.

Curry, First Freedoms at 211. So, for example, Madison and Patrick Henry, on opposite sides of the propriety of the general assessment, "used the same words to describe establishment." *Id.* at 213. Finally, recovering the meaning of the words and the intentions of the Framers requires an appreciation of the social fact that "Americans enunciated their Church-State principles within a framework wherein Protestant Christianity and American culture intertwined," a culture in which the line between the religious and the secular was either absent or greatly blurred. *Id.* at 218.

The search for meaning in history is also a consequence of the Supreme Court's power to invalidate governmental action based on the commands of the Constitution. If, however, the framers never intended subsequent generations to be bound by the intentions of the framers, should this search be abandoned? Whether the framers intended future generations to be bound by their intent is the subject of H. Jefferson Powell's article, *The Original Understanding of Original Intent*, 98 Harv. L. Rev. 885 (1986). Even if the framers intended future generations to be bound by their understanding of the text of the Constitution, should future generations accept that limitation on interpretation?

> The search for original meaning and historical purpose underlying the language has yielded inconclusive results, and it would not be profitable to explore the matter in detail. In the end the Supreme Court is free to give this language the meaning it chooses, whether guided by the court's interpretation of historical purpose or by the court's use of the ambiguous language in accommodating constitutional interpretation to the felt needs of the day.

Paul Kauper, Religion and the Constitution 47 (1964). The option of leaving the Court "free" to interpret the language of the Constitution, even in light of the "felt needs of the day," is regularly resisted, particularly when the Court's interpretation differs from the view held by the critic of the Court.

After only three Supreme Court decisions staking the constitutional boundaries of the relationship between law and religion, Professor Wilber Katz wrote, "One conviction emerges from a study of the various attempts at 'proof.' This is the melancholy conviction that the heat generated by questions concerning religion has made fairness in the handling of historical evidence almost impossible." Wilber G. Katz, *Freedom of Religion and State Neutrality*, 20 U. Chi. L. Rev. 426, 436 (1953). In the 50 years since Katz wrote this statement, the Supreme Court has decided dozens of cases concerning the constitutional boundaries regulating the relationship of government and religion. As you read those cases, consider whether Katz's statement remains an accurate assessment of the study of the historical record.

In speaking of the indeterminacy of the religion clauses, the constitutional scholar Philip Kurland concluded:

> At best, the past is never fully recapturable, and the parts that are recapturable may not be an accurate reflection of what actually occurred. When the quarry is neither recorded words nor events, but rather the state of mind that gave rise to the words or events, and when the state of mind is not of one person but of many persons, the pursuit of the past is almost hopeless.

Philip B. Kurland, *The Origins of the Religion Clauses of the Constitution*, 27 Wm. & Mary L. Rev. 839, 860 (1986).

As your reflect on the historical materials discussed in this section, reconsider the materials in Chapter One §A on "levels of generality." Many of the questions raised in this Chapter are similar to the issues raised in Chapter One. For example, what period of history should be deemed "controlling" with respect to the intent of the Framers? The selection of Virginia during the period 1770–1790 is the selection of a "low," or specific, level of historical generality. Consideration of the entire historical record reflects a much "higher," or less specific, approach. The same point can be made with the question, "Which Framers?" Do you think a court or commentator should be expected to defend the level of linguistic or historical generality on which the analysis is based?

Chapter 3

Law, Religion and Culture in Antebellum America

The history of the United States is a history of transition. The history in America of the relation among law, religion and government mirrors that history. During the late eighteenth century, all southern states ended their formal ties with the Church of England, and included provisions guaranteeing liberty of conscience or the free exercise of religion to all religious believers. Similarly, the middle states of New York and Maryland also severed any formal ties with the Church of England. Only in New England, excepting Rhode Island, did a form of established religion (Congregationalism) continue to exist. Even in New England, the general assessment, the system in which taxes were assessed for the support of the Standing Order, eventually gave way. The New England states first amended the law by granting an exemption from the assessment to Protestant dissenters. Later, largely within the first two decades of the nineteenth century, this system was dismantled throughout New England.

Despite the severing of ties between established faith and state, precepts of Christianity remained a powerful part of the public order. As Tocqueville noted, "For the Americans the ideas of Christianity and liberty are so completely mingled that it is almost impossible to get them to conceive of the one without the other." Alexis de Tocqueville, Democracy in America 293 (J.P. Mayer ed. George Lawrence trans. 1988). Christianity meant Protestant Christianity. State guarantees of liberty of conscience or the free exercise of religion did not mean that non-Protestants or non-Christians were granted civil rights equal to Protestants, nor did those guarantees grant license to nonbelievers to cavil against religion. In this largely Protestant society, public expressions of religious faith, or a lack of religious faith, remained subject to the legal order. Several issues suggesting the role of religion in the public order arose in antebellum America: the requirements of oathtaking to hold public office and to testify in the courtroom; the legitimacy of blasphemy prosecutions; and laws mandating Sunday as a day of rest. All of these issues were related to the question whether Christianity was a part of the common law. In addition, states reflected on the corporate status of religious societies, including the holding of property by such societies. This chapter discusses some the ways in which diffuse Christianity manifested itself in the legal order before the Civil War.

A. Oaths

State guarantees of liberty of conscience included the relatively few Roman Catholics and Jews living in the United States. However, faithful Catholics, to some extent, and

Jews, to a larger extent, were subject to civil disabilities because of their religious faith. Although Pennsylvania, Virginia, Georgia, and South Carolina eliminated religious tests for public office during the late eighteenth century, most states retained such tests. In the nineteenth century, a number of states, including Maryland, Massachusetts, New Hampshire, New Jersey and North Carolina, limited public office to Protestants, and later, to Christians. The religious test for office was eliminated by constitutional amendment in Massachusetts in 1820, and after a protracted effort in Maryland, the so-called "Jew Bill" allowing Jews to hold office was enacted in early 1826. New Jersey amended its constitutional limitation in 1844. North Carolina limited public office to Protestants until 1835, and to "Christians" until 1868, and New Hampshire limited public office to Protestants until 1876. Even after Catholics and Jews were permitted to hold public office, such offices continued to be limited to those who believed in God.

Because Quakers refused to swear an oath, but only affirm, Article VI of the Constitution required that all officeholders "shall be bound by Oath or Affirmation." As expected, Pennsylvania, founded by the Quaker William Penn, permitted Quakers to affirm early in its colonial history. By the time of the American Revolution, most colonies provided the option of affirming to Quakers elected to public office. State constitutions written both before and after the federal Constitution offered this option to all who conscientiously refused to swear an oath, as long as the person who refused to swear was a member of a recognized religious group like the Quakers. Those who were not a member of any organized religious group were not permitted to affirm.

The courtroom was one forum in which the law conditioned benefits on affirmations of religious belief. Although a witness was ordinarily incompetent to testify if he refused to swear an oath on the Bible, Quakers called to testify as witnesses were permitted to affirm rather than swear an oath as early as 1691 in New York. Thomas J. Curry, THE FIRST FREEDOMS: CHURCH AND STATE IN AMERICA TO THE PASSAGE OF THE FIRST AMENDMENT 64 (1986). In 1795, and again in 1798, Maryland amended its Constitution to permit Quakers and members of other religious sects opposed to oaths to affirm rather than swear when called as trial witnesses. Francis Newton Thorpe, III THE FEDERAL AND STATE CONSTITUTIONS 1702 (7 vols. 1909). Section 2 of the latter amendment conditioned the privilege of affirming upon a finding that the court "shall be satisfied, by such testimony as they may require, that such person is one of those who profess to be conscientiously scrupulous of taking an oath." *See also Commonwealth v. Mann*, 9 Mass. 107 (1812) (reversing ancient Massachusetts practice and permitting Quakers to serve on grand juries despite refusal to swear an oath). Although permitting a Quaker to affirm, courts restricted the application of this exemption. In an early federal case arising from the District of Columbia, the Circuit Court refused to permit a witness to affirm because, even though the witness agreed with Quakers in religious principle, met with them in religious worship and had applied for formal membership, he was not an "acknowledged member" "in regard to civil privileges and moral discipline." *King v. Fearson,* Fed. Cas. 7,790 (3 Cranch C.C. 435) (C.C. D.C. 1829). The witness was ordered to swear. Judge Cranch dissented, arguing that Maryland's constitutional provision specifically allowing Quakers, Tunkers and Menonists to affirm should be given a liberal construction, and thus affirmation should be available to anyone whose beliefs approximated the belief of those sects named in Maryland's Constitution. *See also Bryan's Case,* Fed. Cas. No. 2,063 (C.C. D.C. 1804) (forbidding Methodist to affirm rather than swear); *M'Intire's Case,* Fed. Cas. No. 8,824 (C.C. D.C. 1803) (forbidding prospective witness, not a Quaker and not attached to any sect, from affirming).

Although Jews were forbidden in 1737 to testify as witnesses by the New York Assembly, Anson Phelps Stokes, III CHURCH AND STATE IN THE UNITED STATES 144 (3 vols. 1950), and although Asser Levy's service as a juror in 1671 made him "one of the few Jews in colonial times to be accorded that privilege," Jacob R. Marcus, I THE COLONIAL AMERICAN JEW, 1492–1776 247 (3 vols. 1970), those disabilities rarely existed by the time of the Revolution.

In the famous English case of *Omichund v. Barker,* 1 Atk. 45 (1744), an "infidel" (Hindu) was permitted to swear an oath even though he was not Christian. The witness was deemed competent because he "believe[d] in a God and future rewards and punishments." *See* 3 John Henry Wigmore, A TREATISE ON THE SYSTEM OF EVIDENCE IN TRIALS AT COMMON LAW § 1817 (4 vols. 1st ed.1904). At the same time, *Omichund* held incompetent any persons who believed neither in God nor in a future state of rewards and punishments. This permitted Muslims, Jews, Catholics and other religious believers to testify. An early case in Connecticut, decided while the standing order remained, followed *Omichund*: "And every person who believes in the obligation of an oath, etc. whatever may be his religious creed, whether *Christian, Mahommedan, or Pagan,* or whether he disbelieves them all, is an admissible witness...." *Curtiss v. Strong,* 4 Day 51, 55 (1809).

On the other hand, any prospective witness who did not believe in God or in a future state of rewards or punishments was incompetent to testify. The following case offers both the reasons for this rule, as well as the manner of proof of incompetence.

Jackson ex dem. Tuttle v. Gridley

18 Johns. 98 (N.Y. 1820)

[In an ejectment action, the defendant offered the testimony of Amos Gridley to prove usury in the mortgage security. Before hearing Gridley's testimony, two witnesses testified that Gridley had recently said that "he did not believe in a future state of rewards and punishments; that man was like the beasts; when he died, there was an end of him; and that he knew of no superior being to man." A third witness testified that, only a week before trial, Gridley had stated that "he had formerly embraced the principles of the Universalists, and rather believed it was right." After Gridley stated "that he did not know that he had any reason to doubt that there was an afterstate of rewards and punishments," the trial court ordered Gridley sworn. After Gridley testified, however, the trial court instructed the jury that Gridley "ought not to be believed; and that his statement was not deserving of any credit." Despite this instruction, the jury returned a verdict in favor of the defendant.]

SPENCER, C.J.

By the law of England, which has been adopted in this State, it is fully and clearly settled, that infidels who do not believe in a God, or if they do, do not think that he will either reward or punish them in the world to come, cannot be witnesses in any case, nor under any circumstances—because an oath cannot possibly be any tie or obligation upon them. Mahometans may be sworn on the Koran; Jews on the Pentateuch, and Gentoos and others according to the ceremonies of their religion, whatever may be the form. It is appealing to God to witness what we say, and invoking punishment, if what we say be false. On this subject we have, also, express legislative recognition of the common law. Every person believing in the existence of a Supreme Being, and a future state of rewards and punishments, having conscientious scruples against taking an oath, shall be admitted to an affirmation.

But how is it to be ascertained whether a person offered as a witness disbelieves in the existence of a God, or in a state of future rewards and punishments? In *Curtiss v. Strong,* it was decided that the incompetency of the witness could be proved from his declarations out of court, concerning his opinions and principles; and it was also decided that he could not be admitted to deny or explain in court the declarations imputed to him, as it would be incongruous to admit a man to his oath, for the purpose of ascertaining whether he had the necessary qualifications to be sworn. I fully concur in the opinion expressed in *Curtiss v. Strong*, that it would be incongruous to admit a man to his oath, to ascertain whether an oath had any binding influence on his conscience. If he had no idea of the sanction which the appeal to Heaven, by taking an oath, creates, what is there to prevent his swearing falsely in preliminary inquiry? [I]t does appear to me, that upon principle, after it is proved that a witness offered is, at the time he is offered, an infidel, that he can neither be sworn to disprove the fact, nor be permitted, without oath, to make himself competent. If the declarations were made some time before, and it could be proved by external signs that there had been a change of mind, such as a pious and devout attention to religious worship, and declarations in the belief of God, and a future state of rewards and punishments, such proof might reinstate the witness, and entitle him to be sworn.

It would be strange if the law admitted a man to be a witness, that the same law should declare he was not to be believed on account of the obliquity of his mind and because he was incapable of being bound by any religious tie, to speak the truth. The very fact that a person possesses such an awful creed as renders him unworthy of credit, establishes that he should not be heard.

Religion is a subject on which every man has a right to think according to the dictates of his understanding. It is a solemn concern between his conscience and his God, with which no human tribunal has a right to meddle. But in the development of facts, and the ascertainment of truth, human tribunals have a right to interfere. They are bound to see that no man's rights are impaired or taken away, but through the medium of testimony entitled to belief, and no testimony is entitled to credit, unless delivered under the solemnity of an oath, which comes home to the conscience of the witness, and will create a tie arising from his belief that false swearing would expose him to punishment in the life to come. On this great principle rest all our institutions, and especially the distribution of justice between man and man.

There must be a new trial, with costs to abide the event.

Notes

1. The eventual resolution of the issue of witness incompetence for lack of religious belief in New York tells us much about the role of religion in the public order in the nineteenth century. Only a year after the decision in *Jackson v. Gridley*, New York held a constitutional convention. Although the convention was not focused on issues of religion, delegate Erastus Root moved: "The judiciary shall not declare any particular religion to be the law of the land; nor exclude any witness on account of his religious faith." DEMOCRACY, LIBERTY, AND PROPERTY: THE STATE CONSTITUTIONAL CONVENTIONS OF THE 1820's 234 (Merrill D. Peterson ed. 1966). Root's motion was intended to overturn both Chancellor James Kent's decision in the blasphemy case of *People v. Ruggles*, excerpted below, as well as *Jackson v. Gridley*. Root later divided his motion, the second part of which then read: "No witness shall be questioned as to his religious faith." John Webb Pratt, RELIGION, POLITICS, AND DIVERSITY: THE CHURCH-STATE THEME IN NEW YORK HISTORY 143 (1967). In support of his motion, Root claimed that he wanted to "purify the morals of the people and the incorrect practice of our courts." He "wished all men might be religious, but not hypocrites and liars, for there was

enough of them in all conscience." After a rejoinder from Chancellor Kent, who was also a delegate, Root's motion was defeated, 94–8. *Id.* at 144. In 1823, a Universalist was deemed a competent witness, although he did not believe in eternal punishments for perjury, *Butts v. Swartwood,* 2 Cow. 431 (N.Y. 1823), and five years later, the New York legislature deemed competent any witness who believed in a state of rewards and punishments, whether in the present or the hereafter. Pratt, at 150. In *People v. M'Garren,* 17 Wend. 460 (N.Y. 1837), the court upheld the trial court's ruling that an objection to a witness's incompetence for lack of religious belief must be made before the witness was sworn, although evidence of the witness's lack of religious belief was admissible to discredit the witness's credibility. In 1846, New York held another constitutional convention, and the issue of witness competence again arose. Although a committee of revision proposed no changes to the state's religious liberty provision, a motion to eliminate the requirement of a belief in God, or in a future state of rewards and punishments was offered on the floor. By a vote of 63–46, the convention voted to approve an amendment that "no person shall be rendered incompetent to be a witness on account of his opinions on matters of religious belief." *See* V Thorpe, at 2653. A related issue involved credibility. Even if the witness was competent to testify, could the witness's lack of religious belief be use to attack the witness's credibility? The sponsor of the competency amendment moved to amend his motion permitting such examination. This motion was soundly defeated, 92–12. Pratt, at 152. Despite this sentiment, the Court of Appeals of New York, in *Stanbro v. Hopkins,* 28 Barb. 265 (N.Y. 1858), permitted the jury to evaluate a witness's credibility based on the witness's religious beliefs. *Stanbro* was not formally overruled until 1903, in *Brink v. Stratton,* 175 N.Y. 150, 68 N.E. 148 (1903).

2. Courts in the United States almost universally followed the rule in *Omichund.* On more than one occasion while riding circuit, Supreme Court Justice Joseph Story held incompetent a witness who did not believe in a future state of rewards and punishments. *See Wakefield v. Ross,* Fed. Cas. No. 17,050 (5 Mason 16) (1827); *United States v. Coolidge,* Fed. Cas. No. 14,858 (2 Gall. 364) (C.C. Mass. 1815) (holding in contempt a witness who, though not a Quaker, refused to swear an oath because option of affirming belonged only to those who were members of the sect called Quakers). *Accord Norton v. Ladd,* 4 N.H. 444 (1828); *Smith v. Coffin,* 18 Me. (6 Shep.) 157 (1840); *Blocker v. Burness,* 2 Ala. 355 (1841). *See also State v. Cooper,* 2 Tenn. 96 (1807). The most stringent interpretation of the rule in *Omichund* was by Connecticut Supreme Court Justice David Daggett in *Atwood v. Welton,* 7 Conn. 66 (1828). Daggett, who had argued the incompetence of the witness in *Curtiss v. Strong,* suggested that Jews were not competent witnesses under the proper interpretation of *Omichund* and concluded that the witness, a Universalist, was not competent because he did not believe in a future state of rewards and punishments. (Universalists believed that after death all persons would ascend to Heaven.) The court was equally divided, however, and a new trial was ordered. Daggett presided over that trial, and a note after *Atwood* states that after the testimony of a number of witnesses, Daggett concluded that the witness "was a believer in future, though not endless punishment. He was, therefore, admitted." *Atwood,* at 86. Two years later, Connecticut enacted a law explicitly making Universalists competent witnesses. In Massachusetts, in part because of the Supreme Judicial Court's Unitarian bias and in part because of the more secular understanding of the oath, a witness's lack of religious belief initially went only to credibility, not competence. *Hunscom v. Hunscom,* 15 Mass. 184 (1818) (allowing witness in divorce action to testify to husband's adultery despite claim that witness was a nonbeliever). However, *Hunscom* was overruled thirty years later in *Thurston v. Whitney,* 56 Mass. (2 Cush.) 104 (1848). In *Thurston,* the Court held

an atheist was an incompetent witness. It rejected the atheist's claim that the religious liberty provision of Massachusetts's Constitution applied to an atheist, concluding, "But an atheist is without any religion, true or false." *Id.* at 110. Even after nonbelievers were deemed competent witnesses, courts permitted a witness's credibility to be attacked based on a lack of religious belief. Such credibility attacks largely ended about the turn of the century. For a critical historical overview, see Frank Swancara, OBSTRUCTION OF JUSTICE BY RELIGION (1936).

3. The court in *Jackson v. Gridley* bars the prospective witness from testifying to his religious beliefs, concluding that "it would be incongruous to admit a man to his oath, to ascertain whether an oath had any binding influence on his conscience. If he had no idea of the sanction which the appeal to Heaven, by taking an oath, creates, what is there to prevent his swearing falsely in preliminary inquiry?" The only proof of the prospective witness's belief in God are "external signs that there had been a change of mind." The court refused to recognize that this manner of proof could be applied to the "character" witnesses as well, thus leading to the absurd result that additional character witnesses could be called to testify to the lack of religious belief of the "original" character witnesses, a never ending spiral. Not all courts accepted that testimonial bar. *See United States v. White,* Fed. Cas. No. 16,675 (5 Cranch C.C. 38) (C.C.D.C. 1836) (allowing testimony of witness despite evidence of prior statements indicating lack of belief in God based on witness's testimony that he now believed in God, and that his children attended Sunday school).

B. Legal Privileges Accorded Catholics and Jews

For those professing their faith as Catholics and Jews, two other courtroom issues arose. Wigmore's 1904 TREATISE noted that the English common law provided no evidentiary privilege for confidential communications between a Roman Catholic priest and penitent. 4 Wigmore, TREATISE at §2394. The dilemma for Jews was the fact that courts were in session on Saturdays, the Jewish Sabbath.

The following case, officially unreported, was the first to allow such a privilege.

People v. Phillips

New York, Court of General Sessions (1813),
reprinted in 1 Cath. Law. 199 (1955)

[Daniel Phillips and his wife were charged with the misdemeanor of receiving the stolen property of James Keating (spelled Cating in the *Catholic Lawyer* reprint). After filing his complaint, Keating's property was returned, and he apparently wished to drop the matter. After being threatened "with a commitment to bridewell," and told that it was his duty "on his oath to reveal the whole truth," Keating stated that he had received his property from "his pastor, the Reverend Mr. Kohlmann, Rector of Saint Peter's." Kohlmann refused to testify to the Grand Jury, but it indicted Phillips, his wife and others. 1 Cath. Law. at 199. At the trial, Kohlmann "in a very becoming manner entreated that he might be excused." *Id.* at 200.]

CLINTON, MAYOR.

The question then is, whether a Roman catholic priest shall be compelled to disclose what he has received in confession—in violation of his conscience, of his clerical engagements, and of the canons of his church, and with a certainty of being stripped of his sacred functions, and cut off from religious communion and social intercourse with the denomination to which he belongs.

This is an important enquiry; It is important to the church upon which it has a particular bearing. It is important to all religious denominations, because it involves a principle which may in its practical operation affect them all; we have therefore, devoted the few moments which we could spare, to an exposition of the reasons that have governed our unanimous opinion.

It is a general rule, that every man when legally called upon to testify as a witness, must relate all he knows. This is essential to the administration of civil and criminal justice.

After carefully examining this subject, we are of opinion that such a witness ought not to be compelled to answer. The benevolent and just principles of the common law, guard with the most scrupulous circumspection, against temptations to perjury, and against a violation of moral feeling; and what greater inducement can there be for the perpetration of this offence, than placing a man between Scylla and Charybdis, and in such an awful dilemma that he must either violate his oath, or proclaim his infamy in the face of day, and in the presence of a scoffing multitude? And is there not something due to the feelings of human nature, which revolt with horror at an avowal that must exclude the witness from the pale of decent society, and subject him to that degradation which is as frequently the cause as the consequence of crimes?

There can be no doubt but that the witness does consider, that his answering on this occasion, would be such a high handed offence against religion, that it would expose him to punishment in a future state—and it must be conceded by all, that it would subject him to privations and disgrace in this world. It is true, that he would not be obnoxious to criminal punishment, but the reason why he is excused where he would be liable to such punishment, applies with greater force to this case, where his sufferings would be aggravated by the compunctious visitings of a wounded conscience, and the gloomy perspective of a dreadful *hereafter.*

It cannot therefore, for a moment be believed, that the mild and just principles of the common law would place the witness in such a dreadful predicament; in such a horrible dilemma, between perjury and false swearing: If he tells the truth he violates his ecclesiastical oath—If he prevaricates he violates his judicial oath—Whether he lies, or whether he testiffes [sic] the truth he is wicked, and it is impossible for him to act without acting against the laws of rectitude and the light of conscience.

The only course is, for the court to declare that he shall not testify or act at all. And a court prescribing a different course must be governed by feelings and views very different from those which enter into the composition of a just and enlightened tribunal, that looks with a propitious eye upon the religious feelings of mankind, and which dispenses with an equal hand the universal and immutable elements of justice.

[After concluding that nothing in English law is contrary to this ruling, Clinton continues:]

But this is a great constitutional question, which must not be solely decided by the maxims of the common law, but by the principles of our government: We have considered it in a restricted shape, let us now look at it upon more elevated ground—upon the ground of the constitution, of the social compact, and of civil and religious liberty.

Religion is an affair between God and man, and not between man and man. The laws which regulate it must emanate from the Supreme Being, not from human institutions. Established religions, deriving their authority from man, oppressing other denominations, prescribing creeds of orthodoxy, and punishing non-conformity, are repugnant to the first principles of civil and political liberty, and in direct collision with the divine spirit of Christianity. Although no human legislator has a right to meddle with religion, yet the history of the world, is a history of oppression and tyranny over the consciences of men. And the sages who formed our constitution, with this instructive lesson before their eyes, perceived the indispensable necessity of applying a preventative, that would forever exclude the introduction of calamities, that have deluged the world with tears and with blood, and the following section was accordingly engrafted in our state constitution.

It is essential to the free exercise of a religion, that its ordinances should be administered—that its ceremonies as well as its essentials should be protected. The sacraments of a religion are its most important elements. We have but two in the Protestant Church—Baptism and the Lord's Supper—and they are considered the seals of the covenant of grace. Suppose that a decision of this court, or a law of the state should prevent the administration of one or both of these sacraments, would not the constitution be violated, and the freedom of religion be infringed? Every man who hears me will answer in the affirmative. Will not the same result follow, if we deprive the Roman catholic of one of his ordinances? Secrecy is of the essence of penance. The sinner will not confess, nor will the priest receive his confession, if the veil of secrecy is removed: To decide that the minister shall promulgate what he receives in confession, is to declare that there shall be no penance, and this important branch of the Roman catholic religion would be thus annihilated.

We speak of this question, not in a theological sense, but in its legal and constitutional bearings. Although we differ from the witness and his brethren, in our religious creed, yet we have no reason to question the purity of their motives, or to impeach their good conduct as citizens. They are protected by the laws and constitution of this country, in the full and free exercise of their religion, and this court can never countenance or authorize the application of insult to their faith, or of torture to their consciences.

There being no evidence against the Defendants, they were acquitted.

Notes

1. Although unreported, the *Phillips* case was well known. William Sampson, a lawyer for the Phillipses, published a book about the case called *The Catholic Question in America* (1813 repr. 1974). Four years later, *Phillips* was cited in *People v. Smith,* 1 Am. St. Tr. 799, 2 City Hall Rec. (Rogers) 77 (N.Y. Ct. Oyer & Term. 1817), *reprinted in* 1 Cath. Law. 209 (1955). In *Smith*, the defendant was charged with manslaughter. While in jail, he spoke with the Reverend Peter J. Van Pelt in confidence. When offered by the state as a witness, defense counsel objected, citing *Phillips.* Before testifying the court asked Van Pelt "if he had any objection to state the communication made by the prisoner?" *Id.* at 211. "The witness answered, that he had not." *Id.* The court then held the

testimony admissible because, unlike the confession by Phillips, the statements made by Smith to Van Pelt were not made in the course of church discipline, but merely in confidence to a friend and advisor. *Phillips* was also cited in support of a priest-penitent privilege in a code of evidence proposed in 1825 for the state of Louisiana, *Introductory Report to the Code of Evidence* in I THE COMPLETE WORKS OF EDWARD LIVINGSTON, and was reprinted in 1 Western L.J. 109 (1843).

2. In 1828, New York revised much of its law. It passed the first statute recognizing a privilege for confidential communications: "No minister of the gospel, or priest of any denomination whatsoever, shall be allowed to disclose any confessions made to him in his professional character, in the course of discipline enjoined by the rules or practice of such denomination." Note, 1 Cath. Law. at 213, *citing* N.Y. Rev. Stat. art. 3, ch. 7, Tit. 3, Sec. 72 (1828). Additionally, the legislature passed a law limiting attacks on the competence of witness based on a lack of religious belief. It was not until 1835 that the next state, Missouri, statutorily adopted the priest-penitent privilege, and it did so as a result of adopting a great deal of New York law. In 1855, a Catholic priest in Virginia heard the confession of a dying woman. In a prosecution of her husband for murder, the priest, John Teeling, refused to testify to her statements. The trial court concluded: "To encroach upon the confessional, which is well understood to be a fundamental tenet in the Catholic church, would be to ignore the Bill of Rights, so far as it is applicable to that Church." III Stokes, at 434. (Stokes notes that the court record of this case was destroyed during the Civil War, and cites for authority to the HISTORY OF THE DIOCESE OF RICHMOND.) The privilege was not universally adopted. For example, Massachusetts, without discussion, refused to create a common law penitent privilege. *Commonwealth v. Drake*, 15 Mass. 161 (1818). Only four states had enacted a priest-penitent privilege by mid-century, although the inclusion of such a privilege in the Field Code (N.Y. Commissioners on Practice and Pleadings, CODE OF CIVIL PROCEDURE § 1710(3) (1850)), in part led to the adoption of such a privilege in 25 states by the end of the nineteenth century. *See* 4 Wigmore, *Treatise* at 2395 n.1 (collecting statutes).

3. Mayor DeWitt Clinton justifies his decision not on merely the common law, but on the constitutional right to the free exercise of religion. In examining the common law, Clinton notes that it cannot place "a man between Scylla and Charybdis, and in such an awful dilemma that he must either violate his oath, or proclaim his infamy in the face of day, and in the presence of a scoffing multitude." In the modern interpretation of the First Amendment, Justice Brennan suggested this dilemma compels a constitutional exemption from a state law. *See Sherbert v. Verner*, 374 U.S. 398 (1963), excerpted in Chapter Five. In interpreting the constitutional language, Clinton states, "It is essential to the free exercise of a religion, that its ordinances should be administered—that its ceremonies as well as its essentials should be protected." Is this an invitation to assess the central or "core" aspects of religious faith? Finally, Clinton rejects the "slippery slope" argument that "men under pretence of religion [will] act counter to the fundamental principles of morality, and endanger the well being of the state." *Phillips*, 1 Cath. Law. at 209. Is this fear that harm will come to the state from those cloaking themselves in the garb of religious liberty more likely to arise today than in 1813?

4. Clinton's reasons for adopting the privilege may, in part, include his understanding of the emerging political power of the growing number of (Irish-American) Roman Catholics in New York City. It was Clinton, who, in 1806, while both appointive Mayor of New York City and as a state legislator, maneuvered the elimination of the religious test for public office that barred Catholics from office, thus allowing the first

Irish Catholic legislator to serve in the Assembly. As of 1806, that legislator, Francis Cooper, was a member (and trustee) of St. Peter's Church, the same church at which Father Kohlmann became rector in 1808. Clinton's actions in 1806 were part of his effort to consolidate his downstate power against the power of the Livingstonian Jeffersonians in upstate New York. Pratt, at 124–27. In 1812, Clinton ran for President on the Fusion ticket, but lost to James Madison. At the time the case was decided, Clinton was both Mayor of New York City and Lieutenant Governor of New York, and he later served as Governor of New York.

5. Article 38 of New York's 1777 Constitution, quoted by Clinton in a part of the opinion not excerpted above, limited liberty of conscience by forbidding any construction that would "excuse acts of licentiousness, or justify practices inconsistent with the peace or safety of this state." Clinton first concluded that this proviso did not apply to the case here. He then stated:

> If a religious sect should rise up and violate the decencies of life, by practicing their religious rites, in a state of nakedness; by following incest, and a community of wives. If the Hindoo should attempt to introduce the burning of widows on the funeral piles of their deceased husbands, or the Mahometan his plurality of wives, or the Pagan his bacchanalian orgies or human sacrifices. If a fanatical sect should spring up, as formerly in the city of Munster, and pull up the pillars of society, or if any attempt should be made to establish the inquisition, then the licentious acts and dangerous practices, contemplated by the constitution, would exist, and the hand of the magistrate would be rightfully raised to chastise the guilty agents.

Keep Clinton's limitations of the right to free exercise in mind as you read the Supreme Court's cases of the late nineteenth century, as well as the decisions of the Supreme Court in the late twentieth century.

During the antebellum era, the Supreme Court of Pennsylvania decided two cases concerning the refusal of Jews to testify in court on Saturday. In 1793, in *Stansbury v. Marks*, 2 Dall. 213, the Court's opinion, in its entirety, states:

> In this cause (which was tried on *Saturday*, the 5th of *April)* the defendant offered *Jonas Phillips*, a Jew, as a witness but he refused to be sworn, because it was his *Sabbath*. The Court, therefore, fined him L 10; but the defendant, afterwards, waving [sic] the benefit of his testimony, he was discharged from the fine.

Although the report never mentions the first name of the defendant Marks, it was likely one of two Jewish brothers, Henry or Levy Marks, who lived in Philadelphia. If either Henry or Levy was the defendant in the case, this may explain why Jonas Phillips's testimony was waived. The prospective witness Jonas Phillips named in *Stansbury v. Marks* is the same Jonas Phillips who wrote to the 1787 Constitutional Convention requesting the elimination of religious tests for office. His son Levi is the witness who refused to testify in the following case.

Simon's Executors v. Gratz

2 Pen. & W. (39 Penn.) 412 (Pa. 1831)

[Levi Phillips (spelled Philips in the case report), one of the executors of Joseph Simon's estate, swore in open court on Saturday "that he had scruples of conscience against appearing in court to-day, and attending to any secular business; and that he believes his presence and aid will be material in the progress of the cause." *Id.* at 412. Plaintiff's counsel thus requested a continuance until the next session of the court. The court denied the request for continuance. Phillips then took a nonsuit, and after the court overruled a motion to remove the nonsuit, Phillips appealed. Phillips's counsel Champneys argued on appeal that although the *Updegraph* case, excerpted below, held that Christianity was a part of the common law of Pennsylvania, it also granted religious liberty to Jews. He also argued that an exemption for religious conscience based on *People v. Phillips.* In reply to appellee's argument that the rights of conscience had not been violated, because "[t]here was no coercion to change his faith, or to alter his practice in pursuance of it," *id.* at 415, Champneys urged that "our civil conduct, and social relations often grow out of our religious persuasions, and that the peculiar faith is violated, where the practices necessarily growing out of it, are disregarded." *Id.* at 416.]

GIBSON, C.J.

The religious scruples of persons concerned with the administration of justice, will receive all the indulgence that is compatible with the business of government; and had circumstances permitted it, this cause would not have been ordered for trial on the Jewish Sabbath. But when a continuance for conscience sake, is claimed as a right, and at the expense of a term's delay, the matter assumes a different aspect.

It never has been held except in a single instance, that the course of justice may be obstructed by any scruple or obligation whatever. The sacrifice that ensues from an opposition of conscientious objection to the performance of a civil duty, ought, one would think, to be on the part of him whose moral or religious idiosyncrasy, makes it necessary; else a denial of the lawfulness of capital punishment would exempt a witness from testifying to facts that might serve to convict a prisoner of murder, or to say nothing of the other functionaries of the law, excuse the sheriff, for refusing to execute one capitally convicted. That is an exemption which none would pretend to claim; yet it would inevitably follow from the principle insisted on here. Indeed a more apposite instance of conflict betwixt religious obligation and social duty, can hardly be imagined. Rightly considered, there are no duties half so sacred as those which the citizen owes to the laws. In the judicial investigation of facts, the secrets of no man will be wantonly exposed, nor will his principles be wantonly violated; but a respect for these must not be suffered to interfere with the operations of what organ of the government which has more immediately to do with the protection of person and property: the safety of the citizen, and the very existence of society require that it should not. That every other obligation shall yield to that of the laws, as to a superior moral force, is a tacit condition of membership in every society, whether lay or secular, temporal or spiritual, because no citizen can lawfully hold communion with those who have associated on any other terms; and this ought, in all cases of collision, to be accounted a sufficient dispensation to the conscience. I therefore entirely dissent from the opinion of the Mayor's Court of *New York,* in the case which has been cited. [*People v. Phillips*] No one is more sensible than I, of the benefit derived by society from the offices of the Catholic clergy, or of the policy of protecting the secrets of auricular confession. But considerations of policy address themselves with propriety to the legislature, and not to a magistrate whose course is prescribed not by discretion, but rules already established. On this subject, I expressed my sentiments somewhat more at large in *Lesher v. The Commonwealth,* 17 *Serg. & Rawle,* 160.

[The court set aside the nonsuit for other reasons.]

Notes

1. Chief Justice Gibson's opinion relies in part on his dissent in *Commonwealth v. Lesher,* 17 Serg. & Rawle 155 (Pa. 1828). In *Lesher,* a majority of the court held that it was not error to exclude from a jury a person whose religious beliefs led him to disavow capital punishment. Gibson believed that a citizen was under a duty to abide by the civil law if it contradicted his conscience, and if exemptions from laws were granted "wherever they happen to be in collision with some supposed religious obligation, government would be perpetually falling short of the exigence." *Id.* at 161. A case contrary to *Lesher,* and thus in accord with Gibson's dissent, is *State v. Willson,* 13 S.C.L. (2 McCord) 393 (S.C. 1823), in which the South Carolina Supreme Court held that a religious group known as Covenanters possessed no constitutional right to be exempt from jury service.

2. Chief Justice Gibson's opinion in *Simon's Executors* explicitly disavows the decision in *People v. Phillips.* Why does Gibson reject *People v. Phillips*? After assuring the reader of his devotion to protecting the Catholic auricular confession, Gibson states: "But considerations of policy address themselves with propriety to the legislature, and not to a magistrate whose course is prescribed not by discretion, but rules already established." Is this an early version of judicial restraint? Gibson also makes the broad claims that, "Rightly considered, there are no duties half so sacred as those which the citizen owes to the laws," and "every other obligation shall yield to that of the laws." Is this "positivistic" understanding of duty convincing? Is it more or less convincing in the present United States? What is Gibson expressing when he calls the fulfillment of a secular duty a "sacred" obligation?

3. Champneys did not suggest the applicability of case law and constitutional provisions giving Quakers (and in some states, others as well) the right to affirm rather than swear an oath before testifying. He also does not cite as analogous Pennsylvania's constitutional right for those religiously scrupulous to refuse to bear arms. Is that because providing an affirmation rather than swearing an oath is considered a civil right rather than a natural right? Why isn't this case like the refusal to bear arms, for the armed citizenry was viewed as essential to the maintenance of liberty and the social order? Is that because Pennsylvania chose not to provide affirmatively for this exemption, as it did for pacifists? The exemption pressed here by Phillips and Champneys might have seemed particularly appropriate in Pennsylvania, founded by the Quaker William Penn. Do you think that the fact that Levi Phillips was a Jew made this case less troubling for Gibson, or is this more a case in which the court simply believed that Phillips's more "sacred" duty was to the law than to his religious faith? Is there some middle ground between these positions?

4. In both *Lesher* and *Simon's Executors,* Gibson argues that granting exemptions for reasons of religious conscience may strike at the very existence of society. This is a classic slippery slope argument. Keep in mind Gibson's analysis in *Simon's Executors* when reading the Supreme Court's late twentieth century decisions.

5. The Simons, Gratzes, and Phillipses were all well established Jewish merchants in the Philadelphia area, and closely related by marriage. Joseph Simon's daughters married five Jewish businessmen, including Michael Gratz and Levi Phillips. *See* II Marcus, at 603. As noted above, Levi Phillips was the executor of Joseph Simon's estate, and on behalf of the estate was suing the estate of Michael Gratz. This case was not the only case among the parties, see *Gratz v. Philips,* 2 Pen. & W. (39 Penn.) 410 (1831), and it is possible that Levi Phillips's request to be excused from testifying was an attempt to delay the trial. Unlike the presumably Jewish defen-

dant in *Stansbury v. Marks,* the Jewish defendants in *Simon's Executors* expressed no sympathy to Phillips's request. Does this offer a convincing alternative explanation for Gibson's opinion?

6. The impact of *Simon's Executors* and *People v. Phillips* on modern free exercise jurisprudence is discussed in Michael W. McConnell, *The Origins and Historical Understanding of Free Exercise of Religion,* 103 Harv. L. Rev. 1409, 1503–11 (1990). After a survey of the historical record regarding free exercise exemptions, Professor McConnell suggests that although "exemptions on account of religious scruple should have been familiar to the framers and ratifiers of the free exercise clause," *id.* at 1511, and that "[t]here is no substantial evidence that such exemptions were considered constitutionally questionable, whether as a form of establishment or as an invasion of liberty of conscience," *id.*, it is "more difficult to claim...that the framers and ratifiers specifically understood or expected that the free exercise clause would vest the courts with authority to create exceptions from generally applicable laws on account of religious conscience." *Id.* at 1512. Professor McConnell's interpretation is criticized in Gerard V. Bradley, *Beguiled: Free Exercise Exemptions and the Siren Song of Liberalism,* 20 Hofstra L. Rev. 245 (1991) and Philip A. Hamburger, A *Constitutional Right of Religious Exemption: An Historical Perspective,* 60 Geo. Wash. L. Rev. 915 (1992).

C. Blasphemy

In 1659, a Maryland Jew named Jacob Lumbrozo was charged with blasphemy for denying the divinity of Jesus Christ. According to Marcus, "Lumbrozo is the only Jew known to have ever been called before an American or English court to answer to the crime of blasphemy." I Marcus, at 450. For some reason, Lumbrozo was never tried, and was released from custody. Shortly thereafter, Lumbrozo changed his first name to John, and in 1664, he served as a member of a jury, "a privilege usually reserved to Christians." *Id.* Leonard Levy notes a charge of blasphemy against a Jew named Wolf Hirsh Rosentrauch by a Catholic in New Jersey in 1882. After the jury learned that the complainant had been convicted of murder, and that the complainant and Rosentrauch had had a business dispute, the jury acquitted Rosentrauch after five minutes of deliberation. Leonard W. Levy, BLASPHEMY: VERBAL OFFENSE AGAINST THE SACRED, FROM MOSES TO SALMAN RUSHDIE 508 (1993).

Blasphemy prosecutions were brought against freethinkers whose opinions "reviled Christianity." There are four notable opinions concerning blasphemy prosecutions in antebellum America: *People v. Ruggles,* 8 Johns. 290 (N.Y. 1811); *Commonwealth v. Updegraph,* 11. Serg. & R. (26 Pa. R.) 394 (1824); *State v. Chandler,* 2 Del. (2 Harr.) 553 (1837); and *Commonwealth v. Kneeland,* 37 Mass. (20 Pick.) 206 (1838). In each case, the court upheld the prosecution, and in each case the crucial issue was whether Christianity was a part of the common law. All of the opinions are written by well-regarded judges, including the two best known state judges of the antebellum era, Chancellor (then Chief Judge) James Kent of New York, the author of COMMENTARIES ON AMERICAN LAW, and Chief Justice Lemuel Shaw of Massachusetts. A curious fact about these cases is that only *Kneeland* arose in New England; the other cases arose in the mid-Atlantic states of Pennsylvania, New York and Delaware, where liberty of religious conscience had existed much longer. *Kneeland* itself arose after the disestablishment of the standing order.

People v. Ruggles

8 Johnson 290 (N.Y. 1811)

KENT, Ch. J., delivered the opinion of the court:

The offense charged is, that the defendant below did "wickedly, maliciously and blasphemously utter, in the presence and hearing of divers good and Christian people, these false, feigned, scandalous, malicious, wicked and blasphemous words, to wit," Jesus Christ was a bastard and his mother must be a whore;" and the single question is, whether this be a public offense by the law of the land. After conviction we must intend that these words were uttered in a wanton manner, and, as they evidently import, with a wicked and malicious disposition, and not in a serious discussion upon any controverted point in religion. The language was blasphemous, not only in a popular, but in a legal sense; for blasphemy, according to the most precise definitions, consists in maliciously reviling God, or religion, and this was reviling Christianity through its author.

The authorities show that blasphemy against God, and contumelious reproaches and profane ridicule of Christ or the Holy Scriptures (which are equally treated as blasphemy), are offenses punishable at common law, whether uttered by words or writings. The consequences may be less extensively pernicious in the one case than in the other, but in both instances the reviling is still an offense, because it tends to corrupt the morals of the people, and to destroy good order. Such offenses have always been considered independent of any religious establishment or the rights of the Church. They are treated as affecting the essential interests of civil society.

And why should not the language contained in the indictment be still an offense with us? There is nothing in our manners of institutions which has prevented the application or the necessity of this part of the common law. We stand equally in need, now as formerly, of all the moral discipline, and of those principles of virtue, which help to bind society together. The people of this State, in common with the people of this country, profess the general doctrines of Christianity, as the rule of their faith and practice; and to scandalize the author of these doctrines is not only, in a religious point of view, extremely impious, but, even in respect to the obligations due to society, is a gross violation of decency and good order. Nothing could be more offensive to the virtuous part of the community, or more injurious to the tender morals of the young, than to declare such profanity lawful. It would go to confound all distinction between things sacred and profane.

The free, equal, and undisturbed enjoyment of religious opinion, whatever it may be, and free and decent discussions on any religious subject, is granted and secured; but to revile, with malicious and blasphemous contempt, the religion professed by almost the whole community, is an abuse of that right. Nor are we bound, by any expressions in the constitution, as some have strangely supposed, either not to punish at all, or to punish indiscriminately the like attacks upon the religion of Mahomet or of the Grand Lama; and for this plain reason, that the case assumes that we are a Christian people, and the morality of the country is deeply ingrafted upon Christianity, and not upon the doctrines or worship of those imposters. It is sufficient that the common law checks upon words and actions, dangerous to the public welfare, apply to our case, and are suited to the condition of this and every other people whose manners are refined, and whose morals have been elevated and inspired with a more enlarged benevolence, by means of the Christian religion.

Though the constitution has discarded religious establishments, it does not forbid judicial cognizance of those offenses against religion and morality which have no reference to any such establishment, or to any particular form of government, but are punishable because they strike at the root of moral obligation, and weaken the security of the social ties. The object of the 38th article of the constitution... was never meant to withdraw religion in general, and with it the best sanctions of moral and social obligation from all consideration and notice of the law. It will be fully satisfied by a free and universal toleration, without any of the tests, disabilities, or discriminations, incident to a religious establishment. To construe it as breaking down the common law barriers against licentious, wanton, and impious attacks upon Christianity itself, would be an enormous perversion of its meaning. [T]he framers of the constitution intended only to banish test oaths, disabilities and the burdens, and sometimes the oppressions, of church establishments, and to secure to the people of this State freedom from coercion, and an equality of right, on the subject of religion. This was no doubt the consummation of their wishes. It was all that reasonable minds could require, and it had long been a favorite object, on both sides of the Atlantic, with some of the most enlightened friends to the rights of mankind, whose indignation had been roused by infringements of the liberty of conscience, and whose zeal was inflamed in the pursuit of its enjoyment.

The legislative exposition of the constitution is conformable to this view of it. Christianity, in its enlarged sense, as a religion revealed and taught in the Bible, is not unknown to our law. The statute for preventing immorality consecrates the first day of the week as holy time, and considers the violation of it as immoral. This was only the continuation, in substance, of a law of the colony which declared that the profanation of the Lord's day was "the great scandal of the Christian faith."

The court are accordingly of opinion that the judgment below must be affirmed.

Judgment affirmed.

Notes

1. Kent holds that blasphemy violates the common law, for "[t]he people of this State, in common with the people of this country, profess the general doctrines of Christianity." However, blasphemy prosecutions are limited to reviling Christianity. No prosecution can be sustained for "attacks upon the religion of Mahomet or of the Grand Lama," because "we are a Christian people." The trial judge in *Ruggles* was Ambrose Spencer, the author of the *Gridley* decision. Pratt, at 137.

2. As noted above in the discussion after *Gridley,* Erastus Root attempted to overturn both *Gridley and Ruggles* at New York's 1821 constitutional convention. Root proposed that "the judiciary shall not declare any particular religion the law of the land." Reports of the Proceedings and Debates of the Convention of 1821 462 (1821). As framed, a majority of the convention, including James Kent, the author of *Ruggles,* voted to amend Article 38 of New York's Constitution to include Root's language. In Kent's view, this provision "was perfectly harmless, and might be a security." *Id.* at 465. Less than two weeks later, though, Ambrose Spencer moved to strike the amendment. After a speech by Kent explaining that Ruggles was indicted not because Christianity was established by law, but because "Christianity was, *in fact,* the religion of the people of this state," *id.* at 575, as well as several other speeches, the Root amendment was deleted. It was deleted in large part not because the delegates agreed with Kent, Spencer, and others, but because this course avoided disrupting the convention. Pratt, at 144.

3. There are no other recorded blasphemy convictions in New York. In 1821, Judge William Jay, John Jay's son, instructed a grand jury that freedom of speech "extends equally to religious and political topics," Morton Borden, JEWS, TURKS, AND INFIDELS 99 (1984), and in 1823, the last recorded blasphemy case was tried in New York. Based on a lack of evidence, the court ordered the jury to acquit the defendant. *People v. Porter,* 2 Parker's Crim. 14 (1823).

Updegraph v. Commonwealth

11. Serg. & R. (26 Pa. R.) 394 (1824)

[The defendant Updegraph belonged to a debating society, and during the course of debate, stated that the Bible was a "mere fable." After he was tried and convicted of blasphemy, Updegraph appealed his five shilling fine and conviction, claiming that the United States and Pennsylvania Constitutions protected his remarks. For failing to include the word "profanely" in the indictment, the court reversed the conviction, but only after discussing the authority of the commonwealth to punish blasphemers under an Act of 1700.]

DUNCAN, J.

The bold ground is taken, though it has often been exploded, and nothing but what is trite can be said upon it—it is a barren soil, upon which no flower ever blossomed;—the assertion is once more made, that Christianity never was received as part of the common law of this Christian land; and it is added, that if it was, it was virtually repealed by the constitution of *the United States,* and of this state, as inconsistent with the liberty of the people, the freedom of religious worship, and hostile to the genius and spirit of our government, and, with it, the act against blasphemy; and if the argument is worth any thing, all the laws which have Christianity for their object—all would be carried away at one fell swoop—the act against cursing and swearing, and breach of the Lord's day; the act forbidding incestuous marriages, perjury by taking a false oath upon the book, fornication and adultery—for all these are founded on Christianity—for all these are restraints upon civil liberty, according to the argument—edicts of religious and civic tyranny, "when enlightened notions of the rights of man were not so universally diffused as at the present day."

We will first dispose of what is considered the grand objection—the *constitutionality of Christianity*—for in effect that is *the question.*

Christianity, general Christianity, is, and always has been, a part of the common law of *Pennsylvania;* Christianity, without the spiritual artillery of *European* countries; for this Christianity was one of the considerations of the royal charter, and the very basis of its great founder, *William Penn*; not Christianity founded on any particular religious tenets; not Christianity with an established church, and tithes, and spiritual courts; but Christianity with liberty of conscience to all men. From the time of *Bracton,* Christianity has been received as part of the common law of *England.*

The first legislative act in the colony was the recognition of the Christian religion, and establishment of liberty of conscience. Before this, in 1646, Lord *Baltimore* passed a law in *Maryland* in favour of religious freedom, and it is a memorable fact, that of the first legislators, who established religious freedom, one was a Roman Catholic and the other a Friend.

Every one had the right of adopting for himself whatever opinion appeared to be the most rational, concerning all matters of religious belief, thus, securing by law this inestimable freedom of conscience, one of the highest privileges, and greatest interests of the human race. This is the Christianity of the common law, incorporated into the great law of *Pennsylvania,* and thus, it is irrefragably proved, that the laws and institutions of this state are built on the foundation of reverence for Christianity. Here was complete liberty of conscience, with the exception of disqualification for office of all who did not profess faith in Jesus Christ. This disqualification was not contained in the constitution of 1776; the door was open to any believer in a God, and so it continued under our present constitution, with the necessary addition of a belief in a future state of rewards and punishments. On this the constitution of *the United States* has made no alteration, nor in the great body of the laws which was an incorporation of the common law doctrine of Christianity, as suited to the condition of the colony, and without which no free government can long exist.

All men, of conscientious religious feeling, ought to concede outward respect to every mode of religious worship. Upon the whole, it may not be going too far to infer, from the decisions, that no author or printer, who fairly and conscientiously promulgates the opinions with whose truths he is impressed, for the benefit of others, is answerable as a criminal; that a malicious and mischievous intention is, in such a case, the broad boundary between right and wrong, and that it is to be collected from the offensive levity, scurrilous and opprobrious language, and other circumstances, whether the act of the party was malicious; and since the law has no means of distinguishing between different degrees of evil tendency, if the matter published contains any such evil tendency, it is a public wrong. An offence against the public peace may consist either of an actual breach of the peace, or doing that which tends to provoke and excite others to do it. Within the latter description fall all acts and all attempts to produce disorder, by written, printed, or oral communications, for the purpose of generally weakening those religious and moral restraints, without the aid of which mere legislative provisions would prove ineffectual. No society can tolerate a wilful and despiteful attempt to subvert its religion, no more than it would break down its laws—a general, malicious, and deliberate intent to overthrow Christianity, general Christianity. This is the line of indication, where crime commences, and the offence becomes the subject of penal visitation. The species of offence may be classed under the following heads—1. Denying the Being and Providence of God. 2. Contumelious reproaches of Jesus Christ; profane and malevolent scoffing at the Scriptures, or exposing any part of them to contempt and ridicule. 3. Certain immoralities tending to subvert all religion and morality, which are the foundations of all governments. Without these restraints no free government could long exist. It is liberty run mad, to declaim against the punishment of these offences, or to assert that the punishment is hostile to the spirit and genius of our government. They are far from being true friends to liberty who support this doctrine, and the promulgation of such opinions, and general receipt of them among the people, would be the sure forerunners of anarchy, and finally of despotism. Amidst the concurrent testimony of political and philosophical writers among the Pagans, in the most absolute state of democratic freedom, the sentiments of *Plutarch,* on this subject, are too remarkable to be omitted. Religion he terms the cement of civil union, and the essential support of legislation. No free government now exists in the world, unless where Christianity is acknowledged, and is the religion of the country. Christianity is part of the common law of this state. It is not proclaimed by the commanding voice of any human superior, but expressed in the calm and mild accents of customary law. Its foundations are broad, and strong, and deep: they are laid in the authority, the interest, the affections of the people. Waiving all questions of hereafter, it is the purest system of morality, the firmest auxiliary, and only stable support of all human laws. The plaintiff in error has totally failed to support his grand objection to this indictment, for Christianity is part of the common law. The act against blasphemy is neither obsolete nor virtually repealed, nor is Christianity inconsistent with our free governments or the genius of the people.

No preference is given by law to any particular religious persuasion. Protection is given to all by our laws. It is only the malicious reviler of Christianity who is punished. By general Christianity is not intended the doctrine of worship of any particular church or sect; the law leaves these disputes to theologians; it is not known as a standard by which to decide political dogmas. The worship of the Jews is under the protection of the law, and all prosecutions against Unitarians have been discontinued in *England.* While our own free constitution secures liberty of conscience and freedom of religious worship to all, it is not necessary to maintain that any man should have the right publicly to vilify the religion of his neighbors and of the country. These two privileges are directly opposed. It is open, public vilification of the religion of the country that is punished, not to force conscience by punishment, but to preserve the peace of the country by an outward respect to the religion of the country, and not as a restraint upon the liberty of conscience; but licentiousness endangering the public peace, when tending to corrupt society, is considered as a breach of the peace, and punishable by indictment.

This is the Christianity which is the law of our land, and I do not think it will be an invasion of any man's right of private judgment, or of the most extended privilege of propagating his sentiments with regard to religion, in the manner which he thinks most conclusive. If from a regard to decency and the good order of society, profane swearing, breach of the Sabbath, and blasphemy, are punishable by civil magistrates, these are not punished as sins or offences against God, but crimes injurious to, and having a malignant influence on society; for it is certain, that by these practices, no one pretends to prove any supposed truths, detect any supposed error, or advance any sentiment whatever.

Judgment reversed.

Notes

1. Like Kent's decision in *Ruggles,* Justice Duncan's opinion asserts that "Christianity is a part of the common law." Duncan also explicitly connects the civil order and religion. Religion is so necessary to maintain civic virtue that "[n]o free government now exists in the world, unless where Christianity is acknowledged, and is the religion of the country." As noted in Chapter Two, a number of Anti-Federalists and civic republicans opposed ratification of the Federal Constitution because it did not make clear the dependence of civil institutions on religion, particularly Protestant Christianity. The absence of Christian morality would result in an absence of civic virtue, which would lead to the end of republican institutions and the introduction of tyranny. Madison strongly dissented from this view, and Madisonian republicanism, which downplays the necessity of civic virtue, is one of the hallmarks of the American democratic experiment. But Justice Duncan also disclaims any establishment of religion, for this is a Christianity stripped of the particular beliefs of differing Protestant sects. He also proclaims Pennsylvania's broad liberty of conscience, which the blasphemy law leaves unaffected.

2. Although Christianity is a part of the common law, Duncan appears to acknowledge the liberty of conscience of Jews. At one point in the opinion, Duncan states: "The worship of the Jews is under the protection of the law." In an excised portion of

the opinion, he writes that "persons of a different religion, as *Jews*, though they must necessarily deny the authenticity of other religions, have never been punished as blasphemers or libellers at common law, for so doing." Are these statements inconsistent with the concept of religious liberty, or simply statements of social fact?

3. A mid-twentieth century case strikingly analogous to *Ruggles* and *Updegraph* is *Joseph Burstyn, Inc. v. Wilson,* 101 N.E.2d 665 (N.Y. 1951), in which the New York Court of Appeals refused to overturn a decision of the Board of Regents of the University of the State of New York rescinding licenses for the public exhibition of a motion picture entitled *The Miracle,* on the ground that the Board's decision that the film was "sacrilegious" was neither too indefinite nor a religious term prohibited by the state's Constitution. In its opinion, the court stated, "We are essentially a religious nation" and that "This nation is a land of religious freedom; it would be strange indeed if our Constitution, intended to protect that freedom, were construed as an instrument to uphold those who publicly and sacrilegiously ridicule and lampoon the most sacred beliefs of any religious denomination to provide amusement and for commercial gain." *Id.* at 673. The Supreme Court reversed the decision of the New York Court of Appeals on free speech and press grounds. *Burstyn v. Wilson*, 343 U.S. 495 (1952).

4. In *State v. West*, 263 A.2d 602 (Md. App. 1970), the Maryland Court of Special Appeals reversed a blasphemy conviction and held Maryland's blasphemy law unconstitutional on Establishment Clause grounds. The court concluded that the law lacked any secular purpose. Yet, the opinions in *Ruggles* and *Updegraph* claim there is a secular purpose in enforcing blasphemy laws, for such laws protect society from licentiousness, moral corruption, anarchy and despotism. It appears highly unlikely that any court would ignore the reasoning in *West* and follow *Ruggles* and *Updegraph*, but can a plausible argument be made in favor of the *Ruggles* and *Updegraph* approach? The *West* decision exemplifies a transformation in our understanding both of the role of religion in maintaining social and legal order, and in the division between religious and secular. Assess the benefits and the costs to this transformation in that understanding. For more on the secular/religious divide, see Chapters Ten and Thirteen.

5. In both *Ruggles* and *Updegraph*, the actions and speech of an individual is constrained in favor of the interests of the community. Instead of deciding the case from the perspective of the right of the individual to speak his mind, the courts in those cases focus on the interests of the community, and the interest in preserving moral virtue in the community by forbidding the reviling of Christianity. In modern constitutional rights jurisprudence, the "balance" struck by courts is between the individual's fundamental right to express himself or herself and the state's claim of a compelling interest in preventing that expression. Can the interests of a community, if that community consists merely of a part of the entire society, count as part of the *state's* interest? *See* Robert C. Post, *Cultural Heterogeneity and Law: Pornography, Blasphemy, and the First Amendment*, 76 Cal. L. Rev. 297 (1988).

6. Does it matter that the court in *Updegraph* reverses the judgment of conviction because the state failed to include the word "profanely" in the indictment, and thus did not allege the state of mind element necessary to convict? Should it be constitutionally sufficient that the court permits one to disagree publicly with Christians about the nature of the divinity of Jesus of Nazareth as long as the speaker refrains from uttering his beliefs maliciously? Is this protection of the sensibilities of those Christians who believe Jesus is the Messiah a state interest? Can the state claim such a law is permissible be-

cause it fosters the state's interest in harmonious group relations? *Cf. R.A.V. v. City of St. Paul*, 505 U.S. 377 (1992).

Shortly before *Updegraph* was decided, Thomas Jefferson wrote a letter to the English radical Major John Cartwright. In his letter, the 81-year old Jefferson made his famous statement about constitutional change: "A generation may bind itself as long as its majority continues in life; when that has disappeared, another majority is in place, holds all the rights and powers their predecessors once held, and may change their laws and institutions to suit themselves." *Thomas Jefferson to Major John Cartwright, June 5, 1824*, in THOMAS JEFFERSON: WRITINGS 1490, 1493–94 (Merrill D. Peterson ed. 1984). Jefferson then traced what he claimed was the dubious history of the assertion that "Christianity is a part of the common law."

Letter of Thomas Jefferson to Major John Cartwright

June 5, 1824

I was glad to find in your book a formal contradition [sic], at length, of the judiciary usurpation of legislative powers; for such the judges have usurped in their repeated decisions, that Christianity is a part of the common law. The proof of the contrary, which you have adduced, is incontrovertible—to wit, that the common law existed while the Anglo-Saxons were yet Pagans, at a time when they had never yet heard the name of Christ pronounced, or knew that such a character had ever existed. But it may amuse you, to shew when, and by what means, they stole this law in upon us. In a case of *quare impedit* in the Year-book 34. H. 6. folio 38. (anno 1458), a question was made, how far the ecclesiastical law was to be respected in a common law court? And Prisot, Chief Justice, gives his opinion in these words, 'A tiel leis qu'ils de seint eglise ont en *ancien scripture,* covient à nous à donner credence; car ceo common ley sur quels touts manners leis sont fondés.' Finch in his first book, c. 3. is the first afterwards who quotes this case, and mistakes it thus. 'To such laws of the church as have warrant in holy scripture, our law giveth credence.' And cites Prisot; mistranslating '*ancien scripture,*' into '*holy scripture.*' Whereas Prisot palpably says, 'to such laws as those of holy church have in *ancient writing,* it is proper for us to give credence;' to wit, to their *ancient written* laws. This was in 1613, a century and a half after the dictum of Prisot. Wingate, in 1658, erects this false translation into a maxim of the common law, copying the words of Finch, but citing Prisot. Wing. Max. 3. And Sheppard, title, 'Religion,' in 1675, copies the same mistranslation, quoting the Y.B. Finch and Wingate. Hale expresses it in these words; 'Christianity is parcel of the laws of England.' 1 Ventr. 293. 3 Keb. 607. but he quotes no authority. By these echoings and re-echoings from one to another, it had become so established in 1728, that in the case of the *King vs. Woolston*, 2 Stra. 834, the court would not suffer it to be debated, whether to write against Christianity was punishable in the temporal court at common law? Wood, therefore, 409, ventures still to vary the phrase, and say, that all blasphemy and profaneness are offences by the common law; and cites 2 Stra. Then Blackstone, in 1763, IV. 59, repeats the words of Hale, that 'Christianity is part of the laws of England,' citing Ventris and Strange. And finally, Lord Mansfield, with a little qualification, in Evans' case, in 1767, says, that 'the essential principles of revealed religion are part of the common law.' Thus ingulphing Bible, Testament and all into the common law, without citing any authority. And thus we find this chain of authorities hanging link by link, one upon another, and all ultimately on one and the same hook, and that a mistranslation of the words '*ancien scripture,*' used by Prisot. Finch quotes Prisot; Wingate does the same. Sheppard quotes Prisot, Finch and Wingate. Hale cites nobody. The court in Woolston's case, cite Hale. Wood cites Woolston's case. Blackstone quotes Woolston's case and Hale. And Lord Mansfield, like Hale, ventures it on his own authority. Here I might defy the best read lawyer to produce another scrip of authority for this judiciary forgery; and I might go on further to shew, how some of the Anglo-Saxon priests interpolated into the text of Alfred's law, the 20th, 21st, 22nd and 23rd chapters of Exodus, and the 15th of the Acts of the Apostles, from the 23rd to the 29th verses. But this would lead my pen and your patience too far. What a conspiracy this, between Church and State! Sing Tantarara, rogues all, rogues all, Sing Tantarara, rogues all!

Id. at 1494–95.

Jefferson's views were long held, and his letter to Cartwright was widely published, including in the *Boston Daily Advertiser,* where it was read by Edward Everett, who called the letter to the attention of Supreme Court Justice Joseph Story. James McClellan, Joseph Story and the American Constitution 119 (1971); R. Kent Newmyer, Supreme Court Justice Joseph Story: Statesman of the Old Republic 183 (1985). Both Everett and Story agreed that Jefferson's claims must be rebutted, but that would not occur for five years.

In 1829, when Story was inaugurated as the first Dane Professor of the Harvard Law School, Jefferson had been dead for nearly three years. However, both Jefferson's Memoirs, which virulently attacked both the Marshall Court and Story, and his Reports of Cases Determined in the General Court of Virginia, which included a lengthier "disquisition" concerning the subject of the relation of Christianity and the common law, had been published. (This disquisition is found at page 137 of Jefferson's Reports.) Story attacked Jefferson's "specious objection" to the claim that Christianity was a part of the common law in his Inaugural lecture as Dane Professor. Gerald T. Dunne, Justice Joseph Story and the Rise of the Supreme Court 310 (1970) (*quoting* Joseph Story, Miscellaneous Writings 517 (William W. Story ed. 1852)). Five years later, in the same year as his Commentaries on the Constitution was published, Story published a lengthier response to Jefferson's claims.

J. S., Art. V.—Christianity A Part of the Common Law

9 American Jurist and Law Magazine 346 (1833)

Mr. JEFFERSON, in a letter to Major Cartwright, recently published, insists that the maxim, that Christianity is a part of the common law, has no foundation in the cases cited to support it, they all referring to the year book 34 Henry 6, 38, 40; which he says has no such meaning.

[After discussing the case which gave rise to Prisot's conclusion, as well as its literal translation, Story continues:]

Mr. Jefferson supposes that the words 'ancien scripture' do not refer to the Holy Scriptures or Bible, but to *ancient writings,* or the written code of the church.

But if this be so, how could *Prisot* have said that they were common law, *upon* which *all manner of laws are founded?* Do not these words suppose that he was speaking of some superior law, having a foundation in nature or the Divine appointment, and not merely a positive ancient code of the church?

Mr. Jefferson asserts, that in subsequent cases, which he refers to, the expression has been constantly understood as referring to the Holy Scriptures; but he thinks it a mistake of Prisot's meaning. Now it is some argument in favor of the common interpretation, that it has always been cited as clear—Mr. J.'s interpretation is novel.

Mr. Jefferson quotes sundry cases where this saying has been relied on in proof of the maxim that Christianity is a part of the common law.

Thus in Taylor's case, 1 Vent. 293, indictment for blasphemous words, *Hale,* C.J. said, 'Such blasphemous words are not only an offence against God and religion, but a crime against the laws and government, and therefore punishable in this court; and Christianity is a part of the laws of England; and therefore to reproach the Christian religion is to speak in subversion of the law.' In the same case in 3 Keble, 607, Hale, C.J. is reported to have said, 'Religion is a part of the law itself, therefore injuries to God are as punishable as to the King or any common power.['] The case of 34 Hen. 6, 38, 40, is not here cited by the court as a foundation of their opinion. But it proceeds upon a general principle.

But independently of any weight in any of these authorities, can any man seriously doubt, that Christianity is recognised as *true,* as a revelation, by the law of England, that is, by the common law? What becomes of her whole ecclesiastical establishment and the legal rights growing out of it on any other supposition? What of her test act, and acts perpetually referring to it, as a divine system, obligatory upon all? Is not the reviling of any establishment, created and supported by the public law, held a libel by the common law?

Notes

1. Story initially penned a version of this article in his Common Place Book in 1811. McClellan, at 121 (*citing* I Life and Letters of Joseph Story 431, 434 (2 vols. William W. Story ed. 1851)).

2. Joseph Story was a native of Massachusetts, and, at the beginning of the nineteenth century, was a rare combination of New England lawyer and Republican. Story was a member of the Massachusetts legislature and the House of Representatives before he was 30. He was also, however, a conservative Republican, and a confirmed nationalist, who Thomas Jefferson would later label, in his posthumous Memoirs, a "Tory, a pseudo-republican, and a party deserter." Dunne, at 309. The death of Supreme Court Justice William Cushing created an opening for a New Englander on the Court. After three failed attempts to fill Cushing's seat, and despite Jefferson's opposition to his appointment, President James Madison nominated Story to the Supreme Court. He was then 32. Story was confirmed three days later, and remained a member of the Supreme Court until his death in 1845. *Id.* at 80.

3. From the time of his conversion at Harvard, Story was a "decided Unitarian," Newmyer, at 180, and regularly attended church in Massachusetts and Washington. *Id.* Story served several terms as President of the American Unitarian Association, and shortly before his death, presided over the annual meeting of the Association. He also believed that "religion was the foundation of a stable, moral society." *Id.* at 183. He wondered " 'whether any free government can be permanent where the public worship of God and the support of religion constitute no part of the policy or duty of the State in any assignable shape.' " III Stokes, at 110. In Massachusetts politics, Story successfully worked to retain the standing order at the Massachusetts constitutional convention of 1820. As a Unitarian, however, Story believed that the state had no authority to compel individual conscience or to prefer one sect over another. Thus, although it was neces-

sary to support religion to protect the civil order, it was impermissible for Massachusetts to prefer Congregationalism to Unitarianism.

4. Story rejects Jefferson's claim that Christianity is not a part of the common law by noting that several English decisions relied not on Prisot, but "upon a general principle." Additionally, because the law of England recognized Christianity as true, by requiring officials to swear to the test oath and by calling a libel the reviling of the Christian establishment, it must form a part of the common law. Evaluate Story's claim that Christianity is a part of the common law in light of his opinion in *Girard v. Vidal's Executors*, 3 U.S. [2 How.] 127 (1844), excerpted below.

5. Story is the author of the Supreme Court's opinion in *Terrett v. Taylor*, 9 Cranch 43 (1815), excerpted in Chapter One, which held that the property held by the formerly established Church of England passed not to the Commonwealth of Virginia, but to the Church's legal successor, the Protestant Episcopal Church. His decision in *Terrett* was part of his effort to defend the republican order against the "rising forces of secularism." Newmyer, at 183.

6. Story was not the only political conservative whose liberal religious views seemed inconsistent with declarations that blasphemy was a criminal offense. Zephaniah Swift, a Connecticut politician, treatise writer and state court justice, was also a liberal in religion and a conservative in politics. Like Story, Swift defended Connecticut's blasphemy law as a "'necessary measure to preserve the tranquillity [sic] of a government." Donald F. Gerardi, *Zephaniah Swift and Connecticut's Standing Order: Skepticism, Conservatism, and Religious Liberty in the Early Republic*, 67 N.E. Qtrly. 234, 246 (1994) (*quoting* Zephaniah Swift, II A SYSTEM OF THE LAWS OF CONNECTICUT 322–24 (1795–96)).

If Jefferson was correct, then blasphemy prosecutions were untenable, for such prosecutions were founded on the assertion that Christianity was a part of the common law. In 1826, Delaware enacted a statute outlawing blasphemy. A decade later, the prosecution of the aptly named Thomas Jefferson Chandler for saying "the virgin Mary was a whore and Jesus Christ was a bastard" created the opportunity for further criticism of Jefferson. In *State v. Chandler*, 2 Del. (2 Harr.) 553 (1837), Chief Justice John M. Clayton concluded that Jefferson's view was both incomplete and misleading. *Id.* at 558–62. Although the aphorism was "liable to misconstruction, and has been misunderstood," Christianity was a part of the common law. *Id.* at 562. It was a part of the common law in the sense that "every court in a civilized country is bound to notice in the same way, what is the prevailing religion of the people," *id.*, and that notice protected the people by "punishing any man who outraged the feelings of the people and insulted civil society, by wantonly and maliciously reviling or ridiculing the religion which they had freely preferred, and upon which they had staked all their hopes of happiness both here and hereafter." *Id.* at 563. Clayton then found Chandler's conviction for blasphemy did not violate the state's religious liberty provisions, for, like the *Ruggles* and *Updegraph* courts, the guarantee of liberty of conscience did not permit using words to harm the public order. *Id.* at 564–72.

The last blasphemy case arose in Massachusetts. A freethinker named Abner Kneeland, whose oratorical flourishes drew crowds of up to 2,000 listeners, and whose magazine *Investigator* enjoyed the same number of subscribers, was indicted in late 1833 for blasphemy. Levy, BLASPHEMY at 414. Among other things, Kneeland wrote, "The Universalists believe in a God, which I do not, but believe that their God, with all his moral attributes (aside from nature itself), is nothing else than a chimera of their imagination." *Id.* at 415. After five trials, and after an appeal argued in 1836, the Massachusetts

Supreme Judicial Court, in 1838, upheld the state's 1782 blasphemy law, and thus Kneeland's conviction. *Commonwealth v. Kneeland*, 20 Pick. (37 Mass.) 206 (1838). The lone dissenter, Judge Marcus Morton, in a long and impassioned dissent, concluded Kneeland had "a constitutional right to discuss the subject of God, to affirm or deny his existence." *Id.* at 244. Kneeland served sixty days in jail, and then moved to Iowa, where he died in 1844. He was the only man to be jailed in Massachusetts for the crime of blasphemy. Levy, at 414. The documentary record concerning Abner Kneeland's conviction is found in BLASPHEMY IN MASSACHUSETTS: FREEDOM OF CONSCIENCE AND THE ABNER KNEELAND CASE, A DOCUMENTARY RECORD (Leonard W. Levy ed. 1973).

D. Sunday Laws

Among the first laws passed by the states were laws regulating economic and other pursuits on Sundays. Except for Rhode Island, such laws were universally enacted. Alvin W. Johnson, THE LEGAL STATUS OF CHURCH-STATE RELATIONSHIPS IN THE UNITED STATES, WITH SPECIAL REFERENCE TO THE PUBLIC SCHOOLS 231 (1934 repr. 1982). The purpose of such laws, as noted by an Alabama court, "was evidently to promote morality and advance the interest of religion, by prohibiting all persons from engaging in their common and ordinary avocations of business, or employment, on Sunday." *O'-Donnell v. Sweeney*, 5 Ala. 467, 469 (1843). Like the blasphemy laws, Sunday laws raised the relation of Christianity and the public order. One legal issue was the constitutionality of such laws; a second was whether persons whose Sabbath was on the "seventh day" (Saturday) were exempted from the Sunday law.

Only one supreme court, California's, held a Sunday law unconstitutional. *Ex parte Newman*, 9 Cal. 502 (1858), excerpted below. On the second issue, Virginia, by statute, and Ohio by judicial decision, exempted from the application of Sunday laws those whose Sabbath was not on Sunday.

In a case arising in Pennsylvania before *Updegraph*, the Pennsylvania Supreme Court upheld the conviction of a Jewish merchant for violating the commonwealth's 1794 Sunday law. *Commonwealth v. Wolf*, 3 Serg. & R. (18 Pa.) 47 (1817). Wolf argued was that he was exempt from the law under the religious liberty article of Pennsylvania's Constitution because, as a devout Jew, he was required to work six days a week and rest on Saturday. To this, the court responded:

> [W]e have never heard of the fourth commandment having received this construction by any persons who profess to believe either in the Old or New Testament. And that the Jewish Talmud, containing the traditions of that people, and the Rabbinical constitutions and explications of their law, asserts no such doctrine. The true meaning of the command is uniformly supposed to be, that we should abstain from our usual labour the one seventh part of our time, and devote the same to the worship of the Deity, and the exercise of our religious duties. Upon this subject the sense of the adherents to the *Mosaic* dispensation is strongly evinced by the religious holidays which they keep at the proper seasons.

Id. at 50–51.

A subsidiary argument in opposition to the law was that others might find the Christian Sabbath abhorrent, and thus for reasons of conscience engage in actions on Sundays to demonstrate their abhorrence. The court strongly objected to this argument:

> The invaluable privilege of the rights of conscience, secured to us by the constitution of the Commonwealth, was never intended to shelter those persons, who, out of mere caprice, would directly oppose those laws, for the pleasure of showing their contempt and abhorrence of the religious opinions of the great mass of the citizens.

Id.

Thirty years later, the Pennsylvania Supreme Court again upheld the Sunday law, this time challenged by a member of the "Seventh Day Baptist Congregation."

Specht v. Commonwealth

8 Pa. St. 312 (1848)

[In argument, Specht's counsel rejected the claim that Christianity was a part of the common law, for that "doctrine was promulgated in the worst times, and by the worst men of a government that avowedly united church and state." *Id.* at 315. Counsel then cited several instances in which Sunday laws were held void as applied to those who conscientiously worship on the seventh day. Third, counsel urged, "[s]o far then as the authority of the United States, and of other states goes, this act is unconstitutional." *Id.* at 318. Finally, counsel traced the history of Christian worship back to Constantine.]

BELL, J.

[After noting the precedent of *Commonwealth v. Wolf*, and stating that it would follow it, the court continued:]

The constitution of this state secures freedom of conscience and equality of religious right. No man, living under the protection of our institutions, can be coerced to profess any form of religious belief, or to practise any peculiar mode of worship, in preference to another. In this respect, the Christian, the Jew, the Mohammedan, and the Pagan, are alike entitled to protection. Nay, the Infidel, who madly rejects all belief in a Divine Essence, may safely do so, in reference to civil punishment, so long as he refrains from the wanton and malicious proclamation of his opinions with intent to outrage the moral and religious convictions of a community, the vast majority of whom are Christians. But beyond this, conscientious doctrines and practices can claim no immunity from the operation of general laws made for the government and to promote the welfare of the whole people. Does the act of Assembly in question impinge upon this natural right or on the constitutional declaration which seeks to foster and protect it?

Though it may have been a motive with the law-makers to prohibit the profanation of a day regarded by them as sacred—and certainly there are expressions used in the statute that justify this conclusion—it is not perceived how this fact can vitally affect the question at issue. All agree that to the well-being of society, periods of rest are absolutely necessary. To be productive of the required advantage, these periods must recur at stated intervals, so that the mass of which the community is composed, may enjoy a respite from labour at the same time. They may be established by common consent, or, as is conceded, the legislative power of the state may, without impropriety, interfere to fix the time of their stated return and enforce obedience to the direction. When this happens, some one day must be selected, and it has been said the round of the week presents none which, being preferred, might not be regarded as favouring some one of the numerous religious sects into which mankind are divided. In a Christian community, where a very large majority of the people celebrate the first day of the week as their chosen period of rest from labour, it is not surprising that that day should have received the legislative sanction: and as it is also devoted to religious observances, we are prepared to estimate the reasons why the statute should speak of it as the Lord's day, and denominate the infraction of its legalized rest, a profanation. Yet this does not change the character of the enactment. It is still, essentially, but a civil regulation made for the government of man as a member of society, and obedience to it may properly be enforced by penal sanctions.

[The statute] intermeddles not with the natural and indefeasible right of all men to worship Almighty God according to the dictates of their own consciences; it compels none to attend, erect, or support any place of worship, or to maintain any ministry against his consent; it pretends not to control or to interfere with the rights of conscience, and it establishes no preference for any religious establishment or mode of worship. It treats no religious doctrine as paramount in the state—it enforces no unwilling attendance upon the celebration of Divine worship. It says not to the Jew or Sabbatarian, You shall desecrate the day you esteem as holy, and keep sacred to religion that we deem to be so. It does not, in the slightest degree, infringe upon the Sabbath of any sect, or curtail their freedom of worship. It detracts not one hour from any period of time they may feel bound to devote to this object, nor does it add a moment beyond what they may choose to employ.

Nor can it be objected against the statute that it gives a preference to any religious establishment or mode of worship. It leaves all free alike in the exercise of their distinctive religious tenets, saying to none, What doest thou? As I have said, the selection of the day of rest is but a question of expediency, and if from the choice falling on the first day of the week, the Jew and the Seventh-day Christian suffer the inconvenience of two successive days of withdrawal from worldly affairs, it is an incidental worldly disadvantage, temporarily injurious, it may be to them, but conferring no superior religious position upon those who worship upon the first day of the week.

Notes

1. Bell rests his conclusion on the "common consent" to the proposition that everyone needs one day of rest every seven days. His opinion neither cites *Updegraph,* nor claims that Christianity is a part of the common law. For that reason, Justice Richard Coulter concurred in the result only. He believed the law was constitutional because "it guarded the Christian Sabbath from profanation...and not because of the mere usefullness of the day as a day of rest and cessation from worldly labour." *Id.* at 327. Bell's utilitarian calculus differs from the decidedly religious interpretation given by Coulter. *Specht* was decided after the last conviction for blasphemy was upheld. Does this suggest a judicial change in the understanding of the relation of religion to the public order?

2. The three "precedents" cited in argument by Specht's counsel were the trial court's decision in *City Council v. Benjamin,* 2 Stroh. 508 (S.C. 1846), *rev'd,* 2 Stroh. 521 (S.C. 1848); *City of Cincinnati v. Rice,* 15 Ohio 225 (1846); and Virginia's rejection of a Richmond Sunday ordinance which did not exempt seventh-day worshipers. In *Benjamin,* the Recorder of Charleston found that the ordinance was a religious ordinance, and concluded with a plea for religious liberty for Jews: "Persecuted for so many centuries, the sport of tyranny and oppression in so many climes, shall he not here, at least, be at liberty to worship God in freedom, and find peace and security upon the soil and under the Constitution of South Carolina?" *Benjamin,* at 517. The South Carolina Court of Appeals soundly rejected the Recorder's decision, and justified its decision in part on the claim that Christianity was a part of the common law. Although the court

made a brief appeal to the ordinance's constitutionality as a police regulation, it also stated, "Sunday is our day of rest. We say to him, simply, *respect us,* by ceasing on this day from the pursuit of that trade and business in which you, by the security and protection given to you by our laws, make great gain." *Id.* at 527.

In *City of Cincinnati v. Rice,* 15 Ohio 225 (1846), the Supreme Court of Ohio held the City's Sunday ordinance constitutional, but void as applied to all seventh-day worshipers, as required by Ohio's 1831 Sunday law.

Finally, in Virginia, where the Sunday law was rarely enforced, the City of Richmond, in 1845, passed an ordinance largely to restrict the activities of free Negroes and slaves. Borden, at 119. After several Jews were arrested and complained, the City Council accepted a recommendation to repeal the ordinance. After *Specht* was decided, the Virginia legislature amended the law in 1849 to exempt "any person who conscientiously believed that the seventh day of the week ought to be observed as the Sabbath." *Id.* at 120.

Ex Parte Newman

9 Cal. 502 (1858)

TERRY, C. J.

The questions which arise in the consideration of the case, are:

1. Does the act of the legislature make a discrimination or preference favorable to one religious profession, or is it a mere civil rule of conduct?

2. Has the Legislature the power to enact a municipal regulation which enforces upon the citizen a compulsory abstinence from his ordinary lawful and peaceable avocations for one day in the week?

There is no expression in the act under consideration which can lead to the conclusion that it was intended as a civil rule, as contradistinguished from a law for the benefit of religion. It is entitled "An Act for the better observance of the Sabbath," and the prohibitions in the body of the act are confined to the "Christian Sabbath."

It is contended that a civil rule requiring the devotion of one-seventh of the time to repose is an absolute necessity, and the want of it has been dilated upon as a great evil to society. Such an assumption is not warranted by anything contained in the Sunday law. On the contrary, the intention which pervades the whole act is to enforce, as a religious institution, the observance of a day held sacred by the followers of one faith, and entirely disregarded by all the other denominations within the State. The whole scope of the act is expressive of an intention on the part of the Legislature to require a periodical cessation from ordinary pursuits, not as a civil duty, but in furtherance of the interests, and in aid of the devotions of those who profess the Christian religion.

Now, does our Constitution, when it forbids discrimination or preference in religion, mean merely to guarantee toleration? For that, in effect, is all which [*Specht* and *Benjamin*] seem to award, as the right of a citizen. In a community composed of persons of various religious denominations, having different days of worship, each considering his own as sacred from secular employment, all being equally considered and protected under the Constitution, a law is passed which in effect recognizes the sacred character of one of these days, by compelling all others to abstain from secular employment, which is precisely one of the modes in which its observance is manifested and required by the creed of that sect to which it belongs as a Sabbath. Is not this a discrimination in favor of the one? Does it require more than an appeal to one's common sense to decide that this is a preference? And when the Jew, or Seventh-Day Christian complains of this, is it any answer to say, your conscience is not constrained, you are not compelled to worship or to perform religious rites on that day, nor forbidden to keep holy the day which you esteem as a Sabbath? We think not, however high the authority which decides otherwise.

When our liberties were acquired, our republican form of government adopted, and our Constitution framed, we deemed that we had attained not only toleration, but religious liberty in its largest sense—a complete separation between Church and State, and a perfect equality without distinction between all religious sects.

We come next to the question whether, considering the Sunday law as a civil regulation, it is in the power of the Legislature to enforce a compulsory abstinence from lawful and ordinary occupation for a given period of time, without some apparent civil necessity for such action.

The truth is, however much it may be disguised, that this one day of rest is a purely religious idea. Derived from the Sabbatical institutions of the ancient Hebrew, it has been adopted into all the creeds of succeeding religious sects throughout the civilized world.

[The court then held the law violative of the religious liberty provision of California's Constitution, and discharged Newman from custody.]

FIELD, J. [dissenting]

I cannot perceive any valid ground for declaring the Act of 1858, for the better observance of the Sabbath, unconstitutional.

The inquiry is as to the power of the Legislature, not as to the motives which induced the enactment. If the exercise of this power is not prohibited to the Legislature by the Constitution, either in express terms, or by necessary implication, it is our duty to uphold the statute. Of its wisdom or policy, it is not within our province to judge. In what manner it conflicts with the [constitution] I am unable to perceive. What have the sale of merchandise, the construction of machines, the discount of notes, the drawing of bills of exchange, the purchase of gold, or the business of the artisan, mechanic, or manufacturer, to do with the religious profession or worship? There is no necessary connection between them. The petitioner is an Israelite, engaged in the sale of clothing, and his complaint is, not that his religious profession or worship is interfered with, but that he is not permitted to dispose of his goods on Sunday; not that any religious observance is imposed upon him, but that his secular business is closed on a day on which he does not think proper to rest. In other words, the law, as a civil regulation, by the generality of its provisions, interrupts his acquisition on a day which does not suit him. The law treats of business matters, not religious duties. In fixing a day of rest, it establishes only a rule of civil conduct. In limiting its command to secular pursuits, it necessarily leaves religious profession and worship free. It is absurd to say that the sale of clothing, or other goods, on Sunday, is an act of religion or worship; and it follows that the inhibition of such sale does not interfere with either. Religious profession springs from matters of faith, and religious worship is the adoration of the soul. As to the forms in which that profession or worship shall be exhibited, the law is silent; it utters no command, and it imposes no restraint. It makes no discrimination or preference between the Hebrew and Gentile, the Mussulman and Pagan, the Christian and Infidel, but leaves to all the privilege of worshipping God, or of denying His existence, according to the conclusions of their own judgments, or the dictates of their own consciences. *It does not even allude to the subject of religious profession or worship, in any of its provisions.* It establishes, as a civil regulation, a day of rest from secular pursuits, and that is its only scope and purpose. Upon no subject is there such a concurrence of opinion, among philosophers, moralists, and statesmen of all nations, as on the necessity of periodical cessations from labor. One day in seven is the rule, founded in experience, and sustained by science. There is no nation, possessing any degree of civilization, where the rule is not observed, either from the sanctions of the law, or the sanctions of religion.

That the law operates with inconvenience to some is no argument against its constitutionality. Such inconvenience is an incident to all general laws. A civil regulation can not be converted into a religious institution because it is enforced on a day which a particular religious sect regards as sacred. The Legislature has seen fit, in different enactments, to prohibit judicial and various kinds of official business on Sunday, and yet it has never been contended that these enactments establish any religious observances, or that the compulsory abstinence from judicial or official labor is a discrimination or preference in favor of any religious sect. The law requires notes, when the last day of grace falls on Sunday, to be presented to the maker on Saturday, in order to hold the endorser. Would the complaint of an Israelite, that this was a discrimination in an important class of contracts in favor of the Christian, be listened to for a moment? But why not? In the course of his business it often becomes important to his interest that he should take commercial paper, not given to him in the first instance, and when, therefore, it is not in his power to fix the day of payment; and if the opinion of my associates is law, I see no reason why he should be compelled to have the note presented on Saturday, in order to hold the endorser. And why should he be denied the power of enforcing on that day, by legal process, contracts entered into with him? To be consistent, we ought to hold all this legislation as discriminating and giving a preference in favor of one religious sect, and therefore unconstitutional. The answer consists in the simple fact that the legislation is not based upon any idea of enforcing a religious observance, but of establishing, as a civil regulation, a day of rest from judicial and other official labor.

The fact that the civil regulation finds support in the religious opinions of a vast majority of the people of California is no argument against its establishment. It would be fortunate for society if all wise civil rules obtained a ready obedience from the citizen, not merely from the requirement of the law, but from conscientious or religious convictions of their obligation. The law against homicide is not the less wise and necessary because the Divine command is, "thou shalt do no murder." The legislation against perjury is not the less useful and essential for the due administration of justice because the injunction comes from the Most High, "thou shalt not bear false witness against thy neighbor." The establishment by law of Sunday as a day of rest from labor, is none the less a beneficent and humane regulation, because it accords with the Divine precept that upon that day "thou shalt do no manner of work; thou, and thy son, and thy daughter, the man-servant and thy maid-servant, thy cattle, and the stranger that is within thy gates."

Notes

1. Three years later, a differently constituted California Supreme Court sustained a nearly identical law. *Ex parte Andrews,* 18 Cal. 678 (1861). The *Andrews* opinion began with the statement that, "Probably such strong concurrence of opinion on one leading question affecting the general community cannot be found in the history of American jurisprudence." *Id.* at 681. The court cited *Ex parte Newman* only to assent to Field's dis-

sent. Chief Justice Field silently concurred. In *Bloom v. Richards*, 2 Ohio St. 387 (1853), the Supreme Court of Ohio refused to hold void at common law a contract entered into on Sunday. Additionally, the court upheld enforcement of the contract against a challenge that it was barred by Ohio's Sunday law. The court refused to hold Christianity a part of the common law, but upheld the Sunday law "as a mere municipal or police regulation, whose validity is neither strengthened nor weakened by the fact that the day of rest it enjoins is the Sabbath day." *Id.* at 392. Because the law forbade only "work" and certain types of recreation, and did not extend to all "manner of worldly business," *id.* at 396, the contract was enforceable.

2. In another part of Chief Justice David Terry's opinion, he approvingly cited an 1829 report by Senator Richard M. Johnson concerning the operation of post offices on Sunday. In 1828, a group organizing itself as the General Union for Promoting the Observance of the Christian Sabbath was formed in New York. Petitions from this group, as well as petitions requesting Congress keep post offices open on Sunday, flooded Congress. Johnson's report stated, in part:

> With these different religious views, the committee are of opinion that Congress cannot interfere. It is not the legitimate province of the Legislature to determine what religion is true, or what is false. Our Government is a civil and not a religious institution. Our constitution recognizes in every person the right to choose his own religion, and to enjoy it freely, without molestation. Whatever may be the religious sentiments of citizens, and however variant, they are alike entitled to protection from the Government, so long as they do not invade the rights of others.

II Stokes, at 15.

The campaign to prohibit Sunday mail delivery failed.

3. Terry's opinion strongly distinguishes religious toleration from religious liberty. All persons enjoy the constitutional right to religious liberty, not merely toleration of their religion. Terry also concludes that the law is unconstitutional even though it does not compel a religious believer to do anything contrary to his conscience. In this, Terry foreshadows the Supreme Court's decision over a century later in *Sherbert v. Verner*, 374 U.S. 398 (1963), excerpted in Chapter Five. However, Terry does not discuss the impact of the law on the nonbeliever, only its effect on Jews and Seventh Day Christians.

Field's dissent is strongly reminiscent of recent Supreme Court decisions concerning constitutional exemptions for religious believers from general laws. *See, e.g., Employment Div., Dep't of Human Resources v. Smith,* 494 U.S. 872 (1990), excerpted in Chapter Five. Like the Court in *Smith,* and like Chief Justice Gibson in *Simon's Executors,* Field fears that the granting of an exemption for constitutional reasons will result in many more and varied requests. The cost of exemptions is too high, in Field's view. Is this fear reasonable? How can we tell?

4. One major difference between the blasphemy and Sunday law cases is the latter cases are not justified by resort to the claim that Christianity is a part of the common law. Instead, Sunday laws are justified by the claim of legislative authority over police matters. Why this difference? Is it a result of the fact that Sunday laws are decided nearly a generation after the blasphemy cases? Is it because the blasphemy cases could not otherwise be justified in states in which liberty of conscience was guaranteed in their constitutions? As you consider the materials in the next chapter,

note that the Supreme Court makes the broader claim that the United States is a Christian nation, rather than the narrower claim that Christianity is a part of the common law.

5. Stephen Field became a member of the Supreme Court in late 1863. He served on the court for 34 years, eclipsing the tenure of Chief Justice Marshall. Although Field was the son of a Congregationalist minister, "he was not commonly regarded as a religious man." Carl Brent Swisher, STEPHEN J. FIELD: CRAFTSMAN OF THE LAW 447 (1930). After largely ignoring religion for most of his life, Field turned to it after his retirement. *Id.* His brother was the famous New York lawyer and advocate of codification of the laws, David Dudley Field.

6. David Terry left the California Supreme Court in 1859, the same year in which he killed a man in a duel. He would once again clash with Stephen Field. Nearly three decades later, and shortly after the death of his wife and two sons, Terry became the attorney for, and later the husband of, Sarah Hill. Sarah Hill claimed to be the wife of former Nevada Senator William Sharon, a claim vigorously denied by Sharon, and after his death, by his heirs. In the summer of 1888, while riding circuit, Justice Field delivered an opinion declaring that a purported marriage certificate involving Sharon and Hill was a forgery. After accusing Field of accepting a bribe to decide against her, Hill was ordered from the courtroom. When a marshal began to carry her out, David Terry assaulted him and attempted to pull a Bowie knife from his coat. Both of them were imprisoned for contempt of court. During the ensuing year, the Terrys repeatedly threatened to kill Field when he returned to California. In the summer of 1889, Field returned to California. At breakfast at the Lathrop, California railroad station, Terry saw Field and assaulted him. A federal marshal assigned to protect Field, David Neagle, shot and killed Terry. With Field recusing himself, the Supreme Court held that California could not charge Neagle with murder because his actions were taken under the color of federal authority. *In re Neagle,* 135 U.S. 1 (1890). *See* Swisher, at 321–61.

E. Churches and the Holding of Property

As noted in Chapter One § B, one consequence of the disestablishment was a struggle for the property of those churches. Although Massachusetts allowed the Congregational and Unitarian churches to take ownership of parish churches after the disestablishment of the standing order, the Commonwealth of Virginia claimed ownership of all such property after the failure of the general assessment. The Virginia Court of Appeals held in *Turpin v. Locket,* 6 Call 133 (Va. 1804), that land on which there was no existing church reverted to the state. A decade later, in an opinion by Justice Story, the Supreme Court disagreed, and held that such land was lawfully that of the Protestant episcopal church. *Terrett v. Taylor,* 9 Cranch 43 (1815).

Another consequence of the disestablishment of state churches was the legality of bequests made in trust to a religious organization. In the following cases, the courts take very different views of the legality of such trusts, and of the place of churches in the United States. Like *Turpin v. Locket* and *Terrett v. Taylor,* the divergent views of the capability of religious societies to hold property are given by the Virginia Court of Appeals and the Supreme Court of the United States.

Gallego's Executors v. Attorney General

3 Leigh 487 (Va. 1832)

CARR, J.

This case involves several very important questions, which I shall consider in the order they were discussed at the bar.

First, then, as to the charities. The attorney general filed an information and bill; to have them applied to the objects for which they were bequeathed, and to enforce the execution of the trusts in respect to them; and the chancellor considering them good and valid, decreed them. It was contended in the argument that this decree was erroneous, because the devise and bequests were vague and indefinite, and therefore void. Let us examine this. The pecuniary legacies of 4000 dollars are, in effect, given to *the roman catholic congregation,* but for the building and support of a chapel; and the ground is given to trustees to permit the roman Catholics to build a church on, *for the use of themselves, and all persons of that religion, residing in Richmond.* The bare statement seems sufficient to shew, that under the general rule, as applicable to ordinary legacies, these would be void. Who are the beneficiaries? The roman catholic congregation residing in Richmond. And who are they? Suppose you name them to-day: are those the same persons who constituted the congregation yesterday? Or who will constitute it to-morrow? Will none remove from, or come to Richmond, to reside? Will none be converted to or from the roman catholic religion? For it is to the roman catholic congregation for the time being, that the legacies are given. This however is a point which need not be pressed; for it was not pretended, that they could be supported, as legacies to individual persons. But it was strongly insisted, that as *charitable legacies* they were entitled to the aid and protection of a court of equity; and the practice of the English courts, in similar cases, was referred to in proof of the position. The course of decisions in England was admitted on the other side, but it was contended, that they rested intirely on the statute of charitable uses, 43 Eliz. and did not at all belong to the ordinary powers of a court of equity. This was the only serious question. I certainly shall not discuss it; for I find this completely done to my hand, by chief justice Marshall, in the case of *The Baptist Association v. Hart's Ex'ors.* The cases cited and examined, and the reasons given by him, prove, conclusively to my mind, that in England, charitable bequests, where no legal interest is vested, and which are too vague to be claimed by those for whom the beneficial interest was intended, cannot be established by a court of equity, either exercising its ordinary jurisdiction, or enforcing the prerogative of the king as *parens patriae,* independently of the statute 43 Elizabeth; and as that statute, if ever in force here, was repealed in 1792, I conclude that *charitable* bequests stand on the same footing with us, as all others, and will alike be sustained, or rejected, by courts of equity. I think the bill of the attorney general must be dismissed.

TUCKER, P.

It cannot be denied, that the principal question in this case, is one of the deepest interest and importance.

It is contended, on the one hand, that these several bequests are void and ineffectual, for uncertainty as to the beneficiaries who are to take under them: and, on the other, that they are good as bequests to charitable purposes, which the law will support, and which the court of chancery, upon the general principles of its equitable jurisdiction, will enforce at the instance of the attorney general.

It is obvious, that the bequest here, though for building a church, is a bequest to the roman catholic congregation in Richmond; and it is equally obvious that the testator designed no individual benefit to the members of that congregation: yet, as the society or congregation is not incorporated, it may well be asked, who are to be regarded as the beneficiaries entitled to the advantage of this bequest? Who can present himself as a claimant of this aid designed for the roman catholic religion? If membership of the congregation is to be the test of right, then the title will be in a continual state of flux. What belongs to A. to-day, will by his removal *from* Richmond, or apostacy *from* the church, cease to be his to-morrow; whereas B. by removal *to* the city, or conversion *to* the church, might, by the converse of the principle, acquire to-morrow, a right which he has not to-day. Moreover, who would be the legally constituted triers of the fact of conversion or apostacy, whereby one man is to gain, or another is to lose, the interest in the property? Who, indeed, constitute the society? Whom does the law recognize, or the testator designate, as having the power to decide this essential question? Are all who have been baptized in the church, within the operation of the will? Or those only who are received as partakers of its most solemn ordinances? These, and a multitude of like difficulties, present themselves to the notion of any grant or conveyance to a religious society, or to trustees for their use. In short, there cannot be a trust without a *cestui que trust;* and if it cannot be ascertained who the *cestui que trust* is, it is the same thing as if there was none.

These principles, it is confidently believed, are the general principles of the common law upon this subject. If there are exceptions to these principles, those exceptions may without doubt be shewn. A diligent search has led me to the conviction, that there was no case at common law, in which a bequest or a trust of this *indefinite* character, could be supported; and the learned counsel on both sides, have acknowledged, that they have been unable to discover any case anteriour to the statute 43 Elizabeth, in which the validity of such bequests or trusts has been distinctly recognized by the courts.

That charitable gifts were known and recognized by the law anteriour to the statute of Elizabeth, it is not necessary to deny. The devise in [*Philadelphia Baptist Ass'n v. Hart's Executors*] was not more indefinite than this devise; it was, like this, for religious purposes; and it was pronounced void for its uncertainty. I refer to it, therefore, as presenting a much stronger argument than any I can offer, in support of the position, that these indefinite bequests for charitable purposes, could only be sustained under the statute 43 Elizabeth.

Upon the whole, I am well satisfied, that the whole of the doctrine of the English courts in reference to indefinite charities, springs from the statute of 43 Elizabeth, which is not in force in Virginia. Whether that statute ever was in force here, has been made a question in the cause. If it ever was in force, however, it was repealed in the year 1792, in the general repeal of English statutes. That repeal was no rash or unadvised act. The repeal of this statute must, therefore, be looked upon as an advised act of legislation, and in the same light as if it had been specially repealed by its title.

If I have been correct in this course of argument, there can be no pretence for the enforcing of the charities under this will of Mr. Gallego, as they were void at common law, and are not entitled to the protection of the statute of the 43 Elizabeth.

No man at all acquainted with the course of legislation in Virginia, can doubt, for a moment, the decided hostility of the legislative power to religious incorporations. Its jealousy of the possible interference of religious establishments in matters of government, if they were permitted to accumulate large possessions, as the church has been prone to do elsewhere, is doubtless at the bottom of this feeling. The legislature knows, as was remarked by the counsel, that wealth is power. Hence the provision in the bill of rights; hence, the solemn protest of the act on the subject of religious freedom; hence, the repeal of the act incorporating the episcopal church, and of that other act which invested the trustees appointed by religious societies with power to manage their property: hence too, in part, the law for the sale of the grebe lands: hence the tenacity with which applications for permission to take property in a corporate character (even the necessary ground for churches and graveyards) have been refused. The legislature seems to have been fearful, that the grant of any privilege, however trivial, might serve but as an entering wedge to greater demands. Nor did this apprehension of the dangers of ecclesiastical establishments, spring up for the first time with our republican institutions. The history of ages had attested the proneness of such establishments to vast accumulations of property, and the statute book of England is loaded with statutes of *mortmain,* which were rendered necessary by the rapacity of the clergy, at least in the early periods of the church. So long as there have been church establishments, with power to receive and accumulate property, so long has the tendency to such accumulation been manifested distinctly. The history of the papal see, and the religious houses under its dominion, is but a history of the cupidity of monks and devotees, veiled under the sacred garb of our holy religion. The vast domains of the clergy acquired by the catholic establishment of France, are known to us all. From this fatal source, among others, sprung a revolution, which deluged the fairest country in Europe in blood, and, in its horrible progress, spread desolation over adjoining states, and shook the civilized world to its centre. And in Protestant England, fenced around as it has been with *mortmain* acts, we see a church establishment possessed of overgrown wealth and power, less devoted to the cause of genuine religion, than to pamper the luxury and indolence of the high dignitaries of the church. With these examples before our eyes, it is not wonderful that our statesmen have been cautious. They have been wise in their caution. The evil has not sprung from particular creeds, or the peculiarities of a confession of faith. It grows out of the very nature of the thing. The church, if made capable to take, while it is continually acquiring, from the liberality of the pious, or the fears of the timid, or the credulity of the ignorant, never can part with anything; and thus, like those sustaining powers in mechanics, which retain whatever they once have gained, it advances with a step that never retrogrades. The natural cupidity of the human heart, is watched by the devotee himself, with the less jealousy in his pursuit after acquisitions for the church, since he believes it to be purified from the dross of selfishness, and sanctified by the holy object of his ambition. Thus it is, that however humble in its beginning, accumulation is the natural result of the power vested in any religious society to acquire property. The same influence which enables it to gain from the state its first insignificant privileges, will secure to it, from time to time, new though apparently inconsiderable accessions; until, at last, the power will be acquired which legislative jealousy has apprehended. Property, indeed, it need not ask of the legislature. The power to take and accumulate, alone, is necessary: all time has shewn, that the influence of feelings of devotion will do the rest. I speak of those feelings which exist without any undue influence from the pastor of the society. But, if we go farther, and suppose it possible, that those abuses which once have existed, may exist again, the progress will be more rapid, though not more certain. "What (says the accomplished sir Samuel Romilly) is the authority of a guardian, or even of a parent, compared with the power of religious impressions under the ascendancy of a spiritual advisor, with such an engine to work upon the passions; to inspire (as the object may be best promoted) despair or confidence; to alarm the conscience by the horrors of eternal misery, or support the drooping spirits, by unfolding the prospect of happiness which is never to end."

Such, I conceive, are the general grounds, upon which rests the legislative policy, in relation to the power of acquiring and holding property by religious societies. We have seen, too, a similar policy evinced as to charities generally, in striking at the root of them all, by the repeal of the statute of Elizabeth. It is not (to use the language of one of the counsel) that charity is banished from Virginia. Its benign and salutary influence may warm and animate every heart, and lead to a generous munificence, as the daily habit of our lives, without exposing the state to the evils which have always flowed from what are called conveyances in *mortmain.* It is not necessary here to detail those evils. But it is relevant to observe, that conveyances in *mortmain* to corporations, were not more calculated to produce a pernicious locking up of property, than charitable bequests of this indefinite character. A corporation may be dissolved, and the property may be again taken up into the general circulation, by reverting to the donor. But these charities never die. Experience has justified these complaints, and accordingly about one hundred years ago, the parliament of G. Britain found itself compelled to pass the statute 9 George 2. which, in important particulars, repeals the statute of 43 Elizabeth. It is at this moment, when the country whose laws we have adopted, has partly receded from the wretched policy of permitting the whole property of society to be swallowed up in the insatiable gulph of public charities, that we are called upon to reanimate the pernicious principle, which they now deprecate, and which with us has been sleeping in inaction, for nearly two centuries and an half. And this too, when we have put off the panoply of the *mortmain* acts, by the general repeal of them in 1792. It is said, indeed, that the legislature may pass the necessary laws for regulating these charitable gifts, and thus prevent the evils that might flow from the unlimited permission of them. But I think, under the existing doubts which hang around the subject, and after the lapse of centuries, during which the law respecting charities, if it ever existed here, has been silent and quiescent, it behooves the judiciary to leave to the legislature, the duty of waking it into life.

The result of this view of the subject is, that the interlocutory order of the chancellor must be reversed, and the bill of the attorney general dismissed.

Notes

1. The opinions agree that the bequest of $4000 to the Roman Catholic congregation of Richmond is invalid because such bequests are void at common law, and cannot be established by a court of equity independently of the English statute (43 Elizabeth) allowing bequests for charitable purposes. When the Virginia legislature enacted a "general repeal" of English laws in 1792, the court concludes that it intended specifically to repeal the Act of 43 Elizabeth. Thus, the bequest was invalid in law and equity. Tucker claims that the legislature initiating repeal understood that "wealth is power." Restricting the wealth of religious societies would prevent "the possible interference of religious establishments in matters of government." In the course of his opinion, Tucker states, "The history of the papal see, and the religious houses under its dominion, is but a history of the cupidity of monks and devotees, veiled under the sacred garb of our holy religion." Does this suggest that Tucker's animus is less toward religion than to the influx of the Roman Catholic faith in Virginia? *See* Lawrence M. Friedman, A History of American Law 254 (2d ed. 1985) ("A faint odor of anti-Catholicism also hung over these laws—the fantasy of the evil priest, extorting ransom for the Church as the price of absolution"). Tucker also lambastes the influence of the Church of England in that country. Remember that the Church of England was the established church in colonial Virginia. Later in the opinion, Tucker speaks reverentially about "our holy religion".

What does he mean by that language? Whose interests is Tucker protecting in his opinion? The decision in *Gallego's Executors* was overruled in *Protestant Episcopal Educ. Soc. v. Churchman*, 80 Va. 718 (1885) and *Trustees of the General Assembly of the Presbyterian Church in the United States v. Guthrie*, 10 S.E. 318 (Va. 1889).

The opinions also mention mortmain laws. Mortmain laws, based on an English statute dating from the reign of George II, were laws designed to prevent religious societies from obtaining ownership of lands unless certain conditions were met.

Virginia's constitution, then and now, bars religious societies from incorporating. Does such a provision violate the free exercise clause of the First Amendment?

2. As noted in § D above, Virginia amended its Sunday law in 1849, but did not abolish it. What does the legislature's action suggest about the "interference of religious establishments in matters of government"?

3. *Trustees of Philadelphia Baptist Ass'n v. Hart's Executors,* 4 Wheat. 1 (1819), cited in the opinions in *Gallego's Executors,* involved a legacy to "the Baptist Association that, for ordinary, meets at Philadelphia annually, which I allow to be a perpetual fund for the education of youths of the Baptist denomination, who shall appear promising for the ministry, always giving preference to the descendants of my father's family." The testator was a citizen and resident of Virginia. He died in 1795. The Philadelphia Baptist Association was an unincorporated association at the time of the testator's death, but was incorporated in 1797 in Pennsylvania. Suit was brought against the executors in the United States Circuit Court for the District of Virginia by the Pennsylvania corporation and persons who were members of the unincorporated association at the time of the testator's death. The lower court was divided and a question was certified to the Supreme Court. Chief Justice Marshall held for the Court that the plaintiffs were incapable of taking the legacy for which the suit was instituted. In the following case, Justice Story, who joined the Court's opinion in *Hart's Executors,* determined that a more complete reading of the history of charitable bequests in England permitted such trusts even without statutory support.

4. The influx of Roman Catholics to the United States during the first half of the nineteenth century led to a dramatic expansion of both Roman Catholic parishes and the creation of dioceses governed by bishops. Under Roman Catholic canon law, the bishop was responsible for protecting the temporal goods of the church. State religious incorporation laws were drafted so that members of the congregation or religious society voted to elect trustees, who were responsible to decisions concerning church property. New York first passed a religious incorporation law in 1784, which permitted any church to elect between 3 and 9 trustees to "take charge of the Estate and Property belonging to their respective Churches, Congregations or Societies." *See* Patrick J. Dignan, A History of the Legal Incorporation of Catholic Church Property in the United States, 1784–1932 53 (1935) (quoting Act of April 6, 1784). In 1813, *An Act for the Incorporation of Religious Societies*, which superseded the 1784 act, was adopted. Like the earlier act, it provided that between 3 and 9 trustees were to be elected by a majority of the male persons belonging to the church. These trustees had the legal authority "to transact all affairs relative to the temporalities thereof." The trustees "are hereby authorized and empowered to take into their possession and custody all the temporalities belonging to such church, congregation or society, whether the same consists of real or personal estate, and whether the same shall have been given, granted or devised directly to such church congregation or society, or to any other person for their use... and all other matters relating to the temporal concerns and revenues of such church." *See*

Dignan, at 65. Although the law exempted the Episcopal and Dutch Reformed churches from the requirements of the act, it neither exempted nor included the Roman Catholic Church. For the Roman Catholic hierarchy, this law was unacceptable because it failed to acknowledge the bishop's canonical responsibility to protect church property. Suspicion of the "anti-democratic" nature of the Roman Catholic Church made any amendment to this law impossible for over four decades. After the spectacular decline of the Know Nothing Party in New York in 1856, however, renewed efforts to adopt a church incorporation law amenable to the Roman Catholic church led to the adoption of an act permitting the Roman Catholic church to incorporate and own property through "corporation aggregate." This form of incorporation allowed the bishop, the vicar general and the pastor of a church to act as three members of the corporation. Those three persons (and their successors in office) would then appoint two lay members, and the five constituted a corporation aggregate. States gradually acknowledged Roman Catholic perspectives on the proper locus of control of church property by the end of the nineteenth century.

Blair v. Odin, 3 Tex. R. 288 (1848)—The Bishop of Texas, Jean Marie (anglicized in the opinion as John M.) Odin sued for possession of a lot in Victoria, Texas. When Victoria was laid out in 1832, Texas was a part of Mexico. Pursuant to Mexican law, the lot was designated as the church square, for the use of the established Roman Catholic Church. However, the church actually used by the Catholics for worship in Victoria was located elsewhere in the town, and the lot was never developed or possessed by the Catholic Church. Odin sued after Presbyterians possessed the lot and claimed it for themselves. The lower court held for the Bishop. On appeal to the Supreme Court of Texas, it held that, because the Pope had unwisely made the Spanish monarch the spiritual leader of all Spanish possessions in the Americas, the Roman Catholic Church never held fee simple title to its churches in Texas when Texas was a part of Spain or Mexico, but a usufruct, the right to the benefits of property but not ownership of that property. What, then, was the effect of the revolution that resulted in Texas declaring its independence from Mexico? The court rejected the contention that "the mere act of a change of sovereignty all such tenures were dissolved and became absolutely void." It did so because

> [t]his conclusion is believed not to be sustainable on the sound principles of the liberal and enlightened jurisprudence of the present age. Modern jurists, in this country and in Europe, have harmonized with the progress of public sentiment so far, as almost to have built up an improved international code, one of the maxims of which is, so to construe rights of persons and communities as to cause the least possible injury to result from revolutions or changes in the form of government; whether such changes be brought about peaceably by an expression of the will of the inherent right of the people, or forcibly, by a resort to arms. A conquering general overruns, and reduces to subjection a province of (or the whole of) a neighboring independent government. What is to be the course he will adopt for the government of the conquered people? Is he to destroy at once all municipal law, all their rights of property, their customs and religion? The more expanded sentiments of humanity would furnish an answer in the negative; and would declare that it is his duty to abridge rights and privileges no further than necessity, and a prudent regard to the preservation of his conquest, would dictate. When an integral part of a government, by a successful revolution, establishes its independence, are rights of every description to be less regarded than if the people had been subjugated by a foreign invader? Such a conclusion would be too preposterous to be for a moment thought of;

> nor is it believed that the principles we have been discussing could lead to any embarrassing or pernicious results to the new government.

Id. at 297–98.

Had the Roman Catholic Church taken possession of the lot at issue, it "would have constituted a dedication entitled to the protection of the law." *Id.* at 299. Because it never did so, it could not now claim any ownership interest.

Although the Texas Supreme Court holds against Bishop Odin, it is much more accommodating to the property claim of the Roman Catholic Church than was the Virginia Court of Appeals in *Gallego's Executors.* Is the position taken in *Gallego's Executors* by the Virginia Court of Appeals a consequence of the longstanding suspicion of religious societies by notable Virginians, including Thomas Jefferson?

Vidal v. Girard's Executors

43 U.S. [2 How.] 127 (1844)

[Stephen Girard, a wealthy French immigrant, left 2 million dollars to the city of Philadelphia to create an institution for "poor male white orphan children" with the proviso that "no ecclesiastic, missionary, or minister of any sect whatsoever, shall ever hold or exercise any station or duty whatever in the said college, nor shall any such person ever be admitted for any purpose, or as a visitor, within the premises appropriated to the purposes of the said college." He included this restriction, he stated, not "to cast any reflection upon any sect or person whatsoever; but, as there is such a multitude of sects, and such a diversity of opinion amongst them, I desire to keep the tender minds of the orphans, who are to derive advantage from this bequest, free from the excitement which clashing doctrines and sectarian controversy are so apt to produce." This provision was challenged as "derogatory to the Christian religion."]

Mr. Justice STORY delivered the opinion of the court.

We are, then, led directly to the consideration of the question which has been so elaborately argued at the bar, as to the validity of the trusts for the erection of the college, according to the requirements and regulations of the will of the testator. That the trusts are of an eleemosynary nature, and charitable uses in a judicial sense, we entertain no doubt. Not only are charities for the maintenance and relief of the poor, sick, and impotent, charities in the sense of the common law, but also donations given for the establishment of colleges, schools, and seminaries of learning, and especially such as are for the education of orphans and poor scholars.

The statute of the 43 of Elizabeth, ch. 4, has been adjudged by the Supreme Court of Pennsylvania not to be in force in that state. But then it has been solemnly and recently adjudged by the same court that "it is so considered rather on account of the inapplicability of its regulations as to the modes of proceeding, than in reference to its conservative provisions."

This objection is that the foundation of the college upon the principles and exclusions prescribed by the testator, is derogatory and hostile to the Christian religion, and so is void, as being against the common law and public policy of Pennsylvania; and this for two reasons: First, because of the exclusion of all ecclesiastics, missionaries, and ministers of any sect from holding or exercising any station or duty in the college, or even visiting the same: and Secondly, because it limits the instruction to be given to the scholars to pure morality, and general benevolence, and a love of truth, sobriety, and industry, thereby excluding, by implication, all instruction in the Christian religion.

In considering this objection, the court [is] not at liberty to travel out of the record in order to ascertain what were the private religious opinions of the testator, (of which indeed we can know nothing,) nor to consider whether the scheme of education by him prescribed, is such as we ourselves should approve, or as is best adapted to accomplish the great aims and ends of education. Nor are we at liberty to look at general considerations of the supposed public interests and policy of Pennsylvania upon this subject, beyond what its constitution and laws and judicial decisions make known to us. The question, what is the public policy of a state, and what is contrary to it, if inquired into beyond these limits, will be found to be one of great vagueness and uncertainty, and to involve discussions which scarcely come within the range of judicial duty and functions, and upon which men may and will complexionally differ; above all, when that topic is connected with religious polity, in a country composed of such a variety of religious sects as our country, it is impossible not to feel that it would be attended with almost insuperable difficulties, and involve differences of opinion almost endless in their variety. We disclaim any right to enter upon such examinations, beyond what the state constitutions, and laws, and decisions necessarily bring before us.

It is also said, and truly, that the Christian religion is a part of the common law of Pennsylvania. But this proposition is to be received with its appropriate qualifications, and in connection with the bill of rights of that state, as found in its constitution of government. The constitution of 1790, (and the like provision will, in substance, be found in the constitution of 1776, and in the existing constitution of 1838,) expressly declares, "That all men have a natural and indefeasible right to worship Almighty God according to the dictates of their own consciences; no man can of right be compelled to attend, erect, or support any place of worship, or to maintain any ministry against his consent; no human authority can, in any case whatever, control or interfere with the rights of conscience, and no preference shall ever be given by law to any religious establishments or modes of worship." Language more comprehensive for the complete protection of every variety of religious opinion could scarcely be used; and it must have been intended to extend equally to all sects, whether they believed in Christianity or not, and whether they were Jews or infidels. So that we are compelled to admit that although Christianity be a part of the common law of the state, yet it is so in this qualified sense, that its divine origin and truth are admitted, and therefore it is not to be maliciously and openly reviled and blasphemed against, to the annoyance of believers or the injury of the public. Such was the doctrine of *Updegraff* [sic].

It is unnecessary for us, however, to consider what would be the legal effect of a devise in Pennsylvania for the establishment of a school or college, for the propagation of Judaism, or Deism, or any other form of infidelity. Such a case is not to be presumed to exist in a Christian country; and therefore it must be made out by clear and indisputable proof. Remote inferences, or possible results, or speculative tendencies, are not to be drawn or adopted for such purposes. There must be plain, positive, and express provisions, demonstrating not only that Christianity is not to be taught; but that it is to be impugned or repudiated.

Now, in the present case, there is no pretence to say that any such positive or express provisions exist, or are even shadowed forth in the will. The testator does not say that Christianity shall not be taught in the college. But only that no ecclesiastic of any sect shall hold or exercise any station or duty in the college. Suppose, instead of this, he had said that no person but a layman shall be an instructor or officer or visitor in the college, what legal objection could have been made to such a restriction? And yet the actual prohibition is in effect the same in substance. But it is asked; why are ecclesiastics excluded, if it is not because they are the stated and appropriate preachers of Christianity? The answer may be given in the very words of the testator. "In making this restriction," says he, "I do not mean to cast any reflection upon any sect or person whatsoever. But as there is such a multitude of sects and such a diversity of opinion amongst them, I desire to keep the tender minds of the orphans, who are to derive advantage from this bequest, free from the excitement which clashing doctrines and sectarian controversy are so apt to produce." Here, then, we have the reason given; and the question is not, whether it is satisfactory to us or not; nor whether the history of religion does or does not justify such a sweeping statement; but the question is, whether the exclusion be not such as the testator had a right, consistently with the laws of Pennsylvania, to maintain, upon his own notions of religious instruction. Suppose the testator had excluded all religious instructors but Catholics, or Quakers, or Swedenborgians; or, to put a stronger case, he had excluded all religious instructors but Jews, would the bequest have been void on that account? Suppose he had excluded all lawyers, or all physicians, or all merchants from being instructors or visitors, would the prohibition have been fatal to the bequest? The truth is, that in cases of this sort, it is extremely difficult to draw any just and satisfactory line of distinction in a free country as to the qualifications or disqualifications which may be insisted upon by the donor of a charity as to those who shall administer or partake of his bounty.

But the objection itself assumes the proposition that Christianity is not to be taught, because ecclesiastics are not to be instructors or officers. But this is by no means a necessary or legitimate inference from the premises. Why may not laymen instruct in the general principles of Christianity as well as ecclesiastics. There is no restriction as to the religious opinions of the instructors and officers. They may be, and doubtless, under the auspices of the city government, they will always be, men, not only distinguished for learning and talent, but for piety and elevated virtue, and holy lives and characters. And we cannot overlook the blessings, which such men by their conduct, as well as their instructions, may, nay must impart to their youthful pupils. Why may not the Bible, and especially the New Testament, without note or comment, be read and taught as a divine revelation in the college—its general precepts expounded, its evidences explained, and its glorious principles of morality inculcated? What is there to prevent a work, not sectarian, upon the general evidences of Christianity, from being read and taught in the college by lay-teachers? Certainly there is nothing in the will, that proscribes such studies. Above all, the testator positively enjoins, "that all the instructors and teachers in the college shall take pains to instil into the minds of the scholars the purest principles of morality, so that on their entrance into active life they may from inclination and habit evince benevolence towards their fellow-creatures, and a love of truth, sobriety, and industry, adopting at the same time such religious tenets as their matured reason may enable them to prefer." Now, it may well be asked, what is there in all this, which is positively enjoined, inconsistent with the spirit or truths of Christianity? Are not these truths all taught by Christianity, although it teaches much more? Where can the purest principles of morality be learned so clearly or so perfectly as from the New Testament? Where are benevolence, the love of truth, sobriety, and industry, so powerfully and irresistibly inculcated as in the sacred volume? The testator has not said how these great principles are to be taught, or by whom, except it be by laymen, nor what books are to be used to explain or enforce them. All that we can gather from his language is, that he desired to exclude sectarians and sectarianism from the college, leaving the instructors and officers free to teach the purest morality, the love of truth, sobriety, and industry, by all appropriate means; and of course including the best, the surest, and the most impressive. The objection, then, in this view, goes to this,—either that the testator has totally omitted to provide for religious instruction in his scheme of education, (which, from what has been already said, is an inadmissible interpretation,) or that it includes but partial and imperfect instruction in those truths. In either view can it be truly said that it contravenes the known law of Pennsylvania upon the subject of charities, or is not allowable under the article of the bill of rights already cited? Is an omission to provide for instruction in Christianity in any scheme of school or college education a fatal defect, which avoids it according to the law of Pennsylvania? If the instruction provided for is incomplete and imperfect, is it equally fatal? These questions are propounded, because we are not aware that any thing exists in the constitution or laws of Pennsylvania, or the judicial decisions of its tribunals, which would justify us in pronouncing that such defects would be so fatal. Let us take the case of a charitable donation to teach poor orphans reading, writing, arithmetic, geography, and navigation, and excluding all other studies and instruction; would the donation be void, as a charity in Pennsylvania, as being deemed derogatory to Christianity? Hither to it has been supposed, that a charity for the instruction of the poor might be good and valid in England even if it did not go beyond the establishment of a grammar-school. And in America, it has been thought, in the absence of any express legal prohibitions, that the donor might select the studies, as well as the classes of persons, who were to receive his bounty without being compellable to make religious instruction a necessary part of those studies. It has hitherto been thought sufficient, if he does not require any thing to be taught inconsistent with Christianity.

Looking to the objection therefore in a mere juridical view, which is the only one in which we are at liberty to consider it, we are satisfied that there is nothing in the devise establishing the college, or in the regulations and restrictions contained therein, which are inconsistent with the Christian religion, or are opposed to any known policy of the state of Pennsylvania.

Upon the whole, it is the unanimous opinion of the court, that the decree of the Circuit Court of Pennsylvania dismissing the bill, ought to be affirmed, and is accordingly affirmed with costs.

Notes

1. At one point in the opinion, Story states that it is "unnecessary" to decide the legal effect "of a devise in Pennsylvania for the establishment of a school or college, for the propagation of Judaism, or Deism, or any other form of infidelity." Later in the opinion, however, he suggests that the bequest would not have been void even if "to put a stronger case, [Girard] had excluded all religious instructors but Jews." Is Story suggesting a greater toleration of non-Christians, or some "right" of non-Christians to devise their property in what Story calls "a Christian country"?

2. As should be expected, Story supports the claim that Christianity is a part of the common law of the state, "yet it is so in this qualified sense, that its divine origin and truth are admitted, and therefore it is not to be maliciously and openly reviled and blasphemed against, to the annoyance of believers or the injury of the public." He then approvingly cites *Updegraph*, the blasphemy case. Story's interpretation is consistent

with his view of the role of religion in the public order. The claim that the will violates the law because it disparages Christianity is given short shrift, in part because Story concludes that the teaching of purest principles of morality is not inconsistent with the moral teachings of Christianity. Is Story's decision to sustain Girard's will reflective of his Unitarianism? Of his political views? Both?

3. Stephen Girard's will limited admission to poor male white orphans. In 1957, the Supreme Court, in a *per curiam* opinion, held that refusing to admit black orphans violated the Fourteenth Amendment. *Pennsylvania v. Board of Directors of City Trusts of City of Philadelphia,* 353 U.S. 230, *reh'g denied,* 353 U.S. 989 (1957). *See* Elias Clark, *Charitable Trusts, the Fourteenth Amendment and the Will of Stephen Girard,* 66 Yale L.J. 979 (1957).

4. The Marshall Court decided a case in 1831 concerning both religious liberty and the relation of religion and government, and, more importantly, the legal status of Indians in the United States. Samuel Worcester and Elizur Butler were missionaries sent by the American Board of Commissioners for Foreign Missions to the Cherokee nation to convert the Cherokee to Christianity. Worcester was found guilty by a Georgia court of residing in Cherokee territory without a required license from the state. By this licensing system, Georgia asserted sovereignty over Cherokee territory not acknowledged by the Cherokee nation. Additionally, the federal government at this time had announced a policy of removing the Cherokee. Although offered a pardon, the defendants refused it and filed a writ of error to the Supreme Court. Georgia refused to appear in court, and "publicly announced that it would disregard any decree of the Court overturning the conviction." G. Edward White, THE MARSHALL COURT & CULTURAL CHANGE, 1815–35 731 (Abr. ed. 1991). Worcester and Butler claimed a right under the authority of the President of the United States to "engage in preaching the Gospel to the Cherokee Indians, and in translating the sacred Scriptures into their language." *Worcester v. Georgia,* 6 Pet. (31 U.S.) 515, 529 (1832). Marshall concluded that Worcester and Butler had an individual right to engage in their actions, and condemned Georgia's decision as unconstitutional.

Eight months later, Andrew Jackson was reelected, and showed no interest in enforcing the judgment, which Georgia had refused to accept. Then, the South Carolina nullification crisis erupted. Georgia threatened to declare all federal treaties and statutes concerning the Cherokees void, if Jackson was called upon by the Court to "take care that the laws be faithfully executed." Although Worcester and Butler first pressed their appeal, they dropped it shortly before the beginning of the January 1833 Term, and were shortly thereafter pardoned by the governor of Georgia. White, at 738.

F. Joseph Story, The Antebellum Supreme Court And Religion

Story's opinion in *Vidal* was one of his last opinions, and reflected his view that, properly understood, Christianity was a part of the common law. As both a Supreme Court Justice and as an important figure in Massachusetts politics, Story attempted to ensure that religion remained a part of the public order. His most influential writing on law and religion, however, is found in his 1833 treatise, COMMENTARIES ON THE CONSTITUTION. The COMMENTARIES provide a thorough view of Story's understanding of the great constitutional issues of the day, including the Jeffersonian view of the relation of federal government to state government, and John C. Calhoun's doctrine of interposition. Story also gave his interpretation of the religion clauses in his COMMENTARIES.

Joseph Story, Commentaries on the Constitution

(1833)

§ 1863. Let us now enter upon the consideration of the amendments, which, it will be found, principally regard subjects properly belonging to a bill of rights.

§ 1864. The first is, "Congress shall make no law respecting an establishment of religion, or prohibiting the free exercise thereof, or abridging the freedom of speech, or of the press; or the right of the people peaceably to assemble, and to petition government for a redress of grievances."

§ 1865. And first, the prohibition of any establishment of religion, and the freedom of religious opinion and worship,

How far any government has a right to interfere in matters touching religion, has been a subject much discussed by writers upon public and political law. The right and the duty of the interference of government, in matters of religion, have been maintained by many distinguished authors, as well those, who were the warmest advocates of free governments, as those, who were attached to governments of a more arbitrary character. Indeed, the right of a society or government to interfere in matters of religion will hardly be contested by any persons, who believe that piety, religion, and morality are intimately connected with the well being of the state, and indispensable to the administration of civil justice. The promulgation of the great doctrines of religion, the being, and attributes, and providence of one Almighty God; the responsibility to him for all our actions, founded upon moral freedom and accountability; a future state of rewards and punishments; the cultivation of all the personal, social, and benevolent virtues;—these never can be a matter of indifference in any well ordered community. It is, indeed, difficult to conceive, how any civilized society can well exist without them. And at all events, it is impossible for those, who believe in the truth of Christianity, as a divine revelation, to doubt, that it is the especial duty of government to foster, and encourage it among all the citizens and subjects. This is a point wholly distinct from that of the right of private judgment in matters of religion, and of the freedom of public worship according to the dictates of one's conscience.

§ 1866. The real difficulty lies in ascertaining the limits, to which government may rightfully go in fostering and encouraging religion. Three cases may easily be supposed. One, where a government affords aid to a particular religion, leaving all persons free to adopt any other; another, where it creates an ecclesiastical establishment for the propagation of the doctrines of a particular sect of that religion, leaving a like freedom to all others; and a third, where it creates such an establishment, and excludes all persons, not belonging to it, either wholly, or in part, from any participation in the public honours, trusts, emoluments, privileges, and immunities of the state. For instance, a government may simply declare, that the Christian religion shall be the religion of the state, and shall be aided, and encouraged in all the varieties of sects belonging to it; or it may declare, that the Catholic or Protestant religion shall be the religion of the state, leaving every man to the free enjoyment of his own religious opinions; or it may establish the doctrines of a particular sect, as of Episcopalians, as the religion of the state, with a like freedom; or it may establish the doctrines of a particular sect, as exclusively the religion of the state, tolerating others to a limited extent, or excluding all, not belonging to it, from all public honours, trusts, emoluments, privileges, and immunities.

§ 1867. Now, there will probably be found few persons in this, or any other Christian country, who would deliberately contend, that it was unreasonable, or unjust to foster and encourage the Christian religion generally, as a matter of sound policy, as well as a revealed truth. In fact, every American colony, from its foundation down to the revolution, with the exception of Rhode Island, (if, indeed, that state be an exception,) did openly, by the whole course of its laws and institutions, support and sustain, in some form, the Christian religion; and almost invariably gave a peculiar sanction to some of its fundamental doctrines. And this has continued to be the case in some of the states down to the present period, without the slightest suspicion, that it was against the principles of public law, or republican liberty. Indeed, in a republic, there would seem to be a peculiar propriety in viewing the Christian religion, as the great basis, on which it must rest for its support and permanence, if it be, what it has ever been deemed by its truest friends to be, the religion of liberty.

§ 1868. Probably at the time of the adoption of the constitution, and of the amendment to it, now under consideration, the general, if not the universal, sentiment in America was, that Christianity ought to receive encouragement from the state, so far as was not incompatible with the private rights of conscience, and the freedom of religious worship. An attempt to level all religions, and to make it a matter of state policy to hold all in utter indifference, would have created universal disapprobation, if not universal indignation.

§ 1869. It yet remains a problem to be solved in human affairs, whether any free government can be permanent, where the public worship of God, and the support of religion, constitute no part of the policy or duty of the state in any assignable shape. The future experience of Christendom, and chiefly of the American states, must settle this problem, as yet new in the history of the world, abundant, as it has been, in experiments in the theory of government.

§ 1871. The real object of the amendment was, not to countenance, much less to advance Mahometanism, or Judaism, or infidelity, by prostrating Christianity, but to exclude all rivalry among Christian sects, and to prevent any national ecclesiastical establishment, which should give to an hierarchy the exclusive patronage of the national government. It thus cut off the means of religious persecution, (the vice and pest of former ages) and of the subversion of the rights of conscience in matters of religion, which had been trampled upon almost from the days of the Apostles to the present age.

Notes

1. Story states that the "general, if not the universal" understanding of the first amendment was to protect Christianity, not to hold it in "utter indifference." He further states: "The real object of the amendment was, not to countenance, much less to advance Mahometanism, or Judaism, or infidelity, by prostrating Christianity, but to exclude all rivalry among Christian sects, and to prevent any national ecclesiastical establishment, which should give to an hierarchy the exclusive patronage of the national government." Story's interpretation implicitly rejects the "wall of separation" metaphor of Jefferson, and seems to reflect the older idea of religious toleration rather than religious liberty or right. Is Story's interpretation convincing? What evidence would better allow us to accept or reject Story's interpretation as a historical matter?

2. Story also advances the idea that the state should "foster and encourage the Christian religion generally, as a matter of sound policy, as well as a revealed truth."

Further, "in a republic, there would seem to be a peculiar propriety in viewing the Christian religion, as the great basis, on which it must rest for its support and permanence, if it be, what it has ever been deemed by its truest friends to be, the religion of liberty." In this approach, general Christianity would assist the state, and the state would foster and encourage Christian religion. Is this expression anything more Story's republican ideal?

3. Should Story, who was born in 1779, be considered as a "framer" for purposes of understanding the meaning of the First Amendment? If so, are there others who were not at the Constitutional convention or a member of the first Congress who should also be considered framers? If not, what credit, if any, should Story's views receive?

Permoli v. New Orleans

44 U.S. [3 How.] 589 (1845)

[In 1827, New Orleans passed an ordinance barring the conveying or exposing of any corpse in St. Louis Catholic Church, and requiring all funeral rites to be performed at the obituary chapel on Rampart street. In 1842, after the death of Abbé Moni of St. Louis Church, a dispute between the new curate, the Reverend Maenhant, and the church-wardens arose, as a result of which the Reverend Maenhant refused to say funeral masses in the obituary chapel. He then said several funeral masses at St. Augustin church. The city then amended the ordinance, and barred any Catholic priest from saying any funeral mass anywhere other than at the obituary chapel. The rector at St. Augustin church, a Fr. Bernard Permoli, said a funeral mass there shortly after this amended ordinance became law. At trial, the judge decided the ordinance was illegal, but was reversed on appeal to the City Court. Because there was no further appeal allowed under state law, Permoli appealed to the Supreme Court, alleging a deprivation of his rights under federal law and the federal Constitution.]

Mr. Justice CATRON delivered the opinion of the court.

As this case comes here on a writ of error to bring up the proceedings of a state court, before proceeding to examine the merits of the controversy, it is our duty to determine whether this court has jurisdiction of the matter.

The Constitution makes no provision for protecting the citizens of the respective states in their religious liberties; this is left to the state constitutions and laws: nor is there any inhibition imposed by the Constitution of the United States in this respect on the states. We must therefore look beyond the Constitution for the laws that are supposed to be violated, and on which our jurisdiction can be founded; these are the following acts of Congress. That of February 20, 1811, authorized the people of the territory of Orleans to form a constitution and state government; by sect. 3, certain restrictions were imposed in the form of instructions to the convention that might frame the constitution; such as that it should be republican; consistent with the Constitution of the United States; that it should contain the fundamental principles of civil and religious liberty; that it should secure the right of trial by jury in criminal cases, and the writ of *habeas corpus;* that the laws of the state should be published, and legislative and judicial proceedings be written and recorded in the language of the Constitution of the United States.

By the act of April 8, 1812, Louisiana was admitted according to the mode prescribed by the act of 1811; Congress declared it should be on the conditions and terms contained in the 3d section of that act; which should be considered, deemed and taken, as fundamental conditions and terms upon which the state was incorporated in the union.

All Congress intended, was to declare in advance, to the people of the territory, the fundamental principles their constitution should contain; this was every way proper under the circumstances: the instrument having been duly formed, and presented, it was for the national legislature to judge whether it contained the proper principles, and to accept it if it did; or reject it if it did not. Having accepted the constitution and admitted the state, "on an equal footing with the original states in all respects whatever," in express terms, by the act of 1812, Congress was concluded from assuming that the instructions contained in the act of 1811 had not been complied with.

The principal stress of the argument for [Permoli] proceeded on the [Northwest] ordinance of 1787. The act of 1805, chap. 83, having provided, that from and after the establishment of the government of the Orleans territory, the inhabitants of the same should be entitled to enjoy all the rights, privileges, and advantages secured by said ordinance, and then enjoyed by the people of the Mississippi territory. It was also made the frame of government, with modifications.

In the ordinance, there are terms of compact declared to be thereby established, between the original states, and the people in the states afterwards to be formed north-west of the Ohio, unalterable, unless by common consent—one of which stipulations is, that "no person demeaning himself in a peaceable manner, shall ever be molested on account of his mode of worship, or religious sentiments, in the said territory." For this provision is claimed the sanction of an unalterable law of Congress; and it is insisted the city ordinances above have violated it; and what the force of the ordinance is north of the Ohio, we do not pretend to say, as it is unnecessary for the purposes of this case. But as regards the state of Louisiana, it had no further force, after the adoption of the state constitution, than other acts of organizing, in part, the territorial government of Orleans, and standing in connection with the ordinance of 1787. So far as they conferred political rights, and secured civil and religious liberties, (which are political rights,) the laws of Congress were all superseded by the state constitution; nor is any part of them in force, unless they were adopted by the constitution of Louisiana, as laws of the state. It is not possible to maintain that the United States hold in trust, by force of the ordinance, for the people of Louisiana, all the great elemental principles, or any one of them, contained in the ordinance, and secured to the people of the Orleans territory, during its existence. It follows, no repugnance could arise between the ordinance of 1787 and an act of the legislature of Louisiana, or a city regulation founded on such act and therefore this court has no jurisdiction on the last ground assumed, more than on the preceding ones. In our judgment, the question presented by the record is exclusively of state cognisance, and equally so in the old states and the new ones; and that the writ of error must be dismissed.

Notes

1. In *Barron v. Mayor of Baltimore*, 32 U. S. (7 Pet.) 243 (1833), a unanimous Court held that the Fifth Amendment's just compensation principle did not apply to action taken by state or local authorities. The *Permoli* case does not cite *Barron*, although its decision reaffirms the nonapplicability of the Bill of Rights to the states.

2. As noted above, this case arose as a result of infighting between a Catholic priest and wardens of a church. Counsel for the First Municipality rejects Permoli's claim of religious discrimination by noting that the "great body of Catholic citizens of

New Orleans (other than those of Irish descent) reside in the First Municipality," *Permoli*, at 600, and that "[i]f Catholics are wronged, Catholics have wronged them." *Id.* at 602. Is this sufficient to reject Permoli's claim as a substantive matter?

3. Permoli's lawyer also argued the applicability of the Northwest Ordinance of 1787, which guarantees "[n]o person demeaning himself in a peaceable manner shall ever be molested on account of his mode of worship or religious sentiments." The Court rejects this argument, holding that "as regards the state of Louisiana, it had no further force, after the adoption of the state constitution." "So far as they conferred political rights, and secured civil and religious liberties, (which are political rights,) the laws of Congress were all superseded by the state constitution."

4. Joseph Story participated in the unanimous opinion in *Permoli*. Later that year, on September 10, he died, his last words praising God. Newmyer, at 381.

Chapter 4

Religious Liberty, Pluralism and Government Action

A. Introduction

The issues of religion in the public order that energized the American legal systems during the first half of the nineteenth century changed shape in the latter half of the century. States reformed witness competency requirements, first forbidding inquiries into the religious beliefs of the witness, and later prohibiting credibility attacks based on a lack of religious belief. For example, the initial Constitution of the State of Washington, adopted in 1889, prohibited inquiries into a witness's religious beliefs for either purpose. *See* Francis Newton Thorpe, VII The Federal and State Constitutions 3974 (7 vols. 1909). From 1838, when the Massachusetts Supreme Judicial Court decided *Kneeland v. Commonwealth*, 37 Mass. 206 (1838), until 1882, there were no blasphemy prosecutions in the United States. *See* Leonard W. Levy, Blasphemy 506–08 (1993). From the late nineteenth century through the first two decades of the twentieth century, only a few prosecutions took place, the most notorious being the several prosecutions of Michael Mockus. *See, e.g., State v. Mockus*, 113 A. 39 (Me. 1921). *See also* William Wolkovich, Bay State "Blue" Laws and *Bimba* (1973) (detailing history of failed blasphemy prosecution in 1920s Massachusetts). However, prosecutions for profanity (taking the name of God in vain) were upheld against challenges that such prosecutions violated the religious liberty of the defendant. *See, e.g., Bodenhamer v. State*, 28 S.W. 507 (Ark. 1894); *Taney v. State*, 36 N.E. 295 (Ind. App. 1894). Sunday laws remained in force, and were in some respects strengthened, although new challenges claiming the laws violated the fourteenth amendment were pressed in federal court. Finally, the Supreme Court was asked to decide not whether the established church retained ownership of property after disestablishment, or whether it could receive property in trust, but which of two contending groups divided over the issue of slavery was the rightful owner of church property.

It was not until after the Civil War that the Supreme Court first interpreted the meaning of the declaration that "Congress shall make no law respecting an establishment of religion or prohibiting the free exercise thereof." In rejecting a religious liberty claim of members of the Church of Jesus Christ of Latter-day Saints, also known as Mormons, the Court interpreted the First Amendment based on the history of the events in Virginia in the 1780s regarding the general assessment. In creating a rigid distinction between action and belief, the Court relied on Thomas Jefferson's letter to the Danbury Baptist Association. However, near the end of the nineteenth century, the Court, in language unmistakably like that of the state courts upholding blasphemy convictions, and unmistakably unlike that of Jefferson, concluded, "this is a Christian nation."

Throughout the last half of the nineteenth century, the nation contended with a growing plurality of religious voices. In addition to the continued division and creation of Protestant sects, the United States became the home to a rapidly growing number of Roman Catholics. During the first three decades of the twentieth century, disputes arose between Protestants and Catholics concerning the relationship of government and religion. Additionally, disputes within Protestantism, between Moderns and Fundamentals, and disputes between the religious and the secular, became more prominent. These disputes resulted in several important cases delineating the boundary regulating the permissible interaction of religious faith and government, and presaged the end of the *de facto* Protestant establishment.

One issue created by this emerging pluralism, an issue that first arose before the Civil War, was the reading, ordinarily without comment, of passages from the King James version of the Bible in the common, or public, schools. That this was an issue was in large part a consequence of the increasing immigration of Irish Catholics to the United States.

B. Religious Education and the "Schools" Question Prior to 1920

1. The Bible in the Common School

The first controversy over the reading of the Bible in the common school arose in New York in 1840. Earlier in the century, the state agreed to support education. Those first schools "were as devoted to religious as to secular instruction." John Webb Pratt, RELIGION, POLITICS, AND DIVERSITY 164 (1967). In New York City, aristocratic education reformers created a private organization called the Free School Society to educate the poor children of New York. By 1825, the Free School Society had changed its name to the Public School Society, and operated 11 free schools educating almost 20,000 children. Robert L. Church and Michael W. Sedlak, EDUCATION IN THE UNITED STATES: AN INTERPRETIVE HISTORY 154–69 (1976). Although both Baptists and Methodists requested funds from the state in the early 1820s to teach poor children, a request that was denied, most Protestants found favor with the Public School Society, for "its membership was largely Protestant and its effort was a Protestant one." *Id.* at 159. The reading of the King James Bible, without comment, exemplified the Protestant nature of the Society, and until the immigration from Ireland of persons who were mostly poor, uneducated and Catholic, this system remained unchallenged. To Protestant New Yorkers, Irish immigrants were "different": their poverty, clannishness, and affinity for alcohol and brawling were all grounds to view them suspiciously. But most importantly, their Catholicism marked them as different from the "natives," and this difference helped fuel the American Nativist movement. At the same time, the huge increase in numbers of Irish Catholics in New York made them politically attractive to Democrats, and later, to Whigs.

The directors of the Public School Society insisted that the free schools were nonsectarian. Catholics believed otherwise, and they were led by their Irish-born Bishop, John

Hughes. Whigs in state government were appalled at the number of children, largely Catholic, who were left unschooled in New York City (it is believed that in the late 1830s, only a few hundred of the 12,000 or so Catholic children were taught in the public schools, Diane Ravitch, THE GREAT SCHOOL WARS 32 (1974)), and demanded that the Public School Society get them into schools. On January 7, 1840, William Seward, the Whig Governor of New York, suggested in his opening message to the state legislature that "children of foreigners" be "instructed by teachers speaking the same language and professing the same faith." Pratt, at 161. The Public School Society had tried in the late 1830s to encourage Catholics to send their children to the free schools by deleting material offensive to Catholics and by appointing several Catholics as trustees. On the issue of reading, without comment or interpretation, the King James translation of the Bible, however, the Society would not compromise. For Catholics, then, the Public School Society was a sectarian institution, and one which received funds from the state to operate. Therefore, they believe they deserved state funds to create their own education system just as the Protestants. For Catholics, the free school was not only Protestant, it was godless, for "the Public School Society had banned direct moral instruction and explicit dogmatic training." Church and Sedlak, at 162. For Bishop Hughes, a story in a public school reader which he believed "equated religious beliefs with trivial choices like ways of eating and dressing," Ravitch, at 52, exemplified the godless nature of the public schools. Their hopes raised by Seward's speech, the seven or eight Catholic schools in operation requested a share of common school funds from the Common Council of New York City. After heated nativist reaction to the petition, the Common Council denied the Catholic request for funds on the principle that this would violate the state Constitution by creating "a legal establishment of one denomination over another." Pratt, at 177. Even after Whig losses in the 1840 election and a narrow re-election to office, Seward again called for a local solution to educating Catholic children. A report by Seward's secretary of state John Spencer recommended that the moral values taught the children be decided by the people of the local district. Therefore, the residents of each district would determine "for themselves the kind of religious instruction to be offered." Church and Sedlak, at 167. Legislation to implement the Spencer report was tabled until after the 1841 elections.

The education issue was the main issue in the New York election in the fall of 1841, and the New York City election in the spring of 1842. Democrats, needing the Catholic vote, accepted the Catholic position concerning state funding of Catholic schools, and the Whigs, except for Seward, accepted the Protestant approach to education. The American Protestant Union, a nativist group, was organized in May 1841 "to oppose any Catholic school bill." Pratt, at 183. Bishop Hughes endorsed 10 of the 13 Democrats running for state legislature from New York City. For the other three positions, Hughes endorsed candidates running on a straight Catholic ticket. The ten Democrats endorsed by Hughes won, and the other three seats were won by Whigs. A bill recommending enactment of the Spencer report was passed, although the Senate eliminated the provision granting local residents the authority to determine the religious instruction in the schools. This law created the New York City board of education, with the power to tax as well as receive state funds. The law also forbade the board of education from distributing funds to schools in which sectarian religious instruction was given, thus eliminating Catholic schools from receiving state funds. However, because Bible reading in the free schools was not considered sectarian religious instruction, the King James translation of the Bible continued to be read. In 1842, the election of a bare majority of Whigs to the New York City Council led to the mandatory reading of the King James translation of the Bible for any schools wishing to share in the school fund. The result was that Catholics in New York concentrated on building their own educational system. *See generally* Vincent P. Lannie, PUBLIC MONEY AND PAROCHIAL EDUCATION: BISHOP HUGHES, GOVERNOR SEWARD, AND THE NEW YORK SCHOOL CONTROVERSY (1968).

In late 1842, the Roman Catholic Bishop of Philadelphia, Francis Kentrick, "[i]nspired by the efforts of Bishop Hughes to secure a share of the school fund," Roy Allen Billington, THE PROTESTANT CRUSADE, 1800–1860: A STUDY OF THE ORIGINS OF AMERICAN NATIVISM 221 (1938), wrote to the public school Board of Controllers "complaining that the Protestant Bible was being read to Catholic children and that religious exercises were being made a daily part of the instruction." *Id.* In January 1843, the Board granted Kentrick's request, allowing all students to read from the version of the Bible chosen by their parents. Angry reaction to this accommodation built during all of 1843. In March 1844, Nativists claimed this was an attempt to "banish the bible from our public institutions." *Id.* at 222 (quoting March 11, 1844 resolution of nativist group). Two months later, nativists rioted in Philadelphia against Catholics, riots that resulted in the death of thirteen people, and injuries to fifty more. *Id.* at 230.

A little more than a decade later, the first case asserting the unconstitutionality of Bible reading in public schools was decided, and again the complainants were Catholics who opposed reading from the King James translation of the Bible.

Donahoe v. Richards

38 Me. 379 (1854)

[Bridget Donahoe refused to read from the King James Bible, and was expelled. She brought suit through her father to recover damages against the members of the Ellsworth, Maine school committee for "maliciously, wrongfully and unjustifiably expelling her." *Id.* at 380. After concluding that the school committee was statutorily clothed with complete authority over the general course of instruction, and concluding that the true remedy lay with the election of a new legislature, the court discussed the issue of Donahoe's right to an exemption from the committee's prescribed course of instruction based on her religious conscience.]

APPLETON, J.

The plaintiff den[ies] that the book selected was one in which she could be constitutionally compelled to read upon pain of expulsion, in case of her refusal to obey. She claims exemption from the general duty of obedience, from the particular character of the book in which she was required to read. The question therefore, is whether, if the Legislature should by statute direct any version of the Bible to be read in schools, and should impose the penalty of expulsion, in the case of refusal, such statute would be a violation of the constitution.

The use of the Bible as a reading book is not prohibited by any express language of the constitution.

Is its use for that purpose in opposition to the spirit and intention of that instrument?

If it be not, if it be a book which may be directed within the spirit and meaning of the constitution, to be used in schools, it is obvious that its use may be required of all; for a regulation which any scholar may violate with impunity would cease to have the force and effect of a rule.

The case finds that the superintending school committee directed that the English Protestant version should be used in all the public schools of Ellsworth, and that all who were of sufficient capacity to read therein should be required to read that version in school.

The common schools are not for the purpose of instruction in the theological doctrines of any religion, or of any sect. The State regards no one sect as superior to any other—and no theological views as peculiarly entitled to precedence. It is no part of the duty of the instructor to give theological instruction—and if the peculiar tenet of any particular sect were so taught it would furnish a well grounded cause of complaint on the part of those, who entertained different or opposing religious sentiments.

But the instruction here given is not in fact, and is not alleged to have been, in articles of faith. No theological doctrines were taught. The creed of no sect was affirmed or denied. The truth or falsehood of the book in which the scholars were required to read, was not asserted. No interference by way of instruction, with the views of the scholars, whether derived from parental or sacerdotal authority, is shown.

The Bible was used merely as a book in which instruction in reading was given. But reading the Bible is no more an interference with religious belief, than would reading the mythology of Greece or Rome be regarded as interfering with religious belief or an affirmance of the pagan creeds. A chapter in the Koran might be read, yet it would not be an affirmation of the truth of Mahomedanism, or an interference with religious faith. The Bible was used merely as a reading book, and for the information contained in it, as the Koran might be, and not for religious instruction; if suitable for that, it was suitable for the purpose for which it was selected. No one was required to believe or punished for disbelief, either in its inspiration or want of inspiration; in the fidelity of the translation or its inaccuracy—or in any set of doctrines deducible or not deducible therefrom.

The plaintiff, indeed, makes no objection to the Bible as a book which she may not rightfully be required to read in schools, but only to a particular translation. Indeed, the report finds that she was willing to read from the Douay version. It is apparent that it is highly desirable that in the same class there should be an uniformity of books to be used. But if the book is proper, if consonant to the soundest principles of morality, then is there any translation which can be justly deemed adverse to those principles? Does the version in which the plaintiff was willing to read contravene sound morality, even in the judgment of the defendants? Does the version which the defendants required to read, conflict, even in the opinion of the plaintiff, with pure morality? If not, then the book itself, alike in the judgment of the plaintiff and the defendants, is one which may be read without reasonable grounds of objection in schools.

The catholics deny the accuracy of portions of the version commonly used by protestants. The protestants assert that in some respects the Douay version is erroneous. Different sects of the protestants express dissatisfaction, in some instances, with both. The adoption of one is no authoritative sanction of purity of text or accuracy of translation. School committees could rarely be found competent to settle those questions. It is simply the adoption of a particular version of a work, which from the idiomatic English of the translation, and the sublime morality of its teachings, furnishes the best illustration which the language affords of pure English undefiled, and is best fitted to strengthen the morals and promote the virtues which adorn and dignify social life.

The controversy seems to resolve itself into the inquiry whether there is any thing in the constitution, which in case of different translations of a work fitting and proper for schools, forbids the requirement of the use of a particular version as a reading book by those who may conscientiously believe it to have been, in some respects, erroneously made. If so, it is obvious that the particular version must be entirely prohibited, for if the plaintiff has a constitutional right to be absolved from a regulation of the school requiring its reading, because it is in conflict with her religious conscientious belief, it is not easy to perceive why she has not an equally valid ground of objection to hearing it read. If so, as others may have their consciences, it follows, not merely that no translation of the Bible can be used, but that no book can be used which may contain any proposition opposed to the conscientious belief of any scholar.

The clause in the constitution upon which reliance is specially placed, is, that "no one shall be *hurt, molested* or *restrained* in his person, liberty or estate, for worshiping God in the manner and season most agreeable to the dictates of his own conscience, nor for his *religious professions* or *sentiments*, provided he does not disturb the public peace, nor obstruct others in their religious worship." The object of this clause was to protect all—the Mahomedan and the Brahmin, the Jew and the Christian, of every diversity of religious opinion, in the unrestrained liberty of worship and religious profession, provided the public peace should not thereby be endangered nor the worship of others obstructed. It was to prevent pains and penalties, imprisonment or the deprivation of social or political rights, being imposed as a penalty for religious professions and opinions.

Another clause in the constitution, upon which reliance is placed, is, "that no *subordination nor preference* of any sect or denomination to another shall ever be established by law."

This clause obviously provides for the equality of all sects, and forbids the preference of one over another. It is insisted that here is a preference by law. This relates to an Act of the Legislature, which shall establish the preference of one sect and the subordination of others. The selection of a school book is no preference within this clause. The choice is left entirely to the popular will.

If this were to be regarded as a legislative preference, much more must those laws, by which the Sabbath is established as a day of rest, in which labor, except for necessity, is prohibited being done, be regarded as a subordination of the religious views of all other sects to those holding that day sacred. Indeed this very objection has, in many States, been raised against the constitutionality of such laws.

The Jews and the seventh day Baptists regarding Saturday as divinely set apart for rest, find legal impediments to labor on the Christian Sabbath, when they believe it may be lawfully done, and conscientious scruples to their laboring on the preceding day, so that between the law and their consciences they are compelled to abstain from labor on both days; yet this is not regarded as hurting, molesting or restraining them in their persons, liberties or estates, within the meaning or constitutional prohibitions similar to our own; nor as creating a subordination or preference of one sect over another. Much more, then, should not the selection of the Bible as a book in which reading only is to be taught, be regarded as in the slightest degree in conflict with this portion of the bill of rights.

But the claim of the plaintiff is much more liable to the exception that it is creating the subordination or preference of one sect or denomination over another. Her claim to be exempted from a general regulation of the school rests entirely on her religious belief, and is to the extent that the choice of reading books shall be in *entire subordination to her faith, and because it is her faith.* The preference is manifestly given, if, in the selection to be made, the defendants were bound to defer to the doctrines and authority and teachings of the sect of which she is a member. The right of negation, in its operation, equivalent to that of proposing and establishing. The right of one sect to interdict or expurgate, would place all schools in subordination to the sect interdicting or expurgating.

If the claim is, that the sect of which the child is a member has the right of interdiction, and that any book is to be banished because under the ban of her church, then the preference is practically given to such church, and the very mischief complained of, is inflicted on others.

If Locke and Bacon and Milton and Swift are to be stricken from the list of authors which may be read in schools, because the authorities of one sect may have placed them among the list of heretical writers whose works it neither permits to be printed, nor sold, nor read, then the right of sectarian interference in the selection of books is at once yielded, and no books can be read, to the reading of which it may not assent. Because Galileo and Copernicus and Newton may chance to be found in some prohibitory index, is that a reason why the youth of the country should be educated in ignorance of the scientific teachings of those great philosophers? If the Bible, or a particular version of it, may be excluded from schools, because its reading may be opposed to the teachings of the authorities of any church, the same result may ensure as to any other book. If one sect may object, the same right must be granted to others. This would give the authorities of any sect the right to annul any regulation of the constituted authorities of the State, as to the course of study and the books to be used.

As the existence of conscientious scruples as to the reading of a book can only *be known from the assertion of the child, its mere assertion must suffice for the exclusion of any book* in the reading or in the hearing of which it may *allege* a wrong to be done to its religious conscience. The claim, so far as it may rest on conscience, is a claim to annul any regulation of the State, made by its constituted authorities. As a right existing on the part of one child, it is equally a right belonging to all. As it relates to one book, so it may apply to another—whether relating to science or to morals.

The right as claimed, undermines the power of the State. It is, that the will of the majority shall bow to the conscience of the minority, or of one. If the several consciences of the scholars are permitted to contravene, obstruct or annul the action of the State, then power ceases to reside in majorities, and is transferred to minorities.

But while the constitution recognizes "the goodness of the Sovereign Ruler of the Universe," it does not recognize the superiority of any form of religion or of any sect or denomination. It knows no religion, nor form of religion as such, as having any binding force over its citizens, against its will constitutionally expressed. It regards the Pagan and the Mormon, the Brahmin and the Jew, the Swedenborgian and the Budhist, the Catholic and the Quaker, as all possessing equal rights.

A law is not unconstitutional, because it may prohibit what a citizen may conscientiously think right, or require what he may conscientiously think wrong. The State is governed by its own views of duty. The right or wrong of the State, is the right or wrong as declared by legislative Acts constitutionally passed. It may pass laws against polygamy, yet the Mormon or Mahomedan cannot claim an exemption from their operation, or freedom from punishment imposed upon their violation, because they may believe, however conscientiously, that it is an institution founded on the soundest political wisdom, and resting on the sure foundation of inspired revelation. It may establish a day of rest, as a civil institution, though the effect of it may be to deprive the Jew of one sixth of his time, for purposes of labor or of business.

The claim of exemption from the operation of a general law, as a matter of right, has received the consideration of Courts of the greatest learning and ability. The conscientious belief of religious duty furnishes no legal defence to the doing or refusing to do what the State within its constitutional authority may require. If it were so, the obligations of a statute would depend not upon the will of the State, but upon its conformity with the religious convictions of its members. When a conflict arises, as it may, between the requirements of law and the obligations of conscience, each man must determine his course of action according to his views of duty and of right.

The claim on the part of the plaintiff has been argued as a question of strict right. As such, without reference to what may be wise or expedient, it has been considered and determined by the Court.

Amid the various and conflicting differences on moral, political and religious subjects, there is need of mutual charity and forbearance—of mutual concession and compromise. Large masses of foreign population are among us, weak in the midst of our strength. Mere citizenship is of no avail, unless they imbibe the liberal spirit of our laws and institutions, unless they become citizens in fact as well as in name. In no other way can the process of assimilation be so readily and thoroughly accomplished as through the medium of the public schools, which are alike open to the children of the rich and the poor, of the stranger and the citizen. It is the duty of those to whom this sacred trust is confided, to discharge it with magnanimous liberality and Christian kindness. While the law should reign supreme, and obedience to it commands should ever be required, yet in the establishment of the law which is to control, there is no principle of wider application and of higher wisdom; "All things whatsoever ye would that men should do to you, do ye even so to them, for this is the law and the prophets."

Plaintiff nonsuit.

Notes

1. The *Donahoe* case arose after the school committee in Ellsworth, Maine, required all schoolchildren to read from the King James Bible. A Jesuit missionary, Father John Bapst, urged Catholics in Ellsworth, Maine, to defy this regulation. Fifteen-year old Bridget Donahoe was then directed by her father to refuse to read from the King James Bible, and was expelled for her action. After town members learned of Bapst's involvement, they threatened to tar and feather him if he ever returned to Ellsworth. Two months later, he did, and the townspeople carried out their threat. Leo Pfeffer, CHURCH, STATE, AND FREEDOM 438 (rev. ed. 1967).

2. The Donahoes pressed their claim as one involving liberty of conscience. Thus, when Justice John Appleton rendered the Court's opinion, the issue was framed as involving an exemption from conscience from a generally applicable law. Appleton cited Chief Justice Gibson's opinion in *Simon's Executors v. Gratz,* excerpted in Chapter Three, as authority for the proposition that there existed no constitutional right of exemption from generally applicable laws for reasons of conscience. Additionally, Appleton cited *Stansbury v. Marks* and Gibson's dissenting opinion in *Commonwealth v. Lesher* as support for his position. Appleton did not cite DeWitt Clinton's opinion *People v. Phillips*. In a part of the opinion not reprinted above, Appleton additionally cites for support *Specht v. Commonwealth* and *City Council v. Benjamin*, the Pennsylvania and South Carolina decisions holding constitutional Sunday laws. Does the citation of these authorities in *Donahoe* suggest that states courts were largely in agreement that the religious liberty

provisions of state constitutions did not permit one to claim an exemption from a general law? When the Supreme Court held unconstitutional state-mandated prayer in public schools, it did not hold such laws violative of the free exercise clause, but concluded that the required prayers were laws respecting an establishment of religion. *See Engel v. Vitale*, 370 U.S. 421 (1962); *Abington School Dist. v. Schempp*, 374 U.S. 203 (1963). Is the difference in focus simply a consequence of Donahoe's request that she be allowed to read from the Douay Bible rather than a request to be excused from the exercise?

3. A post-Civil War Vermont case, *Ferriter v. Tyler*, 48 Vt. 443 (1876), raised similar issues concerning any constitutional right of exemption. Several Catholic students enrolled in the Brattleboro common schools informed their teachers on June 3, 1874, that they would be absent the next day to attendance mass to celebrate a Catholic holy day. The teachers objected to the students's absence. The next morning, approximately ten minutes before classes began, the Catholic priest sent a request to the School Committee asking that the Catholic students be excused. The Committee refused to permit the students to be absent, but a number of them left the school pursuant to the priest's orders. When those students returned, they were informed that they were expelled for the remainder of the term, unless they promised to comply with all school rules, including attendance on all school days, even school days that were also Catholic holy days. Several parents refused to so promise, and sued to enjoin the School Committee from enforcing this attendance rule and enrolling the students.

The Vermont court held the Committee's actions permissible against a constitutional challenge. Although the court was unconvinced that "observance of the day is binding on the Catholic conscience," *id.* at 461, the court more broadly concluded that Vermont's religious liberty provision:

> was not designed to exempt any person or persons of any sect, on the score of conscience as to matters of religion, from the operation and obligatory force of the general laws of the state authorized by other portions of the same instrument, and designed to serve the purposes contemplated by such other portions: it was not designed to exempt any persons from the same subjection that others are under to the laws and their administration, on the score that such subjection at times would interfere with the performance of religious rites, and the observance of religious ordinances, which they would deem it their duty to perform and observe but for such subjection.

Id. at 469.

4. In the fall of 1854, the Know-Nothing Party swept elections in the Commonwealth of Massachusetts, and directed its legislative efforts against Catholics and immigrants. Due to the inexperience and incompetence of the members of the Party, however, it "bungled" the attempt to strike a blow against Catholicism. Billington, at 413. Its only successful effort was the passage of a law in 1855 requiring the reading of the Bible "'in the common English version' in the public schools." *Id.* The "common English version" is the King James translation of the Bible.

Five years later, the first case to interpret this law was decided. A school teacher, McLaurin Cooke, was charged with the assault and battery of an eleven-year old student, Thomas Wall. Wall was Catholic, and he had been ordered by his father and his parish priest not to recite from "the Bible in the common English version." For refusing to obey Cooke's command to recite the Ten Commandments, Wall was repeatedly struck on the hands for a period of thirty minutes "with a rattan stick, some three feet in length, and three-eighths of an inch thick." *Commonwealth v. Cooke*, 7 Am. L. Reg.

417, 419 (Police Court, Boston, Mass. 1859). Echoing (but not citing) the language of *Donahoe*, the Court determined that the religious liberty provision of the Massachusetts Constitution was designed "for the protection of all religions—the Buddhist and the Brahmin, the Pagan and the Jew, the Christian and the Turk," *id.* at 422, but that reading the Bible "is no interference with religious liberty." *Id.* at 423. Granting the student the right to read from the Douay version of the Bible would open to the door to sundry other claims of exemption. Additionally, the Massachusetts Constitution forbade the use of state funds for the maintenance of "any religious sect," which meant that if the court granted Wall's request, it would be "favoring the tenets of a particular religion." *Id.* at 424–25. In other words, any exemption would upset the constitutional command of "neutrality" among religious sects. As a result, Cooke had the right to discipline the child, and he was discharged.

In 1862, possibly as a result of the *Cooke* case, Massachusetts law was amended to provide that, upon parental request to the school, no common school student who refused for reasons of religious conscience would be required to read from any particular version of the Bible. Several years later, Ella Spiller refused to bow her head during the morning prayer, and her parents refused to request she be excused. Her expulsion from the school was upheld by the Massachusetts Supreme Judicial Court, which declared the morning Bible reading and prayer was not an impermissible "religious rite," for the school committee "did not compel a pupil to join in the prayer, but only to assume an attitude which was calculated to prevent interruption by avoiding all communication with others during the service." *Spiller v. Inhabitants of Woburn*, 94 Mass. (12 Allen) 127, 129 (1866). Because her parents had not requested she be excused from bowing her head, she had no warrant to complain.

Massachusetts was the only state to mandate by statute Bible reading in the common schools during the nineteenth century.

The only case holding Bible reading unconstitutional before the turn of the century is *State* ex rel. *Weiss v. District Board*, 44 N.W. 967 (Wis. 1890), which follows.

State ex rel. Weiss v. District Board

44 N.W. 967 (Wis. 1890)

LYON, J.

The petitioners are residents and tax-payers of the city of Edgerton, and their children are pupils in the public schools of that city. They allege in their petition that certain of the teachers, employed by the district board having charge of such schools, read daily to the pupils therein, during school hours, certain portions of King James' version of the Bible, selected by the teachers; and that the petitioners have requested the district board to require the teachers to discontinue such practice, but the board refuses to do so.

The constitutional objections urged by the petitioners to the reading of the Bible in the district schools are that (1) it violates the rights of conscience; (2) it compels them to aid in the support of a place of worship against their consent, (section 18, art. 1, Const.;) (3) it is sectarian instruction, (Id. Art. 10, §3.) This opinion will be confined quite closely to a discussion of the question whether the adoption of the Protestant, or King James, version of the Bible, or any version thereof, in the public schools in the city of Edgerton, as a textbook, and the reading of selections therefrom in those schools at the times and in the manner stated in the answer, is sectarian instruction, within the meaning of that term as used in section 3, art. 10, of the constitution, which ordains that no sectarian instruction shall be allowed in the district schools of this state.

In considering whether such reading of the Bible is sectarian instruction, the book will be regarded as a whole; because the whole bible, without exception, has been designated as a text-book for use in the Edgerton schools, and the claims of the school board is substantially (although perhaps not in terms) that the whole contents thereof may lawfully be so read therein, if the teachers so elect. This being so, it is quite immaterial if the portions thereof set out in the return as the only portions thus far read are not sectarian. Yet it should be observed that some of the portions so read seem to inculcate the doctrines of the divinity of Jesus Christ, and the punishment of the wicked after death, which doctrines are not accepted by some religious sects.

Counsel for the school board maintain, in their argument, that the Christian religion is part of the common law of England; that the same was brought to this country by the colonists, and, by virtue of the various colonial charters, was embodied in the fundamental laws of the colonies; that this religious element or principle was incorporated in the various state constitutions, and in the ordinance of 1787 for the government of the North-West Territory, by virtue of which ordinance it became the fundamental law of the territory of Wisconsin. Numerous quotations are given by him from the above documents, from the utterances of congress and legislatures, and from the writings of our early statesmen, to prove these propositions. That the learned counsel have fairly demonstrated their accuracy is freely conceded. More than that, counsel have proved that many, probably most, of those charters, and some of the state constitutions, not only ordained and enforced some of the principles of the Christian religion, but sectarian doctrines as well. They have also attempted, at considerable length, to show that the Church of Rome is hostile to our common-school system. This court neither affirms nor denies the accuracy of this position. Moreover, counsel on both sides have argued, to some extent, as to whether certain religious dogmas are true or false. None of these matters are material or pertinent to the questions to be determined on this appeal.

We come now to the more direct consideration of the merits of the controversy. The term "sectarian instruction," in the constitution, manifestly refers exclusively to instruction in religious doctrines, and the prohibition is only aimed at such instruction as is sectarian; that is to say, instruction in religious doctrines which are believed by some religious sects, and rejected by others. Hence, to teach the existence of a supreme being, of infinite wisdom, power, and goodness, and that it is the highest duty of all men to adore, obey, and love Him, is not sectarian, because all religious sects so believe and teach. The instruction becomes sectarian when it goes further, and inculcates doctrine or dogma, concerning which the religious sects are in conflict. This we understand to be the meaning of the constitutional prohibition. That the reading from the Bible in the schools, although unaccompanied by any comment on the part of the teacher, is "instruction," seems to us too clear for argument. Some of the most valuable instruction a person can receive may be derived from reading alone, without any extrinsic aid by way of comment or exposition. The question, therefore, seems to narrow down to this: Is the reading of the Bible in the schools—not merely selected passages therefrom, but the whole of it—sectarian instruction of the pupils? In view of the fact already mentioned, that the Bible contains numerous doctrinal passages, upon some of which the peculiar creed of almost every religious sect is based, and that such passages may reasonably be understood to inculcate the doctrines predicated upon them, an affirmative answer to the question seems unavoidable. Any pupil of ordinary intelligence who listens to the reading of the doctrinal portions of the Bible will be more or less instructed thereby in the doctrine of the divinity of Jesus Christ, the eternal punishment of the wicked, the authority of the priesthood, the binding force and efficacy of the sacraments, and many other conflicting sectarian doctrines. A most forcible demonstration of the accuracy of this statement is found in certain reports of the American Bible Society of its work in Catholic countries, (referred to in one of the arguments,) in which instances are given of the conversion of several persons from "Romanism" through the reading of the scriptures alone; that is to say, the reading of the Protestant or King James version of the bible converted Catholics to Protestants without the aid of comment or exposition. In those cases the reading of the Bible certainly was sectarian instruction. We do not know how to frame an argument in support of the proposition that the reading thereof in the district schools is not also sectarian instruction. It should be observed, in this connection, that the above views do not, as counsel seemed to think they may, banish from the district schools such text-books as are founded upon the fundamental teachings and extracts therefrom. Such teachings and extracts pervade and ornament our secular literature, and are important elements in its value and usefulness. Such text-books are in the schools for secular instruction, and rightly so; and the constitutional prohibition of sectarian instruction does not include them, even though they may contain passages from which some inferences of sectarian doctrine might possibly be drawn. Furthermore, there is much in the Bible which cannot justly be characterized as sectarian. There can be no valid objection to the use of such matter in the secular instruction of the pupils. Much of it has great historical and literary value, which may be thus utilized without violating the constitutional prohibition. It may also be used to inculcate good morals,—that is, our duties to each other,—which may and ought to be inculcated by the district schools. No more complete code of morals exists than is contained in the New Testament, which reaffirms and emphasizes the moral obligations laid down in the ten commandments. Concerning the fundamental principles of moral ethics, the religious sects do not disagree.

For the reasons above stated, we cannot doubt that the use of the Bible as a text-book in the public schools, and the stated reading thereof in such schools, without restriction, "has a tendency to inculcate sectarian ideas," and is sectarian instruction, within the meaning and intention of the constitution and the statute.

The answer of the respondent states that the relators' children are not compelled to remain in the school-room while the Bible is being read, but are at liberty to withdraw therefrom during the reading of the same. For this reason it is claimed that the relators have no good cause for complaint, even though such reading be sectarian instruction. We cannot give our sanction to this position. When, as in this case, a small minority of the pupils in the public school is excluded, for any cause, from a state school exercise, particularly when such cause is apparent hostility to the Bible, which a majority of the pupils have been taught to revere, from that moment the excluded pupil loses caste with his fellows, and is liable to be regarded with aversion, and subjected to reproach and insult. But it is a sufficient refutation of the argument that the practice in question tends to destroy the equality of the pupils which the constitution seeks to establish and protect, and puts a portion of them to serious disadvantage in many ways with respect to the others.

A number of cases in different states, supposed to have a bearing upon the main question here considered and determined. None of the states in which those decisions were made seem to have in their constitutions a direct prohibition of sectarian instruction in the public schools. Practically, therefore, we are now determining a question of first impression, and it must be determined upon general principles of law. Cases from which only mere inferences, more or less remote, can be deduced, afford but little aid to correct judgment in this case. Hence the cases cited have not been specially referred to in this opinion.

The drift of some remarks in the argument of counsel for the respondent is that the exclusion of Bible reading from the district schools is derogatory to the value of the holy scriptures, a blow to their influence upon the conduct and consciences of men, and disastrous to the cause of religion. We most emphatically reject these views. The priceless truths of the Bible are, best taught to our youth in the church, the Sabbath and parochial schools, the social religious meetings, and, above all, by parents in the home circle. There, these truths may be explained and enforced, the spiritual welfare of the child guarded and protected, and his spiritual nature directed and cultivated, in accordance with the dictates of the parental conscience. The constitution does not interfere with such teaching and culture[.] It only banishes theological polemics from the district schools. It does this, not because of any hostility to religion, but because the people who adopted it believed that the public good would thereby be promoted, and they so declared in the preamble. Religion teaches obedience to law, and flourishes best where good government prevails. The constitutional prohibition was adopted in the interests of good government; and it argues but little faith in the vitality and power of religion to predict disaster to its progress because a constitutional provision, enacted for such a purpose, is faithfully executed.

[Reversed.]

CASSODAY, J., (concurring.)

While the members of any particular sect may be willing to have one of their own number read the Bible in the public schools; yet they are not always willing to concede the same to a member of a sect believing in an opposite faith or doctrine. But the law is impartial, and has given no rights to any one sect that is not equally secured to every other.

The question, therefore, recurs, whether the provisions of our state constitution here involved, when construed with reference to the evils, or supposed evils, thereby sought to be suppressed, and the object or purpose thereby sought to be secured, permitted or prohibited the stated reading of the Bible as a text-book in the public schools. Wisconsin, as one of the later states admitted into the Union, having before it the experience of others, and probably in view of its heterogeneous population, as mentioned in the opinion of my associate, has, in her organic law, probably furnished a more complete bar to any preference for, or discrimination against, any religious sect, organization, or society than any other state in the Union. Our state constitution expressly prohibits any religious test as a qualification for office, or the exclusion of any witness in consequences of his religious opinion. Section 19, art. 1 The decisions of courts in states having no such constitutional prohibition, of course, can have no application to the case at bar. The question thus presented is not one of sectarian predilection, nor of religious belief, nor of theological conception, nor of sentiment, but one of fundamental law.

We neither have nor can have in this state, under our present constitution, any statutes of toleration, nor of union, directly or indirectly, between church and state, for the simple reason that the constitution forbids all such preferences and guaranties all such rights. But the exercise of such rights by one person, or any given number of persons, cannot be so extended as to interfere with the exercise of similar rights by other persons, nor so far as to prevent the legitimate exercise of the police powers of the state in preserving order, securing good citizenship, the administration of law, and the Sabbath as a day of rest. Stansbury v. Marks, 2 Dall. 213; Com. v. Wolf, 3 Serg. & R. 48; Com. v. Lesher, 17 Serg. & R. 155; McGatrick v. Wason, 4 Ohio St. 566; Simon v. Gratz, 23 Amer. Dec. 33; Shover v. State, 10 Ark. 259; Ferriter v. Tyler, 48 Vt. 469; State v.

Judge, 1 South Rep. 437. Such statutes come within no constitutional prohibition, and are founded upon an impregnable basis.

Certainly, the reading of the holy scriptures, as the eternal word of God, in obedience to the often-repeated injunction therein contained, whether by the individual in private, or in the family, or in the public assembly, is an essential part of divine worship. Every sermon is based upon some text of scripture. Most prayers are preceded by the reading of some passage of scripture, as an intelligent guide to the thoughts of the worshiper or worshipers. The sermon on the mount contains the prayer taught by the blessed Lord. Is it possible for any genuine believer in the Christian religion to read, or listen to the reading, of that sermon, and especially that prayer, without being filled with a holy sense of honor, reverence, adoration, and homage to Almighty God, which is the very essence of worship? We must hold that the stated reading of the Bible in the public schools as a text-book may be "worship" within the meaning of the clause of the constitution under consideration. If, then, such reading of the Bible is worship, can there be any doubt but what the schoolroom in which it is so statedly read is a "place of worship," within the meaning of the same clause of the constitution? The mere fact that only a small fraction of the school hours is devoted to such worship, in no way justifies such use, as against an objecting tax-payer. If the right be conceded, then the length of time so devoted becomes a matter of discretion. If such right does not exist, then any length of time, however short, is forbidden.

ORTON, J.

It is not needful that any other opinion should be written, but I thought it proper to state briefly some of the reasons which have induced such concurrence in the decision.

The clause that "no sectarian instruction shall be allowed therein" was inserted *ex industria* to exclude everything pertaining to religion. They are called by those who wish to have not only religion, but their own religion, taught therein, "Godless schools." They are Godless, and the educational department of the government is Godless, in the same sense that the executive, legislative, and administrative departments are Godless. So long as our constitution remains as it is, no one's religion can be taught in our common schools. By religion I mean religion as a system; not religion in the sense of natural law. Religion in the latter sense is the source of all law and government, justice, and truth. Religion, as a system of belief, cannot be taught without offense to those who have their own peculiar views of religion, no more than it can be without offense to the different sects of religion. How can religion, in this sense, be taught in the common schools, without taxing the people for or on account of it? The only object, purpose, or use for taxation by law in this state must be exclusively secular. It is said, if reading the Protestant version of the Bible in school is offensive to the parents of some of the scholars, and antagonistic to their own religious views, their children can retire. They ought not to be compelled to go out of the school for such a reason for one moment. The suggestion itself concedes the whole argument. That version of the Bible is hostile to the belief of many who are taxed to support the common schools, and who have equal rights and privileges in them. It is a source of religious and sectarian strife. That is enough. It violates the letter and the spirit of the constitution. No state constitution ever existed that so completely excludes and precludes the possibility of religious strife in the civil affairs of the state, and yet so fully protects all alike in the enjoyment of their own religion. All sects and denominations may teach the people their own doctrines in all proper places. Our constitution protects all, and favors none. But they must keep out of the common schools and civil affairs. Religion needs no support from the state. It is stronger and much purer without it.

This case is important and timely. It brings before the courts a case of the plausible, insidious, and apparently innocent entrance of religion into our civil affairs, and of an assault upon the most valuable provisions of the constitution. Those provisions should be pondered and heeded by all of our people, of all nationalities, and of all denominations of religion, who desire the perpetuity, and value the blessings, of our free government. That such is their meaning and interpretation no one can doubt, and it requires no citation of authorities to show. It is religion and sectarian instruction that are excluded by them. Morality and good conduct may be inculcated in the common schools, and should be. The connection of church and state corrupts religion, and makes the state despotic.

Notes

1. The *Weiss* case was brought as a result of the efforts of a Catholic lawyer and newspaper editor in Edgerton, Wisconsin named Humphrey Desmond. Joseph A. Ranney, *Aliens and "Real Americans": Law and Ethnic Assimilation in Wisconsin, 1846–1920*, Wis. Law., December 1994, at 28, 29. The Wisconsin court's opinion was given shortly after the state legislature passed the *Bennett Law*, which required all schools to teach children in English, and which restricted students who attended parochial schools to attend only those schools located in their public school district. *Id.* at 30. The uproar by German immigrants led to the electoral defeat of proponents of the law and to the repeal of the statute. *Id.*

2. From the 1850s to the turn of the century, the constitutionality of Bible reading in the public schools was the subject of approximately two cases per decade. Most courts concluded that because the Bible was not "sectarian," reading the Bible in public school did not violate the state's constitution. Cases holding Bible reading constitutional include *Stevenson v. Hanyon*, 7 Pa. Dist. 585 (1898); *Pfeiffer v. Board of Educ.*, 77 N.W. 250 (Mich. 1898); *Nessle v. Hum*, 2 Ohio Dec. 60 (1894); *Hart v. School Dist.*, 2 Lanc. L. Rev. 346 (Pa., Mercer County Ct. 1885); *Moore v. Monroe*, 20 N.W. 475 (Iowa 1884). As suggested by the *Donahoe* case, the primary reason given for holding Bible reading constitutional was the distinction between "broad" Christianity, represented by the King James Bible, which formed the basis for republican institutions, and "narrow" sectarianism, which concerned particular rites of worship. As noted in one case, "We do not understand how the reading of the Bible in the public schools can be termed sectarian. The Bible is not a sectarian book. On its broad foundation Christianity rests. Without it there is no Christianity." *Stevenson v. Hanyon*, at 590.

3. After 1900, the supreme courts in Illinois and Louisiana held Bible reading unconstitutional. *State* ex rel. *Ring v. Board of Educ.*, 92 N.E. 251 (Ill. 1910); *Herold v. Parish Bd.*, 68 So. 116 (La. 1915). Decisions in Nebraska and South Dakota barred particular Bible reading exercises in public schools on nonconstitutional grounds, but permitted Bible reading if certain conditions were met. *State v. Scheve*, 91 N.W. 846 (Neb. 1902) (requiring Bible reading to be nonsectarian and permitting local authorities to determine whether to include Bible reading in schools); *State* ex rel. *Finger v. Weedman*, 226 N.W. 348 (S.D. 1929) (permitting Bible reading only if pupils allowed to absent themselves during the reading). Additionally, a number of western states statutorily prohibited Bible reading, including Arizona, California, Utah, Washington and Wyoming.

4. Although Massachusetts was the only state to require Bible reading in public schools by statute, this changed rapidly beginning shortly after the turn of the century. Starting in 1913 and continuing for twenty years, eleven states and the District of Columbia statutorily required Bible reading in the public schools. The states were Pennsyl-

vania (1913), Delaware (1915), Tennessee (1915), New Jersey (1916), Alabama (1919), Georgia (1921), Maine (1923), Kentucky (1924), Florida (1925), Idaho (1925), District of Columbia (1926) and Arkansas (1930). Alvin W. Johnson, THE LEGAL STATUS OF CHURCH-STATE RELATIONSHIPS IN THE UNITED STATES, WITH SPECIAL REFERENCE TO THE PUBLIC SCHOOLS 23–25 (1934 repr. 1982). As of 1934, ten other states permitted Bible reading in schools by statute. *Id.* at 26–27 (Table). An excellent summary of this history is Otto Templar Hamilton, THE COURTS AND THE CURRICULUM 73–117 (1927).

5. A widely reported case raising a slightly different issue is *Minor v. Board of Educ. of Cincinnati*, 23 Ohio St. 238 (1871). From its organization in 1829, the common schools of Cincinnati began the school day with a reading from the "Holy Scriptures." In 1842, a student was excused from reading the "Protestant Testament and Bible" upon parental request, and a decade later, students were permitted to read from the version of the Bible they preferred. Finally, in 1869 a majority of the Board of Education excluded religious instruction and the reading of religious books, and ended Bible reading. A minority of the Board protested the decision and sued. A majority at the Superior Court of Cincinnati entered an injunction against the Board's decision, on the ground that moral instruction, exemplified by Bible reading without comment, was a necessary part of common school instruction. On appeal, the Supreme Court of Ohio reversed, holding the Board was solely vested with the authority to determine the common school curriculum. The court then justified the Board's action with three related arguments. First, "[t]rue Christianity asks no aid from the sword, of civil authority," *id.* at 247, so the absence of Bible reading would not harm Christianity. Second, the court made an early "marketplace of ideas" argument:

> Let religious doctrines have a fair field, and a free, intellectual, moral, and spiritual conflict. The weakest—that is, the intellectually, morally, and spiritually weakest—will go to the wall, and the best will triumph in the end. This is the golden truth which it has taken the world eighteen centuries to learn, and which has at last solved the terrible enigma of "church and state."

Id. at 251. Finally, the court interpreted the religious guarantee in a peculiarly modern way, noting, "[t]he 'protection' guaranteed by the section in question, means protection to the minority. The majority can protect itself. Constitutions are enacted for the very purpose of protecting the weak against the strong; the few against the many." *Id.*

6. Three other issues concerning religion and the public school arose in the late nineteenth century. They were the leasing of churches and other buildings owned by religious organizations to use as public school facilities, the use of public school buildings on Sundays and at other times school was not in session for religious teaching and worship, and the wearing of religious garb by public schools teachers, largely Catholic nuns.

In three nineteenth century cases, *Scripture v. Burns*, 12 N.W. 760 (Iowa 1882); *Millard v. Board of Educ.*, 10 N.E. 669 (Ill. 1887); and *Swadley v. Haynes*, 41 S.W. 1066 (Tenn. 1897), state courts held permissible the leasing of property owned by religious organizations largely because of the immediate necessity of the public schools for additional space. In *Doerner v. School Dist. No. 5*, 118 N.W. 353 (Wis. 1908), the Wisconsin Supreme Court permitted a school district to lease space in a building jointly housing a Catholic school. In *Doerner*, the facts indicated that all the schoolchildren, whether enrolled in the public or the Catholic school, were all Catholic, "and the public school conducted in the rooms rented by the school district was characterized by certain religious ceremonies, in that certain distinctive prayers of the Catholic church were said at intervals throughout the school day, church hymns were sung, and the teachers were nuns specially designated to the service by the superior of a Catholic sisterhood to which they belonged." 118 N.W. at 354. Because of these facts, the court upheld the trial court's conclusion that the public school was "pervaded and characterized by sectaran instruction contrary to law," but also held that where instruction was nonsectarian, the school district had the discretion to "maintain a common school in a parochial school building." *Contra Knowlton v. Baumhover*, 166 N.W. 202 (Iowa 1918) (holding that combining public school in a parochial school building made public school religious in nature). The second issue was the converse of the first, that is, the right to use the common school building for sectarian worship or for other religious uses. In *Scofield v. Eighth Sch. Dist.*, 27 Conn. 499 (1858), and *Dorton v. Hearn*, 67 Mo. 301 (1878), courts enjoined the use of public school buildings as the site for religious teaching at Sunday school.

The last related issue concerned the wearing of religious garb by teachers in the common schools. When a Catholic school changed its status and became a common school, the teachers, usually Roman Catholic nuns, often remained as teachers at the school. The earliest case concerning the wearing of identifiably religious clothing in the public schools is *Hysong v. Gallitzin Sch. Dist.*, 30 A. 482 (Pa. 1894). The teachers, Roman Catholic nuns whose clothing and insignia symbolized their membership in the Sisterhood of St. Joseph, were held not to be engaged in sectarian teaching by the wearing of identifiably religious garb. The next year, the legislature of Pennsylvania outlawed the wearing of religious garb while teaching in public schools. This act was upheld in 1910 by the Supreme Court of Pennsylvania in *Commonwealth v. Herr*, 78 A. 68 (Pa. 1910). In *Herr*, the Court relied on language in *Hysong* permitting the state to require all teachers to wear "a particular style of dress." Because the law was not a religious test, but merely a reasonable regulation entrusted to the legislature, the law was not unconstitutional. Similarly, in *O'Connor v. Hendrick*, 184 N.Y. 421, 77 N.E. 612 (1906), the Court of Appeals of New York held that a regulation of the superintendent of public schools forbidding the wearing of religious clothing while teaching public schools comported with the state's constitutional command forbidding the use of public funds to aid sectarian influences. *See also Zellers v. Huff*, 55 N.M. 501, 236 P.2d 949 (1951) (holding impermissible the wearing of religious garb by public school teachers). Several courts have held permissible the wearing by public school teachers of religious garb. *Gerhardt v. Heid*, 66 N.D. 444, 267 N.W. 127 (1936); *State* ex rel. *Johnson v. Boyd*, 217 Ind. 348, 28 N.E. 2d 256 (1940) (holding, among other things, that wearing of religious garb by public school teachers did not necessarily constitute sectarian teaching); *Rawlings v. Butler*, 290 S.W.2d 801 (Ky. 1956) (holding United States Constitution not violated simply because Roman Catholic sisters wore religious clothing while teaching public school). For a modern case upholding a ban on the wearing by public school teachers of religious garb, see *Cooper v. Eugene Sch. Dist. 4J*, 301 Or. 358, 723 P.2d 298 (1986), *appeal dismissed*, 480 U.S. 942 (1987), excerpted in Chapter Six. *See also* Chapter Eight.

2. State Financial Support of Religious Schools

During the 1830s, over 200,000 Irish, most of whom were Roman Catholic, immigrated to the United States. By 1840, there were an estimated 663,000 Catholics out of a population of 17 million persons. During the next decade, the potato famine killed 1.5 million people in Ireland, and more than half a million Irish immigrated to the United

States. Joining these immigrants were Catholics from Germanic states. By 1850, the Roman Catholic Church claimed 1.75 million members, a number that doubled in the next decade, and reached 12 million members at the turn of the century. Even by 1850, Roman Catholicism was the largest religious denomination in the United States, and by 1900, Catholics comprised just under 16% of the total population of the United States.

The decisions in New York to permit the reading of the King James Bible and to refuse to allow Catholic schools to receive common school funds directly led to the creation of the system of Catholic schools in New York. Only a few years later, for essentially the same reasons, Catholic primary and secondary schools were organized in the cities of Chicago and Boston. As the number of Catholic schools increased, and as the number of Catholics increased, so did the calls by Catholics for public aid to support these schools. Shortly after the end of the Civil War, "Catholics in many parts of the Northeast and Midwest opened a campaign to eliminate the Protestant tinge that Bible-reading gave to the public schools, [and] to secure for their own parochial schools a share of the funds that the states were providing for education." John Higham, STRANGERS IN THE LAND: PATTERNS OF AMERICAN NATIVISM, 1860–1925 28 (2d ed. 1988). In 1875, desperate for an issue to replace the flagging popularity of Reconstruction, Ohio Republican gubernatorial candidate Rutherford B. Hayes "worked fiercely to smear the Democrats as subservient to Catholic designs." *Id.* Later that year, in a speech to the Army of the Tennessee on September 29, 1875 at Des Moines, Iowa, the Republican President Ulysses S. Grant took up the cudgel against Catholicism:

> The centennial year of our national existence, I believe, is a good time to begin the work of strengthening the foundations of the structure commenced by our patriotic forefathers one hundred years ago at Lexington. Let us all labor to add all needful guarantees for the security of free thought, free speech, a free press, pure morals, unfettered religious sentiments, and of equal rights and privileges to all men, irrespective of nationality, color or religion. Encourage free schools and resolve that not one dollar appropriated for their support shall be appropriated to the support of any sectarian schools. Resolve that neither the state nor the nation, nor both combined, shall support institutions of learning other than those sufficient to afford every child growing up in the land of opportunity of a good common school education, unmixed with sectarian, pagan or atheistical dogmas. Leave the matter of religion to the family altar, the church, and the private school, supported entirely by private contributions. Keep the church and state forever separate.

II Anson Phelps Stokes, CHURCH AND STATE IN THE UNITED STATES 68 (3 vols. 1950).

In December 1875, Grant sent his annual message to Congress, and incorporating the statement above, recommended the passage of a constitutional amendment

> making it the duty of each of the several States to establish and forever maintain free public schools adequate to the education of all the children in the rudimentary branches within their respective limits, irrespective of sex, color, birthplace, or religions; forbidding the teaching in said schools of religious, atheistic, or pagan tenets; and prohibiting the granting of any school funds, or school taxes, or any part thereof, either by legislative, municipal, or other authority, for the benefit or in aid, directly or indirectly, of any religious sect or denomination, or in aid or for the benefit of any other object of any nature or kind whatever.

4 Cong. Rec. 175 (December 7, 1875).

Immediately after this request, Grant focused Congress's attention to the increase in the value of untaxed church property, and suggested "the taxation of all property equally, whether church or corporation, exempting only the last resting-place of the dead, and possibly, with the proper restrictions, church edifices." *Id.* No action was taken on this request.

A week later, James G. Blaine, the recently deposed Speaker of the House and a possible Republican candidate for President in the 1876 election, introduced a constitutional amendment parroting Grant's proposal.

The Blaine Amendment

> No State shall make any law respecting an establishment of religion or prohibiting the free exercise thereof; and no money raised by taxation in any State for the support of public schools, or derived from any public fund therefor, nor any public lands devoted thereto, shall ever be under the control of any religious sect; nor shall any money so raised or lands so devoted be divided between religious sects or denominations.

4 Cong. Rec. 205 (December 14, 1875).

A month later, Democrats introduced a proposal adding a disqualification from political office of any minister of the gospel and forbidding any religious test for office by any state. 4 Cong. Rec. 440–41 (January 17, 1876). This proposal died in the House Judiciary Committee. After the Republican nomination of Ohio's Hayes and the Democratic nomination of New Yorker Samuel J. Tilden for the office of President, support for the Blaine Amendment was divided largely along party lines. On August 4, the House Judiciary Committee, controlled by Democrats, added, "This article shall not vest, enlarge, or diminish legislative power in Congress." *Id.* at 5189 (August 4, 1876). This amendment appeared to absolve Congress of the responsibility of enforcing the amendment, and as amended, it passed 180–7. *Id.* at 5191.

A week later, the Senate Judiciary Committee proposed the following:

> No State shall make any law respecting an establishment of religion, or prohibiting the free exercise thereof; and no religious test shall be required as a qualification to any office or public trust under any State. No public property, and no public revenue of, nor any loan of credit by or under the authority of, the United States, or any State, Territory, District, or Municipal Corporation, shall be appropriated to, or made, or used for the support of any school, educational or other institution, under the control of any religious or anti-religious sect, organization, or denomination or wherein the particular creed or tenets of any religious or anti-religious sect, organization or denomination shall be taught; and no such particular creed or tenets shall be read or taught in any school or institution supported in whole or in part by such revenue or loan of credit; and no such appropriation or loan of credit shall be made to any religious or anti-religious, sect, organization, or denomination or to promote its interests or tenets. This article shall not be construed to prohibit the reading of the Bible in any school or institution; and it shall not have the effect to impair rights of property already vested.
>
> Sec. 2. Congress shall have power, by appropriate legislation to provide for the prevention and punishment of violations of this article.

4 Cong. Rec. at 5453 (August 14, 1876).

In a vote along straight party lines, the Senate voted 28–16 in favor of the Senate's proposed version of the Blaine Amendment, four votes shy of the necessary two-thirds. *Id.* at 5595. Among the twenty-seven Senators who failed to vote on the Amendment was the recently appointed Senator from Maine, James G. Blaine. Steven K. Green, *The Blaine Amendment Reconsidered*, 36 Am. J. Leg. Hist. 38, 67–68 (1992).

Notes

1. Blaine's mother was Catholic, and his father, long a Presbyterian, converted to Catholicism before his death. One of his daughters married a Catholic, and later became a Catholic. Blaine claimed he was raised a Presbyterian, although it was alleged that as a boy he attended Sunday mass at the Catholic church with his mother, a claim that, if true, would demolish Blaine's presidential aspirations. As of 1876 Blaine claimed an allegiance to, although not membership in, Presbyterianism, and also claimed membership in a Congregational church in Maine. He was neither a religious man nor anti-Catholic. *See* Marie Carolyn Klinkhamer, *The Blaine Amendment of 1875: Private Motives for Political Action*, 42 Cath. Hist. Rev. 15, 29–32 (1955). It appears that Blaine viewed his proposed amendment solely as a way to gain a political advantage to obtain the Republican nomination for President, for Blaine showed "a total disregard for the proposal once he had lost the nomination." Green, at 54. Even though he remained an influential member of Congress, Blaine "did not take part in any of the debates surrounding the amendment." *Id.*

In 1884, Blaine wrested the Republican nomination for President, and enjoyed the support of many Irish-Americans until he spoke of the Democratic party as the party of "Rum, Romanism, and Rebellion." His support among Catholic Irish-Americans disappeared, and Blaine lost the election to Grover Cleveland by losing the state of New York, home to a large number of Irish-American Catholics, by 1149 votes.

2. From 1875 to 1907, the proposed amendment was introduced before Congress over twenty times, although it never received more support than it did in 1876. Despite the Republican failure to win the battle concerning the proposed Blaine Amendment, they won the war concerning state aid to sectarian schools. Congress required all states entering the Union after 1876 to include a provision in the state's constitution requiring the state to maintain a nonsectarian public school system. *See* Enabling Act, ch. 189, § 4, 25 Stat. 676, 676–77 (1889) (requiring new states of Washington, North and South Dakota and Montana to provide for "the establishment and maintenance of a system of public schools, which shall be open to all children... and free from sectarian control"). Additionally, from 1877–1913, thirty-three states forbade the expenditure of public monies for the support of "sectarian instruction." *See, e.g., State* ex rel. *Nevada Orphan Asylum v. Hallock*, 16 Nev. 363 (1882) (holding constitutional provision barring aid for "sectarian purposes" forbids state from paying maintenance for orphans at a Catholic Orphanage).

3. Professor Kurt T. Lash suggests that any understanding of the Establishment Clause is incomplete without taking into account the dramatic change in its meaning by 1868. In Professor Lash's view, "[b]y Reconstruction, the common interpretation of the Establishment Clause and its 'counterparts' in the states was that no government had any legitimate power over religion as religion: the state could neither establish a preferred religion, nor could it visit 'disadvantages or penalties' upon disfavored religious

beliefs. Citizens by right were immune from such religious-based persecutions." Kurt T. Lash, *The Second Adoption of the Establishment Clause: The Rise of the Nonestablishment Principle*, 27 Ariz. St. L.J. 1085, 1133 (1995). Although "the original Clause stood for federalism," by the end of the Civil War, the Clause stood for personal freedom. *Id.* at 1135. Based on this interpretation, Lash does not read the Blaine Amendment as a failed effort to apply the Establishment Clause to the states as well as to the federal government. Instead,

> [g]iven the Blaine Amendment's anti-Catholic animus, as well as its substantial amendment of contemporary nonestablishment principles, the rejection of the Amendment seems rather weak evidence against incorporation in general and the Establishment Clause in particular. Indeed, it seems the opposite. Both the text and the debates over the Amendment indicate that the Establishment Clause was understood as the substantive equal of the Free Exercise Clause, and that the principle of nonestablishment applied at both a state and federal level.

Id. at 1150.

Professor Lash also argues that "the Free Exercise Clause was adopted a second time through its incorporation into the Privileges or Immunities Clause of the Fourteenth Amendment and that the scope of the new Free Exercise Clause was intended to include protections un-anticipated at the Founding." This was "a conception of religious liberty vastly different from that intended in 1791 and constitutes a constitutional modification of the original 'rights of conscience.' Religious exemptions from generally applicable laws, considered unnecessary and improbable at the Founding, now became necessary and proper." Kurt T. Lash, *The Second Adoption of the Free Exercise Clause: Religious Exemptions Under the Fourteenth Amendment*, 88 Nw. L. Rev. 1106, 1109 (1994). A major reason for this re-adoption of the free exercise clause was the clash between religiously-motivated abolitionists and the government over slavery. Laws restricting the right of slaves to read, to write, and to assemble all made slavery incompatible with religious liberty. After the Civil War, the Reconstruction Congress looked at the example of generally applicable laws affecting the religious liberty of slaves, which led it to broaden the protection of the Free Exercise Clause.

The Christian Education Amendment of 1888

The claim that the United States was a Christian nation was oft-made. During the Civil War, a number of Protestant organizations urged the passage of an amendment declaring the United States a Christian nation. Eventually organized as the National Reform Association, the organization proposed reorganizing the Preamble of the Constitution to read: "Recognizing Almighty God as the source of all authority and power in civil government, and acknowledging the Lord Jesus Christ as the Governor among the nations, His revealed will as the supreme law of the land, in order to constitute a Christian government...." Morton Borden, *Jews, Turks, and Infidels* 63 (1984). Lincoln met with a delegation of the Association in early 1864, but "took no action endorsing or supporting the National Reform Association." *Id.* at 69. Congress never acted on the proposed amendment. *Id.*

In 1888, Senator Henry W. Blair of New Hampshire introduced the Christian Education Amendment. Blair had long advocated federal aid to nonsectarian schools, and had introduced legislation to that effect since 1881. In urging passage of his bill for federal financial support of nonsectarian education, Blair complained that newspapers had withdrawn their support of the bill because "upon the staff of every great paper of this country to-day is a Jesuit and the business of that man is to see that a blow is struck wherever there is an opportunity to strike at the common-school system of America." 19 Cong. Rec. 1218 (February 15, 1888). Later that year, after the defeat of his bill, Blair introduced the Christian Education Amendment, a modified version of the Blaine Amendment. It stated, in part:

> Section 1. No State shall ever make or maintain any law respecting an establishment of religion or prohibiting the free exercise thereof.
>
> Sec. 2. Each state in this Union shall establish and maintain a system of free public schools adequate for the education of all the children living therein, between the ages of six and sixteen years, inclusive, in the common branches of knowledge, and in virtue, morality, and the principles of the Christian religion. But no money raised by taxation imposed by law, or any money or other property or credit belonging to any municipal organization or to any State or to the United States, shall ever be appropriated, applied, or given to the use or purposes of any school, institution, corporation, or person whereby instruction or training shall be given in the doctrines, tenets, belief, ceremonials, or observances peculiar to any sect, denomination, organization, or society being or claiming to be religious in its character; nor shall such peculiar doctrines, tenets, belief, ceremonials, or observances be taught or inculcated in the free public schools.

19 Cong. Rec. 4615 (May 25, 1888).

Like the Senate's version of the Blaine amendment, which declared Bible reading nonsectarian, Blair's proposed amendment declared teaching the "principles of the Christian religion" consonant with the provision barring the teaching of religious "doctrines, tenets, belief, ceremonials, or observances be taught or inculcated in the free public schools." This amendment died without a vote of the Senate. Proposals to amend the Constitution to proclaim the United States as a Christian nation were made regularly in the late nineteenth century (1894–96) and in the early twentieth century (1908–1910). None of these proposals achieved formal Congressional approval. Alvin W. Johnson and Frank H. Yost, SEPARATION OF CHURCH AND STATE IN THE UNITED STATES 31 n.26 (1934 repr. 1969).

3. Education, Native Americans and Religious Liberty

After the subjugation of American Indians in the West by the Army, and their forced removal to reservations, the process of "Christianizing" and "Americanizing" them began. From the early 1880s until 1910, Protestants and Catholics fought over the education and religious training of Indians. As the historian of this conflict has noted, "one cannot escape the conclusion that in the battles described here the Indians were on the outside.... It seems fair to say, they were but pawns in the hands of the managers of the campaigns." Francis Paul Prucha, THE CHURCHES AND THE INDIAN SCHOOLS, 1888–1912 xii (1979).

Beginning in the 1880s, the federal government contracted with church mission schools to educate Indians, paying an annual amount for each enrolled student. The Catholic mission schools took advantage of this arrangement, and the result "was a dominance of Catholics in Indian missions and receipt by their schools of the overwhelming proportion of contract funds." *Id.* at 4. Protestants viewed this dominance with alarm, and by 1888, the position of the several Protestant Indian welfare organizations was that the federal government should take over the education of Indians. *Id.* at 8–9.

In the mid-1890s, this system of funding was amended. Beginning with the amount appropriated to sectarian schools for the education of Indian schoolchildren in 1895, Congress voted annually from 1896 to 1900 to reduce the appropriation amount paid by the federal government by appropriating only a percentage of the 1895 amount. For the year 1900, Congress appropriated only 15% of the 1895 amount, and provided that this was "'the final appropriation for sectarian schools.'" *Id.* at 40 (*quoting* Act of March 1, 1899, 30 Stats. 942).

After the end of the contract system, Catholic missionaries made the following requests of the federal government: 1) permission for Indians to use their own money (Indian trust and treaty funds) to educate their children in the Catholic schools; 2) elimination of the so-called "Browning Ruling," which denied Indian parents the right to choose the school their children would attend; 3) modification of a Bureau of Indian Affairs rule that an Indian student remained a member of a school until given permission to change schools by the Commissioner of Indian Affairs; and 4) permission for Catholic priests to give religious instruction to Catholic schoolchildren in government schools. *Id.* at 46. Each request was denied.

After the assassination of McKinley, and the succession to the office of President by Theodore Roosevelt, Catholics were granted relief in the form of the end of the Browning Ruling. While Catholics perceived the decision as a victory for liberty of conscience, Protestants "saw in the abrogation of the ruling the sinister specter again of Roman Catholic influence and power." *Id.* at 63. In 1904, Roosevelt permitted tribes, upon request, to use treaty and trust funds for the support of the Catholic mission schools, which stirred a Protestant protest. Among the protesters was a Sioux Indian named Reuben Quick Bear, who wrote the Protestant Indian Rights Association in December 1904 for assistance to prevent the use of Sioux trust funds for the support of the Catholic schools.

In April 1906, the Law Committee of the Indian Rights Association authorized Charles Binney, a lawyer and member of the Committee, to begin a suit challenging the use of the tribal trust funds for the support of the Catholic mission schools. *Id.* at 151. After a discussion with the nominal defendant, Bureau of Indian Affairs Commissioner Francis E. Leupp, Binney determined to challenge the use of both the treaty and trust funds. *Id.* Quick Bear and two other Sioux were chosen as the nominal plaintiffs, and the suit requested an injunction barring the expenditure of $27,000 in treaty and trust funds of the Sioux tribe at the Rosebud, South Dakota reservation claimed by the Bureau of Catholic Indian Missions. Although the Department of Justice defended the suit, the real burden of preparing the defense was left to "special counsel" Edgar H. Gans, a Baltimore lawyer who was paid by the Catholic Marquette League. *Id.* at 154. The Supreme Court of the District of Columbia held that the trust funds, but not the treaty funds, could be used for the Catholic schools. Both parties appealed to the Court of Appeals, which held that all funds of the Indian tribes could be used to pay the Bureau of Catholic Indian Missions. *Quick Bear v. Leupp*, 30 U.S. App. D.C. 151 (1907). In so concluding, the court stated:

> The first amendment to the Constitution...has shackled the hands of legislation against aid or hindrance to creeds and faiths; so be it that they live and flourish, die or wither; they go untouched, unmoved, unstirred by law; against

> them it speaks not, nor in their favor; in their field each human creature stands unlawed—a sovereign, supreme,—to turn which way he will; not only the white and black, but the red man as well; to prohibit an Indian from a particular faith, or from rearing his children in its schools is as far outside the law as in case of the Caucasian; and this is the result, if Indian education in a sectarian school of his own choice, paid for by his own money, is to be prohibited and the right denied. The "treaty" and "trust" moneys are the only moneys that the Indians can lay claim to as matter of right; the only sums on which they are entitled to rely as theirs for education; and while these moneys are not delivered to them in hand, yet the money must not only be provided, but be expended, for their benefit and in part for their education. It seems inconceivable that Congress shall have intended to prohibit them from receiving religious education at their own cost, if they desire it; such an intent would be one to "prohibit the free exercise of religion" amongst the Indians; and such would be the effect of the construction for which the complainants contend.

Id. at 163–64.

The Indian Rights Association appealed to the Supreme Court.

Quick Bear v. Leupp

210 U.S. 50 (1908)

Mr. Chief Justice FULLER delivered the opinion of the court.

The validity of the contract for $27,000 is attacked on the ground that all contracts for sectarian education among the Indians are forbidden by certain provisos contained in the Indian Appropriation Acts of 1895, 1896, 1897, 1898 and 1899. But if those provisos relate only to the appropriations made by the Government out of the public moneys of the United States raised by taxation from persons of all creeds and faiths, or none at all, and appropriated gratuitously for the purpose of education among the Indians, and not to "Tribal Funds," which belong to the Indians themselves, then the contract must be sustained. The difference between one class of appropriations and the other has long been recognized in the annual appropriation acts. The gratuitous appropriation of public moneys for the purpose of Indian education has always been made under the heading "Support of Schools," whilst the appropriation of the "Treaty Fund" has always been under the heading "Fulfilling Treaty Stipulations and Support of Indian Tribes," and that from the "Trust Fund" is not in the Indian Appropriation Acts at all. One class of appropriations relates to public moneys belonging to the Government; the other to moneys which belong to the Indians and which is administered for them by the Government.

From the history of appropriations of public moneys for education of Indians, set forth in the brief of counsel for appellees and again at length in the answer, it appears that before 1895 the Government for a number of years had made contracts for sectarian schools for the education of the Indians, and the money due on these contracts was paid, in the discretion of the Commission of Indian Affairs, from the "Tribal Funds" and from the gratuitous public appropriations. But in 1894 opposition developed against appropriating public moneys for sectarian education. Accordingly, in the Indian Appropriation Act of 1894, under the heading of "Support of Schools," the Secretary of the Interior was directed to investigate the propriety of discontinuing contract schools and to make such recommendations as he might deem proper. The Secretary suggested a gradual reduction in the public appropriations on account of the money which had been invested in these schools, with the approbation of the Government. He said: "It would be scarcely just to abolish them entirely—to abandon instantly a policy so long recognized," and suggested that they should be decreased at the rate of not less than twenty per cent a year. Thus in a few years they would cease to exist, and during this time the bureau would be gradually prepared to do without them, while they might gather strength to continue without Government aid.

Accordingly Congress introduced in the appropriation act of 1895 a limitation on the use of public moneys in sectarian schools. This act appropriated under the heading "Support of Schools for the support of Indian and industrial schools and for other purposes...$1,164,350,...Provided, That the Secretary of the Interior shall make contracts, but only with the present contract schools for the education of Indian pupils during the fiscal year ending June 30, 1896, to an extent not exceeding eighty per cent of the amount so used in the fiscal year 1895, and the Government shall as early as practicable make provision for the education of the Indians in Government schools."

This limitation of eighty per cent was to be expended for contract schools, which were those that up to that time had educated Indians through the use of public moneys, and had no relations and did not refer to "Tribal Funds."

In the appropriation act of 1896, under the same heading, "Support of Schools," the appropriation of public money of $1,235,000 was limited by a proviso that contracts should only be made at places where non-sectarian schools cannot be provided for Indian children to an amount not exceeding fifty per cent of the amount so used for the fiscal year 1895, and immediately following the appropriation of public money appears the expression, "and it is hereby declared to be the settled policy of the Government to hereafter make no appropriation whatever for education in any sectarian school." This limitation, if it can be given effect as such, manifestly applies to the use of public moneys gratuitously appropriated for such purpose, and not to moneys belonging to the Indians themselves. In the appropriation act of 1897 the same declaration of policy occurs as a limitation on the appropriation of public moneys for the support of schools, and the amount applicable to contract schools was limited to forty per cent of the amount used in 1895. In the act of 1898 the amount applicable to contract schools was limited to thirty per cent, and in the act of 1899 the amount so applicable was limited to fifteen per cent, these words being added: "this being the final appropriation for sectarian schools." The declaration of the settled policy of the Government is found only in the acts of 1896 and 1897, and was entirely carried out by the reductions provided for.

Since 1899 public moneys are appropriated under the heading "Support of Schools" or the support of Indian and industrial schools and for the other educational purposes, without saying anything about sectarian schools. This was not needed, as the effect of the legislation was to make subsequent appropriations for education mean that sectarian schools were excluded in sharing in them, unless otherwise provided.

As has been shown, in 1868 the United States made a treaty with the Sioux Indians, under which the Indians made large cessions of land and other rights. In consideration of this the United States agreed that for every thirty children a house should be provided and a teacher competent to teach the elementary branches of our English education should be furnished for twenty years. In 1877, in consideration of further land cessions, the United States agreed to furnish all necessary aid to assist the Indians in the work of civilization and furnish them schools and instruction in mechanical and agricultural arts, as provided by the Treaty of 1868. In 1889 Congress extended the obligation of the treaty for twenty years, subject to such modifications as Congress should deem most effective, to secure the Indians equivalent benefits of such education. Thereafter, in every annual Indian appropriation act, there was an appropriation to carry out the terms of this treaty, under the heading "Fulfilling Treaty Stipulations with and Support of Indian Tribes."

These appropriations rested on different grounds from the gratuitous appropriations of public moneys under the heading "Support of Schools." The two subjects were separately treated in each act, and, naturally, as they are essentially different in character. One is the gratuitous appropriation of public moneys for the purpose of Indian education, but the "Treaty Fund" is not public money in this sense. It is the Indians' money, at least as dealt with by the Government as if it belonged to them, as morally it does. It differs from the "Trust Fund" in this: The "Trust Fund" has been set aside for the Indians and the income expended for their benefit, which expenditure required no annual appropriation. The whole amount due the Indians for certain land cessions was appropriated in one lump sum by the act of 1889, 25 Stat. 888, chap. 405. This "Trust Fund" is held for the Indians and not distributed *per capita*, being held as property in common. The money is distributed in accordance with the discretion of the Secretary of the Interior, but really belongs to the Indians. The President declared it to be the moral right of the Indians to have this "Trust Fund" applied to the education of the Indians in the schools of their choice, and the same view was entertained by the Supreme Court of the District of Columbia and the Court of Appeals of the District. But the "Treaty Fund" has exactly the same characteristics. They are moneys belonging really to the Indians. They are the price of land ceded by the Indians to the Government. The only difference is that in the "Treaty Fund" the debt to the Indians created and secured by the treaty is paid by annual appropriations. They are not gratuitous appropriations of public moneys, but the payment, as we repeat, of a treaty debt in installments. We perceive no justification for applying the proviso or declaration of policy to the payment of treaty obligations, the two things being distinct and different in nature and having no relation to each other, except that both are technically appropriations.

Some reference is made to the Constitution, in respect to this contract with the Bureau of Catholic Indian missions. It is not contended that it is unconstitutional, and it could not be. *Roberts v. Bradfield*, 12 App. D.C. 475; *Bradfield v. Roberts*, 175 U.S. 291. But it is contended that the spirit of the Constitution requires that the declaration of policy that the Government "shall make no appropriation whatever for education in any sectarian schools" should be treated as applicable, on the ground that the actions of the United States were to always be undenominational, and that, therefore, the Government can never act in a sectarian capacity, either in the use of its own funds or in that of the funds of others, in respect of which it is a trustee; hence that even the Sioux trust fund cannot be applied for education in Catholic schools, even though the owners of the fund so desire it. But we cannot concede the proposition that Indians cannot be allowed to use their own money to educate their children in the schools of their own choice because the Government is necessarily undenominational, as it cannot make any law respecting an establishment of religion or prohibiting the free exercise thereof. The Court of Appeals well said:

"The 'Treaty' and 'Trust' moneys are the only moneys that the Indians can lay claim to as matter of right; the only sums on which they are entitled to rely as theirs for education; and while these moneys are not delivered to them in hand, yet the money must not only be provided, but be expended, for their benefit and in part for their education; it seems inconceivable that Congress should have intended to prohibit them from receiving religious education at their own cost if they so desired it; such an intent would be one 'to prohibit the free exercise of religion' amongst the Indians, and such would be the effect of the construction for which the complainants contend."

The *cestuis que trust* cannot be deprived of their rights by the trustee in the exercise of power implied.

Decree affirmed.

Note

The solicitousness of the government for the religious education of American Indians was limited to Indians whose religious beliefs were Christian. In 1889 and 1890, the evangelist Wovoka, a Paiute, proclaimed from Nevada an eternal future without white men. Robert M. Utley, The Lance and the Shield 282 (1993). Wovoka's words were heard by Kicking Bear, a Miniconjou, who was invited by Sitting Bull, Chief of the Lakota (Sioux), for a visit. Kicking Bear claimed that "the Messiah would lift on high all Indian believers in the Ghost Dance, all who had danced and sang and prayed and practiced the tenets of the faith." *Id.* at 284. In October, the Ghost Dance began on the Lakota reservations in South Dakota. On the morning of December 15, 1890, in order to end the Ghost Dance, Sitting Bull was arrested, and during the ensuing confrontation between his followers and Indian police, was shot and killed. *Id.* at 300–02. Less than two weeks later, the Wounded Knee massacre occurred.

C. Protestantism and Minority Religions

1. Introduction

After the Civil War, the first case touching the issue of religious liberty to come before the Supreme Court was a consequence of that War. The state of Missouri, one of four slave states to remain in the Union, passed a law requiring a number of professionals, including clergy, to swear an oath of loyalty to the Constitution. Article II, § 9 stated in part: "No person shall . . . be competent as a bishop, priest, deacon, minister, elder, or other clergyman of any religious persuasion, sect, or denomination, to teach or preach, or solemnize marriages, unless such person shall have first taken, subscribed, and filed said [loyalty] oath." IV Thorpe, at 2197. A Catholic priest named Cummings was fined $500 and sentenced to jail until the fine was paid for preaching and teaching without taking the loyalty oath. In *Cummings v. Missouri*, 71 U.S. [4 Wall.] 277 (1866), Justice Stephen Field, for a bare majority of the Court, held that the Missouri constitutional provisions violated the *ex post facto* and bill of attainder provisions of the United States Constitution, even though the Missouri provisions appeared formally not to violate those clauses. Field concluded that the Court was required to look at the substance of the provisions, and not just their form, and in doing so, the unconstitutionality of the provisions was clear. Because *Cummings* was decided before the Fourteenth Amendment was ratified, the majority was unable to rely on the guarantees of the due process, privileges and immunities, and equal protection clauses of the Amendment.

Although Missouri remained in the Union during the Civil War, there were a number of proponents of secession in Missouri, and the issue divided the state. For Justice Field, "the fierce passions which that struggle aroused" was a reason to declare the law unconstitutional. Field spent little time discussing the legal implications of requiring a test oath of both "public" officers and "private" persons, including members of the clergy. Does this suggest anything about the "public" role of religion or of clergy in the mid-nineteenth century?

The next case decided by the Court also arose as a consequence of the Civil War. In *Watson v. Jones*, 80 U.S. [13 Wall.] 679 (1872), the legal issue was the rightful owner of the Third (or Walnut) Street Presbyterian Church in Louisville, Kentucky. The parties were pro- and anti-slavery factions of the church. The Court eventually sided with the anti-slavery faction. Although the case did not require the Court to interpret the language of the First Amendment, Justice Samuel Miller's opinion included the following language concerning religious freedom:

> In this country the full and free right to entertain any religious belief, to practice any religious principle, and to teach any religious doctrine which does not violate the laws of morality and property, and which does not infringe personal rights, is conceded by all. The law knows no heresy, and is committed to the support of no dogma, the establishment of no sect.

Id. at 728. *Watson* is discussed in greater detail in Chapter Seven.

Less than two decades later, when the Court faced the third in its trilogy of cases involving the Church of Jesus Christ of Latter-day Saints (Mormons), Justice Joseph Bradley explicated Justice Miller's "morality and property" limitation on the exercise of religious liberty. Writing for the majority, he stated: "The State has a perfect right to prohibit all open offenses against the enlightened sentiment of mankind, notwithstanding the pretense of religious conviction by which they may be advocated and practiced." *The Late Corp. of the Church of Jesus Christ of Latter Day Saints v. United States*, 136 U.S. 1, 50 (1890).

2. Defining the Common Culture

a) Law, Religion and the Supreme Court

Church of the Holy Trinity v. United States

143 U.S. 457 (1892)

[In 1887, the Church of the Holy Trinity hired as its rector and pastor an Englishman, E. Walpole Warren. The United States claimed that the church had violated federal law by paying Warren's transportation expenses to enable him to move from England to the United States "to perform service or labor of any kind in the United States." The act made no exception for the payment of transportation expenses of a minister to the United States. The lower court held the law applied to the action of the Church of the Holy Trinity.]

Mr. Justice BREWER delivered the opinion of the court.

[W]e cannot think Congress intended to denounce with penalties a transaction like that in the present case. It is a familiar rule, that a thing may be within the letter of the statute and yet not within the statute, because not within its spirit, nor within the intention of its makers. This has been often asserted, and the reports are full of cases illustrating its application. This is not the substitution of the will of the judge for that of the legislator, for frequently words of general meaning are used in a statute, words broad enough to include an act in question, and yet a consideration of the whole legislation, or of the circumstances surrounding its enactment, or of the absurd results which follow from giving such broad meaning to the words, makes it unreasonable to believe that the legislator intended to include the particular act.

We find, therefore, that the title of the act, the evil which was intended to be remedied, the circumstances surrounding the appeal to Congress, the reports of the committee of each house, all concur in affirming that the intent of Congress was simply to stay the influx of this cheap unskilled labor.

But beyond all these matters no purpose of action against religion can be imputed to any legislation, state or national, because this is a religious people. This is historically true. From the discovery of this continent to the present hour, there is a single voice making this affirmation. The commission to Christopher Columbus, prior to his sail westward, is from "Ferdinand and Isabella, by the grace of God, King and Queen of Castile," etc., and recites that "it is hoped that by God's assistance some of the continents and islands in the ocean will be discovered," etc. The first colonial grant, that made to Sir Walter Releigh in 1584, was from "Elizabeth, by the grace of God, of England, Fraunce and Ireland, queene, defender of the faith," etc.; and the grant authorizing him to enact statutes for the government of the proposed colony provided that "they be not against the true Christian faith nowe professed in the Church of England." The first charter of Virginia, granted by King James I in 1606, after reciting the application of certain parties for a charter, commenced the grant in these words: "We, greatly commending, and graciously accepting of, their Desires for the Furtherance of so noble a Work, which may, by the Providence of Almighty God, hereafter tend to the Glory of his Divine Majesty, in propagating of Christian Religion to such People, as yet live in Darkness and miserable Ignorance of the true Knowledge and Worship of God, and may in time bring the Infidels and Savages, living in those parts, to human Civility, and to a settled and quiet Government; DO, by these our Letters-Patents, graciously accept of, and agree to, their humble and well-intended Desires."

Language of similar import may be found in the subsequent charters of that colony, from the same king, in 1609 and 1611; and the same is true of the various charters granted to the other colonies. In language more or less emphatic is the establishment of the Christian religion declared to be one of the purposes of the grant. The celebrated compact made by the Pilgrims in the Mayflower, 1620, recites: "Having undertaken for the Glory of God, and Advancement of the Christian Faith, and the Honour of our King and Country, a Voyage to plant the first Colony in the northern Parts of Virginia; Do by these Presents, solemnly and mutually, in the Presence of God and one another, covenant and combine ourselves together into a civil Body Politick, for our better Ordering and Preservation, and Furtherance of the Ends aforesaid."

The fundamental orders of Connecticut, under which a provisional government was instituted in 1638–1639, commence with this declaration: "Forasmuch as it hath pleased the Allmighty God by the wise disposition of his diuyne pruidence so to Order and dispose of things that we the Inhabitants and Residents of Windsor, Hartford and Wethersfield are now cohabiting and dwelling in and vppon the River of Conectecotte and the Lands thereunto adioyneing; And well knowing where a people are gathered together the word of God requires that to mayntayne the peace and vnion of such a people there should be an orderly and decent Gouerment established according to God, to order and dispose of the affayres of the people at all seasons as occation shall require; doe therefore assotiate and conioyne our selues to be as one Publike State or Commonwelth; and doe, for our selues and our Successors and such as shall be adioyned to vs att any tyme hereafter, enter into Combination and Confederation together, to mayntayne and presearue the liberty and purity of the gospell of our Lord Jesus wch we now professe, as also the disciplyne of the Churches, wch according to the truth of the said gospell is now practised amongst vs."

In the charter of privileges granted by William Penn to the province of Pennsylvania, in 1701, it is recited: "Because no People can be truly happy, though under the greatest Enjoyment of Civil Liberties, if abridged of the Freedom of their Consciences, as to their Religious Profession and Worship; And Almighty God being the only Lord of Conscience, Father of Lights and Spirits; and the Author as well as Object of all divine Knowledge, Faith and Worship, who only doth enlighten the Minds, and persuade and convince the Understandings of People, I do hereby grant and declare," etc.

Coming nearer to the present time, the Declaration of Independence recognizes the presence of the Divine in human affairs in these words: "We hold these truths to be self-evident, that all men are created equal, that they are endowed by their Creator with certain alienable Rights, that among these are Life, Liberty, and the pursuit of Happiness." "We, therefore, the Representatives of the united States of America, in General Congress, Assembled, appealing to the Supreme Judge of the world for the rectitude of our intentions, do, in the Name and by Authority of the good People of these Colonies, solemnly publish and declare," etc.; "And for the support of this Declaration, with a firm reliance on the Protection of Divine Providence, we mutually pledge to each other our Lives, our Fortunes, and our sacred Honor."

If we examine the constitutions of the various States we find in them a constant recognition of religious obligations. Every constitution of every one of the forty-four States contains language which either directly or by clear implication recognizes a profound reverence for religion and an assumption that its influence in all human affairs is essential to the well being of the community. This recognition may be in the preamble, such as is found in the constitution of Illinois, 1870: "We, the people of the State of Illinois, grateful to Almighty God for the civil, political and religious liberty which he hath so long permitted us to enjoy, and looking to Him for a blessing upon our endeavors to secure and transmit the same unimpaired to succeeding generations," etc.

It may be only in the familiar requisition that all officers shall take an oath closing with the declaration "so help me God." It may be in clauses like that of the constitution of Indiana, 1816, Article XI, section 4: "The manner of administering an oath or affirmation shall be such as is most consistent with the conscience of the deponent, and shall be esteemed the most solemn appeal to God." Or in provisions such as are found in Article 36 and 37 of the Declaration of Rights of the Constitution of Maryland, 1867: "That as it is the duty of every man to worship God in such manner as he thinks most acceptable to Him, all persons are equally entitled to protection in their religious liberty; wherefore, no person ought, by any law, to be molested in his person or estate on account of his religious persuasion or profession, or for his religious practice, unless under the color of religion, he shall disturb the good order, peace or safety of the State, or shall infringe the laws of morality, or injure others in their natural, civil or religious rights; nor ought any person to be compelled to frequent or maintain or contribute, unless on contract, to maintain any place of worship, or any ministry; nor shall any person, otherwise competent, be deemed incompetent as a witness, or juror, on account of his religious belief: *provided*, He believes in the existence of God, and that, under His dispensation, such person will be held morally accountable for his acts, and be rewarded or punished therefor, either in this world or the world to come. That no religious test ought ever to be required as a qualification for any office or profit or trust in this State other than a declaration of belief in the existence of God; nor shall the legislature prescribe any other oath of office than the oath prescribed by this constitution." Or like that in Article 2 and 3, of Part 1st, of the Constitution of Massachusetts, 1780: "It is the right as well as the duty of all men in society publicly and at stated seasons, to worship the Supreme Being, the great Creator and Preserver of the universe.... As the happiness of a people and the good order and preservation of civil government essentially depend upon piety, religion and morality, and as these cannot be generally diffused through a community but by the institution of the public worship of God and of public instructions in piety, religion and morality: Therefore, to promote their happiness and to secure the good order and preservation of their government, the people of this commonwealth have a right to invest their legislature shall, from time to time, authorize and require, the several towns, parishes, precincts and other bodies politic or religious societies to make suitable provision, at their own expense, for the institution of the public worship of God and for the support and maintenance of public Protestant teachers of piety, religion and morality in all cases where such provision shall not be made voluntarily." Or as in sections 5 and 14 of Article 7, of the constitution of Mississippi, 1832: "No person who denies the being of a God, or a future state of rewards and punishments, shall hold any office in the civil department of this State.... Religion, morality and knowledge being necessary to good government, the preservation of liberty, and the happiness of mankind, schools and the means of education, shall forever be encouraged in this State." Or by Article 22 of the constitution of Delaware, 1776, which required all officers, besides an oath of allegiance, to make and subscribe the following declaration: "I, A. B., do profess faith in God the Father, and in Jesus Christ His only Son and in the Holy Ghost, one God, blessed for evermore; and I do acknowledge the Holy Scriptures of the Old and New Testament to be given by divine inspiration."

Even the Constitution of the United States, which is supposed to have little touch upon the private life of the individual, contains in the First Amendment a declaration common to the constitutions of all the States, as follows: "Congress shall make no law respecting an establishment of religion, or prohibiting the free exercise thereof," etc. And also provides in Article 1, section 7, (a provision common to many constitutions,) that the Executive shall have ten days (Sundays excepted) within which to determine whether he will approve or veto a bill.

There is no dissonance in these declarations. There is a universal language pervading them all, having one meaning; they affirm and reaffirm that this is a religious nation. These are not individual sayings, declarations of private persons: they are organic utterances; they speak the voice of the entire people. While because of a general recognition of this truth the question has seldom been presented to the courts, yet we find that in *Updegrapyh* [sic] *v. The Commonwealth*, 11 S. & R. 394, 400, it was decided that, "Christianity, general Christianity, is, and always has been, a part of the common law of Pennsylvania;... not Christianity with an established church, and tithes, and spiritual courts; but Christianity with liberty of conscience to all men." And in the *People v. Ruggles*, 8 Johns. 290, 294, 295, Chancellor Kent, the great commentator on American law, speaking as Chief Justice of the Supreme Court of New York, said: "The people of this State, in common with the people of this country, profess the general doctrines of Christianity, as the rule of their faith and practice; and to scandalize the author of these doctrines is not only, in a religious point of view, extremely impious, but, even in respect to the obligations due to society, is a gross violation of decency and good order.... The free, equal and undisturbed enjoyment of religious opinion, whatever it may be, and free and decent discussions on any religious subject, is granted and secured; but to revile, with malicious and blasphemous contempt, the religion professed by almost the whole community, is an abuse of that right. Nor are we bound, by any expressions in the Constitution as some have strangely supposed, either not to punish at all, or to punish indiscriminately, the like attacks upon the religion of *Mahomet* or of the Grand

Lama; and for this plain reason; that the case assumes that we are a Christian people, and the morality of the country is deeply ingrafted upon Christianity, and not upon the doctrines or worship of those impostors." And in the famous case of *Vidal v. Girard's Executors*, 2 How. 127, 198, this court, while sustaining the will of Mr. Girard, with its provision for the creation of a college into which no minister should be permitted to enter, observed: "It is also said and truly, that the Christian religion is a part of the common law of Pennsylvania."

If we pass beyond these matters to a view of American Life as expressed by its laws, its business, its customs and its society, we find everywhere a clear recognition of the same truth. Among other matters note the following: The form of oath universally prevailing, concluding with an appeal to the Almighty; the custom of opening sessions of all deliberative bodies and most conventions with prayer; the prefatory words of all wills, "In the name of God, amen;" the laws respecting the observance of the Sabbath, with the general cessation of all secular business, and the closing of courts, legislatures, and other similar public assemblies on that day; the churches and church organizations, which abound in every city, town and hamlet; the multitude of charitable organizations existing everywhere under Christian auspices; the gigantic missionary associations, with general support, and aiming to establish Christian missions in every quarter of the globe. These, and many other matters, which might be noticed, add a volume of unofficial declarations to the mass of organic utterances that this is a Christian nation. In the face of all these, shall it be believed that a Congress of the United States intended to make it a misdemeanor for a church of this country to contract for the services of a Christian minister residing in another nation?

Suppose in the Congress that passed this act some member had offered a bill which in terms declared that, if any Roman Catholic church in this country should contract with Cardinal Manning to come to this country and enter into its service as pastor and priest; or any Episcopal church should enter into a like contract with Canon Farrar; or any Baptist church should make similar arrangements with Rev. Mr. Spurgeon; or any Jewish synagogue with some eminent Rabbi, such contract should be adjudged unlawful and void, and the church making it be subject to prosecution and punishment, can it be believed that it would have received a minute of approving thought or a single vote? Yet it is contended that such was in effect the meaning of this statute. The construction invoked cannot be accepted as correct. It is a case where there was presented a definite evil, in view of which the legislature used general terms with the purpose of reaching all phases of that evil, and thereafter, unexpectedly, it is developed that the general language thus employed is broad enough to reach cases and acts which the whole history and life of the country affirm could not have been intentionally legislated against. It is the duty of the courts, under those circumstances, to say that, however broad the language of the statute may be, the act, although within the letter, is not within the intention of the legislature, and therefore cannot be within the statute.

The judgment will be reversed and the case remanded for further proceedings in accordance with this opinion.

Notes

1. Justice David Brewer was born in Asia Minor (now Turkey), the son of Congregational missionary parents. (His mother was the sister of Stephen Field, so Brewer was a member of the Supreme Court along with his Uncle until Field's retirement in 1897.) Brewer was a noted and popular public speaker, and among his published lec-

tures were three lectures given at Haverford College published under the title *The United States a Christian Nation* (1905). As the title of the lectures indicates, Brewer asserts more broadly the claim made in *Church of the Holy Trinity*. For Brewer, it was both true that the United States was a Christian nation, and that "the government as a legal organization is independent of all religions." David J. Brewer, The United States a Christian Nation 12 (1905). As he did in *Church of the Holy Trinity*, Brewer looked at the constitutional declarations of states in the eighteenth century, and the declarations by courts in the early nineteenth century as proof of his conclusion. Additionally, Christianity "to-day exists as a mighty factor in the life of the republic." *Id.* at 40. Thus, the claim "of this republic [as] a Christian nation is not a mere pretence but a recognition of an historical, legal and social truth." *Id.* at 46. Although he was accused of fomenting anti-Semitism in his Haverford lectures, it appears that Brewer was neither anti-Semitic nor interested in stirring any animosity toward or hatred of Jews. Michael J. Broadhead, David J. Brewer: The Life of a Supreme Court Justice, 1837–1910 180 (1994).

Brewer never faced a crisis of faith, and remained a Congregationalist his entire life. While a member of the Supreme Court, Brewer "regularly taught Sunday school at his church" in Washington, D.C. Broadhead, at 128. According to Morton Borden, Brewer often lectured for the National Reform Association, which regularly proposed an amendment to the Constitution declaring the United States a Christian nation. Borden, at 73.

Steven Green argues that Brewer's statements in *Church of the Holy Trinity* are best understood as a declaration of the cultural importance and historical significance of Christianity in the United States, and not as a statement linking government to Christian principles or the enforcement of Christian norms by law. Steven K. Green, *Justice Joseph Josiah Brewer and the "Christian Nation" Maxim*, 63 Alb. L. Rev. 427 (1999). Green notes that Brewer opposed most religiously-based legislation, including laws strictly enforcing the command to rest on the Sabbath. *Id.* at 459–60. *See also* J. Gordon Hylton, *David Josiah Brewer and the Christian Constitution*, 81 Marq. L. Rev. 417 (1998) (discussing relationship of Brewer's religious and judicial views). Judicial use of the "Christian nation" maxim became rare after the turn of the century. As the *de facto* Protestant establishment began to give way during this era of enormous immigration of Roman Catholics and Jews to the United States from Europe, the explanatory force of the maxim weakened. It was cited in 1898 to uphold Bible reading in the common school, see *Stevenson v. Hanyon*, 7 Pa. Dist. 585 (1898), and one of its last uses is found in a Virginia case upholding a Sunday law. *Pirkey Bros. v. Commonwealth*, 114 S.E. 764, 766 (Va. 1922).

Interestingly, a modern Justice of the United States, Chief Justice Earl Warren, made remarks similar to those made by Brewer. Shortly after becoming Chief Justice and three months before the Court's decision in *Brown v. Bd. of Educ.*, 347 U.S. 483 (1954), Chief Justice Warren spoke at the Annual Christian Action Conference. Warren stated in part:

> I believe the entire Bill of Rights came into being because of the knowledge our forefathers had of the Bible and their belief in it. Freedom of belief, or expression, of assembly, of petition;—the dignity of the individual, the sanctity of the home, equal justice under law, and the reservation of powers to the people. These things are the very essence of Christianity. They have characterized all our institutions. They have shaped our national life. They have given us our vision for the future.
>
> I like to believe we are living today in the spirit of Christian religion. I like also to believe that as long as we do so, no great harm can come to our country,

> and that the spirit which fortifies our individual wills will strengthen our nation, and make it both spiritually and materially strong and useful, not only to ourselves, but to mankind.
>
> What we are doing for our neighbors throughout the world in these turbulent times should be an assurance to people everywhere that we are, not only a great nation, but a Christian nation which has for its foremost objective—
>
> "Peace on earth-Good will to Men".

Speech delivered by Earl Warren, Chief Justice of the United States, at the Annual Christian Action Conference, sponsored by International Council for Christian Leadership—February 4, 1954.

2. Justice Brewer's history of the relationship among law, government and religion differs greatly from the sources used by Chief Justice Waite to interpret the First Amendment in *Reynolds v. United States*, 98 U.S. 145 (1879), excerpted below. Brewer's conclusion, that "no purpose of action against religion can be imputed to any legislation, state or national, because this is a religious people," is supported by references to religion in the colonial charters, state constitutions, the oath, and cases claiming the religiosity of the American people. After you read Reynolds, in which Waite focuses on Madison's *Memorial and Remonstrance* and Jefferson's letter to the Danbury Baptist Association to interpret the meaning of religious liberty, assess whether either history is both accurate and complete. Can both be used to interpret the language of the First Amendment? Does it make a difference that *Church of the Holy Trinity* is ostensibly about statutory interpretation, and *Reynolds* specifically concerns the interpretation of the Constitution? Is your understanding of *Church of the Holy Trinity* affected by the fact that in the several decades after the decision was published, few courts cited it for its understanding of the relation of law, government and religion?

3. In 1908, Brewer wrote the Court's opinion in *Berea College v. Kentucky*, 211 U.S. 45 (1908). Brewer's opinion concluded that a Kentucky law forbidding private schools from teaching black and white students at the same time did not violate the Constitution. Berea College was incorporated by the Commonwealth of Kentucky. The majority decided the Fourteenth Amendment applied only to natural persons, not "artificial" persons like corporations, and the seven man majority, including Justice Oliver Wendell Holmes, seized on this to deny the College's Fourteenth Amendment claim. The majority did not discuss the religious liberty aspect of Berea College's claim except to note that the original charter of Berea College was to "promote the cause of Christ." *Id.* at 56. In dissent, Justice Harlan, who was from Kentucky, stated, "The capacity to impart instruction to others is given by the Almighty for beneficent purposes." *Id.* at 67. He then continued:

> If the commonwealth of Kentucky can make it a crime to teach white and colored children together at the same time, in a private institution of learning, it is difficult to perceive why it may not forbid the assembling of white and colored children in the same Sabbath school, for the purpose of being instructed in the Word of God, although such teaching may be done under the authority of the church to which the school is attached as well as with the consent of the parents of the children. So, if the state court be right, white and colored children may even be forbidden to sit together in a house of worship or at a communion table in the same Christian church. Will it be said that the cases supposed and the case here in hand are different, in that no government, in this country, can lay unholy hands on the religious faith of the people? The answer

> to this suggestion is that, in the eyes of the law, the right to enjoy one's religious belief, unmolested by any human power, is no more sacred nor more fully or distinctly recognized than is the right to impart and receive instruction not harmful to the public. The denial of either right would be an infringement of the liberty inherent in the freedom secured by the fundamental law.

Id. at 68.

On the importance of Justice Harlan's "Old School" Presbyterian beliefs to his jurisprudence, see James W. Gordon, *Religion and the First Justice Harlan: A Case Study in Late Nineteenth Century Presbyterian Constitutionalism*, 85 Marq. L. Rev. 317 (2001).

Bradfield v. Roberts

175 U.S. 291 (1899)

[Congress passed an act appropriating funds for the operation of the District of Columbia. Among the appropriations was one for the construction of buildings at the site of two hospitals, to be determined by commissioners of the District. The District commissioners subsequently contracted with Providence Hospital. Providence Hospital was incorporated by an act of Congress in 1864. In its opinion, the court notes that, "Nothing is said about religion or about the religious faith of the incorporators of this institution in the act of incorporation." Plaintiffs claimed that Providence Hospital was a private corporation operated by the Sisters of Charity, an order of nuns of the Roman Catholic church. Plaintiffs claimed that the contract was void because it was made with a religious corporation, which violated the Establishment Clause.]

Mr. Justice PECKHAM, after stating the facts, delivered the opinion of the court.

If we were to assume, for the purpose of this question only, that under this appropriation an agreement with a religious corporation of the tenor of this agreement would be invalid, as resulting indirectly in the passage of an act respecting an establishment of religion, we are unable to see that the complainant in his bill shows that the corporation is of the kind described, but on the contrary he has clearly shown that it is not.

The above-mentioned allegations in the complainant's bill do not change the legal character of the corporation or render it on that account a religious or sectarian body. Assuming that the hospital is a private eleemosynary corporation, the fact that its members, according to the belief of the complainant, are members of a monastic order or sisterhood of the Roman Catholic Church, and the further fact that the hospital is conducted under the auspices of said church, are wholly immaterial, as is also the allegation regarding the title to its property. The statute provides as to its property and makes no provision for its being held by anyone other than itself. The facts above stated do not in the least change the legal character of the hospital, or make a religious corporation out of a purely secular one as constituted by the law of its being. Whether the individuals who compose the corporation under its charter happen to be all Roman Catholics, or all Methodists, or Presbyterians, or Unitarians, or members of any other religious organization, or of no organization at all, is of not the slightest consequence with reference to the law of its incorporation, nor can the individual beliefs upon religious matters of the various incorporators be inquired into. Nor is it material that the hospital may be conducted under the auspices of the Roman Catholic Church. To be conducted under the auspices is to be conducted under the influence or patronage of that church. The meaning of the allegation is that the church exercises great and perhaps controlling influence over the management of the hospital. It must, however, be managed pursuant to the law of its being. That the influence of any particular church may be powerful over the members of a nonsectarian and secular corporation, incorporated for a certain defined purpose and with clearly stated powers, is surely not sufficient to convert such a corporation into a religious or sectarian body. That fact does not alter the legal character of the corporation, which is incorporated under an act of Congress, and its powers, duties, and character are to be solely measured by the charter under which it alone has any legal existence. There is no allegation that its hospital work is confined to members of that church or that in its management the hospital has been conducted so as to violate its charter in the smallest degree. It is simply the case of a secular corporation being managed by people who hold to the doctrines of the Roman Catholic Church, but who nevertheless are managing the corporation according to the law under which it exists. The charter itself does not limit the exercise of its corporate powers to the members of any particular religious denomination, but, on the contrary, those powers are to be exercised in favor of anyone seeking the ministrations of that kind of an institution. All that can be said of the corporation itself is that it has been incorporated by an act of Congress, and for its legal powers and duties that act must be exclusively referred to. As stated in the opinion of the court of appeal, this corporation "is not declared the trustee of any church or religious society. Its property is to be acquired in its own name and for its own purposes; that property and its business are to be managed in its own way, subject to no visitation, supervision, or control by any ecclesiastical authority whatever, but only to that of the government which created it. In respect, then, of its creation, organization, management, and ownership of property it is an ordinary private corporation whose rights are determinable by the law of the land, and the religious opinions of whose members are not subjects of inquiry."

[T]he only objection set up [by plaintiffs] is the alleged "sectarian character of the hospital and the specific and limited object of its creation."

The act of Congress, however, shows there is nothing sectarian in the corporation, and "the specific and limited object of its creation" is the opening and keeping a hospital in the city of Washington for the care of such sick and invalid persons as may place themselves under the treatment and care of the corporation. To make the agreement was within the discretion of the commissioners, and was a fair exercise thereof.

Without adverting to any other objections to the maintenance of this suit, it is plain that complainant wholly fails to set forth a cause of action, and the bill was properly dismissed by the Court of Appeals, and its decree will therefore be *affirmed*.

Note

In defending the appropriation, the Court makes a happenstance argument:

> Whether the individual who compose the corporation under its charter *happen to be* all Roman Catholics, or all Methodists, or Presbyterians, or Unitarians, or members of any other religious organization, or of no organization at all, is of not the slightest consequence with reference to the law of its incorporation, nor can the individual beliefs upon religious matters of the various incorporators be inquired into. (italics added.)

What meaning should be ascribed to this language? The Court is concerned solely with the fact that Providence Hospital is a private corporation. It declares irrelevant the fact that title to the property is held in the name of the Sisters of Charity. Is the Court willfully blinding itself to some reality about the operation of hospitals by Roman Catholic organizations, or is the Court properly concluding that the religious faith of those operating the hospital is legally irrelevant? If the former case, what is really going on? If the latter, why is this fact irrelevant?

The language of happenstance suggests a type of formalist reasoning. Should this type of reasoning be declared impermissible when applying the Establishment Clause? A related type of reasoning, often used in cases in which a party requests an exemption from the general law, is the parade of horribles or slippery slope argument. This argument was used earlier in this chapter by Justice Appleton in *Donahoe v. Richards*, the first Bible-reading case. Appleton suggests that if a pupil can use her religious beliefs to refuse to read the King James Bible, then that pupil can banish from the common school the works of Locke, Bacon, Milton, Swift, as well as the scientific teachings of Galileo, Copernicus and Newton. The parade of horribles argument is premised on the belief that the possibility of other, more "extreme" cases requires the court to "hold the line" in the extant case and reject the exemption request. These two arguments are regularly used in modern religious liberty cases. *See, e.g., Employment Div. v. Smith*, 494 U.S. 872 (1990) (parade of horribles); *Board of Educ. of Kiryas Joel Village Sch. Dist. v. Grumet*, 512 U.S. 687 (1994) (happenstance).

b) Sunday Laws in the Supreme Court

The Supreme Court decided several cases concerning the constitutionality of Sunday laws in the late nineteenth century. The first case arose in California, and Justice Stephen Field, the author of the dissenting opinion in *Ex parte Newman*, wrote the unanimous opinion of the Court. *Soon Hing v. Crowley*, 113 U.S. 705 (1885). Field concluded, as he had nearly thirty years earlier in his Newman dissent: "Laws setting aside Sunday as a day of rest are upheld, not from any right of the Government to legislate for the promotion of religious observances, but from its right to protect all persons from the physical and moral debasement which comes from uninterrupted labor." *Id.* at 710. Although Field dismissed the claim that the regulation of the San Francisco Board of Supervisors was discriminatory, a year later a unanimous Court held unconstitutional the ordinance on equal protection grounds. *Yick Wo v. Hopkins*, 118 U.S. 356 (1886).

A decade later, the Court upheld the criminal conviction of the superintendent of the Alabama Great Southern Railroad Company for unlawfully running a freight train on that road on Sunday. *Hennington v. Georgia*, 163 U.S. 299 (1896). The Court concluded that the statute did not intrude on Congress's authority to regulate commerce, and was a permissible object of the state's police power: "It is none the less a civil regulation because the day on which the running of freight trains is prohibited is kept by many under a sense of religious duty." *Id.* at 304. The Court then cited Field's dissenting opinion in *Ex parte Newman*, as well as other state cases holding Sunday laws constitutional. Id. at 304–05. Chief Justice Fuller, joined by Justice Edward White, dissented on commerce clause grounds. Id. at 318. Finally, in *Petit v. Minnesota*, 177 U.S. 164 (1900), the Court held constitutional a Minnesota Sunday law specifically prohibiting keeping open a barber shop against a Fourteenth Amendment challenge that the law was class legislation. Once again, Justice Field's dissent in *Ex parte Newman* was cited as authority for the Court's conclusion. *Id.* at 165.

3. The Challenge of Polygamy

The Supreme Court did not interpret the First Amendment until 1879. At issue was a federal law criminalizing plural or polygamous marriages, a law directed against the members of the Church of Jesus Christ of Latter-day Saints, or Mormons, who had settled in the Territory of Utah.

After the assassination of church founder Joseph Smith in 1844 in Nauvoo, Illinois, the Twelve Apostles, led by Brigham Young, were voted by the congregation as the leaders of the church. Beginning in early 1846, the exodus of Mormons from Nauvoo to the West had begun. Leonard J. Arrington and Davis Bitton, THE MORMON EXPERIENCE: A HISTORY OF THE LATTER-DAY SAINTS 95 (1979). The Mormons settled in what became the Territory of Utah. In 1862, in the same year Utah was denied statehood, legislation outlawing polygamy and divesting the Mormon church of any property in excess of $50,000 was enacted. *Id.* at 172. This legislation, introduced by Representative Justin Morrill, was not enforced for a number of years after enactment. However, in 1871, on the complaint of his first wife, Thomas Hawkins was indicted for violating local law on a charge of adultery. He was convicted by a jury, but his conviction was overturned based on the intervening Supreme Court decision in *Clinton v. Englebrecht*, 80 U.S. [13 Wall.] 434 (1872), which barred the method of selecting jurors used in the Hawkins case. Orma Linford, *The Mormons and the Law: The Polygamy Cases*, 9 Utah L. Rev. 308, 330–31 (1964)(Part I). As a result, prosecutions against Brigham Young and other Church leaders temporarily ceased.

In 1874, after a number of efforts to solve the "Mormon problem" had failed, Congress enacted the Poland Act, which gave the federal judiciary jurisdiction over all civil, criminal, and probate cases in the Territory. Arrington & Bitton, at 176–77.

Although the 1862 federal act had been unenforced, George Reynolds, secretary to Brigham Young, arranged a test case of the constitutionality of the act. After Church leaders met with the United States Attorney for the Territory of Utah, Reynolds, who married his second wife Amelia Schofield on August 3, 1874, volunteered as a defendant. The prosecution offered Schofield's testimony that she was married to Reynolds, and a jury of seven Mormons and five "gentiles" convicted Reynolds. Linford, at 332. After this conviction was reversed, a second trial began, and by this time the prosecution no longer viewed the case as a test case. *Id.* at 333. At this trial, Schofield did not testify, and her previous testimony was admitted. After a second conviction, Reynolds appealed to the Supreme Court.

Reynolds v. United States

98 U.S. 145 (1879)

Mr. Chief Justice WAITE delivered the opinion of the court.

The assignments of error, when grouped, present the following questions:—

5. Should the accused have been acquitted if he married the second time, because he believed it to be his religious duty?

6. Did the court err in that part of the charge which directed the attention of the jury to the consequences of polygamy?

These questions will be considered in their order.

5. As to the defence of religious belief or duty.

On the trial,...the accused proved that at the time of his alleged second marriage he was, and for many years before had been, a member of the Church of Jesus Christ of Latter-Day Saints, commonly called the Mormon Church, and a believer in its doctrines; that it was an accepted doctrine of that church "that it was the duty of the male members of said church, circumstances permitting, to practise polygamy;...that this duty was enjoined by different books which the members of said church believed to be of divine origin, and among others the Holy bible, and also that the members of the church believed that the practice of polygamy was directly enjoined upon the male members thereof by the Almighty God, in a revelation to Joseph Smith, the founder and prophet of said church; that the failing or refusing to practise polygamy by such male members of said church, when circumstances would admit, would be punished, and that the penalty for such failure and refusal would be damnation in the life to come." He also proved "that he had received permission from the recognized authorities in said church to enter into polygamous marriage;... that Daniel H. Wells, one having authority in said church to perform the marriage ceremony, married the said defendant on or about the time the crime is alleged to have been committed, to some woman by the name of Schofield, and that such marriage ceremony was performed under and pursuant to the doctrines of said church."

Upon this proof he asked the court to instruct the jury that if they found from the evidence that he "was married as charged—if he was married—in pursuance of and in conformity with what he believed at the time to be a religious duty, that the verdict must be 'not guilty.'" This request was refused, and the court did charge "that there must have been a criminal intent, but that if the defendant, under the influence of a religious belief that it was right,—under an inspiration, if you please, that it was right,—deliberately married a second time, having a first wife living, the want of consciousness of evil intent—the want of understanding on his part that he was committing a crime—did not excuse him; but the law inexorably in such case implies the criminal intent."

Upon this charge and refusal to charge the question is raised, whether religious belief can be accepted as a justification of an overt act made criminal by the law of the land. The inquiry is not as to the power of Congress to prescribe criminal laws for the Territories, but as to the guilt of one who knowingly violates a law which has been properly enacted, if he entertains a religious belief that the law is wrong.

Congress cannot pass a law for the government of the Territories which shall prohibit the free exercise of religion. The first amendment to the Constitution expressly forbids such legislation. Religious freedom is guaranteed everywhere throughout the United States, so far as congressional interference is concerned. The question to be determined is, whether the law now under consideration comes within this prohibition.

The word "religion" is not defined in the Constitution. We must go elsewhere, therefore, to ascertain its meaning, and nowhere more appropriately, we think, than to the history of the times in the midst of which the provision was adopted. The precise point of the inquiry is, what is the religious freedom which has been guaranteed.

Before the adoption of the Constitution, attempts were made in some of the colonies and States to legislate not only in respect to the establishment of religion, but in respect to its doctrines and precepts as well. The people were taxed, against their will, for the support of religion, and sometimes for the support of particular sects to whose tenets they could not and did not subscribe. Punishments were prescribed for a failure to attend upon public worship, and sometimes for entertaining heretical opinions. The controversy upon this general subject was animated in many of the States, but seemed at last to culminate in Virginia. In 1784, the House of Delegates of that State having under consideration "a bill establishing provision for teachers of the Christian religion," postponed until the next session, and directed that the bill should be published and distributed, and that the people be requested "to signify their opinion respecting the adoption of such a bill at the next session of assembly."

This brought out a determined opposition. Amongst others, Mr. Madison prepared a "Memorial and Remonstrance," which was widely circulated and signed, and in which he demonstrated "that religion, or that duty we owe the Creator," was not within the cognizance of civil government. At the next session the proposed bill was not only defeated, but another, "for establishing religious freedom," drafted by Mr. Jefferson, was passed. In the preamble of this act religious freedom is defined; and after a recital "that to suffer the civil magistrate to intrude his powers into the field of opinion, and to restrain the profession or propagation of principles on supposition of their ill tendency, is a dangerous fallacy which at once destroys all religious liberty," it is declared "that it is time enough for the rightful purposes of civil government for its officers to interfere when principles break out into overt acts against peace and good order." In these two sentences is found the true distinction between what properly belongs to the church and what to the State.

In a little more than a year after the passage of this statute the convention met which prepared the Constitution of the United States. Of this convention Mr. Jefferson was not a member, he being then absent as minister to France. As soon as he saw the draft of the Constitution proposed for adoption, he, in a letter to a friend, expressed his disappointment at the absence of an express declaration insuring the freedom of religion, but was willing to accept it as it was, trusting that the good sense and honest intentions of the people would bring about the necessary alterations. Five of the States, while adopting the Constitution, proposed amendments. Three—New Hampshire, New York, and Virginia—included in one form or another a declaration of religious freedom in the changes they desired to have made, as did also North Carolina, where the convention at first declined to ratify the Constitution until the proposed amendments were acted upon. Accordingly, at the first session of the first Congress the amendment now under consideration was proposed with others by Mr. Madison. It met the views of the advocates of religious freedom, and was adopted. Mr. Jefferson afterwards, in reply to an address to him by a committee of the Danbury Baptist Association, took occasion to say: "Believing with you that religion is a matter which lies solely between man and his God; that he owes account to none other for his faith or his worship; that the legislative powers of the government reach actions only, and not opinions,—I contemplate with sovereign reverence that act of the whole American people which declared that their legislature should 'make no law respecting an establishment of religion or prohibiting the free exercise thereof,' thus building a wall of separation between church and State. Adhering to this expression of the supreme will of the nation in behalf of the rights of conscience, I shall see with sincere satisfaction the progress of those sentiments which tend to restore man to all of his natural rights, convinced he has no natural right in opposition to his social duties." Coming as this does from an acknowledged leader of the advocates of the measure, it may be accepted almost as an authoritative declaration of the scope and effect of the amendment thus secured. Congress was deprived of all legislative power over mere opinion, but was left free to reach actions which were in violation of social duties or subversive of good order.

Polygamy has always been odious among the northern and western nations of Europe, and, until the establishment of the Mormon Church, was almost exclusively a feature of the life of Asiatic and of African people. At common law, the second marriage was always void and from the earliest history of England polygamy has been treated as an offence against society.

In connection with the case we are now considering, it is a significant fact that on the 8th of December, 1788, after the passage of the act establishing religious freedom, and after the convention of Virginia had recommended as an amendment to the Constitution of the United States the declaration in a bill of rights that "all men have an equal, natural, and unalienable right to the free exercise of religion, according to the dictates of conscience," the legislature of that State substantially enacted the statute [banning bigamy] because, as recited in the preamble, "it hath been doubted whether bigamy or polygamy be punishable by the laws of this Commonwealth." From that day to this we think it may safely be said there never has been a time in any State of the Union when polygamy has not been an offence against society, cognizable by the civil courts and punishable with more or less severity. In the face of all this evidence, it is impossible to believe that the constitutional guaranty of religious freedom was intended to prohibit legislation in respect to this most important feature of social life. Marriage, while from its very nature a sacred obligation, is nevertheless, in most civilized nations, a civil contract, and usually regulated by law. Upon it solely may be said to be built, and out of its fruits spring social relations and social obligations and duties, with which government is necessarily required to deal. In fact, according as monogamous or polygamous marriages are allowed, do we find the principles on which the government of the people, to a greater or less extent, rests. Professor Lieber says, polygamy leads to the patriarchal principle, and which, when applied to large communities, fetters the people in stationary despotism, while the principle cannot long exist in connection with monogamy. Chancellor Kent observes that this remark is equally striking and profound. An exceptional colony of polygamists under an exceptional leadership may sometimes exist for a time without appearing to disturb the social condition of the people who surround it; but there cannot be a doubt that, unless restricted by some form of constitution, it is within the legitimate scope of the power of every civil government to determine whether polygamy or monogamy shall be the law of social life under its dominion.

In our opinion, the statute immediately under consideration is within the legislative power of Congress. It is constitutional and valid as prescribing a rule of action for all those residing in the Territories, and in places over which the United States have exclusive control. This being so, the only question which remains is, whether those who make polygamy a part of their religion are excepted from the operation of the statute. If they are, then those who do not make polygamy a part of their religious belief may be found guilty and punished, while those who do, must be acquitted and go free. This would be introducing a new element into criminal law. Laws are made for the government of actions, and while they cannot interfere with mere religious belief and opinions, they may with practices. Suppose one believed that human sacrifices were a necessary part of religious worship, would it be seriously contended that the civil government under which he lived could not interfere to prevent a sacrifice? Or if a wife religiously believed it was her duty to burn herself upon the funeral pile of her dead husband, would it be beyond the power of the civil government to prevent her carrying her belief into practice?

So here, as a law of the organization of society under the exclusive dominion of the United States, it is provided that plural marriages shall not be allowed. Can a man excuse his practices to the contrary because of his religious belief? To permit this would be to make the professed doctrines of religious belief superior to the law of the land, and in effect to permit every citizen to become a law unto himself. Government could exist only in name under such circumstances.

The only defence of the accused in this case is his belief that the law ought not have been enacted. It matters not that his belief was a part of his professed religion: it was still belief, and belief only.

In *Regina v. Wagstaff* (10 Cox Crim. Cases, 531), the parents of a sick child, who omitted to call in medical attendance because of their religious belief that what they did for its cure would be effective, were held not to be guilty of manslaughter, while it was said the contrary would have been the result if the child had actually been starved to death by the parents, under the notion that it was their religious duty to abstain from giving it food. But when the offence consists of a positive act which is knowingly done, it would be dangerous to hold that the offender might escape punishment because he religiously believed the law which he had broken ought never to have been made. No case, we believe, can be found that has gone so far.

6. As to that part of the charge which directed the attention of the jury to the consequences of polygamy.

The passage complained of is as follows: "I think it not improper, in the discharge of your duties in this case, that you should consider what are to be the consequences to the innocent victims of this delusion. As this contest goes on, they multiply, and there are pure-minded women and there are innocent children,—innocent in a sense even beyond the degree of the innocence of childhood itself. These are to be the sufferers; and as jurors fail to do their duty, and as these cases come up in the Territory of Utah, just so do these victims multiply and spread themselves over the land."

While every appeal by the court to the passions or the prejudices of a jury should be promptly rebuked, and while it is the imperative duty of a reviewing court to take care that wrong is not done in this way, we see no just cause for complaint in this case. Congress, in 1862 (12 Stat. 501), saw fit to make bigamy a crime in the Territories. This was done because of the evil consequences that were supposed to flow from plural marriages. All the court did was to call the attention of the jury to the peculiar character of the crime for which the accused was on trial, and to remind them of the duty they had to perform. There was no appeal to the passions, no instigation of prejudice. Upon the showing made by the accused himself, he was guilty of a violation of the law under which he had been indicted: and the effort of the court seems to have been not to withdraw the minds of the jury from the issue to be tried, but to bring them to it; not to make them partial, but to keep them impartial.

Upon a careful consideration of the whole case, we are satisfied that no error was committed by the court below.

Judgment affirmed.

Notes

1. On rehearing, the Court reversed the lower court for imposing a sentence at hard labor, a sentence contrary to the law by which Reynolds was convicted. A petition signed by 32,000 people requesting President Rutherford B. Hayes grant executive clemency to Reynolds because there was an agreement to suspend punishment in case of conviction was ignored. Reynolds spent over eighteen months in jail. Linford, at 339.

2. Because a criminal defendant was constitutionally entitled to a jury, and because the vast majority of prospective jurors were Mormons, for several years after *Reynolds*, polygamy prosecutions were relatively rare, and convictions even more rare.

Arrington & Bitton, at 180. One of those rare convictions was overturned by the Supreme Court, on the ground that admission of the testimony of the "second" wife was error, for she was presumptively the defendant's legal wife, and thus not a competent witness against her husband, the defendant, on the subject of the marriage of her husband to his "first" wife. *Miles v. United States*, 103 U.S. 304 (1881).

3. Chief Justice Waite's opinion relies heavily on Jefferson and Madison to interpret the First Amendment. He first discusses the defeat of the proposed general assessment in Virginia, attributing the defeat to Madison's *Memorial and Remonstrance* in opposition to the assessment, and then notes the passage of Jefferson's bill for religious freedom. Waite then quotes Jefferson's January 1, 1802 letter to the Danbury Baptist Association. As noted in Chapter Two, Jefferson's letter contrasts belief with action, and claims there is a "wall of separation" between church and state. About Jefferson's letter, Waite concludes:

> Coming as this does from an acknowledged leader of the advocates of the measure, it may be accepted almost as an authoritative declaration of the scope and effect of the amendment thus secured. Congress was deprived of all legislative power over mere opinion, but was left free to reach actions which were in violation of social duties or subversive of good order.

Is this "Jeffersonian" interpretation an accurate interpretation of the First Amendment?

It appears that Waite obtained this historical information from the American historian George Bancroft. Bruce R. Trimble, CHIEF JUSTICE WAITE 244–45 (1938). Does the nature of the secondary source for an historical account make a jurist's reading of history more or less plausible as a model for interpreting the First Amendment? At what level of generality is Waite's analysis?

4. In determining whether polygamy is "subversive," Waite concludes that polygamy is "odious among the northern and western nations of Europe." Is this a sufficient charge? Recall that early nineteenth century state courts discussing other issues of religious liberty used the example of polygamy to interpret restrictively state religious liberty provisions. Is Waite's evidence of contemporaneous history, that is, Virginia's decision to criminalize bigamy shortly after passage of the bill for religious freedom and its request for a bill of rights, convincing? Waite then cites "Professor Lieber," and "Chancellor Kent" in support of the proposition that polygamy "fetters the people in stationary despotism." Professor Lieber was Francis Lieber, a noted antebellum political scientist and emigrant from Germany. Chancellor Kent was James Kent, the New York judge who declared blasphemy a common law crime while concluding that Christianity was a part of the common law. *People v. Ruggles*, 8 Johnson 290 (N.Y. 1811), excerpted in Chapter Three. Are these authorities authoritative? What makes an authority "authoritative"?

5. Waite analogizes polygamy to human sacrifice and the Hindu practice of suttee, in which a widow is consumed in her husband's funeral pyre. Are these appropriate analogies? What if the sacrificial victim and Hindu widow "consent" to their deaths? Does the issue become, in the present, one of individual choice as opposed to state interference with individual choice? If Waite's examples are inappropriate, what analogies are appropriate?

6. The *Reynolds* decision has been the subject of much academic criticism. *See, e.g.*, Orma Linford, *The Mormons and the Law: The Polygamy Cases*, 9 Utah L. Rev. 308, 543 (1964–65)(in two parts). Should it be criticized? If so, should the criticism be based on the Court's interpretation of the history of the First Amendment, its rigid belief/conduct distinction (taken from Jefferson), its lack of understanding of "minority" or "out-

sider" religious faiths, or its attempt to "privilege" a particular understanding of Christianity in its opinion? Should such criticism instead focus on the particular impact on the Mormon Church?

In 1882, Congress passed, and President Chester A. Arthur signed into law, the Edmunds Act. The Edmunds Act amended the Anti-Bigamy Act of 1862 by declaring polygamy a felony, disfranchising polygamists, defining unlawful cohabitation, and barring polygamists from serving in office or as jurors. After the passage of the Act, the first sustained effort to eradicate polygamy in Utah began. Arrington & Bitton, at 181. In *Cannon v. United States*, 116 U.S. 55 (1885), the Supreme Court upheld a conviction for unlawfully cohabiting despite a lack of any evidence of sexual relations between the defendant and his second wife. Justices Samuel Miller and Stephen Field dissented on the ground that the lack of evidence of a sexual relationship prohibited a conviction. *Id.* at 79–80. *See also Snow v. United States*, 118 U.S. 346 (1885) (concluding Court was without jurisdiction to review conviction for violation of Edmunds Act). *Cf. In re Snow*, 120 U.S. 274 (1887) (granting habeas corpus petition and holding polygamy a continuous act permitting only one conviction).

Davis v. Beason

133 U.S. 333 (1890)

[Samuel D. Davis was charged with conspiring to violate Section 501 of the Revised Statutes of the Territory of Idaho, which forbade any bigamist, polygamist or person who taught, advised, counseled or encouraged one to become a bigamist or polygamist from holding office. Davis allegedly falsely swore an oath that he was not a bigamist, polygamist or person who advocated those doctrines.]

Mr. Justice FIELD[, after stating the facts,] delivered the opinion of the court.

On this appeal our only inquiry is whether the District Court of the Territory had jurisdiction of the offence charged in the indictment of which the defendant was found guilty. If it had jurisdiction, we can go no farther. [O]n this point there can be no serious discussion or difference of opinion. Bigamy and polygamy are crimes by the laws of all civilized and Christian countries. They are crimes by the laws of the United States, and they are crimes by the laws of Idaho. They tend to destroy the purity of the marriage relation, to disturb the peace of families, to degrade woman and to debase man. Few crimes are more pernicious to the best interests of society and receive more general or more deserved punishment. To extend exemption from punishment for such crimes would be to shock the moral judgment of the community. To call their advocacy a tenet of religion is to offend the common sense of mankind. If they are crimes, then to teach, advise and counsel their practice is to aid in their commission, and such teaching and counselling are themselves criminal and proper subjects of punishment, as aiding and abetting crime are in all other cases. The term "religion" has reference to one's views of his relations to his Creator, and to the obligations they impose of reverence for his being and character, and of obedience to his will. It is often confounded with the *cultus* or form of worship of a particular sect, but is distinguishable from the latter. The first amendment to the Constitution, in declaring that Congress shall make no law respecting the establishment of religion, or forbidding the free exercise thereof, was intended to allow every one under the jurisdiction of the United States to entertain such notions respecting his relations to his Maker and the duties they impose as may be approved by his judgment and conscience, and to exhibit his sentiments in such form of worship as he may think proper, not injurious to the equal rights of others, and to prohibit legislation for the support of any religious tenets, or the modes of worship of any sect. The oppressive measures adopted, and the cruelties and punishments inflicted by the governments of Europe for many ages, to compel parties to conform, in their religious beliefs and modes of worship, to the views of the most numerous sect, and the folly of attempting in that way to control the mental operations of persons, and enforce an outward conformity to a prescribed standard, led to the adoption of the amendment in question. It was never intended or supposed that the amendment could be invoked as a protection against legislation for the punishment of acts inimical to the peace, good order and morals of society. With man's relations to his Maker and the obligations he may think they impose, and the manner in which an expression shall be made by him of his belief on those subjects, no interference can be permitted, provided always the laws of society, designed to secure its peace and prosperity, and the morals of its people, are not interfered with. However free the exercise of religion may be, it must be subordinate to the criminal laws of the country, passed with reference to actions regarded by general consent as properly the subjects of punitive legislation. There have been sects which denied as a part of their religious tenets that there should be any marriage tie, and advocated promiscuous intercourse of the sexes as prompted by the passions of its members. And history discloses the fact that the necessity of human sacrifices, on special occasions, has been a tenet of many sects. Should a sect of either of these kinds ever find its way into this country, swift punishment would follow the carrying into effect of its doctrines, and no heed would be given to the pretence that, as religious beliefs, their supporters could be protected in their exercise by the Constitution of the United States. Probably never before in the history of this country has it been seriously contended that the whole punitive power of the government for acts, recognized by the general consent of the Christian world in modern times as proper matters for prohibitory legislation, must be suspended in order that the tenets of a religious sect encouraging crime may be carried out without hindrance.

[I]n *Murphy v. Ramsey*, 114 U.S. 15, 45, referring to the act of Congress excluding polygamists and bigamists from voting or holding office, the court, speaking by Mr. Justice Matthews, said: "Certainly no legislation can be supposed more wholesome and necessary in the founding of a free, self-governing commonwealth, fit to take rank as one of the coordinate States of the Union, than that which seeks to establish it on the basis of the idea of the family, as consisting in and springing from the union for life of one man and one woman in the holy estate of matrimony; the sure foundation of all that is stable and noble in our civilization; the best guaranty of that reverent morality which is the source of all beneficent progress in social and political improvement. And to this end no means are more directly and immediately suitable than those provided by this act, which endeavors to withdraw all political influence from those who are practically hostile to its attainment."

It is assumed by counsel of the petitioner, that because no mode of worship can be established or religious tenets enforced in this country, therefore any form of worship may be followed and any tenets, however destructive of society, may be held and advocated, if asserted to be a part of the religious doctrines of those advocating and practising them. But nothing is further from the truth. Whilst legislation for the establishment of a religion is forbidden, and its free exercise permitted, it does not follow that everything which may be so called can be tolerated. Crime is not the less odious because sanctioned by what any particular sect may designate as religion.

In our judgment, § 501 of the Revised Statutes of Idaho Territory is not open to any constitutional or legal objection.

The judgment of the court below is therefore

Affirmed.

Notes

1. Justice Field defines religion as referring "to one's views of his relations to his Creator, and to the obligations they impose of reverence for his being and character, and of obedience to his will." Does this theistic definition appear to reflect the idea of religion as understood by the framers? Even if it does, is this definition now outmoded? How do we ascertain when a definition has become "outmoded?" *See* Chapter Thirteen.

2. Field also accepts the clear distinction between belief and action, concluding that "[i]t was never intended or supposed that the [first] amendment could be invoked as a protection against legislation for the punishment of acts inimical to the peace, good order and morals of society." Is this consistent with the view taken by state courts in the late nineteenth century? With earlier decisions of state courts? With the constitutional language adopted by the states in the eighteenth and nineteenth centuries? Is Field implicitly suggesting that actions not inimical to society may be protected by the First Amendment? In addition, Field contends that state sanction for acts "recognized by the general consent of the Christian world in modern times as proper matters for prohibitory legislation"is always permissible. Is this statement an acknowledgment that some diffuse notion of Christianity undergirds the state? Why didn't this idea raise establishment clause concerns? Would it raise such concerns today?

3. *Murphy v. Ramsey*, 114 U.S. 15 (1885), cited in *Davis v. Beason*, involved the legality of actions by the Utah Commission in requiring a test oath for those registering to vote. The Edmunds Act disfranchised all polygamists, and the Commission was appointed to oversee the appointment of voting registration officials. The test oath required the applicant to swear he or she was not a bigamist or polygamist. The Court concluded the test oath was unauthorized by the Edmunds Act, and appeared to forbid the application of the Act against those who were polygamists or bigamists before, but not after, the passage of the Edmunds Act.

4. Justice Field wrote the opinions in both *Cummings v. Missouri* and *Davis v. Beason*. Are they consistent? In *Cummings*, Field stated that the Court was required to look beyond the form of the law to its substance. Does Field arbitrarily limit his authority in *Davis v. Beason* to determining jurisdiction? Is that a consequence of his feelings about the practice of polygamy? About societal norms concerning polygamy?

5. A test oath passed by the Idaho state legislature was held constitutional in *Shepherd v. Grimmett*, 31 P. 793 (Idaho 1892). This statute was even more restrictive than the Territorial statute upheld in *Davis v. Beason*. The only case holding a law disfranchising Mormons unconstitutional is *State* ex rel. *Whitney v. Findley*, 19 P. 241 (Nev. 1888), which relied on the Nevada constitution.

6. In *The Late Corp. of the Church of Jesus Christ of Latter Day Saints v. United States*, 136 U.S. 1 (1890), a divided Supreme Court held constitutional the Edmunds-Tucker Act of 1887, by which Congress effectively dissolved the corporation of the Mormon Church. In an opinion by Justice Joseph Bradley, the Court noted the continuing efforts of Mormons "in preaching, upholding, promoting and defending" polygamy. The opinion continued:

> The existence of such a propaganda is a blot on our civilization. The organization of a community for the spread and practice of polygamy is, in a measure, a return to barbarism. It is contrary to the spirit of Christianity and of the civilization which Christianity has produced in the Western World.

Id. at 49.

Congress passed the 1887 Act to force individual Mormons to comply with the Anti-Bigamy Act and to prevent the Church from organizing or supporting the practice of polygamy. Any church property valued in excess of $50,000 was to be taken by the government and used to finance non-Mormon schools in the Territory of Utah.

7. Three months after this decision was handed down, on September 25, 1890, Church President Wilford Woodruff issued what came to be known as the Manifesto, which states in part:

> OFFICIAL DECLARATION—1
>
> To Whom It May Concern:
>
> Press dispatches having been sent for political purposes, from Salt Lake City, which have been widely published, to the effect that the Utah Commission, in their recent report to the Secretary of the Interior, allege that plural marriages are still being solemnized and that forty or more such marriages have been contracted in Utah since last June or during the past year, also that in public discourses the leaders of the Church have taught, encouraged and urged the continuance of the practice of polygamy—
>
> I, therefore, as President of the Church of Jesus Christ of Latter-day Saints, do hereby, in the most solemn manner, declare that these charges are false. We are not teaching polygamy or plural marriage, nor permitting any person to enter into its practice, and I deny that either forty or any other number of plural marriages have during that period been solemnized in our Temples or in any other place in the Territory.
>
> One case has been reported, in which the parties allege that the marriage was performed in the Endowment House, in Salt Lake City, in the Spring of 1889, but I have not been able to learn who performed the ceremony; whatever was done in the this matter was without my knowledge. In consequence of this alleged occurrence the Endowment House was, by instructions, taken down without delay.
>
> Inasmuch as laws have been enacted by Congress forbidding plural marriages, which laws have been pronounced constitutional by the court of last resort, I hereby declare my intention to submit to those laws, and to use my influence with the members of the Church over which I preside to have them do likewise.
>
> There is nothing in my teachings to the Church or in those of my associates, during the time specified, which can be reasonably construed to inculcate or encourage polygamy; and when any Elder of the Church has used language which appeared to convey any such teaching, he has been promptly reproved. And I now publicly declare that my advice to the Latter-day Saints is to refrain from contracting any marriage forbidden by the law of the land.

The Doctrine and Covenants of the Church of Jesus Christ of Latter-day Saints 291–92 (1981).

On October 6, 1890, the Manifesto was unanimously sustained by the general conference of the church. In 1893, Congress passed a joint resolution ordering the return to the Church of its personal property, and the Supreme Court remanded litigation between the Church and the United States for action consistent with the resolution. Linford at 580. In 1896, Utah entered the Union as a State, and shortly thereafter, the Church's real property was returned to it. *Id.*

D. The Collapse of the *de Facto* Establishment

1. Prohibition

Eliminating the harmful effects of intoxicants by prohibiting the sale or manufacture of alcohol was long a goal of Protestant reformers. The first temperance effort begin in New England in the 1840s, and though initially successful, temperance laws were repealed in most states shortly after the Civil War. The second effort began in the 1870s, and was driven by Frances Willard, who was long associated with the Women's Christian Temperance Union (WCTU). In 1884, Willard urged the WCTU to support the Prohibition party. Although women were prohibited from voting, Willard was accused of siphoning enough votes from the Republican presidential candidate, James G. Blaine, to give victory to the Democrat Grover Cleveland. The final effort began with the formation in 1893 of the Anti-Saloon League. Although only three states were "dry" in 1903, two-thirds of all states were under some prohibition scheme by 1916. Sydney E. Ahlstrom, A Religious History of the American People 870 (1972). Prohibition was, according to the historian of religion Sydney Ahlstrom, "the great Protestant crusade of the twentieth century," unifying both Social Gospellers and Fundamentals. *Id.* at 901.

The extent of the ban on intoxicating liquors differed greatly. Several states proudly declared themselves "bone dry" states. In one such state, Oklahoma, the issue of the use of wine in religious services arose. In *De Hasque v. Atchison, T. & S. F. Ry. Co.*, 173 P. 73 (Okla. 1918), a Catholic priest sued to compel the railway to ship sacramental wine within the state. Based on a literal reading of Oklahoma law, the trial court held that Oklahoma's constitutional provision barring the shipping of intoxicating liquors included sacramental wine. The Supreme Court of Oklahoma reversed, holding that the meaning of the constitutional provision was determined not by a literal interpretation of Oklahoma law, but by the "evil which it was designed to remedy." *Id.* at 75. The court extensively borrowed from Justice Brewer's *Church of the Holy Trinity* opinion in support of its conclusion that the evil was not "the sacred use of wine in the sacramental service." *Id.* Consequently, wine used for sacramental purposes was not included within the meaning of "intoxicating liquors" in the Oklahoma Constitution. *Id.* at 78.

In December 1917, the Congress voted to send to the states an amendment prohibiting "the manufacture, sale, or transportation of intoxicating liquors." A little more than a year later, prohibition became a part of the Constitution with the adoption of the Eighteenth Amendment. Over President Woodrow Wilson's veto, Congress passed the Volstead Act implementing the Amendment, and prohibition became a reality in January 1920. Unlike the law in Oklahoma, the Volstead Act specifically exempted from prohibition the manufacture, sale or transportation of wine used "for sacramental purposes, or like religious rites." 41 Stats. 311. However, the manufacturer of such wine was required to obtain a permit to engage in such manufacture, and failure to obtain this permit subjected the manufacturer to the confiscation of the wine. Additionally, the commissioner was given the sole discretionary power to determine whether to issue a permit to a "rabbi, minister, or priest to supervise the manufacture of wine to be used for the purposes and rites in this section." *Id.*

Although the 1928 candidacy for President of the "wet" Catholic Democrat Alfred Smith was fatally wounded by Prohibition forces, support for Prohibition weakened as the United States entered the Great Depression. National prohibition was repealed in 1933 with the ratification of the Twenty-first Amendment.

2. Evolution, the *Scopes* Trial and Religion in the 1920s

The 1920s, the decade between the end of World War I and the beginning of the Great Depression, were a time of rapid technological, social and intellectual change. The era of "normalcy" proclaimed by incoming President Warren G. Harding was anything but. The 1920s was both the Age of the Harlem Renaissance and the Age of the revival of the Ku Klux Klan, the era of urbanization and, with the popularity of the automobile, the emerging era of suburbanization, and within Protestantism, the era of both Modernism and Fundamentalism.

As noted at the beginning of this chapter, a number of states passed laws mandating Bible reading in the public schools during the 1910s and 1920s. The effort of the state of Oregon to forbid parents from sending their children to private or sectarian schools, held unconstitutional by the Supreme Court in *Pierce v. Society of Sisters*, 268 U.S. 510 (1925), excerpted in Chapter Six, was simply the most successful of several efforts to outlaw religious education. These efforts, however, paled in comparison with the publicity accorded statutes prohibiting the teaching of evolution in the public schools.

The Darwinian revolution split Protestantism along modernist and fundamentalist lines. Modernists accepted Darwin's theory of evolution, and accepted the Christian Bible not for its literal truth, but for its deeper truths regarding Christianity; fundamentalists rejected Darwin, and, as their name implied, returned to the fundamental belief in the inerrancy of the Bible.

In early 1921, William Jennings Bryan, the populist Nebraskan, thrice-nominated Democratic candidate for President, former Secretary of State, and tireless orator, began giving a speech titled, "The Menace of Darwinism." Edward J. Larson, TRIAL AND ERROR: THE AMERICAN CONTROVERSY OVER CREATION AND EVOLUTION 45 (updated ed. 1989). For Bryan, Darwinism was harmful for several reasons. Darwinism led people away from God and toward materialism, and the result was a decline in morality. *Id.* at 46–47. Additionally, Bryan feared *social* Darwinism, the application of the idea of survival of the fittest to society. Garry Wills, UNDER GOD: RELIGION AND AMERICAN POLITICS 101 (1990). Third, Bryan, the former Secretary of State, believed there was a connection between German militarism (the cause of World War I) and Darwin's thought. More particularly, Bryan saw a connection between Darwin and the German philosopher, the nihilist Friedrich Nietzsche. Nietzsche pronounced the death of God and called for the rise of a Superman who embraced the will to power. *See* George E. Webb, THE EVOLUTION CONTROVERSY IN AMERICA 66–67 (1994).

Bryan proposed "neutrality" regarding the origins of life. If, as appropriate, the Biblical story recounted in Genesis could not be taught, then it was appropriate to bar teachings which attacked the Biblical story. Larson, at 47–48.

Beginning later that year, the crusade against evolution began. In January 1922, legislation outlawing the teaching of evolution was introduced in the Kentucky legislature. Due largely to the work of University of Kentucky President Frank L. McVey, the legislation failed. Webb, at 73.

In 1923, with little fanfare, and without the knowledge of Bryan, the state of Oklahoma passed the first statute concerning the teaching of Darwinism. The statute provided free textbooks to all elementary schoolchildren, but barred the purchase of any books mentioning Darwinism. The law, however, was repealed in 1925, for reasons unrelated to the purpose of the rider concerning Darwinism. The only other state to adopt an anti-evolution stance in 1923 was Florida, Bryan's adopted state. The Florida legislature, at Bryan's suggestion, passed a resolution prohibiting the teaching of Darwinism. The resolution contained no criminal penalty for violating the law, and barred only books that taught evolution as true. *Id.* at 52–53.

Two years later, Tennessee passed its anti-evolution law, which stated in part: "[I]t shall be unlawful for any teacher to teach any theory that denies the Story of Divine Creation of man as taught in the Bible, and to teach instead that man has descended from a lower order of animal." *Id.* at 54. Unlike the Florida resolution, the Tennessee law provided a criminal sanction for its violation. Governor Peay, while doubting it would ever be enforced, signed the bill into law. Four months later, it would be tested in one of the most famous cases in American legal history. Representing the World's Christian Fundamentals Association and acting as special prosecutor for the state was William Jennings Bryan. Defending John T. Scopes, the teacher who had agreed to be criminally prosecuted for violating the Tennessee act, was Clarence Darrow. The organization that advertised for a test case was the American Civil Liberties Union (ACLU), then a new and small civil liberties organization.

It may be appropriate that nearly everything about the story of the *Scopes* case is surreal. John Scopes was a football coach and physics teacher at Dayton High, not a biology teacher. He had taught several biology classes when the high school principal, who regularly taught biology, was ill, but he did not recall actually teaching evolution in class. Because the City of Dayton was vying with others for the honor of holding the trial to determine the statute's constitutionality, this factual impediment failed to impede them. Although the ACLU did not want Clarence Darrow to try the case, nor to try it in state court, he did try it, and he did try it in state court. The court, apparently oblivious of its import, began each day of the trial with a Christian prayer offered by a local fundamentalist minister. Of the eight or so days of trial, the jury spent a total of approximately one hour listening to testimony. Bizarrely, opposing counsel Bryan agreed to be called as an expert witness on the Bible and examined by Darrow. Although the jury was absent from the courtroom during this examination (later ruled inadmissible by the court), the press was at hand, and members of the press wrote dispatches concluding that Bryan was thoroughly trounced by Darrow during their ninety-six minute exchange. To avoid a closing argument by Bryan, Darrow asked the court to instruct the jury to find his client guilty. After nine minutes of deliberation, the jury did as Darrow suggested. Because it did not return a sentence, the court, as customary when the jury did not impose a sentence, imposed the minimum fine, $100. Less than a week after the conclusion of the trial, Bryan died.

On appeal, the Tennessee Supreme Court held constitutional the anti-evolution statute, but reversed Scopes's conviction based on the fiction that the trial judge had imposed the $100 fine rather than the jury, in violation of Tennessee law. *Scopes v. State*, 289 S.W. 363 (1927). Scopes, who had accepted a fellowship at the University of Chicago, was not further prosecuted.

For the northern press, the *Scopes* trial symbolized the "backwards" resistance of fundamentalists to modernism. The "lesson" learned from the trial, according to the press, was that the forces of progress (secular modernism) had routed the forces of superstition (religious fundamentalism), and the most prominent member of the press reporting from Dayton was H.L. Mencken. It was Mencken who continually championed the cause of the defense, and who acted as Darrow's "Consulting Man" during the trial, Wills, at 109, and who proclaimed Darrow's annihilation of Bryan's views during that famous cross-examination, an opinion unthinkingly adopted for over fifty years. It was also Mencken who "relentlessly ridiculed Bryan" in widely reprinted editorials. Larson, at 72.

Both Mencken and Darrow were ardent social Darwinists. In 1908, Mencken published The Philosophy of Friedrich Nietzsche, in which he argued that the Nietzschean superman was an example of the survival of the fittest. Wills, at 101–02. He was the leading popularizer of Nietzsche in the United States. Kevin Tierney, Darrow: A Biography 367 (1979). For Darrow, "Nietzsche struck a chord of theoretical sympathy." *Id.* at 74. In Garry Wills's estimation, Darrow was "an enthusiastic Nietzschean of the Mencken sort. He had a stock Nietzsche lecture that he took out on the Chautauqua lecture circuit when he needed money." Wills, at 106.

In its effort to impugn Bryan and portray the *Scopes* trial as symbolic of the battle between scientific progress and superstitious nonsense, the press, including Mencken, forgot that the anti-evolution law was also symbolic of the battle between social Darwinism, which ridiculed reform efforts and the responsibility of one for the welfare of another, and a morality championed by Bryan, among others, that all persons were bound by a duty to God to aid all those less fortunate than themselves.

For fundamentalists, "[t]he ridicule heaped on Bryan at the Scopes trial in Tennessee in 1925 and his subsequent sudden death marked a turning point for the movement. It quickly lost its position as a nationally influential coalition." George M. Marsden, Fundamentalism and American Culture: The Shaping of Twentieth-Century Evangelicalism, 1870–1925 6 (1980). Although a number of states introduced anti-evolution bills in the three years after Bryan's death, only two states, Mississippi and Arkansas, enacted such bills. Larson, at 72–81. No legislation prohibiting the teaching of evolution would be introduced for thirty years. *Id.* at 81.

For modernists, the result was no better. Textbook publishers downplayed or eliminated references to evolution in biology books. In one estimation, "as far as teaching biology in the high schools was concerned, [evolutionists] had not won; they had lost. Not only did they lose, but they did not even know they had lost." Judith V. Grabiner and Peter D. Miller, *Effects of the Scopes Trial*, 185 Science 832, 836 (September 6, 1974). Although the modernist victory was re-proclaimed in the play (and later a 1960 movie) *Inherit the Wind*, the refusal of evolutionists to attempt to understand the opposition to the teaching of evolution in the public schools would eventually result in a renewed campaign against evolution. In the 1960s, in an effort to preempt this campaign, the constitutionality of the "Monkey Law" would again be tested. *See* Chapter Ten § B.

Chapter 5

The Contours of the Religious Freedom Guarantee

A. Introduction

The religious liberty guarantee in the United States is best understood as a framework in which "the People of the United States" have divided the power and responsibility to protect religious freedom between the States and the federal government. In order to understand that framework, and to grasp the dynamic nature of the relationships it creates, a student needs a firm grasp of historical materials set out in Chapters Two, Three and Four. They are the foundation upon which the American law of religious liberty has been built by State constitutional and statute law, by the decisions of the Supreme Court of the United States, and by the laws and treaties adopted by the United States Congress.

The goal of this chapter is to draw the many strands of the law governing religious liberty in the United States into a coherent overview. Because the conceptual structure is taken directly from the First and Fourteenth Amendments to the Constitution of the United States, the emphasis is on federal law. State and international materials are included when they illustrate differences in approach or emphasis.

B. The Legal Framework

1. The Starting Point: State Constitutions and Laws Protecting Religious Liberty

State laws governing religious liberty were well developed by the time of the Constitutional Convention in 1787, and the materials in Chapter Two show how the demographics, political character, and history of the States affected not only the approach that each took to religious liberty questions, but also the attitudes their delegates brought to the Constitutional Convention. State law thus formed the backdrop against which the debate over religious liberty took place at the Convention, and in the subsequent ratification debates in the states.

The Constitution drafted in Philadelphia barred the use of a religious test as "a qualification to any office or public trust under the United States", U.S. Const. Art. VI, cl. 3, but lacked a Bill of Rights. The presence of the "No Religious Test" provision was thought by some of the framers to be enough for a federal government of limited powers, but it was not enough for many anti-Federalists and for some of the States. Chapter Two recounts that ratification by several of the States was accompanied by a request for a Bill of Rights that would limit the scope of federal power. *Cf. M'Culloch v. Maryland,* 17 U.S. (4 Wheat.) 316, 421 (1819) ("Let the end be legitimate, let it be within the scope of the constitution, and all means which are appropriate, which are plainly adapted to that end, which are not prohibited, but consist with the letter and spirit of the constitution, are constitutional"). One of the primary concerns of those who opposed the Constitution was its lack of a Bill of Rights. Professor Gerard Bradley has observed that the Federalists "drew a nonestablishment sum from the lack of federal jurisdiction over religion plus the test ban," and asserted that "since the oath requirement was the only plausible power one sect might use to gain the upper hand," Article VI was "enough [of a religious liberty guarantee] for a federal government of specific enumerated powers." Gerard Bradley, *The No Religious Test Clause and the Constitution of Religious Liberty: A Machine that Has Gone of Itself,* 37 Case W. Res. L Rev. 674 (1987) *See* Chart 1-2.

This was not enough for either the anti-Federalists (many of whom viewed the Test and Supremacy Clauses as threats to religious liberty) or the States, for it did not state explicitly that the federal government had no enumerated power either to vex religious liberty directly or to set national policy on the subject. "The Address and Reasons of Dissent of the Minority of the convention of Pennsylvania to their Constituents" (December 18, 1787) made the case as follows:

> We entered on the examination of the proposed system of government, and found it to be such as we could not adopt, without, as we conceived, surrendering up your dearest rights. We offered our objections to the convention, and opposed those parts of the plan, which, in our opinion, would be injurious to you, in the best manner we were able; and closed our arguments by offering the following propositions to the convention.
>
> 1. The right of conscience shall be held inviolable, and neither the legislative, executive nor judicial powers of the United States shall have authority to alter, abrogate, or infringe any part of the constitution of the several states, which provide for the preservation of liberty in matters of religion.
>
> 6. That the people have a-right to the freedom of speech, of writing and publishing their sentiments, therefore, the freedom of the press shall not be restrained by any law of the United States.

THE ANTI-FEDERALIST PAPERS AND THE CONSTITUTIONAL CONVENTION DEBATES 239 (Ralph Ketcham, ed, 1986) (attributed to Samuel Bryan, the author of "Centinel").

The substantive and structural provisions of the Bill of Rights reflect those concerns, and leave the States free to adopt and enforce protections that go "beyond" the protection afforded by federal law. State constitutions and statutes thus form a conceptual "bracket" around the federal religious liberty guarantee, and provide a source of additional protection when the federal guarantee is unavailable. *See generally* Angela C. Carmella, *State Constitutional Protection of Religious Liberty: An Emerging Post-*Smith *Jurisprudence,* 1993 B.Y.U. L. Rev. 275. The adoption by several states of Religious Freedom Restoration Acts after the Supreme Court held the federal Religious Freedom Restoration Act (RFRA) unconstitutional in *City of Boerne v. Flores,* 521 U.S. 507 (1997), excerpted in § K below, is one such example. *See also* Chapter Six.

2. The United States Constitution: Text and Structure

The federal Constitution allocates power. The first three Articles confer and allocate powers among the three branches of the federal government, and limit the scope of state authority over matters placed under federal control. Articles IV and V regulate the relationships of the States to one another, and to the federal government. Article VI makes the Constitution "the supreme Law of the Land," binding on all officials, both State and federal.

a) The "No Religious Test" Clause (1787)

The only explicit mention of religion in the Constitution of 1787 is the No Religious Test Clause of Article VI: "no religious Test shall ever be required as a Qualification to any Office or public Trust under the United States." The Test Clause is an important affirmation of the principle of equal citizenship. It is discussed in detail in Chapter Eight, Section G(1), and briefly in Section F below.

b) The Bill of Rights (1791)

The Bill of Rights, ratified in 1791, added both substantive and structural protections to the baseline provided by the Test Clause. Chapter Two recounts the extensive debates during ratification over the extent to which the federal government could use its powers to set policy regarding religious liberty. The adoption of the Bill of Rights ended that debate. The First, Ninth and Tenth Amendments make explicit the position that Congress has no authority to infringe upon either the religious liberty of individuals, or the power of States to set what they consider to be the proper boundaries between church and state.

The interplay between these substantive and structural guarantees is explicit in the text of the first amendment:

> Congress shall make no law respecting an establishment of religion, or prohibiting the free exercise thereof; or abridging the freedom of speech, or of the press; or the right of the people peaceably to assemble, and to petition the Government for a redress of grievances.

The "structural" aspect of the first amendment is embedded in its first word: "Congress." *See* Mark P. Denbeaux, *The First Word of the First Amendment,* 80 Nw. U. L. Rev. 1156 (1986). Although it is "Congress" that "shall make no law," the amendment also implicitly limits the authority of the executive and judicial branches to act in a manner that would violate the amendment. *See* Robert A. Destro, *The Structure of the Religious Liberty Guarantee,* 11 J. L. & Religion 355 (1994). The "substantive" components of First Amendment—the rights protected—are the subjects of each of its clauses, including the Religion Clause itself: "respecting an establishment of religion, or prohibiting the free exercise thereof." The Ninth and Tenth Amendments are rules of construction for the Constitution and Bill of Rights. Each makes explicit that which is implicit in the text of the Constitution itself: the substantive rights enumerated in the amended Constitution do not necessarily preempt rights recognized in state law, or limit either the power of the States, or of the people, to recognize new ones. *Compare* Treaty of Amsterdam amending Treaty of European Union, "Declaration on the Status of Churches and Non-confessional Organisations," OJ 1997 C340/133 ("The European Union respects and does not prejudice the status under national law of churches and religious associations or communities in the Member States. The European Union equally respects the status of philosophical and non-confessional organisations.").

c) The Fourteenth Amendment (1868)

Adopted in the aftermath of the Civil War, the Fourteenth Amendment provides, in relevant part:

> *Section* 1. All persons born or naturalized in the United States, and subject to the jurisdiction thereof, are citizens of the United States and of the State wherein they reside. No State shall make or enforce any law which shall abridge the privileges or immunities of citizens of the United States; nor shall any State deprive any person of life, liberty, or property, without due process of law; nor deny to any person within its jurisdiction the equal protection of the laws.
>
> *Section* 5. The Congress shall have power to enforce, by appropriate legislation, the provisions of this article.

The Fourteenth Amendment does not specifically mention religious liberty. It does, however, expressly recognize the power of Congress to protect the rights of citizens and other persons subject to the jurisdiction of the United States. The explicit reference to state citizenship also reaffirms the States' authority to legislate concerning the rights of their respective citizens and legal residents. *See generally* Robert A. Destro, *"By What Right?": The Sources and Limits of Federal Court and Congressional Jurisdiction Over Matters "Touching Religion,"* 29 Ind. L. Rev. 1, 36–48 (1995).

3. The "Incorporation Doctrine": Relating the Text of the First Amendment to the Text and Structure of the Fourteenth

Is it possible to "apply" the First Amendment to the States? In the antebellum case of *Permoli v. Municipality No. 1 of the City of New Orleans*, 44 U.S. (3 How.) 589, 609 (1845), excerpted in Chapter Three, the Supreme Court of the United States held that the answer is no. With the ratification of the Fourteenth Amendment in 1868, however, it became possible to argue that the provisions of the Bill of Rights were among "the privileges or immunities of citizens of the United States", and thus binding on the States.

The Supreme Court rejected this argument in the *Slaughterhouse Cases*, 83 U.S. (16 Wall.) 36 (1872), but it did leave open the possibility that the First Amendment might someday be applied to the States. In its view, the Fourteenth Amendment protects (or "incorporates") rights "which are *fundamental*," and illustrated its point by referring to two of the rights protected by the First Amendment: peaceable assembly and petition for redress of grievances. Over the course of the next fifty years, it would often base its decisions on the "fundamental rights" of those challenging State laws, but it would not reconsider the application of the Bill of Rights to the States until 1937.

The Court's decision in *Palko v. Connecticut*, 302 U.S. 319 (1937), marks the beginning of the "Incorporation Doctrine" as we know it today. Its approach, called "selective incorporation," rests on the Court's view that the "liberty" protected by the Due Process Clause of the Fourteenth Amendment incorporates the "fundamental rights" contained in the Bill of Rights, and makes them applicable to the States. Those which are not characterized as "fundamental" are simply rules governing the conduct of the federal government.

Palko was a criminal case, so its specific holding is not relevant here, but the Court's opinion does declare in dictum that religious liberty is a right "so rooted in the traditions and conscience of our people as to be ranked as fundamental." The case thus raises at least two significant questions relevant to the present inquiry: 1) What other rights enumerated in the Bill of Rights are "fundamental"? and 2) Which of these rights takes priority when there is an apparent conflict?

The Court's opinion in *Palko* does not answer these questions directly, but its "selective" approach implicitly adopts the view that there is "an implied hierarchy of constitutional values." Mary Ann Glendon & Raul F. Yanes, *Structural Free Exercise*, 90 Mich. L Rev 477, 479–482 (1991). Otherwise, the Court would have characterized *all* the rights enumerated in the Bill of Rights as "fundamental."

The Incorporation Doctrine also raises two important "structural" questions. The first is *federalism*, which governs the extent to which the federal government, including the Court, may regulate state action alleged to infringe "fundamental rights." The second is *separation of powers*, which affects the distribution of the power to decide whether a right is "fundamental" among the three branches of the federal government.

In *Palko* the Court asserts that it has the power to decide which rights are fundamental, but also implies that Congress, which is given explicit power in Section 5 to enforce the Fourteenth Amendment, may have a similar power. That claim of Congressional authority is controversial. *See City of Boerne v. Flores*, 521 U.S. 507 (1997), excerpted in Section K below.

The Court incorporated the free exercise guarantee in *Cantwell v. Connecticut*, 310 U.S. 296 (1940), and the non-establishment guarantee in *Everson v. Board of Education*, 330 U.S. 1 (1947). The full implications of the Incorporation Doctrine remain to be worked out in the context of religious liberty, but the *fact* of incorporation is no longer open to serious question. Writing for the Court in *Wallace v Jaffree*, 472 U.S. 38, 49 (1985), Justice John Paul Stevens described the incorporation of the First Amendment as an "elementary proposition of law."

With this background in mind, it is now time to look carefully at some of the relationships that arise as a result of incorporation.

4. Envisioning the Structure of the Religious Liberty Guarantee

Because the Bill of Rights applies to the States *through* the Fourteenth Amendment, the jurisprudence of the "incorporated" First Amendment is enormously complex. The text and structure of the Fourteenth Amendment, not the First, is the starting point for the discussion. Professor Akhil Amar observes:

> [T]he Fourteenth Amendment itself often seems to drop out of the analysis [of the Bill of Rights]. We appear to be applying the Bill of Rights directly; the Civil War Amendment is mentioned only in passing or not at all. Like people

> with spectacles who often forget they are wearing them, most lawyers read the Bill of Rights through the lens of the Fourteenth Amendment without realizing how powerfully that lens has refracted what they see.

Akhil R. Amar, *The Bill of Rights as a Constitution*, 100 Yale L.J. 1131, 1136–37 (1991).

The flowchart that follows is an attempt to capture, in graphical form, the following foundational elements of the case law:

- The textual elements—or "clauses"—of the "pre-incorporation" First Amendment.
- The branches of government bound by the Test Clause of Article VI and the pre-incorporation First Amendment.
- The textual elements of Sections One and Five of the Fourteenth Amendment.
- The textual elements—or "clauses"—of Section One of the Fourteenth Amendment.
- The Congressional and State powers affirmed and limited by the Fourteenth Amendment.
- The relationship between state and federal authority under the Fourteenth Amendment, including the impact of federal civil rights legislation on the ability of individuals and groups to bring First Amendment claims pursuant to the general federal civil rights enforcement statute, 42 U.S.C. § 1983.
- The relationship between Congressional and Judicial power under the Fourteenth Amendment.
- The cases in which the Court begins to define the rules embodied in the clauses of the First Amendment.

The organization of the materials in this Chapter follows the basic conceptual structure of the chart.

Thus far, we have looked at the text and constitutional structures that, together, make up the "Religious Liberty Guarantee." We now turn to the case law. As you read each case, consider the following questions.

- Would interpretation of each clause of the First Amendment be any different if the Court had used the Citizenship or Privileges and Immunities Clause as the basis for incorporation?
- How should the Citizenship, Privileges and Immunities, and Equal Protection Clauses affect the Court's reading of the "incorporated" First Amendment?

Chart 5-1
The "Structural" First Amendment

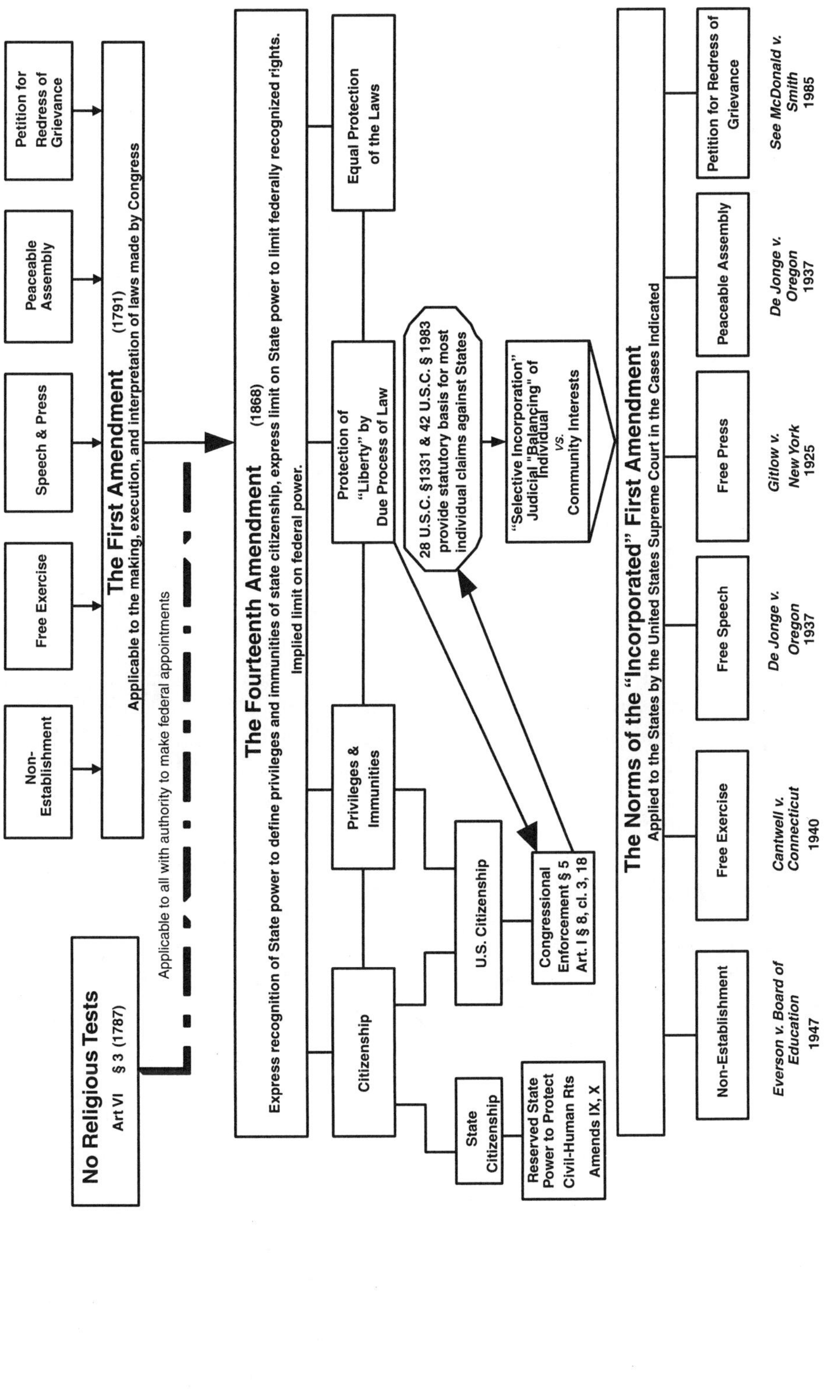

C. The Constitutional Framework

This section is divided into eight parts:

- The Concept of Free Exercise
- Laws "Respecting an Establishment of Religion"
- Religious Freedom and the Ban on Religious Tests
- Freedom of Religious Speech
- Equal Protection as an Aspect of the Religious Liberty Guarantee
- Religious Freedom and Peaceable Assembly
- Religious Freedom and the Right to Petition for Redress of Grievances
- Religious Freedom, Separation of Powers, and Federalism

Chapter One points out that the first task facing a Court asked to review a First Amendment claim is to determine which of its "clauses" applies. In cases involving religion, it is often the case that several may apply. Understanding how the Court "characterized the case" for purposes of analysis is an essential element in understanding what it has decided. There is substantial disagreement among the members of the Court concerning the "proper" meaning of the Religion Clause, and the result is often a marked contrast between the characterization of the issues in the majority, concurring, and dissenting opinions. Even when they agree on the character of the issues to be decided, there are often significant differences among the Justices on the balance that should be struck among the competing parties and interests.

In most cases, we have adopted the characterization used by the majority opinion, and placed the case in that section of the book. Almost all of the decisions of the Supreme Court in this area of constitutional law have been thoroughly criticized by academic commentators, and their reasons are as disparate as they are numerous. The criticism reflects not merely the desire of academics to be contrary, but the contentiousness of the subject matter.

The cases selected are intended to give the student a thorough introduction to the often-meandering and occasionally contradictory course of the Supreme Court's jurisprudence interpreting the Religious Liberty Guarantee. Although quite lengthy, this chapter is introductory only. Specific issues concerning the relation of law, religion and government, are discussed in detail in succeeding chapters. The Supreme Court has addressed some of these issues in detail, and ignored others.

D. The Religious Liberty Guarantee in the Supreme Court of the United States: The Concept of "Free Exercise"

1. "Free Exercise of Religion"

"Free exercise of religion" is a multi-faceted concept. The Second Vatican Council of the Roman Catholic Church (Vatican II) referred to the free exercise of religion as an aspect of the basic human desire "to seek the truth in matters religious in order that [persons] may with prudence form for [themselves] right and true judgments of conscience, under use of all suitable means." Viewed as a matter of individual right, the concept of "free exercise" presupposes that religious liberty has the formative, individual, and communal components summarized in Article 18 of the International Covenant on Civil and Political Rights (ICCPR), ratified by the United States:

1. Everyone shall have the right to freedom of thought, conscience and religion. This right shall include freedom to have or to adopt a religion or belief of his choice, and freedom, either individually or in community with others and in public or private, to manifest his religion or belief in worship, observance, practice and teaching.
2. No one shall be subject to coercion which would impair his freedom to have or to adopt a religion or belief of his choice.
3. Freedom to manifest one's religion or beliefs may be subject only to such limitations as are prescribed by law and are necessary to protect public safety order, health, or morals or the fundamental rights and freedoms of others.
4. The States Parties to the present Covenant undertake to have respect for the liberty of parents and, when applicable, legal guardians to ensure the religious and moral education of their children in conformity with their own convictions.

James Madison offered a more expansive conception of "free exercise of religion" in his *Memorial & Remonstrance Against Religious Assessments*, excerpted in Chapter Two. Religious liberty is the inalienable right "of every man to exercise it as these may dictate," but is an outgrowth of the respect that the *political* community owes to each of its members. For Madison, the protection of religious liberty is a natural outgrowth of an enlightened public policy that protects "every Citizen in the enjoyment of his Religion with the same equal hand which protects his person and his property."

Each of these approaches animates the debate over the meaning of the religious liberty guarantee. The Court's understanding of the concept of "religion" is strikingly similar to that described in Vatican II. *See* Chapter Thirteen. The basic principles of the ICCPR are firmly embedded in both State and federal law. So too is Madison's insight that the protection of religious liberty is both a political function, and an indispensable component of the concept of equal citizenship.

2. Community Demographics: Majority Rule and Protection of Minority Religious Communities

Chapters Two through Four illustrate the close relationship between religious liberty and the ethnic, cultural, political, and religious demographics of the community. Accommodation claims are inevitable in communities undergoing cultural or demographic change, and are often controversial. The social and legal cultures of most local communities were largely Protestant Christian in their origin and orientation, so it should not be surprising that some of the early State constitutions spoke in explicitly Christian terms.

At the turn of the twenty-first century, the United States is a society of extraordinary religious dynamism and diversity. Increased immigration has altered the religious and cultural demographics of many, if not most, of the nation's communities. Since the mid-1970s, there has been a significant resurgence of religious faith and practice in the United States, as well as an increase in the number of Americans professing no religion at all.

3. Early Interpretations of the Free Exercise Clause: Drawing a Bright Line Between "Belief" and "Action"

As we noted in Chapter Four, case law from the mid-1860s through the first three decades of the 20th century is a chronicle of the growth and breadth of religious and cultural diversity in the United States. We summarize below some of that material. We hope it will provide some sense of the degree to which the political majority has reacted to minority claims for religious accommodation.

Every religious liberty case involves the striking of a balance between 1) the power of the political community to legislate for the common good; and 2) the duty of the political community to protect ("accommodate") individual religious believers and religious associations whose beliefs and practices put them at odds with political and other majorities.

The accommodation process begins with the definition of the "common good" that the legislature has embedded in a statute. It is the legislature's balance of the relevant interests that is the starting point for judicial review under the Constitution.

During the years between 1791 and 1940 there were few reported federal cases discussing the meaning of the First Amendment's religious liberty guarantee. Because the amendment applied only to acts of Congress, the few free exercise cases decided by the federal courts before 1940 involved challenges to federal authority.

As noted in Chapter 4 § C(3), the first cases in which the Supreme Court actually interpreted the Free Exercise Clause are rooted in the federal anti-polygamy campaign that began in the mid-nineteenth century. Nearly twenty years after this campaign began, the Supreme Court rejected the proposition that the Free Exercise Clause protected the Mormon practice of plural marriage. In *Reynolds v. United States,* 98 U.S. 145, 164 (1879) and *Davis v. Beason*, 133 U.S. 333 (1890), excerpted in Chapter Four, the Court upheld the Anti-Polygamy Act, and drew on Thomas Jefferson's letter to the Danbury Baptist Association to make the case for distinguishing between belief and action: "Congress was deprived of all legislative power over mere opinion, but was left free to reach actions which were in violation of social duties or subversive of good order. "

The distinction between belief and action has become the focus of most commentaries on the polygamy cases, but another proposition embedded in those cases has an equally distinguished pedigree: the power of majority rule. In *The Late Corporation of the Church of Jesus Christ of Latter Day Saints v. United States*, 136 U.S. 1, 50 (1890), the Court makes the point bluntly: "The State has a perfect right to prohibit... all... open offenses against the enlightened sentiment of mankind, notwithstanding the pretense of religious conviction by which they may be advocated and practiced."

The Court has never fully accepted the proposition that the protection of the public interest, including the definition of religious liberty, is entrusted solely to the political majority, but the Court's jurisprudence does underscore two important points: First, laws are the result of an extended, and highly political, process in which the interests of the public are balanced against the rights of individuals; and, second, except when the Constitution provides clear warrant for judicial intervention, the legislature gets the benefit of the doubt.

4. Incorporating the Free Exercise Clause: Religious Liberty as an Aspect of Personal Liberty

The Court set the stage for the application of the Free Exercise Clause to the States in *Palko v. Connecticut* and *United States v. Carolene Products Co.*, 304 U.S. 144 (1938). Neither case involved the First Amendment, but each informs the religious liberty jurisprudence that has since evolved.

As noted in Section D(3) above, *Palko* used the First Amendment's protection of free exercise of religion, freedom of speech, and freedom of the press as discrete examples of liberty interests the Court was willing to characterize as "fundamental." *Palko* thus set the stage for the Court to define both the substantive *content* of the incorporated Free Exercise Clause, and its *relative importance.*

Chart 5-3 and Chart 1-1 in Chapter One illustrate the way in which the meaning and priority of a norm can change when the Court describes it a higher or lower level of generality. *Carolene Products* illustrates another way in which the meaning of a norm can change: through specification or limitation of its purposes.

The plurality opinion in *Carolene Products* sketches a two-tiered approach to judicial decision-making. In most cases, "the existence of facts supporting the legislative judgment is to be presumed" constitutional because regulatory legislation "is not to be pronounced unconstitutional unless in the light of the facts made known or generally assumed it is of such a character as to preclude the assumption that it rests upon some rational basis within the knowledge and experience of the legislators." *Carolene Products*, at 152.

When the facts show that the Constitution may have been violated, a "more searching judicial inquiry" into the reasons for the legislation is warranted. The plurality mentioned several instances when such a "searching judicial inquiry" (or "higher standard of review") may be warranted:

1. When "legislation appears on its face to be within a specific prohibition of the Constitution, such as those of the first ten Amendments, which are deemed equally specific when held to be embraced within the Fourteenth;"
2. When there are facts tending to show that the legislation in question "restricts those political processes which can ordinarily be expected to bring about repeal of undesirable legislation;"
3. When there are facts tending to show that the statute is "directed at particular religious, or racial minorities;" and
4. When the facts tend to show that "the operation of those political processes ordinarily to be relied upon to protect minorities" may not work because of the unique types of prejudice that affect "discrete and insular minorities."

As you review the cases summarized and excerpted below, which, if any, of these categories apply? You should also consider the possibility that that more than one might be involved.

5. Preaching & Teaching as Free Exercise: Jehovah's Witnesses

The legal problems of the Jehovah's Witnesses gave the Court its first opportunity to determine the parameters of an "incorporated" free exercise norm.

Cantwell v. Connecticut, 310 U.S. 296 (1940), the first free exercise case to use the Court's new approach, invalidated a statute making it a crime to "solicit money, services, subscriptions or any valuable thing for any alleged religious, charitable or philanthropic cause," unless the person solicited was a member of the organization and the solicitation occurred in the county where the organization was located. Holding that the liberties guaranteed by the First Amendment are embraced within the concept of "liberty" protected by the Fourteenth, the Court began a case-by-case process that would define the *operative* content of the incorporated Free Exercise Clause.

Justice Roberts began by reaffirming the belief-action distinction made in *Reynolds:* "[Free exercise] embraces two concepts," he wrote, "freedom to believe and freedom to act. The first is absolute, but in the nature of things, the second cannot be. [In] every case the power to regulate must be so exercised as not, in attaining a permissible end, unduly to infringe the protected freedom." *Id.* at 303–04. Thus, some religiously motivated actions were protected, including evangelization, for it violated both "the free exercise of religion [] and [] freedom to communicate information and opinion."

The shift in emphasis was subtle, but its impact was to be substantial. After *Cantwell,* the State no longer had "a perfect right to prohibit [] all [] open offenses against the enlightened sentiment of mankind." Even when "attaining a permissible end," a state may not unduly infringe a protected freedom. States would have to justify both the nature and degree of the burdens their laws imposed on religious exercise.

Other early cases involving the Witnesses arose in the public schools, and thus inevitably involved actions that could be characterized as either "free exercise," "freedom of thought and speech," or both. For a Witness, a mandatory flag salute pays homage to a graven image. When the Witness children refused to participate in the mandatory flag salutes, they were expelled. *Minersville Sch. Dist. v. Gobitis,* 310 U.S. 586 (1940), and *West Virginia Bd. of Educ. v. Barnette,* 319 U.S. 624 (1943) summarized in Chapter One, illustrate some of the assumptions the Court makes when it attempts to balance "conflicting claims of liberty and authority." In *Gobitis,* the Court focused on the distinction between belief and action, just as it did in *Reynolds.:*

> When does the constitutional guarantee compel exemption from doing what society thinks necessary for the promotion of some great common end, or from a penalty for conduct which appears dangerous to the general good?

The students lost, but *Gobitis* was reconsidered three years later in *Barnette.* This time, the Court posed the conflict in terms of "freedom of thought and speech," and the students won.

> The sole conflict is between authority and rights of the individual. The State asserts power to condition access to public education on making a prescribed sign and profession and at the same time to coerce attendance by punishing both parent and child. The latter stand on a right of self-determination in matters that touch individual opinion and personal attitude. *Barnette,* at 630–631.

Other cases involving the Witnesses during the 1940s also turned on the interplay between the regulatory powers of the government, free exercise, and "freedom of thought and speech." In both ***Murdock v. Pennsylvania***, 319 U.S. 105 (1943), and ***Follett v. McCormick***, 321 U.S. 573 (1944), the Court invalidated flat license and bookseller's taxes imposed on Jehovah's Witnesses who offered religious books and pamphlets for sale during the course of their ministry. In the Court's view, the "taxes imposed...can hardly help but be as severe and telling in their impact on the freedom of the press and religion as the 'taxes on knowledge' at which the First Amendment was partly aimed." *See also Martin v. City of Struthers*, 319 U.S. 141 (1943) (overturning the conviction of a Witness proselytizing door-to-door notwithstanding an ordinance prohibiting door-to-door leafleting because "[f]reedom to distribute information to every citizen wherever he desires to receive it is so clearly vital to the preservation of a free society," even though the content of the speech and materials was highly offensive to those being proselytized).

By the late 1940s, a free exercise standard was beginning to emerge. The Court would assert federal authority to protect "freedom of thought and speech" when State laws and regulations imposed "undue burdens" on these fundamental rights. Such laws would be subject to a "searching judicial scrutiny," in which the Court the nature and importance of the rights involved would be balanced against the regulatory interests of the State. If the burden imposed were reasonable under the circumstances, the Justices would defer to legislative or executive authority. If the burden was deemed excessive, the law was unconstitutional.

6. From *Sherbert* to *Smith*: Free Exercise as a 'Sensible Balance Between Religious Liberty and Competing State Interests'

The foundation for the religious liberty jurisprudence of the Supreme Court was laid down in a series of cases decided between 1945 and 1964. Today, these cases are generally classified as either "Establishment Clause" or "Free Exercise" cases, but every religious liberty case involves at least two of the norms of the incorporated First Amendment, and sometimes more.

Because the First and Fourteenth Amendments are *limitations* on legislative, executive, and judicial powers, three primary questions frame the debate over the meaning of the religious liberty guarantee:

- *To what extent, if any, does the Constitution permit official legal structures or institutions to reflect the religious beliefs, practices, and sensibilities of a community's political majority*? We will call these "structural accommodations." Most such cases are litigated under the Establishment Clause, but have significant free exercise and equal protection components.
- *To what extent, if any, does the Constitution permit the legislature to protect individual or group religious liberty interests without running afoul of other constitutional limitations*? We will refer to these questions as "legislative accommodations." Legislative accommodation cases usually raise First and Fourteenth Amendment issues, and often raise significant separation of powers and federalism questions as well.

- *To what extent, if any, does the Constitution either permit or require judicial recognition of free exercise exemptions from neutral rules of general applicability?* "Judicial accommodation" occurs when the legislative or executive authority is either unwilling or unable to accommodate a religious liberty interest. Judicial accommodations proceed case-by-case, and the rules announced by the Court often raise important equal protection, federalism and separation of powers questions.

Most of the litigation between 1945 and 1964 focused on two public institutions, each of which had a venerable political and cultural pedigree: Sunday closing laws and public schools. Sunday closing laws, sometimes called "Blue Laws," structured the official workweek around the majority's observance of the Christian Sabbath. Public schools required Bible reading without comment and recitation of the Lord's Prayer.

Observant Jews and others challenged the constitutionality of Sunday closing laws on several different constitutional grounds. In *McGowan v. Maryland*, 366 U.S. 420 (1961), the Court upheld the law against a challenge based on the Establishment and Equal Protection Clauses. In *Braunfeld v. Brown*, 366 U.S. 599, 603 (1961), a plurality rejected the proposition that the Free Exercise Clause requires an exemption whenever a burden is proved, but suggested that it might make adjustments on a case-by-case basis. The plurality noted that "[t]o strike down, without the most critical scrutiny, legislation which imposes only an indirect burden on the exercise of religion, *i.e.*, legislation which does not make unlawful the religious practice itself, would radically restrict the operating latitude of the legislature." The plurality also concluded that "[i]f the purpose or effect of a law is to impede the observance of one or all religions or is to discriminate invidiously between religions, that law is constitutionally invalid even though the burden may be characterized as being only indirect." *Id.* at 606–607. *See* Chapter Six.

The Court's theory of judicial accommodation was developed in the following case. Just as in most of the earlier free exercise cases, the complaining party was a member of a small, Christian sect whose members' religious beliefs and practices put them at odds with law, social custom, and "mainstream" Christian practice. Like their Jewish fellow-citizens, Seventh-day Adventists observe the Sabbath the seventh day of the week, on Saturday.

Sherbert v. Verner

374 U.S. 398 (1963)

Mr. Justice BRENNAN delivered the opinion of the Court.

Appellant, [Adell Sherbert,] a member of the Seventh-day Adventist Church, was discharged by her South Carolina employer because she would not work on Saturday, the Sabbath Day of her faith. When she was unable to obtain other employment because from conscientious scruples she would not take Saturday work, she filed a claim for unemployment compensation benefits under the South Carolina Unemployment Compensation Act. That law provides that, to be eligible for benefits, a claimant must be "able to work and * * * available for work"; and, further, that a claimant is ineligible for benefits "[i]f * * * he has failed, without good cause * * * to accept available suitable work when offered him by the employment office or the employer * * *." The appellee Employment Security Commission, in administrative proceedings under the statute, found that appellant's restriction upon her availability for Saturday work brought her within the provision disqualifying for benefits insured workers who fail, without good cause, to accept "suitable work when offered * * * by the employment office or the employer...." We reverse the judgment of the South Carolina Supreme Court and remand for further proceedings not inconsistent with this opinion.

I.

The door of the Free Exercise Clause stands tightly closed against any governmental regulation of religious *beliefs* as such, *Cantwell.* Government may neither compel affirmation of a repugnant belief, *Torcaso v. Watkins*, 367 U.S. 488 (1961), nor penalize or discriminate against individuals or groups because they hold religious views abhorrent to the authorities, *Fowler v. Rhode Island,* 345 U.S. 67 (1953); nor employ the taxing power to inhibit the dissemination of particular religious views. On the other hand, the Court has rejected challenges under the Free Exercise Clause to governmental regulation of certain overt acts prompted by religious beliefs or principles, for "even when the action is in accord with one's religious convictions, [it] is not totally free from legislative restrictions."

Plainly enough, appellant's conscientious objection to Saturday work constitutes no conduct prompted by religious principles of a kind within the reach of state legislation. If, therefore, the decision of the South Carolina Supreme Court is to withstand appellant's constitutional challenge, it must be either because her disqualification as a beneficiary represents no infringement by the State of her constitutional rights of free exercise, or because any incidental burden on the free exercise of appellant's religion may be justified by a "compelling state interest...."

II.

We turn first to the question whether the disqualification for benefits imposes any burden on the free exercise of appellant's religion. We think it is clear that it does. In a sense the consequences of such a disqualification to religious principles and practices may be only an indirect result of welfare legislation within the State's general competence to enact; it is true that no criminal sanctions directly compel appellant to work a six-day week. But this is only the beginning, not the end, of our inquiry. For "[i]f the purpose or effect of a law is to impede the observance of one or all religions or is to discriminate invidiously between religions, that law is constitutionally invalid even though the burden may be characterized as being only indirect." *Braunfeld v. Brown*, 366 U.S. 599 (1961). Here not only is it apparent that appellant's declared ineligibility for benefits derives solely from the practice of her religion, but the pressure upon her to forego that practice is unmistakable. The ruling forces her to choose between following the precepts of her religion and forfeiting benefits, on the one hand, and abandoning one of the precepts of her religion in order to accept work, on the other hand. Governmental imposition of such a choice puts the same kind of burden upon the free exercise of religion as would a fine imposed against appellant for her Saturday worship.

[T]o condition the availability of benefits upon this appellant's willingness to violate a cardinal principle of her religious faith effectively penalizes the free exercise of her constitutional liberties.

Significantly South Carolina expressly saves the Sunday worshipper from having to make the kind of choice which we here hold infringes the Sabbatarian's religious liberty. When in times of "national emergency" the textile plants are authorized by the State Commissioner of Labor to operate on Sunday, "no employee shall be required to work on Sunday * * * who is conscientiously opposed to Sunday work; and if any employee should refuse to work on Sunday on account of conscientious * * * objections he or she shall not jeopardize his or her seniority by such refusal or be discriminated against in any other manner." S.C. Code, §64-4. No question of the disqualification of a Sunday worshipper for benefits is likely to arise, since we cannot suppose that an employer will discharge him in violation of this statute. The unconstitutionality of the disqualification of the Sabbatarian is thus compounded by the religious discrimination which South Carolina's general statutory scheme necessarily effects.

III.

In these respects, then, the state interest asserted in the present case is wholly dissimilar to the interests which were found to justify the less direct burden upon religious practices in *Braunfeld.* The Court recognized that the Sunday closing law which that decision sustained undoubtedly served "to make the practice of [the Orthodox Jewish merchants'] religious beliefs more expensive." But the statute was nevertheless saved by a countervailing factor which finds no equivalent in the instant case—a strong state interest in providing one uniform day of rest for all workers. That secular objective could be achieved, the Court found, only by declaring Sunday to be that day of rest. Requiring exemptions for Sabbatarians, while theoretically possible, appeared to present an administrative problem of such magnitude, or to afford the exempted class so great a competitive advantage, that such a requirement would have rendered the entire statutory scheme unworkable. In the present case no such justifications underlie the determination of the state court that appellant's religion makes her ineligible to receive benefits.

IV.

In holding as we do, plainly we are not fostering the "establishment" of the Seventh-day Adventist religion in South Carolina, for the extension of unemployment benefits to Sabbatarians in common with Sunday worshippers reflects nothing more than the governmental obligation of neutrality in the face of religious differences, and does not represent that involvement of religious with secular institutions which it is the object of the Establishment Clause to forestall. Nor does the recognition of the appellant's right to unemployment benefits under the state statute serve to abridge any other person's religious liberties. Nor do we, by our decision today, declare the existence of a constitutional right to unemployment benefits on the part of all persons whose religious convictions are the cause of their unemployment. This is not a case in which an employee's religious convictions serve to make him a nonproductive member of society. Finally, nothing we say today constrains the States to adopt any particular form or scheme of unemployment compensation. Our holding today is only that South Carolina may not constitutionally apply the eligibility provisions so as to constrain a worker to abandon his religious convictions respecting the day of rest. This holding but reaffirms a principle that we announced a decade and a half ago, namely that no State may "exclude individual Catholics, Lutherans, Mohammedans, Baptists, Jews, Methodists, Non-believers, Presbyterians, or the members of any other faith, *because of their faith, or lack of it,* from receiving the benefits of public welfare legislation." *Everson.*

Reversed and remanded.

Mr. Justice DOUGLAS, concurring.

It seems obvious to me that this law does run afoul of that [free exercise] clause.

Religious scruples of Moslems require them to attend a mosque on Friday and to pray five times daily. Religious scruples of a Sikh require him to carry a regular or a symbolic sword. *Rex v. Singh*, 39 A.I.R. 53 (Allahabad, 1952). Religious scruples of a Jehovah's Witness teach him to be a colporteur, going from door to door, from town to town, distributing his religious pamphlets. See *Murdock v. Pennsylvania*, 319 U.S. 105 [1943]. Religious scruples of a Quaker compel him to refrain from swearing and to affirm instead. See *King v. Fearson*, Fed. Cas. No. 7,790, 14 Fed. Cas. 520; 1 U.S.C. § 1; Federal Rules of Civil Procedure, Rule 43(d); *United States v. Schwimmer*, 279 U.S. 644, 655 [1929] (dissenting opinion). Religious scruples of a Buddhist may require him to refrain from partaking of any flesh, even of fish.

The examples could be multiplied, including those of the Seventh-day Adventist whose Sabbath is Saturday and who is advised not to eat some meats.

These suffice, however, to show that many people hold beliefs alien to the majority of our society—beliefs that are protected by the First Amendment but which could easily be trod upon under the guise of "police" or "health" regulations reflecting the majority's views.

This case is resolvable not in terms of what an individual can demand of government, but solely in terms of what government may not do to an individual in violation of his religious scruples. The fact that government cannot exact from me a surrender of one iota of my religious scruples does not, of course, mean that I can demand of government a sum of money, the better to exercise them. For the Free Exercise Clause is written in terms of what the government cannot do to the individual, not in terms of what the individual can exact from the government.

Mr. Justice STEWART, concurring in the result.

Although fully agreeing with the result which the Court reaches in this case, I cannot join the Court's opinion. This case presents a double-barreled dilemma, which in all candor I think the Court's opinion has not succeeded in papering over. The dilemma ought to be resolved.

I.

I am convinced that no liberty is more essential to the continued vitality of the free society which our Constitution guarantees than is the religious liberty protected by the Free Exercise Clause explicit in the First Amendment and imbedded in the Fourteenth. And I regret that on occasion, and specifically in *Braunfeld*, the Court has shown what has seemed to me a distressing insensitivity to the appropriate demands of this constitutional guarantee. By contrast I think that the Court's approach to the Establishment Clause has on occasion... been not only insensitive, but positively wooden, and that the Court has accorded to the Establishment Clause a meaning which neither the words, the history, nor the intention of the authors of that specific constitutional provision even remotely suggests.

But my views as to the correctness of the Court's decisions in these cases are beside the point here. The point is that the decisions are on the books. And the result is that there are many situations where legitimate claims under the Free Exercise Clause will run into head-on collision with the Court's insensitive and sterile construction of the Establishment Clause. The controversy now before us is clearly such a case.

Because the appellant refuses to accept available jobs which would require her to work on Saturdays, South Carolina has declined to pay unemployment compensation benefits to her. Her refusal to work on Saturdays is based on the tenets of her religious faith. The Court says that South Carolina cannot under these circumstances declare her to be not "available for work" within the meaning of its statute because to do so would violate her constitutional right to the free exercise of her religion.

Yet what this Court has said about the Establishment Clause must inevitably lead to a diametrically opposite result. If the appellant's refusal to work on Saturdays were based on indolence, or on a compulsive desire to watch the Saturday television programs, no one would say that South Carolina could not hold that she was not "available for work" within the meaning of its statute. That being so, the Establishment Clause as construed by this Court not only *permits* but affirmatively *requires* South Carolina equally to deny the appellant's claim for unemployment compensation when her refusal to work on Saturdays is based upon her religious creed.

To require South Carolina to so administer its laws as to pay public money to the appellant under the circumstances of this case is thus clearly to require the State to violate the Establishment Clause as construed by this Court. This poses no problem for me, because I think the Court's mechanistic concept of the Establishment Clause is historically unsound and constitutionally wrong. I think the process of constitutional decision in the area of the relationships between government and religion demands considerably more than the invocation of broad-brushed rhetoric of the kind I have quoted. And I think that the guarantee of religious liberty embodied in the Free Exercise Clause affirmatively requires government to create an atmosphere of hospitality and accommodation to individual belief or disbelief. In short, I think our Constitution commands the positive protection by government of religious freedom—not only for a minority, however small—not only for the majority, however large—but for each of us.

[W]e do not have before us a situation where a State provides unemployment compensation generally, and singles out for disqualification only those persons who are unavailable for work on religious grounds. This is not, in short, a scheme which operates so as to discriminate against religion as such. But the Court nevertheless holds that the State must prefer a religious over a secular ground for being unavailable for work.

Yet in cases decided under the Establishment Clause the Court has decreed otherwise. It has decreed that government must blind itself to the differing religious beliefs and traditions of the people. With all respect, I think it is the Court's duty to face up to the dilemma posed by the conflict between the Free Exercise Clause of the Constitution and the Establishment Clause as interpreted by the Court.

Mr. Justice HARLAN, whom Mr. Justice WHITE joins, dissenting.

Since virtually all of the mills in the Spartanburg areas were operating on a six-day week, the appellant was "unavailable for work," and thus ineligible for benefits, when personal considerations prevented her from accepting employment on a full-time basis in the industry and locality in which she had worked. The fact that these personal considerations sprang from her religious convictions was wholly without relevance to the state court's application of the law. Thus in no proper sense can it be said that the State discriminated against the appellant on the basis of her religious beliefs or that she was denied benefits *because* she was a Seventh-day Adventist. She was denied benefits just as any other claimant would be denied benefits who was not "available for work" for personal reasons.

With this background, this Court's decision comes into clearer focus. What the Court is holding is that if the State chooses to condition unemployment compensation on the applicant's availability for work, it is constitutionally compelled to *carve out an exception*—and to provide benefits—for those whose unavailability is due to their religious convictions. Such a holding has particular significance in two respects.

First, despite the Court's protestations to the contrary, the decision necessarily overrules *Braunfeld v. Brown*, which held that it did not offend the "Free Exercise" Clause of the Constitution for a State to forbid a Sabbatarian to do business on Sunday.

Second, the implications of the present decision are far more troublesome than its apparently narrow dimensions would indicate at first glance. The meaning of today's holding, as already noted, is that the State must furnish unemployment benefits to one who is unavailable for work if the unavailability stems from the exercise of religious convictions. The State, in other words, must *single out* for financial assistance those whose behavior is religiously motivated, even though it denies such assistance to others whose identical behavior (in this case, inability to work on Saturdays) is not religiously motivated.

My own view, however, is that at least under the circumstances of this case it would be a permissible accommodation of religion for the State, if it *chose* to do so, to create an exception to its eligibility requirements for persons like the appellant. The constitutional obligation of "neutrality," is not so narrow a channel that the slightest deviation from an absolutely straight course leads to condemnation. There are too many instances in which no such course can be charted, too many areas in which the pervasive activities of the State justify some special provision for religion to prevent it from being submerged by an all-embracing secularism.

[H]owever, I cannot subscribe to the conclusion that the State is constitutionally *compelled* to carve out an exception to its general rule of eligibility in the present case. Those situations in which the Constitution may require special treatment on account of religion are, in my view, few and far between, and this view is amply supported by the course of constitutional litigation in this area.

Notes

1. *Sherbert* requires a twofold inquiry: First, a court must determine whether the law "burdens" the free exercise of religion. If so, the law may be justified only if there exists a "compelling state interest" that justifies an "incidental" burden on the applicant's exercise of her religion.

Under the post-*Sherbert* case law, a burden exists if either the purpose *or effect* of the law impinges the practice of religion or religious belief. Justice Harlan's dissent in *Sherbert* would have limited the reach of the Free Exercise Clause to intentional discrimination against religious believers.

2. The distinction between "purpose" and "effect" is often used in First and Fourteenth Amendment cases. *See, e.g., Washington v. Davis*, 426 U.S. 229 (1976) (proof of "effects" alone will not support a finding that the Equal Protection Clause has been violated); *Lemon v. Kurtzman*, 403 U.S. 602, 612–13 (1971) (holding "purpose or primary effect" of law must neither advance nor inhibit religion).

3. The majority in *Sherbert* conceded that the *purpose* of the South Carolina statute was not to burden Adell Sherbert's religious practices, but it held that the *effect* of the law was burdensome because it "forces her to choose between following the precepts of her religion and forfeiting benefits, on the one hand, and abandoning one of the precepts of her religion in order to accept work, on the other hand. Governmental imposition of such a choice puts the same kind of burden upon the free exercise of religion as would a fine imposed against appellant for her Saturday worship." Is the Court's analogy to a fine imposed by the state for worshiping on Saturday persuasive? What result if the state refused to grant *any* exemptions?

4. The concurrence of Justice Douglas, the author of the *Murdock* and *Follett* decisions, is based on the idea that "[t]his case is resolvable not in terms of what an individual can demand of government, but solely in terms of what government may not do to an individual in violation of his religious scruples." Is this formal distinction between the demands of the individual and the dictates of government helpful to understanding the breadth of Free Exercise exemptions? In keeping with the views expressed in *Carolene Products*, Justice Douglas suggests that the purpose of the Free Exercise Clause is to give members of minority groups a tool with which to challenge the outcomes of the majoritarian political process. Should the relative size or political strength of the religious institution (or group) affect the Court's interpretation of the Religion Clause? That is, should the Court be more solicitous of claims made by persons who are members of smaller religious organizations than of larger ones? If so, are the Court's "affirmative action" decisions relevant here?

5. Justice Harlan's dissent limits the reach of the Free Exercise Clause to purposeful discrimination against religious believers. Is it possible to argue that South Carolina *had* engaged in "purposeful discrimination" by exempting only Sunday observers?

6. Consider the issue of characterization. What would be the best way to characterize Adell Sherbert's constitutional problem?

- Is it a "free exercise case" because of the burden the denial of unemployment benefits imposed on her religious practice, or an "equal protection case" because the burden arose because South Carolina had two rules governing exemptions for religious practice, one for Sunday observers and another for those whose religions select another day? If both, is it necessary to decide which norm should take priority?
- Does the decision in *Sherbert* create a preference for persons who refuse to work for religious reasons? Would it be appropriate to read the exemption mandated by the Court as "disfavoring" those who refuse to work for nonreligious reasons? If so, how would you characterize the claim of an individual denied unemployment compensation when the administrator decides that his nonreligious reason for failing to accept available suitable work does not measure up under the statute's "good cause" standard? Does it violate the Establishment Clause because it favors religious observance over secular activity? Can an argument be made that it violates the Equal Protection Clause? If so, on what basis is the line drawn? Are all Sabbatarians included in the exemption, or does it cover only those who can prove that they actually observe the Sabbath?

7. In *Everson v. Board of Educ.*, 330 U.S. 1 (1947), excerpted below in §E, the majority opinion states that

> The "establishment of religion" clause of the First Amendment means at least this: Neither a state nor the Federal Government...can pass laws which aid one religion, aid all religions, or prefer one religion over another. Neither can force nor influence a person to go to or to remain away from church against his will or force him to profess a belief or disbelief in any religion. No person can be punished for entertaining or professing religious beliefs or disbeliefs, for church attendance or non-attendance.

In a later case involving the Establishment Clause, *Walz v. Tax Comm'n*, 397 U.S. 664 (1970), Justice Harlan argued in a concurrence that "neutrality" and "voluntarism" are "related and mutually reinforcing concepts" that serve as a "short-form for saying that the Government must neither legislate to accord benefits that favor religion over nonreligion."

Given this background, should *Sherbert* be read as permitting statutory exemptions limited to religious believers in areas other than unemployment compensation? After *Sherbert*, does the Free Exercise Clause forbid statutory exemptions that distinguish between religious traditions, but permit those that distinguish religious and nonreligious activities? If so, why?

8. Equal protection analysis examines the legitimacy of the criteria government uses to draw legal classifications. Is a rule that distinguishes between religious and nonreligious activities a legitimate way to achieve an otherwise legitimate State purpose? If the protection of religious liberty is a legitimate goal of government, how are we to determine whether drawing a distinction between religious and nonreligious activities is a legitimate means to that end? The cases can be read both ways.

- In *Murdock* and *Follett*, discussed above, the Supreme Court held that city ordinances that required Jehovah's Witnesses to pay a flat licensing or occupational tax violated the First Amendment even though the laws were not purposefully directed at religious believers, religious speech, or at Jehovah's Witnesses.
- Nearly fifty years later, and more than twenty-five years after *Sherbert*, the Supreme Court invalidated a Texas statute granting a sales tax exemption to "[p]eriodicals that are published or distributed by a religious faith and that consist wholly of writings sacred to a religious faith." Tex. Tax Code Ann. § 151.312 (amended 1989). In the Court's view, the exclusive tax exemption for religious publications violated both the Establishment and the Free Press Clauses because its purpose was to promote religion, and it did so by discriminating on the basis of the publication's content. *See Texas Monthly v. Bullock*, 489 U.S. 1, 11 (1989), excerpted in Chapter Nine.

How can the difference in approach be explained? Part of the answer can be found in the way the factions within the *Texas Monthly* plurality characterized the question. In *Texas Monthly*, Texas argued that the tax exemption was justified as an accommodation of the religious publishers' rights under the Free Exercise Clause. *Texas Monthly* argued that, whatever the result under Religion Clause analysis, the exemption was forbidden by the Speech and Press Clause. The Court thus faced what might be called a "true categorical conflict": one norm or the other would have to yield. Justices Brennan, Stevens, and Marshall resolved the conflict by holding that the Establishment Clause does not permit legislative exemptions unless it can first be proved that "inclusion in the program actually burdens the claimant's freedom to exercise religious rights." *Id.* at 18. Justices Blackmun and O'Connor agreed that *this* Texas tax exemption violated the Establishment Clause, but would not rule out the theoretical possibility that "the Free Exercise Clause requires a tax exemption for the sale of religious literature by a religious organization." For Justice White, the controlling norm was the Speech and Press Clause, and it is clear from his vote to strike the exemption that he rejected Texas' claim that content-based discrimination can be justified on free exercise grounds. *Id.* at 26 (1989) (White, J., concurring). *See generally* Michael Ariens, *On the Road of Good Intentions: Justice Brennan and the Religion Clauses*, 27 Cal. W. L. Rev. 311 (1991).

* * *

The individualized nature of unemployment cases was evident in three cases that clarify the principal free exercise holding in *Sherbert*. In ***Thomas v. Review Board***, 450 U.S. 707 (1981), the Court rejected Indiana's contention that a Jehovah's Witness who left his job at a munitions factory because of his religious objections to war had done so "voluntarily." In ***Hobbie v. Unemployment Appeals Comm'n of Florida***, 480 U.S. 136 (1987), the Court upheld the free exercise rights of an employee who had converted to Seventh-Day Adventism after having worked for her employer for more than two years. "The First Amendment protects the free exercise rights of employees who adopt religious beliefs or convert from one faith to another after they are hired. The timing of Hobbie's conversion is immaterial to our determination that her free exercise rights have been burdened; the salient inquiry under the Free Exercise Clause is the burden involved." *Id.* at 144 [footnote omitted.] In ***Frazee v. Illinois Dep't of Employment Sec.***, 489 U.S. 829 (1989) (reversing Illinois' refusal of benefits because Frazee's beliefs that a Christian "could not work on the 'Lord's day'" was not "based on some tenets or dogma... of some church, sect, or denomination."), the Court reaffirmed the principle of law that government may examine the sincerity of belief, but not its substantive content. *See Ballard v. United States*, 329 U.S. 187 (1946), excerpted in Chapter 13.

Wisconsin v. Yoder

406 U.S. 205 (1972)

Mr. Chief Justice BURGER delivered the opinion of the Court.

On petition of the State of Wisconsin, we granted the writ of certiorari in this case to review a decision of the Wisconsin Supreme Court holding that respondents' convictions for violating the State's compulsory school-attendance law were invalid under the Free Exercise Clause of the First Amendment to the United States Constitution made applicable to the States by the Fourteenth Amendment. For the reasons hereafter stated we affirm.

Respondents Jonas Yoder and Wallace Miller are members of the Old Order Amish religion, and respondent Adin Yutzy is a member of the Conservative Amish Mennonite Church. They and their families are residents of Green County, Wisconsin. Wisconsin's compulsory school-attendance law required them to cause their children to attend public or private school until reaching age 16 but the respondents declined to send their children, ages 14 and 15, to public school after they completed the eighth grade. The children were not enrolled in any private school, or within any recognized exception to the compulsory-attendance law, and they are conceded to be subject to the Wisconsin statute.

On complaint of the school district administrator for the public schools, respondents were charged, tried, and convicted of violating the compulsory-attendance law in Green County Court and were fined the sum of $5 each. Respondents defended on the ground that the application of the compulsory-attendance law violated their rights under the First and Fourteenth Amendments. The trial testimony showed that respondents believed, in accordance with the tenets of Old Order Amish communities generally, that their children's attendance at high school, public or private, was contrary to the Amish religion and way of life. They believed that by sending their children to high school, they would not only expose themselves to the danger of the censure of the church community, but, as found by the county court, also endanger their own salvation and that of their children. The State stipulated that respondents' religious beliefs were sincere.

In support of their position, respondents presented as expert witnesses scholars on religion and education whose testimony is uncontradicted. They expressed their opinions on the relationship of the Amish belief concerning school attendance to the more general tenets of their religion, and described the impact that compulsory high school attendance could have on the continued survival of Amish communities as they exist in the United States today. The history of the Amish sect was given in some detail, beginning with the Swiss Anabaptists of the 16th century who rejected institutionalized churches and sought to return to the early, simple, Christian life de-emphasizing material success, rejecting the competitive spirit, and seeking to insulate themselves from the modern world. As a result of their common heritage, Old Order Amish communities today are characterized by a fundamental belief that salvation requires life in a church community separate and apart from the world and worldly influence. This concept of life aloof from the world and its values is central to their faith.

A related feature of Old Order Amish communities is their devotion to a life in harmony with nature and the soil, as exemplified by the simple life of the early Christian era that continued in America during much of our early national life. Amish beliefs require members of the community to make their living by farming or closely related activities. Broadly speaking, the Old Order Amish religion pervades and determines the entire mode of life of its adherents. Their conduct is regulated in great detail by the *Ordnung*, or rules of the church community. Adult baptism, which occurs in late adolescence, is the time at which Amish young people voluntarily undertake heavy obligations, not unlike the Bar Mitzvah of the Jews, to abide by the rules of the church community.

Amish objection to formal education beyond the eighth grade is firmly grounded in these central religious concepts. They object to the high school, and higher education generally, because the values they teach are in marked variance with Amish values and the Amish way of life; they view secondary school education as an impermissible exposure of their children to a "worldly" influence in conflict with their beliefs. The high school tends to emphasize intellectual and scientific accomplishments, self-distinction, competitiveness, worldly success, and social life with other students. Amish society emphasizes informal learning-through-doing; a life of "goodness," rather than a life of intellect; wisdom, rather than technical knowledge; community welfare, rather than competition; and separation from, rather than integration with, contemporary worldly society.

Formal high school education beyond the eighth grade is contrary to Amish beliefs, not only because it places Amish children in an environment hostile to Amish beliefs with increasing emphasis on competition in class work and sports and with pressure to conform to the styles, manners, and ways of the peer group, but also because it takes them away from their community, physically and emotionally, during the crucial and formative adolescent period of life. During this period, the children must acquire Amish attitudes favoring manual work and self-reliance and the specific skills needed to perform the adult role of an Amish farmer or housewife. They must learn to enjoy physical labor. Once a child has learned basic reading, writing, and elementary mathematics, these traits, skills, and attitudes admittedly fall within the category of those best learned through example and "doing" rather than in a classroom. And, at this time in life, the Amish child must also grow in his faith and his relationship to the Amish community if he is to be prepared to accept the heavy obligations imposed by adult baptism.

The Amish do not object to elementary education through the first eight grades as a general proposition because they agree that their children must have basic skills in the "three R's" in order to read the Bible, to be good farmers and citizens, and to be able to deal with non-Amish people when necessary in the course of daily affairs. They view such a basic education as acceptable because it does not significantly expose their children to worldly values or interfere with their development in the Amish community during the crucial adolescent period. While Amish accept compulsory elementary education generally, wherever possible they have established their own elementary schools in many respects like the small local schools of the past. In the Amish belief higher learning tends to develop values they reject as influences that alienate man from God.

On the basis of such considerations, Dr. Hostetler testified that compulsory high school attendance could not only result in great psychological harm to Amish children, because of the conflicts it would produce, but would also, in his opinion, ultimately result in the destruction of the Old Order Amish church community as it exists in the United States today. The testimony of Dr. Donald A. Erickson, an expert witness on education, also showed that the Amish succeed in preparing their high school age children to be productive members of the Amish community. He described their system of learning through doing the skills directly relevant to their adult roles in the Amish community as "ideal" and perhaps superior to ordinary high school education. The evidence also showed that the Amish have an excellent record as law-abiding and generally self-sufficient members of society.

I

There is no doubt as to the power of a State, having a high responsibility for education of its citizens, to impose reasonable regulations for the control and duration of basic education. Providing public schools ranks at the very apex of the function of a State. Yet even this paramount responsibility was, in *Pierce*, made to yield to the right of parents to provide an equivalent education in a privately operated system. [T]he values of parental direction of the religious upbringing and education of their children in their early and formative years have a high place in our society.

It follows that in order for Wisconsin to compel school attendance beyond the eighth grade against a claim that such attendance interferes with the practice of a legitimate religious belief, it must appear either that the State does not deny the free exercise of religious belief by its requirement, or that there is a state interest of sufficient magnitude to override the interest claiming protection under the Free Exercise Clause. Long before there was general acknowledgment of the need for universal formal education, the Religion Clauses had specifically and firmly fixed the right to free exercise of religious beliefs, and buttressing this fundamental right was an equally firm, even if less explicit, prohibition against the establishment of any religion by government.

The essence of all that has been said and written on the subject is that only those interests of the highest order and those not otherwise served can overbalance legitimate claims to the free exercise of religion.

II

[T]he Amish religious faith and their mode of life are, as they claim, inseparable and interdependent. A way of life, however virtuous and admirable, may not be interposed as a barrier to reasonable state regulation of education if it is based on purely secular considerations; to have the protection of the Religion Clauses, the claims must be rooted in religious belief. Although a determination of what is a "religious" belief or practice entitled to constitutional protection may present a most delicate question, the very concept of ordered liberty precludes allowing every person to make his own standards on matters of conduct in which society as a whole has important interests. Thus, if the Amish asserted their claims because of their subjective evaluation and rejection of the contemporary secular values accepted by the majority, much as Thoreau rejected the social values of his time and isolated himself at Walden Pond, their claims would not rest on a religious basis. Thoreau's choice was philosophical and personal rather than religious, and such belief does not rise to the demands of the Religion Clauses.

[T]he traditional way of life of the Amish is not merely a matter of personal preference, but one of deep religious conviction, shared by an organized group, and intimately related to daily living. As the expert witness explained, the Old Order Amish religion pervades and determines virtually their entire way of life, regulating it with the detail of the Talmudic diet through the strictly enforced rules of the church community.

The respondents freely concede, and indeed assert as an article of faith, that their religious beliefs and what we would today call "life style" have not altered in fundamentals for centuries. Their way of life in a church-oriented community, separated from the outside world and "worldly" influences, their attachment to nature and the soil, is a way inherently simple and uncomplicated, albeit difficult to preserve against the pressure to conform. Their rejection of telephones, automobiles, radios, and television, their mode of dress, of speech, their habits of manual work do indeed set them apart from much of contemporary society; these customs are both symbolic and practical.

As the society around the Amish has become more populous, urban, industrialized, and complex, particularly in this century, government regulation of human affairs has correspondingly become more detailed and pervasive. The Amish mode of life has thus come into conflict increasingly with requirements of contemporary society exerting a hydraulic insistence of conformity to majoritarian standards. So long as compulsory education laws were confined to eight grades of elementary basic education imparted in a nearby rural schoolhouse, with a large proportion of students of the Amish faith, the Old Order Amish had little basis to fear that school attendance would expose their children to the worldly influence they reject. But modern compulsory secondary education in rural areas is now largely carried on in a consolidated school, often remote from the student's home and alien to his daily home life. As the record so strongly shows, the values and programs of the modern secondary school are in sharp conflict with the fundamental mode of life mandated by the Amish religion; modern laws requiring compulsory secondary education have accordingly engendered great concern and conflict. The conclusion is inescapable that secondary schooling, by exposing Amish children to worldly influences in terms of attitudes, goals, and values contrary to beliefs, and by substantially interfering with the religious development of the Amish child and his integration into the way of life of the Amish faith community at the crucial adolescent stage of development, contravenes the basic religious tenets and practice of the Amish faith, both as to the parent and the child.

The impact of the compulsory-attendance law on respondents' practice of the Amish religion is not only severe, but inescapable, for the Wisconsin law affirmatively compels them, under threat of criminal sanction, to perform acts undeniably at odds with fundamental tenets of their religious beliefs. As the record shows, compulsory school attendance to age 16 for Amish children carries with it a very real threat of undermining the Amish community and religious practice as they exist today; they must either abandon belief and be assimilated into society at large, or be forced to migrate to some other and more tolerant region.

In sum, the unchallenged testimony of acknowledged experts in education and religious history, almost 300 years of consistent practice, and strong evidence of a sustained faith pervading and regulating respondents' entire mode of life support the claim that enforcement of the State's requirement of compulsory formal education after the eighth grade would gravely endanger if not destroy the free exercise of respondents' religious beliefs.

III

Wisconsin concedes that under the Religion Clauses religious beliefs are absolutely free from the State's control, but it argues that "actions," even though religiously grounded, are outside the protection of the First Amendment. But our decisions have rejected the idea that religiously grounded conduct is always outside the protection of the Free Exercise Clause. [T]o agree that religiously grounded conduct must often be subject to the broad police power of the State is not to deny that there are areas of conduct protected by the Free Exercise Clause of the First Amendment and thus beyond the power of the State to control, even under regulations of general applicability. This case, therefore, does not become easier because respondents were convicted for their "actions" in refusing to send their children to the public high school; in this context belief and action cannot be neatly confined in logic-tight compartments.

A regulation neutral on its face may, in its application, nonetheless offend the constitutional requirement for governmental neutrality if it unduly burdens the free exercise of religion. *Sherbert.* The Court must not ignore the danger that an exception from a general obligation of citizenship on religious grounds may run afoul of the Establishment Clause, but that danger cannot be allowed to prevent any exception no matter how vital it may be to the protection of values promoted by the right of free exercise.

The State advances two primary arguments in support of its system of compulsory education. It notes, as Thomas Jefferson pointed out early in our history, that some degree of education is necessary to prepare citizens to participate effectively and intelligently in our open political system if we are to preserve freedom and independence. Further, education prepares individuals to be self-reliant and self-sufficient participants in society. We accept these propositions.

However, the evidence adduced by the Amish in this case is persuasively to the effect that an additional one or two years of formal high school for Amish children in place of their long-established program of informal vocational education would do little to serve those interests.

Whatever their idiosyncrasies as seen by the majority, this record strongly shows that the Amish community has been a highly successful social unit within our society, even if apart from the conventional "mainstream." Its members are productive and very law-abiding members of society; they reject public welfare in any of its usual modern forms. The Congress itself recognized their self-sufficiency by authorizing exemption of such groups as the Amish from the obligation to pay social security taxes.[11]

11. Title 26 U.S.C. § 1402(h) authorizes the Secretary of Health, Education, and Welfare to exempt members of "a recognized religious sect" existing at all times since December 31, 1950, from the obligation to pay social security taxes if they are, by reason of the tenets of their sect, opposed to receipt of such benefits and agree to waive them, provided the Secretary finds that the sect makes reasonable provision for its dependent members. The history of the exemption shows it was enacted with the situation of the Old Order Amish specifically in view. H.R. Rep. No. 213, 89th Cong., 1st Sess., 101–102 (1965).

The record in this case establishes without contradiction that the Green County Amish had never been known to commit crimes, that none had been known to receive public assistance, and that none were unemployed.

The State argues that if Amish children leave their church they should not be in the position of making their way in the world without the education available in the one or two additional years the State requires. However, on this record, that argument is highly speculative.

There is nothing in this record to suggest that the Amish qualities of reliability, self-reliance, and dedication to work would fail to find ready markets in today's society. Absent some contrary evidence supporting the State's position, we are unwilling to assume that persons possessing such valuable vocational skills and habits are doomed to become burdens on society should they determine to leave the Amish faith, nor is there any basis in the record to warrant a finding that an additional one or two years of formal school education beyond the eighth grade would serve to eliminate any such problem that might exist.

Insofar as the State's claim rests on the view that a brief additional period of formal education is imperative to enable the Amish to participate effectively and intelligently in our democratic process, it must fall. The Amish alternative to formal secondary school education has enabled them to function effectively in their day-to-day life under self-imposed limitations on relations with the world, and to survive and prosper in contemporary society as a separate, sharply identifiable and highly self-sufficient community for more than 200 years in this country. In itself this is strong evidence that they are capable of fulfilling the social and political responsibilities of citizenship without compelled attendance beyond the eighth grade at the price of jeopardizing their free exercise of religious belief.

IV

Finally, the State, on authority of *Prince v. Massachusetts*, 321 U.S. 158 (1944), argues that a decision exempting Amish children from the State's requirement fails to recognize the substantive right of the Amish child to a secondary education, and fails to give due regard to the power of the State as *parens patriae* to extend the benefit of secondary education to children regardless of the wishes of their parents.

This case, of course, is not one in which any harm to the physical or mental health of the child or to the public safety, peace, order, or welfare has been demonstrated or may be properly inferred. The record is to the contrary, and any reliance on that theory would find no support in the evidence.

V

For the reasons stated we hold, with the Supreme Court of Wisconsin, that the First and Fourteenth Amendments prevent the State from compelling respondents to cause their children to attend formal high school to age 16.

Mr. Justice POWELL and Mr. Justice REHNQUIST took no part in the consideration or decision of this case. The concurring opinions of Justices Stewart and Brennan are omitted.

Mr. Justice WHITE, with whom Mr. Justice BRENNAN and Mr. Justice STEWART join, concurring.

Cases such as this one inevitably call for a delicate balancing of important but conflicting interests. This would be a very different case for me if respondents' claim were that their religion forbade their children from attending any school at any time and from complying in any way with the educational standards set by the State. Since the

Amish children are permitted to acquire the basic tools of literacy to survive in modern society by attending grades one through eight and since the deviation from the State's compulsory education law is relatively slight, I conclude that respondents' claim must prevail, largely because "religious freedom—the freedom to believe and to practice strange and, it may be, foreign creeds has classically been one of the higher values of our society." *Braunfeld v. Brown*, 366 U.S. [at] 612 (Brennan, J., concurring and dissenting).

Decision in cases such as this and the administration of an exemption for Old Order Amish from the State's compulsory school-attendance laws will inevitably involve the kind of close and perhaps repeated scrutiny of religious practices which the Court has heretofore been anxious to avoid. But such entanglement does not create a forbidden establishment of religion where it is essential to implement free exercise values threatened by an otherwise neutral program instituted to foster some permissible, nonreligious state objective. I join the Court because the sincerity of the Amish religious policy here is uncontested, because the potentially adverse impact of the state requirement is great, and because the State's valid interest in education has already been largely satisfied by the eight years the children have already spent in school.

Mr. Justice DOUGLAS, dissenting in part.

I

I agree with the Court that the religious scruples of the Amish are opposed to the education of their children beyond the grade schools, yet I disagree with the Court's conclusion that the matter is within the dispensation of parents alone.

Although the lower courts and a majority of this Court assume an identity of interest between parent and child, it is clear that they have treated the religious interest of the child as a factor in the analysis.

Religion is an individual experience. It is not necessary, nor even appropriate, for every Amish child to express his views on the subject in a prosecution of a single adult. Crucial, however, are the views of the child whose parent is the subject of the suit. Frieda Yoder has in fact testified that her own religious views are opposed to high-school education. I therefore join the judgment of the Court as to respondent Jonas Yoder. But Frieda Yoder's views may not be those of Vernon Yutzy or Barbara Miller. I must dissent, therefore, as to respondents Adin Yutzy and Wallace Miller as their motion to dismiss also raised the question of their children's religious liberty.

II

This issue has never been squarely presented before today. These children are "persons" within the meaning of the Bill of Rights. We have so held over and over again. On this important and vital matter of education, I think the children should be entitled to be heard. While the parents, absent dissent, normally speak for the entire family, the education of the child is a matter on which the child will often have decided views. He may want to be a pianist or an astronaut or an oceanographer. To do so he will have to break from the Amish tradition.

It is the future of the student, not the future of the parents, that is imperiled by today's decision. It is the student's judgment, not his parents', that is essential if we are to give full meaning to what we have said about the Bill of Rights and of the right of students to be masters of their own destiny. If he is harnessed to the Amish way of life by those in authority over him and if his education is truncated, his entire life may be stunted and deformed.

III

I think the emphasis of the Court on the "law and order" record of this Amish group of people is quite irrelevant. The Court rightly rejects the notion that actions, even though religiously grounded, are always outside the protection of the Free Exercise Clause of the First Amendment.

Action, which the Court deemed to be antisocial, could be punished even though it was grounded on deeply held and sincere religious convictions. What we do today, at least in this respect, opens the way to give organized religion a broader base than it has ever enjoyed; and it even promises that in time *Reynolds* will be overruled. In another way, however, the Court retreats when in reference to Henry Thoreau it says his "choice was philosophical and personal rather than religious, and such belief does not rise to the demands of the Religion Clauses."

Notes

1. Chief Justice Burger's opinion in *Yoder* stresses the communal aspect of the Amish faith. Justice Douglas's dissent, by contrast, declares "religion is a personal experience." Does this matter? The Court's concludes that "compulsory school attendance to age 16 for Amish children carries with it a very real threat of undermining the Amish community and religious practice as they exist today; they must either abandon belief and be assimilated into society at large, or be forced to migrate to some other and more tolerant region." Does the First Amendment protect communities from state attempts to change their character? *See Boy Scouts of America v. Dale*, 530 U.S. 640, 654 (2000) ("to come within [the] ambit [of the First Amendment right of expressive association], a group must engage in some form of expression, whether it be public or private."); *Roberts v. United States Jaycees*, 468 U.S. 609, 622 (1984) ("implicit in the right to engage in activities protected by the First Amendment" is "a corresponding right to associate with others in pursuit of a wide variety of political, social, economic, educational, religious, and cultural ends.")

2. Does the State have an interest in the development of a child's religious identity? Justice Douglas dissented in *Yoder* because there was no evidence in the record that all of the Amish children involved in the case agreed with their parents' decision to end their formal education in the eighth grade. Should are the views of children be relevant in a criminal prosecution of their parents for noncompliance with State compulsory education laws? Justice Douglas implies that the State's interest as *parens patriae* includes protecting the religious liberty of a child who wishes "to break from the Amish tradition." If so, at what point in a child's religious upbringing would State intervention to determine the child's interests be justified? Does Justice Douglas' dissent suggest that a function of compulsory education through high school is to serve as a counterweight to values that are contrary to the "right of students to be masters of their own destiny"?

3. Justice Douglas also disagreed with the Court's conclusion that there is a meaningful distinction between religious and secular reasons for withdrawing from the world. In the Court's view, "Thoreau's choice was philosophical and personal rather than religious, and such belief does not rise to the demands of the Religion Clauses." Justice Douglas described this position as "a retreat." Should the sincerity or strength with which an individual holds philosophical and personal views make them "religious"? Would it be accurate to characterize religious views "philosophical and personal"? *See* Chapter Thirteen.

4. Courts are not receptive to arguments that the First Amendment requires an exemption from general taxation. In *United States v. Lee*, 455 U.S. 252, 257, 260 (1982), excerpted in Chapter Nine, the Court accepted an Amish employer's "contention that both payment and receipt of social security benefits is forbidden by the Amish faith," but held that "the broad public interest in maintaining a sound tax system is of such a high order, religious belief in conflict with the payment of taxes affords no basis for resisting the tax." Congress included a statutory exemption for self-employed individuals who are members of "a recognized religious sect or division thereof and [are] adherent[s] of established tenets or teachings of such sect or division by reason of which he is conscientiously opposed to acceptance of the benefits of any private or public insurance." *See* 26 U.S.C. § 1402(g). In the Court's view, the legislative exemption left no room for judiciary: "Congress has accommodated, to the extent compatible with a comprehensive national program, the practices of those who believe it a violation of their faith to participate in the social security system." *Id.* at 260.

7. Native American Religions and the Religious Liberty Guarantee

Cases concerning Native American religious beliefs and practices provide an interesting, but enormously difficult, vantage point from which to examine the Supreme Court's understanding of religious liberty. The federal government has a unique relationship with the Indian tribes, and with Native Americans generally. Traditional Native American religious beliefs and practices

> interweave and integrate all aspects of human and spiritual existence. Most Indian languages do not possess a word translatable as "religion." Rather, the concept of religion permeates one's existence and is indistinguishable from one's cultural, political, and economic existence. Western religion, on the other hand, is understood and referenced to a linear concept of time and to the celebration of important messiahs, prophets, and sacred events.
>
> The rituals of many Indian religions are required to maintain the spiritual and earthly harmony and balance of nature, the community, and the person. As Deward Walker has explained, "American Indian culture ... entails actually entering sacredness rather than merely praying to it or propitiating it." For a society accustomed to primarily attending services on Sundays and to worship at any of several locations, it is most difficult to appreciate a non-Western religion that requires the performance of a ritualistic act at a certain time and in a certain place.

Sharon L. O'Brien, *Freedom of Religion in Indian Country*, 56 Mont. L. Rev. 451, 453–454 (1995).

As a result, the structure within which questions relating to Native American religious practice is different than most other religious liberty cases. Tribal members have the same privileges and immunities as other citizens of the United States, and, as members of communities whose sovereignty predates the Constitution, they are also beneficiaries the Trust Doctrine, which creates a complex sovereign-to-sovereign relationship between tribes and the federal government. *See United States v. Kagama*, 188 U.S. 375 (1886) (Congress has plenary power over Indian affairs); *Cherokee Nation v. United States*, 30 U.S. (5 Pet.) 1, 17 (1831) (describing the tribes as "domestic dependent nations" whose relationship to the United States "resembles that of a ward to his guardian.").

Thus, the actual location of the alleged religious liberty violation may make a crucial difference. If the case arises on federal property or is otherwise within federal jurisdiction, the federal constitution, the American Indian Religious Freedom Act, 42 U.S.C. § 1996 (2001) (AIRFA), specific treaty obligations, the Trust Doctrine, or other laws may apply. If the case arises within a state's jurisdiction, then AIRFA, treaty obligations, and any applicable state law may apply. Finally, if the case arises within tribal jurisdiction, the Indian Civil Rights Act [ICRA] may be applicable. The Indian Civil Rights Act is discussed briefly below.

Native American religious practices have not fared well before the Supreme Court. *See* O'Brien, *Freedom of Religion in Indian Country, supra*; David C. Williams & Susan H. Williams, *Volitionalism and Religious Liberty*, 76 Cornell L. Rev. 769 (1991).

a) Federal Actions Impinging on Native American Religious Practice

In ***Bowen v. Roy***, 476 U.S. 693 (1986), the parents of Little Bird of the Snow Roy applied for and received Aid to Families with Dependent Children and Food Stamps. One of the eligibility conditions imposed by Congress was that all applicants furnish their social security numbers to their respective State welfare departments. Mr. Roy refused to obtain a number for Little Bird of the Snow, arguing on the basis of his Native American religious beliefs that obtaining and using a unique identifier would "'rob the spirit' of his daughter and prevent her from attaining greater spiritual power."

There were two issues: 1) Can the Social Security Administration assign a Social Security number without violating the Free Exercise rights of either Little Bird of the Snow or her parents? and 2) May Congress condition the receipt of public assistance on conduct that their religious beliefs forbids?

An eight-member majority Court held that: "The Free Exercise Clause simply cannot be understood to require the Government to conduct its own internal affairs in ways that comport with the religious beliefs of particular citizens." *Id.* at 699. A plurality of the Court also rejected the proposition that the requirement that the Roys provide the number violated their Free Exercise rights:

> We conclude then that government regulation that indirectly and incidentally calls for a choice between securing a governmental benefit and adherence to religious beliefs is wholly different from governmental action or legislation that criminalizes religiously inspired activity or inescapably compels conduct that some find objectionable for religious reasons. *Id.* at 706.

In **Lyng v. Northwest Indian Cemetery Protective Ass'n**, 485 U.S. 439 (1988), the issue was the preservation of a sacred site: the Chimney Rock section of the Six Rivers National Forest. A study commissioned by the Forest Service as a part of an environmental impact statement found that the Chimney Rock area was an integral and indispensable part of Indian religion and practice, and that Forest Service plans to build a six-mile stretch of road through it should be shelved. When the Forest Service went ahead, the cemetery association sued.

Writing for a five-Justice majority, Justice O'Connor assumed that "the Indian respondents' beliefs are sincere and that the Government's proposed actions [would] have severe adverse effects on the practice of their religion," but rejected the contention that the government has any obligation to alter a proposed course of actions simply because "'the challenged government action would interfere significantly with private persons' ability to pursue spiritual fulfillment according to their own religious beliefs." *Id.* at 449.

The majority drew a distinction the "incidental effects of [otherwise lawful] government programs, which may make it more difficult to practice certain religions but which have no tendency to prohibit religious exercise or coerce individuals into acting contrary to their religious beliefs," and programs that discriminate against certain religious viewpoints, or prohibit or coerce action inconsistent with religious faith. "[W]e have no reason to doubt that the logging and road-building projects at issue in this case could have devastating effects on traditional Indian religious practices, but... the Constitution simply does not provide a principle that could justify upholding respondents' legal claims."

Justices Brennan, Marshall and Blackmun dissented:

> In the final analysis, the Court's refusal to recognize the constitutional dimension of respondents' injuries stems from its concern that acceptance of respondents' claim could potentially strip the Government of its ability to manage and use vast tracts of federal property. In addition, the nature of respondents' site-specific religious practices raises the specter of future suits in which Native Americans seek to exclude all human activity from such areas. These concededly legitimate concerns lie at the very heart of this case, which represents yet another stress point in the longstanding conflict between two disparate cultures—the dominant Western culture, which views land in terms of ownership and use, and that of Native Americans, in which concepts of private property are not only alien, but contrary to a belief system that holds land sacred. Rather than address this conflict in any meaningful fashion, however, the Court disclaims all responsibility for balancing these competing and potentially irreconcilable interests, choosing instead to turn this difficult task over to the Federal Legislature.
>
> The question for the courts, then, is... whether the Native American claimants have discharged their burden of demonstrating, as the Amish did with respect to the compulsory school law in *Yoder*, that the land-use decision poses a substantial and realistic threat of undermining or frustrating their religious practices.

Notes

1. In both *Roy* and *Lyng*, the Court holds that a showing of religious discrimination, coercion, or prohibition is crucial to a finding that a "burden" on free exercise exists, and that no such burden existed. Is the majority suggesting that the text of the First Amendment, which forbids laws "prohibiting" the free exercise of religion means just that? Is such a reading of the incorporated Free Exercise Clause too "formalistic," because it makes judges powerless to evaluate both the actual nature of the claim, and the extent of the harm suffered by the Native American plaintiffs? On the evanescent nature of free exercise burdens, see Ira C. Lupu, *Where Rights Begin: The Problem of Burdens on the Free Exercise of Religion*, 102 Harv. L. Rev. 933 (1989).

2. In neither *Sherbert* nor *Lyng* was there any claim that the government intended to prohibit the free exercise of religion. In *Sherbert*, the decision to refuse benefits was compared with a fine for worshiping. In *Lyng*, by contrast, the Court found no principle in the Constitution that would support the cemetery association's claim, even if it assumed that the completion of the road would "virtually destroy the... Indians' ability to practice their religion." *Lyng*, 485 U.S. at 451. Why the difference in approach?

3. The federal government knew of the impact of the road on Native American religious belief and practice before it began constructing the road, and both AIRFA and the Trust Doctrine impose a fiduciary duty to preserve and protect Native American lands, traditions, and culture. Does that knowledge, coupled with the fiduciary duty to protect sacred places, make *Lyng* a case involving purposeful harm to Native American beliefs and practices that has no analogy in the case of any other faiths? If so, should the case have been litigated under the Free Exercise Clause at all?

4. The Court holds that "[n]owhere in the [AIRFA] is there so much as a hint of any intent to create a cause of action or any judicially enforceable individual rights," and quotes its sponsor's statement that AIRFA "has no teeth in it." *Id.* at 455. If it is clear that Congress intended the federal government to protect and preserve Native American religious traditions and sacred sites, why does the Court balk at using the Free Exercise Clause to protect legally protected rights unique to adherents of Native American religions?

5. *Lyng* was decided against the backdrop of an intense political debate concerning the role of the judiciary in the American democratic experiment. The majority and dissent are sharply divided on the role of the judiciary in resolving this kind of dispute. The majority restricts the types of governmental action that constitute a free exercise "burden" in order to avoid determining what governmental interests may be "compelling." By necessary implication, it leaves that balancing process to Congress. The dissent claims that the majority, by failing to "address this conflict in any meaningful fashion," "disclaims all responsibility for balancing these competing and potentially irreconcilable interests, choosing instead to turn this difficult task over to the federal legislature." Who makes the better argument? How *should* Congress' "plenary power" over matters affecting Native Americans influence the Court's understanding of its judicial role in their free exercise cases?

6. Before the Supreme Court decided *Lyng*, it refused in two specific contexts to extend the *Sherbert* compelling state interest analysis. In *Goldman v. Weinberger*, 475 U.S. 503 (1986), the Court assessed the military regulation banning the wearing of religious clothing, including yarmulkes, in light of its "reasonableness." A general challenge to the regulation was rejected without resort to the *Sherbert* test. Similarly, the Court deferred to prison authorities who refused to exempt from work a prisoner who wished to attend religious services: "[P]rison regulations alleged to infringe constitutional rights are judged under a 'reasonableness' test less restrictive than that ordinarily applied to alleged infringements of fundamental constitutional rights." *O'Lone v. Estate of Shabazz*, 482 U.S. 342, 349 (1987). In both cases, the Court permitted a burden on religious exercise without subjecting the governmental action to the compelling governmental interest test because of the "restricted" environment in which the claimant desired to engage in that exercise.

b) State Actions Impinging on Native American Religious Practice

The controversy that led to the Supreme Court's watershed decision in *Employment Div. v. Smith*, excerpted below, has its roots in the sometimes convoluted relationships between federal and State policy, and in the ongoing separation of powers debate over which branch has the final word in religious liberty cases. *See* Destro, *By What Right?*, at 36–48. In *Smith*, *three* sets of policies were at issue: federal and state policies regarding certain addictive drugs; federal and state policies affecting Native Americans; and federal and state policies governing religious freedom.

From the perspective of the individual believer, it makes little practical difference why a policy inhibiting religious liberty is voided. For believers, the issue is liberty against a government's attempt to interfere with legitimate religious activity. All that matters is the exemption itself.

For students of constitutional law, however, it is often the rationale, not merely the result, which is important. There is quite a large difference, for both analytical and political purposes, among religious liberty cases whose outcome turns on pre-emption because Congress has plenary power over matters affecting Native Americans; on Congressional exercise of its power under §5 of the Fourteenth Amendment; on the Court's interpretation of a specific provision of the Bill of Rights; or on a State's interpretation of its own religious liberty guarantee.

This, of course, is why *Employment Div. v. Smith* is such an important case. In *Smith v. Employment Div.*, 301 Or. 209, 215, 721 P.2d 445 (1986), the Oregon Supreme Court held that denial of unemployment benefits to a drug counselor who was discharged for using peyote during religious services in the Native American Church did *not* violate Oregon's religious liberty guarantee because the policy was "completely neutral with respect to religious motivations for misconduct." But because the *Sherbert* line of cases required a balancing of the burden on the individual's ability to practice his or her religion against the interests of the State, denial of benefits *did* violate the Free Exercise Clause. Oregon's appeal to the Supreme Court raised the following question:

> Does the Free Exercise Clause compel a state to award unemployment benefits to a drug rehabilitation counselor who agrees to refrain from using illegal drugs as a condition of his employment and is fired for misconduct after illegally ingesting peyote as part of a religious ceremony?

Petition for *Certiorari*, *Employment Div. v. Smith*, No. 86-947 (Dec. 2, 1986).

In *Employment Div. v. Smith*, 485 U.S. 660, 672 (1988) (*Smith* I), the Court refused to answer the question until the Oregon court determined whether *religious* use of peyote was illegal under Oregon law. The case was remanded to the Oregon Supreme Court, which held in *Smith v. Employment Div.*, 307 Or. 68, 75, 763 P.2d 146, 149 (1988), that sacramental use of peyote was illegal in Oregon, but that Congress had "unmistakably adopted the view that the use of peyote in the Native American Church is the kind of free exercise of religion that the First Amendment protects."

Oregon appealed again. This time, the question was posed as follows:

> Does the Free Exercise Clause of the first amendment to the United States Constitution protect a person's religiously motivated use of peyote from the reach of a state's general criminal law prohibition?

Brief for Petitioners, *Employment Div. v. Smith*, 1988 U.S. Briefs (LEXIS) 1213.

Employment Division, Department of Human Resources of Oregon v. Smith

494 U.S. 872, *reh'g denied*, 496 U.S. 913 (1990)

Justice SCALIA delivered the opinion of the Court.

This case requires us to decide whether the Free Exercise Clause of the First Amendment permits the State of Oregon to include religiously inspired peyote use within the reach of its general criminal prohibition on use of that drug, and thus permits the State to deny unemployment benefits to persons dismissed from their jobs because of such religiously inspired use.

I

Oregon law prohibits the knowing or intentional possession of a "controlled substance" unless the substance has been prescribed by a medical practitioner. The law defines "controlled substance" as a drug classified in Schedules I through V of the Federal Controlled Substances Act, as modified by the State Board of Pharmacy. Persons who violate this provision by possessing a controlled substance listed on Schedule I are "guilty of a Class B felony." As compiled by the State Board of Pharmacy under its statutory authority, Schedule I contains the drug peyote.

Respondents Alfred Smith and Galen Black were fired from their jobs with a private drug rehabilitation organization because they ingested peyote for sacramental purposes at a ceremony of the Native American Church, of which both are members. When respondents applied to petitioner Employment Division for unemployment compensation, they were determined to be ineligible for benefits because they had been discharged for work-related "misconduct."

On appeal to the Oregon Supreme Court, petitioner argued that the denial of benefits was permissible because respondents' consumption of peyote was a crime under Oregon law. The Oregon Supreme Court reasoned, however, that the criminality of respondents' peyote use was irrelevant to resolution of their constitutional claim. Citing our decisions in *Sherbert* and *Thomas*, the court concluded that respondents were entitled to payment of unemployment benefits.

Before this Court in 1987, petitioner continued to maintain that the illegality of respondents' peyote consumption was relevant to their constitutional claim. We agreed, concluding that "if a State has prohibited through its criminal laws certain kinds of religiously motivated conduct without violating the First Amendment, it certainly follows that it may impose the lesser burden of denying unemployment compensation benefits to persons who engage in that conduct." *Employment Div., Dept. of Human Resources of Oregon v. Smith*, 485 U.S. 660, 670 (1988) (*Smith I*). Being "uncertain about the legality of the religious use of peyote in Oregon," we determined that it would not be "appropriate for us to decide whether the practice is protected by the Federal Constitution." *Id.* at 673. Accordingly, we vacated the judgment of the Oregon Supreme Court and remanded for further proceedings.

On remand, the Oregon Supreme Court held that respondents' religiously inspired use of peyote fell within the prohibition of the Oregon statute, which "makes no exception for the sacramental use" of the drug. It then considered whether that prohibition was valid under the Free Exercise Clause, and concluded that it was not.

We again granted certiorari.

II

Respondents' claim for relief rests on our decisions in *Sherbert*, *Thomas*, and *Hobbie*, in which we held that a State could not condition the availability of unemployment insurance on an individual's willingness to forgo conduct required by his religion. As we observed in *Smith I*, however, the conduct at issue in those cases was not prohibited by law. Now that the Oregon Supreme Court has confirmed that Oregon does prohibit the religious use of peyote, we proceed to consider whether that prohibition is permissible under the Free Exercise Clause.

A

The free exercise of religion means, first and foremost, the right to believe and profess whatever religious doctrine one desires. Thus, the First Amendment obviously excludes all "governmental regulation of religious *beliefs* as such." *Sherbert.* The government may not compel affirmation of religious belief, punish the expression of religious doctrines it believes to be false, impose special disabilities on the basis of religious views or religious status, or lend its power to one or the other side in controversies over religious authority or dogma.

But the "exercise of religion" often involves not only belief and profession but the performance of (or abstention from) physical acts: assembling with others for a worship service, participating in sacramental use of bread and wine, proselytizing, abstaining from certain foods or certain modes of transportation. It would be true, we think (though no case of ours has involved the point), that a state would be "prohibiting the free exercise [of religion]" if it sought to ban such acts or abstentions only when they are engaged in for religious reasons, or only because of the religious belief that they display. It would doubtless be unconstitutional, for example, to ban the casting of "statues that are to be used for worship purposes," or to prohibit bowing down before a golden calf.

Respondents in the present case, however, seek to carry the meaning of "prohibiting the free exercise [of religion]" one large step further. They contend that their religious motivation for using peyote places them beyond the reach of a criminal law that is not specifically directed at their religious practice, and that is concededly constitutional as applied to those who use the drug for other reasons. They assert, in other words, that "prohibiting the free exercise [of religion]" includes requiring any individual to observe a generally applicable law that requires (or forbids) the performance of an act that his religious belief forbids (or requires). As a textual matter, we do not think the words must be given that meaning. It is no more necessary to regard the collection of a general tax, for example, as "prohibiting the free exercise [of religion]" by those citizens who believe support of organized government to be sinful, than it is to regard the same tax as "abridging the freedom...of the press" of those publishing companies that must pay the tax as a condition of staying in business. It is a permissible reading of the text, in the one case as in the other, to say that if prohibiting the exercise of religion (or burdening the activity of printing) is not the object of the tax but merely the incidental effect of a generally applicable and otherwise valid provision, the First Amendment has not been offended.

Our decisions reveal that the latter reading is the correct one. We have never held that an individual's religious beliefs excuse him from compliance with an otherwise valid law prohibiting conduct that the State is free to regulate. On the contrary, the record of more than a century of our free exercise jurisprudence contradicts that proposition. We first had occasion to assert that principle in *Reynolds.*

Subsequent decisions have consistently held that the right of free exercise does not relieve an individual of the obligation to comply with a "valid and neutral law of general applicability on the ground that the law proscribes (or prescribes) conduct that his religion prescribes (or proscribes)." *United States v. Lee*, 455 U.S. 252, 263 n.3 (1982).

The only decisions in which we have held that the First Amendment bars application of a neutral, generally applicable law to religiously motivated action have involved not the Free Exercise Clause alone, but the Free Exercise Clause in conjunction with other constitutional protections, such as freedom of speech and of the press. [*Citing* to *Cantwell*, *Follett*, *Murdock*, *Pierce* and *Yoder.*] Some of our cases prohibiting compelled expression, decided exclusively upon free speech grounds, have also involved freedom of religion.

The present case does not present such a hybrid situation, but a free exercise claim unconnected with any communicative activity or parental right. Respondents urge us to hold, quite simply, that when otherwise prohibitable conduct is accompanied by religious convictions, not only the convictions but the conduct itself must be free from governmental regulation. We have never held that, and decline to do so now. There being no contention that Oregon's drug law represents an attempt to regulate religious beliefs, the communication of religious beliefs, or the raising of one's children in those beliefs, the rule to which we have adhered ever since *Reynolds* plainly controls.

B

Respondents argue that even though exemption from generally applicable criminal laws need not automatically be extended to religiously motivated actors, at least the claim for a religious exemption must be evaluated under the balancing test set forth in *Sherbert.* Under the *Sherbert* test, governmental actions that substantially burden a religious practice must be justified by a compelling governmental interest. Applying that test we have, on three occasions, invalidated state unemployment compensation rules that conditioned the availability of benefits upon an applicant's willingness to work under conditions forbidden by his religion. We have never invalidated any governmental action on the basis of the *Sherbert* test except the denial of unemployment compensation. Although we have sometimes purported to apply the *Sherbert* test in contexts other than that, we have always found the test satisfied. In recent years we have abstained from applying the *Sherbert* test (outside the unemployment compensation field) at all. In *Bowen v. Roy*, we declined to apply *Sherbert* analysis to a federal statutory scheme that required benefit applicants and recipients to provide their Social Security numbers. In *Lyng*, we declined to apply *Sherbert* analysis to the Government's logging and road construction activities on lands used for religious purposes by several Native American Tribes, even though it was undisputed that the activities "could have devastating effects on traditional Indian religious practices." In *Goldman v. Weinberger*, 475 U.S. 503 (1986), we rejected application of the *Sherbert* test to military dress regulations that forbade the wearing of yarmulkes. In *O'Lone v. Estate of Shabazz*, 482 U.S. 342 (1987), we sustained, without mentioning the *Sherbert* test, a prison's refusal to excuse inmates from work requirements to attend worship services.

Even if we were inclined to breathe into *Sherbert* some life beyond the unemployment compensation field, we would not apply it to require exemptions from a generally applicable criminal law.

Whether or not the decisions are that limited, they at least have nothing to do with an across-the-board criminal prohibition on a particular form of conduct. We conclude today that the sounder approach, and the approach in accord with the vast majority of our precedents, is to hold the test inapplicable to such challenges. To make an individual's obligation to obey such a law contingent upon the law's coincidence with his religious beliefs, except where the State's interest is "compelling"—permitting him, by virtue of his beliefs, "to become a law unto himself," *Reynolds*—contradicts both constitutional tradition and common sense.

Any society adopting such a system would be courting anarchy, but that danger increases in direct proportion to the society's diversity of religious beliefs, and its determination to coerce or suppress none of them. Precisely because "we are a cosmopolitan nation made up of people of almost every conceivable religious preference," *Braunfeld*, and precisely because we value and protect that religious divergence, we cannot afford the luxury of deeming *presumptively invalid*, as applied to the religious objector, every regulation of conduct that does not protect an interest of the highest order. The rule respondents favor would open the prospect of constitutionally required religious exemptions from civic obligations of almost every conceivable kind—ranging from compulsory military service, [*Gillette v. United States*, 401 U.S. 437 (1971)] to the payment of taxes, [*Lee*] to health and safety regulation such as manslaughter and child neglect laws, *Funkhouser v. State*, 763 P.2d 695 (Okla. Crim. App. 1988), compulsory vaccination laws, see, *e.g.*, *Cude v. State*, 237 Ark. 927, 377 S.W.2d 816 (1964), drug laws, see, *e.g.*, *Olsen v. Drug Enforcement Administration*, 279 U.S. App. D.C. 1, 878 F.2d 1458 (1989), and traffic laws, see *Cox v. New Hampshire*, 312 U.S. 569 (1941); to social welfare legislation such as minimum wage laws, [*Tony and Susan Alamo Foundation*, 471 U.S. 290 (1985)], child labor laws, [*Prince v. Massachusetts*, 321 U.S. 158 (1944)], animal cruelty laws, *Church of the Lukumi Babalu Aye Inc. v. City of Hialeah*, 723 F. Supp. 1467 (S.D. Fla. 1989), cf. *State v. Massey*, 229 N.C. 734, 51 S.E.2d 179, appeal dism'd, 336 U.S. 942 (1949), environmental protection laws, see *United States v. Little*, 638 F. Supp. 337 (Mont. 1986), and laws providing for equality of opportunity for the races, [*Bob Jones University v. United States*, 461 U.S. 574 (1983)]. The First Amendment's protection of religious liberty does not require this.[5]

Values that are protected against government interference through enshrinement in the Bill of Rights are not thereby banished from the political process. Just as a society that believes in the negative protection accorded to the press by the First Amendment is likely to enact laws that affirmatively foster the dissemination of the printed word, so also a society that believes in the negative protection accorded to religious belief can be expected to be solicitous of that value in its legislation as well. It is therefore not surprising that a number of States have made an exception to their drug laws for sacramental peyote use. But to say that a nondiscriminatory religious-practice exemption is permitted, or even that it is desirable, is not to say that it is constitutionally required, and that the appropriate occasions for its creation can be discerned by the courts. It may fairly be said that leaving accommodation to the political process will place at a relative disadvantage those religious practices that are not widely engaged in; but that unavoidable consequence of democratic government must be preferred to a system in which each conscience is a law unto itself or in which judges weigh the social importance of all laws against the centrality of all religious beliefs.

Because respondents' ingestion of peyote was prohibited under Oregon law, and because that prohibition is constitutional, Oregon may, consistent with the Free Exercise Clause, deny respondents unemployment compensation when their dismissal results from use of the drug. The decision of the Oregon Supreme Court is accordingly reversed.

---

5. Justice O'Connor contends that the "parade of horribles" in the text only "demonstrates… that courts have been quite capable of strik[ing] sensible balances between religious liberty and competing state interests." Justice O'Connor mistakes the purpose of our parade: it is not to suggest that courts would necessarily permit harmful exemptions from these laws (though they might), but to suggest that courts would constantly be in the business of determining whether the "severe impact" of various laws on religious practice (to use Justice Blackmun's terminology) or the "constitutiona[l] significan[ce]" of the "burden on the particular plaintiffs" (to use Justice O'Connor's terminology) suffices to permit us to confer an exemption. It is a parade of horribles because it is horrible to contemplate that federal judges will regularly balance against the importance of general laws the significance of religious practice.

Justice O'CONNOR, with whom Justice BRENNAN, Justice MARSHALL, and Justice BLACKMUN join as to Parts I and II, concurring in the judgment.

Although I agree with the result the Court reaches in this case, I cannot join its opinion. In my view, today's holding dramatically departs from well-settled First Amendment jurisprudence, appears unnecessary to resolve the question presented, and is incompatible with our Nation's fundamental commitment to individual religious liberty.

II

A

Because the First Amendment does not distinguish between religious belief and religious conduct, conduct motivated by sincere religious belief, like the belief itself, must therefore be at least presumptively protected by the Free Exercise Clause.

The Court today, however, interprets the Clause to permit the government to prohibit, without justification, conduct mandated by an individual's religious beliefs, so long as that prohibition is generally applicable. A person who is barred from engaging in religiously motivated conduct is barred from freely exercising his religion. Moreover, that person is barred from freely exercising his religion regardless of whether the law prohibits the conduct only when engaged in for religious reasons, only by members of that religion, or by all persons. It is difficult to deny that a law that prohibits religiously motivated conduct, even if the law is generally applicable, does not at least implicate First Amendment concerns.

The First Amendment does not distinguish between laws that are generally applicable and laws that target particular religious practices. Indeed, few States would be so naive as to enact a law directly prohibiting or burdening a religious practice as such. Our free exercise cases have all concerned generally applicable laws that had the effect of significantly burdening a religious practice. If the First Amendment is to have any vitality, it ought not be construed to cover only the extreme and hypothetical situation in which a State directly targets a religious practice.

To say that a person's right to free exercise has been burdened, of course, does not mean that he has an absolute right to engage in the conduct. The compelling interest test effectuates the First Amendment's command that religious liberty is an independent liberty, that it occupies a preferred position, and that the Court will not permit encroachments upon this liberty, whether direct or indirect, unless required by clear and compelling governmental interests "of the highest order," *Yoder*.

The Court endeavors to escape from our decisions in *Cantwell* and *Yoder* by labeling them "hybrid" decisions, but there is no denying that both cases expressly relied on the Free Exercise Clause, and that we have consistently regarded those cases as part of the mainstream of our free exercise jurisprudence. Moreover, in each of the other cases cited by the Court to support its categorical rule, we rejected the particular constitutional claims before us only after carefully weighing the competing interests. That we rejected the free exercise claims in those cases hardly calls into question the applicability of First Amendment doctrine in the first place. Indeed, it is surely unusual to judge the vitality of a constitutional doctrine by looking to the win-loss record of the plaintiffs who happen to come before us.

B

Respondents, of course, do not contend that their conduct is automatically immune from all governmental regulation simply because it is motivated by their sincere religious beliefs. Rather, respondents invoke our traditional compelling interest test to argue that the Free Exercise Clause requires the State to grant them a limited exemption from its general criminal prohibition against the possession of peyote. The Court today, however, denies them even the opportunity to make that argument.

In my view, however, the essence of a free exercise claim is relief from a burden imposed by government on religious practices or beliefs, whether the burden is imposed directly through laws that prohibit or compel specific religious practices, or indirectly through laws that, in effect, make abandonment of one's own religion or conformity to the religious beliefs of others the price of an equal place in the civil community. A State that makes criminal an individual's religiously motivated conduct burdens that individual's free exercise of religion in the severest manner possible, for it "results in the choice to the individual of either abandoning his religious principle or facing criminal prosecution." *Braunfeld*. I would have thought it beyond argument that such laws implicate free exercise concerns.

There is nothing talismanic about neutral laws of general applicability or general criminal prohibitions, for laws neutral toward religion can coerce a person to violate his religious conscience or intrude upon his religious duties just as effectively as laws aimed at religion. [T]he First Amendment unequivocally makes freedom of religion, like freedom from race discrimination and freedom of speech, a "constitutional nor[m]," not an "anomaly." The Court's parade of horribles not only fails as a reason for discarding the compelling interest test, it instead demonstrates just the opposite: that courts have been quite capable of applying our free exercise jurisprudence to strike sensible balances between religious liberty and competing state interests.

Finally, the Court today suggests that the disfavoring of minority religions is an "unavoidable consequence" under our system of government and that accommodation of such religions must be left to the political process. In my view, however, the First Amendment was enacted precisely to protect the rights of those whose religious practices are not shared by the majority and may be viewed with hostility.

III

The Court's holding today not only misreads settled First Amendment precedent; it appears to be unnecessary to this case. I would reach the same result applying our established free exercise jurisprudence.

A

Under Oregon law, as construed by that State's highest court, members of the Native American Church must choose between carrying out the ritual embodying their religious beliefs and avoidance of criminal prosecution. That choice is, in my view, more than sufficient to trigger First Amendment scrutiny.

There is also no dispute that Oregon has a significant interest in enforcing laws that control the possession and use of controlled substances by its citizens. As we recently noted, drug abuse is "one of the greatest problems affecting the health and welfare of our population" and thus "one of the most serious problems confronting our society today." In light of our recent decisions holding that the governmental interests in the collection of income tax, *Hernandez v. Commissioner*, 490 U.S. 680, 699–700 (1989), a comprehensive social security system, see *Lee*, and military conscription, see *Gillette*, are compelling, respondents do not seriously dispute that Oregon has a compelling interest in prohibiting the possession of peyote by its citizens.

B

Thus, the critical question in this case is whether exempting respondents from the State's general criminal prohibition "will unduly interfere with fulfillment of the governmental interest." Because the health effects caused by the use of controlled substances exist regardless of the motivation of the user, the use of such substances, even for religious purposes, violates the very purpose of the laws that prohibit them. Cf. *State v. Massey*, 229 N.C. 734, 51 S.E.2d 179 (denying religious exemption to municipal ordinance prohibiting handling of poisonous reptiles), appeal dism'd *sub nom. Bunn v. North Carolina*, 336 U.S. 942 (1949). Moreover, in view of the societal interest in preventing trafficking in controlled substances, uniform application of the criminal prohibition at issue is essential to the effectiveness of Oregon's stated interest in preventing any possession of peyote.

Respondents contend that any incompatibility is belied by the fact that the Federal Government and several States provide exemptions for the religious use of peyote. But other governments may surely choose to grant an exemption without Oregon, with its specific asserted interest in uniform application of its drug laws, being *required* to do so by the First Amendment.

Accordingly, I concur in the judgment of the Court.

Justice BLACKMUN, with whom Justice BRENNAN and Justice MARSHALL join, dissenting.

The Court over the years painstakingly has developed a consistent and exacting standard to test the constitutionality of a state statute that burdens the free exercise of religion. Such a statute may stand only if the law in general, and the State's refusal to allow a religious exemption in particular, are justified by a compelling interest that cannot be served by less restrictive means.

I

In weighing... [respondents'] clear interest... in the free exercise of their religion against Oregon's asserted interest in enforcing its drug laws, it is important to articulate in precise terms the state interest involved. It is not the State's broad interest in fighting the critical "war on drugs" that must be weighed against respondents' claim, but the State's narrow interest in refusing to make an exception for the religious, ceremonial use of peyote. Failure to reduce the competing interests to the same plane of generality tends to distort the weighing process in the State's favor.

The State's interest in enforcing its prohibition, in order to be sufficiently compelling to outweigh a free exercise claim, cannot be merely abstract or symbolic. The State cannot plausibly assert that unbending application of a criminal prohibition is essential to fulfill any compelling interest, if it does not, in fact, attempt to enforce that prohibition. Oregon has never sought to prosecute respondents, and does not claim that it has made significant enforcement efforts against other religious users of peyote.

Similarly, this Court's prior decisions have not allowed a government to rely on mere speculation about potential harms, but have demanded evidentiary support for a refusal to allow a religious exception. In this case, the State's justification for refusing to recognize an exception to its criminal laws for religious peyote use is entirely speculative.

The State proclaims an interest in protecting the health and safety of its citizens from the dangers of unlawful drugs. It offers, however, no evidence that the religious use of peyote has ever harmed anyone. The factual findings of other courts cast doubt on the State's assumption that religious use of peyote is harmful.

The fact that peyote is classified as a Schedule I controlled substance does not, by itself, show that any and all uses of peyote, in any circumstance, are inherently harmful and dangerous. The Federal Government, which created the classifications of unlawful drugs from which Oregon's drug laws are derived, apparently does not find peyote so dangerous as to preclude an exemption for religious use.[5] Moreover, other Schedule I drugs have lawful uses.

The carefully circumscribed ritual context in which respondents used peyote is far removed from the irresponsible and unrestricted recreational use of unlawful drugs.[6] The Native American Church's internal restrictions on, and supervision of, its members' use of peyote substantially obviate the State's health and safety concerns. Far from promoting the lawless and irresponsible use of drugs, Native American Church members' spiritual code exemplifies values that Oregon's drug laws are presumably intended to foster.

The State also seeks to support its refusal to make an exception for religious use of peyote by invoking its interest in abolishing drug trafficking. There is, however, practically no illegal traffic in peyote. Peyote simply is not a popular drug; its distribution for use in religious rituals has nothing to do with the vast and violent traffic in illegal narcotics that plagues this country.

Finally, the State argues that granting an exception for religious peyote use would erode its interest in the uniform, fair, and certain enforcement of its drug laws. The State fears that, if it grants an exemption for religious peyote use, a flood of other claims to religious exemptions will follow. It would then be placed in a dilemma, it says, between allowing a patchwork of exemptions that would hinder its law enforcement efforts, and risking a violation of the Establishment Clause by arbitrarily limiting its religious exemptions. This argument, however, could be made in almost any free exercise case. This Court, however, consistently has rejected similar arguments in past free exercise cases, and it should do so here as well.

That the State might grant an exemption for religious peyote use, but deny other religious claims arising in different circumstances, would not violate the Establishment Clause. Though the State must treat all religions equally, and not favor one over another, this obligation is fulfilled by the uniform application of the "compelling interest" *test* to all free exercise claims, not by reaching uniform *results* as to all claims.

---

5. See 21 CFR § 1307.31 (1989) ("The listing of peyote as a controlled substance in Schedule I does not apply to the nondrug use of peyote in bona fide religious ceremonies of the Native American Church, and members of the Native American Church so using peyote are exempt from registration. Any person who manufactures peyote for or distributes peyote to the Native American Church, however, is required to obtain registration annually and to comply with all other requirements of law").

Moreover, 23 States, including many that have significant Native American populations, have statutory or judicially crafted exemptions in their drug laws for religious use of peyote.

6. In this respect, respondents' use of peyote seems closely analogous to the sacramental use of wine by the Roman Catholic Church. During Prohibition, the Federal Government exempted such use of wine from its general ban on possession and use of alcohol. See National Prohibition Act, Title II, § 3, 41 Stat. 308. However compelling the Government's general interest in prohibiting the use of alcohol may have been, it could not plausibly have asserted an interest sufficiently compelling to outweigh Catholics' right to take communion.

II

Respondents believe, and their sincerity has *never* been at issue, that the peyote plant embodies their deity, and eating it is an act of worship and communion. Without peyote, they could not enact the essential ritual of their religion.

If Oregon can constitutionally prosecute them for this act of worship, they, like the Amish, may be "forced to migrate to some other and more tolerant region." This potentially devastating impact must be viewed in light of the federal policy—reached in reaction to many years of religious persecution and intolerance—of protecting the religious freedom of Native Americans.

I dissent.

***

Church of the Lukumi Babalu Aye v. City of Hialeah, 508 U.S. 520 (1993)—The Supreme Court considered a series of ordinances adopted by the City of Hialeah, Florida after the City learned that adherents of Santeria were planning to establish a church, school, and cultural center there. Santeria, "the way of the Saints," is a fusion of the traditional West African religious beliefs and practices with significant elements of Roman Catholicism. One of its principal forms of devotion is animal sacrifice.

Over the course of several months, the Hialeah city council adopted a series of resolutions and ordinances that "reiterate[d] its commitment to a prohibition against any and all acts of any and all religious groups which are inconsistent with public morals, peace or safety." One resolution took note of "its residents' great concern regarding the possibility of public ritualistic animal sacrifices." Another resolution observed "that certain religions may propose to engage in practices which are inconsistent with public morals, peace or safety," declared it city policy "to oppose the ritual sacrifices of animals" within Hialeah, and announced that any person or organization practicing animal sacrifice "will be prosecuted" under Florida's statutes prohibiting cruelty to animals. *Id.* at 527.

In September 1987, it codified these concerns in several ordinances that, when read together, explicitly forbade "any person, persons, corporations or associations to sacrifice any animal within the corporate limits of the City of Hialeah, Florida;" prohibited the ritual slaughter of animals not "specifically raised for food purposes" by anyone other than a licensed slaughterhouse; and provided criminal penalties for each violation. The combined effect of the ordinances was to limit *only* ritual slaughter associated with animal sacrifice. Ritual slaughter associated with licensed food production was exempt.

The Court unanimously concluded that suppressing a central element of the Santeria worship service was the goal of the ordinances. Just as in *Smith*, however, disagreement over the content of the Free Exercise norm led to disagreements over the proper analytical framework.

Because *Smith* rests on a nondiscrimination principle, Justice Kennedy's opinion for the Court contains an extended discussion of the relationship between "neutrality" and "general applicability." In his view,

> Neutrality and general applicability are interrelated, and failure to satisfy one requirement is a likely indication that the other has not been satisfied. A law failing to satisfy these requirements must be justified by a compelling governmental interest and must be narrowly tailored to advance that interest.
>
> All laws are selective to some extent, but categories of selection are of paramount concern when a law has the incidental effect of burdening religious

> practice. The Free Exercise Clause "protect[s] religious observers against unequal treatment," and inequality results when a legislature decides that the governmental interests it seeks to advance are worthy of being pursued only against conduct with a religious motivation.

Id. at 531–532, 542–543. The purpose of the factual inquiry is to determine the object of the law. The court must therefore examine the proffered goals of the statute, the means employed to effectuate them, and the "fit" between the specific means utilized and the ends the State seeks to accomplish. The bulk of Justice Kennedy's opinion is devoted to an examination of the connection between means and ends, and concludes that, when viewed in context, "[t]he ordinances 'ha[ve] every appearance of a prohibition that society is prepared to impose upon [Santeria worshippers] but not upon itself.'" *Id.* at 546.

Justices Scalia, Souter, and Blackmun, each writing separately, emphasized the differences in their approach to the factual inquiry. For Justice Scalia

> [T]he defect of lack of neutrality applies primarily to those laws that *by their terms* impose disabilities on the basis of religion (*e.g.*, a law excluding members of a certain sect from public benefits); whereas the defect of lack of general applicability applies primarily to those laws which, though neutral in their terms, through their design, construction, or enforcement target the practices of a particular religion for discriminatory treatment.

Id. at 557–558. For Justice Souter, the proper inquiry is not simply unequal *treatment*, but also refusal to *exempt* conduct from laws that burden religious exercise.

> Hialeah's animal-sacrifice ordinances are not neutral under any definition, any more than they are generally applicable.... The extent to which the Free Exercise Clause requires government to refrain from impeding religious exercise defines nothing less than the respective relationships in our constitutional democracy of the individual to government and to God. "Neutral, generally applicable" laws, drafted as they are from the perspective of the non-adherent, have the unavoidable potential of putting the believer to a choice between God and government. Our cases now present competing answers to the question when government, while pursuing secular ends, may compel disobedience to what one believes religion commands. The case before us is rightly decided without resolving the existing tension, which remains for another day when it may be squarely faced.

Id. at 563–564, 576. Justice Blackmun, by contrast, was willing to face that tension:

> [U]nlike the majority, I do not believe that "[a] law burdening religious practice that is not neutral or not of general application must undergo the most rigorous of scrutiny." In my view, regulation that targets religion in this way, *ipso facto,* fails strict scrutiny. Otherwise, however, "[t]he First Amendment... does not distinguish between laws that are generally applicable and laws that target particular religious practices." Because respondent here does single out religion in this way, the present case is an easy one to decide.
>
> A harder case would be presented if petitioners were requesting an exemption from a generally applicable anticruelty law. This case does not present, and I therefore decline to reach, the question whether the Free Exercise Clause would require a religious exemption from a law that sincerely pursued the goal of protecting animals from cruel treatment.

Id. at 579–580.

Notes

1. Justice Souter's discussion of the precedents includes the following reference to *Reynolds v. United States*: "*Reynolds* has been read as consistent with the principle that religious conduct may be regulated by general or targeting law only if the conduct 'pose[s] some substantial threat to public safety, peace or order.'" (*quoting Sherbert v. Verner*). What substantial threat to public safety, peace or order did polygamy pose in *Reynolds*? In *Yoder*, Justice Douglas suggested that *Reynolds* should be overruled. Is *Reynolds* too old, or too often cited, to escape reconsideration in light of the Court's more recent precedent? *See* Keith E. Sealing, *Polygamists Out of the Closet: Statutory and State Constitutional Prohibitions Against Polygamy Are Unconstitutional Under the Free Exercise Clause*, 17 Ga. St. U. L. Rev. 691 (2001) (arguing that the Morrill Act and State constitutions adopted during the campaign against polygamy targeted Mormon belief and practice and are unconstitutional).

2. Justice Kennedy's opinion for the majority concludes with the statement, "The Free Exercise Clause commits government itself to religious tolerance." Is "tolerance" the right concept? Recall that a draft of the 1776 Virginia Declaration of Rights by George Mason granted "the fullest toleration in the exercise of religion." James Madison successfully substituted language granting all men the right "to the free exercise of religion." Madison disparaged the word "tolerance" because it indicated that religious worship was an act that took place at the sufferance of the community, not a duty owed God. Is the Court's use of the concept of "tolerance" in *Lukumi* an indication of a generalized retreat from a stronger position in the *Sherbert-Yoder* line of cases? Professor Stephen Carter has argued that "[t]olerance without respect means little." Stephen L. Carter, The Culture of Disbelief: How American Law and Politics Trivialize Religious Devotion 93 (1993). Does the approach in *Lukumi* suggest that the Court favors tolerance without respect?

3. Justice Blackmun's opinion concurring in the judgment leaves open the question whether a State interest in preventing cruelty to animals constitutes a compelling interest. Reconsider Justice Kennedy's approach to the facts in *Lukumi*. Given the exceptions in Florida law, would it be possible to write a "neutral and generally applicable" law preventing cruelty to animals? Try to write one.

8. The Content of the Free Exercise Norm After *Smith & Lukumi*

Much of the criticism of *Smith* focuses on the Supreme Court's rejection of a standard of review focused on multi-factor balancing in favor of an inquiry focused on neutrality and general applicability. For Justice O'Connor, changing the standard of review was tantamount to changing the content of the free exercise norm itself: "The compelling interest test effectuates the First Amendment's command that religious liberty is an independent liberty, [and] that it occupies a preferred position." *Smith*, at 895 (O'Connor, Brennan & Blackmun, JJ., concurring).

But what *is* the substantive content of the free exercise norm? A review of the commentary indicates that the content of the free exercise norm was the subject of some controversy even before *Smith*. Speaking critically of *Smith* in 1992, Judge John T. Noonan, Jr. noted that the Supreme Court has *never* used the Free Exercise Clause to support a ruling that an act of Congress is unconstitutional. John T. Noonan, Jr., *The End of Free Exercise?*, 42 De Paul L. Rev. 567, 575 (1992). That statement remains true today. Of the list of State laws held unconstitutional by the Court prior to *Smith*, Noonan observes: "It is not a notable list of freedoms. Very few of them relate to any substantial community activity; the majority are negative." *Id.* Professor Mark Tushnet supported the result in *Smith*, but argued that the primary reason was "[his] discomfort with the rhetoric of free exercise discourse under the pre-*Smith* regime, in which generous promises of sensitivity to eccentric religious practices were routinely betrayed." Mark Tushnet, *The Rhetoric of Free Exercise Discourse*, 1993 B.Y.U. L. Rev. 117, 117. At this writing, the debate continues. *Compare* Cedric Merlin Powell, *The Scope of National Power and the Centrality of Religion*, 38 Brandeis L.J. 643 (2000) *with* Richard F. Duncan, *Free Exercise is Dead, Long Live Free Exercise*: Smith, Lukumi *and the General Applicability Requirement*, 3 U. Pa. J. Const. L. 850 (2001).

These criticisms suggest the need for a clarification of the substantive *content* of the incorporated Free Exercise Clause. Consider these options:

- *Justice Scalia's majority opinion* in *Smith* holds that "if prohibiting the exercise of religion... is not the object of the [contested law] but merely the incidental effect of a generally applicable and otherwise valid provision, the *First Amendment* has not been offended." (emphasis added). Does this mean that, after *Smith* and *Lukumi*, the baseline, or norm, of the *First Amendment* (not just the Free Exercise Clause) is "neutrality"?
- *Justice O'Connor's concurring opinion* in *Smith* asserts that "the essence of a free exercise claim is relief from a burden imposed by government on religious practices or beliefs, whether the burden is imposed directly through laws that prohibit or compel specific religious practices, or indirectly through laws that, in effect, make abandonment of one's own religion or conformity to the religious beliefs of others the price of an equal place in the civil community." Because many laws can impose such burdens, it would follow that "the critical question" in every case where a burden is found is whether exempting the individual from a rule of general applicability "will unduly interfere with fulfillment of the governmental interest." Justice O'Connor also wrote that "'[t]he compelling' interest test effectuates the First Amendment's command." Does this mean that the *content* of the free exercise norm is a rule that seeks to preserve "an equal place in the civil community" for adherents of minority or disfavored faiths?
- The *dissenting opinion* in *Smith* by Justices Blackmun, Brennan, and Marshall argues that "the State must treat all religions equally, and not favor one over another, [and that] this obligation is fulfilled by the uniform application of the "compelling interest" *test* to all free exercise claims, not by reaching uniform *results* as to all claims." (emphasis in the original). Does this mean that the free exercise *norm* is a balancing test? If so, what is its purpose? Is it designed only to mitigate "the severe impact of a State's restrictions on the adherents of a minority religion" who cannot otherwise protect themselves in the political process, *cf.*, *Carolene Products*, or is it equally applicable to the concerns of any faith whose beliefs or practices may put them on the wrong side of the law?

The Religious Freedom Restoration Act, 42 U.S.C. §§2000bb–2000bb-4 (2001) (RFRA), later held unconstitutional as applied to the states in *City of Boerne v. Flores*,

521 U.S. 507 (1997), appears to have adopted the broadly stated vision of the free exercise norm embodied in the *Smith* dissent. *See Kikumura v. Hurley*, 242 F.3d 950, 959 (10th Cir. 2001) ("The RFRA standard was so out of proportion to any substantive constitutional violation that it could not be considered remedial or preventive legislation.") The decision in *Boerne* thus confirms that the majority opinion in *Smith* states the current understanding of the free exercise norm: Without a showing of intent to discriminate or attain some other illegitimate goal, neutral rules of general application do not violate the First Amendment.

How close is the Supreme Court's understanding of the concept of "free exercise of religion" to that embodied in Article 18 of the ICCPR, discussed in § D(1)? How does the Court's jurisprudence compare with the understanding of the constitutional courts of other nations? For the Canadian Supreme Court's approach, see *R.B. and B.B. v. Children's Aid Society of Metropolitan Toronto*, 122 D.L.R. (4th) 1 (1995) (refusal to provide blood transfusion for religious reasons: state may properly interfere in situations in which parental conduct falls below a standard that is considered socially acceptable. In doing so, it is limiting the constitutional rights of parents, not vindicating the constitutional rights of children); *R. v. Big M Drug Mart Ltd.*, [1985] 1 S.C.R. 295 (striking down Canada's Sunday closing laws and rejecting the government's efforts justify then on the basis of a uniform day of rest). The High Court of Australia's opinions in *Church of the New Faith v Commissioner of Pay-roll Tax (Victoria)*, 154 CLR 120, 49 ALR 65, 57 ALJR 785 (1982)(religious liberty under Australian law is not limited to theistic religions); and *Adelaide Company of Jehovah's Witnesses Inc. v The Commonwealth*, 67 CLR 116, [1943] ALR 193, 17 ALJ 134 (upholding regulation of "subversive" speech by Jehovah's Witnesses during World War II) also provide a useful contrast.

9. *The Structural Components of the Free Exercise Norm*

a) Federalism, Separation of Powers and Free Exercise

Much of the discussion of religious liberty centers on the standards that should be used by the courts to limit the discretion of political majorities. The structural questions of separation of powers and federalism play a central role in this debate.

The federalism question makes state law the "starting point" for discussions of the religious liberty guarantee. Nearly thirty years before *Employment Div. v. Smith*, the Supreme Court of California refused to apply the state's criminal law in cases in which peyote was used for purposes of religious worship. *People v. Woody*, 40 Cal. Rptr. 69, 394 P.2d 813 (1964). Had the Oregon Supreme Court relied on its own constitution to protect Mr. Smith, the case would not have reached the Supreme Court.

The separation of powers question is deceptively simple: To whom must a request for an accommodation be addressed—the legislator or the judge? The answer, however, is wickedly complex. We have already seen several references to the limits the Establishment Clause imposes on legislative accommodations. In structural terms, the assertion is that the judiciary has the final word on the permissible scope of legislative accommodations, even those that might be a legitimate response to inequality. But to whom does an aggrieved person complain if the scope of *judicial* accommodation is too narrow? In *Smith*, the Court indicates that such grievances are to be resolved by the legislature.

The political response to *Employment Div. v. Smith* (II) was swift and negative. The preamble to RFRA explicitly stated that Congress' goal was to "restore the compelling interest test as set forth in *Sherbert v. Verner*, 374 U.S. 398 (1963) and *Wisconsin v. Yoder*, 406 U.S. 205 (1972)". 42 U.S.C. § 2000bb(b)(1). Congress put teeth into AIRFA in the American Indian Religious Freedom Act Amendments of 1994, Pub. L. 103-344, *codified at* 42 U.S.C. § 1996a. AIRFA now operates as both a legislative accommodation for individuals, and a preemptive limit on State power to regulate the religious practices of Native Americans. 42 U.S.C. § 1996a (b)(1) provides:

> Notwithstanding any other provision of law, the use, possession, or transportation of peyote by an Indian for bona fide traditional ceremonial purposes in connection with the practice of a traditional Indian religion is lawful, and shall not be prohibited by the United States or any State.

Several States also acted to limit the impact of *Smith*, either through judicial interpretation of the state constitution, or legislative action adopting local versions of RFRA. The Oregon legislature reacted by modifying its drug laws. Persons charged with "manufacture, possession or delivery of that plant of the genus *Lophophora* commonly known as peyote" can now claim an affirmative defense to criminal prosecution if the peyote was used, or intended for use, "[i]n connection with the good faith practice or a religious belief," "[a]s directly associated with a religious practice; and [i]n a manner that is not dangerous to the health of the user or others who are in the proximity of the use." *See* Or. Rev. Stats. § 475.992(5) (2001).

According to Professor Steven D. Smith, the result has been to leave most individuals and groups needing accommodations for their religious beliefs and practices in precisely the same position as they were before *Smith,* before the legislature, not the courts:

> Although before *Employment Division v. Smith* (the peyote decision) the federal judiciary theoretically stood ready to require free exercise accommodation in some cases, in reality such accommodation almost always came not from the courts but rather from legislatures. The most significant accommodations to religious freedom are found in state and federal tax exemptions, in the military conscription law, and in federal employment statutes—all legislatively adopted. Indeed, courts seemed more inclined to invalidate legislatively mandated accommodation on establishment grounds than to order such accommodation on free exercise grounds. This experience suggests that a judicial withdrawal from the field might not detract from, and indeed might amount to a net gain for, religious freedom.

Steven D. Smith, Foreordained Failure: The Quest for a Constitutional Principle of Religious Freedom 126 (1995) (footnotes omitted). *See also* Frank B. Cross, *Institutions and Enforcement of the Bill of Rights*, 85 Cornell L. Rev. 1529, 1535 (2000) (proposing "a system that justifies the circumstances under which any of the [branches of government] might merit the last word in interpretation of the Bill of Rights.")

b) The Free Exercise Norm as a Component of the Religious Liberty Guarantee

The Court's decisions in *Smith* and *Lukumi* highlight the relationship of the Free Exercise Clause to the other norms of the incorporated First Amendment, and to the norms of Section One of the Fourteenth Amendment. Justice O'Connor concludes that "religious liberty is an independent liberty, [and] that it occupies a preferred position." Justice Scalia's appears to agree that the Free Exercise Clause is an "independent" limit on government discretion, but indicates that there are times when it is insufficient, standing alone, to raise the standard of judicial review. Can we ascertain the "independent" significance of the Free Exercise Clause, or its "preferred position" (rank) *vis á vis* the other norms of the First Amendment and the Bill of Rights?

Even though it has not been well-received by commentators and courts, Justice Scalia's "hybrid" case involving more than one constitutional norm may provide a partial answer to this question. Professor Richard F. Duncan has noted that "[e]ven if no single strand of the constitutional interests at stake in a case like *Yoder* is sufficient to trigger heightened constitutional protection, it is possible to argue that the cumulative effect of all these interests is sufficient." Duncan, *Free Exercise is Dead*, at 858.

Professor Duncan's observation finds support in the Incorporation Doctrine itself. As a theoretical matter, *all* judicial review of State action under the incorporated First Amendment is based on more than one constitutional norm. The First Amendment does not, by its terms, apply to the States, and the Fourteenth Amendment does not speak directly to issues of religious liberty, speech and press, petition, or peaceable assembly. *See Pierce v. Society of Sisters*, 268 U.S. 510 (1925) (relying on the principle of liberty to support the right of parents to select a religious school); *Meyer v. Nebraska*, 262 U.S. 390 (1923) (teaching a foreign language in a religious school as an aspect of personal liberty). But when the norms of both amendments are read *in conjunction with* one another—as "hybrids"—the Court has a powerful tool with which to control State action deemed inconsistent with the principles of equal liberty, citizenship, and protection embodied in the Fourteenth Amendment.

Both pre- and post-incorporation religious liberty cases demonstrate that the nature of religious belief and practice often require that the Court draw upon more than one constitutional norm for the rule of decision. *See. e.g., Quick Bear v. Leupp*, 210 U.S. 50 (1908) (noting both Establishment and Free Exercise Clause concerns in construing federal statute). *Cantwell*, *Yoder* and other cases involving either proselytization or teaching can easily be characterized as "free exercise cases," "free speech cases," or both (hybrids). Because of the differential treatment of Sunday and Sabbath observers in *Sherbert*, *Braunfeld*, and *McGowan v. Maryland*, each can be characterized as a "free exercise," "establishment," or "equal protection" case. In *Texas Monthly v. Bullock*, the Establishment and Free Speech Clauses were used by the Court as limits on the scope of permissible legislative accommodation of the free exercise interests of religious publishers, and in *Lukumi*, the Court draws upon "an equal protection mode of analysis" to determine whether the statute was a neutral statute of general applicability. *See also* Cross, *Institutions and Enforcement of the Bill of Rights*, at 1604-1604 (noting that "conflicts [between rights] are not typical of Bill of Rights jurisprudence, but neither are they uncommon.")

It is possible to read the cases in a way that supports Justice O'Connor's position that the free exercise norm has both "independent significance" and a "preferred position." It is also possible to read the cases in a way that supports Justice Scalia's view that the free exercise norm does not, of its own accord, require religious exemptions from neutral laws of general applicability. The task of the legal advisor or advocate is to read the Court's decisions for the guidance the opinions provide regarding specific fact situations.

Chart 5-2
The Development of the Free Exercise Norm Since 1890

Late Corporation v. United States (1890) →	Cantwell v. Connecticut (1940) →	Sherbert v. Verner (1963) ↓ Wisconsin v. Yoder (1972) →	Employment Div. v. Smith (1991) ↓ Church of Lukumi Babalu Aye v. City of Hialeah (1993)
The state has a perfect right to prohibit ... all ... open offenses against the enlightened sentiment of mankind, notwithstanding the pretense of religious conviction by which they may be advocated and practiced.	"Strict judicial security" will be utilized to protect fundamental rights, such as "freedom of thought and speech," when State laws impose "undue burdens."	Only state interests "of the highest order and those not otherwise served can overbalance legitimate claims" that religiously motivated conduct is protected.	Laws burdening religious exercise or practice will be scrutinized to determine whether the express or implied object of the law is the regulation of religious exercise. If so, they are presumptively invalid. Laws that are religiously neutral and generally applicable are presumptively valid, even if they have the "incidental effect" of burdening religious belief or practice.

c) The Current Meaning of the Free Exercise Norm

Consider the rules announced in the free exercise cases decided since the late nineteenth century. Does Chart 5-2 above accurately portray the development of the Court's understanding of the content of the free exercise norm?

Consider now each of these decisions using the "level of generality" materials discussed in Chapter One § A. What are the *possible* meanings of the concept of "free exercise" in light of those decisions? If we arrange the list of possible meanings in an order that places the most "specific" understanding of the free exercise norm at the bottom of Chart 5-3 and the more abstract definitions at the top, the following range of options for defining the "free exercise liberty" appears:

Chart 5-3
Characterizing the Free Exercise Norm

	Possible Meanings of the "Free Exercise Liberty"
Abstract (high level)	Personal liberty.
	Freedom to act in a manner consistent with public order.
↓	Freedom of conscience.
	Religious autonomy.
Level	No state compelled association with repugnant beliefs or practices.
of	Freedom to act in a manner consistent with religious beliefs or practices.
Generality	Freedom to practice in accordance with one's beliefs, religion, or tradition.
↑	Freedom to worship.
Specific	Freedom to hold religious beliefs.
(low level)	Toleration.

How many of these possible meanings has the Court included in its interpretation of the incorporated Free Exercise Clause? Is the Court's understanding of the free exercise norm affected by the provisions of Section One of the Fourteenth Amendment *other than* the Due Process Clause?

E. Laws "Respecting an Establishment of Religion"

In this section, we explore the meanings that can be attributed to the part of the religious liberty guarantee embodied in the First Amendment's command that "Congress shall make no law respecting an establishment of religion." This section addresses the language that has animated much of the Court's jurisprudence, ("respecting an establishment of religion" and "separation of church and state"), explores the principles and methods on which much of the case law is based, and discusses the non-establishment norm as a component of the religious liberty guarantee.

1. The Conceptual Framework

The guarantee that "Congress shall make no law respecting an establishment of religion" assured critics of the new Constitution that the federal government could not use its power to make laws infringing State or individual prerogatives regarding religion. The federal government was barred from attempting to establish a national religion and eliminating any official status granted to some religious denominations by a few States. Those state establishments, with but a few exceptions, soon ended. As noted in Chapter Four, however, the end of state establishments of religion did not end the *de facto* Protestant establishment.

In *Everson v. Board of Educ.*, 330 U.S. 1 (1947), excerpted below, the Court held that the Due Process Clause of the Fourteenth Amendment makes the ban on laws "respecting an establishment of religion" enforceable against the States. Over the next fifty years, the Court has considered the meaning of the non-establishment norm on many occasions, and, in the process, has defined the scope of federal power to control state policies on the subject of religious liberty.

a) "Respecting an Establishment of Religion"

The phrase "respecting an establishment of religion" has more than one possible meaning. Politically, "an establishment of religion" is a legally recognized part of the political power structure. As such, an "establishment of religion" has many, if not most, of the characteristics of a government agency or political party: state financing, political control of religious affairs and appointments, preferential hiring and treatment of adherents of the established religion, and harmonization of the policies of the church and the state. *See, e.g., Capitol Square Review and Advisory Bd. v. Pinette*, 515 U.S. 753, 813 (Stevens, J. dissenting) (noting the official status of religious establishments in colonial charters); THE FEDERALIST No. 83 (Alexander Hamilton) (referring to "judicial establishments"). *See also* 2 & 3 Edward VI, c. 1 ("An Act for Uniformity of Service and Administration of the Sacraments throughout the Realm") (1548); and 3 & 4 Edward VI, c. 10 (1549) ("An Act for the abolishing and putting away of divers Books and Images") (authorizing the Anglican Book of Common Prayer).

Another understanding emerges when the phrase is recast as "religious establishment." In this view, a "religious establishment" is a structure used by organized religion to attain its religious goals: religious organizations, including churches and schools, as well as social and cultural structures that foster religious purposes or development. *See, e.g.*, Ariz. Const. art. II § 12 (2001) (forbidding appropriation of public funds or property "to the support of any religious establishment"). Interpreted in this fashion, laws "respecting" religious organizations are prohibited. *See County of Allegheny v. ACLU*, 492 U.S. 573, 648 (1989) (Stevens, Brennan, & Marshall, JJ., concurring in part and dissenting in part) ("'[R]especting' means concerning, or with reference to. But it also means with respect—that is, 'reverence,' 'good will,' 'regard'—to. Taking into account this richer meaning, the Establishment Clause, in banning laws that concern religion, especially prohibits those that pay homage to religion.") (footnote omitted).

b) A "Wall of Separation" Between Church and State

The phrase "separation of church and state" does not appear in the Constitution, but the concept is implicit in both its text and structure. "Separation" is a structural device designed to protect religious liberty. The framers of the Constitution included a ban on religious tests because they wanted the federal government to be open to all its citizens. *See* THE FEDERALIST No. 57 (Alexander Hamilton or James Madison). They opposed a Bill of Rights, in part because they rejected the assertion that the federal government was given any powers to create, administer, or regulate any church or spiritual life in general. *See* THE FEDERALIST No. 69 (Alexander Hamilton) (noting that the President "has no particle of spiritual jurisdiction"). The call of some states for a Bill of Rights that included a specific guarantee for religious liberty reflected their political fear that the federal government might be dominated by factions inhospitable to the rights of individuals and local communities, and which would use federal powers in ways inconsistent with religious liberty. *See* Destro, *Religious Liberty Guarantee,* at 397 (*quoting* sources).

The "wall of separation" metaphor is from Thomas Jefferson's Letter to the Danbury Baptist Association, excerpted in Chapter Two. The phrase was first quoted in *Reynolds* in order to draw a distinction between the power of Congress and the right of an individual act in accordance with his or her religious beliefs.

Writing for the Court in *Everson v. Board of Educ.*, Justice Hugo Black interpreted the phrase more broadly:

> The 'establishment of religion' clause of the First Amendment means at least this: Neither a state nor the Federal Government can set up a church. Neither can pass laws which aid one religion, aid all religions, or prefer one religion over another. Neither can force nor influence a person to go to or to remain away from church against his will or force him to profess a belief or disbelief in any religion. No person can be punished for entertaining or professing religious beliefs or disbeliefs, for church attendance or non-attendance. No tax in any amount, large or small, can be levied to support any religious activities or institutions, whatever they may be called, or whatever from they may adopt to teach or practice religion. Neither a state nor the Federal Government can, openly or secretly, participate in the affairs of any religious organizations or groups and vice versa. In the words of Jefferson, the clause against establishment of religion by law was intended to erect 'a wall of separation between Church and State.'

Everson, 330 U.S. at 15–16.

Justice Black's understanding of this metaphor provides hints that the Court's understanding of the no-establishment norm would be difficult to apply in practice. *See*

McCollum v. Board of Educ., 333 U.S. 203, 238 (1948) (Reed, J., dissenting) ("[a] rule of law" relating to religious liberty "should not be drawn from a figure of speech"). Human character and culture are multi-dimensional, and the legal ordering of faith-related issues is a difficult question in a pluralistic society committed to individual liberty. In *McGowan v. Maryland,* Justice Felix Frankfurter's separate opinion in observes that:

> '[S]eparation' is not a self-defining concept. '(A)greement, in the abstract, that the First Amendment was designed to erect a 'wall of separation between Church and State,' does not preclude a clash of views as to what the wall separates.' By its nature, religion—in the comprehensive sense in which the Constitution uses that word—is an aspect of human thought and action which profoundly relates the life of man to the world in which he lives. Religious beliefs pervade, and religious institutions have traditionally regulated, virtually all human activity. It is a postulate of American life, reflected specifically in the First Amendment to the Constitution but not there alone, that those beliefs and institutions shall continue, as the needs and longings of the people shall inspire them, to exist, to function, to grow, to wither, and to exert with whatever innate strength they may contain their many influences upon men's conduct, free of the dictates and directions of the state.

366 U.S. 420, 46-462 (1961) (citations omitted) (separate opinion of Frankfurter and Harlan, JJ). After years of wrestling with the concept, Court recognized both the difficulty of the issue and the dynamic nature of these relationships by describing Jefferson's metaphorical "wall of separation" as a "blurred, indistinct and variable barrier depending on all the circumstances of a particular relationship," and abandoned it. *Lemon v. Kurtzman*, 403 U.S. 602, 614 (1971).

2. Setting the Contours of Establishment Clause Jurisprudence

Before 1947, the Supreme Court addressed the meaning of the ban on laws "respecting an establishment of religion" on only two occasions. ***Bradfield v. Roberts***, 175 U.S. 291 (1899), excerpted in Chapter Four, concerned a challenge to an appropriation for the construction of "an isolating building or ward for the treatment of minor contagious diseases" on the grounds of Providence Hospital in Washington, D.C. The Court rejected the Establishment Clause challenge by concluding that the hospital's legal charter made it a secular corporation, and the fact that the hospital was operated by a religious organization did not make it a religious corporation. *See also Quick Bear v. Leupp*, 210 U.S. 50 (1908) (rejecting claim that Establishment Clause forbids payment of tribal funds held in trust by the Bureau of Indian Affairs for education of Sioux children at religious schools), excerpted in Chapter Four.

Everson v. Board of Education

330 U.S. 1 (1947)

Mr. Justice BLACK delivered the opinion of the Court.

A New Jersey statute authorizes its local school districts to make rules and contracts for the transportation of children to and from schools. The appellee, a township board of education, acting pursuant to this statute authorized reimbursement to parents of money expended by them for the bus transportation of their children on regular busses operated by the public transportation system. Part of this money was for the payment of transportation of some children in the community to Catholic parochial schools. These church schools give their students, in addition to secular education, regular religious instruction conforming to the religious tenets and modes of worship of the Catholic Faith. The superintendent of these schools is a Catholic priest.

[A]ppellant filed suit in a State court challenging the right of the Board to reimburse parents of parochial school students. He contended that the statute and the resolution passed pursuant to it violated both the State and the Federal Constitutions. That court held that the legislature was without power to authorize such payment under the State constitution. The New Jersey Court of Errors and Appeals reversed, holding that neither the statute nor the resolution passed pursuant to it was in conflict with the State constitution or the provisions of the Federal Constitution in issue.

The only contention here is that the state statute and the resolution, in so far as they authorized reimbursement to parents of children attending parochial schools, violate the Federal Constitution in these two respects, which to some extent, overlap. First. They authorize the State to take by taxation the private property of some and bestow it upon others, to be used for their own private purposes. This, it is alleged violates the due process clause of the Fourteenth Amendment. Second. The statute and the resolution forced inhabitants to pay taxes to help support and maintain schools which are dedicated to, and which regularly teach, the Catholic Faith. This is alleged to be a use of state power to support church schools contrary to the prohibition of the First Amendment which the Fourteenth Amendment made applicable to the states.

First. [The due process argument is omitted.]

Second. The New Jersey statute is challenged as a "law respecting an establishment of religion." The First Amendment, as made applicable to the states by the Fourteenth, commands that a state "shall make no law respecting an establishment of religion or prohibiting the free exercise thereof." These words of the First Amendment reflected in the minds of early Americans a vivid mental picture of conditions and practices which they fervently wished to stamp out in order to preserve liberty for themselves and for their posterity. Doubtless their goal has not been entirely reached; but so far has the Nation moved toward it that the expression "law respecting an establishment of religion," probably does not so vividly remind present-day Americans of the evils, fears, and political problems that caused that expression to be written into our Bill of Rights. Whether this New Jersey law is one respecting the "establishment of religion" requires an understanding of the meaning of that language, particularly with respect to the imposition of taxes. Once again, therefore, it is not inappropriate briefly to review the background and environment of the period in which that constitutional language was fashioned and adopted.

A large proportion of the early settlers of this country came here from Europe to escape the bondage of laws which compelled them to support and attend government favored churches. The centuries immediately before and contemporaneous with the colonization of America had been filled with turmoil, civil strife, and persecutions; generated in large part by established sects determined to maintain their absolute political and religious supremacy. With the power of government supporting them, at various times and places, Catholics had persecuted Protestants, Protestants had persecuted Catholics, Protestant sects had persecuted other Protestant sects, Catholics of one shade of belief had persecuted Catholics of another shade of belief, and all of these had from time to time persecuted Jews. In efforts to force loyalty to whatever religious group happened to be on top and in league with the government of a particular time and place, men and women had been fined, cast in jail, cruelly tortured, and killed. Among the offenses for which these punishments had been inflicted were such things as speaking disrespectfully of the views of ministers of government-established churches, nonattendance at those churches, expressions of non-belief in their doctrines, and failure to pay taxes and tithes to support them.

These practices of the old world were transplanted to and began to thrive in the soil of the new America. The very charters granted by the English Crown to the individuals and companies designated to make the laws which would control the destinies of the colonials authorized these individuals and companies to erect religious establishments which all, whether believers or non-believers, would be required to support and attend. An exercise of this authority was accompanied by a repetition of many of the old world practices and persecutions. Catholics found themselves hounded and proscribed because of their faith; Quakers who followed their conscience went to jail; Baptists were peculiarly obnoxious to certain dominant Protestant sects; men and women of varied faiths who happened to be in a minority in a particular locality were persecuted because they steadfastly persisted in worshipping God only as their own consciences dictated. And all of these dissenters were compelled to pay tithes and taxes[8] to support government-sponsored churches whose ministers preached inflammatory sermons designed to strengthen and consolidate the established faith by generating a burning hatred against dissenters.

These practices became so commonplace as to shock the freedom-loving colonials into a feeling of abhorrence.[9] The imposition of taxes to pay ministers' salaries and to build and maintain churches and church property aroused their indignation. It was these feelings which found expression in the First Amendment. No one locality and no one group throughout the Colonies can rightly be given entire credit for having aroused the sentiment that culminated in adoption of the Bill of Rights' provisions embracing religious liberty. But Virginia, where the established church had achieved a dominant influence in political affairs and where many excesses attracted wide public attention, provided a great stimulus and able leadership for the movement. The people there, as elsewhere, reached the conviction that individual religious liberty could be achieved best under a government which was stripped of all power to tax, to support, or otherwise to assist any or all religions, or to interfere with the beliefs of any religious individual or group.

The movement toward this end reached its dramatic climax in Virginia in 1785–86 when the Virginia legislative body was about to renew Virginia's tax levy for the support of the established church. Thomas Jefferson and James Madison led the fight against

8. Almost every colony exacted some kind of tax for church support. See e.g. Cobb, [Religious Liberty in America], 110 (Virginia); 131 (North Carolina); 169 (Massachusetts); 270 (Connecticut); 304, 310, 339 (New York); 386 (Maryland); 295 (New Hampshire).

9. Madison wrote to a friend in 1774: "That diabolical, hell-conceived principle of persecution rages among some. * * * This vexes me the worst of anything whatever. There are at this time in the adjacent country not less than five or six well-meaning men in close jail for publishing their religious sentiments, which in the main are very orthodox. I have neither patience to hear, talk, or think of anything relative to this matter; for I have squabbled and scolded, abused and ridiculed, so long about it to little purpose, that I am without common patience. So I must beg you to pity me, and pray for liberty of conscience to all." I Writings of James Madison (1900) 18, 21.

this tax. Madison wrote his great Memorial and Remonstrance against the law. In it, he eloquently argued that a true religion did not need the support of law; that no person, either believer or non-believer, should be taxed to support a religious institution of any kind; that the best interest of a society required that the minds of men always be wholly free; and that cruel persecutions were the inevitable result of government-established religions. Madison's Remonstrance received strong support throughout Virginia[12], and the Assembly postponed consideration of the proposed tax measure until its next session. When the proposal came up for consideration at that session, it not only died in committee, but the Assembly enacted the famous "Virginia Bill for Religious Liberty" originally written by Thomas Jefferson.

This Court has previously recognized that the provisions of the First Amendment, in the drafting and adoption of which Madison and Jefferson played such leading roles, had the same objective and were intended to provide the same protection against governmental intrusion on religious liberty as the Virginia statute. *Reynolds v. United States*, 98 U.S. 145 (1879); *Watson v. Jones*, 80 U.S. [13 Wall.] 679 (1872); *Davis v. Beason*, 133 U.S. 333 (1890). Prior to the adoption of the Fourteenth Amendment, the First Amendment did not apply as a restraint against the states. Most of them did soon provide similar constitutional protections for religious liberty. But some states persisted for about half a century in imposing restraints upon the free exercise of religion and in discriminating against particular religious groups. In recent years, so far as the provision against the establishment of a religion is concerned, the question has most frequently arisen in connection with proposed state aid to church schools and efforts to carry on religious teachings in the public schools in accordance with the tenets of a particular sect. Some churches have either sought or accepted state financial support for their schools. Here again the efforts to obtain state aid or acceptance of it have not been limited to any one particular faith. The state courts, in the main, have remained faithful to the language of their own constitutional provisions designed to protect religious freedom and to separate religions and governments. Their decisions, however, show the difficulty in drawing the line between tax legislation which provides funds for the welfare of the general public and that which is designed to support institutions which teach religion.

The meaning and scope of the First Amendment, preventing establishment of religion or prohibiting the free exercise thereof, in the light of its history and the evils it was designed forever to suppress, have been several times elaborated by the decisions of this Court prior to the application of the First Amendment to the states by the Fourteenth. The broad meaning given the Amendment by these earlier cases has been accepted by this Court in its decisions concerning an individual's religious freedom rendered since the Fourteenth Amendment was interpreted to make the prohibitions of the First applicable to state action abridging religious freedom. There is every reason to give the same application and broad interpretation to the "establishment of religion" clause. The interrelation of these complementary clauses was well summarized in a statement of the Court of Appeals of South Carolina, quoted with approval by this Court, in *Watson v. Jones*: "The structure of our government has, for the preservation of civil liberty,

---

12. In a recently discovered collection of Madison's papers, Madison recollected that his Remonstrance "met with the approbation of the Baptists, the Presbyterians, the Quakers, and the few Roman Catholics, universally; of the Methodists in part; and even of not a few of the Sect formerly established by law." Madison, Monopolies, Perpetuities, Corporations, Ecclesiastical Endowments, in Fleet, *Madison's "Detached Memoranda,"* 3 William and Mary Q. (1946) 534, 551, 555.

rescued the temporal institutions from religious interference. On the other hand, it has secured religious liberty from the invasions of the civil authority."

The "establishment of religion" clause of the First Amendment means at least this: Neither a state nor the Federal Government can set up a church. Neither can pass laws which aid one religion, aid all religions, or prefer one religion over another. Neither can force nor influence a person to go to or to remain away from church against his will or force him to profess a belief or disbelief in any religion. No person can be punished for entertaining or professing religious beliefs or disbeliefs, for church attendance or non-attendance. No tax in any amount, large or small, can be levied to support any religious activities or institutions, whatever they may be called, or whatever form they may adopt to teach or practice religion. Neither a state nor the Federal Government can, openly or secretly, participate in the affairs of any religious organizations or groups and vice versa. In the words of Jefferson, the clause against establishment of religion by law was intended to erect "a wall of separation between Church and State."

We must consider the New Jersey statute in accordance with the foregoing limitations imposed by the First Amendment. New Jersey cannot consistently with the "establishment of religion" clause of the First Amendment contribute tax-raised funds to the support of an institution which teaches the tenets and faith of any church. On the other hand, other language of the amendment commands that New Jersey cannot hamper its citizens in the free exercise of their own religion. Consequently, it cannot exclude individual Catholics, Lutherans, Mohammedans, Baptists, Jews, Methodists, Non-believers, Presbyterians, or the members of any other faith, *because of their faith, or lack of it*, from receiving the benefits of public welfare legislation. While we do not mean to intimate that a state could not provide transportation only to children attending public schools, we must be careful, in protecting the citizens of New Jersey against state-established churches, to be sure that we do not inadvertently prohibit New Jersey from extending its general state law benefits to all its citizens without regard to their religious belief.

Measured by these standards, we cannot say that the First Amendment prohibits New Jersey from spending tax-raised funds to pay the bus fares of parochial school pupils as a part of a general program under which it pays the fares of pupils attending public and other schools. It is undoubtedly true that children are helped to get to church schools. There is even a possibility that some of the children might not be sent to the church schools if the parents were compelled to pay their children's bus fares out of their own pockets when transportation to a public school would have been paid for by the State. The same possibility exists where the state requires a local transit company to provide reduced fares to school children including those attending parochial schools, or where a municipally owned transportation system undertakes to carry all school children free of charge. Moreover, state-paid policemen, detailed to protect children going to and from church schools from the very real hazards of traffic, would serve much the same purpose and accomplish much the same result as state provisions intended to guarantee free transportation of a kind which the state deems to be best for the school children's welfare. And parents might refuse to risk their children to the serious danger of traffic accidents going to and from parochial schools, the approaches to which were not protected by policemen. Similarly, parents might be reluctant to permit their children to attend schools which the state had cut off from such general government services as ordinary police and fire protection, connections for sewage disposal, public highways and sidewalks. Of course, cutting off church schools from these services, so separate and so indisputably marked off from the religious function, would make it far more difficult for the schools to operate. But such is obviously not the purpose of the

First Amendment. That Amendment requires the state to be a neutral in its relations with groups of religious believers and non-believers; it does not require the state to be their adversary. State power is no more to be used so as to handicap religions, than it is to favor them.

This Court has said that parents may, in the discharge of their duty under state compulsory education laws, send their children to a religious rather than a public school if the school meets the secular educational requirements which the state has power to impose. It appears that these parochial schools meet New Jersey's requirements. The State contributes no money to the schools. It does not support them. Its legislation, as applied, does no more than provide a general program to help parents get their children, regardless of their religion, safely and expeditiously to and from accredited schools.

The First Amendment has created a wall between church and state. That wall must be kept high and impregnable. We could not approve the slightest breach. New Jersey has not breached it here.

Affirmed.

Mr. Justice JACKSON, dissenting.

I find myself, contrary to first impressions, unable to join in this decision. I have a sympathy, though it is not ideological, with Catholic citizens who are compelled by law to pay taxes for public schools, and also feel constrained by conscience and discipline to support other schools for their own children. Such relief to them as this case involves is not in itself a serious burden to taxpayers and I had assumed it to be little serious in principle. Study of this case convinces me otherwise. The Court's opinion marshals every argument in favor of state aid and puts the case in its most favorable light, but much of its reasoning confirms my conclusions that there are no good grounds upon which to support the present legislation. In fact, the undertones of the opinion, advocating complete and uncompromising separation of Church from State, seem utterly discordant with its conclusion yielding support to their commingling in educational matters. The case which irresistibly comes to mind as the most fitting precedent is that of Julia who, according to Byron's reports, "whispering 'I will ne'er consent,'—consented."

I.

The Court sustains this legislation by assuming two deviations from the facts of this particular case; first, it assumes a state of facts the record does not support, and secondly, it refuses to consider facts which are inescapable on the record.

The Court concludes that this "legislation, as applied, does no more than provide a general program to help parents get their children, regardless of their religion, safely and expeditiously to and from accredited schools," and it draws a comparison between "state provisions intended to guarantee free transportation" for school children with services such as police and fire protection, and implies that we are here dealing with "laws authorizing new types of public services * * *" This hypothesis permeates the opinion. The facts will not bear that construction.

The Township of Ewing is not furnishing transportation to the children in any form; it is not operating school busses itself or contracting for their operation; and it is not performing any public service of any kind with this taxpayer's money. All school children are left to ride as ordinary paying passengers on the regular busses operated by the public transportation system. What the Township does, and what the taxpayer complains of, is at stated intervals to reimburse parents for the fares paid, provided the children attend either public schools or Catholic Church schools. This expenditure of tax funds has no possible effect on the child's safety or expedition in transit. As passengers on the public busses they travel as fast and no faster, and are as safe and no safer, since their parents are reimbursed as before.

In addition to thus assuming a type of service that does not exist, the Court also insists that we must close our eyes to a discrimination which does exist. The resolution which authorizes disbursement of this taxpayer's money limits reimbursement to those who attend public schools and Catholic schools. That is the way the Act is applied to this taxpayer.

The New Jersey Act in question makes the character of the school, not the needs of the children determine the eligibility of parents to reimbursement.

If we are to decide this case on the facts before us, our question is simply this: Is it constitutional to tax this complainant to pay the cost of carrying pupils to Church schools of one specified denomination?

II.

Whether the taxpayer constitutionally can be made to contribute aid to parents of students because of their attendance at parochial schools depends upon the nature of those schools and their relation to the Church. The Constitution says nothing of education. It lays no obligation on the states to provide schools and does not undertake to regulate state systems of education if they see fit to maintain them. But they cannot, through school policy any more than through other means, invade rights secured to citizens by the Constitution of the United States. *West Virginia Board of Educ. v. Barnette*, 319 U.S. 624 (1943). One of our basic rights is to be free of taxation to support a transgression of the constitutional command that the authorities "shall make no law respecting an establishment of religion, or prohibiting the free exercise thereof."

The function of the Church school is a subject on which this record is meager. It shows only that the schools are under superintendence of a priest and that "religion is taught as part of the curriculum." But we know that such schools are parochial only in name—they, in fact, represent a worldwide and age-old policy of the Roman Catholic Church. Under the rubric "Catholic Schools," the Canon Law of the Church by which all Catholics are bound, provides:

> "1215. Catholic children are to be educated in schools where not only nothing contrary to Catholic faith and morals is taught, but rather in schools where religious and moral training occupy the first place. * * * (Canon 1372.)"
>
> "The young people who attend the higher schools are to receive a deeper religious knowledge, and the bishops shall appoint priests qualified for such work by their learning and piety. (Canon 1373.)"
>
> "1217. Catholic children shall not attend non-Catholic, indifferent, schools that are mixed, that is to say, schools open to Catholic and non-Catholics alike. The bishop of the diocese only has the right, in harmony with the instructions of the Holy See, to decide under what circumstances, and with what safeguards to prevent loss of faith, it may be tolerated that Catholic children go to such schools. (Canon 1374.)"
>
> "1224. The religious teaching of youth in any schools is subject to the authority and inspection of the Church."

"The local Ordinaries have the right and duty to watch that nothing is taught contrary to faith or good morals, in any of the schools of their territory."

"They, moreover, have the right to approve the books of Christian doctrine and the teachers of religion, and to demand, for the sake of safeguarding religion and morals, the removal of teachers and books. (Canon 1381.)"

It is no exaggeration to say that the whole historic conflict in temporal policy between the Catholic Church and non-Catholics comes to a focus in their respective school policies. The Roman Catholic Church, counseled by experience in many ages and many lands and with all sorts and conditions of men, takes what, from the viewpoint of its own progress and the success of its mission, is a wise estimate of the importance of education to religion. It does not leave the individual to pick up religion by chance. It relies on early and indelible indoctrination in the faith and order of the Church by the word and example of persons consecrated to the task.

Our public school, if not a product of Protestantism, at least is more consistent with it than with the Catholic culture and scheme of values. It is a relatively recent development dating from about 1840. It is organized on the premise that secular education can be isolated from all religious teaching so that the school can inculcate all needed temporal knowledge and also maintain a strict and lofty neutrality as to religion. The assumption is that after the individual has been instructed in worldly wisdom he will be better fitted to choose his religion. Whether such a disjunction is possible, and if possible whether it is wise, are questions I need not try to answer.

I should be surprised if any Catholic would deny that the parochial school is a vital, if not the most vital, part of the Roman Catholic Church. If put to the choice, that venerable institution, I should expect, would forego its whole service for mature persons before it would give up education of the young, and it would be a wise choice. Its growth and cohesion, discipline and loyalty, spring from its schools. Catholic education is the rock on which the whole structure rests, and to render tax aid to its Church school is indistinguishable to me from rendering the same aid to the Church itself.

III.

It is of no importance in this situation whether the beneficiary of this expenditure of tax-raised funds is primarily the parochial school and incidentally the pupil, or whether the aid is directly bestowed on the pupil with indirect benefits to the school. The state cannot maintain a Church and it can no more tax its citizens to furnish free carriage to those who attend a Church. The prohibition against establishment of religion cannot be circumvented by a subsidy, bonus or reimbursement of expense to individuals for receiving religious instruction and indoctrination.

It seems to me that the basic fallacy in the Court's reasoning, which accounts for its failure to apply the principles it avows, is in ignoring the essentially religious test by which beneficiaries of this expenditure are selected. A policeman protects a Catholic, of course—but not because he is a Catholic; it is because he is a man and a member of our society. The fireman protects the Church school—but not because it is a Church school; it is because it is property, part of the assets of our society. Neither the fireman nor the policeman has to ask before he renders aid "Is this man or building identified with the Catholic Church." But before these school authorities draw a check to reimburse for a student's fare they must ask just that question, and if the school is a Catholic one they may render aid because it is such, while if it is of any other faith or is run for profit, the help must be withheld. To consider the converse of the Court's reasoning will best disclose its fallacy. That there is no parallel between police and fire protection and this plan of reimbursement is apparent from the incongruity of the limitation of this Act if applied to police and fire service. Could we sustain an Act that said police shall protect pupils on the way to or from public schools and Catholic schools but not while going to and coming from other schools, and firemen shall extinguish a blaze in public or Catholic school buildings but shall not put out a blaze in Protestant Church schools or private schools operated for profit? That is the true analogy to the case we have before us and I should think it pretty plain that such a scheme would not be valid.

The Court's holding is that this taxpayer has no grievance because the state has decided to make the reimbursement a public purpose and therefore we are bound to regard it as such. I agree that this Court has left, and always should leave to each state, great latitude in deciding for itself, in the light of its own conditions, what shall be public purposes in its scheme of things. It may socialize utilities and economic enterprises and make taxpayers' business out of what conventionally had been private business. It may make public business of individual welfare, health, education, entertainment or security. But it cannot make public business of religious worship or instruction, or of attendance at religious institutions of any character. There is no answer to the proposition more fully expounded by Mr. Justice Rutledge that the effect of the religious freedom Amendment to our Constitution was to take every form of propagation of religion out of the realm of things which could directly or indirectly be made public business and thereby be supported in whole or in part at taxpayers' expense. That is a difference which the Constitution sets up between religion and almost every other subject matter of legislation, a difference which goes to the very root of religious freedom and which the Court is overlooking today. This freedom was first in the Bill of Rights because it was first in the forefathers' minds; it was set forth in absolute terms, and its strength is its rigidity. It was intended not only to keep the states' hands out of religion, but to keep religion's hands off the state, and above all, to keep bitter religious controversy out of public life by denying to every denomination and advantage from getting control of public policy or the public purse. Those great ends I cannot but think are immeasurably compromised by today's decision.

[W]e cannot have it both ways. Religious teaching cannot be a private affair when the state seeks to impose regulations which infringe on it indirectly, and a public affair when it comes to taxing citizens of one faith to aid another, or those of no faith to aid all. If these principles seem harsh in prohibiting aid to Catholic education, it must not be forgotten that it is the same Constitution that alone assures Catholics the right to maintain these schools at all when predominant local sentiment would forbid them. [*Pierce v. Society of Sisters*, 268 U.S. 510 (1925)]. But I do not think that those who have done so well without this aid would want to see this separation between Church and State broken down. If the state may aid these religious schools, it may therefore regulate them.

I cannot read the history of the struggle to separate political from ecclesiastical affairs, well summarized in the opinion of Mr. Justice Rutledge in which I generally concur, without a conviction that the Court today is unconsciously giving the clock's hands a backward turn.

Mr. Justice FRANKFURTER joins in this opinion.

Mr. Justice RUTLEDGE, with whom Mr. Justice FRANKFURTER, Mr. Justice JACKSON and Mr. Justice BURTON agree, dissenting.

"Congress shall make no law respecting an establishment of religion, or prohibiting the free exercise thereof. * * *." U.S. Const. Am. Art. I.

"Well aware that Almighty God hath created the mind free; * * * that to compel a man to furnish contributions of money for the propagation of opinions which he disbelieves, is sinful and tyrannical; * * *

"We, the General Assembly, do enact, That no man shall be compelled to frequent or support any religious worship, place, or ministry whatsoever, nor shall be enforced, restrained, molested, or burthened in his body or goods, nor shall otherwise suffer on account of his religious opinions or belief. * * *"

I cannot believe that the great author of those words, or the men who made them law, could have joined in this decision. Neither so high nor so impregnable today as yesterday is the wall raised between church and state by Virginia's great statute of religious freedom and the First Amendment, now made applicable to all the states by the Fourteenth. New Jersey's statute sustained is the first, if indeed it is not the second breach to be made by this Court's action. That a third, and a fourth, and still others will be attempted, we may be sure. For just as *Cochran v. Louisiana State Board of Education,* 281 U.S. 370 (1930), has opened the way by oblique ruling for this decision, so will the two make wider the breach for a third. Thus with time the most solid freedom steadily gives way before continuing corrosive decision.

This case forces us to determine squarely for the first time what was "an establishment of religion" in the First Amendment's conception; and by that measure to decide whether New Jersey's action violates its command.

I.

Not simply an established church, but any law respecting an establishment of religion is forbidden. The Amendment was broadly but not loosely phrased. It is the compact and exact summation of its author's views formed during his long struggle for religious freedom. In Madison's own words characterizing Jefferson's Bill for Establishing Religious Freedom, the guaranty he put in our national charter, like the bill he piloted through the Virginia assembly, was "a Model of technical precision, and perspicuous brevity." Madison could not have confused "church" and "religion," or "an established church" and "an establishment of religion."

The Amendment's purpose was not to strike merely at the official establishment of a single sect, creed or religion, outlawing only a formal relation such as had prevailed in England and some of the colonies. Necessarily it was to uproot all such relationships. But the object was broader than separating church and state in this narrow sense. It was to create a complete and permanent separation of the spheres of religious activity and civil authority by comprehensively forbidding every form of public aid or support for religion. In proof the Amendment's wording and history unite with this Court's consistent utterances whenever attention has been fixed directly upon the question.

"Religion" appears only once in the Amendment. But the word governs two prohibitions and governs them alike. It does not have two meanings, one narrow to forbid "an establishment" and another, much broader, for securing "the free exercise thereof."" "Thereof" brings down "religion" with its entire and exact content, no more and no less, from the first into the second guaranty, so that Congress and now the states are as broadly restricted concerning the one as they are regarding the other.

No one would claim today that the Amendment is constricted, in "prohibiting the free exercise" of religion, to securing the free exercise of some formal or creedal observance, of one sect or of many. It secures all forms of religious expression, creedal, sectarian or nonsectarian wherever and however taking place, except conduct which trenches upon the like freedoms of others or clearly and presently endangers the community's good order and security. And on this basis parents have been held entitled to send their children to private, religious schools. [*Pierce*] Accordingly, daily religious education commingled with secular is "religion" within the guaranty's comprehensive scope. So are religious training and teaching in whatever form. The word connotes the broadest content, determined not by the form or formality of the teaching or where it occurs, but by its essential nature regardless of those details.

"Religion" has the same broad significance in the twin prohibition concerning "an establishment." The Amendment was not duplicitous. "Religion" and "establishment" were not used in any formal or technical sense. The prohibition broadly forbids state support, financial or other, of religion in any guise, form or degree. It outlaws all use of public funds for religious purposes.

II.

No provision of the Constitution is more closely tied to or given content by its generating history than the religious clause of the First Amendment. It is at once the refined product and the terse summation of that history. The history includes not only Madison's authorship and the proceedings before the First Congress, but also the long and intensive struggle for religious freedom in America, more especially in Virginia,[11] of which the Amendment was the direct culmination. In the documents of the times, particularly of Madison, who was leader in the Virginia struggle before he became the Amendment's sponsor, but also in the writings of Jefferson and others and in the issues which engendered them is to be found irrefutable confirmation of the Amendment's sweeping content.

[Rutledge then discussed the struggle for religious freedom in Virginia from 1776 to 1786, concluding with Madison's Memorial and Remonstrance and the passage of Jefferson's bill for establishing religious freedom.]

The next year [1787] Madison became a member of the Constitutional Convention. Its work done, he fought valiantly to secure the ratification of its great product in Virginia as elsewhere, and nowhere else more effectively. Madison was certain in his own mind that under the Constitution "there is not a shadow of right in the general government to intermeddle with religion" and that "this subject is, for the honor of America, perfectly free and unshackled. The Government has no jurisdiction over it...." Nevertheless he pledged that he would work for a Bill of Rights, including a specific guaranty of religious freedom, and Virginia, with other states, ratified the Constitution on this assurance.

Ratification thus accomplished, Madison was sent to the first Congress. There he went at once about performing his pledge to establish freedom for the nation as he had done in Virginia. Within a little more than three years from his legislative victory at home he had proposed and secured the submission and ratification of the First Amendment as the first article of our Bill of Rights.

All the great instruments of the Virginia struggle for religious liberty thus became warp and woof of our constitutional tradition, not simply by the course of history, but by the common unifying force of Madison's life, thought and sponsorship. He epito-

---

11. Conflicts in other states, and earlier in the colonies, contributed much to generation of the Amendment, but none so directly as that in Virginia or with such formative influence on the Amendment's content and wording.

mized the whole of that tradition in the Amendment's compact, but nonetheless comprehensive, phrasing.

As the Remonstrance discloses throughout, Madison opposed every form and degree of official relation between religion and civil authority. For him religion was a wholly private matter beyond the scope of civil power either to restrain or to support. Denial or abridgment of religious freedom was a violation of rights both of conscience and of natural equality. State aid was no less obnoxious or destructive to freedom and to religion itself than other forms of state interference. "Establishment" and "free exercise" were correlative and coextensive ideas, representing only different facets of the single great and fundamental freedom. The Remonstrance, following the Virginia statute's example, referred to the history of religious conflicts and the effects of all sorts of establishments, current and historical, to suppress religion's free exercise. With Jefferson, Madison believed that to tolerate any fragment of establishment would be by so much to perpetuate restraint upon that freedom. Hence he sought to tear out the institution not partially but root and branch, and to bar its return forever.

In no phase was he more unrelentingly absolute than in opposing state support or aid by taxation. Not even "three pence" contribution was thus to be exacted from any citizen for such a purpose. Tithes had been the life blood of establishment before and after other compulsions disappeared. Madison and his coworkers made no exceptions or abridgments to the complete separation they created. Their objection was not to small tithes. It was to any tithes whatsoever. Not the amount but "the principle of assessment was wrong." And the principle was as much to prevent "the interference of law in religion" as to restrain religious intervention in political matters.

In view of this history no further proof is needed that the Amendment forbids any appropriation, large or small, from public funds to aid or support any and all religious exercises. But if more were called for, the debates in the First Congress and this Court's consistent expressions, whenever it has touched on the matter directly, supply it.

By contrast with the Virginia history, the congressional debates on consideration of the Amendment reveal only sparse discussion, reflecting the fact that the essential issues had been settled. Indeed the matter had become so well understood as to have been taken for granted in all but formal phrasing. Hence, the only enlightening reference shows concern, not to preserve any power to use public funds in aid of religion, but to prevent the Amendment from outlawing private gifts inadvertently by virtue of the breadth of its wording. In the margin are noted also the principal decisions in which expressions of this Court confirm the Amendment's broad prohibition.[35]

35. The decision most closely touching the question, where it was squarely raised, is Quick Bear v. Leupp, 210 U.S. 50. The ruling was that the latter could be disbursed to private, religious schools at the designation of those patrons for paying the cost of their education. But it was stated also that such a use of public moneys would violate both the First Amendment and the specific statutory declaration involved, namely, that "it is hereby declared to be the settled policy of the government to hereafter make no appropriation whatever for education in any sectarian school." 210 U.S. at page 79. *Cf. Ponce v. Roman Catholic Apostolic Church*, 210 U.S. 296, 322. And see *Bradfield v. Roberts*, 175 U.S. 291, an instance of highly artificial grounding to support a decision sustaining an appropriation for the care of indigent patients pursuant to a contract with a private hospital.

III.

Compulsory attendance upon religious exercises went out early in the process of separating church and state, together with forced observance of religious forms and ceremonies. Test oaths and religious qualification for the office followed later. These things none devoted to our great tradition of religious liberty would think of bringing back. Hence today, apart from efforts to inject religious training or exercises and sectarian issues into the public schools, the only serious surviving threat to maintaining that complete and permanent separation of religion and civil power which the First Amendment commands is through use of the taxing power to support religion, religious establishments, or establishments having a religious foundation whatever their form or special religious function.

Does New Jersey's action furnish support for religion by use of the taxing power? Certainly it does, if the test remains undiluted as Jefferson and Madison made it, that money taken by taxation from one is not to be used or given to support another's religious training or belief, or indeed one's own. Today as then the furnishings of "contributions of money for the propagation of opinions which he disbelieves" is the forbidden exaction; and the prohibition is absolute for whatever measure brings that consequence and whatever [a]mount may be sought or given to that end.

The funds used here were raised by taxation. The Court does not dispute nor could it that their use does in fact give aid and encouragement to religious instruction. It only concludes that this aid is not "support" in law. But Madison and Jefferson were concerned with aid and support in fact not as a legal conclusion "entangled in precedents." Remonstrance, Par. 3. Here parents pay money to send their children to parochial schools and funds raised by taxation are used to reimburse them. This not only helps the children to get to school and the parents to send them. It aids them in a substantial way to get the very thing which they are sent to the particular school to secure, namely, religious training and teaching.

Believers of all faiths, and others who do not express their feeling toward ultimate issues of existence in any creedal form, pay the New Jersey tax. When the money so raised is used to pay for transportation to religious schools, the Catholic taxpayer to the extent of his proportionate share pays for the transportation of Lutheran, Jewish and otherwise religiously affiliated children to receive their non-Catholic religious instruction. Their parents likewise pay proportionately for the transportation of Catholic children to receive Catholic instruction. Each thus contributes to "the propagation of opinions which he disbelieves" in so far as their religions differ, as do others who accept no creed without regard to those differences. Each thus pays taxes also to support the teaching of his own religion, an exaction equally forbidden since it denies "the comfortable liberty" of giving one's contribution to the particular agency of instruction he approves.

New Jersey's action therefore exactly fits the type of exaction and the kind of evil at which Madison and Jefferson struck. Under the test they framed it cannot be said that the cost of transportation is no part of the cost of education or of the religious instruction given. That it is a substantial and a necessary element is shown most plainly by the continuing and increasing demand for the state to assume it. Nor is there pretense that it relates only to the secular instruction given in religious schools or that any attempt is or could be made toward allocating proportional shares as between the secular and the religious instruction. It is precisely because the instruction is religious and relates to a particular faith, whether one or another, that parents send their children to religious schools under the *Pierce* doctrine. And the very purpose of the state's contribution is to defray the cost of conveying the pupil to the place where he will receive not simply secular, but also and primarily religious, teaching and guidance.

Indeed the view is sincerely avowed by many of various faiths,[40] that the basic purpose of all education is or should be religious, that the secular cannot be and should not be separated from the religious phase and emphasis. Hence, the inadequacy of public or secular education and the necessity for sending the child to a school where religion is taught. But whatever may be the philosophy or its justification, there is undeniably an admixture or religious with secular teaching in all such institutions. That is the very reason for their being. Certainly for purposes of constitutionality we cannot contradict the whole basis of the ethical and educational convictions of people who believe in religious schooling.

Yet this very admixture is what was disestablished when the First Amendment forbade "an establishment of religion." Commingling the religious with the secular teaching does not divest the whole of its religious permeation and emphasis or make them of minor part, if proportion were material. Indeed, on any other view, the constitutional prohibition always could be brought to naught by adding a modicum of the secular.

An appropriation from the public treasury to pay the cost of transportation to Suday school, to weekday special classes at the church or parish house, or to the meetings of various young people's religious societies, such as the Y.M.C.A., the Y.W.C.A., the Y.M.H.A., the Epworth League, could not withstand the constitutional attack. This would be true, whether or not secular activities were mixed with the religious. If such an appropriation could not stand, then it is hard to see how one becomes valid for the same thing upon the more extended scale of daily instruction. Surely constitutionality does not turn on where or how often the mixed teaching occurs.

Finally, transportation, where it is needed, is as essential to education as any other element. Its cost is as much a part of the total expense, except at times in amount, as the cost of textbooks, of school lunches, of athletic equipment, of writing and other materials; indeed of all other items composing the total burden. Hardly can it be maintained that transportation is the least essential of these items, or that it does not in fact aid, encourage, sustain and support, just as they do, the very process which is its purpose to accomplish.

For me, therefore, the feat is impossible to select so indispensable an item from the composite of total costs, and characterize it as not aiding, contributing to, promoting or sustaining the propagation of beliefs which it is the very end of all to bring about. No rational line can be drawn between payment for such larger, but not more necessary, items and payment for transportation. The only line that can be so drawn is one between more dollars and less. Certainly in this realm such a line can be no valid constitutional measure. Now, as in Madison's time, not the amount but the principle of assessment is wrong.

IV.

[E]ducation which includes religious training and teaching, and its support, have been made matters of private right and function not public, by the very terms of the First

40. See Bower, Church and State in Education (1944) 58: " * * * the fundamental division of the education of the whole self into the secular and the religious could not be justified on the grounds of either a sound educational philosophy or a modern functional concept of the relation of religion to personal and social experience."

Amendment. That is the effect not only in its guaranty of religion's free exercise, but also in the prohibition of establishments. It was on this basis of the private character of the function of religious education that this Court held parents entitled to send their children to private, religious schools. Now it declares in effect that the appropriation of public funds to defray part of the cost of attending those schools is for a public purpose. If so, I do not understand why the state cannot go farther or why this case approaches the verge of its power.

In truth this view contradicts the whole purpose and effect of the First Amendment as heretofore conceived. The "public function"— "public welfare"—"social legislation" argument seeks in Madison's words, to "employ Religion [that is, here, religious education] as an engine of Civil policy." It is of one piece with the Assessment Bill's preamble, although with the vital difference that it wholly ignores what that preamble explicitly states.

Our constitutional policy is exactly the opposite. It does not deny the value or the necessity for religious training, teaching or observance. Rather it secures their free exercise. But to that end it does deny that the state can undertake or sustain them in any form or degree.

It is not because religious teaching does not promote the public or the individual's welfare, but because neither is furthered when the state promotes religious education, that the Constitution forbids it to do so. Both legislatures and courts are bound by that distinction. Legislatures are free to make, and courts to sustain, appropriations only when it can be found that in fact they do not aid, promote, encourage or sustain religious teaching or observances, be the amount large or small. No such finding has been or could be made in this case. The Amendment has removed this form of promoting the public welfare from legislative and judicial competence to make a public function. It is exclusively a private affair.

The reasons underlying the Amendment's policy have not vanished with time or diminished in force. Now as when it was adopted the price of religious freedom is double. It is that the church and religion shall live both within and upon that freedom. There cannot be freedom of religion, safeguarded by the state, and intervention by the church or its agencies in the state's domain or dependency on its largesse. Madison's Remonstrance, Par. 6, 8. The great condition of religious liberty is that it be maintained free from sustenance, as also from other interferences, by the state. For when it comes to rest upon that secular foundation it vanishes with the resting. *Id.*, Par. 7, 8. Public money devoted to payment of religious costs, educational or other, brings the quest for more. It brings too the struggle of sect against sect for the larger share or for any. Here one by numbers alone will benefit most, there another. That is precisely the history of societies which have had an established religion and dissident groups. *Id.*, Par. 8, 11. It is the very thing Jefferson and Madison experienced and sought to guard against, whether in its blunt or in its more screened forms. *Ibid.* The end of such strife cannot be other than to destroy the cherished liberty. The dominating group will achieve the dominant benefit; or all will embroil the state in their dissensions. *Id.*, Par. 11.

Exactly such conflicts have centered of late around providing transportation to religious schools from public funds. The issue and the dissension work typically, in Madison's phrase, to "destroy that moderation and harmony which the forbearance of our laws to intermeddle with Religion, has produced amongst its several sects." *Id.*, Par. 11. This occurs, as he well knew over measures at the very threshold of departure from the principle. *Id.*, Par. 3, 9, 11.

In these conflicts wherever success has been obtained it has been upon the contention that by providing the transportation the general cause of education, the general welfare, and the welfare of the individual will be forwarded; hence that the matter lies within the realm of public function, for legislative determination. State courts have divided upon the issue, some taking the view that only the individual, others that the institution receives the benefit. A few have recognized that this dichotomy is false, that both in fact are aided.

The majority here does not accept in terms any of those views. But neither does it deny that the individual or the school, or indeed both, are benefited directly and substantially. On the contrary, the opinion concedes that the children are aided by being helped to get to the religious schooling. By converse necessary implication as well as by the absence of express denial, it must be taken to concede also that the school is helped to reach the child with its religious teaching. The religious enterprise is common to both, as is the interest in having transportation for its religious purposes provided.

Notwithstanding the recognition that this two-way aid is given and the absence of any denial that religious teaching is thus furthered, the Court concludes that the aid so given is not "support" of religion. It is rather only support of education as such, without reference to its religious content, and thus becomes public welfare legislation. To this elision of the religious element from the case is added gloss in two respects, one that the aid extended partakes of the nature of a safety measure, the other that failure to provide it would make the state unneutral in religious matters, discriminating against or hampering such children concerning public benefits all others receive.

As will be noted, the one gloss is contradicted by the facts of record and the other is of whole cloth with the "public function" argument's excision of the religious factor. But most important is that this approach, if valid, supplies a ready method for nullifying the Amendment's guaranty, not only for this case and others involving small grants in aid for religious education, but equally for larger ones. The only thing needed will be for the Court again to transplant the "public welfare—public function" view from its proper nonreligious due process bearing to First Amendment application, holding that religious education is not "supported" though it may be aided by the appropriation, and that the cause of education generally is furthered by helping the pupil to secure that type of training.

This is not therefore just a little case over bus fares. In paraphrase of Madison, distant as it may be in its present form from a complete establishment of religion, it differs from it only in degree; and is the first step in that direction.

V.

No one conscious of religious values can be unsympathetic toward the burden which our constitutional separation puts on parents who desire religious instruction mixed with secular for their children. They pay taxes for others' children's education, at the same time the added cost of instruction for their own. Nor can one happily see benefits denied to children which others receive, because in conscience they or their parents for them desire a different kind of training others do not demand.

But if those feelings should prevail, there would be an end to our historic constitutional policy and command. No more unjust or discriminatory in fact is it to deny attendants at religious schools the cost of their transportation than it is to deny them tuitions, sustenance for their teachers, or any other educational expense which others receive at public cost. Hardship in fact there is which none can blink. But, for assuring to those who undergo it the greater, the most comprehensive freedom, it is one written by design and firm intent into our basic law.

Of course discrimination in the legal sense does not exist. The child attending the religious school has the same right as any other to attend the public school. But he foregoes exercising it because the same guaranty which assures this freedom forbids the public school or any agency of the state to give or aid him in securing the religious instruction he seeks.

Were he to accept the common school, he would be the first to protest the teaching there of any creed or faith not his own. And it is precisely for the reason that their atmosphere is wholly secular that children are not sent to public schools under the *Pierce* doctrine. But that is a constitutional necessity, because we have staked the very existence of our country on the faith that complete separation between the state and religion is best for the state and best for religion. Remonstrance, Par. 8, 12.

That policy necessarily entails hardship upon persons who forego the right to educational advantages the state can supply in order to secure others it is precluded from giving. Indeed this may hamper the parent and the child forced by conscience to that choice. But it does not make the state unneutral to withhold what the Constitution forbids it to give. On the contrary it is only by observing the prohibition rigidly that the state can maintain its neutrality and avoid partisanship in the dissensions inevitable when sect opposes sect over demands for public moneys to further religious education, teaching or training in any form or degree, directly or indirectly. Like St. Paul's freedom, religious liberty with a great price must be bought. And for those who exercise it most fully, by insisting upon religious education for their children mixed with secular, by the terms of our Constitution the price is greater than for others.

The problem then cannot be cast in terms of legal discrimination or its absence. This would be true, even though the state in giving aid should treat all religious instruction alike. Thus, if the present statute and its application were shown to apply equally to all religious schools of whatever faith, yet in the light of our tradition it could not stand. For then the adherent of one creed still would pay for the support of another, the childless taxpayer with others more fortunate. Then too there would seem to be no bar to making appropriations for transportation: and other expenses of children attending public or other secular schools, after hours in separate places and classes for their exclusively religious instruction. The person who embraces no creed also would be forced to pay for teaching what he does not believe. Again, it was the furnishing of "contributions of money for the propagation of opinions which he disbelieves" that the fathers outlawed. That consequence and effect are not removed by multiplying to all-inclusiveness the sects for which support is exacted. The Constitution requires, not comprehensive identification of state with religion, but complete separation.

VI.

Nor is the case comparable to one of furnishing fire or police protection, or access to public highways. These things are matters of common right, part of the general need for safety. Certainly the fire department must not stand idly by while the church burns. Nor is this reason why the state should pay the expense of transportation or other items of the cost of religious education.

Two great drives are constantly in motion to abridge, in the name of education, the complete division of religion and civil authority which our forefathers made. One is to introduce religious education and observances into the public schools. The other, to obtain public funds for the aid and support of various private religious schools. In my opinion both avenues were closed by the Constitution. Neither should be opened by this Court. The matter is not one of quantity, to be measured by the amount of money expended. Now as in Madison's day it is one of principle, to keep separate the separate spheres as the First Amendment drew them; to prevent the first experiment upon our liberties; and to keep the question from becoming entangled in corrosive precedents. We should not be less strict to keep strong and untarnished the one side of the shield of religious freedom than we have been of the other.

The judgment should be reversed.

Notes

1. All of the opinions in *Everson* agree that the Establishment Clause ban on "laws respecting an establishment of religion" should be interpreted in light of Thomas Jefferson's "wall of separation" metaphor. The Justices also agree that "the provisions of the First Amendment, in the drafting and adoption of which Madison and Jefferson played such leading roles, had the same objective and were intended to provide the same protection against governmental intrusion on religious liberty as the Virginia statute [for Establishing Religious Freedom]," and thus Madison's *Memorial and Remonstrance Against Religious Assessments* should be viewed as a statement of principles incorporated into the non-establishment norm. Why, then, do they disagree on the result?

2. *Everson* applies the Establishment Clause to the States through the Due Process Clause of the Fourteenth Amendment. Is it possible to extract from *Everson* an understanding of how the principle of "separation of church and state" relates to the individual "liberty" protected by the Due Process Clause of the Fourteenth Amendment? Consider the tension between the non-establishment and free exercise norms highlighted in these two excerpts from Justice Black's opinion.

Everson alleged that his liberty interests under the First Amendment were violated because

> The statute and the resolution forced inhabitants to pay taxes to help support and maintain schools which are dedicated to, and which regularly teach, the Catholic Faith. This is alleged to be a use of state power to support church schools contrary to the prohibition of the First Amendment which the Fourteenth Amendment made applicable to the states.

Everson, 330 U.S. at 5. The Court accepted the proposition that "New Jersey cannot consistently with the "establishment of religion" clause of the First Amendment contribute tax-raised funds to the support of an institution which teaches the tenets and faith of any church," but noted that the Free Exercise Clause may limit the reach of that principle:

> On the other hand, other language of the amendment commands that New Jersey cannot hamper its citizens in the free exercise of their own religion. Consequently, it cannot exclude individual Catholics, Lutherans, Mohammedans, Baptists, Jews, Methodists, Non-believers, Presbyterians, or the members of any other faith, *because of their faith, or lack of it*, from receiving the benefits of public welfare legislation. While we do not mean to intimate that a state could not provide transportation only to children attending public schools, we must be careful, in protecting the citizens of New Jersey against state-established churches, to be sure that we do not inadvertently prohibit New Jersey from extending its general state law benefits to all its citizens without regard to their religious belief.

Id. at 16. (emphasis in the original). How, then, would you summarize the "rule" announced in *Everson*?

3. Justice Black's opinion in *Everson* contains a detailed list of actions that the Establishment Clause forbids. Some are very specific, others more general. Consider the rule announced in *Everson* using the "level of generality" materials discussed in Chapter One. If we arrange that list in an order that places the "specific" prohibitions at the bottom and the more "general" ones at the top, the following range of options appears:

Chart 5-4
Characterizing the Non-establishment Norm

Possible Meanings of the Phrase "laws respecting an establishment of religion"

Abstract (high level)	No state compelled association of individuals with any organized religion, sect, or activity.
	No recognition of religion by the state for any purpose.
↓	No collaboration by the state for any purpose with religious individuals or associations.
Level of Generality	No state participation in religious affairs, or participation by religious individuals and groups in politics.
	No aid to any activity characterized as "religious" or "sectarian."
	No public assistance for religious organizations.
↑	No tax support for churches.
	No preference among churches or religions.
Specific	No compulsion or punishment in matters of religious belief or exercise.
(low level)	No "official" church, churches, or religions.

Which of these formulations best describes the outcome in *Everson?*

4. All of the Justices who wrote opinions in *Everson* relied heavily on history to justify their conclusions. In light of the materials excerpted in earlier chapters, is the Court's reliance on history convincing? Sufficient? Authoritative? Controlling?

5. Does the Court's decision to incorporate the Establishment Clause rest on a sound historical footing? Should its decision to incorporate also depend on the intent of Reconstruction Congress and the States that ratified the Fourteenth Amendment?

6. Embedded in the Court's decision to incorporate the Establishment Clause are a number of important federalism and separation of powers questions. Does the First Amendment also apply to the Court as well as Congress? *See* Destro, *Religious Liberty Guarantee* (yes). If so, does § 5 of the Fourteenth Amendment permit *Congress* to make "laws respecting an establishment of religion" that are necessary, in its judgment, to protect the substantive rights protected by § 1 of the Amendment? *See* § K, p. 384, below.

7. Several of the Justices in *Everson* use the terms "neutral" or "neutrality." As we have seen in the context of free exercise cases, the concept of neutrality is not easily defined. *See generally* Martha Nussbaum, Loving v. Virginia *and the Literary Imagination*, 17 QLR 337 (1997) ("When people approach an issue of equal protection externally and formally, without using their imaginations to try to understand the human meaning and impact of the laws in question, they are apt to be obtuse about equality, taking formal neutrality to be sufficient for equal protection."); Abner S. Greene, Kiryas Joel *and Two Mistakes About Equality*, 96 Colum. L. Rev. 1 (1996) ("The Court's increasing tendency to reject special treatment for minority groups—under either the "equality" or "neutrality" rubric, under either the Equal Protection Clause or the Establishment

Clause—is deeply problematic."); Robert A. Destro, *Equality, Social Welfare and Equal Protection*, 9 Harv. J. Law & Pub. Pol. 53 (1986).

Does the majority explain what the term "neutral" means in the context of church-state relations? Justice Black argues that government must be "neutral in its relations with groups of religious believers and non-believers." Justice Jackson asserts that "[o]ur public school... is organized on the premise that secular education can be isolated from all religious teaching so that the school can inculcate all needed temporal knowledge and also maintain a strict and lofty neutrality as to religion." Justice Rutledge claims "it does not make the state unneutral to withhold what the Constitution forbids it to give." Given the importance of the term in both establishment and free exercise cases, what *should be* the meaning of "neutrality" for First Amendment purposes?

8. An essay by philosopher Michael Sandel suggests that the Court views religious liberty from a "voluntarist" perspective, enfolding religious liberty into broader notions of autonomy. In other words, the Court has treated such questions as concerning "choice" rather than "conscience." *See* Chart 1-1 in Chapter One. In equating claims of religious liberty with claims of the right to choose one's own interests and ends, Sandel says the Court "confuses the pursuit of preferences with the exercise of duties and so forgets the special concern of religious liberty with the claims of conscientiously encumbered selves." Michael J. Sandel, *Freedom of Conscience or Freedom of Choice*, in ARTICLES OF FAITH, ARTICLES OF PEACE: THE RELIGIOUS LIBERTY CLAUSES AND THE AMERICAN PUBLIC PHILOSOPHY 91 (James Davison Hunter & Os Guinness eds. 1990). Can the Court, as an arm of government, view individuals as other than individuals who "choose" their own destinies? That is, can the Court accept a view of individuals *not* premised on liberal political theory, and remain true to the Constitution? If so, of what relevance is the concept of "community" that finds expression in the words of the Preamble, the structure of federalism, and in the First Amendment's recognition of a right "peaceably to assemble"?

9. No discussion of *Everson* would be complete without a discussion of its facts and of the political context in which it arose. We examine the factual setting of *Everson* in the next section, and its political context in §G below.

3. Proving an Establishment Clause Claim

a) *Standard of Review: Development and Transition from 1947–1971*

A "careful examination and weighing of all the relevant circumstances" is necessary whenever allegations are made that State action violates the Constitution. *Palazzolo v. Rhode Island*, 533 U.S. 606, 121 S.Ct. 2448, 2467 (2001) (O'Connor J., concurring). The function of the standard of review is to organize the investigation and presentation of the facts. In the Establishment Clause context, the standard of review should determine: 1) what evidence is necessary to make or defend a claim under the incorporated Establishment Clause; and 2) who bears the burden of proving that the Establishment Clause has been violated.

There is widespread agreement that the incorporated Establishment Clause "requires the state to be a neutral in its relations with groups of religious believers and non-believers; it does not require the state to be their adversary. State power is no more to be used so as to handicap religions, than it is to favor them." *Everson v. Board of Educ.*, 330

U.S. 1, 18 (1947). There is also widespread agreement that the standard of review should organize the fact-finding process around the ultimate question of "constitutional fact" in an Establishment Clause case: "Is the policy of the state 'neutral'?"

The Court, however, has used the terms "neutral" and "neutrality" to characterize state action in at least four different contexts: 1) to describe a state of equipoise, or equilibrium, where government policy neither encourages nor discourages religion; 2) to draw a distinction between the types of rules and programs that are otherwise within the power of government to enact (*i.e.,* those that are "secular" or "neutral") and those that are forbidden ("religious" or "ideological"); 3) to describe criteria for government action (*e.g.*, "evenhanded" or "nondiscriminatory"); and 4) to describe a relationship between the government and religious associations characterized by mutual independence or separation. *See, e.g., Mitchell v. Helms*, 530 U.S. 793, 879–882 (2001) (Souter, J., dissenting); *Employment Div. v. Smith*, 494 U.S. 872 (1990) (discussing neutral laws of general applicability).

The Court itself has recognized that among the "limitations inherent in formulating general principles on a case-by-case basis" is a risk of "considerable internal inconsistency in [its] opinions." *Walz v. Tax Commission,* 397 U.S. 664, 667 (1970). Understanding that the Court continues to disagree *in principle* on the meaning of the non-establishment norm helps to explain many of the differences in the Justices' reasoning and results.

Consider, for example, *Bradfield v. Roberts*, 175 U.S. 291 (1899), excerpted in Chapter Four, and *Everson v. Board of Education*, excerpted above. The taxpayers who sued to stop the hospital construction contract in *Bradfield* and the transportation reimbursement payments in *Everson* alleged that the Establishment Clause prohibits both direct and indirect payments that support the organized religious efforts of others. The Justices in both cases considered the nature of the service for which the government paid, the identity of the recipients, and the criteria the government used to select the recipients. The *result* was identical: the Court upheld both programs, but differences in principle led to significant differences in the published opinions.

In *Bradfield*, the Court did not address the "neutrality" question directly. Instead, asked four questions designed to help elicit facts relevant to the inquiry:

1. Does Congress have the power to enact the program at issue?
2. What is the legal character of the recipient?
3. Is there any evidence to indicate that it will violate the law?
4. Will it "exercise its powers... in favor of anyone seeking the ministrations of that kind of an institution"?

Absent some indication that the hospital corporation would violate the law, "the fact that its members... are members of a monastic order or sisterhood of the Roman Catholic [Church], and the further fact that the hospital is conducted under the auspices of said church, are wholly immaterial." 175 U.S. at 297–300.

In *Everson,* by contrast, both the majority and the dissent assumed that the institutional affiliation of the school to which the students were transported was a relevant factor in the analysis, but took very different positions on whether the Establishment Clause should make the students ineligible for transportation assistance. For the majority, neutrality was to be understood in terms of the government's "relations with groups of religious believers and non-believers." *Everson,* 330 U.S. at 18. From this perspective, the neutrality required by the Establishment Clause requires answers to three questions of fact:

1. Does the law "contribute tax-raised funds to the support of an institution which teaches the tenets and faith of any church"?;
2. Is the benefit part of "public welfare legislation"?; and
3. If so, would a federal rule banning the benefit "prohibit [a State] from extending its general State law benefits to all its citizens without regard to their religious belief"? *Id.*, 330 U.S. at 6–8, 16.

The *Everson* dissenters, by contrast, define neutrality by asking one question:

> "Does [the State's] action furnish support for religion by use of the taxing power?" 330 U.S. at 44 (Rutledge, Burton, Jackson, & Frankfurter, dissenting).

From this perspective, the constitutionality of a program that creates a relationship between the state and religious associations "depends upon the nature of [the associations] and their relation to the Church." 330 U.S. at 22 (Jackson, Rutledge, Frankfurter & Burton, JJ., dissenting).

As you review the materials that follow, bear in mind that the Court has yet to resolve these basic differences in principle, and that differences in principle will inevitably affect the formulation of the standard of review.

b) The Development of the "Lemon Test"

The two cases that follow, *Walz v. Tax Commission* and *Lemon v. Kurtzman*, 403 U.S. 602 (1971), establish a standard of review for Establishment Clause cases known as the "*Lemon* test." In order to pass muster against an Establishment Clause challenge, the state action (1) must have a secular purpose; (2) its principal or primary effect must be one that neither advances nor inhibits religion; and (3) it cannot result in an excessive government entanglement with religion. Each of these factors is best understood as a synthesis of the "cumulative criteria developed by the Court over many years." *Lemon*, 403 U.S. at 612.

As you read the cases in this chapter, consider the role that fact-finding plays in the litigation or settlement process. Whenever State action is alleged to violate the neutrality principle, a decision-maker will need to know the answers to at least four questions:

1) What specific actions has the state taken, or refused to take, that are alleged to violate the Establishment Clause?
2) What is the nature of the specific benefit or harm caused by the state's action?
3) Is the harm alleged unique or specific to the complaining party?
4) In what way does the state action affect either the institutional relationship between church and state, or the relationship of the government to a class of individuals or associations that is defined by reference to religion?

Consider as well whether there is disagreement among the Justices regarding the answers to these questions.

Walz v. Tax Commission

397 U.S. 664 (1970)

Mr. Chief Justice BURGER delivered the opinion of the Court.

Appellant, owner of real estate in Richmond County, New York, sought an injunction in the New York courts to prevent the New York City Tax Commission from granting property tax exemptions to religious organizations for religious properties used solely for religious worship. The exemption from state taxes is authorized by Art. 16, § 1, of the New York Constitution, which provides in relevant part:

> "Exemptions from taxation may be granted only by general laws. Exemptions may be altered or repealed except those exempting real or personal property used exclusively for religious, educational or charitable purposes as defined by law and owned by any corporation or association organized or conducted exclusively for one or more of such purposes and not operating for profit."

I

It is sufficient to note that for the men who wrote the Religion Clauses of the First Amendment the "establishment" of a religion connoted sponsorship, financial support, and active involvement of the sovereign in religious activity. In England, and in some Colonies at the time of the separation in 1776, the Church of England was sponsored and supported by the Crown as a state, or established, church; in other countries "establishment" meant sponsorship by the sovereign of the Lutheran or Catholic Church.

The Establishment and Free Exercise Clauses of the First Amendment are not the most precisely drawn portions of the Constitution. The sweep of the absolute prohibitions in the Religion Clauses may have been calculated; but the purpose was to state an objective, not to write a statute. In attempting to articulate the scope of the two Religion Clauses, the Court's opinions reflect the limitations inherent in formulating general principles on a case-by-case basis. The considerable internal inconsistency in the opinions of the Court derives from what, in retrospect, may have been too sweeping utterances on aspects of these clauses that seemed clear in relation to the particular cases but have limited meaning as general principles.

The Court has struggled to find a neutral course between the two Religion Clauses, both of which are cast in absolute terms, and either of which, if expanded to a logical extreme, would tend to clash with the other.

The course of constitutional neutrality in this area cannot be an absolutely straight line; rigidity could well defeat the basic purpose of these provisions, which is to insure that no religion be sponsored or favored, none commanded, and none inhibited. The general principle deducible from the First Amendment and all that has been said by the Court is this: that we will not tolerate either governmentally established religion or governmental interference with religion. Short of those expressly proscribed governmental acts there is room for play in the joints productive of a benevolent neutrality which will permit religious exercise to exist without sponsorship and without interference.

Each value judgment under the Religion Clauses must therefore turn on whether particular acts in question are intended to establish or interfere with religious beliefs and practices or have the effect of doing so.

Adherents of particular faiths and individual churches frequently take strong positions on public issues including, as this case reveals in the several briefs *amici*, vigorous advocacy of legal or constitutional positions. Of course, churches as much as secular bodies and private citizens have that right. No perfect or absolute separation is really possible; the very existence of the Religion Clauses is an involvement of sorts—one that seeks to mark boundaries to avoid excessive entanglement.

II

The legislative purpose of a property tax exemption is neither the advancement nor the inhibition of religion; it is neither sponsorship nor hostility. New York, in common with the other States, has determined that certain entities that exist in a harmonious relationship to the community at large, and that foster its "moral or mental improvement," should not be inhibited in their activities by property taxation or the hazard of loss of those properties for nonpayment of taxes. It has not singled out one particular church or religious group or even churches as such; rather, it has granted exemption to all houses of religious worship within a broad class of property owned by nonprofit, quasi-public corporations which include hospitals, libraries, playgrounds, scientific, professional, historical, and patriotic groups. The State has an affirmative policy that considers these groups as beneficial and stabilizing influences in community life and finds this classification useful, desirable, and in the public interest. Qualification for tax exemption is not perpetual or immutable; some tax-exempt groups lose that status when their activities take them outside the classification and new entities can come into being and qualify for exemption.

Governments have not always been tolerant of religious activity, and hostility toward religion has taken many shapes and forms—economic, political, and sometimes harshly oppressive. Grants of exemption historically reflect the concern of authors of constitutions and statutes as to the latent dangers inherent in the imposition of property taxes; exemption constitutes a reasonable and balanced attempt to guard against those dangers. The limits of permissible state accommodation to religion are by no means co-extensive with the noninterference mandated by the Free Exercise Clause. To equate the two could be to deny a national heritage with roots in the Revolution itself.

We find it unnecessary to justify the tax exemption on the social welfare services or "good works" that some churches perform for parishioners and others—family counselling [sic], aid to the elderly and the infirm, and to children. [T]he use of a social welfare yardstick as a significant element to qualify for tax exemption could conceivably give rise to confrontations that could escalate to constitutional dimensions.

Granting tax exemptions to churches necessarily operates to afford an indirect economic benefit and also gives rise to some, but yet a lesser, involvement than taxing them. In analyzing either alternative the questions are whether the involvement is excessive, and whether it is a continuing one calling for official and continuing surveillance leading to an impermissible degree of entanglement. Obviously a direct money subsidy would be a relationship pregnant with involvement and, as with most governmental grant programs, could encompass sustained and detailed administrative relationships for enforcement of statutory or administrative standards, but that is not this case. The hazards of churches supporting government are hardly less in their potential than the hazards of government supporting churches; each relationship carries some involvement rather than the desired insulation and separation. We cannot ignore the instances in history when church support of government led to the kind of involvement we seek to avoid.

All of the 50 States provide for tax exemption of places of worship, most of them doing so by constitutional guarantees. For so long as federal income taxes have had any potential impact on churches—over 75 years—religious organizations have been expressly exempt from the tax. Such treatment is an "aid" to churches no more and no less in principle than the real estate tax exemption granted by States. Few concepts are more deeply embedded in the fabric of our national life, beginning with pre-Revolutionary colonial times, than for the government to exercise at the very least this kind of benevolent neutrality toward churches and religious exercise generally so long as none was favored over others and none suffered interference.

It is significant that Congress, from its earliest days, has viewed the Religion Clauses of the Constitution as authorizing statutory real estate tax exemption to religious bodies. In 1802 the 7th Congress enacted a taxing statute for the County of Alexandria, adopting the 1800 Virginia statutory pattern which provided tax exemptions for churches. 2 Stat. 194. As early as 1813 the 12th Congress refunded import duties paid by religious societies on the importation of religious articles. During this period the City Council of Washington, D.C., acting under congressional authority, Act of Incorporation, §7, 2 Stat. 197 (May 3, 1802), enacted a series of real and personal property assessments that uniformly exempted church property. In 1870 the Congress specifically exempted all churches in the District of Columbia and appurtenant grounds and property "from any and all taxes or assessments, national, municipal, or county." Act of June 17, 1870, 16 Stat. 153.

Nothing in this national attitude toward religious tolerance and two centuries of uninterrupted freedom from taxation has given the remotest sign of leading to an established church or religion and on the contrary it has operated affirmatively to help guarantee the free exercise of all forms of religious belief. Thus, it is hardly useful to suggest that tax exemption is but the "foot in the door" or the "nose of the camel in the tent" leading to an established church.

Affirmed.

Mr. Justice BRENNAN, concurring.

I

The existence from the beginning of the Nation's life of a practice, such as tax exemptions for religious organizations, is not conclusive of its constitutionality. But such practice is a fact of considerable import in the interpretation of abstract constitutional language. On its face, the Establishment Clause is reasonably susceptible of different interpretations regarding the exemptions. History is particularly compelling in the present case because of the undeviating acceptance given religious tax exemptions from our earliest days as a Nation.

Thomas Jefferson was President when tax exemption was first given Washington churches, and James Madison sat in sessions of the Virginia General Assembly that voted exemptions for churches in that Commonwealth. I have found no record of their personal views on the respective Acts. The absence of such a record is itself significant. It is unlikely that two men so concerned with the separation of church and state would have remained silent had they thought the exemptions established religion. The adoption of the early exemptions without controversy, in other words, strongly suggests that they were not thought incompatible with constitutional prohibitions against involvements of church and state.

The exemptions have continued uninterrupted to the present day. They are in force in all 50 States. No judicial decision, state or federal, has ever held that they violate the Establishment Clause.

II

Government has two basic secular purposes for granting real property tax exemptions to religious organizations. First, these organizations are exempted because they, among a range of other private, nonprofit organizations contribute to the well-being of the community in a variety of nonreligious ways.

Appellant assumes, apparently, that church-owned property is used for exclusively religious purposes if it does not house a hospital, orphanage, weekday school, or the like. Any assumption that a church building itself is used for exclusively religious activities, however, rests on a simplistic view of ordinary church operations. As the appellee's brief cogently observes, "the public welfare activities and the sectarian activities of religious institutions are... intertwined.... Often a particular church will use the same personnel, facilities and source of funds to carry out both its secular and religious activities."

Second, government grants exemptions to religious organizations because they uniquely contribute to the pluralism of American society by their religious activities. Government may properly include religious institutions among the variety of private, nonprofit groups that receive tax exemptions, for each group contributes to the diversity of association, viewpoint, and enterprise essential to a vigorous, pluralistic society. The scheme is not designed to inject any religious activity into a non-religious context, as was the case with school prayers. No particular activity of a religious organization—for example, the propagation of its beliefs—is specially promoted by the exemptions. They merely facilitate the existence of a broad range of private, nonprofit organizations, among them religious groups, by leaving each free to come into existence, then to flourish or wither, without being burdened by real property taxes.

III

General subsidies of religious activities would, of course, constitute impermissible state involvement with religion. Tax exemptions and general subsidies, however, are qualitatively different. Though both provide economic assistance, they do so in fundamentally different ways. A subsidy involves the direct transfer of public monies to the subsidized enterprise and uses resources exacted from taxpayers as a whole. An exemption, on the other hand, involves no such transfer. Tax exemptions, accordingly, constitute mere passive state involvement with religion and not the affirmative involvement characteristic of outright governmental subsidy.

Whether Government grants or withholds the exemptions, it is going to be involved with religion.

Opinion of Mr. Justice HARLAN.

I

Two requirements frequently articulated and applied in our cases for achieving this goal are "neutrality" and "voluntarism." See *Schempp*, (concurring opinion of Mr. Justice Goldberg); *Engel*. These related and mutually reinforcing concepts are short-form for saying that the Government must neither legislate to accord benefits that favor religion over nonreligion, nor sponsor a particular sect, nor try to encourage participation in or abnegation of religion. In the vast majority of cases the inquiry, albeit an elusive one, can end at this point. Neutrality and voluntarism stand as barriers against the most egregious and hence divisive kinds of state involvement in religious matters.

II

This legislation neither encourages nor discourages participation in religious life and thus satisfies the voluntarism requirement of the First Amendment. The statute also satisfies the requirement of neutrality. Neutrality in its application requires an equal protection mode of analysis. The Court must survey meticulously the circumstances of governmental categories to eliminate, as it were, religious gerrymanders. In any particular case the critical question is whether the circumference of legislation encircles a class so broad that it can be fairly concluded that religious institutions could be thought to fall within the natural perimeter. I would hold the present exemption neutral because New York has created a general class so broad that it would be difficult to conclude that religious organizations cannot properly be included in it.

To the extent that religious institutions sponsor the secular activities that this legislation is designed to promote, it is consistent with neutrality to grant them an exemption just as other organizations devoting resources to these projects receive exemptions. I think, moreover, in the context of a statute so broad as the one before us, churches may properly receive an exemption even though they do not themselves sponsor the secular-type activities mentioned in the statute but exist merely for the convenience of their interested members. As long as the breadth of exemption includes groups that pursue cultural, moral or spiritual improvement in multifarious secular ways, including, I would suppose, groups whose avowed tenets may be antitheological, atheistic, or agnostic, I can see no lack of neutrality in extending the benefit of the exemption to organized religious groups.

Mr. Justice DOUGLAS, dissenting.

Petitioner is the owner of real property in New York and is a Christian. But he is not a member of any of the religious organizations, 'rejecting them as hostile.' The New York statute exempts from taxation real property 'owned by a corporation or association organized exclusively for * * * religious * * * purposes' and used 'exclusively for carrying out' such purposes. Yet nonbelievers who own realty are taxed at the usual rate. The question in the case therefore is whether believers—organized in church groups—can be made exempt from real estate taxes, merely because they are believers, while non-believers, whether organized or not, must pay the real estate taxes.

My Brother HARLAN says he 'would suppose' that the tax exemption extends to 'groups whose avowed tenets may be antitheological, atheistic, or agnostic.' If it does, then the line between believers and nonbelievers has not been drawn. But, with all respect, there is not even a suggestion in the present record that the statute covers property used exclusively by organizations for 'antitheological purposes,' 'atheistic purposes,' or 'agnostic purposes.'

There is a line between what a State may do in encouraging 'religious' activities, and what a State may not do by using its resources to promote 'religious' activities, or bestowing benefits because of them. Yet that line may not always be clear. Closing public schools on Sunday is in the former category; subsidizing churches, in my view, is in the latter.

With all due respect the governing principle is not controlled by *Everson v. Board of Education*. This case is quite different. Education is not involved. The financial support rendered here is to the church, the place of worship. A tax exemption is a subsidy.

Churches perform some functions that a State would constitutionally be empowered to perform. I refer to nonsectarian social welfare operations such as the care of orphaned children and the destitute and people who are sick. Under the First Amendment a State may not, however, provide worship if private groups fail to do so. That is a major difference between churches on the one hand and the rest of the nonprofit organizations on the other. Government could provide or finance operas, hospitals, historical societies, and all the rest because they represent social welfare programs within the reach of the police power. In contrast, government may not provide or finance worship because of the Establishment Clause any more than it may single out 'atheistic' or 'agnostic' centers or groups and create or finance them.

If believers are entitled to public financial support, so are nonbelievers. A believer and nonbeliever under the present law are treated differently because of the articles of their faith. I conclude that this tax exemption is unconstitutional.

Notes

1. Just before the excerpt from *Walz,* we raised four basic questions of fact that arise in every Establishment Clause case. Consider how each group of Justices responded in *Walz* to each of the four questions. In some cases, the answers are virtually identical; in others they are very different. How, if at all, do you think their answers to these questions affected their judgment?

- ***What specific actions has the state taken, or refused to take, that are alleged to violate the Establishment Clause?***

Majority opinion: The state grants "tax exemptions to religious organizations for religious properties used solely for religious worship."

Justice Brennan: The state grants "real property tax exemptions to religious organizations."

Justice Harlan: The state grants "tax exemptions to religious organizations."

Justice Douglas: The state grants tax exemptions for "real property 'owned by a corporation or association organized exclusively for ... religious ... purposes' and used 'exclusively for carrying out' such purposes.'"

- ***What is the specific nature of the benefit or harm caused by the state's action?***

Majority opinion: The exemption benefits "all houses of religious worship within a broad class of property owned by nonprofit, quasi-public corporations which include hospitals, libraries, playgrounds, scientific, professional, historical, and patriotic groups."

Justice Brennan: The exemption benefits "the variety of private, nonprofit groups that receive tax exemptions."

Justice Harlan: The exemption benefits "nonprofit organizations."

Justice Douglas: The exemption benefits only "believers—organized in church groups."

- ***What is the nature of the harm that is unique or specific to the complaining party?***

Majority opinion: "Grant of an exemption to church property indirectly requires the appellant to make a contribution to religious bodies."

Justice Brennan does not address the question directly. His focus is on the nature of the relationship between church and state.

Justice Harlan does not address the question directly. His focus is on the nature of the relationship between church and state.

Justice Douglas: "Believers—organized in church groups—can be made exempt from real estate taxes, merely because they are believers, while non-believers, whether organized or not, must pay the real estate taxes."

- ***In what way does the state action affect either the institutional relationship between church and state, or the relationship of a class of individuals or associations that is defined by reference to religion?***

Majority opinion: "Grants of exemption historically reflect the concern of authors of constitutions and statutes as to the latent dangers inherent in the imposition of property taxes; exemption constitutes a reasonable and balanced attempt to guard against those dangers."

Justice Brennan: "The exemptions have continued uninterrupted [from the founding period] to the present day."

Justice Harlan: "New York has created a general class so broad that it would be difficult to conclude that religious organizations cannot properly be included in it."

Justice Douglas: "[S]ubsidies either through direct grant or tax exemption for sectarian causes, whether carried on by church qua church or by church qua welfare agency, must be treated differently, lest we in time allow the church qua church to be on the public payroll, which, I fear, is imminent."

2. Why do you suppose that the focus in the opinions of Justices Brennan and Justice Harlan was on nature of the church-state relationship rather than the harm to the dissenting taxpayer? *See, e.g.*, Carl H. Esbeck, *The Establishment Clause as a Structural Restraint on Governmental Power,* 84 Iowa L. Rev. 1, 98 (1998) (arguing that "the purpose of the Establishment Clause is not to safeguard individual religious rights").

3. In *Walz*, Chief Justice Burger asserts that: "The Court has struggled to find a neutral course between the two Religion Clauses, both of which are cast in absolute terms, and either of which, if expanded to a logical extreme, would tend to clash with the other." Is the "clash" between the Free Exercise and Establishment Clauses a consequence of the framers' *design* of the First Amendment, or a result of the Court's *interpretation* of the amendment? *See* Mary Ann Glendon & Raul Yanes, *Structural Free Exercise*, 90 Mich. L. Rev. 477 (1991) (arguing that it results from an inadequate theory of "incorporation"); Esbeck, *The Establishment Clause as a Structural Restraint on Governmental Power, supra* note 2, 84 Iowa L. Rev. 1 at 3–4 (arguing that "the Supreme Court's case law is more easily understood when the Establishment Clause is conceptualized as a structural restraint on the government's power to act on certain matters pertaining to religion" rather than as a protection for individual rights).

4. **Pluralism:** Justice Brennan's concurring opinion in *Walz* offers two "secular" reasons justifying the state's decision to grant tax exemptions for churches. The first is that churches offer help to the community in nonreligious ways. The second is that churches "uniquely contribute to the pluralism of American society by their religious activities." In *County of Allegheny v. ACLU*, 492 U.S. 573 (1989), summarized in Section C below, the majority relied on "pluralism" as one of the reasons to support a display of a menorah and Christmas tree in a holiday display on the grounds of the county building. Justice Brennan disagreed: "I discern [no] theory under which the government is permitted to appropriate particular holidays and religious objects to its own use in celebrating 'pluralism.'" Are the factual settings in *Walz* and *County of Allegheny* different in kind, or different in degree? Justice Brennan's opinion in *Walz* relies on the *absence* of opposition to tax exemptions by Jefferson and Madison as one justification for his conclusion that exemptions are constitutional. Justice Harlan also noted that exemptions are not as politically controversial as direct subsidies. Should the constitutionality of a governmental attempt to accommodate religious pluralism depend on the amount of

political opposition it engenders, or on the basis of a judicial determination of how "pluralistic" the accommodation appears to be? Or should the case be decided on the basis of a factual finding that the officials who crafted the challenged program intended to foster pluralism? If "intent" is the key, should the court also require proof that the program actually fostered pluralism? *Cf. American Civil Liberties Union of New Jersey v. Schundler*, 931 F.Supp. 1180 (D.N.J. 1995) (enjoining a holiday display that did not include both the Christmas crèche and a menorah, but permitting the city to modify the display to include Santa and reindeer), *aff'd in part and vacated in part and remanded*, 104 F.3d 1435 (3rd Cir. 1997) (holding that display of crèche and menorah violated the Establishment Clause, and that additional figures did not "demystify" the religious symbols), *cert. denied*, 520 U.S. 1265 (1997), *appeal after remand*, 168 F.3d 92 (3rd Cir. 1999) (upholding a modified holiday display that included a crèche, a menorah, a 4' tall plastic figure of Santa Claus, a 3' 10" tall plastic figure of Frosty the Snowman, a 4' tall sled, Kwanzaa symbols on the tree, and two signs, each approximately 2' by 3', stating: "Through this display and others throughout the year, the City of Jersey City is pleased to celebrate the diverse cultural and ethnic heritages of its peoples.")

5. How *should* the Court understand the function of a tax exemption? In *Walz*, the majority asserts that tax exemptions provide "an indirect economic benefit" to eligible taxpayers. Justice Brennan asserts that "[t]ax exemptions and general subsidies... are qualitatively different." Justice Harlan, by contrast, agreed with Justice Douglas "that exemptions do not differ from subsidies as an economic matter", but noted important political differences between exemptions and subsidies. In *Regan v. Taxation with Representation of Washington*, 461 U.S. 540 (1983), the Court was nearly unanimous in its view that "[an income] tax exemption has much the same effect as a cash grant to the organization of the amount of tax it would have to pay on its income," but hastened to point out that "[i]n stating that exemptions and deductions,... are *like* cash subsidies,..., we of course do not mean to assert that they are in all respects identical." *id.* at 544 & n.5 (emphasis added). Is the question "What is a tax exemption?" a question of "fact," a question of "economic theory," or both? For a detailed discussion of the relationship between constitutional law and tax theory, see Chapter Nine § E (discussing constitutional limits on the exercise of the taxing power).

Lemon v. Kurtzman

403 U.S. 602 (1971)

Mr. Chief Justice BURGER delivered the opinion of the Court.

These two appeals raise questions as to Pennsylvania and Rhode Island statutes providing state aid to church-related elementary and secondary schools. Both statutes are challenged as violative of the Establishment and Free Exercise Clauses of the First Amendment and the Due Process Clause of the Fourteenth Amendment.

Pennsylvania has adopted a statutory program that provides financial support to nonpublic elementary and secondary schools by way of reimbursement for the cost of teachers' salaries, textbooks, and instructional materials in specified secular subjects. Rhode Island has adopted a statute under which the State pays directly to teachers in nonpublic elementary schools a supplement of 15% of their annual salary. Under each statute state aid has been given to church-related educational institutions. We hold that both statutes are unconstitutional.

I

The Rhode Island Statute

In order to be eligible for the Rhode Island salary supplement, the recipient must teach in a nonpublic school at which the average per-pupil expenditure on secular education is less than the average in the State's public schools during a specified period. Appellant State Commissioner of Education also requires eligible schools to submit financial data.

The Act also requires that teachers eligible for salary supplements must teach only those subjects that are offered in the State's public schools. They must use "only teaching materials which are used in the public schools." Finally, any teacher applying for a salary supplement must first agree in writing "not to teach a course in religion for so long as or during such time as he or she receives any salary supplements" under the Act.

The Pennsylvania Statute

The statute authorizes appellee state Superintendent of Public Instruction to "purchase" specified "secular educational services" from nonpublic schools. Under the "contracts" authorized by the statute, the State directly reimburses nonpublic schools solely for their actual expenditures for teachers' salaries, textbooks, and instructional materials. A school seeking reimbursement must maintain prescribed accounting procedures that identify the "separate" cost of the "secular educational service." These accounts are subject to state audit. The funds for this program were originally derived from a new tax on horse and harness racing, but the Act is now financed by a portion of the state tax on cigarettes.

There are several significant statutory restrictions on state aid. Reimbursement is limited to courses "presented in the curricula of the public schools." It is further limited "solely" to courses in the following "secular" subjects: mathematics, modern foreign languages, physical science, and physical education. Textbooks and instructional materials included in the program must be approved by the state Superintendent of Public Instruction. Finally, the statute prohibits reimbursement for any course that contains "any subject matter expressing religious teaching, or the morals or forms of worship of any sect."

It appears that some $5 million has been expended annually under the Act. The State has now entered into contracts with some 1,181 nonpublic elementary and secondary schools with a student population of some 535,215 pupils—more than 20% of the total number of students in the State. More than 96% of these pupils attend church-related schools, and most of these schools are affiliated with the Roman Catholic church.

II

Candor compels acknowledgment, moreover, that we can only dimly perceive the lines of demarcation in this extraordinarily sensitive area of constitutional law.

The language of the Religion Clauses of the First Amendment is at best opaque, particularly when compared with other portions of the Amendment. Its authors did not simply prohibit the establishment of a state church or a state religion, an area history shows they regarded as very important and fraught with great dangers. Instead they commanded that there should be "no law *respecting* an establishment of religion." A law may be one "respecting" the forbidden objective while falling short of its total realization. A law "respecting" the proscribed result, that is, the establishment of religion, is not always easily identifiable as one violative of the Clause. A given law might not *establish* a state religion but nevertheless be one "respecting" that end in the sense of being a step that could lead to such establishment and hence offend the First Amendment.

Every analysis in this area must begin with consideration of the cumulative criteria developed by the court over many years. Three such tests may be gleaned from our cases. First, the statute must have a secular legislative purpose, second, its principal or primary effect must be one that neither advances nor inhibits religion, [and] finally, the statute must not foster "an excessive government entanglement with religion."

Inquiry into the legislative purposes of the Pennsylvania and Rhode Island statutes affords no basis for a conclusion that the legislative intent was to advance religion. On the contrary, the statutes themselves clearly state that they are intended to enhance the quality of the secular education in all schools covered by the compulsory attendance laws.

We need not decide whether these legislative precautions restrict the principal or primary effect of the programs to the point where they do not offend the Religion Clauses, for we conclude that the cumulative impact of the entire relationship arising under the statutes in each State involves excessive entanglement between government and religion.

III

Our prior holdings do not call for total separation between church and state; total separation is not possible in an absolute sense. Some relationship between government and religious organizations is inevitable. *Zorach*; *Sherbert* (Harlan, J., dissenting). Fire inspection, building and zoning regulations, and state requirements under compulsory school-attendance laws are examples of necessary and permissible contacts. Indeed, under the statutory exemption before us in *Walz*, the State had a continuing burden to ascertain that the exempt property was in fact being used for religious worship. Judicial caveats against entanglement must recognize that the line of separation, far from being a "wall," is a blurred, indistinct, and variable barrier depending on all the circumstances of a particular relationship.

This is not to suggest, however, that we are to engage in a legalistic minuet in which precise rules and forms must govern. A true minuet is a matter of pure form and style, the observance of which is itself the substantive end. Here we examine the form of the relationship for the light that it casts on the substance.

(a) *Rhode Island program*

The church schools involved in the program are located close to parish churches. This understandably permits convenient access for religious exercises since instruction in faith and morals is part of the total educational process. The school buildings contain identifying religious symbols such as crosses on the exterior and crucifixes, and religious paintings and statutes either in the classrooms or hallways. Although only approximately 30 minutes a day are devoted to direct religious instruction, there are religiously oriented extracurricular activities. Approximately two thirds of the teachers in these schools are nuns of various religious orders. Their dedicated efforts provide an atmosphere in which religious instruction and religious vocations are natural and proper parts of life in such schools. Indeed, as the District Court found, the role of teaching nuns in enhancing the religious atmosphere has led the parochial school authorities to attempt to maintain a one-to-one ratio between nuns and lay teachers in all schools rather than to permit some to be staffed almost entirely by lay teachers.

On the basis of these findings the District Court concluded that the parochial schools constituted "an integral part of the religious missions of the Catholic Church." The various characteristics of the schools make them "a powerful vehicle for transmitting the Catholic faith to the next generation." This process of inculcating religious doctrine is, of course, enhanced by the impressionable age of the pupils, in primary schools particularly. In short, parochial schools involve substantial religious activity and purpose.

The substantial religious character of these church-related schools gives rise to entangling church-state relationships of the kind the Religion Clauses sought to avoid. Although the District Court found that concern for religious values did not inevitably or necessarily intrude into the content of secular subjects, the considerable religious activities of these schools led the legislature to provide for careful governmental controls and surveillance by state authorities in order to ensure that state aid supports only secular education.

In our view the record shows these dangers are present to a substantial degree. The Rhode Island Roman Catholic elementary schools are under the general supervision of the Bishop of Providence and his appointed representative, the Diocesan Superintendent of Schools. Religious authority necessarily pervades the school system.

The schools are governed by the standards set forth in a "Handbook of School Regulations," which has the force of synodal law in the diocese. It emphasizes the role and importance of the teacher in parochial schools: "The prime factor for the success or the failure of the school is the spirit and personality, as well as the professional competency, of the teacher * * *." The Handbook also states that: "Religious formation is not confined to formal courses; nor is it restricted to a single subject area." Finally, the Handbook advises teachers to stimulate interest in religious vocations and missionary work. Given the mission of the church school, these instructions are consistent and logical.

Several teachers testified, however, that they did not inject religion into their secular classes. And the District Court found that religious values did not necessarily affect the content of the secular instruction. But what has been recounted suggests the potential if not actual hazards of this form of state aid. The teacher is employed by a religious organization, subject to the direction and discipline of religious authorities, and works in a system dedicated to rearing children in a particular faith. These controls are not lessened by the fact that most of the lay teachers are of the Catholic faith. Inevitably some of a teacher's responsibilities hover on the border between secular and religious orientation.

We need not and do not assume that teachers in parochial schools will be guilty of bad faith or any conscious design to evade the limitations imposed by the statute and the First Amendment. We simply recognize that a dedicated religious person, teaching in a school affiliated with his or her faith and operated to inculcate its tenets, will inevitably experience great difficulty in remaining religiously neutral. Doctrines and faith are not inculcated or advanced by neutrals. With the best of intentions such a teacher would find it hard to make a total separation between secular teaching and religious doctrine. What would appear to some to be essential to good citizenship might well for others border on or constitute instruction in religion. Further difficulties are inherent in the combination of religious discipline and the possibility of disagreement between teacher and religious authorities over the meaning of the statutory restrictions.

We do not assume, however, that parochial school teachers will be unsuccessful in their attempts to segregate their religious beliefs from their secular educational responsibilities. But the potential for impermissible fostering of religion is present. The Rhode Island Legislature has not, and could not, provide state aid on the basis of a mere assumption that secular teachers under religious discipline can avoid conflicts. The State must be certain, given the Religion Clauses, that subsidized teachers do not inculcate religion—indeed the State here has undertaken to do so. To ensure that no trespass occurs, the State has therefore carefully conditioned its aid with pervasive restrictions. An eligible recipient must teach only those courses that are offered in the public schools and use only those texts and materials that are found in the public schools. In addition the teacher must not engage in teaching any course in religion.

A comprehensive, discriminating, and continuing state surveillance will inevitably be required to ensure that these restrictions are obeyed and the First Amendment otherwise respected. Unlike a book, a teacher cannot be inspected once so as to determine the extent and intent of his or her personal beliefs and subjective acceptance of the limitations imposed by the First Amendment. These prophylactic contacts will involve excessive and enduring entanglement between state and church.

(b) *Pennsylvania program*

As we noted earlier, the very restrictions and surveillance necessary to ensure that teachers play a strictly non-ideological role give rise to entanglements between church and state. The Pennsylvania statute, like that of Rhode Island, fosters this kind of relationship. Reimbursement is not only limited to courses offered in the public schools and materials approved by state officials, but the statute excludes "any subject matter expressing religious teaching, or the morals or forms of worship of any sect." In addition, schools seeking reimbursement must maintain accounting procedures that require the State to establish the cost of the secular as distinguished from the religious instruction.

The Pennsylvania statute, moreover, has the further defect of providing state financial aid directly to the church-related school.

IV

A broader base of entanglement of yet a different character is presented by the divisive political potential of these state programs. In a community where such a large number of pupils are served by church-related schools, it can be assumed that state assistance will entail considerable political activity. Partisans of parochial schools, understandably concerned with rising costs and sincerely dedicated to both the religious and secular educational missions of their schools, will inevitably champion this cause and promote political action to achieve their goals. Those who oppose state aid, whether for constitutional, religious, or fiscal reasons, will inevitably respond and employ all of the usual political campaign techniques to prevail. Candidates will be forced to declare and voters to choose. It would be unrealistic to ignore the fact that many people confronted with issues of this kind will find their votes aligned with their faith.

Ordinarily political debate and division, however vigorous or even partisan, are normal and healthy manifestations of our democratic system of government, but political division along religious lines was one of the principal evils against which the First Amendment was intended to protect. To have States or communities divide on the issues presented by state aid to parochial schools would tend to confuse and obscure other issues of great urgency. We have an expanding array of vexing issues, local and national, domestic and international, to debate and divide on. It conflicts with our whole history and tradition to permit questions of the Religion Clauses to assume such importance in our legislatures and in our elections that they could divert attention from the myriad issues and problems that confront every level of government. The highways of church and state relationships are not likely to be one-way streets, and the Constitution's authors sought to protect religious worship from the pervasive power of government. The history of many countries attests to the hazards of religion's intruding into the political arena or of political power intruding into the legitimate and free exercise of religious belief.

Of course, as the Court noted in *Walz*, "[a]dherents of particular faiths and individual churches frequently take strong positions on public issues." We could not expect otherwise, for religious values pervade the fabric of our national life. But in *Walz* we dealt with a status under state tax laws for the benefit of all religious groups. Here we are confronted with successive and very likely permanent annual appropriations that benefit relatively few religious groups. Political fragmentation and divisiveness on religious lines are thus likely to be intensified.

V

Finally, nothing we have said can be construed to disparage the role of church-related elementary and secondary schools in our national life. Their contribution has been and is enormous. Nor do we ignore their economic plight in a period of rising costs and expanding need. Taxpayers generally have been spared vast sums by the maintenance of these educational institutions by religious organizations, largely by the gifts of faithful adherents.

The merit and benefits of these schools, however, are not the issue before us in these cases. The sole question is whether state aid to these schools can be squared with the dictates of the Religion Clauses. Under our system the choice has been made that government is to be entirely excluded from the area of religious instruction and churches excluded from the affairs of government. The Constitution decrees that religion must be a private matter for the individual, the family, and the institutions of private choice, and that while some involvement and entanglement are inevitable, lines must be drawn.

Mr. Justice DOUGLAS, whom Mr. Justice BLACK joins, concurring. [Opinion omitted.]

Mr. Justice BRENNAN, concurring. [Opinion omitted.]

Mr. Justice WHITE, concurring and dissenting.

The issue is fairly joined. It is precisely the kind of issue the Constitution contemplates this Court must ultimately decide. This is true although neither affirmance nor reversal of any of these cases follows automatically from the spare language of the First Amendment, from its history, or from the cases of this Court construing it and even though reasonable men can very easily and sensibly differ over the import of that language.

But, while the decision of the Court is legitimate, it is surely quite wrong in overturning the Pennsylvania and Rhode Island statutes on the ground that they amount to an establishment of religion forbidden by the First Amendment.

Our prior cases have recognized the dual role of parochial schools in American society: they perform both religious and secular functions. Our cases also recognize that legislation having a secular purpose and extending governmental assistance to sectarian schools in the performance of their secular functions does not constitute "law[s] respecting an establishment of religion" forbidden by the First Amendment merely because a secular program may incidentally benefit a church in fulfilling its religious mission. That religion may indirectly benefit from governmental aid to the secular activities of churches does not convert that aid into an impermissible establishment of religion.

It is enough for me that the states and the Federal Government are financing a separable secular function of overriding importance in order to sustain the legislation here challenged.

The Establishment Clause, however, coexists in the First Amendment with the Free Exercise Clause and the latter is surely relevant in cases such as these. Where a state program seeks to ensure the proper education of its young, in private as well as public schools, free exercise considerations at least counsel against refusing support for students attending parochial schools simply because in that setting they are also being instructed in the tenets of the faith they are constitutionally free to practice.

The Court thus creates an insoluble paradox for the State and the parochial schools. The State cannot finance secular instruction if it permits religion to be taught in the same classroom; but if it exacts a promise that religion not be so taught—a promise the school and its teachers are quite willing and on this record able to give—and enforces it, it is then entangled in the "no entanglement" aspect of the Court's Establishment Clause jurisprudence.

---

c) Notes on "The Lemon Test"

The "*Lemon* test" is one of at least "three complementary (and occasionally overlapping) tests" used by the Supreme Court in cases raising Establishment Clause issues. *See Doe v. Santa Fe Indep. Sch. Dist.*, 168 F.3d 806, 816 (5th Cir.1999), *aff'd* 530 U.S. 290 (2000). Because the *Lemon* test is a synthesis of the cumulative criteria the Court has developed over the years, it should not be surprising that each of its three components has been supplemented, modified, and clarified many times in the more than thirty years since *Lemon* was decided. A brief summary of each of the three *Lemon* factors appears below, followed by a discussion of the "complementary (and occasionally overlapping)" factors that have been added over the years.

1) Does the state action have a "secular purpose"?

What does it mean to allege that a state action has "no secular purpose"? Such an allegation could mean that the state intended by its action to accomplish a religious goal such as encouraging attendance at religious services, or that the legislature had religious reasons for the way that it resolved a disputed issue of public policy, such as a ban on further use of the death penalty. In general, the Court has looked at the "secular purpose" inquiry in much the same way that it uses the "any rational basis" standard of review. Unless some facts appear in the record that call the actual purpose of the statute into doubt, the courts will generally presume that the purpose the legislature sought to achieve is within its powers. *See Wallace v. Jaffree*, 472 U.S. 38, 56 (1985) (concluding that the actual purpose was to foster prayer); *Edwards v. Aguillard*, 482 U.S. 578, 592 (1987) (concluding that the actual purpose was to prefer a particular religious doctrine), excerpted in Chapter Ten. The term "secular purpose" therefore appears to be synonymous with "otherwise legitimate public purpose." Is protecting religious freedom a "secular purpose"?

2) Does the state action have a principal or primary effect that neither advances nor inhibits religion?

How does a court determine whether the "principal or primary effect" of a government policy advances or inhibits religion? The case law does not provide a direct answer to this question, but it is possible to formulate one by looking at two important "process issues" that arise in all civil litigation. The first of these issues relates to the evidence required to establish the principal or primary effect. The second involves the burden of proof: Who should bear the burden of proving that a violation of the Establishment Clause has occurred?

In § E(3)(a) above, we noted that the way that judges, Justices, or commentators will answer these questions depends, in large part, on how they understand and apply the concept of "neutrality." That understanding will, in turn, affect the type of evidence required in order to make the case that a given program is, or is not, "neutral."

(A) What evidence is relevant to the proof of that the principal or primary effect of government policy advances or inhibits religion?

In order to support a claim that the "principal or primary effect" of state action "neither advances nor inhibits religion" the parties will need to produce evidence concerning both the specific program at issue and the institutional context in which it occurs. The case law makes it very clear that the Establishment Clause requires that government *programs* must be neutral with respect to religion, but the Court has long been divided over whether, and under what circumstances, *institutions* receiving government assistance must also be religiously neutral. The Court resolved the issue by a 5-4 vote in *Zelman v. Simmons-Harris*, 122 S.Ct. 2460 (2002), in which it held that religious institutions can participate in government programs offering "true private choice" among a wide range of organizations and institutions.

Program neutrality is a question of fact that can be proved or disproved with evidence illustrating the purpose, effect, scope, and administration of specific government programs. *See, e.g., Everson v. Board of Educ.* (reimbursement was limited to cost of public transportation to and from school); *Walz v. Tax Comm'n* (tax exemptions for churches were part of a larger program granting exemptions to charities and other nonprofit organizations). ***Institutional neutrality*** is also a question of fact, the proof or disproof of which turns on evidence concerning the character of the organization, the nature of its programs, and the identity of its personnel and participants. *Compare Lemon v. Kurtzman* (evidence regarding the character, staffing, and operations of Catholic elementary and secondary schools) *with Tilton v. Richardson*, 403 U.S. 672, 682 (1971) (plurality opinion) (evidence concerning the character, staffing, and operations of religiously affiliated colleges).

(B) Which party must prove that the principal or primary effect of the challenged state action neither advances nor inhibits religion?

In ordinary civil litigation, the party who carries the burden of proof will lose if the evidence is insufficient to persuade the judge that the claim or defense rests on a solid factual footing. *See generally* Ronald J. Allen, *Burdens of Proof, Uncertainty, and Ambigu-*

ity in Modern Legal Discourse, 17 Harv. J.L. & Pub. Pol'y 627 (1994) (noting that imposing the burden of persuasion on the party legally responsible for making the claim "merely provides the decision rule" in cases of uncertainty). Adjustments made in the burden or allocation of proof can therefore have a significant impact on the outcome of the case. *See, e.g., New York Times v. Sullivan*, 376 U.S. 254 (1964) (increasing the burden of proof for a public figure alleging libel).

A party who claims that state action violates the Establishment Clause bears the burden of proving the claim, but the Supreme Court has made the task a bit easier by permitting courts to refer to facts and secondary sources outside the trial record. In its view, a decision that state's action either advances or inhibits religion is "not merely one of historical fact, but rather 'in large part a legal question to be answered on the basis of judicial interpretation of social facts.'" *Brooks v. City of Oak Ridge*, 222 F.3d 259, 264 n. 4 (6th Cir. 2000), quoting *Lynch v. Donnelly*, 465 U.S. 668, 693–94 (1984) (O'Connor, J., concurring); and *County of Allegheny v. ACLU*, 492 U.S. 573 at 614 n.60 (1989) (opinion of Blackmun, J).

During the fifty years that elapsed between *Everson*, decided in 1947, and *Agostini v. Felton*, 521 U.S. 203 (1997), the Court relied repeatedly on factual assumptions and generalizations outside the trial record to support a conclusive (or "irrebuttable") presumption that any generalized support for the educational mission of a religiously affiliated elementary or secondary school would inevitably have the impermissible effect of advancing religion. *Mitchell v. Helms*, 530 U.S. 793, 858 (2000) (O'Connor, J., concurring) (tracing the development of the "presumption of indoctrination"). *See Meek v. Pittenger*, 421 U.S. 349, 365–366 (1975) ("[I]t would simply ignore reality to attempt to separate secular educational functions from the predominantly religious role performed by many...church-related elementary and secondary schools."); *Committee for Public Education and Religious Liberty v. Nyquist*, 413 U.S. 756, 767 (1973) (using "a number of pertinent generalizations" about religious schools because no record had been developed in the District Court). *See also* Chapter Six ("Religion in the Classroom"). As a result, lower courts and litigators now commonly assume that they "need not refer to the parties' evidentiary submissions alone in [an] Establishment Clause analysis." *Brooks v. City of Oak Ridge*, 222 F.3d at 264 n.4.

The Court, however, appears to have drawn the opposite conclusion. In *Agostini v. Felton*, for example, it revised the *Lemon* test's inquiry into the "principal or primary effect" of state action by making it more fact-specific, and by requiring the parties to produce evidence of wrongdoing on the part of the state. After *Agostini*, the Court will no longer presume that support for the educational mission of religiously affiliated elementary or secondary school "will inevitably and impermissibly support religious indoctrination." *Agostini*, 521 U.S. at 886 (Souter, Stevens & Ginsburg, JJ., dissenting). *Accord Bowen v. Kendrick*, 487 U.S. 589 (1988) (requiring evidence of indoctrination in a federally funded sex education program); *Tilton v. Richardson*, 403 U.S. 672, 682 (1973) (requiring evidence of indoctrination in a challenge to a higher education program supported by federal funds).

The Court now uses three fact-specific criteria to determine whether a government-aid program impermissibly advances religion: (1) whether the aid results in governmental indoctrination, (2) whether the aid program defines its recipients by reference to religion, and (3) whether the aid creates an excessive entanglement between government and religion. *Agostini*, 521 U.S. at 234. *See Mitchell v. Helms*, 530 U.S. 793, 809 (2000) (discussing the circumstances under which indoctrination can be attributed to government action); *id.* at 858 (O'Connor, J., concurring) (rejecting an "irrebuttable presumption" of indoctrination based on the character of the school); *Good News Club v. Milford Cent. Sch.*, 533 U.S. 98, 121 S.Ct. 2093, 2111 (2001) (Breyer, J., concurring in part) (noting the need for a careful review of the evidence in the record before drawing a conclusion that the Establishment Clause has been violated). A presumption, by contrast, "imposes on the party against whom it is directed the burden of going forward with evidence to rebut" the facts assumed to exist, Fed. R. Evid. 301, and in an Establishment Clause case forces the party against whom it is directed to *disprove* the facts that a court may mistakenly assume are undisputed. *See, e.g., Lemon*, 403 U.S. at 618–619 (assuming, in the face of evidence to the contrary in the record, that a "dedicated religious person, teaching in a school affiliated with his or her faith and operated to inculcate its tenets, will inevitably experience great difficulty in remaining religiously neutral"); *Good News Club*, 533 U.S. 98, 121 S.Ct. 2093, 2104 (refusing to accept unsupported assertions of fact that would support the state's position); *id.* at 2111 (Breyer, J., concurring in part) (noting that the District Court erred when it assumed that there were no material issues of fact in dispute).

In sum, the parties themselves bear the burden of proving every element of a claim or defense based on the Establishment Clause, and judges should not assume what has not been proved. *See generally* Robert A. Destro, *Litigating Constitutional Defenses to Tort Claims: Do the Courts Take the First Amendment Seriously?*, 37 Cath. Law. 101 (1997).

(C) Does a "principal or primary effect that inhibits religion" violate the Establishment Clause, the Free Exercise Clause, or both?

Most of the case law under the second "prong" or inquiry of the *Lemon* test involves state action that is alleged to *advance* religion. There is very little case law that addresses the other part of the inquiry. *See Smith v. Raleigh Dist. of North Carolina Conf. of United Methodist Church*, 63 F.Supp.2d 694 (E.D.N.C. 1999) (refusing to dismiss a sexual harassment suit against a church, but acknowledging that the Establishment Clause might bar litigation of a case where the administration of the church's "spiritual functions" was at issue). This is so, in part, because most cases in which a claim is made that state action "inhibits" religion are characterized as free exercise claims, but in the few cases in which the courts have been asked to elaborate on the *Lemon* test's requirement that state action must not "inhibit" religion, they have refused to do so. *See, e.g., Strout v. Albanese*, 178 F.3d 57, 64 (1st Cir.), *cert. denied* 528 U.S. 931 (1999) (First Circuit professed to be "at a loss to understand why plaintiff-appellants believe that the Establishment Clause gives them a basis for recovery" in a case where the State Legislature changed a neutral rule of general applicability into one that discriminates on the basis of religion); *Bagley v. Raymond Sch. Dep't*, 728 A.2d 127, 133–135, 144–245 (Me.), *cert. denied*, 528 U.S. 947 (1999) (finding that the statute singled out only religious schools for adverse treatment without considering whether intentional discrimination on the basis of religion or religious viewpoint has "a purpose or primary effect that...inhibits religion").

3) Will the state action or policy result in an "excessive entanglement" between church and state?

The case law indicates that there are three distinct forms of "entanglement": 1) doctrinal; 2) administrative; and 3) political. As you review each form, consider what facts an attorney might use to prove that the entanglement is "excessive."

- ❑ *Doctrinal entanglement* occurs when a court or governmental body must make a decision that passes judgment on the doctrines or "ministerial" operations of a church or religious body. These issues most commonly arise when a court is called upon to resolve an intra-church dispute. Examples include disputes over internal church discipline or governance, see Chapter Seven § C, employment disputes where a religious employer relies on religious doctrine as a reason for making an employment decision that adversely affects an employee, see Chapter Eight § E (the religious workplace), and cases where the parties in civil litigation call expert witnesses to testify about the content of religious beliefs or doctrines, see Chapter Eleven § D (religion as an affirmative defense to government regulation). There is widespread agreement that doctrinal entanglement is absolutely forbidden by both the Establishment and Free Exercise Clauses, but there are significant differences of opinion over how to avoid it. This is particularly problematic in cases where application of a neutral rule of general applicability will change the character of an organization, or set civil standards for the conduct of religious affairs. *See, e.g.*, Carl H. Esbeck, *Tort Claims Against Churches and Ecclesiastical Officers: The First Amendment Considerations*, 89 W. Va. L. Rev. 1, 76-113 (1986). *See also* § H(2) below (discussing the right of "expressive association").

- ❑ ***Administrative entanglement*** occurs when the State has an oversight role in the day-to-day operations of churches and church-related institutions. Because the Court recognizes that civil oversight is "inevitable," how does a judge (or public official) determine that the amount of entanglement is "excessive"? Does it depend on the type and amount of information sought, the nature of the institution, or the government's purpose in seeking the information? Most of the cases where excessive entanglement is cited as a reason for striking down the program involve aid to education. In the labor, tax, and fiscal oversight contexts, including bankruptcy, the courts have been unsympathetic to allegations that *Lemon* requires invalidation of a continuing oversight role. In these cases, both courts and legislatures have crafted special rules that limit the scope of permissible oversight of the internal administrative and personnel operations of religious organizations. *See* Chapters Seven (discussing fiscal oversight of religious charities by the attorney general), Eight (judicially created limits on labor-management laws) and Nine (discussing the Church Audit Procedures Act, 26 U.S.C. § 7611 (2002)).

- ❑ ***Political entanglement, or "divisiveness"*** are concepts the Court used in *Lemon* to describe a "[a] broader base of entanglement of yet a different character" that focuses on "the divisive political potential of these state programs." The theory is that the Court has a special responsibility in construing the Establishment Clause to protect against political division along religious lines, and it has sparked considerable debate in the literature. *Compare e.g.*, Ronald C. Kahn, *God Save Us From the Coercion Test: Constitutive Decisionmaking, Polity Principles, and Religious Freedom*, in Symposium: *Religion and the Public Schools After* Lee v. Weisman, 43 Case W. Res. L. Rev. 983, 1017–1020 (1993) *with e.g.*, Edward M. Gaffney, *Political Divisiveness Along Religious Lines: The Entanglement of the Court in Sloppy History and Bad Public Policy*, 24 St. Louis U. L.J. 205 (1980). In the years since *Lemon*, the Court has recognized that the potential for political divisiveness cannot be used as an independent factor that would invalidate an otherwise constitutional policy. *See Lee v. Weisman*, 505 U.S. 577, 577–578 (1992) ("Divisiveness, of course, can attend any state decision respecting religions, and neither its existence nor its potential necessarily invalidates the State's attempts to accommodate religion in all cases."); *Lynch v.*

Donnelly, 465 U.S. 668, 684 (1984) ("This Court has never held that political divisiveness alone can serve to invalidate otherwise permissible conduct."); *id.* at 689 (O'Connor, J., concurring) (political divisiveness is "an evil addressed by the Establishment Clause," but the ultimate inquiry must always focus on "the character of the government activity that might cause such divisiveness"). The First Amendment implications of using the divisiveness doctrine as an Establishment Clause limit on political activism by religious factions are discussed in Section I (Religion and the Right to Petition for Redress of Grievances).

Now that you have reviewed the *Lemon* test in some detail, consider Justice White's dissent in that case. His criticism was that the Court's approach "creates an insoluble paradox for the State and the parochial schools" because the steps they must take to avoid the forbidden "effects" lead inexorably to "excessive entanglements." Is this a fair reading of the majority's opinion in *Lemon*? If so, is there any way to avoid the problem? We consider some alternative formulations of the standard of review in the following section.

d) Other Formulations of the Standard

Although it has been "widely criticized and occasionally ignored" by both the Supreme Court and lower courts, the *Lemon* test remains the standard of review most often applied in Establishment Clause cases. Because it is a synthesis of the factors the Court has taken into account in cases raising Establishment Clause issues, the perspectives and concerns of individual Justices have played an important role in its evolution. The case law indicates that the Court is very sensitive to arguments based in history, and to allegations that state action threatens political equality, individual liberty, or and equal protection of the laws.

Summarized below are four additional factors that the Court utilizes in Establishment Clause cases: history, endorsement analysis, coercion, and equal treatment. As you will see from the discussion, some of the Justices treat them as independent inquiries; others integrate them into their understanding of the *Lemon* test. This section concludes with a brief summary of the main criticisms of the *Lemon* test.

1) History

History is rarely determinative in Establishment Clause litigation, but it is influential. Historical materials have two basic functions in Establishment Clause litigation. The first is to illuminate the practices the Establishment Clause was designed to eliminate. *See, e.g., Wallace v. Jaffree*, 472 U.S. 38, 91 (1985) (Rehnquist, J., dissenting) (thirty-one references to history); *Marsh v. Chambers*, 463 U.S. 783, 795 (1983) (Brennan, J., dissenting) (thirteen references to history). *See generally* Robert L. Cord, *The Separation of Church and State: A Debate*, 1987 Utah L. Rev. 895 (recounting these and other uses of history by the Court in Establishment Clause litigation). The second function of historical material is to provide the factual background and context of a specific practice or policy. An accurate understanding of historical context is essential if the court must draw conclusions regarding the purpose or the primary effect of the government's actions. *Compare Lynch v. Donnelly*, 465 U.S. at 692 (O'Connor, J., concurring) (finding that there was a secular purpose for the display of a city-owned crèche in a municipal Christmas display), *with City of Elkhart v. Books*, 121 S.Ct. 2209, 2211 (2001)

(Rehnquist, C.J., Scalia and Thomas, JJ., dissenting from denial of *certiorari*) (arguing that the Court should "decide whether a monument which has stood for more than 40 years, and has at least as much civic significance as it does religious, must be physically removed from its place in front of the city's Municipal Building.").

2) Endorsement

Noting that "[i]t has never been entirely clear... how the three parts of the [*Lemon*] test relate to the principles enshrined in the Establishment Clause," Justice Sandra Day O'Connor has suggested that a focus "on institutional entanglement and on endorsement or disapproval of religion clarifies the *Lemon* test as an analytical device." *Lynch v. Donnelly*, 465 U.S. at 687–689 (O'Connor, J., concurring).

> The Establishment Clause prohibits government from making adherence to a religion relevant in any way to a person's standing in the political community. Government can run afoul of that prohibition in two principal ways. One is excessive entanglement with religious institutions, which may interfere with the independence of the institutions, give the institutions access to government or governmental powers not fully shared by nonadherents of the religion, and foster the creation of political constituencies defined along religious lines. *E.g., Larkin v. Grendel's Den*, 459 U.S. 116 (1982). The second and more direct infringement is government endorsement or disapproval of religion. Endorsement sends a message to nonadherents that they are outsiders, not full members of the political community, and an accompanying message to adherents that they are insiders, members of the political community. Disapproval sends the opposite message. *See generally Abington School District v. Schempp*, 374 U.S. 203 (1963).

Two factors are critical in an endorsement analysis. The first is the nature of the relationship between the government and any religious organizations involved in the case. The second is the content of the "message" embodied in the policy or practice under scrutiny. In both inquiries, a conclusion concerning "neutrality" is "in large part a legal question to be answered on the basis of judicial interpretation of social facts," and the outcome will often turn on the perspective of the reviewing court. *Lynch v. Donnelly*, 465 U.S. 668, 693–94 (1984) (O'Connor, J., concurring).

Recognizing that judges and Justices are affected by their own biases on these issues, Justice O'Connor suggests that the assessment of political neutrality should be made from the point of view of a fictional "objective observer, acquainted with the text, legislative history, and implementation of the statute." *Wallace v. Jaffree*, 472 U.S. 38, 68, 76 (O'Connor, J., concurring in the judgment). If the objective observer would find that the practices at issue foster political inequality, the state has violated the First Amendment.

Justice O'Connor has been consistent in her use of the approach. Other members of the Court have adopted it when it supports their analysis. *See, e.g., Santa Fe Indep. Sch. Dist. v. Doe*, 530 U.S. 290, 308 (2000); *County of Allegheny v. American Civil Liberties Union*, 492 U.S. 573 (1989) (plurality opinion) (using endorsement analysis as a factor to be considered as a part of the "principal or primary effect" inquiry of the *Lemon* test).

Justice O'Connor's endorsement analysis has provoked a lively debate among academic commentators. Because an endorsement analysis posits that the Establishment Clause is a guarantee of political equality, it would make little difference to a reviewing court that "[t]he risk of significant religious or denominational control over our democratic processes—or even of deep political division along religious lines—is remote...." *Wolman v. Walter*, 433 U.S. 229, 263 (1977) (opinion of Powell, J.). Political equality is required even when there is no division along religious lines. *See, e.g.*, Gary C. Leedes, *Rediscovering the Link Between the Establishment Clause and the Fourteenth Amendment: The Citizenship Declaration*, 26 Ind. L. Rev. 469, 507 (1993) (arguing that endorsement "violates enduring American traditions of justice"); Kenneth L. Karst, *The First Amendment, the Politics of Religion and the Symbols of Government*, 27 Harv. C.R.-C.L. L. Rev. 503, 517–18 (1992) (noting the difficulties were endorsement to be used as a general inquiry, but recognizing its utility in cases involving public symbols); Donald L. Beschle, *The Conservative as Liberal: The Religion Clauses, Liberal Neutrality, and the Approach of Justice O'Connor*, 62 Notre Dame L. Rev. 151, 171–82 (1987) (praising the approach and construing neutrality as nonendorsement). Her focus on the "message" conveyed to the citizen by the law or practice being challenged has not been so warmly received. *See, e.g.*, Steven D. Smith, *Symbols, Perceptions, and Doctrinal Illusions: Establishment Neutrality and the "No Endorsement" Test*, 86 Mich. L. Rev. 266, 283–91 (1987) (criticizing the approach); William P. Marshall, *"We Know It When We See It": The Supreme Court and Establishment*, 59 S. Cal. L. Rev. 495, 514–516, 537 (1986) (arguing that endorsement analysis is best understood in symbolic terms, but noting that "the test [is] incomprehensible"). *See generally* Matthew D. Adler, *Expressive Theories of Law: A Skeptical Overview*, 148 U. Pa. L. Rev. 1363 (2000) (arguing that it is difficult to ascribe "meaning" or find a "message" in most laws).

One critic of endorsement analysis suggests that Justice O'Connor is "the natural heir to Justice Black and to the political language of the 1940s." Winifred Fallers Sullivan, PAYING THE WORDS EXTRA: RELIGIOUS DISCOURSE IN THE SUPREME COURT OF THE UNITED STATES (1994) at 121.

> For O'Connor, as for Black, the central meaning of the religion clauses is neither protection of religion nor protection of religious liberty for their own sakes, but protection of the political rights of individuals against despotic government. While her constitutional piety lacks the emotional intensity of Justice Black's, the location of her faith, like his, is in law, in the Constitution, not in religion.... Like Black, religion, as religion, does not interest or worry her very much.

Id. at 123–24.

Is Professor Sullivan's criticism well taken? Is it, in fact, a criticism at all? As we noted at the beginning of this chapter, James Madison's *Memorial and Remonstrance* argued that the protection of religious liberty is a natural outgrowth of an enlightened public policy that protects "every Citizen in the enjoyment of his Religion with the same equal hand which protects his person and his property."

Consider, in this regard, the No Religious Test Clause of Article VI, discussed in detail in Chapter Eight § G(1). It provides that "no religious Test shall ever be required as a Qualification to any Office or public Trust under the United States." Is the goal of the Test Clause to protect religion or religious liberty "for their own sakes," or to guarantee political equality? Would a conclusion that the Test Clause was designed primarily as a guarantee of political equality diminish its value as a means of protecting religion and religious liberty, or enhance it?

Now consider the First Amendment as a whole. Does it protect religious liberty, speech and press, peaceable assembly, and petition for redress of grievances "for their own sake"? If so, why does it mention only Congress? Can it also be argued that the federalism component of the First Amendment is a guarantor of political equality? If so, how does it do so? Does Section One of the Fourteenth Amendment protect religious liberty "for its own sake," or does it accomplish that goal through language that was originally designed to foster equality?

3) Coercion

Like Justice O'Connor, Justice Anthony Kennedy has suggested that the *Lemon* test fails to capture the central purpose of the Establishment Clause. In *Lee v. Weisman*, 505 U.S. 577, 587 (1992), he observed that:

> It is beyond dispute that, at a minimum, the Constitution guarantees that government may not coerce anyone to support or participate in religion or its exercise, or otherwise act in a way which "establishes a [state] religion or religious faith, or tends to do so."

While coercion has been an important element for maintaining a government preferences for religion, the Court has never required evidence of coercion as a precondition for holding state action unconstitutional on Establishment Clause grounds. Nor has it spent much time considering what the characteristics of an established state religion or religious faith might be. Its focus has been on the ways government provides support for religion.

> An Establishment Clause standard that prohibits only "coercive" practices or overt efforts at government proselytization, but fails to take account of the numerous more subtle ways that government can show favoritism to particular beliefs or convey a message of disapproval to others, would not, in my view, adequately protect the religious liberty or respect the religious diversity of the members of our pluralistic political community.

County of Allegheny v. ACLU, 492 U.S. 573, 627–628 (1989) (O'Connor, Brennan & Stevens, JJ. concurring in part and concurring in the judgment).

How, for example, should the Court deal with "passive and symbolic accommodation of religious beliefs," such as making Christmas a national holiday, including religious symbols in public war memorials, special rules for protecting Native American religious beliefs and traditions, or public displays that have both religious and cultural significance? In Justice Kennedy's view, passive and symbolic accommodation of religious beliefs present minimal Establishment Clause concerns if no coercion is present, and judicial decrees mandating government indifference to the religious dimension of the lives of many Americans is tantamount to a "callous indifference" toward religion. Justice O'Connor's endorsement analysis, by contrast, would see coercion as only one form of endorsement.

What result in each of the following cases? Placement in a public park of a war memorial "Friendship Bell" cast in Japan in accordance with Buddhist ritual and tradition? *See Brooks v. City of Oak Ridge*, 222 F.3d 259 (6th Cir. 2000) (permitted). Placement in a downtown public square and maintenance at public expense of a sculpture of the Plumed Serpent deity, Quetzalcoatl? *See Alvarado v. City of San Jose, California*, 94 F.3d 1223 (9th Cir. 1996) (permitted); Placement and maintenance of a large Latin cross in a public war memorial? *See Separation of Church & State Committee v. City of Eugene of Lane County, Oregon*, 93 F.3d 617 (9th Cir. 1996) (forbidden). What explains the difference in outcomes? Does Justice Kennedy's assertion that a judicial decree requiring the elimination of non-coercive symbols or practices in public space demonstrates a "callous indifference toward religion" suggest that the Court is sending a "message of disapproval" of the religious character and customs of believers when it orders such symbols removed?

Which of these views—endorsement or coercion—is more consistent with the Incorporation Doctrine? Can there be a violation of the Fourteenth Amendment *without* state action that infringes individual liberty or denies equal protection of the laws? If neither individual liberty nor equal protection is at issue, why is there any concern for "neutrality"?

4) Equal Treatment

In *Agostini v. Felton*, discussed in Chapter Six § E(2), the Court adopted three criteria for determining whether the principal or primary effect of a government program is to advance or inhibit religion. *See* Section E(3) above. The second of these criteria is whether the government utilizes religion as a factor in the selection of recipients or participants, or in the allocation of benefits. *See Mitchell v. Helms*, 530 U.S. 793, 825 (2001); *Agostini*, 521 U.S. at 234.

Whether, and to what extent, the government may consider the religious beliefs, affiliations, practices, or teachings of individuals and associations as eligibility criteria for any program, benefit, office, or public trust is one of the most contentious issues in the jurisprudence of the Religious Liberty Guarantee. It arises in government aid programs; in hiring, appointments, and public contracting; in the formulation of laws and regulations of general applicability; and in access to property and fora owned or operated by the government.

In *Mitchell v. Helms*, four Justices suggested that "the religious nature of a recipient should not matter to the constitutional analysis, so long as the recipient adequately furthers the government's secular purpose." 530 U.S. at 827. (opinion of Thomas, Kennedy, and Scalia, JJ., and Rehnquist, C.J.) In their view, it is the *government's* purpose, actions, and programs that must be "neutral," not those of the recipient. The dissenters take precisely the opposite position. It is the religious character *of the institution or endeavor receiving assistance* that is critical. "[I]f we looked no further than evenhandedness, and failed to ask what activities the aid might support, or in fact did support," there would be no occasion to consider whether the *effect* of the government's action is support for the religious mission or objective. *Id.* at 885 (Souter, Stevens and Ginsburg, JJ., dissenting). *See* Part 3(c)(2) above.

This is not a new debate. *Compare Bradfield v. Roberts*, 175 U.S. 291 (1899) (religious character of an association alone is an insufficient reason to exclude either the association or its members) *with Everson v. Board of Educ.*, 330 U.S. 2, 59–60 (Jackson, Rutledge, Frankfurter & Burton, JJ., dissenting) ("the state can maintain its neutrality and avoid partisanship" only by drawing lines that distinguish religious from "wholly secular" endeavors).

As you review the cases excerpted in this chapter, consider how, if at all, the nondiscrimination norms of the Fourteenth Amendment affect the Court's interpretation of the substantive norms of the incorporated First Amendment. Should equality, neutrality, and equal protection be the starting points for the interpretation of *all* of the First Amendment's clauses? Does Justice Clarence Thomas' concurring opinion in *Zelman v. Simmons-Harris*, 122 S.Ct. 2460 (2002) suggest that such a standard should govern Establishment Clause cases? *See, e.g., Employment Div. v. Smith*, 494 U.S. 872 (1990). If so, what happens to religious minorities who may need special accommodations because of the majority's propensity to view its own religious practices as normative? *See* Abner S.

Greene, Kiryas Joel *and Two Mistakes About Equality*, 96 Colum. L. Rev. 1 (1996) ("The Court's increasing tendency to reject special treatment for minority groups—under either the "equality" or "neutrality" rubric, under either the Equal Protection Clause or the Establishment Clause—is deeply problematic.") *See generally* Robert A. Destro, *Equality, Social Welfare and Equal Protection*, 9 Harv. J. Law & Pub. Pol. 53 (1986).

5) Eliminating the Lemon Test

Justice Antonin Scalia is the most outspoken critic of the *Lemon* test. Concurring in *Lamb's Chapel v. Center Moriches Union Free Sch. Dist.*, 508 U.S. 384 (1993), he compared it to a "ghoul in a late-night horror movie that repeatedly sits up in its grave and shuffles abroad, after being repeatedly killed and buried." In his view, the *Lemon* test used, not so much to analyze, but to determine the outcome.

> It is there to scare us (and our audience) when we wish it to do so, but we can command it to return to the tomb at will. When we wish to strike down a practice it forbids, we invoke it, *see, e.g., Aguilar v. Felton*; when we wish to uphold a practice it forbids, we ignore it entirely, *see Marsh v. Chambers.* Sometimes, we take a middle course, calling its three prongs "no more than helpful signposts," *Hunt v. McNair*, 413 U.S. 734, 741 (1973). Such a docile and useful monster is worth keeping around, at least in a somnolent state; one never knows when one might need him.

508 U.S. at 398–99 (Scalia, J., concurring). *See also Tangipahoa Parish Board Of Educ. v. Freiler*, 530 U.S. 1251, 120 S.Ct. 2706, 2708 (2000) (Scalia & Thomas, JJ., and Rehnquist, C.J., dissenting from the denial of *certiorari*) (arguing that the Court should have granted certiorari "if only to take the opportunity to inter the *Lemon* test once and for all.")

Despite the criticism the *Lemon* test has received from a number of the Justices, and despite the criticism leveled at it from legal scholars representing most legal and political perspectives, the Court has not voted to eliminate or replace it. It thus remains the law of the Establishment Clause, and is regularly used by lower courts to decide many cases that never reach the Supreme Court.

* * *

In the sections that follow, we will examine the implications of the Court's approach to the non-establishment norm. The remainder of this Section will examine several specific instances where the government itself engages in action alleged to advance religion. In Sections F through I, we will examine the government's attempts to "maintain a strict and lofty neutrality as to religion" in the "marketplace of ideas," in political affairs, and in its oversight of the associations that play an important role in defining the character of American culture. Sections J and K will return to the structural theme with which the Chapter began, and reexamine the federal government's role in the enforcement of the equal protection and religious liberty guarantees.

4. Official Sponsorship of Religious Activity

The cases discussed in this section consider the following question: *When, and under what circumstances, does the non-establishment guarantee permit government officials to use prayer, religious symbolism, or religious teachings as an official component of govern-*

ment activities? As you review them, you should reconsider Charts 5-3 on page 250 and Chart 5-4 on page 271. Both charts examine the level of generality at which it is possible to understand the constitutional norms governing government behavior affecting religious belief and practice. Ask yourself what these cases tell you about the operational, or "as applied," meaning of the free exercise and non-establishment norms in the day-to-day operations of government? Does the setting in which officially sponsored religious activity take place make a difference in the constitutional analysis? Should it?

a) Official Prayers

Marsh v. Chambers

463 U.S. 783 (1983)

Chief Justice BURGER delivered the opinion of the Court.

The question presented is whether the Nebraska Legislature's practice of opening each legislative day with a prayer by a chaplain paid by the State violates the Establishment Clause of the First Amendment.

I

The Nebraska Legislature begins each of its sessions with a prayer offered by a chaplain who is chosen biennially by the Executive Board of the Legislative Council and paid out of public funds. Robert E. Palmer, a Presbyterian minister, has served as chaplain since 1965 at a salary of $319.75 per month for each month the legislature is in session.

Ernest Chambers is a member of the Nebraska Legislature and a taxpayer of Nebraska. Claiming that the Nebraska Legislature's chaplaincy practice violates the Establishment Clause of the First Amendment, he brought this action.

Applying the three-part test of *Lemon* the [C]ourt [of Appeals] held that the chaplaincy practice violated all three elements of the test: the purpose and primary effect of selecting the same minister for 16 years and publishing his prayers was to promote a particular religious expression; use of state money for compensation and publication led to entanglement. Accordingly, the Court of Appeals prohibited the State from engaging in any aspect of its established chaplaincy practice.

We granted certiorari limited to the challenge to the practice of opening sessions with prayers by a state-employed clergyman, and we reverse.

II

The opening of sessions of legislative and other deliberative public bodies with prayer is deeply embedded in the history and tradition of this country. From colonial times through the founding of the Republic and ever since, the practice of legislative prayer has coexisted with the principles of disestablishment and religious freedom. In the very courtrooms in which the United States District Judge and later three Circuit Judges heard and decided this case, the proceedings opened with an announcement that concluded, "God save the United States and this Honorable Court."

The tradition in many of the Colonies was, of course, linked to an established church, but the Continental Congress, beginning in 1774, adopted the traditional procedure of opening its sessions with a prayer offered by a paid chaplain. *See, e.g.*, 1 J. Continental Cong. 26 (1774); 2 *id.* at 12 (1775); 5 *id.* at 530 (1776); 6 *id.* at 887 (1776); 27 *id.* at 683

(1784). Although prayers were not offered during the Constitutional Convention, the First Congress, as one of its early items of business, adopted the policy of selecting a chaplain to open each session with prayer. Thus, on April 7, 1789, the Senate appointed a committee "to take under consideration the manner of electing Chaplains." S. Jour., 1st Cong., 1st Sess., 10 (1820 ed.). On April 9, 1789, a similar committee was appointed by the House of Representatives. On April 25, 1789, the Senate elected its first chaplain, *id.* at 16; the House followed suit on May 1, 1789, H.R. Jour., 1st Cong., 1st Sess., 26 (1826 ed.). A statute providing for the payment of these chaplains was enacted into law on September 22, 1789. 2 Annals of Cong. 2180; §4, 1 Stat. 71.

On September 25, 1789, three days after Congress authorized the appointment of paid chaplains, final agreement was reached on the language of the Bill of Rights, S. Jour., *supra*, at 88; H. R. Jour., *supra*, at 121. Clearly the men who wrote the First Amendment Religion Clauses did not view paid legislative chaplains and opening prayers as a violation of that Amendment, for the practice of opening sessions with prayer has continued without interruption ever since that early session of Congress. It has also been followed consistently in most of the states, including Nebraska, where the institution of opening legislative sessions with prayer was adopted even before the State attained statehood.

Standing alone, historical patterns cannot justify contemporary violations of constitutional guarantees, but there is far more here than simply historical patterns. In this context, historical evidence sheds light not only on what the draftsmen intended the Establishment Clause to mean, but also on how they thought that Clause applied to the practice authorized by the First Congress—their actions reveal their intent.

It can hardly be thought that in the same week Members of the First Congress voted to appoint and to pay a chaplain for each House and also voted to approve the draft of the First Amendment for submission to the states, they intended the Establishment Clause of the Amendment to forbid what they had just declared acceptable. [I]t would be incongruous to interpret that Clause as imposing more stringent First Amendment limits on the states than the draftsmen imposed on the Federal Government.

This unique history leads us to accept the interpretation of the First Amendment draftsmen who saw no real threat to the Establishment Clause arising from a practice of prayer similar to that now challenged.... In light of the unambiguous and unbroken history of more than 200 years, there can be no doubt that the practice of opening legislative sessions with prayer has become part of the fabric of our society. To invoke Divine guidance on a public body entrusted with making the laws is not, in these circumstances, an "establishment" of religion or a step toward establishment; it is simply a tolerable acknowledgment of beliefs widely held among the people of this country. As Justice Douglas observed, "[w]e are a religious people whose institutions presuppose a Supreme Being." *Zorach.*

III

We turn then to the question of whether any features of the Nebraska practice violate the Establishment Clause. Beyond the bare fact that a prayer is offered, three points have been made: first, that a clergyman of only one denomination—Presbyterian—has been selected for 16 years; second, that the chaplain is paid at public expense; and third that the prayers are in the Judeo-Christian tradition.[14] Weighed against the historical background, these factors do not serve to invalidate Nebraska's practice.

---

14. Palmer characterizes his prayers as "nonsectarian," "Judeo-Christian," and "with elements of the American civil religion." App. 75 and 87 (deposition of Robert E. Palmer). Although some of his

The unbroken practice for two centuries in the National Congress and for more than a century in Nebraska and in many other states gives abundant assurance that there is no real threat "while this Court sits," *Panhandle Oil Co. v. Mississippi ex rel. Knox*, 277 U.S. 218, 223 (1928) (Holmes, J., dissenting).

The judgment of the Court of Appeals is *Reversed.*

Justice BRENNAN, with whom Justice MARSHALL joins, dissenting.

I now believe that the practice of official invocational prayer, as it exists in Nebraska and most other state legislatures, is unconstitutional. It is contrary to the doctrine as well the underlying purposes of the Establishment Clause, and it is not saved either by its history or by any of the other considerations suggested in the Court's opinion. I respectfully dissent.

I

The Court makes no pretense of subjecting Nebraska's practice of legislative prayer to any of the formal "tests" that have traditionally structured our inquiry under the Establishment Clause. That it fails to do so is, in a sense, a good thing, for it simply confirms that the Court is carving out an exception to the Establishment Clause rather than reshaping Establishment Clause doctrine to accommodate legislative prayer. For my purposes, however, I must begin by demonstrating what should be obvious: that, if the Court were to judge legislative prayer through the unsentimental eye of our settled doctrine, it would have to strike it down as a clear violation of the Establishment Clause.

That the "purpose" of legislative prayer is pre-eminently religious rather than secular seems to me to be self-evident. "To invoke Divine guidance on a public body entrusted with making the laws," is nothing but a religious act. The "primary effect" of legislative prayer is also clearly religious. As we said in the context of officially sponsored prayers in the public schools, "prescribing a particular form of religious worship," even if the individuals involved have the choice not to participate, places "indirect coercive pressure upon religious minorities to conform to the prevailing officially approved religion...." *Engel.* More importantly, invocations in Nebraska's legislative halls explicitly link religious belief and observance to the power and prestige of the State.

Finally, there can be no doubt that the practice of legislative prayer leads to excessive "entanglement" between the State and religion. In the case of legislative prayer, the process of choosing a "suitable" chaplain, whether on a permanent or rotating basis, and insuring that the chaplain limits himself or herself to "suitable" prayers, involves precisely the sort of supervision that agencies of government should if at all possible avoid. Second, excessive "entanglement" might arise out of "the divisive political potential" of a state statute or program. The controversy between Senator Chambers and his colleagues, which had reached the stage of difficulty and rancor long before this lawsuit was brought, has split the Nebraska Legislature precisely on issues of religion and religious conformity.

Justice STEVENS, dissenting.

In a democratically elected legislature, the religious beliefs of the chaplain tend to reflect the faith of the majority of the lawmakers' constituents.... I would not expect to find a Jehovah's Witness or a disciple of Mary Baker Eddy or the Reverend Moon serv-

---

earlier prayers were often explicitly Christian, Palmer removed all references to Christ after a 1980 complaint from a Jewish legislator. Id., at 49.

ing as the official chaplain in any state legislature. Regardless of the motivation of the majority that exercises the power to appoint the chaplain, it seems plain to me that the designation of a member of one religious faith to serve as the sole official chaplain of a state legislature for a period of 16 years constitutes the preference of one faith over another in violation of the Establishment Clause of the First Amendment.

Notes

1. Chief Justice Burger, the architect of the *Lemon* test, purposefully avoids employing it in *Marsh*. Justice Brennan's dissent avoids history and analyzes the case exclusively "through the unsentimental eye of our settled doctrine" (*i.e.*, the *Lemon* test). Who offers the better argument, and why?

2. Controversies over the appointment of legislative chaplains are not confined to state legislatures. In 1999, a controversy erupted over the appointment of a new chaplain for in the United States House of Representatives. *See* Amy Keller, "Rev. Ford to Leave House Chaplaincy," *Roll Call*, Thursday, May 27, 1999, 1999 WL 14665474; Ben Macintyre, "Congress Post Divides Churches," *The Times of London*, Friday, December 3, 1999, p. 23, 1999 WL 29523560; Reps. Earl Pomeroy & Tom Bliley, Letter to Members of the House of Representatives & attached "Final Report, Chaplain Search Committee, January 2000" (January 14, 2000).

3. Would the Court have the authority to order either the House or the Senate to eliminate the post of chaplain? *See* Art. I, §5 cl. 2; *Powell v. McCormack*, 395 U.S. 486 (1969). In *Engel v. Vitale*, 370 U.S. 421 (1962), the school prayer case, Justice Brennan joined Justice William O. Douglas in a concurring opinion stating that the employment of chaplains by the Congress was constitutional. *Id.* at 437 n.1 (Douglas, J., concurring). By the time *Marsh* was decided in 1983, Justice Brennan had changed his mind. Does the rationale of his dissent in *Marsh* apply to the *practice* of opening the House and Senate with a prayer led by an unpaid "guest" chaplain who is invited to do so by his or her representative or senator? Can such a practice be considered a "law respecting an establishment of religion"? What about a proclamation issued by the President urging prayers for the Nation?

4. In *Katcoff v. Marsh*, 755 F.2d 223 (2d Cir. 1985), excerpted in Chapter Ten, the Second Circuit held the Army's military chaplaincy system constitutional. Two chaplains who worked on the litigation have written a book on the history of the controversy. *See* Israel Drazin & Cecil B. Currey, For God and Country: The History of a Constitutional Challenge to the Army Chaplaincy (1985).

A Note on Prayer in Schools

In *Engel v. Vitale*, 370 U.S. 421 (1962), and *Abington Sch. Dist. v. Schempp*, 374 U.S. 203 (1963), excerpted in Chapter Six §D(4), the Court held that government-sponsored prayer in public schools is unconstitutional. In both cases, the Court relied heavily on Jefferson's "wall of separation" metaphor to hold that the Establishment Clause forbids state sponsorship of religious ceremonies. The Court specifically rejected the argument that a violation of the Establishment Clause requires coercion. In the Court's view, a state-mandated opening exercise including prayers and Bible readings were "a religious ceremony and was intended by the State to be so," and that finding alone was sufficient to hold that "the exercises and the law requiring them are in violation of the Establishment Clause." *Schempp*.

In *Lee v. Weisman*, 505 U.S. 577 (1992), also discussed in Chapter Six §D(4), the Court held that an invocation given by a rabbi at a junior high school graduation violated the Establishment Clause. In its view, the decision of the school principal to request an invocation was, "from a constitutional perspective...as if a state statute decreed that the prayers must occur." *Id.* at 587. Although the students were neither coerced to pray nor to participate in the prayer, the Court believed that "given our social conventions, a reasonable dissenter in this milieu could believe that the group exercise signified her own participation or approval of it." *Id.* at 593.

The Court reaffirmed and extended *Lee v. Weisman* in *Santa Fe Indep. Sch. Dist. v. Doe*, 530 U.S. 290 (2000). Writing for a six-member majority, Justice Stevens held that a Santa Fe, Texas School Board policy permitting student-led, student-initiated prayer at football games was a facial violation of the Establishment Clause. The policy adopted by the School Board permitted the students to vote by secret ballot on whether to include an invocation at football games, and to select, also by secret ballot, the individual who would give the invocation.

The Court rejected the assertion that the Board had created a limited public forum for private, student speech. In its view, the Board made the microphone available to only one student, who would use it to convey a religious message approved by both the Board and the majority of the student body. Expanding on its rationale in *Lee*, the majority rejected the Board's argument that an invocation was a proper way to solemnize a public gathering. In its view, permitting an invocation under these circumstances "invites and encourages religious messages," and rendered the asserted secular purpose "a sham." *Id.* at 308. It also held that the football game setting was, by its very nature, a coercive one that conveyed a clear message of state endorsement of prayer. Students unwilling to pray, the Court held, could not be forced to make a "choice between whether to attend these games or to risk facing a personally offensive religious ritual." *Id.* at 312. Chief Justice Rehnquist, joined by Justices Scalia and Thomas, dissented. In their view, the Court's opinion ignored the teachings of history, "bristles with hostility to all things religious in public life," *Id.* at 318, and imposes "a new requirement" under the Establishment Clause: that government policies regarding the selection of speakers and topics "be completely neutral as to content or be considered one that endorses religion."

Official school prayers are discussed in detail in Chapter Six § D(4). The rights of public school students and others to use school facilities for privately initiated, voluntary prayer are discussed in Section G, below.

b) Official Displays

Lynch v. Donnelly, 465 U.S. 668 (1984)—The Court held that the display of a city-owned crèche on a private park in the City of Pawtucket, Rhode Island during the annual during Christmas holiday display did not violate the Establishment Clause. Writing for the Court, Chief Justice Burger noted that the crèche was displayed alongside a "Santa Clause house, reindeer pulling Santa's sleigh, candy-striped poles, a Christmas tree, carolers, cut-out figures representing such characters as a clown, an elephant, and a teddy bear, hundreds of colored lights, a large banner that reads 'SEASON'S GREETING,'...." His opinion relied heavily on the historical recognition of "the role of religion in American life from at least 1789." He cited presidential proclamations, the hiring of Chaplains by Congress, the releasing from work on Christmas and Thanksgiving of federal employees, the statutorily mandated motto "In God We Trust" on our coins and the addition of the phrase "one nation under God" to the Pledge of Allegiance in 1954. In Burger's view, the crèche satisfied the secular purpose of celebrating the holiday and depicting its origins. The city's purpose in including the crèche was not "some kind of subtle advocacy of a particular religious message."

Justice O'Connor concurred, suggesting for the first time that the Court's Establishment Clause jurisprudence would be clarified if the Court examined the state's policy from the perspective of an objective observer, and determined whether its intent was to "endorse" religion. Looking at the display in light of an endorsement analysis, she concluded that Pawtucket had not "endorsed" a view favoring religion, or particular religious beliefs, over non-religion, and thus the display was constitutional. Justice Brennan dissented, joined by Justices Marshall, Blackmun and Stevens. Justice Blackmun also wrote a separate dissent in which he concluded that Pawtucket's victory "is a Pyrrhic one," and that the City's use of the crèche in such a setting was "a misuse of a sacred symbol."

An interesting critique of the opinions that examines the religious and theological premises and bases for much of the language of the opinions in *Lynch* is Winnifred Fallers Sullivan, PAYING THE WORDS EXTRA: RELIGIOUS DISCOURSE IN THE SUPREME COURT OF THE UNITED STATES (1994). For a history of the case, see Wayne R. Swanson, THE CHRIST CHILD GOES TO COURT (1990).

County of Allegheny v. American Civil Liberties Union

492 U.S. 573 (1989)

Justice BLACKMUN announced the judgment of the Court and delivered the opinion of the Court with respect to Parts III-A, IV, and V, an opinion with respect to Parts I and II, in which Justice O'CONNOR and Justice STEVENS join, an opinion with respect to Part III-B, in which Justice STEVENS joins, and an opinion with respect to Part VI.

This litigation concerns the constitutionality of two recurring holiday displays located on public property in downtown Pittsburgh. The first is a crèche placed on the Grand Staircase of the Allegheny County Courthouse. The second is a Chanukah menorah placed just outside the City-County Building, next to a Christmas tree and a sign saluting liberty. The Court of Appeals for the Third Circuit ruled that each display violates the Establishment Clause of the First Amendment because each has the impermissible effect of endorsing religion. We agree that the crèche display has that unconstitutional effect but reverse the Court of Appeals' judgment regarding the menorah display.

I

A

The county courthouse is owned by Allegheny County and is its seat of government. Since 1981, the county has permitted the Holy Name Society, a Roman Catholic group, to display a crèche in the county courthouse during the Christmas holiday season. Christmas, we note perhaps needlessly, is the holiday when Christians celebrate the birth of Jesus of Nazareth, whom they believe to be the Messiah. Western churches have celebrated Christmas Day on December 25 since the fourth century. As observed in this Nation, Christmas has a secular as well as a religious dimension.

The crèche in the County Courthouse, like other crèches, is a visual representation of the scene in the manger in Bethlehem shortly after the birth of Jesus, as described in the Gospels of Luke and Matthew. The crèche includes figures of the infant Jesus, Mary, Joseph, farm animals, shepherds, and wise men, all placed in or before a wooden representation of a manger, which has at its crest an angel bearing a banner that proclaims "Gloria in Excelsis Deo!"

During the 1986–87 holiday season, the crèche was on display on the Grand Staircase from November 26 to January 9. Altogether, the crèche, the fence, the poinsettias, and the trees occupied a substantial amount of space on the Grand Staircase. No figures of Santa Claus or other decorations appeared on the Grand Staircase. Cf. *Lynch.*

The county uses the crèche as the setting for its annual Christmas-carol program. During the 1986 season, the county invited high school choirs and other musical groups to perform during weekday lunch hours from December 3 through December 23.

B

The City-County Building is separate and a block removed from the County Courthouse and, as the name implies, is jointly owned by the city of Pittsburgh and Allegheny County.

For a number of years, the city has had a large Christmas tree under the middle arch outside the Grant Street entrance. Following this practice, city employees on November 17, 1986, erected a 45-foot tree under the middle arch and decorated it with lights and ornaments. A few days later, the city placed at the foot of the tree a sign bearing the Mayor's name and entitled "Salute to Liberty."

At least since 1982, the city has expanded its Grant Street holiday display to include a symbolic representation of Chanukah, an 8-day Jewish holiday that begins on the 25th day of the Jewish lunar month of Kislev. The 25th of Kislev usually occurs in December, and thus Chanukah is the annual Jewish holiday that falls closest to Christmas Day each year. In 1986, Chanukah began at sundown on December 26.

According to Jewish tradition, on the 25th of Kislev in 164 B.C.E. (before the common era), the Maccabees rededicated the Temple of Jerusalem after recapturing it from the Greeks, or, more accurately, from the Greek-influenced Seleucid Empire, in the course of a political rebellion. Chanukah is the holiday which celebrates that event. The early history of the celebration of Chanukah is unclear; it appears that the holiday's central ritual—the lighting of lamps—was well established long before a single explanation of that ritual took hold.

The Talmud[13] explains the lamp-lighting ritual as a commemoration of an event that occurred during the rededication of the Temple. The Temple housed a seven-branch menorah, which was to be kept burning continuously. When the Maccabees rededicated the Temple, they had only enough oil to last for one day. But, according to the Talmud, the oil miraculously lasted for eight days (the length of time it took to obtain additional oil). To celebrate and publicly proclaim this miracle, the Talmud prescribes that it is a mitzvah (i.e., a religious deed or commandment) for Jews to place a lamp with eight lights just outside the entrance to their homes during the eight days of Chanukah. Where practicality or safety from persecution so requires, the lamp may be placed in a window or inside the home. The Talmud also ordains certain blessings to be recited each night of Chanukah before lighting the lamp.

Although Jewish law does not contain any rule regarding the shape or substance of a Chanukah lamp (or "hanukkiyah"), it became customary to evoke the memory of the

---

13. The Talmud (specifically the Babylonian Talmud) is a collection of rabbinic commentary on Jewish law that was compiled by the sixth century. See 14 Encyclopedia of Religion, "Talmud," at 256–259.

Temple menorah. The Temple menorah was of a tree-and-branch design; it had a central candlestick with six branches. In contrast, a Chanukah menorah of tree-and-branch design has eight branches—one for each day of the holiday—plus a ninth to hold the shamash (an extra candle used to light the other eight). Also in contrast to the Temple menorah, the Chanukah menorah is not a sanctified object; it need not be treated with special care.

Chanukah, like Christmas, is a cultural event as well as a religious holiday. Indeed, the Chanukah story always has had a political or national as well as a religious dimension: it tells of national heroism in addition to divine intervention. Also, Chanukah, like Christmas, is a winter holiday; according to some historians, it was associated in ancient times with the winter solstice. Just as some Americans celebrate Christmas without regard to its religious significance, some nonreligious American Jews celebrate Chanukah as an expression of ethnic identity, and "as a cultural or national event, rather than as a specifically religious event."

The cultural significance of Chanukah varies with the setting in which the holiday is celebrated. In contemporary Israel, the nationalist and military aspects of the Chanukah story receive special emphasis. In this country, the tradition of giving Chanukah gelt has taken on greater importance because of the temporal proximity of Chanukah to Christmas. Indeed, some have suggested that the proximity of Christmas accounts for the social prominence of Chanukah in this country. Whatever the reason, Chanukah is observed by American Jews to an extent greater than its religious importance would indicate: in the hierarchy of Jewish holidays, Chanukah ranks fairly low in religious significance. This socially heightened status of Chanukah reflects its cultural or secular dimension.

On December 22 of the 1986 holiday season, the city placed at the Grant Street entrance to the City-County Building an 18-foot Chanukah menorah of an abstract tree-and-branch design. The menorah was placed next to the city's 45-foot Christmas tree, against one of the columns that supports the arch into which the tree was set. The menorah is owned by Chabad, a Jewish group, but is stored, erected, and removed each year by the city.

II

Distinguishing *Lynch v. Donnelly*, the [Court of Appeals] panel majority determined that the crèche and the menorah must be understood as endorsing Christianity and Judaism. The court observed: "Each display was located at or in a public building devoted to core functions of government." Because the impermissible effect of endorsing religion was a sufficient basis for holding each display to be in violation of the Establishment Clause under *Lemon*, the Court of Appeals did not consider whether either one had an impermissible purpose or resulted in an unconstitutional entanglement between government and religion.

III

A

This Nation is heir to a history and tradition of religious diversity that dates from the settlement of the North American continent. Sectarian differences among various Christian denominations were central to the origins of our Republic. Since then, adherents of religions too numerous to name have made the United States their home, as have those whose beliefs expressly exclude religion.

Precisely because of the religious diversity that is our national heritage, the Founders added to the Constitution a Bill of Rights, the very first words of which declare: "Congress shall make no law respecting an establishment of religion, or prohibiting the free exercise thereof...." Perhaps in the early days of the Republic these words were understood to protect only the diversity within Christianity, but today they are recognized as guaranteeing religious liberty and equality to "the infidel, the atheist, or the adherent of a non-Christian faith such as Islam or Judaism." *Wallace v. Jaffree*, 472 U.S., at 52.

In the course of adjudicating specific cases, this Court has come to understand the Establishment Clause to mean that government may not promote or affiliate itself with any religious doctrine or organization, may not discriminate among persons on the basis of their religious beliefs and practices, may not delegate a governmental power to a religious institution, and may not involve itself too deeply in such an institution's affairs.

In *Lemon*, the Court sought to refine these principles by focusing on three "tests" for determining whether a government practice violates the Establishment Clause. Our subsequent decisions further have refined the definition of governmental action that unconstitutionally advances religion. In recent years, we have paid particularly close attention to whether the challenged governmental practice either has the purpose or effect of "endorsing" religion, a concern that has long had a place in our Establishment Clause jurisprudence.

Of course, the word "endorsement" is not self-defining. Rather, it derives its meaning from other words that this Court has found useful over the years in interpreting the Establishment Clause. Whether the key word is "endorsement," "favoritism," or "promotion," the essential principle remains the same. The Establishment Clause, at the very least, prohibits government from appearing to take a position on questions of religious belief or from "making adherence to a religion relevant in any way to a person's standing in the political community." *Lynch* (O'Connor, J., concurring).

B

The rationale of the majority opinion in *Lynch* is none too clear: the opinion contains two strands, neither of which provides guidance for decision in subsequent cases. First, the opinion states that the inclusion of the crèche in the display was "no more an advancement or endorsement of religion" than other "endorsements" this Court has approved in the past, but the opinion offers no discernible measure for distinguishing between permissible and impermissible endorsements. Second, the opinion observes that any benefit the government's display of the crèche gave to religion was no more than "indirect, remote, and incidental,"—without saying how or why.

Although Justice O'Connor joined the majority opinion in *Lynch*, she wrote a concurrence that differs in significant respects from the majority opinion. The main difference is that the concurrence provides a sound analytical framework for evaluating governmental use of religious symbols.

First and foremost, the concurrence squarely rejects any notion that this Court will tolerate some government endorsement of religion. Second, the concurrence articulates a method for determining whether the government's use of an object with religious meaning has the effect of endorsing religion. The effect of the display depends upon the message that the government's practice communicates: the question is "what viewers may fairly understand to be the purpose of the display." That inquiry, of necessity, turns upon the context in which the contested object appears: "a typical museum setting, though not neutralizing the religious content of a religious painting, negates any message of endorsement of that content." *Id.*

[D]espite divergence at the bottom line, the five Justices in concurrence and dissent in *Lynch* agreed upon the relevant constitutional principles: the government's use of religious symbolism is unconstitutional if it has the effect of endorsing religious beliefs, and the effect of the government's use of religious symbolism depends upon its context. These general principles are sound, and have been adopted by the Court in subsequent cases. Accordingly, our present task is to determine whether the display of the crèche and the menorah, in their respective "particular physical settings," has the effect of endorsing or disapproving religious beliefs.

IV

We turn first to the county's crèche display. There is no doubt, of course, that the crèche itself is capable of communicating a religious message. Indeed, the crèche in this lawsuit uses words, as well as the picture of the nativity scene, to make its religious meaning unmistakably clear. "Glory to God in the Highest!" says the angel in the crèche—Glory to God because of the birth of Jesus. This praise to God in Christian terms is indisputably religious—indeed sectarian—just as it is when said in the Gospel or in a church service.

Under the Court's holding in *Lynch*, the effect of a crèche display turns on its setting. Here, unlike in *Lynch*, nothing in the context of the display detracts from the crèche 's religious message. The *Lynch* display comprised a series of figures and objects, each group of which had its own focal point. Santa's house and his reindeer were objects of attention separate from the crèche, and had their specific visual story to tell. Similarly, whatever a "talking" wishing well may be, it obviously was a center of attention separate from the crèche. Here, in contrast, the crèche stands alone: it is the single element of the display on the Grand Staircase.

The floral decoration surrounding the crèche cannot be viewed as somehow equivalent to the secular symbols in the overall *Lynch* display. The floral decoration surrounding the crèche contributes to, rather than detracts from, the endorsement of religion conveyed by the crèche. Its contention that the traditional Christmas greens negate the endorsement effect of the crèche fares no better. Nor does the fact that crèche was the setting for the country's annual Christmas carol-program diminish its religious meaning.

Furthermore, the crèche sits on the Grand Staircase, the "main" and the "most beautiful part" of the building that is the seat of county government. No viewer could reasonably think that it occupies this location without the support and approval of the government. Thus, the county sends an unmistakable message that it supports and promotes the Christian praise to God that is the crèche 's religious message.

The fact that the crèche bears a sign disclosing its ownership by a Roman Catholic organization does not alter this conclusion. On the contrary, the sign simply demonstrates that the government is endorsing the religious message of that organization, rather than communicating a message of its own. But the Establishment Clause does not limit only the religious content of the government's own communications. It also prohibits the government's support and promotion of religious communications by religious organizations. Indeed, the very concept of "endorsement" conveys the sense of promoting someone else's message. Thus, by prohibiting government endorsement of religion, the Establishment Clause prohibits precisely what occurred here: the government's lending its support to the communication of a religious organization's religious message.

Finally, the county argues that it is sufficient to validate the display of the crèche on the Grand Staircase that the display celebrates Christmas, and Christmas is a national holiday. This argument obviously proves too much. It would allow the celebration of the Eucharist inside a courthouse on Christmas Eve. The government may acknowledge Christmas as a cultural phenomenon, but under the First Amendment it may not observe it as a Christian holy day by suggesting that people praise God for the birth of Jesus.

In sum, *Lynch* teaches that government may celebrate Christmas in some manner and form, but not in a way that endorses Christian doctrine. Here, Allegheny County has transgressed this line. It has chosen to celebrate Christmas in a way that has the effect of endorsing a patently Christian message: Glory to God for the birth of Jesus Christ. Under *Lynch*, and the rest of our cases, nothing more is required to demonstrate a violation of the Establishment Clause. The display of the crèche in this context, therefore, must be permanently enjoined.

V

Justice Kennedy and the three Justices who join him would find the display of the crèche consistent with the Establishment Clause. Justice Kennedy's reasons for permitting the crèche on the Grand Staircase and his condemnation of the Court's reasons for deciding otherwise are so far-reaching in their implications that they require a response in some depth.

A

In *Marsh*, the Court relied specifically on the fact that Congress authorized legislative prayer at the same time that it produced the Bill of Rights. Justice Kennedy, however, argues that *Marsh* legitimates all "practices with no greater potential for an establishment of religion" than those "accepted traditions dating back to the Founding." Otherwise, the Justice asserts, such practices as our national motto ("In God We Trust") and our Pledge of Allegiance (with the phrase "under God," added in 1954, Pub.L. 396, 68 Stat. 249) are in danger of invalidity.

Our previous opinions have considered in dicta the motto and the pledge, characterizing them as consistent with the proposition that government may not communicate an endorsement of religious belief. We need not return to the subject of "ceremonial deism," because there is an obvious distinction between crèche displays and references to God in the motto and the pledge. However history may affect the constitutionality of nonsectarian references to religion by the government,[52] history cannot legitimate practices that demonstrate the government's allegiance to a particular sect or creed.

Justice Kennedy's reading of *Marsh* would gut the core of the Establishment Clause, as this Court understands it. The history of this Nation, it is perhaps sad to say, contains numerous examples of official acts that endorsed Christianity specifically. Some of these examples date back to the Founding of the Republic, but this heritage of official discrimination against non-Christians has no place in the jurisprudence of the Establishment Clause. Whatever else the Establishment Clause may mean (and we have held it to mean no official preference even for religion over nonreligion), it certainly means

52. It is worth noting that just because Marsh sustained the validity of legislative prayer, it does not necessarily follow that practices like proclaiming a National Day of Prayer are constitutional. Legislative prayer does not urge citizens to engage in religious practices, and on that basis could well be distinguishable from an exhortation from government to the people that they engage in religious conduct. But, as this practice is not before us, we express no judgment about its constitutionality.

at the very least that government may not demonstrate a preference for one particular sect or creed (including a preference for Christianity over other religions). There have been breaches of this command throughout this Nation's history, but they cannot diminish in any way the force of the command.

B

[For] Justice Kennedy, would it be enough of a preference for Christianity if that city each year displayed a crèche for 40 days during the Christmas season and cross for 40 days during Lent (and never the symbols of other religions)? If so, then what if there were no cross but the 40-day crèche display contained a sign exhorting the city's citizens "to offer up their devotions to God their Creator, and his Son Jesus Christ, the Redeemer of the world"?

The point of these rhetorical questions is obvious. In order to define precisely what government could and could not do under Justice Kennedy's "proselytization" test, the Court would have to decide a series of cases with particular fact patterns that fall along the spectrum of government references to religion (from the permanent display of a cross atop city hall to a passing reference to divine Providence in an official address).

Indeed, perhaps the only real distinction between Justice Kennedy's "proselytization" test and the Court's "endorsement" inquiry is a burden of "unmistakable" clarity that Justice Kennedy apparently would require of government favoritism for specific sects in order to hold the favoritism in violation of the Establishment Clause.

Our cases, however, impose no such burden on demonstrating that the government has favored a particular sect or creed. Thus, when all is said and done, Justice Kennedy's effort to abandon the "endorsement" inquiry in favor of his "proselytization" test seems nothing more than an attempt to lower considerably the level of scrutiny in Establishment Clause cases. We choose, however, to adhere to the vigilance the Court has managed to maintain thus far, and to the endorsement inquiry that reflects our vigilance.

C

Although Justice Kennedy repeatedly accuses the Court of harboring a "latent hostility" or "callous indifference" toward religion, nothing could be further from the truth, and the accusations could be said to be as offensive as they are absurd. Justice Kennedy apparently has misperceived a respect for religious pluralism, a respect commanded by the Constitution, as hostility or indifference to religion. No misperception could be more antithetical to the values embodied in the Establishment Clause.

Justice Kennedy's accusations are shot from a weapon triggered by the following proposition: if government may celebrate the secular aspects of Christmas, then it must be allowed to celebrate the religious aspects as well because, otherwise, the government would be discriminating against citizens who celebrate Christmas as a religious, and not just a secular, holiday. This proposition, however, is flawed at its foundation. The government does not discriminate against any citizen on the basis of the citizen's religious faith if the government is secular in its functions and operations. On the contrary, the Constitution mandates that the government remain secular, rather than affiliating itself with religious beliefs or institutions, precisely in order to avoid discriminating among citizens on the basis of their religious faiths.

A secular state, it must be remembered, is not the same as an atheistic or antireligious state. A secular state establishes neither atheism nor religion as its official creed. Justice Kennedy thus has it exactly backwards when he says that enforcing the Constitution's requirement that government remain secular is a prescription of orthodoxy. It follows directly from the Constitution's proscription against government affiliation with religious beliefs or institutions that there is no orthodoxy on religious matters in the secular state. Although Justice Kennedy accuses the Court of "an Orwellian rewriting of history," perhaps it is Justice Kennedy himself who has slipped into a form of Orwellian newspeak when he equates the constitutional command of secular government with a prescribed orthodoxy.

To be sure, in a pluralistic society there may be some would-be theocrats, who wish that their religion were an established creed, and some of them perhaps may be even audacious enough to claim that the lack of established religion discriminates against their preferences. But this claim gets no relief, for it contradicts the fundamental premise of the Establishment Clause itself. The antidiscrimination principle inherent in the Establishment Clause necessarily means that would-be discriminators on the basis of religion cannot prevail.

For this reason, the claim that prohibiting government from celebrating Christmas as a religious holiday discriminates against Christians in favor of nonadherents must fail. Celebrating Christmas as a religious, as opposed to a secular, holiday, necessarily entails professing, proclaiming, or believing that Jesus of Nazareth, born in a manger in Bethlehem, is the Christ, the Messiah. If the government celebrates Christmas as a religious holiday (for example, by issuing an official proclamation saying: "We rejoice in the glory of Christ's birth!"), it means that the government really is declaring Jesus to be the Messiah, a specifically Christian belief. In contrast, confining the government's own celebration of Christmas to the holiday's secular aspects does *not* favor the religious beliefs of non-Christians over those of Christians. Rather, it simply permits the government to acknowledge the holiday without expressing an allegiance to Christian beliefs, an allegiance that would truly favor Christians over non-Christians.

Of course, not all religious celebrations of Christmas located on government property violate the Establishment Clause. It obviously is not unconstitutional, for example, for a group of parishioners from a local church to go caroling through a city park on any Sunday in Advent or for a Christian club at a public university to sing carols during their Christmas meeting. The reason is that activities of this nature do not demonstrate the government's allegiance to, or endorsement of, Christian faith.

Equally obvious, however, is the proposition that not all proclamations of Christian faith located on government property are permitted by the Establishment Clause just because they occur during the Christmas holiday season, as the example of a Mass in the courthouse surely illustrates. And once the judgment has been made that a particular proclamation of Christian belief, when disseminated from a particular location on government property, has the effect of demonstrating the government's endorsement of Christian faith, then it necessarily follows that the practice must be enjoined to protect the constitutional rights of those citizens who follow some creed other than Christianity.

VI

The display of the Chanukah menorah in front of the City-County building may well present a closer constitutional question. The menorah, one must recognize, is a religious symbol: it serves to commemorate the miracle of the oil as described in the Talmud. But the menorah's message is not exclusively religious. The menorah is the primary visual symbol for a holiday that, like Christmas, has both religious and secular dimensions.

Moreover, the menorah here stands next to a Christmas tree and a sign saluting liberty. While no challenge has been made here to display of the tree and the sign, their presence is obviously relevant in determining the effect of the menorah's display. The necessary result of placing a menorah next to a Christmas tree is to create an "overall holiday setting" that represents both Christmas and Chanukah—two holidays, not one.

The mere fact that Pittsburgh displays symbols of both Christmas and Chanukah does not end the constitutional inquiry. If the city celebrates both Christmas and Chanukah as religious holidays, then it violates the Establishment Clause. The simultaneous endorsement of Judaism and Christianity is no less constitutionally infirm than the endorsement of Christianity alone.

Conversely, if the city celebrates both Christmas and Chanukah as secular holidays, then its conduct is beyond the reach of the Establishment Clause. Because government may celebrate Christmas as a secular holiday, it follows that government may also acknowledge Chanukah as a secular holiday.

Accordingly, the relevant question for Establishment Clause purposes is whether the combined display of the tree, the sign, and the menorah has the effect of endorsing both Christian and Jewish faiths, or rather simply recognizes that both Christmas and Chanukah are part of the same winter-holiday season, which has attained a secular status in our society. Of the two interpretations of this particular display, the latter seems far more plausible and is also in line with *Lynch.*

The Christmas tree, unlike the menorah, is not itself a religious symbol. Although Christmas trees once carried religious connotations, today they typify the secular celebration of Christmas. Indeed, a 40-foot Christmas tree was one of the objects that validated the crèche in *Lynch.*

The tree, moreover, is clearly the predominant element in the city's display. The 45-foot tree occupies the central position beneath the middle archway in front of the Grant Street entrance to the City-County Building; the 18-foot menorah is positioned to one side. Given this configuration, it is much more sensible to interpret the meaning of the menorah in light of the tree, rather than *vice versa.* In the shadow of the tree, the menorah is readily understood as simply a recognition that Christmas is not the only traditional way of observing the winter-holiday season. In these circumstances, then, the combination of the tree and the menorah communicates, not a simultaneous endorsement of both Christian and Jewish faith, but instead, a secular celebration of Christmas coupled with an acknowledgement of Chanukah as a contemporaneous alternative tradition.

Although the city has used a symbol with religious meaning as its representation of Chanukah, this is not a case in which the city has reasonable alternatives that are less religious in nature. It is difficult to imagine a predominantly secular symbol of Chanukah that the city could place next to its Christmas tree. An 18-foot dreidel would look out of place, and might be interpreted by some as mocking the celebration of Chanukah. The absence of a more secular alternative symbol is itself part of the context in which the city's actions must be judged in determining the likely effect of its use of the menorah. Where the government's secular message can be conveyed by two symbols, only one of which carries religious meaning, an observer reasonably might infer from the fact that the government has chosen to use the religious symbol that the government means to promote religious faith. But where, as here, no such choice has been made, this inference of endorsement is not present.

The Mayor's sign further diminishes the possibility that the tree and the menorah will be interpreted as a dual endorsement of Christianity and Judaism. The sign states that during the holiday season the city salutes liberty. Moreover, the sign draws upon the theme of light, common to both Chanukah and Christmas as winter festivals, and links that theme with this Nation's legacy of freedom, which allows an American to celebrate the holiday season in whatever way he wishes, religiously or otherwise. While no sign can disclaim an overwhelming message of endorsement, an "explanatory plaque" may confirm that in particular contexts the government's association with a religious symbol does not represent the government's sponsorship of religious beliefs.

Given all these considerations, it is not "sufficiently likely" that residents of Pittsburgh will perceive the combined display of the tree, the sign, and the menorah as an "endorsement" or "disapproval of their individual religious choices." The Christmas tree alone in the Pittsburgh location does not endorse Christian belief; and, on the facts before us, the addition of the menorah "cannot fairly be understood to" result in the simultaneous endorsement of Christian and Jewish faiths. On the contrary, for purposes of the Establishment Clause, the city's overall display must be understood as conveying the city's secular recognition of different traditions for celebrating the winter-holiday season.

The conclusion here that, in this particular context, the menorah's display does not have an effect of endorsing religious faith does not foreclose the possibility that the display of the menorah might violate either the "purpose" or "entanglement" prong of the *Lemon* analysis. These issues were not addressed by the Court of Appeals and may be considered by that court on remand.

VII

The judgment of the Court of Appeals is affirmed in part and reversed in part, and the cases are remanded for further proceedings.

It is so ordered.

Justice O'CONNOR, with whom Justice BRENNAN and Justice STEVENS join as to Part II, concurring in part and concurring in the judgment.

I

The constitutionality of the two displays at issue in this case turns on how we interpret and apply the holding in *Lynch v. Donnelly*, in which we rejected an Establishment Clause challenge to the city of Pawtucket's inclusion of a crèche in its annual Christmas holiday display. The seasonal display reviewed in *Lynch* was located in a privately-owned park in the heart of the shopping district.

I joined the majority opinion in *Lynch* because, as I read that opinion, it was consistent with the analysis set forth in my separate concurrence, which stressed that "[e]very government practice must be judged in its *unique circumstances* to determine whether it constitutes an endorsement or disapproval of religion." (Emphasis added.) Moreover, I joined the Court's discussion in Part II of *Lynch* concerning government acknowledgments of religion in American life because, in my view, acknowledgments such as the legislative prayers upheld in *Marsh*, and the printing of "In God We Trust" on our coins serve the secular purposes of "solemnizing public occasions, expressing confidence in the future and encouraging the recognition of what is worthy of appreciation in society." Because they serve such secular purposes and because of their "history and ubiquity," such government acknowledgments of religion are not understood as conveying an endorsement of particular religious beliefs.

For the reasons stated in Part IV of the Court's opinion in this case, I agree that the crèche displayed on the Grand Staircase of the Allegheny County Courthouse conveys a message to nonadherents of Christianity that they are not full members of the political community, and a corresponding message to Christians that they are favored members of the political community. In contrast to the crèche in *Lynch*, which was displayed in a private park in the city's commercial district as part of a broader display of traditional secular symbols of the holiday season, this crèche stands alone in the County Courthouse. The display of religious symbols in public areas of core government buildings runs a special risk of "mak[ing] religion relevant, in reality or public perception, to status in the political community." *Lynch*.

II

An Establishment Clause standard that prohibits only "coercive" practices or overt efforts at government proselytization, but fails to take account of the numerous more subtle ways that government can show favoritism to particular beliefs or convey a message of disapproval to others, would not, in my view, adequately protect the religious liberty or respect the religious diversity of the members of our pluralistic political community. Thus, this Court has never relied on coercion alone as the touchstone of Establishment Clause analysis.

I continue to believe that the endorsement test asks the right question about governmental practices challenged on Establishment Clause grounds, including challenged practices involving the display of religious symbols. Moreover, commentators in the scholarly literature have found merit in the approach.

The question under endorsement analysis, in short, is whether a reasonable observer would view such longstanding practices as a disapproval of their particular religious choices, in light of the fact that they serve a secular purpose rather than a sectarian one and have largely lost their religious significance over time. Although the endorsement test requires careful and often difficult line-drawing and is highly context-specific, no alternative test has been suggested that captures the essential mandate of the Establishment Clause as well as the endorsement test does, and it warrants continued application and refinement.

Clearly, the government can *acknowledge* the role of religion in our society in numerous ways that do not amount to an endorsement. Moreover, the government can *accommodate* religion by lifting government-imposed burdens on religion. Indeed, the Free Exercise Clause may mandate that it do so in particular cases. Allegheny County has neither placed nor removed a governmental burden on the free exercise of religion but rather, for the reasons stated in Part IV of the Court's opinion, has conveyed a message of governmental endorsement of Christian beliefs. This the Establishment Clause does not permit.

III

For reasons which differ somewhat from those set forth in Part VI of Justice Blackmun's opinion, I also conclude that the city of Pittsburgh's combined holiday display of a Chanukah menorah, a Christmas tree, and a sign saluting liberty does not have the effect of conveying an endorsement of religion. I agree with Justice Blackmun, that the Christmas tree, whatever its origins, is not regarded today as a religious symbol. Although Christmas is a public holiday that has both religious and secular aspects, the Christmas tree is widely viewed as a secular symbol of the holiday, in contrast to the crèche which depicts the holiday's religious dimensions. A Christmas tree displayed in front of city hall, in my view, cannot fairly be understood as conveying government endorsement of Christianity. Although Justice Blackmun's opinion acknowledges that a Christmas tree alone conveys no endorsement of Christian beliefs, it formulates the question posed by Pittsburgh's combined display of the tree and the menorah as whether the display "has the effect of endorsing *both* Christian and Jewish faiths, or rather simply recognizes that both Christmas and Chanukah are part of the same winter-holiday season, which has attained a secular status in our society."

That formulation of the question disregards the fact that the Christmas tree is a predominantly secular symbol and, more significantly, obscures the religious nature of the menorah and the holiday of Chanukah. The opinion is correct to recognize that the religious holiday of Chanukah has historical and cultural as well as religious dimensions, and that there may be certain "secular aspects" to the holiday. But that is not to conclude, however, as Justice Blackmun seems to do, that Chanukah has become a "secular holiday" in our society. The Easter holiday celebrated by Christians may be accompanied by certain "secular aspects" such as Easter bunnies and Easter egg hunts; but it is nevertheless a religious holiday. Similarly, Chanukah is a religious holiday with strong historical components particularly important to the Jewish people. Moreover, the menorah is the central religious symbol and ritual object of that religious holiday. In my view, the relevant question for Establishment Clause purposes is whether the city of Pittsburgh's display of the menorah, the religious symbol of a religious holiday, next to a Christmas tree and a sign saluting liberty sends a message of government endorsement of Judaism or whether it sends a message of pluralism and freedom to choose one's own beliefs.

In characterizing the message conveyed by this display as either a "double endorsement" or a secular acknowledgment of the winter holiday season, the opinion states that "[i]t is distinctly implausible to view the combined display of the tree, the sign, and the menorah as endorsing Jewish faith alone." That statement, however, seems to suggest that it would be implausible for the city to endorse a faith adhered to by a minority of the citizenry. Regardless of the plausibility of a putative governmental purpose, the more important inquiry here is whether the governmental display of a minority faith's religious symbol could ever reasonably be understood to convey a message of endorsement of that faith. A menorah standing alone at city hall may well send such a message to nonadherents, just as in this case the crèche standing alone at the Allegheny County Courthouse sends a message of governmental endorsement of Christianity, whatever the county's purpose in authorizing the display may have been. Thus, the question here is whether Pittsburgh's holiday display conveys a message of endorsement of Judaism, when the menorah is the only religious symbol in the combined display and when the opinion acknowledges that the tree cannot reasonably be understood to convey an endorsement of Christianity. One need not characterize Chanukah as a "secular holiday" or strain to argue that the menorah has a "secular dimension," in order to conclude that the city of Pittsburgh's combined display does not convey a message of endorsement of Judaism or of religion in general.

In setting up its holiday display, which included the lighted tree and the menorah, the city of Pittsburgh stressed the theme of liberty and pluralism by accompanying the exhibit with a sign bearing the following message: "'During this holiday season, the City of Pittsburgh salutes liberty. Let these festive lights remind us that we are the keepers of the flame of liberty and our legacy of freedom.'" This sign indicates that the city intended to convey its own distinctive message of pluralism and freedom. By accompanying its display of a Christmas tree—a secular symbol of the Christmas holiday season—with a salute to liberty, and by adding a religious symbol from a Jewish holiday also celebrated at roughly the same time of year, I conclude that the city did not endorse Judaism or religion in general, but rather conveyed a message of pluralism and freedom of belief during the holiday season.

The message of pluralism conveyed by the city's combined holiday display is not a message that endorses religion over nonreligion. Here, by displaying a secular symbol of the Christmas holiday season rather than a religious one, the city acknowledged a public holiday celebrated by both religious and nonreligious citizens alike, and it did so without endorsing Christian beliefs. A reasonable observer would, in my view, appreciate that the combined display is an effort to acknowledge the cultural diversity of our country and to convey tolerance of different choices in matters of religious belief or nonbelief by recognizing that the winter holiday season is celebrated in diverse ways by our citizens.

In sum, I conclude that the city of Pittsburgh's combined holiday display had neither the purpose nor the effect of endorsing religion, but that Allegheny County's crèche display had such an effect. Accordingly, I join Parts I, II, III-A, IV, V, and VII of the Court's opinion and concur in the judgment.

Justice BRENNAN, with whom Justice MARSHALL and Justice STEVENS join, concurring in part and dissenting in part.

I had previously explained at some length my views on the relationship between the Establishment Clause and government-sponsored celebrations of the Christmas holiday. I continue to believe that the display of an object that "retains a specifically Christian [or other] religious meaning," is incompatible with the separation of church and state demanded by our Constitution. I therefore agree with the Court that Allegheny County's display of a crèche at the county courthouse signals an endorsement of the Christian faith in violation of the Establishment Clause, and join in Parts III-A, IV, and V of the Court's opinion. I cannot agree, however, that the city's display of a 45-foot Christmas tree and an 18-foot Chanukah menorah at the entrance to the building housing the Mayor's office shows no favoritism towards Christianity, Judaism, or both. Indeed, I should have thought that the answer as to the first display supplied the answer to the second.

[T]he decision as to the menorah rests on three premises: the Christmas tree is a secular symbol; Chanukah is a holiday with secular dimensions, symbolized by the menorah; and the government may promote pluralism by sponsoring or condoning displays having strong religious associations on its property. None of these is sound.

I

The first step toward Justice Blackmun's conclusion is the claim that, despite its religious origins, the Christmas tree is a secular symbol. [W]hile acknowledging the religious origins of the Christmas tree, Justices Blackmun and O'Connor dismiss their significance. In my view, this attempt to take the "Christmas" out of the Christmas tree is unconvincing. That the tree may, without controversy, be deemed a secular symbol if found alone, does not mean that it will be so seen when combined with other symbols or objects.

The notion that the Christmas tree is necessarily secular is, indeed, so shaky that, despite superficial acceptance of the idea, Justice O'Connor does not really take it seriously.... [T]he "pluralism" to which Justice O'Connor refers is *religious* pluralism, and the "freedom of belief" she emphasizes is freedom of *religious* belief.[17] The display of the tree and the menorah will symbolize such pluralism and freedom only if more than one religion is represented; if only Judaism is represented, the scene is about Judaism, not about pluralism. Thus, the pluralistic message Justice O'Connor stresses *depends on* the tree's possessing some religious significance.

In asserting that the Christmas tree, regardless of its surroundings, is a purely secular symbol, Justices Blackmun and O'Connor ignore the precept they otherwise so enthusiastically embrace: that context is all-important in determining the message conveyed by particular objects.

Positioned as it was, the Christmas tree's religious significance was bound to come to the fore. Even though the tree alone may be deemed predominantly secular, it can hardly be so characterized when placed next to such a forthrightly religious symbol. Consider a poster featuring a star of David, a statue of Buddha, a Christmas tree, a mosque, and a drawing of Krishna. There can be no doubt that, when found in such company, the tree serves as an unabashedly religious symbol.

Justice Blackmun believes that it is the tree that changes the message of the menorah, rather than the menorah that alters our view of the tree. After the abrupt dismissal of the suggestion that the flora surrounding the crèche might have diluted the religious character of the display at City Hall, his quick conclusion that the Christmas tree had a secularizing effect on the menorah is surprising. The distinguishing characteristic, it appears, is the size of the tree.

As a factual matter, it seems to me that the sight of an 18-foot menorah would be far more eye-catching than that of a rather conventionally sized Christmas tree. It also seems to me likely that the symbol with the more singular message will predominate over one lacking such a clear meaning. Given the homogenized message that Justice Blackmun associates with the Christmas tree, I would expect that the menorah, with its concededly religious character, would tend to dominate the tree. And, it is highly relevant that the menorah was lit during a religious ceremony complete with traditional religious blessings. With such an openly religious introduction, it is most likely that the religious aspects of the menorah would be front and center in this display.

I would not, however, presume to say that my interpretation of the tree's significance is the "correct" one, or the one shared by most visitors to the City-County Building. I

---

17. If it is not religious pluralism that the display signifies, then I do not know what kind of "pluralism" Justice O'Connor has in mind. Perhaps she means the cultural pluralism that results from recognition of many different holidays, religious and nonreligious. In that case, however, the display of a menorah next to a giant firecracker, symbolic of the Fourth of July, would seem to be equally representative of this pluralism, yet I do not sense that this display would pass muster under Justice O'Connor's view. If, instead, Justice O'Connor means to approve the pluralistic message associated with a symbolic display that may stand for either the secular or religious aspects of a given holiday, then this view would logically entail the conclusion that the display of a Latin cross next to an Easter bunny in the springtime would be valid under the Establishment Clause; again, however, I sense that such a conclusion would not comport with Justice O'Connor's views. The final possibility, and the one that seems most consonant with the views outlined in her opinion is that the pluralism that Justice O'Connor perceives in Pittsburgh's display arises from the recognition that there are many different ways to celebrate "the winter holiday season." But winter is "*the* holiday season" to Christians, not to Jews, and the implicit message that it, rather than autumn, is the time for pluralism sends an impermissible signal that only holidays stemming from Christianity, not those arising from other religions, favorably dispose the government towards "pluralism."

do not know how we can decide whether it was the tree that stripped the religious connotations from the menorah, or the menorah that laid bare the religious origins of the tree. Both are reasonable interpretations of the scene the city presented, and thus both, I think, should satisfy Justice Blackmun's requirement that the display "be judged according to the standard of a 'reasonable observer.'" I shudder to think that the only "reasonable observer" is one who shares the particular views on perspective, spacing, and accent expressed in Justice Blackmun's opinion, thus making analysis under the Establishment Clause look more like an exam in Art 101 than an inquiry into constitutional law.

II

The second premise on which today's decision rests is the notion that Chanukah is a partly secular holiday, for which the menorah can serve as a secular symbol. It is no surprise and no anomaly that Chanukah has historical and societal roots that range beyond the purely religious. I would venture that most, if not all, major religious holidays have beginnings and enjoy histories studded with figures, events, and practices that are not strictly religious. It does not seem to me that the mere fact that Chanukah shares this kind of background makes it a secular holiday in any meaningful sense. The menorah is indisputably a religious symbol, used ritually in a celebration that has deep religious significance. That, in my view, is all that need be said.

I cannot, in short, accept the effort to transform an emblem of religious faith into the innocuous "symbol for a holiday that... has both religious and secular dimensions."

III

I know of no principle under the Establishment Clause that permits us to conclude that governmental promotion of religion is acceptable so long as one religion is not favored. We have, on the contrary, interpreted that Clause to require neutrality, not just among religions, but between religion and nonreligion.

Nor do I discern the theory under which the government is permitted to appropriate particular holidays and religious objects to its own use in celebrating "pluralism." The message of the sign announcing a "Salute to Liberty" is not religious, but patriotic; the government's use of religion to promote its own cause is undoubtedly offensive to those whose religious beliefs are not bound up with their attitude toward the Nation.

The uncritical acceptance of a message of religious pluralism also ignores the extent to which even that message may offend. Many religious faiths are hostile to each other, and indeed, refuse even to participate in ecumenical services designed to demonstrate the very pluralism Justices Blackmun and O'Connor extol. To lump the ritual objects and holidays of religions together without regard to their attitudes toward such inclusiveness, or to decide which religions should be excluded because of the possibility of offense, is not a benign or beneficent celebration of pluralism: it is instead an interference in religious matters precluded by the Establishment Clause.

December is not the holiday season for Judaism. Thus, the city's erection alongside the Christmas tree of the symbol of a relatively minor Jewish religious holiday, far from conveying "the city's secular recognition of different traditions for celebrating the winter-holiday season," has the effect of promoting a Christianized version of Judaism. The holiday calendar they appear willing to accept revolves exclusively around a Christian holiday. And those religions that have no holiday at all during the period between

Thanksgiving and New Year's Day will not benefit, even in a second-class manner, from the city's once-a-year tribute to "liberty" and "freedom of belief." This is not "pluralism" as I understand it.

Justice STEVENS, with whom Justice BRENNAN and Justice MARSHALL join, concurring in part and dissenting in part.

In my opinion the Establishment Clause should be construed to create a strong presumption against the display of religious symbols on public property. There is always a risk that such symbols will offend nonmembers of the faith being advertised as well as adherents who consider the particular advertisement disrespectful. Some devout Christians believe that the crèche should be placed only in reverential settings, such as a church or perhaps a private home; they do not countenance its use as an aid to commercialization of Christ's birthday. In this very suit, members of the Jewish faith firmly opposed the use to which the menorah was put by the particular sect that sponsored the display at Pittsburgh's City-County Building. The Establishment Clause does not allow public bodies to foment such disagreement.

For example, a carving of Moses holding the Ten Commandments, if that is the only adornment on a courtroom wall, conveys an equivocal message, perhaps of respect for Judaism, for religion in general, or for law. The addition of carvings depicting Confucius and Mohammed may honor religion, or particular religions, to an extent that the First Amendment does not tolerate any more than it does "the permanent erection of a large Latin cross on the roof of city hall." Placement of secular figures such as Caesar Augustus, William Blackstone, Napoleon Bonaparte, and John Marshall alongside these three religious leaders, however, signals respect not for great proselytizers but for great lawgivers. It would be absurd to exclude such a fitting message from a courtroom, as it would to exclude religious paintings by Italian Renaissance masters from a public museum.

I cannot agree with the Court's conclusion that the display at Pittsburgh's City-County Building was constitutional. Standing alone in front of a governmental headquarters, a lighted, 45-foot evergreen tree might convey holiday greetings linked too tenuously to Christianity to have constitutional moment. Juxtaposition of this tree with an 18-foot menorah does not make the latter secular. Rather, the presence of the Chanukah menorah, unquestionably a religious symbol, gives religious significance to the Christmas tree. The overall display thus manifests governmental approval of the Jewish and Christian religions. Although it conceivably might be interpreted as sending "a message of pluralism and freedom to choose one's own beliefs," the message is not sufficiently clear to overcome the strong presumption that the display, respecting two religions to the exclusion of all others, is the very kind of double establishment that the First Amendment was designed to outlaw. I would, therefore, affirm the judgment of the Court of Appeals in its entirety.

Justice KENNEDY, with whom The Chief Justice [REHNQUIST], Justice WHITE, and Justice SCALIA join, concurring in the judgment in part and dissenting in part.

The majority holds that the County of Allegheny violated the Establishment Clause by displaying a crèche in the county courthouse, because the "principal or primary effect" of the display is to advance religion within the meaning of *Lemon v. Kurtzman.* This view of the Establishment Clause reflects an unjustified hostility toward religion, a hostility inconsistent with our history and our precedents, and I dissent from this holding. The crèche display is constitutional, and, for the same reasons, the display of a menorah by the city of Pittsburgh is permissible as well. On this latter point, I concur in the result, but not the reasoning, of Part VI of Justice Blackmun's opinion.

I

In keeping with the usual fashion of recent years, the majority applies the *Lemon* test to judge the constitutionality of the holiday displays here in question. I am content for present purposes to remain within the *Lemon* framework, but do not wish to be seen as advocating, let alone adopting, that test as our primary guide in this difficult area. Substantial revision of our Establishment Clause doctrine may be in order; but it is unnecessary to undertake that task today, for even the *Lemon* test, when applied with proper sensitivity to our traditions and our case law, supports the conclusion that both the crèche and the menorah are permissible displays in the context of the holiday season.

The only *Lemon* factor implicated in this case directs us to inquire whether the "principal or primary effect" of the challenged government practice is "one that neither advances nor inhibits religion." Taken to its logical extreme, some of [this] language would require a relentless extirpation of all contact between government and religion. But that is not the history or the purpose of the Establishment Clause. Government policies of accommodation, acknowledgment, and support for religion are an accepted part of our political and cultural heritage.

Rather than requiring government to avoid any action that acknowledges or aids religion, the Establishment Clause permits government some latitude in recognizing and accommodating the central role religion plays in our society. Any approach less sensitive to our heritage would border on latent hostility toward religion, as it would require government in all its multifaceted roles to acknowledge only the secular, to the exclusion and so to the detriment of the religious. A categorical approach would install federal courts as jealous guardians of an absolute "wall of separation," sending a clear message of disapproval. In this century, as the modern administrative state expands to touch the lives of its citizens in such diverse ways and redirects their financial choices through programs of its own, it is difficult to maintain the fiction that requiring government to avoid all assistance to religion can in fairness be viewed as serving the goal of neutrality. Our cases reflect this understanding.

The ability of the organized community to recognize and accommodate religion in a society with a pervasive public sector requires diligent observance of the border between accommodation and establishment. Our cases disclose two limiting principles: government may not coerce anyone to support or participate in any religion or its exercise; and it may not, in the guise of avoiding hostility or callous indifference, give direct benefits to religion in such a degree that in fact "establishes a [state] religion or religious faith, or tends to do so." *Lynch*. These two principles, while distinct, are not unrelated, for it would be difficult indeed to establish a religion without some measure of more or less subtle coercion, be it in the form of taxation to supply the substantial benefits that would sustain a state-established faith, direct compulsion to observance, or governmental exhortation to religiosity that amounts in fact to proselytizing.

It is no surprise that without exception we have invalidated actions that further the interests of religion through the coercive power of government. The freedom to worship as one pleases without government interference or oppression is the great object of both the Establishment and the Free Exercise Clauses. Barring all attempts to aid religion through government coercion goes far toward attainment of this object.

As Justice Blackmun observes, some of our recent cases reject the view that coercion is the sole touchstone of an Establishment Clause violation. That may be true if by "coercion" is meant *direct* coercion in the classic sense of an establishment of religion that the

Framers knew. But coercion need not be a direct tax in aid of religion or a test oath. Symbolic recognition or accommodation of religious faith may violate the Clause in an extreme case. I doubt not, for example, that the Clause forbids a city to permit the permanent erection of a large Latin cross on the roof of city hall. This is not because government speech about religion is *per se* suspect, as the majority would have it, but because such an obtrusive year-round religious display would place the government's weight behind an obvious effort to proselytize on behalf of a particular religion. Speech may coerce in some circumstances, but this does not justify a ban on all government recognition of religion.

This is most evident where the government's act of recognition or accommodation is passive and symbolic, for in that instance any intangible benefit to religion is unlikely to present a realistic risk of establishment. Absent coercion, the risk of infringement of religious liberty by passive or symbolic accommodation is minimal.

In determining whether there exists an establishment, or a tendency toward one, we refer to the other types of church-state contacts that have existed unchallenged throughout our history, or that have been found permissible in our case law. Non-coercive government action within the realm of flexible accommodation or passive acknowledgment of existing symbols does not violate the Establishment Clause unless it benefits religion in a way more direct and more substantial than practices that are accepted in our national heritage.

II

These principles are not difficult to apply to the facts of the case before us. In permitting the displays on government property of the menorah and the crèche, the city and county sought to do no more than "celebrate the season," and to acknowledge, along with many of their citizens, the historical background and the religious as well as secular nature of the Chanukah and Christmas holidays. This interest falls well within the tradition of government accommodation and acknowledgment of religion that has marked our history from the beginning. It cannot be disputed that government, if it chooses, may participate in sharing with its citizens the joy of the holiday season, by declaring public holidays, installing or permitting festive displays, sponsoring celebrations and parades, and providing holiday vacations for its employees. All levels of our government do precisely that. As we said in *Lynch*, "Government has long recognized—indeed it has subsidized—holidays with religious significance."

If government is to participate in its citizen's celebration of a holiday that contains both a secular and a religious component, enforced recognition of only the secular aspect would signify the callous indifference toward religious faith that our cases and traditions do not require; for by commemorating the holiday only as it is celebrated by nonadherents, the government would be refusing to acknowledge the plain fact, and the historical reality, that many of its citizens celebrate its religious aspects as well. Judicial invalidation of government's attempts to recognize the religious underpinnings of the holiday would signal not neutrality but a pervasive intent to insulate government from all things religious. The Religion Clauses do not require government to acknowledge these holidays or their religious component; but our strong tradition of government accommodation and acknowledgment permits government to do so.

There is no suggestion here that the government's power to coerce has been used to further the interests of Christianity or Judaism in any way. No one was compelled to observe or participate in any religious ceremony or activity. Neither the city nor the county contributed significant amounts of tax money to serve the cause of one religious faith. The crèche and the menorah are purely passive symbols of religious holidays.

Passersby who disagree with the message conveyed by these displays are free to ignore them, or even to turn their backs, just as they are free to do when they disagree with any other form of government speech.

There is no realistic risk that the crèche or the menorah represent an effort to proselytize or are otherwise the first step down the road to an establishment of religion. *Lynch* is dispositive of this claim with respect to the crèche, and I find no reason for reaching a different result with respect to the menorah. Both are the traditional symbols of religious holidays that over time have acquired a secular component. If Congress and the state legislatures do not run afoul of the Establishment Clause when they begin each day with a state-sponsored prayer for divine guidance offered by a chaplain whose salary is paid at government expense, I cannot comprehend how a menorah or a crèche, displayed in the limited context of the holiday season, can be invalid.

If *Lynch* is still good law—and until today it was—the judgment below cannot stand. I accept and indeed approve both the holding and the reasoning of Chief Justice Burger's opinion in *Lynch*, and so I must dissent from the judgment that the crèche display is unconstitutional. On the same reasoning, I agree that the menorah display is constitutional.

III

The majority invalidates display of the crèche, not because it disagrees with the interpretation of *Lynch* applied above, but because it chooses to discard the reasoning of the *Lynch* majority opinion in favor of Justice O'Connor's concurring opinion in that case. It has never been my understanding that a concurring opinion "suggest[ing] a clarification of our... doctrine," could take precedence over an opinion joined in its entirety by five Members of the Court. Since the majority does not state its intent to overrule *Lynch*, I find its refusal to apply the reasoning of that decision quite confusing.

[Justice Kennedy's critique of endorsement analysis is omitted.]

IV

The approach adopted by the majority contradicts important values embodied in the Clause. Obsessive, implacable resistance to all but the most carefully scripted and secularized form of accommodation requires this Court to act as a censor, issuing national decrees as to what is orthodox and what is not. What is orthodox, in this context, means what is secular; the only Christmas the State can acknowledge is one in which references to religion have been held to a minimum. The Court thus lends its assistance to an Orwellian rewriting of history as many understood it. I can conceive of no judicial function more antithetical to the First Amendment.

A further contradiction arises from the majority's approach, for the Court also assumes the difficult and inappropriate task of saying what every religious symbol means. Before studying this case, I had not known the full history of the menorah, and I suspect the same was true of my colleagues. More important, this history was, and is, likely unknown to the vast majority of people of all faiths who saw the symbol displayed in Pittsburgh. Even if the majority is quite right about the history of the menorah, it hardly follows that this same history informed the observers' view of the symbol and the reason for its presence. This Court is ill-equipped to sit as a national theology board, and I question both the wisdom and the constitutionality of its doing so. Indeed, were I required to choose between the approach taken by the majority and a strict separationist view, I would have to respect the consistency of the latter.

The suit before us is admittedly a troubling one. It must be conceded that, however neutral the purpose of the city and county, the eager proselytizer may seek to use these symbols for his own ends. The urge to use them to teach or to taunt is always present. It is true that some devout adherents of Judaism or Christianity may be as offended by the holiday display as the nonbelievers, if not more so. To place these religious symbols in a common hallway or sidewalk, where they may be ignored or even insulted, must be distasteful to many who cherish their meaning.

For these reasons, I might have voted against installation of these particular displays were I a local legislative official. But we have no jurisdiction over matters of taste within the realm of constitutionally permissible discretion. Our role is enforcement of a written Constitution. In my view, the principles of the Establishment Clause and our Nation's historic traditions of diversity and pluralism allow communities to make reasonable judgments respecting the accommodation or acknowledgment of holidays with both cultural and religious aspects. No constitutional violation occurs when they do so by displaying a symbol of the holiday's religious origins.

Notes

1. There are pronounced differences in the reasoning among the Justices in *County of Allegheny*. One majority of the Court holds unconstitutional the placement of a crèche on the Grand Staircase of the County Courthouse. Another upholds the placement at the City-County Building of a Christmas tree, a menorah, and a sign saluting religious liberty. Only Justices Blackmun and O'Connor are in the majority in both instances, and they disagree about the status of the menorah. Justice Blackmun concludes that because the tree is a secular symbol, and because the tree informs the meaning of the menorah, in this case the menorah must be understood as a secular symbol. Justice O'Connor concludes that the menorah is a religious symbol, but the combination of the secular tree and the message saluting liberty do not endorse Judaism, but send a message of pluralism and liberty. Does either conclusion seem a sensible as matter of fact? What would an "objective observer" think of the differences in their approach? Isn't it just as plausible to conclude that the entire display endorses religion over non-religion?

This is Justice Brennan's argument. He agrees that the tree, menorah and sign send a message of "pluralism," but argues that the message promotes only *religious* pluralism. Is sending such a message a bad thing generally, or just when the government does so by using religious symbols? Is it possible that the County was trying to promote religious tolerance and pluralism by adding the menorah to its traditional display? If so, what "message" is conveyed, and to whom? *See American Civil Liberties Union of New Jersey v. Schundler*, 168 F.3d 92 (3rd Cir. 1999) (upholding a modified holiday display that included a crèche, a menorah, a 4' tall plastic figure of Santa Claus, a 3' 10" tall plastic figure of Frosty the Snowman, a 4' tall sled, Kwanzaa symbols on the tree, and two signs, each approximately 2' by 3', stating: "Through this display and others throughout the year, the City of Jersey City is pleased to celebrate the diverse cultural and ethnic heritages of its peoples.")

2. How seriously should the Court take the argument that judicial efforts to eliminate public displays of religious symbols will be perceived as hostility toward religion? If a public entity has traditionally placed a Christmas tree and a menorah on public

property for a lengthy period of time, would an objective observer view a demand by those who object to the tree and the menorah—or to the celebration of the a particular "holiday" itself—as government favoritism for those who find public displays of religious belief objectionable? *See, e.g., Ganulin v. United States*, 71 F. Supp. 2d 824 (S.D. Ohio 1999) (recognition of Christmas as national holiday does not violate Establishment Clause because it has acquired a secular character). *See also Bridenbaugh v. O'Bannon*, 185 F.3d 796 (7th Cir. 1999) (Good Friday upheld as paid state holiday because Indiana articulated secular reasons for the designation).

3. *County of Allegheny* raises important questions about both the characterization of symbols as "religious" or "secular," and the use of such symbols in public life. Do these factors make the case less important to those concerned with issues of religious liberty, as suggested by Justice Kennedy, or more important? In *Lynch*, Justice Brennan, although dissenting, noted, "government cannot be completely prohibited from recognizing in its public actions the religious beliefs and practices of the American people as an aspect of our national history and culture." *Lynch v. Donnelly*, 465 U.S. 668, 716 (1984) (Brennan, J., dissenting). *See also* Arlin Adams & Charles J. Emmerich, A NATION DEDICATED TO RELIGIOUS LIBERTY: THE CONSTITUTIONAL HERITAGE OF THE RELIGION CLAUSES 83 (1990) ("To remove religious symbols from public life would change the substance of American culture. This may or may not be a valid goal, but in a democratic society such a change must be wrought by the people, not compelled by one branch of government. That, at least, is the lesson that the principle of federalism would teach."). Recall that Justice Felix Frankfurter, a strict separationist in Establishment Clause matters, noted in upholding the flag salute in *Minersville Sch. Dist. v. Gobitis*, 310 U.S. 586, 596 (1940), that "[w]e live by symbols," and in joining the Court's holding that released time religious instruction in public schools was unconstitutional, declared, "[t]he public school is at once the symbol of our democracy and the most pervasive means for promoting our common destiny." *Illinois* ex rel. *McCollum v. Bd. of Educ.*, 333 U.S. 203, 231 (1948). Does the use of arguably religious symbols in public life create or diminish political divisiveness based on religion? Do symbols define who we are? In *Texas v. Johnson*, 491 U.S. 397 (1989), the Court held unconstitutional on Free Speech grounds a law criminalizing flag burning. Chief Justice Rehnquist's dissenting opinion claimed that because the flag was a unique symbol of the nation, government should be permitted to prohibit "symbolic speech" that defiles it.

4. Although Justice Kennedy suggests that his approach in *County of Allegheny* is consistent with a proper concept of accommodation of religion, one prominent scholar supportive of accommodation contends that his "conception of accommodation does *not* include government action that acknowledges or expresses the prevailing religious sentiments of the community, such as the display of a religious symbol on public property or the delivery of a prayer at public ceremonial events." Michael W. McConnell, *Accommodation of Religion: An Update and a Response to Critics*, 60 Geo. Wash. L. Rev. 685, 687 (1992). *Cf.* Michael W. McConnell, *Religious Freedom at a Crossroads*, 59 U. Chi. L. Rev. 115, 193 (1992) ("It is impossible to tell whether a particular event, symbol, statement, or item is an indication of [permissible] diversity or of [impermissible] favoritism if it is viewed without regard to wider context.").

5. Justices Kennedy and Scalia are identified as Roman Catholic, as was the late Justice Brennan. The opinions of Justices Kennedy and Brennan in *County of Allegheny* suggest that their approach to Establishment Clause issues was very different. Is it possible to determine whether the religious beliefs of a Justice or judge affects his or her ap-

proaches to a case? Is there a "Catholic" or "Protestant" or "Jewish" approach to interpreting law, or to interpreting the Establishment Clause? *See generally* Sanford Levinson, *The Confrontation of Religious Faith and Civil Religion: Catholics Becoming Justices*, 39 DePaul L. Rev. 1047 (1990). Professor George Kannar suggests that the jurisprudence of Justice Scalia is best understood in light of his experiences as a pre-Vatican II Roman Catholic. George Kannar, *The Constitutional Catechism of Antonin Scalia*, 99 Yale L. J. 1297 (1990); *cf.* Donald L. Beschle, *Catechism or Imagination: Is Justice Scalia's Judicial Style Typically Catholic?*, 37 Vill. L. Rev. 1329, 1359 (1992) (concluding that "to the extent that religion correlates with the kind of imagination one brings to the bench, there is no reason to consider Justice Scalia as a typical representative of Catholic analytical style").

c) *Religious Education for Public School Students*

Dissenting in *Everson v. Board of Educ.*, Justice Robert Jackson observed that "[o]ur public school... is organized on the premise that secular education can be isolated from all religious teaching so that the school can inculcate all needed temporal knowledge and also maintain a strict and lofty neutrality as to religion. 330 U.S. at 23 (Jackson, Rutledge, Frankfurter, & Burton JJ., dissenting). It was thus inevitable that programs seeking to provide religious education during the school day for children enrolled in the public schools would be challenged as a violation of the Establishment Clause.

Chapter Six, "Religion in the Classroom," is a detailed examination of the relationship between religion and education (§ B), and the wide variety of ways that state action in the controlled environment of the classroom can implicate the Religious Liberty Guarantee (§§ C, D & E).

Illinois ex rel. McCollum v. Board of Education

333 U.S. 203 (1948)

Mr. Justice BLACK delivered the opinion of the Court.

This case relates to the power of a state to utilize its tax-supported public school system in aid of religious instruction insofar as that power may be restricted by the First and Fourteenth Amendments to the Federal Constitution.

Appellant's petition for mandamus alleged that religious teachers, employed by private religious groups, were permitted to come weekly into the school buildings during the regular hours set apart for secular teaching, and then and there for a period of thirty minutes substitute their religious teaching for the secular education provided under the compulsory education law.

[T]he following facts are shown by the record without dispute. In 1940 interested members of the Jewish, Roman Catholic, and a few of the Protestant faiths formed a voluntary association called the Champaign Council on Religious Education. They obtained permission from the Board of Education to offer classes in religious instruction to public school pupils in grades four to nine inclusive. Classes were made up of pupils whose parents signed printed cards requesting that their children be permitted to attend; they were held weekly, thirty minutes for the lower grades, forty-five minutes for the higher. The council employed the religious teachers at no expense to the school authorities, but the instructors were subject to the approval and supervision of the superintendent of schools. The classes were taught in three separate religious groups by Protestant teachers, Catholic priests, and a Jewish rabbi, although for the past several years there have apparently been no classes instructed in the Jewish religion. Classes were conducted in the regular classrooms of the school building. Students who did not choose to take the religious instruction were not released from public school duties; they were required to leave their classrooms and go to some other place in the school building for pursuit of their secular studies. On the other hand, students who were released from secular study for the religious instructions were required to be present at the religious classes. Reports of their presence or absence were to be made to their secular teachers.

This is beyond all question a utilization of the tax-established and tax-supported public school system to aid religious groups to spread their faith. And it falls squarely under the ban of the First Amendment (made applicable to the States by the Fourteenth) as we interpreted it in *Everson.*

[Appellees] argue that historically the First Amendment was intended to forbid only government preference of one religion over another, not an impartial governmental assistance of all religions. In addition they ask that we distinguish or overrule our holding in the *Everson* case that the Fourteenth Amendment made the "establishment of religion" clause of the First Amendment applicable as a prohibition against the States. After giving full consideration to the arguments presented we are unable to accept either of these contentions.

To hold that a state cannot consistently with the First and Fourteenth Amendments utilize its public school system to aid any or all religious faiths or sects in the dissemination of their doctrines and ideals does not, as counsel urge, manifest a governmental hostility to religion or religious teachings. A manifestation of such hostility would be at war with our national tradition as embodied in the First Amendment's guaranty of the free exercise of religion. For the First Amendment rests upon the premise that both religion and government can best work to achieve their lofty aims if each is left free from the other within its respective sphere. Or, as we said in the *Everson* case, the First Amendment has created a wall between Church and State which must be kept high and impregnable.

This is not separation of Church and State. *Reversed and remanded.*

Mr. Justice FRANKFURTER delivered the following opinion, in which Mr. Justice JACKSON, Mr. Justice RUTLEDGE and Mr. Justice BURTON join.

[T]he public school system of Champaign actively furthers inculcation in the religious tenets of some faiths, and in the process sharpens the consciousness of religious differences at least among some of the children committed to its care. These are consequences not amenable to statistics. But they are precisely the consequences against which the Constitution was directed when it prohibited the Government common to all from becoming embroiled, however innocently, in the destructive religious conflicts of which the history of even this country records some dark pages.

If it were merely a question of enabling a child to obtain religious instruction with a receptive mind the thirty or forty-five minutes could readily be found on Saturday or Sunday. If that were all, Champaign might have drawn upon the French system, known in its American manifestation as "dismissed time," whereby one school day is shortened to allow all children to go where they please, leaving those who so desire to go to a religious school.

Separation means separation, not something less. Jefferson's metaphor in describing the relation between Church and State speaks of a "wall of separation," not of a fine line easily overstepped. The public school is at once the symbol of our democracy and the most pervasive means for promoting our common destiny.

If nowhere else, in the relation between Church and State, "good fences make good neighbors."

Mr. Justice JACKSON, concurring.

While we may and should end such formal and explicit instruction as the Champaign plan and can at all times prohibit teaching of creed and catechism and ceremonial and can forbid forthright proselyting in the schools, I think it remains to be demonstrated whether it is possible, even if desirable, to comply with such demands as plaintiff's completely to isolate and cast out of secular education all that some people may reasonably regard as religious instruction. Perhaps subjects such as mathematics, physics or chemistry are, or can be, completely secularized. But it would not seem practical to teach either practice or appreciation of the arts if we are to forbid exposure of youth to any religious influences. Music without sacred music, architecture minus the cathedral, or painting without the scriptural themes would be eccentric and incomplete, even from a secular point of view. Yet the inspirational appeal of religion in these guises is often stronger than in forthright sermon. Even such a "science" as biology raises the issue between evolution and creation as an explanation of our presence on this planet. Certainly a course in English literature that omitted the Bible and other powerful uses of our mother tongue for religious ends would be pretty barren. And I should suppose it is a proper, if not an indispensable, part of preparation for a worldly life to know the roles that religion and religions have played in the tragic story of mankind. The fact is that, for good or for ill, nearly everything in our culture worth transmitting, everything which gives meaning to life, is saturated with religious influences, derived from paganism, Judaism, Christianity—both Catholic and Protestant—and other faiths accepted by a large part of the world's peoples. One can hardly respect a system of education that would leave the student wholly ignorant of the currents of religious thought that move the world society for a part in which he is being prepared.

But how one can teach, with satisfaction or even with justice to all faiths, such subjects as the story of the Reformation, the Inquisition, or even the New England effort to found "a Church without a Bishop and a State without a King," is more than I know. It is too much to expect that mortals will teach subjects about which their contemporaries have passionate controversies with the detachment they may summon to teaching about remote subjects such as Confucius or Mohammed. When instruction turns to proselyting and imparting knowledge becomes evangelism is, except in the crudest cases, a subtle inquiry.

It is idle to pretend that this task is one for which we can find in the Constitution one word to help us as judges to decide where the secular ends and the sectarian begins in education. Nor can we find guidance in any other legal source. It is a matter on which we can find no law but our own prepossessions. If with no surer legal guidance we are to take up and decide every variation of this controversy, raised by persons not subject to penalty or tax but who are dissatisfied with the way schools are dealing with the problem, we are likely to have much business of the sort. And, more importantly, we are likely to make the legal "wall of separation between church and state" as winding as the famous serpentine wall designed by Mr. Jefferson for the University he founded.

Mr. Justice REED, dissenting.

By directing attention to the many instances of close association of church and state in American society and by recalling that many of these relations are so much a part of our tradition and culture that they are accepted without more, this dissent may help in an appraisal of the meaning of the clause of the First Amendment concerning the establishment of religion and of the reasons which lead to the approval or disapproval of the judgment below.

The phrase "an establishment of religion" may have been intended by Congress to be aimed only at a state church. When the First Amendment was pending in Congress in substantially its present form, "Mr. Madison said, he apprehended the meaning of the words to be, that Congress should not establish a religion, and enforce the legal observation of it by law, nor compel men to worship God in any manner contrary to their conscience." Passing years, however, have brought about acceptance of a broader meaning, although never until today, I believe, has this Court widened its interpretation to any such degree as holding that recognition of the interest of our nation in religion, through the granting, to qualified representatives of the principal faiths, of opportunity to present religion as an optional, extracurricular subject during released school time in public school buildings, was equivalent to an establishment of religion. A reading of the general statements of eminent statesmen of former days, referred to in the opinions in this and *Everson* will show that circumstances such as those in this case were far from the minds of the authors. The words and spirit of those statements may be wholeheartedly accepted without in the least impugning the judgment of the State of Illinois.

Mr. Jefferson, as one of the founders of the University of Virginia, a school which from its establishment in 1819 has been wholly governed, managed and controlled by the State of Virginia, was faced with the same problem that is before this Court today: The question of the constitutional limitation upon religious education in public schools. In his annual report as Rector, to the President and Directors of the Literary Fund, dated October 7, 1822, approved by the Visitors of the University of whom Mr. Madison was one, Mr. Jefferson set forth his views at some length.[11] These suggestions of Mr. Jefferson were adopted, and provided that:

---

11. 19 The Writing of Thomas Jefferson (Memorial ed. 1904)], pp. 414–17:"It was not, however, to be understood that instruction in religious opinion and duties was meant to be precluded by the public authorities, as indifferent to the interests of society. On the contrary, the relations which exist between man and his Maker, and the duties resulting from those relations, are the most interesting and important to every human being, and the most incumbent on his study and investigation. The want of instruction in the various creeds of religious faith existing among our citizens presents, therefore, a chasm in a general institution of the useful sciences * * *. A remedy, however, has been suggested of promising aspect, which, while it excludes the public authorities from the domain of religious freedom, will give to the sectarian schools of divinity the full benefit the public provisions made for instruction in the other branches of science * * *. It has, therefore, been in contemplation, and suggested by some pious individuals, who perceive the advantages of associating other studies with those of religion, to establish their religious schools on the confines of the University, so as to give to their students ready and convenient access and attendance on the scientific lectures of the University; and to maintain, by that means, those destined for the religious professions on as high a standing of science, and of personal weight and respectability, as may be obtained by others from the benefits of the University. Such establishments would offer the further and greater advantage of enabling the students of the University to attend religious exercises with the professor of their particular sect, either in the rooms of the building still to be erected, and destined to that purpose under impartial regulations, as proposed in the same report of the commissioners, or in the lecturing room of such professor * * *. Such an arrangement would complete the circle of the useful sciences, embraced by this institution, and would fill the chasm now existing, on principles which would leave inviolate the constitutional freedom of religion, the most inalienable and sacred of all human rights, over which the people and authorities of this state, individually and publicly, have ever manifested the most watchful jealousy; and could this jealousy be now alarmed, in the opinion of the legislature, by what is here suggested, the idea will be relinquished on any surmise of disapprobation which they might think proper to express."

Mr. Jefferson commented upon the report on November 2, 1822, in a letter to Dr. Thomas

"Should the religious sects of this State, or any of them, according to the invitation held out to them, establish within, or adjacent to, the precincts of the University, schools for instruction in the religion of their sect, the students of the University will be free, and expected to attend religious worship at the establishment of their respective sects, in the morning, and in time to meet their school in the University at its stated hour."

Thus, the "wall of separation between church and State" that Mr. Jefferson built at the University which he founded did not exclude religious education from that school. The difference between the generality of his statements on the separation of church and state and the specificity of his conclusions on education are considerable. A rule of law should not be drawn from a figure of speech.

Mr. Madison's *Memorial and Remonstrance against Religious Assessments*, relied upon by the dissenting Justices in *Everson*, is not applicable here. Mr. Madison was one of the principal opponents in the Virginia General Assembly of *A Bill Establishing a Provision for Teachers of the Christian Religion*. The conclusive legislative struggle over this act took place in the fall of 1785 before the adoption of the Bill of Rights. The *Remonstrance* had been issued before the General Assembly convened and was instrumental in the final defeat of the act which died in committee. Throughout the *Remonstrance*, Mr. Madison speaks of the "establishment" sought to be effected by the act. It is clear from this historical setting and its language that the *Remonstrance* was a protest against an effort by Virginia to support Christian sects by taxation. Issues similar to those raised by the instant case were not discussed. Thus, Mr. Madison's approval of Mr. Jefferson's report as Rector gives, in my opinion, a clearer indication of his views on the constitutionality of religious education in public schools than this general statements on a different subject.

[A]ll churches receive "aid" from government in the form of freedom from taxation. The *Everson* decision itself justified the transportation of children to church schools by New Jersey for safety reasons. It accords with *Cochran v. Louisiana State Board of Education* where this Court upheld a free textbook statute of Louisiana against a charge that it aided private schools on the ground that the books were for the education of the children, not to aid religious schools. Likewise the National School Lunch Act aids all school children attending tax exempt schools. In *Bradfield v. Roberts*, this Court held proper the payment of money by the Federal Government to build an addition to a hospital, chartered by individuals who were members of a Roman Catholic sisterhood, and operated under the auspices of the Roman Catholic Church. This was done over the objection that it aided the establishment of religion. While obviously in these instances the respective churches, in a certain sense, were aided, this Court has never held that such "aid" was in violation of the First or Fourteenth Amendments.

The practices of the federal government offer many examples of this kind of "aid" by the state to religion. The Congress of the United States has a chaplain for each House who daily invokes divine blessings and guidance for the proceedings. The armed forces have commissioned chaplains from early days. They conduct the public services in accordance with the liturgical requirements of their respective faiths, ashore and afloat, employing for the purpose property belonging to the United States and dedicated to the services of religion. Under the Servicemen's Readjustment Act of 1944, eligible veterans may receive training at government expense for the ministry in denominational schools.

Cooper, as follows: "And by bringing the sects together, and mixing them with the mass of other students, we shall soften their asperities, liberalize and neutralize their prejudices, and make the general religion a religion of peace, reason, and morality." 12 Ford, The Works of Thomas Jefferson (Ford ed., 1905) 272.

The schools of the District of Columbia have opening exercises which "include a reading from the Bible without note or comment, and the Lord's prayer."

In the United States Naval Academy and the United States Military Academy, schools wholly supported and completely controlled by the federal government, there are a number of religious activities. Chaplains are attached to both schools. Attendance at church services on Sunday is compulsory at both the Military and Naval Academies. At West Point the Protestant services are held in the Cadet Chapel, the Catholic in the Catholic Chapel, and the Jewish in the Old Cadet Chapel; at Annapolis only Protestant services are held on the reservation, midshipmen of other religious persuasions attend the churches of the city of Annapolis. These facts indicate that both schools since their earliest beginnings have maintained and enforced a pattern of participation in formal worship.

[I]n the light of the meaning given to those words by the precedents, customs, and practices which I have detailed above, I cannot agree with the Court's conclusion that when pupils compelled by law to go to school for secular education are released from school so as to attend the religious classes, churches are unconstitutionally aided. When actual church services have always been permitted on government property, the mere use of the school buildings by a non-sectarian group for religious education ought not to be condemned as an establishment of religion. The prohibition of enactments respecting the establishment of religion do not bar every friendly gesture between church and state. Devotion to the great principle of religious liberty should not lead us into a rigid interpretation of the constitutional guarantee that conflicts with accepted habits of our people. This is an instance where, for me, the history of past practices is determinative of the meaning of a constitutional clause not a decorous introduction to the study of its text. The judgment should be affirmed.

Notes

1. The lone dissenter, Justice Stanley Reed, rested his interpretation of the Establishment Clause on an assessment of Jefferson's report to the Board of Visitors of the University of Virginia in 1822. Does that report raise issues analogous to those involved in *McCollum*? If so, what conclusions do the analogies suggest?

2. What do you make of the majority's argument that the public educational setting is the sphere of the state? Does this mean that the content of education—and the role and treatment of religion as a part of the educational program—is, by definition, under the control of the political majority? Justice Reed mentions the existence of daily readings from the Bible in the District of Columbia public schools as one example of accommodation of religion in the public schools, but the practice of Bible reading without comment was a itself political compromise that caused of considerable unrest and litigation over the rights of dissenting parents and students. *See* Chapters Three, Four and Six. Many Catholic scholars applauded Justice Reed's interpretation of the Establishment Clause, not only because of the traditional Catholic view that religion is an integral part of a well-rounded education, but also because they viewed plans like that adopted by Champaign as an accommodation of their own religious liberty interests in a public school system that was hostile to their beliefs. *See Everson*, 330 U.S. at 23 (Jackson, Rutledge, Frankfurter & Burton, JJ. dissenting) ("Our public school system, if not a product of Protestantism, at least is more consistent with it than with the Catholic culture and scheme of values.") *See* F. William O'Brien, S.J., Justice Reed and the First Amendment: The Religion Clauses

(1958). There is only one brief mention of his religious faith in any biography of Reed. Biographer John D. Fassett notes that as a Maysville, Kentucky lawyer, Reed and his wife belonged to the Trinity United Methodist Church. John D. Fassett, New Deal Justice: The Life of Stanley Reed of Kentucky 28 (1994). At his confirmation hearings, a Senator from his home state referred to him as a "clean, high-class Christian gentleman." The Supreme Court of the United States: Hearings and Reports on Successful and Unsuccessful Nominations of Supreme Court Justices by the Senate Judiciary Committee, 1916–1972 15 (Roy M. Mersky & J. Myron Jacobstein eds. 1975).

According to Professor O'Brien, "Reed always manifested his greatest air of triumph when he discussed his dissent in *McCollum v. Board of Education....*" Francis William O'Brien, *Foreword*, 69 Ky. L.J. 721, 728 (1980–81). Reed told O'Brien that the number of favorable letters received from his opinion in *McCollum* was "'ten times more than any other'" opinion he wrote. *Id.* at 729 (quoting interview with Justice Reed, December 2, 1955). Reed had silently joined the majority the year before in *Everson*. Yet no other justice joined his dissent. Why?

3. The *McCollum* case was the first to hold a state or federal legislative enactment unconstitutional on the basis of the incorporated Establishment Clause. Several noted scholars attacked the Court's decision. In a *Religion and the State* symposium, political scientist Edward S. Corwin, philosopher Alexander Meiklejohn, and the Jesuit theologian John Courtney Murray all criticized the Court's decision. *See Religion and the State*, 14 Law & Contemp. Probs. 1 *et seq.* (1949). Murray, then the most prominent American Catholic writing on the subject of church-state relations, used Justice Jackson's statement that this was "a matter on which we can find no law but our own prepossessions," for the title of his essay. John Courtney Murray, *Law or Prepossessions*, 14 Law & Contemp. Probs. 23 (1949). Murray criticized the Court's historical analysis, its reliance on Madison's absolute conception of church and state, which Murray argued was grounded itself in "a sectarian idea of religion," and Justice Frankfurter's attempt in *McCollum* to use the public school as a symbol as he had in the overruled *Gobitis* decision (the public school as a "symbol of our secular unity"). As might be expected, the Roman Catholic Church strongly opposed *McCollum.* The Catholic Church's opposition to this "American" approach to issues of church-state relations did not change until the early 1960s, after Vatican II. Murray, who was silenced in the mid-1950s by his superiors for his "pluralist" approach to these problems, see Donald E. Pelotte, John Courtney Murray: Theologian in Conflict 34–58 (1975), and was instrumental in drafting the Second Vatican Council's Declaration on Religious Freedom, which announced the change in the Church's position. *Id.* at 82–100.

Not all commentators were critical. *See* Milton R. Konvitz, *Separation of Church and State: The First Freedom*, 14 Law & Contemp. Probs. 44 (1949) and Paul Blanshard, American Freedom and Catholic Power, 94–96 (1949). In addition, before *McCollum* was decided, a number of religious organizations filed *amicus* briefs urging the Court to hold the Champaign released time program unconstitutional. However, one commentator noted that "over 3,000 communities in forty-six states" had created such programs. Russell N. Sullivan, *Religious Education in the Schools*, 14 Law & Contemp. Probs. 92, 107 (1949). Professor Sullivan noted that the *McCollum* decision created rather than dissipated uncertainty about the constitutionality of released time programs. The Court heard another dispute involving a slightly different released time program in the following case.

Zorach v. Clauson

343 U.S. 306 (1952)

Mr. Justice DOUGLAS delivered the opinion of the Court.

New York City has a program which permits its public schools to release students during the school day so that they may leave the school buildings and school grounds and go to religious centers for religious instruction or devotional exercises. A student is released on written request of his parents. Those not released stay in the classrooms. The churches make weekly reports to the schools, sending a list of children who have been released from public school but who have not reported for religious instruction.

This "released time" program involves neither religious instruction in public school classrooms nor the expenditure of public funds. All costs, including the application blanks, are paid by the religious organizations. The case is therefore unlike *McCollum v. Board of Education*. In that case the classrooms were turned over to religious instructors.

Appellants... challenge the present law, contending it is in essence not different from the one involved in the *McCollum* case. Their argument, stated elaborately in various ways, reduces itself to this: the weight and influence of the school is put behind a program for religious instruction; public school teachers police it, keeping tab on students who are released; the classroom activities come to a halt while the students who are released for religious instruction are on leave; the school is a crutch on which the churches are leaning for support in their religious training; without the cooperation of the schools this "released time" program, like the one in the *McCollum* case, would be futile and ineffective.

[O]ur problem reduces itself to whether New York by this system has either prohibited the "free exercise" of religion or has made a law "respecting an establishment of religion" within the meaning of the First Amendment.

It takes obtuse reasoning to inject any issue of the "free exercise" of religion into the present case. No one is forced to go to the religious classroom and no religious exercise or instruction is brought to the classrooms of the public schools. A student need not take religious instruction. He is left to his own desires as to the manner or time of his religious devotions, if any.

[W]e do not see how New York by this type of "released time" program has made a law respecting an establishment of religion within the meaning of the First Amendment. There is much talk of the separation of Church and State in the history of the Bill of Rights and in the decisions clustering around the First Amendment. See *Everson*; *McCollum*. There cannot be the slightest doubt that the First Amendment reflects the philosophy that Church and State should be separated. And so far as interference with the "free exercise" of religion and an "establishment" of religion are concerned, the separation must be complete and unequivocal. The First Amendment within the scope of its coverage permits no exception; the prohibition is absolute. The First Amendment, however, does not say that in every and all respects there shall be a separation of Church and State. Rather, it studiously defines the manner, the specific ways, in which there shall be no concert or union or dependency one on the other. That is the common sense of the matter. Otherwise the state and religion would be aliens to each other—hostile, suspicious, and even unfriendly. Churches could not be required to pay even property taxes. Municipalities would not be permitted to render police or fire protection to religious groups. Policemen who helped parishioners into their places of worship would violate the Constitution. Prayers in our legislative halls; the appeals to the Almighty in the message of the Chief Executive; the proclamations making Thanksgiving Day a holiday; "so help me God" in our courtroom oaths—these and all other references to the Almighty that run through our laws, our public rituals, our ceremonies would be flouting the First Amendment. A fastidious atheist or agnostic could even object to the supplication with which the Court opens each session: "God save the United States and this Honorable Court."

We would have to press the concept of separation of Church and State to these extremes to condemn the present law on constitutional grounds. The nullification of this law would have wide and profound effects. A Catholic student applies to his teacher for permission to leave the school during hours on a Holy Day of Obligation to attend a mass. A Jewish student asks his teacher for permission to be excused for Yom Kippur. A Protestant wants the afternoon off for a family baptismal ceremony. In each case the teacher requires parental consent in writing. In each case the teacher, in order to make sure the student is not a truant, goes further and requires a report from the priest, the rabbi, or the minister. The teacher in other words cooperates in a religious program to the extent of making it possible for her students to participate in it. Whether she does it occasionally for a few students, regularly for one, or pursuant to a systematized program designed to further the religious needs of all the students does not alter the character of the act.

We are a religious people whose institutions presuppose a Supreme Being. We guarantee the freedom to worship as one chooses. We make room for as wide a variety of beliefs and creeds as the spiritual needs of man deem necessary. We sponsor an attitude on the part of government that shows no partiality to any one group and that lets each flourish according to the zeal of its adherents and the appeal of its dogma. When the state encourages religious instruction or cooperates with religious authorities by adjusting the schedule of public events to sectarian needs, it follows the best of our traditions. For it then respects the religious nature of our people and accommodates the public service to their spiritual needs. To hold that it may not would be to find in the Constitution a requirement that the government show a callous indifference to religious groups. That would be preferring those who believe in no religion over those who do believe. Government may not finance religious groups nor undertake religious instruction nor blend secular and sectarian education nor use secular institutions to force one or some religion on any person. But we find no constitutional requirement which makes it necessary for government to be hostile to religion and to throw its weight against efforts to widen the effective scope of religious influence. The government must be neutral when it comes to competition between sects. It may not thrust any sect on any person. It may not make a religious observance compulsory. It may not coerce anyone to attend church, to observe a religious holiday, or to take religious instruction. But it can close its doors or suspend its operations as to those who want to repair to their religious sanctuary for worship or instruction. No more than that is undertaken here.

This program may be unwise and improvident from an educational or a community viewpoint. That appeal is made to us on a theory, previously advanced, that each case must be decided on the basis of "our own prepossessions." Our individual preferences, however, are not the constitutional standard. The constitutional standard is the separation of Church and State. The problem, like many problems in constitutional law, is one of degree.

We cannot read into the Bill of Rights such a philosophy of hostility to religion.

Affirmed.

Mr. Justice BLACK, dissenting.

I see no significant difference between the invalid Illinois system and that of New York here sustained.

I am aware that our *McCollum* decision on separation of Church and State has been subjected to a most searching examination throughout the country. Probably few opinions from this Court in recent years have attracted more attention or stirred wider debate.

The Court's validation of the New York system rests in part on its statement that Americans are "a religious people whose institutions presuppose a Supreme Being." This was at least as true when the First Amendment was adopted; and it was just as true when eight Justices of this Court invalidated the released time system in *McCollum* on the premise that a state can no more "aid all religions" than it can aid one. [I]t is only by wholly isolating the state from the religious sphere and compelling it to be completely neutral, that the freedom of each and every domination and of all nonbelievers can be maintained. It is this neutrality the Court abandons today when it treats New York's coercive system as a program which *merely* "encourages religious instruction or cooperates with religious authorities." The abandonment is all the more dangerous to liberty because of the Court's legal exaltation of the orthodox and its derogation of unbelievers.

Under our system of religious freedom, people have gone to their religious sanctuaries not because they feared the law but because they loved their God. Before today, our judicial opinions have refrained from drawing invidious distinctions between those who believe in no religion and those who do believe. The First Amendment has lost much if the religious follower and the atheist are no longer to be judicially regarded as entitled to equal justice under law.

Mr. Justice FRANKFURTER, dissenting.

The pith of the case is that formalized religious instruction is substituted for other school activity which those who do not participate in the released-time program are compelled to attend. The school system is very much in operation during this kind of released time. If its doors are closed, they are closed upon those students who do not attend the religious instruction, in order to keep them within the school. That is the very thing which raises the constitutional issue. It is not met by disregarding it. Failure to discuss this issue does not take it out of the case.

The deeply divisive controversy aroused by the attempts to secure public school pupils for sectarian instruction would promptly end if the advocates of such instruction were content to have the school "close its doors or suspend its operations"—that is, dismiss classes in their entirety, without discrimination—instead of seeking to use the public schools as the instrument for securing attendance at denominational classes. The unwillingness of the promoters of this movement to dispense with such use of the public schools betrays a surprising want of confidence in the inherent power of the various faiths to draw children to outside sectarian classes—an attitude that hardly reflects the faith of the greatest religious spirits.

Mr. Justice JACKSON, dissenting.

As one whose children, as a matter of free choice, have been sent to privately supported Church schools, I may challenge the Court's suggestion that opposition to this plan can only be antireligious, atheistic, or agnostic. My evangelistic brethren confuse an objection to compulsion with an objection to religion. It is possible to hold a faith with enough confidence to believe that what should be rendered to God does not need to be decided and collected by Caesar.

The day that this country ceases to be free for irreligion it will cease to be free for religion—except for the sect that can win political power. The same epithetical jurisprudence used by the Court today to beat down those who oppose pressuring children into some religion can devise as good epithets tomorrow against those who object to pressuring them into a favored religion. And, after all, if we concede to the State power and wisdom to single out "duly constituted religious" bodies as exclusive alternatives for compulsory secular instruction, it would be logical to also uphold the power and wisdom to choose the true faith among those "duly constituted." We start down a rough road when we begin to mix compulsory public education with compulsory godliness.

A number of Justices just short of a majority of the majority that promulgates today's passionate dialectics joined in answering them in *McCollum*. The distinction attempted between that case and this is trivial, almost to the point of cynicism, magnifying its nonessential details and disparaging compulsion which was the underlying reason for invalidity. A reading of the Court's opinion in that case along with its opinion in this case will show such difference of overtones and undertones as to make clear that the *McCollum* case has passed like a storm in a teacup. The wall which the Court was professing to erect between Church and State has become even more warped and twisted than I expected. Today's judgment will be more interesting to students of psychology and of the judicial processes than to students of constitutional law.

Notes

1. What is the basis for the understanding of neutrality Justice Douglas elaborates in *Zorach*? Would the aid for religion have been any less significant if the school had closed down entirely for the *purpose* of allowing children to attend religion classes? Justice Douglas suggests that the New York released time program permissibly "accommodates" religious belief, and describes the opposing approach as "callous indifference." Justice Jackson's dissent describes this juxtaposition as "epithetical jurisprudence." Given the command of the Free Exercise Clause, how *should* a state-run education system accommodate the religious education needs of parents and children?

Zorach is one of very few First Amendment cases in which Justices Black and Douglas disagreed. Professors Ball and Cooper suggest that Black's background led him to remain primarily interested in "develop[ing] a definition of 'establishment.'" Douglas, on the other hand, "was troubled by freedom of religion questions and the difficulty of working out the clash between free-exercise protections and the ban against establishment." Howard Ball and Philip J. Cooper, OF POWER AND RIGHT 229–30 (1991). Black's view is clearly "categorical." How would you describe that of Douglas?

2. The most famous statement in *Zorach*, and one of the most controversial statements in Establishment Clause jurisprudence, is Justice Douglas's statement, "We are a religious people whose institutions presuppose a Supreme Being." In *McGowan v. Maryland*, 366 U.S. 420 (1961), a case upholding Sunday closing laws against a challenge that they violated the Establishment Clause, Justice Douglas explained that his statement in *Zorach* simply meant that the Puritan influence in America "helped shape our constitu-

tional law and our common law." *Id.* at 563 (Douglas, J., dissenting). A year later, in *Engel v. Vitale*, 370 U.S. 421 (1962), while reiterating his statement in *Zorach*, Justice Douglas interpreted it to mean that "[t]he First Amendment leaves the Government in a position not of hostility to religion but of neutrality." *Id.* at 443 (Douglas, J., concurring).

5. Delegation of Government Functions

Larkin v. Grendel's Den, Inc., 459 U.S. 116 (1982)—The Supreme Court struck down a Massachusetts statute granting schools and churches the authority to veto liquor license applications of establishments located within a five hundred foot radius of the school or church. Holding that Jefferson's metaphorical "wall" was "substantially breached by vesting discretionary governmental powers in religious bodies," the Court used the *Lemon* test to examine a number of factors that led it to conclude that the delegation was unconstitutional. Among them were: 1) there were no standards for the exercise of the delegated discretion; 2) there was no guarantee that that the delegated power "will be used exclusively for secular, neutral, and nonideological purposes"; 3) the "mere appearance of a joint exercise of legislative authority by Church and State provides a significant symbolic benefit to religion in the minds of some by reason of the power conferred;" and 4) such a delegation of power impermissibly "enmeshes churches in the processes of government," and thus violates "the core rationale underlying the Establishment Clause[:] "a fusion of governmental and religious functions." *Id.* at 123–127. Justice Rehnquist dissented. In his view, the majority expressly conceded that a flat ban on the sale of liquor within reasonable prescribed distances from churches, schools, hospitals, and similar institutions is a valid exercise of the state's zoning authority, but would be far more restrictive of local businesses than the law invalidated. In his view, a discretionary system whereby local organizations of this type could determine for themselves whether their operations were adversely affected seem "to be the sort of legislative refinement that we should encourage, not forbid in the name of the First Amendment." *Id.* at 128 (Rehnquist, J., dissenting).

Larkin was not the first time a court has ruled that the government had unconstitutionally delegated power to a church. *See State v. Celmer*, 80 N.J. 405, 404 A.2d 1 (1979) (invalidating the delegation of legislative and judicial power to the Ocean Grove Camp Meeting Association of the United Methodist Church). Later cases dealing with the same issue follow *Larkin. See State of Oregon v. City of Rajneeshpuram*, 598 F. Supp. 1208 (1984) (invalidating the grant of a municipal charter to a religious group); *Ran-Dav's County Kosher, Inc. v. State*, 129 N.J. 141, 608 A.2d 1353 (1992), *cert. denied sub nom National Jewish Com'n on Law & Public Affairs (COLPA) v. Ran-Dav's County Kosher, Inc.*, 507 U.S. 952 (1993) (invalidating state kosher regulations because they impose substantive religious standards for kosher products industry and authorize civil enforcement of those standards with the assistance of clergy).

In ***Board of Education of Kiryas Joel Village School District v. Grumet***, 512 U.S. 687 (1994), the Court invalidated a New York statute that created a special public school district, the only function of which was to accommodate the special religious and cultural needs of a group of learning disabled children who were Satmar Hasidim, practitioners of a strict form of Judaism. 1989 N.Y.Laws, ch. 748. The New York Legislature created the special district after a series of events indicating that there was considerable cultural friction between the Village of Kiryas Joel and the surrounding Monroe-Woodbury Central School District.

Like the Amish in *Wisconsin v. Yoder*, the Court recognized that the "residents of Kiryas Joel are vigorously religious people who make few concessions to the modern world and go to great lengths to avoid assimilation into it. They interpret the Torah strictly; segregate the sexes outside the home; speak Yiddish as their primary language; eschew television, radio, and English-language publications; and dress in distinctive ways that include headcoverings and special garments for boys and modest dresses for girls. Children are educated in private religious schools, most boys at the United Talmudic Academy where they receive a thorough grounding in the Torah and limited exposure to secular subjects, and most girls at Bais Rochel, an affiliated school with a curriculum designed to prepare girls for their roles as wives and mothers." Special education services for the children were provided by the Monroe-Woodbury Central School District in an annex to the Village's religious school.

After the Supreme Court decided that public school teachers could not provide services on the premises of religious schools, *Aguilar v. Felton*, 473 U.S. 402 (1985) and *Ball v. School Dist. of Grand Rapids*, 473 U.S. 373 (1985), the Monroe-Woodbury District refused to continue the practice, and the children from Kiryas Joel were forced to take their special education courses in the public school. The experience was not a happy one for either the Satmarer families or the Monroe-Woodbury schools. The Village petitioned for, and the Legislature created, a special school district.

Writing for the Court, Justice David Souter held that the creation of such a school district violated the Establishment Clause because it was "tantamount to an allocation of political power on a religious criterion and neither presupposes nor requires governmental impartiality toward religion."

Though the Court recognized that the facts in *Kiryas Joel* could be distinguished from those in *Larkin* because "the delegation...of civic power [was] the 'qualified voters of the village of Kiryas Joel,' as distinct from a religious leader such as the village rov [chief rabbi], or an institution of religious government like the formally constituted parish council in *Larkin*," it held that "this distinction turns out to lack constitutional significance."

In its view, "the State's manipulation of the franchise for this district limited it to Satmars, giving the sect exclusive control of the political subdivision," and that "the difference between thus vesting state power in the members of a religious group as such instead of the officers of its sectarian organization is one of form, not substance." Though New York did not delegate power by express reference to the religious belief of the Satmar community, the Court held that "the context here persuades us that Chapter 748 effectively identifies these recipients of governmental authority by reference to doctrinal adherence, even though it does not do so expressly."

> Not even the special needs of the children in this community can explain the legislature's unusual Act, for the State could have responded to the concerns of the Satmar parents without implicating the Establishment Clause, as we explain in some detail further on. We therefore find the legislature's Act to be substantially equivalent to defining a political subdivision and hence the qualification for its franchise by a religious test, resulting in a purposeful and forbidden "fusion of governmental and religious functions."

Id. at 702.

Justices Blackmun, Stevens, and Ginsburg concurred, describing the State's response to "parental concern that children suffered 'panic, fear and trauma'...with a solution that affirmatively supports a religious sect's interest in segregating itself and preventing its children from associating with their neighbors." In their view, in "creating a school district that is specifically intended to shield children from contact with others who have 'different ways,' the State provided official support to cement the attachment of young adherents to a particular faith." *Id.* at 711.

Justice O'Connor's opinion concurring in part and concurring in the judgment focused on the tension between the Establishment Clause and the government's desire to accommodate the religious beliefs of its people. Tracing the history of the difficulties between the communities, she emphasized that New York had several ways in which it could have accommodated the special needs of the Satmarer children, and that "the Religion Clauses—the Free Exercise Clause, the Establishment Clause, the Religious Test Clause, Art. VI, cl. 3, and the Equal Protection Clause as applied to religion—all speak with one voice on this point: Absent the most unusual circumstances, one's religion ought not affect one's legal rights or duties or benefits." *Id.* at 715. In her view, "[t]here is nothing improper about a legislative intention to accommodate a religious group, so long as it is implemented through generally applicable legislation."

Justice Kennedy's concurring opinion, by contrast, focused on the shortcomings of the main opinions. In his view,

> the Court's opinion can be interpreted to say that an accommodation for a particular religious group is invalid because of the risk that the legislature will not grant the same accommodation to another religious group suffering some similar burden. This rationale seems to me without grounding in our precedents and a needless restriction upon the legislature's ability to respond to the unique problems of a particular religious group. The real vice of the school district, in my estimation, is that New York created it by drawing political boundaries on the basis of religion. I would decide the issue we confront upon this narrower theory, though in accord with many of the Court's general observations about the State's actions in this case.

Id. at 722.

For the dissenters, Justices Scalia, Thomas and Chief Justice Rehnquist, the fact that the Kiryas Joel Village School District was a *public* school should have disposed of the Establishment Clause issue.

> If a State can furnish services to a group of sectarian students on a neutral site adjacent to a private religious school, or even *within* such a school, how can there be any defect in educating those same students in a public school? As the Court noted in *Wolman* [*v. Walter*], the constitutional dangers of establishment arise "from the nature of the institution, not from the nature of the pupils." There is no danger in educating religious students in a public school.

Id. at 733–34.

In their view, Justice Souter's majority opinion, "steamroll[ed] the difference between civil authority held by a church, and civil authority held by members of a church," and ignored the long history of legislative and constitutional accommodations for particular religious groups.

> When a legislature acts to accommodate religion, particularly a minority sect, "it follows the best of our traditions." *Zorach.* The Constitution itself contains an accommodation of sorts. Article VI, cl. 3, prescribes that executive, legisla-

> tive and judicial officers of the Federal and State Governments shall bind themselves to support the Constitution "by Oath or Affirmation." Although members of the most populous religions found no difficulty in swearing an oath to God, Quakers, Moravians, and Mennonites refused to take oaths based on Matthew 5:34's injunction "swear not at all." The option of affirmation was added to accommodate these minority religions and enable their members to serve in government.

Id. at 744.

Notes

1. Shortly after the Court's decision, and in response to it, the New York legislature passed two bills, both of which Governor Mario Cuomo signed. One repealed Chapter 748, the law held unconstitutional by the Court in *Grumet*, 1994 N.Y. Ass'y Bill 12229 (signed July 6, 1994), and the other, Chapter 241 of the 1994 Laws of New York, authorized municipalities to create school districts when required by the educational interests of the community. 1994 N.Y. Ass'y Bill 12230 (signed July 6, 1994). Within a month of the Supreme Court's decision, a new Kiryas Joel Union Free School District had been created. Shortly thereafter, the law permitting the creation of new school districts by municipalities was challenged on Establishment Clause grounds. The New York Supreme Court, the state's trial court, held the act constitutional after a *Lemon* analysis, but its ruling was later reversed on appeal. *See Grumet v. Cuomo*, 164 Misc.2d 644, 625 N.Y.S.2d 1000 (N.Y. Sup. Ct. 1995), *rev'd* 225 A.D.2d 4, 647 N.Y.S. 2d 565 (3d Dept. 1996), *aff'd*, *Grumet v. Cuomo*, 659 N.Y. 57, 69, 681 N.Y.S. 2d 173, 681 N.E. 2d 340 (1997).

2. Justice Souter, like all of the Justices before him, acknowledges that one of the crucial goals of the Court's Establishment Clause jurisprudence is achieving neutrality. Because this "benefit flows to a single sect," the statute cannot be held neutral. Can a distinction be made in this case that the benefits flow to children who are all members of a single sect rather than to the sect itself? Is this tenable, or a merely formal distinction? There was no dispute in *Kiryas Joel* that the children had been exposed to a hostile environment; the issue was how to solve that problem. In the administrative state, how should the Court analyze whether state benefits permissibly aid children who are religious or impermissibly aid the religion of the children? Can it?

In *Wisconsin v. Yoder*, the Supreme Court determined that the Amish enjoyed a Free Exercise right to an exemption from Wisconsin's mandatory attendance school law. Should the Satmar Hasidim, whose way of life bears striking similarities to the Amish, be treated in the same way as the Amish? If the Amish had been granted an exemption from Wisconsin's mandatory attendance law, and this law was challenged by one who claimed that such a law violated the Establishment Clause, would the statute be constitutional under the reasoning of *Grumet*? Is the difference a difference of active involvement between religion and government rather than passive acquiescence by the state of religious actions? Is a categorical distinction between passive and active relationships an acceptable approach in an age of balancing?

3. The language of happenstance is used to justify conclusions in the majority opinion by Justice Souter and the dissenting opinion by Justice Scalia. Justice Souter writes, "That individuals who *happen to be* religious may hold public office does not mean that a state may deliberately delegate discretionary power to an individual in-

stitution or community on the grounds of religious identity." (emphasis added.) Justice Scalia writes, "The proper analogy to chapter 748 is not the Court's hypothetical law providing school buses only to Christian students, but a law providing extra buses to rural school districts (which *happen to be* predominantly Southern Baptist)." (emphasis added.) Similar language can be found in Justice O'Connor's opinion: "A [school] district created under a generally applicable scheme would be acceptable even though it coincides with a village which was consciously created by its voters as an enclave for their religious group." Chapter One recounts that Justice Felix Frankfurter used the same language when he stated, "I was not a Jewish professor at the Harvard Law School, but I was a Harvard Law School professor who happened to be a Jew." Harlan Phillips, FELIX FRANKFURTER REMINISCES 37 (1960). Does the use of happenstance suggest a disassociation between the individual and his status as a religious believer; that is, as something irrelevant both to the individuals involved as well as to the legal issues to be decided? In Frankfurter's case, the language of coincidence is the language of the accident of birth. That is possibly the case in Justice Scalia's analogy as well—if the children are considered Baptists only because their parents are Baptists. Does Justice Souter's opinion use the phrase in the same way?

4. Is Justice Scalia's complaint that *Larkin* is inapposite to *Kiryas Joel* persuasive? Is Justice Souter's attempt to analogize the two cases by focusing on their similarities rather than their formal differences a more convincing approach? Is the Village of Kiryas Joel a "church"?

5. Justice O'Connor wrote "[t]hat the government is acting to accommodate religion should generally not change this analysis. What makes accommodation permissible, even praiseworthy, is not that the government is making life easier for some particular religious group as such. Rather, it is that the government is accommodating a deeply held belief." Does this explanation of accommodation adequately distinguish permissible accommodation from impermissible government endorsement of religion? By stating that the "government is accommodating a deeply held belief," and thus not modifying "belief" with the word "religious," is Justice O'Connor raising the level of generality to the point where the fact that the belief is religious is irrelevant? Is it necessary to do so because the Court, since *Everson,* has interpreted the Establishment Clause to forbid favoritism of religion over nonreligion? Does such an effort diminish the specifically religious beliefs of those who are accommodated? Recall that in *County of Allegheny*, Justice O'Connor also avoided using the word "religious" when she concluded that the placement of a Christmas tree, a menorah and a sign saluting liberty was justified as promoting pluralism. Justice Brennan strenuously objected to this omission, which he suggested indicated an implicit and impermissible favoritism of religion over nonreligion.

6. Religious Associations & the Public Purse

a) Exemptions

In the introduction to Chapter Nine, in which we discuss the subject tax policy affecting churches and religious associations in great detail, we note that the conventional wisdom has it that "churches do not pay taxes." It is also generally assumed that all tax exemptions are "subsidies." A good lawyer or accountant, by contrast, will report that the answer to both of these questions "depends" on character of the tax, the type of organization, the types of activity in which it engages, the types of property it holds and uses, whom they employ, and a host of other factors defined by the law governing a particular tax or taxing jurisdiction.

Generally speaking, taxes are mandatory charges imposed by law on a specified "subject": an individual, property, or an activity, and they are measured by a formula set by the legislature. Thus, when we speak of an "income tax," the *subject* of the tax is generally income-producing *activity*, and the amount of the tax is measured by the amount defined by the law as "income." The same analysis holds true for property taxes, excise and sales taxes, or taxes on specified transactions such as land transfers or imports.

Taxes are creatures of statute. Exemptions, by contrast, can be embedded in the structure of the tax, written into the tax law, or derived from the constitution. *See, e.g.*, U.S. Const., art. I, § 9 cl. 5–6 (1787) (requiring uniformity); Pa. Const. art. VIII, § 2(a)(v) (exempting "institutions of purely public charity"). In order to ascertain the impact of the Religious Liberty Guarantee on a specific tax policy or program, one must first become familiar with the theory, law, and practice governing the administration of the tax in question.

There is very little in the case law of the Religious Liberty Guarantee that *requires* the exemption of churches or religious organizations. *Cf. Minneapolis Star & Tribune Co. v. Minnesota Commissioner of Revenue*, 460 U.S. 575 (1983), and one case that seems to indicate that there are times when they may be forbidden. *See Texas Monthly v. Bullock*, 489 U.S. 1 (1989), excerpted in Chapter Nine § E(5). There is, however, a substantial body of case law that leaves the matter to the discretion of the legislature. *See, e.g., Jimmy Swaggart Ministries v. Board of Equalization of California*, 493 U.S. 378 (1990) (churches may be compelled to collect and remit state sales taxes); *United States v. Lee*, 455 U.S. 252 (1982) (Free Exercise Clause does not require tax exemption), both excerpted in Chapter Nine; *Walz v. Tax Comm'n*, 397 U.S. 664 (1970), excerpted in § E(3), above.

b) Schools, Churches, and Other Religiously-Affiliated Organizations

Most of the jurisprudence of the incorporated Establishment Clause developed in litigation over the role of religion in schools. Dubbed "The School Question" in the late nineteenth century, the constitutionality of public support for religious education in both public and private schools has a long and interesting history in the United States and abroad. It has been an issue at the State level from colonial times, and at the federal level since the 1870s. Background materials are provided in Chapters Three, Four, and Six §§ A–D. Comparative law materials are referenced in Chapter Six § F. Key federal and state cases dealing specifically with school finance are excerpted and summarized in Chapter Six § F. The rules governing the eligibility of churches and other religious organizations to participate in generally available public programs rest on the same cases and principles. *See, e.g., Bowen v. Kendrick*, 487 U.S. 589 (1988); *Tilton v. Richardson*, 403 U.S. 672, 682 (1971); *Columbia Union College v. Oliver*, 254 F.3d 496 (4th Cir. 2001).

From the perspective of the *government*, "support" for churches and religious associations is best understood as a continuum. At one end of the spectrum are "inherently religious" uses such as the costs associated with worship and the acquisition of sacred texts. At the other end of the spectrum are "non-religious" (or "secular") uses, such as the "ordinary and necessary" expenses associated with providing a community soup kitchen, hospital, day-care center, or school. Some religious groups share this orientation, and can draw a line between their "religious" and "secular" activities. For others, however, there is no distinction. *All* activities are part and parcel of their organization's religious identity and mission. For policy makers, then, the primary problem is to write a set of generally applicable criteria that define the characteristics and qualifications of individuals, associations, or projects eligible to participate in a publicly financed program or activity.

The Supreme Court has been unanimous with respect to subsidies of inherently religious uses: they are forbidden. It has been equally consistent in its approach to the participation by churches and religious institutions in public welfare programs: they are eligible to participate on the same terms as others. *See, e.g., Bowen v. Kendrick* 487 U.S. 589 (1988); *Hunt v. McNair*, 413 U.S. 734 (1973) ("Whatever may be its initial appeal, the proposition that the Establishment Clause prohibits any program which in some manner aids an institution with a religious affiliation has consistently been rejected."). Virtually all of the debate has centered on the need to assure that public funds will support only activities that fall on the "secular" side of the line. *See, e.g., Mitchell v. Helms*, 530 U.S. 793, 820–825 (2000) (discussing the claim that "aid to religious schools [must] not be impermissibly religious in nature or be divertible to religious use."); *Lemon v. Kurtzman*, 403 U.S. 602, 619 (1971) ("The State must be certain, given the Religion Clauses, that subsidized teachers do not inculcate religion.")

There are two possible approaches to such a fact-finding inquiry. The first is to require direct evidence that the recipient of public funds is using them for a "specifically religious activity" such as worship or religious teaching. This was the approach taken by the six of the Justices in *Mitchell v. Helms* : the plurality opinion of Justices Thomas, Scalia, Kennedy and Chief Justice Rehnquist, and the concurring opinion of Justices O'Connor and Breyer.

The second approach is to presume that the aid will support specifically religious activity where the nature of the institution is such that separating its "specifically religious" and non-religious activities would be impossible. This was the approach taken by the Court from *Lemon* until *Agostini,* and is the preferred approach of the dissenters in *Mitchell v. Helms*, Justices Souter, Stevens and Ginsburg.

> Aid normally may be thought to have a primary effect of advancing religion when it flows to an institution in which religion is so pervasive that a substantial portion of its functions are subsumed in the religious mission or when it funds a specifically religious activity in an otherwise substantially secular setting. *Hunt v. McNair*, 413 U.S. at 743.

The case law uses the term *pervasively sectarian* to describe such institutions, and assumes that the religious and secular aspects of their activities are so "inextricably intertwined" that aid to the secular activity "inescapably" supports the religious one. *Wolman v. Walter*, 433 U.S. 229, 250 (1977). Until *Mitchell v. Helms*, a finding that the institution was "pervasively sectarian" eliminated its eligibility to participate. After *Mitchell v. Helms*, participation is possible, but by no means assured.

In *Mitchell,* Justices O'Connor and Breyer expressly joined the four-Justice plurality in a decision to overrule *Wolman v. Walter. Mitchell*, 530 U.S. at 837 (O'Connor and Breyer, JJ. concurring in the judgment). They suggested that three factors should guide a court's determination concerning the eligibility of religious education programs: 1) neutrality of criteria for participating in the aid program; 2) no actual use of government funds for religious purposes; and 3) a caution that "presumptions of religious indoctrination" inherent in the pervasively sectarian analysis "are normally inappropriate when evaluating neutral school-aid programs under the Establishment Clause." *Id.* at 858. The four-Justice plurality, by contrast, found the "pervasively sectarian" inquiry "offensive" and suggested that it should be "buried now." In their view, courts should not be "trolling though a person's or institution's religious beliefs" as a precondition for their participation in public welfare programs. They also noted that the term "sectarian" has acquired a pejorative meaning with roots in the 1870s, described by the plurality as "a time of pervasive hostility to the Catholic Church and to Catholics in general[. I]t was an open secret that 'sectarian' was code for 'Catholic.'" *Mitchell*, 530 U.S. at 827 (plurality opinion), *citing* Green, *The Blaine Amendment Reconsidered*, 36 Am. J. Legal Hist. 38 (1992). *See generally* Richard A. Baer, Jr., *The Supreme Court's Discriminatory Use of the Term "Sectarian,"* 6 J.L. & Pol. 449 (1990).

Because fragmented decisions such as *Mitchell* are not uncommon, the Court held in *Marks v. United States*, 430 U.S. 188, 193 (1977) that

> When a fragmented Court decides a case and no single rationale explaining the result enjoys the assent of five Justices, 'the holding of the Court may be viewed as that position taken by those Members who concurred in the judgments on the narrowest grounds....' *Gregg v. Georgia*, 428 U.S. 153, 169 n.15 (1976).

The resulting "rule of the case" in *Mitchell* is therefore the three-part factual inquiry suggested by Justices O'Connor and Breyer:

1. Are the criteria for participating in the aid program neutral, both on their face and as applied?
2. Has the party invoking the Establishment Clause proved the actual use or diversion of public funds or property for religious purposes? and
3. Is there any evidence to support a finding that the nature of the institution makes it inevitable that aid to the secular activity will also support its specifically religious activities?

Accord Columbia Union College v. Oliver, 254 F.3d 496 (4th Cir. 2001) (state was unable to make the required showing of actual diversion because Columbia Union had received no money); *DeStefano v. Emergency Housing Group, Inc.*, 247 F.3d 397 (2nd Cir., 2001) (plaintiff was required to prove the level of employee involvement in Alcoholics Anonymous, which, for purposes of the Establishment Clause was treated as a "religion"); *Doe v. Beaumont Indep. Sch. Dist.*, 240 F.3d 462 (5th Cir. 2001) (The District Court "can and should examine the targeted program in its full context, viewing it as it actually operates in its setting, including other programs similar in purpose and functions.").

Zelman v. Simmons-Harris, 122 S.Ct. 2460 (2002), excerpted in Chapter 6 §F(2), confirms that the Court will no longer assume that the funding of religious institutions, including schools, is a violation of the Establishment Clause. The "full context" must be examined, and specific findings must be entered regarding both the neutrality of the government's selection criteria, and the actual use of the funds. If there are other facts that would be relevant to the court's inquiry regarding a specific institutional recipient, the burden of proof is on the party raising the Establishment Clause objection.

F. The Religious Liberty Guarantee and the Ban on Religious Tests

> ". . [N]o religious Test shall ever be required as a Qualification to any Office or public Trust under the United States."
>
> U.S. Const. Art VI cl. 3 (1789)

The No Religious Test Clause of Article VI is the only explicit guarantee of religious freedom contained in the original Constitution. It is also the Nation's first law prohibiting religion-based discrimination employment and public contracting. State constitutions have similar provisions. *See, e.g.*, Colo. Const., art. VIII, §5 (2001) ("No religious test or qualification shall ever be required of any person as a condition of admission into any public educational institution of the state, either as a teacher or student . . ."); Utah Const. art. I, §4 (2001) ("no religious test shall be required as a qualification for any office of public trust or for any vote at any election; nor shall any person be incompetent as a witness or juror on account of religious belief or the absence thereof."). We examine the Test Clause in detail in Chapter Eight §G ("The Government Workplace"), and only a few key points need be mentioned here.

The most obvious—and historic—form of religious test was the oath required under the Act of Supremacy, 26 Hen. VIII, c. 1 §8 (1534). Codified in "An Act to restore to the Crown the ancient Jurisdiction over the Estate Ecclesiastical and Spiritual, and abolishing all foreign Powers repugnant to the same," 1 Eliz., ch. 1, §§1, 18 (1558), the impact of the English Test Oath was immortalized in Robert Bolt's portrait of Sir Thomas More in *A Man for All Seasons* (1962). The Act is reprinted in Documents Illustrative of English Church History, at 243 ff. (H. Gee & W. Hardy eds. 1921). In most instances, however, a "religious test" is simply a device that screens out those whose religious beliefs or practices, including the taking of oaths, are thought, for reasons of policy or prejudice, to be undesirable.

Given the large numbers of persons employed at the federal, state, and local levels of government, and the large number of projects funded in whole or in part though government contracts and grants, the Test Clause is an under-appreciated tool in the arsenal of those who wish to participate in government programs, but feel that they have been excluded because of discrimination on the basis of religion.

An inquiry under the Test Clause has several parts. The practice must be:

- A religious test
- Used as a Qualification for;
- Any Office or public Trust under the United States.

See Chapter Eight §G(1).

Most religious tests are prohibited in government employment by the operation of Title VII of the Civil Rights Act or its counterparts in state law. In situations where the relationship of the individual to the government is not one of "employer-employee" under Title VII or relevant state employment law—as in the case of a potential a government contractor or grant recipient, the Test Clause is both relevant, and possibly controlling.

The case law discussing the Test Clause is sparse. *See, e.g.*, *Girouard v. United States*, 328 U.S. 61 (1946) (relying in part on the Test Clause as a guide for construing the obligation of an applicant for naturalization to swear to "defend" the United States, though it was not directly applicable); *Ex parte Garland*, 71 U.S. (4 Wall.) 333 (1866) (distinguishing a Test Oath from other forms of oath taking).

The Supreme Court has decided two cases that *would have* raised issues under the Test Clause had they involved federal offices. *McDaniel v. Paty*, 435 U.S. 618 (1978), *rev'g Paty v. McDaniel*, 547 S.W.2d 897 (Tenn. 1977) (holding unconstitutional a Tennessee constitutional provision excluding ministers of the gospel from the state legislature), excerpted in Chapter Ten; *Torcaso v. Watkins*, 367 U.S. 488 (1961) (holding unconstitutional a state constitutional provision which prohibited religious tests for public office, "other than a declaration of belief in the existence of God"), excerpted in Chapter Eleven. Because both cases involved State offices, the Court applied the incorporated First Amendment. As a result, it is difficult to state with any degree of certainty whether or not the Test Clause forms a part of the religious liberty guarantees "incorporated" *via* the Fourteenth Amendment, or stands alone as a limit on federal power only. In *Torcaso v. Watkins*, Justice Black's opinion expressly stated that the Court "[found] it unnecessary to consider [the] contention that this provision applies to state as well as federal offices," *Torcaso*, 367 U.S. at 489 n.1. Notwithstanding this statement, some commentators are of the opinion that it has been incorporated "in effect." *See* Gerard V. Bradley, *The No Religious Test Clause and the Constitution of Religious Liberty: A Machine that Has Gone of Itself*, 37 Case W. Res. L. Rev. 674, 718 (1987) ("*Torcaso*, if it is to be grasped at all, affects an 'incorporation' of article VI as much as if the Court expressly said so."). *See generally* Michael W. McConnell, *The Origins and Historical Understanding of Free Exercise of Religion*, 103 Harv. L. Rev. 1410 (1990).

What impact, if any, should the No Religious Test Clause have on the Court's understanding of the Religion Clause of the First Amendment? Justice O'Connor's "endorsement analysis" rests, in part, on her view that one's religion should not be relevant to one's standing in the political community. Does the No Religious Test Clause make the same point? How relevant is the No Religious Test Clause in cases involving federal aid to public welfare programs run by religious organizations? How would you construct the argument? In cases involving State laws, is the imposition of a religious test for a "public trust" such as a government contract a violation of the Establishment Clause, the Free Exercise Clause, or both?

G. Freedom of Religious Speech & Press

> "Congress shall make no law...abridging the freedom of speech, or of the press..."
>
> U.S. Const. amend I (1789)

Even were the two concepts not inextricably intertwined in the First Amendment, religious liberty and freedom of speech and of the press would go hand-in-hand. *Compare Cantwell v. Connecticut*, 310 U.S. 296 (1940)(reversing criminal conviction for activities related to prosyletization) *with Kokkinakis v. Greece*, (1994) 17 E.H.R.R. 397 (European Ct. Human Rts.) (same, under European Convention on Human Rights). For some, the "First Freedom" is religious liberty, because it is in the realm of conscience and ethics that individuals and groups formulate conceptions of "the good" that will later be translated into the ideas, words, and phrases that animate political action. For others, it is freedom of speech and the press, because these two rights make it possible to mobilize the political community to protect all of the others.

Most cases arising under the Speech and Press Clause involve a careful examination of the government's interest in regulating the content or perspective of the written or spoken word. Others discuss the government's interest in regulating "expressive conduct," "expressive association," and the right *not* to speak, to publish, or otherwise to associate with ideas one finds abhorrent. Chart 5-5 provides applies the general principles of characterization to freedom of religious speech and press. Bear in mind as you examine the chart, that the character of the right ("religious speech and press") will depend on how the nature of its subject ("religion") is characterized.

Chart 5-5
Characterizing the Rights of Religious Speech and Press

	Speech & Press
Abstract	Personal autonomy.
(high level)	Non-association with disagreeable messages.
↓	Freedom to learn about religious ideas.
Level	Access to religious information and ideas.
of	Freedom of inquiry, information, and media.
Generality	Freedom to communicate religious ideas.
	Freedom of religious expression and ritual.
↑	Communication of religious ideas or perspectives through symbolic representations.
Specific	Personal speech or publication of religious perspectives on any legitimate subject.
(low level)	Personal speech or publication about religion, including prayer and prosyletization.

The cases excerpted or discussed in this section can be characterized as "hybrids": they involve both religious liberty *and* freedom of speech and press.

1. A Note on Analysis under the Speech & Press Clause

The corpus of law developed by the United States Supreme Court under the Speech and Press Clause is enormous, but the principles of law embodied in the case law reflects focus on one basic question: *What is the nature and extent of the government's interest in regulating the time, place, manner, content, or perspective the written or spoken word, or of other forms of expressive activity?*

The Court does not answer this question directly. Rather, it first decides whether the particular speech is "protected" or "unprotected." Within the "unprotected" category are communicative activities that fall clearly within the government's regulatory authority, such as libel, fraud, copyright, and incitement to violent crime. Speech or publication that falls within the "protected" category can also be regulated, but the scope of the government's authority to do so depends upon its ability to prove that either the setting, or the risk of a specific harm, requires regulation in the public interest. *See generally* Eugene Volokh, The First Amendment: Problems, Cases & Policy Arguments (2001). When the government *itself* is either the speaker, or the purchaser of services where third parties speak on its behalf or on behalf of others, the questions presented are not properly understood as involving the government's interest in "regulation," but rather its own interests in controlling the content of its own messages, image, or associations. *See also* Chapter Six § D(4) ("The State as Educator"), Chapter Eight § G ("The Government Workplace"); Chapter Nine § E(3) ("Subsidy Theory").

In the cases excerpted below, we examine the government's authority to regulate or control the dissemination of "messages" that are religious in content, perspective, or character. Because the general "test" for constitutionality in a speech and press context is the "compelling state interest" standard of review, we begin with a set of questions common to all cases arising under the Speech and Press Clause.

1. What is the subject and character of the speech, publication, or other form of communication? [*i.e.* Is the speech "protected" or "unprotected"?]
2. What is the setting in which the speech, publication, or other form of communication occurs? [*i.e.* What is the government's interest in asserting or protecting control of the forum?]
3. What laws or constitutional provisions serve as the source of the government's power to regulate either the communication itself, or the setting in which it takes place?
4. What, specifically, does the applicable law permit or forbid?
5. What constitutional provisions support the rationale used by the government to restrict the exercise of rights protected by the Speech & Press Clause or its counterparts under state law?
6. What facts, if any support the government's position?

The Court's conclusions concerning the "constitutional fact" in issue—whether a "compelling state interest" exists under these circumstances—will depend upon the answers to these questions.

2. Religious Speech in Public Fora

There are two types of public fora: "traditional public fora" such as parks, sidewalks, and the capitol grounds, and "limited public fora," such as civic auditoria, schools, and other public facilities made available for the use of the public. In the case of the traditional public forum, the government's interests are limited to preserving order through generally applicable "time, place and manner" restrictions. In the case of a "limited public forum," the scope of the public license to use the facility is defined by the statute or regulation that opens it for public use.

In *Capitol Square Review and Advisory Bd. v. Pinette*, 515 U.S. 753 (1995), summarized below, the Ohio Capitol Square was a traditional public forum where unattended public displays were permitted, but governed by generally applicable permit requirements. In *Good News Club v. Milford Central School*, 533 U.S. 98 (2001), summarized after *Pinette*, the parties agreed that the forum at issue was a "limited public forum," the parameters of which were defined by New York Law and School Board regulations.

Capitol Square Review and Advisory Bd. v. Pinette, 515 U.S. 753 (1995)—On the same day in November 1993 that the Capitol Square Review and Advisory Board granted a rabbi permission to place a menorah celebrating Hanukkah on the grounds of the Capitol Squire adjacent to the state capitol building in Columbus, a member of the Ohio Ku Klux Klan applied for permission to erect a cross on the lawn across from it. The Klan's display was to run from December 8 through December 23. The Board denied the permit on the advice of legal counsel. Shortly thereafter, Pinette, the Ohio Klan's leader, successfully sought an injunction requiring the Board to issue the permit. The United States Court of Appeals for the Sixth Circuit affirmed. A majority of the Supreme Court concluded that the unattended display of a privately owned cross in a public park during the Christmas holiday season did not violate the Establishment Clause. Citing, among other cases, *Widmar v. Vincent* and *Lamb's Chapel,* summarized below, the majority concluded that the Court's prior cases "establish[] that private religious speech, far from being a First Amendment orphan, is as fully protected under the Free Speech Clause as secular private expression." *Id.* at 760.

Writing for a four-Justice plurality, Justice Scalia rejected the application of an "endorsement" analysis to private religious speech, and concluded that "[r]eligious expression cannot violate the Establishment Clause where it (1) is purely private and (2) occurs in a traditional or designated public forum, publicly announced and open to all on equal terms." *Id.* at 768. Concurring in part and concurring in the judgment, Justice O'Connor observed that the central question in the case was whether "the State's relationship to [private expression] violates the Establishment Clause." In her view, it is not only *possible* for "a neutral state policy toward private religious speech in a public forum" to violate the Establishment Clause, it is the Court's "*duty* to hold the practice invalid" when the government permits private speech to occur in a setting where a reasonable observer could conclude that the government is "endorsing religion or any particular creed." *Id.* at 772–777 (O'Connor, Souter & Breyer, JJ., concurring in part and concurring in the judgment).

Justices Stevens and Ginsburg dissented. Justice Ginsburg's approach was direct: "If the aim of the Establishment Clause is genuinely to uncouple government from church, see *Everson*, a State may not permit, and a court may not order, a display of this character." *Id.* at 817. Justice Stevens, by contrast, rejected a *per se* rule of exclusion in favor of a fact-based approach: "The Establishment Clause should be construed to create a strong presumption against the installation of unattended religious symbols on public property." *Id.* at 797. He agreed that an endorsement analysis is appropriate when private speech is challenged under the Establishment Clause, but would apply a lower standard of proof than Justices O'Connor, Souter and Breyer: "I think it is enough that *some* reasonable observers would attribute a religious message to the State." *Id.* at 807 (Stevens, J., dissenting)(emphasis in the original). In his view, "the sequence of sectarian displays disclosed by the record in this case illustrates the importance of rebuilding the 'wall of separation between church and State' that Jefferson envisioned." *Id.*

Given the fractured nature of the Court's judgment in *Pinette*, it is important to understand the rationale of the Justices who concurred on the "narrowest grounds." Because four Justices held that the endorsement test should be applied, and four held that it should not be, it appears that the "narrowest ground" for the judgment is the Court's reading of the facts under the standards applicable to Speech and Press Clause cases. All nine Justices agree that "compliance with the Establishment Clause is a state interest sufficiently compelling to justify content-based restrictions on speech," Id. at 761–762 (plurality opinion), and eight agreed that any content or perspective based manipulation of the access rules governing the public forum would be relevant to its determination of whether the government had *administered the forum* in a manner that violated the Establishment Clause. Because the factions in the plurality also split evenly over whether the State must take steps to *disassociate* itself from a private party's religious message in a fairly administered public forum, perhaps the most that can be said about *Pinette* is that a majority agreed that *this particular display* did not violate the Establishment Clause. *Compare id.* at 769 (plurality opinion) ("[T]he State may not, on the claim of misperception of official endorsement, ban all private religious speech from the public square, or discriminate against it by requiring religious speech alone to disclaim public sponsorship." *with id.* at 776–780 (opinion of O'Connor, Souter, and Breyer, JJ.) ("To the plurality's consideration of the open nature of the forum and the private ownership of the display, however, I would add the presence of a sign disclaiming government sponsorship or endorsement on the Klan cross, which would make the State's role clear to the community.... The reasonable observer would recognize the distinction between speech the government supports and speech that it merely allows in a place that traditionally has been open to a range of private speakers accompanied, if necessary, by an appropriate disclaimer.").

Good News Club v. Milford Central School, 533 U.S. 98, 121 S.Ct. 2093 (2001), is also discussed Chapter Six § B. The Court held (6-3) that the Milford Central School violated the Speech and Press Clause when it created a limited public forum by opening its school building for use by the residents of the community after the close of the school day. Among the uses permitted by both school board policy and New York State law were "instruction in any branch of education, learning or the arts," and "social, civic and recreational meetings and entertainment events, and other uses pertaining to the welfare of the community, provided that such uses shall be nonexclusive and shall be opened to the general public." In accordance with the Board's stated policy, the Good News Club, "a private Christian organization for children ages 6 to 12... submitted a request to [the] interim superintendent of the district, in which they sought permission to hold the Club's weekly after school meetings in the school cafeteria." *Id.,* 121 S.Ct. at 2098. Attorneys for the Good News Club described its activities as follows:

> The club opens its session with Ms. Fournier taking attendance. As she calls a child's name, if the child recites a Bible verse the child receives a treat. After attendance, the Club sings songs. Next Club members engage in games that involve, *inter alia,* learning Bible verses. Ms. Fournier then relates a Bible story and explains how it applies to Club members' lives. The Club closes with prayer. Finally, Ms. Fournier distributes treats and the Bible verses for memorization.

Id. The Superintendent denied the request because "the kinds of activities proposed to be engaged in by the Good News Club were not a discussion of secular subjects such as child rearing, development of character and development of morals from a religious perspective, but were in fact the equivalent of religious instruction itself." The Milford Board of Education affirmed the Superintendent's judgment in a resolution rejecting the Club's request to use the Milford School facilities "for the purpose of conducting religious instruction and Bible study." *Id.*

Writing for the Court in an opinion joined by the Chief Justice and Justices Scalia, O'Connor, and Kennedy, Justice Thomas observed that because there was no dispute that the state had created a "limited public forum," the questions before the Court were: 1) "[W]hether Milford Central School violated the free speech rights of the Good News Club when it excluded the Club from meeting after hours at the school", and 2) "whether any such violation is justified by Milford's concern that permitting the Club's activities would violate the Establishment Clause."

Concluding that "that Milford's restriction violates the Club's free speech rights," *Id.,* 121 S. Ct. at 2097, the Court applied the general rule that the determination concerning the constitutionality of a State's excluding "a private speaker from use of a public forum depend on the nature of the forum." *Id.* at 2099, citing *Perry Ed. Assn. v. Perry Local Educators' Assn.*, 460 U.S. 37, 44 (1983). Relying on its holdings in *Rosenberger v. Rector and Visitors of Univ. of Va.*, 515 U.S. 819, 829 (1995) and *Lamb's Chapel v. Center Moriches Union Free School Dist.*, 508 U.S. 384 (1993), discussed below, the Court found that "any group that 'promote[s] the moral and character development of children' is eligible to use the school building." The Good News Club was excluded even though an examination of the content of its activities demonstrated that the "Club sought to address a subject otherwise permitted under the rule, the teaching of morals and character, from a religious standpoint." *Id.* 121 S. Ct. at 2101. The "exclusion of the Club on the basis of its religious perspective" was therefore "unconstitutional viewpoint discrimination." *Id.* 121 S. Ct. at 2100 n.2.

For the dissenters in *Good News Club*, the critique of the majority's approach begins with the level of generality chosen to describe the type of speech involved. *See* Chapter One §A, Chart 1-1, on page 14 and Chart 5-5, on page 346, above. In the view of the dissenters, there is a difference between speech about secular subjects from a religious viewpoint, and speech that is an integral part of religious practice, ritual, prosyletization, or evangelism. Justice Stevens' dissent draws the distinctions as follows:

> Speech for "religious purposes" may reasonably be understood to encompass three different categories. First, there is religious speech that is simply speech about a particular topic from a religious point of view. Second, there is religious speech that amounts to worship, or its equivalent. Third, there is an intermediate category that is aimed principally at proselytizing or inculcating belief in a particular religious faith.... The novel question that this case presents concerns the constitutionality of a public school's attempt to limit the scope of a public forum it has created. *More specifically, the question is whether a school can, consistently with the First Amendment, create a limited public forum that admits the first type of religious speech without allowing the other two.*

Id. at 2112–2113 (Stevens, J., dissenting) (emphasis added). Justice Souter's dissent agrees that these are real distinctions, and takes the majority to task for not grappling with them directly: "The majority avoids [the problem that this is a worship service that calls for religious conversion of the participants] only by resorting to the bland and general characterization of Good News's activity as 'teaching of morals and character, from a religious standpoint.'" *Id.* at 2117 (Souter & Ginsburg, JJ., dissenting). Justice Stevens agrees: "[T]he majority elides the distinction between religious speech on a particular topic and religious speech that seeks primarily to inculcate belief." *Id.* at 2114 n.3.

The majority, by contrast, simply "disagree[d] that something that is 'quintessentially religious' or 'decidedly religious in nature' cannot also be characterized properly as the teaching of morals and character development from a particular viewpoint."

> What matters for purposes of the Free Speech Clause is that we can see no logical difference in kind between the invocation of Christianity by the Club and the invocation of teamwork, loyalty, or patriotism by other associations to provide a foundation for their lessons. It is apparent that the unstated principle... that any time religious instruction and prayer are used to discuss morals and character, the discussion is simply not a "pure" discussion of those issues.

Id. at 2102 (majority opinion).

The Votes in *Good News Club* indicate that the Justices take the following positions concerning the use of the Establishment Clause as a defense in public forum cases:

Chief Justice Rehnquist & Justices Scalia, O'Connor, Kennedy & Thomas	When the limited forum is public and fairly administered, the Establishment Clause is not a defense to a charge of content or viewpoint discrimination.
Justice Breyer	Neutrality is only one factor to be examined in a speech case with Establishment Clause elements. A further endorsement analysis is also required.
Justice Stevens	The government may not exclude from a limited public forum either religious speech that is simply speech about a particular topic from a religious point of view, or religious speech that amounts to worship, but may exclude proselytizing religious speech that does not amount to worship.
Justices Souter & Ginsburg	The government may—and perhaps must—exclude prosyletization and worship from a limited public forum conducted on public school premises.

3. Limited and Nonpublic Fora

In addition to traditional and limited public fora, the Court has recognized that there are other, more limited, fora whose parameters render them open only to a certain group of individuals (*e.g.*, students at a state university, or faculty and administrative staff of a public school), or open only to specific types of messages (*e.g.*, faculty mailboxes at a state university that are designated "for official use only"). Just as in the case of public fora, the Court looks to the parameters that define the character of the forum, and the manner in which the State enforces them.

The two cases summarized below, *Widmar v. Vincent*, 454 U.S. 263 (1981) and *Rosenberger v. Rector and Visitors of the University of Virginia*, 515 U.S. 819 (1995), provide two examples of limited, nonpublic fora. In *Widmar*, access to University facilities was limited to registered student groups, but the University of Missouri did not otherwise attempt to regulate the content or perspectives of the speech in which they could engage. In *Rosenberger*, the forum was a University program that paid for printing costs incurred by qualified student organizations from a fund derived from mandatory student activities fees. The forum was therefore "access-limited" (to qualified organizations), subject to certain procedural requirements, and subject to the general qualification that expenses must be "related to the educational purpose of the University."

Widmar v. Vincent, 454 U.S. 263 (1981)—*Widmar* is the first "equal access" case to be decided by the Supreme Court. The question presented was whether a state university that makes its facilities generally available for the activities of registered student groups may refuse access to a registered student group that intended to use the facilities for religious worship and religious discussion. From 1972–1977, a religious student group, Cornerstone, held regular meetings in the University's facilities, but in 1977, University administrators began to enforce a regulation, adopted by the University's Board of Curators in 1972, that prohibited the use of University buildings or grounds "for purposes of religious worship or religious teaching."

Writing for the Court, Justice Powell held that when the University created a forum generally open for use by student groups, it "assumed an obligation to justify its discriminations and exclusions under applicable constitutional norms." As in *Good News*, the University argued that its discrimination against religious speech and worship was justified by its "compelling interest in maintaining strict separation of church and State," and pointed to the "Establishment Clauses" of both the federal and Missouri Constitutions.

Rejecting the Establishment Clause defense, the Court held that

> The University's argument misconceives the nature of this case. The question is not whether the creation of a religious forum would violate the Establishment Clause. The University has opened its facilities for use by student groups, and the question is whether it can now exclude groups because of the content of their speech. In this context we are unpersuaded that the primary effect of the public forum, open to all forms of discourse, would be to advance religion.... It is possible—perhaps even foreseeable—that religious groups will benefit from access to University facilities. But this Court has explained that a religious organization's enjoyment of merely "incidental" benefits does not violate the prohibition against the "primary advancement" of religion.

Missouri also argued that even if the federal constitution required the University to grant equal access once it had opened the forum for general student use, the Missouri Constitution forbids even indirect state support for religion. Because the Missouri courts had not ruled on the permissibility of the University's practice, the Court saw no occasion to address the Supremacy Clause issue Missouri had raised. *See* § K, below.

Justice White dissented. In his view, the case should be characterized as a "free exercise" matter, and analyzed under the Court's pre-*Smith* "balancing" approach. In his view, characterizing the case as one implicating the Speech and Press Clause "is plainly wrong."

> A large part of respondents' argument, accepted by the court below and accepted by the majority, is founded on the proposition that because religious worship uses speech, it is protected by the Free Speech Clause of the First Amendment. Not only is it protected, they argue, but religious worship *qua* speech is not different from any other variety of protected speech as a matter of constitutional principle. I believe that this proposition is plainly wrong. Were it right, the Religion Clauses would be emptied of any independent meaning in circumstances in which religious practice took the form of speech....This case involves religious worship only; the fact that worship is accomplished through speech does not add anything to respondents' argument. That argument must rely upon the claim that the State's action impermissibly interferes with the free exercise of respondents' religious practices. Although this is a close question, I conclude that it does not.

Shortly after the decision in *Widmar*, Congress passed the Equal Access Act [EAA], 20 U.S.C. §§4071 *et seq.* (1984). The EAA bars high schools from refusing access to religious and philosophical groups if they grant access to other non-curricular organizations. The text of the Act is discussed in § K ("Religious Freedom, Separation of Powers, and Federalism") below.

Rosenberger v. Rector and Visitors of the University of Virginia, 515 U.S. 819 (1995)—student organizations at the University of Virginia were allowed to use University meeting rooms and computer facilities. Upon meeting the requirements necessary to qualify as a "Contracted Independent Organization," or CIO, a student organization could request that the University pay debts it owed third-party contractors for work on student activities projects. Agreements between the University and each CIO stated that all CIOs were independent of University control.

The plaintiff in *Rosenberger* was a CIO named "Wide Awake Productions" (WAP), which was formed by University of Virginia student Ronald Rosenberger in 1990. Its goals, in the organizers' own words, were to "publish a magazine of philosophical and religious expression," "facilitate discussion which fosters an atmosphere of sensitivity to and tolerance of Christian viewpoints," and "provide a unifying focus for Christians of muticultural backgrounds." *Id.* at 825–826. In keeping with those goals, WAP published a paper that offered "a Christian perspective on both personal and community issues, especially those relevant to college students at the University of Virginia." It was distributed free to students.

During the 1990–91 academic year, WAP was one of 343 qualified CIOs, and one of 118 CIOs to receive funding support from a Student Activities Fund (SAF). The SAF was, in turn, supported by revenues from a mandatory student fee of $14 per semester per student. In accordance with the University's rules for CIOs, WAP requested that the SAF pay $5,862 for the cost of printing the paper. The Appropriations Committee of the Student Council refused because the paper promoted the idea of belief in a deity, and was therefore a "religious activity."

The majority opinion, written by Justice Kennedy, held that the Student Council's refusal to pay the debt incurred by WAP was based on impermissible viewpoint discrimination and a violation of the Speech and Press Clause. It also concluded, without any reliance on *Lemon*, that the Establishment Clause was not a defense to WAP's claim. The SAF program was "neutral toward religion" because there was no evidence that the University intended to promote religion SAF's funding mechanism of the SAF, *id.* at 840, and that neutrality also "distinguishes the student fees from a tax levied for the direct support of a church or group of churches," which, "of course, would run contrary to Establishment Clause concerns dating from the earliest days of the Republic." *Id.*

The fact that payments were made on behalf of a religious newspaper was, in the Court's view, irrelevant. Because the payments were made to a third-party contractor, and not directly to WAP, the majority rejected the dissent's claim that these expenditures were the functional equivalent of direct payments to sectarian institutions. The Court further distinguished a fund derived from general taxation from the SAF, which was funded by a mandatory student fee designed to support the wide-ranging inquiry and debate that mark university life. In its view, "[o]ur decision, then, cannot be read as addressing an expenditure from a general tax fund." *Id.* For the majority, *Rosenberger* was simply a logical extension of the principles recognized in *Widmar v. Vincent*, 454 U.S. 263 (1981), *Board of Educ. v. Mergens*, 496 U.S. 226 (1990), and *Lamb's Chapel v. Center Moriches Union Free School Dist.*, 508 U.S. 384 (1993). In its view, "[t]here is no difference in logic or principle, and no difference of constitutional significance, between a school using its funds to operate a facility to which students have access, and a school paying a third-party contractor to operate the facility on its behalf." *Id.*

Justice O'Connor, concurring, offered the view that "[t]his case lies at the intersection of the principle of governmental neutrality and the prohibition on state funding of religious activities." *Id.* at 846. Therefore, "[w]hen two bedrock principles so conflict, understandably neither can provide the definitive answer." *Id.* In her view, resolution of this case required drawing lines based on the particular facts of the case, and depended "on the hard task of judging—sifting through the details and determining whether the challenged program offends the Establishment Clause." *Id.* Crucial facts included the independence of the CIOs from the University, a payment scheme that ensured the proper use of SAF funds because the SAF directly paid the third-party contractor, the improbability that any financial support of WAP would be viewed as an endorsement of WAP's religious message, and the possibility that offended students might, unlike the normal taxpayer, enjoy the right to opt out of supporting WAP's message through a reduction of their mandatory assessment. She concluded, "The Court's decision today therefore neither trumpets the supremacy of the neutrality principle nor signals the demise of the funding prohibition in Establishment Clause jurisprudence." *Id.* at 851–52. Noting that "our Establishment Clause jurisprudence is in hopeless disarray....," Justice Thomas also concurred "to express [his] disagreement with the historical analysis put forward by the dissent." *Id.* at 860.

Justice Souter dissented, joined by Justices Stevens, Ginsburg and Breyer. In his view, the jurisprudence of the Establishment Clause contains

> two general rules: that whenever affirmative government aid ultimately benefits religion, the Establishment Clause requires some justification beyond evenhandedness on the government's part; and that direct public funding of core sectarian activities, even if accomplished pursuant to an evenhanded program, would be entirely inconsistent with the Establishment Clause and would strike at the very heart of the Clause's protection.
>
> *Id.* at 877.

For Justice Souter, the primary principle was "no-aid." In his view, this is the "heart" of the Establishment Clause, but the "no aid" principle "does not answer the questions that occur at the margins of the Clause's application." *Id.* at 878. Answering these "marginal" questions requires an inquiry into both the "evenhandedness" of the program and the effect that it has on religion. That inquiry permits judicial line drawing for the purpose of determining whether specific "incidental benefits" to religion violate the Establishment Clause. "Evenhandedness," however, was not to be used in cases involving direct public funding.

For Justice Souter, the payments made to the printer on WAP's behalf were "direct aid" forbidden by the Establishment Clause. Evenhandedness was a relevant factor, but not "a sufficient condition of constitutionality for direct financial support of religious proselytization." In his view, the Establishment Clause was not "a mere prohibition against unequal direct aid," *id.* at 880, but rather a violation of the very principle upon which Madison had based the *Memorial and Remonstrance Against Religious Assessments*: that payment of even "three pence...of his property for the support of any one establishment, may force him to conform to any other establishment in all cases whatsoever." *Id.* at 882.

Justice Souter distinguished *Mueller v. Allen*, 463 U.S. 388 (1983), *Witters v. Washington Dept. of Services for the Blind*, 474 U.S. 481 (1986), and *Zobrest v. Catalina Foothills Sch. Dist.*, 509 U.S. 1 (1993) (all discussed in Chapter Six), as cases involving the *indirect* funding of religion because the individual recipient of governmental funds got them without regard to religion, and support of religion was the result of the recipients voluntarily and independent choice, not the government's decision to do so as a matter of policy.

Pinette, Good News Club, Mitchell v. Helms, and *Rosenberger* suggest that the present balance of power in Establishment Clause cases lies with Justice O'Connor. This further suggests that, although *Lemon* formally remains the accepted approach to Establishment Clause doctrine, it is likely to be supplanted in some cases (largely those involving schools) by Justice O'Connor's contextualized, fact-driven endorsement analysis, and by a more "categorical" analysis in cases arising under the Speech and Press Clause. *See* Chapter One § A.

Consider, at this point, Justice Stevens' and Ginsburg's reliance in *Pinette* on *Everson*, and Justice Souter's claim in *Rosenberger* that the heart of the Establishment Clause is the "no-aid" principle. Consider as well the assumption in the dissenting opinions of these Justices in *Good News Club* that the Court can, and perhaps must, try to parse religious speech to determine if it is forbidden prosyletization, worship, or merely religious speech on a topic from a religious perspective. *Compare Kokkinakis v. Greece*, (A/2600A) (1994) 17 E.H.R.R. 397 (European Ct. Human Rts.) (discussing the nature of proselytism and the relationship between the right to "manifest" one's religion protected by Article 9 of the European Convention and the rights of expression protected by Article 10.) Does this mean that the dissenters believe that the majority in these cases has gone "too far," and that the only way to clarify matters is to revive an Establishment Clause analysis based on a "strict" enforcement of the wall of separation? Would such a result put the Establishment and Speech Clauses on a collision course with one another?

4. Discrimination the Basis of Content or Perspective

Texas Monthly v. Bullock, 489 U.S. 1 (1989), excerpted in Chapter Nine—Shortly before deciding *County of Allegheny*, the Court decided *Texas Monthly*. Like *County of Allegheny*, no opinion commanded a majority, but the Court did invalidate a Texas statute exempting from its sales tax "[p]eriodicals...published or distributed by a religious faith and that consist wholly of writings promulgating the teaching of the faith and books that consist wholly of writings sacred to a religious faith." Tex. Tax Code Ann. § 151.312 (1982). Justice Brennan concluded for a plurality that "when confined exclusively to publications advancing the tenets of a religious faith, the exemption runs afoul of the Establishment Clause." This was so, according to Justice Brennan, because the law violated the primary effect aspect of *Lemon* by advancing religious over nonreligious publications. He distinguished *Walz* on the ground that the tax exemption in that case was broadly based and not exclusively granted to religious organizations, and rejected a Free Exercise Clause "accommodation" argument on the grounds that such accommodation is only required when a "concrete need to accommodate religious activity has been shown." *Id.* at 18.

Justice Blackmun, joined by Justice O'Connor, concurred in the judgment:

> The Free Exercise Clause value suggests that a State may not impose a tax on spreading the gospel. The Establishment Clause value suggests that a State may not give a tax break to those who spread the gospel that it does not also give to others who actively might advocate disbelief in religion.
>
> The Free Exercise Clause suggests that a special exemption for religious books is required. The Establishment Clause suggests that a special exemption for religious books is forbidden. This tension between mandated and prohibited religious exemptions is well recognized. Of course, identifying the problem does not resolve it.
>
> Justice Brennan's opinion...would resolve the tension between the Free Exercise and Establishment Clause values simply by subordinating the Free Ex-

> ercise value, even, it seems to me, at the expense of longstanding precedents. Justice Scalia's opinion, conversely, would subordinate the Establishment Clause value. This position, it seems to me, runs afoul of the previously settled notion that government may not favor religious belief over disbelief.
>
> Perhaps it is a vain desire, but I would like to decide the present case without necessarily sacrificing either the Free Exercise Clause value or the Establishment Clause value. It is possible for a State to write a tax-exemption statute consistent with both values: for example, a state statute might exempt the sale not only of religious literature distributed by a religious organization but also of philosophical literature distributed by nonreligious organizations devoted to such matters of conscience as life and death, good and evil, being and nonbeing, right and wrong.
>
> To recognize this possible reconciliation of the competing First Amendment considerations is one thing; to impose it upon a State as its only legislative choice is something else. We in the judiciary must be wary of interpreting these three constitutional clauses in a manner that negates the legislative role altogether.
>
> I believe we can avoid most of these difficulties with a narrow resolution of the case before us. We need decide here only whether a tax exemption *limited to* the sale of religious literature by religious organizations violates the Establishment Clause. I conclude that it does.

Id. at 26–28.

Justice Scalia, joined by Chief Justice Rehnquist and Justice Kennedy, dissented. He first noted that the impact of this case likely included the laws of forty five states that exempted religious groups from the application of laws without providing similar exemptions for other nonprofit institutions, as well as the IRS exemption from gross income to "ministers of the gospel" for the rental value of their parsonages. Justice Scalia then argued, "*Walz* is utterly dispositive of the Establishment Clause claim before us here." It was dispositive because *Walz* did not require a "breadth" of exemption, but allowed "legislation that exempted *religion alone*." He then noted that Justice Brennan's concurring opinion in *Walz* permitted the exemption

> because religions, like the other types of non-profit organizations exempted, "contribute to the well-being of the community in a variety of nonreligious ways," and (incomprehensibly) because they "uniquely contribute to the pluralism of American society by their religious activities," (I say incomprehensibly because to favor religion for its "unique contribution" is to favor religion as religion.)

Id. at 37.

Finally, Justice Scalia suggested that prohibiting through the Establishment Clause any accommodation of religion that was not required by the Free Exercise Clause "would completely block off the already narrow 'channel between the Scylla [of what the Free Exercise Clause demands] and the Charybdis [of what the Establishment Clause forbids] through which any state or federal action must pass in order to survive constitutional scrutiny.' " *Id.* at 42.

Justice Brennan's opinion also limited the holdings in two cases involving proselytizing by Jehovah's Witnesses in the mid-1940s. In *Murdock v. Pennsylvania*, 319 U.S. 105 (1943) and *Follett v. McCormick*, 321 U.S. 573 (1944), the Court held violative of the

Free Exercise Clause the imposition of flat license and bookseller's taxes on Jehovah's Witnesses who offered religious books and pamphlets for sale. Although there was "no doubt that the First Amendment prevents both the States and the Federal Government from imposing a special occupation tax exclusively on those who devote their days to spreading religious messages," "[t]o the extent that our opinions in *Murdock* and *Follet* might be read to suggest that the States and the Federal Government may never tax the sale of religious or other publications, we reject those dicta." *Bullock*, 489 U.S. at 23.

Once again, it is important to bear in mind the cautionary rule the Court has imposed for cases in which the Court's decision is fractured. It is the "narrowest" rationale used to decide the case that governs. Which of the Justices has expressed it? See Watchtower Bible and Tract Society of New York, Inc. v. Village of Stratton, __ U.S. __ (June 17, 2002).

H. Religious Freedom and Peaceable Assembly

> *"Congress shall make no law... abridging the right of the people peaceably to assemble..."*

U.S. Const. amend I (1789)

1. The Concept of "Peaceable Assembly"

Like many of the concepts embodied in the Constitution's Preamble, the right of peaceable assembly speaks directly to the communal aspects of the American democratic experiment. Without explicit recognition of a right to organize for a common purpose, it would be far more difficult to gather an audience for a speaker, form political parties, churches, schools, and interest groups, or to use business associations as a means of fostering interstate and international commerce.

> An association consists simply in the public assent which a number of individuals give to certain doctrines; and in the engagement which they contract to promote in a certain manner the spread of those doctrine. The right of associating with such views is very analogous to the liberty of unlicensed printing; but societies thus formed posses more authority than the press. When an opinion is represented by a society, it necessarily assumes a more exact and explicit form. It numbers its partisans, and compromises them in its cause; they, on the other hand, become acquainted with each other, and their zeal is increased by their number. An association unites into one channel the efforts of diverging minds, and urges them vigorously towards the one end which it clearly points out.

Alexis de Tocqueville, DEMOCRACY IN AMERICA 95–96 (1832) (Richard D. Heffner ed., 1956) In *Federalist No. 10*, James Madison referred to such associations as "factions."

> By a faction, I understand a number of citizens, whether amounting to a majority or a minority of the whole, who are united and actuated by some common impulse of passion, or of interest, adversed to the rights of other citizens, or to the permanent and aggregate interests of the community.

Alexander Hamilton, James Madison, John Jay, THE FEDERALIST PAPERS, No. 10 (Madison).

Viewed from Madison's political perspective, "peaceable assembly" is one way of describing the individual and collective interests that coalesce in the formation, maintenance, and growth of associations having unique identities and purposes. The right of peaceable assembly is thus a critical, if under-appreciated, component of the Religious Liberty Guarantee. Though it is certainly possible to make an argument that the Free Exercise Clause protects the collective and communal rights of churches and religious associations, and that the non-establishment and no religious test principles protect them from discrimination and compelled association, the argument for religious freedom is far easier to make—and much more clearly understood—when it is seen "in context." *See* Chart 5-1, on page 207 (graphic illustrating the legal relationships between and among the non-establishment, free exercise, no religious test, and norms).

2. Peaceable Assembly in the Courts

How *should* the Court interpret and apply "the right of the people peaceably to assemble"? The first step in the process is for the court to select the proper characterization from a range of possibilities. As you consider the following list, ask whether any others are possible, or preferable.

Chart 5-6
Characterizing the Right to Peaceable Assembly

	Peaceable Assembly
Abstract	Personal autonomy.
(high level)	Non-association with disagreeable individuals or groups.
↓	Intimate association.
Level	Collective action for any otherwise legitimate purpose.
of	Association or membership in an organizarion for any legitimate purpose.
Generality	Association or membership in an organization for expressive purposes.
	Association or membership in political organizations.
↑	Peaceable assembly for any purpose.
Specific	Peaceable assembly for political purposes.
(low level)	Peaceable assembly at the seat of government for political purposes.

Where, for example, would you place de Tocqueville's formulation of the right? Madison's?

3. Freedom of Association

The right of "peaceable assembly," as such, is rarely discussed in the case law, but the United States Supreme Court has recognized a related *concept*—that of "freedom of association."

> Our decisions have referred to constitutionally protected "freedom of association" in two distinct senses. In one line of decisions, the Court has concluded that choices to enter into and maintain certain intimate human relationships

> must be secured against undue intrusion by the State because of the role of such relationships in safeguarding the individual freedom that is central to our constitutional scheme. In this respect, freedom of association receives protection as a fundamental element of personal liberty. In another set of decisions, the Court has recognized a right to associate for the purpose of engaging in those activities protected by the First Amendment—speech, assembly, petition for the redress of grievances, and the exercise of religion. The Constitution guarantees freedom of association of this kind as an indispensable means of preserving other individual liberties.

Roberts v. United States Jaycees, 468 U.S. 609, 617–618 (1984).

The right of peaceable assembly is thus one of a package of rights subsumed under the substantive due process rubric of freedom of expression. *See, e.g., Hague v. CIO*, 307 U.S. 496 (1939). *See generally* Volokh, THE FIRST AMENDMENT, at 589–666; John E. Nowak & Ronald D. Rotunda, CONSTITUTIONAL LAW §16.54 (6th ed. 2000). Consider the following excerpt from an opinion by Judge Richard Posner.

> The purpose of the free-speech clause and of its judge-made corollary the right of association is to protect the market in ideas, *Abrams v. United States,* 250 U.S. 616, 630, (Holmes, J., dissenting), broadly understood as the public expression of ideas, narratives, concepts, imagery, opinions—scientific, political, or aesthetic—to an audience whom the speaker seeks to inform, edify, or entertain. Casual chit-chat between two persons or otherwise confined to a small social group is unrelated, or largely so, to that marketplace, and is not protected. Such conversation is important to its participants but not to the advancement of knowledge, the transformation of taste, political change, cultural expression, and the other objectives, values, and consequences of the speech that is protected by the First Amendment.

Swank v. Smart, 898 F.2d 1247, 1250–1251 (7th Cir. 1990). How, for example, would a meeting involving only two persons engaged in private prayer or meditation fit into this analysis?

4. Peaceable Assembly and Religious Associations

Neither the "church" nor the "state" exists in the abstract. Both are collective entities formed for a common purpose that defines its identity and character. Each is comprised of associations of individuals and groups who are committed, to some degree, to the attainment of that common purpose. Thus, whether known as the right of "expressive association," or the right of peaceable assembly, the interests it protects "include[] the right to express one's attitudes or philosophies by membership in a group, or affiliation with it or by other lawful means." *Griswold v. Connecticut,* 381 U.S. 479, 483 (1965).

By examining the Religious Liberty Guarantee through the lens of the Peaceable Assembly Clause, the following aspects of religious liberty are brought into relatively sharp focus:

1. The right of religiously motivated individuals to enter into associations consistent with their beliefs and aspirations, and to decline associations that may be inconsistent with them.

2. The right of religious associations to define and project a unique institutional character and mission.
3. The rationales used by government to justify differential treatment of individuals and associations.

a) Distinguishing Individual from Associational Activity

It is by no means self-evident from the text of the Constitution that rules developed for the protection of individuals should also apply to organizations and associations. An organization's identity is often distinct from that of its individual members, and its managers exercise delegated authority.

The initial question, therefore, is whether the *fact* that individuals are operating as an association justifies differential treatment of their rights under the first amendment and No Religious Test Clause. The Peaceable Assembly Clause appears to answer this question in the negative, but the case law—and the attitudes of the Founders themselves—indicate that there is a profound ambivalence on this important question. Developing an answer requires a two-part inquiry. The first examines the stated purposes and goals of the organization; the second relates the form of the organization to its function.

b) The Significance of Organizational Purpose

Affinity, mutual benefit and support, common beliefs and goals, and efficiency, are only a few of the reasons why individuals organize themselves into groups, but few organizations state their *raisons d'être* in explicit terms.

> In no country in the world has the principle of association been more successfully used, or applied to a greater multitude of objects, than in America. Besides the permanent associations, which are established by law, under the names of townships, cities, and counties, a vast number of others are formed and maintained by the agency of private individuals.... In the United States, associations are established to promote the public safety, commerce, industry, morality, and religion. There is no end which the human will despairs of attaining through the combined power of individuals united into a society.

Alexis de Tocqueville, DEMOCRACY IN AMERICA at 95–96.

One of the most important functions of a business, for example, is to make money, but nothing in the law requires that the profit motive be its only purpose. *See* 26 U.S.C. § 212 (2001) (permitting tax deductions for any expenses relating to the production of income). How *should* the courts treat a business corporation that is clearly engaged in business for profit, and but whose owners consider themselves to be engaged primarily in a religious ministry? *Compare EEOC v. Townley Engineering & Manufacturing Co.*, 859 F.2d 610, 615 (9th Cir. 1988), *cert. denied*, 489 U.S. 1077 (1989) (holding that "[it] is a legitimate supposition" that Title VII of the Civil Rights Act of 1964 "posits a gain-seeking [corporate] employer exclusively concerned with preserving and promoting its economic efficiency.") *with id.* at 622 (Noonan, J. dissenting) ("The First Amendment does not say that only religious corporations or only not-for-profit corporations are protected.... All persons—and under our Constitution all corporations are persons—are free. A statute cannot subtract from their freedom.").

Churches, mosques, or synagogues, by contrast, are clearly organized for religious purposes. Does the *fact* that the religious activity is carried on in an associational context mean that they are entitled to any less protection than a business or nonprofit? James Madison and his fellow Virginians were particularly concerned about concentrations of wealth and political power in the hands of religious corporations. *See* Va. Const, Art 4 § 14 (2001) ("The general assembly shall not grant a charter of incorporation to any church or religious denomination."); *Trustees of the General Assembly of the Presbyterian Church v Guthrie*, 10 S.E. 318, 321 (Va. 1889). *See also* David P. Currie, *God & Caesar & President Madison*, 3 Green Bag 2d. 11 (1999) (recounting the early disputes involving Jefferson and Madison concerning the incorporation of church associations). *See generally* Chapter One § B, Chapter Two. Insuring that their other significant activities, both spiritual and temporal, remain accountable is the subject of Chapters Seven, Eight, Nine, and Eleven.

Labels, such as "business," nonprofit, charitable, public and religious, are useful, but not always determinative. *See generally* Chapter Seven § A.

c) The Significance of Organizational Form

Associations adopt a form or structure that reflects the character of their membership, constituencies, and purposes. As a result, there is an inherent relationship between the function of the organization and the form it adopts. *See* Chapter Seven. Attempts to draw clear lines on the basis of either alone can be problematic. From a first amendment perspective, there are two distinct, but related, concerns about organizational activity: accountability and concentration of power. These concerns are often referenced as justifications for differential treatment of the first amendment rights of associations. *See, e.g., Austin v. Michigan Chamber of Commerce*, 494 U.S. 652 (1990). *See The Federalist*, No. 10.

An unincorporated association, for example, functions as the *alter ego* of its members, both as a matter of fact, and as a matter of law, but the synergistic effect of the interactions between and among the individuals and factions within such a group will eventually give it an organizational identity and character distinct from that of its individual members or management. Although a corporation can also function as the *alter ego* of its majority stockholders or management, the corporate form creates a "juridical person" that has a distinct legal identity, with rights, obligations, and a term of existence separate from those of its constituents.

These distinctions are significant, and provide important perspectives on the law of religious liberty. The recognition that organizations and associations are greater than the sum of their constituent parts, for example, provided the impetus for some of the examples of "separation of church and state." In the early American colonial period, the local unit of government was the territorial parish, the boundaries of which were contiguous with those of the parish church. Without some means of separating the identity of the territorial parish as a unit of government from that of the parish church as an association of believers resident in the community, the church as an association of believers could not receive endowments or hold property in its own right.

The common law solved the problem by borrowing the concept of *person ecclesiae*—the corporation sole—from the canon law of the church. A pragmatic mixture of form and function, the corporation sole invests the legal identity of the church in the person of the incumbent minister, who, during his tenure, owns the church's property and has the power to transmit it to his successor. The law governing nonreligious organizations has precisely the same pragmatic character. Corporations are "artificial being[s], invisible, intangible, and existing only in contemplation of law." *Trustees of Dartmouth College v. Woodward*, 17 U.S. (4 Wheat.) 518, 636 (1810). In fact, they are "merely associations of individuals united for a special purpose, and permitted to do business under a particular name, and have a succession of members without dissolution." *Pembina Consol. Silver Min. & Milling Co. v. Commonwealth of Pennsylvania*, 125 U.S. 181, 189 (1888). *See also Gulf, C. & S. F. Ry. Co. v. Ellis*, 165 U.S. 150, 154 (1897) (calling them "artificial entities."). In sum, no association of persons who gather together for a common purpose, has an *independent* legal existence ("juridical personality") until the law specifically grants it. *See* Chapter Seven.

d) Creating and Preserving an Organizational Identity

It is traditional for government agencies to distinguish between and among religious associations by reference to the degree to which they maintain or exhibit their religious character. *See, e.g., EEOC v. Kamehameha Schools*, 990 F.2d 458 (9th Cir. 1993), *cert. denied*, 510 U.S. 963 (1993), excerpted in Chapter Eight. Associations of believers, including church organizations, however, do not generally draw the kinds of fine distinctions between and among their activities that make sense to regulators and courts. For many such organizations, *all* of their activities are part and parcel of their religious mission. Such differences in perception can cause the significant practical and definitional problems described in this chapter, and in Chapters Seven, Eight and Nine. *Compare, e.g.*, Va. Const. art. 4 § 14 (2001) (forbidding the incorporation of "any church or religious denomination") *with Foundation of Human Understanding v. Commissioner*, 88 T.C. 1341, 1356 (1987) ("We can only approach [the definition of the term "church"] with care for all of us are burdened with the baggage of our own unique beliefs and perspectives.").

e) Maintaining a Personal or Institutional "Identity"

The Supreme Court has recognized that the religious liberty interests of individual religious believers and associations include freedom from direct or indirect government compulsion to associate with, or support, the religious beliefs of others. The right of individual "non-association" has been recognized in the individual context in two contexts: 1) when the individual is required to associate with disagreeable messages, see, e.g., *Wooley v. Maynard*, 430 U.S. 705 (1977) (prosecution for covering state motto on license plate); and 2) forced association with individuals and organizations with which he or she disagrees. *See, e.g., Board of Regents of the University of Wisconsin System v. Southworth*, 529 U.S. 217 (2000); *Abood v. Detroit Board of Education*, 431 U.S. 209 (1977). *See generally* FREEDOM OF ASSOCIATION (Amy Gutmann ed. 1998).

An *organization*'s right to maintain its identity through selective association remains a hotly disputed issue. In ***Hurley v. Irish-American Gay Lesbian and Bisexual Group of Boston***, 515 U.S. 557 (1995), the Court unanimously held that the unincorporated association sponsoring Boston's St. Patrick's Day Parade could not be forced "to include among the marchers a group imparting a message the organizers do not wish to convey." *Id.* at 559. At issue were the rights of two organizations. The sponsors of the parade, the South Boston Allied War Veterans Council, are an unincorporated association comprised of individuals elected by South Boston veterans groups. The members of the group seeking permission to march, GLIB, were gay, lesbian, and bisexual descendants of the Irish immigrants and other supporters who sought to convey a number of messages, including "pride in their Irish heritage as openly gay, lesbian, and bisexual individuals, [a message] that there are such men and women among those so descended, and...their solidarity with like individuals who sought to march in New York's St. Patrick's Day Parade."

When the Council refused permission, GLIB sought an injunction, alleging that the parade is a "place of public accommodation, resort or amusement" under the State's public accommodation law, Mass. Gen. Laws §272:98 (1992), which bars "any distinction, discrimination or restriction on account of...sexual orientation." The Superior Court sided with GLIB, holding that "the lack of genuine selectivity in choosing participants and sponsors demonstrates that the Parade is a public event." *Id.* at 561. It rejected the Council's argument that the Parade "expresses traditional religious and social values," holding that exclusion of GLIB because of its values and messages "was not only violative of the public accommodations law but 'paradoxical' as well, since 'a proper celebration of St. Patrick's and Evacuation Day requires diversity and inclusiveness.'" *Id.* at 562. Because the Parade organizers made no attempt to focus the message of the Parade, the Superior Court found it "impossible to discern any specific expressive purpose entitling the Parade to protection under the First Amendment." *Id.* The Supreme Judicial Court of Massachusetts affirmed. *Irish-American Gay, Lesbian and Bisexual Group of Boston v. Boston,* 418 Mass. 238, 242–248, 636 N.E.2d 1293, 1295–1298 (1994).

The Supreme Court reversed. It began its analysis by observing that the "the word 'parade' [indicates] marchers who are making some sort of collective point, not just to each other but to bystanders along the way." The issue presented, therefore, was whether Massachusetts public accommodations law could be used to force a group such as the Council to associate with a message it rejects. *Id.* at 567–568.

After a brief review of the history of public accommodations laws, the Court drew a distinction between a decision "to exclude homosexuals as such," from the Parade, and the refusal of the Parade's sponsors to permit "the admission of GLIB as its own parade unit carrying its own banner." *Id.* at 572. To compel association with GLIB's message "violates the fundamental rule of protection under the First Amendment, that a speaker has the autonomy to choose the content of his own message." *Id.* at 572.

> "Since *all* speech inherently involves choices of what to say and what to leave unsaid," *Pacific Gas & Electric Co. v. Public Utilities Comm'n of Cal.,* 475 U.S. 1, 11 (1986) (plurality opinion) (emphasis in original), one important manifestation of the principle of free speech is that one who chooses to speak may also decide "what not to say," *id.,* at 16. Although the State may at times "prescribe what shall be orthodox in commercial advertising" by requiring the dissemination of "purely factual and uncontroversial information," outside that context it may not compel affirmance of a belief with which the speaker disagrees, *Barnette,* 319 U.S., at 642. Indeed this general rule, that the speaker has the right to tailor the speech, applies not only to expressions of value, opinion, or endorsement, but equally to statements of fact the speaker would rather avoid, subject, perhaps, to the permissive law of defamation, [*New York Times Co. v. Sullivan; Gertz v. Robert Welch, Inc.*; *Hustler Magazine, Inc. v. Falwell*]. Nor is the rule's benefit restricted to the press, being enjoyed by business corporations generally and by ordinary people engaged in unsophisticated expression as well as by professional publishers.

Id. at 573–574. It rejected GLIB's contention that use of civil rights laws to compel expressive association is a legitimate "means to produce speakers free of the biases, whose expressive conduct would be at least neutral toward the particular classes, obviating any future need for correction." *Id.* at 579.

> The very idea that a noncommercial speech restriction be used to produce thoughts and statements acceptable to some groups or, indeed, all people, grates on the First Amendment, for it amounts to nothing less than a proposal to limit speech in the service of orthodox expression. The Speech Clause has no more certain antithesis. While the law is free to promote all sorts of conduct in place of harmful behavior, it is not free to interfere with speech for no better reason than promoting an approved message or discouraging a disfavored one, however enlightened either purpose may strike the government.

Id. at 580.

The Court affirmed and refined its holding in *Hurley* in ***Boy Scouts of America v. Dale***, 530 U.S. 640 (2000), in which it held (5-4) that New Jersey could not compel the Boy Scouts of America to retain James Dale after he publicly announced his homosexuality. The majority accepted the Boy Scouts' assertion "that it does 'not want to promote homosexual conduct as a legitimate form of behavior,'" and noted that it "need not inquire further to determine the nature of the Boy Scouts' expression with respect to homosexuality." It did, however, examine the written record of the Boy Scouts' position "as instructive, if only on the question of the sincerity of the professed beliefs." *Id.* at 651.

Responding to the New Jersey Supreme Court's finding that "Boy Scout members do not associate for the purpose of disseminating the belief that homosexuality is immoral," *Id.* at 652, *quoting* 160 N.J., at 612, 734 A.2d, at 1223, the Court made several points:

> First, associations do not have to associate for the "purpose" of disseminating a certain message in order to be entitled to the protections of the First Amendment. An association must merely engage in expressive activity that could be impaired in order to be entitled to protection.
>
> Second,...the First Amendment protects the [association's] method of expression. If the Boy Scouts wishes Scout leaders to avoid questions of sexuality and teach only by example, this fact does not negate the sincerity of its belief discussed above.
>
> Third, the First Amendment simply does not require that every member of a group agree on every issue in order for the group's policy to be "expressive association."

Id. at 655–656.

Writing for the four dissenting Justices, Justice Stevens acknowledged that New Jersey's understanding of the concept of public accommodation was "expansive," but viewed it as a "courageous" social experiment. In their view, "every state law prohibiting discrimination is designed to replace prejudice with principle," and should be granted a presumption of constitutionality. *Id.* at 664 (Stevens, Souter, Ginsburg, & Breyer, JJ., dissenting). Unlike the majority, the dissenters did not accept the Boy Scouts' statements concerning the content of their educational message. Performing their own review of the Boy Scouts' published materials, they concluded that "[i]n light of BSA's self-proclaimed ecumenism,...it is...difficult to discern any shared goals or common moral stance on homosexuality." *Id.* at 670. In their view,

> The relevant question is whether the mere inclusion of the person at issue would "impose any serious burden," "affect in any significant way," or be "a substantial restraint upon" the organization's "shared goals," "basic goals," or "collective effort to foster beliefs." Accordingly, it is necessary to examine what, exactly, are BSA's shared goals and the degree to which its expressive activities would be burdened, affected, or restrained by including homosexuals.

Id. at 683–684. The dissenters also took issue with the majority's conclusion that the association's written statements concerning the content of its own expression should be given deference. In their view, a court "must inquire whether the group is, in fact, expressing a message (whatever it may be) and whether that message (if one is expressed) is significantly affected by a State's antidiscrimination law. More critically, that inquiry requires our *independent* analysis, rather than deference to a group's litigating posture." *Id.* at 685.

> To prevail in asserting a right of expressive association as a defense to a charge of violating an antidiscrimination law, the organization must at least show it has adopted and advocated an unequivocal position inconsistent with a position advocated or epitomized by the person whom the organization seeks to exclude.

Id. at 687.

For a discussion of the ways in which the rights of peaceable assembly and expressive association apply to the interests of religious employers, see Chapter Eight § E.

I. Religious Freedom and the Right to Petition for a Redress of Grievances

> *"Congress shall make no law... abridging... the right of the people... to petition the Government for a redress of grievances."*

U.S. Const. amend I (1789)

1. The Petition Clause

When individuals and interest groups have social, legal, or political grievances, they engage in all the classic forms of political behavior: they contact their representatives, speak, publish, and organize. The right to petition for a redress of grievances includes all of these efforts. It "extends to all departments of the Government" and to all parts of the community. *California Motor Transport Co. v. Trucking Unlimited,* 404 U.S. 508, 510 (1972) (petitions to administrative agencies). *See McDonald v. Smith*, 472 U.S. 479 (1985) (correspondence with executive branch and representatives); *Bill Johnson's Restaurants, Inc. v. NLRB,* 461 U.S. 731, 741 (1983) (lawsuits in state courts); *NAACP v. Claiborne Hardware Co.*, 458 U.S. 886, 909–912 (1982) (peaceful economic boycott of local business community); *Edwards v. South Carolina,* 372 U.S. 229, 235 (1963) (peaceful protest in public fora).

Perhaps the best known organizing effort for religious liberty was the coalition of churches, religious groups, and advocates for religious liberty formed in 1785–1786 to lobby against Virginia's proposed tax levy to support the salaries of ministers. Led by James Madison, that lobbying effort produced one of the most famous petitions for a redress of grievances published during the founding period: Madison's *Memorial and Remonstrance Against Religious Assessments.*

The historical materials contained in Chapters One § B, Two through Four, and Six recount the important role that the grievances of religiously motivated individuals and religious interest groups have played in the development and maintenance of a political culture that values religious liberty. In this section we consider some of the political dimensions of that process.

2. Interest Group Litigation to Enforce the Religious Liberty Guarantee

Prior to *Cantwell* and *Everson*, the primary fora available for redress of religious liberty grievances were the State legislatures, courts, executive agencies, and local government bodies. Professor Karst has observed that conflicts over religious liberty can arise when "two cultural groups with conflicting values contend in the political arena, each seeking to use the power of the state to impose its values on the other." Kenneth L. Karst, *Paths To Belonging: The Constitution and Cultural Identity*, 64 N.C. L. Rev. 303, 310 (1986). The cases excerpted and summarized in Chapters Two, Three, Four, and Six recount that State political struggles over religious liberty issues were often centered on they key culture forming institutions in the community: the church, the schools, and the family. The case law also indicates that they were intensely fought at each level of government, and that the accommodations reached, if any, generally reflected the relative political strengths of the contending factions.

The Court's decisions in *Cantwell v. Connecticut*, 310 U.S. 296 (1943), and *Everson v. Board of Education*, 330 U.S. 1 (1947), were major developments in the history of American constitutional law because of their structural effect on the distribution of power within the federal system. The immediate effect of the decision to incorporate the Religion Clause was to shift supervisory power over religious liberty from the States to the federal government, and from the legislatures to the courts. *See* Kurt T. Lash, *The Second Adoption of the Establishment Clause: The Rise of the Nonestablishment Principle*, 27 Ariz. St. L.J. 1085 (1995); Akhil Reed Amar, *The Case of the Missing Amendments*, 106 Harv. L. Rev. 124 (1992); Alex Kozinski & Eugene Volokh, *A Penumbra Too Far*, 106 Harv. L. Rev. 1639 (1993). The jurisdictional boundaries of the new federal forum are discussed in § K, below. *See generally* Robert A. Destro, *By What Right? The Sources and Limits of Federal Court and Congressional Jurisdiction Over Matters "Touching Religion,"* 29 Ind. L. Rev. 1 (1995).

Opening the federal courts to complaints that State policies violate the incorporated first amendment created a judicial forum in which lawyers and their clients could debate the contours of a preemptive federal policy specifically governing religious liberty. In *Pierce v. Society of Sisters*, 268 U.S. 510 (1925) and *Meyer v. Nebraska*, 262 U.S. 390 (1923), the Court had relied on a generalized concept of religious liberty to invalidate Oregon's attempt to close religious schools and Nebraska's attempt to stop religious schools from teaching foreign languages. Since *Everson*, the litigation of religious liberty cases in federal courts has become "a continuation of cultural politics by other means." *See* Karst, *Paths to Belonging*, 64 N.C. L. Rev. at 340. *Cf.*, *Lynch v. Donnelly*, 465 U.S. 668, 693–94 (1984) (O'Connor, J., concurring) (noting that a conclusion in Establishment Clause litigation is "in large part a legal question to be answered on the basis of judicial interpretation of social facts").

a) Everson *and the Politics of Religious Liberty, circa 1947.*

Everson arose at a time of increasing political tensions between Protestants and Catholics. It was not a popular decision in either community. Professor Richard Morgan has written that the uproar over the Court's decision was a consequence of "heightened Protestant-Catholic antipathies" arising just after the end of World War II, in which "Catholics were behaving like parvenus[1], Protestants were over-reacting, and the old flames of animosity were fanned."

In mid-1946, a few months before the oral argument in *Everson*, another of the periodic disputes over the permissibility and political wisdom of the United States having an official representative at the Vatican erupted. John Adams had first discussed the issue in a country-by-country diplomatic survey written for the Confederation Congress in 1779, and political controversy over the relationship with the Holy See would occur on a fairly regular basis over the next 200 years. At issue in 1946 was the reappointment of Myron Charles Taylor as President Harry Truman's personal representative. Mr. Taylor had served as Franklin Roosevelt's personal representative to the Vatican, with the rank of ambassador. The Federal (now National) Council of Churches of Christ in America, an organization of Protestant churches, sent a delegation to speak with President Truman about the appointment. The delegation, led by Methodist Bishop G. Bromley Oxnam, complained that appointing such a representative represented a wedge in the principle of the separation of church and state. *See Controversies Aroused in U.S. by Taylor Mission*, United States News, June 28, 1946, at 19. Shortly after the decision in *Everson*, the Council of Bishops of the Methodist Church accused the Roman Catholic Church of actions in the United States and elsewhere that "'amounted to bigotry and denial of religious liberty.'" Richard E. Morgan, THE SUPREME COURT AND RELIGION 82 (1972) (quoting *New York Times*, May 8, 1947). Oxnam later was one of the founders of Protestants and Other Americans United for the Separation of Church and State. *Id.* at 86. Richard E. Morgan, THE POLITICS OF RELIGIOUS CONFLICT: CHURCH AND STATE IN AMERICA 28–29 (1968).

Tensions between the communities increased with a series of articles that appeared in *The Nation* in early 1948. Written by a lawyer named Paul Blanshard, the articles suggested that the Catholic clergy was a threat to American democracy. Echoing the main argument of the State of Oregon in *Pierce v. Society of Sisters*, Blanshard argued that Catholic schools were a key component of this threat because "[i]n the name of religion... [the Catholic Church] segregates Catholic children from the rest of the community in a separate school system, and censors the cultural diet of these children." Paul Blanshard, AMERICAN FREEDOM AND CATHOLIC POWER 4 (1949) (revised version of articles first published in late 1947 and early 1948). *Compare* Brief of Appellee, *Pierce v. Society of Sisters*, 268 U.S. 466 (1925) at 97 (quoting Oregon's Official Ballot Summary), excerpted in Chapter Six §C(2). Blanshard's reported that "a tremendous revival of anti-Catholic feeling is taking place in the United States and that its focal point is the educational policy of the Church." *Id.* at 59. Part of this feeling was related to the implementation by nineteen states of policies permitting public funding for the transportation of parochial schoolchildren to and from school. *Id.* Justice Jackson's dissenting

1. Note by the editors: Parvenu, from the French parvenir—to arrive—is defined as "a person who has suddenly acquired wealth or power, especially one who fails to conform to the established forms, customs, and habits of the class into which he has risen; person considered an upstart." WEBSTER'S NEW WORLD DICTIONARY OF THE AMERICAN LANGUAGE, 1068 (College Ed.).

opinion in *Everson* makes several similar points. *See Everson*, 330 U.S. at 22 ("It is no exaggeration to say that the whole historic conflict in temporal policy between the Catholic Church and non-Catholics comes to a focus in their respective school policies.... Our public school, if not a product of Protestantism, at least is more consistent with it than with the Catholic culture and scheme of values.") *See also* Chapter Four § B(2) (discussing the proposed Blaine and "Christian Education" Amendments to the federal constitution).

Blanshard's book "was unquestionably the most widely read anti-Catholic polemic of the post-World War II years." Frank J. Sorauf, THE WALL OF SEPARATION: THE CONSTITUTIONAL POLITICS OF CHURCH AND STATE 34 (1976). Blanshard was one of the founders, and later a long-time staff member, of Protestants and Other Americans United for Separation of Church and State. *Id.* Justice Black's fear of the Catholic Church led him to read Blanshard's anti-Catholic polemics. Rogers Newman, HUGO BLACK: A BIOGRAPHY 521 (1994).

In 1949, tensions between Catholics and Protestants again arose as a result of another Congressional fight over federal aid for education. The former first lady, Eleanor Roosevelt, twice wrote in her syndicated column in opposition to extending any federal aid to Catholic schools, and the Archbishop of New York, Terence Cardinal Spellman, in what Morgan called "an utterly graceless response," accused Mrs. Roosevelt of writings "unworthy of an American mother." Morgan, SUPREME COURT AND RELIGION, at 93–94. After that conflict, President Harry Truman's decision in 1950 to nominate General Mark Clark as his personal representative to the Vatican led to more intense Protestant-Catholic conflict. The Senate eventually refused to consent to the nomination, and Truman made no further nominations of a representative to the Vatican. *Id.* at 85. A similar controversy arose in 1986, when various religious groups challenged the decision of President Ronald Reagan to establish diplomatic ties with the Vatican. Both cases were dismissed on standing and political question grounds. *Americans United for Separation of Church and State v. Reagan*, 786 F.2d 194 (3d Cir.), *cert. denied sub. nom. American Baptist Churches in the U.S.A. v. Reagan*, 479 U.S. 914 (1986), *reh'g denied*, 479 U.S. 1012 (1986); *Phelps v. Reagan*, 812 F.2d 1293 (10th Cir. 1987).

b) The Religious Demographics of the Everson *Court*

Justice Hugo Black, the author of the majority opinion in *Everson*, was an Alabamian whose religious training included attending Sunday school at the local Baptist church in the morning and the local Methodist church in the afternoon. Howard Ball & Phillip J. Cooper, OF POWER AND RIGHT: HUGO BLACK, WILLIAM O. DOUGLAS, AND AMERICA'S CONSTITUTIONAL REVOLUTION 15 (1992). According to Professors Ball and Cooper, the two key influences in his early intellectual life were the writings of Thomas Jefferson and the commands of the Old Testament. His biographer, Roger K. Newman, however, reports that by the early 1960s, "A more formally irreligious man [than Black] would have been hard to find." Although he and his second wife Elizabeth "sometimes" attended religious services at the All Souls Unitarian Church, Newman quotes Black as saying, "'I can't exactly believe and I can't exactly not believe." Newman, HUGO BLACK at 521. Despite his negative personal views of the Roman Catholic Church, Justice Hugo Black was excoriated for supporting Catholicism in his *Everson* opinion. At the same time, Black complained: "the most severe and consistent criticisms of the opinion have come from leading Catholics." Newman, at 364.

The relationship between Justice Robert H. Jackson and Justice Black was strained. *See* Dennis J. Hutchinson, *The Black-Jackson Feud*, 1988 S.Ct. Rev. 203. The feud arose in part from Jackson's desire to be named Chief Justice after the death of Harlan Fiske Stone. That hope was not realized because, Jackson believed, of Black's actions, and in part because of Black's refusal to recuse himself in a case in which Black's former law partner represented a party before the Court. A year before *Everson* was decided, their feud became public knowledge. Although their personal relationship later became civil, their professional disagreements became more pronounced.

Justice Wiley Rutledge was the son of a Baptist minister. Fowler V. Harper, JUSTICE RUTLEDGE AND THE BRIGHT CONSTELLATION 1 (1965). In addition to his liberal quotations from Madison's *Memorial and Remonstrance*, Justice Rutledge appended it to his dissent.

Justice Felix Frankfurter was the only Jewish member of the Court. Frankfurter was a religious skeptic, rather than an observant Jew. However, possibly because he declared himself to the Protestant theologian Reinhold Niebuhr to be a "believing unbeliever," he requested the Kaddish be said at his burial. According to Black biographer Gerald Dunne, Frankfurter decided early on that *Everson* was a case "on which he should not be heard." Gerald T. Dunne, HUGO BLACK AND THE JUDICIAL REVOLUTION 264 (1977). Instead, Frankfurter worked with both Jackson and Rutledge on their dissents: "Rutledge eventually turned out eight drafts of his opinion and Black responded with six." *Id.* at 266.

The only Roman Catholic on the Court in 1947 was Justice Frank Murphy. Murphy was a former Mayor of Detroit and Governor of Michigan, and served as Attorney General before his nomination to the Court. Murphy's thoroughgoing support of the New Deal, and the death of Roman Catholic Justice Pierce Butler, led to his appointment to the Court's "Catholic" seat by President Franklin Roosevelt. Justice Murphy was an ardent defender of religious and civil liberties, as shown by his votes in a number of cases, including those involving the Jehovah's Witnesses.

Everson was decided by a vote of 5-4, with Murphy silently in the majority. Justice Felix Frankfurter attempted to play on the fact that Murphy was Catholic to get him to change his mind and speak forcefully for the "great American doctrine of Church and State," *see* J. Woodford Howard, Jr., MR. JUSTICE MURPHY: A POLITICAL BIOGRAPHY 450 (1968) (quoting undated letter from Frankfurter to Murphy), but Murphy was not persuaded. Frankfurter did not believe that Murphy deserved to be on the Court, and, as noted in Chapter One, derisively referred to him in letters to others as the "Saint."

Twenty three years later, in *Walz v. Tax Commission*, 397 U.S. 664 (1970), excerpted in § E(3) above, another of the five members in the *Everson* majority, Justice William O. Douglas, retracted his *Everson* vote. Like Rutledge before him, he appended Madison's *Memorial and Remonstrance* to his *Walz dissent.*

c) *Interest Group Litigation: Protestant, Catholic and Jewish Views*

Religious interest groups have long supported litigation, lobbying, and other political action by, or on behalf of, their co-religionists. *See* § J and K, below. In *Everson*, for example, the taxpayer-plaintiff, Arch Everson, opposed the reimbursement program adopted by the Ewing Township School Board. The ACLU and other interest groups provided litigation support. The defendant school board was represented not only by the state attorney general's office, but also by Porter R. Chandler, the attorney for Francis Cardinal Spellman of New York.

Because most free exercise cases are based on hostile action by the state directed at specific individuals or organizations, petitions to the courts for a redress of free exercise grievances are generally "defensive" in nature. *See, e.g., Cantwell v. Connecticut,* 310 U.S. 296 (1940) (criminal prosecution for preaching door-to-door); *Pierce v. Society of Sisters,* 268 U.S. 510 (1925) (closure of religious schools); *The Late Corporation of the Church of Jesus Christ of Latter Day Saints v. United States,* 136 U.S. 1, 50 (1890) (revoking the corporate charter of the LDS Church). Where the grievance is an alleged violation of the nonestablishment principle, the petition asks the court to invalidate legislative or executive action that either supports or "endorses" religion. *See generally* Carl H. Esbeck, *The Establishment Clause as a Structural Restraint on Governmental Power,* 84 Iowa L. Rev. 1, 98 (1998) (arguing that "the purpose of the Establishment Clause is not to safeguard individual religious rights"); Kathleen Sullivan, *Religion and Liberal Democracy,* 59 U. Chi. L. Rev. 195, 198 (1992) ("The correct baseline... is not unfettered religious liberty, but rather religious liberty insofar as it is consistent with the establishment of the secular public moral order.").

The conflict over the meaning of the Establishment Clause has largely been described as a dispute between "separationists" and "accommodationists," but neither term is accurately characterizes the positions taken by the contending factions. Though most Protestant and Jewish organizations have been characterized as "separationist," and Catholics and some others as "accommodationist," their positions vary. A more accurate picture emerges if one examines the coalitions formed on an issue-by-issue basis over the long term: *e.g.,* school prayer, public finance, tax policy, church autonomy, and free exercise.

1) Protestant Organizations

Shortly after *Everson,* a group of liberal and conservative Protestant clergy founded Protestants and Other Americans United for the Separation of Church and State (in 1972, the organization changed its name to Americans United for the Separation of Church and State). According to a former President of Americans United (AU), it

> was shocked into existence. Bishops of the largest denomination of the United States, the Roman Catholic, had denounced Separation of Church and State as the "shibboleth of doctrinaire secularism." They summoned their people to work "patiently, persistently and perseveringly" for its destruction.

Morgan, Politics of Religious Conflict, at 52 (quoting Louie D. Newton from undated AU pamphlet entitled "Wake Up America!").

As suggested by the quote, AU originally was formed to counteract perceived Catholic desires to "destroy" the Jefferson's metaphorical wall separating church and state. Although originally an effort of both liberal and conservative Protestants, AU eventually began to "speak[] the separationism of conservative, traditionalist, and fundamentalist Protestantism." This separationism was driven by "an underlying, pervasive fear of Roman Catholic social and political power." Sorauf, Wall of Separation, at 33. *See also* Morgan, Politics of Religious Conflict, at 52–53. During the first quarter-century of its existence, AU's strict "separationist" stance was considered part and parcel of its fear of Roman Catholicism. Since 1972, AU's strict separationist approach has remained, although its anti-Catholic rhetoric, as partly indicated by its name change, has lessened.

Several other Protestant organizations have also been active in Establishment Clause litigation and in legislative efforts to maintain a "strict" separation of church and state: The National Council of Churches' Commission on Religious Liberty; the Seventh-day

Adventists' International Religious Liberty Association, and the Baptist Joint Committee on Public Affairs.

2) *Jewish Organizations*

The American Jewish Congress (Jewish Congress) was formed in the aftermath of World War I. Since that time, it has supported many significant religious liberty cases. In Professor Frank Sorauf's view

> [t]he separationism of the American Jewish Congress springs directly from the experience of Reform and Conservative Judaism. The public alliances with religion in the United States have almost invariably been alliances with Christian religions. Jewish separationism is, in short, impelled by the vulnerabilities of a religious minority that understands that accommodations between church and state have in the past too often served as vehicles of majority religious intolerance.

Sorauf, WALL OF SEPARATION, at 33.

For nearly four decades, the most important church-state strategist and litigator at the Jewish Congress was Leo Pfeffer. Perhaps the most famous of all advocates in Establishment Clause matters, Mr. Pfeffer was born in Austria-Hungary. At the age of two, he emigrated with his family to the United States when his father, an Orthodox Rabbi, obtained a rabbinate in New York. He became a staff member of the Commission on Law and Social Action of the American Jewish Congress in October 1945, and eventually served for a time as its Director. His "books, articles and briefs constitute the most polished expression of the strict separationist constitutional position." Morgan, POLITICS OF RELIGIOUS CONFLICT, at 55.

For reasons relating New York politics, the American Jewish Congress did not join the *Everson* litigation, but the next year, Pfeffer wrote an *amicus* brief urging the Court to hold unconstitutional the released-time program of the public schools in Champaign, Illinois. (*McCollum*) During the next thirty years, Pfeffer's work as counsel for the American Jewish Congress, and his scholarly work in the area of church-state relations, made him the most influential lawyer in the United States on Religion Clause cases. For details on his career, *see* Leo Pfeffer, *An Autobiographical Sketch*, in RELIGION AND THE STATE: ESSAYS IN HONOR OF LEO PFEFFER 487, 488, 492–93 (1985). Pfeffer, who died in 1993, was a self-described "strict separationist." *Id.* at 531.

Equally active in both litigation and legislative affairs is the American Jewish Committee (AJC). Its traditional focus has been on service to the Jewish community on matters of community interest, including religious liberty, and significant efforts to eradicate religious discrimination and bigotry. It also serves the community at large with education, outreach, and coalition building efforts in support of civil and human rights.

3) *Catholic Organizations*

The Catholic Church is organized in hierarchical form. *See* Chapter Seven. Each Bishop answers only to the Pope, and each has the authority to retain counsel to defend the interests of Catholics within his diocese. For approximately twenty-five years after *Everson*, then-Archbishop of New York, Francis Cardinal Spellman, directed his personal attorney, Porter Chandler, of the New York City law firm of Davis, Polk & Wardwell, to join in defending the interests of Catholics in cases where the actions of governmental bodies were challenged as violations of the Establishment Clause. Morgan,

Supreme Court and Religion, at 91. The legal representation of Catholic interests was coordinated at the federal level through the legal and policy staff of the National Catholic Welfare Conference, later to be called the United States Catholic Conference (USCC), and recently renamed the United States Conference of Catholic Bishops (USCCB). Its legal and policy offices employ full-time counsel to advise the Bishops on a wide range of civil law issues, to evaluate and testify on pending legislation in Congress and the State legislatures, to engage, when necessary, in litigation, and to submit *amicus* briefs in both state and federal litigation.

During the period between 1970 and his death in early 1999, the best-known litigator representing Catholic interests was the late William Bentley Ball of Pennsylvania, who also represented the Amish respondents in both *Wisconsin v. Yoder* and *United States v. Lee.*

4) Other Organizations

The American Civil Liberties Union (ACLU) is not an organization whose primary focus is on religious liberty, but it has played a major role in shaping the contours of the jurisprudence of the first amendment. The ACLU's efforts at the local, state, and national levels have supported a "strict separation" between church and state, and have had a profound effect on the Supreme Court's interpretation of the Establishment Clause. In many cases, the ACLU's separationism has centered on the protection of dissenters who view a purely "secular" state as the best protection for religious liberty.

The formation of the Christian Legal Society's Center for Law and Religious Freedom (CLS) in 1975 marked the beginning of a new activism among religiously motivated religious freedom activists. Reacting in part to what they considered to be inconsistencies in the Court's religious liberty jurisprudence, CLS and other organizations like it began an aggressive litigation and legislative effort to ensure that religious groups were not deprived of equal access to otherwise public space. *See, e.g., Widmar v. Vincent*, 454 U.S. 263 (1981); Equal Access Act 20 U.S.C. §§4071 *et seq.* (1984). Some of these organizations focus on protecting the interests of Protestant Christians, while others focus on the protection of the religious freedom interests of Catholics, Orthodox Jews, Mormons, and other religious minorities. *See generally* Mark Curriden, *Defenders of the Faith*, ABA J., December 1994, at 86. Those professing no religion have also been active in litigation under the Establishment Clause. Among them are the American Atheists and the Freedom from Religion Foundation.

For a more up-to-date summary of the activities of the organizations mentioned, consult the websites of those that maintain them: American Atheists (www.atheists.org); American Center for Law and Justice (www.aclj.org); American Civil Liberties Union (www.aclu.org); American Jewish Committee (www.ajc.org); American Jewish Congress (www.ajcongress.org); Americans United for Separation of Church and State (www.au.org); Baptist Joint Committee on Public Affairs (www.bjcpa.org); Becket Fund for Religious Liberty (www.becketfund.org); Catholic League for Religious and Civil Rights (www.catholicleague.org); Christian Legal Society (www.clsnet.org); Freedom from Religion Foundation (www.ffrf.org); Rutherford Institute (www.rutherford.org); and United States Conference of Catholic Bishops (www.usccb.org).

5) Religiously Motivated Individuals

Individuals have also played an important role in Establishment Clause litigation. An animal lover who apparently believed that rabbis and Catholic priests had scuttled a proposed New York law requiring the humane slaughter of animals in kosher slaughterhouses, Frederick Walz, bought a six-hundred square foot parcel of land to establish taxpayer status, and then commenced litigation urging the unconstitutionality of tax exemptions, see *Walz v. Tax Commission*, 397 U.S. 664 (1970), excerpted in Section E(3) above. A lawyer, Walz conducted his own litigation until the case came before the Supreme Court. Sorauf, at 137. Two Harvard Law School students, apparently energized by their learning in a Constitutional Law class, began a suit challenging the army chaplaincy, and refused assistance from outside organizations. *See* Israel Drazin & Cecil B. Currey, For God and Country: The History of a Constitutional Challenge to the Army Chaplaincy 1 (1995).

3. Access to the Courts: Standing

Standing to sue in the federal courts is a complex topic with constitutional, statutory, and prudential underpinnings. *See generally* William W. Buzbee, *Standing and the Statutory Universe*, 11 Duke Envtl. L. & Pol'y F. 247 (2001). Standing to sue in state courts is a creature of common, statute, and constitutional law. *See generally* Helen Hershkoff, *State Courts and the "Passive Virtues": Rethinking the Judicial Function*, 114 Harv. L. Rev. 1833 (2001); Steven H. Steinglass, *Litigating Section 1983 Actions in State Courts*, 618 PLI/Lit 45 (1999).

In order to gain access to the courts, an individual or association must show some personal "injury-in-fact" to a legally protected interest. In cases arising under the Free Exercise Clause, such injuries are not difficult to show. In Establishment Clause cases where individuals are compelled to participate personally in activities with which they disagree, injury-in-fact is also readily discernable. Where the injury is to a more generalized public interest, or a violation of a structural restraint on government action, it is difficult for an individual or group to make the case that there is a *personal* injury-in-fact. This is particularly true in cases involving federal funds, religious displays on public property, or state actions that are perceived to "endorse" religion.

In *Frothingham v. Mellon*, 262 U.S. 447 (1923), the Court held that federal taxpayers did not have standing to challenge the constitutionality of a federal statute, but in *Flast v. Cohen*, 392 U.S. 83 (1968), the Court "decide[d that] the *Frothingham* barrier should be lowered when a taxpayer attacks a federal statute on the ground that it violates the Establishment and Free Exercise Clauses of the First Amendment." *Id.* at 85.

The federal taxpayer must make a two-part showing. First, there must be a nexus between the taxpayer's status as a taxpayer and the source of the power Congress used to adopt the legislation under scrutiny. Thus, a federal taxpayer has standing to challenge legislation adopted under the Taxing and Spending Clause, but not, for example, under the Property Clause, U.S. Const. Article IV, § 3, cl. 2. *Valley Forge Christian Academy v. Americans United for Separation of Church and State*, 454 U.S. 464 (1982). Second, "the taxpayer must establish a nexus between that status and the precise nature of the constitutional infringement alleged. Under this requirement, the taxpayer must show that the challenged enactment exceeds specific constitutional limitations imposed upon the exercise of the congressional taxing and spending power and not simply that the enactment is generally beyond the powers delegated to Congress by Art. I, § 8." *Flast*, 392 U.S. at 102–103. Citing Madison's *Memorial and Remonstrance Against Religious Assessments*, Chief Justice Earl Warren held that "[t]he Establishment Clause... operates as a specific constitutional limitation upon the exercise by Congress of the taxing and spending power conferred by Art. I, § 8." *Id.* at 104. Justices Douglas and Stewart concurred. Justice Harlan dissented.

The Court has "consistently adhered to *Flast* and the narrow exception it created to the general rule against taxpayer standing established in *Frothingham*." *Bowen v. Kendrick*, 487 U.S. 589 (1988). It has not, however, taken up the issues presented by cases involving "expressive harm" caused by public displays that are alleged to "endorse" religion. *See City of Edmond v. Robinson*, 517 U.S. 1201 (1996) (Rehnquist, C.J. & Scalia and Thomas, JJ., dissenting from the denial of *certiorari*) (noting that there is "disagreement among the Courts of Appeals about whether *Valley Forge* allowed standing to a plaintiff alleging direct injury by being exposed to a state symbol that offends his beliefs.") *See generally* Note, *Expressive Harms and Standing*, 112 Harv. L. Rev. 1313 (1999). *See also* Jay S. Bybee, *Common Ground: Robert Jackson, Antonin Scalia, and a Power Theory of the First Amendment*, 75 Tul. L. Rev. 251 (2000).

How *should* the Court interpret and apply "the right of the people ... to petition the Government for a redress of grievances"? As you consider the following list, ask whether any others are possible, or preferable.

Chart 5-7
Possible Meanings of the Liberty
"to Petition the Government for a Redress of Grievances"

Abstract	personal autonomy regarding any type of grievance, public or private
Formulation	non-association with disagreeable advocacy
(high level)	collective support of political campaigns
↓	personal support of political campaigns
Level	lobbying by hired proxy
of	collective, issue-oriented political action or activity
Generality	collective, issue-oriented litigation
↑	personal communication with any legislator on any issue
Specific	personal communication with one's own Congressional representatives
Formulation	communication with federal administrators or the courts regarding personal
(low level)	interests

J. Equal Protection & the Religious Liberty Guarantee

In *Cantwell* and *Everson*, the Court "incorporated" the First Amendment and applied it to the States via the Due Process Clause of the Fourteenth. As a result, there is a necessary relationship between the norms (or "clauses") of the First Amendment and the equality norms of the Fourteenth. The Court, however, has only recently begun to examine the implications of this important relationship. "[T]he Civil War Amendment is mentioned only in passing or not at all," and the result is that "we appear to be applying the First Amendment directly" when, actually, we are not. Amar, *The Bill of Rights as a Constitution*, 100 Yale L.J. at 1136–37. See § B(1), above.

In this section, we explore the how, if at all, the Equal Protection Clause affects the Court's interpretation of the religious liberty guarantees embedded in the No Religious Test Clause and the First Amendment.

1. Religious Discrimination

Religious discrimination and prejudice, like their counterparts in the field of race and gender relations, have a long and sordid pedigree in this country. *De jure* religious discrimination led to Roger Williams' exile from Massachusetts and the founding of Rhode Island. The laws of Great Britain and the Colonies demonstrate that unequal citizenship is the organizing principle of "an establishment of religion" that seeks political control of the social and cultural life of the community. *See* James Madison, *Memorial & Remonstrance Against Religious Assessments* ("[T]he Bill violates that equality which out to be the basis of every law.") Deeply ingrained in the fabric of community life, religious discrimination was common in the States even after the adoption of post-colonial laws designed to guarantee religious liberty. The vestiges of that discrimination have played a major role in national and local political struggles ever since. *See* Chapter Four.

Over forty million immigrants entered the United States from Europe during the century between 1820 and 1920. Their foreign ways, languages, and loyalties put enormous pressure on the social and political culture into which they would eventually be assimilated. Historians recount that the politics of the period were tainted by overt religious, ethnic, and racial animus. *See generally* Chapters Three and Four. The constitutional, statute, and case law of the period also bears witness to the intensity of the politics of cultural, ethnic, and religious identity. *See Witters v. State Comm'n for the Blind*, 112 Wash. 2d 363, 373, 771 P.2d 1119 (Wash. 1989) (Utter, J., dissenting) (discussing the impact of religious prejudice on the text of the 1889 Washington State Constitution), *reaffirming on state constitutional grounds* on remand from *Witters v. Washington Dep't of Servs. for the Blind*, 474 U.S. 481 (1986), *rev'g* 102 Wash.2d 624, 689 P.2d 53 (1984), excerpted in Chapter Six § F.

Discrimination on the basis of race, national origin (which is often equated with race), and religion (which is often associated with nationality) was practiced openly through much of American history. A wide range of discriminatory legal policies neutral on their face, but discriminatory in both purpose and effect were adopted. *See Pierce v. Society of Sisters*, 268 U.S. 510 (1925), excerpted in Chapter Six § B. *See also St. Francis College v. Al-Khazraji*, 481 U.S. 604, 613 (1987) (defining "race discrimination" under 42 U.S.C. § 1981, as applied to persons of Arab descent); *Shaare Tefila Congregation v. Cobb*, 481 U.S. 615, 617–18 (1987) (defining of "race discrimination" under 42 U.S.C. §§ 1981 & 1982, as applied to persons of Jewish descent).

Vestiges of religious discrimination are also apparent in today's case law. *See* Richard A. Baer, Jr., *The Supreme Court's Discriminatory Use of the Term "Sectarian,"* 6 J.L. & Pol. 449 (1990). *See also* Chapter Six (discussing the "schools question"). So too is the prejudice and intolerance suffered by adherents of the religious traditions of recent immigrants arriving in the United States from Africa, the Caribbean Basin, Central and South America, the Pacific Rim, and the Indian subcontinent. *See, e.g., Church of Lukumi Babalu Aye, Inc. v. City of Hialeah*, 508 U.S. 520 (1993)(Caribbean and African religious traditions); *State v. Singh*, 117 Ohio App.3d 381, 690 N.E.2d 917 (Ohio App. 1996) (prosecution of Sikh for carrying ceremonial dagger).

2. Religion as a "Suspect Classification"

The law of the Equal Protection Clause focuses on the classifications the government utilizes to make policy. Because all policy making requires line drawing, the courts will look carefully at the basis for the government's action. If the lines are drawn on the basis of criteria that define the scope of the government's regulatory interest, the courts will apply only a minimal, or "rational basis," standard of review. *Lindsley v. Natural Carbonic Gas Co.*, 220 U.S. 61 (1911). Where the lines are drawn on the basis of personal characteristics such as race, sex, age, national origin, the classification is subject to a "heightened" level of scrutiny. The result is a "two-tiered" standard of review. *See City of Cleburne v. Cleburne Living Center, Inc.*, 473 U.S. 432, 440–41 (1985).

Characteristics that are almost always irrelevant to government action, such as race and national origin, are deemed "inherently suspect." Those that are sometimes relevant to legitimate government regulatory or social welfare interests, such as age and sex, are subject to a more flexible, or "intermediate," level of scrutiny. In either case, the inquiry is the same: 1) What are the *precise* reasons why the government has elected to classify persons in this manner? and 2) What is the nexus, or "fit," between the goals the government is seeking to accomplish and the classifications used to attain them?

Whether, and under what circumstances, the government may use religion as the basis for decision-making is thus a matter of concern under the No Religious Test Clause of Article VI, the Religion Clause, *and* the Equal Protection Clause. Because religious discrimination is often at least one factor in the grievance to be redressed in a religious liberty case, an "equal protection approach" to a factual finding that religious discrimination occurred would begin with the following question: *Is religion an "inherently suspect" classification under the Equal Protection Clause?*

The case law appears to answer this question in the affirmative, but the materials in this chapter indicate that the Court does not generally use equal protection analysis when it decides petitions for redress of grievances that can be resolved under the Religion Clause. Although there is case law that indicates that religion is a "suspect classification," the Court has never used that term in a case in which it actually found that intentional religious discrimination had taken place. *Compare Burlington Northern Railroad Co. v. Ford,* 504 U.S. 648, 651 (1992) (stating that religion is a suspect classification), *and City of New Orleans v. Dukes,* 427 U.S. 297, 303 (1976) (dictum stating that religion is a suspect-classification) *with Church of Lukumi Babalu Aye, Inc. v. City of Hialeah,* excerpted in §D(1) (Free Exercise Clause violation based on finding of intentional discrimination against Santeria religious practices) and *Sherbert v. Verner*, 374 U.S. 398 (1963) (Free Exercise Clause violation premised on "burden" rather than the statute's unequal treatment of Sabbatarians and Sunday observers).

How *should* the Court deal with laws that draw distinctions on the basis of religion? The case law supplies four possible approaches, and that the choice of approach appears to depend on the facts of the case.

Although the Court has never so held, the Test Clause of Article VI, which forbids religious tests for "any office or public trust under the United States," may support an argument that religious belief or affiliation can *never* be the sole criterion for government action. *See* §F, above, and Chapter Eight §G. *See generally* T. Jeremy Gunn, A Standard for Repair: The Establishment Clause, Equality and Natural Rights, 177–186 (1992). Such a rule would require the government prove that religion, religious affiliation, or lack thereof played no role whatever in its decisions. Some of the Court's cases under the Establishment and Speech and Press Clauses appear to rest on this approach. *See, e.g., Good News Club v. Milford Cent. Sch.*, 533 U.S. 98 (2001) (holding religious content restrictions in a public forum violate the Speech and Press Clause); *Texas*

Monthly v. Bullock, 489 U.S. 1, 11 (1989), excerpted in Chapter Nine (holding that a tax exemption for religious publications violates the Establishment and Speech and Press Clauses); *Lynch v. Donnelly*, 465 U.S. 668, 693–94 (1984)) (O'Connor, J., concurring) (concluding Establishment Clause forbids "making adherence to a religion relevant in any way to a person's standing in the political community.")

The second approach is to treat religion, like race and national origin, as an "inherently suspect" criterion under the Equal Protection Clause. A finding that the classification is based on religion would trigger a presumption that the law is unconstitutional unless the State bears the burden of proving that it is justified by a clearly articulated, "compelling" state interest. The Court appears to have adopted this standard under the Free Exercise Clause. *See, e.g., Lukumi* and *Employment Div. v. Smith*, excerpted in §D(1) above.

A third approach analyzes religious discrimination using the same "intermediate" standard of review that the Court uses in sex discrimination cases. The Court would assume at the outset that some classifications based on religion are reasonable and that others are invalid because they are based on stereotypes or prejudice. Examination of the factual context in which the classification is employed then becomes critical. *Compare J.E.B. v. Alabama* ex rel. *T.B.*, 511 U.S. 127 (1994) (holding that courts may not permit gender-based peremptory challenges to jurors) *with e.g., State v. Davis*, 504 N.W.2d 767 (Minn., 1994), *cert. denied* 511 U.S. 1115 (1994) (permitting religion-based peremptory challenges to potential jurors) *and People v. Martin*, 64 Cal.App.4th 378, 75 Cal.Rptr.2d 147, 150 (1998) (strikes based on affiliation alone, as distinguished from religious beliefs that will affect a juror's judgment, violate California constitution), *and State v. Martinez*, 196 Ariz. 451, 999 P.2d 795, 800 (2000), *cert. denied*, 531 U.S. 934 (2000) (noting the difference between a peremptory challenges based on religion alone and those based on the prospective juror's responses to questions about potential bias). Whether or not the Test Clause would be determinative when the public office or trust is federal has not been decided. *See Card v. United States*, 776 A.2d 571 (D.C. 2001) (indicating that religion-based challenges to potential jurors are unconstitutional without referring to the Test Clause).

A fourth approach, found only in Establishment Clause cases, assumes that religion can be a *legitimate* criterion for government action where the concern is that equal treatment will "advance" religion. *See, e.g., Mitchell v. Helms*, 530 U.S. 793, 879–882 (2001) (Souter, Stevens & Ginsburg, JJ., dissenting)("There is no rule of religious equal protection to the effect that any expenditure for the benefit of religious school students is necessarily constitutional so long as public school pupils are favored on ostensibly identical terms."); *Capitol Square Review and Advisory Bd. v. Pinette*, 515 U.S. 753 (1995) (Ginsburg, J., dissenting) ("If the aim of the Establishment Clause is genuinely to uncouple government from church, [see *Everson*], a State may not permit, and a court may not order, a [religious] display [unattended in close proximity to Ohio's Statehouse.]").

3. Religious Exemptions and Accommodations

Much of the debate over the Supreme Court's decision in *Employment Div. v. Smith*, centered on its holding that the government has no obligation to remedy burdens on religious belief or practice that result from a "valid and neutral law of general applicability." Before the judiciary will intervene, there must be a showing of intentional discrimination or an otherwise invalid attempt to regulate the exercise of another protected right (a "hybrid"). *Accord Washington v. Davis*, 426 U.S. 229 (1976) (proof of "effects" alone will not support a finding that the Equal Protection Clause has been violated). Legislatures, however, are free to write legislation in a way that avoids the disproportionate impact that facially neutral laws can have on religious believers.

Such a development leaves advocates for religious liberty and the Court in a tight bind. Legislation *intended* to accommodate religious belief and practice is subject to challenge under the Establishment Clause. The Court has invalidated an accommodation that "singles out a particular religious sect for special treatment." *Board of Educ. of Kiryas Joel Village Sch. Dist. v. Grumet*, 512 U.S. 687, 707 (1994). It struck down a Connecticut law requiring employers to accommodate the Sabbath preferences of their employees because the accommodation "impermissibly advances a particular religious practice," *Estate of Thornton v. Caldor, Inc.*, 472 U.S. 703, 709–710 (1985), and it rejected a Texas sales tax exemption designed to accommodate religious publishers because the State showed "[n]o concrete need to accommodate religious activity." *Texas Monthly*, 489 U.S. 1, 18 (1989). *Cf. Corporation of Presiding Bishop v. Amos*, 483 U.S. 327, 348 (1987) (upholding provision of federal labor law permitting certain religious organizations to use religious criteria in hiring).

Read together, the cases elaborate a jurisprudence very much like the one applied in Equal Protection cases. Where an individual is in need of *protection* from state-sponsored discrimination or its effects, either the Court or the legislature can step in. Two points remain unsettled: 1) When does the need for protection arise? and 2) Who has the final word on the need for protection? We address both questions in the final section of this chapter, §K, below.

4. Mandating Equal Access

a) Voluntary Prayer, Bible Reading & Religious Instruction

Viewed against the backdrop of history, the Supreme Court's 1962 decision in *Engel v. Vitale*, 370 U.S. 421 (1962) to ban compulsory prayer and Bible reading in public schools might be termed the "mid-point" of the long-running battle over prayer in the public schools. Chapter Four §B(1) recounts that the first controversy over these practices arose in 1840, when the New York City's Public School Society reached an impasse with Catholics who would not send their children to the free "common schools" unless there was a compromise on the daily practice of reading from the King James Version of the Bible without comment or interpretation. The Public School Society refused. Bible reading without comment or interpretation was one of the linchpins holding Protestant support for the common schools together. The King James Version was acceptable to Protestants, but commentary or interpretation was viewed as "sectarian." For Catholics, who used the Douay Version, compulsory reading from the King James Bible was unacceptable. In their view, the "common school" practice was inconsistent with the rights of their children, and the School Society's refusal to compromise confirmed their view that the public schools were, in fact, what they had long suspected: sectarian institutions supported by public funds.

Over the course of the next 120 years, many public schools maintained the fiction that compulsory recitation of the Lord's Prayer and a verse from the King James Bible was "nonsectarian." *See Donahoe v. Richards*, 38 Me. 379 (1854) (confirming expulsion of Catholic student who refused to read from the King James Version). *Compare Stevenson v. Hanyon*, 7 Pa. Dist. 585 (1898) (holding practice nonsectarian); *Pfeiffer v. Board of Educ.*, 77 N.W. 250 (Mich. 1898) (same) *with State* ex rel. *Weiss v. District Board*, 44 N.W. 967 (Wis. 1890), excerpted in Chapter Four (holding practice sectarian). *See also Minor v. Board of Educ. of Cincinnati*, 23 Ohio St. 211 (1872) (upholding School Board's decision to eliminate practice on the grounds that it was sectarian). Until the early 1900s, Massachusetts was the only state to require the practice by statute. After 1913, the pattern changed. Eleven states and the District of Columbia enacted statutes requiring Bible reading in the public schools. *See* Chapter Four § B(1) & notes following.

After *Engel*, most schools complied, but questions concerning the scope of the ruling continued until the Court decided *Lee v. Weisman* in 1992. Others, most recently the public schools in Santa Fe, Texas, have resisted up to the present day. *Santa Fe Indep. Sch. Dist. v. Doe*, 530 U.S. 290, 308 (2000). A few others took exactly the opposite view: that any and all public "prayer in schools"—by any person—is forbidden. *See Widmar v. Vincent*, 454 U.S. 263 (1981) (invalidating a University of Missouri-Kansas City policy forbidding prayer meetings in spaces otherwise available for student use).

By the early 1980s, it had become clear that some high schools were hostile to student-initiated voluntary prayer, and that some courts were not sympathetic either. *Brandon v. Board of Educ.*, 635 F.2d 971, 979 (2d Cir. 1980), *cert. denied*, 454 U.S. 1123 (1981) (upholding the exclusion of a student prayer group); *Trietley v. Board of Educ. of Buffalo*, 65 A.D.2d 1, 409 N.Y.S.2d 912 (1978) (same). Building on the rationale in *Widmar*, and adjusting for the Court's jurisprudence in the school aid cases discussed in Chapter Six § F, Congress responded by passing the Equal Access Act.

The Equal Access Act

20 U.S.C. §§ 4071 *et seq.* (1984)

§ 4071. Denial of equal access prohibited

(a) *Restriction of limited open forum on basis of religious, political, philosophical, or other speech content prohibited*

It shall be unlawful for any public secondary school which receives Federal financial assistance and which has a limited open forum to deny equal access or a fair opportunity to, or discriminate against, any students who wish to conduct a meeting within that limited open forum on the basis of the religious, political, philosophical, or other content of the speech at such meetings.

(b) *"Limited open forum" defined*

A public secondary school has a limited open forum whenever such school grants an offering to or opportunity for one or more noncurriculum related student groups to meet on school premises during noninstructional time.

(c) *Fair opportunity criteria*

Schools shall be deemed to offer a fair opportunity to students who wish to conduct a meeting within its limited open forum if such school uniformly provides that—

(1) the meeting is voluntary and student-initiated;

(2) there is no sponsorship of the meeting by the school, the government, or its agents or employees;

(3) employees or agents of the school or government are present at religious meetings only in a nonparticipatory capacity;

(4) the meeting does not materially and substantially interfere with the orderly conduct of educational activities within the school; and

(5) nonschool persons may not direct, conduct, control, or regularly attend activities of student groups.

(d) Federal or State authority nonexistent with respect to certain rights

Nothing in this subchapter shall be construed to authorize the United States or any State or political subdivision thereof—

(1) to influence the form or content of any prayer or other religious activity;

(2) to require any person to participate in prayer or other religious activity;

(3) to expend public funds beyond the incidental cost of providing the space for student-initiated meetings;

(4) to compel any school agent or employee to attend a school meeting if the content of the speech at the meeting is contrary to the beliefs of the agent or employee;

(5) to sanction meetings that are otherwise unlawful;

(6) to limit the rights of groups of students which are not of a specified numerical size; or

(7) to abridge the constitutional rights of any person.

(e) Unaffected Federal financial assistance to schools

Notwithstanding the availability of any other remedy under the Constitution or the laws of the United States, nothing in this subchapter shall be construed to authorize the United States to deny or withhold Federal financial assistance to any school.

(f) Authority of schools with respect to order-and-discipline, well-being, and voluntary-presence concerns

Nothing in this subchapter shall be construed to limit the authority of the school, its agents or employees, to maintain order and discipline on school premises, to protect the well-being of students and faculty, and to assure that attendance of students at meetings is voluntary.

§ 4072. Definitions

As used in this subchapter—

(1) The term "secondary school" means a public school which provides secondary education as determined by State law.

(2) The term "sponsorship" includes the act of promoting, leading, or participating in a meeting. The assignment of a teacher, administrator, or other school employee to a meeting for custodial purposes does not constitute sponsorship of the meeting.

(3) The term "meeting" includes those activities of student groups which are permitted under a school's limited open forum and are not directly related to the school curriculum.

(4) The term "noninstructional time" means time set aside by the school before actual classroom instruction begins or after actual classroom instruction ends.

§ 4073. Severability

If any provision of this subchapter or the application thereof to any person or circumstances is judicially determined to be invalid, the provisions of the remainder of the subchapter and the application to other persons or circumstances shall not be affected thereby.

§ 4074. Construction

The provisions of this subchapter shall supersede all other provisions of Federal law that are inconsistent with the provisions of this subchapter.

The Supreme Court upheld the Equal Access Act in ***Board of Educ v. Mergens***, 496 U.S. 226 (1990). Writing for the majority, Justice O'Connor held that the Act did not violate the Establishment Clause. Three years later, in *Lamb's Chapel v. Center Moriches Union Free Sch. Dist.*, 508 U.S. 384 (1993), the Court held that denial of equal access to public school facilities during after school hours because of the religious content of the messages to be conveyed at the meetings violated the Free Speech Clause, and that nondiscriminatory access for religious and nonreligious groups did not violate the Establishment Clause. *Good News Club v. Milford Cen. Sch.,* 533 U.S. 98 (2001), confirms and extends that rationale to after-school prayer meetings at a public elementary school.

b) Equal Opportunity to Participate in Government Assistance Programs

In 1996, Congress extended the rationale of the Equal Access Act to public welfare programs. *See* Personal Responsibility and Work Opportunity Reconciliation Act of 1996, Pub. L. No. 104-193, 110 Stat. 2105 (codified as amended in scattered sections of 42 U.S.C.). Known as "Charitable Choice," the equal access provision is codified at 42 U.S.C. § 604a (2001). Its purpose is explicit. Section 604a(b), provides:

> The purpose of this section is to allow States to contract with religious organizations, or to allow religious organizations to accept certificates, vouchers, or other forms of disbursement under any program described in subsection (a)(2) of this section, on the same basis as any other nongovernmental provider without impairing the religious character of such organizations, and without diminishing the religious freedom of beneficiaries of assistance funded under such program.

Charitable Choice

§ 604a. Services provided by charitable, religious, or private organizations

(a) In general

(1) State options

A State may—

(A) administer and provide services under the programs described in subparagraphs (A) and (B)(i) of paragraph (2) through contracts with charitable, religious, or private organizations; and

(B) provide beneficiaries of assistance under the programs described in subparagraphs (A) and (B)(ii) of paragraph (2) with certificates, vouchers, or other forms of disbursement which are redeemable with such organizations.

(2) Programs described

The programs described in this paragraph are the following programs:

(A) A State program funded under part A of title IV of the Social Security Act [42 U.S.C.A. §601 *et seq.*] (as amended by section 103(a) of this Act).

(B) Any other program established or modified under title I or II of this Act, that—

(i) permits contracts with organizations; or

(ii) permits certificates, vouchers, or other forms of disbursement to be provided to beneficiaries, as a means of providing assistance.

(b) Religious organizations

The purpose of this section is to allow States to contract with religious organizations, or to allow religious organizations to accept certificates, vouchers, or other forms of disbursement under any program described in subsection (a)(2) of this section, on the same basis as any other nongovernmental provider without impairing the religious character of such organizations, and without diminishing the religious freedom of beneficiaries of assistance funded under such program.

(c) Nondiscrimination against religious organizations

In the event a State exercises its authority under subsection (a) of this section, religious organizations are eligible, on the same basis as any other private organization, as contractors to provide assistance, or to accept certificates, vouchers, or other forms of disbursement, under any program described in subsection (a)(2) of this section so long as the programs are implemented consistent with the Establishment Clause of the United States Constitution. Except as provided in subsection (k) of this section, neither the Federal Government nor a State receiving funds under such programs shall discriminate against an organization which is or applies to be a contractor to provide assistance, or which accepts certificates, vouchers, or other forms of disbursement, on the basis that the organization has a religious character.

(d) Religious character and freedom

(1) Religious organizations

A religious organization with a contract described in subsection (a)(1)(A) of this section, or which accepts certificates, vouchers, or other forms of disbursement under subsection (a)(1)(B) of this section, shall retain its independence from Federal, State, and local governments, including such organization's control over the definition, development, practice, and expression of its religious beliefs.

(2) Additional safeguards

Neither the Federal Government nor a State shall require a religious organization to—

(A) alter its form of internal governance; or

(B) remove religious art, icons, scripture, or other symbols;

in order to be eligible to contract to provide assistance, or to accept certificates, vouchers, or other forms of disbursement, funded under a program described in subsection (a)(2) of this section.

(e) Rights of beneficiaries of assistance

(1) In general

If an individual described in paragraph (2) has an objection to the religious character of the organization or institution from which the individual receives, or would receive, assistance funded under any program described in subsection (a)(2) of this section, the State in which the individual resides shall provide such individual (if otherwise eligible for such assistance) within a reasonable period of time after the date of such objection with assistance from an alternative provider that is accessible to the individual and the value of which is not less than the value of the assistance which the individual would have received from such organization.

(2) Individual described

An individual described in this paragraph is an individual who receives, applies for, or requests to apply for, assistance under a program described in subsection (a)(2) of this section.

(f) Employment practices

A religious organization's exemption provided under section 2000e-1 of this title regarding employment practices shall not be affected by its participation in, or receipt of funds from, programs described in subsection (a)(2) of this section.

(g) Nondiscrimination against beneficiaries

Except as otherwise provided in law, a religious organization shall not discriminate against an individual in regard to rendering assistance funded under any program described in subsection (a)(2) of this section on the basis of religion, a religious belief, or refusal to actively participate in a religious practice.

(h) Fiscal accountability

(1) In general

Except as provided in paragraph (2), any religious organization contracting to provide assistance funded under any program described in subsection (a)(2) of this section shall be subject to the same regulations as other contractors to account in accord with generally accepted auditing principles for the use of such funds provided under such programs.

(2) Limited audit

If such organization segregates Federal funds provided under such programs into separate accounts, then only the financial assistance provided with such funds shall be subject to audit.

(i) Compliance

Any party which seeks to enforce its rights under this section may assert a civil action for injunctive relief exclusively in an appropriate State court against the entity or agency that allegedly commits such violation.

(j) Limitations on use of funds for certain purposes

No funds provided directly to institutions or organizations to provide services and administer programs under subsection (a)(1)(A) of this section shall be expended for sectarian worship, instruction, or proselytization.

(k) Preemption

Nothing in this section shall be construed to preempt any provision of a State constitution or State statute that prohibits or restricts the expenditure of State funds in or by religious organizations.

Notes

1. Consider the sections of the statute individually in light of *Zelman v. Simmons-Harris*, 122 S.Ct. 2460 (2002), and answer the following questions for each one:

   a) What is the subject of each provision? For example, §604a(h)(2)(j) prohibits the use of funds for "sectarian worship, instruction, or proselytization."

   b) Why was it necessary or useful to include a provision of this type?

   c) What specific legal or practical problems does it seek to address or solve?

   d) What, if any, constitutional problems does it cause? For whom?

2. There is a growing literature on the topic of equal treatment. *See, e.g.*, Alan E. Brownstein, *Evaluating School Voucher Programs Through a Liberty, Equality, and Free Speech Matrix*, 31 Conn. L. Rev. 871 (1999); Stanley W. Carlson-Thies, *"Don't Look To Us": The Negative Responses of the Churches to Welfare Reform*, 11 Notre Dame J.L. Ethics & Pub. Pol'y 667 (1997); Susanna Dokupil, *A Sunny Dome with Caves of Ice: The Illusion of Charitable Choice*, 5 Tex. Rev. L. & Pol. 149 (2000); Carl H. Esbeck, *Charitable Choice and the Critics*, in Symposium on *The Legal Frontier of Religious Freedom: Religion and State in the Twenty-First Century* 57 N.Y.U. Ann. Surv. Am. L. 17 (2000); Harlan A. Loeb, *Suffering In Silence: Camouflaging The Redefinition Of The Establishment Clause*, 77 Or. L. Rev. 1305 (1998); Ira C. Lupu, *The Case Against Legislative Codification of Religious Liberty*, in Symposium: *State and Federal Religious Liberty Legislation: Is It Necessary? Is It Constitutional? Is It Good Policy?*, 21 Cardozo L. Rev. 565 (1999); Julie A. Segal, *Welfare for Churches: Buyers and Beneficiaries Beware*, 5 Geo. J. on Fighting Poverty 71 (1997); Eugene Volokh, *Equal Treatment Is Not Establishment*, 13 Notre Dame J.L. Ethics & Pub. Pol'y 341 (1999).

3. At this writing, there is only one reported opinion on "Charitable Choice." *Freedom from Religion Foundation v. McCallum*, 179 F. Supp. 2d 950 (W.D. Wis. 2002) (invalidating a specific grant because the recipient of the grant was a "pervasively sectarian" organization).

4. For a comparative law perspective on equal treatment, see Shimon Shetreet, *State and Religion: Funding of Religious Institutions—The Case of Israel in Comparative Perspective*, 13 Notre Dame J.L. Ethics & Pub. Pol'y 421 (1999).

K. Separation of Powers & Federalism: The Structural Components of the Religious Liberty Guarantee

To this point in the chapter, the focus has been on the religious liberty jurisprudence of the Supreme Court of the United States. In this section, we take a brief look at the "structural" components of the Religious Liberty Guarantee: separation of powers and federalism. There are three basic questions:

1) What are the sources and limits of State authority to legislate on the subject of religious liberty?
2) What are the sources and limits of Congressional authority to legislate on the subject of religious liberty?
3) How, if at all, do the substantive and structural components of the Religious Liberty Guarantee limit the powers of the Supreme Court?

These questions raise both "structural" and "jurisdictional" issues. The jurisdictional issues arise because the Constitution divides the power of the "People of the United States" to ensure that religious liberty is protected among Congress, the Executive, and the States. The structural issues arise because the "judicial power of the United States" extends only to the case or controversy before the Court. In all other cases, the rule of decision announced stands as a precedent binding on lower courts, and provides guidance to policy makers outside the Judicial Branch. Congress and the States, by contrast, are policymakers in their own right. Their powers function as checks and balances, and permit each to use its own authority to modify, clarify, or mitigate the impact of Supreme Court decisions on those who were not parties to the case in which the rule was announced.

1. State Power to Protect Religious Liberty

At the beginning of this chapter, we noted that State laws, including their constitutions, form a conceptual "bracket" around the federal religious liberty guarantee. This is so for two reasons. First, the debates over the structure of the Constitution were not debates over "*which* rights existed, or *whether* rights existed, but how to design a government that would not infringe upon those rights." Gunn, A STANDARD FOR REPAIR at 142. The first seven words of the Preamble to the Constitution of the United States—"We, the People of the United States"—assume that the People themselves, acting in community, have both the power and the responsibility to protect the inalienable rights of individual, including religious freedom.

Second, the federalism embraced by the Constitutional Convention of 1787 and reaffirmed by the Fourteenth Amendment in 1868, was a structural device designed to guard against the possibility that the federal government could come to be dominated by factions inhospitable to the rights of individuals and local communities. *See* Remarks of Luther Martin in response to Oliver Ellsworth, March 18, 1788, in THE DOCUMENTARY HISTORY OF THE RATIFICATION OF THE CONSTITUTION: COMMENTARIES ON THE CONSTITUTION, PUBLIC AND PRIVATE 16:418 (John P. Kaminski & Gaspare J. Saldino eds. 1986), *quoted in* Gunn, at 161–162 n. 98 (noting that state governments are more immediately responsible, and responsive, to the direct will of the people).

For the Framers, the debate was over *which* group of legislators was better suited to safeguard the rights of the People: the State legislatures or Congress. Madison, who, as "Publius," wrote eloquently of the merits of both separation of powers and federalism in *The Federalist,* did not embrace either concept at the Constitutional Convention. Madison did not believe that the States were able to control factions. In his view, the task could be accomplished only at the national level, and required a representative body diverse enough to produce "disinterested majorities, strongly disposed to seek the general good of the society." Charles F. Hobson, *The Negative on State Laws: James Madison, the Constitution, and the Crisis of Republican Government*, 36 Wm. & Mary Q 215, 232–234 (3d ser. 1979). The Anti-federalists, by contrast, put their trust in political decision-making at a level of government closer to the people, and their faith in representatives known to and trusted by their local communities. *See, e.g.*, "The Address and Reasons of Dissent of the Minority of the convention of Pennsylvania to their Constituents" (December 18, 1787) (attributed to Samuel Bryan, the author of "Centinel"), *in* Ralph Ketcham, The Anti-Federalist Papers and the Constitutional Convention Debates 237, 239 (1986). For them, recognition of the States as distinct political communities and the inclusion of a Bill of Rights in the Constitution were complementary "safeguards... interposed between [the People] and the magistrate who exercises sovereign power." 1 *Annals of Congress* 433 (June 8, 1789) (remarks of James Madison). *Accord, e.g.,* Ariz. Const. Art. 2 § 8 (protecting informational privacy); Fla. Const. Art. 1 § 23 (same); Wash. Const. art 1 § 7 (same); *Roberts v United States Jaycees*, 468 U.S. 609 (1984) (upholding Minnesota's ban on sex-discrimination as applied to a private association).

Although the Fourteenth Amendment is generally viewed as limiting the powers of the States over matters of individual rights, the Citizenship Clause actually reaffirms the position of the anti-Federalists that the primary obligation to protect and defend the rights of the people lies in the political communities in which they have a controlling voice: the States. Made necessary by the Supreme Court's holding in *Dred Scott v. Sandford*, 60 U.S. (19 How.) 393 (1856), the Citizenship Clause repudiates the Supreme Court's holding that Congress and the States are not the primary guardians of the rights of all persons entrusted to their care. By conferring state citizenship as an incident of residency, the Citizenship Clause restored the power of the States to enact and enforce general laws to protect the civil and human rights of all persons who reside within their jurisdiction.

Thus, by virtue of the Fourteenth Amendment itself, the explicit federalism embodied in the First, Ninth and Tenth Amendments remains as a "structural" protection designed to limit the impact of a narrow federal vision on the people's understanding of their rights.

The power of the States to "expand upon" the federal vision of the limits of religious freedom is well settled, but the federalism boundaries of the Religious Liberty Guarantee are not. Part B(9)(a) of this Chapter—"Federalism, Separation of Powers and Free Exercise"—points out that one of the most important results of *Employment Div. v. Smith*, 494 U.S. 872 (1990) was the political response of Congress and the legislatures of several States. Their goal was simple: to "restore" the protection that the Supreme Court of the United States had eliminated when it rejected the "compelling state interest" standard of review for cases involving free exercise challenges to the burdens imposed by neutral laws of general applicability.

The federal response to *Smith* is discussed in the next section, but Congress did not act alone. Several States acted to limit the impact of *Smith*, either through judicial interpretation of the state constitution, or legislative action adopting local versions of the Religious Freedom Restoration Act (RFRA), discussed in subsection (b)(5) below.

Another, equally important, component of this discussion appears in Chapter Six § F(2)(b)(2)—"The Structural Aspects of the Non-Establishment Guarantee." State constitutional provisions governing aid to religiously affiliated schools and other institutions are often far more explicit than the rules developed by the Supreme Court since *Everson v. Board of Educ.*, 330 U.S. 1 (1947). Whether, and to what extent, a State may restrict the participation of religiously motivated individuals and institutions in otherwise neutral programs of general applicability is an open question. *See Witters v. Washington Comm'n for the Blind*, 112 Wash.2d 363, 771 P.2d1119 (en banc, 1989), *on remand from*, 474 U.S. 481 (1986), *cert. denied*, 493 U.S. 850 (1989), excerpted in Chapter Six § F(2).

2. Congressional Power to Protect Religious Liberty

Congress is the branch of the federal government charged with the power to make laws conducive to the general welfare. Although it has no explicit power to protect religious liberty, it can adopt general legislation mandating the protection of individual rights whenever doing so can be justified as a "necessary and proper" means of attaining an otherwise legitimate goal. *See, e.g., Corporation of Presiding Bishop v. Amos* (discussing forms religious discrimination regulated through Title VII of the Civil Rights Act of 1964); *Katzenbach v. McClung*, 379 U.S. 294 (1964) (upholding laws prohibiting race discrimination); *Heart of Atlanta Motel, Inc. v. United States*, 379 U.S. 241 (1964) (upholding laws prohibiting discrimination in public accommodations).

The Fourteenth Amendment both reaffirmed and expanded the scope of Congressional power to legislate protection for the rights of individuals. Read together with the Citizenship Clause, the Privileges and Immunities and Enforcement Clauses confer unquestioned power upon the Congress to enact legislation designed to protect citizens of the United States against State action. U.S. Const. Amend. XIV § 5. Like the Bill of Rights, the provisions of Article I, §§ 9 and 10, and Article IV §§ 1 and 2, the Privileges and Immunities, Due Process and Equal Protection Clauses of the Fourteenth Amendment specify the particular evils their respective framers sought to avoid.

3. The Judicial Branch & Religious Liberty

The Constitution assigns a single role to the federal judiciary: the decision of discrete cases or controversies. U.S. Const. Art. III, § 2. In contrast with norms fixed by legislation, rules developed through a case-by-case analysis tend to be fact-specific and remain "in process" over a long period of time. Sections C through J of this chapter recount the development of the law of religious liberty at the federal level since 1890.

The case law applying the First Amendment to both Congress and the States is best understood as a reflection of the federal judiciary's vision of two related, but distinct, topics: 1) the substantive balance to be struck between religious liberty and the demands of organized society, and 2) the appropriate political balance to be struck between and among those charged with the responsibility to protect individual rights: the federal judiciary, the Congress, and the States. *See Planned Parenthood v. Casey*, 505 U.S. 833, 850 (1992) (plurality opinion), adopting the rationale of Justice Harlan's dissent *Poe v. Ullman*, 367 U.S. 497, 542–43 (1961)(noting that the meaning of "liberty" in the Due Process Clause "has represented the balance which our Nation, built upon postulates of respect for the liberty of the individual, has struck between that liberty and the demands of organized society").

When a plausible case can be made that a rule announced by the Supreme Court is wrong, or that it exceeds the scope of the Court's authority, there are only two places aggrieved citizens can go for a remedy: to Congress, or to their State of residence. Separation of powers and federalism thus provide the fora in which citizens can petition for redress when their grievances arise from an exercise of "the judicial power of the United States." Given the inherently political nature of the process by which constitutional norms are developed and the case-by-case nature of constitutional adjudication, it should not be surprising that Congress and the States *regularly* use their powers to test the limits of the Court's rulings. *See, e.g.*, Equal Access Act, 20 U.S.C. §§4071 *et seq.* (2001), discussed in §G(2), above.

4. Resolving Federalism and Separation of Powers Disputes Over the Meaning of the Incorporated Religious Liberty Guarantee

a) The Structure of a Separation of Powers Analysis

The text of the Fourteenth Amendment is an important, but generally overlooked, factor in religious liberty cases. The Court has claimed the language of Section One as the source of judicial authority to "incorporate" the Bill of Rights, including the Religion Clause, but Section One also subjects *the Court itself* to the checks and balances imposed by Congressional and State powers to protect individual rights. When a dispute arises over the Court's interpretation of the free exercise or non-establishment norms, the primary focus of the controversy will be on the separation of powers and federalism "boundaries" set out by the *Fourteenth* Amendment, not the First.

In *Oregon v. Mitchell*, 400 U.S. 112, 264 n.37 (1970), Justice Brennan noted that:

> the framers of the [Fourteenth] Amendment were not always clear whether they understood it merely as a grant of power to Congress or whether they thought, in addition, that it would confer power upon the courts, which the courts would use to achieve equality of rights. Since §5 is clear in its grant of power to Congress and we have consistently held that the Amendment grants power to the courts, this issue is of academic interest only.

When the issue is the legitimacy of Congressional or State action that seeks to "remedy" an error committed *by the Court*, however, the nature and scope of the power granted to the federal judiciary is hardly "academic." It becomes the central focus of the inquiry because the Court's *Fourteenth Amendment* powers are limited by those the amendment specifically grants or restores to Congress and the States. *See Youngstown Sheet & Tube v. Sawyer*, 343 U.S. 579, 637–638 (1952) (Jackson, J., concurring). It is therefore necessary to distinguish the Court's powers under Article III from the powers granted to Congress by the Fourteenth Amendment, and the powers restored to the States by the Citizenship Clause.

b) The Fourteenth Amendment and Its Impact on the Powers of Congress, the Federal Judiciary, and the States

The language of the Fourteenth Amendment is, for the most part, phrased in the negative. It assumes that an exercise of federal lawmaking authority will occasionally be necessary to provide a remedy for those aggrieved by State or federal action. The amendment thus provides a firm footing for enforcing otherwise valid federal rules protecting the citizenship and equality interests of those subject to the jurisdiction of the United States. *See Civil Rights Cases*, 109 U.S. 3, 11 (1883)(Section 5 does not "authorize Congress to create a code of municipal law for the regulation of private rights; but to provide modes of redress against the operation of state laws, and the action of state officers when these are subversive of the fundamental rights specified in the amendment.").

The Court has concluded from these factors, and from the legislative history of the amendment itself, that Congress' powers under the Fourteenth Amendment are "remedial." Thus, when Congress acts under Section 5 of the Fourteenth Amendment, it must have a rational basis for concluding that remedial legislation of the type and scope proposed is necessary to resolve the grievances of those seeking its protection.

States, by contrast, do not derive *any* power from the Fourteenth Amendment. The Citizenship Clause simply restores the power to define the privileges and immunities of *state* citizenship that were limited by the Supreme Court's decision in *Dred Scott.* When a *State* adopts legislation, amends its constitution, or announces a judicial rule designed to alter the effect of a Supreme Court decision in its courts or executive agencies, it need only show that its law is not *inconsistent* with the United States Constitution. Because the Court has held that the Fourteenth Amendment "confer[s] power upon the courts, which the courts would use to achieve equality of rights," the federalism boundary between the States and the Court thus appears to be the point at which a State's definition of equal rights or equal citizenship would deny the equality of citizenship or protection mandated by either the Fourteenth Amendment or an act of Congress.

The separation of powers boundary between Congress and the Court is much more difficult to pinpoint. The Fourteenth Amendment can be read two ways. If it provides rules of decision that guide the Court in the normal exercise of its Article III power to decide cases or controversies, the Court's powers are also remedial. The Court can intervene when it decides that a State law or policy violates the equality provisions embedded in either the Constitution, or the laws passed by Congress to enforce them. *See Employment Div. v. Smith.* If, however, the Fourteenth Amendment is read to confer power that *enhances* its pre-existing Article III authority to "say what the law is," the Court need not demonstrate that its holdings are "remedial" in nature. It can use its Article III power "to say what the law is" as an invitation to look to sources beyond the Constitution and laws of the United States for the purpose of "achieve[ing] equality of rights." *See Poe v. Ullman*, 367 U.S. 497, 543 (1961) (Harlan, J., dissenting) ("" [T]he full scope of the liberty guaranteed by the Due Process Clause cannot be found in or limited by the precise terms of the specific guarantees elsewhere provided in the Constitution.... It is a rational continuum which, broadly speaking, includes a freedom from all substantial arbitrary impositions and purposeless restraints,...and which also recognizes,...

that certain interests require particularly careful scrutiny of the state needs asserted to justify their abridgment.").

5. The Religious Freedom Restoration Act

All of these issues came together in the controversy over the Supreme Court's decision in *Employment Div. v. Smith.* The case reached the Supreme Court because neither the Oregon legislature nor the Oregon Supreme Court were willing to use their own authority modify Oregon's drug-control laws to permit the sacramental use of peyote in Native American religious rituals. The Oregon Supreme Court was willing to hold that the *federal* constitution requires such an accommodation, but was unwilling to interpret the state constitution to provide that relief. *Smith v. Employment Div.*, 301 Or. 209, 215, 721 P.2d 445 (1986). The Supreme Court remanded for clarification of the State's position. On remand, the Oregon Supreme Court held that state law *did* prohibit the religious use of peyote, but that the Free Exercise Clause required an accommodation. *Smith v. Employment Div.*, 307 Or. 68, 75–76, 763 P.2d 146, 149–150 (1988)(per curiam). The Supreme Court reversed, holding that there is nothing in the Free Exercise Clause that prohibits Oregon from enforcing an otherwise valid law of "general applicability," notwithstanding the burden imposed on the ability of adherents of the Native American Church to practice their faith. *Smith* is summarized in detail in § D(7), above.

The reaction to *Smith* among religious freedom advocates and civil libertarians was both swift and intense. They petitioned both Congress and the States for a redress of a grievance rooted in the *Court's* interpretation of the First Amendment.

The State courts that disagreed with the Court's holding in *Smith* were the first to act. Although recognizing the power of the Supreme Court to construe the United States Constitution, they explicitly retained the Supreme Court's *Sherbert v. Verner* "compelling state interest test" as the rule of decision for cases governed by their own State constitutions. In *State v. Hershberger*, 462 N.W. 2d 393, 396 (Minn. 1990), for example, the Minnesota Supreme Court held that members of the Amish faith having a sincere religious belief that forbids use of the "slow-moving vehicle" symbol on their horse-drawn vehicles could not be prosecuted.

> Only the government's interest in peace or safety or against acts of licentiousness will excuse an imposition on religious freedom under [Art. I § 16 of] the Minnesota Constitution. Conversely, the free exercise clause of the first amendment has been interpreted to allow varied government interests to justify such an imposition. [citing *Bowen v. Roy* and *Goldman v. Weinberger*]

Accord First Covenant Church v. City of Seattle, 840 P.2d 174 (Wash. 1992) (assessing historic preservation ordinance as applied to church in light of compelling state interest test). *But see First Church of Christ v. Historic District Commission*, 737 A.2d 989 (Conn. App. 1999), *cert. denied*, 742 A.2d 358 (Conn. 1999) (upholding denial of application to install vinyl siding on historic church against state RFRA claim). *See* Angela C. Carmella, *State Constitutional Protection of Religious Exercise: An Emerging Post-*Smith *Jurisprudence*, 1993 B.Y.U. L. Rev. 275; Tracey Levy, Comment, *Rediscovering Rights: State Courts Reconsider the Free Exercise Clauses of Their Own Constitutions in the Wake of* Employment Division v. Smith, 67 Temple L. Rev. 1017 (1994) (listing reactions by state courts to *Smith*).

There was considerable political activity as well. Opponents of *Smith* immediately began lobbying both Congress and the State legislatures for the passage of the Religious Freedom

Restoration Act, 42 U.S.C. §§2000bb–2000bb-4 (Supp. V 1993), popularly known as "RFRA." At this writing, approximately ten States have adopted laws patterned on RFRA, and Alabama has amended its constitution to provide additional protection for the religious liberty interests of its citizens. *See, e.g.*, Thomas C. Berg, *The Alabama Religious Freedom Amendment: An Interpretive Guide*, 31 Cumb. L. Rev. 47 (2000–2001); Lisle A. Stalter, *A Practical Overview of Illinois' Religious Freedom Restoration Act*, 88 Ill. B.J. 96 (2000).

Although passage of the federal RFRA was delayed by some bickering among large religious organizations over the impact of the proposed statute on access to abortion and the interpretation of the Establishment Clause, Congress adopted it in late 1993, a little more than three years after *Smith* was decided.

Religious Freedom Restoration Act

42 U.S.C. §§2000bb–2000bb-4 (Supp. V 1993)

42 U.S.C. §2000bb. Congressional findings and declaration of purposes

(a) Findings

The Congress finds that—

(1) the framers of the Constitution, recognizing free exercise of religion as an unalienable right, secured its protection in the First Amendment to the Constitution;

(2) laws "neutral" toward religion may burden religious exercise as surely as laws intended to interfere with religious exercise;

(3) governments should not substantially burden religious exercise without compelling justification;

(4) in *Employment Division v. Smith*, 494 U.S. 872 (1990) the Supreme Court virtually eliminated the requirement that the government justify burdens on religious exercise imposed by laws neutral toward religion; and

(5) the compelling interest test as set forth in prior Federal court rulings is a workable test for striking sensible balances between religious liberty and competing prior governmental interests.

(b) Purposes

The purposes of this chapter are—

(1) to restore the compelling interest test as set forth in *Sherbert v. Verner*, 374 U.S. 398 (1963) and *Wisconsin v. Yoder*, 406 U.S. 205 (1972) and to guarantee its application in all cases where free exercise of religion is substantially burdened; and

(2) to provide a claim or defense to persons whose religious exercise is substantially burdened by government.

§2000bb-1. Free exercise of religion protected

(a) In general

Government shall not substantially burden a person's exercise of religion even if the burden results from a rule of general applicability, except as provided in subsection (b) of this section.

(b) Exception

Government may substantially burden a person's exercise of religion only if it demonstrates that application of the burden to the person—

(1) is in furtherance of a compelling governmental interest; and

(2) is the least restrictive means of furthering that compelling governmental interest.

(c) Judicial relief

A person whose religious exercise has been burdened in violation of this section may assert that violation as a claim or defense in a judicial proceeding and obtain appropriate relief against a government. Standing to assert a claim or defense under this section shall be governed by the general rules of standing under Article III of the Constitution.

§ 2000bb-2. Definitions

As used in this chapter—

(1) the term "government" includes a branch, department, agency, instrumentality, and official (or other person acting under color of law) of the United States, a State, or a subdivision of a State;

(2) the term "State" includes the District of Columbia, the Commonwealth of Puerto Rico, and each territory and possession of the United States;

(3) the term "demonstrates" means meets the burden of going forward with the evidence and of persuasion; and

(4) the term "exercise of religion" means the exercise of religion under the First Amendment to the Constitution.

§ 2000bb-3. Applicability

(a) In general

This chapter applies to all Federal and State law, and the implementation of that law, whether statutory or otherwise, and whether adopted before or after November 16, 1993.

(b) Rule of construction

Federal statutory law adopted after November 16, 1993, is subject to this chapter unless such law explicitly excludes such application by reference to this chapter.

(c) Religious belief unaffected

Nothing in this chapter shall be construed to authorize any government to burden any religious belief.

§ 2000bb-4. Establishment clause unaffected

Nothing in this chapter shall be construed to affect, interpret, or in any way address that portion of the First Amendment prohibiting laws respecting the establishment of religion (referred to in this section as the "Establishment Clause"). Granting government funding, benefits, or exemptions, to the extent permissible under the Establishment Clause, shall not constitute a violation of this chapter. As used in this section, the term "granting", used with respect to government funding, benefits, or exemptions, does not include the denial of government funding, benefits, or exemptions.

The Supreme Court invalidated RFRA in ***City of Boerne, Texas v. Flores***, 521 U.S. 507 (1997), a case that pitted the historic preservation interests of the City of Boerne against the needs of the congregation of St. Peter's Roman Catholic Church. The parish needed to expand the church building to accommodate its growing congregation, but the City refused to grant a building permit because of its fear that the expansion would destroy the mission-style architecture of the original building and detract from the preservation efforts it was fostering in Boerne's central business district. Archbishop Flores sued, relying on RFRA as the basis of his claim for relief. The United States District Court for the Western District of Texas held that RFRA was an unconstitutional attempt by Congress to "intrud[e] on the power and duty of the judiciary." *Flores v. City of Boerne*, 877 F. Supp. 355, 356–57 (W.D. Tex. 1995).

In a 6-3 decision written by Justice Kennedy and joined by Justices Ginsburg, Thomas, Scalia (in part), and Chief Justice Rehnquist, the Supreme Court affirmed. Justice Kennedy observed that that Congress enacted RFRA in direct response to the Court's decision in *Smith*, that "[m]any [members of Congress] criticized the Court's reasoning, and [that] this disagreement resulted in the passage of RFRA." *Id.* at 514–515. The majority agreed that Congress has extensive powers to adopt "legislation which deters or remedies constitutional violations…, even if in the process it prohibits conduct which is not itself unconstitutional and intrudes into legislative spheres of autonomy previously reserved to the States." *Id.* at 518. It also agreed that Congress has the power to enforce the constitutional right to the free exercise of religion because the "'provisions of this article,' to which §5 refers, include the Due Process Clause of the Fourteenth Amendment." *Id.* at 519.

Drawing a clear distinction between the power of the Court and the power of Congress, the majority flatly rejected "[a]ny suggestion that Congress has a substantive, non-remedial power under the Fourteenth Amendment" as "not supported by our case law." *Id.* at 527. Justice Kennedy observed that

> Congress' power to enforce the Free Exercise Clause follows from our holding in *Cantwell v. Connecticut* that the "fundamental concept of liberty embodied in [the Fourteenth Amendment's Due Process Clause] embraces the liberties guaranteed by the First Amendment."
>
> Congress' power under §5, however, extends only to "enforc[ing]" the provisions of the Fourteenth Amendment. The design of the Amendment and the text of §5 are inconsistent with the suggestion that Congress has the power to decree the substance of the Fourteenth Amendment's restrictions on the States. Legislation which alters the meaning of the Free Exercise Clause cannot be said to be enforcing the Clause. Congress does not enforce a constitutional right by changing what the right is. It has been given the power "to enforce," not the power to determine what constitutes a constitutional violation. Were it not so, what Congress would be enforcing would no longer be, in any meaningful sense, the "provisions of [the Fourteenth Amendment]."

Id. at 519. He acknowledged that the line between remedial or preventive measures and those that change the governing law "is not easy to discern," and conceded that the explicit grant of power to Congress means that it "must have wide latitude in determining where it lies," but emphasized that "the distinction exists and must be observed." *Id.* at 519–520. The test, wrote Justice Kennedy, is whether there is a "congruence and proportionality between the injury to be prevented or remedied and the means adopted to that end." Without such a connection, "legislation may become substantive in operation and effect." *Id.* at 520.

In the Court's judgment, RFRA failed the test of "congruence and proportionality" for two related reasons. First, in contrast to the Voting Rights Act, "RFRA's legislative record lacks examples of modern instances of generally applicable laws passed because of religious bigotry.... Rather, the emphasis of the hearings was on laws of general applicability which place incidental burdens on religion." *Id.* at 530. Second, and more important, "RFRA is so out of proportion to a supposed remedial or preventive object that it cannot be understood as responsive to, or designed to prevent, unconstitutional behavior. It appears, instead, to attempt a substantive change in constitutional protections." *Id.* at 531.

> The substantial costs RFRA exacts, both in practical terms of imposing a heavy litigation burden on the States and in terms of curtailing their traditional general regulatory power, far exceed any pattern or practice of unconstitutional conduct under the Free Exercise Clause as interpreted in *Smith.* Simply put, RFRA is not designed to identify and counteract state laws likely to be unconstitutional because of their treatment of religion. If a state law disproportionately burdened a particular class of religious observers, this circumstance might be evidence of an impermissible legislative motive. Cf. *Washington v. Davis,* 426 U.S. 229, 241 (1976). RFRA's substantial-burden test, however, is not even a discriminatory effects or disparate-impact test.... When the exercise of religion has been burdened in an incidental way by a law of general application, it does not follow that the persons affected have been burdened any more than other citizens, let alone burdened because of their religious beliefs.

Id. at 534–535.

Justices Stevens agreed that RFRA was unconstitutional, but would have held RFRA violative of the Establishment Clause. In his view, "the statute has provided the [Catholic] Church with a legal weapon that no atheist or agnostic can obtain. This governmental preference for religion, as opposed to irreligion, is forbidden by the First Amendment." *Id.* at 537. Most of Justice Scalia's concurring opinion is an extended response to the dissenters' claim in *Boerne* that the historical record proves that the Court was wrong in *Smith, see id.* at 537–544, but his conclusion highlights the issue of federalism. Unlike the majority, however, he does not focus on the federalism boundary between Congress and the States, but rather on the boundary between the people and the Court.

> The issue presented by *Smith* is, quite simply, whether the people, through their elected representatives, or rather this Court, shall control the outcome of those concrete cases. For example, shall it be the determination of this Court, or rather of the people, whether (as the dissent apparently believes) church construction will be exempt from zoning laws? The historical evidence put forward by the dissent does nothing to undermine the conclusion we reached in *Smith*: It shall be the people.

Justices O'Connor, Souter, and Breyer dissented. In Justice O'Connor's view, *Smith* was wrongly decided, and the Court should have used the situation in *Boerne* to reexamine that holding. "If the Court were to correct the misinterpretation of the Free Exercise Clause set forth in *Smith,*... [w]e would then be in a position to review RFRA in light of a proper interpretation of the Free Exercise Clause." *Id.* at 545. Making it clear that she agreed with most of the Court's interpretation of Section 5, she noted that "if [she] agreed with the Court's standard in *Smith,* [she] would join the opinion." *Id.* Justice Breyer did not concur with Justice O'Connor on this point because, in his view, it was not "necessary to consider the question whether, assuming *Smith* is correct, §5 of the Fourteenth Amendment would authorize Congress to enact the legislation before us." *Id.* at 566. Justice Souter, believing that the Court had not properly considered the issues in *Smith*, would have dismissed the writ of *certiorari* as improvidently granted. Id. (Souter, J., dissenting.)

Notes

1. The *pre-* and *post-Boerne* commentary on RFRA has been extensive. For a review of the arguments prior to *Boerne, compare, e.g.,* Douglas Laycock & Oliver S. Thomas, *Interpreting the Religious Freedom Restoration Act,* 73 Tex. L. Rev. 209 (1994) *and* Thomas C. Berg, *What Hath Congress Wrought? An Interpretive Guide to the Religious Freedom Restoration Act,* 39 Vill. L. Rev. 1 (1994) *with, e.g.,* Marci A. Hamilton, *The Religious Freedom Restoration Act: Letting the Fox into the Henhouse Under Cover of Section 5 of the Fourteenth Amendment,* 16 Cardozo L. Rev. 357 (1994) (arguing that RFRA violates separation of powers) *and* Jed Rubenfeld, *Antidisestablishmentarianism: Why RFRA Really Was Unconstitutional,* 95 Mich. L. Rev. 2347 (1997) (RFRA violates the Establishment Clause). *See also Symposium on RFRA,* 56 Mont. L. Rev. 5 *et seq.* (1995).

2. Although the Court held that RFRA is unconstitutional as applied to the States, the lower courts are divided on its constitutionality as applied to the federal government. Congress has taken the position that it remains applicable to federal action. *See* Religious Liberty and Charitable Donations Protection Act of 1998, P.L. 105-183, §6 (noting that nothing in the Act "is intended to limit the applicability of" RFRA). Among the cases upholding RFRA as applied to federal action are: *EEOC v. Catholic Univ.*, 83 F.3d 455, 469–70 (D.C. Cir. 1996) (pre-*Boerne*); *Christians v. Crystal Evangelical Free Church,* 141 F.3d 854 (8th Cir. 1998); *Sutton v. Providence St. Joseph Med. Center,* 192 F.3d 826 (9th Cir. 1999); and *Kikumura v. Hurley,* 242 F.3d 950, 957–61 (10th Cir. 2001). Cases taking the opposite view are include: *La Voz Radio de la Communidad v. FCC,* 223 F.3d 313, 319 (6th Cir. 2000) (noting the court's "doubt" that RFRA is constitutional as applied to the federal government); *Waguespack v. Rodriguez,* 220 B.R. 31, 36–37 (W.D. La. 1998) (holding that RFRA "was declared unconstitutional in its totality and for all purposes"); *In re Saunders,* 215 B.R. 800, 803–06 (Bankr. D. Mass. 1997) (application of RFRA in bankruptcy cases violates the Establishment and Free Exercise Clauses). *See generally* Gregory P. Magarian, *How to Apply the Religious Freedom Restoration Act to Federal Law Without Violating the Constitution,* 99 Mich. L. Rev. 1903 (2001); Michael K. Sabers, Note, *Well, It Depends on What Your Definition of "Unconstitutional" Is: The Eighth Circuit's Misinterpretation of* Flores *in* Christians v. Crystal Evangelical Free Church, 44 S.D. L. Rev. 432 (1999).

3. In the years since *Boerne* was decided, the Supreme Court has invalidated numerous statutes because their application to the States exceeds the scope of Congressional power under Section 5. *See, e.g., Board of Trustees of University of Alabama v. Garrett,* 531 U.S. 356 (2001) (Americans with Disabilities Act); *United States v. Morrison,* 529 U.S. 598 (2000) (Violence Against Women Act of 1994); *Kimel v. Florida Bd. of Regents,* 528 U.S. 62 (2000) (Age Discrimination in Employment Act). *See also Alden v. Maine,* 527 U.S. 706 (1999) (Eleventh Amendment does not permit Congress to abrogate state immunity from suit on federal claims in state courts). *See generally* Evan H. Caminker, *Appropriate—Means-Ends Constraints on Section 5 Powers,* 53 Stan. L. Rev. 1127 (2001); Roger C. Hartley, Alden *Trilogy: Praise and Protest,* 23 Harv. J.L. & Pub. Pol'y 323, 373–75 (2000).

4. For a review of the impact of state RFRAs, see Jack S. Vaitayanonta, *In State Legislatures We Trust? The "Compelling Interest" Presumption and Religious Free Exercise Challenges To State Civil Rights Laws*, 101 Colum. L. Rev. 886 (2001); Richard F. Duncan, *Free Exercise Is Dead, Long Live Free Exercise:* Smith, Lukumi *and the General Applicability Requirement*, 3 U. Pa. J. Const. L. 850 (2001); Alvin C. Lin, Note, *Sexual Orientation Antidiscrimination Laws and the Religious Liberty Protection Act: The Pitfalls of the Compelling State Interest Inquiry*, 89 Geo. L.J. 719 (2001).

5. In September 2000, Congress adopted the Religious Land Use and Institutionalized Persons Act of 2000, 42 U.S.C.A. §§2000cc–2000cc-5 (2000) [RLUIPA]. Based in part on RFRA, RLUIPA narrowly targets two classes of cases where determinations are made on a case-by-case basis: 1) land use decisions affecting churches and religious institutions; and 2) decisions affecting persons institutionalized in facilities owned or operated by a federal, state or local government. *See* 42 USC § 1997 (2001)(defining "institution"). Does the "case-by-case" analysis take RLUIPA out of the rule of *Smith*?

6. After *Boerne*, what power does Congress have to protect religious liberty? Does it rest on Congress' Article I powers to define the privileges and immunities of citizens of the United States, or is it contingent upon the Court's holdings in *Cantwell* and *Everson*? Could Congress, for example, prohibit *all* discrimination against religious associations seeking federal contracts? *Cf.* "Charitable Choice," 42 U.S.C. §604a (2001), discussed in §J(4)(b), above.

7. For a discussion of the separation of powers boundary between Congress and the Judicial Branch in a dispute with an administrative agency over access to the courts, *see BE & K Construction Co. v. N.L.R.B.*, 122 S.Ct. 2390 (2002) (holding that the NLRB may not limit an employer's right to petition the courts for a redress of grievances, but reserving the question of whether proof of an improper motive for the suit would justify such a limitation).

Chapter 6

Religion in the Classroom

A. Introduction

Education plays a critical role in shaping the lives, beliefs, and behavior of both children and adults. Because it is the means by which families and communities transmit culture, philosophy, and religion to the next generation of adult citizens, education has long been a central concern of parents, churches, and the community at large. The Book of Proverbs, 22:6, for example, offers the following suggestion: "Train up a child in the way he should go, and when he is old he will not depart from it."

Most of the key cases dealing with church-state relations in the United States are rooted in disputes over the respective roles of the church, the state, and the family in matters of education. The organization of this Chapter is designed to highlight the contours of that struggle.

The clearest examples of community-based attempts to teach and foster religious observance among the citizenry at large are found in the practices of the Colonies concerning the support of ministers of the established church. The justification for Virginia General Assessment Bill, the target of Madison's *Memorial and Remonstrance Against Religious Assessments*, was that "the general diffusion of Christian knowledge hath a natural tendency to correct the morals of men, restrain their vices, and preserve the peace of society;" and that this laudable goal could not "be effected without a competent provision for learned teachers, who may be thereby enabled to devote their time and attention to the duty of instructing such citizens, as from their circumstances and want of education, cannot otherwise attain such knowledge." The Massachusetts Constitution of 1780 took a similar approach, stating that "the happiness of a people, and the good order and preservation of civil government" are "essential[ly] depend[ent] on piety, religion, and morality." To that end, it provided that the legislature should provide, and, if necessary, could compel "suitable provision at [the expense of each town], for the institution of the public worship of God, and for the support and maintenance of public Protestant teachers of piety, religion, and morality...."

Although the purpose of Virginia's General Assessment Bill was to raise money to be "appropriated to a provision for a Minister or Teacher of the Gospel [of each religious denomination in the community], or the providing of places of divine worship, *and to none other use whatsoever*" (emphasis added), its reference to "Christian teachers" has been interpreted by the Supreme Court as a reference to anyone in a position to teach religion at public expense. *See* Chapter Five § E. That interpretation has, in turn, become the baseline for its understanding of the incorporated First Amendment's commands concerning the place of religion in publicly funded education.

The Court's interpretation has been a source of much debate for several related, but conceptually distinct, reasons. The most common of these relates to the Court's use of history, and the manner in which it has developed a set of rules based on its understanding of the "Virginia experience" during the founding period. *See* Section E(2), below. These controversies have important substantive and federalism components, for they relate not only to the Court's understanding of the substantive commands of the First Amendment, but also the scope of its authority to supervise the content of state-funded education programs. The federalism questions are discussed at length in Chapter Five § B, and the relationship of the Speech and Press Clause to the Religious Liberty Guarantee in Chapter Five § G.

Another line of inquiry focuses on the manner in which the Court differentiates that which is "religion" or "religious" from that which is "secular." In the Free Exercise context, the definitional problem is how to identify what beliefs are entitled to accommodation. In the non-establishment context issues arise because "secular" and "value-neutral" are not identical concepts. These questions are addressed at greater length in Chapter Thirteen.

The importance—and difficulty—of definitional problems such as these is immediately apparent in cases relating to educational policy. To the extent that schools are a forum for inculcating the values of citizenship and morality, schools funded at public expense are required by current case law to differentiate religious from nonreligious ideas concerning morality and ethics, and to teach only the latter. Not surprisingly, this raises "preference" issues that are the inverse of those in the free exercise context. *See City of Boerne v. Flores*, 521 U.S. 507, 537 (1997) (Stevens, J., concurring) ("This governmental preference for religion, as opposed to irreligion, is forbidden by the First Amendment.") Is it legitimate for the government to prefer "secular" value systems to religious ones in publicly funded education systems? *Compare Remarks by President William J. Clinton on Religious Liberty in America*, July 12, 1995 (arguing that "most Americans are disturbed if they think that our government is becoming anti-religious, instead of adhering to the firm spirit of the First Amendment—don't establish, don't interfere with, but respect.... The First Amendment does not—I will say again—does not convert our schools into religion-free zones.") *with* Kathleen Sullivan, *Religion and Liberal Democracy*, 59 U. Chi. L. Rev. 195, 199–201 (1992) (arguing that "the affirmative implications of the Establishment Clause...entail[] the establishment of a...culture of liberal democracy" even though such a culture "may well function as a belief system with a substantive content, rather than a neutral and transcendent arbiter among other belief systems"). *See also* Chapter Thirteen.

The dynamic nature of disputes over the relationship of religion to education is illustrated by examining the three basic "interests" involved in any discussion of the relationship of religion to education.

1. The parents' obligation to educate their children, and their interest in raising them in the tenets of their faith or other system of belief;
2. A child's need to be educated and socialized as a member of a larger social, economic, moral, and political community, and the rights of the young adult to make educational choices consistent with his or her needs and aspirations;
3. The State's interest in the health, safety and welfare of children, in the preservation and integrity of the family, and in the preservation of a common culture, language, and political tradition.

Much of the state and federal case law defining the substantive parameters of religious liberty has its roots in disputes within and among communities over the balance to be struck among these interests. As you read the cases, take note of the dates on which they were decided. As the cases themselves make clear, each is a chapter in an ongoing debate that stretches back to discussions in colonial settlements over the suitability of candidates for the post of schoolmaster or teacher.

1. Characterization: Selecting an Appropriate Level of Generality and Mode of Interpretation

The task of this Chapter is to illustrate some of the ways in which religious liberty issues arise in the educational context. Because of the multiplicity of issues involved, and the pervasiveness of state action in the funding, oversight, and control of education, these cases invariably raise issues that can be characterized in a number of different ways. It will be appropriate, therefore, to consider a few of the ways in which to classify them.

The following chart contains a list of *possible* ways to describe the issues in a case having both educational and religious elements. Can you think of any others?

Chart 6-1
Possible Characterizations of the Issues—and of the Case—in a Case Involving Education

First Amendment	Family	Liberty	Equal Protection	Federalism
Non-establishment	Custody	Parental rights	Discrimination on the basis of religious belief or preference	Federal preemption of state policy governing religious liberty
Free exercise	Control of religious education	Children's rights	Discrimination on the basis of religion, expression or association	Federal preemption v. state constitutional law
Freedom of speech and press	Captive audience	Academic freedom	Discrimination on the basis of content or perspective	Federal preemption v. state education policy and content
Freedom of assembly association and non-association	Intimate association: custodial rights of parents	Expressive association	Discrimination on the basis of expressive association	Federal preemption v. control of state property and associations

Exercise: *Characterizing a Case Having Religious & Educational Elements*

Consider the following statement of facts from the Supreme Court's opinion in *Good News Club v. Milford Central School District*, 533 U.S. 98, 121 S.Ct. 2093, 2097–2098 (2001). As you do so, make a chart of the questions that should be asked and answered under each of the possible characterizations of the issues. The goal is to give you a sense of the *process* of characterization in a case having both educational and religious elements. Once the characterizations are chosen, evaluation of the legal and constitutional implications can begin.

> **Facts:** The State of New York authorizes local school boards to adopt regulations governing the use of their school facilities. In particular, N.Y. Educ. Law §414 enumerates several purposes for which local boards may open their schools to public use. In 1992, Milford enacted a community use policy adopting seven of §414's purposes for which its building could be used after school. Two of the stated purposes are relevant here. First, district residents may use the school for "instruction in any branch of education, learning or the arts." Second, the school is available for "social, civic and recreational meetings and entertainment events, and other uses pertaining to the welfare of the community, provided that such uses shall be nonexclusive and shall be opened to the general public."
>
> Stephen and Darleen Fournier reside within Milford's district and therefore are eligible to use the school's facilities as long as their proposed use is approved by the school. Together they are sponsors of the local Good News Club, a private Christian organization for children ages 6 to 12. Pursuant to Milford's policy, in September 1996 the Fourniers submitted a request to Dr. Robert McGruder, interim superintendent of the district, in which they sought permission to hold the Club's weekly after school meetings in the school cafeteria. The next month, McGruder formally denied the Fourniers' request on the ground that the proposed use—to have "a fun time of singing songs, hearing a Bible lesson and memorizing scripture,"—was "the equivalent of religious worship." According to McGruder, the community use policy, which prohibits use "by any individual or organization for religious purposes," foreclosed the Club's activities.
>
> In response to a letter submitted by the Club's counsel, Milford's attorney requested information to clarify the nature of the Club's activities. The Club sent a set of materials used or distributed at the meetings and the following description of its meeting:
>
>> The Club opens its session with Ms. Fournier taking attendance. As she calls a child's name, if the child recites a Bible verse the child receives a treat. After attendance, the Club sings songs. Next Club members engage in games that involve, *inter alia,* learning Bible verses. Ms. Fournier then relates a Bible story and explains how it applies to Club members' lives. The Club closes with prayer. Finally, Ms. Fournier distributes treats and the Bible verses for memorization.
>
> McGruder and Milford's attorney reviewed the materials and concluded that "the kinds of activities proposed to be engaged in by the Good News Club were not a discussion of secular subjects such as child rearing, development of character and development of morals from a religious perspective, but were in fact the equivalent of religious instruction itself." In February 1997, the Milford Board of Education adopted a resolution rejecting the Club's request to use Milford's facilities "for the purpose of conducting religious instruction and Bible study."

The process of sorting the facts begins with a relatively straightforward question: Which facts are relevant to what issues? Chart 6-2 illustrates the process by vetting one issue—the State's policy opening its property open discussion "in any branch of education"—and using *each* of the possible characterizations as the basis for a series of ques-

Chart 6-2
Questions Arising from Alternative Characterizations of Issues in Cases Involving Education

Characterization	Questions Arising from Characterization	Relevant Questions of Fact
Non-establishment	1. Can the Board's policy permitting "instruction in any branch of education, learning or the arts" include instruction in religion?	1. What facts, if any, exist that would indicate Board approval or endorsement of the content of program offered under the policy? 2. What facts, if any, exist that would indicate Board approval or endorsement of the content of this program?
	2. How does the Board differentiate between appropriate and inappropriate discussions of religion?	3. To whom has the initial power to grant or refuse permission been delegated? 4. Are there published criteria to guide the exercise of administrative discretion? 5. What programs have been permitted under the policy? 6. What programs have been refused ? 7. In cases in which permission was refused, what specific reasons were given?
Free Exercise	3. Did the Board engage in intentional discrimination against either religion in general, a specific religion, a group of specific believers, or religious expression?	8. What was the stated rationale for the decision? 9. Are there any facts or statements on the part of the Board or its members that would indicate prejudice? 10. Other than a ban, did the Board consider any other options that would address its concerns? 11. If so, what specific options were considered?
Free speech and press	4. What kind of forum for speech has the Board created by adopting this rule?	12. What are the eligibility criteria for access to the forum? 13. What guidelines, if any, exist governing the use of this forum? 14. Are there any exceptions?
	5. Does either the stated rationale for the Board's decision, or the rule governing the forum, discriminate against individuals or community groups on the basis of the content or perspective of their speech?	15. To what extent, if at all, does the Board scrutinize the programs or syllabi of educational programs? 16. Assuming that there is a program review, what criteria guide the reviewers? 17. What topics, if any, are excluded? 18. Is any discussion of religion permitted under these guidelines?

Characterization	Questions Arising from Characterization	Relevant Questions of Fact
		19. If so, how does the Board differentiate between forbidden religious "instruction" and permitted religious "discussion"? 20. If not, what is the rationale for the content restriction? 21. What is the Board's definition of the term "Bible study"? 22. How does the Board differentiate between "Bible study" and use of the Bible as reading material?
Peaceable Assembly, Association and Non-association	6. Is the Board's policy a direct or indirect attempt to control the membership in an association?	23. What is the meaning of the requirement that that "such uses shall be nonexclusive"? 24. Does the Board's policy create a "space" for private association and peaceable assembly?
	7. Is the Board's policy a direct or indirect attempt to control the expressive character of an association?	25. What persons or groups, if any, can be legitimately excluded from this forum, either by the State or by the private parties who use it? 26. How shall the state accommodate the interests of taxpayers who may object to the use of public property for purposes with which they disagree?
Petition for Redress of Grievances	8. Who has standing to complain under these facts?	27. Which parties are aggrieved? The parents? The children? Parents of other children enrolled in the school?
	9. Which forum, federal or state?	28. What are the advantages and disadvantages of filing in a state federal court?
	10. What remedy?	29. Will there be a request for an an injunction, a declaration of rights, damages, or some combination of remedies?

tions that will highlight *one* constitutional issue. Bear in mind that not every possible characterization of an issue will be either useful or plausible, but the exercise is valuable because it forces recognition of issues that might be overlooked because of either preconceived notions about the equities in the case, or unstated biases that might lead an advocate to ignore unpleasant, but relevant, facts. Bear in mind as well that facts will be relevant to the proof or defense of more than one claim.

Once the process of characterization of each issue is complete, a more complete "picture" of the case begins to emerge. It is then possible to draw some conclusions about the best characterization of the case *as a whole*. Try some of the other issues in the case.

2. Differentiating State and Federal Roles

The regulatory framework in which education takes place is a creature of *State* law. *See, e.g.*, Wisconsin. Const., Art. X § 3 (2002). Not surprisingly, it is a framework that reflects the cultural identity, history and priorities of each State. Its basic outlines are found in state constitutions, and the operational framework in state statutory and administrative law. The edifice generally reflects the multiplicity of the state and local interests (or factions) whose efforts have given it shape and substance. The process is intensely political, not only because it involves the welfare of children, but also because it involves enormous sums of money. Review of the case law and the commentary indicate that litigation is an important strategic tool. *See, e.g., Board of Educ. of the Kiryas Joel Village School District v. Grumet*, 512 U.S. 687 (1994); *Grumet v. Cuomo*, 164 Misc.2d 644, 625 N.Y.S.2d 1000 (N.Y. Sup. Ct. 1995), *rev'd* 225 A.D.2d 4, 647 N.Y.S. 2d 565 (3d Dept. 1996), *aff'd, Grumet v. Cuomo*, 659 N.Y. 57, 69, 681 N.Y.S. 2d 173, 681 N.E. 2d 340 (1997); *Zelman v. Simmons-Harris*, 122 S.Ct. 2460 (2002), *cert. granted* 121 S.Ct. 23 (2001). *See also* Chapter Five §§ J(4) and § E and F (1) below.

The United States Constitution makes no provision for the creation or maintenance of an educational system, either public or private. As a result, the Supreme Court views control of educational policy and finance as among the powers reserved to the States by the Tenth Amendment. *See generally United States v. Lopez*, 514 U.S. 549 (1995) (discussing limits imposed by the Commerce Clause on the power of the federal government to regulate education at the local level); *San Antonio Sch. Dist. v. Rodriguez*, 411 U.S. 1 (1973) (rejecting claims that the federal constitution requires equal state educational funding levels).

Although federal policies governing educational matters are pervasive, the jurisdiction of the federal government to make such policies is limited to situations in which Congress has general regulatory power, or in which it has provided funds for education and has attached conditions on their use. The tax, labor, and employment law policies discussed in Chapters Eight and Nine are good examples of generally applicable federal regulatory policies that apply to many schools. Federal civil rights laws also provide an important source of preemptive federal authority, including the authority to apply the First Amendment to the operations of public schools. *See* U.S. Const. Amend. XIV § 5; 42 U.S.C. §§ 1981–1985(3), 1988 (2001) (enforcement of civil rights). "Voluntary" submission to federal authority occurs when Congress, acting pursuant to its authority under the Spending and Necessary and Proper Clauses, authorizes the promulgation of substantive education standards as a condition for federal assistance. *See, e.g.*, Title VI of the Civil Rights Act of 1964, 42 U.S.C. § 2000(d) (2002) ("No person in the United States shall, on the ground of race, color, or national origin, be excluded from participation in, be denied the benefits of, or be subjected to discrimination under any program or activity receiving Federal financial assistance."); *Lau v. Nichols*, 414 U.S. 563 (1974) (obliging school districts to provide bilingual education under the Civil Rights Act of 1964); Title IX of the Education Amendments of 1972, 20 U.S.C. §§ 1681 *et seq.* (2002)(forbidding to sex discrimination in federally funded educational programs).

The division of constitutional authority over educational matters is important. Discussions of the constitutional law governing education generally tend to focus, as this one does, on the case law developed in the Supreme Court. Because state constitutional law often tracks the trends set by the Supreme Court, much of the law dealing with what are generally termed "First Amendment interests" will be the same at the State and federal levels. *See generally* James Gardner, *The Failed Discourse of State Constitutional-*

ism, 90 Mich. L. Rev. 761 (1992) (arguing that state courts have not developed an independent jurisprudence of state constitutional law). But a focus on federal standards will rarely give a complete picture of the complex regulatory framework that governs both state and private education. State constitutional law on education is both well developed and critical to an understanding of the matrix in which education disputes take place. Some of the issues and holdings will be familiar. *E.g.*, Cal. Const. Art. 9, §8 (2002) ("nor shall any sectarian or denominational doctrine be taught, or instruction thereon be permitted, directly or indirectly, in and of the common schools of this State"); Fla. Const. Art. I §3; Art. IX §6 (2002) ("No revenue of the state or any political subdivision or agency thereof shall ever be taken from the public treasury directly or indirectly in aid of any church, sect, or religious denomination or in aid of any sectarian institution."); Nev. Const. Art. 11, §9 (2002) ("No sectarian instruction shall be imparted or tolerated" in the public schools). *See Bush v. Holmes*, 767 So. 2d 668 (Fla. App. 2000) *review denied*, 790 So. 2d 1104 (Fla. 2001) (school choice program not unconstitutional on its face); *Witters v. Washington Dept. of Serv. for the Blind*, 112 Wash. 2d 363, 771 P.2d 1119, *cert. denied*, 493 U.S. 850 (1989), excerpted in Section F below. *See generally* Note, *Beyond the Establishment Clause: Enforcing Separation of Church and State Through State Constitutional Provisions*, 71 Va. L. Rev. 625, 632–33 (1985). Others, however, have no analogy in federal law. *See, e.g.*, *DeRolfe v. State*, 754 N.E.2d 1184(Ohio 2001)(construing the "thorough and efficient" requirement of Ohio Const. art. VI §2); *Kukor v. Grover*, 148 Wis.2d 469, 436 N.W.2d 568 (1989) (construing the "uniformity" provision of the Wisconsin Constitution).

The following questions should be kept in mind:

1. To what extent do the United States or State constitutions mandate non-interference with a religiously imposed duty to educate one's children in accordance with the tenets of one's sincerely held religious beliefs? *Cf. Wisconsin v. Yoder*, excerpted in Chapter Five.
2. To what extent do state and federal interests in universal education mandate governmental regulation of education programs run by religious associations?
3. To what extent is the parent's right to choose an alternative source of educational values, materials, and environments an affirmative limitation on the power of a State to mandate "uniform" education for students of school age? The answer to this question will affect the degree to which the State will permit accommodation of those interests. *Cf. Pierce v. Society of Sisters*, 268 U.S. 510 (1925), excerpted below in §C. *See, e.g.*, Ohio Const. art VI, §2 (2002) ("it is the duty of the legislature to establish a general and uniform system of public schools") *and Simmons-Harris v. Goff*, 86 Ohio St.3d 1, 711 N.E.2d 203, 214 (Ohio 1999) (construing the section); Wis. Const. art. X, §3 (2002) ("The legislature shall provide by law for the establishment of district schools, which shall be as nearly uniform as practicable; and such schools shall be free and without charge for tuition to all children between the ages of 4 and 20 years."); *Davis v. Grover*, 166 Wis.2d 501, 480 N.W.2d 460 (1992) (construing this section).
4. To what extent does, or should, the First Amendment or a state "Religious Freedom Restoration Act" limit the State's discretion to control the state's policy choices respecting religious education? *See* Chapter Five §K.
5. To what extent are the independent, personal interests of individual children relevant to discussions of educational policy?

B. The Relationship of Religion to Public and Private Education

It is common in educational policy to draw a sharp distinction between public and private education, especially that which is conducted under the auspices of religious institutions. Today, however, the better approach is to look at the entire "educational marketplace" as a continuum that ranges on one end from purely private schools that receive no public funding or support, to purely public schools that receive no private support. Spread out along the continuum is the vast majority of American schools. There exist public-private partnerships that provide scholarships for low-income children, corporate sponsorship of public school facilities, community or charter schools, shared-time and open-enrollment programs, and private endowments for public educational systems. *See, e.g.*, John Schomberg, *Equity v. Autonomy: The Problems of Private Donations to Public Schools*, 1998 Annual Survey of American Law 143.

When the subject is "Religion in the Classroom," an attempt to draw bright line distinctions between public and private educational institutions is not particularly useful. It may, in fact, be misleading. The purpose of state-run educational institutions (public and some charter schools) is identical to that of schools which exist in the private sector: to educate the young by providing them with skills, knowledge, and a firm grasp of the culture and values of the community. As a result, one of the purposes of this Chapter is to examine *why* the educational environment, the source of a school's financial support, the content of its educational program, or the viewpoint from which that program is presented, make a difference for First Amendment purposes. We begin, therefore, with the nature of education itself, and will, in turn, consider philosophical, environmental, and financial issues.

1. The Nature of Education

Education is, by its nature, an inherently value-laden process. David Nyberg, *Teaching Values in School: The Mirror and the Lamp*, 92 Teachers College Record 595 (1990) ("all education is—whatever else it is—in some ways moral."); Carl Bereiter, *Schools Without Education*, 42 Harv. Educ. Rev. 391 (1972). Books must be selected, teachers hired and their performance evaluated, lessons formulated, and students taught. Each of these tasks involves the making of value judgments and the transmission of both values and moral perspective. *See, e.g.*, Md. Educ. Code Ann. §6-202(a) (2001) (permitting dismissal of teachers on grounds of, among other things, "(i) Immorality; (ii) Misconduct in office...; (iii) Insubordination; (iv) Incompetency; or (v) Willful neglect of duty.").

The Supreme Court has recognized that when the state "determines the content of the education it provides, it is the [state] speaking" whether or not it provides the education itself or "enlists private entities to convey its own message," *Rosenberger v. Rector and Visitors of Univ. of Va.*, 515 U.S. 819, 833 (1995), *citing Rust v. Sullivan*, 500 U.S. 173 (1991). It has also described the task of educators, both public and private, as "awakening the child to cultural values, [] preparing him for later professional training, and [] helping him to adjust normally to his environment," *Brown v. Board of Educ.*, 347 U.S. 483, 493 (1954).

Before turning to a specific discussion of the relationship of religion to education, it is useful to consider several views on the purposes of education. John Dewey, whose educational philosophy has been a significant influence in American public education, believed "that the school is primarily a social institution, [and that e]ducation being a social process, the school is simply that form of community life in which all those agencies are concentrated that will be most effective in bringing the child to share in the inherited resources of the race, and to use his own powers for social ends." John Dewey, *My Pedagogic Creed in* "MY PEDAGOGIC CREED BY PROFESSOR JOHN DEWEY AND THE DEMANDS OF SOCIOLOGY UPON PEDAGOGY (ca. 1898)" *in* Kendig Brubaker Culley, BASIC WRITINGS IN CHRISTIAN EDUCATION (1960). He is not alone in this view:

> Central to [a Jewish view of teaching and learning] is Judaism's concept of man, which holds his nature to be a blending of body and soul, of matter and of spirit.... Education is a means, not the end. Though prizing knowledge above all earthly possessions, Judaism ascribes no worth to study for study's sake alone.... The implications of this conception of the understanding of education's task is clear. Its function is all-encompassing. It cannot be divided in any manner or restricted in any fashion. One cannot refine the competence of the mind while oblivious to the needs and potentialities of body or blind to the values and final purposes which are born of a man's spirit. The development of the total man is every teacher's concern. All life is education's proper province.

Alexander M. Schindler, *Reform Judaism and Education*, in David W. Beggs & R. Bruce McQuigg, AMERICA'S SCHOOLS AND CHURCHES: PARTNERS IN CONFLICT 112–13 (1966).

Stanley Ballinger has suggested, however, that it may be useful to distinguish two general conceptions:

> 1. Education as the preservation and transmission of a body of traditional beliefs, practices, ideas, and attitudes [; and]
> 2. Education as the provision of the younger generation with the resources and tools for the intelligent reconstruction of the complexly multiple heritages of cultural achievement evolved by past generations.

Stanley E. Ballinger, *Teaching About Religion: Some Questions* in Beggs & McQuigg at 133. Though Ballinger believed that virtually all "pre-college programs of religious education are essentially indoctrinative: shunting the learner away from the avenues of free inquiry rather than opening them up for him," *id.*, the distinction between the transmission of ideas, and the formation of the individual is a common theme in commentaries on the nature of education. Consider, for example, the Declaration on Christian Education of the Roman Catholic Church, *Gravissimum Educationis* (October 28, 1965), *in* VATICAN COUNCIL II, THE CONCILIAR AND POST CONCILIAR DOCUMENTS (1975–1992):

> In nurturing the intellectual faculties, which is its special mission, [the school] develops a capacity for sound judgment and introduces the pupils to the cultural heritage bequeathed to them by former generations. It fosters a sense of values and prepares them for professional life. By providing for friendly contacts between pupils of different characters and backgrounds it encourages mutual understanding. Furthermore it constitutes a center in whose activity and growth not only the families and teachers but also the various associations

> for the promotion of cultural, civil and religious life, civic society, and the entire community should take part.

Id. at 730–31. *See also* George Albert Coe, "WHAT IS A CHRISTIAN EDUCATION?" 23–24 (1929) *in* Kendig Brubaker Culley, BASIC WRITINGS IN CHRISTIAN EDUCATION 333 (1960) ("Accordingly, the Christian teacher's practical dilemma takes this form: Shall the primary purpose of Christian education be to hand on a religion, or to create a new world?"); Arthur L. Miller, *A Lutheran Looks at Religion and Education in* Beggs & McQuigg, at 72–75.

As long as all education is both private and privately funded, the balance to be struck between the various interests involved is largely a matter of private choice. State intervention, to the extent that it occurs at all, will be directed at discrete aspects of the operations of private schools, such as curriculum content, educational philosophy, "time, place, and manner," and other administrative concerns. Some of these issues, such as state attempts to regulate the content or perspective of education in private schools, raise First Amendment concerns; others, typically the "time, place, and manner" regulations which govern all elementary and secondary education programs, rarely do. These issues are discussed at length in § D (1) below. When the state undertakes the role of educator, the First Amendment problems are more complex, but their contours are relatively straightforward. These problems are discussed in greater detail in §§ D–F below.

The public school is the place "in which child and state (personalities vastly unequal in power) encounter each other." William B. Ball, *Religion and Public Education: The Post-Schempp Years, in* RELIGION & PUBLIC EDUCATION 146 (Theodore R. Sizer 1967). The same is true in the context of a religiously affiliated school, a place in which the child encounters the church as an institution. In the public school context, the problem "seems to be how to have the schools non-religious and still imparting values," Ball, *supra*; Lawrence Kohlberg, *Moral and Religious Education and the Public Schools: A Developmental View, in* Sizer, at 164, while in the private school setting the problem is how to differentiate between the teaching of moral values and the teaching of religious doctrine. *See, e.g., Good News Club v. Milford Central Sch. Dist.*, 533 U.S. 98 (2001); *Bowen v. Kendrick*, 487 U.S. 589 (1988); *Wolman v. Walter*, 433 U.S. 229 (1977); *Meek v. Pittenger*, 421 U.S. 349 (1975).

The importance of these questions to the development of the law on religion and education cannot be overstated. Dissenting in *Everson v. Board of Educ.*, 330 U.S. 1 (1947), Justice Robert Jackson argued that public schools are "organized on the premises that secular education can be isolated from all religious training," and raised the question of "whether such a disjunction is possible, and, if possible, whether it is wise." 330 U.S. 1, 23–24 (Jackson, J. dissenting). Thomas Jefferson struggled with precisely the same questions as he formulated his 1779 "Bill for the More General Diffusion of Knowledge" (No. 79 of the Virginia Revision) and his 1817 "Bill for Establishing a System of Public Education." Robert D. Heslep notes that:

> In formulating his plans for public education in Virginia, Jefferson was compelled to entertain three questions concerning freedom. The first was how to preserve the students' religious freedom.... The second question concerned the limits of academic freedom... [and t]he third question was how much control [over education] Jefferson thought the public should have. On the one hand, Jefferson's political theory implied that the public educational institutions of a republic ought not to provide any religious doctrine; and the numerous religious groups of Virginia were equally insistent that public schools should not

> impart any teaching contrary to their respective creeds. On the other hand, Jefferson believed that it would be unfeasible to try to purge all possible religious observances and subject matters from the states' public schools and university. Therefore, he decided (as reflected by the general education bill of 1817) that all that was needed was to forbid the obvious possible threat to any religious group's doctrine: no ecclesiastical official should be appointed as public education supervisor; no religious reading, instruction, or exercise ought to be prescribed or practiced in the public educational institutions that would be inconsistent with the tenets of any religious sect or denomination; and there should be no professor of divinity at the University of Virginia.

Robert D. Heslep, THOMAS JEFFERSON & EDUCATION 107–110 (1969).

Academic freedom and local control were equally difficult problems. In Jefferson's view, local school boards should be appointed by state authorities so as to assure the quality and *political* orthodoxy of the education provided, but fiscal control should be left with local communities, or wards, because public schools, including the University of Virginia, were the means by which Virginia's citizens would assure the continuity of America's commitment to republican democracy:

> Although Jefferson extolled the pursuit of truth and the freedom of expression as natural rights, he regarded the public schools and university in Virginia as institutions of Virginia's society and maintained that they be limited as such. Thus, far from granting autonomy to the University of Virginia, he stipulated that the state legislature might enact laws governing the Rector and the Board of Visitors and, more broadly, that the university "should in all things, and at all times, be subject to the control of the Legislature." When, as rector, Jefferson gave consideration to establishing the university's professorship of law, he argued that the law curriculum must be favorable to Virginia's republican institutions; in fact, he even prescribed the text to be employed by the professor of law.

Heslep, at 108.

Given the inherent tension among the goals involved, is it possible to formulate a coherent policy concerning the relationship among the non-establishment, free exercise, free speech and petition for redress of grievances norms of the First Amendment? For example, Jefferson wanted to assure *political*, but not religious, orthodoxy among school authorities appointed by the state. Would such a test for public office be consistent with today's understanding of rights of academic freedom and non-association? Might it also be possible that *political* orthodoxy can be measured in religious terms? What would be your evaluation of a school board screening policy for new teachers that carefully scrutinized the candidate's views on the role of religion and religious beliefs in education? If the candidate indicates that religion and morality are important components of education, can he or she be excluded from further consideration? *See* U.S. Const. Art. VI cl. 3; Chapter Eight § G.

Can secular education be isolated from all religious teaching? From the teaching of morality? From preaching or the teaching of religious doctrine? Until the Supreme Court began to mandate the separation of religion from the curriculum, and from public ritual in schools, how accurate was Justice Jackson's observation that American public education is organized around the premise that religion and education can be separated? *See* § D (4) below.

Consider another thorny question: How important in the context of education policy are definitions of the concepts of "religion" and "morality"? *See* Chapter Thirteen. Is it possible, for example, to teach morality or ethics in public schools without teaching someone's concept of "religion"? It might be argued that attempts to teach a form of generic "morality" or "ethics" are similar in form and substance to the states' attempts to craft religiously generic prayers, such as the "Regents' Prayer" struck down in *Engel v. Vitale*, 370 U.S. 421 (1962). Do you agree? *See generally* Thomas L. Shaffer & Robert F. Cochran, Jr., *Lawyers, Clients and Moral Responsibility* 56–61 (1994) (discussing the derivation and character of moral values relevant to law practice).

Is there a difference between simple "neutrality" and a "strict and lofty" one? *See* Brian J. Serr, *A Not-So-Neutral "Neutrality:" An Essay on the State of The Religion Clauses on the Brink of the Third Millennium*, 51 Baylor L. Rev. 319 (1999); Douglas Laycock, *Formal, Substantive, and Disaggregated Neutrality Toward Religion*, 39 DePaul L. Rev. 993 (1990). Does it help the analysis if the concept of "religion" is broken down into a series of component parts, such as dogma, structure, social function, theological discourse, and inter-group relations, all in an attempt to distill a common core of morality and what philosophers describe as "the good"? How did the Supreme Court view the matter in the following case?

Stone v. Graham

449 U.S. 39 (1980)

PER CURIAM.

A Kentucky statute requires the posting of a copy of the Ten Commandments, purchased with private contributions, on the wall of each public classroom in the State. Petitioners, claiming that this statute violates the Establishment and Free Exercise Clauses of the First Amendment, sought an injunction against its enforcement. The state trial court upheld the statute, finding that its "avowed purpose" was "secular and not religious," and that the statute would "neither advance nor inhibit any religion or religious group" nor involve the State excessively in religious matters.

The pre-eminent purpose for posting the Ten Commandments on schoolroom walls is plainly religious in nature. The Ten Commandments are undeniably a sacred text in the Jewish and Christian faiths, and no legislative recitation of a supposed secular purpose can blind us to that fact. The Commandments do not confine themselves to arguably secular matters, such as honoring one's parents, killing or murder, adultery, stealing, false witness, and covetousness. *See* Exodus 20: 12–17; Deuteronomy 5: 16–21. Rather, the first part of the Commandments concerns the religious duties of believers: worshipping the Lord God alone, avoiding idolatry, not using the Lord's name in vain, and observing the Sabbath Day. *See* Exodus 20: 1–11; Deuteronomy 5: 6–15.

The petition for a writ of certiorari is granted, and the judgment below is reversed.

THE CHIEF JUSTICE [BURGER] and Justice BLACKMUN dissent. They would grant certiorari and give this case plenary consideration.

Justice STEWART dissents from this summary reversal of the courts of Kentucky, which, so far as appears, applied wholly correct constitutional criteria in reaching their decisions.

Justice REHNQUIST, dissenting.

With no support beyond its own *ipse dixit*, the Court concludes that the Kentucky statute involved in this case "has *no* secular legislative purpose," (emphasis supplied), and that "[t]he pre-eminent purpose for posting the Ten Commandments on schoolroom walls is plainly religious in nature". This even though, as the trial court found, "[t]he General Assembly thought the statute had a secular legislative purpose and specifically said so." The Court's summary rejection of a secular purpose articulated by the legislature and confirmed by the state court is without precedent in Establishment Clause jurisprudence.

The Court rejects the secular purpose articulated by the State because the Decalogue is "undeniably a sacred text". It is equally undeniable, however, as the elected representatives of Kentucky determined, that the Ten Commandments have had a significant impact on the development of secular legal codes of the Western World. The trial court concluded that evidence submitted substantiated this determination. Certainly the State was permitted to conclude that a document with such secular significance should be placed before its students, with an appropriate statement of the document's secular import. *See also* Opinion of the Justices, 108 N.H. 97, 228 A.2d 161 (1967) (upholding placement of plaques with the motto "In God We Trust" in public schools).[3]

The Establishment Clause does not require that the public sector be insulated from all things which may have a religious significance or origin. This Court has recognized that "religion has been closely identified with our history and government," *Abington School District.* The history of man is inseparable from the history of religion," *Engel v. Vitale.* Kentucky has decided to make students aware of this fact by demonstrating the secular impact of the Ten Commandments. The words of Justice Jackson, concurring in *McCollum v. Board of Education*, merit quotation at length:

> "I think it remains to be demonstrated whether it is possible, even if desirable, to comply with such demands as plaintiff's completely to isolate and cast out of secular education all that some people may reasonably regard as religious instruction. Perhaps subjects such as mathematics, physics or chemistry are, or can be, completely secularized. But it would not seem practical to teach either practice or appreciation of the arts if we are to forbid exposure of youth to any religious influences. Music without sacred music, architecture minus the cathedral, or painting without the scriptural themes would be eccentric and incomplete, even from a secular point of view....I should suppose it is a proper, if not an indispensable, part of preparation for a worldly life to know the roles that religion and religions have played in the tragic story of mankind. The fact is that, for good or for ill, nearly everything in our culture worth transmitting, everything which gives meaning to life, is saturated with religious influences, derived from paganism, Judaism, Christianity—both Catholic and Protestant—and other faiths accepted by a large part of the world's peoples. One can hardly respect the system of education that would leave the student wholly ignorant of the currents of religious thought that move the world society for a part in which he is being prepared."

I therefore dissent from what I cannot refrain from describing as a cavalier summary reversal, without benefit of oral argument or briefs on the merits, of the highest court of Kentucky.

---

3. The Court's emphasis on the religious nature of the first part of the Ten Commandments is beside the point. The document as a whole has had significant secular impact, and the Constitution does not require that Kentucky students see only an expurgated or redacted version containing only the elements with directly traceable secular effects.

Notes

1. Justice Jackson argued in *Everson* that American education is organized around the premise that religion and education can be separated in the educational setting. Does *Stone v. Graham* indicate that the Court has decided that the First Amendment *itself* imposes that premise on the operations of the public schools? If so, such a holding limits what can be offered as a part of the curriculum in public schools, does it not? Is it the role of the federal government to scrutinize public school curricula for forbidden content? If so, what other kinds of content can be excluded? Does Congress share the responsibility for curriculum oversight, or is the job one for judges alone? In either case, what definition of "religious" should be used to determine what is "religious" and what is not? *See* Chapter Ten.

2. Is it desirable to remove all official references to religion from the schools? What, for example, should schools do or say about time periods that hold great significance to religious groups in the community, such as Christmas and Easter, Passover and High Holy Days, and Ramadan? If the schools refuse to acknowledge them, they ignore the cultural and religious heritage of the communities they serve. If such holidays are recognized in some official way, they can be charged with advancing religion. What should be the school's response? *Compare Koenick v. Felton*, 190 F.3d 259 (4th Cir. 1999) *cert. denied*, 528 U.S. 1118 (2000) (Maryland statute creating a public school holidays on the Friday before Easter through the Monday following does not violate Establishment Clause) *and Cammack v. Waihee*, 932 F.2d 765 (9th Cir. 1991) (closing Hawaii public schools over Easter weekend does not violate Establishment Clause) *with Metzl v. Leininger*, 57 F.3d 618 (7th Cir. 1995) (Illinois statute closing schools over Easter weekend was unconstitutional because the State did not articulate a secular purpose). *See generally* Chapter Eight §F(4)(discussing mandatory accommodation in the workplace). Does it help when a school system tries to recognize the importance of a particular day, but decides to rename it so as to avoid mention of its religious significance or origin? For example, one school now refers to St. Patrick's Day as "Ethnic Awareness Day."

3. Do arguments supporting the removal of religious influences and teaching from public schools also apply to private schools? If the focus is on educational philosophy, the answer to this question would be "yes." This, in fact, was part of the Oregon's argument for eliminating private schools altogether. *See Pierce v. Society of Sisters,* excerpted below.

4. Consider the views of Dr. Lawrence Kohlberg, an eminent psychologist famous for his studies of the moral development of children and young adults.

> [A]s a psychologist I have attempted to formulate a conception of moral education in the public schools based on research findings, a conception in which a complete separation of moral and religious education is implicit. In essence, then, I am arguing that [William B.] Ball's interpretation [that the teaching of morals in public schools inevitably entails the teaching of religion] is possible only if morality or ethics is confused with "value systems" in general, and if it is not recognized that the core of morality is justice. Unless one recognizes the core status of justice, any conscious concern about the school's responsibility for developing the basic values of the society and making citizens as well as scholars will run into difficulties as soon as one tries to define the exact content of these basic values.
>
> The problems as to the legitimacy of moral education in the public schools disappear, then if the proper content of moral education is recognized to be

> the values of justice which themselves prohibit the imposition of beliefs of one group upon another. Although philosophers have been unable to agree upon any single ultimate principle which would define "correct" moral judgments, most philosophers concur on the characteristics which make a judgment a genuine moral judgment. [A] developmental moral education would stimulate the child's application of his own moral judgment (not the teacher's) to his actions. The effort to force a child to agree that an act of cheating is very bad when he does not really believe it will only encourage morally immature tendencies toward expedient outward compliance. In contrast, a more difficult but more valid approach involves getting the child to examine the pros and cons of his conduct in his own terms (as well as introducing more developmentally advanced considerations).
>
> Our evidence of culturally universal moral stages... is also direct evidence against the view that the development of moral ideologies depends upon the teachings of particular religious belief systems.

Lawrence Kohlberg, *Moral and Religious Education and the Public Schools: A Developmental View in* Sizer, at 164–65, 178–180.

William B. Ball, whose essay in the Sizer anthology is paired with Kohlberg's, agrees that part of the problem is definitional, but urges that Kohlberg's approach to the teaching of morality is just as religious, or "sectarian," as the approach Kohlberg rejects. In Ball's view, assigning the public school a role with respect to moral and religious upbringing contains within itself a

> tension between concepts which... is similar to that faced by public education in the nineteenth century. The problem then was how to have the schools Protestant and still non-sectarian. The problem today seems to be how to have the schools non-religious and still imparting values (never forgetting, in this connection, what "religion" has come to mean [in the case law]). Our Protestant forebears solved their problem in crude but effective fashion by permitting (or requiring) a commonly Protestant religious infusion into the public schools and pretending that it was non-sectarian.... The earlier attempt of public education to straddle simultaneously Protestantism and non-sectarianism was succeeded by a similar effort to embrace religious neutrality, but "wholesome" neutrality—implying that a *species* of neutrality is the mandate, viz., one that is "conducive to moral or general well-being" (if we may accept a dictionary definition of "wholesome").
>
> [W]here assertions of a "unifying role" [for the public schools] go beyond mere intermixture [of diverse children] and become doctrinal, we must ask whether it is a proper role for the public school to be a school which promises cultural unity. I would answer that it is not, and for two reasons. First, I am not sure what is meant by "cultural unity"; second, I do not know to what end, or about what consensus, our children are to be unified. *If*, in other words, public education conceives that it is charged with providing a child with a working philosophy of life, if it feels that it must address itself to those ultimate questions of the child which were always deemed religious, I do not think that the answer it gives can constitutionally be one which is agreeable to me as a Christian or agreeable to... an Ethical Culturist.

Ball, in Sizer at 157. There is an immense amount of literature on the topic. *See, e.g.*, Susan H. Bitensky, *A Contemporary Proposal for Reconciling the Free Speech Clause with Curricular Values Inculcation in the Public Schools*, 70 Notre Dame L. Rev. 769 (1995) (discussing morals education through elementary and secondary level curricula); IN SEARCH OF A NATIONAL MORALITY: A MANIFESTO FOR EVANGELICALS AND CATHOLICS (William B. Ball ed. 1992); Dudley Plunkett, SECULAR AND SPIRITUAL VALUES (1990); Harvey G. Neufeldt, *Religion, Morality and Schooling: Forging the Nineteenth Century Protestant Consensus*, in RELIGION AND MORALITY IN AMERICAN SCHOOLING 3 (1981); Nyberg, *Teaching Values in School*; William Brickman, *The Teaching of Secular Moral Values in the Twentieth Century*, 12 Paedogogica Historica 370 (1972); Theron B. Maxon, *Religion in the Schools: A Presbyterian's View*, in Beggs & McQuigg, at 56. *See also* John Dewey, THEORY OF THE MORAL LIFE (Arnold Isenberg ed. 1960); Jesse A. Mann, *North American Philosophical Background for Moral Education Theory* in PHILOSOPHICAL FOUNDATIONS FOR MORAL EDUCATION AND CHARACTER DEVELOPMENT (George F. McLean & Frederick E. Ellrod, eds. 1992); Emile Durkheim, *Moral Education: A Study in* THEORY AND APPLICATION OF THE SOCIOLOGY OF EDUCATION 129–281 (1961) (discussing the formation of morality in the child).

5. Given all this, what *ought* to be the role of the state with respect to the training of citizens in morality and values? Can the task be accomplished without compromise? Whose? Does the First Amendment supply an answer? Does it mandate one? What control, if any, should parents and children have in the process?

6. In *McCollum v. Board of Educ.*, §D (4), and *Schempp*, §D (4) below, the Supreme Court began the task of dismantling the last vestiges of what the late Professor Mark DeWolfe Howe has described as America's *de facto* establishment of Protestant Christianity. *See* Mark DeWolfe Howe, THE GARDEN AND THE WILDERNESS 11 (1965) ("The evangelical principle of separation endorsed a host of favoring tributes to faith—tributes so substantial that they have produced in the aggregate what may fairly be described as a *de facto* establishment of religion.") *See generally* Robert S. Alley, *The Protestant Establishment in* JAMES MADISON ON RELIGIOUS LIBERTY (Robert S. Alley ed. 1991); David Boles, THE BIBLE, RELIGION, AND THE PUBLIC SCHOOLS 35 (1961); Robert F. Utter & Edward Larson, *Church and State on the Frontier: The History of the Establishment Clauses in the Washington State Constitution*, 15 Hastings Const. L.Q. 451, 458–67 (1988).

7. Selective use of history has had a profound effect on the Supreme Court's understanding of the religious liberty guarantee. A search for the "original intent" of the non-establishment guarantee has been an important component in the Court's interpretation, but it has given little attention to the "original intent" of either the Free Exercise or Test Clauses. The "original intent" of the Fourteenth Amendment with respect to matters of religious liberty has not been discussed at all. *See* Chapter Five §B(4).

The most obvious problem with the Court's approach is conceptual. To the extent that an historical perspective is used as the grounding for the Court's interpretation of any constitutional provision, it is necessary to have a complete (or as near to complete as possible) understanding of the evil at which that provision was directed. If the historical understanding is incomplete, so too will be the vision of what that provision of the Constitution requires or prohibits. Without historical grounding, the language will be infused with whatever meaning seems appropriate to the time and circumstances. *See* John T. Noonan, Jr., THE BELIEVER AND THE POWERS THAT ARE xiii (1987) ("It is not only a matter of grasping the intentions of the Founding Fathers.... It is also a matter of empathetically appropriating the experience that undergirds the constitutional principles of free exercise and no establishment.")

But this raises a question: *Whose* history, and *when*? Chapter One §A contains a discussion of the importance of characterization and the "level of generality" in language.

A similar problem exists with respect to the selection of an appropriate *historical* point of reference. *See, e.g., Mitchell v. Helms*, 530 U.S. 793, 828 (2000) (plurality opinion of Thomas, Scalia, and Kennedy, JJ. and Rehnquist, C.J.) (noting "pervasive hostility to the Catholic Church and to Catholics in general," of the late nineteenth century, and that "it was an open secret that [the term] 'sectarian' was code for 'Catholic.'"); *Wallace v. Jaffree*, 472 U.S. 38 (1985) (discussing the importance of history in light of past precedent); *Marsh v. Chambers*, 463 U.S. 783 (1983) (holding constitutional prayers given prior to the opening of the state legislature based on history, dissenters argue principles drawn from history).

A Note on Use of History in Education Cases

Some courts go even farther. The United States Court of Appeals for the Second Circuit, for example, has held that "[t]he drafting and adoption of the First Amendment, in which Madison and Jefferson played leading roles, can *only* be understood in light of the Virginia experience," and describes legal arguments that challenge the prevailing reliance on the Virginia experience as "scholarship born of advocacy" which present a "treatment of history [that] is selective and one-sided." *Lamont v. Woods*, 948 F.2d 825, 836–37 (2d Cir. 1991) [emphasis added].

A notable exception to this view is the concurring opinion of Judge Bownes in *Weisman v. Lee*, 908 F.2d 1090 (1st Cir. 1990), *aff'g* 728 F. Supp. 68 (D.R.I.). In his view, "the 'plain meaning' of the [constitutional] text is of little help in determining results in [cases involving school prayer]...[T]he interpretation and practice that has evolved throughout the past two hundred years" is determinative. After dismissing both the "intent of the framers" and the teachings of history in both the ratification period and the nineteenth century, he concludes that

> It is useless to rehash this continuing debate. The ground has been trodden so much that it is barren of meaning and persuasive power. The "historical record" is inconclusive on the various cross-currents in the minds of the framers. Because of the tangled and often conflicting historical record, it is unlikely that, as an empirical matter, we can ever know the original intention of the authors of the Constitution. Even if we could reconstruct the framers' intent, that would not necessarily be determinative in this case, given our two hundred years of experience with the Constitution and changing circumstances.

Id. at 1093 (footnote omitted).

Whatever the merits of this debate, several things are certain. First, the substantive content of the norms of conduct embodied in the First Amendment must come from *somewhere*, and history is universally acknowledged to be at least a relevant guide to the meaning of the constitutional text. *See Michael H. v. Gerald D.*, 491 U.S. 110 (1989); Michael Kent Curtis, *Critics of "Free Speech" and the Uses of the Past*, 12 Const. Comm. 29 (1995). Second, the "original intent" of the non-establishment guarantee is, for some of the Justices, the touchstone of its interpretation. Third, the history of the struggle for religious liberty in States other than Virginia has never figured prominently in the Supreme Court's interpretation of either the non-establishment or the free exercise norms. *See* Chester J. Antieau, Arthur T. Downey & Edward C. Roberts, FREEDOM FROM FEDERAL ESTABLISHMENT: FORMATION AND EARLY HISTORY OF THE FIRST AMENDMENT RELIGION CLAUSES 161–63 (1964) (discussing developments in the States from 1776–1825). *See generally* Hans W. Baade, *"Original Intent" in Historical Perspective: Some Critical Glosses*, 69

Tex. L. Rev. 1001 (1991). *See* Chapters Two through Four. The relationship history and intent of the Fourteenth Amendment, the conduit through which the First Amendment's norms are applied to the States, is rarely mentioned at all. *See* Chapter Five § B(4).

The traditional approach to historical analysis is limited largely to attempts to discern the views of James Madison and Thomas Jefferson, and to extrapolate from their writings both before and after the adoption of the First Amendment their "intent" with respect to questions of contemporary education policy. There are three basic approaches.

Some writers claim that the rejection of the Virginia General Assessment Bill should be read as an endorsement of Jefferson's position as "a rigid separationist utterly opposed to government support of religion, including any form of religion in public education." Others claim him "as an advocate of impartial government support for religion and religious education." *See* Healey at 10. A third view, espoused by Anson Phelps Stokes in CHURCH AND STATE IN THE UNITED STATES, "imputes to Jefferson the double interest common to most of the [founding] fathers: to support religion, because Jefferson was himself religious and felt that without religion democracy could not succeed, and to support religious freedom by doing away with any form of interference by the government in religious matters." Healey at 10–11.

Keeping in mind the admonition of the Second Circuit that challenges to the prevailing reliance on the Virginia experience may be viewed by some judges as "scholarship born of advocacy" which present a "treatment of history [that] is selective and one-sided," *Lamont v. Woods*, 948 F.2d at 836–37, to what extent should scholarship that challenges the prevailing interpretation be used by the courts as they seek to discern the meaning of the incorporated First Amendment? Should the history of religious liberty in states other than Virginia, such as Pennsylvania, be relevant to controversies over the place of religion in education, and the state or federal government's role with respect to both? There is no question that they are "relevant;" the interpretive question for the Supreme Court is the degree to which they should be deemed controlling. *See generally* Robert A. Destro, *The Structure of the Religious Liberty Guarantee*, 11 J. Law & Religion 355 (1995).

The same historical questions would arise if the analysis were conducted under the Speech and Press Clause. Should the funding of public education be considered "government speech"? *See Board of Regents of the University of Wisconsin System v. Southworth*, 529 U.S. 217 (2000) (noting that where the speech is financed by the government and it has control of the content, "the case might be evaluated on the premise that the government itself is the speaker.") *Cf. Board of Educ. v. Pico*, 457 U.S. 853 (1982), excerpted below. If so, governmental policies that inculcate children and young adults with the values the State considers central to the American democratic experiment raise some very interesting questions under not only the First Amendment, but the Fourteenth as well.

It is well known, for example, that discrimination based on race, religion and national origin have been pervasive in systems of public education. The Supreme Court has made it clear that discrimination on the basis of race and ethnicity is not constitutionally permissible, *Brown v. Board of Educ.*, 347 U.S. 483 (1954) (prohibiting racial discrimination in public schools), and has required that the vestiges of discrimination be eliminated "root and branch," *Green v. County Sch. Bd. of New Kent County*, 391 U.S. 430, 437 (1968). It has given little, if any, consideration to the history of religious discrimination in the public schools. *Compare Washington v. Davis*, 426 U.S. 229 (1976) *with Witters v. Washington Dep't of Serv. for the Blind*, 102 Wash.2d 624, 689 P.2d 53 (1984), *rev'd*, 474 U.S. 481 (1986), *reaffirmed on state constitutional grounds*, 112 Wash.2d 363, 771 P.2d 1119, *cert. denied*, 493 U.S. 850 (1989); and *Cooper v. Eugene Sch. Dist.*, excerpted below. What lessons relevant to the First Amendment can be drawn from the materials in Chapter Four?

Publicly funded education of the type we know today was not available in Virginia until after the Civil War, but Madison, Jefferson and others were intimately involved with debates over the content and control of publicly funded education during the period from 1780–1840. Some of this history is recounted in § F(1) below, but the courts rarely, if ever, refer to it. They prefer to rely on the views of the framers concerning special tax assessments to support the salaries of Virginia's Christian ministers. *See* Sadie Bell, The Church, The State, and Education in Virginia 334 (1969) (noting that Thomas Jefferson's attempts to create a public school system in Virginia were rejected, and that the rejection of his proposals had the effect of encouraging the growth of denominational Sunday schools which were later supported with public money).

2. What Are the State's Interests in Education?

It is often stated that the public schools are "a principal instrument in awakening the child to cultural values, in preparing him for later professional training, and in helping him to adjust normally to his environment." *Brown v. Board of Educ.*, 347 U.S. 483, 493 (1954). In so stating, the Court is drawing yet another lesson from the considerable influence of Thomas Jefferson.

Although Jefferson's views concerning the relationship of religion to education were not widely shared during his lifetime, and remain a subject of debate today, there is very little controversy over the need to educate the young concerning the values, traditions, and responsibilities of citizens in a democratic republic. The questions Jefferson raised relate to the method and content of education, and the role religious training and ritual should play in it.

From the time of the Pilgrims through the early 1800s, Americans looked to their churches to provide education. Spanish Catholic missionaries in Florida and New Mexico founded the first schools in what is now the United States between 1594 and 1630. The school of the Dutch Reformed Church opened in what is now New York City in 1633, and the Boston Latin School followed in 1635. At the time the First Amendment was adopted, neither Virginia nor any other colony had a system of public education comparable to that which exists today. As noted in Chapter Four, a public mandate for universal, free and compulsory education did not develop until well into the nineteenth century, and its progress was neither rapid nor unopposed. *See* Charles Ramsdell Lingley, The Transition in Virginia from Colony to Commonwealth (1967) (noting that Jefferson's "Bill for the More General Diffusion of Knowledge" through universal public education at the elementary and secondary schools levels met with the same fate as the General Assessment Bill. It was rejected each time it was offered.)

Political and demographic differences among the States led to considerable diversity in content and approach to education. It continues to do so today. The religious demographics of the new nation were overwhelmingly Protestant Christian, and the schools that served its communities reflected their respective religions and cultures. In Virginia, for example, there were no public schools until after 1870, but the early nineteenth century witnessed the development of a widespread system of denominational Sunday Schools designed to teach both reading and a form of "Common Christianity."

In the East, long-standing cultural and religious practices were of great influence in shaping not only the culture of the public schools, but also the political and social controversies that followed their establishment. *See* Chapter Four. *See generally* James M. O'Neill, CATHOLICISM AND AMERICAN FREEDOM 6 (1952) (noting that the influx of Catholic and Jewish immigrants changed forever the Protestant majority's attitudes concerning the relationship of churches to schools). In the West, communities were more diverse and far-flung. Teachers, books, and time for educational pursuits were in short supply, and the programs were structured accordingly. As we shall see in the notes covering the growing practice of "home schooling," the struggle over the form and content of the education of the young is a continuing one. See § D(1) below.

But none of this can be fully understood without some consideration the profound changes wrought by "The Great Atlantic Migration." Immigration changed America's religious demographics, and was a driving force in the development of the movement for "common schools." Chapter Two recounts that in 1790 Catholics numbered only about 35,000 out of a total population of over four million. Together, Catholics and Jews amounted to only about 0.1 percent of the population. Figures from the 1990 Census and data supplied by 133 religious groups show how much that has changed over time. Eighty six percent of the population identifies itself as "Christian." Catholics now account for approximately 26.2 percent of the population over eighteen years of age, and are the majority religious group in the Northeast, Southwest and coastal Southern California. Although Protestants (of all denominations) remain in the majority, the Roman Catholic Church is now the Nation's single largest denomination. The Jewish population stands at 1.8 percent of the population, down from approximately 3 percent twenty-five years ago, and Islam has become one of the Nation's fastest growing religious faiths. Muslims now account for approximately one-half of one percent (.5%) of Americans over the age of eighteen. For detailed surveys on religious affiliations and other data in the United States and elsewhere, see The American Religion Data Archive, at http://www.thearda.com.

Legal developments in the field of church, state and education have been driven by these factors. As Chapters Four and Five indicate, demographic factors have affected the Supreme Court's understanding of church-state doctrine. The materials in this Chapter will illustrate just how influential those factors have been.

C. Questions of Control

It is against this backdrop that we turn to an examination of what might be termed "control" issues; that is, *who* is ultimately in charge of the education of children, under what circumstances, and for what purposes? There have long been struggles between parents and educators over the sum and substance of education. The correspondence which deals with his 1779 "Bill for the More General Diffusion of Knowledge" (No. 79 of the Virginia Revision) and his 1817 "Bill for Establishing a System of Public Education" demonstrates that Jefferson was concerned not only with freedom of conscience, but also with the formation of a republican consciousness as well. *See* Healey, chs. 9–10. In this view, he was not alone. *Cf.* Herbert Spencer, SOCIAL STATICS pt. ii, ch. 17 at 4

(1850) (stating that "[e]ducation has for its object the formation of character."); Benjamin Disraeli, *Comments in the House of Commons, 15 June 1874*, in OXFORD DICTIONARY OF QUOTATIONS (stating that "[u]pon the education of the people of this country the fate of this country depends"). Commenting on Jefferson's desire that an individual of suitably orthodox political beliefs be hired as the law professor at the University of Virginia, James Madison wrote to his friend and political ally that "the true doctrines of liberty, as exemplified in our Political System, should be inculcated on those who are to sustain and may administer it." *Letter from James Madison to Thomas Jefferson (Feb. 8, 1825) in* WRITINGS OF JAMES MADISON 218 (Gaillard Hunt ed. 1900–1910).

The large, centralized, state-supported systems of primary and secondary education we know today are rooted in the demographic changes brought about by the first great waves of immigration in the 1820s. Not only were there concerns about the preservation of national identity and culture that accompany any great influx of immigrants (including those being experienced today in the United States and Western Europe), there was the very practical need to socialize the new arrivals, teach them English, and provide them with the knowledge necessary to become active citizen-members of the political community.

The States responded to these mid-nineteenth century concerns by amending their constitutions to provide authority for their legislatures to create, fund, and regulate uniform system of free, or "common," schools. As populations grew, the demographics became more diverse. Greater diversity created greater demands on the system, and this, in turn, led to greater centralization. Today's debates over bilingual education and access to the public schools by children whose families are illegally present in the United States reflect many of the same concerns.

The trend toward centralization continues today. Though the communities in which they serve elect more than three-quarters of public school board members, school boards have only those powers granted by statute or rule, and are subject to significant oversight. *See* § C (1) below. There are periodic, and perennially controversial, attempts to garner support for uniform national standards for student achievement. *See, e.g.*, National Public Radio, Talk of the Nation, "Standardized Testing in Our Public Schools," Thursday, March 21, 2002, 2002 WL 3296869; Michael Heise, *Goals 2000: Educate America Act: The Federalization and Legalization of Educational Policy*, 63 Fordham L. Rev. 345, 376–77 (1994). The consolidation and merger of rural schools into "union" school districts has continued in many states, see *Bd. of Educ. of the Kiryas Joel Village Sch. Dist. v. Grumet*, 512 U.S. 687 (1994) (relying, in part, on the existence of such a trend to attribute an illicit purpose to the New York Legislature's creation of a special school district), and litigation aimed at eliminating reliance on the local tax base for education funding may have the unintended purpose of eliminating the last clear vestige of community control of local education as well. *See* § F (1) below.

1. Who Controls Education?

a) State Law Issues

For purposes of this discussion it is necessary to differentiate among three types of authority: 1) the natural right of parents to control the custody, education and upbringing of their children; 2) the powers vested in state governments by their respective constitutions and compulsory education laws; and 3) the powers conferred on the federal government by the United States Constitution.

The popular view of state authority over education is one that emphasizes the role of the parents. Because schools are viewed as agencies of local self-government to whom the parents entrust their children for purposes of education, many of the controversies over educational philosophy, curricula, and activities will involve at least some variant of the argument that schools should reflect the needs, aspirations, and values of the community which supports them. *Compare Wisconsin v. Yoder*, 406 U.S. 205 (1972), excerpted in Chapter Five (looking to the character of the local community) *with Bd of Educ. Island Trees Union Free Sch. Dist. No. 26 v. Pico*, 457 U.S. 853 (1982) (holding local values regarding education relevant but not determinative), excerpted below.

Under state constitutional law, however, education is a *state* function. Article XIII § 1 of the Minnesota Constitution, for example, provides that:

> The stability of a republican form of government depending mainly upon the intelligence of the people, it is the duty of the legislature to establish a general and uniform system of public schools. The legislature shall make such provisions by taxation or otherwise as will secure a thorough and efficient system of public schools throughout the state.

It follows from provisions such as these that the popular conception of the relationship between state and parental authority, on the one hand, and between state and local authority on the other, stands in tension with the traditional view of the courts. The case law is unanimous on the point: "The maintenance of public schools is a matter, not of local, but of state, concern," and ultimate authority to make educational policy reposes in the state legislature. *Associated Schools of Indep. Dist., No. 63 of Hector, Renville County v. Sch. Dist. No. 83 of Renville County*, 122 Minn. 254, 257–258, 142 N.W. 335, 328 (1913) (collecting state cases). *Accord Board of Educ. of Aberdeen-Huntington Local Sch. Dist. v. State Bd. of Educ.*, 116 Ohio App. 515, 189 N.E. 2d 81 (1962) (approving the revocation of local school board's charter by state education authorities). In this view, parental rights are important, but not controlling, and local communities have only as much control over their schools as state law gives them. *See generally* James A. Rapp, Education Law § 3.02 (3)(a); Robert C. O'Reilly & Edward T. Green, School Law for the 1990s (1992).

b) Federal Authority over State Education Policy

The federal government's authority over matters of education derives from two basic sources: the powers of Congress under Article I, and the power of the judicial branch to interpret and enforce the limits on State authority under the Constitution and laws of the Untied States. Those powers and limits are discussed in greater detail below. For present purposes, however, the focus will remain on the distribution of authority among parents, the states, and the federal government.

In *New Jersey v. T.L.O.*, 469 U.S. 325 (1985), a Fourth Amendment challenge to the right of public school administrators to search student lockers, the Supreme Court discussed the theory that schools are delegates of parental responsibility, as well as its own basic understanding of the contours of parental rights. Justice Byron White wrote that

> the Court has recognized that "the concept of parental delegation" as a source of school authority is not entirely "consonant with compulsory education laws." Today's public school officials do not merely exercise authority voluntarily conferred on them by individual parents; rather, they act in furtherance of publicly mandated educational and disciplinary policies. [citations omitted.]

As a result, the federal courts consistently hold that the decisions of educational authorities authorized under state law to resolve a particular issue are entitled to deference absent any suggestion that the rule violates a federal law or constitutional guarantee such as the First Amendment. *Davis v. Monroe County Bd. of Educ.*, 526 U.S. 629 (1999) (setting out standards for right of private action against school board for failure to prevent sexual harassment of students by other students) *Cf. Ambach v. Norwick*, 441 U.S. 68 (1979) (sustaining under the Equal Protection Clause a New York law prohibiting employment of teachers in publicly operated elementary or secondary schools who were not citizens unless the person had indicated an intention to apply, or was not yet eligible to do so). The position taken was summarized succinctly by Justice Scalia's majority opinion in *Vernonia Sch. Dist. 47j v. Acton,* 515 U.S. 646, 655–56 (1995): "[W]hile children assuredly do not "shed their constitutional rights... at the schoolhouse gate," *Tinker v. Des Moines Indep. Comm. Sch. Dist.*, 393 U.S. 503, 506 (1969), the nature of those rights is what is appropriate for children in school."

But who, in the end, decides what rights are "appropriate for children in school?" The case law is very clear that control of the educational system resides in the state legislatures, and that it is for state educational authorities to determine the policies that will govern the time, place and manner of education. This is what has made state educational policy governing the relationship of religion and education such a controversial topic. There are very significant religious and philosophical differences of opinion over the role of religion in the education of children and young adults, and clashes between the two basic schools of thought on this issue are most clearly in evidence in issues central to the control of educational policy: curriculum content and school finance.

2. The Rights of Parents and Children in American Constitutional Law

The leading federal cases on the subject of "parental rights" in education are *Meyer v. Nebraska*, 262 U.S. 390 (1923); *Pierce v. Society of Sisters*, 268 U.S. 510 (1925); and *Wisconsin v. Yoder,* excerpted in Chapter Five. Though both *Meyer* and *Pierce* are now characterized as "First Amendment" cases, they were decided before the Court began the task of selectively incorporating the Bill of Rights. *See* Chapter One §A. As you read each of the cases excerpted below, consider the possible ways in which the issue(s) in the case can, or should, be characterized for purposes of constitutional analysis. Chart 6-1 on page 399 may be useful in this regard. How, if at all, would the analysis differ under each of the possible characterizations?

Meyer v. Nebraska

262 U.S. 390 (1923)

[Meyer was an instructor at a school maintained by Zion Evangelical Lutheran Congregation. A Nebraska statute adopted in 1919 made it a misdemeanor punishable by a fine and or prison for up to thirty (30) days for "[any] person, individually or as a teacher,..., in any private, denominational, parochial or public school, [to] teach any subject to any person in any language than the English language." Under the terms of the statute "Languages, other than [English could] be taught as languages only after a pupil shall have attained and successfully passed the eighth grade as evidenced by a certificate of graduation issued by the county superintendent of the county in which the child resides." Meyer was tried and convicted for using a collection of Biblical stories to teach a 10 year old boy, Raymond Parpart, "the German language as a distinct subject."

The conviction was affirmed. In the view of the Nebraska Supreme Court

> The salutary purpose of the statute is clear. The Legislature had seen the baneful effects of permitting foreigners, who had taken residence in this country, to rear and educate their children in the language of their native land. The result of that condition was found to be inimical to our own safety. To allow the children of foreigners, who had emigrated here, to be taught from early childhood the language of the country of their parents was to rear them with that language as their mother tongue. It was to educate them so that they must always think in that language, and, as a consequence, naturally inculcate in them the ideas and sentiments foreign to the best interests of this country. The obvious purpose of this statute was that the English language should be and become the mother tongue of all children reared in this state."

Meyer appealed.]

Mr. Justice McREYNOLDS delivered the opinion of the Court.

The problem for our determination is whether the statute as construed and applied unreasonably infringes the liberty guaranteed to [Meyer] by the Fourteenth Amendment: "No state * * * shall deprive any person of life, liberty or property without due process of law."

While this court has not attempted to define with exactness the liberty thus guaranteed, the term has received much consideration and some of the included things have been definitely stated. The established doctrine is that this liberty may not be interfered with, under the guise of protecting the public interest, by legislative action that is arbitrary or without reasonable relation to some purpose within the competency of the state to effect.

The American people have always regarded education and acquisition of knowledge as matters of supreme importance which should be diligently promoted. The Ordinance of 1787 declares: 'Religion, morality and knowledge being necessary to good government and the happiness of mankind, schools and the means of education shall forever be encouraged.'

Corresponding to the right of control, it is the natural duty of the parent to give his children education suitable to their station in life; and nearly all the states, including Nebraska, enforce this obligation by compulsory laws.

Practically, education of the young is only possible in schools conducted by especially qualified persons who devote themselves thereto. The calling always has been regarded as useful and honorable, essential, indeed, to the public welfare. Mere knowledge of the German language cannot reasonably be regarded as harmful. Heretofore it has been commonly looked upon as helpful and desirable. [Meyer] taught this language in school as part of his occupation. His right thus to teach and the right of parents to engage him so to instruct their children, we think, are within the liberty of the amendment.

The challenged statute forbids the teaching in school of any subject except in English; also the teaching of any other language until the pupil has attained and successfully passed the eighth grade, which is not usually accomplished before the age of twelve. The Supreme Court of [Nebraska] has held that 'the so-called ancient or dead languages' are not 'within the spirit or the purpose of the act.' *Nebraska District of Evangelical Lutheran Synod, etc., v. McKelvie* et al. (Neb.) 187 N. W. 927 (April 19, 1922). Latin, Greek, Hebrew are not proscribed; but German, French, Spanish, Italian, and every other alien speech are within the ban.

It is said the purpose of the legislation was to promote civic development by inhibiting training and education of the immature in foreign tongues and ideals before they could learn English and acquire American ideals, and 'that the English language should be and become the mother tongue of all children reared in this state.' It is also affirmed that the foreign born population is very large, that certain communities commonly use foreign words, follow foreign leaders, move in a foreign atmosphere, and that the children are thereby hindered from becoming citizens of the most useful type and the public safety is imperiled.

That the state may do much, go very far, indeed, in order to improve the quality of its citizens, physically, mentally and morally, is clear; but the individual has certain fundamental rights which must be respected.

The desire of the Legislature to foster a homogeneous people with American ideals prepared readily to understand current discussions of civic matters is easy to appreciate. But the means adopted, we think, exceed the limitations upon the power of the state.

The power of the state to compel attendance at some school and to make reasonable regulations for all schools, including a requirement that they shall give instructions in English, is not questioned. Nor has challenge been made of the state's power to prescribe a curriculum for institutions which it supports. We are constrained to conclude that the statute as applied is arbitrary and without reasonable relation to any end within the competency of the state.

Reversed.

Mr. Justice Holmes and Mr. Justice Sutherland, dissent.

Notes

1. The decision in *Meyer* is neither a ringing endorsement of parental rights in education, nor a direct challenge to the power of local educational authorities to set minimum competency standards for either students or teachers. Although the case is now understood as involving First Amendment issues, the Court's reasoning was simply that Nebraska's rules on the teaching of foreign languages to young children were "arbitrary and without reasonable relation to any end within the competency of the state."

2. The importance of characterization—the process by which we describe the holding in a case—is obvious when we pose the following question: How should the holding in *Meyer* be understood for purposes of constitutional analysis? It could be characterized as a free speech case because the teacher was prosecuted for the content of his speech. It can also be viewed as a free exercise case because the school was Lutheran, and the children were being taught to read, among other things, the German translation of the Bible. It can be characterized as an equal protection case because of the anti-immigrant, and particularly anti-German, animus led to the passage of the law. It can also be characterized as a parental rights case. These distinctions make a difference for purposes of constitutional analysis.

At bottom though, *Meyer* is a dispute over curriculum content. Nebraska's educational authorities tried to eliminate the teaching of foreign languages from *all* elementary education programs: private, religiously affiliated, and public. If such a case were to arise today, which of the possible characterizations would provide a litigator with the best facts and the best legal arguments?

Consider, for example, the question of how, if at all, the rationale of *Meyer* might apply in the context of a *public* school, where the authority of the state to control curriculum content is undisputed. Do you think that its rationale would support statutes or regulations designed to make it easier for parents to arrange for religious instruction during the public school day?

In *Dilger v. School District*, 222 Or. 108, 352 P.2d 564 (1960), the Oregon Supreme Court considered the constitutionality of a 1925 Oregon Statute which provided that "Any child attending the public school, on application of his guardian or either of his parents, may be excused from such school for a period or periods not exceeding 120 minutes in any week to attend weekday schools giving instruction in religion." Oregon Rev. Stats. § 336.260. The Dilgers petitioned the school authorities to permit their children to attend religious instruction, but the district refused on the grounds that the statute was unconstitutionally vague and that accommodation of multiple parental requests for accommodation would be too disruptive to the school's program.

Upholding the statute, the court stated that it "regard[ed] the statute as vesting in the pupil's parent or guardian and not the school officials, the power to determine whether the pupil will spend a part of his school time not exceeding 120 minutes in any week in religious instruction." The dissenting Justices concluded that the First Amendment required a different balancing of the interests of parents, children and the State.

> The constitution of this state provides: "The Legislative Assembly shall provide by law for the establishment of a uniform, and general system of common schools." Oregon Const., Art. VIII, § 3.
>
> It is thus clear that the primary and mandatory duty placed upon the legislature by the people is that it provide for the public education of its citizens, and, therefore, the legislature may not pass any mandatory act that may in anywise interfere with this primary objective.
>
> There can be no question but that the moral fiber inculcated into the youth of this nation through religious education is of very great value in creating responsible citizenship, but the state is prohibited under the first amendment of the constitution from compelling religious instruction. To interpret the act as 'shall' instead of 'may' seems to me to be in direct conflict with the powers of the legislature, because the mandatory 'shall' places, if necessary, the requirement of honoring the religious excuse above the requirement to provide for a common school education.
>
> There is undoubtedly the right of the parent to exercise parental control over the child, but I would have no doubt of the unconstitutionality of any act which would place in the hands of the parent the power of the state to require that the child be compelled to receive the religious instruction chosen by the parent.

222 Or. 108, 136–137, 352 P.2d 564, 576–577 (Perry, Warner & Sloan, JJ., dissenting).

It is often difficult to distinguish questions of content from questions of control. The Oregon court was content to leave the issue to the discretion of the parents. The dissenters, by contrast, believe that *the First Amendment itself* "constitutionalizes" the premise that education of the young should take place in a wholly secular environment, and that religion is a subject that should be taught outside the confines of the school day. *Compare Illinois* ex rel. *McCollum v. Board of Educ.*, 333 U.S. 203 (1948) (forbidding, as a matter of federal constitutional law, on-public school premises religious instruction by non-school employees, notwithstanding the decision of local authorities to permit it) *with Zorach v. Clauson*, 343 U.S. 306 (1952) (permitting off-public school premises "released time" programs).

3. To what extent, if at all, is *Meyer* relevant to discussions about the propriety of mandatory bilingual and multicultural education programs in public schools? The rationale of the Nebraska Supreme Court certainly appears similar to the arguments opposing bilingual education heard throughout the 1990s. *See* Social Studies Review and Development Committee, *One Nation, Many Peoples: A Declaration of Cultural Interdependence: The Report of the New York State Social Studies Review and Development Committee* (New York State Education Dept., 1991). *Cf. Ambach v. Norwick*, 441 U.S. 68 (1979). *But cf. California Teachers Ass'n v. State Bd. of Educ.*, 271 F.3d 1141(9th Cir., 2001) (upholding requirement that students be taught "in English"); *Ruiz v. Hull*, 191 Ariz. 441, 957 P.2d 984 (1998)(invalidating, on equal protection and petition for redress grounds, Arizona state constitutional amendment requiring the government to "act" only in English). Is there anything in *Meyer* that could be used by a private school to oppose a plan by state authorities to mandate that private schools offer, at their own expense, a state-approved curriculum of multicultural education?

Two years after *Meyer*, the Supreme Court considered an Oregon statute that sought a more direct and tangible form of control over the education of the State's children: it required that all students be educated in public schools. The Official Ballot Summary's "affirmative" argument framed the issue as follows:

> What is the purpose of our public schools,...? Because they are the creators of true citizens by common education which teaches the ideals and standards upon which our government rests. * * * Mix those with prejudices for a few years while their minds are plastic, and finally bring out the finished product—a true American....Our children must not under any pretext, be it based upon money, creed or social status, be divided into antagonistic groups, there to absorb the narrow views of life, as they are taught.

quoted in Brief of Appellee, *Pierce v. Society of Sisters*, 268 U.S. 466 (1925) at 97.

The State of Oregon's brief was more direct concerning the purpose of the statute:

> The early history of the colonies reveals much of intolerance in religious matters. In the gradual evolution of political and religious matters in the nation,..., the state and the church have ever been maintained as separate... institutions.
>
> * * *
>
> The necessity for any other kind of school than that provided by the state has ceased to exist.... [The only deprivation alleged by the schools is [the law] has deprived them of an opportunity to impart sectarian religious instruction... in the schools. Having in mind the...separation of church and state...and the legal struggles which have arisen over the question of sectarian instruction in the public schools, we submit that [the need for this legislation is apparent.]

* * *

> The great majority of American youth receive their religious instruction in purely sectarian institutions or in the home, separate and apart from their common school education or training, and it has been settled that sectarian religious instruction in our public schools will not be tolerated. The right demanded by [the schools] is denied to all whose children attend the public schools.
>
> The voters in Oregon might also have based their action...upon the alarm which they felt at the rising tide of religious suspicions in this country, and their belief that the basic cause of such...feelings was the separation of children along religious lines during the most susceptible years of their lives, with the inevitable awakening of a consciousness of separation, and a distrust and suspicion of those from whom they were so carefully guarded.

Brief of Appellant, William Pierce (Governor of Oregon), *Pierce v. Society of Sisters*, at 70–73, 40.

As you consider the opinion in *Pierce*, excerpted below, please reconsider the note questions raised after *Meyer v. Nebraska*. Does *Pierce* support the assertion that a generalized set of "parental rights" exist with respect to education? Whatever those rights, are they separate and distinct from those of the State?

Pierce v. Society of the Sisters of the Holy Names of Jesus and Mary

268 U.S. 510 (1925)

Mr. Justice McREYNOLDS delivered the opinion of the Court.

The challenged act...requires every parent, guardian, or other person having control or charge or custody of a child between 8 and 16 years to send him 'to a public school.' There are exemptions—not specially important here—for children who are not normal, or who have completed the eighth grade, or whose parents or private teachers reside at considerable distances from any public school, or who hold special permits from the county superintendent. The manifest purpose is to compel general attendance at public schools [, and] without doubt[,] enforcement of the statute would seriously impair, perhaps destroy, the profitable features of appellees' business and greatly diminish the value of their property.

No question is raised concerning the power of the state reasonably to regulate all schools, to inspect, supervise and examine them, their teachers and pupils; to require that all children of proper age attend some school, that teachers shall be of good moral character and patriotic disposition, that certain studies plainly essential to good citizenship must be taught, and that nothing be taught which is manifestly inimical to the public welfare.

The inevitable practical result of enforcing the act under consideration would be destruction of appellees' primary schools, and perhaps all other private primary schools for normal children within the state of Oregon.

Under the doctrine of *Meyer v. Nebraska*, we think it entirely plain that the Act of 1922 unreasonably interferes with the liberty of parents and guardians to direct the upbringing and education of children under their control. The fundamental theory of liberty upon which all governments in this Union repose excludes any general power of the state to standardize its children by forcing them to accept instruction from public teachers only. The child is not the mere creature of the state; those who nurture him and direct his destiny have the right, coupled with the high duty, to recognize and prepare him for additional obligations.

Appellees are corporations, and therefore, it is said, they cannot claim for themselves the liberty which the Fourteenth Amendment guarantees. Generally, it is entirely true, as urged by counsel, that no person in any business has such an interest in possible customers as to enable him to restrain exercise of proper power of the state upon the ground that he will be deprived of patronage. But the injunctions here sought are not against the exercise of any proper power. Appellees asked protection against arbitrary, unreasonable, and unlawful interference with their patrons and the consequent destruction of their business and property.

The decrees below are affirmed.

Notes

1. What is the nature of the rights recognized by the Court in *Pierce* and *Meyer*? There are quite a few possibilities, and the language used by the Court can support several equally plausible characterizations. As you ponder the answers to the questions raised below, you may find it helpful to refer to Chart 6-1 "Possible Characterizations of the Issues—and of the Case—in a Case Involving Education" on page 399.

2. The first step is to consider *whose* rights were defined in *Pierce* and *Meyer*. The possibilities are: the State, the schools and the associations that sponsored them, the teachers, the parents, the children, and families. Does this exhaust the possibilities?

3. The second step in the process is to determine *which* interests are protected. That task is accomplished by taking note, in turn, of the interests of each of the parties involved in the case.

4. *State Interests:* In *Pierce*, the Court assumed the existence of state power to regulate education:

> No question is raised concerning the power of the state reasonably to regulate all schools, to inspect, supervise and examine them, their teachers and pupils; to require that all children of proper age attend some school, that teachers shall be of good moral character and patriotic disposition, that certain studies plainly essential to good citizenship must be taught, and that nothing be taught which is manifestly inimical to the public welfare.

Should the Court have made this assumption? How much discretion do the States have under this standard? *See Nebraska v. Faith Baptist Church*, excerpted below in § D(2).

5. In order to determine *what rights* the Court protected in *Pierce*, it is necessary to examine the interests of each of the parties in light of the limitations the constitution imposes on the exercise of State discretion. Because it is the Due Process Clause of the fourteenth amendment that "incorporates" the norms of the first, the task begins by asking "what liberties" can be claimed by each of the parties. Consider the possibilities illustrated in Chart 6-3 on page 427.

6. **Is *Pierce* a "religious liberty" case?** It took nearly sixty years for the Supreme Court to characterize *Pierce* as a religious liberty case. *See Board of Educ. v. Allen*, 392 U.S. 236, 245 (1968) In the Court's view, Oregon's law "unreasonably interfere[d] with the liberty of parents and guardians to direct the upbringing and education of children

Chart 6-3

Characterizing the Interests in *Meyer v. Nebraska* & *Pierce v. Society of Sisters*

	Liberty Interests						Liberty & Equality	Equality Interests	
Party	Contract economic	Free Exercise	Speech	Press	Peaceable Assembly	Petition	Non-establishment	Equal Citizenship	Equal Protection
Meyer	X	X	X	X	X	N/A	X	X	X
Sisters of the Holy Name	X	X	X	X	X	N/A	X	X	X
Hill Military Academy	X		X	X	X	N/A	X	X	X
Parents (religious schools)	X	X	X	X	X	N/A	X	X	X
Parents (non-religious schools)	X	N/A	X	X	X	N/A	X	X	X
Children (religious schools)	N/A	X	X	X	X	N/A	X	X	X
Children (nonreligious schools)	N/A	N/A	X	X	X	N/A	X	X	X
Teachers in religious schools	X	X	X	X	X	N/A	X	X	X
Teachers in non-religious schools	X	N/A	X	X	X	N/A	X	X	X

X denotes plausible characterization

under their control." It did not rely on either the First Amendment "in general" or any part of the Religious Liberty Guarantee in reaching its conclusion, but it did indicate that "[t]he fundamental theory of liberty upon which all governments in this Union repose excludes any general power of the state to standardize its children by forcing them to accept instruction from public teachers only." That rationale is equally applicable to the parents and students who chose the Hill Military Academy as their preferred educational environment. Dictum in *Meyer*, however, indicates that the Court believed that the liberty protected in the Fourteenth Amendment also protected the right "to worship God according to the dictates of his own conscience." 286 U.S. at 399. Reading the cases together would seem to indicate that the Court was certainly aware that religious liberty was involved in *Pierce*, but that the interests of the parties to the case were sufficiently diverse to require resting the decision on a more generalized constitutional principle. *See also Farrington v. Tokushige*, 273 U.S. 284 (1927) (Territory of Hawaii's law barring private schools teaching in languages other than English violates Fourteenth Amendment).

7. ***Pierce* as a "hybrid" case:** Is it necessary to utilize a single characterization for cases in which educational issues are involved, or might it be more useful to recognize that each case involves several important interests? In *Employment Div. v. Smith*, excerpted in Chapter Five § D, the Supreme Court refers to *Pierce* and other cases involving conflicts between the state and parents concerning the content of religious speech or the education of children as "hybrid" cases because they involve both religious liberty and other First Amendment values, such as freedom of speech and press. In the Court's view, religious liberty will not, standing alone, support a claim for an exemption from a neutral rule of general applicability. *See Smith*, 494 U.S. 872, at 881–82 & n.1. Does consideration of cases such as *Meyer, Pierce* and *Yoder* as "speech" cases make a difference to your analysis? *See* Stephen Arons, *The Separation of School and State:* Pierce *Reconsidered*, 46 Harv. Ed. Rev. 76 (1976). *See also* FREEDOM & EDUCATION: PIERCE V. SOCIETY OF SISTERS RECONSIDERED (Donald P. Kommers & Michael J. Wahoske eds. 1978).

8. What, if any, significance should be attached to the Court's statement that the purpose of the law at issue in *Pierce* was to "standardize [Oregon's] children by forcing them to accept instruction from public teachers only"? Was that the state's purpose? Is the State's goal of ensuring that its children would learn from a common "secular" curriculum a legitimate one? *See* Brief of Appellant, William Pierce (Governor of Oregon), *Pierce v. Society of Sisters,* at 70–73, 40, quoted above.

9. Is it fair to assert that *one* of the purpose of the public schools is to "standardize" children, at least insofar as training them in the basics of American citizenship and other aspects of civic culture and virtue? If so, how would you describe the nature of the State's interest with respect to these issues? Can the States require all schools to provide a "common curriculum" on these topics? If so, to what extent do the First and Fourteenth Amendments permit them to control both the content and perspective of the materials? *Cf. Tinker v. Des Moines Indep. Comm. Sch. Dist.*, 393 U.S. 503 (1969); *West Virginia Bd. of Educ. v. Barnette*, 319 U.S. 624 (1943); *Minersville Sch. Dist. v. Gobitis*, 310 U.S. 586 (1940). *See generally* William G. Ross, FORGING NEW FREEDOMS: NATIVISM, EDUCATION, AND THE CONSTITUTION, 1917–1927 (1994).

10. There are many child custody cases in which the central issue is the legitimacy of the custodial parent's decision regarding religious education. Does the principle recognized in *Pierce*—that the State may not standardize the education of children—affect the power of a family court to enforce parental obligations concerning the religious upbringing of children when disputes arise between them on these issues? Which spe-

cific "hybrid" rights are relevant in the case of parent-child relationships? *Cf.* Richard W. Garnett, *The Family, Religious Education, and Harm to Children*, in Symposium *Taking* Pierce *Seriously*, 76 Notre Dame L. Rev. 109 (2000); Emily Buss, *The Adolescent's Stake in the Allocation of Educational Control Between Parent and State*, 67 U. Chi. L. Rev. 1233 (2000).

11. How, if at all, do the interests of children fit into this analysis? *Cf. Plyler v. Doe*, 457 U.S. 202 (1982) (holding unconstitutional exclusion from the public schools of children who are undocumented aliens because of the negative impact lack of primary and secondary education has on the children and society). Justice McReynolds, a strong proponent of substantive due process, was the author of the Court's unanimous opinion in *Pierce*, and the case was decided during the heyday of substantive due process.

12. Some commentators have argued that it is illegitimate, in this or any other context, to speak of parental "rights" at all. Consider James G. Dwyer, *Parents' Religion and Children's Welfare: Debunking the Doctrine of Parents' Rights*, 82 Calif. L. Rev. 1371, 1426–1430 (1994) (footnotes omitted):

> [E]ven if the assertions [concerning the capacity of children to make rational, informed decisions, the needs of children for stable relationships with their parents, and the "conventional wisdom" that parents "know best" what is good for their children] have some core of truth, it simply does not follow from them that parents should have child-rearing rights, including plenary rights to effectuate their own ideologically-based judgment concerning how a child's life should proceed.

See also Yochai Benkler, *Siren Songs and Amish Children: Autonomy, Information, and Law*, 76 N.Y.U. L. Rev. 23 (2001); Barbara Bennett Woodhouse, *Hatching the Egg: A Child-Centered Perspective on Parents' Rights*, 14 Cardozo L. Rev. 1747 (1993).

13. How, if at all, should the law view the interests of a school (public or private)? There are several different ways to describe a school, each of which has significant consequences. If we assume that a school (or school system) is a community, the discussion will turn immediately to the question of institutional mission, identity, and character. There will be a distinct difference if the identity and character of the school is to be defined by the parents, by those who teach in or operate the school, or by public authorities. When parents decide upon a school for their children, the law recognizes that they accept the authority of the school to define the character of its program. In *Vernonia School District, 41j v. Acton*, 515 U.S. 646, 54–55(1995), Justice Scalia wrote:

> Traditionally at common law, and still today, unemancipated minors lack some of the most fundamental rights of self-determination—including even the right of liberty in its narrow sense, *i.e.*, the right to come and go at will. They are subject, even as to their physical freedom, to the control of their parents or guardians. See 59 Am. Jur. 2d § 10 (1987). When parents place minor children in private schools for their education, the teachers and administrators of those schools stand *in loco parentis* over the children entrusted to them. In fact, the tutor or schoolmaster is the very prototype of that status. As Blackstone describes it, a parent "may... delegate part of his parental authority, during his life, to the tutor or schoolmaster of his child; who is then in loco parentis, and has such a portion of the power of the parent committed to his charge, viz. that of restraint and correction, as may be necessary to answer the purposes for which he is employed." 1 W. Blackstone, *Commentaries on the Laws of England* 441 (1769).

14. Governmental attempts to classify on the basis of race or national origin have long been held by the Court to be "inherently suspect." John E. Nowak, Ronald D. Rotunda, J. Nelson Young, CONSTITUTIONAL LAW §§ 14.8–14.13 (6th ed. 2000). The courts however, are divided on the topic of religion. *See Cooper v. Eugene Sch. Dist., No. 4J*, excerpted below; *Davis v. Minnesota*, 504 N.W. 2d 767 (Minn. 1993), excerpted in Chapter Twelve (permitting religion-based peremptory challenges to jurors). *Cf. Shaare Tefila Congregation v. Cobb*, 481 U.S. 615 (1987) (holding discrimination on the basis of Jewish ancestry racial discrimination under 42 U.S.C. §§ 1981–1982). Should *Pierce* and *Meyer* be characterized as involving *de jure* religious discrimination and analyzed as equal protection cases? *See* Richard W. Garnett, *Brown's Promise, Blaine's Legacy*, 17 Const. Comm. 651 (2000).

As noted in the Court's opinion, the Oregon law was passed as a ballot initiative in 1922. The vote was 115,506–103,685, and its passage was considered "a political upset." *See* David B. Tyack, *The Perils of Pluralism: The Background of the* Pierce *Case*, 74 Am. Hist. Rev. 74, 90–91 (1968). The initiative was a joint effort of the newly revived Ku Klux Klan and the Scottish Rite Masons, and although they comprised only 8% of the population, Catholics clearly "were the chief targets of the bill." *Id.* at 86. Tyack notes that the KKK made other attempts in the West to compel children to attend common schools, but none became law. Two ironies of this case include the attendance at the Hill Military Academy of the son of Fred Gifford, one of the KKK's leaders of the initiative, *id.* at 87, and the decision by an influential Oregon priest to contact the American Civil Liberties Union for legal assistance. *Id.* at 92.

If *Pierce* is, at bottom, an expression of state-sanctioned racial, ethnic, or religious prejudice, how would such a view affect your understanding of state policies which attempt to standardize the education of children? *Cf. Hunter v. Erickson*, 393 U.S. 385 (1969) (striking down, on equal protection grounds, a local ballot initiative requiring voter approval of fair housing legislation).

15. What is, or should be, the role of the federal government, including the Supreme Court, in cases involving education at the local level? *See United States v. Lopez*, 514 U.S. 549 (1995) (rejecting Commerce Clause nexus to local educational concerns). Is the role of the Court limited by the terms of the First Amendment? If so, how? *See generally* Robert A. Destro, *By What Right?: The Sources and Limits of Federal Court and Congressional Jurisdiction Over Matters "Touching Religion,"* 29 Ind. L. Rev. 1 (1996). If, as the Court has made clear since *Lopez,* the federal government has no generalized power to make either education or family law policy, to what extent does the Fourteenth Amendment permit the Court to "balance" the interests of parents and children in the manner suggested in the excerpt from by Professor Dwyer in note 12 above? *See generally* Chapter Five § K.

16. *Board of Educ. of Kiryas Joel Village Sch. Dist. v. Grumet*, 512 U.S. 687 (1994), summarized in Chapter Five § E(6), illustrates the degree to which cultural differences and animosities such as those presented in *Pierce* remain a problem. *Grumet* was the culmination of the second phase of a long-running battle between the public schools of New York's Monroe-Woodbury School District, and a community of Satmar Hasidic Jews who had incorporated the Village of Kiryas Joel.

Because the Satmar are a religious group with a distinctive culture and lifestyle, there was considerable friction. Not unlike the Amish in *Yoder*, the Satmar parents concluded that the environment of the local public schools was hostile to their children, their customs, and their beliefs. Unlike the Amish, however, the Satmar had no intention of relinquishing their entitlement to publicly funded education. They demanded that the Monroe-Woodbury School District provide an environment in which the children could feel comfortable. The School Board, however, believed that it would be unconstitutional to accommodate such a distinctive set of religious and cultural needs.

After much, largely fruitless, litigation, the Satmar took their case to the New York Legislature. They petitioned for, and received, a "redress of grievances" in the form of a public school district with boundaries contiguous with the borders of the Village. That accommodation—the creation of a local school district for a community so identifiably religious—then became the subject of the continuing litigation control of the educational environment for the disabled children who live in the village of Kiryas Joel.

Both the New York Court of Appeals and the Supreme Court of the United States held that the creation of a special school district for the Village of Kiryas Joel alone created an unconstitutional delegation of the discretionary administration of a public school system to a group defined by its character as a religious community. In the view of the Supreme Court, such an action constitutes the merger of "civic and religious authority," and violates the Establishment Clause. *See Grumet v. Board of Educ. of Kiryas Joel Village Sch. Dist.*, 81 N.Y.2d 518, 618 N.E.2d 94, 601 N.Y.S.2d 61 (1993), *aff'd Board of Educ. of Kiryas Joel Village Sch. Dist. v. Grumet*, 512 U.S. 687 (1994). In response to these decisions, the New York Legislature amended the law creating the Kiryas Joel district to permit the formation of smaller districts, thus eliminating the apparent preference for the Satmar. Local public school authorities challenged the creation of the Kiryas Joel Village district again, but this time the trial court held that there was no evidence that the law discriminated in their favor. *Grumet v. Cuomo*, 164 Misc.2d 644, 625 N.Y.S.2d 1000 (N.Y. Sup. 1995). That opinion was reversed on appeal because the appellate courts concluded that "[n]otwithstanding its facial neutrality, we interpret [the amended statute, Chapter 241] as having the nonneutral effect of allowing the religious community of Kiryas Joel, but no other group at this time and probably ever, to create its own school district." This, in the court's view, "confer[s] special benefits on the Village of Kiryas Joel alone, as against virtually all other groups be they religious or nonreligious, [and] effectively conveys a message of impermissible governmental endorsement." *Grumet v. Cuomo*, 659 N.Y. 57, 69, 681 N.Y.S. 2d 173, 681 N.E. 2d 340 (1997).

3. International Law: The Emerging Contours of the Rights of Children and their Parents

On November 20, 1989, the United Nations adopted the Convention on the Rights of the Child ("CRC" or "the Convention") and proposed its ratification by all member nations. Convention on the Rights of the Child, *done at* New York, Nov. 20, 1989, *opened for signature* Jan. 26, 1990, U.N.G.A. Res. 25 (XLIV), 44 U.N. GAOR, Supp. No. 49, U.N. Doc. A/RES/44/25 (1989) *reprinted in* 28 I.L.M. 1448 (1989) (*entered into force* Sept. 2, 1990). Over 150 countries have either signed or ratified the Convention. Karen A. McSweeney, Note, *The Potential for Enforcement of the United Nations Convention on Rights of the Child: The Need to Improve the Information Base*, 16 B.C. Int'l & Comp. L. Rev. 467, 468 n.8 (1993). At this writing, the United States has signed but not ratified the Convention.

The CRC contains substantive provisions that protect children's economic, social, cultural, civil, political, and humanitarian rights. Article 43 of the Convention also establishes an international panel of experts known as the "Committee on the Rights of the Child" to monitor compliance, to assess the condition of children around the world and to make recommendations on their behalf. *See generally* Cynthia Price Cohen, *Introductory Note: United Nations Convention on the Rights of the Child*, 28 I.L.M. 1448 (1989).

The following provisions of the Convention should be considered in light of the materials excerpted above.

Article 14

1. States Parties shall respect the right of the child to freedom of thought, conscience and religion.
2. States Parties shall respect the rights and duties of the parents and, when applicable, legal guardians, to provide direction to the child in the exercise of his or her right in a manner consistent with the evolving capacities of the child.

Article 15

1. States Parties recognize the rights of the child to freedom of association and to freedom of peaceful assembly.
2. No restrictions may be placed on the exercise of these rights other than those imposed in conformity with the law and which are necessary in a democratic society in the interest of national security or public safety, public order (*ordre public*), the protection of public health or morals or the protection of the rights and freedoms of others.

Article 16

1. No child shall be subjected to arbitrary or unlawful interference with his or her privacy, family, home or correspondence, nor to unlawful attacks on his or her honour and reputation.
2. The child has the right to the protection of the law against such interference or attacks.

Article 17

States Parties recognize the important function performed by the mass media and shall ensure that the child has access to information and material from a diversity of national and international sources, especially those aimed at the promotion of his or her social, spiritual and moral well-being and physical and mental health. To this end, States Parties shall:

(a) Encourage the mass media to disseminate information and material of social and cultural benefit to the child and in accordance with the spirit of article 29;

(b) Encourage international co-operation in the production, exchange and dissemination of such information and material from a diversity of cultural, national and international sources;

(c) Encourage the production and dissemination of children's books;

(d) Encourage the mass media to have particular regard to the linguistic needs of the child who belongs to a minority group or who is indigenous;

(e) Encourage the development of appropriate guidelines for the protection of the child from information and material injurious to his or her well-being, bearing in mind the provisions of articles 13 and 18.

To what extent would ratification of this Convention by the United States have an impact on the interpretation of domestic law governing the respective rights of parents, children and the State? Because the United States is the "state party" signatory, would the Convention "federalize" the issue of parental vs. children's rights to an even greater extent than the Court has done under the rubric of substantive due process? The answers to many of these questions under current doctrine depend on the Senate resolution that ratifies the treaty. If the Senate follows the pattern of all recent human rights treaties and includes in the resolution of ratification a declaration to the effect that the treaty is not self-executing, additional Congressional action to implement the terms of the agreement may be required. *See* Louis Henkin, *U.S. Ratification of Human Rights Conventions: The Ghost of Senator Bricker*, 89 Am. J. Int'l Law 341 (1995). *See generally* Carlos Manuel Vazquez, *The Four Doctrines of Self-Executing Treaties*, 89 Am. J. Int'l L. 695 (1995). *See also* John Norton Moore, *Treaty Interpretation, the Constitution and the Rule of Law*, 42 Va. J. Int'l L. 163–263 (2001); Virginia H. Johnson, Note, *Application of the Rational Basis Test to Treaty-Implementing Legislation: The Need for a More Stringent Standard Of Review*, 23 Cardozo L. Rev. 347 (2001).

Consider Article 14's guarantee to the *child* of freedom of thought, conscience and religion. States have the duty to respect the parental role to "provide direction," and to respect the child's rights. What, if any, impact would the ratification of the Convention have on a case like *Wisconsin v. Yoder*? Would, or should, it modify in any way domestic constitutional or statute law concerning the role of religion in education, or in the public schools? *See, e.g.*, Constitution of Spain, Art. 27 (3) ("The public authorities guarantee the right of parents to ensure that their children receive religious and moral instruction that is in accordance with their own convictions.") What do you make of the Convention's provisions concerning the role of the mass media with the inculcation of values for the "social, spiritual, and moral well-being, and physical and mental health" of children?

The laws of other nations and international instruments provide useful comparisons. The Constitution of the Republic of Poland, for example, speaks explicitly to the issue of parental rights to guide the religious upbringing of their children:

Article 48

1. Parents shall have the right to rear their children in accordance with their own convictions. Such upbringing shall respect the degree of maturity of a child as well as his freedom of conscience and belief and also his convictions.
2. Limitation or deprivation of parental rights may be effected only in the instances specified by statute and only on the basis of a final court judgment.

Article 53

1. Freedom of faith and religion shall be ensured to everyone....
3. Parents shall have the right to ensure their children a moral and religious upbringing and teaching in accordance with their convictions. The provisions of Article 48, para. 1 shall apply as appropriate.

4. The religion of a church or other legally recognized religious organization may be taught in schools, but other peoples' freedom of religion and conscience shall not be infringed thereby....
6. No one shall be compelled to participate or not participate in religious practices.
7. No one may be compelled by organs of public authority to disclose his philosophy of life, religious convictions or belief.

http://www.sejm.gov.pl/english/konstytucja/ek3.htm (2002); European Convention on Human Rights, Art. 8(1) ("Everyone has the right to respect for his private and family life, his home and his correspondence.); Art. 9 (1) ("Everyone has the right to freedom of thought, conscience and religion; this right includes freedom to change his religion or belief and freedom, either alone or in community with others and in public or private, to manifest his religion or belief, in worship, teaching, practice and observance."); *Attorney-General (Vict.)*, ex rel. *Black v The Commonwealth*, 146 CLR 559, 55 ALJR 155; 33 ALR 321 (High Court of Australia, 2 Feb 1981) (construing Section 116 of the Commonwealth Constitution, regarding Australia's establishment and free exercise clauses).

D. "Opting-In" vs. "Opting Out:" The Substantive Implications of *Meyer, Pierce and Yoder*

This section is divided into four parts. Section D(1) contains a brief discussion of the "uniformity" requirements governing the education policies in many states and their relationship to debates over state control of the religious content of both public and private education. Sections D(2) and (3) examine the First Amendment issues that arise when the state regulates the educational programs and activities of religiously affiliated schools, and D(4) deals with state control of the key components of *public* education in which religious activity or content has been identified as raising First Amendment problems: students, teachers, curricula, and the educational environment.

The remaining "control of education" issues deal with public finance. The case law summarized in Sections E and F(1) below indicates that the right to "opt out" of the public school system carries with it a hefty price tag. State and federal discretion to fund all or part of a parent's choice to seek an education not conducted under the auspices of state authorities is severely circumscribed, not only by the Supreme Court's interpretation of the Establishment Clause, but also by state constitutional provisions permitting subsidies only for children enrolled in public schools. State constitutional law on the topic of education finance is introduced in Chapter Four, and some of the case law arising under these provisions is summarized in §§ E and F.

1. The Requirement that the States Maintain a "Uniform" System of Public Education

The three main cases excerpted in § C indicate that the States' interest in universal, compulsory education is rarely questioned in cases arising under the First Amendment.

Controversies over educational policy tend, instead, to focus on the content or viewpoint of the educational experiences that are provided. A brief summary of those cases will illustrate the point.

a) The Concept of "Uniformity"

As early as 1846, the framers of the Wisconsin Constitution supported the proposition that "[a] general system of education was the only system on which we could depend for the preservation of our liberties." *Kukor v. Grover*, 148 Wis.2d 469, 488, 436 N.W.2d 568 (1989) *quoting* Journal and Debates of the Constitutional Convention 238 (1847–48). Uniform public education was viewed as a unifying force for the many citizens of diverse heritage who lived on the frontier that was to become the State of Wisconsin. *See* "Universal Education," *Milwaukee Sentinel & Gazette* (August 22, 1846), *reproduced in* Milo M. Quaife, The Movement for Statehood 188 (1918); Erik LeRoy, Comment, *The Egalitarian Roots of the Education Article of the Wisconsin Constitution: Old History, New Interpretation,* Buse v. Smith *Criticized,* 1981 Wis. L. Rev. 1325, 1344–50.

The push for universal education resulted in the adoption of Article X §3 of the 1848 Wisconsin Constitution. In present form, it provides that:

> The legislature shall provide by law for the establishment of district schools, which shall be as nearly uniform as practicable; and such schools shall be free and without charge for tuition to all children between the ages of 4 and 20 years; and no sectarian instruction shall be allowed therein; but the legislature by law may, for the purpose of religious instruction outside the district schools, authorize the release of students during regular school hours.

Wisconsin Const. Art. X §3 (2002). Other states have similar provisions. *See, e.g.*, Arizona Const. Art. 11 §1 (2002) ("The legislature shall enact such laws as shall provide for the establishment and maintenance of a general and uniform public school system..."); Ohio Const. Art. VI §2 (2002) ("The general assembly shall make such provisions, by taxation, or otherwise, as, with the income arising from the school trust fund, will secure a thorough and efficient system of common schools throughout the State."); Wyoming Const. Art. 7 §1 (2002) ("The legislature shall provide for the establishment and maintenance of a complete and uniform system of public instruction....").

b) Uniformity Requirements and Disputes Over Control & Financing

A constitutional command that laws must be "uniform" speaks not only to the geographic reach of the laws, but also to their interpretation, operation, and effect on those who are governed by them. *See, e.g.*, U.S. Const. art. I §8 cl. 1, 4 (1787) (requiring that "Duties, Imposts and Excises shall be uniform throughout the United States" and providing for "uniform" rules of bankruptcy and naturalization). State constitutional provisions requiring the creation, financing, and maintenance of a uniform educational system available to all children have been the subject of much litigation on each of these topics. *See, e.g.*, *Bush v. Holmes*, 767 So.2d 668 (Fla. App. 1st Dist. 2000) (financial assistance to students attending private schools is not unconstitutional on its face); *Leandro v. State,* 346 N.C. 336, 488 S.E.2d 249 (1997) (standards are qualitative); *DeRolph v. State*, 78 Ohio St.3d 193, 677 N.E.2d 733 (1997) (financing and quality disparities);

Seattle Sch. Dist. No. 1 v. State, 90 Wash.2d 476, 496, 585 P.2d 71 (1978) (financing, substance, and content); *Serrano v. Priest* (I), 5 Cal.3d 584, 96 Cal. Rptr. 601, 487 P.2d 1241 (1971) (financial disparities).

Allowing a child to opt-out of a "uniform" system of public schools, and to select an alternative model of education, raises a number of questions regarding the "substantive" meaning of "uniformity." A narrow reading of the term limits its reach to an examination of the programs and services the *state* provides in the schools it operates. A broad reading would make the state the guarantor of uniform educational *experience* for all children in the state. The State of Oregon's brief in *Pierce* made that point explicitly: "The necessity for any other kind of school than that provided by the state has ceased to exist." Brief of Appellant, William Pierce (Governor of Oregon), *Pierce v. Society of Sisters*, at 71.

The experience of the State of Wisconsin in the years following *Pierce* illustrates the practical importance of this question. Under Wisconsin's compulsory education law, Wis. Stats. § 118.115 (2002), parents are required to send their children aged 6 to 18 to a public or private school. Private schools are, in turn, required to offer a program of instruction very similar in structure and content to that which is offered in the public schools. *See* Wis. Stats. §§ 188.115(3r); 118.165 (2002).

In ***Wisconsin v. Yoder***, 406 U.S. 205 (1972), the State of Wisconsin prosecuted Amish parents who chose *neither* a public or private school to educate their high-school age children. Instead, they opted for the "long-established program of informal vocational education" favored by their faith community. In the State's view, the parents' choice violated its compulsory attendance law because the Amish approach not only failed to measure up to the uniform standards the State set for public and private schools, it "foster[ed] 'ignorance' from which the child must be protected by the State." *Wisconsin v. Yoder*, 402 U.S. 605, 622 (1972). Defending their right to opt-out, the Yoders argued that "conventional formal education of the *type* provided by a certified high school" was objectionable "because it comes at the child's crucial adolescent period of religious development," and that ceding control to the State at this point would harm the parents' ability to pass their religious beliefs to their children. *Id.* at 623 (emphasis added.)

The Court held for the Yoders, noting that it was "neither fair nor correct to suggest that the Amish are opposed to education beyond the eighth grade level." *Id.* at 623. By holding that parents cannot be prosecuted for choosing an educational programs that differ in material respects from those offered in conventional educational programs, the Court underscored the point made in Chart 6-1 on page 399: most education cases do not turn on *whether* a child will be educated, but rather the far more controversial question of *who* should control the content of the child's education. *Cf. Roman Catholic Welfare Corp. of San Francisco v. City of Piedmont*, 45 Cal.2d 325, 289 P.2d 438 (1955) (invalidating city's refusal to grant building permits to nonpublic schools).

Much of the discussion of the "proper" role of religion in *public* and publicly financed education focuses on precisely the same question: the right of a parent or child to challenge attempts by the state to structure a curriculum or educational environment that is either inconsistent with, or hostile to, the religious training of children provided at church or in the home. In the public school setting, the state has both physical control of the children, and control of the most important components an educational program: its philosophy, curriculum, physical and social environment, and teachers. When the issue is public financing of private education, there are two related, but distinct, issues. The first issue is the nature of the services and materials purchased with public funds. Cases raising this issue are generally characterized as raising issues under the Establishment Clause or its state equivalents. These cases are summarized in § F, below. The second issue is the degree of control over the program and operations of a private school the state may demand as a condition of its purchase of services. The characterization of these cases will depend on the nature of the specific condition involved.

In **Davis v. Grover**, 166 Wis.2d 501, 480 N.W.2d 460 (1992), decided twenty years after *Yoder* and discussed at greater length in § F(2) below, Wisconsin created an experimental school finance program. It permitted children in certain low-income neighborhoods of the City of Milwaukee to take a portion of the state funds allocated to their education in the public schools and use them to pay for tuition at the nonsectarian private school of their choice. The program was challenged on a number of state constitutional grounds, including the language of Article X § 3. In the view of the groups opposed the program, the plan was unconstitutional because "tax money earmarked for the public schools is transferred to private schools, enabling them to compete directly with public schools in supplying basic primary education." *Id.* at 558, 480 N.W.2d at 482 (Abrahamson, J., dissenting).

The majority in *Davis v. Grover* held that the uniformity requirement refers "to the 'character of instruction' given, rather than to the means by which the [school districts] are established and their boundaries fixed." *Id.* at 537, 480 N.W.2d at 472, *citing Kukor v. Grover*, 148 Wis.2d 469, 486, 436 N.W.2d 568 (1989). The dissenting opinions, by contrast, argued that Art. X § 3 "prohibits the legislature from diverting state support for the district schools to a duplicate, competitive private system of schools.... [P]ublic education was intended to be the only general school instruction to be supported by taxation." 166 Wis.2d at 556, 480 N.W.2d at 481 (Abrahamson, J., dissenting).

Although the facts and the specific state constitutional provisions vary, most courts considering uniformity questions have reached similar results. In *Simmons-Harris v. Goff*, 86 Ohio St.3d 1, 11 & n. 2, 711 N.E.2d 203, 212 & n.2 (1999), for example, the Ohio Supreme Court stated:

> Section 2, Article VI of the Ohio Constitution also states that "[t]he general assembly shall make such provisions, by taxation, or otherwise, as, with the income arising from the school trust fund, will secure a thorough and efficient system of common schools throughout the State." In *DeRolph v. State (1997), 78* Ohio St.3d 193, *677 N.E.2d 733*, this court held that the state has an obligation to establish a "thorough and efficient system of common schools." It can be argued that implicit within this obligation is a prohibition against the establishment of a system of uncommon (or nonpublic) schools financed by the state.
>
> Private schools have existed in this state since before the establishment of public schools. They have in the past provided and continue to provide a valuable alternative to the public system. However, their success should not come at the expense of our public education system or our public school teachers. We fail to see how the School Voucher Program, at the current funding level, undermines the state's obligation to public education. The School Voucher Program does not violate this clause of Section 2, Article VI of the Ohio Constitution.[2] [[2]. It is possible that a greatly expanded School Voucher Program or similar program could damage public education. Such a program could be subject to a renewed constitutional challenge.]

See also Roman Catholic Welfare Corp. of San Francisco v. City of Piedmont, 45 Cal.2d 325, 337, 289 P.2d 438, 445–446 (1955) (Schauer, J., dissenting) (arguing that the California Constitution favors public schools); *Bush v. Holmes*, 767 So. 2d 668, 676 (Fla. App. 1st Dist., 2000) (the Florida constitution does not, on its face, forbid taxpayer support of private education); *Snyder v. Charlotte Public School Dist., Eaton County*, 421 Mich. 517, 365 N.W.2d 151 (1984) (requiring public schools to offer nonpublic student shared time program and rejecting Establishment Clause claim).

2. "Opting-Out"—Regulating Church-Based Education: Reconsidering the Concept of "Absolute Separation"

The relationship between parents, churches, and state educational authorities is the central theme of this section. When parents and children choose private, religiously affiliated schools, they remain bound by state laws governing certification of private schools. When disputes arise over program content or the operation, management, and financing of religiously affiliated schools, the characterization of the issues will vary according to the facts of the specific case, but will generally fall into four categories: Establishment, Free Exercise, Speech and Press, or Peaceable Assembly cases. *See* Chapters Five, Seven § C ("Resolving Disputes within and among Religious Groups"), and Eight § E ("The Religious Workplace"). When parents elect to take advantage of the educational opportunities offered in public schools, the same *types* of questions arise, but must be viewed in a context where the government carries significant additional obligations under the Equal Protection Clause of the Fourteenth Amendment, the No Religious Test Clause of Article VI, and state constitutional law doctrines governing the public school system.

Please reconsider *Wisconsin v. Yoder*, 406 U.S. 205 (1972) excerpted in Chapter Five § C(6).

Notes

1. Five years before *Yoder*, the Kansas Supreme Court upheld the application of a Kansas statute that required all school children to attend a school, public or private, "taught by a competent instructor, in which all instruction shall be given in the English language only...for such period as the public school of the district...is in session." *State v. Garber*, 197 Kan. 567, 419 P. 2d 896 (1966), *cert. denied* 389 U.S. 51 (1967). Just as they did in *Yoder*, the Old Order Amish parents complained that the compulsory education requirement violated their rights under the First Amendment. Although their daughter was enrolled first in a home school program and later in an Amish school taught part-time by a local farmer, the Kansas Supreme Court refused to make any exception to the statute, holding that "the natural rights of a parent to the custody and control of his child are subordinate to the police power of the state and may be restricted and regulated by municipal law providing minimum education standards. The question of how long a child should attend school is not a religious question, no matter how sincere he may be the individual cannot be permitted on religious grounds to be the judge of his duty to obey laws enacted in the public interest." 419 P.2d at 900. In so ruling, the court placed its decision on the religious freedom issue on the distinction between "belief" and "action."

2. Does *Yoder* overrule *Garber* in its entirety? What impact, if any, does *Employment Div. v. Smith* have on your answer?

3. Would *Yoder* permit a state to prescribe the curriculum in an Amish school? Does it permit parental "opt-out" whenever there is a claim by parents that the content or method of state-supported education hampers their ability to inculcate religious beliefs in their children? *See generally*, Note, *Compulsory High School Attendance and the Old Order Amish: A Commentary on* State v. Garber, 16 Kan. L. Rev. 423 (1968); Stephen Knudson, *The Education of the Amish Child*, 62 Calif. L. Rev. 1506 (1974); Note, *Adjudicating What* Yoder *Left Unresolved: Religious Rights for Minors After* Danforth *and* Carey, 126 U. Pa. L. Rev. 1135 (1978).

The States exert control over private schools and the educators who work in them through two basic mechanisms: certification and regulation of private schools, and compulsory education laws that require parents to send their children to schools whose facilities, teachers, and curriculum meet state standards. The courts have adopted the same prudential rules governing judicial oversight as apply in the public school context. Absent some showing that substantive constitutional rights are burdened or otherwise at risk, the courts will generally defer to the judgment of state educational authorities.

In **Nebraska *ex rel.* Douglas v. Faith Baptist Church,** 207 Neb. 802, 301 N.W.2d 571 (1981), for example, the Nebraska Attorney General sued the Faith Baptist Church of Louisville, Nebraska and certain individual officers and employees seeking to enjoin the operation of an elementary and secondary school because there had been no compliance with State's school laws. Those rules provided, among other things,

1. Every person having charge or control of any child between the ages of 7 and 16 "shall cause such child to attend regularly the public, private, denominational, or parochial day schools each day that such schools are open and in session...."
2. The State Board of Education shall have the power and duty to provide "supervision of the state school system"; to "establish...procedures for classifying, approving, and accrediting schools...for the continued legal operation of all schools"; and to "cause to be published laws and regulations governing the schools."
3. "Only school systems approved for continued legal operation by the State Board of Education are considered to be providing a program of instruction which is in compliance with the compulsory attendance laws", and prescribed in detail :
    a. Curriculum content,
    b. Necessary materials and equipment,
    c. Length of the school day and year,
    d. Requirements relating to health and safety,
    e. Filing a "Fall Approval Report" and an "Annual Term Summary Report," and,
    f. Each professional staff member employed by the school must "hold a valid Nebraska certificate or permit issued by the State Board of Education legalizing him or her to teach the grades or subjects to which elected," and that each staff member have a baccalaureate degree.

The curriculum of the Faith Christian School was supplied by Accelerated Christian Education (A.C.E.), and consisted of a series of Bible-oriented booklets called the Packet of Accelerated Christian Education (PACE). Each booklet contained instructional information and self-test questions in various subjects at different instructional levels. Students were to work at their own speed while completing each PACE, and were required to attain a grade of at least 80 percent on the self-test and the PACE test given under the supervision of the supervisor before moving on to the next sequentially numbered PACE. The teachers served as supervisors and monitors, administering the tests and making themselves available to help individual students having difficulty.

The Church defended on both statutory and constitutional grounds, arguing, among other things, that enforcement of the school laws violated the parents' Ninth Amendment rights to bear, raise, and educate their children as they see fit, and the First Amendment rights of both the Church and the parents. From the Church's perspective, "secular humanism [was] the basic philosophy of the public educational system," and the State Department of Education was biased against a religiously inspired approach to Christian "teaching [as] a way of life and not simply a 5-hours-a-day, 5-days-a-week proposition." They argued that the Church could not submit to State control and inspection "because the State has no right to inspect God's property."

The District Court granted the injunction. The Nebraska Supreme Court reversed. Writing for the court, Justice Hastings acknowledged the deep philosophical divide between the State and the defendants, but observed that "the method of instruction [was] not unlike a correspondence course, with the addition of helping supervisors." Such an approach was unacceptable, and so too was the Church's challenge to the State's power "to compel attendance at some school and to make reasonable regulations for all schools." In the court's view, the main issue presented was "the extent to which the State can, if at all, restrict [parental First and Ninth Amendment] rights in the interest of assuring all children a quality basic education."

In its view, neither *Pierce v. Society of Sisters* nor *Wisconsin v. Yoder* supported the Church's broad based attack on State authority to regulate religiously affiliated education programs. It specifically noted that *Pierce* did not question "the power of the State reasonably to regulate all schools, to inspect, supervise, and examine them, their teachers and pupils; to require that all children of proper age attend some school, that teachers shall be of good moral character and patriotic disposition, that certain studies plainly essential to good citizenship must be taught, and that nothing be taught which is manifestly inimical to the public welfare." *Yoder*, in its view, was limited to its facts. *See also State v. Whisner*, 47 Ohio St. 2d 181, 351 N.E.2d 750 (1976) (state regulations were so onerous that they destroyed distinction between public and nonpublic schools).

Chief Justice Krivosha dissented from the part of the majority opinion upholding the rule that all elementary and secondary teachers, public or private, must hold a baccalaureate degree before a student's attendance at such school may satisfy the State's compulsory attendance laws. In his view, the State's claim on this point was just as overbroad as that of the Church: "neither can the State regulate or control all action of a group under the bald assertion that such regulation is necessary to preserve and maintain the health, safety, or welfare of such group."

Notes

1. Was the Nebraska court correct when it limited *Yoder* to its facts? ? Its construction *Yoder* is typical in state cases involving the application of school laws to religious schools. In *State v. DeLaBruere*, 154 Vt. 237, 249 (1990), for example, the Vermont Supreme Court held that *Yoder* should be understood to mean that "the party asserting the violation has the initial burden of proving that the state requirement or restriction imposes a burden on religious belief or practice." The North Dakota

Supreme Court adopted this view in *State v. Shaver*, 294 N.W.2d 883, 892 (N.D. 1980), another challenge to certification requirements, when it held that "[t]o establish a burden '[i]t is incumbent on the challenger to the statute to show the coercive effect of the enactment on the practice of religion." *Id.* at 895. *See generally Roloff Evangelistic Enterprises, Inc. v. Texas*, 556 S.W.2d 856 (Tex. Civ. App., 1977) (requiring religious day care center to obtain state license); *Oxford v. Hill*, 558 S.W.2d 557 (Tex. Civ. App. 1977) (Texas Child Care Licensing Act did not violate Free Exercise Clause as applied to a religious organization which operated a home for boys). Would the church schools have been better served by making an argument that the state was "excessively entangled" in the affairs of church-related schools? *Cf. Lemon v. Kurtzman*, Chapter Five § E.

2. The Nebraska Supreme Court reaffirmed *Douglas* in *Sileven v. Tesch*, 212 Neb. 880, 326 N.W.2d 850 (1982), in which the pastor of the Faith Baptist Church sought a writ of habeas corpus seeking release from custody brought about because the church continued to operate in defiance of the injunction issued in the litigation recounted in the case summarized above. The Rev. Sileven contended that the court had not decided all the constitutional questions in *Douglas*, but the court rejected the contention as follows:

> We are totally at a loss to understand how he can reach that conclusion. [The First and Ninth amendment issue]... is no longer an open question in this jurisdiction and our decision in *Faith Baptist* has declared the law,... no matter what anyone may argue to the contrary. We have already found that Sileven and the Faith Baptist Church do not have a first amendment right to ignore the state's school laws. It is Sileven's choice to continue violating the lawful orders of the court which has resulted in his being held in contempt. Sileven is simply wrong if he believes that he may consistently and continually flout the law by merely declaring that it is contrary to his religious beliefs, no matter how sincerely held.

212 Neb. at 885, 326 N.W. 2d at 853.

3. Consider ***State v. Whisner,*** 47 Ohio St.2d 181, 351 N.E.2d 750 (1976), an opinion criticized by the Nebraska Supreme Court. *Whisner* is one of the few cases in which a state's education requirements were struck down by a court, and it is often cited to support the proposition that pervasive state regulation of religious schools is unconstitutionally burdensome to the free exercise of religion. *See, e.g., Shaver,* 294 N.W.2d at 898. In the Nebraska court's view, the Ohio Supreme Court relied too heavily on the writings of Henry David Thoreau. Consider its facts.

The Whisners were convicted of violating the Ohio's compulsory attendance law after they refused to send their children to a state-approved school. Their defense was a Free Exercise challenge to the application of Ohio's minimum education standards to church operated schools. The Ohio Supreme Court recognized that

> a substantial body of case law has confirmed the power of the States to insist that attendance at private schools, if it is to satisfy state compulsory-attendance laws, be at institutions which provide minimum hours of instruction, employ teachers of specified training, and cover prescribed subjects of instruction... [and that] if the State must satisfy its interest in secular education through the instrument of private schools, it has a proper interest in the manner in which those schools perform their secular educational function.'" *Id.* 47 Ohio St.2d at 197 (citing *Board of Educ. v. Allen,* footnote omitted).

The court noted, however, that in Free Exercise challenges to state regulations, courts must "accord the requisite judicial deference to the veracity" of the parent's religious beliefs, and held that neither of the lower courts had done so. *Id.* 47 Ohio St.2d at 199. In fact, the Court of Common Pleas had concluded that:

> the testimony of Rev. Whisner...however well meant, is inadequate to justify on religious grounds a complete departure from the minimum standards of the state Department of Education...[because] his testimony reflects the subjective attitudes of the members of his congregation, and his reasoning is based essentially upon a subjective interpretation of Biblical language.

Id.

Reversing the lower courts, the Ohio Supreme Court held that "at this date and time in the history of our nation, it is crystal clear that neither the validity of what a person believes nor the reasons for so believing may be contested by an arm of the government." *Id.*

Is this a dispute over religion, or over educational philosophy? Aren't *all* religious beliefs based upon "subjective interpretations" of relevant religious texts or other sources, such as direct revelation? Is it possible to argue that educators also make "subjective interpretations" of the basic works of educational philosophy when they set minimum standards? If so, would (or should) it make any difference in a case challenging those standards on religious liberty grounds? See Chapter Five § D.

4. The regulations at issue in *Whisner* prescribed both the content of the curriculum and the time allocations for teaching each class. They defined the length of each school day; required that "[a]ll activities shall conform to policies adopted by the board of education," 47 Ohio St.2d at 201, and required that each religious school "cooperate with elements of the community in which it exists." *Id.*, 47 Ohio St.2d at 209. The parents challenged each as a burden on their religious practice.

Among the findings of the Ohio Supreme Court were that the regulation that allocated instructional time "almost to the minute," "invariably results in further control of the educational policies of a non-public religious school in a manner that we cannot say is compelled by the enabling legislation pursuant to which the 'minimum standards' were adopted." *Id.*, 47 Ohio St.2d at 206. The regulation mandating that the school conform its policies to those of the public school would cause the state to violate the Establishment Clause by "requir[ing] all activities of a non-public religious school, which, of necessity, must include religious activities, to conform to the policies of a purportedly 'neutral' [school] board[.]" *Id.*, 47 Ohio St.2d at 207. The regulation requiring the school to cooperate with the community "infringes upon the rights of these appellants, consistent with their religious beliefs, to engage in complete, or nearly complete, separation from community affairs." *Id.*, 47 Ohio St.2d at 209.

The court quoted extensively from the trial court record, including the testimony of an expert in non-public education who stated:

> that he [was] 'of the firm position that the state has some far-reaching fundamental educational responsibilities,' but that 'the state can fulfill all its fundamental responsibilities in education without prescribing how people must be educated; where they must be educated; what kind of buildings they must be educated in; what must be in the program; and what must be the nature of the individual who instructs them.'

Id., 47 Ohio St.2d at 191. He also testified that in his opinion "the [minimum education] standards are not neutral in that a philosophy of 'secular humanism' is espoused therein [and] that enforcement of the standards would 'in effect take away from the school the right to run its own philosophy'" *Id.* at 192. The Ohio Supreme Court agreed:

> In our view, these standards are so pervasive and all-encompassing that total compliance with each and every standard by a non-public school would effectively eradicate the distinction between public and non-public education, and thereby deprive these appellants of their traditional interest as parents to direct the upbringing and education of their children.

Id., 47 Ohio St.2d at 211–212.

The Ohio Supreme Court reaffirmed *Whisner* in *State* ex rel. *Nagle v. Olsen,* 64 Ohio St.2d 341, 415 N.E.2d 279 (1980), in which a Christian parent chose to send his daughter to an Amish school which had not complied with the 1979 Minimum Standards challenged in *Whisner.* Although the evidence regarding Mr. Nagle's need to send his daughter to the unaccredited school was equivocal, the Court was willing to find an undue burden on his religious liberty interests because of the "all encompassing nature of the standards, which purport to govern every aspect of the educational process." 415 N.E.2d at 286–87. The *Nagle* court noted that although the state's interest is an important one, "it can not be viewed as compelling when a free exercise claim is at stake unless 'the state's interest cannot be otherwise served.'" *Id.* at 287. The Ohio Supreme Court observed that less burdensome regulations could be formulated, and suggested the following guidelines:

> [T]he issuance of state approval upon a showing that (1) all teachers are legally certified, (2) courses are offered in a prescribed range of secular subjects, and (3) the school is in compliance with all municipal and state health, fire and safety laws.
>
> [U]ntil such time as...minimum standards which go no further than necessary to assure the state's legitimate interest in the education of children in private...schools, the balance is weighted, *ab initio*, in favor of a First Amendment claim to religious freedom.

Id., 415 N.E.2d at 288. *But see Ohio Ass'n of Indep. Sch. v. Goff,* 92 F.3d 419 (6th Cir. 1996) (*Whisner* does not prohibit a uniform proficiency examination).

5. *Vermont v. LaBarge,* 134 Vt. 276, 357 A.2d 121 (1976) was decided the same year as *Whisner.* Like the minister in *Whisner*, the parents were prosecuted under the truancy statute because the state department of education had not approved the private school they had chosen. The major difference in the two cases, however, is that *LaBarge* rests upon a statutory foundation. The school had applied for approval, but the state had made no finding of "equivalency" as required by the statute. (V.S.A. § 1121(b)). Because the statute required "equivalent" rather than approved education, the truancy statute could not be read as requiring the latter. Moreover, the Court noted, "in light of what is involved in 'approval', the state would be hard put to constitutionally justify" requiring such approval. "[C]ompulsory attendance even on an equivalent basis, must yield to First Amendment concerns." *Id.* at 280.

7. Control over the operations of church-related private schools is not always accomplished through enforcement of state truancy laws. In *City of Concord v. New Testament Baptist Church,* 118 N.H. 56, 382 A.2d 337 (1978), local authorities denied a petition for a zoning variance that would have permitted the church to extend its teaching ministry from Sundays to the entire week. Before the trial court heard the case, the

complaint was amended to allege that no variance was necessary under the zoning ordinance because it permitted "facilities usually connected with a church." The New Hampshire Supreme Court reversed the denial, holding that "[w]hile every church may not 'usually' have a school associated, we hold that [the school] is a... permitted use connected with... the [church]." *Id.* at 60. *But cf., Open Door Baptist Church v. Clark County,* 140 Wash.2d 143, 995 P.2d 33 (2000) (church and school could be compelled to obtain temporary use permit).

7. State law can also provide for defenses not found at the federal level. Section 5 of the Kentucky Constitution provides, in relevant part, "nor shall any man be compelled to send his child to any school to which he might be conscientiously opposed." In *Kentucky State Bd. of Educ. v. Rudasill*, 589 S.W.2d 877 (Ky. 1979), Christian schools sought declaratory relief under this section upon learning that the state intended to apply its textbook approval and teacher certification standards to them. The Kentucky Court of Appeals held that it need not "ride with the Federales to reach a decision[, because]... it is obvious that Section 5... is more restrictive of the power of the state to regulate private and parochial schools than is the first amendment to the federal constitution as it has been applied to the states." 589 S.W.2d at 879 and n.3.

Because the provision was intended to restrict the power of the state in the area of compulsory education, the Court of Appeals held that Kentucky's interests are "to prepare children of the Commonwealth to intelligently participate as citizens in a democracy, *i.e.,* to exercise the elective franchise, but not to develop them socially and morally in the same educational mold." *Id.* at 883. It noted that the state possessed the power to prove that the school was not educating the children, or that the entity was not a school within the meaning of the constitution, but that to allow state educational authorities to go beyond "reasonable health, fire, and safety regulations" in the course of the required "approval," and to include textbook approval, would be "[t]o say that one may not be compelled to send a child to a public school but that the state may determine the basic texts to be used in the private or parochial schools is to require hay be fed in the field as it is in the barn. Section 5 protects a diversified diet." *Id.* at 884.

3. Regulating Church-Related and Home Schools

There has been considerable growth in the number and diversity of religious education and home school programs since *Whisner* and *Faith Baptist Church* were decided. In 1983, the number of children being educated at home was estimated to be between 60,000 and 125,000. Patricia Lines, *Home Instruction: The Size and Growth of the Movement*, in HOME SCHOOLING: POLITICAL, HISTORICAL, AND PEDAGOGICAL PERSPECTIVES 10 (Jane Van Galen & Mary Anne Pittman eds. 1991). Estimates for the 1999 school year placed the number of children in some form of home education program at approximately 850,000. *See* National Center for Education Statistics, *Home Schooling in the United States, 1999* (NCES 2001-033, July 2001). As might be expected, these developments have fueled litigation over the impact of state education policies. *See, e.g., Port Arthur Independent School Dist. v. Klein & Associates Political Relations*, 2002 WL 225908 (Tex. App. Beaumont, Feb 14, 2002) (school district argued, unsuccessfully, that it should be permitted to sue for defamation because "the increasing competition among public, private, charter, and home schools for students" makes its reputation a valuable asset).

a) Immunity from Regulation

In *Johnson v. Charles City Community Schools Bd. of Educ.*, 368 N.W.2d 74 (Iowa 1985), the trial court's findings of fact included this assertion from the school's head: "the church school is a 'ministry' or essential religious function of the church and that the state has no more authority to control or regulate the Monday through Friday church school than it has to regulate the Sunday church school." *Id.* at 77. Parents who home school often base their arguments for immunity on their belief that they have a recognized fundamental right to direct the education of their children. *See, e.g., State v. Melin*, 428 N.W.2d 227 (N.D. 1988); *People v. DeJonge*, 442 Mich. 266, 501 N.W.2d 127 (1993).

b) Selecting an Appropriate Level of Generality

1) When are the State's Interests "Compelling"?

The state's interest in the education of children is often stated at a high level of generality. So too, are the parents' interests. In *Wisconsin v. Yoder*, for example, the Supreme Court stated:

> There is no doubt as to the power of a State, having a high responsibility for education of its citizens, to impose reasonable regulations for the control and duration of basic education. Providing public schools ranks at the very apex of the function of a State.

Yoder, 406 U.S. at 213.

What does this quotation tell you concerning the nature of the state interest in regulating the character and content of private education? In most cases involving the regulation of private or home schooling, the parents concede the state's right to ensure that their children are being educated. *See Johnson*, 368 N.W.2d at 79. The real issue in these cases is the *nature* and *extent* of the state's interest, and the degree to which the regulation furthers the specified interest. If, for example, the state is merely interested in ensuring the adequacy of the education received, how much regulation of content and process is consistent with the First Amendment? Is this a situation where "time, place and manner" analysis should apply? What if the state authorities admit that the education offered by the school in question is clearly adequate, and may even be superior to the secular educational program offered in the local public schools? *See People v. DeJonge*, 442 Mich. 266, 501 N.W.2d 127 (1993); *State v. Shaver*, 294 N.W.2d 883 (N.D. 1980). *See generally* Bruce D. Page, Jr., *Changing Our Perspective: How Presumptive Invalidity of Home School Regulations Will Further the State's Interest in an Educated Citizenry*, 14 Regent U. L. Rev. 181 (2001–2002).

2) Which Parental Interests Are Protected?

The belief that they are "in the world, but not of the world" causes many parents to liken themselves to the Old Order Amish in *Wisconsin v. Yoder*. In that case, the Amish parents argued successfully that their children would not be entering general society, and that the education sought by the state was unnecessary for these particular children. Does this mean that *Yoder* is, or should be, limited to situations in which the children will not be entering the general society after leaving school?

Because most religious groups do not segregate themselves from society to the degree that the Amish do, many courts decline to offer them the same level of protection.

For example, in *Fellowship Baptist Church v. Benton*, 815 F.2d 485 (8th Cir. 1987), the court found:

> Plaintiffs... do not segregate themselves from modern communities. They live in ordinary residential neighborhoods and they interact with their neighbors and others not of their faith. They believe they are called by God to perform certain occupations in life, but these include ordinary occupations such as nurse, lawyer, engineer and accountant. They own and use radios, televisions, motor vehicles and other modern conveniences and advancements. Their dress and lifestyle, while conservative, is not distinctive.

Id. at 489. Why are such factors relevant?

Courts rarely permit parents to determine the content of an "adequate" education for their children, but they do accept the argument that decisions affecting the formation of their children's intellect and character involve liberty interests protected by the Fourteenth Amendment. In *Whisner*, for example, the Ohio court's holding on the Free Exercise claim was bolstered by its views on the nature of the state's interest in education. "[E]qually difficult to imagine, is a state interest sufficiently substantial to sanction abrogation of appellants' liberty to direct the education of their children." *Whisner*, at 218.

The more common view is that the scope of the parental rights recognized in *Yoder* is limited by a broad conception of state power in the field of education:

> The Court placed strong emphasis upon the unique sociological position the Amish maintained in relation to other religious sects, and stressed the fact that the Amish were not a group which claimed to have recently discovered a more progressive or enlightened means by which to raise their children. The Court determined that the Amish parents had convincingly demonstrated the interrelationship between their sincerely-held religious beliefs and their mode of life, as well as the hazards presented by the enforcement of Wisconsin's compulsory school attendance law to them."

Shaver, 294 N.W.2d at 899. *See also Swanson v. Guthrie Indep. Sch. Dist. No. I-L*, 135 F.3d 694, 699 (10th Cir. 1998) ("[P]arents simply do not have a constitutional right to control each and every aspect of their children's education and oust the state's authority over that subject."). How does *Employment Div. v. Smith* affect this reasoning? Are school regulations neutral laws of general applicability? Might they also present hybrid situations in which the Free Exercise norm is bolstered by another constitutional provision? *See* Chapter Five § G.

(A) Submission to State Authority, Generally

The most commonly cited burden to the exercise of religious belief is the requirement that the school or home-school parent submit an educational plan to government authorities for review. *See e.g., State v. Shaver*; *State* ex rel. *Douglas v. Bigelow*, 214 Neb. 464, 334 N.W.2d 444 (1983); *Johnson v. Charles City Community Schools Bd. of Educ.*, 368 N.W.2d 74 (Iowa 1985); *State v. DeLaBruere*, 154 Vt. 237, 577 A.2d 254 (1990). This argument is based not so much on the particularities involved in complying with state law, but rather on the premise that the only legitimate authority over a church, and the only authority to which churches will submit, is God. *Shaver*, 294 N.W.2d at 887; *Charles City*, 368 N.W.2d at 77.

In *State v. DeLaBruere*, 154 Vt. 237, 577 A.2d 254 (1990), parents charged with a violation of Vermont's truancy statute for sending their son to a non-state approved church school challenged the application of that statute to them under the Free Exercise Clause. The Court found that, though the parents argued that their religious beliefs were burdened by the particular reporting requirements found in the statute, their objections really centered on a "symbolic, but not actual, burden" because the church school would have been found to have met the state requirements if it had applied to the state for approval. *Id.* at 251.

> [W]e note that virtually every conflict between a state and parents who claim the right to be free of state control of the education of their children because of an interference with religious beliefs involves the fact that state regulation exists at all and not the content of the regulation.

Id.

Courts have mixed reactions to the argument that merely submitting to state authority is a burden on religious beliefs. Some courts are skeptical:

> Although the tenets of the Bible Baptist Church do not forbid public school education, the Church is vehemently opposed to securing state approval required by state law. No attempt was made at trial to show how compliance with the law would affect the religion of the parents or their children.

Shaver, at 893. *See also State v. Schmidt,* 29 Ohio St.3d 32, 505 N.E.2d 627 (1987). Like the *DeLaBruere* court, most concede that a burden exists.

> [W]e resist the state's invitation to hold there is no burden because our view of what is a necessary conflict differs from that of defendants. We must accept on face value that the symbols of state regulation are as religiously important to defendants as the actuality of state control over their religious education.

DeLaBruere, 154 Vt. at 252.

The courts seem more comfortable resolving the issue by balancing the asserted Free Exercise claim against the state's interest in pre-clearance, with the state interest almost always weighing more heavily. Perhaps the strongest repudiation came from the court in *Johnson v. Charles City Community Schools,* in which the court reasoned:

> Sincere persons such as these plaintiffs are often unpersuaded by legal authorities. Religious views prompt them to think they must answer to some authority higher than the law. Over the centuries our legal system has become relatively tolerant in accommodating even those who reject it, especially those who do so for religious reasons. But a point is reached after which the accommodation must be offered by the dissenting citizen rather than the state.

Charles City, 368 N.W.2d at 79. After determining that a state has the right to enact minimum educational standards and to enforce them under the compulsory education statutes, the court went on to state that "[a] citizen must submit to them, persuade society to change them, or join a society without them." *Id.*

In *State v. Schmidt,* 29 Ohio St.3d 32, 505 N.E.2d 627 (1987), parents attempting to educate their children at home refused to seek approval of their home education program from the local school superintendent. The court refused to apply a balancing test, ruling that without a submission of their proposal to the superintendent there was "no way to balance appellants' right to the free exercise of their religion... against the state's interest." *Schmidt,* at 35. The court endorsed the state's right to control education in a footnote, citing as authority the Supreme Judicial Court of Maine:

> For the state to allow home education without imposing some standards as to quality and duration would be, in many cases, to allow parents to deprive their children of any education whatsoever. Not all parents who would hold their children out of school under such an unlimited exception to the compulsory education statute would have the sincere desire, which is no doubt present in the instant case, to provide their children with adequate instruction. Furthermore, many parents, even though they have a sincere desire to educate their children at home, lack the necessary training and facilities to do so.

Schmidt, 29 Ohio St.3d at 35 n.9, quoting *State v. McDonough*, 468 A.2d 977, 980 (Me.1983).

The case law is thus fairly consistent. Courts take a dim view of parental claims for across-the-board exemptions from the operation of compulsory attendance laws, but are fairly sympathetic to claims that state educational authorities have exceeded the scope of their legitimate authority. *See, e.g., Barrow v. Greenville Indep. Sch. Dist.*, 2002 WL 255484 (N.D. Tex. Feb 20, 2002) (refusing to dismiss a civil rights action against a public school administrator who refused interview to an applicant for a position in public school because her children were enrolled in private, Christian school); *Peterson v. Minidoka County Sch. Dist. No. 331,* 118 F.3d 1351 (9th Cir. 1997), as amended, 132 F.3d 1258 (9th Cir. 1997) (public school principal could not be demoted because he home schooled his own children); *Brunelle v. Lynn Public Schools,* 428 Mass. 512, 702 N.E.2d 1182 (1998) (public schools could not condition home school exemption on home visits by school authorities). *But see Kaptein By and Through Kaptein v. Conrad Sch. Dist.*, 251 Mont. 152, 931 P.2d 1311 (Mont. 1997) (public schools may exclude home school students from athletic teams).

(B) Teacher Certification

Prior to the explosive growth of religiously-affiliated schools in the Protestant Christian community during the 1970s and 1980s, compulsory education statutes typically required that every teacher had to be certified by the state in order for the school to be approved. Certification often included a bachelor's degree from an accredited institution and coursework in both teaching methods and child psychology. *See, e.g., Fellowship Baptist Church v. Benton,* 815 F.2d 485 (8th Cir. 1986). Many States' home school regulations during this period also required that children be taught by a certified teacher. *See, e.g., State v. Melin,* 428 N.W.2d 227 (N.D. 1988), *cert. denied,* 488 U.S. 942 (1988).

The growth of private and home schooling has had its political effect in the state legislatures, and regulations vary. *See, e.g.,* Ala. Code §§16-28-1(2); 16-28-5 (2002) (requiring certification of teachers and "private tutors," but exempting "church schools"); *Lawrence v. South Carolina Bd. of Educ.*, 412 S.E.2d 394 (S.C. 1991) (rule requiring home schooling parents pass an basic skills examination in addition to having a high school diploma is unreasonable); *Delconte v. State,* 313 N.C. 384, 329 S.E.2d 636 (1985) (construing N.C. Const. Art. IX §3 to include parental right to home school). If the parent is the home schoolteacher, most states have no qualification requirements whatsoever. *See generally* Elizabeth Reilly, Symposium, *Education and the Constitution: Shaping Each Other & the Next Century*, 34 Akron L. Rev. 1 (2000).

Although the primary argument against teacher certification statutes has been grounded in the notion that religious educators should not be required to submit to state licensure at all, a number of church schools, including those in the Nebraska case, objected to certification mandates based on their perceptions concerning state control over the philosophical viewpoint which a teacher would bring to the classroom. In *Fellowship Baptist Church v. Benton,* the church objected to the "supervision of certified teachers by the Iowa Professional Teaching Practices Commission" and to the requirement that every applicant "take a human relations course designed to 'contribute to the development of sensitivity to and understanding of the values, beliefs, life styles and attitudes of individuals and the diverse groups found in a pluralistic society.'" *Id.* at 492. In response, the court professed skepticism that these requirements constituted a burden on the free exercise of the plaintiff's religion:

> Plaintiffs believe that licensure wrongfully interferes with a teacher's calling to God to teach, yet they apparently do not object to the licensure of those in their church called by God to other occupations, such as doctor or lawyer, nor do they object to obtaining a driver's license for those serving in their bus ministry, even though Pastor Jaspers testified that none of the churches' ministries could be properly regulated by government.

Id. at 493. What is the court's point?

Like many of the churches involved in regulation controversies with state educational authorities, the Fellowship Baptist School had argued that its pupils were comparable to those involved in *Yoder.* The Iowa court, however, found a distinction, in that "[u]nlike the Old Order Amish...plaintiffs expect and encourage their children to attend college and have no objection to college-educated teachers *per se.*" *Id.* Additionally, the court found the coercion element to be missing from certification requirements:

> Iowa's certification process does not prevent teachers in plaintiff schools from teaching from a Biblical perspective nor does it prevent plaintiff schools from hiring only those teachers who meet their religious criteria.

Id.

Most courts, including the court in *Benton,* have been reluctant to find that *no* burden exists in the application of state requirements. Instead, they use a balancing test. Unlike the school in *Faith Baptist Church,* many schools have successfully argued that their students are receiving adequate to above average schooling without certified teachers. In *State v. Shaver,* for example, the North Dakota court acknowledged that "[t]he uncontroverted evidence shows that many of the children have displayed remarkable progress since the school doors opened." 294 N.W.2d at 887. Taking an approach similar to that of Justice Krivosha's dissent in *Faith Baptist Church,* some of these courts have found that the state failed to meet its burden of proving that that teacher certification furthers a compelling state interest.

In *Sheridan Road Baptist Church v. Department of Educ.,* 132 Mich. App. 1, 18 (1984) *aff'd,* 426 Mich. 462, *cert. denied* 481 U.S. 1050 (1987), the Michigan Court of Appeals conceded private school arguments that teacher certification does not ensure quality education for students. "Indeed, the effectiveness of certification in this regard is somewhat open to question." *Id.* Nevertheless, the court cited deference to the legislative determination that "teacher certification is an acceptable method of satisfying part of the constitutional mandate to the legislature to properly provide an education for its youth." *Id., citing State v. Rivinius,* 328 N.W.2d 220, 229 (N.D. 1982), *cert. denied,* 460 U.S. 1070 (1983).

When this issue finally reached the Michigan Supreme Court in *People v. DeJonge,* 442 Mich. 266, 501 N.W.2d 127 (1993), the court rejected the state's argument that it had a compelling interest in "education." Substituting a lower level of generality, it recharacterized the state's interest as "teacher certification."

> [T]he state in the instant case has failed to provide evidence or testimony that supports the argument that the certification requirement is essential to the preservation of its asserted interest. Conversely, while the record is barren of evidence supporting the state's claim, it clearly indicates that the DeJonge children are receiving more than an adequate education: they are fulfilling the academic and socialization goals of compulsory education without certified teachers or the state's interference. In sum, the state has failed to provide one scintilla of evidence that the DeJonge children have suffered for the want of certified teachers; it has failed to prove a "clear and present" or "grave and immediate" danger to the welfare of the children that justifies the onerous burden placed upon the DeJonges' exercise of their religious beliefs.

Id. at 292.

(C) Standardized Testing

Standardized tests have long been a part of the experience of high school students, but the adoption of state and national standards for academic achievement in the lower grades is a more recent, and still reasonably controversial, development. During the 1980s, however, such controversies were localized, and many focused on standardized testing for children enrolled in small religious schools or in religiously oriented home school programs.

Facing prosecution or other disciplinary action under compulsory education laws, parents with children in nontraditional educational settings argued that *Pierce* and *Yoder* do not permit the courts to assume that the state's "compelling" interest in compulsory education requires that children be placed only into traditional public or private school settings. Instead, they argued, the question of parental compliance should be treated as a question of fact that could be proved or disproved by the results of standardized tests administered to the children at periodic intervals. If the children passed, the state's had no reason to demand a traditional placement. If not, the state would be entitled to intervene.

The argument was not well received by either public education authorities or the courts. *New Life Baptist Church Academy v. Town of East Longmeadow*, 885 F.2d 940 (1st Cir. 1989), *cert. denied*, 494 U.S. 1066 (1990), provides not only a good example of the courts' approach to such cases during the 1980s, but also "textbook examples" of the importance of the characterization issues discussed in Chapter One § A, and the need for fact-based proof in constitutional litigation discussed in Chapter Five § D.

Writing for the court of appeals, Judge (now Justice) Steven Breyer considered, and rejected, the argument that standardized testing represented less of a burden on the religious liberty interests of the parents and schools than pervasive regulation of the classroom environment. Characterizing the state's interest "broadly" (*i.e.* at a "high" level of generality), the court held that the state was entitled to advance assurance that the children would receive a "quality" education, and the testing program proposed by the parents could not provide it. The court accepted the assertion that many factors affect test scores, and results on a standardized test, especially a voluntary one, would not provide the quality controls the state needed. The court also concluded that the state would have had no recourse should the child test poorly because the

United States Supreme Court's interpretation of the Establishment Clause at the time appeared to "prohibit state-funded counseling, testing, and special remedial education, at least when provided on the private school's premises." *Id.* at 948.

In *Agostini v. Felton*, 521 U.S. 203 (1997), the Supreme Court ruled that state-funded counseling, testing, and special remedial education provided "on premises" raises no constitutional problems. Though it remains a controversial way to measure the quality of educational outcomes as this edition goes to press, standardized testing has also become a regular part of the academic landscape for elementary school children enrolled in public, private, and home schools.

(D) Health and Safety Requirements

In *City of Sumner v. First Baptist Church of Sumner*, 97 Wash.2d 1, 639 P.2d 1358 (1982), the city sought to enjoin the operation of a church school via the application of its building codes and zoning ordinances. The building that housed the school was approved for church use, but failed to meet "safety standards applicable to structures used for educational purposes." *Id.*, 97 Wash.2d at 3. The court found that the "indirect effect" of this regulation would be to "deny to church members the right to guide the education of their children by sending them to their church-operated school, a fundamental and constitutionally protected right." *Id.*, 97 Wash.2d at 7. The Washington Supreme Court remanded the case to the trial court, which was to determine whether "uncompromising and rigid" enforcement of the building code and zoning ordinance was the least restrictive way for the city to meet its compelling interest in safety. *Id.* at 9–10.

(E) Penalties for Noncompliance

When courts discuss "burdens" on free exercise, they generally focus on two separate issues: (1) the burden on the parents' religious beliefs that results from their need to comply with state law; and (2) the burden that results from a parental prosecution for noncompliance. In fact, many education cases involve parents who assert free exercise *defenses* to criminal actions brought against them. *See, e.g., Wisconsin v. Yoder*, 406 U.S. 205 (1972); *State v. Whisner*, 47 Ohio St. 2d 181, 351 N.E.2d 750 (1976). Penalties can be severe, and children can be taken from their parents if the state seeks an adjudication of neglect.

In *Care and Protection of Charles*, 399 Mass. 324, 504 N.E.2d 592 (1987), for example, the town of Canton, Massachusetts filed a petition for the care and protection of three children who were being taught by their parents at home rather than in a public or state-approved school. Had the court agreed, the result would have been removal of the children from their home.

Though Massachusetts law at the time provided for approval of home schooling programs by local school committees, the parents' proposal had been rejected, in part because of the committee's "concern about certain aspects of the parents' proposal, including the parents' objection to school department's testing and evaluation of their children's progress." *Id.* at 327. When the parents continued to keep their children out of an approved school, the town filed the petition and the trial judge issued an order requiring that the children be sent to school. He did not, however, remove them from the custody of their parents.

The Supreme Judicial Court of Massachusetts held that "the judge's order finding the children in need of care and protection was warranted on the evidence," *id.* at 340, but it vacated and remanded with instructions to the trial court to supervise negotiations between the committee and the parents to work out an adequate home schooling arrangement. *Id. See also Cude v. State*, 237 Ark. 927, 377 S.W.2d 816 (1964) (custody granted to state's child welfare division after parents, based on their religious beliefs, refused to allow children to be vaccinated against smallpox, which prevented them from being able to attend school). *See also In re T.M.*, 171 Vt. 1, 756 A.2d 793 (2000) (child properly enrolled in home study program was not in violation of compulsory attendance rule); *In re Interest of Leslie Sue Rice*, 204 Neb. 732, 285 N.W.2d 223 (1979); *State v. Moorhead*, 308 N.W.2d 60 (Iowa 1981).

4. "Opting In:" The State as Educator

The First Amendment issues that arise when the state undertakes the role of educator are often less obvious than when it seeks to regulate the affairs of private or religiously affiliated schools. Because private schools are not agents of the state even if a large proportion of their operating budgets comes from state funds, *Rendell-Baker v. Kohn*, 457 U.S. 830, 840–43 (1982); *Polk County v. Dodson*, 454 U.S. 312, 320–322 (1981), attempts by the government prescribe more than the basic outlines of a curriculum sufficient to qualify under the compulsory education law will be strictly scrutinized.

When the government itself is the educator, however, both the content of the message and the rights of those who utilize its educational resources are subject to a wide range of cross cutting, and sometimes inconsistent, First Amendment interests. Robert D. Heslep's account of Thomas Jefferson's efforts to create a public education system for Virginia notes that the nature of the system to be created "compelled [Jefferson] to entertain three questions concerning freedom. The first was how to preserve the students' religious freedom. The second question concerned the limits of academic freedom... [and t]he third... was how much control... the public should have." Heslep, THOMAS JEFFERSON & EDUCATION, at 107–110. Charts 6-1 and 6-3 on pages 399 and 427 summarize these interests. How do these interests relate to each other?

A system of fully subsidized elementary and high schools run by the state and the partial subsidy of state college and university education are public benefits of great economic and social value, not only to the children and young adults who use them, but also to the communities served by these institutions. There is a considerable body of literature that seeks to measure the economic costs and benefits of state and federally funded education programs, and little doubt that community and business development is closely tied to the quality and stability of the educational system. For present purposes, however, the inquiry will focus on whether or not it is possible to measure, or even to describe accurately, the First Amendment trade-offs inherent in such programs, both for the taxpayers who purchase educational services from the state with their tax dollars, and for the students and parents who take advantage of the services provided.

The contours of the inquiry can be discerned by reference to the "strings" attached to the benefit. Both *Meyer v. Nebraska* and *Pierce v. Society of Sisters* rest on the explicit assumption that the state has "the power... reasonably to regulate all schools, to inspect, supervise and examine them, their teachers and pupils; to require that all children of proper age attend some school, that teachers shall be of good moral character and patriotic disposition, that certain studies plainly essential to good citizenship must be taught, and that nothing be taught which is manifestly inimical to the public welfare." *Pierce*, 268 U.S. at 534.

When the education takes place in a forum created and funded by the State, however, the analysis, or "standard of review," has been quite different. Because the state itself is the speaker, and both the content and viewpoint are those of the state's choosing, the "reasonability" of the state's actions is a questioned to be determined in light of the goals to be achieved by creating and funding a system of state-run common schools. As a result, the First Amendment "costs" to those who choose state subsidized education are not easily measured in monetary terms. *Cf.* Richard A. Epstein, BARGAINING WITH THE STATE (1993).

The "bargaining risks that are associated with government behavior," Epstein, at 5, can, however, be estimated with some degree of accuracy. This can be done in two ways. The first is by direct comparison of policies and practices that define the First Amendment interests of parents, teachers, and students in private educational settings. The second is to use analytical devices such as the doctrine of "unconstitutional conditions." Such devices seek to answer the question: "What kinds of conditions may the state impose on citizens in the course of their mutual dealings?" *Id.*

As you review the materials in the sections that follow, you should consider not only the nature and source of the state, community and individual interests at stake, but also the level of generality at which they are characterized.

a) Controlling the Content of Education

1) Curriculum & Access to Information

Board of Education, Island Trees Union Free School District No. 26 v. Pico

457 U.S. 853 (1982)

Justice BRENNAN announced the judgment of the Court.

The principal question presented is whether the First Amendment imposes limitations upon the exercise by a local school board of its discretion to remove library books from high school and junior high school libraries.

[The case arose after several members of the school board attended a conference sponsored by a politically conservative organization of parents concerned about education legislation in the State of New York. At the conference, the board members obtained lists of books several of them described as "objectionable," and "improper fare for school students," though they were not obscene. The members determined that the high school library contained nine of the listed books, and that another was in the Junior High School library. A "Book Review Committee," consisting of four Island Trees parents and four members of the Island Trees schools staff read the listed books, and made recommendations to the Board concerning the books' "educational suitability," "good taste," "relevance," and "appropriateness to age and grade level." The Committee recommended that five of the listed books be retained and that two others be removed from the school libraries. As for the remaining four books, the Committee could not agree on two, took no position on one, and recommended that the last book be made available to students only with parental approval. The Board substantially rejected the Committee's report later that month, deciding that only one book should be returned to the High School library without restriction, that another should be made available subject to parental approval, but that the remaining books should "be removed from elementary and secondary libraries and [from] use in the curriculum." The Board gave no reasons for rejecting the recommendations of the Committee that it had appointed.]

II

[T]he issue before us in this case is a narrow one, both substantively and procedurally. It may best be restated as two distinct questions. First, does the First Amendment impose any limitations upon the discretion of petitioners to remove library books from the Island Trees High School and Junior High School? Second, if so, do the affidavits and other evidentiary materials before the District Court, construed most favorably to respondents, raise a genuine issue of fact whether petitioners might have exceeded those limitations? If we answer either of these questions in the negative, then we must reverse the judgment of the Court of Appeals and reinstate the District Court's summary judgment for petitioners. If we answer both questions in the affirmative, then we must affirm the judgment below. We examine these questions in turn.

A

(1)

The Court has long recognized that local school boards have broad discretion in the management of school affairs. [*Meyer, Pierce,* and *Epperson*] reaffirmed that, by and large, "public education in our Nation is committed to the control of state and local authorities," and that federal courts should not ordinarily "intervene in the resolution of conflicts which arise in the daily operation of school systems." *Tinker v. Des Moines School Dist.*, noted that we have "repeatedly emphasized... the comprehensive authority of the States and of school officials... to prescribe and control conduct in the schools." We have also acknowledged that public schools are vitally important "in the preparation of individuals for participation as citizens," and as vehicles for "inculcating fundamental values necessary to the maintenance of a democratic political system." *Ambach v. Norwick.* We are therefore in full agreement with petitioners that local school boards must be permitted "to establish and apply their curriculum in such a way as to transmit community values," and that "there is a legitimate and substantial community interest in promoting respect for authority and traditional values be they social, moral, or political."

At the same time, however, we have necessarily recognized that the discretion of the States and local school boards in matters of education must be exercised in a manner that comports with the transcendent imperatives of the First Amendment.

The nature of students' First Amendment rights in the context of this case requires further examination. *West Virginia Board of Education v. Barnette* is instructive. There the Court held that students' liberty of conscience could not be infringed in the name of "national unity" or "patriotism." We explained that "the action of the local authorities in compelling the flag salute and pledge transcends constitutional limitations on their power and invades the sphere of intellect and spirit which it is the purpose of the First Amendment to our Constitution to reserve from all official control."

Of course, courts should not "intervene in the resolution of conflicts which arise in the daily operation of school systems" unless "basic constitutional values" are "directly and sharply implicate[d]" in those conflicts. *Epperson v. Arkansas.* But we think that the First Amendment rights of students may be directly and sharply implicated by the removal of books from the shelves of a school library. [W]e have recognized that "the State may not, consistently with the spirit of the First Amendment, contract the spectrum of available knowledge." *Griswold v. Connecticut.* In keeping with this principle, we have held that in a variety of contexts "the Constitution protects the right to receive information and ideas." This right is an inherent corollary of the rights of free speech and press that are explicitly guaranteed by the Constitution, in two senses. First, the right to receive ideas follows ineluctably from the sender's First Amendment right to send them: "The right of freedom of speech and press... embraces the right to distribute literature, and necessarily protects the right to receive it." *Martin v. Struthers.* More importantly, the right to receive ideas is a necessary predicate to the recipient's meaningful exercise of his own rights of speech, press, and political freedom.

As we recognized in *Tinker*, students too are beneficiaries of this principle: "In our system, students may not be regarded as closed-circuit recipients of only that which the State chooses to communicate. [S]chool officials cannot suppress 'expressions of feeling with which they do not wish to contend.'"

In sum, just as access to ideas makes it possible for citizens generally to exercise their rights of free speech and press in a meaningful manner, such access prepares students for active and effective participation in the pluralistic, often contentious society in which they will soon be adult members. Of course all First Amendment rights accorded to students must be construed "in light of the special characteristics of the school environment." *Tinker v. Des Moines School Dist.* But the special characteristics of the school library make that environment especially appropriate for the recognition of the First Amendment rights of students.

Petitioners emphasize the inculcative function of secondary education, and argue that they must be allowed unfettered discretion to "transmit community values" through the Island Trees schools. But that sweeping claim overlooks the unique role of the school library. Petitioners might well defend their claim of absolute discretion in matters of curriculum by reliance upon their duty to inculcate community values. But we think that petitioners' reliance upon that duty is misplaced where, as here, they attempt to extend their claim of absolute discretion beyond the compulsory environment of the classroom, into the school library and the regime of voluntary inquiry that there holds sway.

(2)

With respect to the present case, the message of these precedents is clear. Petitioners rightly possess significant discretion to determine the content of their school libraries. But that discretion may not be exercised in a narrowly partisan or political manner.

As noted earlier, nothing in our decision today affects in any way the discretion of a local school board to choose books to add to the libraries of their schools. Because we are concerned in this case with the suppression of ideas, our holding today affects only the discretion to remove books. In brief, we hold that local school boards may not remove books from school library shelves simply because they dislike the ideas contained in those books and seek by their removal to "prescribe what shall be orthodox in politics, nationalism, religion, or other matters of opinion." *West Virginia Board of Education v. Barnette.*

Affirmed.

Justice BLACKMUN, concurring in part and concurring in the judgment.

I

In my view... the principle involved here is both narrower and more basic than the "right to receive information" identified by the plurality. I do not suggest that the State has any affirmative obligation to provide students with information or ideas, something that may well be associated with a "right to receive." And I do not believe, as the plurality suggests, that the right at issue here is somehow associated with the peculiar nature of the school library, if schools may be used to inculcate ideas, surely libraries may play a role in that process. Instead, I suggest that certain forms of state discrimination between ideas are improper. In particular, our precedents command the conclusion that the State may not act to deny access to an idea simply because state officials disapprove of that idea for partisan or political reasons.

Chief Justice BURGER, with whom Justice POWELL, Justice REHNQUIST, and Justice O'CONNOR join, dissenting.

Whatever role the government might play as a conduit of information, schools in particular ought not be made a slavish courier of the material of third parties. If, as we have held, schools may legitimately be used as vehicles for "inculcating fundamental values necessary to the maintenance of a democratic political system," *Ambach v. Norwick*, school authorities must have broad discretion to fulfill that obligation. Presumably all activity within a primary or secondary school involves the conveyance of information and at least an implied approval of the worth of that information. How are "fundamental values" to be inculcated except by having school boards make content-based decisions about the appropriateness of retaining materials in the school library and curriculum? In order to fulfill its function, an elected school board must express its views on the subjects which are taught to its students. In doing so those elected officials express the views of their community; they may err, of course, and the voters may remove them. It is a startling erosion of the very idea of democratic government to have this Court arrogate to itself the power the plurality asserts today.

Justice POWELL, dissenting.

I...view today's decision with genuine dismay. As is evident from the generality of the plurality's "standard" for judicial review, the decision as to the educational worth of a book is a highly subjective one. Judges rarely are as competent as school authorities to make this decision; nor are judges responsive to the parents and people of the school district.

Notes

1. What, after *Island Trees*, is the scope of the school's authority over matters of curriculum? Was the scope of that authority called into question by either the outcome or the reasoning of the case? *See, e.g.*, *Newton v. Slye*, 16 F.Supp.2d 677 (W.D. Va. 2000) (refusing to issue injunction against superintendent's order to remove pamphlet from teacher's door); *Virgil v. Sch. Bd. of Columbia County, Florida*, 677 F. Supp. 1547 (M.D. Fla. 1988) (upholding school board's decision to discontinue use of humanities textbook because of works deemed by the Board to be sexual and vulgar, and holding that decision of school board was reasonably related to its legitimate pedagogical goal of denying students access to "potentially sensitive topics").

2. What discretion should a school board have to include religion in the curriculum? There has been considerable debate over the legitimacy of teaching "about" religion, and considerable criticism in recent years concerning the public schools' treatment—or, more accurately, avoidance—of the subject. Should the courts take a more "hands off" approach to the decisions made by school boards?

3. To what extent do students have a right to be exposed *as a part of the curriculum*, not only to religious ideas, but also to the divergent religious beliefs and practices of

their fellow students? Do cases upholding "voluntary" student prayer on school premises provide an answer, or do they present a different set of question altogether? *See Illinois* ex rel. *McCollum v. Board of Educ.*, 333 U.S. 203 (1948). *Cf. Board of Educ. of Jefferson County Sch. Dist. R-1 v. Wilder*, 960 P.2d 695 (Colo. 1998) (upholding the dismissal of public school teacher for violating county's "controversial learning resources" policy).

4. To what extent do, or should, parent have the right to enforce their objections to the content of the education their children receive from the State? *See, e.g., Parents United For Better Schools, Inc. v. School Dist. of Philadelphia Bd. of Educ.*, 148 F.3d 260 (3rd Cir. 1998) (upholding condom distribution program against claim that it interfered with parental rights to direct the upbringing of children); *Immediato v. Rye Neck Sch. Dist.*, 73 F.3d 454, 461 (2d Cir. 1996) (upholding mandatory community service requirement for high school students); *Brown v. Hot, Sexy and Safer Productions, Inc.*, 68 F.3d 525 (1st Cir. 1995) (mandatory student participation in a sexually explicit AIDS-awareness assembly did not violate the rights of either the students or the parents). *See generally* Molly O'Brien, Symposium: *Free At Last? Charter Schools and The "Deregulated" Curriculum*, 34 Akron L. Rev. 137 (2000). What should be the result if the program is an after-school affair, or involves "guidance" counseling? Should counseling count as "education"? Do parents have the right to know that their children are being counseled or taught so that their right to "opt-out" can be exercised intelligently? *See Dawson v. East Side Union High Sch. Dist.*, 28 Cal. App. 4th 998, 34 Cal. Rptr. 2d 108 (1994); *Alfonso v. Fernandez*, 195 A.D.2d 46, 606 N.Y.S. 2d 259 (2d Dept. 1993); *In re T.W.*, 551 So. 2d 1186 (Fla. 1989); *Doe v. Irwin*, 615 F.2d 1162 (6th Cir. 1980), *rev'g*, *Doe v. Irwin*, 441 F. Supp. 1247 (W.D. Mich., 1977). *Cf.*, Eugene C. Bjorklun, Commentary, *Condom Distribution In The Public Schools: Is Parental Consent Required?*, 91 Ed. Law Rep. 11 (1994); Linda R. Crane, *Family Values And The Supreme Court*, 25 Conn. L. Rev. 427 (1993); Karl J. Sanders, Comment, *Kids and Condoms: Constitutional Challenges to the Distribution of Condoms in Public Schools*, 61 U. Cin. L. Rev. 1479 (1993).

5. With respect to the right of students and parents to "opt-out" of public school curricular programs, see *Mozert v. Hawkins County Bd. of Educ.*, excerpted in Chapter Ten. In *Mozert* the parents complained that the values of the public school system were corrosive of those they were trying to teach their children. *See generally* Jenean M. Klein, *Is Use of the V-Chip in the Public Schools an Exercise of Government-Sponsored Censorship?*, 9-SPG Media L. & Pol'y 11 (2001); Karen C. Daly, *Balancing Act: Teachers' Classroom Speech and The First Amendment*, 30 J.L. & Educ. 1 (2001); James Davison Hunter, CULTURE WARS: THE STRUGGLE TO DEFINE AMERICA (1991).

b) Creating a Religiously "Neutral" Educational Setting: Public Schools

1) Religious Devotions and Ritual

School District of Abington Township v. Schempp

374 U.S. 203 (1963)

Mr. Justice CLARK delivered the opinion of the Court.

I

[In *Schempp*, Pennsylvania law required that "At least ten verses from the Holy Bible shall be read, without comment, at the opening of each public school on each school day.

Any child shall be excused from such Bible reading, or attending such Bible reading, upon the written request of his parent or guardian." The Schempp family objected to the practice, and sought to enjoin the school district from continuing to conduct such readings and recitation of the Lord's Prayer in the public schools of the district pursuant to the statute.

In *Murray*, the Board of School Commissioners of Baltimore City adopted a rule in 1905 that provided for the holding of opening exercises. These exercises consisted primarily of the reading, without comment, of a chapter in the Bible, recitation of the Lord's Prayer, or both. The plaintiffs, Mrs. Madalyn Murray and her son, William J. Murray III, were both professed atheists. It was alleged that William had been excused, but the rule was nevertheless a violation of the petitioners' rights to freedom of religion. They alleged that such practices threaten[ed] "their religious liberty by placing a premium on belief as against non-belief and subjects their freedom of conscience to the rule of the majority; it pronounces belief in God as the source of all moral and spiritual values, equating these values with religious values, and thereby renders sinister, alien and suspect [their] beliefs and ideals..., [thus] promoting doubt and question of their morality, good citizenship and good faith." 374 U.S. at 211.]

III.

Almost a hundred years ago in *Minor v. Board of Education of Cincinnati*[7], Judge Alphonso Taft, father of the revered Chief Justice, in an unpublished opinion stated the ideal of our people as to religious freedom as one of

> 'absolute equality before the law, of all religious opinions and sects....' The government is neutral, and, while protecting all, it prefers none, and it disparages none.

Before examining this 'neutral' position in which the Establishment and Free Exercise Clauses of the First Amendment place our Government it is well that we discuss the reach of the Amendment under the cases of this Court.

First, this Court has decisively settled that the First Amendment's mandate that 'Congress shall make no law respecting an establishment of religion, or prohibiting the free exercise thereof' has been made wholly applicable to the States by the Fourteenth Amendment.

Second, this Court has rejected unequivocally the contention that the Establishment Clause forbids only governmental preference of one religion over another.

> 'The (First) Amendment's purpose was not to strike merely at the official establishment of a single sect, creed or religion, outlawing only a formal relation such as had prevailed in England and some of the colonies. Necessarily it was to uproot all such relationships. But the object was broader than separating church and state in this narrow sense. It was to create a complete and permanent separation of the spheres of religious activity and civil authority by comprehensively forbidding every form of public aid or support for religion.'

7. Superior Court of Cincinnati, February 1870. The opinion is not reported but is published under the title, The Bible in the Common Schools (1870). Judge Taft's views, expressed in dissent, prevailed on appeal. See Board of Education of Cincinnati v. Minor, 23 Ohio St. 211, 253 (1872), in which the Ohio Supreme Court held that:

> The great bulk of human affairs and human interests is left by any free government to individual enterprise and individual action. Religion is eminently one of these interests, lying outside the true and legitimate province of government.

[*Everson:* Justices Rutledge, Frankfurter, Jackson and Burton, dissenting]

IV.

[I]n *Everson,* this Court...held that the Amendment 'requires the state to be a neutral in its relations with groups of religious believers and non-believers; it does not require the state to be their adversary. State power is no more to be used so as to handicap religions, than it is to favor them.' And Mr. Justice Jackson, in dissent, declared that public schools are organized

> 'on the premise that secular education can be isolated from all religious teaching so that the school can inculcate all needed temporal knowledge and also maintain a strict and lofty neutrality as to religion. The assumption is that after the individual has been instructed in worldly wisdom he will be better fitted to choose his religion.' *Id.,* 330 U.S., at 23–24, 67 S.Ct., at 515, 91 L.Ed. 711.

Moreover, all of the four dissenters, speaking through Mr. Justice Rutledge, agreed that

> 'Our constitutional policy...does not deny the value or the necessity for religious training, teaching or observance. Rather it secures their free exercise. But to that end it does deny that the state can undertake or sustain them in any form or degree. For this reason the sphere of religious activity, as distinguished from the secular intellectual liberties, has been given the twofold protection and, as the state cannot forbid, neither can it perform or aid in performing the religious function. The dual prohibition makes that function altogether private.' Id., 330 U.S., at 52, 67 S.Ct., at 529, 91 L.Ed. 711.

V.

The distinction between the two clauses is apparent—a violation of the Free Exercise Clause is predicated on coercion while the Establishment Clause violation need not be so attended.

Applying the Establishment Clause principles to the cases at bar we find that the States are requiring the selection and reading at the opening of the school day of verses from the Holy Bible and the recitation of the Lord's Prayer by the students in unison. The trial court in [*Schempp*] has found that such an opening exercise is a religious ceremony and was intended by the State to be so. We agree with the trial court's finding as to the religious character of the exercises. Given that finding, the exercises and the law requiring them are in violation of the Establishment Clause.

The conclusion follows that in both cases the laws require religious exercises and such exercises are being conducted in direct violation of the rights of the appellees and petitioners. Nor are these required exercises mitigated by the fact that individual students may absent themselves upon parental request, for that fact furnishes no defense to a claim of unconstitutionality under the Establishment Clause.

[We reject the argument that] unless these religious exercises are permitted a 'religion of secularism' is established in the schools. We agree of course that the State may not establish a 'religion of secularism' in the sense of affirmatively opposing or showing hostility to religion, thus 'preferring those who believe in no religion over those who do believe.' We do not agree, however, that this decision in any sense has that effect. Nothing we have said here indicates that...study of the Bible or of religion, when presented objectively as part of a secular program of education, may not be effected consistently with the First Amendment. But the exercises here do not fall into those categories. They are religious exercises, required by the States in violation of the command of the First Amendment that the Government maintain strict neutrality, neither aiding nor opposing religion.

The place of religion in our society is an exalted one, achieved through a long tradition of reliance on the home, the church and the inviolable citadel of the individual heart and mind. We have come to recognize through bitter experience that it is not within the power of government to invade that citadel, whether its purpose or effect be to aid or oppose, to advance or retard. In the relationship between man and religion, the State is firmly committed to a position of neutrality.

It is so ordered.

Mr. Justice STEWART, dissenting.

Specifically, I cannot agree that on these records we can say that the Establishment Clause has necessarily been violated.[1] But I think there exist serious questions under both that provision and the Free Exercise Clause—insofar as each is imbedded in the Fourteenth Amendment—which require the remand of these cases for the taking of additional evidence.

I.

The First Amendment declares that 'Congress shall make no law respecting an establishment of religion, or prohibiting the free exercise thereof * * *.' It is, I think, a fallacious oversimplification to regard these two provisions as establishing a single constitutional standard of 'separation of church and state,' which can be mechanically applied in every case to delineate the required boundaries between government and religion. We err in the first place if we do not recognize, as a matter of history and as a matter of the imperatives of our free society, that religion and government must necessarily interact in countless ways. Secondly, the fact is that while in many contexts the Establishment Clause and the Free Exercise Clause fully complement each other, there are areas in which a doctrinaire reading of the Establishment Clause leads to irreconcilable conflict with the Free Exercise Clause.

II.

As a matter of history, the First Amendment was adopted solely as a limitation upon the newly created National Government. The events leading to its adoption strongly suggest that the Establishment Clause was primarily an attempt to insure that Congress not only would be powerless to establish a national church, but would also be unable to interfere with existing state establishments. Each State was left free to go its own way and pursue its own policy with respect to religion.

I accept without question that the liberty guaranteed by the Fourteenth Amendment against impairment by the States embraces in full the right of free exercise of religion protected by the First Amendment. I accept too the proposition that the Fourteenth Amendment has somehow absorbed the Establishment Clause, although it is not without irony that a constitutional provision evidently designed to leave the States free to go their own way should now have become a restriction upon their autonomy. But I can-

1. It is instructive, in this connection, to examine the complaints in the two cases before us. Neither complaint attacks the challenged practices as 'establishments.' What both allege as the basis for their causes of actions are, rather, violations of religious liberty.

not agree with what seems to me the insensitive definition of the Establishment Clause contained in the Court's opinion.

III.

That the central value embodied in the First Amendment—and, more particularly, in the guarantee of 'liberty' contained in the Fourteenth—is the safeguarding of an individual's right to free exercise of his religion has been consistently recognized. It is this concept of constitutional protection embodied in our decisions which makes the cases before us such difficult ones for me. For there is involved in these cases a substantial free exercise claim on the part of those who affirmatively desire to have their children's school day open with the reading of passages from the Bible.

It might also be argued that parents who want their children exposed to religious influences can adequately fulfill that wish off school property and outside school time. With all its surface persuasiveness, however, this argument seriously misconceives the basic constitutional justification for permitting the exercises at issue in these cases. For a compulsory state educational system so structures a child's life that if religious exercises are held to be an impermissible activity in schools, religion is placed at an artificial and state-created disadvantage. Viewed in this light, permission of such exercises for those who want them is necessary if the schools are truly to be neutral in the matter of religion. And a refusal to permit religious exercises thus is seen, not as the realization of state neutrality, but rather as the establishment of a religion of secularism, or at the least, as government support of the beliefs of those who think that religious exercises should be conducted only in private.

What seems to me to be of paramount importance, then, is recognition of the fact that the claim advanced here in favor of Bible reading is sufficiently substantial to make simple reference to the constitutional phrase 'establishment of religion' as inadequate an analysis of the cases before us as the ritualistic invocation of the nonconstitutional phrase 'separation of church and state.' What these cases compel, rather, is an analysis of just what the 'neutrality' is which is required by the interplay of the Establishment and Free Exercise Clauses of the First Amendment, as imbedded in the Fourteenth.

IV.

Our decisions make clear that there is no constitutional bar to the use of government property for religious purposes. But insofar as the *McCollum* decision rests on the Establishment rather than the Free Exercise Clause, it is clear that its effect is limited to religious instruction—to government support of proselytizing activities of religious sects by throwing the weight of secular authority behind the dissemination of religious tenets.

The dangers both to government and to religion inherent in official support of instruction in the tenets of various religious sects are absent in the present cases, which involve only a reading from the Bible unaccompanied by comments which might otherwise constitute instruction. Indeed, since, from all that appears in either record, any teacher who does not wish to do so is free not to participate, it cannot even be contended that some infinitesimal part of the salaries paid by the State are made contingent upon the performance of a religious function.

In the absence of coercion upon those who do not wish to participate—because they hold less strong beliefs, other beliefs, or no beliefs at all—such provisions cannot, in my view, be held to represent the type of support of religion barred by the Establishment Clause. For the only support which such rules provide for religion is the withholding of state hostility—a simple acknowledgment on the part of secular authorities that the Constitution does not require extirpation of all expression of religious belief.

V.

I have said that these provisions authorizing religious exercises are properly to be regarded as measures making possible the free exercise of religion. But it is important to stress that, strictly speaking, what is at issue here is a privilege rather than a right. In other words, the question presented is not whether exercises such as those at issue here are constitutionally compelled, but rather whether they are constitutionally invalid. And that issue, in my view, turns on the question of coercion.

It is clear that the dangers of coercion involved in the holding of religious exercises in a schoolroom differ qualitatively from those presented by the use of similar exercises or affirmations in ceremonies attended by adults. Even as to children, however, the duty laid upon government in connection with religious exercises in the public schools is that of refraining from so structuring the school environment as to put any kind of pressure on a child to participate in those exercises; it is not that of providing an atmosphere in which children are kept scrupulously insulated from any awareness that some of their fellows may want to open the school day with prayer, or of the fact that there exist in our pluralistic society differences of religious belief.

These are not, it must be stressed, cases like *Brown v. Board of Education*, 347 U.S. 483, in which this Court held that, in the sphere of public education, the Fourteenth Amendment's guarantee of equal protection of the laws required that race not be treated as a relevant factor. A segregated school system is not invalid because its operation is coercive; it is invalid simply because our Constitution presupposes that men are created equal, and that therefore racial differences cannot provide a valid basis for governmental action. Accommodation of religious differences on the part of the State, however, is not only permitted but required by that same Constitution.

The governmental neutrality which the First and Fourteenth Amendments require in the cases before us, in other words, is the extension of evenhanded treatment to all who believe, doubt, or disbelieve—a refusal on the part of the State to weight the scales of private choice. In these cases, therefore, what is involved is not state action based on impermissible categories, but rather an attempt by the State to accommodate those differences which the existence in our society of a variety of religious beliefs makes inevitable. The Constitution requires that such efforts be struck down only if they are proven to entail the use of the secular authority of government to coerce a preference among such beliefs.

[R]eligious exercises are not constitutionally invalid if they simply reflect differences which exist in the society from which the school draws its pupils. They become constitutionally invalid only if their administration places the sanction of secular authority behind one or more particular religious or irreligious beliefs.

VI.

What our Constitution indispensably protects is the freedom of each of us, be he Jew or Agnostic, Christian or Atheist, Buddhist or Freethinker, to believe or disbelieve, to worship or not worship, to pray or keep silent, according to his own conscience, uncoerced and unrestrained by government. It is conceivable that these school boards, or even all school boards, might eventually find it impossible to administer a system of religious exercises during school hours in such a way as to meet this constitutional standard—in such a way as completely to free from any kind of official coercion those who do not affirmatively want to participate. But I think we must not assume that school boards so lack the qualities of inventiveness and good will as to make impossible the achievement of that goal.

I would remand both cases for further hearing.

Lee v. Weisman

505 U.S. 577 (1992)

Justice KENNEDY delivered the opinion of the Court.

School principals in the public school system of the city of Providence, Rhode Island, are permitted to invite members of the clergy to offer invocation and benediction prayers as part of the formal graduation ceremonies for middle schools and for high schools. The question before us is whether including clerical members who offer prayers as part of the official school graduation ceremony is consistent with the Religion Clauses of the First Amendment, provisions the Fourteenth Amendment makes applicable with full force to the States and their school districts.

II

These dominant facts mark and control the confines of our decision: State officials direct the performance of a formal religious exercise at promotional and graduation ceremonies for secondary schools. Even for those students who object to the religious exercise, their attendance and participation in the state-sponsored religious activity are in a fair and real sense obligatory, though the school district does not require attendance as a condition for receipt of the diploma.

The degree of school involvement here made it clear that the graduation prayers bore the imprint of the State and thus put school-age children who objected in an untenable position. We turn our attention now to consider the position of the students, both those who desired the prayer and she who did not.

To endure the speech of false ideas or offensive content and then to counter it is part of learning how to live in a pluralistic society, a society which insists upon open discourse towards the end of a tolerant citizenry. And tolerance presupposes some mutuality of obligation. It is argued that our constitutional vision of a free society requires confidence in our own ability to accept or reject ideas of which we do not approve, and that prayer at a high school graduation does nothing more than offer a choice. This argument cannot prevail, however. It overlooks a fundamental dynamic of the Constitution.

The First Amendment protects speech and religion by quite different mechanisms. Speech is protected by insuring its full expression even when the government participates, for the very object of some of our most important speech is to persuade the government to adopt an idea as its own. The method for protecting freedom of worship and freedom of conscience in religious matters is quite the reverse. In religious debate or expression the government is not a prime participant, for the Framers deemed religious establishment antithetical to the freedom of all.

As we have observed before, there are heightened concerns with protecting freedom of conscience from subtle coercive pressure in the elementary and secondary public schools. The concern may not be limited to the context of schools, but it is most pronounced there.

We need not look beyond the circumstances of this case to see the phenomenon at work. The undeniable fact is that the school district's supervision and control of a high school graduation ceremony places public pressure, as well as peer pressure, on attending students to stand as a group or, at least, maintain respectful silence during the Invocation and Benediction. This pressure, though subtle and indirect, can be as real as any overt compulsion. Of course, in our culture standing or remaining silent can signify adherence to a view or simple respect for the views of others. And no doubt some persons who have no desire to join a prayer have little objection to standing as a sign of respect for those who do. But for the dissenter of high school age, who has a reasonable perception that she is being forced by the State to pray in a manner her conscience will not allow, the injury is no less real. There can be no doubt that for many, if not most, of the students at the graduation, the act of standing or remaining silent was an expression of participation in the Rabbi's prayer. That was the very point of the religious exercise. It is of little comfort to a dissenter, then, to be told that for her the act of standing or remaining in silence signifies mere respect, rather than participation. What matters is that, given our social conventions, a reasonable dissenter in this milieu could believe that the group exercise signified her own participation or approval of it.

Finding no violation under these circumstances would place objectors in the dilemma of participating, with all that implies, or protesting. We do not address whether that choice is acceptable if the affected citizens are mature adults, but we think the State may not, consistent with the Establishment Clause, place primary and secondary school children in this position. Research in psychology supports the common assumption that adolescents are often susceptible to pressure from their peers towards conformity, and that the influence is strongest in matters of social convention. Brittain, *Adolescent Choices and Parent-Peer Cross-Pressures*, 28 Am. Sociological Rev. 385 (June 1963); Clasen & Brown, The *Multidimensionality of Peer Pressure in Adolescence*, 14 J. of Youth and Adolescence 451 (Dec. 1985); Brown, Clasen, & Eicher, *Perceptions of Peer Pressure, Peer Conformity Dispositions, and Self-Reported Behavior Among Adolescents*, 22 Developmental Psychology 521 (July 1986). To recognize that the choice imposed by the State constitutes an unacceptable constraint only acknowledges that the government may no more use social pressure to enforce orthodoxy than it may use more direct means.

The injury caused by the government's action, and the reason why Daniel and Deborah Weisman object to it, is that the State, in a school setting, in effect required participation in a religious exercise. That the intrusion was in the course of promulgating religion that sought to be civic or nonsectarian rather than pertaining to one sect does not lessen the offense or isolation to the objectors. At best it narrows their number, at worst increases their sense of isolation and affront.

Our society would be less than true to its heritage if it lacked abiding concern for the values of its young people, and we acknowledge the profound belief of adherents to many faiths that there must be a place in the student's life for precepts of a morality higher even than the law we today enforce. We express no hostility to those aspirations, nor would our oath permit us to do so. A relentless and all-pervasive attempt to exclude religion from every aspect of public life could itself become inconsistent with the Constitution. We recognize that, at graduation time and throughout the course of the educational process, there will be instances when religious values, religious practices, and religious persons will have some interaction with the public schools and their students. But these matters, often questions of accommodation of religion, are not before us. The sole question presented is whether a religious exercise may be conducted at a graduation ceremony in circumstances where, as we have found, young graduates who object are induced to conform. No holding by this Court suggests that a school can persuade or compel a student to participate in a religious exercise. That is being done here, and it is forbidden by the Establishment Clause of the First Amendment.

For the reasons we have stated, the judgment of the Court of Appeals is

Affirmed.

Justice BLACKMUN, with whom Justice STEVENS and Justice O'CONNOR join, concurring.

Nearly half a century of review and refinement of Establishment Clause jurisprudence has distilled one clear understanding: Government may neither promote nor affiliate itself with any religious doctrine or organization, nor may it obtrude itself in the internal affairs of any religious institution. The application of these principles to the present case mandates the decision reached today by the Court.

Justice SOUTER, with whom Justice STEVENS and Justice O'CONNOR join, concurring. [Opinion omitted.]

Justice SCALIA, with whom THE CHIEF JUSTICE [RHENQUIST], Justice WHITE, and Justice THOMAS join, dissenting.

[T]oday's opinion... [is] conspicuously bereft of any reference to history. In holding that the Establishment Clause prohibits invocations and benedictions at public-school graduation ceremonies, the Court—with nary a mention that it is doing so—lays waste a tradition that is as old as public-school graduation ceremonies themselves, and that is a component of an even more long-standing American tradition of nonsectarian prayer to God at public celebrations generally. As its instrument of destruction, the bulldozer of its social engineering, the Court invents a boundless, and boundlessly manipulable, test of psychological coercion, which promises to do for the Establishment Clause what the *Durham* rule did for the insanity defense. See *Durham v. United States*, 94 U.S. App. D.C. 228, 214 F.2d 862 (1954). Today's opinion shows more forcefully than volumes of argumentation why our Nation's protection, that fortress which is our Constitution, cannot possibly rest upon the changeable philosophical predilections of the Justices of this Court, but must have deep foundations in the historic practices of our people.

Notes

1. What is the nature of the constitutional violation when prayers and Bible reading take place in the public schools? *See Doremus v. Board of Educ. of Borough of Hawthorne*, 5 N.J. 435, 75 A.2d 880 (1950), *appeal dismissed*, 342 U.S. 429 (1952) (taxpayer suit against religious practices in public schools dismissed for want of an appealable question). In the pre-*Schempp* cases upholding the practice, there were two basic rationales. In some cases, the practice of prayer and Bible reading were upheld because there was no objection from any of the affected students or teachers. *See, e.g., Millard v. Board of Education*, 121 Ill. 297, 10 N. E. 669 (1887) (upholding the recitation of a Roman Catholic prayer, the *Angelus*, when school closed at noon). In others, as noted in Chapters Four and Five § J(4)(a), courts simply held that the Bible was "nonsectarian." *Donahoe v. Richards*, 38 Me. 379, 61 Am. Dec. 256 (Me., 1854); *Spiller v. Inhabitants of Woburn*, 12 Allen [Mass.] 127 (1866); *Pfeiffer* v. *Board of Educ. of Detroit*, 118 Mich. 560, 77 N. W. 250, 42 L. R. A. 536 (1898); *Moore v. Monroe*, 64 Iowa 367, 20 N.W. 475

(1884); *Hackett v. Brooksville Sch. Dist.*, 120 Ky. 608, 87 S.W. 792 (1905); *Billard v. Board of Educ.*, 69 Kan. 53 (1904); *Church v. Bullock*, 104 Tex. 1, 109 S.W. 115 (1908). Why was the practice of prayer and Bible reading struck down in *Schempp*?

2. The decisions in *Schempp* and *Weisman* raise several questions concerning the command of the Establishment Clause in the educational setting. There are at least three possible reasons why the Establishment Clause might require the abandonment of religious devotions and rituals as a part of the official school day: (1) coercion of dissenting students; (2) a breach of the neutrality required in the public schools, even if no coercion is present; and (3) such practices constitute tangible support for religion or religious education. Do the opinions in *Schempp* and *Lee v. Weisman* provide a clear answer?

3. What else, if anything, does the rationale of these cases tell us about the command of the First Amendment in the school setting? The public schools have long been embroiled in controversies over public rituals, and religious beliefs (including non-belief) have been at the heart of most of them. Perhaps the most famous pair of cases are those excerpted in Chapter One, *Minersville Sch. Dist. v. Gobitis*, 310 U.S. 586 (1940), and *West Virginia Bd. of Educ. v. Barnette*, 319 U.S. 624 (1943). *Gobitis* upheld the practice of compulsory pledging of allegiance to the flag against a free exercise claim on the grounds that coercion of this sort is part of the price to be paid for living in a free society. *Gobitis* was reversed in *Barnette*, but the controversy over official rituals involving the flag has not subsided. *See, e.g., Lipp v. Morris*, 579 F.2d 834 (3d Cir. 1978) (successful challenge by a high school student to requirement that she show full respect to the flag while the pledge is being given merely by standing at attention during the flag salute and recitation of the Pledge of Allegiance); *Opinions of the Justices to the Governor*, 372 Mass. 874, 363 N.E.2d 251 (1977) (advisory opinion holding that, as applied to teachers, a bill that would require each teacher at the commencement of the first class of each day in all grades in all public schools to lead the class in a group recitation of the Pledge of Allegiance violates the First Amendment, even if under the proposed bill there would be no criminal penalties against teachers who refuse to comply, because there would still be an element of compulsion on a teacher inherent in the existence of the statutory mandate). *See also* Laurie Allen Gallancy, *Teachers and the Pledge of Allegiance*, 57 U. Chi. L. Rev. 929, 939 (1990).

In *Sherman v. Community Consolidated School District 21 of Wheeling Township*, 980 F.2d 437, 443–445 (7th Cir. 1992), the panel opinion by Judge Frank Easterbrook rejected a claim that daily recitation of the Pledge of Allegiance, led by the school principal, is inherently coercive. Discussing the concept of "coercion" in the school setting, he wrote:

> [P]erhaps the rationale of *Barnette*, when joined with the school-prayer cases, equates social pressure with legal pressure. If as *Barnette* holds no state may require anyone to recite the Pledge, and if as the prayer cases hold the recitation by a teacher or rabbi of unwelcome words is coercion, then the Pledge of Allegiance becomes unconstitutional under all circumstances, just as no school may read from a holy scripture at the start of class.
>
> Consider what a general assimilation of religion to patriotism and other values would mean for the public schools. A pupil who takes exception to the prescribed curriculum of the public schools—whether the textbooks or the class discussions or the civic ceremonies—such as the Pledge of Allegiance—is asserting a right to accommodation of his political or religious beliefs. Humane government often calls for accommodation; programs such as tuition vouchers serve this interest without offending other constitutional norms. Government

> nonetheless retains the right to set the curriculum in its own schools and insist that those who cannot accept the result exercise their right under *Pierce v. Society of Sisters* and select private education at their own expense. The private market supports a profusion of schools, many tailored to religious or cultural minorities, making the majoritarian curriculum of the public schools less oppressive.
>
> We agree with Judge Boggs [in *Mozert*] that "school boards may set curricula bounded only by the Establishment Clause" even though pupils may find the books and classroom discourse offensive or immoral. By remaining neutral on religious issues, the state satisfies its duties under the free exercise clause. *Employment Division v. Smith.* All that remains is *Barnette* itself, and so long as the school does not compel pupils to espouse the content of the Pledge as their own belief, it may carry on with patriotic exercises. Objection by the few does not reduce to silence the many who want to pledge allegiance to the flag "and to the Republic for which it stands".

Contra Newdow v. U.S. Congress, __ F.3d __ (9th Cir., June 26, 2002) (holding unconstitutional the words "under God" in the Pledge of Allegiance).

Has the Seventh Circuit accurately stated the content of the Religion Clause as applied to education? If the issue is curriculum, rather than officially sanctioned prayers, ritual or devotion, how does the state "remain neutral" on matters that are heavily value-laden, such as sex-education, the role of religion in society, or the nature of religion itself? *Cf.* James P. Madigan, *Questioning the Coercive Effect of Self-Identifying Speech*, 87 Iowa L. Rev. 75 (2001). For example, may a public school teach the theory of evolution, but ban any discussion of the view that God created the world in the manner described in the Bible? May a public school teacher use his or her classroom to promote "critical thinking" concerning specific religious doctrines without violating the Establishment Clause? *See generally* Chapter Ten.

4. There have been few decisions of the Supreme Court as controversial as those banning prayer from the list of official rituals practiced in the public schools. Examination of the case law indicates that school districts and school officials have gone to great lengths to accommodate the interests of parents and children who wish to engage in teacher-sponsored prayer during school or officially sponsored school programs. Such practices have been invalidated in most instances, but the phenomenon illustrates an important political point. Chapters Two through Four illustrate the close relationship between religious liberty and the ethnic, cultural, political, and religious demographics of the community. Accommodation claims are inevitable in communities undergoing cultural or demographic change, and are often controversial.

Mitchell v. Helms, 530 U.S. 290 (2001) is, quite literally, a "textbook case." Decided nearly forty years after *Engel v. Vitale*, 370 U.S. 421 (1962), *Helms* underscores an important political point made by James Madison's *Memorial and Remonstrance Against Religious Assessments*: Religious liberty is the inalienable right "of every man to exercise it as these may dictate," but is an outgrowth of the respect that the *political* community owes to each of its members. For Madison, the protection of religious liberty is a natural outgrowth of an enlightened public policy that protects "every Citizen in the enjoyment of his Religion with the same equal hand which protects his person and his property."

Set aside for a moment the constitutional rules developed by the Court, and focus instead on the political dynamics of the debate over prayer and Bible reading in schools. What *political* lessons about religious liberty, control of the public schools, political compromise, majority rule, and federalism can one learn from these controversies? *See* John C. Jeffries, Jr. & James E. Ryan, *A Political History of the Establishment Clause*, 100 Mich. L. Rev. 279 (2001).

Do the Equal Access Act, 20 U.S.C. §§4071–4074 (2002), excerpted in Chapter Five §G, and "moment of silence" laws represent a political compromise between those who view religion as an integral part of daily life, and those who oppose any formal religious practices in public schools? *See Brown v. Gilmore*, 258 F.3d 265 (4th Cir. 2001), *cert. denied*, 122 S.Ct. 465 (2001) (upholding Virginia's "minute of silence" statute, Va. Code Ann. §22.1-203 (2000)). *See generally* Ira C. Lupu & Robert Tuttle, *The Distinctive Place of Religious Entities in our Constitutional Order*, 47 Vill. L. Rev. 37 (2002); James L. Underwood, *Applying the* Good News Club *Decision in a Manner that Maintains the Separation of Church and State in Our Schools*, 47 Vill. L. Rev. 281 (2002);. Douglas Laycock, *Equal Access and Moments of Silence: The Equal Status of Religious Speech by Private Speakers*, 81 Nw. U. L. Rev. 1 (1986); Ruti Teitel, *When Separate is Equal: Why Organized Religious Exercises, Unlike Chess, Do Not Belong in the Public Schools*, 81 Nw. U. L. Rev. 174 (1986).

The Equal Access Act requires that public secondary schools receiving federal financial assistance it may not discriminate against or deny equal access to student groups based on the religious or other content-based nature of the speech at their proposed meetings in all cases where school policy creates a "limited open forum" for student speech. 20 U.S.C. §4071(a). A limited open forum, in turn, is created whenever a school allows "one or more noncurriculum related student groups to meet on school premises during noninstructional time." 20 U.S.C. §4071(b).

The meaning of the EAA's "non-curriculum-related student group" was determined in *Board of Educ. of the Westside Community Schools v. Mergens*, 496 U.S. 226, 236–38 (1990). Holding that the EAA was constitutional as applied, the Court found two points significant. First, that "the purpose of granting equal access is to prohibit discrimination between religious or political clubs," and second, "that the Act...was passed by wide, bipartisan majorities in both the House and the Senate [and] reflects at least some consensus [concerning] perceived widespread discrimination against religious speech in public schools, *see* H.R. Rep. No. 98-710, p. 4 (1984); S. Rep. No. 98-357, pp. 10–11 (1984)."

> In light of this legislative purpose, we think that the term "noncurriculum related student group" is best interpreted broadly to mean any student group that does not directly relate to the body of courses offered by the school. In our view, a student group directly relates to a school's curriculum if the subject matter of the group is actually taught, or will soon be taught, in a regularly offered course; if the subject matter of the group concerns the body of courses as a whole; if participation in the group is required for a particular course; or if participation in the group results in academic credit. We think this limited definition of groups that directly relate to the curriculum is a commonsense interpretation of the Act that is consistent with Congress' intent to provide a low threshold for triggering the Act's requirements.

496 U.S. at 239–40.

Although some school districts attempted to evade both the Act and the implications of the Court's holding in *Mergens*, see, e.g., *Pope by Pope v. East Brunswick Bd. of Educ.*, 12 F.3d 1244, 1254 (3rd Cir. 1993) (holding that "East Brunswick attempted to restructure its existing student groups, striving mightily not to trigger the Act...however,...it has indeed triggered it."); *Garnett v. Renton Sch. Dist. No. 403*, 987 F.2d 641 (9th Cir.

1993) (rejecting claim that states can "evade" the EAA by relying on their state constitutional proscriptions concerning religious influences in public schools). Current case law and commentary tends to focus on the nature of the setting, the identity of the speaker, the character of other student groups permitted to use the forum, and the possibility of coercion. *See, e.g., East High Sch. Prism Club v. Seidel*, 95 F.Supp. 2d 1239 (D. Utah 2000) (gay student groups); *Colin* ex rel. *Colin v. Orange Unified School Dist.*, 83 F.Supp.2d 1135(C.D. Cal. 2000) (same). *See generally* Ralph D. Mawdsley, *The Equal Access Act and Public Schools: What Are the Legal Issues Related to Recognizing Gay Student Groups?*, 2001 B.Y.U. Educ. & L.J. 1 (2001).

5. Much of the federal case law permitting student-initiated prayer in public schools turns on a free speech analysis, rather than religious liberty. *See Widmar v. Vincent*, 454 U.S. 263 (1981); *See also Good News Club v. Milford Central Sch. Dist.*, 533 U.S. 98 (2001). Why do you suppose the Court took that route? Does "forum" analysis preserve the discretion of the school authorities more effectively than recognition of a free exercise "right" to engage in prayer or religious ritual? How? See Chapter Five § G.

c) Access to Religious Materials & Information

Public school officials have broad discretion to control the educational environment and the content of materials available for student use. *Bethel Sch. Dist. No. 403 v. Fraser*, 478 U.S. 675 (1986) (content of student speech during assembly); *Hazelwood Sch. Dist. v. Kuhlmeier*, 484 U.S. 260 (1988) (content of school newspaper). Although the Supreme Court's decision in *Board of Educ. v. Pico* is cast in terms of a right to receive information, all of the opinions seem to indicate that the powers of the school board, while not unlimited, are at their peak when the issue is control over the classroom. *Roberts v. Madigan*, excerpted briefly below, presents an interesting "twist" on *Pico*: removal of the Bible from the school and a classroom library. Other cases have challenged the distribution of religious literature on the premises of public schools by both students and adults, with results similar to those found in the prayer cases.

In *Jabr v. Rapides Parish Sch. Bd.* ex rel. *Metoyer*, 171 F.Supp.2d 653 (W.D. La. 2001), for example, Muslim parents sued for redress after their children were given Bibles as Christmas presents by the school principle, acting on behalf of the School Board. *Accord Berger v. Rensselaer Cent. Sch. Corp.*, 982 F.2d 1160 (7th Cir. 1993), *cert. denied*, 508 U.S. 911 (1993). *But see Sherman v. Community Consol. Sch. Dist. 21 of Wheeling Twp.*, 8 F.3d 1160 (7th Cir. 1993), *cert. denied*, 508 U.S. 950 (1994)(refusing to enjoin the school's practice of permitting the Boy Scouts of America (BSA) from using the school premises, hanging posters on the walls, and distributing its materials in the school, notwithstanding the plaintiffs' claim that the BSA discriminates on the basis of religion, and requires its members to profess belief in God.) *See also Boy Scouts of America, South Florida Council v. Till*, 136 F. Supp.2d 1295 (S.D. Fla. 2001) (upholding First Amendment claim of Boy Scouts against school board rule excluding organization because of its policies concerning homosexual scoutmasters).

5. Limiting Religious Influences in the School and Classroom Setting

The controversy concerning religion in the public school setting can only be understood if placed in an historical context. As the materials in this chapter point out, the public, or "common," schools in the United States were intended not only to provide the basic components of education, but to socialize our children, and assimilate them into the social, political and cultural life of the community. Reflecting the majority culture, most public schools were culturally, if not religiously, Protestant Christian. *See, e.g., Washegesic v. Bloomingdale Public Schools*, 33 F. 3d 679 (6th Cir. 1994) (ordering school district to remove donated picture of Jesus Christ from school premises*); People* ex rel. *Ring v. Bd. of Educ. of District 24*, 245 Ill. 334, 92 N.E. 251 (1910) (Catholic parents complaining of preference for Protestant religion).

Because the school system and teacher are state employees who "speak" in a forum created and maintained by the State, the courts have held that the free exercise rights of individuals, particularly teachers and staff members, must yield in the controlled environment of the public school. *See generally Goldman v. Weinberger*, 475 U.S. 503 (1986) (same, as applied to a military officer); *LaRocca v. Lane*, 37 N.Y.2d 575, 376 N.Y.S.2d 93, 338 N.E.2d 606 (1975), *cert. denied,* 424 U.S. 968 (1976) (same, as applied to a courtroom attorney). *See also* Chapter Eight (regarding the rights of employees).

Cooper v. Eugene School District, No. 4J

301 Or. 358, 723 P.2d 298 (1986), *appeal dismissed,* 480 U.S. 942 (1987)

LINDE, Justice.

When Janet Cooper, a special education teacher in the Eugene public schools, became a Sikh, she donned white clothes and a white turban and wore them while teaching her sixth and eighth grade classes. In a letter to the staff of the school where she taught, she wrote that she would wear the turban and often wear white clothing as part of her religious practice, and that she had explained this and other changes in her life to her students. She continued to wear her white garb after being warned that she faced suspension if she violated a law against wearing religious dress at her work. The law provides, in ORS 342.650:

> "No teacher in any public school shall wear any religious dress while engaged in the performance of duties as a teacher."

and, in ORS 342.655:

> "Any teacher violating the provisions of ORS 342.650 shall be suspended from employment by the district school board. The board shall report its action to the Superintendent of Public Instruction who shall revoke the teacher's teaching certificate."

Pursuant to these statutes, the school superintendent, acting for the school board, suspended Cooper from teaching and reported this action to the Superintendent of Public Instruction, who, after a hearing, revoked Cooper's teaching certificate. This order was challenged on constitutional grounds in the Court of Appeals, which set aside the revocation of the teaching certificate as an excessive sanction under the court's understanding of federal First Amendment doctrine. *Cooper v. Eugene Sch. Dist. No. 4J*, 76 Or. App. 146, 708 P.2d 1161 (1985). On petitions by the school district and the Superintendent of Public Instruction, we allowed review.

II. OREGON'S GUARANTEES OF RELIGIOUS FREEDOM

Cooper's case is not one of declining to comply with an otherwise valid law on grounds of personal religious belief. The law here at issue is not a general regulation, neutral toward religion on its face and in its policy, like the unemployment benefits standards that we sustained against attack under the Oregon Constitution (though not under the First Amendment) by claimants who had been discharged for religiously motivated conduct in *Smith v. Employment Division*, 301 Or. 209, 721 P.2d 445 (1986) and *Black v. Employment Division*, 301 Or. 221, 721 P.2d 451 (1986). The cases would be comparable if a school regulation prescribed how teachers should dress while on duty without taking account of religious considerations. Then we would have only an issue of statutory authority to make such a regulation...and an individual claim to exemption on religious grounds. But ORS 342.650 is not neutral toward religion. On the contrary, the religious significance of the teacher's dress is the specific target of this law. The law singles out a teacher's religious dress because it is religious and to the extent that its religious significance is apparent when the wearer is engaged in teaching. The issue therefore is whether the law infringes the right guaranteed to "all men"[10] by Article I, section 2, of the Oregon Constitution "to worship Almighty God according to the dictates of their own consciences," or "control[s] the free exercise, and enjoyment of religious opinions, or interfere[s] with the rights of conscience" contrary to Article I, section 3.

This court sometimes has treated these guarantees and the First Amendment's ban on laws prohibiting the free exercise of religion as "identical in meaning," ...but identity of "meaning" or even of text does not imply that the state's laws will not be tested against the state's own constitutional guarantees before reaching the federal constraints imposed by the Fourteenth Amendment, or that verbal formulas developed by the United States Supreme Court in applying the federal text also govern application of the state's comparable clauses. What is at issue in a constitutional dispute rarely is what a constitutional text "means" but how to effectuate that meaning in the disputed setting. Judicial formulas or "factors" are not themselves the law but aids to analysis that a court from time to time may employ, rephrase, or replace with a better interpretation of their constitutional source.

The guarantees of religious freedom in Article I provide:

> *Section 2.* All men shall be secure in the Natural right, to worship Almighty God according to the dictates of their own consciences.
>
> *Section 3.* No law shall in any case whatever control the free exercise, and enjoyment of religious (sic) opinions or interfere with the rights of conscience.
>
> *Section 4.* No religious test shall be required as a qualification for any office of trust or profit.
>
> *Section 5.* No money shall be drawn from the Treasury for the benefit of any religious (sic), or theological institution, nor shall any money be appropriated for the payment of any religious (sic) services in either house of the Legislative Assembly.
>
> *Section 6.* No person shall be rendered incompetent as a witness, or juror in consequence of his opinions on matters of religion (sic); nor be questioned in any Court of Justice touching his religious (sic) belief to affect the weight of his testimony.

10. Even the most committed strict constructionist of the constitutional text doubtless would fail the challenge to read "men" to exclude "women," at least unless there were a clear record of such an intention. See *State v. Chase*, 106 Or. 263, 271, 211 P. 920 (1922) (women became "freemen" and the "peers" of men for jury service upon gaining political rights).

> *Section 7.* The mode of administering an oath, or affirmation shall be such as may be most consistent with, and binding upon the conscience of the person to whom such oath or affirmation may be administered."

The religion clauses of Oregon's Bill of Rights, Article I, sections 2, 3, 4, 5, 6 and 7, are more than a code. They are specifications of a larger vision of freedom for a diversity of religious beliefs and modes of worship and freedom from state-supported official faiths or modes of worship. The cumulation of guarantees, more numerous and more concrete than the opening clause of the First Amendment, reinforces the significance of the separate guarantees. Article I, section 4, for instance, forbids religious tests specifically "as a qualification for any office of trust or profit"; but in the total context of sections 2, 3, 6 and 7 it would be difficult to argue that the government could impose a religious test on employment in a position that technically is not an "office of trust or profit," for instance in the public schools, on the grounds that such employment is a mere privilege.

Likewise, the present law cannot be sustained simply on grounds that it does not interfere with the free exercise of religion because it regulates conduct rather than religious beliefs or verbal expression of opinion and worship. Thus, a law restricting dress specifically for being "religious dress" cannot stand as a regulation of "conduct" rather than "belief" or "worship." If such a law is to be valid, it must be justified by a determination that religious dress necessarily contravenes the wearer's role or function at the time and place beyond any realistic means of accommodation.

The compatibility of religious dress with the role of public school teachers is an old issue under state laws and constitutions. Generally it involved teaching by nuns while wearing the habits of their orders. It is, of course, a different question whether a constitution itself is claimed to forbid the display of the teacher's religious commitment in the public school or whether a ban on religious dress adopted by law or properly delegated rule contravenes the teacher's religious freedom.

III. RELIGIOUS NEUTRALITY IN PUBLIC SCHOOLS

Here the policy choice was made by the legislature. There is no reason to believe that when the Legislative Assembly enacted ORS 342.650 in its present form in 1965, it had any aim other than to maintain the religious neutrality of the public schools, to avoid giving children or their parents the impression that the school, through its teacher, approves and shares the religious commitment of one group and perhaps finds that of others less worthy. It would be easy to show that this aim has equal constitutional standing with the teacher's religious self-expression if Oregon, like many states, had adopted an explicit constitutional guarantee against sectarian influence in the public schools.[13] Such a provision was omitted from the education article, Article VIII, of the Oregon Constitution.

Nonetheless, the aim of maintaining the religious neutrality of the public schools furthers a constitutional obligation beyond an ordinary policy preference of the legisla-

---

13. Many state constitutions expressly forbid sectarian influence in the public schools. Characteristic phrases are found in California's Art. 9, § 8 ("nor shall any sectarian or denominational doctrine be taught, or instruction thereon be permitted, directly or indirectly, in and of the common schools of this State"); Nevada's Article 11, § 9 ("No sectarian instruction shall be imparted or tolerated" in the public schools); Washington's Article 9, § 4 (Public schools "shall be forever free from sectarian control or influence"). *See generally*, Antieau, Carroll & Burke, Religion Under the State Constitutions (1965).

ture. It is the obligation stated in Article VIII, section 3, to provide for "a uniform, and general system of Common Schools," which must be done without imposing on the religious freedom under Article I, sections 2 and 3, of the children who attend those schools.

Recognition that freedom of religion for all implies official sponsorship of none has grown with the growing diversity of the nation itself. The main battleground has been the public schools, as the cases under the constitutional proscriptions of "sectarian influence" and later under the First Amendment show. Parents and lawmakers may and do assume that the hours, days, and years spent in school are the time and the place when a young person is most impressionable by the expressed and implicit orthodoxies of the adult community and most sensitive to being perceived as different from the majority of his or her peers; famous constitutional cases have involved this socializing rather than intellectual function of the schools. In excluding teachers whose dress is a constant and inescapable visual reminder of their religious commitment, laws like ORS 342.650 respect and contribute to the child's right to the free exercise and enjoyment of its religious opinions or heritage, untroubled by being out of step with those of the teacher.

The principle is most obvious when the teacher represents the community's dominant religion, but it cannot be limited to that situation. From the "Know-Nothing" nativism of the mid-19th century, through the battle over the "Blaine Amendment," to recent times, contention centered on the role of Catholicism in public schools, symbolized by the dress of priests and nuns, as distinct from mainstream Protestantism, represented by school prayers and the King James translation of the Bible. It may be a far cry from these historic conflicts to perceive any threat of sectarian influence in the dress of a sect that, in this country, may seem an exotic curiosity. But we are examining the validity of the law against a charge that it denies teachers the freedom to adopt the dress of their respective religions. Neither their religious freedom nor that of their students can depend on calculations which faiths are more likely than others to snatch a young soul from a rival creed. The tides of immigration and of homegrown religions have changed before and are changing again, and what is exotic today may tomorrow gain many thousands of adherents and potential majority status in some communities.

In other contexts we have held that expression that could not constitutionally be prohibited outright may nevertheless be found incompatible with the performance of an official professional role. We conclude that ORS 342.650 does not impose an impermissible requirement for teaching in the public schools if it is properly limited to actual incompatibility with the teaching function.

IV. THE PERMISSIBLE REACH OF ORS 342.650

The Court of Appeals recognized the need to limit the potential reach of ORS 342.650. Compliance with the statute demands some sacrifice of religious self-expression by a teacher. The statute, of course, does not forbid the wearing of religious dress outright, but it does forbid doing so while teaching. The law could be described either as denying a teacher's right to practice her religion or as denying a person demonstratively committed to a religious vocation the opportunity to teach in the public schools. The two descriptions may invite different responses, but the issue should not hinge on semantics.

The Court of Appeals stated this greater significance as follows:

The additional element not stated in the opinion of the Court of Appeals is the continual or frequent repetition of a teacher's appearance in specifically religious (not merely ethnic) dress. The religious influence on children while in the public school that laws like ORS 342.650, in their concern with the employment of nuns wearing their special garb as public school teachers, legitimately seek to prevent is not the mere knowledge that a teacher is an adherent of a particular religion. Their concern is that the teacher's appearance in religious garb may leave a conscious or unconscious impression among young people and their parents that the school endorses the particular religious commitment of the person whom it has assigned the public role of teacher. This is what makes the otherwise privileged display of a teacher's religious commitment by her dress incompatible with the atmosphere of religious neutrality that ORS 342.650 aims to preserve, or so the school authorities may decide. The statute therefore would not be violated whenever a teacher makes an occasional appearance in religious dress, for instance on her way to or from a seasonal ceremony. It is the same distinction as that between an occasional religious meeting, parade or brief display in a public park or building and the permanent erection of a religious symbol. Only wearing religious dress as a regular or frequently repeated practice while teaching is grounds for disqualification.

V. CONCLUSION

We conclude that, when correctly interpreted and applied, ORS 342.650 survives challenge under Oregon's guarantees of religious freedom. As interpreted in this opinion, we believe it also does not violate the federal First Amendment.

The decision of the Court of Appeals is reversed.

Notes

1. As noted in Chapter Four, religious garb statutes have their genesis in the late nineteenth century, and were designed to prevent Catholic nuns from wearing their habits as public school teachers. Shortly after the Supreme Court of Pennsylvania held that the wearing of religious garb did not constitute sectarian teaching, *Hysong v. Gallitzin Sch. Dist.*, 164 Pa. 629, 30 A. 482 (1894), the Pennsylvania legislature enacted a religious garb law similar to the Oregon law upheld in *Cooper.* That law was sustained in *Commonwealth v. Herr*, 229 Pa. 132, 78 A. 68 (1910) on the ground that the regulation was not a "religious test." Shortly before *Herr,* the New York Court of Appeals held constitutional a regulation of the superintendent of public schools forbidding a teacher to wear religious garb. *O'Connor v. Headrick*, 184 N.Y. 421, 77 N.E. 612 (1906). In addition to the cases cited in Chapter Four, see *New Haven v. Torrington*, 132 Conn. 194, 43 A.2d 455 (1945) and *Moore v. Board of Educ.*, 4 Ohio Misc. 257, 212 N.E.2d 833 (Ohio App. 1965) (both holding permissible the wearing of religious garb).

2. *Harfst v. Hoegen*, 349 Mo. 808, 163 S.W.2d 609, 614 (1942), is a case involving the incorporation of a school formerly run by the Catholic church into the public school system. Most of the teachers in the school were members of an order of Roman Catholic nuns. Relying on Art. II, §7 of the Missouri Constitution, which provides, in relevant part, that "no money shall ever be taken from the public treasury, directly or indirectly, in aid of any church, sect or denomination of religion, or in aid of any priest, preacher, minister or teacher thereof, as such," the Missouri Supreme Court held that the nuns could not be paid from state funds if they taught in the schools. It based this holding on testimony of the Mother Superior of the religious order, which it determined compelled the conclusion "that the members of her religious order, their lives dedicated to the training of children both in religion and education, come within this

constitutional interdiction as teachers of religion and payment to them from public school funds is forbidden."

The conclusion that the Missouri court's intent was in *Harfst* was to bar all nuns from public school classrooms may be bolstered by the same court's decision in *Berghorn v. Reorganized Sch. Dist. No. 8, Franklin County*, 364 Mo. 121, 260 S.W.2d 573 (1953), in which the court held that two Catholic schools incorporated into the public school system retained their Catholic identity and thus were not free public schools and ineligible to receive state monies. The court's conclusion that the schools remained Catholic was based, in part, on the presence of Catholic nuns as teachers. The lower court concluded that, because of the vows a nun took, no Catholic nun could teach in a public school, a conclusion the appellate court formally neither rejected nor accepted. Would it make a difference if the nuns involved had decided to wear no identifiably religious garb, or should the decision be based on the perception of the court that their religious vows are incompatible with public service as teachers? Would such a rationale violate the No Religious Test Clause of Article VI? See Chapter Eight §G ("The Government Workplace").

3. Does Title VII of the Civil Rights Act of 1964, which forbids an employer to discriminate against an employee on the basis of the employee's religion, unless the employer demonstrates that a reasonable accommodation would cause an "undue hardship on the conduct of the employer's business," require public schools to permit its teachers to wear religious garb while teaching? In *United States v. Board of Educ. for the Sch. Dist. of Philadelphia*, 911 F.2d 882 (3d Cir. 1990), the Third Circuit held that the application of Pennsylvania's religious garb statute to a devout Muslim and substitute public school teacher who clothed her entire body except for her face and hands did not violate Title VII. The Third Circuit concluded that the summary dismissal for want of a federal question by the Supreme Court in *Cooper* required it to hold that religious garb statutes serve a "compelling interest in maintaining the appearance of religious neutrality in the public school classroom." *Id.* at 889. Because the "undue hardship" standard was an easier standard to meet than the compelling state interest standard, the Title VII claim failed. *See* Chapter Eight §F ("The Secular Workplace").

4. Does, or should, it make a difference that the religious garb statute was originally adopted with discriminatory animus toward persons of other faiths? *See Washington v. Davis*, 426 U.S. 229 (1976). Does the fact that a legislature re-enacts a religious garb statute immunize it from a charge that such statutes perpetuate religious stereotypes? What facts must be shown before a court is justified in concluding that the re-enactment was untainted by any vestige of past or present discriminatory intent? Does the case law support an argument that a desire on the part of the State to eliminate religious symbolism from the classroom is sufficient to overcome the religious liberty interests of the teacher? *See* Chapter Eight §G ("The Government Workplace"). Would your answer be different if the school involved were private? Why?

5. Is it permissible under the rationale in *Tinker v. Des Moines Sch. Dist.*, 393 U.S. 503 (1969), to exclude a *student* who desires to wear religious garb or symbols in the classroom?

6. Does the fact that a teacher wears a religious symbol or religious garb "convey a message of endorsement" as that phrase is used by Justice O'Connor in her endorsement analysis? Would it be permissible to apply the same rule to the wearing of political campaign buttons by teachers?

7. In *Employment Div. v. Smith*, 494 U.S. 872 (1990), the Court indicated that free exercise challenges might be available to those who could show that "individualized determinations" were available under the terms of the relevant statute(s). *See Sherbert v. Verner*, 374 U.S. 398 (1963). Would it make a difference if it could be shown that the only extant dress code for teachers and staff was one requiring "proper dress and decorum"?

8. Are religious garb statutes discriminatory on their face? Are they supported by a compelling state interest? Which? What impact, if any, does *Church of Lukumi Babalu Aye v. City of Hialeah*, 508 U.S. 520 (1993), noted in Chapter Five, have on your answer? Does Justice Linde's opinion concede that the statute is discriminatory?

9. The Oregon Supreme Court's rationale in *Cooper* is that the First Amendment rights of the teacher must bend to the extent that the exercise of those rights is "incompatible with the performance of an official professional role." What other exercises of First Amendment rights might be "incompatible with the professional role of a teacher"? Does a judgment on that proposition depend on one's views concerning the relationship of religion to the teaching function? *See, e.g., Russo v. Central Sch. Dist. No. 1*, 469 F.2d 623 (2nd Cir. 1972) (teacher could not be disciplined for refusal to participate in Pledge of Allegiance, even though school regulations required her to participate). What about other "messages" conveyed by teacher conduct? *See National Gay Task Force v. Board of Educ. of Oklahoma City*, 729 F.2d 1270 (10th Cir. 1984) *aff'd by equally divided Court*, 470 U.S. 903 (1985) (upholding statute permitting dismissal of teachers for "public homosexual activity," but invalidating the statute insofar as it restricts the rights of teachers to advocate their views in a manner which did not disrupt the school or classroom).

What, for example, should be the outcome in a case where the teacher's private sexual conduct becomes known to the students? *Compare Ponton v. Newport News Sch. Bd.*, 632 F. Supp. 1056 (E.D. Va. 1986) (upholding constitutional and Title VII claims of an unmarried teacher who claimed her constitutional right to privacy and her statutory rights under Title VII were violated when she was forced to take a leave of absence after she became pregnant. The court held that "even if plaintiff's students would have known that she was single, the mere knowledge that their teacher had gotten pregnant out of wedlock would seem to have a fairly minimal impact on them. There was no evidence that plaintiff intended to proselytize her students regarding the issue of unwed pregnancy.") *with Pettit v. State Bd. of Educ.*, 10 Cal.3d 29, 109 Cal. Rptr. 665, 513 P.2d 889 (1973) (upholding State Board of Education's revocation of teaching credential of teacher who had joined a "swingers" club and engaged in acts of sexual intercourse and oral copulation with men other than her husband and had appeared on television programs while facially disguised and discussed nonconventional sexual behavior, even though her principal found her teaching to be satisfactory and school district was willing to rehire her).

10. Is the Oregon Supreme Court's analogy to the professional responsibilities of attorneys and others appropriate in a case where the state seeks to justify imposing limitations on the First Amendment rights of public school teachers?

In *Burt v. Blumenauer*, 299 Or. 55, 74, 699 P.2d 168 (1985), the Oregon Supreme Court held that public officials can be held personally liable for expending public funds to oppose a ballot measure. Does the imposition of personal liability infringe upon the official's liberty interests, or does it impose the full cost of political advocacy on the individual? In *Re Lasswell*, 296 Or. 121, 673 P.2d 855 (1983), the Oregon court held that a disciplinary rule prohibiting a prosecutor's extra-judicial comments on a pending trial is constitutional because the state could show an actual incompatibility between the out of court statements and the prosecutor's official function. Are these appropriate analogies to the situation of a teacher? Don't they depend, at least in part, on the view that the alleged incompatibility arises from a conflict of interest between the professional and personal interests of the professionals involved? *See also LaRocca v. Lane*, 37 N.Y.2d 575, 376 N.Y.S.2d 93, 338 N.E.2d 606 (1975), *cert. denied*, 424 U.S. 968 (1976), excerpted in Chapter Twelve § E.

Is conflict of interest what the Oregon Supreme Court had in mind when it held that a teacher's decision to wear religious garb is incompatible with the professional function of the teacher? If so, to whom does the professional duty of the teacher run? To the students, or to the public school employer? Is it also possible to explain the result as a state-imposed rule of conduct that seeks to control the symbolic content of the classroom environment? Which is the better explanation? *See generally* Thomas Kamm, "The New Battle of Poitiers: France Sees Muslim Youths Turn to Fundamentalism, And Fear of Violence Grows," *The Wall Street Journal Europe*, Thursday, January 5, 1995, at 1 (reporting that the decision of many French Muslim students at the University of Poitiers to wear the veil led to a university ban of the practice).

11. In *Roberts v. Madigan*, 921 F.2d 1047 (10th Cir. 1989), the plaintiffs were a fifth grade school teacher and several of his students who objected when the Adams County, Colorado school authorities removed the Bible from the school library and ordered a teacher to remove religious materials from his classroom bookshelf, to refrain from reading the Bible during silent reading periods, and to keep his personal Bible, which he kept on his desk, out of sight during school hours. They asserted that the school board's actions violated their First Amendment rights of free speech, academic freedom, and access to information. Plaintiffs also claimed that these actions violated the Establishment Clause by treating Christianity in a non-neutral, disparaging manner. The district court dismissed the students and their parents from the case on standing grounds, ordered the school authorities to replace the Bible in the school library, and rejected the teacher's First Amendment claims in their entirety. *Roberts v. Madigan*, 702 F. Supp. 1505 (D. Colo. 1989).

The Tenth Circuit affirmed the trial court's dismissal of the students' claims on the ground that since they had not been in the teacher's class at the time of the actions taken by the Board, they had no standing to challenge its actions. It rejected the disparagement claim as well, holding that "the district court... properly concluded that [the teacher's] actions, when viewed in their entirety, had the primary effect of communicating a message of endorsement of a religion to the impressionable ten-, eleven-, and twelve-year-old children in his class."

Judge Barrett dissented, arguing that "the activities here were passive and *de minimis*. If the condemned activities in this case could, by simple inference, be held to be violative of the principle of separation of church and state, reliance would necessarily have to weigh almost entirely on the proposition that Mr. Roberts' fifth graders were ages 10 or 11 and thus easily proselytized." His concern was that "[n]o students or parents testified in support of Principal Madigan or the School District. No witness protested that Mr. Roberts' practice of reading from his Bible or the maintenance in his classroom library of the two condemned books were motivated by Mr. Roberts' intention to promote belief in Christianity. Under these circumstances and on the record made, I would hold that the activities did not amount to an intrusion on the separation of church and state principle."

What do you think of the majority's rationale and outcome? Is it consistent with the reasoning and outcome in *Island Trees*?

12. In *Doe v. Beaumont Indep. Sch. Dist.*, 240 F.3d 462 (5th Cir. 2001), the United States Court of Appeals for the Fifth Circuit considered a "Clergy in the Schools" volunteer effort undertaken by the Beaumont, Texas School Independent School District. Under the Program, the school district invites members of the local clergy to provide volunteer counseling to students at the schools during school hours. Although individual members of the clergy can participate in the general volunteer program, the "Clergy in the Schools" program is open only to clergy. The school district defended its program on the grounds that it is designed to take advantage of the special listening and communication skills members of the clergy bring to their work. The challenged program is related to a larger School Volunteer Program designed to bring community resources and expertise into the schools, but is administered separately.

School personnel train the clergy volunteers, and provide them with written guidelines. Volunteer clergy are encouraged to discuss civic values, dress codes, the reasons why communities have rules, violence, peer pressure, racial issues, stereotyping, jealousy, unity, self-esteem, self-discipline, setting goals, divorce, diversity, gossip, harassment, alcohol, drugs and respect. The volunteers are to refuse to discuss prohibited subjects, such as sex and abortion. The published guidelines explicitly instruct that clergy volunteers are not to (1) discuss religion, (2) quote religious materials, (3) provide information about church services, (4) identify their church affiliation, (5) wear distinctive garb that would reveal their religious affiliation, or (6) pray or offer to pray with students. Any student who asks for prayer should be encouraged to share that need with a parent or with a member of the clergy outside school.

The District Court held that the program did not violate the Establishment Clause, but did not hold a hearing at which the facts were explored in detail. A divided panel of the Fifth Circuit reversed, holding that the program "advanced" and "endorsed" religion in violation of the Establishment Clause. On hearing *en banc*, the full Fifth Circuit vacated the panel decision and remanded for trial. Holding that the "plan presents a novel configuration of Establishment Clause issues," the court noted the importance of a full factual record in a case where the school district was well-aware that it "was walking a legal high wire": "[P]erhaps because the parties did not squarely engage each other on the merits, they have produced an uncertain record burdened with genuine issues of material fact, including the place of the clergy program in the District's larger overall volunteer program." 240 F.3d at 464. In its view, "ultimate question in this Establishment Clause case is equality of treatment: whether the school board preferred religion over non-religion." *Id.*

E. Dual Enrollment Programs

1. Religious Training for Students Enrolled in Public Schools—Off-Premises "Released Time"

Church groups and state officials have responded in a variety of ways to the assertion that public schools are organized on the premise that secular education can be isolated from all religious training. Clearly doubting, in Justice Jackson's words, "whether such a disjunction is possible, and, if possible, whether it is wise," parents and church authorities have been very creative in their attempts to have religious training included in the course of their children's daily schedule. In order to differentiate clearly between the religious education purposes of programs designed to include religious training during the course of a child's normal school day, the children are "released" to the custody of their parents or church authorities to attend religious education classes or programs. As required by the compulsory education laws, children who do not attend such programs remain in school.

The concept of "released time" illustrates the tension between compulsory education laws and the desires of religiously observant parents and churches to have their children exposed to religious training during the course of the normal school day. The Supreme Court's cases exclude religious education from the public schools because children and young adults are open to all forms of education. Because they are children, however, their attention spans are limited. If the state-controlled curriculum takes up the whole school day, children will likely be too tired to pay attention, or will resent being forced to give up the normal course of after school activities. Limiting religious education to weekends defeats the parents' purpose.

In *Pierce*, the State of Oregon was explicit on this point. The very purpose of its decision to shut down "sectarian" schools was to eliminate sectarian strife, and one way to accomplish that purpose was take control of the education of young children, so as to shield them from the feelings of "distrust and separation" children acquire through instruction in alternative educational settings.

> Having in mind the... separation of church and state... and the legal struggles which have arisen over the question of sectarian instruction in the public schools, we submit that [the need for this legislation is apparent.]
>
> The great majority of American youth receive their religious instruction in purely sectarian institutions or in the home, separate and apart from their common school education or training, and it has been settled that sectarian religious instruction in our public schools will not be tolerated. The right [to teach religion] demanded by [the private schools] is denied to all whose children attend the public schools.
>
> The voters in Oregon might also have based their action... upon the alarm which they felt at the rising tide of religious suspicions in this country, and their belief that the basic cause of such... feelings was the separation of children along religious lines during the most susceptible years of their lives, with the inevitable awakening of a consciousness of separation, and a distrust and suspicion of those from whom they were so carefully guarded.

Brief of Appellant, William Pierce (Governor of Oregon), *Pierce v. Society of Sisters*, *supra*, at 70–73, 40.

For those committed to sending their children to public schools, the most logical approach to this problem are programs that bring religious education to the children on the premises of the public schools themselves. As noted in Chapter Five, on-premises "released time" programs using teachers and materials provided by the parents and churches supporting the programs were held unconstitutional in *Illinois* ex rel. *McCollum v. Board of Educ.*, 333 U.S. 203 (1948). The parents and churches responded by creating programs that bring public school students to off-premises religion classes. Those programs were challenged as well, but upheld in *Zorach v. Clauson*, 343 U.S. 306 (1952).

The history of Establishment Clause litigation indicates that the same creativity is at work in cases involving children attending religiously affiliated schools. The parents, for obvious financial reasons, seek to take advantage of their child's rights under state constitutional law to education at public expense, but for reasons personal to themselves, enroll their children in private schools.

In some of these cases, public school teachers were sent to the religiously-affiliated schools to teach non-religious curricular offerings, in other cases students enrolled at private and religiously-affiliated schools were sent to neighboring public schools to take advantage of the courses offered others.

The cases excerpted below raise several questions. First, to what extent should such cooperation between church organizations and the state be permitted? Second, does the First Amendment or state law require such cooperation if the public school authorities refuse? And finally, why are such programs problematic at all? Do they represent a challenge to the premise on which the public schools are founded; that is, do they represent a creative attempt to "get around" the First Amendment, or do they reflect a continuing struggle by religiously motivated parents to exercise some control over the funds allocated under state law for the education of their children?

Lanner v. Wimmer

662 F.2d 1349 (10th Cir. 1981)

McKAY, Circuit Judge.

This case is a challenge to a school "released-time" program which permits students to take church-sponsored seminary classes off school premises during school hours. The challenge is based on the establishment and free exercise clauses of the first amendment.

Facts

The Logan School District has implemented a permissive released-time program for public school students in grades nine through twelve. The released-time program is available to any student who wishes to enroll in a course sponsored by any religious organization. There is evidence in the record that non-religious activities may also be approved in the released-time program. Except for some occasional enrollment in released-time classes sponsored by several Protestant churches in the community, however, the overwhelming use of the program is by persons attending released-time classes offered by a seminary operated by the Church of Jesus Christ of Latter-Day Saints (L.D.S. Church). The trial court carefully summarized the administration of the released-time program as follows:

> *Administration of the Release Time Program and Integration Between Schools*
>
> Registration at Logan Senior High School and Junior High School occurs in the spring preceding the school year in which the classes are to be taken. Although differing in many respects, registration for the release-time program is generally similar. Each student completes and returns to the high school or junior high a preregistration form or class schedule. If such student desires to attend seminary he or she indicates such a desire by requesting released time on the pre-registration form. The students or their parents are furnished forms by the seminary or ecclesiastical officers of the L.D.S. Church, on which parents may request permission from the school to have their children released for one period during the school-day throughout the school year to take a course at the L.D.S. seminary. Those forms are then returned to the seminary which in turn

forwards them to the high school or the junior high. The slips are checked by the public schools to insure that there is a completed form for each student who has requested release-time for participation in the L.D.S. Seminary Program. The permission slips are kept on file for approximately 3 years.

Schedules for classes, school catalogues and registration forms at Logan High School do not contain any schedules of release-time classes. However, the preregistration for students of Logan Junior High School lists "Release Time" as a course option. Registration for the release-time programs in the junior and senior high schools differs significantly in one respect. The Logan Junior High School officials do not permit the student to determine which hour of the day the student will be excused but make such determination themselves so as to maintain better control over the student program. The senior high students are responsible for designating the hour they wish to be released on their final submitted class schedule. The high school and junior high school each make a daily attendance check of all students enrolled in each school. The attendance slips for each class are collected by a student who participates in an office practice class and who personally visits each classroom and obtains a list of those students who are absent from class. A similar check is made of those students attending LDS seminary by picking up a list, on a form furnished by the public school, of those students absent from seminary class. If students are repeatedly absent from regular school classes or seminary classes, their parents are contacted by public school personnel, in order to maintain overall discipline and be apprised of the whereabouts of its students; but parents are not contacted by public school officials merely to report absences from Seminary. Attendance is not reported on any permanent record but absences appear on the students' administrative records which are stored in school files for several years.

The high school records a student's grade in the Old and New Testament courses on his or her permanent records. Since credit is not given for any classes taken in the ninth grade no such procedure is followed in the junior high schools. Neither the seminary grade nor attendance record is recorded on a student's public school report card. Each of the public school buildings is equipped with a public address system over which announcements are made to the students and a bell system which rings to denote the beginning and ending of each class period. The LDS seminaries have an attachment to the public address systems so that announcements in the junior high school or senior high school as well as the class bells can be heard in the Seminary buildings. However, no announcements can be made from the seminary into the school system nor is the seminary permitted to make any announcement over the school system. The cost of installation and maintenance of the public address system extensions has been paid by the seminaries. Teachers in the LDS programs hold parent-teacher conferences in the seminary buildings on the same dates and times as such conferences are held by the teachers in the public schools. It appears that this is done as a matter of convenience and accommodation for the public and all concerned rather than by specific prearrangement between the school officials and Seminary personnel. At both the junior and senior high schools the LDS seminary has access during school hours to a box in which notices are placed regarding school programs or changes in school schedules, which may affect the daily routine of the public schools. The seminary may then adjust its schedule to accommodate the school and student by permitting

> the public school to preempt the time for which a student is otherwise released. Any mail addressed to the seminary which is mistakenly delivered to the school is also placed in the box rather than being returned to the post office. The seminary facultymen, as members of the general public, are requested from time to time to assist in public school activities such as taking tickets at school events, handling line markers at football games, and timing events in track meets. Release-time personnel are also allowed to eat in the junior or senior high school cafeterias, as are any of the citizens of Logan City, but seminary staff and faculty who utilize the cafeteria are required to pay for their meals at the standard rate for the public. Senior students at the high school are permitted to list their extracurricular or other activities in the annual yearbook, including their participating in seminary. This reference to seminary is neither sanctioned nor encouraged by the school, but is left to the discretion of the students. Many of the other activities listed in the yearbook by the students are unrelated to school functions.
>
> The Logan City School Board's rules require that students in the junior high school be accounted for during regular school hours each day and be enrolled in seven (7) class periods per day unless released at the request of the parents to attend L.D.S. Seminary. Students in the senior high school are eligible to participate in interschool activities, honor roll and student body elections only if they are attending six (6) class periods per day. Enrollment in any of the four release-time courses is accepted by the school as a class period in partial fulfillment of that requirement. The junior and senior high schools receive from the State public funds for their operation and maintenance, based upon the number of students in attendance each day. In order to be counted for the purpose of receipt of state funds by a school, a student must attend four (4) class periods of the day. Attendance in any of the release-time courses by a student is not necessarily counted as "attending" for the purpose of determining entitlement to state funds, but the method used in the past for counting attendance resulted in counting such release-time attendance.
>
> Other contacts between the public school and the seminary which have occurred in recent years include: the offering of a prayer by a seminary official at a school function; voting and collecting votes by the student body for public school elections during seminary class; references to seminary activities in the student paper; the appointment of a seminary faculty member to serve on a public school committee; and the use of seminary classes as homerooms for the public school. These activities, however, were either isolated events or were discontinued prior to the initiation of this suit.

Plaintiffs represent the class of parents of present and future students of Logan High School and Logan Junior High School. They challenge the released-time program under both the establishment clause and the free exercise clause. The trial court held that a released-time program *per se* does not violate the first amendment, but held that certain aspects of this program violate the establishment clause. The trial court enjoined the granting of credit for completion of the Old Testament and New Testament courses offered by the L.D.S. seminary, the collecting of seminary attendance reports by the schools, the recognition of enrollment in seminary classes in fulfillment of minimum hour attendance requirements, and the counting of seminary attendance in the formula for the school district's eligibility for state funds.

IV. The Constitutionality of the Released-Time Program

Notwithstanding continuing scholarly debate, it is clear that released-time programs permitting attendance at religious classes off school premises do not *per se* offend the establishment and free exercise clauses. *Lemon v. Kurtzman*, and its progeny, which established the three-pronged test of constitutionality, do not impair this conclusion.

The trial court enjoined the attendance-gathering procedure, under which student aides must go to the seminary buildings to pick up attendance slips which have been prepared and provided by the public schools. In the released-time program approved in *Zorach*, the churches involved made weekly attendance reports to the schools. In this case, the schools bear more of the administrative responsibility for preparing and gathering attendance reports.

We agree with the trial court that this is "an admittedly minor matter." However, any released-time program, by its very nature, presents the potential for unconstitutional entanglement of public schools with religious institutions. For this reason, the least entangling administrative alternatives must be elected when a released-time program is instituted.

The public school's assumption of the burden of gathering these attendance reports, however, overlooks less entangling alternatives. It is less entangling but as solicitous of the state's interests to require released-time personnel to transmit attendance reports to the public school. Because the alternative chosen by the public schools here is not the least entangling, it must fall.

Putting aside for a moment the question of credit... we agree with the trial court that the other challenged aspects of the released-time program do not violate the establishment clause.

Plaintiffs maintain, however, that defendants' program is more constitutionally pernicious than that in *Zorach*. They point out that the L.D.S. Church's seminary buildings are architecturally similar to the public school buildings they are adjacent to. We do not perceive a problem of constitutional magnitude in the way a church chooses to build its chapels or other buildings on its property. Indeed, a serious constitutional issue would arise were we to presume to tell a church how or where it may fashion its places of worship.

Plaintiffs also note that participating students in Logan's junior and senior high schools are released one hour per day to receive L.D.S. instruction, whereas in *Zorach* students were released approximately one hour per week. The *Zorach* Court did not find the amount of time a student is allowed to spend under religious tutelage to be dispositive of or even relevant to its decision. Although accommodation may slip into abdication at some point, defendants have not reached that point here.

Plaintiffs object to the intercom system through which public school announcements and bells can be heard in seminary classes and also object to boxes in the public school buildings where seminary personnel can obtain school notices and information. These aspects of the released-time program satisfy the three-pronged test and are therefore permissible.

The primary effect of these aspects of the program is simply to make the school's administration of the released-time system convenient and to avoid unnecessary conflicts with school classes and activities. The seminaries pay for the installation and maintenance of the intercom system, and the cost of the boxes is presumably negligible. These aspects of the program neither advance nor inhibit religion.

Neither do these aspects of the program foster an excessive government entanglement with religion. The intercom system does not allow the seminary to make announcements to the schools. It merely allows the school to inform students attending released-time classes of school announcements, activities, and scheduling. The boxes provide seminary personnel with the same information so the seminary can adjust its schedule and permit the school to preempt the time for which a student is otherwise released. Neither the intercom system nor the boxes create such symbolic identification between the schools and the seminaries as to render these aspects of the program unconstitutional.

The district court was also correct in holding that plaintiffs' rights under the free exercise clause are not denied by operation of the released-time program. Plaintiffs complain of social pressures but do not allege that this peer pressure is participated in or sanctioned by defendants.

V. Credit

As in this case, numerous aspects of state and school requirements are defined in terms of hours and "credit." "Credit," as the term is used in this case, has multiple definitions. A proper adjudication of the constitutionality of defendants' activities requires an understanding of the various uses for which the term is employed.

First, "credit" is used to measure the number of hours or units of instruction required for graduation from Logan Senior High School. No released-time courses may count toward the satisfaction of these eight and one-half units. The balance of seven and one-half units required for graduation may be satisfied by "elective" courses. Two released-time units in Bible history courses may be counted as "elective" hours.

The Utah Board of Education's most recent policy statement, adopted in 1969, provides:

> Credits for work taken in released-time classes should be recognized by public schools only upon an official transcript of credits from the institution conducting such classes, and upon evaluation on the same basis that similar credits from established private high schools are evaluated. The State board has authorized high schools to recognize not to exceed two units of Bible history for work taken in private seminaries or schools. Such credit may be counted as an "elective" but may not fill any requirements for required instruction in the fields of social studies, English or literature. No credit is to be given to courses devoted mainly to denominational instruction.

The district court was concerned that "(t)he public school policy of granting credit for those courses which are not 'mainly denominational' presupposes that there must be monitoring by the public school authorities to insure that the classes do not become sectarian in nature." Since the State Board of Education's released-time policy statement apparently requires such monitoring, it implicates an unconstitutional entanglement between school authorities and religious institutions. *Lemon.*

Also, a purely religious test for determining what is not "mainly denominational," and therefore credit-worthy, is not to be left to the state. The constitutional problem with the administration of "elective credit" when such credit is granted to some released-time courses but not to others based upon a religious test is that it requires the public school officials to entangle themselves excessively in church-sponsored institutions by examining and monitoring the content of courses offered there to insure that they are not "mainly denominational."[12]

---

12. It is of course unavoidable that the state must supervise the content of courses in public schools to insure that it is not sponsoring religion in its own classrooms. It lacks the same power to

The state can, however, require that released-time courses for which credit is granted fulfill certain secular criteria. A state's requirement that church-sponsored schools meet certain secular standards if attendance at them is to satisfy state compulsory education laws does not unconstitutionally involve the state in religious institutions, even though it does implicate some entanglement. This *de minimis* entanglement could also be used to determine what courses are properly transferable for "credit" when a private religious school student transfers to a public school. These inquiries, however, could not be designed simply to ferret out religious courses.

If the school officials desire to recognize released-time classes generally as satisfying some elective hours, they are at liberty to do so if their policy is neutrally stated and administered. Recognizing attendance at church-sponsored released-time courses as satisfying graduation requirements advances religion no more than recognizing attendance at released-time courses or full-time church-sponsored schools as satisfying state compulsory attendance laws.

The trial court therefore properly enjoined the practice of granting "credit" in satisfaction of "elective" courses insofar as the program required a judgment as to whether the courses were "mainly denominational" in content. In approving this portion of the judgment we do not prohibit or require the state to recognize for purposes of "elective credit" any released-time classes which are available to all students on terms that do not require any test for religious content.

"Credit" is also used to measure satisfaction of the general compulsory school attendance requirement—that is, the daily and annual hours a student is required to be in the custody of an educational institution. For our purposes we refer to this kind of "credit" as "custodial credit." State statute provides that:

> Every...person having control of any minor between six and eighteen years of age shall be required to send such minor to a public or regularly established private school during the regularly established school year of the district in which he resides."

Utah Code Ann. §53-24-1. The state and school officials have an interest in insuring that students are not drifting about unsupervised during the hours that school is open. The granting of "credit" for this custodial purpose does not offend the Constitution in the released-time context any more than it does in the context of full-time private religious schools.

The senior high school also requires six "credit" hours per day in order for a student to be eligible for extracurricular activities and to be a candidate for the school's honor roll. We refer to this kind of credit as "eligibility credit." Just as in the case of "custodial credit" and "elective credit," the hours spent in lawful released-time classes may be recognized for this purpose so long as no test of religious content is employed.

Finally, "credit" is used to measure the school's eligibility for state financial aid. This eligibility is based on daily pupil attendance. Apparently, an hour spent in a released-time course is counted as an hour in attendance for purposes of measuring the district's eligibility for these state grants. None of these grant funds go to the released-time institutions. The funds do not in any way support or enhance the released-time classes. If giving "funding credit" for attendance at released-time classes in allocating state subsidies has any ef-

---

supervise content when churches teach courses because of the entanglement of public officials with church-sponsored institutions that such supervision necessarily entails.

fect, its sole effect is to increase funds available to the public schools. While the practice may assist the public schools, it neither enhances nor inhibits the church-sponsored released-time courses. Therefore, to the extent that the district court's order enjoins the counting of released-time attendance in measuring eligibility for state funds, it is reversed.

VII. Conclusion

The district court's judgment is affirmed insofar as it holds unconstitutional defendants' procedure of having public school students pick up attendance slips from released-time courses. The district court is reversed insofar as it holds the public school's preparation and provision of the attendance slips to the released-time courses unconstitutional. As pertaining to "credit," the district court's judgment is affirmed insofar as it enjoins defendants' system for granting "elective credit." The district court is reversed insofar as it holds unconstitutional the neutral granting of "custodial," "eligibility," and "funding" credit.

All other aspects of the district court's judgment are affirmed.

2. Sharing the Cost and Responsibility for Providing Nonreligious Education Services for Students Enrolled in Private Schools

Programs in which the state defrays some part of the cost of education for children enrolled in private schools have a long pedigree. Prior to the creation of the public school systems we know today, all schools were "private," in the sense that they were not controlled by the government. Many, if not most, of these schools were run either by churches, or by individuals associated with the church who had some education—usually the minister himself, or the "reader" of the parish.

In the Carolinas, for example, the parish clerks, or "readers", did much of the teaching in the community. These individuals were not always clerics, and taught the rudiments of reading and arithmetic because they had both the time and at least some minimal qualifications to do the job. In early eighteenth century Carolina, the churches "seldom ha[d] orthodox Clergymen," but "[t]he want of these Protestant clergy, [was] generally supply'd by some School Masters" who served as readers. Guy Fred Wells, PARISH EDUCATION IN COLONIAL VIRGINIA 7–8 & n.12 (1969), *quoting* J. Brickell, NATURAL HISTORY OF NORTH CAROLINA 25 (1737) and F. Dalcho, HISTORY OF THE EPISCOPAL CHURCH IN SOUTH CAROLINA 271 (1820). The experience in Colonial Virginia was largely the same:

> Except for the occasional payment of apprenticeship premiums by local parishes there was practically no expenditure of public funds for educational purposes in Colonial Virginia. There was not the strong religious demand for the teaching of reading which was an essential factor in the development of public schools in New England, and the uniformity of belief in the principles of the Established Church meant that there wasn't the same interest as there was in England in providing orthodox instruction so as to combat the influence of competing sects....When, in 1779 Thomas Jefferson undertook his project of establishing a scheme of public education in Virginia there was no precedent upon which he could depend except the custom of parish and county participation in the administration of poor law apprenticeship and en-

> dowed schools for the poor. Back of the practice there was an idea that the public should be concerned with the education of the poor, but there was no general feeling of real public responsibility and no sense of an obligation to do anything which might involve the levying of taxes. While what was done in colonial Virginia in the way of public interference in the education of the poor may be viewed as a step toward the later development of common schools, it probably was an obstacle rather than a help. The association of the idea of public education with that of provision for the poor alone made it seem natural in the early part of the federal period to confine the efforts made to an improvement of arrangements for the poor.

Wells, at 91.

In 1805, New York lawmakers approved the incorporation of "The Society for Establishing a Free School in the City of New York for the Education of Poor Children as do not Belong To or Are Not Provided for By Any Religious Society." Later known as the Free School Society (subsequently, the Public School Society) the law provided that the Society should allocate the educational funds at its disposal to, among others, "such incorporated religious societies in said city, as now support or hereafter shall establish charity schools within the said city, who may apply for the same." Things went well until Catholic and Jewish groups, frustrated by what they considered to be Protestant sectarianism in the public schools, requested their share of the tax moneys allocated to the schools of other religious denominations. Wilber G. Katz, Religion and the American Constitution 63 (1964). The resulting political uproar led to a change in the law. As amended, the law made any school that taught "sectarian doctrine" ineligible for public funding. In practice, the schools deemed "sectarian" were those run by Catholics and Jews. Much of the history of these controversies is recounted in Chapter Four. *See also* Charles Beals, Brass Knuckle Crusade 45–77 (1960); Wm. Oland Bourne, History of the Public School Society of the City of New York 7, 31, 45 (1870). A similar issue arose in Virginia when the State's "Literary Fund" began to support denominational Sunday Schools. The history of that debate is recounted briefly in § F(1) below.

Parents were thus left with one of two possible choices. They could (1) place their children in an educational environment that was at best indifferent, and, at worst, hostile to their children's religious beliefs, or (2) they could form privately-funded schools that would provide a setting more conducive to their religious and cultural needs.

Many chose the latter course of action, and the demographic growth of the immigrant populations made it inevitable that states with large populations of children attending private and parochial schools would eventually experience political pressures to allocate at least some share of state education funds to these children. As Chapter Four recounts, many of the "Blaine" style amendments to state constitutions were adopted in anticipation of precisely this development.

Five years after *Pierce* was decided, the Supreme Court considered such a program in *Cochran v. Louisiana St. Bd. of Educ.*, 281 U.S. 370 (1930). The Louisiana law at issue in *Cochran* required public school boards to purchase all books for schoolchildren, even those children attending religiously affiliated schools. In Louisiana, as in most other parts of the country at the time, the Catholic Church operated most such schools. Because the Court had not yet "incorporated" the First Amendment, the law was challenged on a substantive due process theory that the allocation of tax money to students enrolled in non-public schools violates the taxpayer's rights under the Due Process Clause. Writing for a unanimous Court, Chief Justice Charles Evans Hughes rejected the claim and affirmed the position taken by the Louisiana Supreme Court. That position, known as the "child benefit theory," differentiates benefits given directly to schoolchildren from benefits directed toward the school.

The "child benefit" theory has remained controversial ever since. The majority in *Everson v. Board of Educ.*, 330 U.S. 1 (1947) adopted it when it permitted New Jersey to reimburse parents for the cost of transporting their children to and from Catholic schools, and has applied it in a number of other cases summarized in § F(1) below. The child benefit theory has been offered as a justification for a number of state programs, but has met with mixed success. Chart 6-4 catalogues the cases decided by the Supreme Court of the United States and the types of aid that the states would have permitted.

Why do you think the "child benefit theory" has been so controversial? Isn't the child entitled to a free education at public expense under most state constitutions? Is aid to the child *always* aid to the religious purpose of the school? Can you formulate a test to differentiate aid to the child from aid to the school? Is the debate over public funding of some part of the cost of education for children enrolled in private schools simply another battle in the struggle for control over American education?

In *Matthews v. Quinton*, 362 P.2d 932 (Alaska 1961), the Alaska Supreme Court rejected the child-benefit theory on the grounds that any aid to the child inevitably aids the school, and without children, non-public schools could not flourish. Does such a rationale assume that providing funds for educational alternatives is not in the best interests of the state? Is it inconsistent with *Pierce*? How, if at all, do you think that increasing enrollment and diversity of private school enrollments will affect the Supreme Court's willingness to accept cost sharing of this type in the future? It appears certain that this development will be significant at the state level as well. *See* § F(2) below.

a) Public School Training for Students Enrolled in Private Schools — "Shared Time" on Public School Premises

Just as they have in the case of "released time" programs designed to permit public school students to take advantage of off-campus opportunities to obtain religious training, parents have been creative in their demands that the states provide their children with at least some portion of the educational benefits to which they are entitled under state and federal law. Because the programs and benefits involved in these cases are an integral part of the *public* school curriculum, they are referred to as "shared time" programs.

"Shared time" programs take either of two forms: providing non-religious education on the premises of private schools by sending teachers and other materials to the children, or physically moving the children between public and private school premises as in *Lanner v. Wimmer.*

Cross-registration programs like the one involved in *Lanner* have been controversial for several reasons. First, they increase the costs incurred by the public schools, and add another dimension to debates over the adequacy of public school budgets. Second, they are often viewed as an unwarranted attempt to "pick and choose" from a "menu" of public educational services, and as an implicit rejection of the state's authority in matters of education. Finally, there is the issue of government support for religious education. In those states in which entitlement to education at public expense is a personal right, it has been argued that exclusionary policies impose an unconstitutional condition on the exercise of one's constitutionally protected right to opt out of the public school system. In states in which the constitution specifically forbids state support of schools which teach "sectarian doctrine," any assistance which "frees up" resources for the teaching of religion is viewed as support of the religious mission.

Parents attempting to enroll their children as part-time students have met with mixed success. At one extreme is the view of some courts that a parental decision to exercise the freedom of choice protected by the *Meyer-Pierce-Yoder* line of case ends the analysis. In *Cook v. Griffin*, 364 N.Y.S. 2d 632, 47 A.D.2d 23 (1975), for example, the New York Supreme Court held that the state was not required to make field trips on school buses available to non-public school students.

> While there is no question that parents clearly have the right to send their children to non-public schools [*Pierce*], there is no corresponding right to equal aid or even to any aid at all in the absence of specific legislative authorization [*Norwood v. Harrison*; *San Antonio Independent School District v. Rodriguez*; *Lemon v. Kurtzman*]. All children, regardless of religious affiliation or economic status in life, have an equal opportunity to attend public schools. The fact that a child, or his parent on his behalf, elects to forego that opportunity deprives him of nothing by state action. (*Brusca v. Missouri*, 332 F. Supp. 275 (D.C. Mo.), *aff'd.*, 405 U.S. 1050, 92 S.Ct. 1493, 31 L.Ed.2d 786, *supra*).

Id. at 637.

At the other end of the spectrum are cases holding that it is religious discrimination for the state to adopt an irrebuttable presumption that exercise of the right to attend a nonpublic school operates as an express waiver of statutory and constitutional rights. In *State* ex rel. *School Dist. of Hartington v. Nebraska Bd. of Educ.*, 188 Neb. 1, 195 N.W.2d 161 (1972), *cert. denied*, 409 U.S. 921 (1972), for example, the Nebraska Supreme Court upheld the right of private school students to participate in publicly-funded school programs on the grounds that Art. VII, § 11 of the Nebraska Constitution provides that no religious test or qualification shall be required of any student for admission to any public school.

Squarely in the middle of the spectrum are cases where the schools are *required* by State or federal law to provide certain services to all students, regardless of the school in which they are enrolled. *See* Individuals with Disabilities Education Act ("IDEA"), 20 U.S.C. §§ 1400–1487 (2002). In *Mitchell v. Helms*, 530 U.S. 793 (2000), *Agostini v. Felton*, 521 U.S. 203 (1997), and *Zobrest v. Catalina Foothills Sch. Dist.*, 509 U.S. 1 (1993), the Supreme Court held that supplying special education teachers (*Agostini*), auxiliary services such as sign language interpreters (*Zobrest*), and educational equipment such as computers (*Mitchell v. Helms*) did not violate the Establishment Clause. The Courts of Appeals that have considered the issue since then have reached similar conclusions. *See, e.g., Peck by Peck v. Lansing Sch. Dist.*, 148 F.3d 619 (6th Cir. 1998) (physical and occupational therapy services); *Veschi v. Northwestern Lehigh Sch. Dist.*, 772 A.2d 469, 473 (Pa. Cmwlth. 2001) (noting that while public schools need not provide the services on the premises of the nonpublic school, they may not discriminate against a child based on his parents choice of an alternative education without violating *Pierce* and *Yoder*).

Where the services are *not* required by statute, cases like **Thomas v. Allegany County Board of Education**, 51 Md. App. 312, 443 A.2d 622 (Ct. Spec. App. 1982), provide some insight concerning the degree to which local school boards are empowered to adopt an "all or nothing" approach to the right to an education at public expense.

The right of Maryland students to free education in the public schools is guaranteed by Article VIII § 1 of the Maryland Constitution. It provides that "The General Assembly shall... by Law establish throughout the State a thorough and efficient System of Free Public Schools." That requirement is implemented by Maryland Education Code § 7-101(a), which provides that "all individuals who are 5 years old or older and under 21 shall be admitted free of charge to the public schools of this State."

In *Thomas*, the private school students argued that "inasmuch as the[y] are residents of Allegany County and are within the age limits specified in § 7-101(a), they are entitled not merely to be admitted to the public schools of this state, but to any part or portion of the public school system which they choose." Holding that such a construction of the Education Code is "strained," the Maryland Court of Special Appeals held that dual enrollment programs of the sort suggested by the students would place an "unreasonable burden... on the efficient administration of the public school system." *Id.* at 320, 445 A.2d at 627.

The program at issue in *Thomas* was the "All-County High School Band." In 1978 and 1979, students enrolled at Bishop Walsh High School and the Calvary Christian Academy were permitted to participate, but in 1980, the School Board decided to limit eligibility to those enrolled in the Allegany County Public School System. Members of the band were chosen after an individual audition with music professors from neighboring universities who were paid by the Board. The professors analyzed each student's performance, suggested techniques for improvement, and ultimately rated the student on a scale from 1 to 6. Students with the highest ratings were selected for participation, and academic credit was given.

The Board of Education conceded that each of the students would have been eligible to audition for the All-County Music Program had they been full-time students in the public school system. In fact, three of the students who participated in the 1981 auditions for the band pursuant to the trial court's preliminary order had participated in prior years, and received the highest rating in the 1981 competition. There was no doubt that they would have been seated as members of the band if the prior policies had been continued. The Board admitted that it permitted cross-registration in vocational education programs. It defended the discrepancy on the grounds that the federal government required equal opportunity for private school students in vocational education programs, but that no law required them to do so in other parts of the academic program.

Holding that the exclusionary policy at issue "neither prohibits a parent from enrolling the child in a private school, nor deters the students from following the practices of their faith," the Maryland Court of Special Appeals rejected the students' equal protection and free exercise claims.

In the court's view, "[t]he rule merely prevents a child from reaping the benefits of a public school activity once the constitutional right to a private school education is exercised." *Id.* at 316, 445 A.2d at 625. Acknowledging that

> the administrative impact of a decision mandating the participation of the private students into this public school program appears to us to be trivial, the precedent as it affects the broader spectrum of school administration is of a far more deleterious nature. With the opening of such "Pandora's box", there would be no device to preclude, for example, a private school having difficulty securing a qualified chemistry teacher from unilaterally deciding to transport the entire student body to a nearby public school for their chemistry education. The potential for administrative disruption is obvious. Thus, while we may agree that little

> if any administrative hardship would inure to the Board in permitting these three students to participate in the All-County Band, it is not for this Court to hold that the Board must admit them, in view of the broader implications involved.

Id.

The Court of Special Appeals also rejected the equal protection claim, even though the only schools affected were those affiliated with religious groups. In the court's view, states need only show a rational basis when they decide to exclude nonpublic school children from the benefits of public programs, but opined that even were the compelling state interest test applicable, it would have been "met [in this case] in view of the *de minimis* burden on the appellant's freedom of religion and the legitimate interest in avoiding administrative inefficiency." *Id.* at 317, 445 A.2d at 626. See *Denis J. O'Connell High School v. Virginia High Sch. League*, 581 F.2d 81 (4th Cir. 1978) (upholding league rules which excluded parochial schools from membership on the grounds that they did not draw from defined geographic boundaries); *Valencia v. Blue Hen Conference*, 476 F. Supp. 809 (D. Del. 1979) (no violation of either free exercise or equal protection rights because of the state's interest in maintaining "competitive balance" among the teams in the league).

Notes

1. The case law in the States remains in conflict on the question of cross-registration. In *Snyder and Attorney General of the St. of Michigan v. Charlotte Public Sch. Dist.*, 421 Mich. 517, 365 N.W.2d 151 (1985), the Michigan Supreme Court held that local school boards are constitutionally *required* to offer opportunities for cross-enrollment. The Michigan Supreme Court specifically considered—and rejected—the view of the Maryland Court of Special Appeals in *Thomas v. Allegany County School District.* It cited two primary considerations in support of its conclusion: 1) non-discrimination on the basis of religion; and 2) the obligation of the state to educate all children within the district.

In *Special District for the Educ. and Training of Handicapped Children of St. Louis County v. Wheeler*, 408 S.W.2d 60 (Mo. 1966) (en banc), by contrast, the Missouri Supreme Court held that the practice of busing hearing-impaired private school children to the premises of a public school for special education services during the normal school day violated both the state constitution's requirement that public funds be spent only for the benefit of the public schools, and the state's compulsory education law. Unlike the Maryland Court of Special Appeals in *Thomas*, the Missouri court's rationale would make it impossible for students enrolled in nonpublic schools to take advantage of publicly funded programs. The only exception would appear to be cases in which federal law mandates a policy of nondiscrimination. *Cf.* 20 U.S.C.A. § 1415 (2002) (education of handicapped children); 20 U.S.C. § 5886 (2002) (programs for the systemic improvement of the education system). *Accord Kaptein by and through Kaptein v. Conrad Sch. Dist.*, 931 P.2d 1311, 1313 (Mont. 1997) (affirming school board refusal to permit student enrolled in religiously affiliated school to play on public school athletic teams); *Archbishop Walsh High Sch. v. Section VI of New York State Pub. High Sch. Athletic Ass'n, Inc.*, 629 N.Y.S.2d 346, 347 (A.D. 4th Dept. 1995) (rejecting private high school's contention that subjecting it to a vote before permitting it to participate in public high school athletic association violated its right to equal protection).

2. What do you make of the Michigan Supreme Court's nondiscrimination rationale? The case on which the court relied for its holding is *Traverse City Sch. Dist. v. At-*

torney General, 384 Mich. 390, 411, 185 N.W.2d 9 (1971), decided five years prior to the Supreme Court's holding in *Washington v. Davis*, 426 U.S. 229 (1976). In *Traverse City*, the Michigan Supreme Court considered what was widely known in Michigan as the "anti-parochiaid" amendment to the Michigan Constitution of 1963, Art. 8, §2. That amendment provided that:

> No public monies or property shall be appropriated or paid, or any public credit utilized, by the legislature or any other political subdivision or agency of the state directly or indirectly to aid or maintain any private, denominational or other nonpublic, preelementary, elementary, or secondary school. No payment, credit, tax benefit, exemption or deductions, tuition voucher, subsidy, grant or loan of public monies or property shall be provided, directly or indirectly, to support the attendance of any student or the employment of any person at any such nonpublic school or at any location or institution where instruction is offered in whole or in part to such nonpublic school students. The legislature may provide for the transportation of students to and from any school.

Michigan Const. Art. 8 §2, *quoted in Snyder v. Charlotte County Sch. Dist.*, 421 Mich. at 531, 365 N.W.2d at 157.

Rejecting as "shocking" a Michigan Attorney General opinion which construed the phrase "any location or institution where instruction is offered in whole or in part to such nonpublic school students" to include *public* schools, the *Traverse City* court held that such a construction would violate both the Equal Protection and Free Exercise Clauses. *Traverse City*, 384 Mich. at 412, 185 N.W.2d at 18. In the view of the Michigan court, the proposition was clearly intended to discriminate against students attending religiously affiliated schools.

In *Washington v. Davis*, the Supreme Court of the United States held that a showing of "intent" to discriminate against minorities is essential to make out a *prima facie* case under the Equal Protection Clause. Disparate impact is not enough. How, if at all, does the rationale of *Washington v. Davis* apply to exclusionary policies such as those involved in *Thomas* and *Wheeler*? Is it relevant that religious antagonisms have not been far below the surface in many of the struggles over the proper place of religion in the classroom? *See* Chapters Four and Ten. What factors should be considered by a local school board that asks your advice concerning a proposal to restrict ongoing cross-registration? Would your advice be the same if the proposal were designed to permit it for the first time?

3. To what extent do the values that animate the Test Clause of Article VI control the outcomes of these cases? In *Thomas v. Allegany School Board*, the Maryland Court of Special Appeals found that the burden on the school authorities was "trivial," but held that they had a rational basis for excluding part-time students because of the "Pandora's Box" that cross-registration would create. Is "rational basis" the appropriate standard of review in a claim against a school board for discrimination on the basis of religion or other prohibited classification? *See Church of Lukumi Babalu Aye, Inc. v. Hialeah*, 508 U.S. 520 (1993) (evidence of religious discrimination mandates application of high level review); *City of Cleburne v. Cleburne Living Center, Inc.*, 473 U.S. 432 (1985) (invalidating exclusionary zoning because it was based on stereotype, not facts). If not, what facts would be necessary to raise it to a higher level?

4. To the extent that history is relevant to your analysis of "shared-time" programs, see Healey, Jefferson on Religion in Public Education, at 202–226 (dis-

cussing Jefferson's proposals concerning the inclusion of religion in the curricula of the College of William and Mary, and the University of Virginia, as well as his proposal for theological "Schools on the Confines" of the campus).

5. What are the implications of the new information technologies on the question of "shared-time?" Many public school systems offer regular curricular offerings via digital data, video and voice links to children in remote locations, must they also open them to children enrolled in nonpublic schools? *See, e.g.*, Mississippi's online education program, EDNET (*http://www.msednet.org*) ("EDNET now provides two channels, broadcasting a wide variety of educational programs designed for use at home or in the classroom free of charge."). How do *Mitchell v. Helms, Agostini v. Felton,* and *Zobrest v. Catalina Foothills Sch. Dist.* affect your response?

b) Sharing the Cost and Responsibility for Providing Secular Educational Services—"Shared Time" on the Premises of Religiously Affiliated Schools

There are four ways for the State to deliver secular educational services to children enrolled in nonpublic schools: 1) reimburse the nonpublic schools for the costs they incur in providing specified secular services ("purchase of services"); 2) contract with nonpublic school teachers to provide the necessary services ("contracting out"); 3) hire teachers to deliver services to students on the premises of nonpublic schools ("distributed services" or "shared time"); and 4) provide the services directly to students on the premises of the public school system ("direct services").

"Purchase of services" and "contracting out" were the central features of the Pennsylvania and Rhode Island programs invalidated in *Lemon v. Kurtzman*, 403 U.S. 602 (1971), excerpted in Chapter Five § E(3)(b). The Pennsylvania program reimbursed nonpublic schools for the cost of teachers' salaries, textbooks, and instructional materials in specified secular subjects. The Rhode Island program paid a 15% salary supplement directly to teachers in nonpublic elementary schools as compensation for teaching secular subjects. Such programs are the most advantageous for both the students in nonpublic schools, and to the schools themselves. Because the students' regular teachers provide the services during the school day, there is no need for special classes, at least some portion of the cost of these services is borne by the State, and the nonpublic school maintains control of its own educational environment. All three of these factors led the Court to hold the Rhode Island and Pennsylvania programs unconstitutional.

After *Lemon*, the States and the federal government tried the "distributed services" model. In *Ball v. Sch. Dist. of Grand Rapids*, 473 U.S. 373 (1985), the State of Michigan created a "shared time" program that involved a lease of space in religiously affiliated school buildings that gave the State control over the learning environment, and the provision of regular public school teachers who would provide the services in the leased premises. In *Aguilar v. Felton*, 473 U.S. 402 (1985), federal funds were used to hire teachers who would provide special education programs to learning disabled children on the premises of nonpublic schools.

Although the record in *Aguilar* demonstrated that "in 19 years there ha[d] never been a single incident in which a Title I instructor 'subtly or overtly' attempted to 'indoctrinate the students in particular religious tenets at public expense,'" and one of the Justices who voted to invalidate the program conceded that it "ha[d] done so much good and little, if any, detectable harm," both programs were invalidated. *Id.* at 423 (O'Connor and Rehnquist JJ., dissenting), *quoting Ball v. School District of Grand Rapids*, 473 U.S. 373, 397 (1985); *id.* at 415 (Powell, J. concurring). The majority in *Aguilar* gave three reasons:

1. "[F]irst, state-paid teachers conducting classes in a sectarian environment might inadvertently (or intentionally) manifest sympathy with the sectarian aims [of the school] to the point of using public funds for religious educational purposes,"
2. "Second, the government's provision of secular instruction in religious schools produced a symbolic union of church and state that tended to convey a message to students and to the public that the State supported religion," and
3. [F]inally, the...program subsidized the religious functions of the religious schools by assuming responsibility for teaching secular subjects the schools would otherwise be required to provide.

Agostini v. Felton, 521 U.S. 203, 241–242 (Souter, Ginsburg, & Stevens, JJ., dissenting) (quoting *Aguilar*). The only alternative left was the most expensive for both the students and the public schools: transport the children eligible for services to the premises of the public schools and provide the services outside the normal school day.

Twelve years later, the defendants in *Aguilar* petitioned the Supreme Court for relief from the prospective effects of the District Court's injunction. Their first argument was that "the exorbitant costs of complying with the...injunction constitute a significant factual development warranting modification." 521 U.S. at 215–216. Second, they argued that the validity of *Aguilar* had been called into doubt by three "equal treatment" cases decided during the intervening years: *Witters v. Washington Dep't of Services for Blind*, 474 U.S. 481 (1986); *Zobrest v. Catalina Foothills Sch. Dist.*, 509 U.S. 1 (1993); and *Rosenberger v. Rector and Visitors of Univ. of Va.*, 515 U.S.819, 833 (1995). Their final argument was based on the statement of five Justices in *Board of Educ. of Kiryas Joel Village Sch. Dist. v. Grumet*, 512 U.S. 687 (1994) calling for *Aguilar* to be overruled.

In ***Agostini v. Felton***, 521 U.S. 203 (1997), a five-member majority agreed, and overruled both *Aguilar* and *Grand Rapids*. Writing for the Court, Justice O'Connor observed that its cases "have undermined the assumptions upon which *Ball* and *Aguilar* relied," but noted that "the general principles we use to evaluate whether government aid violates the Establishment Clause have not changed...What has changed since we decided *Ball* and *Aguilar* is our understanding of the criteria used to assess whether aid to religion has an impermissible effect." 521 U.S. 203.

Agostini is significant because of its reaffirmation of the evidentiary and remedial holdings in *Bowen v. Kendrick*, 487 U.S. 589, 614, 621–622 (1988), in which the Court held that churches and religiously-affiliated schools may participate in the development and implementation of publicly-funded sex-education programs for elementary and secondary school children that are general in their scope and religiously-neutral in their content. In *Bowen*, the Court held that it was not enough for plaintiffs to prove that an organization is "religiously-inspired" or affiliated with a religious organization to make it ineligible to participate in public welfare programs. The evidence must also demonstrate that the government actually engaged in unconstitutional behavior. After *Agostini*, the Court will no longer presume that support for the educational mission of religiously affiliated elementary or secondary school "will inevitably and impermissibly support religious indoctrination." *Agostini*, 521 U.S. at 886 (Souter, Stevens & Ginsburg, JJ., dissenting).

The judicial role envisioned in *Agostini* rests on a procedural due process model. Denial of the benefits under the statutory entitlement cannot take place until there is notice and an opportunity for the beneficiary to be heard, and proof that an illegal expenditure has been made. Writing for the dissenters, Justice Souter disagreed:

> I believe *Aguilar* was a correct and sensible decision, and my only reservation about its opinion is that the emphasis on the excessive entanglement produced by monitoring religious instructional content obscured those facts that independently called for the application of two central tenets of Establishment Clause jurisprudence. The State is forbidden to subsidize religion directly and is just as surely forbidden to act in any way that could reasonably be viewed as religious endorsement.

521 U.S. at 242 (Souter, Ginsburg, and Stevens, JJ. dissenting).

Cases such as these highlight the differences in approach between those Justices who object on Establishment Clause grounds to any assistance to children or to the schools, and those who view such programs as social welfare programs which should be equally available to all. *Cf. Capitol Square Rev. and Advisory Bd. v. Pinette*, 515 U.S. 753 (1995) (religious speech may not be excluded from a public forum); *Rosenberger* (university may not discriminate against religious viewpoints). The dissenters in *Pinette* and *Rosenberger* were of the view that content-based discrimination is constitutionally required whenever the circumstances are such that disclaimers would not be adequate to the task of dispelling the impression that the state supports the religious message. *See Pinette,* 515 U.S. at 817 (Ginsburg, J., dissenting) *and id.* at 797 (Stevens, J., dissenting). Writing for himself and Justices O'Connor and Breyer, Justice Souter took aim at the nondiscrimination principle that lies at the heart of the opinion written by Justice Scalia for the four-Justice plurality in *Pinette.*

> I disagree [with the plurality] that '[i]t has radical implications for our public policy to suggest that neutral laws are invalid whenever hypothetical observers may—*even reasonably*—confuse an incidental benefit to religion with State endorsement.' [citation omitted] On the contrary, when the reasonable observer would view a government practice as endorsing religion, I believe that it is our duty to hold the practice invalid.

Id. at 776–77 (Souter, O'Connor, and Breyer, JJ., concurring in part and concurring in the result). Do you agree? Does the application of such a rule in the context of education put a premium on the views of the hypothetical "reasonable observer" concerning the place of religion in the classroom, or on his or her definition of the concept of "religion" itself? *See generally* Chapters Ten and Thirteen.

F. Financing Educational Options

1. Public Financing and Religious Schools: The View of the Supreme Court, Circa 1968–1980

a) Legal and Historical Background

Before embarking on a detailed review of the Supreme Court's views on the issue of public support of religious schools, it will be useful to review a number of points made earlier in this Chapter.

Education is, by common agreement, one of the most important tasks undertaken by a community on behalf of itself and its children. In the words of the Supreme Court, the schools in a community are "a principle instrument in awakening the child to cultural values, in preparing him for later professional training, and in helping him to adjust normally to his environment." *Brown v. Board of Educ.*, 347 U.S. 483, 493 (1954). That view is echoed in state constitutions and statutes.

Article VI of the Ohio Constitution provides a useful example:

> §1 The principal of all funds, arising from the sale, or other disposition of lands, or other property, granted or entrusted to this state for educational and religious purposes, shall forever be preserved inviolate, and undiminished; and, the income arising therefrom, shall be faithfully applied to the specific objects of the original grants, or appropriations.
>
> §2 The general assembly shall make provisions by taxation, or otherwise, as, with the income arising from the school trust fund, will secure a thorough and efficient system of common schools throughout the state; but no religious or other sect, or sects, shall ever have any exclusive right to, or control of, any part of the school funds of this state.
>
> §3 Provision shall be made by law for the organization, administration and control of the public school system of the state supported by public funds: provided, that each school district embraced wholly or in part within any city shall have the power by referendum vote to determine for itself the number of members and the organization of the district board of education, and provision shall be made by law for the exercise of this power by such school districts.
>
> §4 There shall be a state board of education which shall be selected in such manner and for such terms as shall be provided by law. There shall be a superintendent of public instruction, who shall be appointed by the state board of education. The respective powers and duties of the board and of the superintendent shall be prescribed by law.

This provision has several objects: it creates a school trust fund; it mandates the creation *and maintenance* of a "thorough and efficient system of common schools throughout the state"; it seeks to eliminate any possibility that any sect, or sects, religious or otherwise, will control the school funds of the state; and it determines that, in most circumstances, the power to manage the system rests in the sound discretion of the state government. Ohio Const. Art. VI §§1–4 (1995). Other state constitutions contain similar provisions. *See, e.g.*, Arizona Const. Art. XI §6 (1995) ("The Legislature shall provide for a system of common schools by which a free school shall be established and maintained in every school district for at least six months in each year, which school shall be open to all pupils between the ages of six and twenty-one years.") Disputes over funding and control issues are frequent. *See generally* Michael Heise, *State Constitutions, School Finance Litigation, and the "Third Wave": From Equity to Adequacy*, 68 Temp. L. Rev. 1 (1995); William H. Clune, *Educational Adequacy: A Theory and Its Remedies*, 28 U. Mich. J.L. Ref. 481 (1995); Paul Freund, Comment, *Public Aid to Parochial Schools*, 82 Harv. L. Rev. 1680, 1692 (1969). Except for disputes relating to religiously affiliated schools and the many issues arising under the civil rights laws, most financing and control issues are litigated in state courts. *Compare San Antonio School Dist. v. Rodriguez*, 411 U.S. 1 (1973) (rejecting claims that the federal constitution requires equal state educational funding levels) *with Missouri v. Jenkins*, 495 U.S. 33 (1990) (addressing tax-related remedial powers of a court implementing a desegregation remedy) *and Plyler v. Doe*, 457 U.S. 202 (1982) (mandating the education of children who are undocumented aliens). *See Opinion of the Justices*, 624 So.2d 107 (Ala.

1993) (holding Alabama's school financing formula unconstitutional and mandating legislative change); *Serrano v. Priest* (I), 5 Cal.3d 584, 96 Cal. Rptr. 601, 487 P.2d 1241 (1971) (holding California's financing system unconstitutional); *Serrano v. Priest* (II), 18 Cal.3d 728, 135 Cal. Rptr. 345, 557 P.2d 929 (same); *Jenkins v. Leininger*, 277 Ill.App.3d 313, 659 N.E.2d 1366 (1st Dist. 1995) (rejecting the claim); *Campaign for Fiscal Equity, Inc. v. State*, 86 N.Y.2d 307, 655 N.E.2d 661, 631 N.Y.S.2d 565 (1995) (dismissing the New York constitutional claim, but remanding for trial on claims arising under Title VI of the Civil Rights Act of 1964), *on remand*, 187 Misc.2d 1, 719 N.Y.S.2d 475 (Sup. Ct. 2001) (holding that the financing system violates Title VI, but remanding to the Legislature); *DeRolfe v. State*, 677 N.E.2d 733, 742 (Ohio 1997) (*DeRolfe I*), *reh'g and clarification*, 678 N.E.2d 886 (Ohio 1997), *clarification*, 699 N.E.2d 518 (Ohio 1998) (invalidating Ohio's system under the State constitution and remanding to the legislature), *DeRolfe v. State*, 728 N.E.2d 993 (Ohio 2000) (*DeRolfe II*) (requiring further changes), *DeRolfe v. State* (*DeRolfe* III), 754 N.E.2d 1184 (Ohio 2001) (accepting legislative changes); *Carrollton-Farmers Branch Independent School Dist. v. Edgewood Independent School Dist.*, 826 S.W.2d 489 (Tex. 1992). *See generally* John Dayton, Serrano *and Its Progeny: An Analysis of 30 Years of School Funding Litigation*, 157 Ed. Law Rep. 447 (2001); Michael Heise, *State Constitutional Litigation, Educational Finance, and Legal Impact: An Empirical Analysis*, 63 U. Cin. L. Rev. 1735(1995).

Although it has long been assumed that the states organized their public schools on the premise that secular education can be isolated from all religious training, the intense debates over the constitutionality of organized and voluntary school prayer, the teaching of evolution, and Bible reading in public schools cast considerable doubt on the accuracy of that assumption. *See* Chapter Four § A. Commenting on the Supreme Court's decision to ban New York's "Regent's Prayer," *Engle v. Vitale*, 370 U.S. 421 (1962), the June 27, 1962 edition of *The Wall Street Journal* observed that

> [if] the majority doctrine stands, then anything that smacks of religious instruction or the subtle imparting of a religious viewpoint in the public schools becomes suspect. Do not suppose this to be fanciful exaggeration. Already the Bible is banned from some schoolrooms. Already a Florida court decision has declared school observances of Easter and Christmas to be unconstitutional, and similar efforts are afoot elsewhere.

The Wall Street Journal, June 27, 1962, *quoted in* Religious Liberty in the Supreme Court: The Cases that Define the Debate over Church and State 138 (Terry Eastland ed. 1993).

Debates over the closely related topics of educational finance, local control, the content of education, and the role of religion in the schools have been going on since the founding period. The Northwest Ordinance of 1787 contains the now-famous observation that "Religion, morality, and knowledge [are] necessary to good government and the happiness of mankind, [and that] schools and the means of education shall forever be encouraged." Northwest Ordinance, Article III § 14, 1 Stat. 51 (1787). Except for Virginia, which did not have a public school system until 1871, the states made provisions for support of education at the local level, and in many of them, the link between religion and education was palpable. *See* Herbert W. Titus, *1991–1992 Church/State Symposium: No Taxation or Subsidization: Two Indispensable Principles of Freedom of Religion*, 22 Cumb. L. Rev. 505 (1992).

In Virginia, where the only education provided at public expense was designed to assure that pauper children would not become charges on the community, the Assembly twice rejected Thomas Jefferson's proposals to create a free public school system. It did, however, create the State's "Literary Fund" in 1810 to provide public assistance to various educational endeavors. Jefferson was determined to devise an elementary school system which was funded by general tax revenues, and which would be as free of sectarian influence as the politics of the time might permit. "A Bill for Establishing a System of Public Education" § 11, *in* Roy J. Honeywell, The Educational Work of Thomas Jefferson 233–235 (1963).

Jefferson lost in his attempt to head off the political movement to provide funding to the Sunday Schools out of the Literary Fund, and overt public funding of Sunday Schools soon followed. *See* Sadie Bell, The Church, The State, and Education in Virginia 334 (1969). By the 1840s, a number of Virginia's counties were reporting grants of public assistance to support the many denominational Sunday Schools that had been formed to help eliminate illiteracy by teaching both children and adults to read the Bible.

By the time the Civil War ended, however, there was considerable debate over using public funds to finance schools which were identified with a specific faith tradition, and by the end of World War I, attempts were made to eliminate religious and other private schools altogether. *See Pierce v. Society of Sisters*, 268 U.S. 466 (1925), excerpted in § C above, and the materials on the proposed Blaine and "Christian Education" amendments in Chapter Four § B.

The states have taken a number of approaches to this question. They are summarized briefly in § F(2) below.

b) Everson v. Board of Education*: The Supreme Court "Federalizes" the Issue of Public School Finance*

In *Everson v. Board of Educ.*, 330 U.S. 1 (1947), the Supreme Court assumed federal control over state attempts to defray some of the education-related costs incurred by parents who opt out of the public school system. At issue was the decision of New Jersey educational authorities to reimburse parents for the cost of bus transportation for children enrolled in public and non-profit private schools. The case is significant for three reasons relevant to this discussion:

- It marks the first time the Establishment Clause was applied to the states via the Due Process Clause of the Fourteenth Amendment, see Chapter Five § C, and sets the tone for later cases which develop a jurisprudence of the clause which centers on school finance litigation. See Chart 6-4 below.
- The Supreme Court accepted the proposition that a dissenting taxpayer states a claim under the United States Constitution when tax funds are used to support religious education; and
- The Court held, by a 5-4 margin, that free bus transportation was a public service akin to police and fire protection, and that states could provide such services to students in religiously affiliated schools if they chose to do so.

Nevertheless, the fault lines within the Court were clearly drawn in *Everson*. The majority in *Everson* adopted the "child benefit" theory, and viewed transportation services for school children and part and parcel of a public safety program. The dissenting Justices refused to draw that distinction. In their view, aid to the students is aid to the school. And because, in their view, the school is an essential component of the religious mission of the church, they were of the view that the First Amendment prohibits *any* aid to religious schools.

Drawing heavily on the Virginia experience in the disestablishment struggle of the 1780s to bolster their position, the dissenting Justices in *Everson* argued that any aid to religiously affiliated schools is taxation for the support of religion. In their view, the state may support only secular education, notwithstanding Justice Robert Jackson's point that there is a divergence of view on the question of "whether such a disjunction [between religious and secular education] is possible, and, if possible, whether it is wise." *Everson* 330 U.S. at 23–24 (Jackson, J., dissenting).

The importance of this philosophical distinction should not be underestimated. Consider, once again, the words of Justice Jackson in *Everson*:

> It is no exaggeration to say that the whole historic conflict in temporal policy between the Catholic Church and non-Catholics comes to a focus in their respective school policies. The Roman Catholic Church, counseled by experience in many ages and many lands and with all sorts and conditions of men, takes what, from the viewpoint of its own progress and the success of its mission, is a wise estimate of the importance of education to religion. It does not leave the individual to pick up religion by chance. It relies on early and indelible indoctrination in the faith and order of the Church by the word and example of persons consecrated to the task.
>
> Our public school, if not a product of Protestantism, at least is more consistent with it than with the Catholic culture and scheme of values. It is a relatively recent development dating from about 1840. [citing to Cubberley, PUBLIC EDUCATION IN THE UNITED STATES, ch. VI (1934); Knight, EDUCATION IN THE UNITED STATES, ch. VIII (1941)] It is organized on the premise that secular education can be isolated from all religious teaching so that the school can inculcate all needed temporal knowledge and also maintain a strict and lofty neutrality as to religion. The assumption is that after the individual has been instructed in worldly wisdom he will be better fitted to choose his religion. Whether such a disjunction is possible, and if possible whether it is wise, are questions I need not try to answer."

Everson 330 U.S. at 23–24.

But what if the reason Catholics and other minority religious groups in the United States formed their own schools was that they viewed the religion and culture of the public school system as either overtly hostile to their religious beliefs, or unwilling to accommodate them? There is no question that officially-sanctioned hostility to immigrants in general, and to Catholic immigrants in particular, was a key component of the attempt by the State of Oregon to close all non-public schools, see *Pierce v. Society of Sisters*, §C above, and the argument of the State of Wisconsin in *Wisconsin v. Yoder*, excerpted in Chapter Five, was that children educated in the Amish tradition would grow up to be "ignorant." *See also* Chapter Four. Would laws permitting "equal access" be constitutional as a remedy for past, intentional discrimination on the basis of religion or viewpoint?

c) *Taxpayer Standing: Articulating a Basis for Finding a Constitutionally Cognizable Interest*

Taxpayers do not generally have standing in the federal courts to challenge expenditures they believe to be either constitutionally infirm or fiscally unwise. In *Frothingham v. Mellon*, 262 U.S. 447 (1923), the Supreme Court rejected a constitutional challenge to the federal Maternity Act by a taxpayer who alleged that she was injured in that capacity because "the effect of the appropriations complained of will be to increase the burden of future taxation and thereby to take her property without due process of law." *Id.* at 486. Rejecting the theory of the lawsuit, the Court held that the taxpayer in could not, at least in this case, demonstrate

> not only that the statute is invalid, but that [s]he has sustained or is in immediate danger of sustaining some direct injury as a result of its enforcement, and not merely that he suffers in some indefinite way in common with people generally.

262 U.S. at 488.

In *Flast v. Cohen*, 392 U.S. 83 (1968), however, the Court faced a challenge by federal taxpayers to the Elementary and Secondary Education Act of 1965, which would have permitted federal financing of textbooks, and the teaching of reading, arithmetic, and other subjects in both public and private schools. Holding that the taxpayers had standing, the Court announced a two-part inquiry to determine whether a "logical nexus" existed between the plaintiff's status (taxpayer) and the claim to be adjudicated (support for students at religiously affiliated schools).

> The nexus demanded of federal taxpayers has two aspects to it. First, the taxpayer must establish a logical link between that status and the type of legislative enactment attacked. Thus, a taxpayer will be a proper party to allege the unconstitutionality only of exercises of congressional power under the taxing and spending clause of Art. I, §8, of the Constitution. It will not be sufficient to allege an incidental expenditure of tax funds in the administration of an essentially regulatory statute...Secondly, the taxpayer must establish a nexus between that status and the precise nature of the constitutional infringement alleged. Under this requirement, the taxpayer must show that the challenged enactment exceeds specific constitutional limitations imposed upon the exercise of the congressional taxing and spending power and not simply that the enactment is generally beyond the powers delegated to Congress by Art. I, §8. When both nexuses are established, the litigant will have shown a taxpayer's stake in the outcome of the controversy and will be a proper and appropriate party to invoke a federal court's jurisdiction.

392 U.S. at 102–103.

The Court held that the challenge in *Flast*, and by implication all challenges to direct expenditures by federal or state authorities for religiously affiliated schools, met the nexus requirement. The effect has been to permit a wide range of federal cases challenging state and federal funding designed to defray part of the costs associated with religiously affiliated education.

The Court, however, has consistently *refused* to find standing under the *Flast* rationale in controversies other than those challenging government spending powers under the Establishment Clause. *See United States v. Richardson*, 418 U.S. 166 (1974) (Accounting Clause of Art. I §9, cl. 7); *Schlesinger v. Reservists Committee to Stop the War*, 418 U.S. 208 (1974) (Incompatibility Clause, Art. I §6, cl. 2); *Simon v. Eastern Kentucky Welfare Rights Organization*, 418 U.S. 26 (1976) (rejecting standing where plaintiffs alleged that an IRS Revenue Ruling was not authorized by Internal Revenue Code).

Most recently, in *Valley Forge Christian College v. Americans United for Separation of Church and State,* 454 U.S. 464 (1982), the Court found that the taxpayers had not met their burden under *Flast* even though the Establishment Clause was alleged to control the outcome. The action at issue was the transfer of surplus federal property—77 acres of real estate—to a college that trained Christian laymen and ministers. Holding that the plaintiffs had not satisfied the first prong of the *Flast* nexus requirement, the Court found it significant that the challenge was to the transfer of specific property by the Secretary of Health, Education and Welfare, rather than to the substance of the Congressional enactment on which it rested.

This result raises a question: Does taxpayer standing exist in any context *outside* the Establishment Clause? The answer, at least to this point, appears to be "no." *Cf. Allen v. Wright,* 468 U.S. 737 (1984) (parents of black school children attending public schools undergoing desegregation did not have standing to challenge IRS actions granting tax exempt status to racially discriminatory private schools). *See* Chapter Nine § D.

d) The Supreme Court on Aid to Religious Schools, 1968–2002

The case law on aid to students enrolled in religiously affiliated schools has developed at a fairly steady pace since 1968. Close examination of the cases, and of the many opinions filed by the Justices in each, indicates that several themes are involved in each: (1) the important role that education plays in the life of a community; (2) the character of education as a parental responsibility subject to control and oversight by state authorities; (3) the impressionability and youth of children, at least through secondary school, which makes them particularly susceptible to indoctrination; (4) the political importance of the "common school" experience in training future citizens in a pluralistic democracy; (5) the view that church authorities are making authority claims concerning the role of religion in education which are fundamentally at odds with those made by state education authorities; (6) the view that deviation from the common school model will lead to political divisiveness along religious lines; (7) the view that "neutrality" in education is at best, an aspiration, and, at worst, inconsistent with the very concept of liberal education; and (8) a difference of view concerning the federal oversight role in matters of educational funding and philosophy, whether exercised on behalf of parents and children, or in favor of dissenting taxpayers who do not wish to see their tax dollars spent for education which is not subject to the control of the community.

There are two basic positions within the Court on the topic of state support for students enrolled in religiously-affiliated schools: Some Justices take the position that the First Amendment requires the state remain neutral between and among religions, and between religions and secular points of view concerning the role of religion in education. This faction will generally permit the state to allocate educational benefits to all students, regardless of their school of enrollment, as long as the assistance is provided in a religiously neutral public benefits program. Their view is best characterized as one that permits "formal" neutrality in the distribution of public benefits. *Cf.* Douglas Laycock, *Formal, Substantive and Disaggregated Neutrality Toward Religion,* 39 DePaul L. Rev. 993, 993–1018 (1990). Such an approach favors the decentralization of control over education.

Other Justices are of the view that the Establishment Clause was intended to eliminate any form or vestige of official government support for religion, and to eliminate the possibility that the body politic will be divided along religious lines. In their view, the public schools are to be viewed as a religiously neutral educational setting, and that, to the extent children or parents desire to take advantage of publicly funded educational opportunities, they must do so in the public schools. This approach views education as a state function, and federalizes a set of philosophical norms concerning the role of religion, religious training, and religious ritual, in the education of primary and secondary school children.

Review of the case law indicates that there are as many variations on these themes as there are Justices willing to write opinions. Some Justices will distinguish aid given to the institution from that given to the students or their parents; others will not. Some Justices will examine the demographics, program, and character of the particular institutions involved in an attempt to determine whether the aid flows to an institution which is "pervasively sectarian," while others will simply assume that the religious character of the institution is enough to invalidate the assistance. In the few cases involving aid to college and university level students or their schools, in fact, the Court has even been willing to consider the maturity level of the students as a factor relevant to the "sectarian" character of the institution. *See Columbia Union College v. Oliver*, 254 F.3d 496 (4th Cir. 2001); *Tilton v. Richardson*, 403 U.S. 672 (1971) (holding that college students are less susceptible to religious indoctrination than younger children, and that aid to religiously-affiliated colleges simply did not present the same danger of government support for the religious mission of the supporting churches as was present in cases involving religious primary and secondary schools). State case law follows much the same pattern.

What do you make of the Court's holdings? Consider the materials on "characterization" and the Incorporation Doctrine from Chapter One § A. The Court "incorporated" the Establishment Clause via the Due Process Clause of the Fourteenth Amendment. What kind of "liberty" interest does it protect?

When viewed from the perspective of a dissenting taxpayer, the nature of the injury to one's liberty interests appears to be limited to a non-association claim, in which the dissenter complains that he or she is being forced to participate in programs or activities which his or her conscience will not permit, see *Abood v. Detroit Bd. of Educ.*, 431 U.S. 209 (1977) (dissenting union member could not be forced to pay union dues used for political purposes); *Wooley v. Maynard*, 430 U.S. 705 (1977) (government may not compel driver to display state motto against his wishes). Whether described as a free exercise right, or a generalized non-association claim, the claim centers on the assault on individual conscience suffered by the dissenting taxpayer. The case law is summarized below:

Chart 6-4 The Supreme Court on Support for Students Enrolled at Religiously Affiliated Schools (1947–2002)

Case	Permits	Forbids	Reason
Everson v. Bd. of Ed. 330 U.S. 1 (1947)	Reimbursement to parents of transportation costs		Generally available, neutral public welfare program for children
Bd. of Ed. v. Allen 392 U.S. 236 (1968)	Loan of secular textbooks		Aid to children
Lemon v. Kurtzman 403 U.S. 602 (1971)	Loan of secular textbooks	Teacher salary supplements	Excessive administrative entanglement
Tilton v. Richardson 403 U.S. 672 (1971)	Grants to religiously-affiliated colleges under federal program supporting construction of college facilities used for secular purposes		Schools were not "pervasively sectarian," college students are less susceptible to religious indoctrination than younger children, and nature of aid did not lead to excessive entanglement.
Hunt v. McNair 413 U.S. 734 (1973)	Use of state bonding authority to finance secular program facilities at religiously affiliated colleges		School was not so sectarian as to make it impossible to separate religious and secular components of its program.
Comm. for Public Ed. v. Nyquist 413 U.S. 756 (1973)		Tuition tax credit to parents	Aids religion, Catholic schools primary beneficiary.
Sloan v. Lemon 413 U.S. 756 (1973)		Tuition reimbursement to parents	Aids religion, Catholic schools primary beneficiary.
Levitt v. Comm. for Pub. Ed. 413 U.S. 472 (1973)		Per capita reimbursement to school of state-mandated service costs	Aids religion, no guarantee that aid would be used to defray only secular costs.
Meek v. Pittenger 421 U.S. 349 (1975)	Loan of secular textbooks		Approved in *Allen*
		On-premises educational services by public school personnel	Possibility that public school teachers might advance religious mission.
		Loan of instructional materials, such as maps, globes, A.V. equipment	Aids religious mission by making schools more viable.
Roemer v. Bd of Public Works 426 U.S. 736 (1976) (overruled: Mitchell)	Annual per-student subsidy to private universities amounting to 15% of the aid given to students in state institutions		Institutions were not so "pervasively sectarian" as to make it impossible to separate religious and secular components of the education program.
		Cost of bus transportation to field trips	Might advance religious mission.

Chart 6-4 *continued* The Supreme Court on Support for Students Enrolled at Religiously Affiliated Schools (1947–2002)

Case	Permits	Forbids	Reason
Wolman v. Walter 433 U.S. 229 (1977)	Off-premises diagnostic/ remedial services		No possible religious effect.
(overruled: Mitchell)	Loan of secular textbooks		Approved in *Allen.*
	Funds to distribute and score standardized tests used in public schools		Important secular purpose, no religious involvement in preparation for tests.
		Loans of instructional materials to students	Might advance religious mission.
New York v. Cathedral Academy 434 U.S. 125 (1977)		Reimbursement to schools under program held invalid in *Levitt*	Advanced religion, fostered excessive entanglement. Reliance on program by schools prior to challenge irrelevant.
Comm. for Public Ed. v. Regan 444 U.S. 646 (1980)	Reimbursement to school for standardized testing and reporting services		No religious effect. Repaid only administrative costs.
Mueller v. Allen 463 U.S. 388 (1983)	Tax deduction for parents' educational expenses at any school		Benefit to taxpayers, not sectarian schools.
Aguilar v. Felton 473 U.S. 402 (1985) (overruled: *Agostini*)		On-premises remedial education for poor children	No guarantee that public officials would not advance religious mission.
Sch. Dist. of Grand Rapids v. Ball 473 U.S. 373 (1985) (overruled: *Agostini*)		"Shared time" public school teachers teaching secular subjects on private school premises	Frees up resources for religious function; creates "symbolic" link between church and state.
Witters v. Wash Dept. of Serv. for the Blind 474 U.S. 481 (1986)	Tuition at school of handicapped college student's choice		College student had right to choose and program was neutral.
Bowen v. Kendrick 484 U.S. 942 (1987)	Grants to churches and religious institutions to develop secular sex education programs approved by federal government		Religious institutions may participate in general social welfare programs, but may not utilize funds to advance religion.
Zobrest v. Catalina Foothills Sch. Dist. 509 U.S. 1 (1993)	On-premises sign-language interpreter for deaf child in religious secondary school		Benefits available in otherwise neutral program.
Agostini v. Felton, 521 U.S. 203 (1997) (overrules *Aguilar & Grand Rapids*)	On premises special education teachers for poor children		Applies methodology of *Bowen v. Kendrick*, and rejects assumptions about indoctrination in favor of fact-based conclusions.
Mitchell v. Helms, 530 U.S. 793 (2000)	Instructional materials, including library books, maps, globes, computer equipment, software, and audio-visual equipment		No evidence that materials were used for "specifically religious activity."

Chart 6-4 *continued* The Supreme Court on Support for Students Enrolled at Religiously Affiliated Schools (1947–2002)

Case	Permits	Forbids	Reason
Zelman v. Simmons-Harris 122 S.Ct. 2460 (2002)	Tuition vouchers for private, public, and religiously affiliated schools		Voucher program offers "true private choice," is "neutral with respect to religion, and provides assistance directly to a broad class of citizens". "*Nyquist* does not govern neutral educational assistance programs that...offer aid directly to a broad class of individual recipients defined without regard to religion."

An alternative formulation of the dissenter's claim would be a "structural" one, which does not necessarily implicate individual rights at all. *See* Chapter One, Chart 1-2, and Chapter Five § E, discussing the contours of current Establishment Clause jurisprudence. Viewed in this fashion the limit imposed by the Establishment Clause might be characterized as "jurisdictional"; that is, it can be violated by government action alone—without regard to its impact on individuals.

Refer, once again, to Charts 1-1 and 1-2 Chapter One § A. How would you characterize the constitutional claims of students or parents who are *denied* public assistance because they or their parents have chosen to opt-out of the secular educational model offered by the state at public expense? Keep in mind that an education at public expense is generally a benefit made available under the state constitution to all children of school age. Does this make a difference? If so, what difference does it make? Would such students, their parents, teachers, or schools have equal protection, Establishment Clause, "conditioned-benefit," and religious test for public trust or office claims as well? *See generally* Chapters One, Five § E, and Eight § G (discussing the No Religious Test Clause, U.S. Const. Art. VI).

The equal protection components of such arguments rest, at least in part, on the long history of religious prejudice that accompanied what some writers have called America's *de facto* establishment of Protestant Christianity. The Establishment Clause components relate to attempts to eliminate any vestige of religion from the public education system, and the inevitable disputes over curriculum, and the occasional discrimination that such attempts will engender. *See, e.g.*, Chapter Five § J (discussing the Equal Protection Clause). The "conditioned benefit" claims arise when the state seeks to place a condition (inculcation from a secular viewpoint) on an otherwise available public benefit (primary and secondary education at public expense). *See Pierce v. Society of Sisters* in § C, above. No Religious Test issues arise when the state places religious conditions on the persons or institutions with whom it will enter into an employment or subcontracting relationship. Such conditions are discussed at greater length in Chapter Eight, §§ F–G.

2. School Choice: Privatization and the Quest for Family Control of Education

a) The Concept of "School Choice"

The term "school choice" covers a wide variety of programs and plans. It is necessary, therefore, to distinguish between and among the wide variety of meanings the term has acquired.

Viewed from the perspective of those who consume educational services (parents, children and taxpayers), education in the United States is not a matter of "choice": it is compulsory. Every State requires children to attend school, and will prosecute parents who refuse or neglect to educate them. *See, e.g.*, Ohio Rev. Code § 3321.38 (2002) and discussion in § E(3) of this chapter. As a result, the first choice is not *whether* to educate the children (that is already required), but *how*.

There are only two widely available choices: attend a school run by the government and funded by tax dollars, or attend a school which is run and funded, either in whole or in part, by the private sector (including home schooling). A third alternative, cross-registration or "shared time," is not widely available. *See Lanner v. Wimmer* and *Thomas v. Allegany County Board of Education*, summarized above, and notes following. Charter and community schools that are publicly funded, but privately managed, are also emerging in communities around the country.

Choices *within* the government run, managed and funded educational system, are: neighborhood choice, inter-district choice, state-wide choice, enrollment lotteries, pairs, clusters and magnet schools, charter schools, and a host of other options designed to make the public school systems more responsive to their constituency, including private management. The debates over these kinds of choices generally relate to equity, political culture, and effectiveness in the existing public school system. *See generally*, Stephen D. Sugarman, Frank R. Kemerer, ed., School Choice and Social Controversy: Politics, Policy, and Law (1999); Thomas L. Good, Jennifer S. Braden, The Great School Debate: Choice, Vouchers, and Charters (2000); Terry M. Moe, Schools, Vouchers, and the American Public (2001). Much of that debate has taken place over the issue of school desegregation and finance reform. *See, e.g.*, John Dayton, Serrano *and Its Progeny: An Analysis of 30 Years of School Funding Litigation*, 157 Ed. Law Rep. 447 (2001); Daniel J. Monti, A Semblance of Justice (1985).

Notes

1. There is an extensive literature in the field. For a general review of the school choice issue from those who advocate for "choice," *see* John E. Coons and Stephen D. Sugarman, Education by Choice: The Case for Family Control (1978); Abigail Thernstrom, School Choice in Massachusetts (1991); John E. Chubb and Terry M. Moe, Politics, Markets, And America's Schools (1990); Sheldon Richman, Separating School and State: How to Liberate America's Families (1994); Denise C. Morgan, *The New School Finance Litigation: Acknowledging that Race Discrimination in Public Education is More than Just a Tort* 96 Nw. U. L. Rev. 99 (2001); Peter W. Cookston, Jr., School Choice: The Struggle for the Soul of American Education (1994). Contrary perspectives can be found in, among others, the following: Elizabeth F. Lugg and R. Andrew Lugg, *Vouchers as School Choice: An Analysis of* Jackson v. Benson—The *Milwaukee Parental Choice Program*, 29 J.L. & Educ. 175 (2000); Andrew Stark, *Moving the Baseline: The Contradiction at the Core of Constitutional Discourse Over State Aid to Parochial Schools*, 42 Wm. & Mary L. Rev. 1437 (2001) (characterizing the problem as one of "incentive" and "fungibility"); Steven K. Green, *The Legal Argument Against Private School Choice*, 62 U. Cin. L. Rev. 37 (1993).

2. To what extent ought school choice be available as a remedy for children in school districts that have not been, or cannot be, effectively desegregated? This is one of

the issues in *Zelman v. Simmons-Harris*, 122 S.Ct. 2460 (2002), excerpted below. Although "choice" became a synonym for resistance to desegregation in a number of Southern states, the choices available at that time were one-sided: Black children had no choice. In the years following *Brown* "choice" also became a rallying cry for some who wished to avoid the desegregation orders of the federal courts. Today, however, the disputes center on whether school choice programs can be structured in a way that provides meaningful choices for minority students. *Compare* Brief of the NAACP Legal Defense and Educational Fund, Inc., and the National Association for the Advancement of Colored People as Amici Curiae in Support of Respondents, *Zelman v. Simmons-Harris*, U.S. Supreme Court 122 S.Ct. 2460 (2002) (opposing the Cleveland voucher plan because it "raises grave dangers of dissipating resources that are essential to the preservation and ultimate improvement of public education in Cleveland and of fostering the resegregation of schooling in Cleveland (developments completely inconsistent with the purposes of the Brown decisions)), *with* Amici Curiae Brief for the Center for Education Reform, et al. in Support of Petitioners, *Zelman v. Simmons-Harris*, U.S. Supreme Court 122 S.Ct. 2460 (2002) (supporting the Cleveland voucher plan because the "Court's holdings under the Establishment, Due Process, and Equal Protection Clauses show that evidence outlining the purpose, operation, and effects of a specific education reform effort is just as essential to an inquiry under the Establishment Clause as it would be to a review of that reform under *Brown v. Board of Education*, 347 U.S. 483 (1954), and its progeny.")

See generally Denise C. Morgan, *The New School Finance Litigation: Acknowledging that Race Discrimination in Public Education is More than Just a Tort*, 96 Nw. U. L. Rev. 99 (2001); Paul Diller, *Integration Without Classification: Moving Toward Race-Neutrality in the Pursuit of Public Elementary and Secondary School Diversity*, 99 Mich. L. Rev. 1999 (2001); Marilyn V. Yarbrough, *Still Separate And Still Unequal*, *in* Symposium: *Brown v. Board of Education After Forty Years: Confronting the Promise*, 36 Wm. & Mary L. Rev. 685 (1995); Greg D. Andres, Comment, *Private School Voucher Remedies In Education Cases*, 62 U. Chi. L. Rev. 795 (1995).

3. One of the more challenging developments in educational reform is the advent of for-profit schools and management of public schools by both profit-making and non-profit organizations such as universities. What makes a "public" school "public"? What is the character of a "common" school? Does its character as a public or "common" school change when private contractors manage it? *See generally* Frank R. Kemerer, and Catherine Maloney, Commentary, *The Legal Framework for Educational Privatization and Accountability*, 150 Ed. Law Rep. 589 (2001); Cheryl L. Wade, *For-Profit Corporations That Perform Public Functions: Politics, Profit, and Poverty*, 51 Rutgers L. Rev. 323 (1999); Lewis D. Solomon, *The Role of For-Profit Corporations in Revitalizing Public Education: A Legal and Policy Analysis*, 24 U. Tol. L. Rev. 883 (1993); Stephen D. Sugarman, Book Review, *Part of the Solution Rather Than Part of the Problem: A Role for American Private Elementary and Secondary Schools in the 1990s*, 31 Wm. & Mary L. Rev. 681 (1990). If a private contractor manages a public school, does the contractor become a "state actor" whose activities are subject to the constraints of the Fourteenth Amendment? *Compare Marsh v. Alabama*, 326 U.S. 501 (1946) (company town) *with Jackson v. Metropolitan Edison Co.*, 419 U.S. 345 (1974) (holding that management of a utility is not a public function) and *Memphis Light, Gas and Water Div. v. Craft*, 536 U.S. 1 (1978) (holding that where utility is operated by government and state law provides that termination of service may only be "for cause" notice and hearing opportunity must be provided).

b) Financing Education at Private Schools: Developing Case Law

The most difficult issue in the lore of school choice is freedom to choose a school in which religion is an integral part of the curriculum. In this context, the developing case law reflects age-old divisions concerning the role of the state with respect to education, the proper relationship of religion to education, and need to avoid close relationships between church and state, especially those which involve the transfer of money from one to the other. Not surprisingly, there is considerable disagreement between the state and federal courts, and among the states.

1) Federal Case Law

The most important inquiries under the Religious Liberty Guarantee taken as a whole—the No Religious Test Clause and the First and Fourteenth Amendments—have been "neutrality" and "equal treatment." Examination of the federal case law since *Everson v. Board of Education*, 330 U.S. 1 (1947), summarized in Chart 6-4, illustrates the difficulty the Court has had in articulating a federal standard based on these criteria.

This, of course, is not a new debate. In *Bradfield v. Roberts*, 175 U.S. 291 (1899), the Court held that the religious character of an association alone is an insufficient reason to exclude either the association or its members, but in *Everson* Justices Jackson, Rutledge, Frankfurter and Burton, argued that "the state can maintain its neutrality and avoid partisanship" only by drawing lines that distinguish religious from "wholly secular" endeavors. *Everson*, 330 U.S. at 59–60. The opinions in *Everson* elaborated three positions regarding "neutrality":

- *Neutrality with respect to religious and non-religious groups*: In the *Everson* majority opinion, Justice Hugo Black argued that *government* must be "neutral in its relations with groups of religious believers and non-believers." *Everson v. Board of Educ.*, 330 U.S. 1, 18 (1947). This approach is the basis of an "equal treatment" rationale.
- *Content Neutrality*: Dissenting in *Everson*, Justice Robert Jackson asserted that the *content* of the educational program must be neutral respecting religion: "Our public school... is organized on the premise that secular education can be isolated from all religious teaching so that the school can inculcate all needed temporal knowledge and also maintain a strict and lofty neutrality as to religion." *Id.* at 29 (Jackson, J. dissenting).
- *Government Actions Can Foster Only Secular Goals*: Justice Wiley Rutledge, by contrast, argued that the Constitution is not neutral. It makes the choice in favor of secular education: "... [E]ducation which includes religious training and teaching, and its support, have been made matters of private right and function not public, by the very terms of the First Amendment," and therefore it "does not make the state unneutral to withhold what the Constitution forbids it to give." *Id.* at 51, 59 (Rutledge, Frankfurter, Jackson & Burton, JJ., dissenting).

In ***Witters v. Washington Department of Services for the Blind***, 474 U.S. 481 (1986), *rev'g* 102 Wash.2d 624, 689 P.2d 53 (1984), the Court held that the Establishment Clause permits the State of Washington to pay for the education of a young, blind ministerial student who qualified for vocational assistance under Washington state law. *Witters* presented essentially two issues for Supreme Court review: First, does the Establishment Clause forbid the state from supplying money for educational purposes which it knows will be used for training in a religiously affiliated institution? Second, would a requirement that an otherwise qualified individual with a disability must forego religious training as a condition for receiving vocational assistance from the state be a burden on the free exercise of religion?

The majority opinion by Justice Thurgood Marshall focused the inquiry on *who* makes the determination regarding the use of the funds: the individual or the state:

> [W]hether... extension of aid to petitioner and the use of that aid by petitioner to support his religious education is a permissible transfer similar to [a] hypothetical salary donation [by a State employee to a church], or is an impermissible "direct" subsidy."

474 U.S. at 488. The focus of the majority opinion in the Washington Supreme Court was precisely the opposite: it is the *use* to which the funds are put which is critical, and any state funds dedicated to religious education, whether by an individual or the state, has the primary effect of advancing religion. *Witters v. State Comm'n for the Blind*, 102 Wash. 2d 624, 629, 689 P. 2d 53, 56 (1984).

Unlike Justice Marshall, Justice Powell took direct aim at the Washington Supreme Court's theory of the case and rejects it on the basis of the holding in *Mueller v. Allen*, 463 U.S. 388 (1983), that the nature and consequences of the challenged educational assistance program must be "viewed *as a whole*." *Witters*, 474 U.S. at 491. In Justice Powell's view, the Court has never taken the position that the Establishment Clause prohibits government aid to individuals who are likely to use it for religious purposes, *Id.*, 474 U.S. at 491 & n. 4, and wrote separately to make the point that the majority opinion's "omission of *Mueller v. Allen*... may mislead courts and litigants by suggesting that *Mueller* is somehow inapplicable to cases such as this one." *Id.* at 490 n. 4. Justice O'-Connor's opinion agreed that *Mueller* controls the outcome of the case because "any aid to religious results from the private decisions of beneficiaries", but pointed out that "[n]o reasonable observer is likely to draw from the facts before us an inference that the state itself is endorsing a religious practice or belief." 474 U.S. at 493

Zelman v. Simmons-Harris

122 S.Ct. 2460 (2002)

[In 1996, after nearly thirty years of desegregation litigation and education reform programs had failed to improve the Cleveland City School District, the Ohio Legislature adopted the Cleveland Scholarship and Tutoring Program. *See Simmons-Harris v. Goff*, 86 Ohio St.3d 1, 711 N.E.2d 203, 214 (Ohio 1999); *Reed v. Rhodes*, 179 F.3d 453 (6th Cir. 1999). Students receiving scholarships may use them to attend an "alternative school," which is defined as a registered private school or a public school located in an adjacent school district, or to hire private tutors. Ohio Rev. Code § 3313.974(G). The amount of the scholarship depends upon the income level of the student. It is fixed at either ninety percent or seventy-five percent of the lesser of the actual tuition charges or an amount not to exceed $2,500 to be established by the State Superintendent of Education. Ohio Rev. Code §§ R.C. 3313.978(A) and (C)(1). The Scholarship payments are made available in the form of checks payable to the parents, who designate the school to which they will be sent. In order to ensure that the money is spent on education, the parents must go to the school and endorse the check. Other provisions of Ohio law set up "community" (charter) schools, and permit statewide, funded inter-district transfers.

The Ohio Supreme Court upheld the program. In its view, "[w]hatever link between government and religion is created by the School Voucher Program is indirect, depending only on the 'genuinely independent and private choices' of individual parents, who act for themselves and their children, not for the government." 83 Ohio St. 3d at 7, 711 N.E. 2d at 209. After an extensive review of the facts and factual context, it "conclude[d] that the School Voucher Program has a secular legislative purpose, does not have the primary effect of advancing religion, and does not excessively entangle government with religion." Id., 83 Ohio St. 3d at 9, 711 N.E. 2d at 211. It also rejected a challenge under Ohio's religious liberty guarantee, Ohio Const. Art. I §7 ("No person shall be compelled to attend, erect, or support any place of worship, or maintain any form of worship, against his consent; and no preference shall be given, by law, to any religious society; nor shall any interference with the rights of conscience be permitted.")

The plaintiffs in *Goff* then filed suit in the United States District Court for the Northern District of Ohio, and obtained a ruling that the program violated the Establishment Clause. *Simmons-Harris v. Zelman*, 54 F.Supp. 2d 725 (N.D. Ohio 1999). Disagreeing with the Ohio Supreme Court's conclusion that "money goes to religious institutions as a result of a " 'genuinely independent and private choice of individuals' ", 54 F. Supp. 2d at 740, the federal District Court held the program unconstitutionally "advances religion" because the "overwhelming majority of schools from which a student may choose are sectarian and... no adjacent public school has chosen to participate in the Program." The United States Court of Appeals for the Sixth Circuit affirmed. 234 F. 3d 945 (6th Cir, 2000).

The State of Ohio asked the United States Supreme Court to resolve the following constitutional question:

> *Whether the Establishment Clause prohibits Ohio's program from authorizing parents to use the scholarships at any private school, whether religious or not?* (Brief of Petitioner, State of Ohio, *Zelman v. Simmons-Harris*, 2001 WL 1576498.)

In order to provide an answer to the question, the majority had to answer several specific questions raised by those challenging the statute:

1. *Whether the moneys the Voucher Program provides to participating sectarian private schools are "properly attributable to the State," as a form of "an impermissible 'direct [State] subsidy'" to the schools, or are "a permissible [parental] transfer" to the schools "similar to [a] hypothetical salary donation" by a government employee from a government paycheck to a religious institution?*
2. *Whether the Voucher Program has "the [impermissible] effect of advancing religion by creating a financial incentive to undertake religious indoctrination"?*
3. *Whether the Voucher Program impermissibly "confer[s] a[ ] message of [S]tate endorsement of religion"?*

Brief of Respondents, Doris Simmons-Harris, *et al.*, 2001 WL 1636772.]

Chief Justice REHNQUIST delivered the opinion of the Court.

The State of Ohio has established a pilot program designed to provide educational choices to families with children who reside in the Cleveland City School District. The question presented is whether this program offends the Establishment Clause of the United States Constitution. We hold that it does not.

There are more than 75,000 children enrolled in the Cleveland City School District. The majority of these children are from low-income and minority families. Few of these families enjoy the means to send their children to any school other than an inner-city public school. For more than a generation, however, Cleveland's public schools have been among the worst performing public schools in the Nation. In 1995, a Federal District Court declared a "crisis of magnitude" and placed the entire Cleveland school district under state control. See *Reed v. Rhodes*, No. 1:73 CV 1300 (ND Ohio, Mar. 3, 1995). Shortly thereafter, the state auditor found that Cleveland's public schools were in the midst of a "crisis that is perhaps unprecedented in the history of American education." Cleveland City School District Performance Audit 2-1 (Mar.1996). The district had failed to meet any of the 18 state standards for minimal acceptable performance. Only 1 in 10 ninth graders could pass a basic proficiency examination, and students at all levels performed at a dismal rate compared with students in other Ohio public schools. More than two-thirds of high school students either dropped or failed out before graduation. Of those students who managed to reach their senior year, one of every four still failed to graduate. Of those students who did graduate, few could read, write, or compute at levels comparable to their counterparts in other cities.

It is against this backdrop that Ohio enacted, among other initiatives, its Pilot Project Scholarship Program. The program provides financial assistance to families in any Ohio school district that is or has been "under federal court order requiring supervision and operational management of the district by the state superintendent." Cleveland is the only Ohio school district to fall within that category.

The program provides two basic kinds of assistance to parents of children in a covered district. First, the program provides tuition aid for students in kindergarten through third grade, expanding each year through eighth grade, to attend a participating public or private school of their parent's choosing. Second, the program provides tutorial aid for students who choose to remain enrolled in public school.

The program has been in operation within the Cleveland City School District since the 1996–1997 school year. In the 1999–2000 school year, 56 private schools participated in the program, 46 (or 82%) of which had a religious affiliation. None of the public schools in districts adjacent to Cleveland have elected to participate. More than 3,700 students participated in the scholarship program, most of whom (96%) enrolled in religiously affiliated schools. Sixty percent of these students were from families at or below the poverty line. In the 1998–1999 school year, approximately 1,400 Cleveland public school students received tutorial aid. This number was expected to double during the 1999–2000 school year.

The program is part of a broader undertaking by the State to enhance the educational options of Cleveland's schoolchildren in response to the 1995 takeover. That undertaking includes programs governing community and magnet schools. Community schools are funded under state law but are run by their own school boards, not by local school districts. For each child enrolled in a community school, the school receives state funding of $4,518, twice the funding a participating program school may receive. Magnet schools are public schools operated by a local school board that emphasize a particular subject area, teaching method, or service to students. For each student enrolled in a magnet school, the school district receives $7,746, including state funding of $4,167, the same amount received per student enrolled at a traditional public school.

[The procedural history of the case is summarized above.]

The Establishment Clause of the First Amendment, applied to the States through the Fourteenth Amendment, prevents a State from enacting laws that have the "purpose" or "effect" of advancing or inhibiting religion. *Agostini v. Felton*. There is no dispute that the program challenged here was enacted for the valid secular purpose of providing educational assistance to poor children in a demonstrably failing public school system. Thus, the question presented is whether the Ohio program nonetheless has the forbidden "effect" of advancing or inhibiting religion.

To answer that question, our decisions have drawn a consistent distinction between government programs that provide aid directly to religious schools, *Mitchell v. Helms*; *Agostin*; *Rosenberger* (collecting cases), and programs of true private choice, in which government aid reaches religious schools only as a result of the genuine and independent choices of private individuals, *Mueller*; *Witters*; *Zobrest*. While our jurisprudence with respect to the constitutionality of direct aid programs has "changed significantly" over the past two decades, our jurisprudence with respect to true private choice programs has remained consistent and unbroken. Three times we have confronted Establishment Clause challenges to neutral government programs that provide aid directly to a broad class of individuals, who, in turn, direct the aid to religious schools or institutions of their own choosing. Three times we have rejected such challenges.

Mueller, Witters, and *Zobrest* make clear that where a government aid program is neutral with respect to religion, and provides assistance directly to a broad class of citizens who, in turn, direct government aid to religious schools wholly as a result of their own genuine and independent private choice, the program is not readily subject to challenge under the Establishment Clause. A program that shares these features permits government aid to reach religious institutions only by way of the deliberate choices of numerous individual recipients. The incidental advancement of a religious mission, or the perceived endorsement of a religious message, is reasonably attributable to the individual recipient, not to the government, whose role ends with the disbursement of benefits. As a plurality of this Court recently observed:

> "[I]f numerous private choices, rather than the single choice of a government, determine the distribution of aid, pursuant to neutral eligibility criteria, then a government cannot, or at least cannot easily, grant special favors that might lead to a religious establishment."

It is precisely for these reasons that we have never found a program of true private choice to offend the Establishment Clause.

We believe that the program challenged here is a program of true private choice, consistent with *Mueller, Witters,* and *Zobrest,* and thus constitutional. As was true in those cases, the Ohio program is neutral in all respects toward religion. It is part of a general and multifaceted undertaking by the State of Ohio to provide educational opportunities to the children of a failed school district. It confers educational assistance directly to a broad class of individuals defined without reference to religion, *i.e.*, any parent of a school-age child who resides in the Cleveland City School District. The program permits the participation of *all* schools within the district, religious or nonreligious. Adjacent public schools also may participate and have a financial incentive to do so. Program benefits are available to participating families on neutral terms, with no reference to religion. The only preference stated anywhere in the program is a preference for low-income families, who receive greater assistance and are given priority for admission at participating schools.

There are no "financial incentive[s]" that "ske[w]" the program toward religious schools. *Witters, supra,* at 487–488. Such incentives "[are] not present...where the aid is allocated on the basis of neutral, secular criteria that neither favor nor disfavor religion, and is made available to both religious and secular beneficiaries on a nondiscriminatory basis." The program here in fact creates financial *dis* incentives for religious schools, with private schools receiving only half the government assistance given to community schools and one-third the assistance given to magnet schools. Adjacent public schools, should any choose to accept program students, are also eligible to receive two to three times the state funding of a private religious school. Families too have a financial disincentive to choose a private religious school over other schools. Parents that choose to participate in the scholarship program and then to enroll their children in a private school (religious or nonreligious) must copay a portion of the school's tuition. Families that choose a community school, magnet school, or traditional public school pay nothing. Although such features of the program are not necessary to its constitutionality, they clearly dispel the claim that the program "creates... financial incentive[s] for parents to choose a sectarian school." *Zobrest.*

Respondents suggest that even without a financial incentive for parents to choose a religious school, the program creates a "public perception that the State is endorsing religious practices and beliefs." But we have repeatedly recognized that no reasonable observer would think a neutral program of private choice, where state aid reaches religious schools solely as a result of the numerous independent decisions of private individuals, carries with it the *imprimatur* of government endorsement. *Mueller*; *Witters,*; *Zobrest.* The argument is particularly misplaced here since "the reasonable observer in the endorsement inquiry must be deemed aware" of the "history and context" underlying a challenged program. *Good News Club v. Milford Central School,*. See also *Capitol Square Review and Advisory Bd. v. Pinette,* 515 U.S. 753, 780, 115 S.Ct. 2440, 132 L.Ed.2d 650 (1995) (O'CONNOR, J., concurring in part and concurring in judgment). Any objective observer familiar with the full history and context of the Ohio program would reasonably view it as one aspect of a broader undertaking to assist poor children in failed schools, not as an endorsement of religious schooling in general.

There also is no evidence that the program fails to provide genuine opportunities for Cleveland parents to select secular educational options for their school-age children. Cleveland schoolchildren enjoy a range of educational choices: They may remain in public school as before, remain in public school with publicly funded tutoring aid, obtain a scholarship and choose a religious school, obtain a scholarship and choose a nonreligious private school, enroll in a community school, or enroll in a magnet school. That 46 of the 56 private schools now participating in the program are religious schools does not condemn it as a violation of the Establishment Clause. The Establishment Clause question is whether Ohio is coercing parents into sending their children to religious schools, and that question must be answered by evaluating *all* options Ohio provides Cleveland schoolchildren, only one of which is to obtain a program scholarship and then choose a religious school.

Respondents and JUSTICE SOUTER claim that even if we do not focus on the number of participating schools that are religious schools, we should attach constitutional significance to the fact that 96% of scholarship recipients have enrolled in religious schools. They claim that this alone proves parents lack genuine choice, even if no parent has ever said so. We need not consider this argument in detail, since it was flatly rejected in *Mueller,* where we found it irrelevant that 96% of parents taking deductions for tuition expenses paid tuition at religious schools. The constitutionality of a neutral educational aid program simply does not turn on whether and why, in a particular area, at a particular time, most private schools are run by religious organizations, or most recipients choose to use the aid at a religious school. As we said in *Mueller,* "[s]uch an approach would scarcely provide the certainty that this field stands in need of, nor can we perceive principled standards by which such statistical evidence might be evaluated."

Respondents finally claim that we should look to *Committee for Public Ed. & Religious Liberty v. Nyquist,* 413 U.S. 756 (1973), to decide these cases. We disagree for two reasons. First, the program in *Nyquist* was quite different from the program challenged here. *Nyquist* involved a New York program that gave a package of benefits exclusively to private schools and the parents of private school enrollees. Although the program was enacted for ostensibly secular purposes, we found that its "function" was "*unmistakably* to provide desired financial support for nonpublic, sectarian institutions," (emphasis added). Indeed, the program flatly prohibited the participation of any public school, or parent of any public school enrollee. Ohio's program shares none of these features.

Second, were there any doubt that the program challenged in *Nyquist* is far removed from the program challenged here, we expressly reserved judgment with respect to "a case involving some form of public assistance (*e.g.*, scholarships) made available generally without regard to the sectarian-nonsectarian, or public-nonpublic nature of the institution benefited." That, of course, is the very question now before us, and it has since been answered, first in *Mueller,* 463 U.S., at 398–399, then in *Witters,* and again in *Zobrest.* To the extent the scope of *Nyquist* has remained an open question in light of these later decisions, we now hold that *Nyquist* does not govern neutral educational assistance programs that, like the program here, offer aid directly to a broad class of individual recipients defined without regard to religion.

In keeping with an unbroken line of decisions rejecting challenges to similar programs, we hold that the program does not offend the Establishment Clause.

The judgment of the Court of Appeals is reversed. *It is so ordered.*

Justice O'CONNOR, concurring.

While I join the Court's opinion, I write separately for two reasons. First, although the Court takes an important step, I do not believe that today's decision, when considered in light of other longstanding government programs that impact religious organizations and our prior Establishment Clause jurisprudence, marks a dramatic break from the past. Second, given the emphasis the Court places on verifying that parents of voucher students in religious schools have exercised "true private choice," I think it is worth elaborating on the Court's conclusion that this inquiry should consider all reasonable educational alternatives to religious schools that are available to parents. To do otherwise is to ignore how the educational system in Cleveland actually functions.

I

These cases are different from prior indirect aid cases in part because a significant portion of the funds appropriated for the voucher program reach religious schools without restrictions on the use of these funds. The share of public resources that reach religious schools is not, however, as significant as respondents suggest. These statistics do not take into account all of the reasonable educational choices that may be available to students in Cleveland public schools. When one considers the option to attend community schools, the percentage of students enrolled in religious schools falls to 62.1 percent. If magnet schools are included in the mix, this percentage falls to 16.5 percent. See J. Greene, The Racial, Economic, and Religious Context of Parental Choice in Cleveland 11, Table 4 (Oct. 8, 1999), App. 217a (reporting 2,087 students in community schools and 16,184 students in magnet schools).

Even these numbers do not paint a complete picture. The Cleveland program provides voucher applicants from low-income families with up to $2,250 in tuition assistance and provides the remaining applicants with up to $1,875 in tuition assistance. In contrast, the State provides community schools $4,518 per pupil and magnet schools, on average, $7,097 per pupil. Even if one assumes that all voucher students came from low-income families and that each voucher student used up the entire $2,250 voucher, at most $8.2 million of public funds flowed to religious schools under the voucher program in 1999–2000.

Although $8.2 million is no small sum, it pales in comparison to the amount of funds that federal, state, and local governments already provide religious institutions. [Justice O'Connor's discussion of the value of tax exemptions and credits for religious institutions, Medicare, Medicaid, Pell Grants, and other aid payments to individuals that reach religious institutions is omitted.]

Against this background, the support that the Cleveland voucher program provides religious institutions is neither substantial nor atypical of existing government programs. While this observation is not intended to justify the Cleveland voucher program under the Establishment Clause, it places in broader perspective alarmist claims about implications of the Cleveland program and the Court's decision in these cases. See (STEVENS, J., dissenting); (SOUTER, J., dissenting); (BREYER, J., dissenting).

II

Nor does today's decision signal a major departure from this Court's prior Establishment Clause jurisprudence. A central tool in our analysis of cases in this area has been the *Lemon* test. The test today is basically the same as that set forth in *School Dist. of Abington Township v. Schempp* over 40 years ago.

The Court's opinion in these cases focuses on a narrow question related to the *Lemon* test: how to apply the primary effects prong in indirect aid cases? Courts are instructed to consider two factors: first, whether the program administers aid in a neutral fashion, without differentiation based on the religious status of beneficiaries or providers of services; second, and more importantly, whether beneficiaries of indirect aid have a genuine choice among religious and nonreligious organizations when determining the organization to which they will direct that aid. If the answer to either query is "no," the program should be struck down under the Establishment Clause.

[Justice O'Connor's discussion of "neutrality" is omitted.]

Based on the reasoning in the Court's opinion, which is consistent with the realities of the Cleveland educational system, I am persuaded that the Cleveland voucher program affords parents of eligible children genuine nonreligious options and is consistent with the Establishment Clause.

Justice THOMAS, concurring. [all footnotes are omitted]

Frederick Douglass once said that "[e]ducation... means emancipation. It means light and liberty. It means the uplifting of the soul of man into the glorious light of truth, the light by which men can only be made free." Today many of our inner-city public schools deny emancipation to urban minority students. Despite this Court's observation nearly 50 years ago in *Brown v. Board of Education,* that "it is doubtful that any child may reasonably be expected to succeed in life if he is denied the opportunity of an education," 347 U.S. 483, 493, 74 S.Ct. 686, 98 L.Ed. 873 (1954), urban children have been forced into a system that continually fails them. These cases present an example of such failures. Besieged by escalating financial problems and declining academic achievement, the Cleveland City School District was in the midst of an academic emergency when Ohio enacted its scholarship program.

The dissents and respondents wish to invoke the Establishment Clause of the First Amendment, as incorporated through the Fourteenth, to constrain a State's neutral efforts to provide greater educational opportunity for underprivileged minority students. Today's decision properly upholds the program as constitutional, and I join it in full.

I

I agree with the Court that Ohio's program easily passes muster under our stringent test, but, as a matter of first principles, I question whether this test should be applied to the States.

The Establishment Clause of the First Amendment states that "Congress shall make no law respecting an establishment of religion." On its face, this provision places no limit on the States with regard to religion. The Establishment Clause originally protected States, and by extension their citizens, from the imposition of an established religion by the Federal Government. Whether and how this Clause should constrain state action under the Fourteenth Amendment is a more difficult question.

The Fourteenth Amendment fundamentally restructured the relationship between individuals and the States and ensured that States would not deprive citizens of liberty without due process of law. As Justice Harlan noted, the Fourteenth Amendment "added greatly to the dignity and glory of American citizenship, and to the security of personal liberty." *Plessy v. Ferguson,* 163 U.S. 537, 555 (1896) (dissenting opinion). When rights are incorporated against the States through the Fourteenth Amendment they should advance, not constrain, individual liberty.

Consequently, in the context of the Establishment Clause, it may well be that state action should be evaluated on different terms than similar action by the Federal Government. "States, while bound to observe strict neutrality, should be freer to experiment with involvement [in religion]—on a neutral basis—than the Federal Government." Thus, while the Federal Government may "make no law respecting an establishment of religion," the States may pass laws that include or touch on religious matters so long as these laws do not impede free exercise rights or any other individual religious liberty interest. By considering the particular religious liberty right alleged to be invaded by a State, federal courts can strike a proper balance between the demands of the Fourteenth Amendment on the one hand and the federalism prerogatives of States on the other.

Whatever the textual and historical merits of incorporating the Establishment Clause, I can accept that the Fourteenth Amendment protects religious liberty rights. But I cannot accept its use to oppose neutral programs of school choice through the incorporation of the Establishment Clause. There would be a tragic irony in converting the Fourteenth Amendment's guarantee of individual liberty into a prohibition on the exercise of educational choice.

II

The wisdom of allowing States greater latitude in dealing with matters of religion and education can be easily appreciated in this context. Respondents advocate using the Fourteenth Amendment to handcuff the State's ability to experiment with education. But without education one can hardly exercise the civic, political, and personal freedoms conferred by the Fourteenth Amendment.

Although one of the purposes of public schools was to promote democracy and a more egalitarian culture, failing urban public schools disproportionately affect minority children most in need of educational opportunity. At the time of Reconstruction, blacks considered public education "a matter of personal liberation and a necessary function of a free society." J. Anderson, Education of Blacks in the South, 1860–1935, p. 18 (1988). Today, however, the promise of public school education has failed poor inner-city blacks. While in theory providing education to everyone, the quality of public schools varies significantly across districts. Just as blacks supported public education during Reconstruction, many blacks and other minorities now support school choice programs because they provide the greatest educational opportunities for their children in struggling communities. pponents of the program raise formalistic concerns about the Establishment Clause but ignore the core purposes of the Fourteenth Amendment.

While the romanticized ideal of universal public education resonates with the cognoscenti who oppose vouchers, poor urban families just want the best education for their children, who will certainly need it to function in our high-tech and advanced society. As Thomas Sowell noted 30 years ago: "Most black people have faced too many grim, concrete problems to be romantics. They want and need certain tangible results, which can be achieved only by developing certain specific abilities." Black Education: Myths and Tragedies 228 (1972). The same is true today. An individual's life prospects increase dramatically with each successfully completed phase of education. The failure to provide education to poor urban children perpetuates a vicious cycle of poverty, dependence, criminality, and alienation that continues for the remainder of their lives. If society cannot end racial discrimination, at least it can arm minorities with the education to defend themselves from some of discrimination's effects.

* * *

Ten States have enacted some form of publicly funded private school choice as one means of raising the quality of education provided to underprivileged urban children. These programs address the root of the problem with failing urban public schools that disproportionately affect minority students. Society's other solution to these educational failures is often to provide racial preferences in higher education. Such preferences, however, run afoul of the Fourteenth Amendment's prohibition against distinctions based on race. See *Plessy,* 163 U.S., at 555 (Harlan, J., dissenting). By contrast, school choice programs that involve religious schools appear unconstitutional only to those who would twist the Fourteenth Amendment against itself by expansively incorporating the Establishment Clause. Converting the Fourteenth Amendment from a guarantee of opportunity to an obstacle against education reform distorts our constitutional values and disserves those in the greatest need.

As Frederick Douglass poignantly noted "no greater benefit can be bestowed upon a long benighted people, than giving to them, as we are here earnestly this day endeavoring to do, the means of an education."

Justice STEVENS, dissenting.

Is a law that authorizes the use of public funds to pay for the indoctrination of thousands of grammar school children in particular religious faiths a "law respecting an establishment of religion" within the meaning of the First Amendment? In answering that question, I think we should ignore three factual matters that are discussed at length by my colleagues.

First, the severe educational crisis that confronted the Cleveland City School District when Ohio enacted its voucher program is not a matter that should affect our appraisal of its constitutionality. Of course, the emergency may have given some families a powerful motivation to leave the public school system and accept religious indoctrination that they would otherwise have avoided, but that is not a valid reason for upholding the program.

Second, the wide range of choices that have been made available to students *within the public school system* has no bearing on the question whether the State may pay the tuition for students who wish to reject public education entirely and attend private schools that will provide them with a sectarian education.... [I]t is the State's decision to fund private school education over and above its traditional obligation that is at issue in these cases.

Third, the voluntary character of the private choice to prefer a parochial education over an education in the public school system seems to me quite irrelevant to the question whether the government's choice to pay for religious indoctrination is constitutionally permissible. Today, however, the Court seems to have decided that the mere fact that a family that cannot afford a private education wants its children educated in a parochial school is a sufficient justification for this use of public funds.

For the reasons stated by JUSTICE SOUTER and JUSTICE BREYER, I am convinced that the Court's decision is profoundly misguided. Admittedly, in reaching that conclusion I have been influenced by my understanding of the impact of religious strife on the decisions of our forbears to migrate to this continent, and on the decisions of neighbors in the Balkans, Northern Ireland, and the Middle East to mistrust one another. Whenever we remove a brick from the wall that was designed to separate religion and government, we increase the risk of religious strife and weaken the foundation of our democracy.

I respectfully dissent.

Justice SOUTER, with whom Justice STEVENS, Justice GINSBURG, and Justice BREYER join, dissenting.

The applicability of the Establishment Clause to public funding of benefits to religious schools was settled in *Everson v. Board of Ed. of Ewing,* which inaugurated the modern era of establishment doctrine. The Court stated the principle in words from which there was no dissent:

> "No tax in any amount, large or small, can be levied to support any religious activities or institutions, whatever they may be called, or whatever form they may adopt to teach or practice religion." *Id.,* at 16. The Court has never in so many words repudiated this statement, let alone, in so many words, overruled *Everson.*

Today, however, the majority holds that the Establishment Clause is not offended by Ohio's Pilot Project Scholarship Program. Public tax money will pay at a systemic level for teaching the covenant with Israel and Mosaic law in Jewish schools, the primacy of the Apostle Peter and the Papacy in Catholic schools, the truth of reformed Christianity in Protestant schools, and the revelation to the Prophet in Muslim schools, to speak only of major religious groupings in the Republic.

How can a Court consistently leave *Everson* on the books and approve the Ohio vouchers? The answer is that it cannot. [Justice Souter's summary of the case law is omitted.]

II

Although it has taken half a century since *Everson* to reach the majority's twin standards of neutrality and free choice, the facts show that, in the majority's hands, even these criteria cannot convincingly legitimize the Ohio scheme.

A

Consider first the criterion of neutrality. Neutrality in this sense refers, of course, to evenhandedness in setting eligibility as between potential religious and secular recipients of public money. *Mitchell v. Helms* (SOUTER, J., dissenting). In order to apply the neutrality test, then, it makes sense to focus on a category of aid that may be directed to religious as well as secular schools, and ask whether the scheme favors a religious direction. Here, one would ask whether the voucher provisions, allowing for as much as $2,250 toward private school tuition (or a grant to a public school in an adjacent district), were written in a way that skewed the scheme toward benefiting religious schools.

This, however, is not what the majority asks. The majority looks not to the provisions for tuition vouchers, but to every provision for educational opportunity: "The program permits the participation of *all* schools within the district, [as well as public schools in adjacent districts], religious or nonreligious." *Ante,* at 11 (emphasis in original). The majority then finds confirmation that "participation of *all* schools" satisfies neutrality by noting that the better part of total state educational expenditure goes to public schools, thus showing there is no favor of religion.

The illogic is patent. If regular, public schools (which can get no voucher payments) "participate" in a voucher scheme with schools that can, and public expenditure is still predominantly on public schools, then the majority's reasoning would find neutrality in a scheme of vouchers available for private tuition in districts with no secular private schools at all. Why the majority does not simply accept the fact that the challenge here is to the more generous voucher scheme and judge its neutrality in relation to religious use of voucher money seems very odd. It seems odd, that is, until one recognizes that comparable schools for applying the criterion of neutrality are also the comparable schools for applying the other majority criterion, whether the immediate recipients of voucher aid have a genuinely free choice of religious and secular schools to receive the voucher money. And in applying this second criterion, the consideration of "*all* schools" is ostensibly helpful to the majority position.

B

The majority addresses the issue of choice the same way it addresses neutrality, by asking whether recipients or potential recipients of voucher aid have a choice of public schools among secular alternatives to religious schools. Again, however, the majority asks the wrong question and misapplies the criterion. The question is whether the private hand is genuinely free to send the money in either a secular direction or a religious one. The majority now has transformed this question about private choice in channeling aid into a question about selecting from examples of state spending (on education) including direct spending on magnet and community public schools that goes through no private hands and could never reach a religious school under any circumstance.... Confining the relevant choices to spending choices, on the other hand, is not vulnerable to comparable criticism.

If, contrary to the majority, we ask the right question about genuine choice to use the vouchers, the answer shows that something is influencing choices in a way that aims the money in a religious direction: 96.6% of all voucher recipients go to religious schools, only 3.4% to nonreligious ones. Unfortunately for the majority position, there is no explanation for this that suggests the religious direction results simply from free choices by parents.

Of course, the obvious fix would be to increase the value of vouchers so that existing nonreligious private and non-Catholic religious schools would be able to enroll more voucher students, and to provide incentives for educators to create new such schools given that few presently exist. And to get to that hypothetical point would require that such massive financial support be made available to religion as to disserve every objective of the Establishment Clause even more than the present scheme does.

III

I do not dissent merely because the majority has misapplied its own law, for even if I assumed *arguendo* that the majority's formal criteria were satisfied on the facts, today's conclusion would be profoundly at odds with the Constitution.

A

The scale of the aid to religious schools approved today is unprecedented, both in the number of dollars and in the proportion of systemic school expenditure supported. The consequences of "substantial" aid hypothesized in *Meek* are realized here: the majority makes no pretense that substantial amounts of tax money are not systematically underwriting religious practice and indoctrination.

B

It is virtually superfluous to point out that every objective underlying the prohibition of religious establishment is betrayed by this scheme, but something has to be said about the enormity of the violation. Jefferson described [the first objective, freedom of conscience] it as the idea that no one "shall be compelled to... support any religious worship, place, or ministry whatsoever," A Bill for Establishing Religious Freedom, even a "teacher of his own religious persuasion," and Madison thought it violated by any "'authority which can force a citizen to contribute three pence... of his property for the support of any... establishment.'" Memorial and Remonstrance & para;3. "Any tax to establish religion is antithetical to the command that the minds of men always be wholly free". Madison's objection to three pence has simply been lost in the majority's formalism.

As for the second objective, to save religion from its own corruption, Madison wrote of the "'experience... that ecclesiastical establishments, instead of maintaining the purity and efficacy of Religion, have had a contrary operation.'" The risk is already being realized.

When government aid goes up, so does reliance on it; the only thing likely to go down is independence. [Is there not] reason to wonder when dependence will become great enough to give the State of Ohio an effective veto over basic decisions on the content of curriculums? A day will come when religious schools will learn what political leverage can do, just as Ohio's politicians are now getting a lesson in the leverage exercised by religion.

[S]tate mandates to moderate religious teaching may well be the most obvious response to the third concern behind the ban on establishment, its inextricable link with social conflict. Religious teaching at taxpayer expense simply cannot be cordoned from taxpayer politics, and every major religion currently espouses social positions that provoke intense opposition. Not all taxpaying Protestant citizens, for example, will be content to underwrite the teaching of the Roman Catholic Church condemning the death penalty. Nor will all of America's Muslims acquiesce in paying for the endorsement of the religious Zionism taught in many religious Jewish schools, which combines "a nationalistic sentiment" in support of Israel with a "deeply religious" element. Nor will every secular taxpayer be content to support Muslim views on differential treatment of the sexes, or, for that matter, to fund the espousal of a wife's obligation of obedience to her husband, presumably taught in any schools adopting the articles of faith of the Southern Baptist Convention. Views like these, and innumerable others, have been safe in the sectarian pulpits and classrooms of this Nation not only because the Free Exercise Clause protects them directly, but because the ban on supporting religious establishment has protected free exercise, by keeping it relatively private. With the arrival of vouchers in religious schools, that privacy will go, and along with it will go confidence that religious disagreement will stay moderate.

* * *

If the divisiveness permitted by today's majority is to be avoided in the short term, it will be avoided only by action of the political branches at the state and national levels... now that they know a federal court will not save them. My own course as a judge on the Court cannot, however, simply be to hope that the political branches will save us from the consequences of the majority's decision. I hope that a future Court will reconsider today's dramatic departure from basic Establishment Clause principle.

Justice BREYER, with whom Justice STEVENS and Justice SOUTER join, dissenting.

I join JUSTICE SOUTER's opinion, and I agree substantially with JUSTICE STEVENS. I write separately, however, to emphasize the risk that publicly financed voucher programs pose in terms of religiously based social conflict. I do so because I believe that the Establishment Clause concern for protecting the Nation's social fabric from religious conflict poses an overriding obstacle to the implementation of this well-intentioned school voucher program.

I

When it decided [its] 20th century Establishment Clause cases, the Court did not deny that an earlier American society might have found a less clear-cut church/state separation compatible with social tranquility. Indeed, historians point out that during the early years of the Republic, American schools—including the first public schools—were Protestant in character. Their students recited Protestant prayers, read the King James version of the Bible, and learned Protestant religious ideals. Those practices may have wrongly discriminated against members of minority religions, but given the small number of such individuals, the teaching of Protestant religions in schools did not threaten serious social conflict.

The 20th century Court was fully aware, however, that immigration and growth had changed American society dramatically since its early years. By 1850, 1.6 million-Catholics lived in America, and by 1900 that number rose to 12 million. There were similar percentage increases in the Jewish population. Not surprisingly, with this increase in numbers, members of non-Protestant religions, particularly Catholics, began to resist the Protestant domination of the public schools. Scholars report that by the mid-19th century religious conflict over matters such as Bible reading "grew intense," as Catholics resisted and Protestants fought back to preserve their domination. "Dreading Catholic domination," native Protestants "terrorized Catholics." P. Hamburger, *Separation of Church and State* 219 (2002). In some States "Catholic students suffered beatings or expulsions for refusing to read from the Protestant Bible, and crowds... rioted over whether Catholic children could be released from the classroom during Bible reading." Jeffries & Ryan, 100 Mich. L.Rev., at 300.

The 20th century Court was also aware that political efforts to right the wrong of discrimination against religious minorities in primary education had failed; in fact they had exacerbated religious conflict. Catholics sought equal government support for the education of their children in the form of aid for private Catholic schools. But the "Protestant position" on this matter, scholars report, "was that public schools must be 'nonsectarian' (which was usually understood to allow Bible reading and other Protestant observances) and public money must not support 'sectarian' schools (which in practical terms meant Catholic)." *Id.,* at 301. And this sentiment played a significant role in creating a movement that sought to amend several state constitutions (often successfully), and to amend the United States Constitution (unsuccessfully) to make certain that government would not help pay for "sectarian" (*i.e.,* Catholic) schooling for children. *Id.,* at 301–305. See also Hamburger, *supra,* at 287.

These historical circumstances suggest that the Court, applying the Establishment Clause through the Fourteenth Amendment to 20th century American society, faced an interpretive dilemma that was in part practical. The Court appreciated the religious diversity of contemporary American society. See *Schempp,* (Brennan, J., concurring). It realized that the status quo favored some religions at the expense of others. And it understood the Establishment Clause to prohibit (among other things) any such favoritism. Yet *how* did the Clause achieve that objective? Did it simply require the government to give each religion an equal chance to introduce religion into the primary schools—a kind of "equal opportunity" approach to the interpretation of the Establishment Clause? Or, did that Clause avoid government favoritism of some religions by insisting upon "separation"—that the government achieve equal treatment by removing itself from the business of providing religious education for children? This interpretive choice arose in respect both to religious activities in public schools and government aid to private education.

In both areas the Court concluded that the Establishment Clause required "separation," in part because an "equal opportunity" approach was not workable. With respect to religious activities in the public schools,...there were too many religions, too diverse a set of religious practices, too many whose spiritual beliefs denied the virtue of formal religious training. This diversity made it difficult, if not impossible, to devise meaningful forms of "equal treatment" by providing an "equal opportunity" for all to introduce their own religious practices into the public schools.

The upshot is the development of constitutional doctrine that reads the Establishment Clause as avoiding religious strife, *not* by providing every religion with an *equal opportunity* (say, to secure state funding or to pray in the public schools), but by drawing fairly clear lines of *separation* between church and state—at least where the heartland of religious belief, such as primary religious education, is at issue.

II

The principle underlying these cases—avoiding religiously based social conflict—remains of great concern. As religiously diverse as America had become when the Court decided its major 20th century Establishment Clause cases, we are exponentially more diverse today. Under these modern-day circumstances, how is the "equal opportunity" principle to work—without risking the "struggle of sect against sect" against which Justice Rutledge warned? If so, just how is the State to resolve the resulting controversies without provoking legitimate fears of the kinds of religious favoritism that, in so religiously diverse a Nation, threaten social dissension?

I recognize that other nations, for example Great Britain and France, have in the past reconciled religious school funding and religious freedom without creating serious strife. Yet British and French societies are religiously more homogeneous—and it bears noting that recent waves of immigration have begun to create problems of social division there as well. In a society as religiously diverse as ours, the Court has recognized that we must rely on the Religion Clauses of the First Amendment to protect against religious strife, particularly when what is at issue is an area as central to religious belief as the shaping, through primary education, of the next generation's minds and spirits.

III

I concede that the Establishment Clause currently permits States to channel various forms of assistance to religious schools. School voucher programs differ, however, in both *kind* and *degree* from aid programs upheld in the past. They differ in kind because they direct financing to a core function of the church: the teaching of religious truths to young children. For that reason the constitutional demand for "separation" is of particular constitutional concern.

IV

Parental choice cannot help the taxpayer who does not want to finance the religious education of children. It will not always help the parent who may see little real choice between inadequate nonsectarian public education and adequate education at a school whose religious teachings are contrary to his own. It will not satisfy religious minorities unable to participate because they are too few in number to support the creation of their own private schools. It will not satisfy groups whose religious beliefs preclude them from participating in a government-sponsored program, and who may well feel ignored as government funds primarily support the education of children in the doctrines of the dominant religions. And it does little to ameliorate the entanglement problems or the related problems of social division that Part II, *supra*, describes. [T]he fact that the parent may choose which school can cash the government's voucher check does not alleviate the Establishment Clause concerns.

V

In a society composed of many different religious creeds, I fear that this present departure from the Court's earlier understanding risks creating a form of religiously based conflict potentially harmful to the Nation's social fabric. Because I believe the Establishment Clause was written in part to avoid this kind of conflict, and for reasons set forth by JUSTICE SOUTER and JUSTICE STEVENS, I respectfully dissent.

Notes

1. Both Justice Breyer and Justice Souter argue in *Zelman* that public financing carries with it the risk that the government will seek to control the content and perspective of the education provided in religious schools. Do private schools (religious or secular) have a First Amendment argument *against* such controls? Compare *National Endowment for the Arts v. Finley*, 524 U.S. 569 (1998); *Arkansas Educ. Television Com'n v. Forbes*, 523 U.S. 666 (1998); *F.C.C. v. League of Women Voters of California*, 468 U.S. 364 (1984). Would the same arguments be available to public school systems?

2. One of the more challenging developments in educational reform is the advent of for-profit schools and management of public schools by both profit-making and non-profit organizations such as universities. What makes a "public" school "public"? What is the character of a "common" school? Does its character as a public or "common"

school change when it is managed by private contractors? *See generally* Frank R. Kemerer, Ph.D. and Catherine Maloney, M.A., Commentary, *The Legal Framework for Educational Privatization and Accountability*, 150 Ed. Law Rep. 589 (2001); Cheryl L. Wade, *For-Profit Corporations That Perform Public Functions: Politics, Profit, and Poverty*, 51 Rutgers L. Rev. 323 (1999). If a public school is managed by a private contractor, does the contractor become a "state actor" whose activities are subject to the constraints of the Fourteenth Amendment? *Compare Marsh v. Alabama*, 326 U.S. 501 (1946) (company town) *with Jackson v. Metropolitan Edison Co.*, 419 U.S. 345 (1974) (holding that management of a utility is not a public function) and *Memphis Light, Gas and Water Division v. Craft*, 536 U.S. 1 (1978) (holding that where utility is operated by government and state law provides that termination of service may only be "for cause" notice and hearing opportunity must be provided).

2) State Case Law: Federalism & the Establishment Clause

(A) The Structural Aspects of the Non-Establishment Guarantee

In Chapter Five §§B and K, we noted that federalism provides an important structural protection for religious liberty. Because the No Religious Test Clause of Article VI applies only to offices and public trusts "under the United States," and the First Amendment applies by its terms only to Congress, State constitutions and statutes form a conceptual "bracket" around the liberty aspects of the federal religious liberty guarantee. In this understanding, the States are free to supply protection for religious liberty when the federal religious liberty guarantee does not require it. *See* U.S. Const., Amend. IX, X (1791). *See, e.g.*, Angela C. Carmella, *State Constitutional Protection of Religious Liberty: An Emerging Post-*Smith *Jurisprudence*, 1993 B.Y.U. L. Rev. 275.

When the United States Supreme Court applied the First Amendment to the States via the Incorporation Doctrine, its provisions became part and parcel of the Court's understanding of the Fourteenth Amendment. Unlike the First Amendment, the Fourteenth Amendment *is* an explicit limit on the powers of the States. When a *State* adopts legislation, amends its constitution, or announces a judicial rule designed to alter the effect of a Supreme Court decision in its courts or executive agencies, it need only show that its law is not *inconsistent* with the United States Constitution. Since the Court has held that the Fourteenth Amendment "confer[s] power upon the courts, which the courts would use to achieve equality of rights," the federalism boundary between the States and the federal government appears to be the point at which a State's definition of equal rights or equal citizenship would deny the equality of citizenship or protection mandated by either the Fourteenth Amendment, or an act of Congress. *See* Chart 5-1 on page 207.

(B) State Constitutional Provisions Governing Aid to Religious Schools

State constitutions vary on the topic of aid to religiously affiliated schools. The Ohio Constitution, quoted in Section F(1) above, mandates only that "no religious or other sect, or sects, shall ever have any exclusive right to, or control of, any part of the school funds of this state," Ohio Const., Art. VI §4 (2002), whereas the Alabama Constitution states that "No money raised for the support of the public schools shall be appropriated to or used for the support of any sectarian or denominational school." Ala. Const. Art. XIV §263 (2002). The Alaska and California Constitution are more comprehensive. *See* Alaska Const. Art. VII §1, cl. 2 (2002) ("No money shall be paid from public funds for the direct benefit of any religious or other private educational institution.").

The California Constitution is very explicit:

> No public money shall ever be appropriated for the support of any sectarian or denominational school, or any school not under the exclusive control of the officers of the public schools; nor shall any sectarian or denominational doctrine be taught, or instruction thereon be permitted, directly or indirectly, in any of the common schools of this State.

Cal. Const. Art. 9 §8, Art. 16 §5 (2002)

> Neither the Legislature, nor any county, city and county, township, school district, or other municipal corporation, shall ever make an appropriation, or pay from any public fund whatever, or grant anything to or in aid of any religious sect, church, creed, or sectarian purpose, or help to support or sustain any school, college, university, hospital, or other institution controlled by any religious creed, church, or sectarian denomination whatever; nor shall any grant or donation of personal property or real estate ever be made by the state, or any city, city and county, town, or other municipal corporation for any religious creed, church, or sectarian purpose whatever; provided, that nothing in this section shall prevent the Legislature granting aid pursuant to Section 3 of Article XVI.

Cal. Const. Art. 16 §5 (2002).

(C) Framing the Issues Under State Constitutional Law

It is common for both courts and commentators to describe a court's conclusions on a non-establishment issue as either a "strict" or "narrow" interpretation of the Establishment Clause or analogous provisions of a State constitution. Chapter One §A points out, however, that characterizations of this type can have the effect of deciding an issue before it is litigated.

A more analytical approach is to focus first on the language of the constitutional provision at issue. State judicial holdings on the meaning of state constitutional law governing aid to religiously affiliated schools reflect not only differences in the language of their respective constitutions and the willingness of state courts to construe their constitutions in a way that differs from the United States Supreme Court's interpretation of the First Amendment, but also the attitudes of the state's electorate concerning aid to religious institutions, particularly schools.

The section of the New York Constitution governing aid to religiously affiliated schools, Article XI §3 (2002), provides a good example of all three of these factors. It provides:

> Neither the state nor any subdivision thereof, shall use its property or credit or any public money, or authorize or permit either to be used, directly or indirectly, in aid or maintenance, other than for examination or inspection, of any school or institution of learning wholly or in part under the control or direction of any religious denomination, or in which any denominational tenet or doctrine is taught, but the legislature may provide for the transportation of children to and from any school or institution of learning.

Described by the New York Court of Appeals as a "Blaine Amendment," Article XI §3 does at the state level what the federal Blaine Amendment would have done had it been adopted. It forbids any form of aid to schools controlled or directed by a religious denomination, or where religion is taught as a part of the curriculum. See Chapter Four.

In *Judd v. Board of Educ.*, 278 N.Y. 200, 212, 15 N.E.2d 576 (1938), the Court of Appeals held that Art. XI §3 forbids free bus transportation for students enrolled in religious schools because "[t]he purpose of the transportation is to promote the interests of the private school or religious or sectarian institution that controls and directs it." Later that year, New York voters amended Art. XI §3 to permit "the transportation of children to and from any school or institution of learning." In *Board of Ed. of Cent. Sch. Dist. No. 1, Towns of East Greenbush Rensselaer County v. Allen*, 20 N.Y.2d 109, 114, 228 N.E.2d 791, 793, 281 N.Y.S.2d 799, 803 (1967), *aff'd* 392 U.S. 236 (1968), the Court of Appeals upheld a New York statute that permitted school boards to purchase textbooks approved for use in the public schools and loan them to students enrolled in religiously affiliated schools. In its view, the "architecture reflected in *Judd* would impede every form of legislation, the benefits of which, in some remote way, might inure to parochial schools. It is our view that the words 'direct' and 'indirect' relate solely to the means of attaining the prohibited end of aiding religion as such." *See also Opinion of the Justices*, 291 Ala. 301, 280 So.2d 547 (1973) (holding that a proposed grant program for college students would be unconstitutional to the extent that it included students enrolled at religiously-affiliated colleges and universities, but relying on federal precedent); *Cecrle v. Illinois Educational Facilities Authority*, 52 Ill.2d 312, 288 N.E.2d 399 (1972) (rejecting a challenge under Art. X §3 of the Illinois Constitution to a tax-exempt financing of construction at a religiously affiliated college on the basis of precedent from federal and other state courts).

Matthews v. Quinton, 362 P.2d 932 (Alaska 1961), is a good illustration of the process by which state courts set their own course. In an opinion that contains an extensive review of the case law at the federal and state levels, the Alaska Supreme Court concluded that that public school authorities were required to exclude a child enrolled in a religiously affiliated school from a public school bus route. Unlike the New York Court of Appeals and the Supreme Court of the United States in *Board of Education v. Allen*, its view was that the cost of transportation is "direct" aid to the school. *But see Quinn v. School Committee of Plymouth*, 332 Mass. 410, 125 N.E.2d 410 (1955) (refusing to allow the school committee to question the constitutionality of a statute providing transportation for all eligible students in the district, and holding that mandamus would lie to compel the committee to furnish transportation regardless of the school in which they are enrolled). California's approach is similar to that of Alaska. *See California Teachers Assn. v. Riles*, 29 Cal.3d 794, 632 P.2d 953, 176 Cal. Rptr. 300 (1981) (state could not loan textbooks to children enrolled in religiously affiliated schools); *California Educational Facilities Authority v. Priest*, 12 Cal.3d 593, 116 Cal. Rptr. 361, 526 P.2d 513 (1974) (permitting the issuance of tax exempt bonds to finance construction at religiously affiliated colleges because the bonds were not obligations of the state and the administrative costs were borne by the institution); *Bowker v. Baker*, 73 Cal.App.2d 653, 657, 167 P.2d 256 (1956) (permitting bus transportation).

Ohio's provision, which focuses on issues of control of the school fund rather than subsidy to the schools, has been interpreted to permit forms of aid that would likely be forbidden in Alaska, Alabama, or California. *See Simmons-Harris v. Goff*, 86 Ohio St.3d 1, 711 N.E.2d 203 (Ohio 1999) (upholding the Cleveland Scholarship and Tutoring Grant Program at issue in *Zelman v. Simmons-Harris*, 122 S.Ct. 2460 (2002); *Protestants and Other Americans United for Separation of Church and State v. Essex*, 28 Ohio St. 2d 79, 275 N.E.2d 603 (1971) (payments for instructional materials and programs for children attending church-related schools did not violate Article VI §2).

The diversity of viewpoints among the States on these issues underscores the impact of federalism on the "operational" definition of the non-establishment norm. One of the clearest examples of a case in which a State supreme court has drawn a clear distinction between the command of the Establishment Clause and analogous provisions of a State constitution is *Witters v. Washington Commission for the Blind*, 112 Wash.2d 363, 711 P.2d 1119 (1989), *on remand from* 474 U.S. 481 (1986), *rev'g* 102 Wash.2d 624, 689 P.2d 53 (1984), excerpted below. When the United States Supreme Court decided that the Establishment Clause did not make it unconstitutional for Washington State to pay for Larry Witters' vocational education program at the Inland Empire School of the Bible in Spokane, it remanded the case to the Washington Supreme Court. On remand, the Washington Supreme Court considered the constitutionality of the payments under the Washington Constitution.

Witters v. Washington Commission for the Blind

112 Wash.2d 363, 771 P.2d 1119 (en banc)
cert. denied, 493 U.S. 850 (1989)

ANDERSEN, Justice.

In this case we consider for the second time whether error was committed when a visually handicapped student was denied state financial assistance to enable him to attend a private bible college with the goal of becoming a pastor, missionary or church youth director. We hold that when a person "*is getting a religious education*" (italics ours), to use the words of his attorney, that person comes squarely within the express prohibition contained in the Constitution of the State of Washington that "*[n]o public money... shall be appropriated for or applied to any religious... instruction*". (Italics ours.) Const. art. 1, § 11 (part). Accordingly, the Washington State Commission for the Blind and the Superior Court for Spokane County did not err when they denied state financial assistance for his education. Phrasing it a bit differently, our state constitution prohibits the taxpayers from being put in the position of paying for the religious instruction of aspirants to the clergy with whose religious views they may disagree.

Appellant Larry Witters, who will be referred to herein as the "applicant", applied for vocational rehabilitation funds from the Washington State Commission for the Blind (Commission) in 1979. He planned to use the funds to pursue a course of study that would prepare him for a career as a pastor, missionary or youth director. At the time of his request, the applicant was enrolled at the Inland Empire School of the Bible in Spokane pursuing a 3-year Bible diploma. Later, he switched to a 4-year program that would earn him a biblical studies degree from Inland Empire School of the Bible and a bachelor of arts degree from Whitworth College. His curriculum included Old and New Testament studies, ethics, speech and church administration.

The applicant qualifies as a legally blind person under the physical and medical eligibility requirements specified in [state law]. Funding for the Commission's assistance program is provided by both federal (80 percent) and state (20 percent) moneys. The Commission denied the applicant's request on the basis of its policy statement, which states: "Private institutions or out-of-state institutions: The Washington State Constitution forbids the use of public funds to assist an individual in the pursuit of a career or degree in theology or related areas." [The trial court affirmed its decision on state constitutional grounds.]

In 1984, this court affirmed the decision of the Commission and the Superior Court holding that "the provision of state aid to a person studying to be a pastor, missionary, or church youth director violates the establishment clause of the first amendment to the United States Constitution." *Witters v. Commission for the Blind*, 102 Wash.2d 624, 626,

689 P.2d 53 (1984), *rev'd sub nom. Witters v. Washington Dep't of Servs. for the Blind,* 474 U.S. 481 (1986). This court did not reach the state constitutional grounds on which both the Commission and the Superior Court had relied. Instead, it based its decision on the United States Supreme Court's 3-part test for determining the constitutionality of state aid under the establishment clause of the first amendment to the United States Constitution:

> First, the statute must have a secular legislative purpose; second, its principal or primary effect must be one that neither advances nor inhibits religion…; finally, the statute must not foster "an excessive government entanglement with religion."

Lemon v. Kurtzman, 403 U.S. 602, 612–13 (1971), quoted in *Witters,* 102 Wash.2d at 628, 689 P.2d 53. After concluding that the first criterion was met, this court held that the second criterion, primary effect, was not. The court declined to address entanglement, the third *Lemon* criterion. Finally, this court rejected the applicant's free exercise clause argument and declined to address his equal protection clause argument.

In 1986, the United States Supreme Court reversed this court's 1984 decision. It rejected this court's analysis of the second *Lemon* criterion and remanded the case to us for further proceedings. Pursuant to that remand, we now address three principal issues.

ISSUES

ISSUE ONE. Does the Constitution of the State of Washington prohibit the Commission from granting vocational rehabilitation funds to a visually handicapped applicant to use at a religious institution for a course of study designed to prepare him for a career as a pastor, missionary or youth director?

ISSUE TWO. If the Constitution of the State of Washington is a bar to the applicant's request for educational assistance, is such denial of funds a violation of the free exercise clause of the First Amendment?

ISSUE THREE. If the Constitution of the State of Washington is a bar to the applicant's request, is the denial of funds to the applicant a violation of the Fourteenth Amendment equal protection clause?

DECISION

ISSUE ONE—CONCLUSION. The Commission and the Superior Court did not err in denying state financial assistance for the applicant to use for religious instruction; the Constitution of the State of Washington, article 1, section 11, prohibits this.

[The] United States Supreme Court…held that "[o]n remand, the state court is of course free to consider the applicability of the 'far stricter' dictates of the Washington State Constitution. Article 1, section 11 of the Constitution of the State of Washington provides in pertinent part:

> No public money or property shall be appropriated for *or applied to* any religious worship, exercise or *instruction,* or the support of any religious establishment…

(Italics ours.) Here, the applicant is asking the State to pay for a religious course of study at a religious school, with a religious career as his goal. This falls precisely within the clear language of the state constitutional prohibition against applying public moneys to any religious instruction. Indeed, as counsel for the applicant summarized at oral argument before this court:

> *We would concede that Larry Witters is getting a religious education.*

(Italics ours.) Our state constitution prohibits the use of public moneys to pay for such religious instruction.

This court has twice construed the term "religious instruction".

In *State ex rel. Dearle v. Frazier*, 102 Wash. 369, 373, 173 P. 35 (1918), the court struck down a school board resolution giving high school credits for Bible study done outside of school, even though the course of study covered only the "historical, biographical, narrative and literary features of the Bible". On the other hand, the court upheld the teaching of "English 390: The Bible as Literature" at the University of Washington in *Calvary Bible Presbyterian Church v. Board of Regents*, 72 Wash.2d 912, 919, 436 P.2d 189 (1967), *cert. denied*, 393 U.S. 960 (1968). In *Calvary*, the court interpreted "religious instruction" as used in article 1, section 11 to mean "instruction that is devotional in nature and designed to induce faith and belief in the student." The court went on to say:

> There can be no doubt that our constitutional bars are absolute against *religious* instruction and indoctrination in specific religious beliefs or dogma; but they do not proscribe open, free, critical, and scholarly examination of the literature, experiences, and knowledge of mankind.

Calvary, at 919, 436 P.2d 189.

In this case, Inland Empire School of the Bible is a Christian college. The applicant's course of study is designed to prepare him for a career promoting Christianity. His Bible study and church courses necessarily provide indoctrination in the specific beliefs of Christianity. Thus, for the Commission to provide vocational assistance funds to the applicant as he requests would violate article 1, section 11 of the [Washington Constitution] because public money would be applied to religious instruction.

The applicant urges that we examine the vocational rehabilitation program as a whole and not focus on his individual participation in the program. His argument ignores the "sweeping and comprehensive" language of art. 1, § 11, which prohibits not only the *appropriation* of public money for religious instruction, but also the *application* of public funds to religious instruction. Herein lies a major difference between our state constitution and the establishment clause of the first amendment to the United States Constitution. It follows that to apply federal establishment clause analysis to article 1, section 11 of the state constitution as the applicant urges would be inappropriate.

Having concluded... that Constitution of the State of Washington prohibits the funding of the applicant's vocational rehabilitation plan, we need not consider the parameters of article 9, section 4 of the state constitution.[12]

ISSUE TWO—CONCLUSION. Neither the applicant's freedom to believe nor his freedom to act in a manner consistent with his beliefs is being encroached by the article 1, section 11 ban on expenditure of state funds for religious instruction. The applicant's right to free exercise of religion has not been violated.

ISSUE THREE—CONCLUSION. Denial of vocational assistance funds to the applicant herein is not a violation of the equal protection clause of the Fourteenth Amendment.

The classification here at issue is the Commission's policy of denying vocational funding of any student's religious studies. This classification is directly related to the state's interest in ensuring the separation of church and state, as required by the Consti-

---

12. "All schools maintained or supported wholly or in part by the public funds shall be forever free from sectarian control or influence." Washington Const. art. 9 § 4.

tution of the State of Washington. The state has a compelling interest in maintaining the strict separation of church and state set forth in Const. art. 1, § 11. The applicant's individual interest in receiving a religious education must therefore give way to the state's greater need to uphold its constitution.

In any event, the denial of tuition for religious instruction is but a refusal of state funds to advance religion in a constitutionally impermissible way; the Commission has not discriminated against the applicant because he is religious, but has refused to use state moneys to pay for his religious activities.

Callow, C.J., and Brachtenbach, Pearson and Smith, JJ., concur.

UTTER, Justice (dissenting).

The majority's analysis of Const. art. 1, § 11 is contrary to the meaning and purpose of this provision in our state constitution. The decision by the Washington State Commission for the Blind to exclude Mr. Witters from the vocational rehabilitation program is not required by the language in our constitution, our previous holdings, or the evidence in this case. It also jeopardizes public funding for students who study nonreligious courses at religious institutions. Additionally, as Justice Dolliver states in his dissenting opinion, and as I have previously stated, the State's attempt to condition the receipt of vocational rehabilitation assistance on the absence of a "religious" career goal unconstitutionally abridges the recipient's right under the United States Constitution to freely exercise his faith. For these reasons, I dissent.

The majority holds that an individual who meets all of the state and federal legislative criteria for participating in the vocational rehabilitation program for the blind must be excluded entirely from the program because some of his vocational training may involve "religious" instruction. Yet the State has completely failed to show that Mr. Witters' vocational training constitutes such instruction or that public funding in his case is forbidden.

Const. art. 1, § 11 states: (1) no "public money" (2) shall be "appropriated…or applied" by the state (3) to "religious…instruction". A careful examination of these three clauses reveals three major defects in the majority opinion. First, "public money" refers only to those funds emanating from the state treasury; since state money contributes only 20 percent of the funding for this vocational rehabilitation program, the state constitution affects only that portion. Second, application of these funds for instruction at a religious institution is the result of a personal decision by the individual recipient, not the state; therefore, the state would not be "appropriating or applying" the funds. Third, this court has previously defined "religious instruction" to be that instruction which is devotional in nature and is intended to induce faith in the pupil. There is no evidence in the record to support the majority's conclusion that all or any of Mr. Witters' training will involve such instruction.

I

Const. art. 1, § 11 prohibits the state from appropriating "public money" for religious worship or instruction. The term 'public money' refers only to those revenues raised by the state government, not those raised by the federal government. The definition of "public money" as that term is used in Const. art. 1, § 11 is well settled. As this court stated in *Washington Health Care Facilities Auth. v. Spellman*, 96 Wash.2d 68, 73, 633 P.2d 866 (1981):

> The reasonable meaning of "public money" in article 1, section 11 is money from the treasury of this state or its municipalities, not some other governmental exchequer.

The constitutional constraints apply only to those funds appropriated by the state; in this case, money from the state treasury represents only 20 percent of the program. The state constitution does not prohibit a state agency from disbursing federal funds to Mr. Witters. Therefore, at a minimum, Mr. Witters is entitled to vocational rehabilitation funding in proportion to the federal funds involved in this program.

II

Const. art. 1, § 11 prohibits the state from "appropriating or applying" public money for religious instruction. In granting Mr. Witters money for his vocational training, the state is neither appropriating nor applying funds for religious instruction. The state is merely appropriating public funds for a neutral vocational rehabilitation program designed to assist the visually handicapped in developing skills necessary for employment. The decision to apply those funds for instruction at a religious or secular school is made by the individual aid recipient, not the state.

The majority suggests that in order to determine whether the application of public funds violates Const. art. 1, § 11 we must examine how the individual recipient of such funds chooses to apply the money. The majority provides no precedent for such a microscopic examination of the use of public assistance funds. Such an approach lacks any support in our case law and will have serious unintended consequences.

It is far more reasonable and consistent to confine our analysis to the nature of the public assistance program itself. If the program itself does not violate the constitution, then our inquiry should end. The purpose of the constitutional prohibition against appropriating or applying public funds for religious instruction is to constrain state government actions not individual decisions. For the same reasons that the State does not now attempt to prevent a salaried public official or recipient of unemployment compensation from giving their public money for "religious worship, exercise or instruction", the state should not be allowed to control the career choices of a recipient of vocational rehabilitation funds.

III

The majority now says that Mr. Witters must be excluded from the rehabilitation program not because of his vocational objectives per se but because his vocational training may involve some "religious instruction". This conclusion is not supported by the record. The State has introduced no evidence describing the nature of the instruction Mr. Witters is receiving.

There is only one case in Washington law that defines "religious instruction" as that phrase is used in Const. art. 1, § 11. In *Calvary Bible Presbyterian Church v. Board of Regents*, 72 Wash.2d 912, 436 P.2d 189 (1967), *cert. denied*, 393 U.S. 960 (1968), this court stated that

> the framers of our constitution did not intend the word "instruction" to be construed without limit, but that the proscribed field be confined to that category of instruction that resembles worship and manifests a devotion to religion and religious principles in thought, feeling, belief, and conduct, *i.e., instruction that is devotional in nature and designed to induce faith and belief in the student.*

(Italics mine.) *Calvary*, at 919, 436 P.2d 189.

The *Calvary* court demonstrated that the only way to determine whether any instruction is "religious" is to examine the instruction itself and see whether it is objective or devotional in manner. *Calvary,* at 920–21, 436 P.2d 189. Finding that the teaching of "English 390: The Bible as Literature" at the University of Washington was not designed to induce faith and belief in the student, the court held that this course was not "religious instruction".

Mr. Witters' curriculum includes courses in Old and New Testament, ethics, speech, and church administration. Aside from this general information, we know little about the vocational training Mr. Witters is receiving. The State has produced no evidence regarding the manner of instruction. The parties stipulated only that the "classwork consists of classes instructional in nature for which he pays tuition. There are also devotional chapel services at the school for which he pays nothing." Petitioner's Proposed Factual Stipulation, Aug. 11, 1980 (signed by counsel for both parties). The parties also stipulated that the college Mr. Witters wished to attend was not a denominational or sectarian institution. Verbatim Report of Proceedings, at 6.

Given the absence of any evidence regarding Mr. Witters' other courses and the manner of instruction, the majority's conclusion that his program of study amounts to "religious instruction" rests on no more than speculation. The state has constitutional authority to exclude Mr. Witters from the vocational rehabilitation program only for that portion of his training which involves "religious instruction". Because the evidence does not indicate that any of Mr. Witters' vocational training will include "religious instruction", he is entitled to the full amount of state and federal benefits under the program.

IV

In *State v. Gunwall,* this court announced several nonexclusive neutral guidelines to assist courts in deciding whether to interpret state constitutional provisions differently than the United States Supreme Court's interpretation of analogous provisions of the United States Constitution. *State v. Gunwall,* 106 Wash.2d at 56–61, 720 P.2d 808. These guidelines were articulated to facilitate state constitutional analysis and prevent result-oriented jurisprudence.

The court listed six nonexclusive criteria: (1) textual language of the state constitution; (2) significant differences in the texts of parallel provisions of the federal and state constitutions; (3) state constitutional and common law history; (4) preexisting state law; (5) differences in structure between the federal and state constitutions; and (6) matters of particular state interest or local concern. *Gunwall,* at 61–62, 720 P.2d 808. Inexplicably, the majority discusses none of the *Gunwall* criteria. Thus, we have no principled analysis to explain why this court chooses to interpret the state establishment clause to prohibit that which a unanimous United States Supreme Court has expressly approved under the establishment clause of the federal constitution. Without such analysis, the resort to independent state grounds to reach a different result in this case appears to spring from the "pure intuition" that this court rightly scorned in *Gunwall.* A close examination of [these] criteria demonstrates why application of the state constitution in this instance should not lead to a different result than [in] the United States Supreme Court.

A. LANGUAGE

The first two criteria of *Gunwall* direct the court to consider the language of the state constitution and the parallel provision of the federal constitution. There is no question that the language of the federal and state establishment clauses is different. The First Amendment provides in relevant part:

> Congress shall make no law respecting an establishment of religion, or prohibiting the free exercise thereof...

Const. art. 1, § 11 provides:

> No public money or property shall be appropriated for or applied to any religious worship, exercise or instruction, or the support of any religious establishment...

While the language of the state constitution appears to be more specific in prohibiting the state from appropriating funds for religious instruction, it is not necessarily any more or less restrictive in application to specific fact situations than the federal establishment clause.

The majority suggests a different result than that reached by the United States Supreme Court is mandated by the "far stricter" language of the state constitution. This characterization of the Washington establishment clause does not by itself support the conclusion that the state constitution must differ from the federal constitution on this particular issue. The doctrinaire rigidity with which the majority attempts to interpret Const. art. 1, § 11 is not justified by the document's purpose and history and has received well-deserved criticism in the scholarly literature. *See* Conklin & Vache, *The Establishment Clause and the Free Exercise Clause of the Washington Constitution—A Proposal to the Supreme Court,* 8 U. Puget Sound L. Rev. 411 (1985) (suggesting that the rigid ideological interpretation of Const. art. 1, § 11 reflected in some of this court's previous opinions owes more to anti-Mormon and anti-Catholic sentiment in the late 19th century than to any careful examination of its terms). Differences in language between the state and federal establishment clauses do not support a different result in every case. The majority does not present a reasonable argument that such differences compel a contrary result in this case.

B. CONSTITUTIONAL AND COMMON LAW HISTORY

Courts must often resort to extrinsic sources in order to determine the meaning of constitutional terms. In *State ex rel. Mason Cy. Logging Co. v. Wiley,* 177 Wash. 65, 74, 31 P.2d 539 (1934), this court declared that "'the public history of the times should be consulted, and should have weight'" in giving meaning to the terms used. A variety of sources are available to assist this court in determining the meaning and purpose of the "religious instruction" clause of Const. art. 1, § 11. Two very useful sources are the Enabling Act, through which the federal government authorized the citizens of the Washington Territory to call a constitutional convention and proceed to statehood, and the *Journal of the State Constitutional Convention, 1889* (B. Rosenow ed. 1962). In addition, this court has used contemporary newspapers' accounts of the state constitutional convention to supplement the official minutes since no verbatim record of the convention exists. Consideration of these various historical sources demonstrates that the sole purpose of the "religious instruction" clause of Const. art. 1, § 11 was to prevent public schools from giving sectarian religious instruction and to prevent the use of public funds to support private parochial schools. *See* Utter & Larson, *Church and State on the Frontier: The History of the Establishment Clauses in the Washington State Constitution,* 15 Hastings Const. L.Q. 451 (1988). There is no evidence of any intent by those who drafted and ratified our state constitution to prohibit the use of public money for the purposes proposed by Mr. Witters.

The federal Enabling Act of 1889 which authorized the Washington Constitutional Convention contained a significant limitation in the area of religious freedom. The Enabling Act required that the state constitution include a provision for the "establishment and maintenance of systems of public schools, which shall be open to all the children... and free from sectarian control." Enabling Act, ch. 180, § 4, 25 Stat. 676 (approved Feb. 22,

1889), *reprinted in* Revised Code of Washington, vol. 0 at 20 (1987). This provision reflected a widespread concern about the contemporary practice of Bible reading and other sectarian religious instruction in the public primary and secondary schools. *See* D. Boles, *The Bible, Religion, and the Public Schools* 35 (1961); Utter & Larson, 15 Hastings Const. L. Q. at 458–67. Such practices were particularly offensive to the recent waves of Catholic and Jewish immigrants who objected to their children receiving compulsory instruction in the majority Protestant faith. *See* B. Parkany, *"Religious Instruction" in the Washington Constitution* (1965) (thesis available in the Washington State Library); D. Boles, *supra.*

The general consensus in Washington and the rest of the country was that public schools should not give sectarian religious instruction, and that private schools should not be supported by public funds. *See* B. Parkany, pt. 2, at 14; D. Boles, at 23–27, 33. This attitude was reflected in many state constitutions, including Washington's, that were written in the last half of the 19th century. D. Boles, at 33–34.

The Washington Constitutional Convention met in Olympia on July 4, 1889. That the Convention was concerned with forced religious instruction in public primary and secondary schools and public aid to parochial schools is supported by a number of circumstances surrounding the adoption of the "religious instruction" clause itself. On July 17, 1889, the Seattle Post-Intelligencer and the Tacoma Morning Globe both printed the Bill of Rights Committee's first draft of Const. art. 1, § 11. At that point, this provision contained no reference to "religious instruction." B. Parkany, pt. 1, at 6.

Two days later, on July 19, the Portland Oregonian, which was one of the most widely read newspapers in Washington Territory, ran an editorial concerning "religious instruction" in public schools. The editorial used the phrase "religious instruction" six times, and concluded with a strong stand:

> In order that liberty of conscience may remain inviolate... there must be an absolute separation of church and state, religion and public schools... [I]t is necessary to keep the public schools free from religious influences, from theological disputes and sectarian teachings....
>
> * * *
>
> ...Religious instruction in the public school means a gradual retrogression to the union of church and state, and this union means a tyrannical government and a corrupt priesthood.... [I]f liberty of conscience is valued at all, keep religion away from public schools.

The Oregonian, July 19, 1889, at 4, col. 2. On the same date, a Spokane newspaper also used the phrase "religious instruction" in an article summarizing the views of eminent clergymen on both sides of the debate. Spokane Falls [Daily] Review, July 19, 1889, at 3.

On July 25, a few days after the flurry of newspaper editorials, articles and letters to the editor on religious instruction in the public primary and secondary schools, the Bill of Rights Committee submitted its amended report to the Convention. The new draft, which was later adopted by the Republican-dominated Convention without debate, read in pertinent part as follows:

> Absolute freedom of conscience in all matters of religious sentiment, belief, and worship, shall be guaranteed to every individual... No public money or property shall be appropriated for, or applied to any religious worship, exercise or instruction, or the support of any religious establishment...

Journal of the Washington State Constitutional Convention, 1889, at 500 (B. Rosenow ed. 1962); B. Parkany, pt. 1, at 1.

The circumstantial evidence is strong that the phrase "religious instruction" that had been added by the Bill of Rights Committee was borrowed from the various newspaper articles published between the first and last drafts of its report. The frequent use of this phrase in the popular press and in the context of discussions relating to religious instruction in the public primary and secondary schools provides uncontradicted evidence as to the "common and ordinary meaning" of the phrase among those who drafted and ratified the constitution in 1889.

This evidence is considerable and leads to only one conclusion: the historic purpose of the "religious instruction" clause of Const. art. 1, § 11 was to prevent public aid to parochial schools and to prohibit religious instruction in public primary and secondary schools. Neither of these concerns is implicated here. Although historical analysis is not necessarily dispositive in a question of state constitutional interpretation, the majority does not suggest that current values and conditions conflict with the historical intent of this provision.

C. PREEXISTING STATE LAW AND DIFFERENCES IN STRUCTURE

Neither of the fourth or fifth *Gunwall* criteria appear to be applicable in this case.

D. PARTICULAR STATE OR LOCAL CONCERN

Gunwall also advises the court to examine whether the matter is of particular state or local interest. Neither the history of Const. art. 1, § 11 nor the vocational training program at issue in this case reflect any particular state interest. As discussed above, the language of Const. art. 1, § 11 reflected a national consensus in the late 19th century to restrict sectarian religious instruction in the public schools and to prohibit public funding of sectarian institutions. This is the context in which the phrased "religious instruction" was used by the local popular press of 1889.

Applying the *Gunwall* criteria, I can only conclude that public funding of religious instruction, as that term was commonly understood by those who ratified our state constitution, is not involved in this case. Therefore, there is no basis for reaching a result contrary to the one reached by the United States Supreme Court under the federal establishment clause.

V

I would hold that the granting of vocational rehabilitation assistance to Mr. Witters would not violate Const. art. 1, § 11. So long as the choice of which institution to attend for vocational training is that of the individual, the state's role in appropriating the funds is insufficient to come within the constraints of Const. art. 1, § 11.

DOLLIVER and DORE, JJ., concur.

DOLLIVER, Justice (dissenting).

By holding Larry Witters ineligible to receive funds to develop his employment skills merely because he made the personal choice to pursue a religious career, the court denies Witters his religious freedom as protected by the free exercise clause of the United States Constitution and diminishes his rights as a citizen.

I do not believe the state constitution ever meant to prohibit the individual choice of an adult in such a case as this (see dissent by Utter, J.). But even assuming the majority interpretation of the meaning of "religious instruction" is correct, it cannot supersede the free exercise clause. *See Reynolds v. Sims*, 377 U.S. 533, 584 (1964).

Witters chooses to carry out his religious beliefs by studying theology and becoming a minister. He became eligible for aid because of a physical handicap and is still eligible for that reason. Witters does not ask for an exception to the general rule of eligibility. He only asks the general rule to be applied with equality, not for his choice of training to be disqualified because of its religious content.

The majority says Witters is not being denied benefits because of conduct arising from his religious beliefs. The argument that being a minister is a "career or calling" and is not a religious act within the protection of the free exercise clause has already been rejected by the Supreme Court. As Justice Brennan wrote in his eloquent concurrence:

> The [Tennessee] court stated that "[i]t is not religious belief, but the career or calling [of ministry], by which one is identified as dedicated to the full time promotion of the religious objectives of a particular religious sect, that disqualifies."...
>
> The characterization of the exclusion [of ministers or priests as delegates to a constitutional convention] as one burdening appellant's "career or calling" and not religious belief cannot withstand analysis. Clearly freedom of belief protected by the Free Exercise Clause embraces freedom to profess or practice that belief, even including doing so to earn a livelihood. One's religious belief surely does not cease to enjoy the protection of the First Amendment when held with such depth of sincerity as to impel one to join the ministry.

(Footnotes omitted.) *McDaniel v. Paty* 435 U.S. 618, 630–31 (1978) (Brennan, J., concurring).

The only reason given for denying Witters his education is the need for greater separation of church and state than is provided under the First Amendment, which the majority believes can be found in the Washington Constitution. This is not enough. In a case originating in the state of Missouri, a student group wanted to use university facilities for religious activity. The Supreme Court found that once a public forum is created the First Amendment protection of free speech requires there be no discrimination based on the religious content of the speech. The Court ruled it was a compelling interest of the state to meet the requirements of the establishment clause, but that an equal access policy adequately met that requirement. *Widmar v. Vincent.*

In the words of the Supreme Court:

> Arguing that the State of Missouri has gone further than the Federal Constitution in proscribing indirect state support for religion, the University claims a compelling interest in complying with the applicable provisions of the Missouri Constitution.
>
> * * *
>
> ... [T]he state interest asserted here—in achieving greater separation of church and State than is already ensured under the Establishment Clause of the Federal Constitution—is limited by the Free Exercise Clause and in this case by the Free Speech Clause as well. In this constitutional context, we are unable to recognize the State's interest as sufficiently "compelling" to justify content-based discrimination against respondents' religious speech.

(Footnotes omitted.) *Widmar v. Vincent,* at 275–76.

In an age of government benefits, balancing separation of church and state and freedom of religion is complex and cannot be done by placing our state establishment clause above the federal free exercise clause.

In this case the statute as applied is not facially neutral. It has only one exclusion, as indicated in the policy statement by the Commission, which is for those who use the funds "in pursuit of a career or degree in theology or related areas." Here a religious classification triggers the disqualification, and under these circumstances, even the recent cases would apply the strict scrutiny test of requiring a compelling state interest.

To require Witters to abandon his religious vocation in order to retain his funding as a handicapped person—to require him to make such a choice—is to deprive him of the full benefits of citizenship. It is just such a diminishing of citizenship that the free exercise clause was meant to prevent. I dissent.

Justice Durham's dissent is omitted.

Notes

1. Justice Andersen's majority opinion concludes that there is no violation of the Equal Protection Clause when the State excludes otherwise eligible persons because they are "getting a religious education." In its view, the "classification is directly related to the state's interest in ensuring the separation of church and state, as required by the Constitution of the State of Washington." What is the precise nature of Washington state's interest in ensuring the separation of church and state in a case such as this one? The Court provides the answer: "Phrasing it a bit differently, our state constitution prohibits the taxpayers from being put in the position of paying for the religious instruction of aspirants to the clergy with whose religious views they may disagree."

2. Is Justice Dolliver correct when he asserts that *McDaniel v. Paty*, 435 U.S. 618 (1978) is the controlling case? *McDaniel*, which is excerpted in Chapter Ten, invalidated a Tennessee constitutional provision excluding ministers of the gospel from the state legislature.

3. Does the Washington Supreme Court hold that art. 1 § 11 is, in effect, a non-association norm? If so, would it be relevant to the equal protection analysis to determine whether other dissenting taxpayers' non-association interests are protected to the same degree? Is there something other than the Washington Constitution itself that makes the protection of a dissenting taxpayer's non-association interests more compelling than those of an otherwise eligible blind student who is denied benefits on the basis of his choice of a religious career path? *See State* ex rel. *Gallwey v. Grimm*, 2002 WL 1293054 (Wash., June 13, 2002) (upholding tuition grants at religious colleges and universities because the grant program "requires that the student *not* 'be enrolled for any program that include any religious worship, exercise, or instruction'") (emphasis in original).

4. Justice Utter's dissent contains a short history of Washington State's art. 1 § 11, and suggests that "the rigid ideological interpretation of Const. art. 1, § 11 reflected in some of this court's previous opinions owes more to anti-Mormon and anti-Catholic sentiment in the late 19th century than to any careful examination of its terms." Does the existence of such sentiment at the time the State constitution was adopted provide support for an argument that religious animus tainted the provision *ab initio*? Is it relevant to the equal protection argument?

(D) State Cases Decided After 1990: Calculating the Effect of Smith

The Washington Supreme Court decided the remand of *Witters* less than a year before the United States Supreme Court decided *Employment Div. v. Smith*, 494 U.S. 872 (1990). After *Smith*, *Lukumi*, and *Rosenberger* could the State of Washington exclude Larry Witters from participation in a generally applicable social welfare program because of his choice to use the benefits to prepare for a career in ministry?

In *Jackson v. Benson*, 218 Wis.2d 835, 578 N.W.2d 602, 617–19 (1998), *cert. denied*, 525 U.S. 997 (1998), the Wisconsin Supreme Court upheld a funded school choice program that permitted low income students in the City of Milwaukee to enroll in any school, private or public, and receive state assistance, but in *Bagley v. Raymond Sch. Dep't*, 728 A.2d 127, 133–35, 144–45 (Me.), *cert. denied*, 528 U.S. 947 (1999), the Maine Supreme Court upheld Maine's education tuition program, which explicitly *excludes* religious schools from receipt of state funds. *Accord Strout v. Albanese*, 178 F.3d 57 (1st Cir.), *cert. denied*, 528 U.S. 931 (1999) (upholding constitutionality of state statute authorizing direct grants to nonsectarian high schools for reimbursement of tuition for students that had no public education facilities available).

Some State courts are revisiting the issue. Reversing its prior holding that payment of tuition at religiously-affiliated schools violates the Establishment Clause, *Swart v. South Burlington Town Sch. Dist.*, 122 Vt. 177, 167 A.2d 514, *cert. denied*, 366 U.S. 925 (1961), the Vermont Supreme Court held that "that jurisprudence has evolved greatly since 1961 and in directions unpredictable at that time." *Campbell v. Manchester Bd. of Sch. Dir.*, 161 Vt. 441, 448, 641 A. 2d 352, 357 (1994). Like many courts considering the issue, the Vermont court found itself in a quandary: "If *Mueller* and *Witters* [v. *Washington State Commission for the Blind*] are the controlling precedents, there may be no Establishment Clause barrier to reimbursing plaintiff for tuition paid to a private school. If [*Committee for Pub. Educ. & Religious Liberty v. Nyquist*, 413 U.S. 756 (1993)], is the controlling precedent, there may be a barrier." *Id.* at 451, 641 A. 2d at 358.

Choosing *Mueller* and *Witters* as the controlling precedent, the Vermont court identified several criteria that led it to conclude that the reimbursement scheme was constitutional and that *Swart* should be overruled:

> First, plaintiff has already paid the tuition in question and is looking for reimbursement; thus, no payment will go directly to a sectarian school. [A]lthough the relevant statute appears to contemplate payment directly to the private high school selected by the parent of the pupil[,] see 16 V.S.A. §822(a)(1), [and] direct payments to a sectarian institution may raise additional considerations, we do not address the validity of a direct payment to a sectarian institution [in this case].
>
> Second, defendant does not maintain a high school and pays tuition for all high school pupils, as required by statute. This is not a case in which a school district both maintains an appropriate school and allows some students to go elsewhere by paying tuition for them.
>
> Third, there is no allegation that defendant's decision not to maintain a high school represents a desire to aid sectarian education. From the state perspective, the main evidence that the tuition reimbursement system is not intended to aid religious education is its history. If aiding religious education was the intent of the reimbursement system originally, that intent did not survive *Swart*

> in 1961. Instead, the system has continued for the past thirty years with the only change being the resulting limitation on parental choice.
>
> Fourth, unlike *Nyquist*, there is no indication that the result of defendant's policy will be to send any substantial number of children to sectarian schools. We have no indication, however, of the extent to which tuition might be paid for out-of-state schools.
>
> Fifth, the extent of state regulation, or other involvement with, St. Andrews Academy will not be affected by the outcome of this case. The school is already an "approved" independent school. *See* 16 V.S.A. § 166(b).
>
> Sixth, in this case, the subsidy scheme does not operate to promote sectarian education. The school district of the student's residence must reimburse for the full tuition charged by a public school. For a private school, reimbursement is only at the "average announced tuition of Vermont union high schools for the year of attendance" unless the school meets Vermont public school approval standards or the paying district votes a higher rate. 16 V.S.A. § 824(b)–(c). There is no indication of a higher rate here, and St. Andrews Academy, because it is not a Vermont institution, cannot meet Vermont public approval standards. *See* id. § 11(a)(8).

Id. at 452–454, 641 A.2d at 359–61. *But see Asociacion de Maestros de Puerto Rico v. Torres*, 1994 WL 780744 (P.R. 1994) (holding scholarship program for needy children unconstitutional under the Establishment Clause because aid to the student is aid to the school, and because students attending private and religious schools received a cash payment, while students who chose to use their payments within existing public schools were "credited" with a payment). *See also Kotterman v. Killian*, 972 P.2d 606, 612–15 (Ariz.), *cert. denied*, 528 U.S. 921 (1999) (upholding $500 tuition tax credit against challenges under the Establishment Clause and Arizona Constitution); *Jenkins v. Leininger*, 277 Ill.App.3d 313, 659 N.E.2d 1366 (1995) (rejecting arguments for school choice based on parental rights of care and control of the education of their children, and holding that the manner in which education funds are to be applied rests with the discretion of the Illinois Legislature).

Now that the Supreme Court has upheld the constitutionality of the Cleveland Scholarship Program involved in *Zelman v. Simmons-Harris*, it is likely that opponents of funded school choice will seek state-by-state rulings invalidating the practice. Those who support school choice will also seek state-by-state rulings invalidating state laws and constitutional provisions that restrict the practice. Eventually, however, the United States Supreme Supreme Court will be called upon to resolve the "next generation" of issues relating to school finance. What theories will be raised, both for and against, publicly-funded parental choice? See *Zelman v. Simmons-Harris*, 122 S.Ct. 2460 (2002) (Thomas, J. concurring); id. (Breyer, J. dissenting).

Chapter 7

The Structure, Management & Property of Churches and Religious Organizations

A. Introduction

Religious organizations choose to adopt a civil law corporate form for many of the same reasons that businesses organized for profit do: to limit liability, to own and control property in the name of the organization, and to take advantage of benefits available to corporations under tax and other regulatory provisions of state and federal law. Due to religious freedom guarantees, however, religious organizations, whether incorporated or operating in some other form, are not just another kind of "business". Currently, each of the United States allows a number of different ways for churches and religious organizations to organize themselves for legal purposes. Most states provide special statutes to govern the corporate life of a religious organization; others provide a more generalized opportunity to acquire legal status under state codes governing nonprofit corporations and unincorporated associations. *See e.g.* Cal. Corp. Code §§9110, *et seq.* (Supp. 2001); Mass. Gen. L. ch. 67 §55 (2001) (providing special rules for the incorporation of Orthodox churches); N.Y. Not-for-Profit Corp. Law §201 (2001) (defining corporations incorporated for religious purposes as "type B" non-profit corporations).

In an 1880 *ultra vires* action, a Maine court offered the following view of its own and other states' statutes allowing for the incorporation of religious organizations:

> The statutes relating to this subject differ in the various states. In some a large majority of such societies are incorporated, while in others, as in this State, the societies themselves (using church and society as synonymous), are incorporated bodies with certain officers, on whom is conferred by statute, a corporate succession, holding the legal title of the property.... The object of the statute is to prevent property belonging to the church, but held by the trustees, from descending, at the decease of the latter, to their heirs, and save the trouble and expense of causing new trustees to be appointed by the courts, and conveyances made to new trustees. This the law effects by clothing the persons holding the office of trustees for the time being, though frequently changing by death, removal or otherwise, with the character of perpetuity and unbroken continuance, which is the peculiar attribute of a corporation.

Bailey v. Trustees of Methodist Episcopal Church of Freeport, 71 Me. 472, 476–77 (1880).

B. Organizational Types

1. Common law forms

a) The Territorial Parish

Under the law of England, corporations could exist only upon grant of charter by the King. These concepts were transferred to New England and to the rest of the United States during the period when a number of the States had established churches. In the States where established churches were found, the "territorial parish" concept took root.

Like the English models on which they were based, the parish in Colonial Virginia or New England "was a local governmental institution which administered both church and local affairs without a distinction being made between the two in either law or custom." Membership privileges and obligations came with residence within the parish, and the Vestry controlled many aspects of local affairs. Seventeenth century New Englanders dubbed their parish administration the "town meeting." Virginians, by contrast, used the term "vestry meeting." *See generally* Guy Fred Wells, Parish Education in Colonial Virginia (1969).

b) The Common Law Corporation Sole

The common law corporation sole is also a reflection of the practical needs of the Anglican Establishment in America, and Virginia was one of the colonies to adopt the device as a means of governing the affairs of the Episcopal Church in that State. Because the Church was organized by territorial parish, the common law needed to recognize that the Church had an existence independent from that of the parish, and should be capable of receiving endowments and holding property in its own right. The common law device utilized for this purpose was that of the *person ecclesiae*, the sole corporation embodied in the minister who, during his tenure, was seized of the freehold of its property and who was capable of transmitting such inherited property to his successor. This common law form has been recognized in some states to apply to the Roman Catholic Church as well. *See Municipality of Ponce v. Roman Catholic Apostolic Church*, 210 U.S. 296, 318 (1908); *Terrett v. Taylor*, 13 U.S. (9 Cranch) 43, 46 (1815) (common law of Virginia), excerpted in Chapter One § B; *Reid v. Barry*, 93 Fla. 849, 887, 112 So. 846, 860 (1927); *Blanc v. Alsbury*, 63 Tex. 489 (1885) (Roman Catholic).

2. Statutory Organization Forms

a) Nonprofit Corporation Law: An Overview

A nonprofit corporation is generally understood to be "a corporation, no part of the income or profit of which is distributable to its members, directors or officers," Model Nonprofit Corp. Act § 2(a) (1964).[1] Though this is no longer the legal definition of the

1. This definition of "nonprofit" is not included in the Revised Act. Colorado's official commentary on the definition explains its reasoning for not including one. "A common definition—it is an association whose net gains do not inure to the benefit of its members and which makes no distribution to its members, except on dissolution—does not work for all nonprofit associations. Consumer cooperatives, for example, make distributions to their members; but they are not for-profit

term, the nonprofit form is one of the most common organizational structures utilized by religious and religiously affiliated corporations. Because the requirements for nonprofit and charitable status vary from state to state, the specifics of the nonprofit corporation law of a church or religious corporation's domicile should be consulted with respect to all matters relevant to its organization and structure: *e.g.*, matters of form, management, membership and voting rights, meetings, property rights, mergers, dissolution, and qualification as a "charity" for tax and other purposes.

The Revised Model Nonprofit Corporation Act (the "Revised Act") represents the greatest departure yet from standard business corporation statutes and was modeled somewhat after California's nonprofit corporation statute. *See* Cal. Corp. Code §§5002–12000 (2001). The differences between the Revised Act and the prior version were characterized as follows by one of the drafters: "While the earlier model nonprofit corporation statutes were designed to be primarily enabling, i.e., to give the nonprofit community an opportunity to obtain limited liability through a general incorporation statute, the Revised Act is both an enabling and a regulatory statute. It emerged as something of a hybrid between the California Act and the Revised Model Business Corporation Act." Lizabeth A. Moody, *The Who, What and How of the Revised Model Nonprofit Corporation Act*, 16 N. Ky. L. Rev. 251, 265 (1988).

Nonprofits incorporating under the Revised Act must designate themselves as either (1) a mutual benefit corporation; (2) a public benefit corporation; or (3) a religious corporation. Nonprofits already in existence when the Revised Act was adopted were designated by statute in light of the purposes for which they were organized. A categorical approach was employed by the drafters of the Revised Act because of the weaknesses that appear whenever the law seeks to impose a uniform set of rules on different of types of nonprofit corporations. Thomas F. Blackwell, *The Revolution is Here: The Promise of a Unified Business Entity Code*, 24 J. Corp. L. 333 (1999) (noting the need for special treatment of nonprofits).

This is particularly true in the case of churches and religious organizations. The application of "general" principles of nonprofit or business corporation law to these organizations can create a host of legal and constitutional problems. Although these models function well in the non-religious sector, the control and accountability structures they envision are not well adapted to the diversity that exists among churches and religious organizations. The Revised Act avoids the "one size fits all" problem by requiring a newly organized nonprofit to choose which of the three categories best describes the purpose for which it is being organized. Under the Revised Act, that description is binding. No outside authority is given authority to review the designation, and the Act contains no definition of the terms "public," "mutual benefit," and "religious."

One major source of controversy for the drafters of the Revised Act was whether to include a separate category for religious corporations. Those favoring a separate category argued that religious corporations did not fit neatly into either of the other two available categories, and further, that certain tax and constitutional issues compelled a separate category. In a somewhat grudging example of deference to First Amendment concerns, the drafters included the following language in §1802(b):

> If religious doctrine governing the affairs of a religious corporation is inconsistent with the provisions of this Act on the same subject, the religious doctrine

---

organizations. Those consumer cooperatives not organized under specific state or federal laws need the benefits of this Act." Colo. Stats. 7-30-101 (2001)(Official Comment).

> shall control to the extent and only to the extent, required by the Constitution of the United States or the constitution of this state or both.

Why do you suppose there was such resistance to a special category for religious organizations? Does this language mean that religious doctrine governs only when the Free Exercise Clause or its state constitutional equivalent *mandates* accommodation? Note the reference in the statute to religious *doctrine*. Would, or should, the same considerations apply to cases involving church legal systems such as the canon law of the Anglican, Catholic, or Presbyterian churches? See *Korean United Presbyterian Church v. Presbytery of the Pacific*, 230 Cal. App. 3d 480, 503, 281 Cal.Rptr. 396 (1991) (holding that canon law governs when incorporated into the organic documents). Based on your reading of *Texas Monthly v. Bullock*, noted in Chapter Five and excerpted in Chapter Nine, and *Employment Div. v. Smith*, excerpted in Chapter Five, is it possible to argue that such a situation would *ever* arise? *See generally* Catherine M. Knight, Comment, *Must God Regulate Religious Corporations? A Proposal for Reform of the Religious Corporation Provisions of the Revised Model Nonprofit Corporation Act*, 42 Emory L.J. 721 (1993).

b) The Charter Form

Prior to the adoption of modern incorporation statutes, all corporations were formed by direct grant of authority from the State. Under modern incorporation statutes, the corporation comes into existence when certain filing and registration requirements are met. In states that retain the charter form, a church applies for a charter in a manner similar to old-style incorporation practice. It must obtain formal approval by the appropriate authority, often a court, before its charter becomes effective.

Because the charter is a document allowing for the incorporation of a specific religious organization, and the procedure requires formal review *and certification* that the organization is being formed for a proper purpose, this form of incorporation raises a number of constitutional issues that are not present in statutory incorporation settings where incorporations are handled administratively. Examples of states that permit this form of corporate existence include Pennsylvania, 10 Pa. Cons. Stat. Ann. § 81 (2001); Maine, Maine Rev. St. Ann. tit. 13 § 41 *et seq.* (2001); and New York, N.Y. Relig. Corp. Law § 180 (2001). Consider the following cases:

Application for Charter of the Conversion Center, Inc.

388 Pa. 239, 130 A.2d 107 (1957)

CHIDSEY, Justice

This appeal is from the order of the court below refusing to grant a charter under the provisions of the Nonprofit Corporation Law to The Conversion Center, Inc. Article II, § 201 of the Act provides:

> Five or more natural persons of full age and of either sex, married or single, at least three of whom are residents of the Commonwealth and citizens of the United States, its territories or possessions, may form a nonprofit corporation under the provisions of this act *for any purpose or purposes which are lawful and not injurious to the community.* (Emphasis supplied.)

Appellants qualified as incorporators and complied with all procedural requirements of the Act[]. The pertinent portion of Article II, § 207 of the Act is as follows:

...The court shall consider the application. It may hear evidence, if any there be, on behalf of the applicants and against the application, or it may refer the application to a master to make report as to the propriety of granting the application. In such case, upon the filing of the master's report, the court shall grant the applicants and protestants a hearing, if exceptions are filed by either of them. If the court shall find the articles to be in proper form and within the provisions of this act, *and the purpose or purposes given in the articles to be lawful and not injurious to the community, the court shall so certify on the articles*, and *shall* order and decree thereon that the articles are approved and that, upon the recording of the articles and the order, the corporation shall come into existence for the purpose or purposes and upon the terms stated therein; otherwise, the court shall refuse the application for a charter. (Emphasis supplied.)

The purpose of the formation of the corporation as set forth in the articles of incorporation is as follows:

> "*Third:* The purpose of this corporation shall be to promote the Gospel of Our Lord and Savior, Jesus Christ; to foster, promote and encourage understanding and good will among members of all religious faiths, and to discourage the use of violence, boycotts and sanctions by adherents of one religion against adherents of another by holding religious meetings and conferences; by radio and television broadcasting; by the imprinting of Gospel messages on records and transcriptions; by producing and distributing Gospel motion pictures; by printing and publishing religious literature; by employing and contributing to the support of missionaries; by conducting forums and instruction classes; by operating a library, and by conducting such other activities as promote the said purpose."
>
> "This corporation will place particular emphasis on the evangelization and conversion of adherents of the Roman Catholic faith, providing spiritual, temporal and financial assistance, especially to their converted clergy."
>
> "This is to be a nonprofit corporation and does not contemplate pecuniary gain incidental, or otherwise, to its members."

The function of the court was to satisfy itself that the purposes set forth in the proposed articles are "lawful and not injurious to the community." However, in its opinion denying the application the court stated its reasons to be that to grant the charter "... would in effect place the blanket of approval of this court on such activity," and "... might well lead to a condition of unrest in the community...." Both of these reasons were predicated upon the second paragraph of the purpose clause which stated that the corporation would place particular emphasis on the evangelization and conversion of adherents of the Roman Catholic faith, providing spiritual, temporal and financial assistance, especially to their converted clergy.

It may be immediately observed that whether the court, because of personal predilection on the subject, does not wish it to appear that it approves of the purposes of the corporation is beside the point. The court does not state that the purposes of the incorporators are unlawful or injurious to the public. The [trial] court's position in effect was that the proposed incorporation could concentrate its efforts toward the conversion of adherents of the Roman Catholic Church but that it should not say so in its charter.[1] Certainly a true and frank statement of the purposes of incorporation is desir-

1. In its opinion the court states: "...such exclusion does not take away any privileges of proselytizing the corporate members might desire to indulge in, either among Roman Catholics and their Priesthood or any other group now existing or to come into existence."

able and contemplated by the Act of Assembly. Charters will be refused where the real or ultimate purpose of incorporation is not disclosed in its articles of incorporation and is found to be an unlawful one.

Neither in the court below nor in this Court did anyone appear in opposition to the grant of the charter. [The court below also] inquir[ed] as to the necessity of the incorporation. While in our opinion a sufficient answer to this inquiry was given, if the purposes are lawful and not injurious to the public, the absence of necessity for a charter of incorporation is not a valid reason for refusing its grant. It clearly appeared that the incorporators, who were not all of the same religious denomination, were reputable citizens. The court did not question the sincerity of any of them.

The 14th Amendment [and] Article I, Section 3 of the Constitution of Pennsylvania [guarantee that] a citizen [is not only] entitled to the free expression of his religious beliefs, but he may by peaceful persuasion endeavor to convert others thereto, and we are aware of no bar to individuals organizing to effectuate their guaranteed rights in this regard.

Nothing in the purpose clause of the proposed incorporation or in the evidence adduced indicates that the activities of the corporation would consist of or include acts inimical to the peace, good order or morals of society, but quite clearly established the contrary.

The order is reversed and the record remanded to the court below with direction to grant the charter as applied for.

MUSMANNO, Justice (dissenting),

If there is one thing that the world needs less than anything else it is religious controversy; if there is one thing that the United States symbolizes more than any other thing it is religious freedom; if there is one thing that the judiciary of this country should frown upon, it is any attempt to obtain the approval of the Courts to stir up strife, discord, wrangling and violence over creed, dogma, and doctrine. Yet this Court is doing that very thing by ordering the Court of Common Pleas of Delaware County to grant a charter to an organization whose incorporators are intent on unleashing the winds of intolerance, the gales of prejudice, and the forces of hate and ignorance.

No one, of course, with the slightest respect for the Constitution, would for a moment deny to the incorporators the right to make peaceful overtures to members of any organized religious organization to leave their church and join whatever organization the incorporators hold out as the salvation of the world. This right is guaranteed specifically by Article I, Section 3 of our Pennsylvania Constitution.

However, it is to be noted that the very phraseology of this constitutional provision interdicts this Court from doing what it is about to do, for if government cannot interfere with the right of man to worship Almighty God according to the dictates of his own conscience, it certainly cannot authorize a corporation to interfere with that indefeasible right. By granting such an authorization the government would be entering a field in which it has no right to be whatsoever.

The seven men of the Conversion Center do not need the approval of any Court to set about proselytizing Catholics. The incorporators of the Conversion Center apparently doubted they had sufficient talents in the arts of persuasion to achieve the fulfillment of their proselytizing desires, so they turned to the Court of Common Pleas of Delaware County to assist them in the realization of their plans.

The majority opinion says that the incorporators are 'reputable citizens.' Without casting any reflection upon the character of the incorporators, it may be said that the pages of history are stained with the chronicles of acts of heart-shattering injustices accomplished by 'reputable citizens.' The killings of the so-called witches in Salem, Massachusetts, as well as in England up to the dawn of the Eighteenth Century were urged, instigated, and executed by 'reputable citizens.' The burning of Joan of Arc was done by 'reputable citizens.' The French Reign of Terror, with its emphasis on atheism, was headed by 'reputable citizens.' Many who manned the guillotine were 'reputable citizens.'

What is reputable citizenship? While it is a cloak of dignity which proclaims that its wearer is law-abiding and respectable, it does not conclusively guarantee that it may not conceal the bolo of intolerance and the falchion of fanaticism.

If the incorporators really wished to "foster, promote and encourage understanding and good will among all members of all religious faiths," they could do so without a corporation. They have functioned so far without incorporation. Why must they have the imprimatur of the Court to do what no one could legally object to their doing?

Notes

1. While most cases involving corporate charters involve mere form requirements, cases like *Application of Conversion Center* raise questions concerning the degree to which the State ought to be in the business of supervising either the day-to-day business of religious organizations, or the reasons for which they are formed. Some cases, however, fit into both categories. In *Application of New York Soul Clinic*, 208 Misc. 612, 615–616, 144 N.Y.S. 2d 543, 546 (1955), for example, a charter was denied for two reasons. The first was that the name "Soul Clinic" might be misleading. In the court's view the term *clinic* "has such a commonly accepted [medical] meaning that one would not ordinarily say that it connotes the idea of church or religion." The second reason was more substantial, and focused on the doctrines of the proposed church. The court stated

> It may be that the desire and intent of the proposed society is to establish a free church: and in that sense, perhaps, that is its "purpose." But what religious doctrine this free church elects to expound and teach is nowhere stated. I do not mean that the creed thus purposed must necessarily be one of the established faiths. What I do mean to say is that whatever the basic creedal purpose of this free church, the petitioners should adequately formulate and articulate it in the certificate presented for filing. And there is nothing in the present certificate which indicates what the purpose of the incorporators is.

What is, or should be, the nature of the court's inquiry into the "purpose" of the incorporators? Is it similar to the task which faces revenue agents charged with the task of determining whether or not an organization qualifies as a "church" or religious organization under the Internal Revenue Code or state tax laws? *See* Chapter Nine § D.

2. Do you agree with Justice Musmanno's position that a church that expressly devotes itself to the conversion of adherents of a specific faith should not be granted a corporate charter because the charter conveys "the imprimatur of the Court"? Would an

incorporation statute that did not require court approval avoid the appearance of an "imprimatur" by the state?

3. What *legitimate* interests do states have when they regulate the organization and operations of churches? Do they differ substantially, if at all, from the interests they have when they oversee the operations of a business corporation or a non-religious charity? To what extent do the unique characteristics of churches warrant a special set of regulations tailored to their specific needs?

c) Trustee Corporation

The trustee form of incorporation grew from the common law practice of using trustees to hold the assets of an unincorporated association. Incorporating the trustees allowed for perpetual succession of the property without changing the existing legal relationships. The use of the trustee form solved the common law problem that unincorporated associations had no legal existence. *See Hunt v. Adams*, 111 Fla. 164, 149 So. 24 (1933) (rejecting breach of contract action against members of building committee of an unincorporated church because plaintiff was aware of the church's legal status). *See generally* Claude D. Morgan, *The Significance of Church Organizational Structure in Litigation and Government Action*, 16 Val. U. L. Rev. 145 (1981); Paul G. Kauper and Stephen C. Ellis, *Religious Corporations and the Law*, 71 Mich. L. Rev. 1499 (1973).

A variant of this form of church organization is described in *Robertson v. Bullions*, 11 N.Y. 243, 264 (1854) and *Petty v. Tooker*, 21 N.Y. 267 (1860), in which the New York Court of Appeals added a majority rule requirement to the basic rules governing trusteeship. By 1872, however, the Supreme Court of the United States had rejected both the implied trust and departure from doctrine rules in favor of congregational and hierarchical models of church management structures. *Watson v. Jones*, 80 U.S. (13 Wall.) 679 (1871), discussed in §C(1)(b) below.

d) Membership Corporations

Based on the traditional business corporation model, the membership corporate form is readily adaptable to churches having a congregational structure and management. The California Nonprofit Religious Corporation Law, Cal. Corp. Code §§9110, *et. seq.* (2001), is one of the best contemporary examples of this statutory type. Notwithstanding its statutory nature, however, it retains several common law characteristics. The most notable of these is oversight of the corporate board's activities by the Attorney General, who is charged by the Code with the general duty to assure that the assets of charitable corporations are used in accordance with their intended purposes. *See* Cal. Corp. Code §9230 (2001).

e) Corporations Sole

The corporation sole is well suited to the needs of churches organized in hierarchical form. It places corporate governance, assets and other powers of the corporation in one person, who is invested with the right to carry on all the corporation's affairs. *See, e.g.*, Ala. Code §§10-4-1 to 10-4-7 (2001); Ariz. Rev. Stat. Ann. §§10-11901 to 10-11908 (2001); Cal. Corp. Code §§10000–10015 (2001); Hawaii Rev. Stat. §§419-1 to 419-9 (2000).

f) Unincorporated Associations

Many churches and religious organizations simply commence and continue operations, taking no action to obtain an independent legal identity. By remaining unincorporated, however, such organizations have no independent legal or juridical status. Historically, this has meant that they could not, while operating as unincorporated associations, hold property in the name of their association, nor could they sue or be sued. As a practical matter, it also means that the association lacks both the limited liability features of the corporate form, and the tax advantages conferred upon charitable corporations under both state and federal tax laws. *See* Chapter Nine.

Although there are good reasons to adopt the corporate form, there are often doctrinal reasons for avoiding it. As noted in Chapter Six, many religious groups and churches operating schools believe that incorporation indicates an allegiance to the state that poses a conflict with their allegiance to God. For others, tenets of faith do not permit the church to bind itself to any formal organizational model. One such example is Methodism, which "has continued for more than two centuries to proclaim a freedom of spirit as opposed to the bondage of an organization, and its appeal has been based on the reality of a personal experience of spiritual emancipation through faith in Christ." *Barr v. United Methodist Church,* 90 Cal. App. 3d 259, 262 n.2 (1979), excerpted below. In an effort to reconcile faith concerns of this type with the practical necessities and advantages of recognizing some sort of limited legal existence for voluntary associations, many states have enacted legislation dealing specifically with unincorporated associations.

The practical necessity for such legislation is apparent from a reading of the case law. Unless given independent existence by statute, unincorporated associations do not exist as legal entities. As such, gifts of real property to an unincorporated association will fail because no legal entity exists to receive it, and the associations themselves, not being legal entities, could not be liable in tort, contract, or otherwise for conduct taken in their names. Their members, however, could be.

The Uniform Unincorporated Nonprofit Association Act (1992) was intended to serve as a basis for reforming the common law and making uniform throughout the country laws with respect to "unincorporated, nonprofit associations in three basic areas: authority to acquire, hold, and transfer property, especially real property; authority to sue and be sued as an entity; and contract and tort liability of officers and members of the association." Just as in the case of nonprofit corporations, the drafters of the Uniform Act left the term "nonprofit" undefined, concluding that the common definition of nonprofit was too limiting and did not reach all not-for-profit organizations. *See* Comment to § 1.

Several states have adopted versions of the Uniform Unincorporated Nonprofit Association Act. *See, e.g.,* Colo. Rev. Stat. §§ 7-30-101 to 7-30-119 (2000); Idaho Code §§ 53-701 to 53-717 (2000); Wyo. Stat. §§ 17-22-101 to 17-22-115 (2001).

C. Resolving Disputes within and among Religious Groups

Controversies within and among religious groups and organizations pose significant difficulties for the law. Because they are often driven by differences over doctrine or interpretation of church laws or traditions, a civil court called upon to resolve them finds itself in a delicate position. The litigants are entitled by the constitutions and laws of the United States and the states to seek judicial resolution of their controversies, but the courts themselves have no authority to resolve questions that require judicial interpretation of either scripture or religious doctrine.

How then should a court proceed when faced with such a problem? As is the case in many other contexts involving the proper relationship of religion and government, there are three basic possibilities: (1) resolve the doctrinal questions presented, and apply the conclusions in a manner which resolves the case; (2) avoid those questions by applying whatever legal principles that appear to govern the case had it arisen in a non-religious context; or (3) defer to appropriate church authorities to resolve the controversy.

The first possibility, to recognize that it has been drawn into an intra-religious dispute, consider the doctrinal questions on their merits, and resolve them based on the sources deemed by the parties to be relevant, is both the most obvious, and the most problematic from a First Amendment perspective. Nonetheless, it is an option with a considerable historical pedigree.

The roots of much of the current law of church management and property are deeply embedded in the law of charitable trusts. Because a trust could not be enforced without specific, identifiable beneficiaries, the common law permitted charitable trustees to hold the property for the benefit of a specific purpose. In *Attorney General v. Pearson*, [1817], 3 Merivale 353, 35 Eng. Rep. 135, Lord Eldon extended this rule to assets held in trust for a church, and impressed them with an implied trust in favor of the doctrines in force at the time the contributions were made. Known as *Lord Eldon's Rule*, the holding provides that it is "the duty of the Court in such cases to inquire and decide for itself, not only what was the nature and power of these church judicatories, but what is the true standard of faith in the church organization, and which of the contending parties before the Court holds to this standard." *Watson v. Jones*, 80 U.S. (13 Wall.) 679, 727 (1871), *citing Attorney General v. Pearson,* [1817], 3 Merivale 353. Known in the United States as the "Departure from Doctrine Rule," it permitted the court to supervise the trustees and to assure that church property was devoted to the uses to which the congregation had dedicated it. *See Presbyterian Church in the United States v. Mary Elizabeth Blue Hull Memorial Presbyterian Church*, 393 U.S. 440 (1969) [*Hull Church*]. The First Amendment limitations imposed on this mode of supervision are developed in this Section.

The second option is for a court to view the case as a non-religious dispute and resolve the case based on whatever non-religious principles seem to apply under the circumstances. Though such an approach to intra-religious dispute resolution will appeal to a court which is bound by the Constitution to leave the resolution of doctrinal questions to religious authorities, its seeming "neutrality" is accomplished by the courts' refusal to take into account facts which are both important to the parties, and often critical to an accurate resolution of their dispute.

The last option is for the court to abstain from deciding the controversy altogether. But this is only possible when it is possible for a court to find that the case is actually governed by the internal law or doctrinal principles of the church, and that there are church authorities charged with the responsibility of deciding such disputes. Such an approach requires the parties to seek their remedies within the structures provided by the church. *See, e.g., Decker* ex rel. *Decker v. Tschetter Hutterian Brethren, Inc.*, 1999 S.D.

62, 594 N.W.2d 357, 365 (1999) (refusing to intervene in an intra-communal dispute because the "record indicates there is no separation of religious life from a secular life in a Hutterite colony because there is no separate secular life").

As you consider the cases below, ask yourself what, if any, changes in the governing documents of the churches involved might have prevented civil court intervention in the dispute in the first place.

1. The Search for Judicially Manageable Standards

a) The "Neutral Principles" Approach

Jones v. Wolf

443 U.S. 595 (1979)

Mr. Justice BLACKMUN delivered the opinion of the Court.

This case involves a dispute over the ownership of church property following a schism in a local church affiliated with a hierarchical church organization. The question for decision is whether civil courts, consistent with the First and Fourteenth Amendments to the Constitution, may resolve the dispute on the basis of "neutral principles of law," or whether they must defer to the resolution of an authoritative tribunal of the hierarchical church.

The Vineville Presbyterian Church of Macon, Ga., was organized in 1904, and first incorporated in 1915. Its corporate charter lapsed in 1935, but was revived and renewed in 1939, and continues in effect at the present time.

The property at issue and on which the church is located was acquired in three transactions. The funds used to acquire the property were contributed entirely by local church members. Pursuant to resolutions adopted by the congregation, the church repeatedly has borrowed money on the property.

In the same year it was organized, the Vineville church was established as a member church of the Augusta-Macon Presbytery of the Presbyterian Church in the United States (PCUS). The PCUS has a generally hierarchical or connectional form of government, as contrasted with a congregational form.

On May 27, 1973, at a congregational meeting of the Vineville church attended by a quorum of its duly enrolled members, 164 of them, including the pastor, voted to separate from the PCUS. Ninety-four members opposed the resolution. The majority immediately informed the PCUS of the action, and then united with another denomination, the Presbyterian Church in America. Although the minority remained on the church rolls for three years, they ceased to participate in the affairs of the Vineville church and conducted their religious activities elsewhere.

In response to the schism within the Vineville congregation, the Augusta-Macon Presbytery appointed a commission to investigate the dispute and, if possible, to resolve it. The commission eventually issued a written ruling declaring that the minority faction constituted "the true congregation of Vineville Presbyterian Church," and withdrawing from the majority faction "all authority to exercise office derived from the [PCUS]." The majority took no part in the commission's inquiry, and did not appeal its ruling to a higher PCUS tribunal.

Representatives of the minority faction brought this class action in state court, seeking declaratory and injunctive orders establishing their right to exclusive possession and use of the Vineville church property as a member congregation of the PCUS. The trial court, purporting to apply Georgia's "neutral principles of law" approach to church property disputes, granted judgment for the majority. The Supreme Court of Georgia affirmed.

Georgia's approach to church property litigation has evolved in response to *Presbyterian Church v. Hull Church.* That case was a property dispute between the PCUS and two local Georgia churches that had withdrawn from the PCUS.

On remand, the Georgia Supreme Court concluded that, without the departure-from-doctrine element, the implied trust theory would have to be abandoned in its entirety. *Presbyterian Church v. Eastern Heights Church*, 225 Ga. 259, 167 S.E.2d 658 (1969) (*Presbyterian Church II*). In its place, the court adopted what is now known as the "neutral principles of law" method for resolving church property disputes. The court examined the deeds to the properties, the state statutes dealing with implied trusts, Ga. Code §§ 108-106, 108-107 (1978), and the Book of Church Order to determine whether there was any basis for a trust in favor of the general church. Finding nothing that would give rise to a trust in any of these documents, the court awarded the property on the basis of legal title, which was in the local church. Review was again sought in this Court, but was denied.

The neutral-principles analysis was further refined by the Georgia Supreme Court in *Carnes v. Smith*, 236 Ga. 30, 222 S.E.2d 322, *cert. denied*, 429 U.S. 868 (1976). That case concerned a property dispute between The United Methodist Church and a local congregation that had withdrawn from that church. As in *Presbyterian Church II*, the court found no basis for a trust in favor of the general church in the deeds, the corporate charter, or the state statutes dealing with implied trusts. The court observed, however, that the constitution of The United Methodist Church, its Book of Discipline, contained an express trust provision in favor of the general church. On this basis, the church property was awarded to the denominational church.

In the present case, the Georgia courts sought to apply the neutral-principles analysis of *Presbyterian Church II* and *Carnes* to the facts presented by the Vineville church controversy. Here, as in those two earlier cases, the deeds conveyed the property to the local church. Here, as in the earlier cases, neither the state statutes dealing with implied trusts, nor the corporate charter of the Vineville church, indicated that the general church had any interest in the property. And here, as in *Presbyterian Church II*, but in contrast to *Carnes*, the provisions of the constitution of the general church, the Book of Church Order, concerning the ownership and control of property failed to reveal any language of trust in favor of the general church. The courts accordingly held that legal title to the property of the Vineville church was vested in the local congregation.

The only question presented by this case is which faction of the formerly united Vineville congregation is entitled to possess and enjoy the property located at 2193 Vineville Avenue in Macon, Ga.

[T]he First Amendment prohibits civil courts from resolving church property disputes on the basis of religious doctrine and practice. As a corollary to this commandment, the Amendment requires that civil courts defer to the resolution of issues of religious doctrine or polity by the highest court of a hierarchical church organization. Subject to these limitations, however, the First Amendment does not dictate that a State must follow a particular method of resolving church property disputes.

At least in general outline, we think the "neutral principles of law" approach is consistent with the foregoing constitutional principles.

The primary advantages of the neutral-principles approach are that it is completely secular in operation, and yet flexible enough to accommodate all forms of religious organization and polity. The method relies exclusively on objective, well-established concepts of trust and property law familiar to lawyers and judges. It thereby promises to free civil courts completely from entanglement in questions of religious doctrine, polity, and practice. Furthermore, the neutral-principles analysis shares the peculiar genius of private-law systems in general: flexibility in ordering private rights and obligations to reflect the intentions of the parties. Through appropriate reversionary clauses and trust provisions, religious societies can specify what is to happen to church property in the event of a particular contingency, or what religious body will determine the ownership in the event of a schism or doctrinal controversy. In this manner, a religious organization can ensure that a dispute over the ownership of church property will be resolved in accord with the desires of the members.

This is not to say that the application of the neutral-principles approach is wholly free of difficulty. The neutral-principles method, at least as it has evolved in Georgia, requires a civil court to examine certain religious documents, such as a church constitution, for language of trust in favor of the general church. In undertaking such an examination, a civil court must take special care to scrutinize the document in purely secular terms, and not to rely on religious precepts in determining whether the document indicates that the parties have intended to create a trust. In addition, there may be cases where the deed, the corporate charter, or the constitution of the general church incorporates religious concepts in the provisions relating to the ownership of property. If in such a case the interpretation of the instruments of ownership would require the civil court to resolve a religious controversy, then the court must defer to the resolution of the doctrinal issue by the authoritative ecclesiastical body.

On balance, however, the promise of nonentanglement and neutrality inherent in the neutral-principles approach more than compensates for what will be occasional problems in application. We therefore hold that a State is constitutionally entitled to adopt neutral principles of law as a means of adjudicating a church property dispute.

The neutral-principles approach cannot be said to "inhibit" the free exercise of religion, any more than do other neutral provisions of state law governing the manner in which churches own property, hire employees, or purchase goods. Under the neutral-principles approach, the outcome of a church property dispute is not foreordained. At any time before the dispute erupts, the parties can ensure, if they so desire, that the faction loyal to the hierarchical church will retain the church property. They can modify the deeds or the corporate charter to include a right of reversion or trust in favor of the general church. Alternatively, the constitution of the general church can be made to recite an express trust in favor of the denominational church. The burden involved in taking such steps will be minimal. And the civil courts will be bound to give effect to the result indicated by the parties, provided it is embodied in some legally cognizable form.

It remains to be determined whether the Georgia neutral-principles analysis was constitutionally applied on the facts of this case. Although both the trial court and the Supreme Court of Georgia viewed the case as involving nothing more than an application of the principles developed in *Presbyterian Church II*, and in *Carnes*, the present case contains a significant complicating factor absent in each of those earlier cases. *Pres-*

byterian Church II and *Carnes* each involved a church property dispute between the general church and the entire local congregation. Here, the local congregation was itself divided between a majority of 164 members who sought to withdraw from PCUS, and a minority of 94 members who wished to maintain the affiliation. Neither of the state courts alluded to this problem, however; each concluded without discussion or analysis that the title to the property was in the local church and that the local church was represented by the majority rather than the minority.

Petitioners earnestly submit that the question of which faction is the true representative of the Vineville church is an ecclesiastical question that cannot be answered by a civil court. At least, it is said, it cannot be answered by a civil court in a case involving a hierarchical church, like the PCUS, where a duly appointed church commission has determined which of the two factions represents the "true congregation." Respondents, in opposition, argue in effect that the Georgia courts did no more than apply the ordinary presumption that, absent some indication to the contrary, a voluntary religious association is represented by a majority of its members.

If in fact Georgia has adopted a presumptive rule of majority representation, defeasible upon a showing that the identity of the local church is to be determined by some other means, we think this would be consistent with both the neutral-principles analysis and the First Amendment. Majority rule is generally employed in the governance of religious societies. See *Bouldin v. Alexander*. Furthermore, the majority faction generally can be identified without resolving any question of religious doctrine or polity. Certainly, there was no dispute in the present case about the identity of the duly enrolled members of the Vineville church when the dispute arose, or about the final vote. Most importantly, any rule of majority representation can always be overcome, under the neutral-principles approach, either by providing, in the corporate charter or the constitution of the general church, that the identity of the local church is to be established in some other way, or by providing that the church property is held in trust for the general church and those who remain loyal to it. Indeed, the State may adopt any method of overcoming the majoritarian presumption, so long as the use of that method does not impair free-exercise rights or entangle the civil courts in matters of religious controversy.

Therefore, if Georgia law provides that the identity of the Vineville church is to be determined according to the "laws and regulations" of the PCUS, then the First Amendment requires that the Georgia courts give deference to the presbyterial commission's determination of that church's identity.

This Court, of course, does not declare what the law of Georgia is. Since the grounds for the decision that respondents represent the Vineville church remain unarticulated, the judgment of the Supreme Court of Georgia is vacated, and the case is remanded for further proceedings not inconsistent with this opinion.

It is so ordered.

Mr. Justice POWELL, with whom THE CHIEF JUSTICE [BURGER], Mr. Justice STEWART, and Mr. Justice WHITE join, dissenting.

This case presents again a dispute among church members over the control of a local church's property. Although the Court appears to accept established principles that I have thought would resolve this case, it superimposes on these principles a new structure of rules that will make the decision of these cases by civil courts more difficult. The new analysis also is more likely to invite intrusion into church polity forbidden by the First Amendment.

The question actually presented is which of the factions within the local congregation has the right to control the actions of the titleholder, and thereby to control the use of the property, as the Court later acknowledges.

Since 1872 disputes over control of church property usually have been resolved under principles established by *Watson v. Jones*. Under the new and complex, two-stage analysis approved today, a court instead first must apply newly defined "neutral-principles of law" to determine whether property titled to the local church is held in trust for the general church organization with which the local church is affiliated. If it is, then the court will grant control of the property to the councils of the general church. If not, then control by the local congregation will be recognized. In the latter situation, if there is a schism in the local congregation, as in this case, the second stage of the new analysis becomes applicable. Again, the Court fragments the analysis into two substeps for the purpose of determining which of the fractions should control the property.

As this new approach inevitably will increase the involvement of civil courts in church controversies, and as it departs from long-established precedents, I dissent.

The first stage in the "neutral principles of law" approach operates as a restrictive rule of evidence. Thus, where religious documents such as church constitutions or books of order must be examined "for language of trust in favor of the general church," "a civil court must take special care to scrutinize the document in purely secular terms, and not to rely on religious precepts in determining whether the document indicates that the parties have intended to create a trust." It follows that the civil courts using this analysis may consider the form of religious government adopted by the church members for the resolution of intrachurch disputes *only* if that polity has been stated, in express relation to church property, in the language of trust and property law.

One effect of the Court's evidentiary rule is to deny to the courts relevant evidence as to the religious polity that is, the form of governance—adopted by the church members. The constitutional documents of churches tend to be drawn in terms of religious precepts. Attempting to read them "in purely secular terms" is more likely to promote confusion than understanding.

This limiting of the evidence effectively will have reversed the decisions of doctrine and practice made in accordance with church law. The schism in the Vineville church, for example, resulted from disagreements among the church members over questions of doctrine and practice. Under the Book of Church Order, these questions were resolved authoritatively by the higher church courts, which then gave control of the local church to the faction loyal to that resolution. The Georgia courts, as a matter of state law, granted control to the schismatic faction, and thereby effectively reversed the doctrinal decision of the church courts. This indirect interference by the civil courts with the resolution of religious disputes within the church is no less proscribed by the First Amendment than is the direct decision of questions of doctrine and practice.

The Court's basic neutral-principles suffice to settle only disputes between the central councils of a church organization and a unanimous local congregation. Where, as here, the neutral-principles inquiry reveals no trust in favor of the general church, and the local congregation is split into factions, the basic question remains unresolved: which faction should have control of the local church?

The Court acknowledges that the church law of the Presbyterian Church in the United States (PCUS), of which the Vineville church is a part, provides for the authoritative resolution of this question by the Presbytery. Indeed, the Court indicates that Georgia, consistently with the First Amendment may adopt the *Watson v. Jones* rule of adherence to the resolution of the dispute according to church law: a rule that would necessitate reversal of the judgment for the respondents. But instead of requiring the state courts to take this approach, the Court approves as well an alternative rule of state law: the Georgia courts are said to be free to "adop[t] a presumptive rule of majority representation, defeasible upon a showing that the identity of the local church is to be determined by some other means." This showing may be made by proving that the church has "provid[ed], in the corporate charter or the constitution of the general church, that the identity of the local church is to be established in some other way."

On its face, this rebuttable presumption also requires reversal of the state court's judgment in favor of the schismatic faction. The polity of the PCUS commits to the Presbytery the resolution of the dispute within the local church. Having shown this structure of church government for the determination of the identity of the local congregation, the petitioners have rebutted any presumption that this question has been left to a majority vote of the local congregation.

The Court nevertheless declines to order reversal. In essence, the Court's instructions on remand therefore allow the state courts the choice of following the long-settled rule of *Watson v. Jones* or of adopting some other rule unspecified by the Court that the state courts view as consistent with the First Amendment.

Disputes among church members over the control of church property arise almost invariably out of disagreements regarding doctrine and practice. Because of the religious nature of these disputes, civil courts should decide them according to principles that do not interfere with the free exercise of religion in accordance with church polity and doctrine. The only course that achieves this constitutional requirement is acceptance by civil courts of the decisions reached within the polity chosen by the church members themselves.

[I]n each case involving an intrachurch dispute including disputes over church property the civil court must focus directly on ascertaining, and then following, the decision made within the structure of church governance. By doing so, the court avoids two equally unacceptable departures from the genuine neutrality mandated by the First Amendment. First, it refrains from direct review and revision of decisions of the church on matters of religious doctrine and practice that underlie the church's determination of intrachurch controversies, including those that relate to control of church property. Equally important, by recognizing the authoritative resolution reached within the religious association, the civil court avoids interfering indirectly with the religious governance of those who have formed the association and submitted themselves to its authority.

The principles developed in prior decisions thus afford clear guidance in the case before us. The Vineville church is presbyterian, a part of the PCUS. The presbyterian form of church government, adopted by the PCUS, is [hierarchical].

Thus, while many matters, including the management of the church property, are committed in the first instance to the Session and congregation of the local church, their actions are subject to review by the Presbytery. Here, the Presbytery exercised its authority over the local church, removing the dissidents from church office, asserting direct control over the government of the church, and recognizing the petitioners as the legitimate congregation and Session of the church. It is undisputed that under the established government of the Presbyterian Church accepted by the members of the church before the schism the use and control of the church property have been determined authoritatively to be in the petitioners. Accordingly, under the principles I have thought were settled, there is no occasion for the further examination of the law of

Georgia that the Court directs. On remand, the Georgia courts should be directed to enter judgment for the petitioners.

Notes

1. Since deciding *Jones v. Wolf*, the Supreme Court has not granted *certiorari* in any church property dispute. But as the cases excerpted in the sections of this chapter that follow demonstrate, it is inevitable that the Court will eventually be forced to revisit the issue. *See, e.g., Moses v. Episcopal Diocese of Colorado*, excerpted in Part 2(c) below.

2. Justice Blackmun's opinion for the Court indicates that the "neutral principles" approach "promises to free civil courts completely from entanglement in questions of religious doctrine, polity, and practice." Do you agree? Justice Powell's dissenting opinion argues that, in practice, the requirement that courts review the internal documents of churches without regard to their religious content is inconsistent with religious liberty principles. In his view, "[t]he first stage in the 'neutral principles of law' approach operates as a restrictive rule of evidence[, o]ne effect of [which] is to deny to the courts relevant evidence as to the religious polity that is, the form of governance adopted by the church members." Justice Powell argues that a civil court's attempt that "[a]ttempting to read [the organic documents of churches] 'in purely secular terms' is more likely to promote confusion than understanding." Which opinion presents the better argument?

3. Do you think that the Court's decision in *Jones v. Wolf* should cause attorneys for churches and religious organizations to consider changes in the way the church organizations they represent do business? Lawyers for churches and religious organizations certainly have an obligation under the A.B.A. Model Rules of Professional Conduct to advise their clients concerning the practical and legal problems that can arise because of ambiguities or contradictions in their organic documents (charters, internal law, and constitutions). If these legal documents will not provide adequate guidance to a court that has been asked to resolve an internal controversy, what is their purpose? *Cf. Application of Conversion Center, Inc.*

4. Do you think it would be useful for an attorney representing a church or religious organization to include in the organization's charter or other organic documents references to doctrine or other religious beliefs concerning resolution of civil law disputes? Would it be legitimate? Necessary? *See generally* William W. Bassett, *The American Civil Corporation, The "Incorporation Movement" and the Canon Law of the Catholic Church*, 25 J.C. & U.L. 721 (1999) (noting that the incorporation of many Catholic organizations was accomplished without reference to the obligations imposed by canon law).

5. Does the Court's approach in *Jones v. Wolf* mandate the application of "neutral principles," or merely suggest that neutral principles of law should be utilized to resolve cases which cannot be decided by reference to a clear statement of church policy concerning either the rule of decision, or the identity of the person or persons who can decide on its behalf?

b) What Qualifies as a "Neutral Principle" of Law?

In practice, courts compelled to decide intra-religious disputes use several different approaches. Each has a long historical pedigree, and is a reflection of the law's tendency to accommodate religious diversity when and to the extent possible without compromising other important legal interests.

Watson v. Jones, 80 U.S. (13 Wall.) 679 (1871). *Watson* remains the basic precedent concerning judicial resolution of intra-religious disputes, even though it was decided on the basis of federal common law standards many years before the "incorporation" of the First Amendment.

Watson arose as the result of a dispute within and among the congregation of the Walnut Street Presbyterian Church in Louisville, Kentucky. Throughout the Civil War, the General Assembly of the Presbyterian Church had expressed its support for the policies of the Federal government and President Lincoln, and denounced slavery. In May 1865, after the surrender of the South, the General Assembly announced that any Southerner who had supported slavery (or the Southern Presbyterian denomination) was to repent before being received as a minister or missionary, and being a hierarchical church, it expected that its instructions would be followed in the local churches. The Presbytery of Louisville denounced the General Assembly's actions. In turn, the General Assembly stated that any Presbytery which refused to follow these orders would be dissolved.

The Louisville Presbytery divided as well, with one group joining the Presbyterian Church of the Confederate States. In July, 1865, the Kentucky Synod divided along the same lines. On June 1, 1867, the General Assembly declared that the pro-slavery faction of the Walnut Street Presbyterian Church was excluded from connection with the General Assembly. The result was that a majority of the congregation sided with the General Assembly on the anti-slavery side, while the pro-slavery faction consisted of the majority of the elders and trustees of the Walnut Street Presbyterian Church, a minority of the congregation, the Louisville Presbytery and the Kentucky Synod.

Writing for the majority, Justice Miller found that the Walnut Street Presbyterian Church was a member of a hierarchical church organization, the Presbyterian Church, and as such was subject to the ecclesiastical judgments rendered by that body. "[I]n cases of this character we are bound to look at the fact that the local congregation is itself but a member of a much larger and more important religious organization, and is under its government and control, and is bound by its orders and judgments." 80 U.S. at 726–27. In this case, the General Assembly had determined that the majority of the congregation was entitled to its use.

Justice Miller's opinion, however, was not confined to the narrow question presented by the case.

> The questions which have come before the civil courts concerning the rights to property held by ecclesiastical bodies, may, so far as we have been able to examine them, be profitably classified under three general heads, which of course do not include cases governed by considerations applicable to a church established and supported by law as the religion of the state.
>
> 1. The first of these is when the property which is the subject of the controversy has been, by the deed or will of the donor, or other instrument by which the property is held, by the express terms of the instrument devoted to the teaching, support, or spread of some specific form of religious doctrine or belief.
>
> 2. The second is when the property is held by a religious congregation that, by the nature of its organization, is strictly independent of other

ecclesiastical associations, and so far as church government is concerned, owes no fealty or obligation to any higher authority.

3. The third is where the religious congregation or ecclesiastical body holding the property is but a subordinate member of some general church organization in which there are superior ecclesiastical tribunals with a general and ultimate power of control more or less complete, in some supreme judicatory over the whole membership of that general organization.

1) *The Implied Trust Theory: Does the First Amendment Prohibit Civil Courts from Making Findings Concerning "Religious Facts"?*

Drawing from rules fashioned in the English courts, the *Watson* court identified the implied trust doctrine as the "principle which was at once recognized and has since been uniformly accepted as the true governing rule in all cases of this nature." *Watson,* 80 U.S. at 704.

> That property conveyed for the use of a society for purposes of religious worship, is a trust, which is to be enforced for the purpose of maintaining that religious worship for which the property was devoted, and in the event of schism (the deed making no provision for such case), its uses are to be enforced, not in behalf of a majority of the congregation, nor yet exclusively in behalf of the party adhering to the general body, but in favor of that part of the society adhering to and maintaining the original principles upon which it was founded.

Watson, 80 U.S. at 705.

The application of implied trust theory, as expressed in *Lord Eldon's Rule,* had been troublesome for the courts in two respects. First, it was difficult for the court to determine the principles to which the society was bound to adhere. The second difficulty was aptly stated by the Supreme Court in *Watson,* itself:

> In these matters of religious doctrine, discipline, and church order, who is to be the judge? Who has the right to say conclusively, in case of controversy, that one or the other party has departed from the doctrines of the church? Who shall determine upon the validity of an act or judgment of a church court; upon the status of a member or officer; upon the legality or otherwise of a voluntary or enforced severance of a part from the body of the general organization?

Watson, 80 U.S. at 707.

A variant of the implied trust theory is the "Departure from Doctrine Rule." Rejected by the Supreme Court in *Hull Church,* 393 U.S. at 444 n.3 (1969), it provides that

> when property is devoted to a specific doctrine or purpose, the courts will prevent it from being diverted from the trust.... [A] trust (in favor of the general church) is conditioned upon the general church's adherence to its tenets of faith and practice existing when the local church affiliated with it and...an abandonment of, or departure from, such tenets is a diversion from the trust, which the civil courts will prevent.

The Court in *Hull Church* rejected the rule as a basis for civil court decision-making because:

> The departure-from-doctrine element of the implied trust theory which [the Georgia Supreme Court] applied requires the civil judiciary to determine whether actions of the general church constitute such a 'substantial departure' from the tenets of faith and practice existing at the time of the local churches' affiliation that the trust in favor of the general church must be declared to have terminated. This determination has two parts. The civil court must first decide whether the challenged actions of the general church depart substantially from prior doctrine. In reaching such a decision, the court must of necessity make its own interpretation of the meaning of church doctrines. If the court should decide that a substantial departure has occurred, it must then go on to determine whether the issue on which the general church has departed holds a place of such importance in the traditional theology as to require that the trust be terminated. A civil court can make this determination only after assessing the relative significance to the religion of the tenets from which departure was found. Thus, the departure-from-doctrine element of the Georgia implied trust theory requires the civil court to determine matters at the very core of a religion: the interpretation of particular church doctrines and the importance of those doctrines to the religion. Plainly, the First Amendment forbids civil courts from playing such a role.

Id. at 449–50.

In *Presbyterian Church in United States v. Eastern Heights Presbyterian Church*, 225 Ga. 259, 167 S.E.2d 658 (1969), the Georgia Supreme Court rejected the departure-from-doctrine element of implied trust theories as unworkable in light of the Supreme Court's holding in *Hull Church.* As the Supreme Court notes in *Jones v. Wolf*, the Georgia court developed "what is now known as the 'neutral principles of law' method for resolving church property disputes." By holding that evidence of a trust relationship resolves the matter, the Georgia Supreme Court effectively avoids the question of how to interpret the terms of that trust relationship. It simply finds that a trust relationship exists, and thereafter, deals with the trustee. The Supreme Court's decision, by contrast, requires that the terms of church documents be examined to determine what their secular significance might be.

The practical difficulties of these questions can be illustrated by reference to Rule 52(a) of the Federal Rules of Civil Procedure, which provides that in "all actions tried upon the facts without a jury the court shall find the facts specially and state separately its conclusions of law." Because the court must base its findings on evidence derived from testimony or documentary evidence, what *types* of evidence might be relevant to the court's determination concerning the content and meaning of the church's organic documents? Would it be appropriate, for example, to turn to an "expert" in the field of church law who is acceptable to all the parties if there is a need to obtain evidence concerning the meaning of a disputed word, phrase, or concept? What should be the outcome if the parties *disagree* concerning the reliability or qualifications of the expert witness? *See* F. R. Evid. 702.

Do you think it possible to approach the decision and resolution of cases which turn on the interpretation of internal church law as matters to be governed by the "neutral principles" found in the field of Conflict of Laws? There are a number of religious organizations which have highly well-developed legal systems. What is, or would be, perceived as the problem of dealing with issues of religious law the same way that courts deal with the pleading and proof of foreign (non-U.S.) law?

2) Abstention and Deference to Church Hierarchy: The Significance of Church Structure

Another way to dispose of a controversy without appearing to take sides is to abstain from deciding the controversy whenever there is a legal basis for doing so.

In *Gonzalez v. Roman Catholic Archbishop,* 280 U.S. 1, 3 (1929), "[t]he main questions for decision [were] whether the petitioner is legally entitled to be appointed the chaplain, and whether he shall recover the surplus income accrued during the vacancy." The chaplaincy at issue had been established some one-hundred years earlier by an ancestor of the petitioner and by its terms provided: (1) that a descendant of the donor be appointed chaplain; (2) that sixty Masses be said each year; and (3) that income from the chaplaincy be used to support the appointed chaplain. It was uncontested that the petitioner was a direct descendant of the donor, and that he was willing to take on the duties of the chaplaincy. Church authorities objected for two reasons: the petitioner was only ten years old at the time he requested appointment to the chaplaincy, and the trust fund had, over the years, accumulated an amount far in excess of the needs of the chaplaincy itself (the fund amount was estimated to be $86,862.50).

Based upon the Canon Law of the Roman Catholic Church in effect at the time of the petition, the Archbishop denied the petitioner's appointment, finding that the petitioner was unqualified to be appointed a chaplain. Not only was he too young, but the standards governing the qualification of chaplains had changed over the years and precluded him being appointed to that position. The petitioner argued that he ought be held only to the standards of the Canon Law in effect at the time the foundation was established. "The archbishop's claim [was] that by an implied term of the gift, the property, which was to be held by the church, should be administered in such manner and by such persons as may be prescribed by the church from time to time." 280 U.S. at 16.

Likening churches to other voluntary organizations, the court held:

> [b]ecause the appointment is a canonical act, it is the function of the church authorities to determine what the essential qualifications of a chaplain are and whether the candidate possesses them. In the absence of fraud, collusion, or arbitrariness, the decisions of the proper church tribunals on matters purely ecclesiastical, although affecting civil rights, are accepted in litigation before the secular courts as conclusive, because the parties in interest made them so by contract or otherwise.

Id.

The Court apparently accepted the argument that the donor *intended* for her gift to be in accord with changing church doctrines:

> Neither the foundress, nor the church authorities, can have intended that the perpetual chaplaincy created in 1820 should, in respect to the qualifications of an incumbent, be forever administered according to the canons of the church which happened to be in force at that date. The parties to the foundation clearly contemplated that the archbishop would, before ordination, exercise his judgment as to the fitness of the applicant; and they must have contemplated that, in the course of the centuries, the standard of fitness would be modified.

280 U.S. at 17.

For many years after it was decided, *Gonzalez* was read by parties seeking judicial redress as creating an exception to the general rule that civil courts must defer to the pronouncements by church judicatories in cases in which the evidence showed fraud, collusion, or arbitrariness. That reading, however, was explicitly rejected by the Supreme Court in *Serbian Eastern Orthodox Diocese for the United States of America and Canada v. Milivojevich*, 426 U.S. 696, 712–15 (1976). Civil courts are not permitted to review the decisions of ecclesiastical bodies.

Distinguishing the situation in *Hull Church* from the situation in *Gonzalez*, the Supreme Court stated in *Jones v. Wolf* that:

> The departure-from-doctrine approach is not susceptible of the marginal judicial involvement contemplated in *Gonzalez*. Gonzalez' rights under a will turned on a church decision, the Archbishop's, as to church law, the qualifications for the chaplaincy. It was the archbishopric, not the civil courts, which had the task of analyzing and interpreting church law in order to determine the validity of Gonzalez' claim to a chaplaincy. Thus, the civil courts could adjudicate the rights under the will without interpreting or weighing church doctrine but simply by engaging in the narrowest kind of review of a specific church decision *i.e.*, whether that decision resulted from fraud, collusion, or arbitrariness. Such review does not inject the civil courts into substantive ecclesiastical matters.

Jones v. Wolf, 443 U.S. at 607.

(A) Mandatory Deference: Congregational Churches

In *Watson v. Jones*, the Supreme Court recognized two basic types of church "polities" or structures: congregational and hierarchical, and articulated rules for use by the courts when dealing with them.

When a church is found to be "congregational" the court is to treat the church just as it would any other voluntary association:

> In...cases where there is a schism which leads to a separation into distinct and conflicting bodies, the rights of such bodies to the use of the property must be determined by the ordinary principles which govern voluntary associations. If the principle of government in such cases is that the majority rules, then the numerical majority of members must control the right to the use of the property. If there be within the congregation officers in whom are vested the powers of such control, then those who adhere to the acknowledged organism by which the body is governed are entitled to the use of the property. The minority in choosing to separate themselves into a distinct body, and refusing to recognize the authority of the governing body, can claim no rights in the property from the fact that they had once been members of the church or congregation. This ruling admits of no inquiry into the existing religious opinions of those who comprise the legal or regular organization; for, if such was permitted, a very small minority, without any officers of the church among them, might be found to be the only faithful supporters of the religious dogmas of the founders of the church. There being no such trust imposed upon the property when purchased or given, the court will not imply one for the purpose of expelling from its use those who by regular succession and order constitute the church, because they may have changed in some respect their views of religious truth.

Watson v. Jones, 443 U.S. at 725.

(B) Mandatory Deference to Church Authority: Hierarchical Churches

Where the church is found to have a hierarchical structure, the court is still required to defer to the decision of the appropriate authority. Just as in the case of the congregational church, the internal structure of the organization is relevant to the court's determination concerning the appropriate decision-maker:

> In this class of cases we think the rule of action which should govern the civil courts, founded in a broad and sound view of the relations of church and state under our system of laws, and supported by a preponderating weight of judicial authority is, that, whenever the questions of discipline, or of faith, or ecclesiastical rule, custom, or law have been decided by the highest of these church judicatories to which the matter has been carried, the legal tribunals must accept such decisions as final, and as binding on them, in their application to the case before them.

Watson v. Jones, 443 U.S. at 727.

Notes

1. Is mandatory deference a neutral principle? At least a partial answer to this question can be found by comparing the *types* of church polity against their nearest non-religious counterparts. For example, would it be legitimate to analogize the internal structure of a hierarchical church to that of a non-religious business corporation? Corporate law requires virtually complete deference to be given to a decision otherwise within the discretion of the corporation's board of directors. In the case of congregational polities, the Supreme Court itself makes the comparison to voluntary associations. Because most states presume that the majority rules in voluntary organizations, is there any reason to impose a different rule for congregational churches?

2. In many cases, the distinction between a congregational church and a hierarchical church organization is obvious. The Roman Catholic and Eastern Orthodox Churches, for example, are highly structured organizations, with ultimate power residing in the Holy See in Rome or the Patriarchate. The chain of authority *appears* to descend from the Holy See or the Patriarch to the Bishops and then down to the parishes, but the *actual* authority structure can only be determined by reference to the Canon Law of either church. "Conversely, Baptist churches comprise self-governing congregations, and although these congregations join in denominational bodies for such purposes as the promotion of missionary programs, the bodies exercise no control over the member congregations." Note, *Judicial Intervention in Disputes Over the Use of Church Property,* 75 Harv. L. Rev. 1142, 1159 (1962). Many denominations exhibit characteristics of more than one polity and sometimes characteristics of both congregational and hierarchical organizations.

> Reliable indices of control in such cases are not easy to come by. The lines of authority within polities are apt to be blurred, and the relevant church law chaotic, voluminous and unintelligible to a court. Further, questions of authority are likely to depend on matters of dogma, so that courts may be drawn into the briar patch of theological controversy from which *Watson* sought to save them. It may be reasonably clear although courts have not always thought

> so that the affiliation of Baptist congregations in conventions does not create a hierarchical organization, or that the mere outward presbyterial form *i.e.*, a series of assemblies does not necessarily import a functional hierarchy even where power to ordain ministers is vested in the assemblies.

Note, *Judicial Intervention,* 75 Harv. L. Rev. at 1160.

3. How many kinds of church polity are there? In *Maryland and Virginia Eldership of the Churches of God v. Church of God at Sharpsburg, Inc.*, 249 Md. 650, 241 A.2d 691 (1968), *vacated and remanded*, 393 U.S. 528 (1969), *reaffirmed* 254 Md. 162, 254 A.2d 162 (1969), *appeal dismissed*, 396 U.S. 367 (1970) (per curiam), the Maryland Court of Appeals described *three* types of recognized church polities:

> At least three kinds of internal structure, of 'polity,' may be discerned; congregational, presbyterial, and episcopal. In the congregational form, each local congregation is self-governing. The presbyterial polities are representative, authority being exercised by laymen and ministers organized in an ascending succession of judicatories: presbytery over the session of the local church, synod over presbytery, and general assembly over all. In the episcopal form power reposes in clerical superiors, such as bishops. Roughly, presbyterial and episcopal polities may be considered hierarchical, as opposed to congregational polities, in which the autonomy of the local congregation is the central principle. (Footnotes omitted).

249 Md. at 662, 241 A.2d at 698.

The Maryland court noted that the Sharpsburg church generally followed the presbyterial model: "[T]here is a governing body beyond that of the local congregation consisting of elders, the ordained ministerial elders (teaching elders) and the elected lay persons (ruling elders) and a general eldership over all of the intermediate elderships", but this did not "exclude the use of a congregational polity so far as the use and control of the property of the local congregational is concerned." *Id.* at 664. Factors that the court considered significant to its finding that a congregational polity existed with respect to property matters included (1) that the Constitution of the General Eldership had no provision whatsoever regarding the ownership of property by the local churches; (2) that any statements made by the Eldership regarding local church property ownership were strictly advisory in nature; and (3) that the deeds to the local church property contained no reverter language requiring that, in the event of disassociation, the property would become the property of the Eldership. *Id.* at 664–665.

4. Another common dispute centers on the actual relationship a local church has with its hierarchical parent. In *African Methodist Episcopal Zion Church in America, Inc. v. Zion Hill Methodist Church, Inc.*, 534 So.2d 224 (Ala. 1988), factors the court found significant were that the national organization had sent ministers to the local church for almost a century; that ceremonies (i.e. marriage, funeral, *etc.*) were conducted under the rules and regulations of the national organization; that the national organization financially assisted the local church; and, significantly, that when the local church decided to terminate the relationship with the national organization, "[t]he local church authorized an attorney to write AME Zion to inform AME Zion that Zion Hill had left the denomination. There was no evidence explaining why Zion Hill would leave the denomination if it did not in the first place belong to the denomination." *Id.* at 226. The fact that the local church had not executed a property deed in favor of the national organization, a violation of the AME Zion Discipline, was found insignificant by the court. "This argument, in effect, states that because Zion Hill

broke the rules of the Discipline, Zion Hill should be immune from those rules." *Id.* at 227.

5. In *Kendysh v. Holy Spirit Byelorussian Autocephalic Orthodox Church*, 683 F. Supp. 1501 (E.D. Mich., 1987), *aff'd*, 850 F.2d 692 (6th Cir. 1988), *cert. denied*, 488 U.S. 944 (1988), the court endorsed a "living relationship test" to determine such cases:

> It seems far preferable to look to the lines of church authority as they existed just before the dispute impaired them. Courts using this approach have emphasized such factors as whether the local organization accepted ministers appointed by diocesan executives, regularly sent delegations to denominational convocations, received financial assistance from the general church, or made payments to the funds of the general church. This inquiry has the advantage of directing the courts' attention to the prevailing understanding within the church and of eliciting difficult questions of the construction of ecclesiastical documents. Long-continued renunciation of hierarchical control should be conclusive of autonomy; conversely, acquiescence by the local congregation in the exercise of discipline and the management of its internal affairs by the hierarchy should preclude an assertion of autonomy.

Id. at 1510.

Doesn't this approach actually take sides in the controversy by imposing what is, in effect, a form of majority rule in the local congregation? The "living relationship" test, however, has been recognized as a valid, and "neutral," mechanism for the resolution of property disputes arising from schisms within hierarchical churches. *See, e.g., Church of God in Christ, Inc. v. Graham*, 54 F.3d 522 (8th Cir. 1995); *Southern Ohio State Exec. Offices of Church of God v. Fairborn Church of God*, 61 Ohio App.3d 526, 573 N.E.2d 172 (1989); *St. John Chrysostom Greek Catholic Church of Pittsburgh v. Elko*, 436 Pa. 243, 259 A.2d 419 (1969).

3) Reconsidering the "Neutral Principles Method"

Now that you have had a chance to review the basics of what the Supreme Court describes as the "neutral principles method," what is it about a given principle of law that makes it sufficiently "neutral" to be applied to an intra-religious dispute? Is there a difference between the vision of "neutrality" espoused in *Jones v. Wolf* and the "benevolent neutrality" espoused in *Zorach v. Clauson*, excerpted in Chapter Five, § C? Does the Establishment Clause require that religious disputes be treated just like any other intra-organizational dispute (a "strict" neutrality), or should the Free Exercise Clause be read as mandating a wide, or "benevolent," form of neutrality which is intended to give the church as wide a berth as possible? *Compare* Gerard V. Bradley, *Church Autonomy in the Constitutional Order: The End of Church and State?*, 49 La. L. Rev. 1057, 1086 (1989) (arguing that the autonomy of the institutional church is a value of independent significance under the First Amendment) *with* Laurence H. Tribe, *Bicentennial Blues: To Praise the Constitution Or To Bury It*, 37 Am. U. L. Rev. 1 (1987) (viewing religious liberty as a form of personal autonomy).

Because it is settled that civil courts may not involve themselves in ecclesiastical disputes, whether they relate to the content of doctrine, the enforcement of church law, or the administration of internal church affairs, how should a court actually deal with a claim that the resolution of an affirmative defense based on the First Amendment requires consideration of religious doctrine? Most of the "intra-church" case law has involved disputes over church property, but some have involved intra-church personnel matters as well. *See, e.g.*, *Turner v. Church of Jesus Christ of Latter-day Saints*, 18 S.W.3d 877 (Tex. App. 2000) (rejecting tort claims on both non-establishment and free exercise grounds). This is discussed in greater detail below. In an attempt both to avoid judicial determinations on matters of faith or doctrine, and the difficulties that arise when disputes over property are permitted to fester without resolution, some courts have seized upon the seemingly "objective" standards provided by the law of property, torts, or agency. Drawn from *Hull Church,* 393 U.S. 440, the phrase "neutral principles of law" has, however, acquired, at least in the minds of some courts in the tort context, a more expansive meaning, that of "a law of general applicability."

In *Moses v. Diocese of Colorado,* excerpted below, the Colorado Supreme Court observed that:

> In *Jones v. Wolf,* the Supreme Court of the United States explained, "[t]he neutral-principles approach cannot be said to 'inhibit' the free exercise of religion, any more than do other neutral provisions of state law governing the manner in which churches own property, hire employees, or purchase goods." [W]e noted that during the turn of the century this court had held that religious corporations, "are subject to the principles of the common law and the practice and procedure applicable to corporations under the general incorporation laws, so far as the same are pertinent." We...read [this holding] as general guidance and "as a persuasive statement that *this court should analyze legal issues that arise out of church organizations in the same manner as we would analyze those issues if they arose out of any other corporation or voluntary association.*" (emphasis added)
>
> Application of a secular standard to secular conduct that is tortious is not prohibited by the Constitution. [*Employment Div. v. Smith*]. The Supreme Court has not granted churches broad immunity against being sued in civil courts. Civil actions against clergy members and their superiors that involve claims of a breach of fiduciary duty, negligent hiring and supervision, and vicarious liability are actionable if they are supported by competent evidence in the record. [*DeStefano v. Grabrian*, 763 P.2d 275 (Colo. 1988)]

It will be useful therefore to take a moment to review *why* the "neutral principles of law" approach was approved by the Supreme Court: a State may adopt any one of various approaches for settling church property disputes so long as it involves no consideration of doctrinal matters, whether the ritual and liturgy of worship or the tenets of faith. *Maryland & Va. Churches*, 396 U.S. at 368, at 500. (Brennan, J., concurring).

Though the doctrine makes much sense as a device to avoid doctrinal disputes by "encouraging" churches to see to it that legal documents (such as titles, wills, corporate charters) are specific enough to make the intent of the organization, its leadership, and its members clear, the doctrine is not really designed to resolve what are, in essence, matters of internal church governance. An assumption that *all* laws of general applicability can be deemed "neutral principles of law" has profound implications for religious institutions. *See* Douglas Laycock, *Formal, Substantive and Disaggregated Neutrality Toward Religion,* 39 DePaul L. Rev. 993, 993–1018 (1990).

In *Employment Div. v. Smith,* 494 U.S. 872 (1990), the Supreme Court held that the First Amendment is not implicated when a law of general applicability places a "burden," substantial or otherwise, on the exercise of religion or religiously-motivated conduct. In *Church of Lukumi Babalu Aye, Inc. v. City of Hialeah,* 508 U.S. 520 (1993), the

Court reaffirmed the holding in *Smith*, but held that when a law of general applicability (in this case, an ordinance prohibiting animal sacrifice) was intended to single out a specific religion for discriminatory treatment (in *Lukumi*, practitioners of Santeria), it would be held invalid.

In light of this analysis, does the "neutral principles method" demand that incorporated religious organizations be treated exactly the same as any other business? The same as any other "charitable" organization? If so, is such a view consistent with the fact that most states have enacted legislation especially for the incorporation and governance of religious organizations? Alternatively, would neutrality be violated by forcing religious bodies to conform their respective legal documents to the strictures of their internal and doctrinal rules, and holding them to secular standards if they do not? Such an approach would avoid putting civil courts in the middle of doctrinal disputes, would it not? How should the First Amendment influence your answers to these questions?

A brief exercise:

Place yourself in the role of an attorney for a church or religious organization that desires to raise the First Amendment as an affirmative defense in a pending tort or property case. Which of the following statements accurately reflects your understanding of the law?

- Courts can avoid the First Amendment though application of strictly "neutral" principles of law.
- Application of a single standard of care to all persons, including clergy, and to lay and religious organizations is an example of a "neutral principles" approach.
- An advocate who wishes to rely upon a First Amendment claim or defense in a tort or property case must:
    1. Avoid generalized assertions that the law involved in the case will "burden" (substantially or otherwise) the free exercise of religion. A generalized claim of "burden" will not do.
    2. Produce evidence that the decision making process in the type of case involved proceeds on a discretionary, or case-by-case, basis.
    3. Produce evidence that demonstrates the impact of the proposed liability standard, and the judicial inquiry (including discovery) that will be necessary to develop it in this particular case, on specific religious beliefs and practices.
    4. Allege and make a *prima facie* case that the law, regulation, or practice is either discriminatory on its face or as applied; or the legal or factual inquiries necessary to establish the plaintiff's claims will necessitate civil court scrutiny or resolution of matters that the First Amendment leaves to the discretion of ecclesiastical authorities.

2. Ordinary Civil Liability: Utilizing the First Amendment as a Defense to Liability in Tort or Contract

a) The Nature of the Interests Involved in Tort Litigation

There are at least *three* sets of interests that are involved in tort litigation where legitimate First Amendment claims or defenses can be raised:

- The legal interests of the tort plaintiff;
- The First Amendment interests of the defendant;
- The regulatory interests of the state.

In the usual tort or contract setting, the regulatory interests of the state are assumed to be legitimate. They are, in the language of constitutional law, entitled to "a presumption of constitutionality" because tort and contract policies, like other forms of government regulation, are constitutional if they are "rationally related" to an otherwise legitimate state interest. Because the damage caused by intentional or negligent torts and breaches of contractual obligations are social and economic problems that are otherwise within the power of government to regulate, valid constitutional claims and defenses are difficult to establish. As a result, the only conduct which is relevant to the disposition of the usual tort or contract case is that of the plaintiffs and defendants.

In a case in which First Amendment claims or defenses can be raised, however, the situation is considerably more complex. Though the state's interest in the enforcement of its tort and contract law policies is a strong one, the First Amendment requires that the courts take these important liberty interests into account. The litigation should be conducted in a manner that does not intrude on First Amendment rights, and the relationships (or "law of the case") must be defined in a way that does not intrude on constitutionally protected interests.

b) Defining the Relationships in Tort Cases

A tort is either an intentional act that causes damage to a legally protected interest, or the breach of a legal duty that is the proximate cause of harm to a legitimate interest of another. §4 Restatement (Second) of the law of Torts provides:

> §4. **Duty** The word "duty" is used throughout the Restatement [(Second) of Torts] to denote the fact that the actor is required to conduct himself in a particular manner at the risk that if he does not do so he becomes subject to liability to another to whom the duty is owed for any injury sustained by such other, of which that actor's conduct is a legal cause.

Contractual duties are of a similar character, but with one significant difference. They are voluntary relationships defined by the terms of the contract itself. Only when contracts are governed by well-developed regulatory rules, such as employment contracts and labor agreements, will they raise First Amendment problems. Employment issues are discussed in greater detail in Chapter Eight.

Because a "duty" is defined by the Restatement of Torts as a legal requirement "that the actor is required to conduct himself in a particular manner at the risk that if he does not do so he becomes subject to liability to another to whom the duty is owed," it is important that a trial court in a tort case be put on notice as early as possible that the First Amendment may be relevant to the conduct of *two* "actors," not just one: the church or religiously-motivated actor, and *the court itself*. Though the focus of the judicial inquiry is action taken by individuals alleged to be acting for the church, a court conducting tort litigation is itself an "actor required [by the First Amendment] to conduct [it]self in a particular manner." The task of the advocate is to establish a factual predicate for an assertion that either the inquiry, or the nature of the duty to be imposed on the church ("standard of care") violates the First Amendment.

In *McNair v. Worldwide Church of God*, 197 Cal. App. 3d 363, 242 Cal. Rptr. 823 (1988), for example, the California Court of Appeal held that the Free Exercise Clause requires the application of the "actual malice" standard developed in *New York Times v. Sullivan*, 376 U.S. 254 (1964) for free speech and press cases to allegedly tortious actions of a church. The alleged torts, libel, slander, intentional infliction of severe emotional distress, and invasion of privacy occurred during an explanation of church doctrine on divorce. The minister used plaintiff's divorce—and her alleged responsibility for it as an example of when divorce might be justified under church teachings.

Illustrative Case

Peter Penitent had suffered for years from bouts of deep depression, but had (over the objections of his wife) neglected to get any "professional" help. His only counselor was his confessor, a Catholic priest, Fr. Damien, who had warned Peter in the strongest of terms that suicide is a grave sin, and that he (Peter) had a moral obligation to himself and to his family to seek professional help. Though he could easily have done so, Fr. Damien made no attempt to provide specific referrals. Neither did he make any attempt to "condition" absolution on Peter's willingness to seek treatment.

About six months ago, Peter sought treatment from a psychiatrist, who told him that he had suffered "needlessly" for all these years. He has now filed suit against Fr. Damien for clergy malpractice, breach of fiduciary duty, and negligent infliction of emotional distress.

What "facts" are relevant to the proof of Fr. Damien's First Amendment claim that Penitent's lawsuit and legal theory constitute a grave threat to his right to hear confessions and offer spiritual advice to penitents?

The following are examples:

- That discovery will inevitably require testimony concerning matters covered by priest-penitent privilege;
- That taking testimony on the standard of care for "a reasonably prudent confessor" will inevitably require a civil court to decide questions of religious doctrine;
- That Fr. Damien's conduct in the confessional cannot be considered "unreasonable" without some examination of the practices of other priests in the community;
- That the duty undertaken by a confessor and understood by a penitent is defined by specific provisions of the Canon Law of the Roman Catholic Church, and in its theology of the Sacrament of Reconciliation; and
- That expert testimony on religious matters will be required, and that any disputes over the qualifications of the experts will also raise theological questions.

See, e.g., O'Connor v. Diocese of Honolulu, 77 Hawai'i 383, 885 P.2d 361 (1994) (holding that the court should defer to ecclesiastical authorities, and that such abstention warrants dismissal of claim for wrongful excommunication); *Smith v. Calvary Christian Church*, 462 Mich. 679, 614 N.W.2d 590 (2000) (plaintiff specifically consented to the imposition of church discipline and thus failed to state a tort claim).

c) *Ascending Liability*

Another form of intra-religious dispute arises when a party is injured because of some act or omission on the part of church officials or members. When the injured party is not a member of the affected church, the dispute can be characterized as "intra-church" to the extent that the plaintiff demands that defendants other than those immediately involved in the dispute be joined under "joint and several," common purpose, or *respondeat superior* theories of recovery. An intra-church dispute can also arise when a local church body seeks contribution or indemnity from a body farther up in the hierarchical chain of authority.

The doctrine of ascending liability has been developed in tort and contract actions by plaintiffs who have attempted to reach deeper pockets than those belonging to the person or organization bearing direct responsibility for the injury. Using various agency principles, plaintiffs have attempted with differing degrees of success to hold one person or organization, presumably one with greater assets, responsible for the debts and liabilities incurred by another.

Barr v. The United Methodist Church

90 Cal. App. 3d 259, 153 Cal. Rptr. 322 (1979), *cert. denied sub nom., United Methodist Church v. Barr,* 444 U.S. 973 (1979)

WIENER, Associate Justice.

The guarantees of due process of law and religious freedom under the State and Federal Constitutions do not prohibit the United Methodist Church, a legal entity under Code of Civil Procedure section 388, subdivision (a), from being sued. We reverse the order of the trial court quashing service of summons on the United Methodist Church.[2]

The Procedural Background

Plaintiffs commenced their class action on behalf of approximately 1,950 present and former residents of the 14 retirement homes operated in California, Hawaii and Arizona by Pacific Homes Corporation (Pacific Homes) for equitable relief or damages. The complaint alleged each member of the class had entered into a "continuing care agreement" with Pacific Homes; that on or about February 18, 1977 Pacific Homes pe-

2. The entire text of the minute order is as follows: "The 'United Methodist Church' is an international religious denomination consisting of over 10,000,000 persons who worship in some 43,000 churches and missions throughout the world. The 'United Methodist Church' is a 'connectional' structure maintained through a chain and series of periodic conferences. It has never been incorporated. "A respected unbiased source, 'The Encyclopedia Britannica,' 1959 Ed., Vol. 15, p. 358, states: 'Methodism has continued for more than two centuries to proclaim a freedom of spirit as opposed to the bondage of an organization, and its appeal has been based on the reality of a personal experience of spiritual emancipation through faith in Christ.' "The Court rules that: 'The United Methodist Church' is no more than a 'spiritual confederation' and is not a jural entity or unincorporated association subject to suit under Code of Civil Procedure 388. A contrary ruling would effectively destroy Methodism in this country, and would have a chilling effect on all churches and religious movements by inhibiting the free association of persons of similar religious beliefs. If all members of a particular faith were to be held personally liable for the transgressions of their fellow churchmen, church pews would soon be empty and the pulpits of America silent. "Accordingly, the motion to quash service of process on 'The United Methodist Church' is granted."

titioned for relief under Chapter 11 of the Bankruptcy Act, and that the defendants Pacific and Southwest Annual Conference of the United Methodist Church (PSWAC), a California corporation, the General Council on Finance and Administration of the United Methodist Church (GCFA), and the United Methodist Church (UMC), were each financially responsible for the operations of Pacific Homes. Plaintiffs sought a declaration requiring each of the defendants to specifically perform the continuing care agreements between each plaintiff and Pacific Homes or for damages.

Plaintiffs' bases for jurisdiction over UMC in each cause of action are the allegations which state UMC was an unincorporated association, Pacific Homes was the agent of the defendants PSWAC, GCFA and UMC and in doing the acts alleged was acting within the scope of its authority as agent and with the permission, knowledge and consent of PSWAC, UMC and GCFA; each defendant or predecessor in interest was the agent of each other defendant and in doing the acts alleged, each was acting within the scope of his authority with the permission, knowledge and consent of each other defendant; and Pacific Homes was the alter ego of each defendant.

Persons upon whom service of process was attempted on behalf of UMC moved to quash the service on the grounds that (1) UMC was merely a loose connectional system and not a jural entity capable of being sued; and (2) to permit suit against UMC was unconstitutional as a violation of the due process, free exercise and establishment of religion provisions of the United States and California Constitutions.

The Status of UMC in the Litigation is a Question of Law and Not of Fact.

The initial argument made by UMC is that as an elementary principle of appellate procedure, we must uphold the trial court order if it is supported by any substantial evidence. The first difficulty we encounter with this proposition is it assumes the trial judge made a factual determination. Although there was a plethora of evidence on the issue of whether UMC was an unincorporated association, the trial court explained its holding by reference to two sets of considerations. One was peculiar to Methodism with apparent reliance on the Encyclopedia Britannica as an unbiased source; the other was of general applicability to "all churches and religious movements" with the apparent assumption that the suit against UMC involved the unconstitutional interference with the free exercise of religion. Nothing is contained in the trial court order which suggests a factual determination was made which involved the process of weighing the evidence which was presented. Secondly, the analysis of whether UMC is a jural entity involves a review of data relating to the creation, existence and operation of UMC. The facts contained in the affidavits and declarations submitted, including the information in the Book of Discipline of the United Methodist Church (1976), are not in dispute. The only ostensible factual conflict which arises is related to the ultimate issue expressed in opinions of witnesses on behalf of UMC to the effect that UMC cannot be sued. "In short, this is not a true case of conflicting evidence in which a reviewing court will refuse to disturb findings based thereon." The result which must be reached in this case does not rest on ecclesiastical expertise, but rather on principles of law. The question as to the jural status of UMC is one of law and not of fact.

The Criteria to be Applied to Determine Whether an Entity is Capable of Being Sued as an Unincorporated Association

[The court held that the law in California is that the definition of unincorporated association is "any partnership or other unincorporated organization of two or more persons, whether organized for profit or not...," Corp. Code, § 24000 (a); that such associations are liable to third persons to the same extent as if the association were a natural person, Corp. Code, § 24001; and that each such organization may protect its name and insignia from expropriation by others. Corp. Code, §§ 21300–21310.]

UMC contends an essential element for legal status, the creation of associate liability in furtherance of the common purpose is absent in the instant case because all members and connected bodies of the denomination have not delegated agency authority to Pacific Homes to act on behalf of UMC. This circuitous argument, however, assumes actual agency must be conferred on Pacific Homes before any defendant can be liable. Whether Pacific Homes had actual authority to act on behalf of UMC is unnecessary for the application of doctrines relating to either alter ego or agency. To hold otherwise would permit an unincorporated association to escape liability by the simple technique of requiring express consent from all units of the association.

The Organization of UMC

In resolving intra-church schisms or property disputes, courts have identified at least two categories of church polities; congregational and hierarchal. UMC is not congregational, i.e., the local church is not the highest authority in all matters of doctrine and usage. It is hierarchal; the 43,000 local churches and 114 Annual Conferences are governed through the structure described by the Book of Discipline of the United Methodist Church (Discipline). In United Methodism, "the local church is a part of the whole body of the general church and is subject to the higher authority of the organization and its laws and regulations." (Carnes v. Smith (1976), 236 Ga. 30, 222 S.E.2d 322, 325, cert. den. 429 U.S. 868.)

UMC may be unique in that it has no single chief operating officer, but the clearly defined operating and conceptual levels of responsibility starting with the General Conference, "(t)he legislative body for the entire Church" (Discipline, Glossary, p. 598), the Annual Conference, the District Conference, the Charge Conference, the Local Church Conference and the local church cannot be ignored. Moreover, a persuasive argument can be made that the Council of Bishops is equivalent to the board of directors of UMC. According to the Book of Discipline, the "Council of Bishops is thus the corporate expression of episcopal leadership in the Church" which is required "to meet at stated intervals" in order to oversee "the spiritual and temporal affairs of the whole Church." (Discipline, par. 525.)

Control over the local church ranging from the restrictions on purchase or sale of [real] estate which requires authorization from the Charge Conference and the written consent of the pastor and district superintendent (Discipline, par. 2429, 2431, 2433, pp. 547–549) to the selection of local church pastors is more reflective of a single entity than completely autonomous and independent units.

The day to day operation of UMC is in keeping with the reality of its organization. In applying for a group exemption under section 501(c) of the Internal Revenue Code of 1954, GCFA described itself as "the central treasury and fiscal agent of the United Methodist Church....

The possibility of UMC's liability has not gone unnoticed by those responsible for insurance coverage. UMC is a named insured on a high limit contract of insurance commencing June 1, 1976 to June 1, 1979, with a broad range of fidelity, casualty, property, fire, theft, medical malpractice and comprehensive general liability coverage. The policy as issued describes UMC as a corporation engaged in business as a religious organization.

In summary, UMC is a highly organized religious body working through specific agencies to accomplish laudable goals.

The Relationship Between Pacific Homes and UMC Requires UMC be Recognized as a Legal Entity

Before we examine the circumstances surrounding the activities of Pacific Homes and the alleged involvement of UMC, we wish to stress that our decision in the pleading phase of this litigation does not imply any lack of compassion by UMC or infer liability on its part. Our holding based upon neutral principles of law simply determines UMC is suable. What the outcome of that suit will be or should be is not before us.

Pacific Homes, a non-profit organization, was formed in 1929 by the Southern California Annual Conference (the predecessor of the PSWAC) of the Methodist Episcopal Church. Amended Articles of Incorporation signed in January 1929 expressly provided that the powers of the corporation subject to California law shall be "subject to the uses and Discipline of The Methodist Church as from time to time authorized and declared by the General Conference of said Church and by the Annual Conference within whose bounds the said corporation is located." The articles also provided that before either voluntary or involuntary dissolution, the corporate assets shall be subject to the Annual Conference of the Methodist Church or its successors; by-laws adopted or amended shall not be inconsistent with the Book of Discipline; and membership in the corporation was restricted to the Southern California Arizona Annual Conference of the Methodist Church.

The relationship between Pacific Homes and UMC has continued since 1929 in a similar fashion. Through the years, the Board of Directors of Pacific Homes has been either appointed by the Methodist Church's Annual Conference in Southern California or composed of Methodist ministers and lay persons of the Annual Conference.

The literature prepared by Pacific Homes distributed to persons interested in either a convalescent hospital or a retirement residence expressly stated that Pacific Homes was an agency of the United Methodist Church Southern California Arizona Conference. Plaintiffs' complaint mirrors the literature of Pacific Homes alleging agency, sponsorship and control over Pacific Homes.

The events referred to in the pleadings and described in the documents presented to the trial court refer to activities which not only involve spiritual concerns relating to the health and welfare of either the elderly or infirm, but which are commercial activities. The costs for lodging and the type of accommodations are primarily business decisions. UMC, in fulfilling its commitment to society, has elected to involve itself in worldly activities by participating in many socially valuable projects. It has enjoyed the benefits, both economic and spiritual, of those projects. It has even on occasion filed suit for the protection of its interests. It must now, as part of its involvement in society, be amenable to suit.

The Action Against UMC Does not Violate the Free Exercise and Establishment of Religion Provisions of the United States and California Constitutions

We have previously stated that UMC's status in the context of this appeal is a question of law, thus rejecting the ecclesiastical expertise furnished by persons knowledgeable in the history, development and faith of United Methodism. Whether we may do so is challenged by UMC under both the Federal and State Constitutions. UMC contends the First and Fourteenth Amendments prevent a civil court from independently examining its polity to conclude it is suable contrary to church doctrine.

There are situations specifically in internal church disputes where civil courts are required to accept the decision of the highest body of the church. This rule, however, has not been extended into secular disputes. Clearly the present case is secular. To defer absolutely to authoritative church experts would be to grant immunity to religious organizations in cases which might arise far afield from religious activities with the resultant effect that civil courts would then be subordinate to organizations which might attempt to classify themselves as religious to obtain the benefits of the shield of First Amendment protection.

California cases addressing this issue outside the realm of intra-church disputes have held that civil courts are not bound by a church's constitution or its ecclesiastical doctrine.

To hold UMC suable is not equivalent to a review of its polity thus interfering with its internal affairs in violation of the free exercise clause of the First Amendment. There is no evidence to show that rendering UMC amenable to suit would affect the distribution of power or property within the denomination, would modify or interfere with the modes of worship affected by Methodists or would have any effect other than to oblige UMC to defend itself when sued upon civil obligations it is alleged to have incurred.

We are keenly aware of the church-state separation articulated both in our State Constitution and Federal Constitution.... Nevertheless, nothing either our State or Federal Supreme Court has said has even remotely implied that "under the cloak of religion, persons may, with impunity, commit frauds upon the public." [Cantwell v. Connecticut] To apply a different standard to determine the jural status of religious organizations as opposed to non-religious organizations in purely secular suits might very well constitute a preference for religion in violation of the establishment clause.

The trial court order reflected the concern that if individual members of a church were to be liable there would be a chilling effect on church membership. This concern, legitimate as it may be, is properly placed with the religious body to consider before becoming involved in commercial affairs and is not a consideration which may be considered in our resolution of the issue before us.

Judgment reversed.

STANIFORTH, Acting P. J., and EHRENFREUND, J. concur.

1) Charitable Immunity

At one time, the doctrine of charitable immunity operated to shield charitable organizations from liability for damages under general tort principles. Several theories supported this doctrine. One was the notion that property was donated to a charity for a particular purpose and that it ought not be deviated from that purpose to cover debts or liabilities incurred by the donee. Another theory was that because nonprofit organizations did not profit from the work done by its employees, liability pursuant to the doctrine of *respondeat superior* was not appropriate.

In many states, however, the courts have modified the rules governing charitable immunity, and it is no longer safe for churches and religious organizations to assume that they are protected from suit simply because of their status. *See generally* Scott C. Idleman, *Tort Liability, Religious Entities, and the Decline of Constitutional Protection*, 75 Ind. L.J. 219 (2000); Daniel A. Barfield, Note, *Better to Give Than to Receive: Should Nonprofit Corporations and Charities Pay Punitive Damages?* 29 Val. U. L. Rev. 1193 (1995).

2) A Note on Liability Theories

There are two basic theories by which liability can be asserted against an entity other than the one directly causing injury to an injured plaintiff. The first is *respondeat superior*, in which it is alleged that the actor was acting for the benefit of another; the second is a direct breach of duty. *See generally* Mark Chopko, *Ascending Liability of Religious Entities for the Actions of Others*, 17 Am. J. Trial Advoc. 189 (1993) (collecting cases); Paul J. Morken, *Church Discipline and Civil Tort Claims: Should Ecclesiastical Tribunals Be Immune?*, 28 Idaho L. Rev. 93 (1991/1992); Carl H. Esbeck, *Tort Claims Against Churches and Ecclesiastical Officers: The First Amendment Considerations*, 89 W. Va. L. Rev. 1 (1986).

(A) Respondeat Superior

1. This doctrine derives from the master/servant relationship, and is generally at issue in cases in which an injured party seeks to recover from the employer of the person who is alleged to be responsible for the plaintiff's injury. Its main focus is on the extent to which the "master" has the right to control the servant's activities.

In *Brillhart v. Scheier*, 243 Kan. 591, 758 P.2d 219 (1988), the court was asked to determine whether a priest involved in a car accident was an employee of the diocese acting within the scope of his employment when the accident occurred. The priest had been driving his own car, which he insured, and had been visiting a friend prior to the accident. In determining that the diocese was entitled to judgment as a matter of law, the court first found that the priest was under the ecclesiastical rather than civil control of the bishop:

> The bishop is clearly the pastor's superior under ecclesiastical law. The evidence shows, however, that a pastor's day-to-day activities are within his own discretion and control. He is authorized under Canon Law to do whatever he feels is necessary to carry out his duties. He sets his own hours and vacation. He makes out his own paycheck, and hires or fires any non-priest/non-deacon employee, such as secretaries and janitors. Such salaries, including his own, come from parish receipts. The pastor has complete discretion in purchasing church supplies and paying the bills from parish funds. The details of daily bookkeeping and accounting of sums received and spent by the parish are not reviewed by the diocese.

Id. at 592. The court further found that the priest was not an employee for purposes of *respondeat superior*:

> In contrast to an "employee" under the respondeat superior doctrine, an "independent contractor" is one who contracts to do certain work according to his own methods, without being subject to the control of his employer, except as to the result of his work. An independent contractor therefore represents the will of his employer only in the result, and not as to the means in which it is accomplished. Thus, one who hires such an individual is not liable for that party's negligence.

Id. at 594.

Finally, the court determined that the public policy reasons behind the recognition of *respondeat superior* liability were not present in this case.

> In a typical *respondeat superior* situation, the employee would not be expected to procure insurance to protect against liability for his actions at work. His po-

> tential negligence is viewed by his employer as "a required cost of doing business" which may be shifted to society at large. *See* Prosser and Keeton on Torts § 69. In such a situation, an innocent victim would often not be able to recover damages for negligence unless the employee's negligence was imputed to the employer. The doctrine of *respondeat superior* allows the victim to reach the "deep pocket" which benefits from the risk undertaken, and thus encourages an employer to supervise his employees to prevent injuries to others caused by the employees' negligence. The case at bar is not a typical *respondeat superior* situation where public policy dictates imputed liability.

Id. at 597.

2. Authorities have identified two areas of agency analysis that pose particular problems for courts when deciding questions involving religious organizations. *See generally*, David Frohlich, Note, *Will Courts Make Change for a Large Denomination?: Problems of Interpretation in an Agency Analysis in Which a Religious Denomination is Involved in an Ascending Liability Tort Case*, 72 Iowa L. Rev. 1377 (1987); Edward M. Gaffney and Philip C. Sorensen, ASCENDING LIABILITY IN RELIGIOUS AND OTHER NONPROFIT ORGANIZATIONS (1984). In your consideration of the following materials, try to determine how or whether neutral principles analysis affects the issues being discussed.

Benefit: The fiduciary relationship necessary for an agency relationship to be formed requires that the agent be acting primarily for the benefit of the principal. Restatement (Second) of Agency § 1 cmt. a (1957). Agency principles were developed almost exclusively using for-profit corporations as a model. Consequently, it was usually clear for whose benefit the agent was acting: the corporation and its shareholders. In the nonprofit setting, it has historically been assumed that the activities being undertaken by the nonprofit corporation were for the benefit of society as a whole. However, "[t]he contemporary shift in attitudes toward charitable immunity has been accompanied by a corresponding shift in attitudes about the nature of charitable activities; not that they are held less worthy but that they constitute what is regularly described as the 'business' of charity, and organizational end that is, benefit to be served, the costs of which are to be the responsibility of the organization." Gaffney & Sorensen, at 34–35.

How, then, is it to be determined when a church member is acting for the benefit of the religious organization to which he or she belongs? If church doctrine encourages members to do good works, does a church member who works in a soup kitchen act for the benefit of his or her church, or does this person act as an expression of ideological beliefs shared with the other members of her church? How did the *Barr* court address this issue?

Control: Religious organizations often differ significantly from the for-profit enterprises around which agency theories developed. There are at least two different areas of control where religious organizations create unique problems for the courts.

First, management structures in religious organizations tend operate more loosely than in for-profit institutions. Religious organizations tend to be managed primarily by volunteers rather than paid employees. *See* Frohlich, at 1385–87. High turnover and consequent confusion about the lines of authority is also a major problem.

Second, doctrinal control, which is irrelevant in most for-profit enterprises, can muddy the waters of agency analysis. In *Gibson v. Brewer*, 952 S.W.2d 239, 248 (Mo. en banc 1997), for example, the Missouri Supreme Court recognized a cause of action for "intentional failure to supervise clergy." The court was explicit regarding the implications of the holding: "This cause of action requires a supervisor. The First Amendment does not, however, allow a court to decide issues of church government—whether or not a cleric should have a supervisor." *See also Ambrosio v. Price*, 495 F. Supp. 381, 385 (D. Neb. 1979) (reviewing facts to determine if priest's trip was personal, to satisfy a priestly duty, or to further church business).

3. Following the court's decision in *Barr*, many religious organizations sought to restructure themselves to limit their potential liability. The key to this type of restructuring is to segregate, as much as is possible, assets devoted to one type of activity from assets devoted to another.

The separate incorporation of entities is an attempt to make them and their assets legally distinct from one another. Problems can arise when the civil control structure dictated by the various different incorporation statutes conflicts with the hierarchy or structure of control in the religious organization. For example, note the general outlines of the Catholic Church's hierarchy: parish, diocese (comprised of a group of parishes within a certain geographic area), national bishops' conference, and the Holy See in Rome. Historically, the Catholic Church has preferred control of assets be vested in its hierarchy at the diocese level, a practice incompatible with a corporation utilizing the membership or trustee corporate forms. One way of avoiding the problem of parish level debt and liabilities "ascending" to the diocese level is to incorporate each parish separately. The bishop in this scenario may be appointed either as a director and/or as an officer of the parish corporation. It should be noted, however, that when the bishop is the sole director, or when the bishop and his administrators dominate a board of directors, the argument that the parish entity is legally distinct from the diocese is weakened. *See Doe v. Gelineau*, 732 A.2d 43 (R.I. 1999) (refusing to pierce the corporate veil). *See generally* William F. McCarthy, *Diocesan Asset Management Strategies from the Civil Law Perspective*, National Diocesan Attorneys Association San Antonio Conference, March 1995.

(B) Seeking the "Deep Pocket:" Ascending Liability

There are a number of different ways in which to characterize the duty owed by clerics or religious workers to the members of a congregation and others affected by their work. The cases excerpted in this section deal with those duties in starkly different ways. As you review them you should consider the nature of the duty alleged, the nature of the duty imposed by state law both before and after the decision, and the degree to which the holding comports with the requirements of the First Amendment. The materials on religion-based personal and institutional autonomy claims covered in Chapter Eleven § D(1) are closely related to the materials covered in this section, and should be consulted as well.

Moses v. Diocese of Colorado

863 P.2d 310 (Colo. 1993)

Justice ERICKSON delivered the Opinion of the Court.

This appeal is from a judgment entered on a jury verdict awarding Mary E. Moses $1,216,500 as damages against the Episcopal Diocese of Colorado (Diocese), and Bishop William Frey (Bishop Frey). Tenantry was a parishioner at St. Philip and St. James Episcopal Church in Denver. She sought counseling from Father Paul Robinson

(Father Robinson), who was then an assistant priest at St. Philip and St. James. Although Tenantry had a long history of mental illness, her condition was relatively stable at the time she began her counseling with Father Robinson. While counseling and advising Tenantry, Father Robinson entered into a sexual relationship with her. When her relationship with Father Robinson ended, Tenantry suffered a relapse and aggravation of her mental illness. Shortly thereafter, her marriage ended in divorce. Tenantry is now under psychiatric care which will be required indefinitely.

The jury found that Bishop Frey and the Diocese breached their fiduciary duties to the plaintiff, the Diocese negligently hired and negligently supervised Father Robinson, and was vicariously liable for Robinson's breach of his fiduciary duty to Tenantry. On appeal, the Diocese and Bishop Frey assert that the First Amendment of the United States Constitution forecloses recovery for clergy malpractice and an award against them for the damages sustained by Tenantry. If the First Amendment defense is valid, the remaining issues on appeal are moot.

In our view, the First Amendment does not grant the Diocese and its employees immunity from liability in this case. The Diocese and Bishop Frey also assert that the evidence was insufficient to support the jury's findings. We disagree in part. The evidence was sufficient to support Tenantry's claims for breach of fiduciary duty, negligent hiring, and supervision. The evidence, however, was not sufficient to prove that Robinson was acting within the scope of his employment when he engaged in oral sex with Tenantry; therefore, the Diocese is not vicariously liable for Robinson's sexual acts with Tenantry.

Accordingly, we affirm the judgment of the trial court on Tenantry's claims for breach of fiduciary duty and negligent hiring and supervision. We reverse the judgment for damages against the Diocese and Bishop Frey based upon the claim of vicarious liability, and remand with directions.

I

A

[Plaintiff Tenantry suffered from a multiple personality disorder which allegedly developed as a reaction to sexual abuse by her father. She married Geoffrey Moses (Moses) in 1974. After treatment for her mental illness concluded in 1979, she became an active member of St. Philip and St. James Parish.]

In 1984, the vestry of St. Philip and St. James decided to hire an assistant priest. Father Myers, the Pastor, suggested the vestry interview Father Robinson, a newly ordained priest who would help the vestry accomplish its goal of attracting young families to the parish. Father Myers interviewed Father Robinson during his ordination period and knew that Bishop Frey considered Father Robinson to be "bishop material." Neither Bishop Frey nor the Diocese provided the church vestry with any of the information about Father Robinson contained in the Diocese's personnel files. Included in Father Robinson's personnel file were reports of psychological examinations that were conducted as a result of Father Robinson seeking ordination. These reports indicated Father Robinson had problems with depression, low self-esteem, and possessed a "sexual identification ambiguity."

Father Robinson was selected by the vestry to begin his duties as assistant priest at St. Philip and St. James Parish in June 1984. Tenantry and her husband were among many of the young couples who befriended Father Robinson and his wife.

In September 1984, Tenantry sought counseling with Father Robinson. At the time of these counseling sessions, Father Robinson knew [that] Tenantry...had been sexually abused as a child. Tenantry's counseling sessions with Father Robinson always ended with a prayer and a hug. The hugs eventually led to fondling, and finally, to mutual sex.

[When Tenantry disclosed the relationship to her sister, steps were taken to bring it to an end. Robinson was confronted and eventually admitted that there had been a sexual relationship. The pastor was consulted, but downplayed the incidents and did nothing. Finally, the Bishop was asked to intervene. He scheduled a meeting among the complaining parties, but on the day before the scheduled meeting, he signed a letter which promoted Father Robinson to the position of pastor of the Colorado Springs church.][5]

At the meeting, Father Robinson admitted to a sexual relationship with Tenantry.... Bishop Frey asked Moses if he would be content to let the Bishop supervise "whatever needed to happen." Moses acquiesced to Bishop Frey assuming control of the matter. Bishop Frey arranged to meet with Tenantry in order to resolve the matter. After Moses left, Bishop Frey informed Father Robinson that if this was a one-time episode, he would not mention it to the Colorado Springs parish. The Bishop also gave Father Robinson a book entitled "Affair Prevention" and told him to get counseling and to advise him immediately if the matter came up in the Colorado Springs parish.

Moses returned home and informed Tenantry that Bishop Frey wanted to see her. Tenantry was terrified about the loss of her salvation and feared having to meet with the Bishop. At their meeting, Tenantry described her past to Bishop Frey and explained that she had an intimate sexual relationship with Father Robinson. Tenantry discussed her fear of not having salvation because of her acts and Bishop Frey granted Tenantry absolution. At trial, Bishop Frey testified that at this meeting his impression of Tenantry was that she was fragile and had a sense of guilt that bordered on [being] pathological because she blamed herself for the relationship.

Tenantry explained to Bishop Frey that she still loved Father Robinson. Bishop Frey told Tenantry that if she loved Father Robinson she should not talk to anyone about her relationship with him, never go near the church, and never talk to Father Robinson again. Tenantry received permission from Bishop Frey to speak to a priest or counselor. Tenantry told Bishop Frey that she had discussed the relationship with her sister and asked if she needed to stop talking with her. Bishop Frey stated that the prohibition on talking to people included Tenantry's sister. Tenantry then asked if she could talk to her husband and Bishop Frey gave her permission to talk to him. The Bishop took no further action to assist Tenantry after this meeting.

At trial, mental health experts testified that the discovery of Bishop Frey's promotion of Father Robinson led to the unraveling of Tenantry's personality structure. Tenantry was diagnosed as suffering [from] a recurrence of her multiple personality disorder a post-traumatic stress syndrome.

---

5. Bishop Frey did not inform the vestry of Father Robinson's newly assigned parish about the allegations against Father Robinson despite the fact that Bishop Frey knew that the prior priest assigned to the Colorado Springs parish had left that church because of his illicit sexual relationship with a parishioner. An expert who testified at trial expressed the opinion that the likelihood of a priest repeating sexual relationships with parishioners is fifty percent.

II

For the first time on appeal, the defendants have formulated First Amendment defenses that were not raised in the trial court and allegedly bar Tenantry's claims for the injuries she suffered as a result of the conduct of Father Robinson, Bishop Frey, and the Diocese. The First Amendment issues raised on appeal were not properly preserved in the trial court. However, it is within our discretion to review the First Amendment defenses. The First Amendment to the United States Constitution does not grant religious organizations absolute immunity from tort liability. Liability can attach for breach of a fiduciary duty, negligent hiring and supervision. Destefano v. Grabrian, 763 P.2d 275, 284, 286–87 (Colo.1988).

A

The principle of [the *Watson v. Jones* to *Jones v. Wolf* line of cases] is, as this court has recognized, that courts must not become embroiled in disputes involving a religious organization if the court would be required to interpret or weigh church doctrine. [In] *Bishop and Diocese of Colorado v. Mote*, 716 P.2d 85, 102 (Colo.1986)... [we] held that Colorado law required application of the "neutral principles" doctrine when a court is resolving a religious property dispute. *Id.* at 96.

Even though *Mote* involved a church property dispute, we noted that during the turn of the century this court had held that religious corporations, "are subject to the principles of the common law and the practice and procedure applicable to corporations under the general incorporation laws, so far as the same are pertinent." *Mote*, 716 P.2d at 98 (*quoting Horst v. Traudt*, 43 Colo. 445, 96 P. 259 (1908)). We recognized in *Mote* that *Horst* was not controlling precedent but we read *Horst* as general guidance and "as a persuasive statement that this court should analyze legal issues that arise out of church organizations in the same manner as we would analyze those issues if they arose out of any other corporation or voluntary association." *Mote*, 716 P.2d at 99.

Application of a secular standard to secular conduct that is tortious is not prohibited by the Constitution. The Supreme Court has not granted churches broad immunity against being sued in civil courts.... Civil actions against clergy members and their superiors that involve claims of a breach of fiduciary duty, negligent hiring and supervision, and vicarious liability are actionable if they are supported by competent evidence in the record.

The facts of Tenantry's case indicate that an organization, confronted with the misdeeds of one of its agents, assumed control of the matter and in the process of protecting itself injured a vulnerable individual. The defendants have not argued that Bishop Frey's decision to assume control and resolve the problems created by Father Robinson and Tenantry's relationship was a matter of purely ecclesiastical concern. Tenantry's claims in this case do not involve disputes within the church and are not based solely on ecclesiastical or disciplinary matters which would call into question the trial court's power to render a judgment against the defendants. Our decision does not require a reading of the Constitution and Canons of the Protestant Episcopal Church or any other documents of church governance. Because the facts of this case do not require interpreting or weighing church doctrine and neutral principles of law can be applied, the First Amendment is not a defense against Tenantry's claims.

III

On appeal, Bishop Frey and the Diocese have urged this court to overrule *Destefano v. Grabrian*, 763 P.2d 275 (Colo.1988). The defendants contend the claims of breach of fiduciary duty and clergy malpractice are merely different names for professional liability. Their position is that because we refused to recognize a claim for clergy malpractice in *Destefano,* and all of Tenantry's claims relating to the negligence of the church and the acts of the church's agents are in reality claims for clergy malpractice, Tenantry's case should have been dismissed.

We have declared that breach of fiduciary duty and clergy malpractice are not identical claims and involve different elements.[13] Sufficient evidence existed to allow the jury to find that a fiduciary relationship existed between Bishop Frey and the Diocese and Tenantry and that the breach of the fiduciary duty caused Tenantry's injuries.

A

A prerequisite to finding a fiduciary duty is the existence of a fiduciary relationship. "A fiduciary relation exists between two persons when one of them is under a duty to act for or to give advice for the benefit of another upon matters within the scope of the relation." Restatement (Second) of Torts § 874 cmt. a (1979). A fiduciary relationship may arise where one party occupies a superior position relative to another. Stuart M. Speiser et al., THE AMERICAN LAW OF TORTS, § 36:81 (1983) (stating that there are two ways to find a fiduciary relationship: it may presumed from the relationship of the parties; or, it may exist as a result of the superiority and influence that accompanies a repose of trust); *see also Bailey v. Allstate Ins. Co.*, 844 P.2d 1336 (Colo.App.1992) (recognizing that although some relationships give rise to a fiduciary duty as a matter of law, *e.g.*, attorney-client, the nature of the claim is a relationship of trust, confidence and reliance). Although a professional relationship can be used as evidence that one party has both the position and opportunity to influence the other party, a professional relationship is not a prerequisite to finding a fiduciary relationship. A fiduciary relationship can arise out of a relationship of blood, business, friendship, or association. Speiser et al., *supra*, § 36:81. The claim for breach of fiduciary duty in this case involves a party who used his superior position as a counselor, a bishop, and a final arbiter of problems with the clergy to the detriment of a vulnerable, dependent party.

The clergy-parishioner relationship is not necessarily a fiduciary relationship. It does, however, involve the type of interaction that creates trust and reliance. Courts have recognized the fiduciary nature of the clergy-parishioner relationship. *See, e.g.*, *Destefano*, 763 P.2d at 284 (holding a priest who abuses his role as counselor can be liable for breach of fiduciary duty); *Erickson v. Christenson*, 781 P.2d 383, 386 (Or.App.1989) (same); *Adams v. Moore,* 96 N.C. App. 359, 385 S.E.2d 799, 801 (1989)

---

13. *Destefano* held that a cause of action for breach of fiduciary duty was separate and distinct from a claim of clergy malpractice. The fundamental difference between the two causes of action is the former is a breach of trust and does not require a professional relationship or a professional standard of care, while the latter is an action for negligence based on a professional relationship and a professional standard of care. In *Destefano*, we held the defendant owed a fiduciary duty to the plaintiff that "was created by his undertaking to counsel [the plaintiff]." The position of trust occupied by the defendant, when coupled with his positive act of counseling the plaintiff, resulted in a duty to the plaintiff. The relevant common facts in *Destefano* and Tenantry's case are not the profession of the defendants; the relevant facts are that the defendants in both cases occupied a position of superiority, assumed a duty to act in good faith, and then breached their duty. In Colorado, breach of fiduciary duty is actionable, clergy malpractice is not.

(finding preacher owed fiduciary duty to parishioner and violated that duty by using his position and influence to obtain the deed to parishioner's home).

The existence of the fiduciary relationship is a question of fact for the jury. In this case, the jury was properly instructed on the requisite elements of a fiduciary relationship and determined a fiduciary relationship existed between Bishop Frey and Tenantry.

In the meeting between Bishop Frey and Tenantry the parties did not occupy equal positions. Bishop Frey held a position of authority in the church and had the power to resolve conflicts in the church. In addition, Bishop Frey's role during the meeting was as a counselor to Tenantry, not as a representative of the Diocese or Father Robinson. If Bishop Frey was acting only for the Diocese and Father Robinson, he failed to convey that fact to Tenantry and led her to believe he was acting in her interest.

B

An unequal relationship does not automatically create a fiduciary duty. In order to be liable the superior party must assume a duty to act in the dependent party's best interest. The defendants assert they are not liable because Bishop Frey and the Diocese did not take any action that would allow the jury to conclude they assumed a duty to Tenantry. There is sufficient evidence that the defendants assumed a duty to Tenantry when they acted to resolve the problems that were the result of the relationship between Father Robinson and Tenantry.

One of the fiduciary's duties is the duty to deal "with utmost good faith and solely for the benefit" of the dependent party. *Destefano,* 763 P.2d at 284. Once a member of the clergy accepts the parishioner's trust and accepts the role of counselor, a duty exists to act with the utmost good faith for the benefit of the parishioner. Despite his experience in handling issues of clergy misconduct and his knowledge of Tenantry's extreme vulnerability, Bishop Frey took no action to help Tenantry. Acting as the representative for the Diocese, Bishop Frey failed to assist Tenantry in understanding that she was not the only person responsible for her sexual relationship with Father Robinson. He did not recommend counseling for Tenantry but did recommend counseling for Father Robinson and ordered Father Robinson to make progress reports on the counseling. Bishop Frey's only action in regard to Tenantry was to bind her to secrecy. Thus, Bishop Frey assumed control of a situation that demanded he consider Tenantry's interests and then used Tenantry's trust to her detriment.

IV

Bishop Frey and the Diocese contend that the jury erred in finding the Diocese negligent in hiring and supervising Father Robinson and that the alleged negligence caused Tenantry's injuries. Bishop Frey and the Diocese maintain that there was no employment relationship between the Diocese and Father Robinson and even if there was, there was insufficient evidence in the record to support these negligence claims.

A

An employer may be liable for harm to others for negligently employing an improper person for a task which may involve a risk to others. It is axiomatic that a prerequisite to establishing negligent hiring is an employment or agency relationship. Tenantry produced sufficient evidence to raise a factual dispute on the issue of the relationship between the Diocese and Father Robinson as well as the relationship between Bishop Frey and Father Robinson. Because a dispute existed, the trial court properly submitted the issue to the jury.

The control a principal exercises over the manner of work performed by an agent is evidence that an agency relation exists. The evidence presented at trial shows that the structure of the Episcopal Church is basically hierarchal. A pamphlet distributed by the Episcopalian Church titled "About Being an Episcopalian" (Exhibit 25) contains a chart of the "Structure of the Episcopal Church." The chart graphically shows that the bishop presides over the Diocese and the priests. A priest presides over the parish "subject to the bishop's approval." In "The Episcopal Church: Essential Facts" another pamphlet admitted during the trial (Exhibit 24), the Episcopal Church defines the role of priests: "Priests (also known as presbyters) are ordained and consecrated to assist the bishop in overseeing the Church." The pamphlet sets forth that the diocese "is governed by its bishop and a diocesan convention composed of clergy of the diocese and lay persons elected by the parishes." Vestries call rectors to serve only after consultation with the bishop. Additionally, the bishop signs a letter promoting a priest to a pastor of a parish.

Other evidence presented at trial establishes the relationship among the rector, the bishop, the diocese, and the assistant priest. The rector supervises an assistant priest's counseling duties which are specifically prescribed by regulations promulgated by the Diocese. In addition, the rector in this case stated that he reported to the bishop and that the bishop made final decisions on discipline. Father Robinson testified that when a priest needs pastoral care, the priest looks to the bishop. The Diocese has independent responsibility for the employment of priests. The bishop oversees ordination, discipline, counseling, the maintenance of personnel files and the provision of information with respect to hiring. Vestries rely on the Diocese to prepare and educate candidates, to obtain psychological evaluations of candidates for ordination, and provide information about individuals who are being considered for clergy positions in the parish. While the individual priests and parishes may be independently responsible for their day-to-day activities, the Diocese exercises an employment option in the hiring of its pastors.

B

The jury also found the Diocese was negligent in its supervision of Father Robinson. Both the Diocese and Bishop Frey had previous exposure to the problem of sexual relationships developing between priests and parishioners because the problem had arisen seven times before.

V

The jury determined that the Diocese and Bishop Frey were vicariously liable for Father Robinson's tortious conduct. Father Robinson, however, was not acting within the scope and course of his employment and therefore the Diocese and Bishop Frey are not vicariously liable.

There is no evidence in the record to support Tenantry's contention that Father Robinson was acting in the scope of his employment by engaging in sex with her. In fact, the evidence in the record establishes that Father Robinson was not acting within the scope of his employment by engaging in [sexual activity with her]. Bishop Frey testified that Father Robinson's conduct was a "serious breach of [his] ordination vows." Father Robinson testified that his physical relationship was not within the scope of his employment with the church. Even Tenantry's own experts testified that Father Robinson's sexual conduct was outside the scope of his priestly duties.[29]

The jury's finding that Robinson was acting within the scope of his employment when he had tortious sexual contact with Tenantry is erroneous as a matter of law. The Diocese is not vicariously liable for Robinson's acts with Tenantry. We therefore order the trial court to vacate its judgment holding the Diocese and Bishop Frey vicariously liable for Father Robinson's acts.

VI

The judgment entered by the trial court is affirmed in part and reversed in part.

Chief Justice ROVIRA concurring in part and dissenting in part:

While the majority points to several facts in support of its conclusion that the evidence presented was sufficient to create a factual dispute respecting whether the relationship between the diocese and Father Robinson was one of either agency or employment, those facts do not create such a dispute because they have no bearing on the critical elements needed to establish the existence of either of these legal relationships. Because the evidence pertaining to those decisive elements was undisputed and cannot, as a matter of law, support a finding of an agency or employment relationship, the Diocese of Colorado cannot be held liable for the negligent hiring and supervision of Father Robinson.

The uncontradicted evidence presented at trial established that the diocese neither had the right of continuous control over Father Robinson nor exercised that "right." Indeed, no evidence was presented which created even the inference that the diocese was vested with such power over Father Robinson. Canon 14(a) of the Episcopal Church provides that "[a]ll assistant Clergy... shall be selected by the rector... and shall serve under the authority and direction of the Rector." Constitution & Canons for the Government of The Episcopal Church Title III, canon 14(a) at 80 (1988). Numerous witnesses testified that it was the rector at St. Philip and St. James Parish who gave Father Robinson his assignments and who instructed him as to how to carry out his day-to-day duties. Those same witnesses testified that those day-to-day activities would be supervised and controlled by the rector, and not the diocese or the bishop. Father Charles Farr, Father Meyers, and Gary Schoener, [] all were in complete agreement on these points. In short, the evidence established, as the majority concedes, that individual rectors are "independently responsible for their [assistant priests'] day-to-day activities."

Thus, I am of the opinion that the uncontradicted evidence precludes, as a matter of law, a finding that the diocese and Father Robinson occupied an employer-employee relationship.

---

29. Although it is evident that a priest who engages in tortious sexual contact with a parishioner under the facts in this case is not acting within the scope of his employment, Tenantry nevertheless claims that the Diocese is vicariously liable because it was foreseeable that Robinson would mishandle the transference phenomenon. There is some support for the theory that reasonable foreseeability can establish vicarious liability. Expanding vicarious liability of a religious organization to cover foreseeable acts may well intrude into the First Amendment of the United States Constitution. Rather, the phenomenon of transference is better dealt with in this case through the claim of negligent hiring and supervision

III

The majority, however, points to number of facts about the structure of the Episcopal Church and places primary reliance on the testimony of [the expert] in support of the conclusion that sufficient evidence was presented to create a jury question as to whether Robinson was either an agent or employee of the diocese. In my opinion, none of those facts support the conclusion for which they are enlisted, because none of them relate to the critical elements needed to establish an agency or employment relationship.

The jury was properly instructed that in order to find an employment relation between the diocese and Robinson, they should consider whether: (1) the diocese selected or retained Robinson; (2) wages or other consideration were to be paid by them; (3) the diocese or bishop had the power to terminate Robinson; and (4) the diocese or Bishop Frey had the right to control Robinson. *See supra* (quoting Jury Instruction 23). The majority concedes that the fourth, and "critical," element of control is wanting here because it is the rector who controls an assistant priest's day-to-day activities. Furthermore, the majority nowhere states or concludes that the diocese hired Robinson, had the duty to compensate Robinson, or had the actual ability to terminate Robinson's employment with the parish.

In short, the majority never contends that any of the elements that the jury was instructed to consider in determining whether an employment relation existed between the diocese and Robinson have been met here. Rather, all of the evidence cited establishes only that the bishop and diocese can exert influence over an assistant priest. The jury was not, however, instructed that "influence" alone could either support a finding of an employment relation or that such a fact should even be considered by them. Thus, the fact that such influence exists cannot support the conclusion that sufficient evidence was presented to either create a question for the jury or to support the jury's verdict.

Consequently, I would hold that the trial court erred in denying defendant's directed verdict motion dismissing plaintiff's claim for negligent hiring and supervision. Accordingly, I concur in the result in Part III, concur in Part V, and dissent from Part IV of the majority opinion.

Notes

1. As noted in Chapter Eleven, no court has accepted the premise that a member of the clergy can be sued for "malpractice." *See, e.g., Dausch v. Ryske*, 1993 WL 34873 (N.D.Ill. Feb 10, 1993), *aff'd in part rev'd in part*, 52 F.3d 1425 (7th Cir. 1994); *Schmidt v. Bishop*, 779 F. Supp. 321 (S.D.N.Y. 1991) *Cherepski v. Walker*, 323 Ark. 43, 913 S.W.2d 761 (1996). *See* Mark Chopko, *Ascending Liability of Religious Entities for the Actions of Others*, 17 Am.J. Trial Advoc. 189, 335–36, & nn. 212–219 (1993) (collecting cases), but there are a number of cases, like *Moses*, which indicate that there may be other breaches of duty for which liability can attach, both to the individual and to his or her superiors. *See, e.g., Sanders v. Casa View Baptist Church*, 898 F. Supp. 1169 (N.D. Tex. 1995); *Isely v. Capuchin Province*, 880 F. Supp. 1138 (E.D. Mich. 1995); *Barquin v. Roman Catholic Diocese of Burlington, Vermont, Inc.*, 839 F. Supp. 275 (D. Vt. 1993); *Tichenor v. Roman Catholic Church of Archdiocese of New Orleans*, 665 So. 2d 1307 (La. App. 1995); *Doe v. Redeemer Lutheran Church*, 531 N.W.2d 897 (Minn. App. 1995) (church failed to address problems of minister's behavior); *F.G. v. MacDonell*, 696 A.2d 697 (N.J. 1997) (rejecting clergy malpractice claim based on pastor's sexual misconduct, but recognizing claim for breach of fiduciary duty); *Curran v. Walsh Jesuit High School*, 99 Ohio App.3d

696, 651 N.E.2d 1028 (1995) (concluding liability cannot be predicated on failure to report information concerning alleged abuse of minor). *See generally* Seymour Moskowitz & Michael J. DeBoer, *When Silence Resounds: Clergy and the Requirement to Report Elder Abuse and Neglect*, 49 DePaul L. Rev. 1 (1999); James T. O'Reilly and Joann M. Strasser, *Clergy Sexual Misconduct: Confronting the Difficult Constitutional and Institutional Liability Issues*, 7 St. Thomas L. Rev. 31 (1994).

2. Controversies charging "wrongful baptism" are not unknown, see *Suit Filed Over Girl's Baptism,* Rocky Mtn. News, Oct. 4, 1995, at 19A, and Virginia prison authorities denied a condemned prisoner the right to be re-baptized on the grounds that "once is enough." *See* David Cox, Editorial, Baptism: Salvation is Not a Matter of State, *Roanoke Times & World News*, Feb. 15, 1995, at A-11. What result in the following hypothetical situation?

> Nathan Nurse, a devout Christian, works in the pediatric intensive care unit of a large religiously affiliated hospital. Whenever an infant appears likely to die, Nurse undertakes quietly to baptize it. On one recent occasion, he undertook to baptize the baby of Jewish parents. The baby survived, and Nurse was overheard confiding in a co-worker that he believed that the child had been "reborn in the Spirit, Who had helped her to survive." When the parents found out, they were outraged. They have threatened to sue.

Consider the chart that appears in Chapter Eleven §D(1) summarizing the kinds of complaints raised against members of the clergy and others who work in religious ministry. Do you see the relationship between tort theory and practice in constitutional cases?

D. Zoning and Historic Preservation as Limits on Religious Freedom

1. Zoning & Land Use Planning

Zoning laws were first held constitutional by the Supreme Court in *Euclid v. Ambler Realty Co.*, 272 U.S. 365 (1926). Because zoning ordinances can limit the use of land to residences, the permissible extent of zoning regulation of church buildings is subject to much dispute. Several courts have held zoning regulations that exclude churches violate constitutional provisions concerning religious liberty. *Compare City of Sherman v. Simms*, 143 Tex. 115, 183 S.W.2d 415 (1944); *State* ex rel. *Lake Drive Baptist Church v. Village of Bayside Bd. of Trustees*, 12 Wis. 2d 585, 108 N.W.2d 288 (1961); and *Church of Christ v. Metropolitan Bd. of Zoning Appeals*, 371 N.E.2d 1331 (Ind. App. 1978) (all holding zoning ordinances unconstitutional) *with Corporation of Presiding Bishop v. City of Porterville*, 90 Cal. App. 2d 656, 203 P.2d 823 (1949) and *Miami Beach United Lutheran Church of the Epiphany v. City of Miami Beach*, 82 So.2d 880 (Fla. 1955)(contra). More recent decisions have been more deferential to land use regulations. The reason for this may be the changing perception of the value of churches in communities, as noted in a November 20, 1991 article in the Wall Street Journal by R. Gustav Niebuhr. Niebuhr noted that many residents of the community of Rancho San Diego, California were opposed to the construction of churches in the community because they would contribute to congested traffic, bring a large number of children to the area, and contribute additional noise to the community. These residents utilized zoning restrictions to regulate the churches in the community. R. Gustav Niebuhr, *Here Is the Church; As for the People, They're Picketing It*, Wall Street Journal, November 20, 1991, at 1.

The two excerpted cases discuss the permissible extent of zoning regulation of church property. The first case concerns the free exercise rights of churches when their proposed use of land is barred by zoning laws. The second concerns whether the Establishment Clause bars a city from passing zoning regulations which create different rules for land owned by churches rather than individuals. The Alaska Supreme Court held in *Seward Chapel, Inc. v. City of Seward*, 655 P.2d 1293 (Alaska 1982), that zoning regulations barring the building of a nonpublic school were constitutional. In *Cohen v. City of Des Plaines*, 8 F.3d 484 (7th Cir. 1993), *cert. denied,* 512 U.S. 1236 (1994), Seventh Circuit reversed the district court and held that a city zoning ordinance allowing a different use of property if owned by a church rather than an individual did not violate the Establishment Clause.

Seward Chapel, Inc. v. City of Seward

655 P.2d 1293 (Alaska 1982)

RABINOWITZ, Justice.

I. OVERVIEW

This appeal presents a zoning dispute of constitutional magnitude between Seward Chapel, Inc. and the City of Seward. The principal issue on appeal is whether the federal or Alaska constitutions, or both, compel the city to allow Seward Chapel to operate a parochial school in its church building notwithstanding a zoning ordinance which excludes all nonpublic schools from the residential area in which Seward Chapel's building is located. We conclude that the ordinance is constitutionally permissible.

II. FACTS

The case is set in a residential subdivision of the City of Seward called Forest Acres, an area described by the superior court as "the premier residential subdivision on the Kenai Peninsula." The area has a rural character and, according to the city, affords residents a "peaceful seclusion." From the record it appears that a majority of the residents of Forest Acres would prefer that their peaceful seclusion not be disturbed by a parochial school.

Seward Chapel's dispute with the city over zoning began in 1974, when Pastor Paul Pichotta and Michael Van Deusen of the Abbott Loop Christian Center in Anchorage came to Seward to establish a church. Pastor Pichotta located two adjacent lots in Forest Acres which were owned by a fellow church member and purchased the lots after the city approved his application for a permit to build a church on the lots. Although Pastor Pichotta expressed his intent to operate a parochial school as well as a church on the premises, the city made it clear that a parochial school was not permitted in Forest Acres under the then-existing zoning laws.[5] Notwithstanding the limitation on

5. At a meeting of the Planning and Zoning Commission which occurred a month before Pastor Pichotta acquired the Forest Acres site, the pastor advised the commission that the church expected to operate a "five day a week" school in addition to a church. He was told that a school was not a permissible use of the site. In a letter to Pastor Pichotta the city confirmed its view that the zoning regulations excluded schools. The pastor testified at trial that he was "disappointed...when I found out that we would not be able [to operate a school], but I felt we could pursue that later." Seward Chapel argues that, notwithstanding notice that the site could not be used as a parochial school, the

parochial schools, Seward Chapel constructed a church on the Forest Acres site; the church flourished and, at the time of trial in 1980, had a congregation of ninety to one-hundred members.

The applicable zoning ordinance has been amended several times since Seward Chapel acquired its site in Forest Acres. In 1978 the ordinance, which then allowed churches and accessory uses by permit, was amended to create a new "Rural Residential" ("RR") zone; Forest Acres, which comprises seven to eight percent of the city, was zoned RR, and was the only area so zoned within the city. The RR classification provided for minimum lot sizes of one-half acre and limited the use of lots largely to single-family residences. The pertinent change for purposes of this appeal is that churches and nonpublic schools were excluded from the newly created RR zone and from some other residential zones.

In May 1979, the zoning ordinance was again amended; this amendment restored the earlier provision permitting churches in residential areas after the borough's senior planner advised that zoning ordinances which wholly exclude churches from residential areas occasionally have been declared unconstitutional. The provision excluding nonpublic schools remained unchanged.

In July 1979, Seward Chapel commenced the proceedings which led to this appeal. The church filed suit in superior court, seeking an injunction against enforcement of the zoning restriction on nonpublic schools and a determination that exclusion of parochial schools contravenes the First and Fourteenth Amendments of the federal constitution and Article I, sections 1 and 4 of the Alaska Constitution. Shortly after filing suit Seward Chapel began operating a parochial school with about a dozen students; pending the outcome of a motion for a preliminary injunction, the church operated its school in a carpenter's shop owned by a church member and located several miles from the church rather than in the church building.

In April 1980, the superior court preliminarily enjoined enforcement of the zoning ordinance's prohibition of nonpublic schools in Forest Acres, and Seward Chapel for the first time began operating its school in its church building. The court did not then pass upon the constitutional issues raised by Seward Chapel but instead required the church to apply for a contract zoning agreement which would allow operation of a school on its premises. Seward Chapel's application for a contract zoning agreement was denied; the denial was appealed through appropriate administrative channels and found its way back to the superior court, where it was consolidated with the prior declaratory judgment action. Prior to trial, the city's zoning ordinance was amended a third time in response to Seward Chapel's contention that the city could not exclude

---

church's good faith interpretation of the zoning ordinance was that a school would be permitted as an accessory use to the church building. Although there is nothing in the record indicating that this was in fact Seward Chapel's interpretation of the zoning ordinance when it purchased the Forest Acres site, we agree that that interpretation is not without merit. The zoning ordinance permitted churches and accessory uses and did not specifically address the question of parochial schools; several courts have held that parochial schools are accessory uses within the meaning of zoning ordinances which permit accessory uses to churches. See, e.g., City of Concord v. New Testament Baptist Church, 118 N.H. 56, 382 A.2d 377 (1978) (five day per week school is a facility "usually connected with a church"). Nonetheless, in this case the possibility that a parochial school might be considered an accessory use to the church was foreclosed when the zoning ordinance was amended to address specifically the question of parochial schools, thus removing such schools from the general classification of accessory uses. See Damascus Comm. Church v. Clackamas County, 45 Or.App. 1065, 610 P.2d 273 (1980), appeal dismissed, 450 U.S. 902 (1981).

only nonpublic schools from Forest Acres; the amended ordinance excluded all schools, public and nonpublic, from areas zoned Rural Residential.

The superior court affirmed the administrative denial of Seward Chapel's application for a contract zoning agreement and, after a bench trial, ruled that the zoning ordinance, as finally amended, did not abridge Seward Chapel's rights under the state and federal constitutions. For the reasons set forth below we affirm the superior court's rulings.

IV. FREE EXERCISE

The testimony offered at trial establishes that providing a Christian education for children is an integral aspect of the church members' religious beliefs. Parents whose children attend the Seward Chapel school explained that it is important that their children receive an education from which spiritual values are not excluded. In addition, church members testified about the inconvenience that would be caused by requiring Seward Chapel to operate its school in a facility other than the existing church building in Forest Acres, such as the expense of maintaining a separate facility and the inconvenience caused by requiring the pastor, who also acts as principal of the school, to travel between two locations. Turning first to the federal constitutional issue, the fundamental question is whether the First Amendment requires the city to relieve Seward Chapel of this burden by setting aside its zoning laws.

Rights protected by the First Amendment are not immune from governmental regulation; the city may impose reasonable restrictions on the time, place, and manner in which such rights are exercised. A lengthy discussion of the parameters of the federal constitutional limits of a city's zoning power is unnecessary, however, because the Supreme Court has already answered the question whether conflicts between land use regulations and First Amendment values must be resolved against the regulations. The Court has repeatedly dismissed for want of a substantial federal question appeals from state court decisions upholding the validity of zoning ordinances such as the one involved in this case. *See Corporation of Presiding Bishop v. City of Porterville*, 90 Cal.App.2d 656, 203 P.2d 823 (1949) (zoning ordinance excluding churches from residential districts valid), *appeal dismissed*, 338 U.S. 805 (1949); *Allendale Congregation of Jehovah's Witnesses v. Grosman*, 30 N.J. 273, 152 A.2d 569 (N.J.1959) (per curiam) (denial of permit to build a church did not violate First Amendment where church could not comply with regulations governing parking), *appeal dismissed*, 361 U.S. 536 (1960); *Damascus Community Church v. Clackamas County*, 610 P.2d 273 (Or.App.1980) (no First Amendment prohibition against preventing church from operating a parochial school in its church building), *appeal dismissed*, 450 U.S. 902 (1981). *Cf. State ex rel. Wisconsin Lutheran High School Conference v. Sinar*, 267 Wis. 91, 65 N.W.2d 43 (1954) (sustaining zoning ordinance excluding nonpublic school over due process and equal protection challenges), *appeal dismissed*, 349 U.S. 913 (1955).[6]

Summary dismissal of an appeal for want of a substantial federal question is a disposition on the merits and, as such, it is binding on this court. In light of the fact that the Supreme Court rejected [in *Damascus Community Church*] less than two years ago a constitutional argument virtually identical to the one presented in the case at hand, we

6. We are not unaware that courts of other states have concluded in some instances that zoning restrictions on religious uses of property abridge First Amendment rights. [citations omitted] In our view, however, we are not free to disregard decisions of the Supreme Court which leave us no choice but to conclude that the Court's view is that such zoning restrictions are constitutionally permissible.

are constrained to hold that the First Amendment does not require the city to accommodate the desire of the members of Seward Chapel to provide a Christian education for their children by abandoning the zoning restriction which excludes schools from Forest Acres.

Finally, we address the question whether Article I, section 4 of the Alaska Constitution prevents the city from enforcing its zoning ordinance. Seward Chapel argues that, under our ruling in *Frank v. State*, 604 P.2d 1068 (Alaska 1979), the city must accommodate church members' desire to educate their children in a Christian school and that this duty of accommodation requires the city to permit the Seward Chapel school to operate in Forest Acres.

We do not doubt that the protection accorded religious beliefs by the Alaska Constitution embraces both the right of parents to educate their children in a parochial school and the right of children to attend a parochial rather than public school. Similarly, we agree that had the city attempted a wholesale exclusion of parochial schools from its confines the city's position would be precarious indeed, for the duty of accommodation recognized in *Frank* would surely require the city to provide in its zoning scheme areas where persons may assemble for sectarian purposes. For the reasons expressed below, however, we believe there is a difference of constitutional significance between an outright ban on parochial schools in any area and a zoning scheme which requires that such schools, like a variety of other land uses, be located in areas in which their impact on surrounding parcels is lessened.

In *Frank*, we reversed on constitutional grounds the appellant's conviction for transporting an illegally taken moose in violation of game regulations. We recognized that the appellant's "deeply rooted religious beliefs" required him to supply moose meat for an Athabascan funeral potlatch and concluded that the state could not force him to choose between abandoning his beliefs and violating the law. Our ruling in *Frank* establishes that there are situations in which the Alaska Constitution requires the state or a municipality to except from a facially neutral law persons whose religious beliefs dictate that they not comply with the law. In short, our constitution prevents a governmental entity from creating situations in which persons are faced with a Hobson's choice: complying with the law or abandoning the precepts of their religion. In the case before us now, however, the city's zoning scheme does not force the members of Seward Chapel to make such a choice, nor does it create an otherwise unacceptable burden upon the exercise of their religious beliefs.

First, although we do not question the sincerity of the church members' conviction that their children should be educated in a Christian school, there has been no showing of a religious belief which requires members of Seward Chapel to locate in Forest Acres. Thus, in this case it cannot be said that the city's zoning ordinance forces members of the church to set aside their beliefs in order to comply with the zoning ordinance. The fact that Seward Chapel would find it more convenient to locate its school in Forest Acres does not mean that the city has imposed an impermissible burden upon church members' rights by requiring that the school be located elsewhere.

Second, the inconvenience and economic burden of which Seward Chapel now complains is caused largely by the choice to build in Forest Acres notwithstanding notice prior to acquiring the site that a parochial school would not be permitted in the area.

In sum, we conclude that the duty to accommodate established by our decision in *Frank* is met by a zoning scheme which includes provisions for areas in which parochial schools and other religious uses of land may locate. We do not agree that the duty of accommodation attaches to each and every parcel within the city's borders.

The decision of the superior court is AFFIRMED.

Cohen v. City of Des Plaines

8 F.3d 484 (7th Cir. 1993), *cert. denied*, 512 U.S. 1236 (1994)

KANNE, Circuit Judge.

Harriet Cohen sued the City of Des Plaines, Illinois, and various city officials, claiming that a provision of the city's zoning ordinance regulating the use of church property in a residential district violated the Establishment Clause of the First Amendment as well as her right to equal protection of the laws under the Fourteenth Amendment. The district court agreed, granted Cohen's motion for summary judgment, and subsequently awarded her damages. We find that the ordinance offends neither the First nor Fourteenth Amendment and therefore reverse.

I.

Harriet Cohen owns property in the city of Des Plaines on which stands a building formerly used as a church. The property is located within a district designated "R-2," or single-family residential, under the city's zoning ordinance. R-2 districts are reserved primarily for single-family dwellings, but the city's zoning regime permits other uses of property without requiring a special use permit. Paragraph 3.1.2.2 of the ordinance permits "[p]ublic schools, elementary and high or private schools having a curriculum the same as ordinarily given in a public elementary or high school,... colleges, junior colleges, or universities." In addition, paragraph 3.1.2.6 permits "[c]hurches, temples, religious reading rooms, rectories and parish houses, *including nursery schools operated in any of such buildings*" (emphasis added). Finally, paragraph 3.1.2.16 allows operation of day care centers in R-2 districts only if the operator first obtains a special use permit from the city and complies with the various size, density, signage and safety requirements set forth in paragraphs 3.1.2.16.1 through 3.1.2.16.15.

Cohen owns and operates day care centers in Des Plaines and Arlington Heights, and initially sought to use her R-2 property to open another day care center. To that end, in April 1987, she filed an application for a special use permit with the city. The Des Plaines Plan Commission recommended to the mayor, city council, and Zoning Board of Appeals that the application be denied. The Zoning Board of Appeals then held a public hearing on the matter, at the conclusion of which the Board voted 6–0 to deny the request for a special use permit. On September 21, 1987, the mayor and city council voted unanimously to deny Cohen's application.

Cohen sued the city and various city officials claiming that the city's zoning ordinance violated, among other things, the First Amendment's Establishment Clause and the Fourteenth Amendment's Equal Protection Clause. Both parties moved for summary judgment, which the district court granted to Cohen. *Cohen v. City of Des Plaines*, 742 F.Supp. 458 (N.D.Ill.1990). The court noted that in her Statement of Material Facts, Cohen had listed seven day care facilities that she claimed operated in religiously-affiliated buildings in areas zoned for residential use. Four of the centers were located in R-2 single-family districts, one in an R-4 multi-family district, and two in R-5 multi-family districts. According to Cohen, each of the centers charged a fee for its services, advertised in the local yellow pages, and was licensed by the State to operate as a day care facility. Moreover, at least one was operated by a "for profit corporation." None, however, by virtue of their affiliation with a church, were required to obtain a special use permit from the city.

The city contested that these facilities were day care centers under paragraph 1.2.17 of the zoning ordinance, which defines a "day care center" as

> [a] specifically designed, reconstructed or remodeled structure other than a single-family residence simultaneously occupied by a single family, and licensed by the State of Illinois, providing day care services for compensation for more than eight (8) children during the day.

The city's zoning ordinance does not define "nursery school." The district court found that "there [was] no material difference between the activities engaged in by nursery schools and day care centers." *Cohen*, 742 F.Supp. at 464. The city had "failed to identify any material difference between the manner in which the facilities in church buildings that City calls 'nursery schools' provide child care services for a fee and the manner in which a 'day care center' such as Cohen's would provide those same services." *Id.* at 465.

Turning to the merits of the parties' arguments concerning the equal protection claim, the court determined that... the ordinance violated the Fourteenth Amendment.

The court next considered Cohen's Establishment Clause claim. Applying the test set forth in *Lemon v. Kurtzman*, the court found that the Des Plaines ordinance confers a benefit upon churches operating child care facilities on their premises that is unavailable to others who wish to operate day care centers in residential areas. The court concluded that "the sole effect of City's Ordinance is to lift from religious organizations, without any rational justification, a regulatory burden that is uniformly applicable to day care operators generally." *Id.* Accordingly, the ordinance violated the Establishment Clause.

II.

The City appeals both the merits of the district court's decision as well as the award of damages. We find it necessary only to address the Establishment Clause and equal protection issues. In fact, because we find that an analysis of Cohen's Establishment Clause claim is largely dispositive of her equal protection complaint, we address the issues in that order.

We cannot say that the district court's factual findings are clearly erroneous. Accordingly, we accept the finding that the city has allowed four facilities to provide child care services in R-2 districts without special use permits. We also accept the finding that there is no functional difference between day care centers and nursery schools for purposes of Des Plaines' zoning ordinance. That said, we turn to the merits.

As did the district court, we analyze the plaintiff's argument against the zoning ordinance using the trilogy of tests developed by the Supreme Court in *Lemon*.

According to the *Lemon* test, the Des Plaines ordinance must (1) have a secular purpose; (2) neither advance nor inhibit religion in its principal or primary effect; and (3) not foster an excessive entanglement with religion. The Supreme Court has refined the analysis under the first two prongs of *Lemon*, focusing on "whether the challenged governmental practice either has the purpose or effect of 'endorsing' religion, a concern that has long had a place in [the Court's] Establishment Clause jurisprudence."

We will defer to a municipality's sincere articulation of a secular purpose. This is in keeping with the well settled maxim that courts are "reluctan[t] to attribute unconstitutional motives to the States, particularly when a plausible secular purpose for the State's program may be discerned from the face of the statute." *Mueller v. Allen*, 463 U.S. 388, 394–95 (1983). This is true whether the governing body is a state legislature or a city council.

The sparse legislative history of the city's ordinance reveals precious little about its purpose. Nonetheless, the city asserts that the ordinance, by exempting day care centers operated in churches from the special use permit requirement, reduces governmental interference with religious organizations and their decision making processes.

Cohen challenges this asserted purpose, essentially relying on the district court's determination that City's exemption applies to all day care centers in church buildings regardless of whether they teach religion at all. Furthermore, there is no evidence that any of the facilities operating pursuant to City's exemption view their child care functions as pastoral.

We do not think that whether the ordinance satisfies *Lemon*'s secular purpose requirement can depend on a district court's decision that a particular church does not view its endeavor either to educate or care for young children as sufficiently pastoral. Moreover, we are wary of holding that the Des Plaines' ordinance would pass muster under *Lemon*'s purpose requirement only if it stated that nursery school and day care center activities must be "religious" in nature. First, it is not up to legislatures (or to courts for that matter) to say what activities are sufficiently "religious." Any legislative or judicial attempt at such a definition would surely fail. Worse, it would almost certainly undercut the neutral posture required of every branch of government under the Establishment Clause.

Second, it is clear that the legitimate purpose of minimizing governmental interference with the decision making processes of a religious organization can extend to seemingly secular activities of the organization. *Corporation of the Presiding Bishop of the Church of Latter Day Saints v. Amos,* 483 U.S. 327 (1987), makes precisely this point. There, a building engineer who worked for a nonprofit gymnasium operated by religious entities associated with the Church of Jesus Christ of Latter-day Saints was discharged because he failed to qualify for a certificate that he was a member of the Church and eligible to attend its temples. *Amos*, 483 U.S. at 330. The employee, with others purporting to represent a class, sued the religious entities of the Church operating the gym, alleging religious discrimination in violation of Title VII.

The defendants moved to dismiss the suit on the ground that they were shielded from liability by section 702 of the Act, which exempts religious organizations from Title VII's prohibition of religious discrimination in employment. The Court, employing the *Lemon* test, found that section 702 had a secular purpose because it sought to alleviate "significant governmental interference with the ability of religious organizations to define and carry out their religious missions." *Id.* at 335. Moreover, Congress "acted with a legitimate purpose in expanding the section 702 exemption to cover *all* activities of religious employers." *Id.* at 339 (emphasis added). In so holding, the Court observed that [it is a significant burden on a religious organization to require it, on pain of substantial liability, to predict which of its activities a secular court will consider religious. The line is hardly a bright one, and an organization might understandably be concerned that a judge would not understand its religious tenets and sense of mission. Fear of potential liability might affect the way an organization carried out what it understood to be its religious mission.] *Id.* at 336 (footnote omitted).

Concurring with the Court's decision, Justice Brennan elaborated on this point:

> Determining that certain activities are in furtherance of an organization's religious mission, and that only those committed to that mission should conduct them, is... a means by which a religious community defines itself. Solicitude for a church's ability to do so reflects the idea that furtherance of the autonomy of religious organizations often furthers religious freedom as well.

Id. at 342 (Brennan, J., concurring in the judgment).

We think that Des Plaines' zoning ordinance has the secular purpose of minimizing governmental meddling in religious affairs notwithstanding that the ordinance does not explicitly state that nursery schools (or day care centers) operated in churches in residential areas must give care or instruction defined as "religious." History and common sense teach that the care and education of young children fall within the mission of most, if not all, religious organizations. Sunday schools provide one obvious example of the way churches minister to pre-school youth.

Under the second requirement of *Lemon*, the ordinance must have a "principal or primary effect... that neither advances nor inhibits religion." At the core of this requirement is the notion that government may not be overtly hostile to religion but also that it may not place its prestige, coercive authority, or resources behind a single religious faith or behind religious belief in general, compelling nonadherents to support the practices or proselytizing of favored religious organizations and conveying the message that those who do not contribute gladly are less than full members of the community.

We do not think that the Des Plaines ordinance, by allowing churches to operate nursery schools and day care centers without a special use permit, puts the city in the position of "establishing" religion within the meaning of the First Amendment any more than either the property tax exemption for religious organizations at issue in *Walz v. Tax Comm'n of New York City*, 397 U.S. 664 (1970), or the tax deduction for the expenses of religious education at issue in *Mueller* constituted state establishment of religion. The religious component of child care and education activities in Des Plaines will come from church members or leaders, not from government officials.

We do share the district court's concern about the commercial benefit that the Des Plaines ordinance might confer upon churches in R-2 districts. Specifically, relying on *Texas Monthly* v. *Bullock*, 489 U.S. 1 (1989), the [district] court was concerned that the ordinance provided a subsidy to churches. *See Cohen*, 742 F.Supp. at 471. In *Bullock*, the Supreme Court invalidated a Texas statute that exempted from the state's sales and use tax "periodicals published or distributed by a religious faith consist[ing] entirely of writing promulgating the teaching of the faith, along with books consisting solely of writings sacred to a religious faith...." 489 U.S. at 5–6. In a plurality opinion, Justice Brennan found that the state's subsidy was not required by the Free Exercise Clause and could not "reasonably be seen as removing a significant state-imposed deterrent to the free exercise of religion...." *Id.* at 15. Accordingly, "[i]t [was] difficult to view Texas' narrow exemption as anything but a state sponsorship of religious belief". *Id.* at 15.

We think this case is distinguishable from *Bullock* in two important respects. First, allowing churches to provide child care and educational services coheres with the religious missions of most churches and thus implicates rights protected by the Free Exercise Clause. This country has long recognized the right of religious organizations to educate their youngest members, and while there may be some difference between formal education and learning attendant to child care, we do not think it is a constitutional difference. It cannot be doubted that the same persons who would seek to have their children educated in religious schools (including nursery schools) would also entrust their youngest children to be cared for by those who are adherents of their religious beliefs. By exempting churches (which themselves do not require a special use permit to operate) from the special use requirement in the operation of nursery schools and day care centers, the city has removed a burden to the free exercise of religion.

Second, the Des Plaines zoning ordinance exemption does not require the general populace to subsidize religious organizations. In *Bullock*, the Supreme Court found that the sales and use tax exemption "burden[ed] nonbeneficiaries by increasing their tax bills by whatever amount is needed to offset the benefit bestowed on subscribers to religious publications." 489 U.S. at 18 n.8. In effect, nonbeneficiaries subsidized the efforts of religious organizations to propagate their faiths. By contrast, the Des Plaines zoning ordinance exemption has no such effect. The costs that would otherwise be borne by churches in obtaining the special use permit are not transferred to the public at large by virtue of the exemption.

Nonetheless, we recognize that exemption from the requirements of a special use permit confers some benefit, albeit indirect, on churches not available to others who would seek to establish day care centers in residentially zoned districts. Thus, we believe that, in order to be consistent with the holdings in *Bullock* and in particular *Amos*, the Des Plaines ordinance must be read to require that church operated nursery schools and day care centers be not-for-profit.

We hold that the Des Plaines ordinance does not have the principal or primary effect of advancing religion. Yet, mindful of the well settled principle that statutes should be interpreted to avoid constitutional difficulties, we construe the ordinance to require that, in order to be exempt from the special use requirement, church operated nursery schools or day care centers must be not-for-profit.

We turn next to *Lemon*'s final requirement, that the ordinance "must not foster 'an excessive entanglement with religion.'" 403 U.S. at 613 (*quoting Walz*, 397 U.S. at 674). [I]t is difficult to conceive how the Des Plaines ordinance impermissibly entangles city and church. Indeed, as construed, the ordinance effectuates a separation between the two and avoids intrusive inquiry into religious belief and practice.

[A]ccording to Cohen, under the ordinance's exemption, the city "has the right to determine what constitutes a 'nursery school' operating 'in conjunction with' a 'church operation.'"

[I]t is true that the ordinance does define "day care center" but not "nursery school." However, there is no claim in the record that the city has in fact discriminated among religious organizations in determining what church operated endeavor constituted a "nursery school." Indeed, there is no evidence at all of contact between city officials and religious officials concerning the character of church operated day care or nursery school activities in Des Plaines. In short, the zoning ordinance does not create the kind of government surveillance of religious activities or cooperation between government and religious officials that has been deemed an impermissible administrative entanglement under *Lemon*.

IV.

As applied to not-for-profit nursery schools and day care centers operated by churches located in R-2 single-family residential districts, the Des Plaines zoning ordinance does not violate either the Establishment Clause of the First Amendment or Cohen's right to equal protection of the laws. The decision of the district court granting

Cohen's motion for summary judgment is REVERSED. The city's cross-motion for summary judgment is REMANDED with directions to the district court to enter judgment for the city consistent with this opinion.

Notes

1. The Alaska Supreme Court observes that the Seward Chapel was never permitted by the city's zoning law to build a parochial school. Should this "expectations" argument be dispositive? Is the Alaska court's reliance on the Supreme Court's decisions to dismiss the appeals of a number of church organizations to adverse zoning rulings persuasive? Does it matter that the Court has never stated a reason for dismissing the appeals, or that the Court altered its free exercise framework during this same period of time?

2. As a number of courts have done, the court in *Cohen* creates a constitutional distinction between the commercial and not-for-profit activities of a religious organization. Does this distinction make sense?

3. Do the *Seward Chapel* and *Cohen* cases suggest that municipalities have little room to maneuver when zoning laws have a major impact on the ability of religious organizations to carry out their work? On what basis should the courts evaluate the competing constitutional claims of religious organizations and those who may oppose special exemptions for them? Does, or should, it make a difference if the opponent is a potential "competitor," as in both *Seward Chapel* and *Cohen*? If so, what difference should it make? What if the opponent is simply opposed to the traffic or parking problems such a use will generate? Given the purposes of zoning ordinances, is the distinction between public and nonpublic school a valid one under a zoning ordinance? *Cf. Alpine Christian Fellowship v. County Com'rs of Pitkin County*, 870 F. Supp. 991 (D. Colo. 1994) (denying a permit to operate school in church building violates free exercise rights).

4. In September 2000, Congress adopted the Religious Land Use and Institutionalized Persons Act of 2000, 42 U.S.C.A. §§ 2000cc–2000cc-5 (2000) [RLUIPA]. Based in part on the Religious Freedom Restoration Act, which was ruled unconstitutional in *City of Boerne v. Flores*, 521 U.S. 507 (1997), RLUIPA narrowly targets two classes of cases where determinations are made on a case-by-case basis: 1) land use decisions affecting churches and religious institutions; and 2) decisions affecting persons institutionalized in facilities owned or operated by a federal, state or local government. See 42 USC § 1997 (2001)(defining "institution"). It provides, in relevant part,

> **§ 2000cc. Protection of land use as religious exercise**
>
> (a) Substantial burdens
>
> *(1) General rule*
>
> No government shall impose or implement a land use regulation in a manner that imposes a substantial burden on the religious exercise of a person, including a religious assembly or institution, unless the government demonstrates that imposition of the burden on that person, assembly, or institution
>
> (A) is in furtherance of a compelling governmental interest; and
>
> (B) is the least restrictive means of furthering that compelling governmental interest.
>
> *(2) Scope of application*

This subsection applies in any case in which—

(A) the substantial burden is imposed in a program or activity that receives Federal financial assistance, even if the burden results from a rule of general applicability;

(B) the substantial burden affects, or removal of that substantial burden would affect, commerce with foreign nations, among the several States, or with Indian tribes, even if the burden results from a rule of general applicability; or

(C) the substantial burden is imposed in the implementation of a land use regulation or system of land use regulations, under which a government makes, or has in place formal or informal procedures or practices that permit the government to make, individualized assessments of the proposed uses for the property involved.

(b) Discrimination and exclusion

(1) *Equal terms*

No government shall impose or implement a land use regulation in a manner that treats a religious assembly or institution on less than equal terms with a nonreligious assembly or institution.

(2) *Nondiscrimination*

No government shall impose or implement a land use regulation that discriminates against any assembly or institution on the basis of religion or religious denomination.

(3) *Exclusions and limits*

No government shall impose or implement a land use regulation that

(A) totally excludes religious assemblies from a jurisdiction; or

(B) unreasonably limits religious assemblies, institutions, or structures within a jurisdiction.

How would RLUILPA affect the outcome in either *Seward Chapel* or *Cohen*? At this writing, the case law is just developing. The cases under the Religious Freedom Restoration Act [RFRA] were mixed. *Compare Western Presbyterian Church v. Board of Zoning Adjustment of District of Columbia*, 862 F. Supp. 538 (D.D.C. 1994) (application of zoning ordinance to prohibit feeding of homeless persons on church premises "substantially burdens" free exercise under RFRA) *with Daytona Rescue Mission, Inc. v. City of Daytona Beach*, 885 F. Supp. 1554 (M.D. Fla. 1995) (rejecting claim that denial of permit to operate homeless shelter and food bank "substantially burdens" free exercise under RFRA, and further holding permit denial supported by compelling state interest). For an interesting case alleging discrimination against a specific religious group, see *Al-Salam Mosque Foundation v. City of Palos Heights*, 2001 WL 204772 (March 1, 2001).

5. How should a court approach the case of the "storefront" or "home" church? Many ministers found their churches in small, neighborhood settings, and commence operations by scheduling services, prayer meetings, and other church functions on a regular basis. Is it constitutionally permissible for a locality to ban such uses? Does RLUIPA affect your answer? Because zoning is a matter of state and local law, the impact of *state* "religious freedom restoration acts" should also be taken into account. *See, e.g.*, Florida Religious Freedom Restoration Act, Fla. Stats. §§761.03(1)(a)–(b) (1999); Illinois Religious Freedom Restoration Act, 775 Il. Cons. Stats. §§35/1–35/99 (2001);

See City of Chicago Heights v. Living Word Outreach Full Gospel Church and Ministries, Inc., 302 Ill.App.3d 564, 571, 707 N.E.2d 53, 59 (1st Dist.1999). *Cf. Church of Iron Oak, Inc. ATC v. City of Palm Bay*, Fla., 868 F. Supp. 1361 (M.D. Fla. 1994); *LeBlanc-Sternberg v. Fletcher*, 846 F. Supp. 294 (S.D.N.Y. 1994); *Trinity Resources, Inc. v. Township of Delanco*, 842 F. Supp. 782 (D.N.J. 1994); *United States v. Village of Airmont*, 839 F. Supp. 1054 (S.D.N.Y. 1993).

6. As you consider the materials relating to the use and control of church property, consider as well the strictures imposed on the use of property by fair housing laws. *See* Chapter Ten. *See generally* Jack S. Vaitayanonta, *In State Legislatures We Trust?: The "Compelling Interest" Presumption and Religious Free Exercise Challenges to State Civil Rights Laws*, 101 Colum. L. Rev. 886 (2001); Maureen E. Markey, *The Price of Landlord's "Free" Exercise of Religion: Tenant's Right to Discrimination-Free Housing and Privacy*, 22 Fordham Urb. L.J. 699 (1995).

2. Historic Preservation

In addition to the constitutional problems raised by zoning regulations, the application of historic preservation laws to church property has raised constitutional issues. The following case, *First Covenant Church of Seattle v. City of Seattle*, suggests some of those problems. After the trial court entered summary judgment in favor of City, the church appealed, and the Washington Supreme Court reversed, holding the historic preservation law unconstitutional as applied to church property. *First Covenant Church of Seattle v. City of Seattle*, 114 Wash.2d 392, 787 P.2d 1352 (1990). The Supreme Court of the United States then vacated and remanded the case to the Washington Supreme Court. *Seattle v. First Covenant Church of Seattle*, 499 U.S. 901 (1991). The following is the Washington Supreme Court's decision on remand.

First Covenant Church of Seattle v. City of Seattle

120 Wash. 2d 203, 840 P.2d 174 (1992)

DORE, Chief Justice.

We reinstate our holding in *First Covenant Church v. Seattle*, that applying the City's ordinances to the church violates the free exercise guaranties of the First Amendment to the federal constitution and article 1, Section 11 of the state constitution. We have fully considered the Supreme Court's holding in *Employment Div., Dep't of Human Resources v. Smith*, and we conclude that *Smith* is distinguishable from this case and does not compel a different result.

ISSUE

Whether applying Seattle's Landmarks Preservation Ordinance to First Covenant violated the church's right to free exercise under the state and the federal constitutions?

FACTS

First Covenant owns the church located at Pike and Bellevue Streets in Seattle. First Covenant uses its church exclusively for religious purposes.

The City of Seattle adopted the Landmarks Preservation Ordinance to:

> designate, preserve, [and] protect,...improvements and objects which reflect significant elements of the City's cultural, aesthetic, social, economic, political, architectural, engineering, historic or other heritage...[.]

Seattle Municipal Code (SMC) 25.12.020(B) (1977). Pursuant to that ordinance, the Landmarks Preservation Board nominated First Covenant's church as a landmark in October 1980. First Covenant objected to the nomination at public hearings, but the Board approved designation of the church as a landmark in January 1981. In April 1981, the Board adopted controls to preserve the exterior of the church.

The church and City unsuccessfully negotiated about the controls that the City would impose on the church. The parties appeared before a hearing examiner in June 1981. The church again objected to its designation as a landmark. The hearing examiner recommended that the city council approve the Board's proposed controls in July 1981.

On September 17, 1985, the city council adopted ordinance 112425, which designated First Covenant's church a landmark. The designation ordinance requires that First Covenant get a certificate of approval before it makes certain alterations to the church's exterior. It also provides that:

> [N]othing herein shall prevent any alteration of the exterior when such alterations are necessitated by changes in liturgy, it being understood that the owner is the exclusive authority on liturgy and is the decisive party in determining what architectural changes are appropriate to the liturgy. When alterations necessitated by changes in liturgy are proposed, the owner shall advise the Landmarks Preservation Board in writing of the nature of the proposed alterations and the Board shall issue a Certificate of Approval. Prior to the issuance of any Certificate, however, the Board and owner shall jointly explore such possible alternative design solutions as may be appropriate or necessary to preserve the designated features of the landmark.

First Covenant filed a declaratory judgment action in January 1986. It sought a judgment that the "religious freedom provisions" of the state constitution prohibited application of the Landmarks Preservation Ordinance to active churches and that application of the Landmarks Preservation Ordinance to its church was void.

First Covenant and the City both filed for summary judgment on the free exercise issues. The court granted the City's motion and dismissed First Covenant's free exercise claims as premature, without prejudice to First Covenant's other contentions. A majority of this court concluded, in *First Covenant*, that First Covenant's claims that the Landmarks Preservation and designation ordinances violated the free exercise of religion were not premature. *First Covenant Church v. Seattle*, 114 Wash.2d at 398–400, 787 P.2d 1352. A majority, for different reasons, also concluded that applying the City's ordinances to First Covenant burdened the Church's right of free exercise of religion under the federal and state constitutions. *First Covenant Church v. Seattle, supra* at 405–06, 412, 787 P.2d 1352. And the majority, again for different reasons, concluded that the liturgy exemption did not mitigate the burden on free exercise. *First Covenant Church v. Seattle, supra* at 407, 412, 787 P.2d 1352.

The majority applied the strict scrutiny analysis of *Sherbert v. Verner*, 374 U.S. 398 (1963), when assessing the free exercise claim. It concluded that landmark preservation was not a "compelling interest" that justified the burden on First Covenant's right to free exercise and, therefore, that applying the City's ordinances to First Covenant violated First Covenant's free exercise rights under the state and federal constitutions.

The City appealed. The United States Supreme Court vacated the judgment and remanded it to us for "further consideration in light of *Employment Division, Department of Human Resources of Oregon v. Smith*...".

ANALYSIS

First Covenant and the CLS contend that the City's Landmarks Preservation Ordinances are not neutral or generally applicable because the sites, improvements, and objects they govern are arbitrarily selected, and the selection process requires individual evaluation of each building, site, or improvement.

The Landmarks Preservation Ordinance, SMC 25.12, was passed in 1977. The designation ordinance, 112425, was passed pursuant to the general ordinance. Thus, although it was enacted after SMC 25.12, we consider it part of the general act.

The designation criteria of SMC 25.12 is neutral. It applies to "[a]n object, site or improvement which is more than twenty-five (25) years old" and meets the designation criteria. SMC 25.12.350. The definitions of "object" and "improvement" are also facially neutral. SMC 25.12.190, .140. *See Rector, Wardens, & Members of Vestry of St. Bartholomew's Church v. New York*, 914 F.2d 348, 354 (2d Cir. 1990), *cert. denied*, 499 U.S. 905 (1991). Designation ordinance 112425, however, is not neutral. It alludes to religious facilities in the two references to "liturgy". Because the Landmarks Preservation Ordinances specifically refer to religious facilities, they are not "neutral". *See Health Servs. Div., Health & Env't Dep't v. Temple Baptist Church*, 112 N.M. 262, 266, 814 P.2d 130, 134 (Ct. App. 1991), *cert. denied*, 112 N.M. 235, 814 P.2d 103 (1991).

The landmark ordinances must also be "generally applicable" laws. Justice Scalia contrasted "generally applicable" tax laws with statutes that contain "a system of individualized exceptions", that "create[ ] a mechanism for individualized exemptions" or that lend themselves to "individualized governmental assessment" of the conduct governed. *Smith II*, 494 U.S. at 884. The landmark ordinances at issue here are unlike a general tax law because they invite individualized assessments of the subject property and the owner's use of such property, and contain mechanisms for individualized exceptions. The City's Landmarks Preservation Ordinance is not generally applicable.

The City and the National Trust for Historic Preservation (National Trust) insist that *Rector, Wardens, & Members of Vestry of St. Bartholomew's Church v. New York*, compels a different result. St. Bartholomew's owned a church and a community house. Both buildings were designated landmarks in 1967, pursuant to New York's Landmark Law. The law provides a detailed hearings and appeals process for those who object to designation and exempts from designation "interiors utilized as places of religious worship".

In 1983, St. Bartholomew's asked for a certificate of appropriateness to replace the community house with a 47-story tower, some of which it would use, the rest of which it would rent as commercial property. The New York City Landmarks Preservation Commission (Commission) denied approval. The church alleged that the landmark law violated its right to free exercise and was not neutral or generally applicable because it vested discretion in the Commission. The court concluded that the landmark law did not "demonstrate a lack of neutrality or general applicability" and that, absent proof that the Commission exercised its discretion in a discriminatory way, "there [was] no constitutional relevance" to the church's claim. *St. Bartholomew's Church* at 354–55.

St. Bartholomew's is distinguishable from this case. St. Bartholomew's accepted designation as a landmark, without objection. First Covenant has objected continuously to designation. St. Bartholomew's sought an exception for an adjunct building, not its church building. First Covenant seeks an exception for its church building. St. Bartholomew's sought an exception to use its property for commercial purposes. First Covenant seeks an exemption so that it may continue to use its church for exclusively religious purposes. St. Bartholomew's did not allege that designation reduced its principal asset, only that it impeded its ability to generate additional revenue to expand its programs. Uncontroverted evidence supports First Covenant's claim that designation reduces the values of its principal asset by almost one-half. Finally, the parties in St. Bartholomew's did not challenge the effect of the religious exemption on the New York law's constitutionality, and the religious exemption in the New York law is not "liturgy" based, as is Seattle's. *St. Bartholomew's* is factually distinguishable and does not control this case.

The rule in *Smith II* also does not apply because First Covenant's claim presents a "hybrid situation". The Church's claim is "hybrid" because designation not only violates First Covenant's right to freely exercise religion, it infringes on First Covenant's rights to free speech.

First Covenant claims, and no one disputes, that its church building itself "is an expression of Christian belief and message" and that conveying religious beliefs is part of the building's function. First Covenant reasons that when the State controls the architectural "proclamation" of religious belief inherent in its church's exterior it effectively burdens religious speech. We agree with First Covenant's reasoning. The relationship between theological doctrine and architectural design is well recognized. Pak, *Free Exercise, Free Expression, and Landmark Preservation*, 91 Colum.L.Rev. 1813, 1840–43 (1991); Carmella, *Houses of Worship and Religious Liberty: Constitutional Limits to Landmark Preservation and Architectural Review*, 36 Vill.L.Rev. 401, 490–98 (1991); Crewdson, *Ministry and Mortar: Historic Preservation and the First Amendment After* Barwick, 33 J.Urb. & Contemp.L. 137, 157–58 (1988). The exterior and the interior of the structure are inextricably related. When, as in this case, both are "freighted with religious meaning" that would be understood by those who view it, then the regulation of the church's exterior impermissibly infringes on the religious organization's right to free exercise and free speech. Crewdson, *supra*; *See Society of Jesus v. Boston Landmarks Comm'n*, 409 Mass. 38, 42, 564 N.E.2d 571, 573 (1990); *cf. Murdock v. Commonwealth*, 319 U.S. 105 (1943); *West Va. State Bd. of Educ. v. Barnette*, 319 U.S. 624 (1943); *Follett v. McCormick*, 321 U.S. 573 (1944).

The *Sherbert* Court's "compelling interest" test, therefore, applies to the justiciable controversy before us.

Applying the *Sherbert* "compelling interest" test, we address the church's contention that subjecting it to the controls of the Landmarks Preservation Ordinance burdens its right to freely exercise religion.

The City's ordinances, as this court held earlier, impermissibly burden First Covenant's right to free exercise in two ways. The ordinances burden free exercise "administratively" because they require that First Covenant seek the approval of a government body before it alter the exterior of its house of worship, whether or not the alteration is for a religious reason. Further, they burden First Covenant financially, because they reduce the value of the Church's property by almost half.

The City alleges that financial burdens do not violate the First Amendment, under *Jimmy Swaggart Ministries v. Board of Equalization*, 493 U.S. 378 (1990). The City is mistaken: *Swaggart* does not control this case. *Swaggart* held that imposition of California's sales and use tax on the in-state sales of Jimmy Swaggart Ministries did not violate the free exercise clause because the sales tax was not a "precondition to the exercise of evangelistic activity" and was more "akin to a generally applicable income or property tax". *Swaggart* at 389–90. The Court warned, however, "a more onerous tax rate, even if generally applicable" might violate the constitution if it too severely impeded religious activity. *Swaggart* at 391.

After *Swaggart*, the State may impose on religious activity a neutral, generally applicable tax that does not act as a prior restraint on religious conduct. It is clear, however, that a financial burden on religious activity, if too gross, may unconstitutionally infringe on free exercise. Designation of First Covenant's church so grossly diminishes the value of the Church's principal asset that it impermissibly burdens First Covenant's right to free exercise of religion.

The City urges that the "liturgy exemption" alleviates any burden on the exercise of religion. We do not believe that the exemption cures either the "administrative" or the financial infringements of First Covenant's right to free exercise.

First, the plain and ordinary meaning of the term "liturgy", which we employ absent a statutory definition of that term, does not provide a workable standard that protects the constitutional rights of the church. "Liturgy" is a "rite or series of rites, observances, or procedures prescribed for public worship in the Christian church in accordance with authorized or standard form." Webster's Third New International Dictionary 1323 (1971). "Liturgy" essentially refers to prescribed conduct that occurs within the structure. The liturgy-focused exemption in this case is constitutionally infirm because it allows the City to control any nonliturgical elements of religious conduct that require architectural change. *Carmella* at 475, 507–08. Further, as we previously observed:

> Would a wider door to permit access by handicapped parishioners comprise a liturgical change? Although... widening the door does not relate directly to the rites or procedures of worship in the church, it does facilitate the ability of disabled persons to participate in religious services and activities. The anomalies created by the liturgy exception are cumbersome and would result in... delays in carrying out routine church work.

First Covenant, 114 Wash.2d at 407, 787 P.2d 1352.

Secondly, adopting the City's interpretation of the phrase "necessitated by changes in liturgy" as meaning "for religious purposes" does not resolve the ambiguity. The City still has the right to determine what is or what is not for a religious purpose and it acknowledged at argument that it reserved the right to determine if the 'religious purpose' claim was bona fide. [I]t is clear that the City reserves the right to oversee and challenge First Covenant's decisions about what is liturgy and what is a valid religious purpose. The governmental oversight of church action that the City reserves to itself, under the liturgy exception, impermissibly burdens free exercise.

Ordinance 112425 also requires that First Covenant seek the City's approval before it alters its church, even for presumptively valid "liturgical" purposes. The exemption states that if the Church proposes an alteration "necessitated by changes in liturgy", "the Board and owner shall jointly explore such possible alternative design solutions as may be appropriate or necessary to preserve the designated features of the landmark." The requirement that the Church negotiate with the City constitutes unjustified governmental interference in religious matters and infringes First Covenant's right to free exercise.

Finally, the liturgy exemption does not mitigate the financial burden that designation imposes on First Covenant. Regardless of how the exemption is construed, the Church suffers the same dramatic depreciation in the value of its property and principal asset. In sum, the liturgy exemption does not cure the infringement of free exercise by the Landmarks Preservation Ordinance.

If government action burdens the exercise of religion, but the State demonstrates that it has a compelling interest in enforcing its enactment, that interest will justify the infringement of First Amendment rights. *Sherbert.* The State, through its police power, may regulate the use of land. Landmark preservation laws enacted pursuant to legislative authority regulate land use by conserving structures with historic or esthetic significance that enhance the quality of life of all citizens. Preservation ordinances further cultural and esthetic interests, but they do not protect public health or safety. We hold that the City's interest in preservation of esthetic and historic structures is not compelling and it does not justify the infringement of First Covenant's right to freely exercise religion. The possible loss of significant architectural elements is a price we must accept to guarantee the paramount right of religious freedom.

Upon further consideration, in light of *Smith II*, we conclude that applying the City's preservation ordinances to First Covenant's church violates the church's right to freely exercise religion under the First Amendment.

Although we might distinguish this case from *Smith II*, and base our decision solely on federal grounds, we decline to do so. [W]e eschew the "uncertainty" of *Smith II* and rest our decision also on independent grounds under the Washington constitution.

Article 1, section 11, of the Washington State Constitution provides that:

> Absolute freedom of conscience in all matters of religious sentiment, belief, and worship, shall be guaranteed to every individual, and no one shall be molested or disturbed in person or property on account of religion; but the liberty of conscience hereby secured shall not be so construed as to excuse acts of licentiousness or justify practices inconsistent with the peace and safety of the state.

The first amendment to the United States Constitution provides in part:

> Congress shall make no law respecting an establishment of religion, or prohibiting the free exercise thereof... [.]

The text of the state constitution focuses both on belief and on conduct, as evidenced in the terms "worship", "acts", and "practices". Article 1 clearly protects both belief and conduct.

The language of our state constitution is significantly different and stronger than the federal constitution. The First Amendment limits government action that "prohibits" free exercise. Our state provision "absolutely" protects freedom of worship and bars conduct that merely "disturbs" another on the basis of religion. Any action that is not licentious or inconsistent with the "peace and safety" of the state is "guaranteed" protection.

Our state constitutional and common law history support a broader reading of article 1, section 11, than of the First Amendment. Article 1, section 11, as adopted in 1889 and as amended in 1903, contained the same active, broad language noted above. Further, case law interpreting earlier versions of article 1 endorse a broad interpretation of the free exercise provision.

Free exercise of religion is not a local concern. As noted above, however, our State exhibits a long history of extending strong protection to the free exercise of religion.

Seattle's ordinances, as discussed fully in our First Amendment analysis, impose unconstitutional administrative and financial burdens on First Covenant's free exercise of religion.

We conclude that imposing the City's Landmarks Preservation Ordinance on First Covenant's church violates First Covenant's right to free exercise of religion under article 1, section 11 of our state constitution.

UTTER, DURHAM, GUY and JOHNSON, JJ., concur.

UTTER, Justice (concurring).

I agree with the majority's conclusion that application of the Seattle Landmarks Preservation Ordinance (Seattle Municipal Code (SMC) 25.12 *et seq.*) to the First Covenant Church of Seattle violates the First Amendment of the United States Constitution and article 1, § 11 of the Washington State Constitution. The majority persuasively demonstrates that the United States Supreme Court's opinion in *Employment Div., Dep't of Human Resources v. Smith* does not compel a different result. Nonetheless, I write separately to emphasize certain facts which require this result and to set forth federal and state constitutional standards we should apply in future cases.

I

Only the Second Circuit, in *Rector, Wardens, & Members of the Vestry of St. Bartholomew's Church v. New York*, has concluded that a landmark ordinance was generally applicable for first amendment purposes. The majority factually distinguishes *St. Bartholomew's*. I also cannot agree with the legal analysis in *St. Bartholomew's*.

The Second Circuit's analysis is incorrect. Simply because landmark designations may not be arbitrary enough to be reverse spot zoning, it does not necessarily follow that landmark laws are generally applicable where first amendment rights are also affected. More is at stake here than the investment-backed expectations at issue in the takings context. As the majority correctly notes, the Church's First Amendment rights to free exercise and free speech are also implicated. While we might tolerate such broad governmental discretion where only a takings issue is involved, it does not follow that we should allow it when other liberties, such as free exercise of religion and free speech, are also affected.

II

Although financial burdens on religious entities do not constitute a per se free exercise violation, the United States Supreme Court has indicated that an onerous financial burden can violate the First Amendment. *Swaggart*, 493 U.S. at 392. The financial impact on First Covenant's principal asset, its church, is severe and was not disputed at the trial court level. The Church's uncontroverted affidavit stated that landmark designation reduced the value of the property from $700,000 to $400,000. The dissent's assertion that this is a disputed fact is incorrect.

For future cases, I still believe we should require a specific showing of hardship to justify exemption from land use restrictions. We should follow New York's courts by requiring a landmark designation not prevent or seriously interfere with the carrying out of a church's religious and charitable purposes.

III

I offer an alternative to the majority's analysis of Const. art. 1, § 11 which focuses on the unique text of that provision.

The language of Const. art. 1, § 11 indicates the drafters considered religious belief and practice to be closely related.

This was a wise decision. Religion is to some extent a communal matter. Ritual in many religions is inseparable from one's spiritual experience of faith.

For two additional reasons, protection of religious liberty is stronger under Const. art. 1, § 11 than under the free exercise clause of the First Amendment. First, Const. art. 1, § 11 grants Washington citizens affirmative rights that are absolute. The free exercise clause of the First Amendment only limits government action at the point of prohibiting the exercise of religion. Thus, the text of Const. art. 1, § 11 indicates we should start with the assumption that government may not interfere with sincerely held religious belief and religious practice.

Second, Const. art. 1, § 11 expressly limits the governmental interests that may outweigh the otherwise absolute right to religious liberty. Only the government's interest in peace and safety or in preventing licentious acts can excuse an imposition on religious liberty.

Conversely, the free exercise clause of the first amendment has been interpreted to allow varied government interests to justify such an imposition. Therefore, landmark designation of the church is only valid if it furthers one of the limited, countervailing governmental interests listed in Const. art. 1, § 11: preventing licentious practices or acts that are inconsistent with peace and safety in our state.

Historic preservation does not prevent licentious behavior, or ensure peace or safety. While the Ordinance has a very noble aim, it simply does not further one of the limited governmental interests that the drafters of our state constitution thought important enough to infringe on religious liberty.

JOHNSON, J., concurs.

DOLLIVER, Justice (dissenting).

I cannot agree with the majority's conclusions that *Employment Div., Dep't of Human Resources v. Smith* (*Smith II*) does not apply to this case and that the Landmarks Preservation Ordinance (Seattle Municipal Code (SMC) 25.12 *et seq.*) and the implementing ordinance (ordinance 112425) violate First Covenant's right of free exercise under the federal constitution and article 1, section 11 of the state constitution. Therefore, I dissent.

The Landmarks Preservation Ordinance and its implementing ordinance, like the criminal prohibition against peyote use in *Smith II*, are neutral, generally applicable laws which do not involve other constitutional protections. While the landmark ordinances will affect many religious buildings because of their social and cultural importance, this does not demonstrate a lack of neutrality or general applicability. *See Rector, Wardens, & Members of the Vestry of St. Bartholomew's Church v. New York.* Indeed, the majority admits the designation criteria in the Landmarks Preservation Ordinance are neutral.

The majority, however, asserts the implementing ordinance's two references to "liturgy," which provide an exemption for religiously motivated exterior changes, transform the otherwise neutral ordinance into a non-neutral one. The irony, even the perversity, of this position is apparent. In this case, the Landmarks Preservation Ordinance makes no reference to religious facilities. Only the implementing ordinance, which must necessarily focus on the designated church site, is deemed not neutral because of its exception for liturgically required exterior changes. Yet, the majority uses this exemption as the reason the landmark ordinances fail the neutrality test! Incredible. This is bootstrapping of the most egregious nature.

Contrary to the inference of the majority, *Health Servs. Div. v. Temple Baptist Church*, 112 N.M. 262, 814 P.2d 130, 134 (Ct.App.1991) does not hold references to religious facilities render a statute per se not neutral. Rather, the court looked at the statute as a whole and found

> nothing within these statutes that detracts from their character as being generally applicable and religion-neutral. We find nothing that intimates a legislative intent to discriminatorily burden religious exercise. Likewise, in this case, there is nothing in the ordinances which intimates an intent to discriminatorily burden religious exercise.

Next, the majority contends the Seattle landmark ordinances are not generally applicable and characterize them as being similar to laws in the unemployment compensation field, which remains the only context in which the Court has invalidated laws under the compelling governmental interest test set forth in *Sherbert*. This majority position sweeps broader than *Smith II* justifies, is contrary to the application of *Smith II* by other courts in land use cases, and misconstrues the landmark ordinances as involving a system of individualized exemptions.

Because this case does not involve unemployment compensation and does involve the City's ability to carry out its public policy, the majority's assumption that the *Sherbert* test even applies in this context is erroneous. *See, e.g., Rector, Wardens, & Members of the Vestry of St. Bartholomew's Church v. New York, supra*; *Salvation Army v. Department of Community Affairs*, 919 F.2d 183 (3rd Cir. 1990); *Cornerstone Bible Church v. Hastings*, 740 F. Supp. 654 (D. Minn. 1990) (land use cases since *Smith II* which have not applied the *Sherbert* test).

The legal issue in *St. Bartholomew's* is virtually identical to that presented here. In *St. Bartholomew's*, the New York City Landmarks Preservation Commission denied the church's application to demolish a building designated as a landmark to construct a commercial office tower in its place. The building was designated a landmark pursuant to religion-neutral designation criteria similar to the ordinance in this case. As the court noted, the building

> had a special character, special historical and aesthetic interest and value as part of the development, heritage and cultural aspects of New York City

St. Bartholomew's, 914 F.2d at 351 (citing N.Y.C. Admin. Code § 25-305(a)(1) (1985)). Once designated, the Commission had to approve any alteration or demolition of the building designated as a landmark. St. Bartholomew's argued the Commission's denial of its application for a certificate of appropriateness for the demolition and new construction violated its right of free exercise by substantially limiting its ability to provide space for church programs and raise needed revenue.

The court held *Smith II* applied, noted the landmark law would affect many religious buildings, but concluded the law was a valid, neutral regulation of general applicability because there was no "evidence of an intent to discriminate against, or impinge on, religious belief in the designation of landmark sites." *St. Bartholomew's*, 914 F.2d at 354. Similarly, First Covenant has presented no evidence of such discriminatory intent.

The majority's attempt to distinguish *St. Bartholomew's* on the facts is unconvincing. Free exercise, if applicable at all in the landmark preservation arena, should not depend on when a church objects to a regulation, whether the affected building is an adjunct or a main church building, or whether the claimed financial restrictions are characterized as a reduction in market value or revenue generation. These matters are simply irrelevant under the *Smith II* analysis. Moreover, the landmark law in *St. Bartholomew's* did not have an exception for alterations required by liturgy, which is present here.

[T]he unemployment compensation laws are concerned not only with whether one meets the criteria of unemployment, but also look to the reasons why the person is unemployed. The landmark ordinances, however, apply to all sites and provide, similar to the function of the criminal law, a procedure to determine whether the designating criteria are met. Once the criteria are held to be satisfied, there is no provision in the landmark ordinances which is comparable to the individualized assessments necessarily required by the "good cause" exception to entitlement to unemployment compensation benefits. Nor does this case present the hybrid situation provided for in *Smith II*. Even assuming secular design regulation of the exterior of a church violates free speech, which I am far from convinced it does, the landmark ordinances cannot restrict the church's expression of religious belief because the City has agreed that exterior changes required by liturgy are removed from the landmark regulations.

The church has also failed to show how the Seattle ordinances burden their free exercise, either administratively or financially.

The church has also failed to show an unconstitutional financial burden. Even if the reduction is taken as fact, the church has not shown the alleged reduction prohibits or interferes with religious practice. The central question in identifying an unconstitutional burden is whether the claimant has been denied the ability to practice his religion or coerced in the nature of those practices. *St. Bartholomew*'s, 914 F.2d at 355.

Lastly, I would find no violation of article 1, section 11 of the Washington State Constitution. I would hold the landmark ordinances are neutral, generally applicable laws which neither implicate the free exercise clause of the First Amendment nor violate article 1, section 11 of the Washington State Constitution. The protections afforded by the federal and state religion clauses are not properly invoked when a claimant has not been denied the ability to practice his religion or coerced in the nature of those practices. To hold the religion clauses applicable in this context denigrates their true meaning and unjustifiably limits the City's efforts to preserve the cultural assets of the City in the interest of the general welfare. *See* SMC 25.12.020(A).

SMITH and BRACHTENBACH, JJ., concur.

Notes

1. All three opinions thoroughly discuss the decision in *Rector, Wardens, & Members of Vestry of St. Bartholomew's Church v. New York*, 914 F.2d 348 (2d Cir. 1990), *cert. denied*, 499 U.S. 905 (1991), holding New York's historic preservation law constitutional. Are the factual differences between the two cases suggested by the majority persuasive? Are the legal differences between the two cases suggested by the concurring opinion persuasive? Should the "commercial" nature of the use of the land make a constitutional difference? *See Corporation of the Presiding Bishop of the Church of Jesus Christ of Latter-Day Saints v. Amos*, 483 U.S. 327 (1987) and related cases concerning religious liberty in the employment and labor context, excerpted in Chapter Eight. Should the "financial" impact of the regulation be viewed in absolute or relative terms? Both *First Covenant Church* and *St. Bartholomew's* were decided after the Supreme Court decided *Smith*, and each viewed the applicability of *Smith* differently. Which case more convincingly discusses the applicability of *Smith*?

2. The majority in *First Covenant Church* also relies on its state constitution as an adequate and independent state ground to strike Seattle's landmark ordinance. Such an approach effectively shields the majority's decision from Supreme Court review. Does this approach suggest a disagreement with the Court's interpretation of the First Amendment in *Smith*?

3. To what extent should decisions in zoning and historic preservation cases also be viewed as "takings" cases? Although the Supreme Court held that the application of New York's historic preservation law to Penn Station did not trigger a "taking for public use" within the meaning of the Fifth Amendment's Takings Clause, the Court has since made it clear that such determinations are both fact-specific, and turn on the nature of the rights conferred on the property owner by state law. *See Lucas v. South Carolina Coastal Council*, 505 U.S. 1003 (1992).

4. The majority cites several commentators in its opinion. Professor Angela Carmella's article, *Houses of Worship and Religious Liberty: Constitutional Limits to Landmark Preservation and Architectural Review*, 36 Vill. L. Rev. 401 (1991), suggests that the building itself is an expression of religious faith. The majority accepts this analysis in deciding the case. *City of Boerne v. Flores*, 521 U.S. 507 (1997), in which the Supreme Court invalidated the Religious Freedom Restoration Act, was an historic preservation case. In light of the failure of RFRA, the Congressional enactment of RLUIPA, and the existence of state versions of RFRA, how should an advocate go about making the case "for" or "against" in an historic preservation case? *See* Robert W. Tuttle, *How Firm a Foundation? Protecting Religious Land Uses After* Boerne, 68 Geo. Wash. L. Rev. 861 (2000); Laura S. Nelson, *Remove Not the Ancient Landmark: Legal Protection for Historic Religious Properties in an Age of Religious Freedom Legislation*, 21 Cardozo L. Rev. 721 (1999).

E. Bankruptcy, Receivership & Other Forms of Fiscal or Organizational Oversight

Like their counterparts in the non-religious sector, churches and religious organizations sometimes find themselves in financial difficulty. Such problems arise from precisely the same kinds of events which send others into bankruptcy or receivership: the entry of a judgment on a tort or contract claim; the threat posed by anticipated, but still contingent, liabilities for which insurance will be inadequate or nonexistent; unanticipated revenue shortfalls; and financial mismanagement.

There are two primary means by which the law deals with such problems: bankruptcy, in which the estate of the bankrupt is sequestered by a trustee and either reorganized or liquidated; and receivership, in which the operations of the debtor are administered by a court-appointed receiver.

1. Bankruptcy

a) A Brief Overview

Bankruptcy laws balance two competing interests: justice and mercy. Adopted pursuant to Congress' power to establish "uniform Laws on the subject of Bankruptcies throughout the United States," U.S. Const. Art. I, §8, cl. 4, the bankruptcy code is a comprehensive statutory scheme which seeks to balance the legitimate interests of creditors against the needs of debtors for relief from crushing debt obligations. *See generally* Michael J. Herbert, *Understanding Bankruptcy* (1995).

There are two basic situations in which the religious liberty interests of individuals, churches or religious organization will intersect with the Bankruptcy Code. The first arises when a church or religious organization seeks protection from the Bankruptcy Court. The appointment of a trustee to manage the estate of the bankrupt will inevitably entangle the federally appointed trustee in the internal operations and decision-making processes of the church. In these situations, the affairs of the bankrupt must be managed carefully, so as to avoid problems that which can arise under both the Establishment and Free Exercise Clauses. The second arises when pledges, contributions, or tithes to a church or religious organization become contested items in individual bankruptcies. In some of these cases the bankrupt petitions the court to approve a plan in which tithes are claimed as necessary expenses under Chapter 13 of the Bankruptcy Code. In others, the trustee seeks to reclaim tithes already paid to the church by debtors by invoking his or her power to recapture certain payments made by the debtor in the year prior to the bankruptcy petition.

In a bankruptcy under Chapter 7, the organization itself is liquidated and the assets held for the benefit of creditors. In a bankruptcy under Chapter 13, a debtor is required to devise and submit to a judge for confirmation a budget detailing expenses necessary for the support of the debtor and his or her family. *See* 11 U.S.C. §1325 (b). All other income to the debtor is considered disposable and is to be used for the repayment of the debtor's unsecured creditors. Chapter 13 plans are subject to time limits, after which all of the debtor's remaining debts and obligations are discharged. In order to offset the seemingly unfair practice of allowing debtors to avoid a portion of their debts entirely, unsecured creditors and trustees in bankruptcy are permitted to challenge items listed in the plan as not being "reasonably necessary" expenses. Challenges of this sort are common when debtors include tithes among the expenses deemed "necessary" to their life.

See generally Steven Hopkins, Comment, *Is God A Preferred Creditor? Tithing As An Avoidable Transfer In Chapter 7 Bankruptcies*, 62 U. Chi. L. Rev. 1139 (1995); Aric D. Martin, Comments, *Chapter 13 and the Tithe: Is God a Creditor*? 56 Ohio St. L.J. 307 (1995); Troy S. Anderson, Case Comment, *Christians v. Crystal Evangelical Free Church* (In re Young): *Why Would "Christians" Take Money Out of the Church Offering Plate*?, 4 Regent U. L. Rev. 177 (1994); Leonard J. Long, *Religious Exercise as Credit Risk*, 10 Bankr. Dev. J. 119 (1993/1994); Donald R. Price and Mark C. Rahdert, *Distributing the First Fruits: Statutory and Constitutional Implications of Tithing in Bankruptcy*, 26 U.C. Davis L. Rev. 853 (1993); David W. Case, Comment, *Resolving the Conflict Between Chapter 13 of the Bankruptcy Code and the Free Exercise Clause: In re* Green*: A Step in the Wrong Direction*, 57 Miss. L.J. 163 (1987).

b) Recovery of Tithes and Other Contributions

Bankruptcy judges have had mixed reactions to attempts by bankruptcy trustees and creditors to recover tithes and other contributions for the estate of the bankrupt. In *In re Green*, 73 B.R. 893 (W.D. Mich. 1987), for example, the State of Michigan was an unsecured creditor, and objected to the court's approval of a Chapter 13 plan on the grounds that "if the court confirms a Chapter 13 plan which permits tithing, then the court will be favoring religions which require tithes over those that do not, and favoring these debtors over those debtors who are not required to tithe or who do not practice any religion at all." The court rejected the assertion, and held that to deny confirmation of the plan solely because of the tithe would violate the free exercise rights of the debtors.

A similar conclusion was reached in *In re Bien*, 95 B.R. 281 (D. Conn. 1989), where the trustee objected to inclusion of the tithe as a "reasonably necessary" item of expense "for the maintenance or support of the debtor" under 11 U.S.C. § 1325(b). The debtor, a devout Mormon, was required to tithe, and had done so on a monthly basis for over thirteen years. The trustee argued, however, that the money is part of the debtor's disposable income, and that since he had discretion concerning the decision to tithe in the first place, the funds must be used to make payments under the plan.

In the normal bankruptcy situation, the court applies a two-prong analysis in determining whether a budgeted item of expense satisfies § 1325(b). The court looks first to whether a challenged item serves an appropriate purpose. If it does, the proper amount of the expense is considered. In *In re Bein*, however, the court held that:

> An expense for a religious tithe must be treated differently. Court scrutiny of such expense should include a determination of whether the proposed expense fulfills a *bona fide* personal commitment intended to serve or promote some religious or spiritual purpose, rather than an effort to hinder, delay or defraud creditors, and whether there is a nondiscretionary obligation to pay such expense in a specific amount. Where, as here, the obligation is nondiscretionary [due to a sincerely held religious belief regarding tithing], the amount of such expense is not a proper subject for court scrutiny.

In re Bien, 95 B.R. at 282.

In *Bein*, the court avoided the Free Exercise question by finding that the tithe was nondiscretionary; that is, in order for the debtor to participate fully in his religion, he was required to tithe. The court "observed, however, that if the proposed tithe were discretionary, [it] would then have to determine whether it was unreasonable. A finding that it was would then require a consideration of whether § 1325(b) infringed upon the debtor's First Amendment rights." *Id.* at 282, n.3.

In re Reynolds, 83 B.R. 684 (W.D. Mo. 1988) provides a useful contrast. In this case, the court denied the proposed bankruptcy plan which called for a tithe of $80.00 per month. In its view,

> There is no doubt that, to many, churches (or religions) serve and satisfy a deep and abiding need that exists somewhere in either the consciousness or unconsciousness of *homo sapiens*. By whatever name or rite, man has and will seek some entity or institution that answers the unanswerable questions and assuages the unassuageable doubts and concerns of our human existence. But that is each person's free choice; to seek or not, to believe or not; to contribute or not; and who or what is right is not for this Court or any other branch of the state or federal government to decide. This Court may not and must not say what if any portion of debtor's income shall go to support his personal religious beliefs, but this Court may determine what constitutes those items reasonably necessary "to be expended: (A) for the maintenance or support of a debtor or a dependent."

83 B.R. at 685. The court noted that the determination of whether a tithe was reasonable was a fact specific inquiry, but "that amount will need to be below 3% of gross in-

come unless very unusual circumstances are present." *Id.* The court in *Bein* specifically rejected the kind of judicial oversight exercised in *Reynolds.*

Notes

1. How much oversight should a court exercise in the bankruptcy context? The pre-1998 case law was very clear that debts relating to religious obligations were to be treated like other debts.

In *Newman v. Midway Southern Baptist Church,* 183 B.R. 239 (Bankr. D. Kan. 1995), for example, the court considered a bankruptcy trustee's claim that a church which had received a tithe from a member in arguable violation of the Bankruptcy Code should be forced to pay it over to the estate. The church defended on Free Exercise Clause and RFRA grounds. The section of the Bankruptcy Code which debtors were alleged to have violated, 11 U.S.C. § 548(a), reads as follows:

> **§ 548. Fraudulent transfers and obligations**
>
> (a) The trustee may avoid any transfer of an interest of the debtor in property, or any obligation incurred by the debtor, that was made or incurred on or within one year before the date of the filing of the petition, if the debtor voluntarily or involuntarily: (2)(A) received less than a reasonably equivalent value in exchange for such transfer or obligation; and (B)(i) was insolvent on the date that such transfer was made or such obligation was incurred, or became insolvent as a result of such transfer or obligation.

The court found that the debtors had transferred a total of approximately $2,500 during the year prior to filing the petition for bankruptcy and that they were insolvent at the time of the transfers. The issue in this case was whether or not the debtors "received less than a reasonably equivalent value in exchange for such transfer" for their tithe. The church, as defendant, argued that by requiring the church to return the tithes, the government would be violating the Free Exercise and RFRA rights of the debtors.

Before reaching the First Amendment and RFRA claims, the court first had to determine whether, under the statute, the debtors received something "of reasonably equivalent value" in exchange for their tithe. The court concluded that "the debtors did not receive *anything* in exchange for their tithe and that the religious comfort and support does not constitute value under the Bankruptcy Code" (emphasis added) because "value" under the Bankruptcy Code had been interpreted to mean "tangible benefit or economic value." 183 B.R. at 246–247.

Relying on *Christians v. Crystal Evangelical Free Church* (*In re* Young), 152 B.R. 939 (D. Minn. 1993), the court stated "transfers 'made out of a sense of moral obligation rather than legal obligation' cannot be for reasonably equivalent value.'" In its view, tithes were not "in exchange" for value, even if a "value" could be determined and quantified. Testimony at trial indicated that the church did not keep track of who tithed and who did not. Further, the provision of worship services and the membership requirements of the church did not require members to tithe. *Newman,* 183 B.R. at 247.

Using the Free Exercise analysis developed in *Employment Div. v. Smith,* 494 U.S. 872 (1990), and later restated in *Church of Lukumi Babalu Aye, Inc. v. City of Hialeah,* 508 U.S. 520 (1993) the court found that "[s]ection 548(a)(2) is therefore a generally applicable law, neutral toward religion both in its object and its operation, does not have more than an incidental effect on religion, and therefore does not offend the First Amendment's Free Exercise Clause." 183 B.R. at 250.

Under RFRA, 42 U.S.C. § 2000bb, the court found "the threshold inquiry...is whether the statute in question substantially burdens a person's religious practice." 183 B.R. at 251. The court found no burden because "[t]he statute, by its own operation, does nothing to prevent the debtors' fulfillment of their personally held religious obligation to tithe and, therefore, does not place a 'substantial burden' on the debtors' practice of their religion." 183 B.R. at 251.

In *In re Cadogan*, 4 B.R. 598, 599 (Bankr. W.D. Va. 1980), the court rejected a plan where amounts listed as "tithes" actually included both a 10% tithe and dues for various religious organizations to which one of the debtors belonged. Refusing to confirm the plan "in view of the niggardly manner in which creditors were being treated," the debtor was informed that, "if she wished to continue to make the entire contribution for religious purposes, her other expenditures would have to be reduced." *Id.* at 600. Does this kind of oversight "burden" the free exercise of religion, substantially or otherwise?

2. In 1998, Congress reacted by adopting the Religious Liberty and Charitable Donation Protection Act of 1998, Pub.L. 105-183, § 1, 112 Stat. 517, codified at 11 U.S.C. §§ 544(b), 546(e), 546(f), 546(g), 548(a), 548(d), 707(b) and 1325(b)(2)(A) (2001). The key revisions are to § 544 (trustee's avoidance powers), § 548 (fraudulent transfer), § 707(b) (dismissal for substantial abuse) and § 1325(b)(2)(A) (chapter 13 confirmation). Read together, they provide significant protection for debtors and the religious and charitable organizations to which they contributed prior to filing the bankruptcy petition. For an extensive discussion of the provisions of RLCDPA, see John K. Turner, *Giving God the Unavoidable Preference Tithing and the Religious Liberty and Charitable Donation Protection Act of 1998*, 19-NOV Am. Bankr. Inst. J. 8 (November 2000).

3. Unlike RFRA, which was challenged on both separation of powers and federalism grounds, RLCDPA is both clearly within the scope of Congress power to define the content of the estate of the bankrupt, and an Establishment Clause challenge is unlikely to succeed because 11 U.S.C. § 548 defines the term "qualified charity" in precisely the same inclusive manner as those terms are defined in Section 170(c)(1–2) of the Internal Revenue Code, 26 U.S.C. § 170 (2001). *Accord In re Witt*, 231 B.R. 92 (Bankr. N.D. Okla. 1999) (rejecting Establishment Clause challenge).

F. Operational Oversight by the Attorney General

How should the state respond when allegations are made that those charged with the duty of administering church affairs are guilty of fraud, malfeasance, or other actions inconsistent with their fiduciary duties? Both § B(2)(d) of this chapter, and Chapter Nine § D5 recount that one of the vestiges of the law of charitable trusts that remains applicable to nonprofit and charitable corporations is oversight and, in appropriate cases, supervision by the Attorney General. Oversight occurs on a regular basis with respect to fund-raising, tax status, and other critical aspects of charitable operations and solicitations. When that supervision extends to a church, however, the issues are complex.

Weaver v. Wood

425 Mass. 270, 680 N.E.2d 918 (1997)

MARSHALL, Justice.

Two members of the First Church of Christ, Scientist, in Boston (Church) seek to challenge decisions of the directors of the Church and its publishing arm, The Christian Science Publishing Society (Publishing Society), to expand the Publishing Society's activities in the electronic media. The plaintiffs claim that the defendants failed to abide by the Church's relevant governing documents when they authorized major investments in television ventures in the late 1980's and the early 1990's in violation, it is alleged, of the defendants' fiduciary duties. The defendants moved for summary judgment on several grounds, including that these two individuals do not have standing to bring this action. A judge in the Superior Court denied their motion, concluding, as to standing, that the plaintiffs "are members of the Mother Church in a special and unique manner separate and distinct from any member of the public." The defendants appealed. We conclude under well-settled principles of law long enforced by this court that the plaintiffs do not have standing to obtain judicial redress in this matter.

Central to the plaintiffs' claim is their allegation that the defendants have failed to abide by two deeds of trust executed by Mary Baker G. Eddy, the founder of Christian Science, and the Church by-laws that are contained in a "Manual of The Mother Church" (Manual), also prepared and executed by Eddy.

[Based on a review of the documents creating the Church, the court concluded that] the ultimate fiscal responsibility for the Church rests with the ["Christian Science Board of Directors" (board), a self-perpetuating body.]

In 1898, Eddy executed an additional deed of trust (1898 deed) that established the Publishing Society "for the purpose of more effectually promoting and extending the religion of Christian Science." The Publishing Society trustees are charged with the management of all of its operations, subject to the comprehensive and final authority of the board. The 1898 deed does not grant to any members of the Church any beneficial rights.

Since its inception the Publishing Society has produced many publications including a daily newspaper, The Christian Science Monitor (since 1908), and various radio programs (since the 1930's). Beginning in the mid-1980's the Publishing Society began pursuing the medium of television as a means of accomplishing its mission. In its fiscal year 1986, the Publishing Society initiated a monthly television program in conjunction with the Independent News Network, which became a weekly program in July 1986. The Church also purchased a Boston-area television station, ultimately investing more than $60 million in that venture. From September, 1988, through January, 1992, a daily television program produced by the Church entitled "World Monitor" aired on the cable television's Discovery Channel. From May, 1991, through the end of fiscal year 1992, the Monitor Channel had deficits in excess of $30 million. The Monitor Channel ceased broadcast operations in April, 1992.

The defendants claim that these various television ventures were undertaken to "promote" and "extend" Christian Science, to advance the Church's religious interests and to fulfil its mission as described by Eddy in her 1898 deed. The failure of the television ventures and the accumulation of significant debts in connection with those ventures form the crux of the plaintiffs' allegations against the defendants.

We turn to consider whether the plaintiffs have standing to maintain this action. The plaintiffs describe themselves as "life-long members in good standing" of the Church; they do not claim to be members of the Publishing Society. They have never held office in the Church, nor are they directors of the Church or trustees of the Publishing Society. Is their status as members sufficient-without more-to confer standing on them?

We begin by stating what may seem entirely obvious: the Church is a public charity, established by Eddy under a series of charitable trusts.[8] The 1892 instrument executed by Eddy conveyed land in trust for the purpose of building a "suitable and convenient church edifice," in which to "maintain public worship in accordance with the doctrines of Christian Science in said church." Her second deed, executed in 1898, granted property in trust to the Publishing Society for "promoting and extending the religion of Christian Science." In addition to these two trusts, in the residuary clause of her will Eddy made a further gift to the Church in trust for the "purpose of more effectually promoting and extending the religion of Christian Science." In *Chase v. Dickey*, 212 Mass. 555, 566, 99 N.E. 410 (1912), we concluded that her residuary clause created a charitable trust and that the "[r]elief of spiritual destitution and religious or moral ignorance, intolerance or perversity, is a good public charity."

In the case of a private trust, only a named beneficiary, or one suing on his or her behalf, can maintain an action to enforce a trust. When a trust is charitable, and is created not to benefit one or more individuals but is devoted to purposes that are beneficial to a broader community, the Legislature has determined that the Attorney General is responsible for ensuring that its charitable funds are used in accordance with the donor's wishes; "[t]he attorney general shall enforce the due application of funds given or appropriated to public charities within the commonwealth and prevent breaches of trust in the administration thereof." G.L. c. 12, §8.

We consistently have held that only the Attorney General can bring an action alleging the misuse of charitable assets. It is his duty to see that the public interests are protected and to proceed in the prosecution or to decline so to proceed as those interests may require."

We have on occasion recognized a private plaintiff's standing to make claims against a public charity, but only where the plaintiff asserts "interests in such organizations which are distinct from those of the general public." In each such case the claim has arisen from a personal right that directly affects the individual member, such as where the member has a right to exercise a vote in connection with some aspect of the charity's affairs (a right not present here) and is prohibited from doing so. [I]t is "the exclusive function of the Attorney General to correct abuses in the administration of a public charity."

The judge below concluded that the plaintiffs had standing because they "are members of the Mother Church in a special and unique manner separate and distinct from any member of the public." While the plaintiffs' relationship with the Mother Church is indeed different from a member of the public who is not a member of the Church, we have never held that membership in a public charity, alone, is sufficient to give standing to pursue claims that a charitable organization has been mismanaged or that its officials

8. A charitable trust is "a fiduciary relationship with respect to property arising as a result of a manifestation of an intention to create it, and subjecting the person by whom the property is held to equitable duties to deal with the property for a charitable purpose." Restatement (Second) of Trusts §348 (1959).

have acted ultra vires. The plaintiffs may be of the view that they are "beneficiaries" of Eddy in a religious or theological sense. They have not, however, demonstrated that they are beneficiaries of any of Eddy's trusts in any legal sense. As such, they have no enforceable legal interest in the administration of the charity, and have no standing to pursue such claims.

We vacate the ruling of the judge below denying the defendants' motion for summary judgment, and remand this matter to the Superior Court for entry of a judgment dismissing this action.

So ordered.

* * *

Was the conclusion in *Weaver v. Wood* that the Church of Christ, Scientist is a "public trust" based on Mary Baker Eddy's explicit use of trust instruments when she set up the Church, or on a more fundamental assumption that church assets *in general* are impressed with a public trust? Given the case below, does it matter?

Word of Faith World Outreach Center Church, Inc. v. Morales

787 F. Supp. 689 (W.D. Tex. 1992)

MEMORANDUM OPINION AND ORDER

SPARKS, District Judge.

On November 21, 1991, ABC's Prime Time Live published a television network special involving, in part, the Word of Faith World Outreach Center Church, Incorporated, and Robert G. Tilton, two of the three plaintiffs in this lawsuit. The import of this publication was not flattering to either the church or Mr. Tilton, but the accuracy or inaccuracy of the reporting is not relevant to the issues in this lawsuit.[1] [Attorneys for the church offered to meet with federal and state governmental agencies, including the Texas Attorney General and to permit review and inspection of the church's records for the purpose of demonstrating that the allegations made in Prime Time Live were false. The federal agencies accepted the offer, but the Attorney General declined.]

On January 13, 1992, the Consumer Protection Division of the Office of the Attorney General of Texas sent to the Plaintiffs, by facsimile transmission, a demand for documents pursuant to the Texas Deceptive Trade Practices-Consumer Protection Act. [DTPA] The demand states in the first paragraph:

> The Consumer Protection Division of the Office of the Attorney General has reason to believe that Word of Faith Family Church and World Outreach Center... has engaged in trade practices and charitable solicitations which may violate provisions of state law including the Texas Consumer Protection and Deceptive Trade Practices Act.

[The Attorney General requested a wide range of documents, including the following:

(1) Media plans and insertion data for television presentations and written solicitations made by the Church;

---

1. ... [T]he Attorney General stipulated Word of Faith World Outreach Center Church, Inc. is a bona fide church holding sincere religious beliefs.

(2) All documents, shipping records, memoranda and other materials relating to the handling of prayer requests and any other solicitation material which is claimed to be the subject of any prayer or other entreaty to God by Robert Tilton or any other person employed by the Church from January 1, 1989, to and including the present;

(3) All canceled checks and other documentary material relating to contributions sent to each orphanage, mission, ministry, and charitable organization by Robert Tilton or the Church during the period from January 1, 1989 to and including the present;

(4) Testimonials or complaints from any individuals who have sent money or anything else of value to Robert Tilton, Marte Tilton, the Church, or any other Church entity from January 1, 1989, to and including the present;

(5) List of all Church employees and consultants that have received in excess of $100,000 from the Church or any Church entity from January 1, 1987, to and including the present, including the name, address, and telephone number of each person and amounts received;

(6) List of all persons who have been paid or remunerated in any way in excess of $100,000 from the Church or any Church entity from January 1, 1987, to and including the present, including the name, address, and telephone number of each person;

(7) List of all persons who have sent contributions to the Church and any other Church entity from January 1, 1989, to and including the present, including name, address, telephone number, amount and date of contribution;

(8) List of all vendors and/or contract labor that have received payments in excess of $50,000 from the Church and any other Church entity from January 1, 1987, to and including the present, including name, address, telephone number, and amounts and dates received;

(9) Copies of the minutes of meetings of the board of directors for the Church held since January 1, 1987, to and including the present;

(10) List of all members of Robert Tilton's family who are involved in any way with the production of Robert Tilton's television broadcasts;

(11) A copy of all policy or procedure manuals relating to the method and manner in which the Church, other Church entities, and Robert Tilton solicit contributions;

(12) A copy of every advertisement, brochure, or other document used in the promotion or marketing of the Church and all other Church entities.]

[The Attorney General continued to refuse to meet with the church's attorneys, and sent a copy of the document demand to the press and television media, even though Texas law indicates that information obtained from such a request was confidential and could not be released except by court order. The result was very unfavorable publicity for the church and a decision by the church and the Tilton family not to release any information whatever.]

[Attorneys for the church continued to seek a meeting with the Attorney General's staff, and warned them that they would file a lawsuit seeking a determination of their rights under the First Amendment. Five days before the deadline for production of the documents, the Attorney General filed a petition in *quo warranto* in the Probate Court of Travis County, Texas. The verified petition expressly alleged:]

> This suit is brought in the nature of *quo warranto* against the Defendant corporation...*for the purpose of obtaining a permanent injunction ordering Defendant to produce records as requested by the Attorney General, for forfeiture of Defendant's charter* and dissolution of the corporation, an appointment of a receiver to take possession of the affairs of the Defendant, *to rehabilitate*, to reorganize, conserve, or liquidate *the affairs of the corporation*, as the case may be. *A further purpose of this suit is to obtain*, after notice and hearing, a temporary injunction and *a permanent injunction against the Defendant, its officers*, directors, stockholders, agents, employees, *and representatives whomsoever from conducting any business of the Defendant.* (emphasis added).

* * *

The testimony, the records demand, and the filing of the *quo warranto* petition establish unequivocably that the Attorney General interprets the [Texas Deceptive Trade Practices-Consumer Protection Act and Texas Miscellaneous Corporation Laws Act] as giving the Attorney General complete discretion to request any documents from any corporate entity (including a non-profit corporation which operates as a church with its principal or sole purpose of religious activities).

The Court finds from the evidence that the conduct of the Attorney General and his personnel was neither professional nor responsible, bordering on the unethical, and constitutes "bad faith." This conduct is not what is expected of attorneys charged with the responsibility of being the legal representatives of the State of Texas.

However, the Court does not find this "bad faith" conduct prevents the Attorney General of Texas from appropriately using his authority to investigate the corporate plaintiff to determine if it is truly a non-profit corporation under Texas law.

ABSTENTION

[The court rejected the argument that it should abstain in order to permit the *quo warranto* proceedings in the Probate Court of Travis County to run their course. In part, this finding was based on the fact that the Attorney General filed the state proceedings to preempt the federal lawsuit and to force resolution of the federal issues in state court. The court viewed the entire proceeding as an abuse of power.]

[T]he Plaintiffs specifically seek to enjoin the Attorney General from conducting any civil investigation or investigation of any kind of the Plaintiffs' religion pursuant to the DTPA and the MCLA, and to enjoin [the other relief sought, including forfeiture of the Church's charter and its right to conduct its religious service in the State of Texas.]

TEXAS DECEPTIVE TRADE PRACTICES-CONSUMER PROTECTION ACT

In his brief and in hearings before this Court, the Attorney General continues to maintain the Plaintiffs are subject to the DTPA because it is alleged they solicit and accept donations from members and others, distribute various pamphlets, books, and objects, and make certain representations that are not technically accurate. Plaintiffs, in opposition, argue that the DTPA does not apply as they are not engaged in "trade or commerce" and the contributors to the church ("members") are not "consumers" because no money is required to receive anything from the church or to have Mr. Tilton pray over returned objects or perform other acts and because contributors' donations are not requested for any specific purpose.

This Court agrees the Texas Deceptive Trade Practices-Consumer Protection Act has no applicability in this case. Although no Texas court has considered the applicability of the DTPA to church activities and donations, the language as well as Texas case law make clear the Plaintiffs are not subject to [it].

[The district court held that there were no grounds for a breach of warranty action because "[e]xpress or implied warranties arise out of contracts or sales," and that contributors are not "consumers" under the DPTA because "[in] order to be a consumer, one must purchase or seek to purchase goods or services. Contributors to the church do not seek to purchase goods or services."]

Even if the DTPA were applicable to the Plaintiffs on its face, it still could not be constitutionally applied to the Plaintiffs as interpreted by the Attorney General. The fact that the DTPA has a valid purpose and was not enacted to discriminate against a religion or restrict the free exercise of a religion, does not mean any effects on the Plaintiffs are merely incidental and permissible under the First Amendment. [citing *Wisconsin* v. *Yoder*, *Bates* v. *City of Little Rock*, *N.A.A.C.P.* v. *Alabama*, *Murdock v. Pennsylvania*]. The scope and substance of these requests are clearly unconstitutional. The State has no constitutional authority to know a person's membership in or support of any church. The State has no constitutional authority to know what a person believes, how he or she practices religion, or how he or she supports religious activities. Nor does the State have constitutional authority to probe into the internal operations of a church without limitation or compelling purpose. The First Amendment right to freedom of religious belief and freedom of association protects this kind of information.

During the hearing on injunctive relief before this Court, Assistant Attorney Generals testified that they were not trying to prevent the Plaintiffs from practicing their religion as they see fit or discourage membership in the church, but rather only wanted to investigate as to whether or not "secular statements" made in pamphlets and on television by Mr. Tilton were false or deceptive. For instance, if Mr. Tilton promised to pray over a prayer cloth, did he actually do so? However, the Assistant Attorney Generals fail to take the next logical step. If they apply the DTPA, and if they determine the church or Mr. Tilton have violated the DTPA, the relief granted under the DTPA is injunctive. It is simply not the business of courts or the State to "approve, classify, regulate, or in any manner control sermons delivered at religious meetings" or other forms of religious expressions.

TEXAS MISCELLANEOUS CORPORATION LAWS ACT

[Even though] the Church was incorporated as a non-profit corporation under the Texas Non-Profit Corporation Act[,]...the provisions of the MCLA may not be constitutionally applied to the Plaintiffs. Not only is the discretion of the Attorney General to investigate under the MCLA as broad and unbridled as it is under the DTPA, but the remedies provided under the MCLA and sought by the Attorney General would wholly deprive the Plaintiffs of their right to worship.

Under Article 1302-5.03 [of the MCLA]

> [t]he Attorney General...has the power and authority to make investigation into the *organization, conduct and management* of any corporation...authorized to do business within this State, and has authority to inspect and examine *any* of its said books, records, and other documents, and take such copies thereof as *in his judgment* may show *or tend to show* said corporation has been or is engaged in acts or conduct in violation of its charter rights and privileges, or in violation of any law of this State.

Id. at Art. 1302-5.03(A) (Vernon's 1992 Supp.) (emphasis added).

This is not just unbridled discretion, this is complete discretion. For the same First Amendment freedom of religion and association concerns described above with respect to the DTPA, this Court finds application of these articles to the Plaintiffs unconstitutional.

CHARITABLE TRUSTS LAW

The Attorney General also maintains that the Church is a charitable trust and that, as such, it is the Attorney General's common law duty to protect the public's interest with respect to that charitable trust. Without having to reach the Attorney General's duties over charitable trusts under the common law, this Court finds that the church is not a charitable trust. A church is not organized for a "civic or public purpose". If the Legislature had intended to incorporate any entity described in the Internal Revenue Code, whatever its purpose, it could have easily done so. The church is not a charitable trust, and because jurisdiction in the Travis County Probate Court is based on the church being a charitable trust, that jurisdiction is improper.

TEXAS NON-PROFIT CORPORATION ACT

This Court's finding that the DTPA and MCLA cannot be constitutionally applied to the Plaintiffs and that the *quo warranto* proceeding may not be properly maintained in the Travis County Probate Court does not mean that the Attorney General has no authority to investigate the Plaintiffs.

The Court agrees with the Attorney General that persons may not, "under the cloak of religion" use the First Amendment "with impunity" to "commit frauds upon the public". Nonetheless, the Attorney General cannot, in turn, use allegations of fraud as a sword to violate the Plaintiffs' First Amendment rights either. Lines must be drawn and interests balanced. The DTPA and the MCLA, as interpreted by the Attorney General, are too broad and give too little protection and may not be constitutionally applied to the Plaintiffs. The Texas Non-Profit Corporation Act ("NPCA"), however, may be constitutionally applied.

CONCLUSION

The *quo warranto* proceeding in the Travis County Probate Court, Cause No. 59,268, is permanently enjoined. The Attorney General of Texas is permanently enjoined from pursuing further its January 13, 1992, demand for documents and investigation pursuant to the DTPA and the MCLA, but this order is without prejudice to the Attorney General to appropriately pursue an investigation of the Plaintiffs under the Texas Non-Profit Corporation Act.

* * *

The trial court's holding was reversed in **Word of Faith World Outreach Center Church, Inc. v. Morales**, Attorney General of Texas, 986 F.2d 962 (5th Cir.), *cert. denied*, 510 U.S. 823 (1993):

> The question thus presented is whether the statutes at issue here apply full-force to the church or are susceptible of a limiting construction that would alleviate the unconstitutional burdens the district court found they imposed upon the church. [Finding that the Texas courts offered "an adequate state forum in which to obtain a resolution of the state law issues while preserving its federal constitutional claims,] [w]e venture no opinion as to the correctness of the district court's decision on the constitutional merits, for we need not do so in order to apply the *Pullman* doctrine [*Railroad Comm'n v. Pullman Co.*, 312 U.S. 496 (1941)] to the particulars of this case.

Id. at 967–68.

Notes

1. The *Word of Faith Outreach Center* case presents several important issues, not least of which is the one avoided by the application of *Pullman* abstention. How can the Church recover the cost of litigating an overbroad investigatory demand, made in bad faith? *See* 42 U.S.C. §§ 1983, 1988 (2001) (permitting recovery of damages and attorney fees).

2. How *should* government protect its citizens from fraud practiced under the cover of religion? *See e.g., In re* The Bible Speaks, 73 B.R. 848, (Bankr.D.Mass. 1987), *aff'd, The Bible Speaks v. Dovydenas,* 81 B.R. 750 (D.Mass. 1988), *aff'd in part, rev'd in part In re The Bible Speaks,* 869 F.2d 628 (1st Cir.), *cert. denied sub nom., The Bible Speaks, Inc. v. Dovydenas,* 493 U.S. 816 (1989) (permitting recovery of $5.5 million from church on grounds that it was obtained from the donor through undue influence). *See generally* Jonathan Turley, *Laying Hands On Religious Racketeers: Applying Civil RICO to Fraudulent Religious Solicitation,* 29 Wm. & Mary L. Rev. 441 (1988). In 1995, the Supreme Court of Texas held that the trial court did not abuse its discretion in compelling the production of religious tithing records from Robert Tilton to plaintiffs alleging fraud, intentional infliction of emotional distress and conspiracy nor in refusing to dismiss these claims against him on constitutional grounds. The court found actionable a fraud claim alleging Tilton promised and failed to keep his promise personally to pray over the prayer requests made by the plaintiffs. On rehearing, the Texas Supreme Court reversed itself in large part. The court held that plaintiffs could not sue Tilton for fraudulent and deceitful representations concerning religious beliefs, that intentional infliction of emotional distress claim and related conspiracy claims must be dismissed because they required forbidden inquiry into truth of religious beliefs, and that Tilton should receive relief from trial court's order requiring production of tithing records. A plurality of the court denied mandamus relief to Tilton concerning trial court's decision refusing to dismiss claim that Tilton fraudulently promised to read, touch, and pray over contributors' prayer, and refused to dismiss related conspiracy claims. In calculating damages for those claims, the court held that no damages could be awarded for allegedly unanswered prayers. An award of punitive damages was permissible. *Tilton v. Marshall,* 925 S.W.2d 672 (Tex. 1996).

3. **Unconstitutional Remedies:** Courts forced to decide cases involving mismanagement and waste of the assets of a religious organization face a delicate task. *See generally* Catherine M. Knight, Comment, *Must God Regulate Religious Corporations? A Proposal for Reform of the Religious Corporation Provisions of the Revised Model Nonprofit Corporation Act,* 42 Emory L.J. 721 (1993). Because dissolution of the corporation is generally considered a drastic remedy, courts have discretion to fashion an equitable remedy that protects the interests of all of the stakeholders. *State* ex rel. *Heitkamp v. Family Life Services,* Inc., 2000 N.D. 166, 616 N.W.2d 826 (2000) illustrates the constitutional problems that can arise when a court tries to "save" the corporation rather than dissolve it. *Heitkamp* involved a credit counseling service operated as part of an Evangelical Christian ministry. The North Dakota Attorney General proved "commingling of client trust funds, improper loans to directors and officers, misappropriation of funds, and failure to keep adequate corporate financial records" and sought dissolution of the corporation. The trial court agreed that a drastic remedy was warranted, but fashioned a remedy that required the election of a new board of directors that "would follow the

same religious beliefs and ideology of the founders" of Family Life Services. The North Dakota Supreme Court reversed, and instructed the trial court to dissolve the corporation because "[t]he trial court's attempt to select [a group of electors] that would follow the same religious beliefs and ideology of the founders necessarily involved the court in deciding FLS's religious doctrine and polity and placed the court in an excessive entanglement with religion in conflict with the principles underlying both the Establishment Clause and Free Exercise Clause of the First Amendment." Dissolution was therefore a "less drastic" remedy under the circumstances.

Greek Orthodox Archdiocese of North and South America v. Abrams, Attorney General

162 Misc.2d 850, 618 N.Y.S.2d 504 (Sup. Ct. 1994)

STUART C. COHEN, Justice.

In this proceeding, petitioner, Greek Orthodox Archdiocese of North and South America ("the Archdiocese") seeks an order declaring the validity of a 1987 order issued by the Supreme Court, Westchester County which approved the sale of certain real property owned by the Archdiocese. The Archdiocese also challenges the constitutionality of certain statutes pursuant to which the Attorney General of the State of New York contends that the Archdiocese's actions require further governmental review and approval.

The Archdiocese was incorporated in 1921 under the Religious Corporations Law of the State of New York. It is a church recognized by the Apostolic Historic Eastern Orthodox Patriarchate of Constantinople, as referred to under Section 290 of the New York Religious Corporations Law. The Greek Orthodox Church is the worldwide body of communicants of the Greek Orthodox faith. The Archdiocese states that it is the highest spiritual and governing authority of the church for all communicants of the Greek Orthodox faith in North and South America.

On or about November 24, 1980, the Archdiocese purchased 51 acres of land known collectively as the "Lincoln Rise Property."

In 1986, the Archdiocese decided to sell the Lincoln Rise Property. Proposals were received from several parties as to possible purchase, but these proposals were determined to be insufficient. In late 1986, Chris Demetriades, the Director of Economic Development of the Archdiocese, made a proposal on behalf of his corporation, Demetriades Developers, Inc. ("DDI"), to purchase the property for approximately $10,000,000. On or about February 13, 1987, the Executive Committee of the Archdiocesan Council unanimously passed resolutions approving the proposed sale to DDI.

Paragraphs 6 and 44 of the Contract of Sale expressly conditioned the agreement's enforceability on Court approval thereof as required by Section 12 of the Religious Corporation Law. On or about March 23, 1987, the Archdiocese commenced a proceeding. The Attorney General was not given notice of this proceeding. Nevertheless, on April 3, 1987, an order was entered granting permission to the Archdiocese to sell the Lincoln Rise Property to DDI.

Subsequent to obtaining Court approval of the conveyance, the Archdiocese agreed to modify its contract with DDI. [The modifications were a restructuring of the contingent interest formula of the contract, and a payment by DDI to the Archdiocese of $1,303,275 to release DDI from any further obligations under the contract. Both modifications occurred after DDI complained of financial exigencies related to development of the Lincoln Rise property.]

The Archdiocese neither sought nor obtained Court approval for either of these modifications. In August, 1992, Simos Dimas, a member of the Archdiocese, commenced an Article 78 proceeding against the Archdiocese and DDI alleging, among other things, that the Archdiocese had not properly obtained Court approval for the conveyance of the Lincoln Rise Property to DDI or for any of the modifications to the contract of sale. The Attorney General also alleged that the Archdiocese was required to obtain Court approval for the modifications. As a means of resolving these conflicting claims, the Archdiocese commenced this proceeding.

In the petition, the Archdiocese seeks an order declaring that the 1987 order of the Supreme Court, Westchester County, approving the sale to DDI was valid and that subsequent modification to the contract did not require further Court approval. In the alternative, the Archdiocese contends that Section 12(1) of the Religious Corporation Law ("RCL") is unconstitutional. The Attorney General interposed an answer which includes a counterclaim alleging that the modifications to the contract were consummated in violation of the law and requiring the Archdiocese to seek *nunc pro tunc* approval of the modifications.

Presently before the Court are motions for summary judgment by the Archdiocese and DDI which seek judgment for the relief demanded in the petition. The Attorney General opposes these motions and moves for leave to conduct discovery.

The Archdiocese first seeks a declaration that Religious Corporation Law Section 12(1), the statute mandating Court approval of the sale, does not apply to a church's sale of real property which is not used as a place of worship and, therefore, does not apply to the Archdiocese's sale of the Lincoln Rise Property.

Religious Corporation Law § 12(1) provides, in relevant part:

> A religious corporation shall not sell, mortgage or lease for a term exceeding five years *any of its real property* without applying for and obtaining leave of the court therefor pursuant to section five hundred eleven of the not-for-profit corporation law... [emphasis added].

The language of this provision is clear and unambiguous. By using the words "any of its real property" the legislature did not intend to limit applicability of the statute to property used as a place of worship.

Accordingly, Religious Corporation Law sec. 12(1) applies to the sale mortgage or lease of any real property by a religious corporation, not merely to property used as a place of worship, and the statute therefore applies to the Archdiocese's sale of the Lincoln Rise Property.

The Archdiocese also argues that provisions of the Religious Corporation Law are unconstitutional.

The Archdiocese argues that Religious Corporation Law Sections 12 and 2-b(a)(d-i)—which provide that certain churches are required to notify the Attorney General when obtaining leave of Court to sell, mortgage or lease real property, while other churches are not required to notify the Attorney General—discriminates between religious denominations and religious corporations, is an intrusion into and entanglement with the internal affairs of the Archdiocese in violation of the Establishment Clause and interferes with the Archdiocese's internal procedure for administering itself in violation of the Free Exercise Clause.

The purpose of requiring notice to the Attorney General of the sale of real property by a religious corporation is to insure that such sale is in the best interest of the corporation and its members and that the proceeds are properly disbursed. The purpose of enacting this provision—to protect the interests of members of religious corporations by safeguarding potentially substantial proceeds from sales of property—is secular and there is no evidence to suggest that the statute was motivated by an intent to endorse or disapprove religion.

Additionally, the principal and primary effect of the notice provision neither advances nor inhibits religion. The notice provision does nothing to convey any message whatsoever that could be construed to advance or inhibit any religion or religious belief. This notice requirement does not even remotely involve any indoctrination of particular religious views by the state nor does it convey any message of state support, or inhibition of religion.

Furthermore, the notice requirement does not foster an excessive government entanglement with religion. Routine regulatory interaction, such as the notice requirement, which involves no inquiries into religious doctrine, no delegation of state power to a religious body and no detailed monitoring and close administrative contact between secular and religious bodies, does not violate the non entanglement command.

Accordingly, the provision requiring notice to the Attorney General passes constitutional muster pursuant to the *Lemon* test.

The provisions in the Religious Corporation Law requiring notice to the Attorney when a religious corporation seeks leave of Court to sell, mortgage or lease real property have no effect on, and therefore place no burden on, the members of the Archdiocese to practice their religion: either by pressuring them to commit some act forbidden by their religion or by preventing them from engaging in conduct mandated by their faith. Any inquiry by the Attorney General involves only the terms of a real estate transaction; it involves no inquiry into religious beliefs nor does it involve the regulation or prohibition of conduct undertaken for religious reasons.

The Archdiocese's claim that the Religious Corporation Law discriminates among churches presents a more difficult issue.

Pursuant to Religious Corporation Law sections 2-b and 12, certain religious corporations, which are hierarchically structured, such as the Roman Catholic Church, Protestant Episcopal Church, Ruthenian Catholic Church of the Greek rite, African Methodist Episcopal Zion Church, Presbyterian Church and United Methodist Church, are not required to give notice to the Attorney General when making an application for the sale, lease or mortgage of real property. However, the statutes also provide that before any of these exempted churches may sell, mortgage or lease real property, they must obtain approval by their top executive before submission to the Court. For example, the Roman Catholic Church must obtain the consent of the "archbishop or bishop of the diocese" (Religious Corporation Law sec. 12[3]) while the Protestant Episcopal Church must obtain the consent of the "bishop and standing committee of the diocese" (Religious Corporation Law sec. 12[2]).

In a memorandum for the Governor, dated June 8, 1981, the Attorney General explained the exemption for hierarchical churches as follows:

> "This exemption is based on the theory that there are safeguards already built into the process under section 12 of the Religious Corporation Law for hierarchical churches by requiring approval of the sale by the top executive of the hierarchical

church corporations before submission to the court." (New York State Department of Law, Memorandum for the Governor, Re: Assembly 2442, June 8, 1981).

Conversely, notice to the Attorney General was deemed necessary for those corporations not specified in Religious Corporation Law sec. 2-b in order to afford members of those corporations the same types of safeguards against abuse in the transfer of real property transactions which are afforded to the hierarchical organizations who are required to obtain specific consents to transfer property.

Pursuant to both the Free Exercise and Establishment Clauses, legislation that singles out a particular religious group for special benefits or burdens should be evaluated under a strict scrutiny test, requiring that the law be closely fitted to a compelling State interest.

Here, the State's interests in protecting members of religious corporations—by safeguarding the potentially substantial proceeds from sales of property, and ensuring that the proceeds are properly disbursed—are compelling ones (*Larson* v. *Valente*, 452 U.S. 904 (1982)). The Attorney General also argues that the statutory obligation challenged is narrowly tailored to meet its objectives. The Archdiocese claims that because it is a hierarchical church—and not exempted from giving notice to the Attorney General—the statute is not closely fitted to the government's compelling interest. It is argued that the statute does not exempt all hierarchical churches. Rather it favors specific hierarchical churches while leaving out others, such as the Archdiocese.

The proof submitted by the Archdiocese does not demonstrate as a matter of law that it is a hierarchical church—where the religious congregation is but a subordinate member of some general church organization in which there are superior ecclesiastical tribunals with a general and ultimate power of control more or less complete, in some supreme judiciary over the whole membership of that general organization. Nor has the Archdiocese demonstrated that the structure of its particular church ensures that its members will be protected from abuses in the transfer of real property which are afforded to the hierarchical organizations which are required by statute to obtain specific consents to transfer property.

Where, as here, the structure of a particular church does not assure that its members have an opportunity to review the sale of real property, the statute provides for notice to the Attorney General of the petition in order to allow the Attorney General to perform that role in a particular proceeding. As such, the *de minimus* statutory obligation of notice to the Attorney General is narrowly tailored to meet its objectives. Accordingly, it is declared that the statutory provisions requiring notice to the Attorney General are constitutional pursuant to the Free Exercise and Establishment clauses.

The Attorney General's motion for discovery is granted. The Attorney General has demonstrated "ample need" for such discovery of, among other things, the circumstances surrounding the contract modifications.

Notes

1. Does the approval procedure contemplated by the New York Religious Corporation Law resolve some of the problems associated with operational oversight of the activities of church organizations? What do you make of the court's contention that the Archdiocese had not proven its hierarchical status? Assuming it had done so, would the outcome have been different?

2. One of the most celebrated receivership cases involving a church is *People* ex rel. *Deukmejian v. Worldwide Church of God*, 127 Cal.App.3d 547, 178 Cal.Rptr. 913

(1981), in which a California court issued *ex parte* orders empowering the receiver "to take possession forthwith of all of the funds, assets and property, and all of the books and records" of the Church, College and Foundation, and enjoined the defendants and others from interfering with or obstructing the receiver or withholding from him "any of the funds, assets, properties, books or records of the Church." Though the orders were later overturned, the case itself served to bring attention to the problems lurking in the supervisory powers of attorneys general.

3. In *Surinach v. Pesquera de Busquets*, 604 F.2d 73, 75–78 (1st Cir. 1979), the United States Court of Appeals for the First Circuit found unconstitutional an investigation of operating costs of Catholic schools under a Puerto Rico statute similar to the one involved in *Word of Faith Outreach Center*. The purpose of the statute was to "defend and implement the rights of the consumer, to restrain inflationary trends; as well as the establishment and inspection of a price control over the goods and services for use and consumption." Because the gathering of information was "not viewed as an end in itself," but merely as the first step in imposing controls on what the schools could spend, the Court found that cost limits the Department might impose could interfere with duties the school believed it owed its students. Imposition of cost controls would also necessitate continuing surveillance and an impermissible degree of entanglement.

4. Similar concerns arise in the context of tax audits. In order to control Internal Revenue Service discretion, Congress enacted The Church Audit Procedures Act, 26 U.S.C. §7611 (1995). *See United States* v. *Church of Scientology of Boston, Inc.*, 739 F. Supp. 46 (D. Mass. 1990), *aff'd*, 933 F.2d 1074 (1st Cir. 1991) (holding IRS could not enforce summons without demonstrating compliance with procedural requirements). The Act is discussed in Chapter Nine §E(5). *See generally* Susan N. Gary, *Regulating the Management of Charities: Trust Law, Corporate Law, and Tax Law*, 21 U. Haw. L. Rev. 593 (1999).

G. The "Public Policy" Requirement

Closely related to the issue of state supervision, but legally distinct from it, is the requirement that nonprofit, charitable organizations operate in compliance with "public policy." Different aspects of this topic are discussed at some length in the labor context in Chapter 8 §E(2)(the religious employer) and §F(2) (the secular workplace), and in the tax context in Chapter 9 §b(5) (the common law of charities). It is equally relevant here. In the view of the common law, nonprofit, charitable organizations are to devote themselves to the public interest, and are to refrain from taking actions inconsistent with "public policy." Direct regulation via state, local, and federal civil rights laws raises similar issues. *See, e.g., Silo v. CHW Medical Foundation*, 86 Cal.App.4th 947, 103 Cal.Rptr.2d 825 (Cal. App. 2000), *review granted and opinion superceded*, 107 Cal.Rptr.2d 615, 23 P.3d 1142, (2001) (discussing the relationship between statute law and public policy and holding that a religious hospital could be held liable for religious discrimination notwithstanding the exemption in California's fair employment laws).

In a series of cases that began with the New Jersey Supreme Court's decision in *Falcone v. Middlesex County Medical Society*, 34 N.J. 582, 170 A.2d 791 (1961), the courts have consistently held that when a nonprofit or charitable organization serves as the sole provider or "gatekeeper" for important social functions, the general rule against judicial intervention in intra-associational matters should not apply. In these contexts, the organizations were deemed to be "quasi-public." *Storrs v. Lutheran Hosps. and Homes Soc'y of Am., Inc.*, 609 P.2d 24, 28 (Alaska 1980) is typical of this approach:

> Although Fairbanks Memorial Hospital is not a public hospital, we hold that it is a quasi-public hospital because it is the only hospital serving the community, the construction of the hospital was funded in significant part by state and federal grants, and over twenty-five per cent of the funds received for hospital services comes from governmental sources.

Problems can arise when the organization's internal policy is inconsistent with state policy on the same subject. This is particularly true in the case of health care providers. *See, e.g., Valley Hosp. Ass'n, Inc. v. Mat-Su Coalition for Choice*, 948 P.2d 963 (Alaska 1997) (relying on state policy favoring widespread availability of abortion as the rationale for requiring nonprofit, private hospital to make its facilities available for abortions even though the hospital board unanimously rejected the practice). When the hospital is religious in character, an already-complex set of First Amendment issues becomes nearly unmanageable. These issues are discussed at greater length in Chapters Five (free exercise and association) and Eight (Congressional efforts to protect individual and institutional "conscience"). Cf. *Boy Scouts of America v. Dale*, 530 U.S. 640 (2000), *rev'g on first amendment grounds, Dale v. BSA*, 160 N.J. 562, 734 A.2d 1196 (1999) (holding that the Boy Scouts was a place of "public accommodation" under New Jersey law and subjecting its hiring practices to state antidiscrimination laws). *See generally* William W. Bassett, *Private Religious Hospitals: Limitations Upon Autonomous Moral Choices in Reproductive Medicine*, 17 J. Contemp. Health L. & Pol'y 455 (2001) (summarizing cases and sources); Perry Dane, *The Public, the Private, and the Sacred: Variations on a Theme of Nomos and Narrative*, 8 Cardozo Stud. L. & Literature 15 (1996)(discussing the problems with the public policy rationale).

Chapter 8

Religion in the Workplace

A. Introduction

Labor and employment laws strike a balance between and among the many individual and collective interests that co-exist in the workplace. Because we know that religious beliefs and practices are pervasive influences in the lives of both individuals and communities, it is inevitable that those beliefs will affect the way in which individuals and employers conduct their private and professional lives. Beliefs concerning the place of religion in society will also affect the way in which legislators and judges view the rights and obligations of workers. The goal of this Chapter is to examine the role religion plays in workplace decision-making.

Workplaces are specialized communities, devoted to a common purpose. As a result, the nature of the work done there will be an important consideration in any analysis of the "place" that religion has, or should have, in that particular environment. The organization of this Chapter reflects that fact by differentiating between and among three workplace types: (1) those that are essentially non-religious, or "secular," in character; (2) those that are religious in character, or that view their purpose or mission in religious terms; and (3) the government. We begin with an overview of the major laws and regulations governing the workplace, and then consider the ways in which the religious, non-religious, or governmental character of the working environment affects either the content of policy, or its application.

B. The Law of Workplace Relationships

The workplace is a highly competitive, dynamic market where human creativity, intellect and labor are traded for money, goods or services. For some, workplace participation is purely a matter of trade. Such workers have labor, services, or talent to sell, and expect reasonable compensation in return. For individuals such as these, structure and fairness in the labor market assure an orderly and safe workplace, discourage over-reaching on the part of employers and unions, and otherwise assure their ability to enjoy the fruits of active workplace participation.

For an increasing number of individuals, however, work is "an integral part of our humanity and our intelligence."[1] It serves to provide many employers and employees with a source of pride, self-worth, and "specific dignity."[2] When employers and employees such as these are involved, the stakes in work-related disputes can involve far more than money alone. They affect the very identity of the persons and organizations involved.

Given the importance of workplace relationships and behavior, it is not surprising that a vast and complex web of federal, state, and local laws has arisen to regulate them. Developed over many years, labor and employment discrimination laws reflect a series of judgments concerning the balance to be struck between and among economic efficiency, the interests of capital and labor, and the rights of individuals to be judged on their work-related merits. Political and economic compromise has played, and will continue to play, a large role in that balancing process.

Given these "social facts," employer-employee relationships can be delicate even without consideration of the many issues that can arise when religion becomes a factor in employment decisions. Nevertheless, good relationships between and among employers and employees are critical to the success of any functioning enterprise. They are vitally important to the efficient functioning of the Nation's economy as well. The law has responded accordingly.

C. Terminology

For purposes of this chapter, *labor* law includes all aspects of labor-management relations, including collective bargaining rules, wage and hour provisions, and the obligations that unions owe to their members under federal and state labor codes. *Employment discrimination* law, by contrast, deals primarily with the need to guarantee to all members of our society unfettered access to the labor market, and all of the economic and social benefits that flow from active participation in it. Title VII of the Civil Rights Act of 1964, 42 U.S.C. § 2000e-2(a), for example, provides:

> It shall be an unlawful employment practice for an employer
>
> (1) to fail or refuse to hire or to discharge any individual, or otherwise to discriminate against any individual with respect to his compensation, terms, conditions, or privileges of employment, because of such individual's race, color, religion, sex, or national origin; or
>
> (2) to limit, segregate, or classify his employees or applicants for employment in any way which would deprive or tend to deprive any individual of employ-

---

1. David Meakin has written that: "Work...and not least manual work...is an integral part of our humanity and our intelligence. It dictates not only our relationship to nature, to our environment, but thereby also the working and scope of our consciousness itself, for consciousness is born of that active confrontation with nature." MAN & WORK: LITERATURE & CULTURE IN INDUSTRIAL SOCIETY 1 (1976). Albert Camus made essentially the same point: "Without work, all life goes rotten. But when work is soulless, life stifles and dies." *Id.*

2. Pope John Paul II, Encyclical Letter, *Laborem Exercens* ("On Human Work") 3 ("Man's life is built up every day from work, from work it derives its specific dignity.").

> ment opportunities or otherwise adversely affect his status as an employee, because of such individual's race, color, religion, sex, or national origin.

42 U.S.C. § 2000e-2(a)(2001). Title VII and its state law counterparts guarantee access to, and full participation in, the workplace and the benefits of employment without regard to one's religion. *See, e.g.*, Fla. Stat. § 760.10 (2001). For a good overview of the requirements of state law, see Peter M. Panken, *et al.*, "Religious Discrimination: Multi-State Survey" in *Religion in the Workplace: Respecting Religious Practices and Reconciling Conflicts with Work Requirements*, American Law Institute-American Bar Association Continuing Legal Education (November 16, 2000).

Religion does, however, play a role in defining workplace relationships. Whether it *should* do so is a difficult question, the answer to which depends, at least in part, on the character of the specific workplace at issue. For purposes of this Chapter, we will differentiate between two ways in which job-related religious issues manifest themselves: representation and accommodation.

Discrimination in hiring, promotion or conditions of employment on the basis of race, national origin, sex, and disability are *representation* issues. The inquiry in these cases is whether religion, race, or another legally irrelevant characteristic serves as a barrier to representation in the workforce.

Accommodation becomes an issue when employers learn that an employee has specific needs that must be accommodated if the employee is to preserve both job and other important interests, such as religious faith, family obligations, or in the case of some persons with disabilities, their ability to participate in the labor force at all. An employer facing an accommodation claim is required, to a point, to take affirmative steps to accommodate the otherwise legitimate needs of an employee. *See, e.g.*, Pregnancy Discrimination Act, 42 U.S.C. § 2000e(k) (2001) (prohibiting discrimination "because of or on the basis of pregnancy, child birth, or related medical conditions."); Family and Medical Leave Act, 29 U.S.C. § 2611 *et seq.* (2001) (requiring employer to provide leave for medical and family reasons); Americans with Disabilities Act, 42 U.S.C. § 12101 *et seq.* (2001); 42 U.S.C.A. § 2000e-11 (2001) (preserving the special rights and preferences of veterans under state law). In these contexts, the scope of permissible accommodation requires a careful balancing of priorities, social facts, and issues of fundamental fairness.

D. An Overview of Statutory and Constitutional Rules Prohibiting Religious Discrimination in Employment

The Nation's first law prohibiting religion-based employment discrimination is in the Constitution itself. The Religious Test Clause, U.S. Const. Art. VI, cl. 3, provides that "no religious test shall ever be required as a Qualification to any Office or public Trust under the United States." Whether targeted at classes of believers or non-believers, the imposition of a religious test or oath is one of the purest examples of intentional religious discrimination because it involves inquiry into the substance of personal religious belief and practice. *See McDaniel v. Paty*, 435 U.S. 618 (1978) (holding unconstitutional Tennessee's ban on clergy representation in the legislature), excerpted in

Chapter Ten; *Torcaso v. Watkins*, 367 U.S. 488 (1961) (holding unconstitutional a ban on the appointment of atheists), excerpted in Chapter Eleven. *See generally* Gerard V. Bradley, *The No Religious Test Clause and the Constitution of Religious Liberty: A Machine that Has Gone of Itself*, 37 Case W. Res. L. Rev. 674 (1987). The Test Clause is discussed at greater length in §G ("The Government Workplace").

Before examining other labor and employment law rules governing workplace relationships, it will be useful to consider a series of questions common to all employment cases.

1) Who is the employee or prospective employee?
2) Who is the employer or prospective employer?
3) What is the size and character of the employer?
4) Is there a labor union or other collective bargaining organization involved in the controversy?
5) What is the legal character of the relationship at issue? (employer/employee, management-labor, union-member, employer-applicant)
6) How is religion related to the conflict? (Is it the cause of an adverse employment or hiring action; a condition of employment, retention or promotion; or is it alleged to interfere with the employee's ability to perform required duties?)
7) Is there a federal statute or constitutional provision that regulates the conduct at issue?
8) Is there a state statute or constitutional provision that regulates the conduct at issue?
9) What are the elements of the plaintiff's claim under each available law? What are the elements of a valid defense or counter-claim under these laws?
10) Does the law cover private sector discrimination or is it limited to state action?
11) What exemptions, if any, exist in the law?
12) Does the plaintiff need to prove intent to discriminate in order to make a case?
13) What defenses are available to the defendant (other than attacking the facial constitutionality of the statute or the merits of the plaintiff's claim)? Does the statute provide defenses?
14) Is the law constitutional as applied to this defendant? Is this defendant exempted from the coverage of this statute by constitutional provisions?

Sensitivity to these issues is important because there are times when there will be more than one law or theory under which a claim may be prosecuted. Unless all bases are covered in the preliminary research, a client cannot be advised effectively.

The materials in this section deal only with the requirements of the major federal employment discrimination law, Title VII of the Civil Rights Act of 1964, 42 U.S.C. §§2000e, *et. seq*. The requirements of applicable state fair employment practice laws, and the application of those statutes to federal defense contractors, are issues beyond the current scope of this section. *See, e.g.*, Nebraska Rev. Stat. §48-1104 (2000); Pa. Stat. Ann. tit. 43 §955 (2001); Utah Code Ann. §34A-5-106 (2001). For a discussion of the application of those statutes to religiously affiliated educational institutions, see Thomas C. Berg, *State Religious Freedom Statutes in Private and Public Education*, 32 U.C. Davis L. Rev. 531 (1999); David L. Gregory & Charles J. Russo, *The First Amend-*

ment and the Labor Relations of Religiously-Affiliated Employers, 8 B.U. Pub. Int. L.J. 449 (1999).

1. Constitutional Rules Prohibiting Workplace Discrimination

Constitutional claims, like their statutory counterparts, can take two forms: *jurisdictional* and *operational.* Jurisdictional claims are generally defensive because they are challenges to the power of the government to regulate the activities or policies under attack. Operational claims assume the existence of the power to regulate, and deal specifically with the legality of specific workplace behaviors.

There are three occasions in which the Constitution itself will serve as the basis for workplace-related claims. The first is when the government acts in its capacity as an employer. The second is when it serves as a provider of employment-related social services, such as unemployment benefits, job placement and training, or programs designed to foster the creation and financing of small businesses. The third is when it serves as regulator of workplace relationships in the private sector. Constitutionally-based jurisdictional claims arise only when the government seeks to regulate private workplace relationships. Operational claims can arise in any setting where jurisdiction exists.

Where the government is the employer, the first recourse will generally be to applicable statutes governing federal, state or local government employees and union activities. Where those rules do not provide adequate coverage or relief, constitutional rules governing state and federal action should also be consulted.

The Religion Clause of the First Amendment can be used to bring both jurisdictional and operational claims. In an appropriate case, so too can the No Religious Test Clause of Article VI. As a result, the first critical step is to determine the character of the employer (private or public) and the nature of the behavior thought to be questionable. The incorporated Free Exercise Clause, for example, operates as a generalized limit on the discretion of federal, state, and local governments. In the government workplace or job-related social service setting, it operates in a manner similar to the nondiscrimination and accommodation provisions of Title VII, discussed below. In the private sector, it does not apply at all.

The most common labor relations complaints arising under the Free Exercise Clause are filed by employees seeking accommodation of their religious needs in a government workplace or social welfare program, such as unemployment compensation. *See, e.g., Employment Div. v. Smith,* 494 U.S. 872 (1991) (unemployment compensation), excerpted in Chapter Five; *Hobbie v. Unemployment Appeals Comm'n of Fla.,* 480 U.S. 136 (1987). Such cases can, however, contain elements of religious discrimination as well. *See Sherbert v. Verner,* 374 U.S. 398 (1963)(preference for Sunday observers), excerpted in Chapter Five.

a) The Government Workplace

When the federal government is the employer, the No Religious Test Clause, the First and Fifth Amendments, and Executive Order 11478 (mandating equal opportunity in executive agencies) are sources of protection which exist independently of, and in addition to, the rights guaranteed by Title VII. *See* Title VII of the Civil Rights Act of 1964, 42 U.S.C. §2000e-16(e) (2001); Civil Rights Act of 1991 §117, P.L. 102-166, 105 Stat.

1071 (102nd Cong. 1st Sess.). *See also*, *Davis v. Passman*, 442 U.S. 228 (1979) (employment discrimination suit based directly on the Constitution). When the employer is a state or local government, the First and Fourteenth Amendments and any relevant provisions of state statutory and constitutional law, should be considered sources along with federal and state statutes governing labor and employment discrimination law. *See, e.g.*, 42 U.S.C. §§ 1983, 1985(3). *See* § G, *infra*.

b) The Private Workplace

When government acts in its capacity as regulator of the private workplace, laws and regulations affect the interests of both employers and employees. When the law was written, the legislature struck a series of balances between and among legitimate interests that are sometimes at odds. As a result, the practical result of much First Amendment litigation over workplace rules will be to alter balances struck, in the first instance, by the legislature or by the parties to collective bargaining agreements. Without careful consideration of the justifications for both the initial balance, and the proposed alternative, the possible outcomes will often appear starkly at odds. *See generally* Harlan Loeb & David Rosenberg, *Fundamental Rights in Conflict: The Price of a Maturing Democracy*, 77 N.D.L. Rev. 27 (2001); Note, *Religious Discrimination and the Title VII Exemption for Religious Organizations: A Basic Values Analysis for the Proper Allocation of Conflicting Rights*, 60 S. Cal. L. Rev. 1375 (1987).

Consider, for example, the case of a church or religiously-affiliated private school. Without a series of exemptions from the general rule prohibiting discrimination on the basis of religion, it may be unable to maintain its identifiably religious character. If the statute itself grants an exemption for such organizations, the statute is subject to the charge that it violates either the Establishment Clause or the Equal Protection Clause, or both, because it favors religious over non-religious employee activity. Without such an exemption, however, the general statute is subject to attack under both the Free Exercise and Establishment Clauses because it seeks to regulate the internal demographics of churches and religious institutions.

Every attempt to provide special accommodation for religious beliefs and practices involves the same questions. The Title VII exemption for religious employers, 42 U.S.C. § 2000e-1(a) (2001), for example, indicates that Congress did not intend to regulate the religious demographics of the religious workplace. The statute accomplishes this goal by creating a "religion-specific" exemption to what would otherwise be a neutral law of general applicability. This deviation from strict or "formal" neutrality is equally evident when the judiciary mandates an accommodation under the rubric of the Religion Clause. *See generally* Douglas Laycock, *Formal, Substantive and Disaggregated Neutrality Toward Religion*, 39 DePaul L. Rev. 993–1018 (1990). When the National Labor Relations Board (NLRB) attempted to assert regulatory jurisdiction over religious secondary schools under the National Labor Relations Act (NLRA), the Supreme Court rejected the effort because of concerns arising under the Establishment and Free Exercise Clauses. Even though most such schools are employers who would otherwise be subject to the Board's jurisdiction, the Supreme Court's refusal to allow the exercise of that jurisdiction, *National Labor Relations Board v. Catholic Bishop of Chicago*, 440 U.S. 490 (1979), has the intended effect of creating a "religious schools" exemption to a statute which is otherwise silent on the topic. State versions of the Religious Freedom Restoration Act, 42 U.S.C. § 2000bb, *et seq.* (1996), which was held unconstitutional in *City of Boerne v. Flores*, 521 U.S. 507 (1997), also requires accommodation of religious freedom claims in settings in which the Free Exercise Clause of the state or federal constitution would not, but leaves it to the courts to determine how, and when, to balance competing secular and religious claims. *See, e.g.*, Ill. Stat., ch. 775 §§35/1, et *seq.* (2001).

c) The Supreme Court on Religious Liberty in the Workplace

Disputes over the "proper" role of religion in the workplace date to the earliest days of the Massachusetts Bay Colony, when Roger Williams was imprisoned and later expelled for preaching against legal enforcement of the Sabbath. *See* Chapter Two, § 1. *See also* William G. Torpey, JUDICIAL DOCTRINES OF RELIGIOUS RIGHTS IN AMERICA (1948); AMERICAN STATE PAPERS AND RELATED DOCUMENTS ON FREEDOM IN RELIGION 17–92 (William A. Blakely ed. 1949). Although the specific issues presented have changed due to the increasing religious and cultural diversity of the United States, the underlying issue remains the same: Given the importance of religion in the lives of individuals and communities, what balance, if any, should the Supreme Court permit the government strike between the legitimate needs of the labor market and legitimate concerns for religious liberty?

Braunfeld v. Brown

366 U.S. 599 (1961)

Mr. Chief Justice WARREN announced the judgment of the Court and an opinion in which Mr. Justice BLACK, Mr. Justice CLARK, and Mr. Justice WHITTAKER concur.

This case concerns the constitutional validity of the application to appellants of the Pennsylvania criminal statute, enacted in 1959, which proscribes the Sunday retail sale of certain enumerated commodities. Among the questions presented are whether the statute is a law respecting an establishment of religion and whether the statute violates equal protection. Since both of these questions, in reference to this very statute, have already been answered in the negative, *Two Guys from Harrison-Allentown, Inc., v. McGinley*, and since appellants present nothing new regarding them, they need not be considered here. Thus, the only question for consideration is whether the statute interferes with the free exercise of appellants' religion.

Appellants are merchants in Philadelphia who engage in the retail sale of clothing and home furnishings within the proscription of the statute in issue. Each of the appellants is a member of the Orthodox Jewish faith, which requires the closing of their places of business and a total abstention from all manner of work from nightfall each Friday until nightfall each Saturday.

Appellants contend that the enforcement against them of the Pennsylvania statute will prohibit the free exercise of their religion because, due to the statute's compulsion to close on Sunday, appellants will suffer substantial economic loss, to the benefit of their non-Sabbatarian competitors, if appellants also continue their Sabbath observance by closing their businesses on Saturday; that this result will either compel appellants to give up their Sabbath observance, a basic tenet of the Orthodox Jewish faith, or will put appellants at a serious economic disadvantage if they continue to adhere to their Sabbath.

We also took cognizance, in *McGowan*, of the evolution of Sunday Closing Laws from wholly religious sanctions to legislation concerned with the establishment of a day of community tranquillity, respite and recreation, a day when the atmosphere is one of calm and relaxation rather than one of commercialism, as it is during the other six days of the week. We reviewed the still growing state preoccupation with improving the health, safety, morals and general well-being of our citizens.

Concededly, appellants and all other persons who wish to work on Sunday will be burdened economically by the State's day of rest mandate; and appellants point out that their religion requires them to refrain from work on Saturday as well. Our inquiry then is whether, in these circumstances, the First and Fourteenth Amendments forbid application of the Sunday Closing Law to Appellants.

Certain aspects of religious exercise cannot, in any way, be restricted or burdened by either federal or state legislation. Compulsion by law of the acceptance of any creed or the practice of any form of worship is strictly forbidden. But this is not the case at bar; the statute before us does not make criminal the holding of any religious belief or opinion, nor does it force anyone to embrace any religious belief or to say or believe anything in conflict with his religious tenets.

However, the freedom to act, even when the action is in accord with one's religious convictions, is not totally free from legislative restrictions.

[I]n *Reynolds*, this Court upheld the polygamy conviction of a member of the Mormon faith despite the fact that an accepted doctrine of his church then imposed upon its male members the *duty* to practice polygamy. And, in *Prince v. Massachusetts*, this Court upheld a statute making it a crime for a girl under eighteen years of age to sell any newspapers, periodicals or merchandise in public places despite the fact that a child of the Jehovah's Witnesses faith believed that it was her religious *duty* to perform this work.

It is to be noted that, in the two cases just mentioned, the religious practices themselves conflicted with the public interest. In such cases, to make accommodation between the religious action and an exercise of state authority is a particularly delicate task, because resolution in favor of the State results in the choice to the individual of either abandoning his religious principle or facing criminal prosecution.

But, again, this is not the case before us because the statute at bar does not make unlawful any religious practices of appellants; the Sunday law simply regulates a secular activity and, as applied to appellants, operates so as to make the practice of their religious beliefs more expensive. Furthermore, the law's effect does not inconvenience all members of the Orthodox Jewish faith but only those who believe it necessary to work on Sunday. And even these are not faced with as serious a choice as forsaking their religious practices or subjecting themselves to criminal prosecution. Fully recognizing that the alternatives open to appellants and other similarly situated—retaining their present occupations and incurring economic disadvantage or engaging in some other commercial activity which does not call for either Saturday or Sunday labor—may well result in some financial sacrifice in order to observe their religious beliefs, still the option is wholly different than when the legislation attempts to make a religious practice itself unlawful.

To strike down, without the most critical scrutiny, legislation which imposes only an indirect burden on the exercise of religion, *i.e.*, legislation which does not make unlawful the religious practice itself, would radically restrict the operating latitude of the legislature. Statutes which tax income and limit the amount which may be deducted for religious contributions impose an indirect economic burden on the observance of the religion of the citizen whose religion requires him to donate a greater amount to his church; statutes which require the courts to be closed on Saturday and Sunday impose a similar indirect burden on the observance of the religion of the trial lawyer whose religion requires him to rest on a weekday. The list of legislation of this nature is nearly limitless.

Of course, to hold unassailable all legislation regulating conduct which imposes solely an indirect burden on the observance of religion would be a gross oversimplification. If the purpose or effect of a law is to impede the observance of one or all religions or is to discriminate invidiously between religions, that law is constitutionally invalid even though the burden may be characterized as being only indirect. But if the State regulates conduct by enacting a general law within its power, the purpose and effect of which is to advance the State's secular goals, the statute is valid despite its indirect burden on religious observance unless the State may accomplish its purpose by means which do not impose such a burden.

As pointed out in *McGowan*, we cannot find a State without power to provide a weekly respite from all labor and, at the same time, to set one day of the week apart from the others as a day of rest, repose, recreation and tranquillity.

However, appellants advance yet another means at the State's disposal which they would find unobjectionable. They contend that the State should cut an exception from the Sunday labor proscription for those people who, because of religious conviction, observe a day of rest other than Sunday. By such regulation, appellants contend, the economic disadvantages imposed by the present system would be removed and the State's interest in having all people rest one day would be satisfied.

A number of States provide such an exemption, and this may well be the wiser solution to the problem. But our concern is not with the wisdom of legislation but with its constitutional limitation. Thus, reason and experience teach that to permit the exemption might well undermine the State's goal of providing a day that, as best possible, eliminates the atmosphere of commercial noise and activity. Although not dispositive of the issue, enforcement problems would be more difficult since there would be two or more days to police rather than one and it would be more difficult to observe whether violations were occurring.

Additional problems might also be presented by a regulation of this sort. To allow only people who rest on a day other than Sunday to keep their businesses open on that day might well provide these people with an economic advantage over their competitors who must remain closed on that day; this might cause the Sunday-observers to complain that their religions are being discriminated against. With this competitive advantage existing, there could well be the temptation for some, in order to keep their businesses open on Sunday, to assert that they have religious convictions which compel them to close their businesses on what had formerly been their least profitable day. This might make necessary a state-conducted inquiry into the sincerity of the individual's religious beliefs, a practice which a State might believe would itself run afoul of the spirit of constitutionally protected religious guarantees. Finally, in order to keep the disruption of the day at a minimum, exempted employers would probably have to hire employees who themselves qualified for the exemption because of their own religious beliefs, a practice which a State might feel to be opposed to its general policy prohibiting religious discrimination in hiring. For all of these reasons, we cannot say that the Pennsylvania statute before us is invalid, either on its face or as applied.

Mr. Justice BRENNAN, concurring and dissenting.

I agree with The Chief Justice that there is no merit in appellants' establishment and equal-protection claims. I dissent, however, as to the claim that Pennsylvania has prohibited the free exercise of appellants' religion.

The Court has demonstrated the public need for a weekly surcease from worldly labor, and set forth the considerations of convenience which have led the Commonwealth of Pennsylvania to fix Sunday as the time for that respite. I would approach this case differently, from the point of view of the individuals whose liberty is—concededly—curtailed by these enactments. For the values of the First Amendment, as embodied in the Fourteenth, look primarily towards the preservation of personal liberty, rather than towards the fulfillment of collective goals.

[R]eligious freedom—the freedom to believe and to practice strange and, it may be, foreign creeds—has classically been one of the highest values of our society. Even the most concentrated and fully articulated attack on this high standard has seemingly admitted its validity in principle, while deploring some incidental phraseology. The honored place of religious freedom in our constitutional hierarchy, suggested long ago by the argument of counsel in *Permoli*, and foreshadowed by a prescient footnote in *United States v. Carolene Products Co.*, 304 U.S. 144, 152, n. 4 (1938), must now be taken to be settled. Or at least so it appeared until today. For in this case the Court seems to say, without so much as a deferential nod towards that high place which we have accorded religious freedom in the past, that any substantial state interest will justify encroachments on religious practice, at least if those encroachments are cloaked in the guise of some nonreligious public purpose.

Admittedly, these laws do not compel overt affirmation of a repugnant belief, as in *Barnette*, nor do they prohibit outright any of appellants' religious practices, as did the federal law upheld in *Reynolds*, cited by the Court. That is, the laws do not say that appellants must work on Saturday. But their effect is that appellants may not simultaneously practice their religion and their trade, without being hampered by a substantial competitive disadvantage. Their effect is that no one may at one and the same time be an Orthodox Jew and compete effectively with his Sunday-observing fellow tradesmen. This clog upon the exercise of religion, this state-imposed burden on Orthodox Judaism, has exactly the same economic effect as a tax levied upon the sale of religious literature. And yet, such a tax, when applied in the form of an exercise or license fee, was held invalid in *Follett*. All this the Court, as I read its opinion, concedes.

What, then, is the compelling state interest which impels the Commonwealth of Pennsylvania to impede appellants' freedom of worship? What overbalancing need is so weighty in the constitutional scale that it justifies this substantial, though indirect, limitation of appellants' freedom? It is not the desire to stamp out a practice deeply abhorred by society, such as polygamy, as in *Reynolds*, for the custom of resting one day a week is universally honored, as the Court has amply shown. Nor is it the State's traditional protection of children, as in *Prince*, for appellants are reasoning and fully autonomous adults. It is not even the interest in seeing that everyone rests one day a week, for appellants' religion requires that they take such a rest. It is mere convenience of having everyone rest on the same day. It is to defend this interest that the Court holds that a State need not follow the alternative route of granting an exemption for those who in good faith observe a day of rest other than Sunday.

In fine, the Court, in my view, has exalted administrative convenience to a constitutional level high enough to justify making one religion economically disadvantageous. The Court would justify this result on the ground that the effect on religion, though substantial, is indirect. The Court forgets, I think, a warning uttered during the congressional discussion of the First Amendment itself: "...the rights of conscience are, in their nature, of peculiar delicacy, and will little bear the gentlest touch of governmental hand...."

Mr. Justice STEWART, dissenting.

I agree with substantially all that Mr. Justice Brennan has written. Pennsylvania has passed a law which compels an Orthodox Jew to choose between his religious faith and his economic survival. That is a cruel choice. It is a choice which I think no State can constitutionally demand. For me this is not something that can be swept under the rug and forgotten in the interest of enforced Sunday togetherness. I think the impact of this law upon these appellants grossly violates their constitutional right to the free exercise of their religion.

Notes

1. *Braunfeld* was one of four cases concerning the constitutionality of Sunday closing laws decided on the same day. In addition to *Braunfeld*, the Court decided *McGowan v. Maryland*, 366 U.S. 420 (1961), *Two Guys from Harrison-Allentown, Inc. v. McGinley*, 366 U.S. 582 (1961), and *Gallagher v. Crown Kosher Super Market, Inc.*, 366 U.S. 617 (1961). *McGowan* held constitutional against Equal Protection, Due Process and Establishment Clause challenges a Maryland statute prohibiting the retail sale of most, but not all, goods on Sundays. Part of the justification for the Court's decision in *McGowan* was that shortly after Virginia's "Bill for Establishing Religious Freedom" was passed in 1785, James Madison presented to the Virginia legislature "A Bill for Punishing... Sabbath Breakers," which became law in 1786 and remained in force when the First Amendment was ratified. *McGowan*, 366 U.S. at 438–39. Justice Frankfurter wrote an opinion concurring in *McGowan, Two Guys* and *Gallagher*, but dissenting in *Braunfeld*, which he concluded should be remanded. Including two Appendices his opinion totaled more than 100 pages! *Two Guys* upheld a Pennsylvania statute challenged on the same grounds as the Maryland statute in *McGowan*. *Gallagher* upheld a Massachusetts Sunday Closing Law challenged on Equal Protection, Establishment Clause and Free Exercise Clause grounds.

2. Although the Court did not rely on precedent to justify its decision to hold Sunday laws constitutional, recall from Chapters Three and Four the efforts in the nineteenth century challenging Sunday-closing laws. In those early cases, the courts concluded, as they did in *Braunfeld*, that the selection of Sunday as a mandatory day of rest was an exercise of the state's police power, designed to effectuate essentially secular goals. That the day chosen just happened to coincide with the Christian Sabbath was deemed not controlling.

3. Since the Court decided *Braunfeld* most states have relaxed or abolished their Sunday closing laws. Does this suggest that the justification the Supreme Court found for these statutes—the designation of a weekly day of rest—was not the actual justification? How, if at all, should a state seek to accommodate the needs of workers for time to participate in religious observances?

Estate of Thornton v. Caldor, Inc.

472 U.S. 703 (1985)

Chief Justice BURGER delivered the opinion of the Court.

We granted *certiorari* to decide whether a state statute that provides employees with the absolute right not to work on their chosen Sabbath violates the Establishment Clause of the First Amendment.

In early 1975, petitioner's decedent Donald E. Thornton began working for respondent Caldor, Inc., a chain of New England retail stores; he managed the men's and boys' clothing department in respondent's Waterbury, Connecticut store.

In 1977, following the state legislature's revision of the Sunday-closing laws, respondent opened its Connecticut stores for Sunday business. In order to handle the expanded store hours, respondent required its managerial employees to work every third or fourth Sunday. Thornton, a Presbyterian who observed Sunday as his Sabbath, initially complied with respondent's demand and worked a total of 31 Sundays in 1977 and 1978. In October 1978, Thornton was transferred to a management position in respondent's Torrington store, he continued to work on Sundays during the first part of 1979. In November 1979, however, Thornton informed respondent that he would no longer work on Sundays because he observed that day as his Sabbath; he invoked the protection of Conn. Gen. Stat., §53-303e(b) (1985), which provides:

> No person who states that a particular day of the week is observed as his Sabbath may be required by his employer to work on such day. An employee's refusal to work on his Sabbath shall not constitute grounds for his dismissal.

Thornton rejected respondent's offer either to transfer him to a management job in a Massachusetts store that was closed on Sundays, or to transfer him to a nonsupervisory position in the Torrington store at a lower salary. In March 1980, respondent transferred Thornton to a clerical position in the Torrington store; Thornton resigned two days later and filed a grievance with the State Board of Mediation and Arbitration alleging that he was discharged from his manager's position in violation of Conn. Gen. Stat. §53-303e(b).

After holding an evidentiary hearing the Board evaluated the sincerity of Thornton's claim and concluded it was based on a sincere religious conviction; it issued a formal decision sustaining Thornton's grievance. The Board framed the statutory issue as follows, "[i]f a discharge for refusal to work Sunday hours occurred and Sunday was the Grievant's Sabbath...," §53-303e(b) would be violated; the Board held that respondent had violated the statute by "discharg[ing] Mr. Thornton as a management employee for refusing to work...[on] Thornton's...Sabbath." The Board ordered respondent to reinstate Thornton with backpay and compensation for lost fringe benefits. The Superior Court, in affirming that ruling, concluded that the statute did not offend the Establishment Clause.

The Supreme Court of Connecticut reversed, holding the statute did not have a "clear secular purpose." By authorizing each employee to designate his own Sabbath as a day off, the statute evinced the "unmistakable purpose...[of] allow[ing] those persons who wish to worship on a particular day the freedom to do so." The court then held that the "primary effect" of the statute was to advance religion because the statute "confers its 'benefit' on an explicitly religious basis. Only those employees who designate a Sabbath are entitled not to work on that particular day, and may not be penalized for so doing." The court noted that the statute required the State Mediation Board to decide which religious activities may be characterized as an "observance of Sabbath" in order to assess employees' sincerity, and concluded that this type of inquiry is "exactly the type of 'comprehensive, discriminating and continuing state surveillance'...which creates excessive governmental entanglements between church and state."

We affirm.

Under the Religion Clauses, government must guard against activity that impinges on religious freedom, and must take pains not to compel people to act in the name of any religion. In setting the appropriate boundaries in Establishment Clause cases, the Court has frequently relied on our holding in *Lemon* for guidance, and we do so here.

The Connecticut statute challenged here guarantees every employee, who "states that a particular day of the week is observed as his Sabbath," the right not to work on his chosen day. Conn. Gen. Stat. §53-303e(b) (1985). The State has thus decreed that those who observe a Sabbath any day of the week as a matter of religious conviction must be relieved of the duty to work on that day, no matter what burden or inconvenience this imposes on the employer or fellow workers. The statute arms Sabbath observers with an absolute and unqualified right not to work on whatever day they designate as their Sabbath.

In essence, the Connecticut statute imposes on employers and employees an absolute duty to conform their business practices to the particular religious practices of the employee by enforcing observance of the Sabbath the employee unilaterally designates. The State thus commands that Sabbath religious concerns automatically control over all secular interests at the workplace; the statute takes no account of the convenience or interests of the employer or those of other employees who do not observe a Sabbath. The employer and others must adjust their affairs to the command of the State whenever the statute is invoked by an employee.

There is no exception under the statute for special circumstances, such as the Friday Sabbath observer employed in an occupation with a Monday through Friday schedule—a school teacher, for example; the statute provides for no special consideration if a high percentage of an employer's work force asserts rights to the same Sabbath. Moreover, there is no exception when honoring the dictates of Sabbath observers would cause the employer substantial economic burdens or when the employer's compliance would require the imposition of significant burdens on the employees required to work in place of the Sabbath observers. Finally, the statute allows for no consideration as to whether the employer has made reasonable accommodation proposals.

This unyielding weighting in favor of Sabbath observers over all other interests contravenes a fundamental principle of the Religion Clauses, so well articulated by Judge Learned Hand:

> "The First Amendment... gives no one the right to insist that in pursuit of their own interests others must conform their conduct to his own religious necessities." *Otten v. Baltimore & Ohio R. Co.*, 205 F.2d 58, 61 (CA2 1953).

As such, the statute goes beyond having an incidental or remote effect of advancing religion. The statute has a primary effect that impermissibly advances a particular religious practice.

We hold that the Connecticut statute, which provides Sabbath observers with an absolute and unqualified right not to work on their Sabbath, violates the Establishment Clause of the First Amendment. Accordingly, the judgment of the Supreme Court of Connecticut is

Affirmed.

Justice O'CONNOR, with whom Justice MARSHALL joins, concurring.

The Court applies the test enunciated in *Lemon*, and concludes that Conn. Gen. Stat. §53-303e(b) (1985) has a primary effect that impermissibly advances religion. I agree, and I join the Court's opinion and judgment. In my view, the Connecticut Sabbath law has an impermissible effect because it conveys a message of endorsement of the Sabbath observance.

All employees, regardless of their religious orientation, would value the benefit which the statute bestows on Sabbath observers—the right to select the day of the week in which to refrain from labor. Yet Connecticut requires private employers to confer this valued and desirable benefit only on those employees who adhere to a particular religious belief. The statute singles out Sabbath observers for special and, as the Court concludes, absolute protection without according similar accommodation to ethical and religious beliefs and practices of other private employees. There can be little doubt that an objective observer or the public at large would perceive this statutory scheme precisely as the Court does today. The message conveyed is one of endorsement of a particular religious belief, to the detriment of those who do not share it. As such, the Connecticut statute has the effect of advancing religion, and cannot withstand Establishment Clause scrutiny.

I do not read the Court's opinion as suggesting that the religious accommodation provisions of Title VII of the Civil Rights Act of 1964 are similarly invalid. These provisions preclude employment discrimination based on a person's religion and require private employers to reasonably accommodate the religious practices of employees unless to do so would cause undue hardship to the employer's business. 42 U.S.C. §§ 2000e(j) and 2000e-2(a)(1). Like the Connecticut Sabbath law, Title VII attempts to lift a burden on religious practice that is imposed by *private* employers, and hence it is not the sort of accommodation statute specifically contemplated by the Free Exercise Clause. The provisions of Title VII must therefore manifest a valid secular purpose and effect to be valid under the Establishment Clause. In my view, a statute outlawing employment discrimination based on race, color, religion, sex, or national origin has the valid secular purpose of assuring employment opportunity to all groups in our pluralistic society. Since Title VII calls for reasonable rather than absolute accommodation and extends that requirement to all religious beliefs and practices rather than protecting only the Sabbath observance, I believe an objective observer would perceive it as an anti-discrimination law rather than an endorsement of religion or a particular religious practice.

Justice REHNQUIST dissents.

Note

There are few religious needs more "concrete" than those that relate to Sabbath and other mandatory religious holiday observances. The history of the legislation involved in *Caldor, Inc.* reflects the manner in which the demographics of a changing society affect the courts' judgments concerning the nature and purpose of a statute.

The controversy in *Caldor, Inc.* is deeply rooted in the historical connection of Blue Laws to the *de jure* religious establishments that lasted into 1830s, and the *de facto* religious establishments that lasted well into the 1960s. The Court's holding that mandatory Sunday closing laws did not violate the Establishment Clause, *McGowan v. Maryland*, 366 U.S. 420 (1961), reflects the Court's deference to majoritarian concerns. Its decision in *Braunfeld v. Brown*, excerpted above, reflects similar deference, notwithstanding the differential impact such laws have on non-Sunday observers.

The States, however, were generally sensitive to minority concerns, and tried on a number of occasions to provide legislative accommodations that reflected both the character of the times, and the needs of the community. The Connecticut experience is a case in point.

After a state court held in 1976 that the existing laws were unconstitutionally vague, *State v. Anonymous*, 33 Conn. Supp. 55, 364 A.2d 244 (Com.Pl. 1976), the Connecticut legislature modified the state's Sunday-closing laws to permit certain classes of businesses to remain open. Conn. Gen. Stat. § 53-302a (1985). At the same time, a new provision that prohibited employment of more than six days in any calendar week and guaranteed employees the right not to work on the Sabbath of their religious faith was added to the statute. Soon after it was revised, the part of the law that required businesses other than those exempted to close on Sunday was once again declared unconstitutional. *State v. Anonymous*, 33 Conn. Supp. 141, 366 A.2d 200 (1976). The court did not consider the validity of the other provisions. In 1978, the state legislature enacted yet another Sunday-closing law, but the Supreme Court of Connecticut declared it unconstitutional. The Connecticut court accepted the proposition that a Sunday-Closing Law could be defended on "uniform day of rest" grounds, but held that the increasing number and character of the transactions and businesses exempted rendered the statute irrational under both the Due Process and Equal Protection Clauses of the United States and Connecticut Constitutions. *See Caldor's Inc. v. Bedding Barn, Inc.*, 177 Conn. 304, 417 A.2d 343 (1979). *See also* Conn. Const., art. I §§1, 8, 20.

Once the requirement that businesses close on Sunday was eliminated, the provisions that required accommodation of minority religious practice became the primary source of state law protection for employee religious practices requiring time off from work. The State legislatures were left in a quandary. To the extent that they felt any need to create a legislative accommodation for the religious needs of workers, there were only a few plausible options, which are summarized in Chart 8-1 on page 702. Which of these options do you feel is the most "legitimate"? Why?

Does the Court's opinion in *Caldor, Inc.* suggest that neither the government nor a secular employer may utilize religion as a legitimate basis for employment decisions? Does it hold that that secular concerns must *always* be given equal weight in the balance to be struck between religious and secular concerns?

How useful is the distinction drawn in *Caldor* between the "primary" and "indirect" effects of the law? Wasn't the *intent* of the statute to accommodate religious exercise? Isn't that also the "primary effect" when viewed from the perspective of the "three-pronged test" developed in *Lemon v Kurtzman*? Is this what makes the law unconstitutional? Can it be argued that the intent of the statute was also to create an orderly labor market?

In standard equal protection analysis, it is the *intent* of the statute, rather than its "effect," which controls the analysis. *Washington v. Davis*, 426 U.S. 229 (1976). In *Employment Div. v. Smith*, excerpted in Chapter Five, §B, the Supreme Court relied on *Washington v. Davis* when it held that disparate impact on religious minorities will not, standing alone, state a claim under the Free Exercise Clause. *See Church of Lukumi Babalu Aye, Inc. v. City of Hialeah*, 508 U.S. 520 (1993) (intentional discrimination invalid under Free Exercise Clause). Does this mean that any time a statute intentionally discriminates in favor of religious believers or adherents, it is unconstitutional? *Cf. Texas Monthly v. Bullock*, 489 U.S. 1 (1989), excerpted in Chapter Nine §E (holding unconstitutional religious tax exemption as discriminatory because it was not *necessary* to accommodate religious belief or practice). Would the same analysis hold true when discrimination against religion is mandated by judicial interpretation of the Establishment Clause? *See generally Good News Club v. Milford Central School*, 533 U.S. 98, 121 S.Ct. 2093 (2001) (holding that exclusion of religious children's club from meeting after hours on school property is unconstitutional viewpoint discrimination); *Capitol Square Review and Advisory Board v. Pinette*, 515 U.S. 753 (1995) (holding unconstitutional ban on display of Latin cross in public forum); *Rosenberger v. The Rector & Visitors of the University of Virginia*, 515 U.S. 819 (1995) (holding unconstitutional university ban on funding a student newspaper with religious perspective).

Does Justice O'Connor's "endorsement analysis" provide a useful alternative means of analyzing religious accommodation cases? Her opinion suggests that the Title VII's "reasonable accommodation" standard, discussed below, passes constitutional muster, but that an "absolute accommodation" standard would not. What is the difference between the two? If, for example, an *employer* were to decide, in all cases, to prefer religious over secular reasons, would it be guilty of discrimination under the statute? Should it be?

What makes an accommodation "reasonable" under either Title VII or the Constitution? Does a judge's determination that an accommodation is (or is not) "reasonable" also determine whether its "primary effect" is impermissibly to advance religion? *See* § F(4), *infra* (discussing "reasonable accommodation.")

2. Title VII of the Civil Rights Act of 1964: Equal Employment Opportunity

Title VII of the Civil Rights Act of 1964, 42 U.S.C. § 2000e *et seq.*, is the principal federal statute protecting employees, applicants, and trainees from religious discrimination in the workplace. It forbids disparate treatment, retaliatory actions, hostile work environments, and unwillingness to make reasonable accommodations for religious practice. It applies to employers with fifteen or more employees who operate a business affecting interstate commerce. All of the States, and many local governments, have enacted statutes substantially similar to Title VII.

For purposes of this provision, Congress defines the concept of "religion" broadly:

> The term "religion" includes all aspects of religious observance and practice, as well as belief, unless an employer demonstrates that he is unable to reasonably accommodate to an employee's or prospective employee's religious observance or practice without undue hardship on the conduct of the employee's business.

42 U.S.C. § 2000. This definition prohibits two forms of employment discrimination on the basis of religion:

(1) that which is based on the identity or type of religious belief held or practiced by the employee ("representation"); and

(2) failure to accommodate religious practices where it is possible to do so without "undue hardship" to the employer's business ("accommodation").

A plaintiff does not have to hold traditional or conventional religious beliefs or belong to an organized religious sect in order to be protected under Title VII, as long as the asserted beliefs qualify as "religious" and are sincerely held. *See* Chapter Thirteen (discussing the definition of "religion").

a) Representation Cases

Religious "representation" cases are difficult to find among the reported federal cases. The reasons for the lack of reported cases are not clear, but it is fair to assume that *overt* religious discrimination in the secular and government workplaces occurs, but is not the subject of much reported litigation.

The situation in the religious workplace is more complex. Religious organizations are entitled to discriminate on the basis of religion as a means of preserving their identity and mission, but the scope of their right to do so remains a hotly contested issue in the courts and in academic commentary. *See, e.g.*, *Hall v. Baptist Memorial Health Care*

Corp., 215 F.3d 618 (6th Cir. 2000) (a religiously affiliated health care organization whose purposes included "hospital and health care and education... in line with the traditional and ongoing mission of the Baptist churches" was entitled to claim the Title VII exemption). Defendants can, for example, argue that religion is a *bona fide* occupational qualification (BFOQ), or that employee conduct inconsistent with the religious standards set by the sponsoring religious organization is a legitimate basis for adverse job action.

Covert discrimination on the basis of religion, however, is extremely difficult to measure, and difficult to prove. The burden of proving such discrimination thus falls on the individual complaining of disparate treatment. *See, e.g., Abramson v. William Paterson College of New Jersey*, 260 F.3d 265 (3rd Cir. 2001) (holding that the evidence established discrimination in retention against Jewish faculty member); *Henegar v. Sears, Roebuck and Co.*, 965 F.Supp. 833 (N.D.W.Va. 1997) (discussing various types of claims alleging religious discrimination). The government does not keep detailed statistics on the religious demographics of the nation, and E.E.O.C. Guidelines do not permit employers to inquire about religious beliefs for statistical purposes. *See Blum v. Gulf Oil Corp.*, 597 F.2d 396, 398 (5th Cir. 1979) (defendant denies during discovery that it kept records reflecting religious and sexual preferences of employees); *Equal Employment Opportunity Comm'n v. United States Fidelity and Guaranty Co.*, 14 E.P.D. ¶7528 (D. Md. 1977) (employer defended against subpoena seeking records on religious demographics of the work force by stating that it did not keep such information). *See also* Executive Office of the President, Office of Management and Budget (OMB), Office of Information and Regulatory Affairs, *Interim Notice of Review and Possible Revision of OMB's Statistical Policy Directive No. 15, Race and Ethnic Standards for Federal Statistics and Administrative Reporting: Summary and Analysis of Public Comments and Brief Discussion of Research Agenda*, 60 Fed. Reg. 44674 (1995) (Monday, August 28, 1995) (discussing the legal, social and economic implications of keeping detailed information on the racial, gender, age, religious, and ethnic demographics of the workplace, discussing the need for the demographic information to be collected in the census, and providing a critique of current practice) [hereafter *OMB Notice on Race and Ethic Standards*]; United States Office of Federal Contract Compliance Regulations, 41 C.F.R. § 60-1.-7 (adopting E.E.O.C. categories).

Workplace demographics are important in Title VII enforcement litigation. Though statistics alone will not prove a Title VII violation, 42 U.S.C. § 2000e-2(j), statistical proof is relevant to making a *prima facie* case that the employer utilized improper criteria for the job action in question. *McDonnell Douglas Corp. v. Green*, 411 U.S. 792 (1973). When the charge is that an employer discriminates on the basis of religion, a lack of workplace religious demographics forces an individual claiming religious discrimination to make a *prima facie* case without regard to the inferences that can be drawn from representation statistics.

EEOC Guidelines currently require that employers, labor organizations, and joint labor-management committees keep demographic data in five basic classifications: "White," "Black," "Hispanic," "Asian or Pacific Islander," or "American Indian and Alaskan Native." *See* 29 C.F.R. § 1602.20. Although the guidelines do not carry the force of law and are, therefore, not binding on employers or judges, they are firmly rooted in both precedent and federal agency practice, *see* OMB Notice on Race and Ethic Standards, and the Supreme Court has indicated that they are to be given "great deference." *Griggs v. Duke Power Co.*, 401 U.S. 424, 433–434 (1971).

Although the Bureau of the Census expanded the race and ethnicity categories in preparation for the decennial census conducted in 2000, no active steps to increase the amount of data gathered on religious demographics were taken. This is due, at least in part, to the perception of government agencies that the principle of separation of church and state forbids the collection and dissemination of such data. *See* OMB Notice on Race and Ethnic Standards. In addition, some states prohibit employers from collecting such data. *See, e.g.*, Admin. Code of City of N.Y. § B1-7.0(1)(d) and (1-a)(d); N.Y. Exec. Law §§ 296(1)(d) and (1-a)(d) (1972) (prohibition of discrimination on the basis of "creed"). *Cf. State Div. of Human Rights v. Gorton*, 32 App. Div. 2d 933, 302 N.Y.S. 2d 966 (2nd Dep't. 1969) (discrimination found on the basis of employer's repeated inquiries and constant harassment regarding employee's religion).

b) Disparate Impact

Disparate impact claims are similar to disparate treatment claims. They address the same types of adverse employment actions, but they differ in one crucial respect: intent to discriminate is not a crucial element of the *prima facie* case. Though seen more often in the context of gender and race discrimination, a *prima facie* case of religious discrimination can be shown if a plaintiff is able to demonstrate that a specific employment practice or condition operated to the disadvantage of a specific religious group.

Impact claims generally involve facially neutral policies "fair in form but discriminatory in operation." The burden is on the plaintiff to prove the exclusionary effect of a specific selection device. *Connecticut v. Teal*, 457 U.S. 440 (1980). As a result, a Title VII plaintiff must pay careful attention to the possible means that can be utilized to prove disparate impact.

In *Dothard v. Rawlinson*, 433 U.S. 321 (1977), for example, it was suggested that a plaintiff satisfied the burden by showing the effect of the disputed requirement on a certain class of employees or applicants. A second method of proving impact involves "applicant flow analysis," a statistical device that examines, for each employment requirement, the passage or success rate of each protected class under the statute. *See generally* Fred W. Alvarez, Michael J. Levy, Shirley C. Wang, *Class Actions and Pattern And Practice Claims: Overview of Theories, Defenses, Settlements and The Government's Activist Role*, 591 PLI/Lit 275, n.5 (Practicing Law Institute, October/November 1998) ("Under actual applicant flow analysis, the disparity is measured by comparing the actual number of applicants in the relevant demographic category to the corresponding number of the remaining applicants hired, or subset of applicants hired").

Tagatz v. Marquette University, 861 F.2d 1040 (7th Cir. 1988) provides a good example of the need for careful fact-finding and preparation. In *Tagatz*, a professor charged Marquette University with discrimination against non-Catholics in the allocation of pay raises. His case was based solely on statistical evidence of discrepancies in the pay increases of Catholic and non-Catholic professors. Because the specific discriminatory practices that he believed had a discriminatory effect were neither alleged nor proved, the statistical evidence was rejected as insufficient to make a *prima facie* case.

It is not clear what sort of statistical evidence would satisfy the plaintiff's burden in a religious discrimination case based on a disparate impact theory. Because most disparate impact claims are made in the context of race or gender discrimination where census and other demographics are readily available, it is relatively easy to compare the effects of specific employment actions or requirements on the affected groups. Such evidence is not readily available for either religious groups, or for ethnic groups on which the Bureau of the Census collects no data.

This disparity in demographic data raises three rather important questions. The first question is whether such demographic information should be gathered *at all*. Congress, the courts, the states, and civil rights advocates have answered this question in the affirmative. Demographic data are key indicators of workplace assimilation, even though they will not, standing alone, suffice as proof that an employer or labor union is guilty of illegal practices. Given the importance of workplace demographics to the proof of disparate impact claims, the second question is whether the justifications for permitting impact claims by racial minorities, women and nationality groups for which data are collected are equally applicable to allegations of discrimination on the basis of the two characteristics for which little data exists: religion and national origin. *See Sklenar v. Detroit Bd. of Educ.*, 497 F. Supp. 1154 (E.D. Mich. 1980) (noting lack of statistics in case alleging discrimination against persons of Polish descent). *See also* OMB Notice on Race and Ethic Standards. If there is no qualitative difference between the two types of representation cases for which demographic data is unavailable, the third question is how the difference in treatment can be rationalized under the provisions of the Constitution that guarantee equal treatment under the law. *See* U.S. Const. Amend. I (Religion Clause); Amend. V (equal protection component of Due Process Clause); Amend. XIV §§ 1 (Equal Protection Clause), 5 (enforcement clause). *See also* Christopher A. Ford, *Administering Identity: The Determination of "Race" in Race-Conscious Law*, 82 Cal. L. Rev. 1231 (1994).

c) Hostile Work Environments

Racial slurs and sexual harassment are the most common practices that lead to the creation of a hostile work environment, but an increasing number of cases report instances where racial or sexual innuendo or derogatory comments concerning religion have been alleged to create a hostile environment as well. *See generally* Thomas C. Berg, *Religious Speech in the Workplace: Harassment or Protected Speech?*, 22 Harv. J.L. & Pub. Pol'y 959 (1999); Theresa M. Beiner & John M. A. DiPippa, *Hostile Environments and the Religious Employee*, 19 U. Ark. Little Rock L.J. 577 (1997).

To be cognizable as claims under Title VII, the words or acts which form the basis of the complaint must be highly offensive, continual, or made by supervisors. The employee must show that he or she was subjected to "a discriminatory and offensive work environment so heavily polluted with discrimination as to destroy completely the emotional and psychological stability of minority group workers." This burden is not satisfied by "casual comments or sporadic conversation;" the enmity must be "pervasive." *Man-of-Jerusalem v. Hill*, 769 F. Supp. 97 (E.D.N.Y. 1991). The plaintiff attempting to prove a religiously hostile environment must also be able to show that the hostility is religiously motivated. *Goldberg v. City of Philadelphia*, 1995 WL 472108 (E.D. Pa. 1995).

Hostile work environment claims may also be brought under an accommodation theory. In cases in which an employer was made aware of the situation and refused to remedy it, liability may be found because of the employer's failure to accommodate the reasonable needs of employees to work in a non-hostile environment. As in other Title VII cases, notice to the employer will be an important part of the plaintiff's case. Although the employer may assert any defense appropriate under the circumstances, proof that official policies against harassment were in place is not an adequate defense. Such policies must be enforced if they are to be effective. *See generally* Stephen S. Kao,

The President's Guidelines on Religious Exercise and Religious Expression in the Federal Workplace: A Restatement or Reinterpretation of Law?, 8 B.U. Pub. Int. L.J. 251 (1999); Wayne Lindsey Robbins, Jr., *When Two Liberal Values Collide in an Era of "Political Correctness": First Amendment Protection as a Check on Speech-Based Title VII Hostile Environment Claims*, 47 Baylor L. Rev. 789 (1995); Eugene Volokh, *How Harassment Law Restricts Free Speech*, 47 Rutgers L. Rev. 563 (1995).

3. The National Labor Relations Act

The National Labor Relations Act (NLRA) governs relationships between employers and organized groups of employees. Its basic purpose is to permit employees who so choose to organize and engage in collective bargaining over the terms of their employment relationship. Section 157 of the Act, 29 U.S.C. § 157 (1996), provides that

> Employees shall have the right to self-organization, to form, join, or assist labor organizations, to bargain collectively through representatives of their own choosing, and to engage in other concerted activities for the purpose of collective bargaining or other mutual aid or protection, and shall also have the right to refrain from any or all of such activities except to the extent that such right may be affected by an agreement requiring membership in a labor organization as a condition of employment as authorized in section 158(a)(3) of this title.

Section 158 of the NLRA, 29 U.S.C. § 158 (2001), defines the term "unfair labor practice." It requires, among other things, that employers subject to the Act cooperate in the unionization process, and that they bargain in good faith with the union selected by their employees. It also forbids both direct and indirect union intimidation of workers or employers, and specifies certain procedures to be followed in strikes and collective bargaining. For a general overview of the NLRA and its requirements, see Michael R. Carrell & Christina Heavrin, Labor Relations and Collective Bargaining: Cases, Practice, and Law (6th ed. 2001); Henry H. Perritt, Jr., Civil Rights in the Workplace (3d ed. 2001).

By its terms, the NLRA applies to "any person engaged in commerce or in an industry affecting commerce." *See, e.g.*, 29 U.S.C. §§ 152(7); 158(b)(4)(i) (2001). Unlike Title VII, it makes no exceptions for religious organizations. As a result, one of the most heavily litigated issues under the NLRA is whether Congress intended that the jurisdiction of the National Labor Relations Board (NLRB) extend to religious organizations, and, if so, whether the First Amendment permits regulatory oversight of the internal affairs of a religious organization by an agency of the federal government. This issue is discussed at length in the next section.

E. The Religious Workplace

1. Jurisdictional Issues

When a religious employer makes employment decisions based on religious factors a different set of considerations are implicated than when a secular employer takes the same employment action. Government regulation of religious employers is limited both by the Religion Clauses of the First Amendment, by the terms of federal regulatory statutes, and by state constitutional and statutory provisions.

a) Developing a Theory of Abstention

National Labor Relations Board v. Catholic Bishop of Chicago

440 U.S. 490 (1979)

[The NLRB ordered union elections at Catholic high schools in the Chicago area. After a victory by the Illinois Education Association, the Board certified it as the exclusive representative of the lay faculty for the schools involved. In order to seek judicial review of the Board's representation decision, the employer refused to bargain. In response, the union filed unfair labor practice charges claiming violations of Section 8(a)5 and 8(a)1 of the NLRA, 29 U.S.C. §§ 158(a)5 and 158(a)1 (refusal to bargain and interference with collective bargaining rights). The Board granted the union summary judgment and found the schools in violation. *Id.* at 1115. The Board's Decision and Order, 224 NLRB 1221, 1226 (1976), demanded that the schools "collectively bargain concerning rates of pay, wage, hours, and other terms and conditions of employment with Illinois Educational Association (the union)."

The "terms and conditions" over which bargaining was required were never made specific by the union because the Seventh Circuit agreed with the school's contention that, "the very threshold act of certification of the union necessarily alters and impinges upon the religious character of all parochial schools. No longer would the Bishop be the sole repository of authority as required by church law Canon 1381." *Catholic Bishop of Chicago v. NLRB*, 559 F.2d 1112, 1123 (7th Cir. 1977). The circuit court went on to state that, under the NLRB's decision, the Bishop would be required to consult the lay faculty's representative on all matters bearing upon the employment arrangement.

Rejecting the Board's certification of the union, the Seventh Circuit quoted Professor Brown's article, *Collective Bargaining in Higher Education*, 67 Mich. L. Rev. 1067, 1075 (1969):

> Once a bargaining agent has the weight of statutory certification behind it, a familiar process comes into play. First, the matter of salaries is linked to the matter of workload; workload is then related directly to class size, class size to range of offerings, and range of offerings to curricular policy. Dispute over class size may also lead to bargaining over admission policies. This transmutation of academic policy into employment terms is not inevitable, but it is quite likely to occur.

After outlining potential situations in which the exercise of the Board's oversight jurisdiction might alter the religious character of the institution, the Seventh Circuit found that "these paradigmatic situations proposed... are not merely fanciful horror tales... [but] rather persuasively demonstrated by charges that have actually been filed." *Catholic Bishop v. NLRB*, 559 F.2d at 1125.]

Mr. Chief Justice BURGER delivered the opinion of the Court

This case arises out of the National Labor Relations Board's exercise of jurisdiction over lay faculty members at two groups of Catholic high schools. We granted certiorari to consider two questions: (a) Whether teachers in schools operated by a church to teach both religious and secular subjects are within the jurisdiction granted by the National Labor Relations Act; and (b) if the Act authorizes such jurisdiction, does its exercise violate the guarantees of the Religion Clauses of the First Amendment?

I

One group of schools is operated by the Catholic Bishop of Chicago, a corporation sole; the other group is operated by the Diocese of Fort Wayne-South Bend, Inc. The group operated by the Catholic Bishop of Chicago consists of two schools, Quigley North and Quigley South. Those schools are termed "minor seminaries" because of their role in educating high school students who may become priests. At one time, only students who manifested a positive and confirmed desire to be priests were admitted to the Quigley schools. In 1970, the requirement was changed so that students admitted to these schools need not show a definite inclination toward the priesthood. Now the students need only be recommended by their parish priest as having a potential for the priesthood or for Christian leadership. The schools continue to provide special religious instruction not offered in other Catholic secondary schools. The Quigley schools also offer essentially the same college-preparatory curriculum as public secondary schools. Their students participate in a variety of extracurricular activities which include secular as well as religious events. The schools are recognized by the State and accredited by a regional educational organization.

The Diocese of Fort Wayne-South Bend, Inc., has five high schools. Unlike the Quigley schools, the special recommendation of a priest is not a prerequisite for admission. Like the Quigley schools, however, these high schools seek to provide a traditional secular education but oriented to the tenets of the Roman Catholic faith; religious training is also mandatory. These schools are similarly certified by the State.

In 1974 and 1975, separate representation petitions were filed with the Board by interested union organizations for both the Quigley and the Fort Wayne-South Bend schools; representation was sought only for lay teachers. The schools challenged the assertion of jurisdiction on two grounds: (a) that they do not fall within the Board's discretionary jurisdictional criteria; and (b) that the Religion Clauses of the First Amendment preclude the Board's jurisdiction. The Board rejected the jurisdictional arguments on the basis of its decision in *Roman Catholic Archdiocese of Baltimore*, 216 NLRB 249 (1975). There the Board explained that its policy was to decline jurisdiction over religiously sponsored organizations "only when they are completely religious, not just religiously associated." Because neither group of schools was found to fall within the Board's "completely religious" category, the Board ordered elections.

Notwithstanding the Board's order, the schools declined to recognize the unions or to bargain. The unions filed unfair labor practice complaints with the Board.

The Board concluded that the schools had violated the Act and ordered that they cease their unfair labor practices and that they bargain collectively with the unions.

II

[On appeal, the Court of Appeals] concluded that the Board had not properly exercised its discretion, because the Board's distinction between "completely religious" and "merely religiously associated" failed to provide a workable guide for the exercise of discretion:

> We find the standard itself to be a simplistic black or white, purported rule containing no borderline demarcation of where "completely religious" takes

> over or, on the other hand, ceases. In our opinion the dichotomous "completely religious—merely religiously associated" standard provides no workable guide to the exercise of discretion. The determination that an institution is so completely a religious entity as to exclude any viable secular components obviously implicates very sensitive questions of faith and tradition.

The Court of Appeals recognized that the rejection of the Board's policy as to church-operated schools meant that the Board would extend its jurisdiction to all church-operated schools. The court therefore turned to the question of whether the Board could exercise that jurisdiction, consistent with constitutional limitations. It concluded that both the Free Exercise Clause and the Establishment Clause of the First Amendment foreclosed the Board's jurisdiction.

The court distinguished local regulations which required fire inspections or state laws mandating attendance, reasoning that they did not "have the clear inhibiting potential upon the relationship between teachers and employers with which the present Board order is directly concerned." The court held that interference with management prerogatives, found acceptable in an ordinary commercial setting, was not acceptable in an area protected by, the First Amendment. "The real difficulty is found in the chilling aspect that the requirement of bargaining will impose on the exercise of the bishops' control of the religious mission of the schools."

III

The Board now asserts jurisdiction over all private, nonprofit, educational institutions with gross annual revenues that meet its jurisdictional requirements whether they are secular or religious. In the Board's view, the Association had chosen to entangle itself with the secular world when it decided to hire lay teachers.

When it ordered an election for the lay professional employees at five parochial high schools in Baltimore in 1975, the Board reiterated its belief that exercise of its jurisdiction is not contrary to the First Amendment:

> "[T]he Board's policy in the past has been to decline jurisdiction over similar institutions only when they are completely religious, not just religiously associated, and the Archdiocese concedes that instruction is not limited to religious subjects. That the Archdiocese seeks to provide an education based on Christian principles does not lead to a contrary conclusion. Most religiously associated institutions seek to operate in conformity with their religious tenets." *Roman Catholic Archdiocese of Baltimore*, 216 NLRB, at 250.

The Board also rejected the First Amendment claims in *Cardinal Timothy Manning, Roman Catholic Archbishop of the Archdiocese of Los Angeles*, 223 NLRB 1218, 1218 (1976): "Regulation of labor relations does not violate the First Amendment when it involves a *minimal intrusion* on religious conduct and is necessary to obtain [the Act's] objective." (Emphasis added.)

The Board thus recognizes that its assertion of jurisdiction over teachers in religious schools constitutes some degree of intrusion into the administration of the affairs of church-operated schools. Implicit in the Board's distinction between schools that are "completely religious" and those "religiously associated" is also an acknowledgment of some degree of entanglement. Because that distinction was measured by a school's involvement with commerce, however, and not by its religious association, it is clear that the Board never envisioned any sort of religious litmus test for determining when to assert jurisdiction. Nevertheless, by expressing its traditional jurisdictional standards in First Amendment terms, the Board has plainly recognized that intrusion into this area could run afoul of the Religion Clauses and hence preclude jurisdiction on constitutional grounds.

IV

That there are constitutional limitations on the Board's actions has been repeatedly recognized by this Court even while acknowledging the broad scope of the grant of jurisdiction. The First Amendment, of course, is a limitation on the power of Congress. Thus, if we were to conclude that the Act granted the challenged jurisdiction over these teachers we would be required to decide whether that was constitutionally permissible under the Religion Clauses of the First Amendment.

Although the respondents press their claims under the Religion Clauses, the question we consider first is whether Congress intended the Board to have jurisdiction over teachers in church-operated schools. In keeping with the Court's prudential policy it is incumbent on us to determine whether the Board's exercise of its jurisdiction here would give rise to serious constitutional questions. If so, we must first identify "the affirmative intention of the Congress clearly expressed" before concluding that the Act grants jurisdiction.

V

In recent decisions involving aid to parochial schools we have recognized the critical and unique role of the teacher in fulfilling the mission of a church-related school. The key role played by teachers in such a school system has been the predicate for our conclusions that governmental aid channeled through teachers creates an impermissible risk of excessive governmental entanglement in the affairs of the church-operated schools. For example, in *Lemon*, we wrote:

> "In terms of potential for involving some aspect of faith or morals *in secular subjects*, a textbook's content is ascertainable, but a teacher's handling of a subject is not. We cannot ignore the danger that a teacher under religious control and discipline poses to the separation of the religious from the purely secular aspects of pre-college education. The conflict of functions inheres in the situation." (Emphasis added.)

The Board argues that it can avoid excessive entanglement since it will resolve only factual issues such as whether an anti-union animus motivated an employer's action. But at this stage of our consideration we are not compelled to determine whether the entanglement is excessive as we would were we considering the constitutional issue. Rather, we make a narrow inquiry whether the exercise of the Board's jurisdiction presents a significant risk that the First Amendment will be infringed.

[I] t is already clear that the Board's actions will go beyond resolving factual issues. Inevitably the Board's inquiry will implicate sensitive issues that open the door to conflicts between clergy-administrators and the Board, or conflicts with negotiators for unions. What we said in *Lemon*, applies as well here:

> "[P]arochial schools involve substantial religious activity and purpose.
>
> "The substantial religious character of these church-related schools gives rise to entangling church-state relationships of the kind the Religion Clauses sought to avoid." (Footnote omitted.)

Mr. Justice Douglas emphasized this in his concurring opinion in *Lemon*, noting "the admitted and obvious fact that the *raison d'être* of parochial schools is the propagation of a religious faith."

The church-teacher relationship in a church-operated school differs from the employment relationship in a public or other nonreligious school. We see no escape from conflicts flowing from the Board's exercise of jurisdiction over teachers in church-operated schools and the consequent serious First Amendment questions that would follow. We therefore turn to an examination of the National Labor Relations Act to decide whether it must be read to confer jurisdiction that would in turn require a decision on the constitutional claims raised by respondents.

VI

There is no clear expression of an affirmative intention of Congress that teachers in church-operated schools should be covered by the Act. Admittedly, Congress defined the Board's jurisdiction in very broad terms; we must therefore examine the legislative history of the Act to determine whether Congress contemplated that the grant of jurisdiction would include teachers in such schools.

In enacting the National Labor Relations Act in 1935, Congress sought to protect the right of American workers to bargain collectively. The concern that was repeated throughout the debates was the need to assure workers the right to organize to counterbalance the collective activities of employers which had been authorized by the National Industrial Recovery Act. But congressional attention focused on employment in private industry and on industrial recovery.

Our examination of the statute and its legislative history indicates that Congress simply gave no consideration to church-operated schools. It is not without significance, however, that the Senate Committee on Education and Labor chose a college professor's dispute with the college as an example of employer-employee relations *not* covered by the Act.

[The Court's general discussion of amendments relating to nonprofit hospitals is omitted.]

During the debate [over nonprofit hospitals] there were expressions of concern about the effect of the bill on employees of religious hospitals whose religious beliefs would not permit them to join a union. The result of those concerns was an amendment which reflects congressional sensitivity to First Amendment guarantees:

> "Any employee of a health care institution who is a member of and adheres to established and traditional tenets or teachings of a bona fide religion, body, or sect which has historically held conscientious objections to joining or financially supporting labor organizations shall not be required to join or financially support any labor organization as a condition of employment; except that such employee may be required, in lieu of periodic dues and initiation fees, to pay sums equal to such dues and initiation fees to a nonreligious charitable fund exempt from taxation under section 501(c)(3) of title 26, chosen by such employee from a list of at least three such funds, designated in a contract between such institution and a labor organization, or if the contract fails to designate such funds, then to any such fund chosen by the employee." 29 U.S.C. § 169.

The absence of an "affirmative intention of the Congress clearly expressed" fortifies our conclusion that Congress did not contemplate that the Board would require church-operated schools to grant recognition to unions as bargaining agents for their teachers.

Accordingly, in the absence of a clear expression of Congress' intent to bring teachers in church-operated schools within the jurisdiction of the Board, we decline to construe the Act in a manner that could in turn call upon the Court to resolve difficult and sensitive questions arising out of the guarantees of the First Amendment Religion Clauses.

Affirmed.

Mr. Justice BRENNAN, with whom Mr. Justice WHITE, Mr. Justice MARSHALL, and Mr. Justice BLACKMUN join, dissenting.

The Court today holds that coverage of the National Labor Relations Act does not extend to lay teachers employed by church-operated schools. That construction is plainly wrong in light of the Act's language, its legislative history, and this Court's precedents. It is justified solely on the basis of a canon of statutory construction seemingly invented by the Court for the purpose of deciding this case. I dissent.

II

In construing the Board's jurisdiction to exclude church-operated schools the Court today is faithful to neither the statute's language nor its history. Moreover, it is also untrue to its own precedents. "This Court has consistently declared that in passing the National Labor Relations Act, Congress intended to and did vest in the Board the fullest jurisdictional breadth constitutionally permissible under the Commerce Clause." As long as an employer is within the reach of Congress' power under the Commerce Clause—and no one doubts that respondents are—the Court has held him to be covered by the Act regardless of the nature of his activity. *See, e.g., Polish National Alliance v. NLRB,* 322 U.S. 643 (1944) (nonprofit fraternal organization). Indeed, *Associated Press v. NLRB,* 301 U.S. 103 (1937), construed the Act to cover editorial employees of a nonprofit news-gathering organization despite a claim—precisely parallel to that made here—that their inclusion rendered the Act in violation of the First Amendment. Today's opinion is simply unable to explain the grounds that distinguish that case from this one.

Thus, the available authority indicates that Congress intended to include, not exclude, lay teachers of church-operated schools. The Court does not counter this with evidence that Congress did intend an exception it never stated. Instead, despite the legislative history to the contrary, it construes the Act as excluding lay teachers only because Congress did not state explicitly that they were covered. In Mr. Justice Cardozo's words, this presses "avoidance of A DIFFICULTY ... TO THE POINT OF DISINGENUOUS EVASION." *Moore Ice Cream Co. v. Rose,* 289 U.S., at 379.

Notes

1. The two-step analysis developed by the Court to decide challenges to regulatory jurisdiction under the First Amendment proceeds as follows. First, the court must determine "whether the exercise of the Board's jurisdiction presents a significant risk that the First Amendment will be infringed," 440 U.S. at 502. If such a risk exists, the court must then determine if Congress has expressed an affirmative intention to regulate the activities in question. The purpose of such an inquiry is to avoid judicial resolution of constitutional questions that have not been considered by Congress in the first instance. Where an "affirmative expression" of Congressional intent to regulate exists, the Court then has the benefit of a legislative determination concerning with balance to be struck between religious and governmental interests.

2. Which of the Court's prior decisions under the Religion Clause, if any, determined the result in *Catholic Bishop*? *See* Chapter Five. Was the majority's decision influenced by fears that government regulators would become too enmeshed in the internal affairs of religious schools? If so, how do you explain the rationale of the dissenting opinion? Should the Court's jurisdictional analysis be applied in regulatory contexts beyond labor law? *See, e.g.*, Chapter Seven, §C (taking a mixed approach to cases involving intra-church disputes); Nine, §C (explicitly rejecting a challenge to jurisdiction to tax).

3. What do you make of Justice Brennan's view that the reasoning employed by the majority "presses 'avoidance of a difficulty...to the point of disingenuous evasion'"? Why is it evasive? It seems clear that Congress did not consider the issue. Does this mean that the NLRA is neutral statute of general applicability? Does the NLRB's case-by-case approach to resolving labor disputes affect your answer?

4. Would it have been possible to protect the schools from the "excessive entanglement" that appears to have motivated the majority's decision without also striking down the NLRA as applied to religious institutions? Justice Brennan argued that

> an exemption, available only to church-operated schools, generates a possible Establishment Clause question of its own. *Walz v. Tax Comm'n*, 397 U.S. 664 (1970), does not put that question to rest, for in upholding the property tax exemption for churches there at issue, we emphasized that New York had "not singled out...churches as such; rather, it has granted exemption to all houses of religious worship within a broad class of property owned by nonprofit, quasi-public corporations."

Id. at 673. Does this mean that religious exemptions from neutral laws of general applicability should be viewed as presumptively unconstitutional? *Compare Texas Monthly v. Bullock*, 489 U.S. 1 (1989), excerpted in Chapter Nine, *with Employment Div. v. Smith* 494 U.S. 872 (1991), excerpted in Chapter Five §B.

5. Is the Court's attempt to avoid "excessive entanglement" based on a concern that the NLRB or state labor agency could wander into territory forbidden by the Establishment Clause, or that such "entanglement" would burden the free exercise of religious belief? Consider the following scenario at a hypothetical, unionized religious school:

> Teacher X is assigned by the school to teach a course in sex-education, and is instructed to utilize a curriculum approved by church authorities. She believes, in good faith, that the curriculum is an inadequate treatment of the subject of human sexuality and would like to supplement it with materials approved by the local affiliate of the National Education Association. When the school refuses, she files a grievance under the procedure contemplated by the union contract. The union sides with her, but the school refuses to reconsider the request. It also refuses to submit the matter to arbitration as provided in the contract because it believes that the matter is central to the religious character of the school.

Would labor agency or court intervention in such a controversy "entangle" the government in matters of religious belief or doctrine? How so? Would it burden the school's right to free exercise of religion?

The point of this hypothetical is to prompt reflection on the following question: Does the distinction between the two parts of the Religion Clause make a difference in a religious workplace? *See* Chapter Seven §C (resolution of intra-religious disputes). If so, what *is* the difference between them? Does the fact that teaching and curriculum content involve both speech and religion make cases involving schools "hybrid cases" under *Employment Div. v. Smith*? If so, why is there not a similarly fact-sensitive inquiry into the degree of entanglement required in a case such as *Lemon*? *See* Chapter Six.

6. The Court's finding on the entanglement issue is based on the "critical and unique role of the teacher in fulfilling the mission of a church-operated school." *Catholic Bishop*, 440 U.S. at 501. Drawing a close connection to its conclusion in *Lemon v. Kurtzman*, excerpted in Chapter Five §B, the Court noted "that the key role played by teachers in such a school system has been the predicate for our conclusions that governmental aid channeled through teachers creates an impermissible risk of excessive governmental entanglement in the affairs of church-operated schools." *Catholic Bishop*, 440 U.S. at 501. *See generally Agostini v. Felton*, 521 U.S. 203 (1997); *Wolman v. Walters*, 433 U.S. 229 (1977); *Meek v. Pittenger*, 421 U.S. 349 (1975); *Lemon v. Kurtzman*, 403 U.S. 602 (1971). The Board, however, argued that it could avoid excessive entanglement by resolving only factual issues, such as whether an anti-union animus motivated the religious employer's action. The Seventh Circuit was not sanguine concerning the Board's ability to steer clear of the shoals created by the First Amendment. Judge Sprecher observed that "in attempting to steer a course between the Scylla and Charybdis of the Establishment and Free Exercise Clauses," the NLRB had devised a solution which "collided with one and fallen into the other." *Catholic Bishop of Chicago* v. NLRB, 559 F.2d 1112, 1131 (7th Cir. 1977) (Sprecher, J., concurring).

7. The questions raised in the preceding paragraphs have rather substantial practical implications for religious organizations. If religious exemptions are not available as a matter of course, the alternative is expensive and time-consuming litigation over the degree to which, under the circumstances of the case, the particular "entanglement" is "excessive" as a matter of fact or law. After *Employment Div. v. Smith*, what facts would be needed to establish that a judicially cognizable burden exists under the Free Exercise Clause?

b) Developments Since NLRB v. Catholic Bishop*: Labor Cases*

Though a similar analysis is applied in cases outside the workplace setting, see Chapter Nine (discussing jurisdiction to tax), the analysis required by *Catholic Bishop of Chicago* highlights a number of issues that arise at the point where the values identified by the Supreme Court as animating the Free Exercise and Establishment Clauses appear to come into conflict.

Because the Supreme Court did not reach the merits of the First Amendment issues that can arise when a regulatory agency attempts to strike a balance between the faith-based demands of religious employers and the bargaining rights to which employees are entitled under federal and state labor laws, the practical problem facing both courts and administrators dealing with cases after *Catholic Bishop of Chicago* was to determine *why* and *under what circumstances* abstention is appropriate in disputes between religious employers and their employees. These are not easy questions. Unlike property cases, in which "neutral principles of law" can sometimes be invoked to resolve intra-organizational disputes, labor law disputes turn on a finding that given practice is "unfair" under the circumstances. And, to the extent that the First Amendment guarantees the right of a religious employer to protect either its mission, the integrity of its teachings, or its character as a religious institution identified with the tenets of a particular faith, labor practices designed to effectuate those purposes cannot be viewed as "unfair."

The reported cases since *NLRB v. Catholic Bishop of Chicago* have been fairly consistent. The central holding of the case, that the NLRA may not be applied to bargaining situations involving teachers in religious secondary schools unless they are clearly covered by the Act, has not been challenged, but the cases have largely refused to extend the application of the case beyond those specific facts. In cases where *other* employees and religious institutions, including colleges and universities, are involved, both courts and labor boards appear to prefer the analysis rejected by the Seventh Circuit in *Catholic Bishop of Chicago*: fact-finding designed to determine whether the institution, employment setting, or job category is sufficiently "religious" in character to escape regulation. *See, e.g., Universidad Central de Bayamon v. NLRB*, 778 F.2d 906 (1st Cir. 1985).

The federal courts have also refused to extend *Catholic Bishop of Chicago* to cases in which *state* labor authorities seek to exercise jurisdiction over religious schools. *Catholic High School Association of the Archdiocese of New York v. Culvert*, 753 F.2d 1161 (2d Cir. 1984). *Accord Hill-Murray Federation of Teachers v. Hill-Murray High School*, 487 N.W. 2d 857 (Minn. 1992) (holding that NLRA does not preempt the Minnesota Labor Relations Act and that no principle of state law would require abstention).

With one exception, *NLRB v. Bishop Ford Central Catholic High School*, 623 F.2d 818, 823 (2d Cir. 1980) (extending the holding in *Catholic Bishop of Chicago* to a religiously-affiliated high school that had been transferred from the Roman Catholic Diocese to an independent Board of lay trustees because of "the suffusion of religion into the curriculum and the mandate of the faculty to infuse the students with religious values"), the cases decided after *Catholic Bishop of Chicago* have permitted the NLRB and state labor agencies to exercise jurisdiction in three settings:

1. *When the situation presents no significant risk*: Where the courts find no significant risk that the First Amendment will be implicated by the assertion of jurisdiction, courts will find that *Catholic Bishop of Chicago's* holding that jurisdiction is not appropriate absent a clear expression of congressional intent should not be followed.
2. *When state labor boards assert jurisdiction*: When *state* labor boards assert jurisdiction over religious organizations, courts have refused to interfere on First Amendment grounds; and
3. *When a "clear expression" of congressional intent to regulate the affairs of religious organization is found*: Some courts have found a clear expression of Congressional intent to expand the NLRB's jurisdiction in the 1974 Amendment to the National Labor Relations Act.

The effect of these holdings has been to resolve, for the present at least, First Amendment issues expressly left open in *Catholic Bishop of Chicago*.

As you consider the approaches described above, you should also remember several points drawn from the case law. The first is the impact of *Employment Div. v. Smith* on the law of free exercise. In *Smith*, the Court held that generally applicable and otherwise valid regulatory laws that are not intended to regulate religious conduct or belief do not violate the Free Exercise Clause, even if they result in burdening First Amendment rights. Such inquiries are, by their nature, fact-sensitive. The careful advocate will therefore consider both the environment in which the labor dispute occurs, the degree to which the reviewing agency has discretion, and the degree to which the dispute will turn on principles of church doctrine, law, or custom. *See generally* Chapter Seven §§ B–D (discussing principles applicable to cases involving intra-church disputes) and

Chapter Eleven. These are the settings in which there is a substantial risk of government entanglement in matters of religious doctrine or internal discipline.

No significant risk of First Amendment infringement

NLRB v. Salvation Army of Massachusetts, Dorchester Day Care Center, 763 F.2d 1 (1st Cir. 1985). After the NLRB ordered elections and certified the union at the Salvation Army's day care center, the union and center began collective bargaining. The negotiations broke down when the center proposed an "agency function and management rights" clause that included a provision that read as follows:

> [T]he parties recognize that the [Salvation] Army is an international, religious, and charitable movement, organized and operated as a branch of the Christian Church, based upon a motivation of love of God and a concern for the needs of humanity [as] expressed by a wide variety of social services, including the functions of the Center, which are extended to all persons without discrimination as to race, color, creed or national origin. The parties further recognize that the operation the Center is an integral part of the missions of the Army, and that neither the union nor any employees shall engage in any activity which interferes with, or contests the mission of the Army.

Id. at 3.

The center asserted that the clause was a mandatory subject of bargaining, and if the union refused to negotiate on the subject, it could, in good faith, discontinue all bargaining. The union believed that the clause was not a mandatory subject of bargaining, and refused to include it. It did, however, want to continue negotiating other topics.

Under controlling labor law principles, parties to a labor dispute have a mutual obligation to bargain in good faith with respect to wages, hours, and other genuine terms and conditions of employment. Subject terms, however, are either mandatory or non-mandatory. Mandatory subjects must bear a "direct, significant relationship to... terms or conditions of employment, rather than a remote or incidental relationship." *Id.* at 7, *quoting NLRB v. Massachusetts Nurses Association*, 557 F.2d 894, 898 (1st Cir. 1977). If the term is mandatory, a party is not required to concede its position on the issue as long as that position can be maintained in good faith. If the subject is non-mandatory, the party may propose a clause, but may not in good faith insist upon its inclusion, for to do so would be to refuse to bargain on mandatory subjects. *Id.* at 7.

After holding a hearing in the *Salvation Army* case, the NLRB concluded that the proposed clause was a *non*-mandatory subject and that the day care center could not insist that it be included. In the Board's view, an express recognition of the religious mission of the organization was not necessary to insure the integrity of the day care center's spiritual mission. *Id.* at 8. On appeal, the First Circuit upheld the Board's conclusions on the ground that the courts will overturn only unreasonable or unprincipled decisions concerning mandatory subjects. *Id.* at 7.

The court did note, however, that the religious concerns of the Salvation Army were legitimate. It therefore turned to an analysis of the jurisdictional issue. Holding on the facts that the exercise of the Board's jurisdiction presented no significant risk that the First Amendment would be infringed, the court found that no significant condition of employment at the center was of a religious nature. The staff consisted of nine teachers, one social worker, and a cook, all of whom were selected without regard to religious belief. The children attending the day care center were chosen on the basis of need, rather than religious affiliation, and religious instruction and activities were a part of the day care center's program. The staff received no religious training and were not expected to give religious guidance either to the children or the parents. Under these circumstances, the exercise of jurisdiction by the NLRB was proper. *Id.* at 2–3. *Accord National Labor Relations Board v. St. Louis Christian Home*, 663 F.2d 60 (8th Cir. 1980) (refusing to apply *Catholic Bishop of Chicago* to a church-operated home for neglected children and ordering collective bargaining for child-care workers, maintenance employees and a storeroom clerk); *Denver Post of the National Society of the Volunteers of America v. NLRB*, 732 F.2d 769, 722 (1984) (holding that the "First Amendment problems identified by the court in *Catholic Bishop of Chicago* stemmed not from the church's religious philosophy itself, but from the infusion of that philosophy into the school's functions and the critical role it performed").

Universidad Central de Bayamon v. NLRB, 793 F.2d 383 (1st Cir. 1986), represents a case in which a significant threat to First Amendment interests was found. In its initial review of the Board's action, a divided (2–1) panel granted enforcement of the NLRB's order that the University, controlled by the Dominican Order, a religious society of the Catholic Church, take part in collective bargaining. After a rehearing *en banc*, however, the full-court was unable to enforce the panel's order:

> Since the court is equally divided, it cannot grant the Labor Board's request to enforce its order requiring the university to bargain with its faculty union. Whether this kind of institution of higher education falls within the strictures of *Catholic Bishop* is, in our view, an important, likely recurring question that calls for Supreme Court guidance.

Id. at 401.

The split within the full court is instructive. Half of the judges concluded that the University should fall within *Catholic Bishop of Chicago.* They gave four reasons: First, the language of *Catholic Bishop of Chicago* does not distinguish colleges from primary and secondary schools; second, the risks of entanglement found to exist in *Catholic Bishop of Chicago* are just as great in colleges as they are in primary and secondary schools; third, administration of the Board's orders might require continuing oversight, and thus, impermissible entanglement; and finally, they reject the Board's assertion that the school aid cases drawing a distinction between secondary schools and colleges made it legitimate to exercise jurisdiction over the latter. *See Tilton v. Richardson*, 403 U.S. 672 (1971); *Hunt v. McNair*, 413 U.S. 734 (1973); *Roemer v. Board of Public Works*, 426 U.S. 736 (1976), all noted in Chapter Six. In the view of these judges, the availability of public funding for religiously-affiliated universities does not justify Board scrutiny of unfair labor practice charges, and the inevitable need to distinguish between religious and labor matters. 793 F.2d at 403. The school funding cases are discussed at greater length in Chapter Six § D(2).

The other half of the Court found a significant difference in the risk of entanglement in secondary parochial schools, which receive no government assistance, and "*Tilton*" type colleges, which do. In the view of these judges, the role of the teacher in parochial primary and secondary schools is more religiously oriented than the task assigned university professors. 793 F.2d at 404. In their view, *Catholic Bishop of Chicago* does not apply to colleges and universities at all.

Federal Preemption and the Impact of Catholic Bishop of Chicago *on the Assertion of State Labor Relations Board Jurisdiction*

In *Catholic High School Association of the Archdiocese of New York v. Culvert*, 753 F.2d 1161 (2d Cir. 1985), the Second Circuit held that the National Labor Relations Act did not preempt the New York State Labor Relations Act (SLRA). *Accord Christ the King Regional High School v. Culvert*, 815 F.2d 219 (2d Cir. 1987), *cert. denied*, 484 U.S. 830 (1987); *Ferro v. Association of Catholic Schools*, 623 F. Supp. 1161 (S.D.N.Y. 1985); *Hill-Murray Federation of Teachers v. Hill-Murray High School*, 487 N.W. 2d 857 (Minn. 1992); *South Jersey Catholic School Teachers Organization v. St. Teresa of the Infant Jesus Church Elementary School*, 150 N.J. 575, 696 A.2d 709 (1997). Unlike Congress, the New York Legislature had amended the state labor relations act to include an express grant of jurisdiction over employees of charitable, educational and religious associations. Because the clearly expressed affirmative intent of the legislature absent in *Catholic Bishop of Chicago* was present in *Culvert*, the court reached and resolved a number of issues expressly left open in *Catholic Bishop*.

The first issue was the state labor board's jurisdiction. Applying *Lemon v. Kurtzman*'s "three-pronged" test to resolve the Establishment Clause issues, that court found that the parties agreed that the Act (1) had a secular purpose, and (2) that neither purpose or primary effect was to advance or inhibit religion. *Culvert*, 753 F.2d at 1166. Their dispute centered on the third prong, and whether case-by-case adjudication of SLRA unfair labor practice charges would create excessive entanglement.

The Second Circuit decided that the mere assertion of jurisdiction would not result in excessive entanglement. Distinguishing the comprehensive and continuing surveillance envisioned by the Supreme Court in *Lemon*, *Meek v. Pittenger*, 421 U.S. 349 (1975), and *Wolman v. Walter*, 433 U.S. 229 (1977), it held that no continuing surveillance would be necessary. *Culvert*, 753 F.2d at 1167. Under the SLRA, the unfair labor practices prohibited were secular, the Board could investigate only after a complaint was filed, and its investigations were limited to issues pertaining directly to the charges filed. The court found it relevant that the state Board's orders were not self-enforcing, and that the school would have ample opportunity to assert First Amendment claims as defenses in enforcement proceedings. *Accord Christ the King Regional High School v. Culvert*, 815 F.2d 219 (2d Cir. 1987) (abstention is proper until after the New York State Labor Board concludes its formal investigation).

The school's free exercise claims were rejected as well. The court saw no significant risk of a free exercise violation in the mere exercise of the Board's jurisdiction, and held that whatever incidental burden the assertion of regulatory jurisdiction caused was justified by the compelling state interest of allowing workers the protection afforded by collective bargaining. *Culvert*, 753 F.2d at 1169–71.

Not all of the school's claims were rejected, however. The court cautioned that cases involving "mixed motives" for termination or discipline should be handled with care. Even though termination for anti-union animus was unlawful under the SLRA, a discharge of a lay teacher for religious reasons could not be enjoined unless the state labor board could find that the discharge or discipline would not have occurred "but for" the anti-union bias of the employer. In the court's view, such a rule would ensure the school the right to fire lay teachers for religious reasons without interference from the state labor Board. *See also, Hill-Murray Federation of Teachers v. Hill-Murray High School*, 487 N.W. 2d 857 (Minn. 1992) (holding that no principle of Minnesota law or statutory construction limited the reach of the Minnesota Labor Relation Act (MLRA), and rejecting a free exercise claim because *Employment Div. v. Smith* controls the free exercise analysis).

Catholic Bishop of Chicago assumes that a decision to compel negotiations on the usual mandatory subjects of bargaining would require a church to place its faith's commitments on the bargaining table, and that mandatory negotiations of this type would raise substantial questions under the First Amendment. The case law after *Catholic Bishop*, however, often rejects both the reasoning and result of that case. *See New York State Employment Relations Bd. v. Christian Bros. Academy*, 238 A.D.2d 28, 668 N.Y.S.2d 407 (3d. Dept. 1998) (ordering religious school to bargain "on the secular issues of "rates of pay, wages, hours of employment and other terms and conditions of employment"). There is divergent authority on the question of whether it is possible for a court to distinguish between the "core" religious functions of a religious organization, and those which can be described as ancillary to its central purpose. *Compare NLRB v. Hanna Boys Center*, 940 F.2d 1295 (9th Cir. 1991) (holding that *Catholic Bishop of Chicago* extends only to teachers in church operated schools, not to all employees), *Ecclesiastical Maintenance Services, Inc.*, 325 NLRB 629, 325 NLRB No. 98 (1998) (holding under the facts that a church-run janitorial service was not exempt) *and NLRB v. Jewish Day School of Greater Washington*, 283 NLRB 757 (1987) (NLRB declining to exercise jurisdiction over school whose "purpose and function in substantial part are to propagate a religious faith.") *with Christ the King Regional High School v. Culvert,* 815 F.2d 219 (2d Cir. 1987) (holding that the NLRB has no jurisdiction over a religious school). *See also Central Catholic Education Association v. Archdiocese of Portland,* 133 Or. App. 280, 283, 891 P.2d 1318 (1995), *aff'd* 323 Or. 238, 916 P.2d 303 (1996) (holding that the union could not be certified under Oregon's labor law, Or. Rev. Stats. §663.005(4)(f), because the NLRB has jurisdiction over a religious employer under the jurisdictional amount standards of *Siemons Mailing Service*, 122 NLRB 81 (1958) and *Dilene Answering Service, Inc.,* 216 NLRB 669 (1975) "regardless of whether the relevant body of employees is independently outside the jurisdiction of the NLRB"), *Jacobo Marti and Sons, Inc. v. NLRB*, 676 F.2d 975 (3d. Cir. 1982) (rejecting an assertion that an organization controlled by members of one particular faith is either "religious" or "religiously affiliated"); *Casa Italiana Language School and Washington Italian Teachers Association*, 326 NLRB 40, 326 NLRB No. 14 (1998) (holding on the facts that a parish-run language school should be viewed as a "retail operation operated by religious institution"). *But see Sabatino v. Saint Aloysius Parish*, 280 N.J. Super. 185, 654 A.2d 1033 (1994) (holding First Amendment requires abstention in a breach of contract claim filed by an elementary school principal whose contract was not renewed); *Alicea v. New Brunswick Theological Seminary*, 128 N.J. 303, 608 A.2d 218 (1992) (refusing to intervene in tenure dispute where position involved ministerial functions).

Religious Hospitals and Nursing Homes: Finding a Clear Expression of Congressional Intent to Expand the Jurisdiction of the National Labor Relations Board

When Congress amended the NLRA in 1974 to provide for jurisdiction over religious hospitals and nursing homes, 29 U.S.C. §152, it provided a foundation for resolving some of the constitutional issues left open in *Catholic Bishop of Chicago.* In *Tressler Lutheran Home for Children v. NLRB*, 677 F.2d 302 (3d Cir. 1982), the hospital claimed that ordering it to bargain with a union of maintenance employees, nursing and physiotherapy assistants, clerks, orderlies and nurses would violate both the Establishment and the Free Exercise Clauses of the First Amendment.

Rejecting both claims, the court held that actual conflicts over the commands of religious doctrine were neither inevitable nor probable when NLRB jurisdiction is asserted. In the event they did arise, as in *United States v. Lee*, 455 U.S. 252 (1982), excerpted in Chapter Nine, the free exercise question is resolved against the employer:

> When followers of a particular sect enter into commercial activity as a matter of choice, the limits they accept on their own conduct as a matter of con-

> science and faith are not to be superimposed on the statutory schemes which are binding on others in that activity. Granting an exemption from social security taxes to an employer operates to impose the employer's religious faith on the employee.

Tressler, 677 F.2d at 307 (*quoting United States v. Lee*, 955 U.S. at 259). *Accord St. Elizabeth Community Hospital v. NLRB*, 708 F.2d 1436 (9th Cir. 1983) (hospital service and maintenance employees; holding that the primary functions of hospitals are secular in nature). *See also American Hospital Association v. Hansbarger*, 594 F. Supp. 483 (N.D. W.Va. 1984) (denying a hospital's request for a preliminary injunction against enforcement of W. Va. Code § 16-5b-6a, which required that at least 40% of the board of directors of all non-profit hospitals located in West Virginia be composed of an equal proportion of consumer representatives; failure to prove irreparable harm). *But cf. NLRB v. Lighthouse for the Blind of Houston*, 653 F.2d 206 (5th Cir. 1981) (refusing jurisdiction on the grounds that the primary purpose of employment at the Lighthouse was rehabilitation).

c) *Application of* **Catholic Bishop of Chicago** *in Labor Settings outside the Collective Bargaining Context*

1) *The Fair Labor Standards Act*

Tony and Susan Alamo Foundation v. Secretary of Labor

471 U.S. 290 (1985)

Justice WHITE delivered the opinion of the Court.

The threshold question in this case is whether the minimum wage, overtime, and recordkeeping requirements of the Fair Labor Standards Act, 52 Stat. 1060, as amended, 29 U.S.C. § 201 *et seq.*, apply to workers engaged in the commercial activities of a religious foundation, regardless of whether those workers consider themselves "employees." A secondary question is whether application of the Act in this context violates the Religion Clauses of the First Amendment.

The Tony and Susan Alamo Foundation is a nonprofit religious organization incorporated under the laws of California. Among its primary purposes, as stated in its Articles of Incorporation, are to "establish, conduct and maintain an Evangelistic Church; to conduct religious services, to minister to the sick and needy, to care for the fatherless and to rescue the fallen, and generally to do those things needful for the promotion of Christian faith, virtue, and charity." The Foundation does not solicit contributions from the public. It derives its income largely from the operation of a number of commercial businesses, which include service stations, retail clothing and grocery outlets, hog farms, roofing and electrical construction companies, a recordkeeping company, a motel, and companies engaged in the production and distribution of candy. These activities have been supervised by petitioners Tony and Susan Alamo, president and secretary-treasurer of the Foundation, respectively. The businesses are staffed largely by the Foundation's "associates," most of whom were drug addicts, derelicts, or criminals before their conversion and rehabilitation by the Foundation. These workers receive no cash salaries, but the Foundation provides them with food, clothing, shelter, and other benefits.

In 1977, the Secretary of Labor filed an action against the Foundation, the Alamos, and Larry La Roche, who was then the Foundation's vice president, alleging violations of the minimum wage, overtime, and recordkeeping provisions of the Fair Labor Standards Act.

The District Court rejected petitioners' arguments that application of the Act to the Foundation violated the Free Exercise and Establishment Clauses of the First Amendment, and the court found no evidence that the Secretary had engaged in unconstitutional discrimination against petitioners in bringing this suit.

We affirm.

Petitioners argue that imposition of the minimum wage and recordkeeping requirements will violate the rights of the associates to freely exercise their religion and the right of the Foundation to be free of excessive government entanglement in its affairs. Neither of these contentions has merit.

It is virtually self-evident that the Free Exercise Clause does not require an exemption from a governmental program unless, at a minimum, inclusion in the program actually burdens the claimant's freedom to exercise religious rights. Petitioners claim that the receipt of "wages" would violate the religious convictions of the associates. The Act, however, does not require the payment of cash wages. Section 203(m) defines "wage" to include "the reasonable cost…of furnishing [an] employee with board, lodging, or other facilities." Since the associates currently receive such benefits in exchange for working in the Foundation's businesses, application of the Act will work little or no change in their situation: the associates may simply continue to be paid in the form of benefits. The religious objection does not appear to be to receiving any specified *amount* of wages. Indeed, petitioners and the associates assert that the associates' standard of living far exceeds the minimum. Even if the Foundation were to pay wages in cash, or if the associates' beliefs precluded them from accepting the statutory amount, there is nothing in the Act to prevent the associates from returning the amounts to the Foundation, provided that they do so voluntarily. We therefore fail to perceive how application of the Act would interfere with the associates' right to freely exercise their religious beliefs.

The Foundation's commercial activities, undertaken with a "common business purpose," are not beyond the reach of the Fair Labor Standards Act because of the Foundation's religious character, and its associates are "employees" within the meaning of the Act because they work in contemplation of compensation. Like other employees covered by the Act, the associates are entitled to its full protection. Furthermore, application of the Act to the Foundation's commercial activities is fully consistent with the requirements of the First Amendment. The judgment below is accordingly

Affirmed.

Notes

1. In *Alamo Foundation* a unanimous Supreme Court extended the two-step evaluation process created in *Catholic Bishop of Chicago*, and applied it to a set of workplace regulations closely related to the NLRA: the Fair Labor Standards Act (FLSA). Addressing the jurisdictional question first, it held that the FLSA applied to a religious, nonprofit, commercial organization. It then turned to a consideration of the merits of the First Amendment claims. The Court dismissed them in short order because it "fail[ed] to perceive how application of the Act would interfere with the associates' right to freely exercise their religious beliefs." It also rejected a claim that the recordkeeping requirements of FLSA would create an "excessive government entanglement with religion."

Alamo, 471 U.S. at 304. To what extent should such a two-step approach be applied to other cases arising under the Religion Clause? How, if at all, would it affect the outcome in the school funding cases on which the Court relied in *Catholic Bishop of Chicago? See* Chapter 6 § D.

2. What is the Court's rationale in *Alamo Foundation*? The Court could have chosen from among the following: (1) that the Tony and Susan Alamo Foundation's religious character did not, standing alone, suffice to confer an exemption; (2) that its commercial activities make it unsuited to claim such an exemption; or (3) that no free exercise claim was stated. It appears that, under these facts, the Court saw no free exercise problem at all: "We...fail to perceive how application of the Act would interfere with the associates' right to freely exercise their religious beliefs." Was that the best approach?

3. To what extent do you think that the clearly stated and vigorous opposition of teachers' unions to voucher-style reforms of public education financing systems are based on the difficulties inherent in organization campaigns aimed at religious schools? *See* Chapter Six, § D (2). Although there is no constitutional difficulty when unions seek to organize non-religious private schools, the sheer number of such schools and their relatively small size may much organizing campaigns too expensive to be worth the effort, and cases such as *Catholic Bishop of Chicago* have stood in the way of union campaigns to organize major religious school systems.

2) Jurisdiction Under Title VII of the Civil Rights Act of 1964

Distinguishing Between Exemptions and Claims of Immunity

Because Title VII itself provides an exemption for religious institutions, the resolution of jurisdictional questions under Title VII is a bit more complicated than those arising under the NLRA or FLSA. 42 U.S.C. § 2000e-1(a) provides:

> This subchapter shall not apply to an employer with respect to the employment of aliens outside any State, or to a religious corporation, association, educational institution, or society with respect to the employment of individuals of a particular religion to perform work connected with the carrying on by such corporation, association, educational institution, or society of its activities.

42 U.S.C. § 2000e-2(e) (2001) provides:

> Businesses or enterprises with personnel qualified on basis of religion, sex, or national origin; educational institutions with personnel of particular religion
>
> Notwithstanding any other provision of this subchapter, (1) it shall not be an unlawful employment practice for an employer to hire and employ employees, for an employment agency to classify, or refer for employment any individual, for a labor organization to classify its membership or to classify or refer for employment any individual, or for an employer, labor organization, or joint labor-management committee controlling apprenticeship or other training or retraining programs to admit or employ any individual in any such program, on the basis of his religion, sex, or national origin in those certain instances where religion, sex, or national origin is a bona fide occupational qualification reasonably necessary to the normal operation of that particular business or enterprise, and (2) it shall not be an unlawful employment practice for a school, college, university, or other educational institution or institution of learning to

> hire and employ employees of a particular religion if such school, college, university, or other educational institution or institution of learning is, in whole or in substantial part, owned, supported, controlled, or managed by a particular religion or by a particular religious corporation, association, or society, or if the curriculum of such school, college, university, or other educational institution or institution of learning is directed toward the propagation of a particular religion.

As a result, it is necessary to distinguish between claims that allege that Congress has no power to regulate the relationship, and those which turn on the meaning of the statute itself.

Jurisdictional Claims

McClure v. Salvation Army, 460 F.2d 553 (5th Cir. 1972), held that Sections 702 and 703(a) of Title VII, 42 U.S.C.A. §§2000e-1, 2000-2(a), do not apply to the relationship between a church and its ministers. Mrs. McClure became a minister for the Salvation Army after a two year training program. She was then appointed to a variety of posts and served the Salvation Army until her status as a minister was terminated. She then commenced a civil action against the Salvation Army alleging that she had received less salary and benefits than similarly situated male ministers.

The Salvation Army argued that it was neither an "employer," nor Mrs. McClure an "employee," as those terms are defined by Title VII. Rejecting this contention, the court held that "[o]rganizations affecting commerce may not escape the coverage of social legislation by showing that they were created for fraternal or religious purposes." *Id.* at 557. The Salvation Army then argued that the religious exemption provided by Section 702 should be applied. Rejecting this argument as well, the court looked to both the legislative history of §702 and the language of the statute and concluded that Congress did not intend to exempt religious organizations from liability for discrimination on the basis of race, color, sex or national origin.

Turning to the constitutional question inherent in a government decision to regulate the relationship between a church and its ministers, the court found that "[t]he relationship between an organized church and its ministers is its lifeblood." *Id.* at 558. In its view, issues relating to the selection, payment, placement and assignment of duties to a minister are matters of church administration and government. *Id.* at 554. Citing *Watson v. Jones*, 13 Wall 679 (1871), *Kedroff v. St. Nicholas Cathedral*, 344 U.S. 94, 116 (1954), and *Ashwander v. Tennessee Valley Authority*, 297 U.S. 288 (1936) (Brandeis, J. concurring), the court held that Congress simply did not intend by its general wording of the statute to regulate church-minister relationships. *Id.* at 560, 561. *Accord Gellington v. Christian Methodist Episcopal Church, Inc.*, 203 F.3d 1299 (11th Cir. 2000) (ministerial exception survives *Employment Div. v. Smith*).

Other cases involving attempts to assert jurisdiction over positions that are inherently religious in nature reach the same result. *See Rayburn v. General Conf. of Seventh Day Adventists*, 772 F.2d 1164 (4th Cir. 1985) (pastoral positions which are functionally identical to ministerial ones are exempt from Title VII); *Maguire v. Marquette University*, 627 F. Supp. 1499 (E.D. Wis. 1986) (both Title VII and the First Amendment preclude an inquiry into the suitability of an individual to teach theology); *Van Osdol v. Voght*, 908 P.2d 1122 (Colo. 1996) (dismissing Title VII claim by minister against another minister and church governing board). The courts have been strict, however, in their view that only positions functionally equivalent to those of ministers are exempt.

See Equal Employment Opportunity Commission v. Southwestern Baptist Theological Seminary, 651 F.2d 277, 280 (5th Cir. 1981) (requiring a seminary to file periodic reports describing workplace demographics, and drawing distinctions between and among the faculty, administrative staff, and support personnel, even though it was alleged by the Seminary that all were hired and retained on the basis of "a divinely guided 'spiritual quest' mutually pursued by the Seminary and the prospective employee"); *Equal Employment Opportunity Commission v. Pacific Press Publishing Association*, 676 F.2d 1272 (9th Cir. 1982) (upholding the application of equal pay and retaliatory discharge requirements to a non-profit corporation affiliated with the Seventh Day Adventist Church that required all employees to be members of the church in good standing). In situations where the individual does not, and cannot, function as a minister, the courts take the position that unless doctrine forms the basis for the employment decision and would provide a basis for claiming the statutory exemption, the general norms of Title VII apply. *See Whitney v. Greater N.Y. Corp. of Seventh Day Adventists*, 401 F. Supp. 1363, 1368 (S.D.N.Y. 1975) (nothing in the record showed "that the relationship between the church and its clerical help touches so close to the heart of church administration as to be protected by the First Amendment from the commands of Title VII"); *Ninth & O Street Baptist Church v. EEOC*, 633 F. Supp. 229 (W.D. Ky. 1986) (refusing to issue an injunction of EEOC investigation of complaint alleging unlawful discharge for religious reasons). *But see* Laura L. Coon, Note, *Employment Discrimination By Religious Institutions: Limiting the Sanctuary of the Constitutional Ministerial Exception to Religion-Based Employment Decisions,* 54 Vand. L. Rev. 481 (2001) ("Instead of focusing on whether an employment dispute implicates a ministerial relationship, as courts have done by analyzing the primary duties of the plaintiff in order to determine application of the constitutional ministerial exception, justiciability should be based on whether adjudication of the dispute would actually implicate religious doctrine or practice.")

Exemption Claims

In *Little v. Wuerl*, 929 F.2d 944 (3d Cir. 1991), the United States Court of Appeals for the Third Circuit considered the applicability of the Title VII exemption to Catholic schools in their hiring and retention of employees. A non-Catholic employee of a Catholic school filed a Title VII complaint after the school failed to renew her employment contract because the teacher had entered into a second marriage not recognized as valid by the Catholic Church.

Following the methodology of the cases decided after *Catholic Bishop of Chicago*, the court sought to determine whether application of Title VII to the religiously-motivated dismissal of a teacher in a religious school would implicate substantial constitutional questions. Quoting *Catholic Bishop of Chicago*, the court noted the "the critical and unique role of the teacher in fulfilling the mission of a church-operated school," 929 F.2d at 948, n.6, and held that a strict reading of Title VII would be inconsistent with the church's free exercise rights. The court also concluded that the application of Title VII would be "suspect because it arguably would create excessive government entanglement with religion in violation of the establishment clause." *Id.* at 949.

Having concluded that application of Title VII to church-operated schools would raise serious constitutional concerns, the court proceeded to consideration of the jurisdictional issue: *i.e.*, did Congress clearly intend Title VII to apply to such schools? Because the express language of Title VII allows religiously-affiliated institutions to discriminate on the basis of religion, the jurisdictional question was answered in the affirmative: Title VII *does* apply to such schools. 929 F.2d at 950. But because the teacher in *Little v. Wuerl* was not discharged on the basis of her religion, but rather because she did not conform her behavior to the teachings of the Church, the court was forced to consider, not the Constitution (as it would in the NLRA context), but the scope of the statutory exemption.

Based on an interpretation of the legislative history of the religious institution exemption, the court reasoned that Title VII exempts religious institutions from the prohibition on religious discrimination so that they may "create and maintain communities composed solely of individuals faithful to their doctrinal practices." 929 F.2d at 951. Thus, while the school is subject to Title VII, it is *not a violation* of Title VII for a religious school to discharge an employee who has publicly engaged in behavior regarded by the school as inconsistent with its religious principles.

A similar analysis was followed, though a different result was reached, in *Dolter v. Wahlert High School*, 483 F. Supp. 266 (N.D. Iowa 1980). The issue was whether an unmarried, pregnant Catholic teacher could be fired because of her sexual conduct. Rejecting the school's immunity claim, the court held that even if the school had a moral conduct standard governing the pre- and extra-marital sexual conduct of its teachers based on Catholic doctrine, the First Amendment did not preclude a judicial determination whether the standard it was applied equally to all teachers, regardless of their sex. *Id.* at 270. *Accord Cline v. Catholic Diocese of Toledo*, 206 F.3d 651 (6th Cir. 2000)(remanding for determination of whether termination of contract was because of pregnancy, or because of the premarital sexual activity from which it resulted); *Ritter v. Mount St. Mary's College*, 495 F. Supp. 724 (D. Md. 1980) (tenure dispute alleging sex and age discrimination in the choice of a professor who was a priest; summary judgment was denied until it could be determined whether religion actually played a role in the college's tenure decision).

Mixed motive cases present a particularly difficult question in this context. To what extent may the EEOC or a private litigant seek to prove that the religious claim is a pretext for discrimination that is prohibited by the statute? *See EEOC v. Mississippi College*, 626 F.2d 477, 485 (5th Cir. 1980) (holding that "if a religious institution of the kind described in § 702 presents convincing evidence that the challenged employment practice resulted from discrimination on the basis of religion, § 702 deprives the EEOC of jurisdiction to investigate further to determine whether the religious discrimination was a pretext for some other form of discrimination"). *See also Geary v. Visitation of the Blessed Virgin Mary Parish School*, 7 F.3d 324 (3d Cir. 1993) (same, Age Discrimination in Employment Act (ADEA)).

There can be significant differences between federal and state laws on this topic. While many states adopt the Title VII approach to *pleading and proof* of cases, *see, e.g., Basinger v. Pilarczyk*, 125 Ohio App.3d 74, 707 N.E.2d 1149, 1150–51 (1997) (stating that the *McDonnell Douglas* analysis applies under the Ohio Civil Rights Act when teacher sues a sectarian school), the *substantive* reach of state law may be broader. *See, e.g., Ward v. Hengle*, 124 Ohio App.3d 396, 706 N.E.2d 392 (9th Dist., 1997) (concluding Ohio Civil Rights Act, Ohio Rev. Code § 4112.02, does not exempt church from claims that cannot be justified on BFOQ grounds.).

2. Identifying the Religious Employer

Given the importance of jurisdictional and exemption inquiries, it is not surprising that disputes arise over the religious character of institutions facing charges under Title

VII. Similar questions arose under the NLRA prior to *Catholic Bishop of Chicago.* The two-step inquiry utilized by the courts attempts to distinguish between positions that are central to preserving the religious character of the institution, and those which are merely ancillary to it. Occasionally, however, a case arises where the religious character of the institution itself is called into question.

EEOC v. Kamehameha Schools, 990 F.2d 458 (9th Cir.) (as amended, May 10, 1993), *cert. denied*, 510 U.S. 963 (1993), is one of those cases. The Kamehameha School was created by the will of Bernice Pauahi Bishop, a member of the Hawaiian royal family and, at the time of her death in 1884, the largest landowner in Hawaii. Her will provided that the bulk of her estate should be placed in a charitable trust "to erect and maintain in the Hawaiian Islands two schools, each for boarding and day scholars, one for boys and one for girls, to be known as, and called the Kamehameha Schools." The will also directed that "the teachers of said schools shall forever be persons of the Protestant religion," but made it clear that Mrs. Bishop did "not intend that the choice be restricted to persons of any particular sect of Protestants." 990 F.2d at 459.

When Carole Edgerton, who is not a Protestant, sought a position as a substitute French teacher, she was informed of the Protestant-only requirement. She filed a charge of religious discrimination with EEOC, which attempted conciliation, but the Schools informed the Commission they were bound by the terms of Mrs. Bishop's will. The defense was based on three assertions that Title VII itself permitted its "Protestant-only" hiring policy: first, that it was a religious educational institution; second, that it was entitled to claim the religious curriculum exemption;[3] and third, that religion was a bona fide occupational requirement given the terms of Mrs. Bishop's will. 990 F.2d at 459.

The Ninth Circuit rejected each defense, holding that the religious exemptions are to be narrowly construed, and that the burden of proving that they apply rests upon the institution claiming them. 990 F.2d at 460. Basing its analysis on *EEOC v. Townley Engineering & Mfg. Co.*, excerpted in § F(2) below, the court undertook an analysis of the facts to determine whether the secular characteristics of the school outweighed its religious aspects. The goal is, in the court's words, to determine "whether the 'general picture' of the institution is primarily religious or secular." 990 F.2d at 460. "Mere affiliation" with a religious organization, or the maintenance of a religious environment, is not enough. In the view of the Ninth Circuit, the exemption only applies to schools that are actively involved in the propagation of a particular religion. The court stated:

> the religious characteristics of the Schools consist of minimal, largely comparative religious studies, scheduled prayers and services, quotation of Bible verses in a school publication, and the employment of nominally Protestant teachers for secular subjects. References to Bible verses, comparative religious education, and even prayers and services are common at private schools and cannot suffice to exempt such schools; the addition of nominally Protestant teachers does not alter this conclusion. We conclude the Schools are an essentially secular institution operating within an historical tradition that includes Protestantism, and that the Schools' purpose and character is primarily secular, not primarily religious.

3. The curriculum exemption in 42 U.S.C. § 2000e-2(e)(2) provides that "...it shall not be an unlawful employment practice for a school...to hire and employ employees of a particular religion...if the curriculum of such school...is directed toward the propagation of a particular religion."

990 F.2d at 463–64. *Accord Fike v. United Methodist Children's Home of Va., Inc.*, 547 F. Supp. 286 (E.D. Va. 1982) (exemption does not apply because the home had abandoned its sectarian orientation and become a secular organization although it remained affiliated with the Methodist Church).

Addressing the BFOQ defense, the court observed that:

> The district court held the requirement related to the teachers' ability to perform their job because "the essence or central mission of [the Schools] is to provide native Hawaiians with an education from the Protestant point of view. Similarly, the essence or central mission of the teachers' jobs is to provide that viewpoint." 780 F. Supp. at 1323. The district court defined the central mission of the Schools too narrowly. The record demonstrates the Schools have embraced a broad mandate to help native Hawaiians "participate in contemporary society for a rewarding and productive life" by providing a solid education in traditional secular subjects, instruction in Hawaiian culture and history, and the moral guidance necessary to help students "define a system of values." The requirement of Protestant affiliation in a teacher's past is largely irrelevant to this mission. There is no basis in the record for concluding a nominally Protestant teacher will provide superior instruction or serve as a better moral guide to students. *See* [*UAW v.*] *Johnson Controls*, [499 U.S. 187](employer must show "a high correlation" between a qualification and ability to perform job functions).

990 F.2d at 465–66 (footnote omitted).

Notes

1. *Religion as BFOQ*: Unless an employer is specifically permitted to establish religion as a BFOQ, it would be nearly impossible to prove that religious discrimination is necessary to the effective conduct of the employer's business. The law simply does not permit such "broad brush" classification, see, e.g., *City of Los Angeles Dept. of Water & Power v. Manhart*, 435 U.S. 702 (1978) (sex-based pension annuity tables), and it provides special protection in those few cases where scrutiny of religious belief by an employer is clearly proper. *See E.E.O.C. v. Southwestern Baptist Theological Seminary*, 651 F.2d 277 (5th Cir. 1981) (reporting requirements of Title VII). *Compare* 42 U.S.C. §2000e-2(e)(1) (1995) (BFOQ) *and Phillips v. Martin Marietta Corp.*, 400 U.S. 542 (1971) (standards for BFOQ) *with* 42 U.S.C. §300a-7 (1996) (forbidding discrimination against those opposing abortion by employers and training programs receiving financial assistance from the Public Health Service).

2. What, precisely, did the court decide in *Kamehameha Schools*? That the school was not "Protestant *enough*" to claim the exemption, or that being a Protestant is not a BFOQ for a French teacher? If the decision is read as a finding that the Kamehameha Schools were not really "religious," which, if any, of the Supreme Court's Religion Clause decisions authorize a secular court to make such findings? Is that authorization implicit in the Title VII exemption? The operative language of §2000e-2(e)(2) refers to schools which are "in whole or in substantial part, owned, supported, controlled, or managed by a particular religion or by a particular religious corporation, association, or society," and yet the court holds that "at least where the school is not owned by a church, the courts must determine in each case whether a particular educational institution is a religious organization." *Kamehameha Schools*, 990 F.2d at 460. Does the lan-

guage of the statute support the court's preference for case-by-case analysis in all cases where a religious school is not owned by the church? Does the First Amendment authorize such an inquiry, even if it would be permitted under Title VII? How does § 2000e-1(a) affect your answer?

3. What is the justification for the court's requirement that in order to claim the Title VII religious exemption, a school cannot "merely [be] 'affiliated' with a religious organization?" 990 F.2d 460 (quoting *Townley*, 859 F.2d 610, 617). Is that an accurate description of the Kamehameha Schools?

4. Is there any doubt that the culture of the *Kamehameha Schools* was Protestant, and that they had many, if not all, of the characteristics which would disqualify them for state aid under the Supreme Court's Establishment Clause rulings? (*e.g.*, classroom prayer, the study of religion for its own sake rather than as literature). *See* Chapters Five and Six. Why then were they not religious "enough" to qualify for the exemption for religious educational institutions?

5. In *Pime v. Loyola Univ. of Chicago*, 803 F.2d 351, 358 (7th Cir. 1986), the Seventh Circuit upheld the university's decision to reserve four positions in its Philosophy Department in order to maintain a Jesuit "presence" at the University. The court in *Pime* considered the "long Jesuit tradition," the largely Catholic student body, the character of the school, and the desire of administrators "'that students would *occasionally* encounter a Jesuit,'" (emphasis added), to support its finding that "the educational experience at Loyola would be different if Jesuit presence were not maintained." *Id.* at 354. Would the result have been different if Loyola had decided to reserve the positions for "orthodox," practicing Catholics, regardless of their clerical status?

6. In *UAW v. Johnson Controls, Inc.*, 499 U.S. 187, 202–03 (1991), the Supreme Court held that in order for a discriminatory job qualification to qualify as a BFOQ, it must "affect an employee's ability to do the job," and "must relate to the 'essence' or to the 'central mission of the employer's business.'" In *Kamehameha Schools*, the EEOC took the position that the BFOQ requirement should be applied on a position-by-position basis, and that there was nothing "specific about the subject matter of any given teacher position ... that would make a teacher being Protestant a bona fide occupational qualification." 990 F.2d at 465. Given this reasoning, what practical steps can, or should, a religiously affiliated school take to protect its "religious" character? *See Montrose Christian School Corporation v. Walsh*, 363 Md. 565, 770 A.2d 111 (2001) (holding that First Amendment and Maryland Declaration of Rights bar Montgomery County from limiting the religious exemption in its employment discrimination ordinance to employees hired "to perform purely religious functions").

7. It has been argued in other settings that educational "diversity" requires the creation of a "critical mass" of individuals who share common racial, cultural, or ethnic characteristics. Although the term "critical mass" is used extensively in the literature on diversity in the academic setting, there is little, if any, guidance on what it means. Generally speaking, the concept refers to a certain percentage of individuals who share a common characteristic, such as religion or ethnic heritage. Although there is no agreement on what that percentage should be—it will vary according to the character of the institution—the figure is usually set at a percentage high enough to give that group enough "weight" to overcome what might be called "token" status. *See, e.g.*, Richard Delgado, *The Inward Turn In Outsider Jurisprudence*, 34 Wm. & Mary L. Rev. 741 (1993) ("The term 'critical mass' means a number sufficient to enable the newcomers to offer each other psychological support and avoid being engulfed by de-

mands such as tutoring and counseling"). With this background in mind, is it possible, in your view, for a religious educational institution to be "diverse" if its faculty and staff share a common religious tradition? Would it be legitimate for the state to demand, under compulsion of employment discrimination law, the creation, through hiring practices, of a "critical mass" of members of different religious traditions? Might the same result be obtained by state or federal enactments requiring an atmosphere of "academic freedom"? *See, e.g.*, Colo. Stats. §23-3.5-105 (2001) (defining the term "pervasively sectarian").

8. On which of the characteristics of the Kamehameha Schools did the Ninth Circuit rely to support its determination that the institutions are "primarily secular"?

9. The trend toward greater secularization of society in general, and of educational institutions in particular, has been noted by a number of commentators. *See, e.g.*, Alexandra D. Furth, *Secular Idolatry and Sacred Traditions: A Critique of the Supreme Court's Secularization Analysis*, 146 U. Pa. L. Rev. 579 (1998); George Marsden, The Soul of the American University: From Protestant Establishment to Established Nonbelief (1994); Mark Schwehn, Exiles from Eden: Religion and the Academic Vocation in America (1993); Frederick Mark Gedicks, *Public Life And Hostility To Religion*, 78 Va. L. Rev. 671 (1992). *See also* Apostolic Constitution of the Supreme Pontiff, John Paul II, "On Catholic Universities (*Ex Corde Ecclesiae)*" (August 15, 1990) (United States Catholic Conference Publication no. 399-X). The legal implications of this trend have produced a wide array of commentary. *See generally* Joanne C. Brant, *"Our Shield Belongs to the Lord": Religious Employers and a Constitutional Right to Discriminate*, 21 Hast. Const. L.Q. 275 (1994); Trevor Hodson, *The Religious Employer Exemption Under Title VII: Should a Church Define Its Own Activities?*, 1994 B.Y.U. L. Rev. 571.

10. The trend toward greater secularization has affected law schools as well. *See generally* Sanford Levinson, *Some Reflections on Multiculturalism, "Equal Concern and Respect," and the Establishment Clause of the First Amendment*, 27 U. Rich. L. Rev. 989 (1993); John T. Noonan, Jr., Essay, *A Catholic Law School*, 67 Notre Dame L. Rev. 1037 (1992). *See also* Robert A. Destro, *ABA and AALS Accreditation: What's "Religious Diversity" Got to Do With It?* 78 Marq. L. Rev. 427 (1995) (discussing the impact of accreditation standards of the American Bar Association and the Association of American Law Schools which are more restrictive than those of Title VII); Thomas L. Shaffer, Symposium on Civic and Legal Education, *Erastian and Sectarian Arguments In Religiously Affiliated American Law Schools*, 45 Stan. L. Rev. 1859 (1993).

3. Operational Issues

Religious corporations, associations, educational institutions and societies are not subject to Title VII for employment decisions relating to the "employment of individuals of a particular religion to perform work connected with the carrying on by such corporation, association, educational institution, or society of its activities." 42 U.S.C. §2000e-1(a) (2001). As currently written, the exemption covers *all* of the "activities" of such organizations. Is this what Congress intended, and, if so, does such a broadly-worded exemption violate either the First Amendment, or the equal protection component of the Fifth? Consider the following case.

Corporation of the Presiding Bishop of the Church of Jesus Christ of Latter-Day Saints v. Amos

483 U.S. 327 (1987)

Justice WHITE delivered the opinion of the Court.

Section 702 of the Civil Rights Act of 1964, 78 Stat. 255, *as amended*, 42 U.S.C. § 2000e-1, exempts religious organizations from Title VII's prohibition against discrimination in employment on the basis of religion. The question presented is whether applying the § 702 exemption to the secular nonprofit activities of religious organizations violates the Establishment Clause of the First Amendment. The District Court held that it does, and the case is here on direct appeal.

The Deseret Gymnasium (Gymnasium) in Salt Lake City, Utah, is a nonprofit facility, open to the public, run by the Corporation of the Presiding Bishop of The Church of Jesus Christ of Latter-Day Saints (CPB), and the Corporation of the President of The Church of Jesus Christ of Latter-Day Saints (COP). The CPB and the COP are religious entities associated with The Church of Jesus Christ of Latter-Day Saints (Church), an unincorporated religious association sometimes called the Mormon or LDS Church.

Appellee Mayson worked at the Gymnasium for some 16 years as an assistant building engineer and then building engineer. He was discharged in 1981 because he failed to qualify for a temple recommend, that is, a certificate that he is a member of the Church and eligible to attend its temples.[4]

Mayson and others purporting to represent a class of plaintiffs brought an action against the CPB and the COP alleging, among other things, discrimination on the basis or religion in violation of § 703 of the Civil Rights Act of 1964, 42 U.S.C. § 2000e-2. The defendants moved to dismiss this claim on the ground that § 702 shields them for liability. The plaintiffs contended that if construed to allow religious employers to discriminate on religious grounds in hiring for nonreligious jobs, § 702 violates the Establishment Clause.

The [district] court concluded that Mayson's case involves nonreligious activity.[8]

The court next considered the plaintiffs' constitutional challenge to § 702. Finding that § 702 impermissibly sponsors religious organizations by granting them "an exclusive authorization to engage in conduct which can directly and immediately advance religious tenets and practices," the court declared the statute unconstitutional as applied to secular activity.

The private appellants contend that we should not apply the three-part *Lemon* approach, which is assertedly unsuited to judging the constitutionality of exemption statutes such as § 702. The argument is that an exemption statute will always have the effect of advancing religion and hence be invalid under the second (effects) part of the *Lemon* test, a result claimed to be inconsistent with cases such as *Walz*. The first two of the three *Lemon* factors, however, were directly taken from pre-*Walz* decisions, and

4. Temple recommends are issued only to individuals who observe the Church's standards in such matters as regular church attendance, tithing, and abstinence from coffee, tea, alcohol, and tobacco.

8. The court also considered and rejected the possibility that § 702 could be construed to exempt a religious organization only with respect to employment involving religious activities.

Walz did not purport to depart from prior Establishment Clause cases, except by adding a consideration that became the third element of the *Lemon* test. In any event, we need not reexamine *Lemon* as applied in this context, for the exemption involved here is in no way questionable under the *Lemon* analysis.

Under the *Lemon* analysis, it is a permissible legislative purpose to alleviate significant governmental interference with the ability of religious organizations to define and carry out their religious missions. Appellees argue that there is no such purpose here because § 702 provided adequate protection for religious employers prior to the 1972 amendment, when it exempted only the religious activities of such employers from the statutory ban on religious discrimination. We may assume for the sake of argument that the pre-1972 exemption was adequate in the sense that the Free Exercise Clause required no more. Nonetheless, it is a significant burden on a religious organization to require it, on pain of substantial liability, to predict which of its activities a secular court will consider religious. The line is hardly a bright one, and an organization might understandably be concerned that a judge would not understand its religious tenets and sense of mission. Fear of potential liability might affect the way an organization carried out what it understood to be its religious mission.

We agree with the District Court that this purpose does not violate the Establishment Clause.

The second requirement under *Lemon* is that the law in question have "a principal or primary effect... that neither advances nor inhibits religion." Undoubtedly, religious organizations are better able now to advance their purposes than they were prior to the 1972 amendment to § 702. But religious groups have been better able to advance their purposes on account of many laws that have passed constitutional muster: for example, the property tax exemption at issue in *Walz*, or the loans of school books to school children, including parochial school students, upheld in *Allen*. A law is not unconstitutional simply because it *allows* churches to advance religion, which is their very purpose. For a law to have forbidden "effects" under *Lemon*, it must be fair to say that the *government itself* has advanced religion through its own activities and influence.

The District Court appeared to fear that sustaining the exemption would permit churches with financial resources impermissibly to extend their influence and propagate their faith by entering the commercial, profit-making world. The case before us, however, involves a nonprofit activity instituted over 75 years ago in the hope that "all who assemble here, and who come for the benefit of their health, and for physical blessings, [may] feel that they are in a house dedicated to the Lord." This case therefore does not implicate the apparent concerns of the District Court. Moreover, we find no persuasive evidence in the record before us that the Church's ability to propagate its religious doctrine through the Gymnasium is any greater now than it was prior to the passage of the Civil Rights Act in 1964. In such circumstances, we do not see how any advancement of religion achieved by the Gymnasium can be fairly attributed to the Government, as opposed to the Church.

We find unpersuasive the District Court's reliance on the fact that § 702 singles out religious entities for a benefit. Although the Court has given weight to this consideration in its past decisions, it has never indicated that statutes that give special consideration to religious groups are *per se* inval*id*. That would run contrary to the teaching of our cases that there is ample room for accommodation of religion under the Establishment Clause. Where, as here, government acts with the proper purpose of lifting a regulation that burdens the exercise of religion, we see no reason to require that the exemption comes packaged with benefits to secular entities.

We are also unpersuaded by the District Court's reliance on the argument that § 702 is unsupported by long historical tradition. There was simply no need to consider the scope of the § 702 exemption until the 1964 Civil Rights Act was passed, and the fact that Congress concluded after eight years that the original exemption was unnecessarily narrow is a decision entitled to deference, not suspicion.

[W]e see no justification for applying strict scrutiny to a statute that passes the *Lemon* test. The proper inquiry is whether Congress has chosen a rational classification to further a legitimate end. We have already indicated that Congress acted with a legitimate purpose in expanding the § 702 exemption to cover all activities of religious employers. [I]t suffices to hold—as we now do—that as applied to the nonprofit activities of religious employers, § 702 is rationally related to the legitimate purpose of alleviating significant governmental interference with the ability of religious organizations to define and carry out their religious missions.

It cannot be seriously contended that § 702 impermissibly entangles church and state; the statute effectuates a more complete separation of the two and avoids the kind of intrusive inquiry into religious belief that the District Court engaged in this case. The statute easily passes muster under the third part of the *Lemon* test.

The judgment of the District Court is reversed, and the case is remanded for further proceedings consistent with this opinion.

It is so ordered.

Justice BRENNAN, with whom Justice MARSHALL joins, concurring in the judgment.

I write separately to emphasize that my concurrence in the judgment rests on the fact that this case involves a challenge to the application of § 702's categorical exemption to the activities of a *nonprofit* organization. I believe that the particular character of nonprofit activity makes inappropriate a case-by-case determination whether its nature is religious or secular.

This case presents a confrontation between the rights of religious organizations and those of individuals. Any exemption from Title VII's proscription on religious discrimination necessarily has the effect of burdening the religious liberty of prospective and current employees. An exemption says that a person may be put to the choice of either conforming to certain religious tenets or losing a job opportunity, a promotion, or, as in this case, employment itself. The potential for coercion created by such a provision is in serious tension with our commitment to individual freedom of conscience in matters of religious belief.

At the same time, religious organizations have an interest in autonomy in ordering their internal affairs. For many individuals, religious activity derives meaning in large measure from participation in a larger religious community. Such a community represents an ongoing tradition of shared beliefs, an organic entity not reducible to a mere aggregation of individuals.[3] Determining that certain activities are in furtherance of an organization's religious mission, and that only those committed to that mission should conduct them, is thus a means by which a religious community de-

3. See, e.g., Karl Barth, *The Christian Community and the Civil Community*, in COMMUNITY, STATE AND CHURCH 149 (1960); Robert M. Cover, *The Supreme Court, 1982 Term—Forward: Nomos and Narrative*, 97 Harv. L. Rev. 4 (1983). *Cf.* Michael Perry, *The Authority of Text, Tradition, and Reason: A Theory of Constitutional* "Interpretation," 58 S. Cal. L. Rev. 551, 558 (1985) (tradition represents "a particular history or narrative, in which the central motif is an aspiration to a particular form of life, to certain projects, goals, [and] ideals, and the central discourse... is an argument... about how that form of life is to be cultivated and revised").

fines itself. Solicitude for a church's ability to do so reflects the idea that furtherance of the autonomy of religious organizations often furthers individual religious freedom as well.

The authority to engage in this process of self-definition inevitably involves what we normally regard as infringement on Free Exercise rights, since a religious organization is able to condition employment in certain activities on subscription to particular religious tenets. We are willing to countenance the imposition of such a condition because we deem it vital that, if certain activities constitute part of a religious community's practice, then a religious organization should be able to require that only members of its community perform those activities.

This rationale suggests that, ideally, religious organizations should be able to discriminate on the basis of religion *only* with respect to religious activities, so that a determination should be made in each case whether an activity is religious or secular. This is because the infringement on religious liberty that results from conditioning performance of *secular* activity upon religious belief cannot be defended as necessary for the community's self-definition. Furthermore, the authorization of discrimination in such circumstances... puts at the disposal of religion the added advantages of economic leverage in the secular realm. As a result, the authorization of religious discrimination with respect to nonreligious activities goes beyond reasonable accommodation, and has the effect of furthering religion in violation of the Establishment Clause.

What makes the application of a religious-secular distinction difficult is that the character of an activity is not self-evident. As a result, determining whether an activity is religious or secular requires a searching case-by-case analysis. This results in considerable ongoing government entanglement in religious affairs. Furthermore, this prospect of government intrusion raises concern that a religious organization may be chilled in its Free Exercise activity. While a church may regard the conduct of certain functions as integral to its mission, a court may disagree. A religious organization therefore would have an incentive to characterize as religious only those activities about which there likely would be no dispute, even if it genuinely believed that religious commitment was important in performing other tasks as well. As a result, the community's process of self-definition would be shaped in part by the prospects of litigation. A case-by-case analysis for all activities therefore would both produce excessive government entanglement with religion and create the danger of chilling religious activity.

The risk of chilling religious organizations is most likely to arise with respect to *nonprofit* activities. The fact that an operation is not organized as a profit-making commercial enterprise... makes plausible a church's contention that an entity is not operated simply in order to generate revenues for the church, but that the activities themselves are infused with a religious purpose.

Nonprofit activities therefore are most likely to present cases in which characterization of the activity as religious or secular will be a close question. If there is a danger that a religious organization will be deterred from classifying as religious those activities it actually regards as religious, it is likely to be in this domain. This substantial potential for chilling religious activity makes inappropriate a case-by-case determination of the character of a nonprofit organization, and justifies a categorical exemption for nonprofit activities. While every nonprofit activity may not be operated for religious purposes, the likelihood that many are makes a categorical rule a suitable means to avoid chilling the exercise of religion.

Sensitivity to individual religious freedom dictates that religious discrimination be permitted only with respect to employment in religious activities. Because of the nature of nonprofit activities, I believe that a categorical exemption for such enterprises appropriately balances these competing concerns. As a result, I concur in the Court's judgment that the nonprofit Deseret Gymnasium may avail itself of an automatic exemption from Title VII's proscription on religious discrimination.

Justice BLACKMUN, concurring in the judgment.

[Opinion omitted.]

Justice O'CONNOR, concurring in the judgment.

Although I agree with the judgment of the Court, I write separately to note that this action once again illustrates certain difficulties inherent in the Court's use of the test articulated in *Lemon*. As a result of this problematic analysis, while the holding of the opinion for the Court extends only to non-profit organizations, its reasoning fails to acknowledge that the amended § 702, 42 U.S.C. § 2000e-1, raises different questions as it is applied to profit and nonprofit organizations.

While acknowledging that "[u]ndoubtedly, religious organizations are better able now to advance their purposes than they were prior to the 1972 amendment to § 702," the Court seems to suggest that the "effects" prong of the *Lemon* test is not at all implicated as long as the government action can be characterized as "allowing" religious organizations to advance religion, in contrast to government action directly advancing religion. This distinction seems to me to obscure far more than to enlighten. Almost any government benefit to religion could be recharacterized as simply "allowing" a religion to better advance itself, unless perhaps it involved actual proselytization by government agents. In nearly every case of a government benefit to religion, the religious mission would not be advanced if the religion did not take advantage of the benefit; even a direct financial subsidy to a religious organization would not advance religion if for some reason the organization failed to make any use of the funds. It is for this same reason that there is little significance to the Court's observation that it was the Church rather than the government that penalized Mayson's refusal to adhere to Church doctrine. The Church had the power to put Mayson to a choice of qualifying for a temple recommend or losing his job because *the government* had lifted from religious organizations the general regulatory burden imposed by § 702.

The necessary first step in evaluating an Establishment Clause challenge to a government action lifting from religious organizations a generally applicable regulatory burden is to recognize that such government action *does* have the effect of advancing religion. The necessary second step is to separate those benefits to religion that constitutionally accommodate the free exercise of religion from those that provide unjustifiable awards of assistance to religious organizations. As I have suggested in earlier opinions, the inquiry framed by the *Lemon* test should be "whether government's purpose is to endorse religion and whether the statute actually conveys a message of endorsement."

Because there is a probability that a nonprofit activity of a religious organization will itself be involved in the organization's religious mission, in my view the objective observer should perceive the government action as an accommodation of the exercise of religion rather than as a government endorsement of religion.

It is not clear, however, that activities conducted by religious organizations solely as profit-making enterprises will be as likely to be directly involved in the religious mission of the organization. While I express no opinion on the issue, I emphasize that under the holding of the Court, and under my view of the appropriate Establishment Clause analysis, the question of the constitutionality of the § 702 exemption as applied to for-profit activities of religious organizations remains open.

Notes

1. The Court's decision that Title VII's religious exemption does not violate the Establishment Clause appears to rest on its view that it is permissible for Congress to allow religious organizations to pursue their respective missions without scrutiny by government agencies. It rejected the proposition that religious exemptions "advance religion" under the second prong of the *Lemon* test when the exemption merely permits the religious organization to pursue its mission unfettered by government controls. Although several Justices argued that the holding might not apply in a case where the business had been a taxable, "for-profit" enterprise which funneled its earnings into the activities of a church, the facts did not present such a case, and the Court did not consider the question. Why should an organization's tax status be relevant?

2. Justices Brennan and Marshall suggest that "ideally, religious organizations should be able to discriminate on the basis of religion *only* with respect to religious activities," but concede that "the application of a religious-secular distinction [is] difficult [because] the character of an activity is not self-evident." Given the size and breadth of the activities that are carried on in the nonprofit sector in the United States (over 10% of GDP), is this a meaningful distinction? Does it serve as a useful proxy for the religious-secular distinction?

3. Is it self-evident that the *ideal* is for government to limit the ability of religious organizations to discriminate in their hiring to activities that are "religious" in their character? Putting aside the difficulties inherent in determining the character of any given activity, would it not be reasonable for Congress to require that religious organizations be left alone when the topic is religion? If so, isn't the Court's penchant for "case-by-case" adjudication of such claims an implicit holding that the Establishment Clause forbids what the Free Exercise Clause does not require? *Cf. Texas Monthly v. Bullock*, excerpted in Chapter Nine, E(5).

4. Should the Establishment Clause be construed to forbid exemptions for religious organizations only when the activities exempted are "directly involved in the religious mission of the organization"? Does a "directly involved" standard answer any of the questions posed above? *See Montrose Christian School Corporation v. Walsh*, 363 Md. 565, 770 A.2d 111 (Ct. App. 2001) (holding that First Amendment and Maryland Declaration of Rights do not permit Montgomery County, Maryland to limit the religious exemption in its county ordinance to employees hired "to perform purely religious functions and permitting religious schools solely to hire members of its church.")

5. Justice O'Connor's opinion restates her preference for the "objective observer" standard. What would the "objective observer" perceive to be the intent of a statute (or judicial decree) that would *preclude* religious organizations from discriminating on the basis of religion?

4. The Americans with Disabilities Act and Religious Organizations

The Americans with Disabilities Act ("ADA"), 42 U.S.C. § 12101 *et seq.* (2001), prohibits employers with more than fifteen (15) employees from discriminating against any "otherwise qualified individual" on the basis of their disability. In keeping with its remedial purpose, it is to be liberally construed, see *PGA Tour, Inc. v. Martin,* 531 U.S.

1049 (2001), but it will be applied in accordance with its express terms. *See, e.g., Birchem v. Knights of Columbus*, 113 F.3d 310, 312–313 (8th Cir. 1997) (ADA does not apply to independent contractors).

The ADA contains two important exemptions for "religious organizations or entities controlled by religious organizations including places of worship." Like other employers, religious organizations covered by the Act may not discriminate on the basis of disability in making employment decisions, but may adopt religion-based employment preferences, even if doing so would discriminate against a disabled individual protected under the ADA. Section 12113(c) of the ADA provides:

> (1) *In general*
>
> This subchapter shall not prohibit a religious corporation, association, educational institution, or society from giving preference in employment to individuals of a particular religion to perform work connected with the carrying on by such corporation, association, educational institution, or society of its activities.
>
> (2) *Religious tenets requirement*
>
> Under this subchapter, a religious organization may require that all applicants and employees conform to the religious tenets of such organization.

This provision appears to immunize churches from liability under Title VII for hiring decisions made in order to meet institutional obligations under the ADA. Does the Supreme Court's holding in *Corporation of Presiding Bishop v. Amos, supra,* support such an interpretation? *See Starkman v. Evans*, 198 F.3d 173 (5th Cir. 1999) ("ministerial exception" of Title VII applies to ADA claim by choir director)

Religious organizations are also exempt from the "public accommodations" provisions of Title III of the ADA. 42 U.S.C. § 12187 (2001) provides that "The provisions of this subchapter shall not apply...to religious organizations or entities controlled by religious organizations, including places of worship." Thus, qualifying religious organizations are not required to have all newly built facilities conform to the ADA's accessibility guidelines, are not required to remove architectural barriers in existing facilities that would otherwise be subject to the "public accommodations" requirements, or defend against ADA claims arising from their non-employment program activities. *See White v. Denver Seminary*, F.Supp.2d, 2001 WL 987539 (D. Colo. 2001) (seminary's educational program is immune from suit under ADA's religious exemption). For an extensive discussion of the liability of church-related organizations under ADA and Section 504 of the Rehabilitation Act of 1973, 29 U.S.C. § 794 (2001), see John A. Liekweg, *The Americans with Disabilities Act, Section 504, and Church-Related Institutions*, 37 Cath. Law. 87 (1998). For an interesting comparative analysis of this issue in the educational context, see Ralph D. Mawdsley and Lisa C. Ehrich, Commentary, *Religious K-12 Schools and Disability Discrimination: An Australia-United States Comparison*, 147 Ed. Law Rep. 1 (2000).

F. The Secular Workplace

1. Jurisdiction

Both the federal government and the states regulate the secular workplace. States may choose to regulate workplace behavior, including discrimination based on religion, as part of their general police powers. The federal government's powers are more limited in their scope, but plenary to the extent they are exercised. Both the NLRA and Title VII rest on the Commerce Clause, U.S. Const. art. I, § 8, cl. 3, and apply to employers who are part of an "industry affecting commerce." *See* 29 U.S.C. § 158 (2001); 42 U.S.C. § 2000e(b, h)(2001). They are limited in their application only insofar as the Commerce Clause itself is limited. *See* 42 U.S.C. § 2000e(f)(2001) (applying Title VII to certain State and local employees). *United States v. Lopez*, 514 U.S. 549 (1995).

The First Amendment, however, *is* a limitation on Congress' power under the Commerce Clause, and on the police powers of the States insofar as it is incorporated into the Fourteenth Amendment. How it affects the exercise of state and federal power to regulate the role of religion in the secular workplace is the topic considered in this section.

2. When Is a Workplace "Secular"?

EEOC v. Townley Engineering & Manufacturing Co.

859 F.2d 610 (9th Cir. 1988), *cert. denied*, 489 U.S. 1077 (1989)

SNEED, Circuit Judge:

FACTS AND PROCEEDINGS BELOW

Townley Manufacturing Company (Townley) is a closely held corporation [which] manufactures mining equipment. It was founded in 1963 by J.O. (Jake) and Helen Townley, who still own about 94% of the stock. When they founded the company, Jake and Helen Townley made a covenant with God that their business "would be a Christian, faith-operated business." The Townleys were and are "born again believers in the Lord Jesus Christ" who "are unable to separate God from any portion of their daily lives, including their activities at the Townley company." Appellant's Brief at 6. Townley opened its first plant in Florida; it has since opened other plants, including one in Eloy, Arizona in 1973.

Townley reflects its founders' covenant with God in several ways. For example, the company encloses a Gospel tract in every piece of outgoing mail; it prints Biblical verses on all company invoices, purchase orders, and other commercial documents; it gives financial support to various churches and missionaries; and, of particular importance to this case, it holds a devotional service once a week during work hours.

Townley's Florida plant has had weekly devotional services since its inception. They typically last from thirty to forty-five minutes, and may include prayer, thanksgiving to God, singing, testimony, and scripture reading, as well as discussion of business related matters. Townley required all employees to attend the weekly services; failure to attend was regarded as equivalent to not attending work.

In November 1979, Townley hired Louis Pelvas as a machinist in its Eloy plant. At that time there were no devotional services conducted at the Eloy plant. In December 1982, Townley gave its employees an employee handbook, which stated the company's policies and rules. Under the heading of company rules, the handbook stated: "All employees are required to attend the non-denominational devotional services each Tuesday. Employees are paid for their time while attending these services." Pelvas read the handbook and signed a statement agreeing, *inter alia*, "to abide by all the requirements and policies stated within that handbook, as a condition of my continued employment with Townley... I recognize that failure on my part to keep this agreement may result in my dismissal from the company." Townley did not institute devotional services at its Eloy plant until April 1984. Pelvas attended the services without complaint only until June 1984, when he asked to be excused from the services because he was an atheist. His supervisor told him that attendance was mandatory. The supervisor also stated that Pelvas could sleep or read the newspaper during the services. Pelvas continued to attend the services, but in October 1984 he filed a religious discrimination charge with the Equal Employment Opportunity Commission. In December 1984, Pelvas left the company. Pelvas states that he was constructively discharged; Townley says that Pelvas refused to accept an offer of transfer to another plant.

In July 1986, the EEOC filed this action against Townley. The EEOC charged that Townley violated section 703(a) of the Civil Rights Act of 1964, 42 U.S.C. § 2000e-2(a), (1) by requiring its employees to attend devotional services, [and] (2) by failing to accommodate Pelvas' objection to attending the services. The district court granted the EEOC's motion for summary judgment on the two issues, and issued a permanent injunction prohibiting Townley from continuing the mandatory devotional services at its Eloy plant.

IV.

THE REACH OF TITLE VII

Townley argues both that Title VII was not intended to apply to this employment policy, and that the proposed application of Title VII would violate the Free Exercise Clause of the First Amendment. It is clear that applying Title VII to the devotional services "would give rise to serious constitutional questions." [*Catholic Bishop*] Therefore, we may not find it applicable unless there is an "affirmative intention of Congress clearly expressed" that it should be so applied. We hold that Congress did clearly intend for Title VII to cover Townley's mandatory devotional services. Sections 701(j) and 703(a) of Title VII make clear that requiring employees over their objections to attend devotional services cannot be reconciled with Title VII's prohibition against religious discrimination. Furthermore, we hold that Congress did not intend section 702's exemption for religious corporations to shield corporations such as Townley. We do hold, however, that Jake and Helen Townley have certain rights under the Free Exercise Clause that Title VII cannot infringe.

A. Sections 701(j) and 703 of Title VII

1. *Discrimination on the Basis of Religion in General*

As originally enacted, Title VII of the Civil Rights Act of 1964 simply prohibited employment discrimination on the basis of religion. This prohibition clearly covered discrimination on the basis of religious belief; whether it protected employees' religious practices was less clear. To clarify the point, Congress amended Title VII in 1972 by adding a definition of religion. The definition, contained in section 701(j), states:

> The term "religion" includes all aspects of religious observance and practice, as well as belief, unless an employer demonstrates that he is unable to reasonably accommodate to an employee's or prospective employee's religious observance or practice without undue hardship on the conduct of the employer's business.

42 U.S.C. § 2000e(j). "The intent and effect of this definition was to make it an unlawful employment practice under § 703(a)(1) for an employer not to make reasonable accom-

modations, short of undue hardship, for the religious practices of his employees and prospective employees." *Trans World Airlines, Inc. v. Hardison.* Accommodation by the employer to the employee's religious practices was made a statutory obligation.

On appeal, Townley does not argue that atheistic beliefs are not protected against religious discrimination.

3. *Accommodation*

Townley admits that it has made no effort to accommodate Pelvas' objections to the services. It argues that Title VII does not require accommodation because (1) any attempt at accommodation would have caused it "undue hardship," and (2) Pelvas "waived the accommodation requirement when he voluntarily consented to attending the devotional services at the time he executed the signature page of the Employee Handbook agreeing to comply with all the policies of Townley."

The language in our cases emphasizes that the burden of attempting an accommodation rests with the employer rather than the employee.

Pelvas proposed that Townley accommodate his religious objections to the devotional services by excusing him from attendance. The district court found that "Excusing Pelvas from the mandatory devotional services would have cost Townley nothing in the operation of its business activities, and would not have disrupted other workers." We agree.

Townley argues that the district court should have considered the spiritual hardship the accommodation would have caused. We acknowledge that spiritual costs can exist.... It is very doubtful, however, that such "costs" can impose on a corporate employer the required level of hardship.

The difficulty is that under the statute the employer must show that the accommodation of a religious practice would cause "undue hardship *on the conduct of the employer's business.*" 42 U.S.C. § 2000e(j) (emphasis added). To assert that excusing Pelvas from the services would have inflicted spiritual costs on the company, or on Jake and Helen Townley is not enough. Townley, the corporate entity, must connect the asserted spiritual hardship to an adverse impact on the conduct of the business. The statute, in brief, posits a gain-seeking employer exclusively concerned with preserving and promoting its economic efficiency. This is a legitimate supposition with respect to corporate employers.

It follows that Townley's attempts to link the alleged spiritual hardship to the conduct of the business must fail. It is not enough to argue that Townley was founded to "share with all of its employees the spiritual aspects of the company," and that the proposed accommodation would have a "chilling effect" on that purpose. To "chill" its purpose is irrelevant if it has no effect on its economic well-being.

It is true, of course, that Title VII does not ignore entirely the spiritual objectives of employers, [but i]t is likely that Congress intended section 702 to be the sole recourse of corporations professing to be religious.

However, even if this is not so, any effort in this case by Townley to show that its religious nature makes any accommodation of the religious belief of Pelvas an "undue hardship" under section 701(j) must fail. Its only support for this assertion is Jake and Helen Townley's statement that they cannot separate God from their business. It does not argue that the attempt to separate the secular aspects of the service from the religious would cause hardship to coworkers or disrupt the work routine. Even if undue hardship to Townley's business could be supplied by establishing a high degree of "spiritual hardship," a rather doubtful proposition, Townley has failed to establish that level of hardship.

B. The "Religious Corporation" Exemption of Section 702

Townley next argues that it is a "religious corporation" exempt from Title VII by the terms of section 702, which states in part:

> This subchapter shall not apply... to a religious corporation, association, educational institution, or society with respect to the employment of individuals of a particular religion to perform work connected with the carrying on by such corporation, association, educational institution, or society of its activities.

42 U.S.C. §2000e-1. The district court rejected this argument, as do we.

As the district court noted, the case law on this question is not very helpful. In most cases, the defendant is clearly a "religious corporation, association, educational institution, or society" within the meaning of section 702 of the statute. These cases, like the legislative history, demonstrate that the central function of section 702 has been to exempt churches, synagogues, and the like, and organizations closely affiliated with those entities.[13]

We shall not attempt to outline section 702's precise scope. Rather, each case must turn on its own facts. All significant religious and secular characteristics must be weighed to determine whether the corporation's purpose and character are primarily religious. Only when that is the case will the corporation be able to avail itself of the exemption.[14]

Townley and the EEOC do not dispute the "primarily religious" standard. They differ over whether Townley is primarily religious or secular. On the secular side, the company is for profit. It produces mining equipment, an admittedly secular product. It is not affiliated with or supported by a church. Its articles of incorporation do not mention any religious purpose. Against these elements are the facts that Townley encloses Gospel tracts in its outgoing mail, prints Bible verses on its commercial documents (such as invoices and purchase orders), financially supports churches, missionaries, a prison ministry, and Christian radio broadcasts, and, of course, conducts a weekly devotional service. Underlying these facts, of course, is "the discipleship Jake and Helen Townley have for the Lord Jesus Christ." When viewed together, we have no difficulty in holding that these characteristics indicate that Townley is primarily secular. We do not

---

13. Of course, even without section 702, the First Amendment would limit Title VII's ability to regulate the employment relationships within churches and similar organizations. *See Kedroff v. St. Nicholas Cathedral*, 344 U.S. 94, 107, 73 S.Ct. 143, 150 (1952); *McClure v. Salvation Army*, 460 F.2d 553, 558–61 (5th Cir. 1972).

14. We do not mean to imply that the analysis in a section 702 case is the same as in an Establishment Clause case. Our inquiry here is to determine whether the "general picture" of the institution is primarily religious or secular. In Establishment Clause cases, the "general picture" is only one element for the court to consider in determining whether the government activity in question "fosters excessive government entanglement with religion." In making that determination, a court may have to conduct more particular inquiries into the institution's character than simply deciding whether it is primarily religious or secular. For example, an institution with a substantially, or even primarily, religious character may nevertheless have activities which can be regulated by the government without fear of excessive entanglement. See, e.g., *Tony & Susan Alamo Found. v. Secretary of Labor*, 471 U.S. 290, 305–06; *EEOC v. Pacific Press Publishing Ass'n*, 676 F.2d 1272, 1282 (9th Cir. 1982); *EEOC v. Southwestern Baptist Theological Seminary*, 651 F.2d 277, 286 (5th Cir. 1981).

question the sincerity of the religious beliefs of the owners of Townley. Nor do we question that they regard the conduct of their company as subject to a compact with God. We merely hold that the beliefs of the owners and operators of a corporation are simply not enough in themselves to make the corporation "religious" within the meaning of section 702. We therefore agree with the district court that Townley is not exempt under section 702 from Title VII's prohibition against religious discrimination.

V.

FREE EXERCISE CLAUSE

We now address Townley's contention that this application of Title VII violates its rights under the Free Exercise Clause of the First Amendment. Thus, the rights at issue are those of Jake and Helen Townley.

We accept that ending mandatory attendance at the devotional services would have an impact on the Townley's religious practice. But we do not believe that the impact would be unreasonable and extreme. The EEOC does not seek to enjoin the services altogether; rather, it only objects to their mandatory nature. As the EEOC points out, the Townleys would still be able to share the Gospel with their employees. Nevertheless, viewing the evidence in the light most favorable to the Townleys, it is clear that enjoining the services would make it more difficult for them to impart their religious message to their employees, and therefore to some extent would adversely affect their religious practices.

The strength of the government's interest in eradicating discrimination through Title VII is also clear. Protecting an employee's right to be free from forced observance of the religion of his employer is at the heart of Title VII's prohibition against religious discrimination. Finally, we must consider whether the elimination of mandatory attendance at the devotional services constitutes an application of Title VII that is the "least restrictive means" of furthering the state's goal. Here, there is no doubt that to force the employee Pelvas to attend Townley's devotional services would seriously impede Title VII's goal.

The rights of the Townleys under the Free Exercise Clause do not alter this conclusion.

The transcendent principle in cases of this sort is accommodation. Therefore, we hold that, as applied in this case by the district court, Title VII's requirement of religious accommodation does not unduly burden the Townleys' free exercise rights save in one respect. The district court simply enjoined all mandatory services at Townley's Eloy plant. We believe the district court's decree was too broad. The goal of Title VII is served by protecting only those who have religious objections to the services. To protect those who do not have such objections is not necessary. Nor do we think that to require that the service be voluntary as to all employees, whether that is their wish or not, is necessary to further the purposes of Title VII. Therefore, on remand the district court should frame the injunction accordingly.

We affirm in part and reverse and remand in part.

NOONAN, Circuit Judge, dissenting:

In the performance of its mission in this case, the EEOC is asserting a position that, like the Townley Manufacturing Company's, must find its roots in the First Amendment. To exempt an activity from governmental regulation because of its religious nature is to accord a benefit to religion. *Corporation of Presiding Bishop v. Amos* (O'Connor, J. concurring). The EEOC could not exempt the Townley Manufacturing Company to the disadvantage of Pelvas if the effect of exemption were to coerce Pelvas to practice the company's religion or to give up his own.

No such showing of coercion has been made. According to Pelvas he was explicitly told that if he attended the prescribed meetings he could wear ear plugs and read a book or sleep. Wearing ear plugs, he was not exposed to hearing a word of doctrine subversive of his atheism. Reading a book or sleeping, he was not participating in any form of worship. The Townley Manufacturing Company has already accommodated Pelvas' conscientious unwillingness to participate in its services.

The court appears to gloss §701(j) to mean that the employer must accept the employee's proposed accommodation unless the employee's proposal causes undue hardship. That is not the law. *Ansonia Bd. of Education v. Philbrook.* Accommodation has been accomplished but has not been acknowledged.

Just as a corporation enjoys the right of free speech guaranteed by the First Amendment, *Hague v. CIO*, 307 U.S. 496 (1939), so a corporation enjoys the right guaranteed by the First Amendment to exercise religion.

The First Amendment does not say that only one kind of corporation enjoys this right. The First Amendment does not say that only religious corporations or only not-for-profit corporations are protected. The First Amendment does not authorize Congress to pick and choose the persons or the entities or the organizational forms that are free to exercise their religion. All persons—and under our Constitution all corporations are persons—are free. A statute cannot subtract from their freedom.

If it were otherwise, we would be back to the bad old days when state governments insisted that religious organizations incorporate in accordance with state law if they wanted to enjoy the benefits made available by the state. *E.g., Barnes v. First Parish of Falmouth*, 6 Mass. 401 (1810). Such establishment, such forcing of a governmentally chosen form upon religious activity, is incompatible with the Religious Clauses.

True, Congress may create a bright line and exempt from regulation all of the non-profit activity of religious corporations. That a bright line may constitutionally be created does not mean that on a case-by-case basis other activities, asserted to be religious, may not be found to fall within the First Amendment's protection.

Amos did not pretend to decide whether the business activity of a religious corporation should be exempted; and we do not face here the question unresolved in *Amos*. But we meet a parallel question: what exemption from governmental interference is required by the First Amendment as to the religious activity of a business corporation? The First Amendment by its express terms is directed against Congress prohibiting the free exercise of religion.

Secular men and women take secular values seriously. Men and women of the world believe that the world's business is important. When Congress elevates this business to a national priority it has been all too easy for officers of the government and even judges to ignore the countervailing command of the Constitution. In the Supreme Court, the Constitution has been no shield for the spirit when Congress has ordained that the spirit must yield to secular needs. The result should not be foreordained by Congress choosing a secular value as overriding. The Free Exercise Clause requires solicitude for the religious values that are invaded.

Insensitive to its entry on sacred ground, the EEOC in this case has proceeded as though it had but to invoke the congressional mandate and all opposition should cease.

The EEOC has proceeded in this case as though the defendant was simply one more racist bigot.

The agency and the court appear to assume that there must be a sharp division between secular activity and religious activity. The theological position is that human beings should worship God on Sundays or some other chosen day and go about their business without reference to God the rest of the time. Such a split is attractive to some religious persons. It is repudiated by many, especially those who seek to integrate their lives and to integrate their activities. Among those who repudiate this theology is the Townley Manufacturing Company.

The integration of work and religious purpose that the Townleys and their company seek was captured centuries ago in exquisite devotional verse:

Who sweeps a room as for Thy cause
Makes that, and the action, fine.

George Herbert, "The Elixir," The Writings of George Herbert, 185.

For an agency of the government, or Congress, or a court to say that the Townleys are mistaken in their beliefs or that the Townley Manufacturing Company cannot have the purpose ascribed to it and shall not carry out the program of devotion it has set up is to make a theological judgment—a theological judgment fairly characterized as reflecting either a secularism skeptical of God's existence and power or a species of deism that radically isolates God from the world that believers believe God created and animates and directs. The First Amendment prohibits an agency of government, or Congress, or even a court, from imposing such a theological judgment to curb the free exercise of religion.

Notes

1. There are several ways to interpret the decision in *Townley Engineering:*

The first is that Townley did not comply with Title VII's requirement that all employers must make good faith efforts to accommodate Mr. Pelvas' views on attending the prayer meetings. Do the facts support that interpretation? Would it have made a difference if the meetings the employee had to attend were not overtly religious, but were presented as "inspirational" or "self-help" programs? Would Mr. Pelvas have had a claim of "religious discrimination" in that case? Should Mr. Pelvas have been entitled to an excused absence if the moderator of the meetings had introduced the gatherings as meetings designed to improve sales performance, rather than as explicit attempts to enhance the employees' spiritual well being?

The second possibility is that the accommodation offered by Townley (allowing Mr. Pelvas to sleep or read) could not really preserve his legal interests. If permitting employees who do not want to attend corporate devotions to sleep, read, or do paperwork in the room does not protect their legal interests, how would you describe those interests? If an employee has a right not to participate, permitting the employee to attend but to do something else should be adequate to protect that interest, but if the problem lies in forcing the employee to attend *at all*, the interest in *non*-attendance begins to look a bit like the right of "non-association" recognized in other contexts.

This point raises the third possibility: that the court has construed Title VII's concept of "religious discrimination" to include the "non-association" principles recognized by the Supreme Court in the labor law and general First Amendment contexts. *See Communications Workers v. Beck*, 487 U.S. 735 (1988); *Abood v. Detroit Board of Education*, 431 U.S. 209 (1977); and *Wooley v. Maynard*, 430 U.S. 705 (1977).

2. What do you make of Judge Noonan's argument that corporations have First Amendment rights of their own? *See Austin v. Michigan Chamber of Commerce*, 494 U.S. 652 (1990). Are the rights of the corporation distinguishable from the rights of its shareholders? Does the form of the corporation make a difference (*e.g.*, a single shareholder, or closely-held corporation)? Would it be more accurate to draw the distinction between profit-making activities, which the court in *Townley* appears to hold are "secular" as a matter of law, and those which are not inspired by the profit motive? Does the First Amendment make such distinctions? *See Corporation of the Presiding Bishop of the Church of Jesus Christ of Latter-Day Saints v. Amos*, 483 U.S. 327 (1987).

3. What basis is there, either in Title VII, the structure of labor law, or the Constitution, for the majority's premise that Title VII "posits a gain-seeking employer *exclusively* concerned with preserving and promoting its economic efficiency"? While there is no question that "This is a legitimate supposition with respect to corporate employers," isn't the real question whether or not it was the supposition of *Congress*?

4. How, if at all, would Congress' imposition of significant accommodation costs on the private and the public sector in order to comply with the ADA affect your response to the prior question? Are the religious accommodation and exemption requirements evidence that Congress was not *exclusively* concerned with the promotion of economic efficiency? What of affirmative action requirements? Would a non-unionized employer's decision to accommodate an employee's religious concerns be the basis for a religious discrimination complaint on behalf of the employees whose secular concerns are not accommodated? *See Caldor, Inc.*, discussed in § D (1) above. Should it?

3. Operational Issues

The materials in this section should be considered relevant to all non-religious work settings, including those operated and controlled by the government. While the case excerpted below involves allegations of religious discrimination in a workplace operated by the federal government, the standards applicable under Title VII are identical to those that would be applied in a private sector setting.

Rosen v. Thornburgh

928 F.2d 528 (2d Cir. 1991)

ALTIMARI, Circuit Judge:

Plaintiff-appellant Paul Rosen, proceeding *pro se*, appeals from a judgment granting defendants-appellees' motion for summary judgment. Rosen, who is Jewish, alleges that he was unlawfully dismissed from his position as a Special Agent trainee of the Drug Enforcement Administration ("DEA") in violation of Title VII of the Civil Rights Act of 1964, 42 U.S.C. § 2000e *et seq*. The district court granted summary judgment in favor of the defendants on the ground that Rosen had not established a *prima facie* case of discrimination and, alternatively, that Rosen had failed to rebut the DEA's stated reasons for dismissing him. On this appeal, Rosen contends that the district court failed to consider all of the evidence and to draw permissible inferences in his favor.

For the reasons set forth below, we reverse the judgment of the district court and remand for further proceedings.

BACKGROUND

On March 23, 1983, Paul Rosen was officially offered a position as a DEA Special Agent, contingent upon the successful completion of a twelve-week training program and a one-year probationary period. At the end of April 1983, the DEA sent Rosen to the Federal Law Enforcement Training Center ("FLETC") in Glynco, Georgia for training. The FLETC is part of the Department of the Treasury and provides training to various law enforcement personnel. For the most part, Rosen's instructors and counselors at the FLETC were DEA Special Agents. However, FLETC employees provided driving instruction and evaluated the driving portion of the training program. On June 3, 1983, as a consequence of an allegedly poor performance on a driving examination, Rosen was dismissed from the FLETC and terminated as a DEA Special Agent trainee. Rosen subsequently filed a Title VII action in District Court, naming as defendants various Department of Justice and DEA officials and alleging that the defendants had discriminated against him on the basis of his religion.

According to the defendant [Everett], Rosen's performance was marred by several driving errors, most notably a near collision with another car. As a result, the DEA officials responsible for the FLETC training camp decided that Rosen needed remedial driving instruction and that he would be forbidden from driving a government vehicle until he demonstrated adequate driving skills.

On June 2, Rosen was told to report for remedial training the following day. According to Rosen's remedial driving instructor, the June 3 remedial driving session consisted of two hours of demonstrations and specific instructions on proper driving techniques. Everett then evaluated Rosen's driving skills, based on a two lap test, and concluded that he failed to meet the DEA's driving standards. Consequently, Everett informed the DEA officials that Rosen lacked basic driving skills and that further remedial training would be of no value. Based on Everett's recommendation, the DEA officials decided that Rosen was unable to satisfy DEA training requirements and dismissed him from the program. Less than one week later, the DEA officially terminated Rosen's employment.

The defendants also noted that since April 1983, nine individuals, including Rosen, have been deemed to have failed the vehicle driving portion of the training program. Three of these nine subsequently satisfied the driving requirement; the remaining six were dismissed, in whole or in part, because of their lack of driving proficiency.

Based on the foregoing, the defendants argued that Rosen was not qualified to be a DEA Special Agent and, therefore, could not establish a *prima facie* case of employment discrimination. Further, the defendants asserted that Rosen's failure to pass the driving test was a legitimate, nondiscriminatory reason to dismiss him.

Rosen [argued] that he was capable of satisfying the DEA driving requirement and that the test he failed was improperly administered by DEA and FLETC staff members who were motivated by anti-Jewish animus.

To support his allegations, Rosen provided a detailed affidavit setting forth his version of the relevant events. According to Rosen, upon arrival at the FLETC, the DEA class coordinator, welcomed the new trainees by advising them that the DEA had been "stabbed in the back by Congress, the Courts and other commie pinko fags who were out to destroy this organization." Shortly thereafter, DEA Counselor Patricia McCurdy derisively asked Rosen what kind of name "Rosen" is, and stated that she did not like the name and would henceforth call him "Franklin." During one class, Rosen claims that an instructor questioned him about whether he enjoyed lox and bagels and repeatedly referred to New York as "Rosenland." In another class, apparently as part of a lecture on the cultural diversity that a Special Agent must be prepared to encounter, the instructor explained that Jews only care about their money. Another instructor made derogatory remarks about the Jewish population in Miami, Florida.

Rosen also asserts that his counselors and instructors condoned the anti-Semitic behavior of his DEA classmates. In particular, one trainee called Rosen a "half-breed jew bastard" and made other religious slurs. Although the staff was aware of this trainee's expressed anti-Semitism, Rosen was paired with this individual for various practical training sessions.

[On the advice of his attorney], Rosen informed his DEA counselors that he wished to file a formal discrimination complaint. The counselors advised Rosen against taking any action or publicly discussing his complaints. [This led to an acrimonious meeting with his supervisors concerning the procedure to be followed.] [T]he day after [the] meeting, Rosen was told to report for remedial driving instruction. [He did so, and was later] informed that he was being dismissed from the FLETC because he had been unable to satisfy the DEA's driving requirement. Within one week, Rosen was terminated from his position as a DEA Special Agent.

DISCUSSION

On this appeal, Rosen contends that the district court erred in holding that he failed to adduce sufficient evidence on the issue of his qualification to serve as a DEA Special Agent. Although Rosen concedes that driving proficiency was a legitimate employment requirement, he nevertheless claims that the court below failed to fully comprehend the nature of his complaint, *i.e.,* that he was denied any meaningful opportunity to satisfy the DEA's driving requirement as a consequence of religious discrimination. We agree.

A. *Proof in a Title VII Action and Summary Judgment*

In actions brought under Title VII, the plaintiff bears the burden of initially proving a *prima facie* case. *See Texas Dep't of Community Affairs v. Burdine*, 450 U.S. 248, 252–53 (1981). To establish a prima facie case, the plaintiff must show that he or she: (1) was a member of a protected class; (2) was qualified for the position; (3) was discharged; and (4) the discharge occurred in circumstances giving rise to an inference of discrimination. *See Furnco Constr. Corp. v. Waters*, 438 U.S. 567, 577 (1978); *McDonnell Douglas Corp. v. Green*, 411 U.S. 792, 802 (1973). The burden then shifts to the defendant "to articulate some legitimate, nondiscriminatory reason for the employee's [discharge]." *McDonnell Douglas*, 411 U.S. at 802. Once the defendant advances evidence of a nondiscriminatory basis for its action, the burden again shifts to the plaintiff, who ultimately must establish by a preponderance of the evidence that the nondiscriminatory reasons advanced for plaintiff's rejection are a pretext for discrimination. *See Burdine*, 450 U.S. at 253; *McDonnell Douglas*, 411 U.S. at 804.

Also relevant to this inquiry is our recognition that employment discrimination is often accomplished by discreet manipulations and hidden under a veil of self-declared innocence. An employer who discriminates is unlikely to leave a "smoking gun," such as a notation in an employee's personnel file, attesting to a discriminatory intent. A victim of discrimination is therefore seldom able to prove his or her claim by direct evidence and is usually constrained to rely on the cumulative weight of circumstantial evidence.

Consequently, in a Title VII action, where a defendant's intent and state of mind are placed in issue, summary judgment is ordinarily inappropriate.

B. *The Existence of Triable Issues of Fact*

The defendants' argument in support of summary judgment is predicated on the undisputed fact that Rosen received a failing grade on his driving test. Because Rosen failed the driving test, the defendants claim that he was not qualified to serve as a DEA Special Agent and, therefore, cannot establish a *prima facie* case of employment discrimination. The district court agreed with this analysis, assuming that Rosen had disputed neither the legitimacy of the driving requirement nor his failing grade on the test. Accordingly, the court held that no material issues of fact existed for trial.

The court's analysis, however, misconstrued the nature of Rosen's claims and failed to properly consider whether a triable issue of fact had been presented. In actuality, Rosen's contention is that his driving skills were never properly evaluated and that he was not afforded a fair opportunity to satisfy the DEA's driving proficiency requirement. Thus, the legitimacy of the driving requirement and the fact that Rosen was given a failing grade on the driving test were not disputed. Rather, the central question was whether anti-Jewish animus affected the driving requirement as applied to Rosen. In effect, Rosen believes that the test was a sham.

A variety of circumstantial evidence supports Rosen's assertion that the defendants' evaluation of his driving skills was, at most, a perfunctory exercise. We also find unavailing the defendants' contention that Rosen cannot survive summary judgment because Everett did not know he was Jewish. We believe that a trier of fact might reasonably conclude that Rosen's religion was apparent from his surname as well as from the vocal anti-Semitism engendered by his presence at the FLETC. [E]ven if Everett was unaware of Rosen's religion, he was not the sole individual responsible for Rosen's dismissal. Indeed, the record provides ample evidence that a variety of DEA and FLETC staff members played a role in the ultimate decision.

[A] factual dispute exists regarding whether Rosen was qualified for the position he sought. Since the defendants do not dispute that Rosen has satisfied the remaining conditions for establishing a prima facie case of employment discrimination, we believe that Rosen has produced sufficient evidence to survive the defendants' motion for summary judgment.

Notes

1. In EEOC Decision 72-1114 (reported in 4 F.E.P. (BNA) 842 (1972)), the EEOC found that a supervisor's comments about his religious beliefs subjected employees to discrimination on the basis of religion. In EEOC Decision 91-1 (reported in 1991 WL 77565 (1991)), the EEOC held that employees who objected to attending training programs because the organization leading the programs advanced religious beliefs contrary to their "Christian" beliefs were subjected to discriminatory working conditions after they made their objections known to their employer's president.

2. What result in the following case? A police officer stops a driver for a traffic violation. During the course of the brief interrogation that follows, the driver makes a series of anti-Semitic remarks about the Jewish women living in the neighborhood. The policeman informs the driver that he is Jewish, and the driver indicates that she will "get [his] Jewish wife." He arrests her for the threat, but later drops the charges when she

apologizes. *See Hershinow v. Bonamarte,* 735 F.2d 264 (7th Cir. 1984) (affirming dismissal of police officer's civil rights action alleging that three-day suspension was a punishment for the exercise of his religion).

3. *Rosen* illustrates a point that has not received much attention in the literature: the close connection between claims of religious discrimination, and those based on national origin. Judaism is a religion for purposes of Title VII, but discrimination against persons of Jewish descent may constitute discrimination on the basis of race or national origin as well. *See Board of Educ. of the Kiryas Joel Village Sch. Dist. v. Grumet,* 512 U.S. 687 (1994) (religious and cultural differences led to the creation of a hostile environment in the public school system); *Saint Francis College v. Al-Khazraji,* 481 U.S. 604 (1987) (definition of "race discrimination" under 42 U.S.C. § 1981 as applicable to individual of Arab descent); *Shaare Tefila Congregation v. Cobb,* 481 U.S. 615 (1987) (42 U.S.C. §§ 1981–1982 as applied to racial and religious animus directed at Jewish congregation); *Meyer v. Nebraska,* 262 U.S. 390 (1923) (German language taught in Lutheran school). *See also Chaudhuri v. State of Tennessee,* 886 F. Supp. 1374 (M.D. Tenn. 1995) (rejecting claim of religious and racial discrimination at an historically black university involving a Hindu of Indian descent). There was an extensive discussion of this problem in Washington State at the time its state constitutional rules governing support for religious institutions were enacted. *See Witters v. Washington Department of Services for the Blind,* 112 Wash. 2d 363; 771 P.2d 1119 (1989), *reaffirming on state constitutional grounds,* 102 Wash. 2d 624, 689 P.2d 53 (1984), *rev'd,* 474 U.S. 481 (1986) (Utter J., dissenting) (noting discriminatory animus toward Catholics, Mormons and immigrants). *See* Chapters 1 and 6. *See generally* Charleton Beals, BRASS KNUCKLE CRUSADE 45–77 (1960), *quoted in* Paul A. Fisher, BEHIND THE LODGE DOOR: CHURCH, STATE AND FREEMASONRY IN AMERICA (1988); Wm. Oland Bourne, HISTORY OF THE PUBLIC SCHOOL SOCIETY OF THE CITY OF NEW YORK 7, 31, 45 (1870), *quoted in* Fisher; Wilber G. Katz, *Religion and the American Constitutions* 63 (1964).

4. The interplay between religious and national origin discrimination was evident in two cases involving the educational workplace: *Cooper v. Eugene Sch. Dist. 4J,* excerpted in Chapter Six; and *EEOC v. Sch. Dist. of Philadelphia,* 911 F.2d 882 (3d Cir. 1991). In both cases, the lower courts had held that the No Religious Garb statutes involved had been adopted at a time of great anti-Catholic and anti-immigrant bias. In *School Dist. of Philadelphia,* the teacher was a devout Muslim. In accordance with her beliefs, "she wore while teaching... a head scarf which covered her head, neck, and bosom leaving her face visible and a long loose dress which covered her arms to her wrists." Holding that requiring the school district to permit her to teach notwithstanding the Pennsylvania Garb Statute would be an "undue burden," the court stated;

> In reaching these conclusions, we have not been unmindful of the district court's finding in the present case that "anti-Catholicism was a significant factor in the passage of the Pennsylvania religious garb bill of 1895, now codified as section 11-1112." District Court Findings of Fact P 143. A similar contention was raised in *Cooper,* and in fact the Oregon Supreme Court agreed that considerable anti-Catholic sentiment surrounded the original enactment of the Oregon statutes in 1923, however, the *Cooper* court dismissed this issue by noting that the legislature reenacted the statutes in 1965 in an atmosphere untainted by hostility to any sect, motivated purely by its desire "to maintain the religious neutrality of the public schools, to avoid giving children or their

parents the impression that the school, through its teacher, approves and shares the religious commitment of one group and perhaps finds that of others less worthy." *Id.* As we have noted, the Pennsylvania Garb Statute was similarly reenacted as part of Pennsylvania's Public School Code of 1949. 24 Pa. St. Ann. §§ 1-101 *et seq.* However, the parties in this case tendered no evidence, and the district court made no finding, regarding the circumstances surrounding the reenactment of the statute in 1949.

Since we have already concluded that the School Board has a valid undue hardship defense regardless of the ultimate validity of the Garb Statute, the allegedly impermissible motivation behind that statute is irrelevant to our decision with regard to that defendant. Even if the School Board had had some reason, not reflected in this record, for being suspicious of the motives of the legislature in 1895, we believe that requiring it to litigate over that motivation would itself constitute an undue hardship.

However, we must still consider whether the putatively anti-Catholic motivation behind the Garb Statute is of any greater significance in the context of the case against the Commonwealth. Accepting for the sake of argument the district court's finding of fact that "anti-Catholicism was a significant factor" in the passage of the statute, we conclude that this fact is irrelevant to this Title VII suit against the Commonwealth.

We need not here address what if any importance this "significant factor" finding would have in the context of an establishment clause challenge to the statute; we have no such challenge before us. The Garb Statute plays a role in this litigation only because the Commonwealth asserts that it would be an undue hardship upon its public school system to require it to permit teachers to wear religious attire as they teach. The Garb Statute is significant solely because it evidences a decision on the part of the Commonwealth that barring religious attire is important to the maintenance of an atmosphere of religious neutrality in the classroom.

In this context, where the statute bans all religious attire and is being enforced by the Commonwealth in a non-discriminatory manner with respect to the Muslim teachers as well as Catholics, we conclude that it is irrelevant whether a portion of those who voted for the statute in 1895 were motivated by a desire to bar Catholic habit from the classroom. We therefore accept that the Commonwealth regards the wearing of religious attire by teachers while teaching as a significant threat to the maintenance of religious neutrality in the public school system, and accordingly conclude that it would impose an undue hardship to require the Commonwealth to accommodate Ms. Reardon and others similarly situated.

Id. at 893–94. How should "religious" garb be distinguished from garb reflecting one's ethnic or national identity? How, for example, should a court deal with a Title VII challenge to an order that a teacher of Indian descent may not wear a sari while teaching, or that an African-American teacher may not wear a Kente cloth over his suit? Do the results in these cases suggest that religious garb statutes may effectively bar Orthodox Jews from teaching in the public schools if they wish to wear a yarmulke? *See Goldman v. Weinberger*, 475 U.S. 503 (1986) (holding constitutional military regulation barring wearing of yarmulke by Orthodox Jewish officer).

5. The decisions in *Cooper* and *EEOC v. School District of Philadelphia* raise several additional questions. The latter court assumes, for purposes of the discussion, that

discriminatory animus *did* infect the reenactment of the statute. Setting aside the question of what facts a state needs to show before a court will assume that its current intent is nondiscriminatory, why should the discriminatory animus of the statute be relevant to an Establishment Clause challenge to the Garb Statute, but not to a Title VII challenge? Discriminatory animus *is* relevant to an Equal Protection Clause challenge, *Washington v. Davis*, 426 U.S. 229 (1976), and, after *Employment Div. v. Smith*, to Free Exercise Clause claims as well.

6. Professor David L. Faigman has suggested that a piecemeal approach to such questions is one of the reasons that constitutional interpretation is viewed as being in such disarray. He recommends a more structural approach, which he dubs "Madisonian Balancing":

> Madisonian Balancing begins with the premise that a constitutional injury caused by some government action cannot be described in a piecemeal fashion. An infringement of a due process property right, for example, has greater constitutional significance when it also infringes freedom of speech. A court's evaluation of the constitutionality of a challenged government action must entail a full assessment of the constitutional costs of that action. Madisonian Balancing thus operates with a Constitution-wide perspective, rather than from a right-specific or amendment-specific viewpoint. The metric by which individual liberty is to be balanced against government interests is constitutionality itself. The balance is struck at a transactional level, by comparing the depth of the full constitutional infringement with the government's justification for its action. Madisonian Balancing thus aggregates rights and then balances them against the government's interests, which have always been aggregated for balancing purposes.

David L. Faigman, *Madisonian Balancing: A Theory of Constitutional Adjudication*, 88 Nw. U. L. Rev. 641, 643–44 (1994). *See also* Robert A. Destro, *"By What Right?": The Sources and Limits of Federal Court and Congressional Jurisdiction Over Matters "Touching Religion,"* 29 Ind. L. J. 1 (1996) (suggesting a similar structural approach). *Cf. Employment Div. v. Smith*, excerpted in Chapter Five (suggesting a "hybrid" approach to the resolution of free exercise claims which also implicate the Speech and Press Clause).

7. The EEOC proposed an amendment to its Religious Discrimination Guidelines, 29 CFR § 1609.1, which would have prohibited religious harassment in the workplace. What constitutional and interpretive problems could such a guideline create? What, for example, would be the result when an employee complains that other workers are trying, during their respective lunch breaks, to "convert" him to their faith? *See Finnemore v. Bangor Hydro-Electric Co.*, 645 A.2d 15 (Maine 1994) (religious harassment claim based on sexual comments directed at employee with strong religious views); *Bellini v. University of St. Thomas*, 1994 WL 425166 (Minn. App. Aug 16, 1994) (rejecting claim, on the facts presented, that mandatory attendance at religious services is religious harassment); *Meltebeke v. Bureau of Labor and Industries*, 903 P.2d 351 (Or. 1995); *Vaughn v. Ag Processing, Inc.*, 459 N.W.2d 627, 632 (Iowa 1990) (reference to employee and co-workers as "dumb Catholics" constitutes religious discrimination). *See generally* Wayne Lindsey Robbins, Jr, *When Two Liberal Values Collide in an Era of "Political Correctness": First Amendment Protection as a Check on Speech-Based Title VII Hostile Environment Claims*, 47 Baylor L. Rev. 789 (1995); Eugene Volokh, *How Harassment Law Restricts Free Speech*, 47 Rutgers L. Rev. 563 (1995).

4. An Employer's Duty to Accommodate under Title VII

The goal of Title VII is to reduce or eliminate most religion-based barriers to labor market participation. In 1966, the Equal Employment Opportunity Commission (EEOC) interpreted Title VII's anti-discrimination provision as imposing an affirmative duty upon employers to accommodate the religious practices of employees if accommodation did not cause a "serious inconvenience to the conduct of their business." A year later, the EEOC changed its position and required less from an employer. The amended guidelines required accommodation of an employee's religious practices if it did not impose an "undue hardship on their business." Congress later amended Title VII to reflect the undue hardship requirement. 42 U.S.C. § 2000 (j).

The "Religious Discrimination Guidelines" state that "the Commission will define [the statutory term] 'religious practices' to include moral or ethical beliefs as to what is right and wrong which are sincerely held with the strength of traditional religious views." Thus, a worker need only show that the position of conscience is taken on the basis of beliefs that are sincerely held "with the strength of traditional religious views." It makes no difference whether the teachings are "identifiably" those of the faith to which the worker subscribes. EEOC, Religious Discrimination Guidelines, 29 C.F.R. §§ 1605.1 to 1605.3 (2001). In this regard, the EEOC follows the broad definition of the concept of religion developed in conscious objection cases. *See* Chapter Thirteen.

An employer's duty to attempt accommodation arises at the point where an employee fulfills his or her preliminary obligation to disclose the religious need. From this, it follows that an employer has the right to assume that there are no religious objections to the type of work or duties assigned, religious or otherwise, unless the employee requests an accommodation. Likewise, an employer may not make blanket assumptions during the hiring or promotion process concerning adherents of a particular religion without first ascertaining that the individual involved would be unable or unwilling to do the job. 42 U.S.C. § 2000e-l. *Cf.* 29 C.F.R. § 1605.1 (by negative implication). *City of Los Angeles Dep't of Water & Power v. Manhart*, 435 U.S. 702 (1978); *Griggs v. Duke Power Co.*, 401 U.S. 424 (1971); *Phillips v. Martin Marietta Corp.*, 400 U.S. 542 (1971). Thus, an employer who elects to avoid the burden of accommodation by simply refusing to hire or promote adherents of a given religion would be guilty of a *prima facie* violation of the statute.

An accommodation problem can thus arise only *after* the employer learns of the employee or potential employee's needs. Assuming that the employee and employer can locate an available job within the employer's work force that does not compromise the employee's religious needs, there is no guarantee that the employer will be either willing or able to accommodate the request. *See Minkus v. Metropolitan Sanitary Dist. of Greater Chicago*, 600 F.2d 80 (7th Cir. 1979); *Haring v. Blumenthal*, 471 F. Supp. 1172 (D. D.C. 1979) (employer refusal to accommodate). Simple unwillingness, of course, is not enough, but as the cases excerpted in this section indicate, any legitimate business reason will suffice as long as it is not a pretext for discriminatory conduct. *Accord Oates v. United States Postal Service*, 458 F. Supp. 57 (S.D.N.Y. 1978), *aff'd without opinion*, 591 F.2d 1331 (2d Cir. 1978); *Levine v. Navapache Hospital*, 26 E.P.D. ¶ 32, 103 (D. Ariz. 1981) (anti-Semitic remark insufficient to prove religious discrimination where employee was insubordinate and disruptive; religious discrimination charge would not affect discharge for valid cause).

Accommodation claims can be complex because the statute presupposes an ongoing conversation between employers and the affected employees concerning the nature and scope of the accommodation requested. In order to prevail on an accommodation claim, the employee must first establish a *prima facie* case by showing that: (1) he has a bona fide belief that compliance with an employment requirement is contrary to his religious faith; (2) he informed his employer about the conflict; and (3) he was penalized because of his refusal to comply with the employment requirement. The burden then shifts to the employer to rebut any of the key components of the employee's case on their merits. This can be done, for example, by showing that the employee failed to inform the employer of the conflict, by proving that reasonable accommodation was attempted, or that accommodation is not possible without undue hardship on the business.

If an employer can show she has reasonably accommodated the employee concern, the "statutory inquiry is at an end," but if the employer has failed to accommodate, she can defend her failure to do so by arguing that it would constitute an undue hardship. The undue hardship defense, however, may not be based "merely on speculation," and the "magnitude as well as the fact of hardship" must be determined by reference to the facts of each case. *See, e.g., Protos v. Volkswagen*, 797 F.2d 129 (3d Cir. 1986), *cert. denied*, 479 U.S. 972 (1986); *Bhatia v. Chevron U.S.A. Inc.*, 734 F.2d 1382 (9th Cir. 1984); *EEOC v. Sambo's*, 530 F. Supp. 86 (N.D. Ga. 1981). State employment laws contain similar requirements. *See, e.g., Rankins v. Commission on Professional Competence,* 24 Cal.3d 167, 174, 154 Cal.Rptr. 907, 593 P.2d 852 (1979).

The EEOC has developed a list of possible accommodations an employer can utilize to meet its obligation to accommodate. Among these are: (1) voluntary substitutes and "swaps," in which an employer "promote[s] an atmosphere in which...substitutions are favorably regarded," and provides a central location which will facilitate posting of requests for substitution; (2) flexible scheduling, so that employees requesting accommodation can be served by permitting them flexible arrival and departure times, flexible work breaks, and use of lunch, personal, or vacation time in exchange for early departure; staggering work hours, or allowing an employee to make up lost time due to observing religious practices; and (3) arranging lateral transfers or changing an employee's job assignment. 29 C.F.R. § 1605.2 (d)(1)(i)–(iii).

There are other factual circumstances in which accommodation may be at issue. Accommodation has been required when an employee's religious beliefs prevent him or her from joining a union and paying union dues. In such cases employees are allowed to make a contribution to charity of their choice of an amount equal to the union dues. *See, e.g., Tooley v. Martin-Marietta Corp.*, 648 F.2d 1239 (9th Cir. 1981). Accommodation claims are often the vehicle for employee challenges to employer requirements that interfere with other aspects of religious belief. Among these are uniform dress requirements that interfere with the wearing of religious garb or symbols, the need to pray at intervals during the workday, and the modification of job-related requirements governing non-work time employee behavior. *See, e.g., EEOC v. ADAPT,* Civ. No. C85-6139-E (D. Or. March 5, 1986), Appendix 1 to Brief In Opposition To Petition For Writ Of Certiorari, *Employment Div. v. Smith*, 494 U.S. 872 (1990) (mandating that Smith and Black be rehired, and that ADAPT no longer consider the religious use of peyote by Native American Church members work-related misconduct).

Because Title VII attempts to strike a balance between business and employee needs, an employer is not required to offer a choice among possible accommodations. Once an employer makes a valid attempt to accommodate, it has fulfilled its obligation under the statute. At that point, the employee refuses to cooperate at his or her own risk.

a) *The Scope of the Duty to Accommodate*

Trans World Airlines, Inc. v. Hardison

432 U.S. 63 (1977)

Mr. Justice WHITE delivered the opinion of the Court.

Section 703(a)(1) of the Civil Rights Act of 1964, Title VII, 78 Stat. 255, 42 U.S.C. §2000e-2(a)(1), makes it an unlawful employment practice for an employer to discriminate against an employee or a prospective employee on the basis of his or her religion. At the time of the events involved here, a guideline of the Equal Employment Opportunity Commission (EEOC), 29 CFR 1605.1(b) (1968), required, as the Act itself now does, 42 U.S.C. §2000e(j) (1970 ed., Supp. V), that an employer short of "undue hardship," make "reasonable accommodations" to the religious needs of its employees. The issue in this case is the extent of the employer's obligation under Title VII to accommodate an employee whose religious beliefs prohibit him for working on Saturdays.

Petitioner Trans World Airlines (TWA) operates a large maintenance and overhaul base in Kansas City, Mo. On June 5, 1967, respondent Larry G. Hardison was hired by TWA to work as a clerk in the Stores Department at its Kansas City base. Because of its essential role in the Kansas City operation, the Stores Department must operate 24 hours per day, 365 days per year, and whenever an employee's job in that department is not filled, an employee must be shifted from another department, or a supervisor must cover the job, even if the work in other areas may suffer.

In the spring of 1968 Hardison began to study the religion known as the Worldwide Church of God. One of the tenets of that religion is that one must observe the Sabbath by refraining from performing any work from sunset on Friday until sunset on Saturday. The religion also proscribes work on certain specified religious holidays.

When Hardison informed Everett Kussman, the manager of the Stores Department, of his religious conviction regarding observance of the Sabbath, Kussman agreed that the union steward should seek a job swap for Hardison or a change of days off; that Hardison would have his religious holidays off whenever possible if Hardison agreed to work the traditional holidays when asked; and that Kussman would try to find Hardison another job that would be more compatible with his religious beliefs. The problem was temporarily solved when Hardison transferred to the 11 p.m.–7 a.m. shift. Working this shift permitted Hardison to observe his Sabbath.

The problem soon reappeared when Hardison bid for and received a transfer from Building 1, where he had been employed, to Building 2, where he would work the day shift. The two buildings had entirely separate seniority lists; and while in Building 1 Hardison had sufficient seniority to observe the Sabbath regularly, he was second from the bottom on the Building 2 seniority list.

In Building 2 Hardison was asked to work Saturdays when a fellow employee went on vacation. TWA agreed to permit the union to seek a change of work assignments for Hardison, but the union was not willing to violate the seniority provisions set out in the collective-bargaining contract, and Hardison had insufficient seniority to bid for a shift having Saturdays off.

A proposal that Hardison work only four days a week was rejected by the company. Hardison's job was essential, and on weekends he was the only available person on his shift to perform it. To leave the position empty would have impaired supply shop functions, which were critical to airline operations; to fill Hardison's position with a supervisor or an employee from another area would simply have undermanned another operation; and to employ someone not regularly assigned to work Saturdays would have required TWA to pay premium wages.

When an accommodation was not reached, Hardison refused to report for work on Saturdays. A transfer to the twilight shift proved unavailing since that schedule still required Hardison to work past sundown on Fridays. After a hearing, Hardison was discharged on grounds of insubordination for refusing to work during his designated shift.

Hardison's claim of religious discrimination rested on 1967 EEOC guidelines requiring employers "to make reasonable accommodations to the religious needs of employees" whenever such accommodation would not work an "undue hardship," 29 CFR § 1605.1 (1968), and on similar language adopted by Congress in the 1972 amendments to Title VII, 42 U.S.C. § 2000e(j) (1970 ed., Supp. V).

Because we agree with petitioners that their conduct was not a violation of Title VII, we need not reach the other questions presented.

The Court of Appeals found that TWA had committed an unlawful employment practice under § 703(a)(1) of the Act, 42 U.S.C. § 2000e-2(a)(1), which provides:

> (a) It shall be an unlawful employment practice for an employer—
>
> (1) to fail or refuse to hire or to discharge any individual, or otherwise to discriminate against any individual with respect to his compensation, terms conditions, or privileges of employment, because of such individual's race, color, religion, sex, or national origin.

The emphasis of both the language and the legislative history of the statute is on eliminating discrimination in employment; similarly situated employees are not to be treated differently solely because they differ with respect to race, color, religion, sex, or national origin.

The prohibition against religious discrimination soon raised the question of whether it was impermissible under § 703(a)(1) to discharge or refuse to hire a person who for religious reasons refused to work during the employer's normal workweek. In 1966 an EEOC guideline dealing with this problem declared that an employer had an obligation under the statute "to accommodate to the reasonable religious needs of employees... where such accommodation can be made without serious inconvenience to the conduct of the business." 29 CFR § 1605.1 (1967).

In 1967 the EEOC amended its guidelines to require employers "to make reasonable accommodations to the religious needs of employees and prospective employees where such accommodations can be made without undue hardship on the conduct of the employer's business." 29 CFR § 1605.1 (1968). The EEOC did not suggest what sort of accommodations are "reasonable" or when hardship to an employer becomes "undue."

Congress included the following definition of religion in its 1972 amendments to Title VII:

> The term 'religion' includes all aspects of religious observance and practices, as well as belief, unless an employer demonstrates that he is unable to reasonably

> accommodate to an employee's or prospective employee's religious observance or practice without undue hardship on the conduct of the employer's business." §701(j), 42 U.S.C. §2000e(j) (1970 ed., Supp. V).

The intent and effect of this definition was to make it an unlawful employment practice under §703(a)(1) for an employer not to make reasonable accommodations, short of undue hardship, for the religious practices of his employees and prospective employees. But like the EEOC guidelines, the statute provides no guidance for determining the degree of accommodation that is required of an employer.

With this in mind, we turn to a consideration of whether TWA has met its obligation under Title VII to accommodate the religious observances of its employees.

The Court of Appeals held that TWA had not made reasonable efforts to accommodate Hardison's religious needs under the 1967 EEOC guidelines in effect at the time the relevant events occurred.

We disagree with the Court of Appeals in all relevant respects. It is our view that TWA made reasonable efforts to accommodate and that each of the Court of Appeals' suggested alternatives would have been an undue hardship within the meaning of the statute as construed by the EEOC guidelines.

In summarizing its more detailed findings, the District Court observed:

> TWA established as a matter of fact that it did take appropriate action to accommodate as required by Title VII. It held several meetings with plaintiff at which it attempted to find a solution to plaintiff's problems. It did accommodate plaintiff's observance of his special religious holidays. It authorized the union steward to search for someone who would swap shifts, which apparently was normal procedure.

It is also true that TWA itself attempted without success to find Hardison another job. The District Court's view was that TWA had done all that could reasonably be expected within the bounds of the seniority system.

The Court of Appeals observed, however, that the possibility of a variance from the seniority system was never really posed to the union. This is contrary to the District Court's findings and to the record.

We shall say more about the seniority system, but at this juncture it appears to us that the system itself represented a significant accommodation to the needs, both religious and secular, of all of TWA's employees. As will become apparent, the seniority system represents a neutral way of minimizing the number of occasions when an employee must work on a day that he would prefer to have off. Additionally, recognizing that weekend work schedules are the least popular, the company made further accommodation by reducing its work force to a bare minimum on those days.

We are also convinced, contrary to the Court of Appeals, that TWA itself cannot be faulted for having failed to work out a shift or job swap for Hardison. Both the union and TWA had agreed to the seniority system; the union was unwilling to entertain a variance over the objections of men senior to Hardison; and for TWA to have arranged unilaterally for a swap would have amounted to a breach of the collective-bargaining agreement.

Hardison and the EEOC insist that the statutory obligation to accommodate religious needs takes precedence over both the collective-bargaining contract and the seniority rights of TWA's other employees. We agree that neither a collective-bargaining contract nor a seniority system may be employed to violate the statute, but we do not believe that the duty to accommodate requires TWA to take steps inconsistent with the otherwise valid agreement. Without a clear and express indication from Congress, we cannot agree with Hardison and the EEOC that an agreed-upon seniority system must give way when necessary to accommodate religious observances.

Whenever there are not enough employees who choose to work a particular shift, some employees must be assigned to that shift even though it is not their first choice. Such was evidently the case with regard to Saturday work; even though TWA cut back its weekend work force to a skeleton crew, not enough employees chose those days off to staff the Stores Department through voluntary scheduling. In these circumstances, TWA and IAM agreed to give first preference to employees who had worked in a particular department the longest.

Had TWA nevertheless circumvented the seniority system by relieving Hardison of Saturday work and ordering a senior employee to replace him, it would have denied the latter his shift preference so that Hardison could be given his. The senior employee would also have been deprived of his contractual rights under the collective-bargaining agreement.

It was essential to TWA's business to require Saturday and Sunday work from at least a few employees even though most employees preferred those days off. Allocating the burdens of weekend work was a matter for collective bargaining. In considering criteria to govern this allocation, TWA and the union had two alternatives: adopt a neutral system, such as seniority, a lottery, or rotating shifts; or allocate days off in accordance with the religious needs of its employees. TWA would have had to adopt the latter to assure Hardison and others like him of getting the days off necessary for strict observance of their religion, but it could have done so only at the expense of others who had strong, but perhaps nonreligious, reasons for not working on weekends. There were no volunteers to relieve Hardison on Saturdays, and to give Hardison Saturdays off, TWA would have had to deprive another employee of his shift preference at least in part because he did not adhere to a religion that observed the Saturday Sabbath.

Our conclusion is supported by the fact that seniority systems are afforded special treatment under Title VII itself. Section 703(h) provides in pertinent part:

> Notwithstanding any other provision of this subchapter, it shall not be an unlawful employment practice for an employer to apply different standards of compensation, or different terms, conditions, or privileges of employment pursuant to a bona fide seniority or merit system... provided that such differences are not the result of an intention to discriminate because of race, color, religion, sex, or national origin...." 42 U.S.C. § 2000e-2(h).

Thus, absent a discriminatory purpose, the operation of a seniority system cannot be an unlawful employment practice even if the system has some discriminatory consequences.

There has been no suggestion of discriminatory intent in this case. TWA was not required by Title VII to carve out a special exception to its seniority system in order to help Hardison to meet his religious obligations.

To require TWA to bear more than a *de minimis* cost in order to give Hardison Saturdays off is an undue hardship. [The statute does not contemplate that time off will be] allocated according to religious beliefs.

As we have seen, the paramount concern of Congress in enacting Title VII was the elimination of discrimination in employment. In the absence of clear statutory language or legislative history to the contrary, we will not readily construe the statute to require an employer to discriminate against some employees in order to enable others to observe their Sabbath.

Reversed.

Mr. Justice MARSHALL, with whom Mr. Justice BRENNAN joins, dissenting.

One of the most intractable problems arising under Title VII of the Civil Rights Act of 1964 has been whether an employer is guilty of religious discrimination when he discharges an employee (or refuses to hire a job applicant) because of the employee's religious practices. Particularly troublesome has been the plight of adherents to minority faiths who do not observe the holy days on which most business are closed—Sundays, Christmas, and Easter—but who need time off for their own days of religious observance.

Today's decision deals a fatal blow to all efforts under Title VII to accommodate work requirements to religious practices. The Court holds, in essence, that although the EEOC regulations and the Act state that an employer must make reasonable adjustments in his work demands to take account of religious observances, the regulation and the Act do not really mean what they say. An employer, the Court concludes, need not grant even the most minor special privilege to religious observers to enable them to follow their faith. As a question of social policy, this result is deeply troubling, for a society that truly values religious pluralism cannot compel adherents of minority religions to make the cruel choice of surrendering their religion or their job. [I]f an accommodation can be rejected simply because it involves preferential treatment, then the regulation and the statute, while brimming with "sound and fury," ultimately "signif[y] nothing."

The accommodation issue by definition arises only when a neutral rule of general applicability conflicts with the religious practices of a particular employee. In each instance, the question is whether the employee is to be exempt from the rule's demands. To do so will always result in a privilege being "allocated according to religious beliefs," unless the employer gratuitously decides to repeal the rule *in toto*. What the statute says, in plain words, is that such allocations are required unless "undue hardship" would result.

The Court's interpretation of the statute, by effectively nullifying it, has the singular advantage of making consideration of petitioners' constitutional challenge unnecessary. Moreover, while important constitutional questions would be posed by interpreting the law to compel employers (or fellow employees) to incur substantial costs to aid the religious observer, not all accommodations are costly, and the constitutionality of the statute is not placed in serious doubt simply because it sometimes requires an exemption from a work rule. I think it beyond dispute that the Act does—and, consistently with the First Amendment, can—require employers to grant privileges to religious observers as part of the accommodation process.

What makes today's decision most tragic, however, is not that respondent Hardison has been needlessly deprived of his livelihood simply because he chose to follow the dictates of his conscience. Nor is the tragedy exhausted by the impact it will have on thousands of Americans like Hardison who could be forced to live on welfare as the price they must pay for worshipping their God. The ultimate tragedy is that despite Congress' best efforts, one of this Nation's pillars of strength—our hospitality to religious diversity—has been seriously eroded. All Americans will be a little poorer until today's decision is erased.

I respectfully dissent.

Ansonia Board of Education v. Philbrook

479 U.S. 60 (1986)

Chief Justice REHNQUIST delivered the opinion of the Court.

Petitioner Ansonia Board of Education has employed respondent Ronald Philbrook since 1962 to teach high school business and typing classes in Ansonia, Connecticut. In 1968, Philbrook was baptized into the Worldwide Church of God. The tenets of the church require members to refrain from secular employment during designated holy days, a practice that has caused respondent to miss approximately six school days each year. We are asked to determine whether the employer's efforts to adjust respondent's work schedule in light of his beliefs fulfills its obligation under §701(j) of the Civil Rights Act of 1964, 42 U.S.C. §2000e(j), to "reasonably accommodate to an employee's... religious observance or practice without undue hardship on the conduct of the employer's business."

Since the 1967–68 school year, the school board's collective-bargaining agreements with the Ansonia Federation of Teachers have granted to each teacher 18 days of leave per year for illness, cumulative to 150 and later to 180 days. Accumulated leave may be used for purposes other than illness as specified in the agreement. A teacher may accordingly use five days' leave for a death in the immediate family, one day for attendance at a wedding, three days per year for attendance as an official delegate to a national veterans organization, and the like. With the exception of the agreement covering the 1967–1968 school year, each contract has specifically provided three days' annual leave for observance of mandatory religious holidays, as defined in the contract. Unlike other categories for which leave is permitted, absences for religious holidays are not charged against the teacher's annual or accumulated leave.

The school board has also agreed that teachers may use up to three days of accumulated leave each school year for "necessary personal business." Recent contracts limited permissible personal leave to those uses not otherwise specified in the contract. This limitation dictated, for example, that an employee who wanted more than three leave days to attend the convention of a national veterans organization could not use personal leave to gain extra days for that purpose. Likewise, an employee already absent three days for mandatory religious observances could not later use personal leave for "[a]ny religious activity," or "[a]ny religious observance." Since the 1978–1979 school year, teachers have been allowed to take one of the three personal days without prior approval; use of the remaining two days requires advance approval by the school principal.

The limitations on the use of personal business leave spawned this litigation. Until the 1976–1977 year, Philbrook observed mandatory holy days by using the three days granted in the contract and then taking unauthorized leave. His pay was reduced accordingly. In 1976, however, respondent stopped taking unauthorized leave for religious reasons, and began scheduling required hospital visits on church holy days. He also worked on several holy days. Dissatisfied with this arrangement, Philbrook repeatedly asked the school board to adopt one of two alternatives. His preferred alternative would allow use of personal business leave for religious observance, effectively giving him three additional days of paid leave for that purpose. Short of this arrangement, respondent suggested that he pay the cost of a substitute and receive full pay for additional days off for religious observances. Petitioner has consistently rejected both proposals.

[W]e are asked to address whether the Court of Appeals erred in finding that Philbrook established a prima facie case of religious discrimination and in opining that an employer must accept the employee's preferred accommodation absent proof of undue hardship. We find little support in the statute for the approach adopted by the Court of Appeals, but we agree that the ultimate issue of reasonable accommodation cannot be resolved without further factual inquiry. We accordingly affirm the judgment of the Court of Appeals remanding the case to the District Court for additional findings.

In addressing this question, the Court of Appeals assumed that the employer had offered a reasonable accommodation of Philbrook's religious beliefs. This alone, however, was insufficient in that court's view to allow resolution of the dispute. The court observed that the duty to accommodate "cannot be defined without reference to undue hardship." It accordingly determined that the accommodation obligation includes a duty to accept "the proposal the employee prefers unless that accommodation causes undue hardship on the employer's conduct of his business."

We find no basis in either the statute or its legislative history for requiring an employer to choose any particular reasonable accommodation. By its very terms the statute directs that any reasonable accommodation by the employer is sufficient to meet its accommodation obligation. The employer violates the statute unless it "demonstrates that [it] is unable to reasonably accommodate ... an employee's ... religious observance or practice without undue hardship on the conduct of the employer's business." Thus, where the employer has already reasonably accommodated the employee's religious needs, the statutory inquiry is at an end. The employer need not further show that each of the employee's alternative accommodations would result in undue hardship.

Under the approach articulated by the Court of Appeals the employee is given every incentive to hold out for the most beneficial accommodation, despite the fact that an employer offers a reasonable resolution of the conflict. This approach, we think, conflicts with both the language of the statute and the views that led to its enactment. We accordingly hold that an employer has met its obligation under § 701(j) when it demonstrates that is has offered a reasonable accommodation to the employee.

We think that the school board policy in this case, requiring respondent to take unpaid leave for holy day observance that exceeded the amount allowed by the collective-bargaining agreement, would generally be a reasonable one. In enacting § 701(j), Congress was understandably motivated by a desire to assure the individual additional opportunity to observe religious practices, but it did not impose a duty on the employer to accommodate at all costs. The provision of unpaid leave eliminates the conflict between employment requirements and religious practices by allowing the individual to observe fully religious holy days and requires him only to give up compensation for a day that he did not in fact work.

But unpaid leave is not a reasonable accommodation when paid leave is provided for all purposes *except* religious ones. Such an arrangement would display a discrimination against religious practices that is the antithesis of reasonableness. We do not think that the record is sufficiently clear on this point for us to make the necessary factual findings, and we therefore affirm the judgment of the Court of Appeals remanding the case to the District Court.

It is so ordered.

Justice MARSHALL, concurring in part and dissenting in part.

I agree with the Court's conclusion that, if the school board provides paid leave "for all purposes *except* religious ones," its accommodation of Philbrook's religious needs would be unreasonable and thus violate Title VII. But I do not find the specificity of the personal business leave, or the possibility that it may be used for activities similar to the religious activities Philbrook seeks leave to pursue, necessarily dispositive of whether the board has satisfied its affirmative duty under §701(j), 42 U.S.C. §20000e(j), to reasonably accommodate Philbrook's religious needs.

I do not accept the Court's conclusion that the statute, "[b]y its very terms," relieves the board from this continuing duty to accommodate the special religious practices of its employees where doing so is reasonable and causes no undue hardship. The statute simply creates an affirmative duty to accommodate; it does not specify who must respond to whom.

The EEOC's guidelines on religious discrimination support an interpretation of the statute placing this continuing duty to accommodate on the employer. The EEOC guidelines consider compensation encompassed within the concept of "employment opportunities." 29 CFR §1605.2(c) (1986). A forced reduction in compensation based on an employee's religious beliefs can be as much a violation of Title VII as a refusal to hire or grant a promotion.

In this case, contrary to the Court's conclusion, the school board's accommodation of Philbrook's religious needs by merely allowing unpaid leave does not eliminate the conflict. Rather, the offer forces Philbrook to choose between following his religious precepts with a partial forfeiture of salary and violating these precepts for work with full pay. It is precisely this loss of compensation that entitles Philbrook to further accommodation, if reasonably possible without undue hardship to the school board's educational program. It may be that unpaid leave will generally amount to *a* reasonable accommodation, but this does not mean that unpaid leave will always be *the* reasonable accommodation which *best* resolves the conflict between the needs of the employer and employee. In my view, then, an offer of unpaid leave does not end the inquiry: If an employee, in turn, offers another reasonable proposal that results in a more effective resolution without causing undue hardship, the employer should be required to implement it.

Accordingly, I would remand this case for factual findings on both the intended scope of the school board's leave provision *and* the reasonableness and expected hardship of Philbrook's proposals.

Justice STEVENS, concurring in part and dissenting in part.

Whether respondent's complaint is analyzed as an outright claim that he is entitled to six paid days of leave for religious observances or as an argument that petitioner's employment policies, while facially neutral, fail to accommodate [respondent's] religious beliefs, the record before us plainly disclose that he cannot prevail. In essence, he argues that the employer's practice of requiring him to complete this work, which is an integral part of his job duties as a salaried employee, conflicts with his religious obligation to be absent on the days when he would otherwise have performed this work and been paid for it. An examination of these claims discloses that neither has merit.

Accordingly, I respectfully dissent from the part of the Court's judgment that remands the case for further proceedings.

Notes

1. What is the best way to accommodate the needs of individuals who want the day off to observe their respective Sabbaths? Consider the following alternatives:

Option 1: **Mandatory Accommodation—Uniform Day of Rest**. This option will accommodate the adherents of the religion whose Sabbath is chosen as the day of rest. Costs are borne by the entire population, but religious differences result in a "disparate impact" on those who do not observe that, or any, day. *See McGowan v. Maryland*; *Braunfeld v. Brown*. *See generally* Gary J. Simpson, *Laws Intentionally Favoring Mainstream Religions: An Unhelpful Comparison to Race*, 79 Cornell L. Rev. 514 (1994).

Option 2: **Mandatory Accommodation—Individual Choice.** This option seeks to accommodate everyone whose religious beliefs requires special observance or rest days, but prefers religious reasons to non-religious ones. Costs are borne by non-observing population. *See Estate of Thornton v. Caldor, Inc.*

Option 3: **Negotiated, Voluntary Accommodation.** This option seeks to balance religious and secular needs, but gives preference to secular and economic concerns. Employee needs will be accommodated only if co-workers and employers agree that making the accommodation is otherwise consistent with their needs. Economic and social costs of accommodation are borne by religious adherent. *See TWA v. Hardison.*

Are there other possibilities? Is there a way to better protect those rights without reaching the same result as in *Caldor*? The Americans with Disabilities Act, 42 U.S.C. § 12111 (9), (10) (2001), contains a slightly different, and arguably more stringent, accommodation standard. See Chart 8-1 on page 702.

(9) Reasonable accommodation

The term "reasonable accommodation" may include—

(A) making existing facilities used by employees readily accessible to and usable by individuals with disabilities; and

(B) job restructuring, part-time or modified work schedules, reassignment to a vacant position, acquisition or modification of equipment or devices, appropriate adjustment or modifications of examinations, training materials or policies, the provision of qualified readers or interpreters, and other similar accommodations for individuals with disabilities.

(10) Undue hardship

(A) *In general*

The term "undue hardship" means an action requiring significant difficulty or expense, when considered in light of the factors set forth in subparagraph (B).

(B) *Factors to be considered*

In determining whether an accommodation would impose an undue hardship on a covered entity, factors to be considered include—

(i) the nature and cost of the accommodation needed under this chapter;

(ii) the overall financial resources of the facility or facilities involved in the provision of the reasonable accommodation; the number of persons employed at such facility; the effect on expenses and resources, or the impact otherwise of such accommodation upon the operation of the facility;

(iii) the overall financial resources of the covered entity; the overall size of the business of a covered entity with respect to the number of its employees; the number, type, and location of its facilities; and

Chart 8-1: Mandatory v. Negotiated Accommodations

Sunday Closing (Blue Law) Option	Concerns Accommodated						Cost of Accommodation Borne By
	Business Owner's Concerns			Employee's Concerns			
	Religious Freedom	Purely Economic	Labor Concerns	Religious Freedom	Economic	Secular	
Maintain Blue Law	Sunday Observers only	Limits Ability to Operate on 7-day schedule	Exposes Employer to Increased Unemployment Payments*	Sunday Observers only	Limits Job Opportunities for Non-Sunday Observers	All	Non-Sunday Observers
Repeal Blue Law No Protection for Employee Religious Needs	All	All	Increases Level of Employee Dissatisfaction	Non-Sunday Observers only	Some	None	All Employees
Repeal Blue Law Mandatory Accommodation of Employee-Designated Religious Practice	All	Loss of Employee	Prefers Some Employees over Others, Impact on Seniority System	Yes	Yes	None	Employers, non-observant employees, collective bargaining unit
"Reasonable" Accommodation	All	All	All	Those Negotiated	Those Negotiated	Those Negotiated	Parties to Negotiation

* *E.g.*, Fla. Stat. § 443.131(2) (1996). *See Hobbie v. Unemployment Appeals Comm'n of Florida*, 480 U.S. 136 (1987).

(iv) the type of operation or operations of the covered entity, including the composition, structure, and functions of the workforce of such entity; the geographic separateness, administrative, or fiscal relationship of the facility or facilities in question to the covered entity.

What would this standard accomplish if applied to religious accommodation cases? *Should* the same standard be applied to religious practices? If so, would such a standard survive Establishment Clause scrutiny after *Estate of Thornton v. Caldor, Inc.*?

2. Justices Marshall and Brennan argued in *Hardison* that the Court's reading of Title VII "deals a fatal blow to all efforts under Title VII to accommodate work requirements to religious practices." In their view, the *de minimis* approach taken by the Court is "deeply troubling, for a society that truly values religious pluralism cannot compel adherents of minority religions to make the cruel choice of surrendering their religion or their job." *Hardison,* at 86–87. Do you agree?

3. How much is the decision in *Hardison* affected by the rights of other employees under collective bargaining and other job security arrangements? Title VII makes explicit provisions that immunize otherwise legitimate seniority and collective bargaining plans, and there is no question that an undue hardship can include violating the collective bargaining agreement's seniority provisions. Is this fair? Should collective bargaining agreements provide explicit protection for employee religious concerns? Would negotiating such provisions be otherwise consistent with Title VII and the NLRA?

4. The reasonableness of an accommodation is determined on a case-by-case basis. In assessing undue hardship, courts have been careful to examine whether the employee desiring accommodation performs an "essential" job for the employer, whether the employee can be easily replaced, and whether the employer must pay higher wages in order to hire a replacement. *See, e.g., Thomas v. National Ass'n of Letter Carriers*, 225 F.3d 1149 (10th Cir. 2000) (rejecting accommodation claim against labor union because the employee requesting accommodation did not rebut the claim that collective bargaining agreement prohibited further accommodations). Courts also have looked at non-economic factors, such as safety and health concerns, effect upon morale of fellow employees, whether an accommodation has generated complaints by co-workers, whether the employee has fully exhausted an employer's already existing procedures for accommodation, and whether accommodating an employee would result in violating a state or federal statute. All non-economic factors, however, must be shown to have an "adverse impact on the conduct on the business." *See e.g., Palmer v. Bd. of Educ. of the City of Chicago*, 603 F.2d 1271 (7th Cir. 1979), *aff'g*, 466 F. Supp. 600 (N.D. Ill. 1979) (refusing to take part in essential activities). *See generally* Marianne C. Del Po, *Never on Sunday: Workplace Religious Freedom in the New Millennium*, 51 Me. L. Rev. 341 (1999).

5. EEOC Regulations indicate that if more than one accommodation is available to the employee, and none of the alternatives would impose an undue hardship, the EEOC will examine whether any of the alternatives would "disadvantage the individual with respect to his or her employment opportunities, such as compensation, terms, conditions, or privileges of employment." The employer must offer the alternative that would disadvantage the employee the least. *Hardison* and *Ansonia* cast doubt on this interpretation. Should they?

6. Cases have arisen in which an employee refuses to pay union dues under a union security clause because the employee asserts that his religion prevents him from joining or financially supporting a union. Courts have held that the loss of one em-

ployee's union dues cannot constitute an undue hardship for the union. The EEOC has specified that a union must accommodate the employee by permitting her to "donate a sum equivalent to dues to a charitable organization." 29 C.F.R. § 1605.2 (d)(2). This applies even when an employee does not have a "per se religious objection to labor unions." For example, in *Equal Employment Opportunity Comm'n v. Univ. of Detroit*, 904 F.2d 331 (6th Cir. 1990) an employee was entitled to accommodation because the employee objected to paying dues to the union because it supported "pro-abortion activities." In this regard, the provisions of Title VII mirror the constitutional and labor law rules on this subject. *See Communications Workers of Am. v. Beck*, 487 U.S. 735 (1988); *Abood v. Detroit Bd. of Educ.*, 431 U.S. 209 (1977).

7. The National Labor Relations Act provides a similar provision which allows an "employee who is a member of and adheres to established and traditional tenets or teachings of a bona fide religion, body, or sect which has historically held conscientious objections to joining or financially supporting labor organizations" to donate a sum equal to dues and initiation fees to a "nonreligious, nonlabor organization charitable fund" 29 U.S.C. § 169 (1996). An employer or union cannot require such a "conscientious objector" to join or financially support a labor organization as a condition of employment. The Sixth Circuit has held that this provision of the NLRA is unconstitutional because it requires courts to determine if the religion or sect is "bona fide," and whether it has traditionally held conscientious objections to joining or supporting unions. According to the Sixth Circuit, this inquiry "borders on excessive entanglement with religion." *Wilson v. National Labor Relations Board*, 920 F.2d 1282, 1288 (6th Cir. 1990), *cert. denied*, 505 U.S. 1218 (1992). However, another court has argued that the legislative history of the NLRA indicates that Congress did not intend for the NLRA to supersede Title VII. *See EEOC v. Davey Tree Surgery Co.*, 671 F. Supp. 1260 (N.D. Cal. 1987). Given the case law, which position is the most defensible under the Constitution? *See also E.E.O.C. v. Alliant Techsystems, Inc.*, 1998 WL 777015, 159 L.R.R.M. (BNA) 2664, 74 Empl. Prac. Dec. ¶45,518 (W.D. Va. 1998) (requiring accommodation of employee objections to union membership absent a showing of undue hardship).

b) Statutes Addressing Specific Religious Concerns

There has been a considerable resurgence of interest in religious liberty questions. This trend has been fueled by several social developments, including increasing religious diversity and changing public policy on what have been called "social issues." The result has been increasing sensitivity to issues of workplace religious discrimination and accommodation claims. *See generally* James Davison Hunter, Culture Wars: The Struggle to Define America (1991).

Some of these issues manifest themselves in ways that fit into traditional constitutional categories, such as equal access to public and nonpublic fora by religious speakers and associations. Others arise when Congress seeks to enact changes in the civil rights laws to reflect social concerns about the manner in which public funds are expended. For example, Title IX of the Education Amendments of 1972, 34 U.S.C. §§ 1681, *et seq.*, forbids discrimination "on the basis of sex" to institutions receiving federal funds, and applies to both secular and religious organizations. Title VI of the Civil Rights Act of 1964, 42 U.S.C. §§ 2000d, *et seq.*, forbids discrimination on the basis of race and national origin in federally funded programs, but there is no current legislation that bans religious discrimination in federally-funded programs. (State laws, however, may address the issue.) In the government workplace, issues have arisen when either the government or government contractors attempt to use the BFOQ exception of Title VII to limit employment of religious believers in certain "sensitive" positions where it can be alleged that their beliefs would interfere with the proper functioning of the business. (*e.g.*, defense industries, certain types of health-care facilities).

The cases involving access of religious speakers to public fora are addressed in Chapter Five § B (discussing the Equal Access Act), and the rights of teachers who seek accommodation of their religious beliefs or practices in the respective work setting are addressed in Chapter Six.

One of the most sensitive of these concerns has arisen in the aftermath of the Supreme Court's decision legalizing abortion, *Roe v. Wade*, 410 U.S. 113 (1973). Because of the extensive public funding of health care facilities in the United States, religiously-affiliated hospitals found themselves at risk of being ordered to make their facilities available for sterilizations and abortions. Similar concerns arise under the myriad variations of corporate medicine that have developed since the mid-1980s. *See generally* Daniel Callahan, What Kind of Life: The Limits of Medical Progress (1990); Daniel Callahan, Setting Limits: Medical Goals in an Aging Society (1987); Robert A. Destro, *Targeting the Elderly: A Non-discrimination Perspective on Daniel Callahan's Setting Limits* in Set No Limits: A Rebuttal to Daniel Callahan's Proposal to Limit Health Care for the Elderly (1991). Given recent developments on the issue of assisted suicide and euthanasia, similar issues will arise in this context as well. *See, e.g., Washington v. Glucksberg*, 521 U.S. 702 (1997); Vacco v. Quill, 521 U.S. 793 (1997). *See generally* Michael Ariens, *Suicidal Rights*, 20 Rutgers L.J. 79 (1988); Donald L. Beschle, *Autonomous Decisionmaking and Social Choice: Examining the 'Right to Die'*, 77 Ky. L.J. 319 (1988).

In *Taylor v. St. Vincent's Hospital*, 369 F. Supp. 948 (D. Mont. 1972), *aff'd*, 523 F.2d 75 (9th Cir. 1972), *cert. denied*, 424 U.S. 948 (1976) the United States District Court for the District of Montana enjoined St. Vincent's Hospital from prohibiting Mrs. Taylor's physician from carrying out her desire that he perform a sterilization procedure on her during the delivery of her baby by Cesarean section. The suit to enjoin the hospital from enforcing its religiously-based policy was commenced under 42 U.S.C. § 1983 (which authorizes civil actions for redress of deprivation of civil rights by an person acting under color of law) and 28 U.S.C. § 1343 (which grants the United States district courts jurisdiction of actions (authorized by another law) to redress deprivation, under color of any State law, of a constitutional right). In ruling on the hospital's motion to dismiss for lack of jurisdiction, the court stated that "the fact that the defendant [St. Vincent's Hospital] is the beneficiary of the receipt of Hill-Burton Act [Title VI of the Public Health Service Act] funds is alone sufficient to support an assumption of jurisdiction." 369 F. Supp. at 950 n.1. The court also found that state licensing and tax immunity established a connection between the hospital and the State sufficient to support jurisdiction.

Although this reasoning has been undercut by Supreme Court decisions in the area of state action, *Blum v. Yaretsky*, 457 U.S. 991 (1982) (nursing homes providing care to Medicaid patients are not state actors); *Rendell-Baker v. Kohn*, 457 U.S. 830 (1982) (private school which receives most of its funding from government sources is not state actor), the trend in federal regulation has been to *expand* rather than contract the coverage of federal civil rights laws governing recipients of federal funds.

In keeping with its concern for religious freedom, Congress enacted 42 U.S.C. § 300a-7. It provides protection for all those likely to encounter pressure because of their participation in federally funded programs to conform their views on abortion to those of the administrators of the program. Sections 300a-7[a] and [b] provide protection to institutions and medical personnel, and sections 300a-7[c] and [d] provide protection to individuals whose views conflict with those of program administrators. In relevant part, those sections provide:

> (d) Individual rights respecting certain requirements contrary to religious beliefs or moral convictions. No individual shall be required to perform or assist in the performance of any part of a health service program or research activity funded in whole or in part under a program administered by the Secretary of Health, Education and Welfare [now Health and Human Services], if his performance or assistance in the performance of such part of such program or activity would be contrary to his religious beliefs or moral convictions. 42 U.S.C. §300a-7(d) (1996).
>
> (e) No entity which receives, after the date of enactment of this paragraph, any grant, contract, loan, loan guarantee, or interest subsidy under the Public Health Service Act, the Community Mental Health Centers Act...may deny admission or otherwise discriminate against any applicant (including applicants for internships and residencies) for training or study because of the applicant's reluctance, or willingness, to counsel, suggest, recommend, assist, or in any way participate in the performance of abortion or sterilizations contrary to or consistent with the applicant's religious beliefs or moral convictions. 42 U.S.C. §300a-7(e) (1996).

In order to conform federal policy on this issue, Congress was forced to address the implications of the assumption that abortion must be treated like any other pregnancy-related disability, thus raising the concern that an employer's religiously-based refusal to make health insurance available for abortions on the same terms as childbirth expenses would be deemed "discrimination on the basis of sex" for purposes of Title VII. During the debate over the Pregnancy Disability Act of 1979, P.L. 95-598, Title III §330, 92 Stat. 2679, Congress addressed whether an individual might be guilty of sex discrimination if, on religious grounds, he or she refused to pay for an abortion insurance or otherwise. The result was 42 U.S.C. §2000e(k), amended, which provides:

> The terms 'because of sex' or 'on the basis' include, but are not limited to, because of or on the basis of pregnancy, childbirth, or related medical conditions; This subsection shall not require an employer to pay for health insurance benefits for abortion, except where the life of the mother would be endangered if the fetus were carried to term, or except where medical complications have arisen from abortion. 42 U.S.C. §2000e(k) (1996).

This section was added in committee because many members of Congress "were troubled...by any implication that an employer would have to pay for abortions not necessary to preserve the life of the mother through medical benefits or other fringe benefit programs, even if that employer...harbored religious or moral objections to abortion; such a requirement, it was felt, could compromise the religious freedom of such employers." House Rept. No. 95-948, "Civil Rights Act of 1964-Pregnancy Discrimination," 72-2 U.S. Code Cong. & Admin. News 4749, 4755 (1978).

It should be noted that the rationale of such statutes rests, at least in part, on non-association principles first articulated in the public sector labor union cases, see, e.g., *Abood v. Detroit Bd. of Educ.*, and in cases such as *Wooley v. Maynard*, 430 U.S. 705 (1977) §A. The growth of the non-association principle in employment law has proceeded under the rubric of "accommodation." *See, e.g., Haring v. Blumenthal*, 471 F. Supp. 1172 (D.D.C. 1979), *cert. den. sub. nom. Haring v. Regan*, 452 U.S. 939 (1981) (holding denial of promotion to IRS attorney who refused, on religious grounds, to process the applications of tax exemptions of organizations whose philosophies were religiously repugnant to him not justified as undue burden); *Kenny v. Ambulatory Centre of Miami, Florida, Inc.*, 400 So. 2d 1262 (Fla. 1981) (same, under state law). *But see Erzinger v. Regents of the University of California*, 137 Cal. App. 3d 389, 187 Cal. Rptr. 164 (Fourth Dist. 1982), *cert. denied* 462 U.S. 1133 (1983) (holding §300a-7 does not prohibit funding abortions with mandatory student fees).

Litigation under these sections has been uncommon, but these statutes, as well as those which are in effect in states and cities around the country, are available for use by aggrieved parties. *See, e.g.*, Fla Stat. §§390.001(8) (1996); 458.22(5). The latter section states:

> *Right of Refusal.* —Nothing in this section shall require any hospital or any person to participate in the termination of a pregnancy, nor shall any hospital or any person be liable for such refusal. No person who is a member of, or associated with, the staff of a hospital nor any employee of a hospital or physician in which or by whom the termination of a pregnancy has been authorized or performed, who shall state an objection to such procedure on moral or religious grounds, shall be required to participate in the procedure which will result in the termination of pregnancy. The refusal of any such person or employee to participate shall not form the basis for any disciplinary or other recriminatory action against such person.

For additional cases raising the §300a-7 issue, see *Shelton v. University of Medicine and Dentistry of New Jersey*, 1999 WL 706160 (D.N.J. 1999); *Chrisman v. Sisters of St. Joseph of Peace*, 506 F.2d 308 (9th Cir. 1974); *Watkins v. Mercy Medical Center*, 364 F. Supp. 799 (D. Idaho 1973), *aff'd*, 520 F.2d 894 (9th Cir. 1975). For a discussion contrasting the obligations of religious and non-religious hospitals in this context see Chapter 7, §D, "The Public Policy Requirement." *See generally* William W. Bassett, *Private Religious Hospitals: Limitations Upon Autonomous Moral Choices In Reproductive Medicine*, 17 J. Contemp. Health L. & Pol'y 455 (2001); Lynn D. Wardle, *Protecting the Rights of Conscience of Health Care Providers*, 14 J. Legal Med. 177 (1993); Kathleen M. Boozang, *Deciding the Fate of Religious Hospitals in the Emerging Health Care Market*, 31 Hous. L. Rev. 1429 (1995); Mark E. Chopko, *Religious Access to Public Programs and Governmental Funding*, 60 Geo. Wash. L. Rev. 645 (1992); Carl H. Esbeck, *Government Regulation of Religiously Based Social Services: The First Amendment Considerations*, 19 Hastings Const. L.Q. 343 (1992); Irene Prior Loftus, Note, *I Have a Conscience, Too: The Plight of Medical Personnel Confronting the Right to Die*, 65 Notre Dame L. Rev. 699 (1990); W. Cole Durham, Jr., M.A.Q. Wood & S.J. Condie, *Accommodation of Conscientious Objection to Abortion*, 1982 B.Y.U. L. Rev. 253.

G. The Government Workplace

When an employee works for the government, an additional set of considerations, both constitutional and statutory, must be factored into the labor and employment law equation. Although Congress amended Title VII to cover state and federal employees, not all are subject to its provisions. *See* 2 U.S.C. § 1302 (2001) (applying key labor and employment laws to the legislative branch of the federal government); 2 U.S.C. § 1434 (2001) (soliciting recommendations from the Chief Justice concerning "legislation to provide to employees of the judicial branch the rights, protections, and procedures under the listed laws, including administrative and judicial relief, that are comparable to those available to employees of the legislative branch"); 42 U.S.C. §§ 2000e(f),[4] 2000e-16. There are, in addition, special provisions applicable in the government sector that have no precise equivalent when the private sector is involved. *See, e.g.*, Exec. Order 11478, 34 Fed. Reg. 12985 (August 8, 1969) (prohibiting employment discrimination in the Executive Branch and in those portions of the legislative and judicial branches having employees in the competitive civil service); Exec. Order 11375, 32 Fed. Reg. 14303 (October 13, 1967) (extending Exec. Order 11246 to sex discrimination); Exec. Orders 13087, 63 Fed. Reg. 3009 (May 28, 1998) and 13152, 65 Fed. Reg. 26115 (May 2, 2000) (extending Exec. Order 11478 to discrimination on the basis of sexual orientation and parental status); Exec. Order 11246, 30 Fed. Reg. 12319 (September 24, 1965) (prohibiting employment discrimination by federal agencies and contractors). The provisions of state and local labor and fair employment law should be checked carefully for similar provisions.

When the government is the employer, however, constitutional provisions apply directly. In addition, the nature of the governmental functions with which the employee is charged can affect the outcome of the case, and statutory schemes such as Title VII may require that administrative remedies be pursued before a court case can be filed. Cases brought before the United States Merit Systems Protection Board (MSPB), for example, demonstrate that the jurisdictional issues for wrongful termination actions affecting federal employees can be quite complex. As a practical matter, the lesson for both attorneys and litigants is clear: there is a vast array of administrative procedures about which government employees need to be aware if they are to protect their rights. The benefits of these procedures, however, are equally clear: where the government is the employer there may a greater variety of claims available to the plaintiff than if the employer were operating in the private sector.

1. The Test Clause of Article VI

The Test Clause of Article VI is the Nation's oldest employment discrimination law. It provides that "no religious test shall ever be required as a Qualification to any Office or public Trust under the United States." U.S. Const. Art. VI, cl. 3. The case law discussing the Test Clause is sparse. *See, e.g.*, *Girouard v. United States*, 328 U.S. 61 (1946) (relying in part on the Test Clause as a guide for construing the obligation

4. Section 2000e(f) provides, in relevant part:

The term "employee" means an individual employed by an employer, except that the term "employee" shall not include any person elected to public office in any State or political subdivision of any State by the qualified voters thereof, or any person chosen by such officer to be on such officer's personal staff, or an appointee on the policy making level or an immediate adviser with respect to the exercise of the constitutional or legal powers of the office. The exemption set forth in the preceding sentence shall not include employees subject to the civil service laws of a State government, governmental agency or political subdivision.

of an applicant for naturalization to swear to "defend" the United States, though it was not directly applicable); *Ex parte Garland*, 71 U.S. (4 Wall.) 333 (1866) (distinguishing a Test Oath from other forms of oath taking). State constitutions have similar provisions. *See, e.g.*, Colo. Const., art. VIII, § 5 (2001) ("No religious test or qualification shall ever be required of any person as a condition of admission into any public educational institution of the state, either as a teacher or student"); Ohio Const., art. I, § 7 (2001) ("No religious test shall be required, as a qualification for office, nor shall any person be incompetent to be a witness on account of his religious belief; but nothing herein shall be construed to dispense with oaths and affirmations."); Utah Const. art. I, § 4 (2001) ("no religious test shall be required as a qualification for any office of public trust or for any vote at any election; nor shall any person be incompetent as a witness or juror on account of religious belief or the absence thereof.").

In fact, the two Supreme Court cases to which the test clause would most clearly apply are not within its scope. *See McDaniel v. Paty*, 435 U.S. 618 (1978), *rev'g Paty v. McDaniel*, 547 S.W.2d 897 (Tenn. 1977) (holding unconstitutional a Tennessee constitutional provision excluding ministers of the gospel from the state legislature); *Torcaso v. Watkins*, 367 U.S. 488 (1961) (holding unconstitutional a state constitutional provision which prohibited religious tests for public office, "other than a declaration of belief in the existence of God" as applied to state notary public). As a result, it is difficult to state with any degree of certainty whether or not it forms a part of the religious liberty guarantees "incorporated" via the Fourteenth Amendment, or stands alone as a limit on federal power only. In *Torcaso v. Watkins*, Justice Black's opinion expressly stated that the Court "[found] it unnecessary to consider [the] contention that this provision applies to state as well as federal offices," *Torcaso*, 367 U.S. at 489 n.1, although some commentators are of the opinion that it has been incorporated "in effect." *See* Gerard V. Bradley, *The No Religious Test Clause and the Constitution of Religious Liberty: A Machine that Has Gone of Itself*, 37 Case W. Res. L. Rev. 674, 718 (1987) ("*Torcaso*, if it is to be grasped at all, affects an 'incorporation' of article VI as much as if the Court expressly said so."). *See generally* Michael W. McConnell, *The Origins and Historical Understanding of Free Exercise of Religion*, 103 Harv. L. Rev. 1410 (1990).

Given the large numbers of persons employed at the federal, state and local levels of government, and the large number of projects funded in whole or in part by government money, the Test Clause is an under-appreciated tool in the arsenal of those who believe they have been victims of discrimination on the basis of religion.

An inquiry under the Test Clause has several parts. The practice must be:

- A religious test
- Required as a Qualification for;
- Any Office or public Trust under the United States.

a) What is a "Religious Test or Qualification"?

The most obvious—and historic—form of religious test was the Oath required under the Act of Supremacy, 26 Hen. VIII, c. 1 § 8 (1534). Codified in "An Act to restore to the Crown the ancient Jurisdiction over the Estate Ecclesiastical and Spiritual, and abolishing all foreign Powers repugnant to the same," 1 Eliz., ch. 1, §§ 1, 18 (1558), the impact of the English Test Oath was immortalized in Robert Bolt's portrait of Sir

Thomas More in *A Man for All Seasons* (1962). The Act is reprinted in DOCUMENTS ILLUSTRATIVE OF ENGLISH CHURCH HISTORY, at 243 ff. (H. Gee & W. Hardy eds. 1921).

In most instances, however, a "religious test" is simply a device that operates to screen out those whose religious beliefs or practices, including the taking of oaths, are thought, for reasons of policy or prejudice, to be undesirable. The English Test Oath, for example, operated not only to bar individuals from holding office under the Crown, but from emigrating to certain of the Colonies as well. *See* Finbarr McCarthy, *Participatory Government and Communal Property: Two Radical Concepts in the Virginia Charter of 1606*, 29 U. Rich. L. Rev. 327 (1995) (noting that the Oath was utilized to restrict the emigration of Catholics to Virginia). *See, e.g., Bader v. State*, 344 Ark. 241, 40 S.W.3d 738 (2001) (defendant in a criminal case was not entitled to question jurors on *voir dire* concerning their religion, denomination, and number of times that they attended religious services each month); *Thorson v. State*, 721 So. 2d 590 (Miss. 1998) (Mississippi constitutional and statutory law prohibits religion-based peremptory challenges to potential jurors); *Bacher v. City of North Ridgeville*, 47 Ohio App. 2d 164, 352 N.E.2d 627 (1975) (Jehovah's Witness fireman reinstated after having been fired for refusal to raise the flag over the firehouse); *In the Matter of the Adoption of "E,"* 112 N.J. Super. 326, 271 A.2d 27 (1970) (refusing adoption of a minor child under the age of two years on grounds that it would not be in the child's best interests to be adopted by persons professing no belief in a Supreme Being). *See* Bradley, *The No Religious Test Clause.* As such, most religious tests are already prohibited in government employment by the operation of Title VII of the Civil Rights Act. In situations where the government agency or officer is not an "employer" under Title VII or relevant state employment law, the Test Clause is both relevant, and may be controlling.

b) What is an "Office... under the United States"?

One of the major issues debated at the Constitutional Convention of 1787 was the potential that the newly-created federal government would be staffed and administered in a discriminatory manner. Had either Congress or the President been determined to create a federal "establishment of religion," staffing the Executive and Judicial Branches with individuals of the preferred orthodoxy would have been an important component of the success of such a program. The administration of religious test oaths would have been an essential part of the final screening process.

The Test Clause limits the exercise of State authority as well. The office of Senator is unquestionably a "public Trust under the United States," and until the adoption of the Seventeenth Amendment, U.S. Const. Amend. XVII (1913), the appointing authorities were the State Legislatures. U.S. Const. Art. I §3, cl. 1. Governors have the power to make temporary Senatorial appointments, U.S. Const. Amend. XVII cl. 3 (1913), and the States appoint presidential Electors and set their qualifications. U.S. Const. Art. II §2, cl. 1, 2

The significance of the Test Clause is thus both structural and normative. Its language and structure differentiates between the powers of the newly-created federal government and those of the States, and foreshadows the structural limits contained in the First Amendment. Article VI, clause 3 requires an oath or affirmation in support of the Constitution from all officials and legislators, both State and federal, but only the federal government was prohibited from using religious tests to determine fitness for public office. The States, by contrast, commonly applied such tests to those seeking State offices, and at least one—Tennessee—felt free to do so as late as 1977! *McDaniel v. Paty*,

435 U.S. 618 (1978), *rev'g*, *Paty v. McDaniel*, 547 S.W.2d 897 (Tenn. 1977). *See generally* William G. Torpey, JUDICIAL DOCTRINES OF RELIGIOUS RIGHTS IN AMERICA 16 (1948), *quoting* Sanford H. Cobb, THE RISE OF RELIGIOUS LIBERTY IN AMERICA 510 (1902) (compiling statistics regarding religious qualifications for officeholders in the first thirteen state constitutions.)

c) What is a "Public Trust"?

The phrase "public Trust under the United States" is broader than the term "office," a construction supported by the phrase "office of trust or profit under the United States" which appears in the incompatibility clause of Article II, as well as by Congress' own distinction between individuals "holding an office of trust or profit" and those who may be "discharging an official function *under or in connection with* the United States." 5 U.S.C. §2105(d) (2001) (emphasis added).

Federal case law sheds very little light on this question, but there are a number of State cases construing the phrases "office or public Trust" and "Office of Trust or Profit" which do provide some guidance on the meaning of the term "office of public trust or profit." Those terms are commonly found in the incompatibility provisions of state constitutions and shed some light on the present inquiry. *See, e.g.*, *Pennsylvania v. Dallas*, 4 Dall. 229, 4 U.S. 229, (Pa., Sept. Term 1801) (U.S. Attorney and Recorder of City of Philadelphia); *Begich v. Jefferson*; 441 P.2d 27 (Alaska 1968) (position as state or federal legislator is incompatible with superintendent or teaching positions in state operated school districts); *Commonwealth* ex rel. *Hancock v. Clark*, 506 S.W.2d 503 (Ky. 1974) (postmaster of a fourth class post office was not exercising an office of trust or profit under the United States ineligible to hold or exercise any office of trust or profit under the Kentucky Constitution and so could serve as a member of a county school board). *See also Maxey v. Bell*, 41 Ga. 184 (1870) (holding that the office of guardian is a "public trust" under the Georgia Constitution, and thus subject to the rule that religious tests may not be required). For a more generalized discussion of the term "public trust" as the term was commonly used in the Eighteenth Century see John Louis Lucaites, FLEXIBILITY AND CONSTITUENCY IN EIGHTEENTH-CENTURY ANGLO-WHIGGISM: A CASE STUDY OF THE RHETORICAL DIMENSIONS OF LEGITIMACY (1984).

Given the advent of the modern administrative state, and laws which require federal contractors and grantees of federal funding to comply with federal law in their dealings with the public, it is arguable that the explicit non-discrimination norm of the Test Clause applies not only to federal employment, but also to federal contracting and grant-eligibility considerations as well. *E.g.*, 42 U.S.C. §2000d (Title VI of the Civil Rights Act of 1964); Civil Rights Restoration Act of 1987, Pub. L. 100-259, Mar. 22, 1988, 102 Stat. 28, 20 U.S.C. §§1681 note, 1687, 1687 notes, 1688, 1688 note; 29 U.S.C. §§706, 794; 42 U.S.C. §§2000d-4a, 6107, *Bowen v. Kendrick*, 484 U.S. 942 (1987); *Walz v. Tax Comm'n*, 397 U.S. 664 (1970). *See also Bob Jones University v. United States*, 461 U.S. 574 (1983), excerpted in Chapter Nine.

The federal case law on the topic seems to support a broad reading of the term. The Claims Court has stated that "[t]ransactions relating to the expenditure of public funds require the highest degree of public trust and an impeccable standard of conduct." *Refine Construction Co. v. United States*, 12 Cl. Ct. 56, 63 (1987) (government contracts). Environmental Protection Agency grants for the construction of certain public works projects also constitute a public trust. *See* 40 C.F.R. §§30.120, 33.300; *Town of Fallsburg v. United States*, 22 Cl. Ct. 633, 641 (1991). And finally, the grantee of broadcasting license is considered to be a public trustee; that is, one who must serve the broad goals of the public interest, convenience, and necessity. *Red Lion Broadcasting v. F.C.C.*, 395 U.S. 367, 383 (1969); *Office of Communication of the United Church of Christ v. F.C.C.*, 707 F.2d 1413, 1427–28 (D.C. Cir. 1983).

Notes

1. Reconsider the two charts in Chapter One, § A. How does the Test Clause relate to the equal citizenship provisions of Article IV and the Privileges and Immunities Clause of the Fourteenth Amendment? Should it be viewed as an "incorporated" norm affecting the interpretation of the Due Process and Equal Protection Clauses of the Fourteenth Amendment?

2. Which constitutional norms prohibit intentional discrimination on the basis of religion? The First Amendment alone, or do the Test, Fourteenth Amendment Privileges and Immunities, Citizenship, and Equal Protection Clauses do so as well?

3. To what extent should the Test Clause be applicable to government funding decisions? Is receipt of government funding for a specific purpose (*e.g.*, education, health care) a "public trust"? If so, is it valid to deny funding to religious organizations simply because they are religious? *See Bowen v. Kendrick*, 484 U.S. 942 (1987) (holding that the Establishment Clause did not require the government to exclude religious groups from participation in a government-funded sex education demonstration project).

4. In *Lemon v. Kurtzman*, 403 U.S. 602 (1971), and in *Aguilar v. Felton*, 473 U.S. 402 (1985), the Supreme Court held that neither Congress nor the States may provide funding for secular services and subjects in religiously-affiliated schools on the grounds that, while it could not be presumed that the teachers would violate the law, the Court needed to be *certain* that no public funds would support religious education. Is the requirement of fiscal certainty in such contexts a religious test for a public trust? Does it operate as one?

2. Statutory and Administrative Claims

There are two facets of the government workplace that have no parallel in the private sector. The first relates to the government's law enforcement role and the investigative tasks that accompany it. The second relates to the myriad administrative and procedural requirements that apply to civil service employment. For purposes of this section, only these two aspects of the government workplace will be considered. In most other respects, government employees are governed by the same standards as those governing the private sector secular workplace. *See, e.g.*, *Mann v. Frank, Postmaster General*, 7 F.3d 1365 (8th Cir. 1993) (rejecting a Sabbatarian's claim of discrimination for failure to accommodate because of the seniority system and voluntary nature of the job assignment she had undertaken); *American Postal Workers Union v. Postmaster General*, 781 F.2d 772 (9th Cir. 1986) (applying "undue hardship" standard to a group of postal workers who refused to process draft registration forms on religious grounds); *United States v. City of Albuquerque*, 545 F.2d 110 (10th Cir. 1976) (failure to accommodate Seventh Day Adventist fireman was justified on both public safety and administrative grounds).

a) *Conscientious Objection to Regulatory and Investigatory Assignments*

In *Haring v. Blumenthal*, 471 F. Supp. 1172 (D.D.C. 1979), the employee was an examiner in the Exempt Organizations Section of the Internal Revenue Service. In the course of his employment, he was required to examine and pass upon the validity of requests for tax exemptions by abortion clinics. After being rebuffed by the Service on his legal argument that such organizations were not entitled to exemptions under I.R.C. §501(c)(3), he requested assignments that would not compel him to deal with organizations whose purposes he opposed on moral grounds. Branded a troublemaker and a religious zealot by his supervisors, his requests for accommodation were refused, and he was given less challenging assignments. After the District Court held that he had stated a claim, the matter was settled.

In *Ryan v. U.S. Department of Justice*, 950 F.2d 458 (7th Cir. 1991), by contrast, the nature of the position played an important role in the outcome. Ryan, an FBI agent, refused on religious grounds to investigate non-violent protest groups. He was dismissed from his job for insubordination and appealed to the Merit Systems Protection Board (MSPB). The Board upheld the dismissal. In its view, there were strong public policy reasons for deferring to the FBI's determination that obedience to orders is an essential requirement for agents of law enforcement agencies. On appeal, however, the Seventh Circuit addressed a slightly different question: whether a single, religion-based act of insubordination was sufficient grounds for firing. Upholding the dismissal, the court focused heavily on the special nature of the FBI. It also noted that Ryan had refused to exchange assignments with peers, and had suggested no alternative accommodation to the employer. As a result, he was unable to make a case that he was entitled to accommodation under 42 U.S.C. §2000e-16(a) (1996) (applying Title VII to the Government as an employer).

b) *Procedural Requirements*

The procedural requirements for federal employees raising discrimination complaints are detailed, and vary from agency to agency. The general procedures are contained in 29 C.F.R §§1614.101 through 1614.607 (2001), but the rules governing specific agencies should also be consulted.

Just as the requirements for timely filing under Title VII must be scrupulously observed by private litigants, so too must the statutory and administrative exhaustion requirements which apply only to federal employees. In *Siegel v. Kreps*, 654 F.2d 773 (D.C. Cir. 1981), for example, the primary issue was the plaintiff's failure to exhaust remedies within the agency prior to the commencement of court action under Title VII. Holding that the "principal exhaustion requirement is that the complainant must initially seek relief in the agency which has allegedly discriminated against him," Siegel's claims were dismissed on the ground that he had failed to meet the timing requirements of 42 U.S.C. §2000e-16(c), a provision which applies only to Title VII complaints brought by federal employees. It provides as follows:

> Within 90 days of receipt of notice of final action taken by a department, agency, or unit..., or by the Equal Employment Opportunity Commission upon an appeal from a decision or order of such department, agency, or unit on a complaint of discrimination based on race, color, religion, sex or national origin, brought pursuant to subsection (a) of this section, Executive Order

> 11478 or any succeeding Executive orders, or after one hundred and eighty days from the filing of the initial charge with the department, agency, or unit or with the Equal Employment Opportunity Commission on appeal from a decision or order of such department, agency, or unit until such time as final action may be taken by a department, agency, or unit, an employee or applicant for employment, if aggrieved by the final disposition of his complaint, or by the failure to take final action on his complaint, may file a civil action as provided in section 2000e-5 of this title, in which civil action the head of the department, agency, or unit, as appropriate, shall be the defendant.

Greenberg v. Hove, Acting Chairman, FDIC, 1995 WL 33997 (E.E.O.C.), illustrates another important point concerning the prosecution of discrimination complaints: A timely complaint should state every possible ground for relief. Greenberg sought relief for wrongful termination through the MSPB. After exhausting those remedies for wrongful termination, Greenberg filed a civil suit against the agency for discrimination, but summary judgment for the agency was granted because the plaintiff had failed to file any administrative complaints alleging discrimination. Greenberg then attempted to file such complaints, but these too were dismissed as untimely. Greenberg appealed, but the EEOC upheld the dismissal on the grounds that the complaints were based on a common set of facts which had already been reviewed in the initial MSPB proceeding. By the time he re-filed alleging job discrimination under Title VII, the time for filing had long since passed. *See also Nolen v. Brown, Secretary, Department of Veterans Affairs,* 1995 WL 70240 (E.E.O.C.) (same; enforcement of time limits on EEO complaints). *But see Seely v. Runyon, Postmaster General,* 1995 WL 96295 (E.E.O.C.) (reversing a dismissal on timeliness grounds), in which a "mixed case" complaint (defined as a "complaint of employment discrimination filed with a Federal agency based on race, color, religion, sex, national origin, age or disability related to or stemming from an action that can be appealed to the MSPB") was dismissed by the MSPB on jurisdictional grounds. Because the MSPB declined jurisdiction, the case lost its status as "mixed" and became subject to the normal government EEO process.

Chapter 9

The Taxation of Churches, Charities & Their Affiliates

A. Introduction

It is an article of legal and political faith that "churches do not pay taxes." It is also untrue. Although "churches" and "houses of worship" belonging to institutions recognized by the government as religious are not generally subject to *ad valorem* property taxes, the complex web of federal, state, and local policies governing the taxation and exemption of religious institutions, their income, properties, and activities makes it clear that tax exemptions are the exception, not the rule.

The taxation of churches and religious organizations presents a number of closely related but conceptually distinct questions. The purpose of this chapter is to "unpack" the key issues, and to provide a context in which it is possible to distinguish them from one another. Once that task is accomplished, it will be possible to place questions of statutory construction, economic and tax theory, the law of charities, and questions relating to the administration of the tax system into the general framework of the law governing religious liberty in a pluralistic democracy.

1. Distinguishing Theory and Practice: A Preliminary Note on Methodology

In tax law, just as in other legal disciplines, it is often not enough to know what the law says and how it is administered. Because the "intent" of a statute is often a key component of legal and constitutional analysis, we will sometimes want to know *why* the law was written or is structured in a specific way. At times, we will also need to know whether administrative interpretation and enforcement of the statute is consistent with its text and structure.

In the tax context, such inquiries are exceedingly complex. This is so, in part, because tax laws rarely arise from one cohesive vision of taxation. Rather, the existing tax structure is built up gradually, and reflects the give-and-take of political compromise. Legislators are often far more concerned about whom the tax affects, and the fiscal burdens it will impose, rather than whether the tax provision eventually enacted will fit comfortably into a coherent theory of taxation. *Compare e.g.*, United States Congress,

Joint Committee on Taxation, *Summary of Distributional Effects, By Income Category: Budget Reconciliation (H.R. 5835)—Revenue Provisions As Reported by the Conferees* (October 26, 1990) (Document JCX-46-90) *with* Paul R. McDaniel & James R. Repetti, *Horizontal and Vertical Equity: The Musgrave/Kaplow Exchange*, 1 *Fla. Tax Rev.* 607 (1993).

Because courts must use tax legislation and regulations to resolve actual controversies, judges and scholars study tax measures in an attempt to make interpretive sense of a body of law that has evolved piecemeal from the political process. Though achieving a cohesive synthesis or theory is likely to be impossible, the exercise is valuable because the law cannot be applied or improved without some sense of what it is intended to accomplish. *But see* Mikhail A. Bakunin, *Letters to his Sisters*, November 4, 1882, *quoted in* DICTIONARY OF QUOTATIONS 687 (Bergen Evans ed. 1968) ("Throw theory into the fire; it only spoils life."). So if we are to understand the relationship between tax law and theory, and between tax policy and constitutional law, we must first seek a basic understanding of what each seeks to accomplish in its own sphere. Only then can we attempt a comparison.

2. Ascertaining the Character of the Issue

Legal methodology is determined both by reference to the type of measure being analyzed, and by reference to the purpose of the analysis. The first step, therefore, is to distinguish among the types of issues that can arise in tax controversies.

Most of the tax problems facing churches and other religious institutions and organizations are **statutory** or **administrative**. The resolution of these controversies involves the application of relatively straightforward legal principles to a given set of facts.[1] Careful development of the facts relevant to the specific statute and regulations thought by the tax authorities to be applicable to the controversy is crucial.

Conceptual analysis is required when the issues being debated are **structural**, such as the most effective way to close a specific tax loophole, or whether a specific provision should be characterized as a "loophole" at all. Analysis of structural issues requires a working knowledge of the existing statute and regulations, a thorough understanding of the economic theories on which the particular tax is based, and an appreciation for the sometimes conflicting political and revenue goals the legislature had in mind when it adopted the provisions in question. Whether tax exemptions for churches and religious institutions should be viewed as subsidies to the exempt organization is a question that fits into this category.

A third set of issues is **political**. These include the definition of an appropriate tax base, the merits of progressive or "flat" taxation, or the wisdom of using the tax code as a vehicle for making and implementing social policies in addition to the raising of revenue. Debates over the legitimacy of the economic assumptions that support a proposed tax provision, an assertion that the existing tax code is improperly structured, or is insufficiently "progressive," also fall into this category.

The last set of issues is **jurisdictional**. The focus here is on the manner in which federal and state constitutional provisions allocate and limit the power to tax. Knowledge of the language and structure of the tax code and regulations is useful when such issues

1. Whether or not a specific expenditure is an "ordinary and necessary expense" of a business under Internal Revenue Code [I.R.C.] § 162, or an expense related to the production of income under I.R.C. § 212, are two examples.

are discussed, but the underlying issues are political: (1) Upon whom has the political community conferred the power to levy the specific tax in question? and (2) What limits, if any, have been placed on the exercise of that power?

The tax treatment of churches and religious institutions is a classic example of a problem that involves all four of the categories noted above. At the most basic level, an understanding of the statutes, codes and regulations adopted by Congress and the states is required if one is to provide tax advice to churches, religious institutions, and charitable institutions. When disputes over the meaning or application of those laws and regulations arise, a review of their legislative, administrative and judicial history may be necessary to ascertain the proper interpretation of the statute. It is only when the issue turns on a policy question external to the statute or regulations that the analysis must turn to economics, the law of charities, politics, and constitutional law.

Because the policy arguments relating to the taxation of churches, religious institutions, charities and non-profit institutions are often complex, an attempt to "unpack" them requires a systematic examination of each set of issues: jurisdictional, statutory, conceptual and political.

B. Definitions & Terminology

The starting point of our analysis is definitional. The following questions are common to the analysis of any tax issue:

1. What is the "subject" of the tax in question? (*e.g.*, a tax on individuals, imports, property, *etc.*)
2. What is the tax called? (*e.g.*, a tax, duty, assessment, impost, user fee, *etc.*)
3. Who (or what) is the taxing authority? (*e.g.*, Congress, a State, county, municipality or special taxing district)
4. What is the source of the taxing authority's power to levy the tax in question?
5. What limits, if any, apply to the exercise of the taxing authority's power?
6. How is the tax measured? (*e.g.*, income, value-added, assessed property valuation, flat fee)
7. What are the rules, both statutory and administrative, that govern the administration of the tax?

Questions one through five are **jurisdictional** because they define the power of the taxing authority to levy on the "subject" of the tax. Questions six and seven assume the existence of jurisdiction to tax the person, property, or activity that is the subject of the tax. Constitutional claims will arise at this stage, not because of defects in the tax, but because of the manner in which it is administered. Constitutional and statutory claims that arise at this point are **operational**.

1. What Is a 'Tax'?

Taxes are ubiquitous. Oliver Wendell Holmes viewed taxes as "what we pay for civilized society." *Compania General de Tabacos de Filipinas v. Collector*, 275 U.S. 87, 100

(1927). Ralph Waldo Emerson observed that taxes are, "of all debts[, the one] men are least willing to pay." Ralph Waldo Emerson, ESSAYS: SECOND SERIES 232 (1888).

Whatever they may be called, taxes have the following general characteristics:

1. Taxes represent a charge or levy imposed by the government on individuals or property;
2. Taxes are exacted pursuant to legislation;
3. The objective of a tax is to generate revenue to be used for the needs of the public, and not a "charge primarily imposed for the purpose of regulation;"
4. A tax is an enforced contribution, not a debt, donation, or a payment for some special privilege or service rendered, or other voluntary payment; and
5. A tax is enforceable by levy, attachment or imprisonment, or a combination of these remedies.

See generally Rev. Rul. 57-345, 1957-2 C.B. 132, *revoked on other grounds by* Rev. Rul. 60-366, 1960–2 C.B. 63; Boris Bittker, FEDERAL TAXATION OF INCOME, ESTATES, AND GIFTS ¶ 32.1.2 (1981).

2. Types of Taxes

Taxes come in many forms. They are usually described by reference either to their subject, the method of calculation, or both. (*e.g.*, an *ad valorem* real or personal property tax, a "flat" income tax, or a license tax). By definition, the revenue generated by a tax is intended to benefit the whole community without regard to the benefits received by particular individuals or property. *See* Treas. Reg. § 1.164-4(a), 26 C.F.R. § 1.164-4(a) (2001) (drawing a distinction between taxes that benefit the general public and special assessments that pay for improvements that benefit specific properties).

The *subject* of the tax defines its character and validity. An *assessment*, for example, is a form of taxation that is distinguishable from general taxation because it is imposed on specific individuals or property owners in order to defray the cost of improvements or services that are thought to be of special benefit to them. Because they are a charge for a specific purpose, assessments are calculated or levied as a proportionate share of the cost of the improvement or service received. Among the most common examples of assessments are the charges allocated to abutting property owners for the cost of new sidewalks or street lighting.

Closely related to assessments, but legally and conceptually distinct from them, are *user fees*. User fees are not taxes at all. They are voluntary charges based upon the proprietary right of a governing body to recover the cost of specific services or facilities from those who utilize them. The key difference is that an assessment is a tax that cannot be avoided, whereas a user fee can be avoided by not utilizing the service or facility for which the charge is imposed.

Imposts, duties and excises round out the specific kinds of taxes to be considered at this point in the Chapter. *Impost* is another term for a "tax." The term *duty* also can be used interchangeably with the term "tax," but the term is generally used to refer to a tax on the import or export of goods (tariff). An *excise* is a tax imposed on the manufacture, sale, transfer, or use of goods, or on an occupation, service, or activity. Federal income taxes, which will be considered later in this chapter, are an excise tax income-producing activity. *See* Daniel Q. Posin, FEDERAL INCOME TAXATION 33–40 (1993).

Note

Now that we have looked at the types of taxes, let us reconsider — from a tax perspective — one of the most famous, *un*successful tax proposals in American history: Virginia's "Bill Establishing A Provision for Teachers of the Christian Religion," also known as the "General Assessment Bill." Though it was defeated in committee in 1785, the controversy it engendered has had a significant impact far beyond its specific provisions. *See* Chapter Two § A. Consider the following points:

1. The proposed tax was to be levied "for support of Christian teachers" [*i.e.* ministers].
2. It was to be assessed "on the property within [the] Commonwealth," and was to be paid "by every person chargeable with the said tax at the time the same shall become due."
3. The taxpayer was given the power to direct the money collected under the assessment to whatever "society of Christians" the taxpayer thought deserving. If no designation was made by the taxpayer, the money was to be paid into the public treasury to be used to support schools ("seminaries of learning") in the county from which it had been collected.
4. The money to be raised was to be devoted "by the Vestries, Elders, or Directors of each religious society... to a provision for a Minister or Teacher of the Gospel of their denomination, or the providing of places of divine worship, *and to none other use whatsoever*; except in the denominations of Quakers and Menonists, who may receive what is collected from their members, and place it in their general fund, to be disposed of in a manner which they shall think best calculated to promote their particular mode of worship." (emphasis added).

What can we learn from the specific provisions of this tax proposal? First, the proposed tax is an *assessment*. By its terms, it is intended to defray the cost of a specific service or structure: the support of ministers, places of worship, or both, and for *no other use or purpose whatsoever*. Second, it was "general" because it was to be paid at a uniform rate "by every person chargeable with the said tax at the time the same shall become due." *See generally* Marvin K. Singleton, *Colonial Virginia as First Amendment Matrix: Henry, Madison, and Assessment Establishment*, *in* JAMES MADISON ON RELIGIOUS LIBERTY 162 (Robert S. Alley ed. 1985).

What else can we learn from the structure and language of the tax proposed to support Virginia's Christian ministers? First, observe that the taxpayer had the power to designate the specific beneficiary of the tax. If the taxpayer made a designation to a religious society under this provision, the money designated would be allocated solely for the society so designated and would be available for no other public purposes. (This is what made it an "assessment," rather than a general tax.) Under the current Internal Revenue Code, federal income taxpayers have the ability to contribute up to three dollars of their income tax liability to the Presidential Election Campaign Fund. 26 U.S.C. § 6096(a) (2001). What conceptual and legal differences explain the difference in the Court's approach to the two issues? *See Buckley v. Valeo*, 424 U.S. 1, 92 (1976) (rejecting an analogy between taxation for the support of religion and taxation for the support of political speech).

How does the proposed Virginia tax for the support of ministers' salaries compare with tax support of churches in other countries? The Federal Republic of Germany, for example, has a "church tax." Only church members are liable for the tax, but it is levied and administered by the states (Länder) under their respective taxation systems. *See* Klaus Tipke & Joachim Lang, STEUERRECHT 388, 390 (12th ed. 1989). How do the two systems compare?

Second, "undesignated" money was to be paid into the public treasury, where it was available only for educational purposes within the counties from which it was raised. *See* Chapters Two and Six. For a brief summary of the educational practices in Colonial Virginia, see Chapter Six § F (1). *See generally* Guy Fred Wells, PARISH EDUCATION IN COLONIAL VIRGINIA 7–8 & n.12 (1969) (noting that by the end of the Colonial period, parish record books indicate that frustration with the expense of educating and caring for the poor was becoming as commonplace as frustration with the expense of supporting the Anglican ministry). Today local, state, and federal governments use general tax revenues to support a wide variety of public welfare programs, including job-training, day care, housing, health care, and drug abuse programs. These programs are run by government agencies, by private contractors, or both. Can the government contract with churches and religious organizations to provide these services?

C. Does the State Have the Power to Tax the Church?

1. The Power to Tax

The power to tax is a legislative function. Given its importance, as well as the great potential that the power can be abused, constitutions, both federal and state, are quite specific concerning its contours and limitations. Article I, § 8, cl. 1 of the United States Constitution, for example, gives Congress the power to "[t]o lay and collect Taxes, Duties, Imposts and Excises, to pay the Debts and provide for the common Defence and general Welfare of the United States," but Article I, § 9 clauses 5 and 6 limit Congressional discretion by requiring apportionment of direct taxes, and that "all Duties, Imposts and Excises shall be uniform throughout the United States." *See also* U.S. Const. Amend. XVI (permitting the taxation of incomes without apportionment). State constitutions contain similar provisions limiting the legislature's power to tax. *See* Del. Const. art. VIII, § 1 ("All taxes shall be uniform upon the same class of subjects within the territorial limits of the authority levying the tax, and shall be levied and collected under general laws passed by the General Assembly.").

The starting point for an analysis of the power of Congress or the States to impose taxes on churches and religious institutions is to review of the nature and extent of the legislative power granted by the constitution. If there is no jurisdiction over the taxpayer or the subject of the tax, or if the power is exercised in a manner inconsistent with the grant, the tax is void to the extent that it exceeds the powers granted. *See City of Tampa v. Birdsong Motors, Inc.*, 261 So. 2d 1, 3 (Fla. 1972) ("Doubt as to the powers sought to be exercised must be resolved against the [taxing authority] and in favor of the general public.")

Ascertaining "jurisdiction to tax" is thus the critical first step any tax case. The question is a simple one:

> *Does the taxing authority have jurisdiction to levy on the subject of the tax, and the right to collect it from the putative taxpayer?*

2. State and Federal Jurisdiction to Tax Churches and Religious Activities

The most famous statement concerning the rationale for careful scrutiny of taxes alleged to be imposed in violation of constitutional limitations is John Marshall's observation that "the power to tax involves the power to destroy." *McCulloch v. Maryland*, 19 U.S. (4 Wheat). 316, 431 (1819). This is so because taxes can impose significant economic, administrative, and regulatory burdens on the individuals and institutions called upon to pay them.

Given the nature and degree of burdens which can be imposed by taxes and the myriad regulations which accompany them, it is unsurprising that constitutional provisions place express limits on the power to tax, and speak directly to the type of taxes that may be imposed, the nature of allowable burdens, and the permissible subjects. More generalized constitutional limitations on legislative powers are applicable as well. *See Marchetti v. United States*, 390 U.S. 39 (1968) (privilege against self-incrimination); *Bailey v. Drexel Furniture Co.*, 259 U.S. 20 (1922) (Child Labor Tax Case) (invalidating excise tax as a penalty where Congress lacked power to regulate in the first instance); *McCulloch v. Maryland* (recognizing the doctrine of intergovernmental tax immunity).

Burden alone is rarely, if ever, an argument which will suffice to invalidate an otherwise valid tax. Congress and State legislatures act pursuant to express powers to levy and collect taxes, and the power to tax carries with it a considerable range of powers to legislate in furtherance of the government's fiscal and economic policies. *See, e.g.*, U.S. Const. art. I, § 8, cl. 18 (Necessary and Proper Clause); *McCray v. United States*, 195 U.S. 27, 59 (1904) (upholding tax on oleomargarine set at prohibitive levels). Once jurisdiction to levy on the subject and collect from the taxpayer has been established, tax exemptions are "matters of legislative grace." *See, e.g.*, *Regan v. Taxation With Representation of Washington*, 461 U.S. 540, 549 (1983), *quoting Commissioner v. Sullivan*, 356 U.S. 27, 28 (1958); *Colton v. City of Montpelier*, 71 Vt. 413, 415, 45 A. 1039, 1040 (1899) ("The general right to make exemptions is involved in the right to apportion taxes, and must be understood to exist in the supreme legislative power."). Questions which go to the wisdom of tax policy, such as the appropriateness of a particular subject, the rate charged, or the existence of motives in addition to the desire collect revenue for the use of the government, are issues left to legislative discretion. *See, e.g.*, *Minor v. United States*, 396 U.S. 87, 98 n.13 (1969) (purely regulatory purpose did not invalidate tax statute).

In the present context, John Marshall's observation concerning the ability of a hostile legislature to use the power of taxation in a destructive manner raises two questions: (1) Does the taxing power really invest the legislature with the discretionary power to destroy, regulate, or otherwise inhibit, the free exercise of religion? and (2) If so, what is the best mechanism to protect religious liberty in the tax context?

Unfortunately, it is impossible to answer either of these questions in the abstract. Not only are there different kinds of taxes, there is also a wide range of subjects on which they can be imposed. So before even a preliminary answer can be developed, careful attention must be given to the character of the taxpayer, the nature of the tax, its subjects, its purpose, and the types of burdens it imposes. The dissenting opinion of Justice Frankfurter in *Jones v. City of Opelika*, 319 U.S. 105, 134–35 (1943), is instructive:

> A tax can be a means for raising revenue, or a device for regulating conduct, or both. Challenge to the constitutional validity of a tax measure requires that it be analyzed and judged in all its aspects. We must therefore distinguish between the questions that are before us... and those that are not.

In *McCulloch v. Maryland*, for example, the state of Maryland sought to collect an excise tax on the transactions and operations of the Baltimore office of the Bank of the United States. Maryland law levied a tax on the transactions or operation of "any bank [which] established, or shall, without authority from the state establish any branch, office of discount and deposit, or office of pay and receipt in any part of this state."

On its face, the tax is an excise, levied on the operations of banks operating without official sanction. As applied to banks in general, the tax would likely be valid. The question in *McCulloch* was whether Maryland could collect its tax from the Bank of the United States. Relying on the Supremacy Clause, U.S. Const. art. VI, the Supreme Court held that the Bank, as an instrumentality of the federal government, was immune from state taxes without its consent. Such an approach is *jurisdictional.*

Murdock v. Pennsylvania, 319 U.S. 105 (1943), is a case in which the tax immunity claim was based on the First Amendment. The putative taxpayers in *Murdock* were Jehovah's Witnesses who evangelized door-to-door. During the course of their visits, they preached, delivered religious literature, and sought donations to cover the cost of that literature from those who were willing to accept it. In the view of local tax authorities, their activities involved the "sale" of literature, and the tax authorities accordingly sought to collect the appropriate license tax. An excise, it was imposed on all individuals who engaged in the privilege of "canvassing for or soliciting... orders for goods, paintings, pictures, wares, or merchandise of any kind, or... delivering such articles under orders so obtained or solicited."

Unlike *McCulloch*, in which the immunity sought was due to the federal character of the *taxpayer*, the immunity sought in *Murdock* was due to the protected nature of the *activity* alleged by the taxing authorities to be subject to the excise tax. The Jehovah's Witnesses viewed the tax as an excise on the privilege of door-to-door evangelism and fund-raising. To the tax authorities, the subject of the tax was the distribution of literature for a price. Which was it?

The dissenters in *Murdock* viewed the tax as little more than a general imposition on the distribution and the sale of literature.

> It is altogether incorrect to say that the question here is whether a state can limit the free exercise of religion by imposing burdensome taxes. No claim is made that the effect of these taxes, either separately or cumulatively, has been or is likely to be to restrict the petitioners' religious propaganda activities in any degree. Counsel expressly disclaim any such contention. They insist on absolute immunity from any kind of monetary exaction for their occupation. Their claim is that no tax, no matter how trifling, can constitutionally be laid upon the activity of distributing religious literature, regardless of the actual effect of the tax upon such activity.

Jones v. Opelika, 319 U.S. 105, 134–35 (1943) (Frankfurter, J. dissenting) (companion case to *Murdock*).

The majority in *Murdock*, however, saw the case as "present[ing] a single issue: the constitutionality of an ordinance which as construed and applied requires religious colporteurs to pay a license tax as a condition to the pursuit of their activities." 319 U.S. at 110. The problem, in the view of the majority, was neither the subject of the tax, nor the character of the taxpayer, but rather the *burden* it imposed on the exercise of First Amendment rights. The ordinance was the functional equivalent a tax on "the privilege of delivering a sermon." Such an approach is *prudential*.

Read together, *McCulloch* and *Murdock* raise an important question concerning the nature of tax immunities derived from the First Amendment. Are they *jurisdictional* because the concept of religious liberty embodied in the First Amendment makes religious activity or property an improper *subject* of taxation? Or is the limit imposed by the First Amendment a *prudential* one which turns on a court's perception that the nature and degree of the burden on religious freedom which results from the imposition or administration of the tax is too high?

Jimmy Swaggart Ministries v. Board of Equalization of California

493 U.S. 378 (1990)

Justice O'CONNOR delivered the opinion for a unanimous Court.

This case presents the question whether the Religion Clauses of the First Amendment prohibit a State from imposing a generally applicable sales and use tax on the distribution of religious materials by a religious organization.

I

California's Sales and Use Tax Law requires retailers to pay a sales tax "[f]or the privilege of selling tangible personal property at retail."A "sale" includes any transfer of title or possession of tangible personal property for consideration. The use tax, as a complement to the sales tax, reaches out-of-state purchases by residents of the State. It is "imposed on the storage, use, or other consumption in this state of tangible personal property purchased from any retailer" at the same rate as the sales tax (6 percent). Although the use tax is imposed on the purchaser, it is generally collected by the retailer at the time the sale is made. Neither the State Constitution nor the State Sales and Use Tax Law exempts religious organizations from the sales and use tax, apart from a limited exemption for the serving of meals by religious organizations.

During the tax period in question (1974 to 1981), Jimmy Swaggart Ministries was a religious organization. From 1974 to 1981, [it] conducted numerous "evangelistic crusades"[and] conducted religious services that included preaching and singing. Appellant also sold religious books, tapes, records, and other religious and nonreligious merchandise at the crusades. Appellant also published a monthly magazine, "The Evangelist," which was sold nationwide by subscription.

Based on the sales figures for appellant's religious materials, [California authorities] notified appellant that it owed sales and use taxes of [$166,145.10, including interest and a penalty]. Appellant did not contest the assessment of tax liability for the sale and use of nonreligious merchandise, [but objected to the remainder on the grounds that] the tax on religious materials violated the First Amendment. [Following a hearing and an appeal before the tax authorities, the penalty was dropped, but the amount of tax and interest due was reaffirmed.] Pursuant to state procedural law, appellant paid the amount and filed a petition for redetermination and refund. The [Tax] Board denied appellant's petition, and appellant brought suit in state court, seeking a refund of the tax paid. [The California courts denied a refund.]

II

Appellant's central contention is that the State's imposition of sales and use tax liability on its sale of religious materials contravenes the First Amendment's command, made applicable to the States by the Fourteenth Amendment, to "make no law respecting an establishment of religion, or prohibiting the free exercise thereof." Appellant challenges the Sales and Use Tax Law under both the Free Exercise and Establishment Clauses.

A

The Free Exercise Clause, we have noted, "withdraws from legislative power, state and federal, the exertion of any restraint on the free exercise of religion. Its purpose is to secure religious liberty in the individual by prohibiting any invasions thereof by civil authority." [*Abington School Dist. v. Schempp*]. Indeed, "[a] regulation neutral on its face may, in its application, nonetheless offend the constitutional requirement for governmental neutrality if it unduly burdens the free exercise of religion." [*Wisconsin v. Yoder*]. Our cases have established that "[t]he free exercise inquiry asks whether government has placed a substantial burden on the observation of a central religious belief or practice and, if so, whether a compelling governmental interest justifies the burden." [*Hernandez v. Commissioner*]. Appellant relies almost exclusively on our decisions in *Murdock v. Pennsylvania* and *Follett v. McCormick* for the proposition that a State may not impose a sales or use tax on the evangelical distribution of religious material by a religious organization.

We reject appellant's expansive reading of *Murdock* and *Follett* as contrary to the decisions themselves. In *Murdock*, we considered the constitutionality of a city ordinance requiring all persons canvassing or soliciting within the city to procure a license by paying a flat fee. Reversing the convictions of Jehovah's Witnesses convicted under the ordinance of soliciting and distributing religious literature without a license, we explained:

> The hand distribution of religious tracts is an age-old form of missionary evangelism [and] has been a potent force in various religious movements down through the years. This form of evangelism is utilized today on a large scale by various religious sects whose colporteurs carry the Gospel to thousands upon thousands of homes and seek through personal visitations to win adherents to their faith. It is more than preaching; it is more than distribution of religious literature. It is a combination of both. Its purpose is as evangelical as the revival meeting. This form of religious activity occupies the same high estate under the First Amendment as do worship in the churches and preaching in the pulpits.

Accordingly, we held that "spreading one's religious beliefs or preaching the Gospel through distribution of religious literature and through personal visitations is an age-old type of evangelism with as high a claim to constitutional protection as the more orthodox types."

We extended *Murdock* the following Term by invalidating, as applied to "one who earns his livelihood as an evangelist or preacher in his home town," an ordinance (similar to that involved in *Murdock*) that required all booksellers to pay a flat fee to procure a license to sell books. [*Follett v. McCormick*] Reaffirming our observation in *Murdock* that "'the power to tax the exercise of a privilege is the power to control or suppress its enjoyment,'" we reasoned that "[t]he protection of the First Amendment is not restricted to orthodox religious practices any more than it is to the expression of orthodox economic views. He who makes a profession of evangelism is not in a less preferred position than the casual worker." Our decisions in these cases, however, resulted from the particular nature of the challenged taxes—flat license taxes that operated as a prior restraint on the exercise of religious liberty. In *Murdock*, for instance, we emphasized that the tax at issue was "a license tax—a flat tax imposed on the exercise of a privilege granted by the Bill of Rights," and cautioned that "[w]e do not mean to say that religious groups and the press are free from all financial burdens of government. We have here something quite different, for example, from a tax on the income of one who engages in religious activities or a tax on property used or employed in connection with those activities." In *Follett*, we reiterated that a preacher is not "free from all financial burdens of government, including taxes on income or property" and, "like other citizens, may be subject to general taxation."

Significantly, we noted in both cases that a primary vice of the ordinances at issue was that they operated as prior restraints of constitutionally protected conduct. Our concern in *Murdock* and *Follett*—that a flat license tax would act as a precondition to the free exercise of religious beliefs—is simply not present where a tax applies to all sales and uses of tangible personal property in the State.

Our reading of *Murdock* and *Follett* is confirmed by our decision in *Minneapolis Star & Tribune Co. v. Minnesota Commissioner of Revenue*, where we considered a newspaper's First Amendment challenge to a state use tax on ink and paper products used in the production of periodic publications. In the course of striking down the tax, we rejected the newspaper's suggestion, premised on *Murdock* and *Follett*, that a generally applicable sales tax could not be applied to publications. We do, however, limit[] *Murdock* and *Follett* to apply only where a flat license tax operates as a prior restraint on the free exercise of religious beliefs. As such, *Murdock* and *Follett* plainly do not support appellant's free exercise claim. California's generally applicable sales and use tax is not a flat tax, represents only a small fraction of any retail sale, and applies neutrally to all retail sales of tangible personal property made in California. California imposes its sales and use tax even if the seller or the purchaser is charitable, religious, nonprofit, or state or local governmental in nature. Thus, the sales and use tax is not a tax on the right to disseminate religious information, ideas, or beliefs *per se*; rather, it is a tax on the privilege of making retail sales of tangible personal property and on the storage, use, or other consumption of tangible personal property in California. California treats the sale of a Bible by a religious organization just as it would treat the sale of a Bible by a bookstore; as long as both are in-state retail sales of tangible personal property, they are both subject to the tax regardless of the motivation for the sale or the purchase. There is no danger that appellant's religious activity is being singled out for special and burdensome treatment.

There is no evidence in this case that collection and payment of the tax violates appellant's sincere religious beliefs. California's nondiscriminatory Sales and Use Tax Law requires only that appellant collect the tax from its California purchasers and remit the tax money to the State. The only burden on appellant is the claimed reduction in income resulting from the presumably lower demand for appellant's wares (caused by the marginally higher price) and from the costs associated with administering the tax. As the Court made clear in *Hernandez* [*v. Commissioner*] however, to the extent that imposition of a generally applicable tax merely decreases the amount of money appellant has to spend on its religious activities, any such burden is not constitutionally significant.

Finally, because appellant's religious beliefs do not forbid payment of the sales and use tax, appellant's reliance on *Sherbert v. Verner*, and its progeny is misplaced, because in no sense has the State "'condition[ed] receipt of an important benefit upon conduct proscribed by a religious faith, or denie[d] such a benefit because of conduct mandated by religious belief, thereby putting substantial pressure on an adherent to modify his behavior and to violate his beliefs.'"

We therefore conclude that the collection and payment of the generally applicable tax in this case imposes no constitutionally significant burden on appellant's religious practices or beliefs. The Free Exercise Clause accordingly does not require the State to grant appellant an exemption from its generally applicable sales and use tax. Although it is of course possible to imagine that a more onerous tax rate, even if generally applicable, might effectively choke off an adherent's religious practices, *cf. Murdock*, *supra*, (the burden of a flat tax could render itinerant evangelism "crushed and closed out by the sheer weight of the toll or tribute which is exacted town by town"), we face no such situation in this case. Accordingly, we intimate no views as to whether such a generally applicable tax might violate the Free Exercise Clause.

B

[The Court then rejected the argument that application of a sales and use tax to the sale of religious materials violates the Establishment Clause because it fosters "'an excessive government entanglement with religion,'" under the "three pronged test" announced in *Lemon v. Kurtzman* even though the case "featured on-site inspections of appellant's evangelistic crusades, lengthy on-site audits, examinations of appellant's books and records, threats of criminal prosecution, and layers of administrative and judicial proceedings."]

The Establishment Clause prohibits "sponsorship, financial support, and active involvement of the sovereign in religious activity." [*Walz*]. The "excessive entanglement" prong of the tripartite purpose-effect-entanglement *Lemon* test, requires examination of "the character and purposes of the institutions that are benefited, the nature of the aid that the State provides, and the resulting relationship between the government and the religious authority. "The issue presented, therefore, is whether the imposition of sales and use tax liability in this case on appellant results in "excessive" involvement between appellant and the State and "continuing surveillance leading to an impermissible degree of entanglement."

At the outset, it is undeniable that a generally applicable tax has a secular purpose and neither advances nor inhibits religion, for the very essence of such a tax is that it is neutral and nondiscriminatory on questions of religious belief. Thus, whatever the precise contours of the Establishment Clause, its undisputed core values are not even remotely called into question by the generally applicable tax in this case.

[The Court held that there was no evidence of "excessive entanglement," and that the burdens imposed by administrative and recordkeeping requirements "do not rise to a constitutionally significant level."] The fact that appellant must bear the cost of collecting and remitting a generally applicable sales and use tax—even if the financial burden of such costs may vary from religion to religion—does not enmesh government in religious affairs. Most significantly, the imposition of the sales and use tax without an exemption for appellant does not require the State to inquire into the religious content of the items sold or the religious motivation for selling or purchasing the items, because the materials are subject to the tax regardless of content or motive. From the State's point of view, the critical question is not whether the materials are religious, but whether there is a sale or a use, a question which involves only a secular determination.

Accordingly, because we find no excessive entanglement between government and religion in this case, we hold that the imposition of sales and use tax liability on appellant does not violate the Establishment Clause. The judgment of the California Court of Appeal is affirmed.

It is so ordered.

Notes

1. When the taxpayer is a church or religious institution, or the subject of the tax is property held for religious use or religious activity, the constitutional inquiry should focus initially on the limits imposed by the relevant constitution (federal or state) on the exercise of the taxing power itself. Many state constitutions are specific with respect to the types of taxes which can be imposed on churches, "houses of worship," religious organizations, and properties held for religious or charitable uses. *See* § D below. The United States Constitution, however, does not address the issue. Congress has the power "to lay and collect taxes," and the First Amendment is an express limit on that power.

2. There are two basic variants of the argument that the First Amendment is jurisdictional when the subject of the tax is religious activity or property. Both begin with the premise that the First Amendment embodies Jefferson's concept of a "'high and impregnable wall of separation' between church and state," but reach opposite conclusions on what a regime based on a separationist ideal would look like.

The argument that the First Amendment *forbids the taxation of* religious activities can be expressed as follows: Just as Jefferson's 'wall of separation' should be viewed as a barrier to government support of religious activities, so too should it be viewed as a barrier to government seeking support from the money devoted by the citizenry to religious purposes. *See Matthew* 22:16—21 (New International).[2] Such an argument concedes the existence of the power to tax, but posits that religious activities, properties, and funds are not proper *subjects* of taxation.

Arguments that the First Amendment *forbids tax exemptions* for churches and religious organizations make essentially the same point—that the First Amendment leaves no room for legislative discretion over the subject of the tax. In this view, if the taxing power is exercised at all, the First and Fourteenth Amendments *require* that churches and religious organizations be taxed on the same subjects, in the same manner, and at the same rate, as others. The subject of tax exemptions is addressed at greater length in § E below.

---

2. The Gospel according to Matthew recounts the following exchange between Jesus and those sent to trap Him:[v16] "Teacher," they said, "we know you are a man of integrity and that you teach the way of God in accordance with the truth. You aren't swayed by men, because you pay no attention to who they are. [v17] Tell us then, what is your opinion? Is it right to pay taxes to Caesar or not?" [v18] But Jesus, knowing their evil intent, said, "You hypocrites, why are you trying to trap me? [v19] Show me the coin used for paying the tax." They brought him a denarius, [v20] and he asked them, "Whose portrait is this? And whose inscription?" [v21] "Caesar's," they replied. Then he said to them, "Give to Caesar what is Caesar's, and to God what is God's." [v22] When they heard this, they were amazed. So they left him and went away.'

3. To what extent can the outcome of the *Jimmy Swaggart Ministries* (*JSM*) case be explained on the basis of "neutral principles" of tax law? Consider the following questions:

a) What was the character of the tax at issue? Was it a duty, excise, income tax?

b) What was its "subject"? Was it the Ministry itself, the use by the Ministry of religious items, or the purchase and sale of goods having religious themes?

c) Did JSM actually "pay" the tax, or did it simply "collect" the tax at point of sale from those who bought religious items and remit the proceeds to the state? *See generally* Howard E. Abrams & Richard L. Doernberg, FEDERAL CORPORATE TAXATION ¶ 1.03 at 5–6 (2d ed. 1990). Abrams & Doernberg's treatise contains a useful discussion of the incidence of taxation, and suggests that it is helpful to distinguish between the person who actually "tender[s] payment to the taxing authority" (the "nominal payor") and the individual "who bears the economic burden of the tax, [*i.e.*] who is worse off by reason of that particular tax having been paid" (the *actual* payor).

4. What difference, if any, do (or should) such distinctions make under the First Amendment? If, for example, the economic burden of the tax falls exclusively on the purchaser of the religious items, and that *JSM* is only the "nominal payor," what would be the nature of the *church's* free exercise claim? Would it have one? If not, should it have standing to raise a free exercise claim on the part of its members? *See generally* John E. Nowak *et. al.*, CONSTITUTIONAL LAW §2.12 (6th ed. 2000) (discussing third-party standing).

5. Consider the diverse forms of tax levies, from import duties and excises, to sales and income taxes. Would it be possible, for example, to allege a religious liberty claim when the government imposes duties on the import of religious goods of foreign origin? What about an "occupation tax" (an excise) imposed on all those who engage in the occupation of priest, minister, rabbi or clergy member? Would such taxes operate as prior restraints on the exercise of religion if the religious goods were not manufactured domestically and were absolutely essential for the conducted of religious ritual, or if the penalty for nonpayment of the occupation tax were a jail term?

6. What do you make of the Court's treatment of the "excessive entanglement" argument in *JSM*? Is it not inevitable that there will be "entanglement" between church and state when the government compels the church to become a tax collector? Why did the Court reject the assertion that the accounting oversight required by the tax laws did not breed excessive entanglement? It appears that the Court was persuaded that the entanglement that would result from the imposition of this tax was not really "excessive" because both audit and compliance were relatively straightforward. How, if at all, does such accounting oversight differ from the kind found to breed excessive entanglement in *Lemon v. Kurtzman*, 403 U.S. 602 (1971) and other school-aid cases? *See* Chapters Five and Six.

7. In *JSM* the Court appears to limit the reach of its holdings in *Follett v. McCormick*, 321 U.S. 573 (1944), and *Murdock v. Pennsylvania*, 319 U.S. 105 (1943), to instances where the penalties for noncompliance have the effect of imposing a prior restraint on the exercise of First Amendment rights. It appears to take the same position in *Texas Monthly v. Bullock*, 489 U.S. 1 (1989), excerpted in §E(5) of this Chapter. Should this be the *only* situation in which the Court will intervene in the tax setting? In *Minneapolis Star & Tribune Co. v. Minnesota Commissioner of Revenue*, 460 U.S. 575 (1983), the Court struck down a state use tax on ink and paper products used in the production of periodicals. Although Justice O'Connor notes in *JSM* that "[the Court]

rejected the newspaper's suggestion, premised on *Murdock* and *Follett*, that a generally applicable sales tax could not be applied to publications" to support the proposition that churches and their auxiliary ministries do not have a First Amendment immunity, the *holding* of *Minneapolis Star* is that the First Amendment required the invalidation of the tax at issue. If the tax did not operate as a prior restraint, why was it unconstitutional?

8. Would it have made a difference to the outcome of the free exercise claim in *JSM* if Jimmy Swaggart Ministries had been able to make a *prima facie* case that either the payment or collection of sales and use taxes *did* violate the sincerely held religious beliefs of the organization or its members? On what facts might such a showing be based? Even if they had made such a showing, what remedies would have been available? Can a court enjoin the collection of a tax? Must the taxpayer first tender payment and then sue for a refund? Consider these questions in light of the statutes summarized in the next note.

9. Congress takes a dim view of judicial interference with tax collection activities. Subject to limited exceptions, the anti-tax injunction statute, 26 U.S.C. § 7421 (2001), provides that "no suit for the purpose of restraining the assessment or collection of any tax shall be maintained in any court by any person, whether or not such person is the person against whom such tax was assessed." If the tax in question is federal, the taxpayer can either challenge the assessment in the Tax Court, or pay the tax and seek a refund in the District Court. 28 U.S.C. § 1341 (2001) applies a similar rule for state taxes: "The [United States] district courts shall not enjoin, suspend or restrain the assessment, levy or collection of any tax under State law where a plain, speedy and efficient remedy may be had in the courts of such State." *See Independent Baptist Church of Red Bank v. State of Tennessee*, 468 F. Supp. 71 (E.D. Tenn. 1978) (denying an injunction). These statutes are a fairly clear affirmation that a dissenting taxpayer's options are limited. *But cf. Texas Monthly v. Bullock*, 489 U.S. 1 (1989), excerpted in § E (5) below, in which the taxpayer sought a judicial declaration that a tax exemption was unconstitutional.

10. It is fairly clear after *JSM* that the First Amendment does not impose a *jurisdictional* bar to either federal or state power to tax the church. If the Court's intervention is limited to a *prudential* inquiry when a tax is challenged on Free Exercise grounds, does this not leave us with the question posed by John Marshall? Is the state really invested with a discretionary power to destroy the church through the exercise of its power "to lay and collect taxes"?

11. The answer appears to be "Yes, the state does indeed have that power, but the First Amendment limits its right to exercise it in such a fashion." In keeping with that sentiment, Justice Oliver Wendell Holmes once observed that the power to tax could not be so exercised "while this Court sits." *Panhandle Oil Co. v. State of Mississippi* ex rel. *Knox*, 277 U.S. 218, 223 (1928) (Holmes, J., joined by Brandeis and Stone, JJ., dissenting). Given the general contours of the Free Exercise Clause, how realistic will it be to rely on judicial intervention in tax controversies alleged to pose a threat to religious liberty?

In § B, above, it was noted that constitutional claims can arise at the operational stage; that is, when jurisdiction to tax is conceded, but the taxpayer has a constitutional claim which arises because of the way in which the statute is either interpreted or administered by the taxing authority. *Hernandez v. Commissioner of Internal Revenue*, 490 U.S. 680 (1989), is one of those cases.

Hernandez arose because the teachings of the Church of Scientology require that a person receiving something give something in return. In keeping with the "Doctrine of

Exchange," the Church charged a "fixed donation" for access to its religious educational sessions, known as "auditing" and "training." Because the Commissioner viewed the exchange as a *quid pro quo*, the IRS refused to allow Mr. Hernandez and others to claim the deduction permitted by I.R.C. § 170 for contributions to organizations exempt under I.R.C. § 501(c)(3). After a trial, the Tax Court upheld the IRS position because cases interpreting § 170 of the Internal Revenue Code interpret the term "charitable contribution" as synonymous with the term "gift;" that is, "a *voluntary transfer* of property by the owner to another *without consideration therefor*." 83 T.C. 575, 580 (1984) (emphasis in original), *quoting DeJong v. Commissioner*, 36 T.C. 896, 899 (1961), *aff'd*, 309 F.2d 373 (9th Cir. 1962).

The taxpayers' primary argument was that Congress never intended to tax the income generated by exchanges where the benefit received for a payment is religious, rather than economic, social or financial, and that the language of I.R.C. § 170 makes such payments deductible. In their view, a holding that such exchanges generate taxable income for the church would require the courts to place a monetary value on the "services" received in exchange for the contribution, and to deny a deduction for the value of the amount paid would put the government in the business of ascertaining the "fair market value" of the religious services received.

The federal courts of appeal were equally divided. Three had held that the religious character of the services received was irrelevant to the tax question. In their view, the structure of the transaction, rather than the identity of the recipient or the nature of the services rendered, is controlling. If the transaction is *quid pro quo*, there can be no deduction. The other three had held on statutory grounds that the deduction should be permitted.

Beyond the Scientologist taxpayers' statutory argument, however, were two operational claims concerning the constitutionality of the Commissioner's *application* of the rules under I.R.C. § 170. The Commissioner conceded in *Hernandez* that the IRS has had a long-standing practice of *allowing* deductions for payments to other churches and synagogues. As the Supreme Court itself noted in *Hernandez*: "[a] 1971 ruling, still in effect, states: 'Pew rents, building fund assessments, and periodic dues paid to a church...are all methods of making contributions to the church, and such payments are deductible as charitable contributions within the limitations set out in section 170 of the Code.'" Rev. Rul. 70-47, 1970–1 C.B. 49 *superseding* A.R.M. 2, C.B. 150 (1919). Because the IRS allowed *other* taxpayers to deduct "specified payments for attendance at High Holy Day services, for tithes, for torah readings and for memorial plaques," *Foley v. Commissioner of Internal Revenue*, 844 F.2d 94, 96 (2d Cir. 1988), the Scientologist taxpayers believed that the IRS was guilty of intentional discrimination against a specific church.

The taxpayers' view was that because the practice of the IRS supported their contention concerning the meaning of the statute, the Code should not be construed to permit such a result. If, however, the IRS were permitted to discriminate, the constitutionality of the I.R.C. § 170 itself would be called into question. In support of this argument, the taxpayers alleged that the disallowance of the deductions was but one part of a much larger practice of selective prosecution and discrimination by the IRS against the Church of Scientology itself. In fact, there was considerable support in the record for the assertion that the IRS believed that the Church was really a commercial venture, not a religion. *See* 490 U.S. at 686 n.4, 704 (O'Connor and Scalia, JJ., dissenting).

Five members of a seven-member Court (Justices Kennedy and Brennan did not participate) held that, for statutory purposes, receipt of a *quid pro quo* destroys the character of the payment as a gift. The majority also rejected the claim that Congress intended to give special treatment to payments resulting in access to religious benefits, and hinted broadly that the Establishment Clause might prevent such result even if it did.

The majority also rejected the Establishment and Free Exercise Clause claims which arose from the IRS administration of the statute, holding that *Lemon v. Kurtzman*, 403 U.S. 602 (1971), and *United States v. Lee*, 455 U.S. 252 (1982), provided the appropriate rules of decision. The non-discrimination claim was rejected on the ground that when there is nothing *on the face of the statute* that differentiates among religions, the three-part test of *Lemon v. Kurtzman* provides the framework for analysis. *Cf. Larsen v. Valente*, 456 U.S. 228 (1982) (statute discriminated among religions on its face). *But see Church of Lukumi Babalu Aye, Inc. v. City of Hialeah*, 508 U.S. 520 (1993) (statute discriminatory on its face, but all Justices agreed that both overt and covert forms of intentional discrimination are prohibited by the Free Exercise Clause).

In the Court's view of *Lemon*, the IRS position was unassailable under the Establishment Clause. The Free Exercise claim was rejected under *United States v. Lee*'s holding that "even a substantial burden [on religion] would be justified by the 'broad public interest in maintaining a sound tax system,' free of 'myriad exceptions flowing from a wide variety of religious beliefs,'" 455 U.S. at 260. The Court decided that its conclusion concerning the applicability of *United States v. Lee* was supported by its holding in that case that the alleged burden was not caused by a doctrinal prohibition against paying taxes, but because of the incrementally larger tax burden borne by the taxpayers as a result of the disallowance of the tax deduction.

Justices O'Connor and Scalia dissented, arguing that the record presented a clear case of discrimination against the Church of Scientology. Significantly, they took aim squarely at the majority's holding that there was an insufficient factual record on which to judge the alleged administrative inconsistency of the Commissioner's treatment of other religious organizations:

> On a more fundamental level, the Court cannot abjure its responsibility to address serious constitutional problems by converting a violation of the Establishment Clause into an "administrative consistency argument," (citation omitted), with an inadequate record. It has chosen to ignore both long-standing, clearly articulated IRS practice, and the failure of the Government to offer any cogent, neutral explanation for the IRS' refusal to apply this practice to the Church of Scientology. Instead, the Court has pretended that whatever errors in application the IRS has committed are hidden from its gaze and will, in any event, be rectified in due time.

490 U.S. at 712 (O'Connor and Scalia, JJ., dissenting) (citing the majority opinion's reference to "administrative consistency" at 703).

The dispute in *Hernandez* is larger than it appears. What, for example, do you think the outcome would be if members of minority racial groups alleged that the IRS were systematically engaged in a conspiracy to oppress churches whose members were members of racial minority groups? Do you think the courts would, or should, hold that judicial review of tax decisions is inappropriate across-the-board, or that they would hold that the IRS is not authorized to administer the Code in a racially discriminatory manner? *See, e.g.*, 26 U.S.C. § 7421 (2001) (prohibiting suits in any court to restrain collection of federal taxes); 28 U.S.C. § 1341 (2001) (prohibiting federal court injunctions against the collection of State taxes unless no adequate remedy is available). *See also Bob Jones Univ. v. United States*, 461 U.S. 574 (1983), excerpted in § D(5)(6) below.

The Internal Revenue Code has been amended to deal with the problem faced by the taxpayer in *Hernandez*. I.R.C. § 170(f)(8)(B) provides:

> (B) Content of acknowledgment.—An acknowledgment [of a gift] meets the requirements of this subparagraph if it includes the following information:
>
> (i) The amount of cash and a description (but not value) of any property other than cash contributed.
>
> (ii) Whether the donee organization provided any goods or services in consideration, in whole or in part, for any property described in clause (i).
>
> (iii) A description and good faith estimate of the value of any goods or services referred to in clause (ii) or, if such goods or services consist solely of intangible religious benefits, a statement to that effect.
>
> For purposes of this subparagraph, the term "intangible religious benefit" means any intangible religious benefit which is provided by an organization organized exclusively for religious purposes and which generally is not sold in a commercial transaction outside the donative context.

Does this section raise any questions under the Establishment Clause? It does, after all, distinguish between "intangible religious benefit[s]" and other intangible benefits, such as career counseling, which might be offered by a college in exchange for a contribution. Is it rational for Congress to draw such a distinction, or should the courts hold that the Constitution demands uniform treatment of all *quid pro quo* transactions? If your answer is that such transactions should be subject to tax, how should the government go about setting a value on the intangible benefit received?

United States v. Lee

455 U.S. 252 (1982)

Chief Justice BURGER delivered the opinion of the Court.

Appellee, a member of the Old Order Amish, is a farmer and carpenter. From 1970 to 1977, appellee employed several other Amish to work on his farm and in his carpentry shop. He failed to file the quarterly social security tax returns required of employers, withhold social security tax from his employees, or pay the employer's share of social security taxes.

In 1978, the Internal Revenue Service assessed appellee in excess of $27,000 for unpaid employment taxes; he paid $91—the amount owed for the first quarter of 1973—and then sued... for a refund, claiming that imposition of the social security taxes violated his First Amendment free exercise rights and those of his Amish employees.

The District Court held the statutes requiring appellee to pay social security and unemployment insurance taxes unconstitutional as applied. The court's holding was based on both the exemption statute for the self-employed and the First Amendment; appellee and others "who fall within the carefully circumscribed definition provided in 1402(g) are relieved from paying the employer's share of [social security taxes] as it is an unconstitutional infringement upon the free exercise of their religion."

II

The exemption provided by § 1402(g) is available only to self-employed individuals and does not apply to employers or employees. Thus any exemption from payment of the employer's share of social security taxes must come from a constitutionally required exemption.

A

The preliminary inquiry in determining the existence of a constitutionally required exemption is whether the payment of social security taxes and the receipt of benefits interferes with the free exercise rights of the Amish. It is not within "the judicial function and judicial competence," however, to determine whether appellee or the Government has the proper interpretation of the Amish faith.[4] We therefore accept appellee's contention that both payment and receipt of social security benefits is forbidden by the Amish faith. Because the payment of the taxes or receipt of benefits violates Amish religious beliefs, compulsory participation in the social security system interferes with their free exercise rights.

The conclusion that there is a conflict between the Amish faith and the obligations imposed by the social security system is only the beginning. Not all burdens on religion are unconstitutional. *See, e.g., Prince v. Massachusetts*; *Reynolds v. United States.* The state may justify a limitation on religious liberty by showing that it is essential to accomplish an overriding governmental interest. *Thomas [v. Review Board]*; *Wisconsin v. Yoder*; *Gillette v. United States*; *Sherbert v. Verner.*

B

Because the social security system is nationwide, the governmental interest is apparent. The design of the system requires support by mandatory contributions from covered employers and employees. This mandatory participation is indispensable to the fiscal vitality of the social security system. Moreover, a comprehensive national social security system providing for voluntary participation would be almost a contradiction in terms and difficult, if not impossible, to administer. Thus, the Government's interest in assuring mandatory and continuous participation in and contribution to the social security system is very high.[5]

C

The remaining inquiry is whether accommodating the Amish belief will unduly interfere with fulfillment of the governmental interest. The difficulty in attempting to accommodate religious beliefs in the area of taxation is that "we are a cosmopolitan nation made up of people of almost every conceivable religious preference." [*Braunfeld v. Brown*]. The Court has long recognized that balance must be struck between the values of the comprehensive social security system, which rests on a complex of actuarial fac-

---

4. This is not an instance in which the asserted claim is "so bizarre, so clearly nonreligious in motivation, as not to be entitled to protection under the Free Exercise Clause." Thomas v. Review Bd. of Indiana Employment Security Div., 450 U.S., at 715. At least one other religious organization has sought an exemption under § 1402(g). See also Henson v. Commissioner, 66 T.C. 835 (1976) (member of Sai Baba denied exemption because although opposed to insurance on religious grounds, the faith did not provide for its dependent members).

5. The fiscal soundness of the social security system has been the subject of several studies and of congressional concern.

tors, and the consequences of allowing religiously based exemptions. To maintain an organized society that guarantees religious freedom to a great variety of faiths requires that some religious practices yield to the common good. Religious beliefs can be accommodated, but there is a point at which accommodation would "radically restrict the operating latitude of the legislature." *Braunfeld.*

Unlike the situation presented in *Wisconsin v. Yoder*, it would be difficult to accommodate the comprehensive social security system with myriad exceptions flowing from a wide variety of religious beliefs. The tax system could not function if denominations were allowed to challenge the tax system because tax payments were spent in a manner that violates their religious belief. Because the broad public interest in maintaining a sound tax system is of such a high order, religious belief in conflict with the payment of taxes affords no basis for resisting the tax.

III

When followers of a particular sect enter into commercial activity as a matter of choice, the limits they accept on their own conduct as a matter of conscience and faith are not to be superimposed on the statutory schemes which are binding on others in that activity. Granting an exemption from social security taxes to an employer operates to impose the employer's religious faith on the employees. Congress drew a line in § 1402(g), exempting the self-employed Amish but not all persons working for an Amish employer. The tax imposed on employers to support the social security system must be uniformly applicable to all, except as Congress provides explicitly otherwise.[7]

Accordingly, the judgment of the District Court is reversed, and the case is remanded for proceedings consistent with this opinion.

Justice STEVENS, concurring in the judgment.

The clash between appellee's religious obligation and his civic obligation is irreconcilable. He must violate either an Amish belief or a federal statute. According to the Court, the religious duty must prevail unless the Government shows that enforcement of the civic duty "is essential to accomplish an overriding governmental interest." That formulation of the constitutional standard suggests that the Government always bears a heavy burden of justifying the application of neutral general laws to individual conscientious objectors. In my opinion, it is the objector who must shoulder the burden of demonstrating that there is a unique reason for allowing him a special exemption from a valid law of general applicability.

Nevertheless, I agree with the Court's conclusion that the difficulties associated with processing other claims to tax exemption on religious grounds justify a rejection of this claim.[2] I believe, however, that this reasoning supports the adoption of a different constitutional standard than the Court purports to apply.

---

7. We note that here the statute compels contributions to the system by way of taxes; it does not compel anyone to accept benefits. Indeed, it would be possible for an Amish member, upon qualifying for social security benefits, to receive and pass them along to an Amish fund having parallel objectives. It is not for us to speculate whether this would ease or mitigate the perceived sin of participation.

2. In my opinion, the principal reason for adopting a strong presumption against such claims is not a matter of administrative convenience. It is the overriding interest in keeping the government—whether it be the legislature or the courts—out of the business of evaluating the relative merits of differing religious claims. The risk that governmental approval of some and disap-

The Court's analysis supports a holding that there is virtually no room for a "constitutionally required exemption" on religious grounds from a valid tax law that is entirely neutral in its general application.[3] Because I agree with that holding, I concur in the judgment.

Notes

1. The case law is generally consistent with the view that that tax policy is a matter textually committed to the discretion of Congress and state legislatures, U.S. Const. art. I § 1, § 8, cl. 1; amends. X, XI, XVI. In *McCray v. United States*, 195 U.S. 27 (1904), for example, the Court sustained a tax on oleomargarine that was designed to price it out of the market. It held that the sale of colored oleomargarine was a legitimate subject of taxation. In the Court's view, that finding ended the inquiry, even if the result was to sustain a tax that destroyed the market for the product. "[I]f a tax be within the lawful power, the exertion of that power may not be judicially restrained because of the results to arise from its exercise." *Id.* at 59. At least in some cases, then, the power to tax *is* the power to destroy its subject.

2. With few apparent exceptions since the 1930s, the Supreme Court has declined to accept an oversight role in the field of federal taxation, and its role in state tax cases has generally been limited to questions concerning jurisdiction to tax and the fair apportionment of the tax burden as between in-state and out-of-state taxpayers. With respect to the federal role, compare *Bailey v. Drexel Furniture Co.*, 259 U.S. 20 (1922) (The Child Labor Tax Case) (holding that the imposition was not a 'tax') and *Hill v. Wallace*, 259 U.S. 44 (1922) (same) with *Board of Trade of City of Chicago v. Olsen*, 262 U.S. 1 (1923) (sustaining direct regulation of the subject matter involved in *Hill v. Wallace*), and *Pollock v. Farmer's Loan and Trust Co.*, 157 U.S. 429 (1895) (initial decision), *on rehearing*, 158 U.S. 601 (1895) (invalidating the first income tax). With respect to the Court's oversight of state tax policy, see generally Jesse H. Choper, Richard H. Fallon, Yale Kamisar & Stephen H. Shiffrin, CONSTITUTIONAL LAW: CASES-COMMENTS-QUESTIONS (West 9th ed. 2000).

3. To what extent do the holdings in *JSM* and *United States v. Lee* presage the outcome of *Employment Div. v. Smith*, excerpted in Chapter Five? In *United States v. Lee*, Justice Stevens argued "it is the *objector* who must shoulder the burden of demonstrating that there is a unique reason for allowing him a special exemption from a valid law of general applicability." (emphasis added) Was his reasoning consistent with the interpretation of the Free Exercise Clause in either *Sherbert v. Verner*, 374 U.S. 398 (1963), or *Wisconsin v. Yoder*, 406 U.S. 205 (1972)? *See* Chapter Five.

4. After *JSM*, *United States v. Lee* and *Employment Div. v. Smith*, what facts might demonstrate that the burden of an otherwise valid tax is inconsistent with the Free Ex-

---

proval of others will be perceived as favoring one religion over another is an important risk the Establishment Clause was designed to preclude.

3. Today's holding is limited to a claim to a tax exemption. I believe, however, that a standard that places an almost insurmountable burden on any individual who objects to a valid and neutral law of general applicability on the ground that the law proscribes (or prescribes) conduct that his religion prescribes (or proscribes) better explains most of this Court's holdings than does the standard articulated by the Court today. The principal exception is *Wisconsin v. Yoder*, in which the Court granted the Amish an exemption from Wisconsin's compulsory school-attendance law by actually applying the subjective balancing approach it purports to apply today. The Court's attempt to distinguish *Yoder* is unconvincing because precisely the same religious interest is implicated in both cases, and Wisconsin's interest in requiring its children to attend school until they reach the age of 16 is surely not inferior to the federal interest in collecting these social security taxes.

ercise Clause? An approach which begins with the traditional formulation of the Free Exercise Clause would likely focus on questions of intent or degree, and would ask whether the tax in question targets the church or religious activity, or imposes an undue burden on constitutionally protected activity. Is there any requirement under the Free Exercise Clause that the imposition be "unique" as well? *See* Chapter Five § B.

5. Because the Court has repeatedly rejected the assertion that the First Amendment provides any sort of "subject-matter" tax immunity for either religion or the press, it is accurate to describe its approach as one of judicial deference to the legislature's judgment in matters of tax policy? How should *legislatures* approach the more general problem of tax policy concerning religion and religious institutions? For example, can a state decide that its understanding of religious liberty requires a jurisdictional, rather than prudential, approach? *See* U.S. Const. amend. IX. Would such an approach be consistent with the First Amendment? *See Texas Monthly Inc. v. Bullock*, excerpted in § E(5) below.

6. To what extent are the structural limitations of federalism and separation of powers relevant to the Court's analysis in tax cases? In both of the cases excerpted above the taxpayer was compelled to pay at least a part of the tax and file for a refund because both federal and state laws impose strict limits on the ability of courts to enjoin, or otherwise impede, the levy and collection of taxes.

7. To what extent does the Court either hold or imply in *JSM* or *United States v. Lee* that the Establishment Clause compels its tax rulings? Are they? *See Texas Monthly, Inc. v. Bullock*, excerpted in § E(5) below.

8. Tax exemptions for religious institutions and charities are common throughout the country, and exist at all levels of government: federal, state, and local. Because the jurisdiction of states and local governments to tax churches and religious organizations is defined by state constitutional and statutory law, it would be a mistake to place too much emphasis on the requirements of the First Amendment. Though a state may not permit what the First Amendment forbids, and may not forbid what the First Amendment requires, it may forbid what the First Amendment permits. *See* U.S. Const. amend. IX, X. The nature of state constitutional limits on the power to tax religious activities and property is discussed below.

3. Historical Note on the Origin and Development of Tax Policy Affecting the Property and Activities of Religious Institutions

The exemption of religious institutions from general taxation is neither a strictly American practice, nor is it limited to the traditions of English law inherited by the American colonists. Indeed, the exemption of religious organizations from general taxes seems to be as old as the practice of taxation. John W. Whitehead, *Tax Exemption and Churches: A Historical and Constitutional Analysis*, 22 Cumb. L. Rev. 521, 524 (1992), *citing* Leo Pfeffer, CHURCH, STATE AND FREEDOM 210 (rev. ed. 1967) ("tax exemption of church property is probably as ancient as taxation itself").

In ancient Babylon, the king, nominally the personification of the government, commandeered temple riches at his risk, for the priests "laid terrible curses upon all who should touch, unpermitted, the smallest jot of ecclesiastical property." Whitehead, *supra* at 525, *citing* Will Durant, OUR ORIENTAL HERITAGE 113 (1954). During the reigns of the Egyptian Pharaohs Ramses II (1300–1233 B.C.) and Ramses III (circa 1200 B.C.) the temples owned fifteen percent of the arable land of the Upper and Lower Kingdoms, all of which was exempt from Pharaoh's tax. Whitehead at 526, *citing* Durant at 214; Carroll H. Sierk, *State Tax Exemptions of Non-Profit Organizations*, 19 Cleve. St. L. Rev. 281, 282 (1970). Even during extreme times, temple lands were out of Pharaoh's reach. The Book of Genesis reports "Joseph made it a statute concerning the land of Egypt valid to this day, that Pharaoh should have the fifth; only the land of the priests did not become Pharaoh's." Genesis 47:26. The priests of ancient Israel were also exempt from taxation: "We also inform you that it is not permitted to impose taxes, tributes, or tolls on any priest, Levite, singer, gatekeeper, temple slave, or any other servant of that house of God." Ezra 7:24. In ancient India, land controlled by the Brahman class was exempt from taxation. Whitehead at 528–29, *citing* Durant at 201. Religions and charities received special treatment in both Greece and Rome. Glenn Goodwin, Note, *Would Caesar Tax God? The Constitutionality of Governmental Taxation of Churches*, 35 Drake L. Rev. 383, 384 (1985–86), *citing* Edward Gibbon, THE DECLINE AND FALL OF THE ROMAN EMPIRE, 301 (1952). In the fourth century, the Roman Emperor Constantine exempted the Christian Church from all taxes.

The tax-exempt status of churches and religious institutions in some of the United States has its roots in European tradition. The laws of Texas and California, for example, reflect their Spanish origins, and Louisiana's civil law approach has its origins in the law of France. Not surprisingly, however, the legal traditions and history deemed relevant to the Supreme Court's interpretation of the Constitution reflects the English character and experience of the colonists along the Eastern seaboard. An attempt to describe the social and political underpinnings of the tax exemption of religious institutions in the United States must therefore include at least a passing reference to the manner in which the relationship between church and state developed in English law.

In medieval England, where our common law legal traditions find their firmest roots, the Church was considered an institution separate from the state. From the time of Alfred the Great (871–901) until Henry VIII (1509–1547) began the process of integrating the church into the state, the relationship was marked by varying degrees of conflict and cooperation.

In the land-law of post-Conquest feudal England, the Church held its lands in a form of tenure known as *frankalmoign*. In this form of feudal tenure, the tenant was not required to render any service to any superior lord. By the time of Henry VIII (1509–1547), it is estimated that tenure by frankalmoign accounted for one-third to one-half of the entire wealth of England, thus making the Church the single largest landowner in England. It did not go unnoticed that the Church held its property without obligation to the Crown. Shakespeare's *Henry V* recounts an offer made by the Archbishop of Canterbury to give Henry "a greater sum/Than ever at one time the clergy yet/Did to his predecessors part withal." *Henry V*, Act 1, Scene 1, lines 79–81 (ca. 1599), in 1 THE COMPLETE WORKS OF WILLIAM SHAKESPEARE 416 (W.G. Clark & W. Aldis Wright eds.)

The existence of the church as an institution separate from the English state ended with the Reformation. Henry, eager for political and financial reasons to gain absolute control over the Church and its property in England, promulgated the Act of Supremacy in 1534. 26 Hen. 8 ch. 1 (Eng.). Under the Act, the Crown became the head of the Church in England, the church an arm of the Crown, and church lands, Crown lands.

But even though it lost its land and status as a special landholder free of feudal dues, the English church did not lose its exemption from taxes. The operative part of the Elizabeth I's Act of Supremacy (1558) 1 Eliz., ch. 1, § 8 (Eng.), granted the Crown the right "to exercise, occupy and execute... all manner of jurisdictions, privileges and pre-eminences, in any wise touching or concerning any spiritual or ecclesiastical jurisdiction" within the realm. As one modern writer has noted, no government taxes itself: "The church was an agency of the state, and for the state to tax its own instrumentalities was considered an unsound financial practice." William G. Torpey, JUDICIAL DOCTRINES OF RELIGIOUS RIGHTS IN AMERICA 171 (1948). The exemption of the property of the established church and its activities grew out of the regulations promulgated as part of the English Reformation, and thus became part of the English common law.

The British colonists came from a society in which church and state were inextricably linked. By the middle of the eighteenth century, as many as nine of the colonies had established churches and levied taxes for their support. *See* Chapters Two and Three. In New Hampshire, for example, "places of worship were exempt from taxation as public property by the nature of things, and not by the constitution or by statute" because towns provided for parochial affairs and levied taxes for the support of public worship. Torpey, *supra, quoting Franklin Street Society v. Manchester*, 60 N.H. 342, 349 (1880). Even after the two institutions were separated during the disestablishment struggles of the late eighteenth century, the exemption of church property from general taxation was a constant feature in both state and federal laws.

Because tax exemptions for church property were ubiquitous, the question whether exemptions should be considered constitutional rights or legislative privileges subject to repeal or restriction simply did not occur during the late Colonial and early federal periods. As Torpey notes, "[t]he exemption was so obviously proper and in harmony with public sentiment that it universally prevailed" even though "church meeting houses enjoyed a privilege not formally extended to them and that favorable public reaction enabled the right to endure, even after there had been a complete separation of church and state." Torpey, at 172.

The justification of tax exemptions for churches and church property from taxation began to change in the nineteenth century. Courts were aware that tax exemptions had been founded on long-standing custom, but concluded that additional justification—based on statutory or constitutional authority—was needed to save the exemptions.

It was during this period that tax exemptions for churches were first justified by reference to the public moral and social benefits that accrue to a community because of church-sponsored activities. Chapter Four recounts some of the history of this period, including the suggestion by President Grant that federal and state law be changed to permit "the taxation of all property equally, whether church or corporation, exempting only the last resting-place of the dead, and possibly, with the proper restrictions, church edifices." 4 Cong. Rec. 175.

These suggestions were enormously controversial, and prompted wide-ranging discussions concerning the justification for tax exempt status. Many churches argued that exemptions were so well settled in law and custom that they were, in effect, contracts which the states could not impair. The courts, however, were not persuaded.

Though the courts accepted the proposition that an agreement by a state to exempt certain property could rise to the level of a contract, they were unwilling to find that the government had ever indicated an intent to relinquish its power to tax. In the words of the New Hampshire Supreme Court, "No prescription runs against the sovereign, nor does the state, by omission to use, waive or lose the right to exercise its supreme power, and the citizen can have no vested right in the continuance of any statute of general exemptions." *Franklin Street Society v. Manchester*, 60 N.H. 342, 349–350 (1880). In *Bd. of Directors of Chicago Theological Seminary v. Illinois* ex rel. *Raymond*, 188 U.S. 662, 672 (1903), the Supreme Court noted that "The rule is that, in claims for exemption from taxation under legislative authority, the exemption must be plainly and unmistakably granted; it cannot exist by implication only; a doubt is fatal to the claim."

Because the judicial trend was consistent with the sentiment expressed by the New Hampshire Supreme Court in *Franklin Street Society*, the freedom of church property from taxation could no longer be assured without either legislative or constitutional change. In response to judicial insistence that tax exemptions should be explicitly authorized by either constitution or statute, the discussion turned to possible legislative or constitutional reasons why exemptions should be continued.

Perhaps the most important of these is the "public benefit" theory. In essence, the argument is that "religious organizations are of benefit to society, that they promote the social and moral welfare, and that, to some extent, they are bearing burdens that would otherwise be imposed upon the public to meet by general taxation." Torpey, at 172. *See* §E below. The theory accepts the proposition that legislatures have the power to tax churches, charities, and religious institutions, but argues that to impose such taxes is not consistent with the public interest.

Most states now provide some form of explicit exemptions from taxes for religious activities and property used for religious purposes. In some states, the exemptions are mandatory, but require that exempt property be used *exclusively* for religious purposes or worship in order to qualify;[3] in others, proof that the owner or activity is religious in character is enough to remove the legislature's jurisdiction to levy taxes on it. *See, e.g.*, Minn. Const. art. X, §1 (2002). In still other states, the constitution merely authorizes the legislature to exempt religious property, thus leaving it free to limit or revoke the amount and character of exemptions as it sees fit. *See, e.g.*, Ariz. Const. art. IX, §2 (2002). While in a few others the power to create exemptions is implied from the power to tax in the first instance. *See, e.g.*, Del. Const. art. VIII, §1 (2002).

D. Federal and State Tax Policy Affecting Churches, Charities and Religious Organizations: An Overview

Before looking at the specific instances where federal statutes impose taxes on churches, reconsider the subjects on which Congress may impose taxes. Article I, Section 8, clause 1 permits the levy and collection of "Taxes, Duties, Imposts and Excises," on whatever subjects are otherwise appropriate, as long as the taxes are "uniform" throughout the United States. The Sixteenth Amendment adds the direct taxation of individual incomes "from whatever source derived" to the list of proper subjects of federal

3. *See, e.g.*, Cal. Const., art. 13 §3(f) (exempted from property taxation are, among other types of property, "(f) Buildings, land on which they are situated, and equipment used exclusively for religious worship."; Cal. Const. art. 13 §4(b) (the legislature "may" exempt "(b) Property used exclusively for religious, hospital, or charitable purposes and owned or held in trust by corporations or other entities (1) that are organized and operating for those purposes, (2) that are nonprofit, and (3) no part of whose net earnings inures to the benefit of any private shareholder or individual."

taxation. It also dispenses with the requirement of article I, clause 9 that this particular "direct tax" be apportioned.

This section introduces the reader to the bewildering complexity of the federal government's tax treatment of churches, charities, their auxiliaries, and contributors. Like all statutes, the tax code is subject to interpretation not only by the courts, but also in regulations adopted by the Internal Revenue Service. As you will see from the materials that follow, the statute raises as many questions as it answers. In context, theory may be interesting, but is often not particularly useful.

1. A Short History of the Federal Tax Structure and Its Impact on Religious Organizations

Prior to the enactment of the first permanent income tax in 1894, federal revenues were derived primarily from import duties and excise taxes on businesses and professions. Such taxes were considered "indirect" because they were not levied on the property or person directly, but on the privilege or act of doing business or the act of importing goods. Apportioned direct taxes on real and personal property were occasionally utilized as well.

When Congress elected to impose direct taxes on persons or property, it regularly exempted the property of religious bodies. As early as 1802, Congress followed the state pattern of exempting religious organizations when it incorporated the Virginia tax exemption for churches in a taxing plan for the County of Alexandria. Except for requiring that all lands and dwellings be appraised for tax purposes notwithstanding their exemption under state law, all subsequent taxes expressly or impliedly incorporated state exemptions. Congress also granted tax exemptions for churches in the District of Columbia.

Because duties and excise taxes increase the cost of all goods subject to them, the imposition of these taxes affected religious organizations only indirectly. Unless they were engaged in one of the activities subject to the excise tax, there was no need for an exemption, since neither religious activity nor religious organizations were the subjects of these taxes. When religious groups found themselves involved in taxable activities, such as the importation of printing plates for Bibles or the furnishing of churches with bells, paintings or vestments which had to be imported from Europe, Congress exempted these items from taxes as an accommodation of the special needs of religion.

The first federal income tax statutes were enacted during and after the Civil War, and taxed only the income of individuals. As a result, taxation of "churches" was not an issue. Religious and social communities that held their property in common, however, were another matter. They were not "churches" as such, but were organized for religious or charitable purposes. In 1870 Congress resolved the problem by providing special tax accounting rules for members of such communities. These rules permitted groups within these communities to be treated as families for purposes of apportioning family exemptions. *See, e.g.*, Revenue Act of 1870, 16 Stat. 256, c. 255 §§6–7 (1870).

Business taxes during this period, including those levied on corporations, were excise taxes. Levied on the privilege of conducting specified types of business or manufacturing, they were measured by the value of the goods produced. Corporations were also subject to a flat excise on dividends and interest paid on corporate stock, coupons, or obligations, and any undistributed amounts added to surplus. They could either pay the tax themselves, or withhold it from the account of the person from whom it was due. Until the passage of the Revenue Act of 1894, the corporation served merely as the collector of the tax due on the income attributable to the individual holder of stocks, bonds or coupons.

Two things are apparent from the nature and structure of these pre-1894 federal taxes. First, the revenue base was individual income and the profit of larger, profit-making businesses. Second, taxes on business organizations operated by specific imposition. Prior to 1894, if the law imposed no direct obligation to pay, no taxes were imposed. Exemptions for churches and religious organizations were thus implicit in the structure of the tax code.

a) The Revenue Act of 1894

While it may seem difficult to imagine a federal government financed in its entirety in times of peace by import duties and an occasional apportioned direct tax, this was, in fact, the entire federal revenue base for the first century of the Nation's existence. Only when the immense expenses of war required additional revenue did Congress resort to income and additional levies of direct taxes. The adoption of a graduated income tax applicable to both individuals and businesses was a major turning point in the manner in which the federal government was financed.

Congressman Henry St. George Tucker of Virginia introduced The Revenue Act of 1894 on August 15, 1893. The main controversy over the Act was whether business associations should be taxed at all. Although that particular debate was resolved in favor of the imposition of a tax on businesses operated for profit, the language applicable to business organizations and corporations was phrased in general terms: "all other corporations, companies, or associations [in addition to those named] doing business for profit in the United States, no matter how created and organized." Act of August 27, 1894, ch. 349, §32, 28 Stat. 509, 556–557 (1894).

Because of its breadth, this phrasing prompted much floor debate over who and what should be taxed. It also created, for the first time, a need to make specific mention of those types of organizations, associations, and businesses that would not be subject to the new federal tax. These were to become the first "exempt" organizations.

Review of the extensive debates over the Act in both the House and the Senate indicates that such exemptions have not been controversial in either body. The substance of the 1894 exemption was included in the corporate income tax contained in the Payne-Aldrich Tariff Act of 1909, ch. 6, §38, 36 Stat. 11, 112 (1909), and a similar exemption has been included in every income tax act since the adoption of the Sixteenth Amendment. *See* Revenue Act of 1913, ch. 16, §II(G), 38 Stat. 114, 172 (1913).

b) The Internal Revenue Code

The current version of the Internal Revenue Code (I.R.C.) dates to 1954. Unlike the Revenue Act of 1894, which contained both a list of entities to be taxed and a "catch-all" provision designed to capture those subject to tax but not mentioned, the current Code imposes a general tax on individuals and corporations, and adjusts its coverage by creating exemptions and special taxing categories. Section One of the Internal Revenue Code, 26 U.S.C. §1, imposes a tax on individuals, estates and trusts and measures it by reference to "taxable income." Section 11(a) of the Code, 26 U.S.C. §11(a), imposes a "[a] tax...

for each taxable year on the taxable income of every corporation." Churches and religious organizations are not mentioned in either section. Section 11 then differentiates for purposes of rates and coverage by reference to the type of corporation, the amount of its income, its character as either foreign or domestic, and other business-related factors.

Determining the tax status of church or religious organization, however, is not an easy task. Some churches, synagogues, temples, and mosques are corporations. So organized, they would be subject to the tax imposed by Section 11. Because I.R.C. §7701(a)(3) defines the term 'corporation' to include 'associations,' the same would also be true with respect to churches that operate as unincorporated associations. *See Fifth-Third Union Trust Co. v. Commissioner*, 56 F.2d 767 (6th Cir. 1932). *See generally* Chapter Seven §B (discussing organizational forms of religious bodies).

Although Section 11 imposes a tax on all corporations and associations not specifically mentioned as being subject to other provisions of the Code, the language and history of the entire Code suggests that Congress takes a more "functional" approach. Business associations which operate "for profit" are subject to the corporate double tax. Nonprofit organizations that have no shareholders and retain their net income as a means of furthering the purposes for which they were organized, are subject to a myriad of rules that differentiate on the basis of function. Determining which functions are exempt, and which are subject to tax, requires a close reading of the Code.

In the distinctly non-theological world of federal income tax policy, there are two constant features. The first is that Congress has determined that certain transfers of wealth are to be treated as occasions for the imposition of federal taxes. Among these are payment for goods or services rendered, certain gifts, bequests, and most income-producing activities, including employment, investment, or operation of a trade or businesses. The second is that the Internal Revenue Code recognizes two kinds of taxpayers: (1) individuals, including heads of households and married couples; and (2) juridical entities created for a specific purpose, including, among others, corporations, trusts, estates, partnerships, foundations, unincorporated associations, and insurance companies.

The question to be considered here is: How do churches and religious organizations fit into this structure? Because the topic is quite a large one, the goal of this section is modest: to provide an overview of the key questions relating to federal taxation of churches and religious organizations. A more complete understanding of the topic can be gained by examining either course materials or standard reference works devoted in their entirety to tax policy governing nonprofit groups and exempt organizations. *See, e.g.*, John D. Colombo and Mark A. Hall, The Charitable Tax Exemption (1995); Bruce R. Hopkins, The Law of Tax-Exempt Organizations (7th ed. 1998); Howard L. Oleck, Nonprofit Corporations, Organizations & Associations (5th ed. 1988); United States Congress, House Committee on Ways and Means, Subcommittee on Oversight, *Federal Tax Laws Applicable to the Activities of the Tax-Exempt Charitable Organizations* (103rd Cong., 1st Sess. June 15; August 2, 1993).

2. Which Functions are Exempt?

a) Income Producing Activities

Because the primary purpose of the corporate tax is to raise needed revenue from organizations involved in income-producing activities, Congress has determined that profits (net earnings) distributed to those who own or operate a business will be subject to the corporate double tax. *Cf. Founding Church of Scientology v. United States*, 412 F.2d 1197, 1200 (Ct. Cl. 1969), *cert. denied*, 397 U.S. 1009 (1970). Subchapter F of the Code, which contains the provisions dealing with exempt organizations, provides that the "unrelated business taxable income" of exempt organizations is subject to the Section 11 corporate tax. I.R.C. § 511. *See also* I.R.C. § 502 (for-profit businesses not exempt simply because they "feed" their profits to exempt organizations). *Accord United Church of Religious Science v. Board of Assessors of Attleboro*, 372 Mass. 280, 361 N.E.2d 1254 (1977) (religious property tax exemption did not apply to personal property of manufacturing concern owned by church, the income of which was used for religious programs and reinvestment in the business).

b) Exempt Function Income

Because the corporate tax is an excise imposed on the privilege of doing business "for profit" in the corporate form, see *Flint v. Stone Tracy Co.*, 220 U.S. 107 (1911) (upholding the 1909 corporate income tax as an excise on the privilege of operating in corporate form), it follows that Congress would draw a distinction between organizations which are engaged in profit-making activities, and those which are not. I.R.C. § 501, for example, exempts a wide range of organizations and activities from the corporate tax, and I.R.C. § 115 codifies to some extent the constitutionally-based intergovernmental tax immunity enjoyed by state and local governments by excluding from the definition of "gross income" income "derived from any public utility or the exercise of any essential governmental function and accruing to a State or any political subdivision thereof, or the District of Columbia..." *Helvering v. Therell*, 303 U.S. 218, 223 (1938) (holding that immunity attaches to the performance of "essential governmental duties"). *Cf. United States v. Hatter*, 532 U.S. 557 (2001) (Compensation Clause does not forbid the imposition of nondiscriminatory taxes on the salaries of federal judges); *South Carolina v. Baker*, 485 U.S. 505 (1988) (upholding denial of federal income tax exemption for interest earned on unregistered long-term state and local government bonds). As a result, an organization engaged in an exempt function is not subject to the corporate tax on the income attributable to that function.

3. Religious Activity as an Exempt Function

The Code treats religious activity as an exempt function, see, e.g., I.R.C. §§ 170, 501(c)(3), 6033, and recognizes a wide range of religious organizations as exempt from taxes. It also draws a rather clear line between "churches" and the many kinds of organizations which operate either as a part of a church, or in conjunction with it. "Churches" are not only exempt from taxes on the income generated by their exempt functions, they are also exempt from a number of critical filing requirements. Churches need not file tax returns, I.R.C. § 6033(a, b), and are presumed to be exempt. All other religious organizations must demonstrate their eligibility for exempt status by filing an application on form prescribed by the Secretary of the Treasury, but "churches, their integrated auxiliaries, and conventions or associations of churches" are given a "mandatory exemption" from filing requirements. I.R.C. § 508(a, b).

a) What Is a 'Church'?

In keeping with the materials on characterization discussed in Chapter One, we must first consider what a "church" is for general purposes, and then ask what definition, if any, is supplied by the Code for tax purposes.

At its lowest, or most specific, level of generality, the term "church" can refer either to a building which is devoted to religious worship, or to the "collective membership of persons constituting the congregation of a single permanent place of worship." *Forsberg v. Zehm*, 150 Va. 756, 764–765 143 S.E. 284, 286 (1928); *Bennett v. City of La Grange*, 153 Ga. 428, 112 S.E. 482, 485 (1922) ("an organization for religious purposes, for the public worship of God"). At higher levels of generality, the term can describe both "the great body of persons holding the Christian belief," *Forsberg v. Zehm*, or any organized body or community of believers "united under one form of government by the same profession of the same faith, and the observance of the same ritual and ceremonies." *McNeilly v. First Presbyterian Church in Brookline*, 243 Mass. 331, 137 N.E. 691 (1923). *See* Canon Law Society of America, CODE OF CANON LAW — LATIN-ENGLISH EDITION Canon 515 § 1 (1983) ("A parish is a definite community of the Christian faithful established on a stable basis within a particular church") [available online at http://www.prairienet.org/nrpcatholic/cicmenu.html].

The Internal Revenue Code, however, contains no definition of the term. Congress has not defined it, and regulators take the position that "a rigid regulatory definition of the term 'church' would undoubtedly be unconstitutional." *See* Bruce R. Hopkins, THE LAW OF TAX-EXEMPT ORGANIZATIONS (7th ed. 1998), *quoting Foundation of Human Understanding v. Commissioner*, 88 T.C. 1341, 1356 (1987) ("We can only approach this question with care for all of us are burdened with the baggage of our own unique beliefs and perspectives.")

To the extent that a working definition exists, it has developed over time and must be extracted from a number of statutory, regulatory, and judicial sources. As Hopkins points out, it is more fruitful to focus, not on the term church itself, but rather on the categories of entities that are eligible for *designation* as churches under the Code.

In order to qualify as a church under the Code's working definition, an organization must be able to demonstrate that it has at least some of the following characteristics:

1. Self-identification as a church from its inception;
2. Distinct legal existence;
3. A recognized creed and form of worship;
4. Some form of distinct ecclesiastical government;
5. A formal code of doctrine and discipline;
6. A distinct religious history;
7. A membership not associated with any other church or denomination;
8. Ordained ministers who minister to their congregations and who are selected after completing a prescribed course of study;
9. Its own literature;
10. Established places of worship;
11. A distinct congregation;
12. Regular religious services;

13. Schools for the religious instruction of children; and
14. Schools which train its ministers.

Internal Revenue Manual § 321.3; Rev. Rul. 59-129, 1959 C.B. 58. *See St. Martin Evangelical Lutheran Church v. South Dakota*, 451 U.S. 772 (1981) (rejecting, in the Federal Unemployment Tax Act (FUTA) context, the notion that "church" should be limited to the building, and holding that the term "must be construed, instead to refer to the congregation or the hierarchy itself, that is, the church authorizes who conduct the business of hiring, discharging and directing church employees"); *Pusch v. Commissioner*, 39 T.C.M. 838 (1980), *aff'd* 628 F.2d 1353 (5th Cir. 1980), *cert. denied.* 450 U.S 930, *reh'g denied.* 450 U.S. 1050 (1981); *Puritan Church of America v. Commissioner,* 10 T.C.M. 485 (1951), *aff'd* 209 F.2d 306 (D.C. Cir. 1953), *cert. denied*, 347 U.S. 975 (1954), 350 U.S. 810 (1955), *reh'g denied.* 350 U.S. 890 (1955).

Few organizations of any denomination are described by all these criteria, but the listing does serve two basic purposes. First, it provides the IRS with a list of "objective" criteria against which it can measure a claim that an organization is a "church." Gen. Couns. Mem. 38,982 (Sept. 29, 1982) and Gen. Couns. Mem. 38699 (Apr. 23, 1981). Second, and perhaps more importantly for both statutory and constitutional purposes, it provides IRS examiners with a high degree of flexibility. In fact, the IRS has stated that it will also consider "any other facts and circumstances which may bear upon the organization's claim to church status." Internal Revenue Manual § 321.3.

Occasionally, however, a case arises which demonstrates that flexibility is not without limits.

Church of Eternal Life and Liberty, Inc. v. Commissioner

86 T.C. 916 (Tax Court 1986)

WILLIAMS, Judge:

The Commissioner determined that petitioner does not qualify for exemption from Federal income taxation under section 501(a) as an organization described in section 501(c)(3) or as a church within the meaning of sections 509(a) (1) and 170(b) (1) (A) (i). Petitioner seeks a declaratory judgment of this Court pursuant to section 7428 that it is an exempt organization described in section 501(c)(3) and a church within the meaning of sections 509(a) (1) and 170(b) (1) (A) (i).

FINDINGS OF FACT

Petitioner, the Church of Eternal Life and Liberty, Inc. (CELL), was incorporated on October 1, 1976, in the state of Michigan. Its three incorporators were Patrick Heller (CELL's founder), his brother James Heller, and Anna Bowling. Petitioner is independent of any other organization's control or supervision. Petitioner's articles of incorporation state that petitioner is organized exclusively for religious purposes within the meaning of section 501(c)(3). Its doctrine generally follows that of an organization known as "the First Libertarian Church." The record does not indicate whether the First Libertarian Church is an exempt organization under section 501(c)(3).

The bylaws of petitioner provide that it is to be managed by a board of at least three directors, who are not compensated and who need not be members of CELL. Ministers, however, must be members of CELL, and may be ordained only by the unanimous consent of CELL's ordained ministers. Since its inception CELL has had two ordained ministers—Patrick Heller and Thomas Selene.

To become a member of petitioner an applicant: (1) must not be a member of any political party, unless so required by the state in which the applicant resides; (2) must sign an "oath of devotion";[4] (3) must demonstrate an understanding of CELL's principles and a willingness to promote these principles; and (4) must not voluntarily accept governmental welfare benefits, including Social Security, educational scholarships, Medicare and other forms of governmental assistance. An applicant is evaluated for at least one year by a minister, during which period he or she is classified as a "student." After evaluation the minister submits a recommendation to petitioner's board of directors. The final decision on whether to accept or reject an applicant for membership is made by vote of the board.

Petitioner has only two members—Patrick Heller and Thomas Selene—though petitioner has evaluated approximately 3–5 "students" since its inception, one of whom was Anna Bowling. Some of these individuals have continued as 'students' from year to year, while others have had their applications canceled. None has been approved by petitioner's board as a member of CELL. Petitioner states that potential members and contributors will refrain from participation in the activities of CELL until its tax-exempt status is established.

[The discussion of the close relationship between the church's finances and those of the founders is omitted.]

Petitioner's principal activities include the operation of a library containing about 4,000 items, bi-monthly meetings, the distribution of literature, the sale of merchandise and the publication of a newsletter. The library is open to the public two nights per month for 2.5 hours per night. Petitioner states that appointments may be made by members of the public to use the library. The record does not indicate whether any such appointments were in fact made. The topics of petitioner's bi-monthly meetings are sometimes listed in petitioner's newsletter, and have included political and economic debates, readings of libertarian poetry and discussion of philosophical subjects.

Petitioner's newsletter, published approximately five times per year, is distributed to roughly 150 recipients. It includes a calendar of events deemed of interest to its readers (usually notices of meetings of libertarian organizations, philosophical and political lectures, CELL meetings and related events), slogans and short articles on issues of concern to or activities of CELL.[7]

Petitioner has never filed a Form 1023, "Application for Recognition of Exemption." Pursuant to section 7605(c) of the Internal Revenue Code of 1954, respondent sent a

4. The oath of devotion is as follows: I, as a member of The Church of Eternal Life & Liberty, Inc. affirm my understanding of, support for and desire to promote the following principles: That freedom is self-control—no more, no less. That the ideal of rational existence is to live and let live. That the individual is the only being who knows the totality of his timeplace knowledge and value system, and therefore most capable of knowing what will maximize his happiness. That, in order for an individual to avoid infringing upon the rights of others to life, liberty and property, use of force for aggression and retaliation should be avoided. That each individual, through use of his mind, is capable of recognizing his rights and the rights of others. That immortality is logically possible and that when an individual leads a longer, healthier life, his potential for happiness increases.

7. The newsletter included the following slogans and prayer: "Freedom…self-control…self-responsibility," "Freedom isn't free. Freedom isn't dumb," "May I be strong enough to survive while living my life as I think right. May I love long and freely while I live my life as I think right. The will is within me, I shall live my life right."

written request for information to petitioner in April of 1981 to determine whether petitioner qualified for exemption from Federal income tax. [Based on this information,] Respondent concluded that:

> You are not organized or operated exclusively for religious or any exempt purpose described in section 501(c)(3) of the Code. You are operated in such a manner that part of your net earnings inures to the benefit of certain individuals. In addition, you are operated for private rather than public interests and many of your activities are for non-exempt purposes; for example the publication of a newsletter and the purchase of a company. We have also determined that you are not a church. As we have determined that you are not a church, even if you were to be recognized as exempt under section 501(c)(3) you would not be exempt because you have not satisfied the provisions of section 508(a).

It is on this record that petitioner seeks a declaratory judgment pursuant to section 7428.

OPINION

Section 508(a) requires an organization organized after October 9, 1969 to give notice to the Commissioner that it is applying for recognition of exempt status as an organization described in section 501(c)(3). The parties agree that petitioner has never filed a Form 1023, Application for Recognition of Exemption. Therefore, unless petitioner can establish that one of the exceptions provided by section 508(c) applies to it, petitioner does not qualify as an organization described in section 501(c)(3). Petitioner contends that it is a church, and thus, pursuant to section 508(c)(1) (A), it is not required to give the notice required by section 508(a). For the reasons described below we find petitioner's claims to be without merit.

It is important to note at the outset that an examination of what constitutes a "church" for purposes of applicable provisions of the tax code does not require consideration of whether an organization's beliefs and practices represent a "religion" within the purview of the First Amendment to the Constitution. *See Chapman v. Commissioner*, 48 T.C. 358, 361 (1967). We are not required in this case to reach the difficult question of whether the organization's purposes are religious or non-religious.[10]

Although fundamental to determining whether an organization is a church, religious purposes alone do not serve to establish it as a church. Equally important are the means by which its religious purposes are accomplished. A church is a coherent group of individuals and families that join together to accomplish the religious purposes of mutually held beliefs. In other words, a church's principal means of accomplishing its religious purposes must be to assemble regularly a group of individuals related by common worship and faith. As stated by Tannenwald, J., concurring in *Chapman*: "[T]he word

10. The evidence strongly suggests that petitioner's purposes and activities are not religious but political. See United States v. Seeger, 380 U.S. 163, 176 (1965); First Libertarian Church v. Commissioner, 74 T.C. 396, 405 (1980). Petitioner presented no evidence of the nature or conduct of its purportedly religious services. Cf. United States v. Dykema, 666 F.2d 1096 (7th Cir. 1981). Its newsletter consists primarily of a calendar of events and articles the clear focus of which is to report on and promote libertarian activities. Since our decision is based on our finding that the means by which petitioner seeks to accomplish its stated purposes fail to satisfy the threshold test of fulfilling an associational role and that petitioner, therefore, is not a church within the meaning of section 508(c) (1) (A) for purposes of exemption from the requirements of section 508(a), we need not reach the issue of whether petitioner's promotion of libertarian philosophy is political or religious activity for purposes of section 508(c) (1) (A), or for purposes of our discussion of whether petitioner is an organization described in section 501(c) (3), which follows.

'church' implies that an otherwise qualified organization *brings people together as the principal means* of accomplishing its purpose. The objects of such gatherings need not be conversion to a particular faith or segment of a faith nor the propagation of the views of a particular denomination or sect. The permissible purpose may be accomplished individually and privately * * * but it may not be accomplished in physical solitude. * * *" (48 T.C. at 367; emphasis in original.) To qualify as a church an organization must serve an associational role in accomplishing its religious purposes.

In the present case petitioner fails this threshold test. Petitioner has had only two members since its formation in 1976. While incipient churches may have only "two or three gathered together," a church's membership will grow well beyond those small numbers given the vitality of its associational role. Petitioner, by contrast, seems to have intentionally pursued a policy that discouraged membership for reasons, we believe, that served the private purposes of its founder. Although petitioner generally held bi-monthly meetings, the record is void of evidence of the nature or conduct of these meetings other than listings in petitioner's newsletter of topics for certain meetings, generally involving discussion of libertarian, economic or social issues. The record fails to establish that petitioner serves any associational role for purposes of worship. Therefore, we hold that petitioner is not a church within the meaning of section 508(c)(1) (A).

To reflect the foregoing,

Decision will be entered for the respondent.

* * *

The definition of the term "church" for tax purposes thus appears to be quite similar to the "common parlance" definition. The organization must be "religious" in character, it must appear to be denominational in some sense, and it must engage in what are called "sacerdotal" (priestly or clerical) functions. In short, a church is an "organization established to carry out 'church' functions, under the general understanding of the term." *De La Salle Institute v. United States*, 195 F. Supp. 891, 903 (N.D. Cal. 1961). For an illuminating and detailed discussion of the topic see Bruce R. Hopkins, The Law of Tax-Exempt Organizations, at §§9.1–9.3.

b) What Is a "Religious Organization"?

The term "religious organization" is broader than the term "church." Churches are undoubtedly religious organizations, but not all other organizations whose central purpose is "religious" are churches. Conventions and associations of churches and the "integrated auxiliaries" of churches are given the same tax treatment as "churches," but there are many groups that are closely associated with churches that do not themselves qualify as churches under the Code. Among these are religious orders, apostolic and missionary groups, religious broadcasting stations and production companies, religious publishing houses, bible and tract societies, church-run schools, colleges, universities, and seminaries, hospitals, nursing homes, orphanages, homes for unwed mothers, soup kitchens and food pantries, charitable funds for the support of the poor and homeless, fraternal societies, and cemeteries.

The distinction between church and religious organization is an important one. The Code approaches the taxation of churches in a much more deferential way than it does the taxation of other organizations, and the boundary between the two organizations is critically important. The Internal Revenue Service ordinarily draws the boundary between the two types of organization by reference to the concept of "integrated auxiliary." I.R.C. § 508; Internal Rev. Reg. § 1.6033-2(g) (5). In the view of the IRS, an integrated auxiliary exists in order to carry out the tenets of the church with which it is affiliated, and its operations must directly promote either religious faith or activity among the church's members. Some examples of integrated auxiliaries are theological seminaries, the myriad "societies," "leagues," "sodalities," "youth groups," "funds," "auxiliaries," "boards," "orders," "councils," "legions," "confraternities," and "clubs" which play an important role in the daily life of most faith communities. An "integrated auxiliary" is thus classified as a part of the "church," while a related organization that is considered by a specific church to be an integral part of its ministry may not be. *See also* Chapters Seven and Eleven, discussing the significance of church organizational structure on questions of property ownership, management rights, and civil liability.

Eligibility for the exemptions granted to churches and religious organizations thus turns on both the nature and function of the organization. *See* Internal Rev. Reg. § 1.501(c)(c)-1(a). *See Holy Spirit Ass'n for Unification of World Christianity v. Tax Commission of City of New York*, 55 N.Y.2d 512, 435 N.E.2d 662, 450 N.Y.S.2d 292 (1982); Gen. Couns. Mem. 36,993 (1977) (opining that a witches' coven may qualify as a religious organization under I.R.C. § 501(c)(3), and as a "church" under I.R.C. § 170(b) (1) (A) (i)). To the extent that the organization in question operates independently and has a separate legal existence, it is likely to be considered a separate entity for tax purposes. Where it is supported, operated and controlled by a church or "convention or association" of churches, however, there is strong support for the conclusion that it is part and parcel of the church itself. *See St. Martin Evangelical Lutheran Church v. South Dakota*, 451 U.S. 772 (1981); *Tennessee Baptist Children's Homes, Inc. v. United States*, 604 F. Supp. 210 (M.D. Tenn. 1984), *aff'd*, 790 F.2d 534 (6th Cir. 1986). For a detailed discussion of the tax treatment of church-related and other public benefit organizations, see Hopkins, THE LAW OF TAX-EXEMPT ORGANIZATIONS at § 9.4; Fishman & Schwarz, NONPROFIT ORGANIZATIONS, at 307–579.

4. Other Exempt Activities

Both the Internal Revenue Code and analogous provisions of state statutory and constitutional law recognize a wide range of exempt activities that are not inherently religious. Among these are public and private charity, scientific research, political activity, education, and the endeavors of mutual benefit societies such as labor unions and veterans groups. *See* I.R.C. § 501(c). Both bodies of law also draw careful distinctions between and among exempt activities for purposes of tax and regulatory treatment. Article X, § 1 of the Minnesota Constitution provides a good example:

> Taxes shall be uniform upon the same class of subjects and shall be levied and collected for public purposes, but public burying grounds, public school houses, public hospitals, academies, colleges, universities, all seminaries of learning, all churches, church property, houses of worship, institutions of purely public charity, and public property used exclusively for any public purpose, shall be exempt from taxation except as provided in this section. The legislature by law may define or limit the property exempt under this section other than churches, houses of worship, and property solely used for educational purposes by academies, colleges, universities and seminaries of learning.

See also Regan v. Taxation with Representation of Washington, 461 U.S. 540 (1983) (upholding Congressional discretion to permit veterans organizations exempt under I.R.C. § 501(c)(19) to lobby in pursuit of their exempt activities with tax exempt funds, while organizations exempt under § 501(c)(3) are not); *Hospital Utilization Project v. Commonwealth of Pennsylvania*, 507 Pa. 1, 487 A.2d 1306 (1985) (defining the characteristics of "institutions of purely public charity" under Pa. Const. art. VIII, § 2(a)(v)).

Church organizations often do not draw such fine distinctions. For many churches, *all* of their activities are part and parcel of their religious mission. Differences in perception such as these can cause problems for both church and tax authorities.

The most obvious problems arise when conditions are imposed on the benefits available to exempt organizations under the tax code. Religious, charitable, educational and scientific organizations exempt from tax under § 501(c)(3), for example, are not only exempt from the corporate double tax; Congress encourages individual taxpayers to support their activities. It does so by providing that individual and corporate taxpayers may take a deduction for the amount contributed, up to fifty percent (50%) of adjusted gross income. Depending on the taxpayer's bracket, the deduction has the effect of reducing the amount of income subject to tax (taxable income). I.R.C. § 170 (2001).

Such benefits, however, are not "free;" they come with substantial regulatory and administrative "strings" attached. *See, e.g.*, I.R.C. § 170(c)(2) (2001). The following factors should be considered in every case:

1. The language of the statute(s) or constitutional provision(s) which authorize (or deny) the exemption in question;
2. The construction of that language by the courts; and
3. The manner in which constitutional considerations influence the construction ultimately adopted by the court.

5. What Is a "Charity"?

Society's conception of activities and uses that can validly be described as "charitable" has evolved over time. Read together, *Bob Jones University v. United States*, excerpted below, and more recent cases arising under state constitutional and statutory law illustrate the continuing role that both courts and legislatures have played in defining the concept of "charitable use."

The church has been intimately involved in the process as well. The concept of charity is so tightly bound up with questions of religious obligation that it was, for many years, virtually synonymous with it. *See The Commissioners for Special Purposes of the Income Tax v. Pemsel* [1891] A.C. 559 (holding that the terms "charitable" and "pious" were used in English law as synonyms of the term "godly"); *Mayo Foundation v. Commissioner of Revenue*, 306 Minn. 25, 33, 236 N.W.2d 767, 771 (1975) ("bringing [the] hearts [of an indefinite number of people] under the influence of education or religion, by relieving their bodies from disease, suffering, or constraint, by assisting them to establish themselves for life, or by erecting or maintaining public buildings or works, or otherwise lessening the burdens of government"). Though churches and their auxiliaries, such as convents and monasteries, have long been among the primary providers of charity, so too have towns and civic organizations, such as guilds and trade unions.

Common law courts have struggled for centuries to delineate the characteristics of the activities and purposes which should be recognized as charitable. *See generally* Howard S. Miller, THE LEGAL FOUNDATIONS OF AMERICAN PHILANTHROPY, 1776–1884 (1961). The structure and history of the Statute of Charitable Uses, Stat. 43 Eliz. ch 4 (1602), reflects the long-standing tension between government desires for revenue and the traditional view that moneys and property devoted to religious and charitable uses should not be subject to levy or obligation. *See, e.g., Gallego's Executors v. Attorney General*, 3 Leigh 450 (Va. 1832); *Vidal v. Girard's Executors*, 43 U.S. [2 How.] 127 (1844), both excerpted in Chapter Three.

The Act was adopted at the behest of the Crown in order to control the discretion of the common law courts in charity cases. Not unlike *mortmain* statutes, which were enacted periodically throughout the Middle Ages and designed to limit, if not altogether prohibit, the accumulation of land by the Church through bequests, the Statute of Charitable Uses was captioned "*An Act to redress the misemployment of lands, goods, and stocks of money heretofore given to charitable uses.*"

Listed in the preamble were the uses Parliament regarded as charitable: (1) relief of aged, impotent, and poor people, (2) maintenance of sick and maimed soldiers, (3) schools of learning, (4) free schools, (5) scholars in universities, (6) houses of correction, (7) repair of bridges, (8) repair of ports and havens, (9) repair of causeways, (10) repair of churches, (11) repair of sea banks, (12) repair of highways, (13) education and preferment of orphans, (14) marriage of poor maids, (15) support and help of young tradesmen, (16) support and help of handicraftsmen, (17) support and help of persons decayed, (18) redemption or relief of prisoners or captives, (19) aid or ease of any poor inhabitant concerning payment of fifteens, (20) setting out of soldiers, and (21) other taxes.

The courts, however, did not view the Act as conclusive of the question. After the adoption of the statute, controlling weight was given to the provisions of the Act whenever the particular use or purpose fell within its ambit, but purposes analogous in spirit and "intendment" to those enumerated were deemed "charitable" as well. *See, e.g., In re MacDuff* [1986] 2 Ch. 451; *Morice v. The Bishop of Durham* [1805] 32 E.R. 947. The inquiry turns on the answers to two questions: (1) Is the use for the benefit of the public? and (2) Is the activity to be supported consistent with public policy?

a) The Requirement of "Public Benefit"

1) Generally

The requirement that a charitable use be dedicated to the benefit of the public is well established in both English and American law. *See, e.g., Davis v. United States*, 495 U.S. 472 (1990) (disallowing charitable deduction to parents who provided support for their son while he was serving as a full-time missionary); *In re Christchurch Inclosure Act* [1888] 38 Ch. D. 520, 531 (holding that a gift subject to a condition or trust for the benefit of the inhabitants of a parish or town, or of any particular class of such inhabitants, is a charitable trust); *The President of the United States v. Drummond, cited in Whicker v. Hume* [1858] 7 H.L. Cas. 124, M.R. (gift to the United States to establish the Smithsonian Institution for the purpose of increasing knowledge among men); *Whicker v. Hume* [1858] 7 H.L. Cas. 124 (testamentary trust "for the benefit, advancement, and propagation of education and learning in every part of the world").

Not all public purposes, however, are charitable, either at common law or under the terms of applicable tax law. Philanthropy, for example, is not always viewed by the courts as "charitable," even though the concept of philanthropy is generally understood as "goodwill to mankind at large" or "the giving or pure, unalloyed pleasure to all the world." *See MacDuff v. MacDuff* [1896] 2 Ch. 451 (recognizing that there may be philanthropic purposes which are not charitable). The same is true for organizations which operate in the public interest, but which have a "commercial hue." *See* I.R.C. §501(c)(3) (1996); *American Institute for Economic Research v. Assessors of Great Barrington*, 324 Mass. 509, 87 N.E.2d 186 (1949) (exemption denied to corporation whose purposes included conducting scientific research in economics and disseminating the results); *Battelle Memorial Institute v. Dunn*, 148 Ohio St. 53, 73 N.E.2d 88 (1947) (realty not used exclusively for "charitable" purposes when research done there for compensation was primarily for the pecuniary advantage of those for whom the research was performed).

Religious uses or activities raise similar questions, for not all religious purposes are dedicated to the benefit of the public at large. Because the same is true for many other educational, scientific, and mutual benefit activities, many, if not most, American jurisdictions resolve this problem by exempting a wide range of public, charitable, educational, and religious organizations, activities and properties. Where eligibility requirements for tax exemptions are more tightly drawn, however, both courts and religious institutions must confront the "public benefit" problem directly.

It is at this point that some of the most critical distinctions between federal and state tax laws become apparent. When the issue is eligibility under *state* common and statutory law, the fact that an organization or activity may be exempt under the provisions of Section 501 of the Internal Revenue Code will not be relevant to the state's determination unless the tax statute in question expressly incorporates federal eligibility standards by reference.

2) *"Purely Public" Charities*

Article VIII §2 of Pennsylvania's Constitution provides a good example of a provision which draws careful distinctions between and among the types of uses eligible for tax exemptions. It provides that

> (a) The General Assembly may by law exempt from taxation:
>
> (i) Actual places of regularly stated religious worship; and
>
> (v) Institutions of purely public charity, but in the case of any real property tax exemptions only that portion of real property of such institution which is actually and regularly used for the purposes of the institution.

Construing this provision in *Hospital Utilization Project v. Commonwealth*, 507 Pa. 1, 22, 487 A.2d 1306, 1317 (1985) [*HUP*], the Pennsylvania Supreme Court held that an institution of "purely public charity" is one which has *each* of the following characteristics:

(a) Advances a charitable purpose;

(b) Donates or renders gratuitously a substantial portion of its services;

(c) Benefits a substantial and indefinite class of persons who are legitimate subjects of charity;

(d) Relieves the government of some of its burden; and

(e) Operates entirely free from private profit motive.

Accord North Star Research Institute v. County of Hennepin, 306 Minn. 1, 6, 236 N.W.2d 754, 757 (1975).

Elaborating on the manner in which the phrase "purely public" modifies the common-law concept of "charity," the Pennsylvania Supreme Court held in *HUP* that "institutions of purely public charity" bear a heavy burden of demonstrating both the public nature of their work, and the charitable character of the institution.

The courts appear to divide over two basic questions. The first relates to the amount of free or reduced cost services provided. In *HUP*, the Pennsylvania Supreme Court held that the amount of gratuitous services rendered must be "substantial." Some courts adopt percentages to make the determination. *E.g.*, *Aransas Hospital, Inc. v. Aransas Pass Independent School District*, 521 S.W.2d 685, 691 (Tex. Civ. App. 1975) (not a charity when only 1.9% of admissions in five years were charitable cases). Other courts find percentage formulations too confining, "difficult of application and unsound in theory." *Southern Methodist Hospital & Sanatorium of Tucson v. Wilson*, 51 Ariz. 424, 431, 77 P.2d 458, 462 (1938). *Accord Medical Center Hospital of Vermont, Inc. v. City of Burlington*, 152 Vt. 611, 617, 566 A.2d 1352, 1355 (1989) ("The better inquiry, it seems to us, is whether health care was made available by the plaintiff to all who needed it, regardless of their ability to pay.")

The second dispute is over the meaning of the term "charity" itself. All courts recognize "that the definition of 'charitable organization' need not be locked into the past," *Medical Center Hospital of Vermont*, 152 Vt. 611, 618–619, 566 A.2d 1352 (1989), but there is a divergence of view concerning the function of private charity now that the government has become a major provider of social welfare benefits. In *Evangelical Lutheran Good Samaritan Society v. County of Gage*, 181 Neb. 831, 836, 151 N.W.2d 446, 449 (1967), for example, the Nebraska Supreme Court noted that when few, if any, public welfare programs existed, the primary function of private charities was to provide services and alms for the poor, but "[w]ith the advent of present day social security and welfare programs, this type of charity is not often found because assistance is available to the poor under these programs." In its view, the term "'charity' is 'broad enough to include practical enterprises for the good of humanity operated at a moderate cost to those who receive the benefits.'" *Quoting Young Men's Christian Ass'n v. Lancaster County*, 106 Neb. 105, 111, 182 N.W. 593, 595 (1921)). In *HUP*, by contrast, the Pennsylvania Supreme Court observed that a charity "receiving [an] exemption from taxation... is merely being given a '*quid pro quo*' for its services in providing something which otherwise the government would have to provide." *Hospital Utilization Project v. Commonwealth*, 507 Pa. at 13, 487 A. 2d at 1314, *quoting Young Men's Christian Ass'n of Germantown v. City of Philadelphia*, 323 Pa. 401, 413–14, 187 A. 204, 210 (1936).

The practical impact of such debates is twofold. First, they encourage state and local taxing authorities to construe the term "charitable" as strictly as possible. This forces some charitable institutions to re-examine both the kinds of services they render and the manner in which they operate, down to, and including, the pay scales for their officers, directors and key employees. Second, and perhaps most important, they reopen a debate over the nature and purpose of tax exemptions.

In one view, payment of taxes is a social obligation. Courts adopting this view are prepared to hold that the obligation is met when an organization provides services to the public that the government would otherwise have to provide on it own. The contrasting view is that taxes, while essential to the functioning of the government, are nonetheless an economic burden. In this view, imposition of taxes on not-for-profit organizations involved in charitable activities siphons off funds already devoted to the public, makes them subject to the control of the government, and leads to "an abject dependence upon that superior power—Government" for grants, while "[t]he exemption method leaves the trustees of the institutions fostered untrammeled in their action, and untempted to unworthy arts or mean compliances." *See* Charles William Eliot, VIEWS RESPECTING PRESENT EXEMPTION FROM TAXATION OF PROPERTY USED FOR RELIGIOUS EDUCATIONAL AND CHARITABLE PURPOSES (1874), *quoted in* Fishman & Schwarz, NONPROFIT ORGANIZATIONS at 317–18. In this view, it makes no difference that the services provided may not be of the type or character provided by the government. In fact, that is the point of the argument: their value lies in what they *add* to what is already provided at public expense. *See generally* James J. Fishman & Stephen Schwarz, NONPROFIT ORGANIZATIONS—CASES AND MATERIALS (2000) (summarizing the theories which are used to justify tax exemptions for churches, religious organizations, and charities).

3) Distinguishing Between 'Religious' and 'Charitable' Uses

By the later part of the nineteenth century it was clear that state judges had become hostile to the traditional assumption that "places of worship were exempt from taxation as public property by the nature of things, and not by the constitution or by statute." Torpey, *quoting Franklin Street Society v. Manchester,* 60 N.H. 342, 349 (1880). In response to judicial insistence that tax exemptions should be explicitly authorized by either constitution or statute, most states now provide some form of explicit exemptions from taxes for religious activities and property used for religious purposes. *See* § C(3), above.

Some state constitutional provisions draw rather clear distinctions between and among types of religious activity. Article 13, § 3(f) of the California Constitution, for example, exempts "[b]uildings, land on which they are situated, and equipment used exclusively for religious worship" from property taxes, but leaves it to the discretion of the legislature to determine the exempt status of "[p]roperty used exclusively for religious, hospital, or charitable purposes and owned or held in trust by corporations or other entities (1) that are organized and operating for those purposes, (2) that are nonprofit, and (3) no part of whose net earnings inures to the benefit of any private shareholder or individual." Cal. Const. art. 13, § 4(b) (2001). Minnesota, for example, even restricts the tax exemptions available to *public* property. In order to qualify, it too must be "used exclusively for [a] public purpose." *See* Minn. Const. art. X, § 1 (2001).

The effect of such provisions is to draw a conceptual distinction between what might be termed the "purely religious" function of "worship," and other activities or properties that should not be taxed, such as religious, charitable, and public uses. Not surprisingly, each exemption case must be decided upon its own facts. *Mayo Foundation v. Commissioner of Revenue,* 306 Minn. 25, 236 N.W.2d 767 (1975).

For the same reason that the cases contain no clear definition of the concept of "church," see § D(1)(b) above, courts are equally hesitant to place legal constraints on the either the form or the content of "worship." The cases indicate that the courts are looking to the actual function of the premises, rather than to a concept of "worship" that fails to reflect the actual needs and practices of believers. *See, e.g., Roberts v. Ravenwood Church of WICCA,* 249 Ga. 348, 292 S.E.2d 657 (1982) (allowing exemption for property used for worship services conducted by a church whose members are commonly referred to as witches and warlocks), *World Evangelistic Enterprise Corporation v. Tracy*, 96 Ohio App. 3d 78, 644 N.E.2d 678 (Clark County 1994), *motion to certify denied*, 71 Ohio St. 3d 1412, 641 N.E.2d 1111 (1994) (Christian radio broadcast facility held to be a "house used exclusively for public worship"); *Mount Zion New Life Center v. Board of Assessment and Revision Of Taxes and Appeals*, 94 Pa. Cmwlth. 439, 503 A.2d 1065 (1986) (weekly worship by different groups of worshippers at Christian retreat center qualified the property as "regular place of stated worship"). *But see Wynnefield United Presbyterian Church v. City of Philadelphia*, 348 Pa. 252, 35 A.2d 276 (1944) (exemption denied where parcel adjacent to the church was not clearly needed for the support of church functions).

But the courts are equally clear that not every "religious" function is to be equated with "worship." In *Bright Horizon House, Inc., v. Zoning Board of Appeals of Town of Henrietta, Monroe County*, 121 Misc.2d 703, 469 N.Y.S.2d 851 (1983), a religious group sought a zoning variance and tax exemption for a proposed facility in which its members would study the tenets of their faith in the hope of attaining "personal healing." Though their purpose was unquestionably religious, the proposed facility was deemed neither a church, nor a public hospital. In *Christian Church of Ohio v. Limbach*, 53 Ohio St. 3d 270, 560 N.E.2d 199 (1990), a building used by the church as its regional headquarters was not entitled to a real property tax exemption limited to places of worship, even though most of the support services for ministers of the denomination were provided there. The reason was a simple one: it was an office, and no public worship services were conducted there.

Cases in which the tax-exempt status of parsonage property is questioned show a similar concern for detail. In *Christian Business Men's Committee of Minneapolis, Inc. v. State*, 228 Minn. 549, 38 N.W.2d 803 (1949), for example, the subject premises were used for both religious and non-religious purposes. Because neither function could be described as the "principal" use, but both were "substantial," the Minnesota Supreme Court ordered an apportionment. A similar result was reached in *United Church of Religious Science v. Board of Assessors of Attleboro*, 372 Mass. 280, 361 N.E.2d 1254 (1977), where the church owned a manufacturing plant, the income of which was used for religious programs and reinvestment in the business. A property tax exemption for property owned or held by a religious corporation if the principal or income is used or appropriated for religious, benevolent or charitable purposes was held to be inapplicable because both the property and the income must be used for religious purposes. *See also Supervisor of Assessments of Baltimore County v. Keeler*, 362 Md. 198, 764 A.2d 821 (2001) (undeveloped "green space" portion of larger parcel on which a church was to be built qualifies for the exemption); *State v. Church of Incarnation*, 158 Minn. 48, 196 N.W. 802 (1924) (residence owned and maintained by the church as a rent-free residence for its pastor was used for religious exempt purposes); *Trinity Episcopal Church v. County of Sherburne*, 1991 WL 95745 (Minn. Tax, May 20, 1991) (exemption for parsonage lost when priest did not live on the premises, and house was rented to others); *Holy Trinity Orthodox Church of East Meadow v. O'Shea*, 186 Misc.2d 880, 720 N.Y.S.2d 904 (2001) (choir director was not "officiating clergyman" under the statute, but property was exempt because it was devoted to fostering the religious use). *See* 26 U.S.C. § 107 (2002) as amended by P.L. 107-81 § 2(a), 116 Stat. 783 (May 20, 2002).

In the end, however, the historically close relationship between religious and charitable functions continues to be recognized by the courts.

> The legal meaning of the word "charity" has a broader significance than in common speech and has been expanded in numerous decisions. Charity is broadly defined as a gift, to be applied consistently with existing laws, for the benefit of an indefinite number of persons "by bringing their hearts under the influence of education or religion, by relieving their bodies from disease, suffering, or constraint, by assisting them to establish themselves for life, or by erecting or maintaining public buildings or works, or otherwise lessening the burdens of government."

Rio Vista Non-Profit Housing Corporation v. County of Ramsey, 277 N.W.2d 187, 190 (Minn. 1979), *quoting Mayo Foundation v. Commissioner of Revenue*, 306 Minn. 25, 33, 236 N.W.2d 767, 771 (1975). *See also Assessors of Dover v. Dominican Fathers Province of St. Joseph*, 334 Mass. 530, 137 N.E.2d 225 (1956) (entire grounds in residential area owned and used by religious order to conduct a seminary for training young men for the priesthood including a house used for dormitory purposes as well as extensive wooded acreage used for recreational activities, were within statute exempting from taxation literary, benevolent, charitable or scientific institutions).

b) The Requirement That the Purpose or Activity be "Consistent with Public Policy"

The second requirement imposed by the common law of charities is that a use alleged to be "charitable" must be "consistent with public policy." But what *is* "public policy"? In American law, "public policy" can refer to common, or judge-made, law; to legislation, executive orders and administrative regulations authorized to implement legislative policy; to treaties and other binding international accords; and to constitutional law. *See generally* Dennis Lloyd, PUBLIC POLICY: A COMPARATIVE STUDY OF ENGLISH AND FRENCH LAW (1953).

Until the adoption of the Statute of Charitable Uses in 1602, the development of the law of charities took place in common law courts. Because the intent of Parliament was to correct what it viewed as the "misdirection" of property put to charitable use, the courts gave the Statute controlling effect when it applied. When the proposed use provided a public benefit and was otherwise consistent with the public policy of England—including the Statute of Charitable Uses—judges held the use to be "charitable."

Because federal and state constitutions make taxation a matter of legislative prerogative, see, e.g., U.S. Const. Art. I, §8, cl. 1, ascertaining the content of "public policy" presents a number of complex constitutional and statutory issues. A judicially created rule governing taxation cannot be "consistent with public policy" if it is inconsistent with any aspect of either constitutional law or legislative policy. *See* U.S. Const. Art. VI (Supremacy Clause).

As you read *Bob Jones University v. United States*, excerpted below, consider the following questions:

1) Did the taxpayer qualify for the exemption under the terms of the relevant statute?
2) Aside from the Constitution, what "public policy" *in addition to* that enacted by Congress in the Internal Revenue Code determines the tax status of a corporation or individual?
3) How do the requirements of the Constitution that do not deal specifically with the power to tax affect the power of Congress "to lay and collect taxes," and the power of the Executive to see to it that the tax laws are "faithfully executed"?

4) What powers with respect to taxation does the Constitution confer on the Judicial Branch of the government?

Bob Jones University v. United States

461 U.S. 574 (1983)
Decided together with
Goldsboro Christian Schools, Inc. v. United States

Chief Justice BURGER delivered the opinion of the Court.

We granted certiorari to decide whether petitioners, nonprofit private schools that prescribe and enforce racially discriminatory admissions standards the basis of religious doctrine, qualify as tax-exempt organizations under § 501(c)(3) of the Internal Revenue Code of 1954.

I

A

Until 1970, the Internal Revenue Service granted tax-exempt status to private schools, without regard to their racial admissions policies, under § 501(c)(3) of the Internal Revenue Code, 26 U.S.C. § 501(c)(3), and granted charitable deductions for contributions to such schools under § 170 of the Code, 26 U.S.C. § 170.

On January 12, 1970, a three-judge District Court for the District of Columbia issued a preliminary injunction prohibiting the IRS from according tax-exempt status to private schools in Mississippi that discriminated as to admissions on the basis of race. Thereafter, in July 1970, the IRS concluded that it could "no longer legally justify allowing tax-exempt status [under § 501(c)(3)] to private schools which practice racial discrimination." IRS News Release(7/10/70).

The revised policy on discrimination was formalized in Revenue Ruling 71-447, 1971–2 Cum. Bull. 230:

> "Both the courts and the Internal Revenue Service have long recognized that the statutory requirement of being 'organized and operated exclusively for religious, charitable,... or educational purposes' was intended to express the basic common law concept [of 'charity']. All charitable trusts, educational or otherwise, are subject to the requirement that the purpose of the trust may not be illegal or contrary to public policy." Id. at 230.

Based on the "national policy to discourage racial discrimination in education," the IRS ruled that "a private school not having a racially nondiscriminatory policy as to students is not 'charitable' within the common law concepts reflected in sections 170 and 501(c)(3) of the Code." Id. at 231.[3]

---

3. Revenue Ruling 71-447, 1971–2 Cum.Bull. 230, defined "racially nondiscriminatory policy as to students" as meaning that:

> "[T]he school admits the students of any race to all the rights, privileges, programs, and activities generally accorded or made available to students at that school and that the school does not discriminate on the basis of race in administration of its educational policies, admissions policies, scholarship and loan programs, and athletic and other school-administered programs."

The application of the IRS construction of these provisions to petitioners, two private schools with racially discriminatory admissions policies, is now before us.

B

No. 81-3, Bob Jones University v. United States

Bob Jones University is a nonprofit corporation located in Greenville, South Carolina. Its purpose is "to conduct an institution of learning, giving special emphasis to the Christian religion and the ethics revealed in the Holy Scriptures." Bob Jones University is not affiliated with any religious denomination, but is dedicated to the teaching and propagation of its fundamentalist Christian religious beliefs. It is both a religious and educational institution.

The sponsors of the University genuinely believe that the Bible forbids interracial dating and marriage. To effectuate these views, Negroes were completely excluded until 1971. From 1971 to May 1975, the University accepted no applications from unmarried Negroes, but did accept applications from Negroes married within their race.

Following the decision of the United States Court of Appeals for the Fourth Circuit in *McCrary v. Runyon*, prohibiting racial exclusion from private schools, the University revised its policy. Since 1975, the University has permitted unmarried Negroes to enroll; but a disciplinary rule prohibits interracial dating and marriage. The University [denies] admission to applicants engaged in an interracial marriage or known to advocate interracial marriage or dating.

Until 1970, the IRS extended tax-exempt status to Bob Jones University under §501(c)(3). [In November, 1970], the IRS formally notified the University of the change in IRS policy, and announced its intention to challenge the tax-exempt status of private schools practicing racial discrimination in their admissions policies.

[The tax exemption was revoked in 1971, and the University instituted the present action, seeking to recover $21.00 it had paid to the IRS. The Government counterclaimed for unpaid federal unemployment taxes for the taxable years 1971 through 1975, in the amount of $489,675.59, plus interest.]

[The District Court held that the revocation exceeded the delegated powers of the IRS, was improper under the IRS rulings and procedures, and violated the University's rights under the Religion Clauses of the First Amendment. The Court of Appeals for the Fourth Circuit, in a divided opinion, reversed, concluding that §501(c)(3) must be read against the background of charitable trust law. To be eligible for an exemption under that section, an institution must be "charitable" in the common law sense, and therefore must not be contrary to public policy.]

We granted *certiorari* in both cases, and we affirm in each.

II

A

In Revenue Ruling 71-447, the IRS formalized the policy first announced in 1970, that §170 and §501(c)(3) embrace the common law "charity" concept. Under that view, to qualify for a tax exemption pursuant to §501(c)(3), an institution must show, first, that it falls within one of the eight categories expressly set forth in that section, and second, that its activity is not contrary to settled public policy.

Section 501(c)(3) provides that "[c]orporations... organized and operated exclusively for religious, charitable... or educational purposes" are entitled to tax exemption. Petitioners argue that the plain language of the statute guarantees them tax-exempt status. They emphasize the absence of any language in the statute expressly requiring all exempt organizations to be "charitable" in the common law sense, and they contend that the disjunctive "or" separating the categories in § 501(c)(3) precludes such a reading. Instead, they argue that if an institution falls within one or more of the specified categories it is automatically entitled to exemption, without regard to whether it also qualifies as "charitable." The Court of Appeals concluded that petitioners' interpretation of the statute "tears section 501(c)(3) from its roots."

Section 501(c)(3) therefore must be analyzed and construed within the framework of the Internal Revenue Code and against the background of the Congressional purposes. Such an examination reveals unmistakable evidence that, underlying all relevant parts of the Code, is the intent that entitlement to tax exemption depends on meeting certain common law standards of charity—namely, that an institution seeking tax-exempt status must serve a public purpose and not be contrary to established public policy.

This "charitable" concept appears explicitly in § 170 of the Code. That section contains a list of organizations virtually identical to that contained in § 501(c)(3). In § 170, Congress used the list of organizations in defining the term "charitable contributions." On its face, therefore, § 170 reveals that Congress' intention was to provide tax benefits to organizations serving charitable purposes. The form of § 170 [indicates that] Congress sought to provide tax benefits to charitable organizations, to encourage the development of private institutions that serve a useful public purpose or supplement or take the place of public institutions of the same kind.

Tax exemptions for certain institutions thought beneficial to the social order of the country as a whole, or to a particular community, are deeply rooted in our history, as in that of England. The origins of such exemptions lie in the special privileges that have long been extended to charitable trusts.[11] When the Government grants exemptions or allows deductions all taxpayers are affected; the very fact of the exemption or deduction for the donor means that other taxpayers can be said to be indirect and vicarious "donors." Charitable exemptions are justified on the basis that the exempt entity confers a public benefit—a benefit which the society or the community may not itself choose or be able to provide, or which supplements and advances the work of public institutions already supported by tax revenues. The institution's purpose must not be so at odds with the common community conscience as to undermine any public benefit that might otherwise be conferred.

B

We are bound to approach these questions with full awareness that determinations of public benefit and public policy are sensitive matters with serious implica-

11. The form and history of the charitable exemption and deduction sections of the various income tax acts reveal that Congress was guided by the common law of charitable trusts. See Simon, The Tax-Exempt Status of Racially Discriminatory Religious Schools, 36 Tax L.Rev. 477, 485–489 (1981) (hereinafter Simon). The House Report on the Tax Reform Act of 1969, Pub.L. 91-172, 83 Stat. 487, stated that the § 501(c) (3) exemption was available only to institutions that served "the specified charitable purposes,"... and described "charitable" as "a term that has been used in the law of trusts for hundreds of years." [citation omitted]. We need not consider whether Congress intended to incorporate into the Internal Revenue Code any aspects of charitable trust law other than the requirements of public benefit and a valid public purpose.

tions for the institutions affected; a declaration that a given institution is not "charitable" should be made only where there can be no doubt that the activity involved is contrary to a fundamental public policy. Racially discriminatory educational institutions cannot be viewed as conferring a public benefit within the "charitable" concept discussed earlier, or within the Congressional intent underlying § 170 and § 501(c)(3).[21]

C

[The Court rejected that argument that that the IRS overstepped its lawful bounds in issuing its 1970 and 1971 rulings, holding that "[i]n an area as complex as the tax system, the agency Congress vests with administrative responsibility must be able to exercise its authority to meet changing conditions and new problems."]

III

Petitioners contend that, even if the Commissioner's policy is valid as to nonreligious private schools, that policy cannot constitutionally be applied to schools that engage in racial discrimination on the basis of sincerely held religious beliefs.

This Court has long held the Free Exercise Clause of the First Amendment an absolute prohibition against governmental regulation of religious beliefs. As interpreted by this Court, moreover, the Free Exercise Clause provides substantial protection for lawful conduct grounded in religious belief. However, "[n]ot all burdens on religion are unconstitutional. The state may justify a limitation on religious liberty by showing that it is essential to accomplish an overriding governmental interest."

The Government has a fundamental, overriding interest in eradicating racial discrimination in education.[29] That governmental interest substantially outweighs whatever burden denial of tax benefits places on petitioners' exercise of their religious beliefs.[30]

Affirmed.

Justice POWELL, concurring in part and concurring in the judgment.

I join the Court's judgment, along with part III of its opinion holding that the denial of tax exemptions to petitioners does not violate the First Amendment. I write separately because I am troubled by the broader implications of the Court's opinion with respect to the authority of the Internal Revenue Service (IRS) and its construction of §§ 170(c) and 501(c)(3) of the Internal Revenue Code.

---

21. In view of our conclusion that racially discriminatory private schools violate fundamental public policy and cannot be deemed to confer a benefit on the public, we need not decide whether an organization providing a public benefit and otherwise meeting the requirements of § 501(c)(3) could nevertheless be denied tax-exempt status if certain of its activities violated a law or public policy.

29. We deal here only with religious schools—not with churches or other purely religious institutions; here, the governmental interest is in denying public support to racial discrimination in education. As noted earlier, racially discriminatory schools "exer[t] a pervasive influence on the entire educational process," outweighing any public benefit that they might otherwise provide, *Norwood v. Harrison*, 413 U.S. 455, 469 (1973). *See generally* Simon 495–496.

30. [The Court rejected the argument that denial of tax exemption violates the Establishment Clause by preferring religions whose tenets do not require racial discrimination over those which do not believe in racial intermixing.]

I

Federal taxes are not imposed on organizations "operated exclusively for religious, charitable, scientific, testing for public safety, literary, or educational purposes." 26 U.S.C. § 501(c)(3). The Code also permits a tax deduction for contributions made to these organizations. § 170(c). It is clear that petitioners, organizations incorporated for educational purposes, fall within the language of the statute. It also is clear that the language itself does not mandate refusal of tax-exempt status to any private school that maintains a racially discriminatory admissions policy. Accordingly, there is force in Justice Rehnquist's argument that §§ 170(c) and 501(c)(3) should be construed as setting forth the only criteria Congress has established for qualification as a tax-exempt organization. Indeed, were we writing prior to the history detailed in the Court's opinion, this could well be the construction I would adopt. But there has been a decade of acceptance [of that construction by Congress] that is persuasive in the circumstances of this case, and I conclude that there are now sufficient reasons for accepting the IRS's construction of the Code as proscribing tax exemptions for schools that discriminate on the basis of race as a matter of policy.

I cannot say that this construction of the Code, adopted by the IRS in 1970 and upheld by the Court of Appeals below, is without logical support. The statutory terms are not self-defining, and it is plausible that in some instances an organization seeking a tax exemption might act in a manner so clearly contrary to the purposes of our laws that it could not be deemed to serve the enumerated statutory purposes.

II

I therefore concur in the Court's judgment that tax-exempt status under §§ 170(c) and 501(c)(3) is not available to private schools that concededly are racially discriminatory. I do not agree, however, with the Court's more general explanation of the justifications for the tax exemptions provided to charitable organizations.

With all respect, I am unconvinced that the critical question in determining tax-exempt status is whether an individual organization provides a clear "public benefit" as defined by the Court. Over 106,000 organizations filed § 501(c)(3) returns in 1981. I find it impossible to believe that all or even most of those organizations could prove that they "demonstrably serve and [are] in harmony with the public interest" or that they are "beneficial and stabilizing influences in community life." Nor am I prepared to say that petitioners, because of their racially discriminatory policies, necessarily contribute nothing of benefit to the community. It is clear from the substantially secular character of the curricula and degrees offered that petitioners provide educational benefits.

Even more troubling to me is the element of conformity that appears to inform the Court's analysis. The Court asserts that an exempt organization must "demonstrably serve and be in harmony with the public interest," must have a purpose that comports with "the common community conscience," and must not act in a manner "affirmatively at odds with [the] declared position of the whole government." Taken together, these passages suggest that the primary function of a tax-exempt organization is to act on behalf of the Government in carrying out governmentally approved policies. In my opinion, such a view of § 501(c)(3) ignores the important role played by tax exemptions in encouraging diverse, indeed often sharply conflicting, activities and viewpoints.

I do not suggest that these considerations always are or should be dispositive. In this case I agree with the Court that Congress has determined that the policy against racial discrimination in education should override the countervailing interest in permitting unorthodox private behavior.

I would emphasize, however, that the balancing of these substantial interests is for Congress to perform. I am unwilling to join any suggestion that the Internal Revenue Service is invested with authority to decide which public policies are sufficiently "fundamental" to require denial of tax exemptions. Its business is to administer laws designed to produce revenue for the Government, not to promote "public policy." This Court often has expressed concern that the scope of an agency's authorization be limited to those areas in which the agency fairly may be said to have expertise, and this concern applies with special force when the asserted administrative power is one to determine the scope of public policy.

III

Many questions remain, such as whether organizations that violate other policies should receive tax-exempt status under § 501(c)(3). These should be legislative policy choices. The contours of public policy should be determined by Congress, not by judges or the IRS.

Justice REHNQUIST, dissenting.

The Court points out that there is a strong national policy in this country against racial discrimination. To the extent that the Court states that Congress in furtherance of this policy could deny tax-exempt status to educational institutions that promote racial discrimination, I readily agree. But, unlike the Court, I am convinced that Congress simply has failed to take this action and, as this Court has said over and over again, regardless of our view on the propriety of Congress' failure to legislate we are not constitutionally empowered to act for them.

In approaching this statutory construction question the Court quite adeptly avoids the statute it is construing. [T]here is nothing in the language of § 501(c)(3) that supports the result obtained by the Court. An entity must be (1) a corporation, or community chest, fund, or foundation, (2) organized for one of the eight enumerated purposes, (3) operated on a nonprofit basis, and (4) free from involvement in lobbying activities and political campaigns. Nowhere is there to be found some additional, undefined public policy requirement.

The Court first seeks refuge from the obvious reading of § 501(c)(3) by turning to § 170 of the Internal Revenue Code which provides a tax deduction for contributions made to § 501(c)(3) organizations. Since § 170 is no more than a mirror of § 501(c)(3) and, as the Court points out, § 170 followed § 501(c)(3) by more than two decades, it is at best of little usefulness in finding the meaning of § 501(c)(3).

Making a more fruitful inquiry, the Court next turns to the legislative history of § 501(c)(3) and finds that Congress intended in that statute to offer a tax benefit to organizations that Congress believed were providing a public benefit. I certainly agree. I think [however,] that the legislative history of § 501(c)(3) unmistakably makes clear that Congress has decided what organizations are serving a public purpose and providing a public benefit within the meaning of § 501(c)(3) and has clearly set forth in § 501(c)(3) the characteristics of such organizations.

One way to read the opinion handed down by the Court today leads to the conclusion that when enacting the original 1894 statute Congress intended to adopt a common law term of art, and intended that this term of art carry with it all of the common law baggage which defines it. Such a view, however, leads also to the unsupportable idea that Congress has spent almost a century adding illustrations simply to clarify an already defined common law term.

Another way to read the Court's opinion leads to the conclusion that even though Congress has set forth some of the requirements of a § 501(c)(3) organization, it intended that the IRS additionally require that organizations meet a higher standard of public interest, not stated by Congress, but to be determined and defined by the IRS and the courts. This view I find equally unsupportable.

I have no disagreement with the Court's finding that there is a strong national policy in this country opposed to racial discrimination. I agree with the Court that Congress has the power to further this policy by denying § 501(c)(3) status to organizations that practice racial discrimination.[3] But as of yet Congress has failed to do so. Whatever the reasons for the failure, this Court should not legislate for Congress.[4]

Therefore, it is my view that unless and until Congress affirmatively amends § 501(c)(3) to require more, the IRS is without authority to deny petitioners § 501(c)(3) status. For this reason, I would reverse the Court of Appeals.

Notes

1. The history of the *Bob Jones University* litigation is recounted exhaustively Fishman & Schwarz, Nonprofit Organizations at 359–365. *See also* Miriam Galston, *Public Policy Constraints on Charitable Organizations*, 3 Va. Tax. Rev. 291 (1984); Douglas Laycock, *Observation: Tax Exemptions for Racially Discriminatory Religious Schools*, 60 Tex. L. Rev. 259 (1982); Karla W. Simon, *The Tax-Exempt Status of Racially Discriminatory Religious Schools*, 36 Tax L. Rev. 477 (1981).

2. In *Allen v. Wright*, 468 U.S. 737 (1984), the Supreme Court held that private individuals have no standing to challenge the tax exempt status of racially discriminatory private schools, thus severely limiting the potential reach of the holding in *Bob Jones University*. The plaintiffs in *Wright* were parents whose children were enrolled in school systems subject to desegregation decrees. They alleged two direct harms: (1) the fact of Government financial aid to discriminatory private schools; and (2) that federal tax exemptions to racially discriminatory private schools in their communities allegedly impaired the ability of the communities in which they lived to desegregate their public schools. The Court rejected both assertions, holding that "neither [harm] suffices to support respondents' standing. The first fails under clear precedents of this Court because it does not constitute judicially cognizable injury. The second fails because the alleged injury is not fairly traceable to the assertedly unlawful conduct of the IRS." *Id.* at 753.

3. A similar holding was reached in *In re United States Catholic Conference (USCC)*, 885 F.2d 1020 (2nd Cir. 1989) *cert. denied*, 495 U.S. 918 (1990), in which a number of abortion rights groups sought to challenge the tax exempt status of the Catholic Church on grounds that the IRS was not enforcing the political activity restrictions of I.R.C. § 501(c)(3). The Second Circuit considered, and rejected, theories of "clergy standing" under the Establishment Clause, taxpayer standing, voter standing and "competitive advocate" standing. Although the court was hesitant to "foreclose the

---

3. I agree with the Court that such a requirement would not infringe on petitioners' First Amendment rights.

4. Because of its holding, the Court does not have to decide whether it would violate the equal protection component of the Fifth Amendment for Congress to grant § 501(c)(3) status to organizations that practice racial discrimination. I would decide that it does not. The statute is facially neutral; absent a showing of a discriminatory purpose, no equal protection violation is established. *Washington v. Davis*, 426 U.S. 229, 241–244 (1976).

possibility that political competitors may state a cognizable injury," it held that the plaintiffs in the case had not pleaded a "direct injury in fact." *See generally* Jordana G. Schwartz, Note, *Standing to Challenge Tax Exempt Status: The Second Circuit's Competitive Political Advocate Theory*, 58 Fordham L. Rev. 723 (1990).

4. What did the Court actually hold in *Bob Jones University*? Was BJU ineligible under the terms of the statute, or does the Constitution itself preclude the recognition of an exemption for otherwise-eligible organizations which practice racial discrimination? Reading the case in light of the holding in *Allen v. Wright*, it is possible to conclude that the reach of the holding may be limited to cases involving tax-exempt organizations charged with racial discrimination. Rev. Proc. 75-50, 1975-2 C.B. 587, requiring schools seeking tax exempt status to demonstrate that their policies are nondiscriminatory remains in force, and has been extended to a private charitable trust having a governing instrument which was restricted to "worthy and deserving white persons." *See* Priv. Ltr. Rul. 89-19-991 (Nov. 30, 1988). *See also Calhoun Academy v. Commissioner*, 94 T.C. 284 (1990) (upholding denial of tax exempt status to school which could not demonstrate its nondiscriminatory policy). Should the scope of the Court's decision be limited in this fashion?

5. The Court's opinion in *Bob Jones University* relies heavily on the interplay between I.R.C. §501(c)(3), which grants an exemption from the corporate tax which would otherwise be payable by the entity under Section 11, and I.R.C. §170, which grants individuals a "charitable" deduction from gross income for contributions to the organizations listed in §501(c)(3). What is the significance of the point made by Justices Powell and Rehnquist that, in the absence of a clearly expressed congressional intent to do so, taxes may not be imposed by judicial or administrative action? Is this simply a restatement of the view that the imposition of taxes is a legislative function, or are these Justices raising separation of powers concerns as well?

6. The Court notes in *Bob Jones University* that "Many of the *amici curia*...argue that denial of tax-exempt status to racially discriminatory schools is independently required by the equal protection component of the Fifth Amendment," but states that "[i]n light of our resolution of this case, we do not reach that issue." What are the theoretical underpinnings of such an argument? Does it depend for its validity on the assertion that other taxpayers can be said to be indirect and vicarious "donors" whenever the government grants a tax exemption?

7. What do you make of the Court's argument that the Internal Revenue Code incorporates the common law of charities? Consider the statute itself. I.R.C. §501(c)(3) is written in the disjunctive, and permits an exemption from the corporate tax for

> religious, charitable, scientific, testing for public safety, literary, or educational purposes, or to foster national or international amateur sports competition (but only if no part of its activities involve the provision of athletic facilities or equipment), or for the prevention of cruelty to children or animals, no part of the net earnings of which inures to the benefit of any private shareholder or individual.

Would it be accurate to describe all these functions as "charitable"? Does each of them serve a public purpose?

8. One holding of the *Bob Jones* case is that I.R.C. §§170 and 501(c)(3) should be read in all cases as incorporating the common law of charities. As the opinions Justices Powell and (now Chief) Justice Rehnquist indicate, such a holding would create substantial interpretive problems. One of the most significant of these is the source of com-

mon law on which either the courts or the IRS would rely in administering the statute. *Compare Erie Railroad Co. v. Tompkins*, 304 U.S. 64 (1938), *overruling Swift v. Tyson*, 41 U.S. (16 Pet.) 1 (1842) (holding that there is no federal common law) *with Clearfield Trust Co. v. United States*, 318 U.S. 363 (1943) (holding that federal "common law" arises as a result of the interpretation of statutes). Can Congress, if it so desires, make the Code itself the exclusive source of "public policy" in the tax field?

9. Are §§ 170 and 501(c)(3) statutes of "general applicability" as that term is used in *Employment Div. v. Smith*? If so, is the problem with BJU's tax exemption (a) that the I.R.S. should not have granted it in the first place?; (b) that it has a racially discriminatory effect?; or (c) that it compels dissenting taxpayers to "support" actions or ideas they find morally abhorrent?

E. Does the First Amendment Require the Exercise of the Taxing Power?: Constitutional Limits on the Power of Legislatures to Exempt Churches and Religious Institutions from Taxes of General Applicability

Because the Court has held that tax exemptions are not constitutionally compelled unless the character or operation of the tax presents a clearly articulated danger to interests protected by the First Amendment, *see JSM* in § C(2), above, the initial question for a legislature is not whether churches and religious organizations *can* be taxed, but rather whether they *should* be. *See, e.g.*, Dean M. Kelley, Why Churches Should Not Pay Taxes (1977); D.B. Robinson, Should Churches Be Taxed? (1958); Alfred Balk, The Religion Bu$iness (1968) (collecting statements of religious organizations and discussing the problem of "unrelated business income"); Chester J. Antieau, Arthur T. Downey & Edward C. Roberts, Freedom from Federal Establishment: Formation and Early History of the First Amendment Religion Clauses 175–76 (1964) (discussing Colonial and early state practices).

Viewed from a legislative perspective, the question "Should churches and religious organizations be taxed?" involves a number of competing political, economic, and social values. Does imposing a specific kind of tax on religious organizations make economic sense? Is the revenue to be gained worth the political cost of asserting the government's power to collect it? Is taxing the church consistent the public's views on religious liberty?

Because courts will generally defer to legislative judgment concerning the subjects and levels of taxation, the religious liberty and tax policy questions which arise when a legislature decides *not* to tax religious activities are identical to those which arise when it decides to impose them: Is there any basis in the federal or state constitution for judicial review of a legislative judgment concerning the subject or level of a tax?

Where the issue is the power to *exempt* churches and religious institutions from taxes of general applicability, the federal constitutional question posed is the obverse of that presented in *JSM*: "Do the First and Fourteenth amendments *require* that churches and religious organizations or their activities be taxed?" *See Warren v. Commissioner*, 282 F.3d 1119 (9th Cir. 2002). Because state constitutions contain explicit exemptions for churches and religious organizations, such issues simply do not arise at the state level.

Before turning to a review of the cases, however, it will be necessary to examine several preliminary issues.

- What is a tax exemption, and how does it differ from a tax credit or deduction?
- To what extent should tax exemptions, tax credits, and tax deductions be equated with "subsidies"—the functional or economic equivalent of cash transfer payments—to those receiving them?

1. What Is a Tax "Exemption"?

A tax exemption reflects a decision by the taxing authority *not* to tax the persons, property, organizations, institutions, or activities. The reasons why specific exemptions exist are as varied as the kinds of exemptions themselves. They do, however, have a common purpose: to define the "subject" of the tax by drawing clear lines between and among that which is to be taxed or measured for purposes of taxation, and what is not to be taxed or which should be disregarded when computing the tax at issue.

The contours of exemptions vary in accordance with the nature of the tax and the purpose(s) of the exemption. Duties and excise taxes, for example, tend to be specific levies. The "subject" can be determined either by reference to that which *is* taxed, in which case the list of exemptions is implicit, or by examining the list of exemptions to determine the *actual* subject(s) of the levy in question. The limited exemption from the California Sales and Use Tax for sales of meals by religious organizations in *JSM*, Cal. Rev. & Taxation Code § 6363.5 (1996), provides a good example of this distinction. Standing alone, it can be viewed as a "religious exemption" from a tax on retail sales of meals; read in context, it is but one of a number of exemptions which, when read together, define the term "retail sale." *See* Cal. Rev. & Tax Code § 6361.5 (2001) (exempting student yearbooks); § 6362.3 (2001) (exempting certain newspaper and periodical subscriptions); § 6374 (2001) (exempting sale of meals to low-income elderly by nonprofit organizations); § 6359.3 (2001) (exempting flags sold by qualified veterans organizations); § 6369 (2001) (exempting certain medicines and medical equipment). *See also The Way International v. Limbach*, 50 Ohio St. 3d 76, 552 N.E.2d 908 (1990) (religious organization's sale of books and tapes for more than it paid for such items was not "business" rendering purchases subject to sales tax).

In federal income taxation the *subject* of the tax is the income-producing activity of the taxpayer: individuals and heads of households, corporations, estates and trusts, and other taxable entities. "Income" is the concept utilized to measure the amount of tax liability. Given the nature of an income tax, there are two relevant kinds of exemptions: (1) those that define the class of individuals, entities and organizations subject to the tax; and (2) those that are necessary to arrive at a proper measure of "income."

The first kind of exemption is self-explanatory: Congress differentiates among classes of taxpayers on the basis of its judgments concerning the wisdom (political or otherwise) of taxing them. Some of these exemptions are explicit. I.R.C. § 501 contains an extensive list of organizations that are exempt from the tax on corporations. Along with the organizations exempted by § 501(c)(3) discussed above, the list also includes civic leagues and other non-profit social welfare organizations [§ 501(c)(4)], labor organizations [§ 501(c)(5)], and political organizations [§ 527]. Other exemptions in this category are implicit, such as the exemptions for state governments, which are constitutionally immune, and for taxpayers and corporations in the "zero" bracket.

The second kind of exemption is necessary because of the nature of an income tax. Because the amount of the tax is calculated by reference to an income "base", both law and elemental tax fairness requires that "taxable income" (or the "tax base") be measured accurately. As a result, amounts which are exempt from tax, either by their nature or by legislative fiat, are deducted from gross receipts ("gross income") in order to derive the "taxable income" base upon which the tax is calculated. *See, e.g.,* I.R.C. § 1 (imposing a tax on individuals measured by taxable income); § 151 (personal exemption); § 162 (deduction of ordinary and necessary business expenses).

A *deduction* is thus a device utilized to arrive at a measure of taxable "income." A *credit* is a direct remission of some portion of the amount of tax due, and an *exemption* is a mechanism that helps to define the proper subject(s) of the tax.

2. Subsidy Theory: Are Tax Exemptions Subsidies?

a) Tax Exemptions as "Contributions" to Exempt Organizations

As you read the summary of *Walz v. Tax Commission*, which appears below, consider the economic and constitutional underpinnings of the plaintiff's theory "that the New York City Tax Commission's grant of an exemption to church property indirectly requires the appellant to make a contribution to religious bodies." Does a majority of the Court accept the premise that a tax exemption is the economic equivalent of a cash subsidy? Do you? *Walz* is excerpted in Chapter Five.

In *Walz v. Tax Commission*, 397 U.S. 664 (1970), the Supreme Court considered the constitutionality of Article 16, § 1, of the New York Constitution:

> Exemptions from taxation may be granted only by general laws. Exemptions may be altered or repealed except those exempting real or personal property used exclusively for religious, educational or charitable purposes as defined by law and owned by any corporation or association organized or conducted exclusively for one or more of such purposes and not operating for profit.

As implemented by § 420, subd. 1, of the Real Property Tax Law, the policy of New York was that

> Real property owned by a corporation or association organized exclusively for the moral or mental improvement of men and women, or for religious, bible, tract, charitable, benevolent, missionary, hospital, infirmary, educational, public playground, scientific, literary, bar association, medical society, library, patriotic, historical or cemetery purposes... and used exclusively for carrying out thereupon one or more of such purposes... shall be exempt from taxation as provided in this section.

A New York real property owner sought an injunction in the New York courts to prevent the New York City Tax Commission from granting property tax exemptions to religious organizations for religious properties used solely for religious worship. The essence of appellant's contention was that the New York City Tax Commission's grant of an exemption to church property indirectly requires the appellant to support religious worship and thereby violates the Establishment Clause of the First Amendment. The New York courts rejected the argument, and the Supreme Court affirmed in an opinion written by Chief Justice Warren Burger.

Holding that the "legislative purpose of the property tax exemption is neither the advancement nor the inhibition of religion," the majority considered a number of factors relevant to New York's decision to grant or deny tax exemptions. The state had granted exemptions to a broad class of property owned by nonprofit, quasi-public corporations, which included hospitals, libraries, playgrounds, scientific, professional, historical and patriotic groups. It considered such groups beneficial and stabilizing influences in community life, and provided a mechanism to review the tax status of both new and established organizations.

The Court conceded that "[g]ranting tax exemptions to churches necessarily operates to afford an indirect economic benefit," and that the administration of tax exemptions "also gives rise to some, but yet a lesser, involvement than taxing them," but that these factors alone did not bear any "genuine nexus between tax exemption and establishment of religion." A decision by the legislature to grant an exemption is, in the Court's view, a decision "simply [to[abstain[] from demanding that the church support the state."

> Determining that the legislative purpose of tax exemption is not aimed at establishing, sponsoring, or supporting religion does not end the inquiry, however. We must also be sure that the end result—the effect—is not an excessive government entanglement with religion. The test is inescapably one of degree. Either course, taxation of churches or exemption, occasions some degree of involvement with religion. Elimination of exemption would tend to expand the involvement of government by giving rise to tax valuation of church property, tax liens, tax foreclosures, and the direct confrontations and conflicts that follow in the train of those legal processes.

Given these dangers, and the universal acceptance of tax exemptions for places of worship by Congress and all fifty states, the Court concluded "that federal or state grants of tax exemption to churches were not a violation of the Religion Clauses of the First Amendment."

Concurring, Justice Brennan suggested that the Court's reliance on history was misplaced. He observed that "[t]he existence from the beginning of the Nation's life of a practice, such as exemptions for religious organizations, is not conclusive of its constitutionality," but conceded that "it seems clear that...exemptions [for churches] were not among the evils that the Framers and Ratifiers of the Establishment Clause sought to avoid." Believing that the Court should reconsider the question, he suggested that

> Government has two basic secular purposes for granting real property tax exemptions to religious organizations. First, these organizations are exempted because they, among a range of other private, nonprofit organizations contribute to the well-being of the community in a variety of nonreligious ways, and thereby bear burdens that would otherwise either have to be met by general taxation, or be left undone, to the detriment of the community. [G]overnment [also] grants exemptions to religious organizations because they uniquely contribute to the pluralism of American society by their religious activities.

These benefits, he believed, are the *quid pro quo* that supports the government's decision to grant a *form* of subsidy to religious organizations. But he rejected the taxpayer's claim that exemptions are the *equivalent* of a subsidy. In his view

> Tax exemptions and general subsidies, however, are qualitatively different. Though both provide economic assistance,[9] they do so in fundamentally different ways. A subsidy involves the direct transfer of public monies to the subsidized enterprise and uses resources exacted from taxpayers as a whole. An exemption, on the other hand, involves no such transfer. It assists the exempted enterprise only passively, by relieving a privately funded venture of the burden of paying taxes.

The majority, however, took pains to distance itself from Justice Brennan's rationale.

> We find it unnecessary to justify the tax exemption on the social welfare services or "good works" that some churches perform for parishioners and others. Churches vary substantially in the scope of such services; programs expand or contract according to resources and need. To give emphasis to so variable an aspect of the work of religious bodies would introduce an element of governmental evaluation and standards as to the worth of particular social welfare programs, thus producing a kind of continuing day-to-day relationship which the policy of neutrality seeks to minimize. Hence, the use of a social welfare yardstick as a significant element to qualify for tax exemption could conceivably give rise to confrontations that could escalate to constitutional dimensions.

Dissenting, Justice Douglas zeroed in on the essence of the taxpayer's complaint:

> The financial support rendered here is to the church, the place of worship. A tax exemption is a subsidy. Is my Brother Brennan correct in saying that we would hold that state or federal grants to churches, say, to construct the edifice itself would be unconstitutional? What is the difference between that kind of subsidy and the present subsidy?
>
> State aid to places of worship, whether in the form of direct grants or tax exemption, takes us back to the Assessment Bill and the Remonstrance. The church *qua* church would not be entitled to that support from believers and from nonbelievers alike. Yet the church *qua* nonprofit, charitable institution is one of many that receive a form of subsidy through tax exemption.
>
> Churches perform some functions that a State would constitutionally be empowered to perform. I refer to nonsectarian social welfare operations such as the care of orphaned children and the destitute and people who are sick. A tax exemption to agencies performing those functions would therefore be as constitutionally proper as the grant of direct subsidies to them. Under the First Amendment a State may not, however, provide worship if private groups fail to do so.

Echoing the concerns voiced in the early 1870s by President Grant, Justice Douglas observed that "[t]he religiously used real estate of the churches today constitutes a vast domain. Their assets total over $141 billion and their annual income at least $22 billion.

---

9. In certain circumstances, of course, the economic value of a subsidy exceeds that of an exemption. If the only state assistance received by a religious organization is a real property tax exemption, the church must raise privately every cent that it spends. If, on the other hand, the only state aid to a church is a general subsidy, the church is relieved of the need to support itself to the extent that its subsidy payments from the State exceed its tax payments to the State. Thus, to take the extreme case, a lightly taxed religious organization that received a large, general subsidy could purchase property, construct buildings and maintain its program wholly at public expense. Such dependence on state support is impossible when the only aid provided is a real property tax exemption. [Footnote by Justice Brennan].

And the extent to which they are feeding from the public trough in a variety of forms is alarming."

Notes

1. Most of the controversies involving the constitutionality, political legitimacy, or economic rationality of tax exemptions have been around for many years. One of the first reported cases involving an attempt by a state taxpayer to have the judiciary nullify an exemption statute is *Trustees of Griswold College v. State,* 46 Iowa 275 (1877). The argument in the *Griswold College* case was twofold: first, that the legislature lacked specific constitutional authority to *grant* tax exemptions to churches, and second, that since article I, section 3 of the Iowa Constitution provides that no "person [shall] be compelled to attend any place of worship, pay tithes, taxes, or other rates for building or repairing places of worship, or the maintenance of any minister, or ministry," the legislative grant of a tax exemption had the effect of a compelled contribution to churches. Drawing a distinction between the levying of tithes, assessments, taxes, or other rates for church purposes (the practice in Virginia which led to Madison's *Memorial and Remonstrance Against Religious Assessments*), the Iowa Supreme Court rejected the claim. Other courts have followed suit.

2. Based on your reading of the opinions in *Walz,* how would you answer the following questions?

a) What are the reasons why States grant tax exemptions to churches?

b) What reasons would support a decision by a legislature to *deny* a tax exemption to churches or religious organizations?

c) How, if at all, would the reasons for exempting (or taxing) churches differ from those that apply to charities and educational institutions?

d) To what extent do the reasons identified above constitute a rational basis for distinguishing, for tax purposes, between and among the religious, charitable, educational activities declared exempt under the tax code, and other activities, which are not?

e) You will recall that a legislature can impose a tax selectively by listing the activities, persons, or entities subject to the tax. Those not listed are exempt. It can also impose a general tax, and shape its actual contours, or "subjects" via the creation of explicit exemptions. Does (or should) the *form* of the exemption make a difference in the constitutional analysis?

3. The argument that tax exemptions for churches or religious activities violate the Establishment Clause appears to depend on an assumption that tax exemptions are the functional equivalent of direct subsidies. If we assume, for purposes of analysis, that a majority of tax theorists argue that many, though not all, exemptions and deductions should be viewed as tax preferences which have the same economic effect as indirect cash subsidies, the implicit argument is that the economic *effect* of the exemption, rather than its intended purpose, should determine its constitutionality. *But see Employment Div. v. Smith,* 494 U.S. 872, 878 (1990) ("the First Amendment has not been offended" if generally applicable and otherwise valid legislation has the incidental effect of "prohibiting the free exercise of religion."); *Washington v. Davis,* 426 U.S. 229 (1976) (holding that proof of intent, rather than effect, is essential to an equal protection claim). *Smith* is excerpted in Chapter Five.

4. Should the courts hold that a tax exemption *limited* to religious activities or property violate the Establishment Clause? Why? Does this mean that the legislature *must* tax churches? Would such an exemption violate either the Equal Protection Clause or the equal protection "component" of the Fifth Amendment's Due Process Clause? What rationale supports your conclusion?

5. To what extent should the Free Exercise Clause be viewed as providing a "compelling" justification for relieving religious institutions of the financial burdens that would be created were their activities subject to general taxation? In *Employment Div. v. Smith*, 494 U.S. 872 (1990), the Court took the position that it would not construe the Free Exercise Clause to require exemptions from statutes of general applicability, but that it would permit legislatures to create them. *But see Texas Monthly v. Bullock*, 489 U.S. 1 (1989) (rejecting Texas's argument that its sales tax exemption for sales of religious literature by religious organizations was a legitimate legislative accommodation of free exercise interests), excerpted below. What impact, if any, do these cases have on the vitality of the rule(s) announced in *Walz*?

6. Consider, once again, the characteristics of a "tax." If one of the essential characteristics of a tax is that it be "imposed by legislation," what happens when a dissenting taxpayer obtains a judicial decree holding a tax exemption for religious organizations or activities is unconstitutional? There are several possibilities.

The dissenting taxpayer could claim that the exemption should be expanded, and that a refund of the taxes it has paid under the unconstitutional tax provision is the appropriate remedy. In *Harper v. Virginia Dept. of Taxation*, 509 U.S. 86 (1993), the Supreme Court held that civil decisions of the Court apply retroactively, but reserved the question of whether Virginia owed a refund to federal retirees subjected to an unconstitutional tax on their benefits.

Another possibility is that the organizations or activities covered by the unconstitutional exemption should be subjected to the tax. In *Harper*, the Court held that "[i]n providing such relief, a State may either award full refunds to those burdened by an unlawful tax or issue some other order that 'create[s] *in hindsight* a nondiscriminatory scheme.'" *Id.* at 101 (emphasis added) Given the retroactive effect of judicial decrees, would it be legitimate for Congress or a State to assess and seek back taxes in such a context? Would it be politically expedient to do so if it were? In *United States v. Carleton*, 512 U.S. 26 (1994), the Court upheld Congress's retroactive elimination of a tax provision against a Fifth Amendment Due Process challenge, even though the retroactive change in the law cost the taxpayer involved in that case over $600,000. Though the Court indicated that the nature and extent of the burden were relevant to the analysis, it held, nevertheless, that as long as the retroactivity were rationally related to the government's interest in raising revenue, a Due Process challenge failed. Quoting Justice Stone's opinion in *Welch v. Henry*, 305 U.S. 134, 146–147 (1938), the Court held that "'[s]ince no citizen enjoys immunity from [the] burden [of paying taxes], its retroactive imposition does not necessarily infringe due process.'" 512 U.S. at 33.

The last option is for the legislature to rewrite the tax statute and to provide a remedy that seeks to accommodate all of the divergent interests. Which is the most appropriate remedy? The answer depends, at least in part, on the structure of the tax code itself. In *Harper*, the Court held that that "[t]he constitutional sufficiency of any remedy...turns (at least initially) on whether [state] law 'provide[s] a[n] [adequate] form of "predeprivation process," for example, by authorizing taxpayers to bring suit to enjoin imposition of a tax prior to its payment, or by allowing taxpayers to withhold payment and then interpose their objections as defenses in a tax enforcement proceeding.'" *Harper*, at 101–02.

Such remedies, however, are not always readily available under federal law. Consider, in this context, the importance of legislative prohibitions on judicial decrees that enjoin the collection of a tax. *See* 26 U.S.C. § 7421(a) (1996) (anti-tax injunction provision of Internal Revenue Code); 28 U.S.C. § 1341 ("The district courts shall not enjoin, suspend or restrain the assessment, levy or collection of any tax under State law where a plain, speedy and efficient remedy may be had in the courts of such State."); § 2201 (1996) (granting to district courts the power to issue declaratory judgments "except with respect to Federal taxes other than actions brought under section 7428 of the Internal Revenue Code of 1986").

7. Does an exempt taxpayer become "taxable" by virtue of a judicial decree holding its exemption unconstitutional? The Court has never directly answered this question, but it is important to distinguish cases in which the judiciary interprets the statute authorizing the tax to include the subject organization, and cases in which the judiciary seeks to impose the tax on subjects that the legislature did not intend to tax in the first instance.

The *Bob Jones University* case is an example of the first situation. The Internal Revenue Service took the position that, in addition to the specific requirements of Section 501, the Code *also* contains an implied "non-discrimination" proviso that authorized the revocation of the University's tax exemption. As a result, the University made the decision to pay the tax under protest and file suit for a refund. That strategy had two components. First, it challenged the authority of the IRS to collect the tax by questioning its construction of the statute. Second, and more importantly, the University challenged the authority of Congress to impose such a condition on a religiously affiliated educational institution.

Given the structure of the Internal Revenue Code, the University was in a difficult position. Any incorporated educational organization that does not meet the requirements for exemption under I.R.C. § 501(c)(3) is subject to the general corporate tax imposed by I.R.C. § 11. If the Service were correct in its construction of the statute, the *Code* authorized the collection of the tax *ab initio*. The University's only argument would be a free exercise claim that Congress could not validly prohibit race discrimination by exempt organizations.

The second situation involves cases where the organization, property, or activity is not *subject* to the tax in the first instance. The church property in *Walz* and the exempt-function "income" of churches under the Internal Revenue Code are examples of situations where the elimination of the exemption raises both separation of powers and federalism questions concerning the authority of the courts to mandate that taxes be imposed on subjects the legislature has specifically excluded. Compare *Warren v. Comm'r*, 212 F.3d 1119 (9th Cir. 2002) with P.L. 107-81 § 2(a), 116 Stat. 583 (May 20, 2002) (retroactive amendment to parsonage exclusion embodied in 26 U.S.C. § 107 and at issue in *Warren*).

This issue was addressed in passing in *Pollock v. Farmers' Loan & Trust Co.*, 157 U.S. 429 (1895), *on rehearing*, 158 U.S. 601 (1895), which invalidated the first federal personal income tax. Although the Court reached no conclusion on this question, Justices Field and Harlan did discuss it, and reached opposite conclusions.

Justice Harlan argued that an "unconstitutional part of the statute [is] severable from the remainder." If "the law in question is a general law providing a revenue for the government, their exemption of those items could be disregarded and such property taxed," even though "the legislature... evinced a purpose not to tax [the listed items]." 158 U.S. at 683. His assumption was that Congress would have wanted to impose the tax had it known of the Court's views concerning the exemptions.

Justice Field saw the issue quite differently: "The abrogation or repeal of an unconstitutional or illegal provision does not operate to create and give force to any enactment or part of an enactment which Congress has not sanctioned and promulgated." 157 U.S. at 600 (Field, J., concurring in initial opinion). In Justice Field's view, the Court's precedents stood only for the proposition "that the unconstitutional part of [an] enactment, which was separable from the remainder, could be omitted and the remainder enforced." Severability, he wrote, "is entirely different from the position here taken [by the parties], that exempted things can be taxed by striking out their exemption." For Justice Field, the question of what is to be assessed and collected depends solely upon "what Congress has otherwise affirmatively ordered." His focus was separation of powers:

> Nothing less can have the force of law. This court is impotent to pass any law on the subject. It has no legislative power. I am unable, therefore, to see how we can, by declaring an exemption or exception invalid, thereby give effect to provisions as though they were never exempted. The court by declaring the exemptions invalid cannot by any conceivable ingenuity give operative force as enacting clauses to the exempting provisions. That result is not within the power of man.

157 U.S. at 601 (Field, J. concurring in initial opinion).

As applied to the question raised here—whether religious organizations become taxable by operation of a judicial decree striking their exemptions—which of the two positions do you find to be more persuasive? In *Employment Div. v. Rogue Valley Youth for Christ*, 307 Or. 490, 770 P.2d 588 (1989), the Oregon Supreme Court invalidated Oregon's exclusion of services performed for a church and services performed by a minister of a church from employment covered by the state's unemployment compensation law. Although the state statutory provisions "intentionally mirror the corresponding federal statute," the Oregon court held that, had it been put to the choice, the Oregon legislature would have chosen to impose the tax on churches in order to maintain its tax credit under federal law.

8. Chief Justice Burger's opinion for the Court in *Walz* assumes that a decision to invalidate an exemption for church property would create as many constitutional problems as it solves. Do you agree? Does the approach taken by the Court in *JSM* address any of those problem? How, for example, should a state or local government deal with differences in property valuation attributable to design or ornamentation reflecting religious doctrine or tradition? It seems logical to assume, does it not, that, location aside, a sparsely-furnished Meeting House would be assessed as being worth "less" than a magnificent Gothic-style cathedral? Would it be legitimate to respond to such differentials by imposing a user-fee on churches in lieu of *ad valorem* property taxes? Although churches and "purely private charities" are exempt under Pennsylvania law, the City of Philadelphia has begun to experiment with the concept of "payments in lieu of taxes" in order to defray the costs of government associated with exempt properties. *See* City of Philadelphia, Report of the Mayor's Special Committee on "Payments-in-Lieu-of-Taxes" (PILOTs) and "Services-in-Lieu-of-Taxes" (SILOTs) (June 30, 1994).

9. Might any of the foreseeable consequences of taxing church property result in violations of either the Establishment Clause, the Free Exercise Clause, or the Speech and Press Clause? In *Texas Monthly v. Bullock*, excerpted below, the Court held that *Follett v. McCormick* and *Murdock v. Pennsylvania* should be understood as cases involving

unconstitutional prior restraints on activity protected by the First Amendment? What, for example, would be the free exercise implications of a tax seizure and sale of objects essential to a church's sacramental rituals, or of the books of scripture themselves?

10. In the final analysis, the basis of the Court's holding in *Walz* remains the subject of some dispute. Those who take the position that the First Amendment requires the taxation of churches and religious institutions rely on Justice Brennan's theory that tax exemptions are subsidies warranted only to the extent that they serve a public purpose. Those who take the position that the First Amendment is not offended by legislative decisions to exempt church activities and property, tend to rely on historical and constitutional arguments which rest on equal protection, free exercise, separation of powers, and federalism.

3. "Tax Expenditure" Theory and Its Impact in the Courts

When the Court decided *Walz* in 1970, it was divided over how to characterize tax exemptions for purposes of analysis under the First Amendment. The Court assumed that tax exemptions are a form of "support" for organizations which are not subject to tax, but it was not willing to accept the dissent's assumption that they should be equated with direct cash subsidies. By the time the Court decided *Regan v. Taxation with Representation of Washington*, 461 U.S. 540 (1983) [TWR], however, its ambivalence had disappeared:

> Both tax exemptions and tax deductibility [for 501(c)(3) organizations] are a form of subsidy that is administered through the tax system. A tax exemption has much the same effect as a cash grant to the organization of the amount of tax it would have to pay on its income. Deductible contributions are similar to cash grants of the amount of a portion of the individual's contributions.

Although the Court in *TWR* hastened to point out that "'[i]n stating that exemptions and deductions,... are *like* cash subsidies, we of course do not mean to assert that they are in all respects identical,'" *id.* at 544, n.5. (emphasis added), its assumptions illustrate the important role that tax and economic theory plays in current constitutional analysis. Tax Expenditure Theory (also called "Subsidy Theory") has had a profound impact on the courts' understanding of the economics of exemptions and deductions. Less clear, however, is whether the theory provides an adequate foundation for constitutional decision-making.

a) What Is a "Tax Expenditure"?

A "tax expenditure" is a device used to describe

> those special provisions of the federal income tax system which represent government expenditures made through that system to achieve various social and economic objectives. These special provisions provide deductions, credits, exclusions, exemptions, deferrals, and preferential rates, and serve ends similar in nature to those served by direct government expenditures or loan programs.

Stanley Surrey, *Tax Incentives as a Device for Implementing Government Policy: A Comparison with Direct Government Expenditures*, 83 Harv. L. Rev. 705, 706 (1970).

The concept was developed during the 1950s as an analytical device that seeks to determine the "cost" of government programs which do not involve the direct expenditure of funds. 1968 *Sec'y Treas. Ann. Rep. on the State of the Finances.* "Tax expenditure analysis explicitly recognizes that the federal income tax system consists of two parts. One part provides a structure for the raising of revenue, and the other part carries out social and economic goals that are independent of revenue raising goals." Donna Adler, *Tax Expenditure Analysis in Judicial Decision Making,* 28 Wake Forest L. Rev. 855, 860 (1993). Viewed through the lens of tax expenditure theory, government expenditures are either "direct" or "indirect."

"Direct" expenditures are actual transfer payments to, or on behalf of, persons, real or corporate. Their purposes are specific, and include such diverse expenditures as the purchase of missile systems, payments to farmers for surplus agricultural commodities and the transfer of those commodities to individuals as food assistance, or the payment of educational expenses for school children. The revenues *foregone* as a result of tax provisions designed to encourage socially beneficial activity are scored as "indirect" expenditures.

Because tax expenditure analysis counts revenues *foregone* in order to determine the total cost of government policies and programs, it is important to understand that the central purpose of tax expenditure theory is to define an appropriate "base" for the calculation of tax revenues. Once the appropriate base is determined, the expected revenue stream can be calculated by applying a rate to the base.

Determining whether a specific tax provision should be scored as structural part of the tax in question (and, hence, outside the "base"), or an indirect expenditure designed to make or implement social policy, is no easy task. "Tax expenditures" are any provisions that would not be a part of "the generally accepted structure of an income tax" under "widely accepted definitions of income and standards of business accounting." Surrey, *Tax Incentives* at 706. Thus, an understanding of "[t]ax expenditure analysis[] as applied to a particular tax, requires an understanding of the normative structure of that tax in order to determine whether a provision is a part of the structural or the tax expenditure component." Stanley S. Surrey & Paul R. McDaniel, TAX EXPENDITURES 3–4 (1985). Some tax provisions fall clearly in one category or another; others are a bit more difficult to classify.

b) Differentiating "Revenue" from "Social and Economic" Goals: What Are the Characteristics of a "Tax Expenditure"?

The tools that Congress uses to craft social policy in the tax code are familiar to anyone who has filled out an income tax return: deductions, credits, preferential or punitive tax rates, surtaxes, and other devices used to calculate the amount of tax payable by individual and organizational taxpayers.

The focus of tax expenditure theory is not the *nature* of the tool that is used, but rather the *reason* it is employed. "[T]ax expenditure analysis involves a definitional question: which tax rules are special provisions of the kind described above and therefore tax expenditures, and which tax rules are simply tax rules, that is, constitute the basic structure of an income tax system and thus are integral to having an income tax at all?" Stanley Surrey, *Federal Income Tax Reforms: The Varied Approaches Necessary to Replace Tax Expenditures with Direct Governmental Assistance*, 84 Harv. L. Rev. 352, 354 (1970). If the reason for the exemption or deduction is to arrive at an accurate measure of income, tax expenditure analysis posits that no "expenditure" of revenue otherwise payable to the government is involved. If, on the other hand, the purpose of the device utilized is to foster social policy goals, a provision that results in less revenue for the treasury is classified as "indirect spending" designed to achieve a socially useful goal. Hence, the term: tax "expenditure."

Because the Internal Revenue Code recognizes two kinds of taxpayers: (1) individuals, including heads of households and married couples; and (2) juridical entities created for a specific purpose, including, among others, corporations, trusts, estates, partnerships, foundations, unincorporated associations, and insurance companies, we will provide one example from each class of taxpayers to illustrate the concept *deductions*

Deductions Necessary to Arrive at a Fair Measure of "Taxable Income"

All individual taxpayers are familiar with deductions. The most basic are the standard deduction and personal exemptions permitted to individuals under I.R.C. §§63(c), 151–153, 26 U.S.C. §§63(c). 151–153 (2001) Deducted from one's gross income, their purpose is to arrive at a fair measure of income that takes the basic cost of living into account. The purpose of the deduction for ordinary and necessary business expenses under I.R.C. §162 and §212 is to arrive at an accurate measure of business or other income-producing activities. Unless the basic cost of living and producing income are excluded from the tax "base", an "income tax" becomes a "gross receipts tax."

Deductions that Provide Economic Incentives for Socially Useful Activity

I.R.C. §170, which figures prominently in the *Bob Jones University* case, permits a deduction for gifts to charitable, religious, educational, scientific, and other organizations exempt from tax under I.R.C. §501(c)(3). Because the reasons for allowing the charitable and other discretionary deductions do not reflect any inherent relationship between the deduction and the cost of producing the income generated by the taxpayer's efforts, deductions of this type are not *structural* components of the income tax. Their goal is to reduce the amount of tax payable for those who engage in the activity for which a deduction is permitted. The revenues *foregone* under such deductions are therefore scored as "tax expenditures."

Tax Credits

A tax credit is a rebate of a portion of taxes otherwise due from a taxpayer. It differs from a tax deduction in that the taxpayer's tax liability is calculated without regard to the credit. The tax credit is then applied to the total and reduces the amount due in accordance with a formula established in the legislation creating the credit.

Exempt Organizations

When the taxpayer is an organization, the analysis follows a similar pattern. In order to determine whether an organization is "exempt" from taxes, the analysis should begin with an analysis of the nature and extent of the organization's gross receipts. An organization can be exempt from taxes because it is in the "zero bracket," because it is constitutionally immune, or because the funds received are not counted as "income" for purposes of the Internal Revenue Code. *See, e.g.*, I.R.C. §§102 (excluding gifts); 118 (excluding contributions to the capital of a corporate taxpayer). In these situations, the exemption is "structural," in that, for reasons central to the tax code itself, the organization is not subject to tax.

An organization can also be exempt because Congress has decided that it belongs to a class of associations that should receive special tax treatment. I.R.C. § 501 contains an extensive list of such organizations. *See, e.g.*, I.R.C. § 501(c)(3) (religious, charitable, scientific, testing for public safety, literary, or educational organizations); § 501(c)(4) (civic leagues and other non-profit social welfare organizations); § 501(c)(5) (labor and horticultural organizations); § 527 (political organizations). Just as in the case of individuals, Congress has decided that it will forego, for reasons of public policy, the taxes that would otherwise be due from these organizations. The income *foregone* is therefore scored as a "tax expenditure."

Summing Up

Because its goal is to provide a means by which to measure the economic cost of using the tax code to promote socially useful behavior, tax expenditure theory does not recognize a conceptual difference between direct subsidies and tax expenditures. Its author, Stanley Surrey, believed that direct government expenditures provided a more efficient and open use of resources, and were preferable for that reason. In his view, "[t]he existing tax incentive for charitable giving could also be structured as a direct expenditure program, under which the Government would match an individual's contribution to charity with a proportional contribution of its own to the same charity." *Tax Incentives* at 714.

Surrey saw the problems his theory would cause for tax exempt religious institutions, but did not attempt to resolve them. "Where the charity was a religious institution, a direct government contribution would raise serious questions under the establishment of religion clause of the First Amendment. But such a direct subsidy should be considered constitutional if the present tax provision is, since there is no practical difference between the two." *Id.* at n.9.

Most of the current literature, including recent decisions of the Supreme Court, "accept[s] the basic concept that special exemptions from tax function as subsidies. The current debate focuses on whether particular items are correctly identified as tax expenditures, and whether incentive provisions are more efficient when structured as tax expenditures rather than direct spending programs." Adler, at 862 n.30. *See Rosenberger v. Rector & Visitors of the Univ. of Virginia*, 515 U.S. 819, 859–860 & nn. 4–5 (1995) (Thomas, J., concurring); *Cammarano v. United States*, 358 U.S. 498 (1959); *Slee v. Commissioner*, 42 F.2d 184 (2nd Cir. 1930).

4. The Constitutional Implications of Tax Expenditure Analysis

When the Supreme Court observed in *TWR* that "[i]n stating that exemptions and deductions,...are like cash subsidies,..., we of course do not mean to assert that they are in all respects identical," it drew a distinction between acknowledging tax expenditure theory as a device to prompt discussion of the relative merits of "direct" and "indirect" expenditures thought to be in the public interest, and adopting it as a comprehensive theory of taxation.

Because tax expenditure theory seeks to differentiate the structure of a tax from the economic "costs" incurred when the legislature manipulates the tax base to accomplish goals beyond the generation of revenue, it depends, like all theories, upon certain assumptions concerning both the nature of "income" and the proper scope of the tax base. It then utilizes those assumptions to construct what tax theorists call a "first-best," or economically optimum, approach to analyzing tax policy. *See* Daniel Shaviro, *Selective Limitations on Tax Benefits*, 56 U. Chi. L. Rev. 1189 (1989).

Economic efficiency is not the sole goal of tax policy, however. In some instances, the Constitution immunizes certain subjects from tax. It would not be appropriate, for example, to score the intergovernmental tax immunities shared by the federal and state governments as "tax expenditures" because the Supremacy Clause immunizes the federal government from the taxing power of the States, and the concept of federalism immunizes the governmental functions of the States from Congress's power to tax. A similar analysis would be applicable to exemptions required by the First Amendment. *See, e.g.*, *Follett v. McCormick* (concluding that excise tax on the privilege of preaching is a prior restraint); *Minneapolis Star & Tribune v. Commissioner of Revenue* (invalidating use tax on paper and ink).

In other instances, a political consensus exists that certain properties, transactions, or entities should not be subject to tax, and the reasons for exempting them have little or nothing to do with "encouraging" socially useful activity. The earliest criticism of tax expenditure theory, in fact, was that because no tax is all-inclusive, any attempt to classify all exemptions as subsidies is simply wrong. *See* Bernard Wolfman, *Tax Expenditures: From Idea to Ideology*, 99 Harv. L. Rev. 491 (1985); Boris I. Bittker, *Churches, Taxes and the Constitution*, 78 Yale L.J. 1285 (1969). In this view, tax expenditure theory is an effective way to differentiate the "structural" and "social policy" provisions in the tax code, but it should not be assumed that it provides the *only* legitimate explanation for the existence of tax exemptions.

Other authors challenged Surrey's assumptions, and sought to show that tax expenditure theory did not offer a useful thesis to explain why churches and charities are exempt from taxation. Boris Bittker and George Rahdert, for example, developed an "Income Measurement Theory" which they proffered as a more complete explanation of tax exemptions than tax expenditure theory. Income Measurement Theory posits that nonprofit organizations are exempt from taxation for two basic reasons. The first is that the main source of income of most religious and charitable groups is gifts, which are not taxable, and this fact creates inherent difficulties in measuring their net income. The second reason is the nature of their activity. Their capital inflows are expended in ways that are not motivated by profit, and there are other significant reasons why the organizations themselves should not be subject to income taxation. *See* Boris I. Bittker & George K. Rahdert, *The Exemption of Nonprofit Organizations from Federal Income Taxation*, 81 Yale L.J. 299, 308–310 (1976).

5. Applying Theory to Practice: Tax Subsidy Theory in the Courts

The discussion of Tax Expenditure and Income Measurement Theory indicates that the terminology of debates over tax exemptions has changed since the days when courts and legislatures were attempting to develop a rationale for the tradition of exempting churches, religious organizations and charities from taxes. In fact, the debates over Subsidy Theory can be viewed as part and parcel of a continuing debate over whether such organizations should be taxed. The present-day "economic" approach thus seems to take two points for granted that were very much in issue when most religious and charitable exemptions were initially adopted:

1. That the taxing system is (or can be) used as a system for accomplishing social goals as well as generating revenue; and
2. That exemptions, deductions and credits should be treated as economic equivalents; that is, as alternative means of accomplishing identifiable social goals through the taxing structure.

When Congress enacted the first income tax exemptions for religious organizations in the late nineteenth century, and created the deductions for such organizations in the mid-1930s, the assumption was far more traditional. The floor debates over the Revenue Act of 1894 and the phrasing of the exemptions included in Section 59 of the Act can be read as an indication that Congress did not intend to impose any tax whatever when it granted the exemptions. The exemption applicable to religious institutions was phrased as follows:

> That nothing herein contained *shall apply* to... corporations, companies, or association organized and conducted solely for charitable, religious, or educational purposes... nor to the stocks, shares, funds, or securities held by any fiduciary or trustee for charitable, religious, or educational purposes.

28 Stat. 556 (1894) (Ch. 349, § 32) (emphasis added).

As you review the case that follows, consider the following questions:

1. Has Congress ever considered the question "Should the exempt functions or property of religious organizations be taxed?" on its merits?
2. Would such a decision be necessary in order to impose a tax on those functions?

Most of the cases involving the taxation of churches and religious organizations raise questions that are typical in any tax controversy: *Does the statute imposing the tax actually require the church or religious organization to pay it*? Because many of the issues which arise in tax law contexts turn on very specific statutes and rules, it is important to remember that unless the issue is either jurisdictional or presents other questions relating to the "facial validity" of the tax policy under either federal or state law, it is imperative to examine the statutory framework *before* turning to an examination of constitutional materials.

The same analysis holds true where the funding is alleged to be "indirect" via deductions or credits. Viewing the case as a "tax problem with potential constitutional implications" requires that the operation and outcome of the tax be examined before turning to an analysis of the constitutional issue. *See, e.g., Kotterman v. Killian*, 193 Ariz. 273, 972 P.2d 606 (1999) (en banc) (rejecting the proposition that a tax credit is the constitutional equivalent of an appropriation because the money *would* have entered the treasury "but for" the credit). *See generally* Erika King, *Tax Exemptions and the Establishment Clause*, 49 Syracuse L. Rev. 971 (1999).

Texas Monthly, Inc. v. Bullock

489 U.S. 1 (1989)

Justice BRENNAN announced the judgment of the Court and delivered an opinion, in which Justice MARSHALL and Justice STEVENS join.

Texas exempts from its sales tax "[p]eriodicals that are published or distributed by a religious faith and that consist wholly of writings promulgating the teaching of the faith and books that consist wholly of writings sacred to a religious faith." Tex. Tax Code Ann. § 151.312 (1982). The question presented is whether this exemption violates the Establishment Clause or the Free Press Clause of the First Amendment when the State denies a like exemption for other publications. We hold that, when confined exclusively to publications advancing the tenets of a religious faith, the exemption runs afoul of the Establishment Clause; accordingly, we need not reach the question whether it contravenes the Free Press Clause as well.

I

[In 1985] Appellant, Texas Monthly, Inc. paid sales taxes of $149,107.74 under protest and sued to recover those payments in state court.

The District Court, ruled that an exclusive exemption for religious periodicals had "no basis... other than the promotion of religion itself, a prohibited reason" under the Establishment Clause. The court also found the exemption unconstitutional because it discriminated on the basis of the content of publications, presumably in violation of the Free Press Clause. Declaring itself "without power to rewrite the statute to make religious periodicals subject to tax," the court struck down the tax as applied to nonreligious periodicals and ordered the State to refund the amount of tax Texas Monthly had paid, plus interest.

[Applying the tripartite test of *Lemon v. Kurtzman*, the Texas Court of Appeals reversed. It held that the exemption served the secular purpose of preserving separation between church and state, and that the exemption did not have the primary effect of advancing or inhibiting religion, because "the effect of religious tax exemptions... is to permit religious organizations to be independent of government support or sanction."] We noted probable jurisdiction, and now reverse.

III

In proscribing all laws "respecting an establishment of religion," the Constitution prohibits, at the very least, legislation that constitutes an endorsement of one or another set of religious beliefs or of religion generally. The core notion animating the requirement that a statute possess "a secular legislative purpose" and that "its principal or primary effect... be one that neither advances nor inhibits religion," *Lemon*, is not only that government may not be overtly hostile to religion but also that it may not place its prestige, coercive authority, or resources behind a single religious faith or behind religious belief in general, compelling nonadherents to support the practices or proselytizing of favored religious organizations and conveying the message that those who do not contribute gladly are less than full members of the community.

In [*Widmar v. Vincent*, *Mueller v. Allen*, and *Walz*], we emphasized that the benefits derived by religious organizations flowed to a large number of nonreligious groups as well. Indeed, were those benefits confined to religious organizations, they could not have appeared other than as state sponsorship of religion; if that were so, we would not have hesitated to strike them down for lacking a secular purpose and effect.

[W]e emphasized in *Walz* that the breadth of New York's property tax exemption was essential to our holding that it was "not aimed at establishing, sponsoring, or supporting religion," but rather possessed the legitimate secular purpose and effect of contributing to the community's moral and intellectual diversity and encouraging private groups to undertake projects that advanced the community's well-being and that would otherwise have to be funded by tax revenues or left undone. Moreover, "[t]he scheme

[was] not designed to inject any religious activity into a nonreligious context, as was the case with school prayers. No particular activity of a religious organization—for example, the propagation of its beliefs—[was] specially promoted by the exemptions."

Texas' sales tax exemption lacks sufficient breadth to pass scrutiny under the Establishment Clause. Every tax exemption constitutes a subsidy that affects nonqualifying taxpayers, forcing them to become "indirect and vicarious 'donors.'" [*Bob Jones University v. United States. See also Regan v. Taxation with Representation of Washington*] [W]hen government directs a subsidy exclusively to religious organizations that is not required by the Free Exercise Clause and that either burdens nonbeneficiaries markedly or cannot reasonably be seen as removing a significant state-imposed deterrent to the free exercise of religion, it "provide[s] unjustifiable awards of assistance to religious organizations" and cannot but "conve[y] a message of endorsement" to slighted members of the community. This is particularly true where, as here, the subsidy is targeted at writings that promulgate the teachings of religious faiths. It is difficult to view Texas' narrow exemption as anything but state sponsorship of religious belief, regardless of whether one adopts the perspective of beneficiaries or of uncompensated contributors.

How expansive the class of exempt organizations or activities must be to withstand constitutional assault depends upon the State's secular aim in granting a tax exemption. It is not our responsibility to specify which permissible secular objectives, if any, the State should pursue to justify a tax exemption for religious periodicals. That charge rests with the Texas Legislature. Our task, and that of the Texas courts, is rather to ensure that any scheme of exemptions adopted by the legislature does not have the purpose or effect of sponsoring certain religious tenets or religious belief in general.

IV

A

In defense of its sales tax exemption for religious publications, Texas claims that it has a compelling interest in avoiding violations of the Free Exercise and Establishment Clauses, and that the exemption serves that end. Without such an exemption, Texas contends, its sales tax might trammel free exercise rights, as did the flat license tax this Court struck down as applied to proselytizing by Jehovah's Witnesses in *Murdock v. Pennsylvania*. In addition, Texas argues that an exemption for religious publications neither advances nor inhibits religion, as required by the Establishment Clause, and that its elimination would entangle church and state to a greater degree than the exemption itself.

We reject both parts of this argument. Although Texas may widen its exemption consonant with some legitimate secular purpose, nothing in our decisions under the Free Exercise Clause prevents the State from eliminating altogether its exemption for religious publications. In this case, the State has adduced no evidence that the payment of a sales tax by subscribers to religious periodicals or purchasers of religious books would offend their religious beliefs or inhibit religious activity. The State therefore cannot claim persuasively that its tax exemption is compelled by the Free Exercise Clause in even a single instance, let alone in every case. No concrete need to accommodate religious activity has been shown.[8]

---

8. Texas' tax exemption does not remove a demonstrated and possibly grave imposition on religious activity sheltered by the Free Exercise Clause. Moreover, it burdens nonbeneficiaries by increasing their tax bills by whatever amount is needed to offset the benefit bestowed on subscribers to religious publications. The fact that such exemptions are of long standing cannot shield them from the strictures of the Establishment Clause. As we said in Walz v. Tax Comm'n, 397 U.S., at 678, "no

Moreover, even if members of some religious group succeeded in demonstrating that payment of a sales tax—or, less plausibly, of a sales tax when applied to printed matter—would violate their religious tenets, it is by no means obvious that the State would be required by the Free Exercise Clause to make individualized exceptions for them. [*United States v. Lee*] No one has suggested that members of any of the major religious denominations in the United States—the principal beneficiaries of Texas' tax exemption—could demonstrate an infringement of their free exercise rights sufficiently serious to overcome the State's countervailing interest in collecting its sales tax.

B

Texas' further claim that the Establishment Clause mandates, or at least favors, its sales tax exemption for religious periodicals is equally unconvincing. Not only does the exemption seem a blatant endorsement of religion, but it appears, on its face, to produce greater state entanglement with religion than the denial of an exemption.

On the record before us, neither the Free Exercise Clause nor the Establishment Clause prevents Texas from withdrawing its current exemption for religious publications if it chooses not to expand it to promote some legitimate secular aim.

C

Our conclusion today is admittedly in tension with some unnecessarily sweeping statements in *Murdock* and *Follett*. To the extent that language in those opinions is inconsistent with our decision here, based on the evolution in our thinking about the Religion Clauses over the last 45 years, we disavow it.

In *Murdock*, the Court ruled that a city could not impose a flat license tax payable by "all persons canvassing for or soliciting...orders for goods, paintings, pictures, wares, or merchandise of any kind" on Jehovah's Witnesses who "went about from door to door...distributing literature and soliciting people to 'purchase' certain religious books and pamphlets." In *Follett*, the Court ruled similarly that a Jehovah's Witness who "went from house to house distributing certain books" was exempt under the Free Exercise Clause from payment of a flat business and occupation tax on booksellers. In both cases, the majority stated that the "sale" of religious pamphlets by itinerant evangelists was a form of preaching, and that imposing a license or occupation tax on such a preacher was tantamount to exacting "a tax from him for the privilege of delivering a sermon." The Court acknowledged that imposing an income or property tax on preachers would not be unconstitutional. It emphasized, however, that a flat license or occupation tax poses a greater threat to the free exercise of religion than do those other taxes, because it is "levied and collected as a condition to the pursuit of activities whose enjoyment is guaranteed by the First Amendment" and thus "restrains in advance those constitutional liberties...and inevitably tends to suppress their exercise."

If one accepts the majority's characterization of the critical issues in *Murdock* and *Follett*, those decisions are easily compatible with our holding here. The sales tax that Texas imposes is not an occupation tax levied on religious missionaries. Nor is it a flat tax that "restrains in advance," the free exercise of religion. On the contrary, because the tax is equal to a small fraction of the value of each sale and payable by the buyer, it poses little danger of stamping out missionary work involving the sale of religious publications, and in view of

---

one acquires a vested or protected right in violation of the Constitution by long use, even when that span of time covers our entire national existence and indeed predates it."

its generality it can hardly be viewed as a covert attempt to curtail religious activity. We therefore see no inconsistency between our former decisions and our present holding.

To the extent that our opinions in *Murdock* and *Follett* might be read, however, to suggest that the States and the Federal Government may never tax the sale of religious or other publications, we reject those dicta. Our intervening decisions make clear that even if the denial of tax benefits "will inevitably have a substantial impact" on religious groups, the refusal to grant such benefits does not offend the Free Exercise Clause when it does not prevent those groups "from observing their religious tenets." *Bob Jones University*

V

We conclude that Texas' sales tax exemption for religious publications violates the First Amendment, as made applicable to the States by the Fourteenth Amendment. Accordingly, the judgment of the Texas Court of Appeals is reversed, and the case is remanded for further proceedings.

It is so ordered.

Justice WHITE, concurring in the judgment.

The Texas law at issue here discriminates on the basis of the content of publications. This is plainly forbidden by the Press Clause of the First Amendment.

Justice BLACKMUN, with whom Justice O'CONNOR joins, concurring in the judgment.

The Texas statute at issue touches upon values that underlie three different Clauses of the First Amendment: the Free Exercise Clause, the Establishment Clause, and the Press Clause. As indicated by the number of opinions issued in this case today, harmonizing these several values is not an easy task.

It perhaps is fairly easy to reconcile the Free Exercise and Press Clause values. If the Free Exercise Clause suggests that a State may not tax the sale of religious literature by a religious organization, this fact alone would give a State a compelling reason to exclude this category of sales from an otherwise general sales tax. In this respect, I agree generally with what Justice Scalia says in Part II of his dissenting opinion.

I find it more difficult to reconcile in this case the Free Exercise and Establishment Clause values. The Free Exercise Clause suggests that a special exemption for religious books is required. The Establishment Clause suggests that a special exemption for religious books is forbidden. This tension between mandated and prohibited religious exemptions is well recognized. Of course, identifying the problem does not resolve it.

Justice Brennan's opinion, in its Part IV, would resolve the tension between the Free Exercise and Establishment Clause values simply by subordinating the Free Exercise value. Justice Scalia's opinion, conversely, would subordinate the Establishment Clause value. This position, it seems to me, runs afoul of the previously settled notion that government may not favor religious belief over disbelief.

Perhaps it is a vain desire, but I would like to decide the present case without necessarily sacrificing either the Free Exercise Clause value or the Establishment Clause value. It is possible for a State to write a tax-exemption statute consistent with both values: for example, a state statute might exempt the sale not only of religious literature distributed by a religious organization but also of philosophical literature distributed by nonreligious organizations devoted to such matters of conscience as life and death, good and evil, being and nonbeing, right and wrong. Such a statute, moreover, should survive Press Clause scrutiny because its exemption would be narrowly tailored to meet the compelling interests that underlie both the Free Exercise and Establishment Clauses.

To recognize this possible reconciliation of the competing First Amendment considerations is one thing; to impose it upon a State as its only legislative choice is something else. I believe we can avoid most of these difficulties with a narrow resolution of the case before us. We need decide here only whether a tax exemption limited to the sale of religious literature by religious organizations violates the Establishment Clause. I conclude that it does.

Justice SCALIA, with whom the CHIEF JUSTICE [REHNQUIST] and Justice KENNEDY join, dissenting.

As a judicial demolition project, today's decision is impressive. The machinery employed by the opinions of Justice Brennan and Justice Blackmun is no more substantial than the antinomy that accommodation of religion may be required but not permitted, and the bold but unsupportable assertion... that government may not "convey a message of endorsement of religion."

I dissent because I find no basis in the text of the Constitution, the decisions of this Court, or the traditions of our people for disapproving this longstanding and widespread practice.

I

Justice Brennan explains away *Walz* by asserting that "[t]he breadth of New York's property tax exemption was essential to our holding that it was 'not aimed at establishing, sponsoring, or supporting religion.'" This is not a plausible reading of the opinion. The finding of valid legislative purpose was not rested upon [the breadth of the exemption], but upon the more direct proposition that "exemption constitutes a reasonable and balanced attempt to guard against" the "latent dangers" of governmental hostility towards religion "inherent in the imposition of property taxes."

Moreover, if the Court had intended to rely upon a "breadth of coverage" rationale, it would have had to identify some characteristic that rationally placed religion within the same policy category as the other institutions. The Court's opinion in *Walz*, however, not only failed to conduct such an analysis, but—seemingly in reply to the concurrences—explicitly and categorically disavowed reliance upon it, concluding its discussion of legislative purpose with a paragraph that begins as follows: "We find it unnecessary to justify the tax exemption on the social welfare services or 'good works' that some churches perform for parishioners and others." This should be compared with today's rewriting of *Walz*: "[W]e concluded that the State might reasonably have determined that religious groups generally contribute to the cultural and moral improvement of the community, perform useful social services, and enhance a desirable pluralism of viewpoint and enterprise, just as do the host of other nonprofit organizations that qualified for the exemption." This is a marvelously accurate description of what Justices Brennan and Harlan believed, and what the Court specifically rejected. The Court did not approve an exemption for charities that happened to benefit religion; it approved an exemption for religion as an exemption for religion.

In repudiating what *Walz* in fact approved, they achieve a revolution in our Establishment Clause jurisprudence. Breadth of coverage is essential to constitutionality whenever a law's benefiting of religious activity is sought to be defended not specifically (or not exclusively) as an intentional and reasonable accommodation of religion, but as merely the incidental consequence of seeking to benefit all activity that achieves a particular secular goal. But that is a different rationale—more commonly invoked than accommodation of religion but, as our cases show, not preclusive of it. Where accommodation of religion is the justification, by definition religion is being singled out. However the reconciliation with the *Lemon* [test] is achieved, our cases make plain that it is permissible for a State to act with the purpose and effect of "limiting governmental interference with the exercise of religion." *Corporation of Presiding Bishop.*

It is not always easy to determine when accommodation slides over into promotion, and neutrality into favoritism, but the withholding of a tax upon the dissemination of religious materials is not even a close case. The subjects of the exemption before us consist exclusively of "writings promulgating the teaching of the faith" and "writings sacred to a religious faith." If there is any close question, it is not whether the exemption is permitted, but whether it is constitutionally compelled in order to avoid "interference with the dissemination of religious ideas."

Unlike the Texas exemption for sacred books, which, on its face at least, applies to all sales, the exemption for periodicals applies to material that not only "consist[s] wholly of writings promulgating the teaching of [a religious] faith," but also is "published or distributed by [that] faith." Surely this is material distributed by missionaries. Unless, again, one wishes to trivialize [*Follett* and *Murdock*], whether they are full-time or part-time missionaries can hardly make a difference, nor can the fact that they conduct their proselytizing through the mail or from a church or store instead of door-to-door.

I am willing to acknowledge, however, that *Murdock* and *Follett* are narrowly distinguishable. But what follows from that is not the facile conclusion that therefore the State has no "compelling interest in avoiding violations of the Free Exercise and Establishment Clauses," and thus the exemption is invalid.

The Court has consistently rejected "the argument that any program which in some manner aids an institution with a religious affiliation" violates the Establishment Clause. To be sure, we have set our face against the subsidizing of religion—and in other contexts we have suggested that tax exemptions and subsidies are equivalent. *E.g.*, *Bob Jones University v. United States*; *Regan v. Taxation With Representation of Washington*. We have not treated them as equivalent, however, in the Establishment Clause context, and with good reason.

> In the case of direct subsidy, the state forcibly diverts the income of both believers and nonbelievers to churches. In the case of an exemption, the state merely refrains from diverting to its own uses income independently generated by the churches through voluntary contributions. Giannella, *Religious Liberty, Nonestablishment, and Doctrinal Development*, 81 Harv. L. Rev. 513, 553 (1968).

II

Having found that this statute does not violate the Establishment Clause of the First Amendment, I must consider whether it violates the Press Clause.

The tax exemption at issue in *Arkansas Writer's Project v. Ragland*, which we held to be unconstitutional because content based, applied to trade publications and sports magazines along with religious periodicals and sacred writings, and hence could not be justified as an accommodation of religion. If the purpose of accommodating religion can support action that might otherwise violate the Establishment Clause, I see no reason why it does not also support action that might otherwise violate the Press Clause or the Speech Clause. To hold otherwise would be to narrow the accommodation principle enormously, leaving it applicable to only nonexpressive religious worship. I do not think that is the law. Just as the Constitution sometimes requires accommodation of religious expression despite not only the Establishment Clause but also the Speech and Press Clauses, so also it sometimes permits accommodation despite all those Clauses. Such accommodation is unavoidably content based—because the Freedom of Religion Clause is content based.

Today's decision introduces a new strain of irrationality in our Religion Clause jurisprudence. It is not right—it is not constitutionally healthy—that this Court should feel authorized to refashion anew our civil society's relationship with religion, adopting a theory of church and state that is contradicted by current practice, tradition, and even our own case law. I dissent.

Notes

1. Now that you have had an opportunity to examine the law governing the tax status of churches and religious institutions, what role has tax and economic theory played in the development of the law? Given the inherently political nature of tax policy, it can be argued that the courts should be wary of constitutionalizing economic and political theories that have little to do with the actual practice and politics of tax law. *See generally* Marjorie E. Kornhauser, *The Constitutional Meaning of Income and the Income Taxation of Gifts*, 25 Conn. L. Rev. 1 (1992). A good example is the *Bob Jones University* litigation, in which the courts compelled the IRS to change long-standing policy concerning qualifications for "charitable" status under I.R.C. §501(c)(3). If viewed *purely* as a "race" case, the decision is uncontroversial, for there are few public policies so strongly affirmed in the Constitution as the ban on racial discrimination. If viewed *purely* as a tax case—*i.e.* without the "race" factor, the case raises substantial issues concerning the power of federal judges and tax administrators to create and enforce a "common law" of charities alleged to be lurking within the interstices of the Internal Revenue Code. It was a dispute over IRS and judicial authority to impose conditions on tax exemptions not enacted by Congress, rather than a willingness to countenance race discrimination, which led both Justices Powell and Rehnquist to part company with the majority in *Bob Jones University*. And they raise a valid question: if the Code is clear, what role is there for judicial intervention? *Cf. United States v. Little Lake Misere Land Co., Inc.*, 412 U.S. 580, 593 (1973) (noting that "the inevitable incompleteness presented by all legislation means that interstitial federal lawmaking is a basic responsibility of the federal courts.") *See generally* Paul Mishkin, *The Variousness of "Federal Law": Competence and Discretion in the Choice and National and State Rules for Decision*, 105 U. Pa.L. Rev. 797, 800 (1957) (arguing that "effective Constitutionalism requires recognition of power in the federal courts to declare, as a matter of common law or 'judicial legislation,' rules which may be necessary to fill in interstitially or otherwise effectuate the statutory patterns enacted in the large by Congress.").

2. In Justice Brennan's view, a valid legislative exemption from a tax rule of general applicability needs to remove "a demonstrated and possibly grave imposition on religious activity." Why such a strict standard? Justice Brennan dissented when the Court held, in *Employment Div. v. Smith*, that it would limit the holding in *Sherbert v. Verner* to cases involving "case-by-case" administrative determinations. Does the holding in *Sherbert* require that burdens on free exercise rights be "demonstrated and possibly grave"? Are tax determinations "case-by-case"?

3. Congress is very solicitous of the tax-exempt status of churches. Consider the following excerpt from the Church Audit Procedures Act, 26 U.S.C. §7611 (2001) [CAPA].

§7611. Restrictions on church tax inquiries and examinations

(a) Restrictions on inquiries.—

(1) In general.—

The Secretary may begin a church tax inquiry only if—

(A) the reasonable belief requirements of paragraph (2), and

(B) the notice requirements of paragraph (3), have been met.

(2) reasonable belief requirements.—The requirements of this paragraph are met with respect to any church tax inquiry if an appropriate high-level Treasury official reasonably believes (on the basis of facts and circumstances recorded in writing) that the church—

(A) may not be exempt, by reason of its status as a church, from tax under section 501(a), or

(B) may be carrying on an unrelated trade or business (within the meaning of section 513) or otherwise engaged in activities subject to taxation under this title.

Why do you think churches rate such special treatment? Does it underscore the possibility (because no court has yet addressed the question directly) that the exempt activities of churches are not proper *subjects* for taxation under the Code? *See generally* Wendy Gerzog Shaller, *Churches and their Enviable Tax Status*, 51 U. Pitt. L. Rev. 345 (1990). The Act, however, applies *only* to the church itself. *See, e.g.*, Branch Ministries v. Rossotti, 211 F.3d 137, 141 (D.C. Cir. 2000); *Kerr v. United States*, 801 F.2d 1162 (9th Cir. 1986) (CAPA does not apply to IRS audit of taxpayer who was trustee and founder of church); *In re Faith Missionary Baptist Church*, 174 B.R. 454 (Bkr. E.D. Tex. 1994) (CAPA not applicable to investigation to determine whether a church, organized and operating as an unincorporated association, was the alter ego of individual taxpayers who established the church).

4. Assuming, for purposes of argument, that Congress did *not* intend to tax the religious activities of churches, is it constitutional for Congress to attempt to control what clergy say from the pulpit concerning politics, political parties, and legislation? I.R.C. §§501(c)(3) and 501(h) impose what are commonly known as "political activity restrictions" on organizations exempt under §501(c)(3). Do they apply to churches?

In **Branch Ministries v. Rossotti**, 211 F.3d 137, 141 (D.C. Cir. 2000), the Internal Revenue Service revoked the tax exemption of a church that placed full-page advertisements in *USA Today* and the *Washington Times* four days before the 1992 presidential election. Each advertisement bore the headline "Christians Beware" and asserted that then-Governor Clinton's positions concerning abortion, homosexuality, and the distribution of condoms to teenagers in schools violated Biblical precepts. The ads also bore the legend: "This advertisement was co-sponsored by the Church at Pierce Creek, Daniel J. Little, Senior Pastor, and by churches and concerned Christians nationwide. Tax-deductible donations for this advertisement gladly accepted. Make donations to: The Church at Pierce Creek. [mailing address]."

The church argued that the IRS lacked the statutory authority to revoke the tax exemption of a bona fide church because I.R.C. §501(c)(3) "refers to tax-exempt status for religious organizations, not churches; section 508, on the other hand, specifically exempts 'churches' from the requirement of applying for advance recognition of tax-exempt status, *id.* § 508(c)(1)(A); therefore, according to the Church, its tax-exempt status is derived not from section 501(c)(3), but from the lack of any provision in the Code for the taxation of churches."

Finding this argument "more creative than persuasive" in light of the fact that this particular church had applied for, and been granted, 501(c)(3) status, the D.C. Circuit held that CAPA

> provides authority for revocation of the tax-exempt status of a church through its references to other sections of the Internal Revenue Code. The section of CAPA entitled "Limitations on revocation of tax-exempt status, etc." provides that the Secretary of the Treasury may "determine that an organization is not a church which [ ] (i) is exempt from taxation by reason of section 501(a), or (ii) is described in section 170(c)." 26 U.S.C. § 7611(d)(1)(A)(i), (ii). Both of these sections condition tax-exempt status on non-intervention in political campaigns. Section 501(a) states that "[a]n organization described in subsection (c)... shall be exempt from taxation."

Branch Ministries, 211 F.3d at 141. *See generally* Wendell R. Bird & Thomas O. Kotouc, *Exempt Religious Organizations Have Strict Limits*, 48 Tax'n for Acct. 207 (1992).

The D.C. Circuit also rejected the church's claims under the Free Exercise Clause, holding that

> The sole effect of the loss of the tax exemption will be to decrease the amount of money available to the Church for its religious practices. The Supreme Court has declared, however, that such a burden "is not constitutionally significant." [citing *Swaggart Ministries* and *Hernandez*]. In actual fact, even this burden is overstated. Because of the unique treatment churches receive under the Internal Revenue Code, the impact of the revocation is likely to be more symbolic than substantial. As the IRS confirmed at oral argument, if the Church does not intervene in future political campaigns, it may hold itself out as a 501(c)(3) organization and receive all the benefits of that status. All that will have been lost, in that event, is the advance assurance of deductibility in the event a donor should be audited.
>
> Nor does the revocation necessarily make the Church liable for the payment of taxes. As the IRS explicitly represented in its brief and reiterated at oral argument, the revocation of the exemption does not convert bona fide donations into income taxable to the Church. *See* 26 U.S.C. § 102 ("Gross income does not include the value of property acquired by gift.").

Branch Ministries, 211 F.3d at 142–143. The court also rejected the church's selective prosecution claim, holding that even if it had been able to prove that the IRS took no action on violations by other churches, Branch Ministries "failed to demonstrate that it was similarly situated to any of those other churches [because] [n]one of the reported activities involved the placement of advertisements in newspapers with nationwide circulations opposing a candidate and soliciting tax deductible contributions to defray their cost." *Id.* at 144.

After *Rossotti*, what advice would you give a preacher who wants to preach or write on a political issue or candidate? Because of its facts, the concessions made by the IRS, and the language of the relevant statutes, it seems clear that *Rossotti* will not be the last word on the subject, either by courts or commentators. *See generally* Deirdre Dessingue, *Prohibition in Search of a Rationale: What the Tax Code Prohibits; Why; to What End?*, 42 B.C.L. Rev. 903 (2001); Randy Lee, *When a King Speaks of God; When God Speaks to a King: Faith, Politics, Tax Exempt Status, and the Constitution In The Clinton Administration,* Law & Contemp. Probs. 391 (Winter/Spring 2000); Miriam Galston, *Lobbying and the Public Interest: Rethinking the Internal Revenue Code's Treatment of Legislative Activities*, 71 Tex. L. Rev. 1269 (1993).

Chapter 10

The Secular State, Civil Society and Religious Morality

The conflict of religious values with the values prized by the dominant culture is one of the recurring themes in the history of law and religion in America. One occasion in which this conflict arose was in 1940 in *Minersville Sch. Dist. v. Gobitis*, 310 U.S. 586 (1940), excerpted in Chapter One § B. School children who refused to salute the American flag because of their religious convictions as Jehovah's Witnesses were expelled from school. For Justice Felix Frankfurter, who authored the opinion upholding the expulsion against a constitutional challenge, "[t]he flag is the symbol of our national unity, transcending all internal differences, however large, within the framework of the Constitution." *Gobitis*, 310 U.S. at 596. The use of "transcending," a word of religious devotion, suggests the manner in which Frankfurter manifested his "faith" in the American democratic experiment. The conflict between secular and religious faiths has continued throughout the years since *Gobitis* was issued, and forms the theme of this chapter.

In *Brown v. Board of Educ.*, 347 U.S. 483, 493 (1954), Chief Justice Warren wrote:

> Today, education is perhaps the most important function of state and local governments.... It is the very foundation of good citizenship. Today it is a principal instrument in awakening the child to cultural values, in preparing him for later professional training, and in helping him to adjust normally to his environment. In these days, it is doubtful that any child may reasonably be expected to succeed in life if he is denied the opportunity of an education.

As noted by Chief Justice Warren, education both fosters the transmission of useful knowledge and shapes the values of the youngest members of the community in accordance with the values of the common culture. Nevertheless, in *Wisconsin v. Yoder*, 406 U.S. 205 (1972), excerpted in Chapter Five, the Supreme Court permitted Amish parents to remove their children from school before entering high school despite the legal requirement that children must attend school until at least age sixteen. This was required, according to the Court, because Amish religious values were not inconsistent with the state's interest in the education of the young. When the Constitution requires the state to defer to (or even affirmatively recognize) a claim of religious liberty in conflict with democratic values, and when the Constitution permits the state to ignore or override a claim of religious liberty, is the subject of this chapter.

One recurring issue in law and religion cases is whether the secular state must be neutral on questions of morals or values. Former President Clinton has argued "even though the schools can't advocate religious beliefs,..., they should teach mainstream values and virtues. The fact that some of these values happen to be religious values does not mean that they cannot be taught in our schools." This issue mirrors the broader debate between defenders of liberal political theory and their critics over the legitimacy of the state's decision to promote particular values in law. The cases in this chapter suggest that on some occasions the state must remain neutral, and forego favoring any particular value or virtue. On others it need not. When and why the state must remain neutral, and when and why it may take value-laden positions is often unclear. Whether or not such claims are constitutionally accepted tells us much about the relation of law, religion and government.

A. Political Participation by Religious Adherents

Notes

1. The following case, *McDaniel v. Paty*, concerns the constitutionality of a Tennessee statute barring "ministers of the Gospel" from serving as delegates to a state constitutional convention. Although the entirety of the Court agrees that this provision violates the federal constitution, there is no opinion of the Court. When reading the plurality opinions, analyze why this case so hard for the Court. One possibility may be a conflict of visions concerning the Court's role in interpreting of the Constitution. Another may be a conflict about the most important principles of the Constitution, or more particularly, a conflict about the most important principle of the First Amendment. A third may be a conflict concerning the constitutional command, if any, regarding the proper role of religious discourse in popular government. While one plurality opinion focuses primarily on avoiding political divisiveness by ensuring the separation of church and state, another focuses primarily on the claim of individual liberty, which includes the liberty to be religious and to act on those beliefs, and the third focuses on an equality norm prohibiting a distinction between the religious and the non-religious citizen.

The Court has always declared religious beliefs absolutely protected, and religious actions subject to some regulation. Determine whether the opinions below in *McDaniel v. Paty* clarify the meaning of the belief/action distinction.

Tennessee's statute was based on the prohibition included in its first constitution, adopted in 1796, barring Ministers of the Gospel from holding public office. Both the statute and the constitutional provision are premised on a clear distinction between the "religious" realm and the "secular" realm, and attempt to prevent the former from influencing the latter. Assess whether the opinions are based on the unwillingness of the authors to accept this distinction in whole or part, or whether the opinions are based on the inability of the authors to mark the boundary separating the "religious" from the "secular."

As acknowledged in Chief Justice Burger's plurality opinion, most states included in their earliest constitutions a prohibition against ministers holding public office. Does the Court's decision counsel that history should not be a guide for deciding cases concerning law and religion, or that history is just one of several guides?

2. In the 1960 campaign for President, Democratic nominee John Fitzgerald Kennedy, a Roman Catholic, spoke at a convention of Baptists in Houston, Texas shortly before the election. Among other things, Kennedy declared:

> I believe in an America where the separation of church and state is absolute—where no Catholic prelate would tell the President (should he be a Catholic) how to act and no Protestant minister would tell his parishioners for whom to vote—where no church or church school is granted any public funds or political preference....
>
> I believe in a President whose views on religion are his own private affair, neither imposed upon him by the nation or imposed by the nation upon him as a condition to holding that office.
>
> * * *
>
> I am not the Catholic candidate for President. I am the Democratic Party's candidate for President, who happens also to be a Catholic. I do not speak for my church on public matters—and the church does not speak for me.

John F. Kennedy, *Remarks on Church and State*, in CHURCH AND STATE IN AMERICAN HISTORY 190, 190–92 (2d ed. John F. Wilson & Donald L. Drakeman eds. 1987).

Ironically, Kennedy's election that fall was aided by public support from ministers at a number of black parishes, who appreciated his call to Coretta Scott King, Martin Luther King, Jr.'s wife, while the Rev. King was in jail.

Do Kennedy's remarks on the "private" nature of religious faith, or his claim that he "happens also to be Catholic," suggest that properly understood, religion should be cabined within a particular area of influence, or irrelevant to discussions of public policy? President Clinton also uses the language of "happenstance," but in a different manner: for him, the congruence of "mainstream values" with values that "happen to be religious" does not make the teaching of values constitutionally suspect. Is Kennedy's understanding of religion as a private matter separate from his public duties the kind of separation that the Establishment Clause was designed to ensure? Is Kennedy suggesting that a public official may hold religious convictions as long as they do not affect one's public actions? Then-President Clinton stated, "Religion has a proper place in private and a proper place in public because the public square belongs to all Americans." Do President Clinton's remarks modify the remarks made by then presidential candidate Kennedy? Are the claims made by Kennedy or Clinton themselves theological claims about the role of religion in public life? If Kennedy's or Clinton's claims about the proper "role" of religion in public life is a "theological" or "philosophical" position, is there any way this claim about "role" can be made without privileging either a "theological" or "philosophical" claim?

3. On the relation of the politician's commands of his faith and his duties as a politician, *compare* Mario M. Cuomo, *Religious Belief and Public Morality: A Catholic Governor's Perspective, Address at the University of Notre Dame (Sept. 13, 1984), in* 1 Notre Dame J.L. Ethics & Pub. Pol'y 13 (1984) *with* Henry J. Hyde, *Keeping God in the Closet: Some Thoughts on the Exorcism of Religious Values from Public Life, Address at the University of Notre Dame (Sept. 24, 1984), in id.* at 33. *See also Politics and Morality Are Inseparable, Remarks of President Ronald Reagan to the Ecumenical Prayer Breakfast, Dallas, Texas, August 23, 1984 in id.* at 7; Senator Edward M. Kennedy, *Faith and Freedom*, delivered at Tavern on the Green, New York City, before the Coalition of Conscience, September 10, 1984. *See generally* Edward M. Gaffney, *Biblical Religion and American Politics: Some Historical and Theological Reflections*, 1 J. L. & Rel. 171 (1983). For a discussion of the morality of using religious arguments in debates on political questions,

see Juha Räikkä, *The Place of Religious Arguments in Civic Discussion*, 13 Ratio Jurisp. 162 (2000).

4. If a legislator introduced a bill to regulate abortions, and explicitly argued for the bill's passage on religious grounds, would this violate the First Amendment? What if pressure by religious organizations was brought to bear on legislators to pass such legislation? In 1973, Professor Laurence H. Tribe suggested that there was an impermissible entanglement of religion and government "whenever the views of organized religious groups have come to play a pervasive role in an entire subject's legislative consideration for reasons intrinsic to the subject matter as then understood." Laurence H. Tribe, *The Supreme Court 1972 Term—Foreword: Toward a Model of Roles in the Due Process of Life and Law*, 87 Harv. L. Rev. 1, 23 (1973) (discussing authority of state to decide when life begins for purposes of legislating abortion). Professor Tribe has since concluded that this view is mistaken. *See* Laurence H. Tribe, *American Constitutional Law* § 15-10, at 1349–50 (2d ed. 1988). However, Justice John Stevens made a similar argument in *Webster v. Reproductive Health Serv.*, 492 U.S. 490, 566–72 (1989) (Stevens, J., concurring and dissenting) (concluding that legislative preamble declaring life begins at conception can be supported only by resort to theological premises, which violates Establishment Clause).

Can a right to procreative autonomy, including a right to an abortion, be claimed under the Free Exercise Clause? *See* Ronald Dworkin, Life's Dominion 160–68 (1993) (yes).

Should such arguments also apply to laws regulating assisted suicide and euthanasia? To laws concerning capital punishment? *See* Tom Stacy, *Death, Privacy, and the Free Exercise of Religion*, 77 Cornell L. Rev. 490, 557–63 (1992) (concluding question of death "quintessentially religious" and that Free Exercise interests are implicated in "right to die" cases such as *Cruzan v. Director, Missouri Dep't of Health*, 497 U.S. 261 (1990)).

5. Can or should lawmakers rely on religious arguments or justifications in making laws? An extraordinary amount of thoughtful writing concerning the proper and permissible role of religious convictions in a liberal polity has been published in the last decade. *See, e.g.*, Symposium, *The Religious Voice in the Public Square*, 29 Loy. L. Rev. 1401 (1996), and Symposium, *The Role of Religion in Public Debate in a Liberal Society*, 30 San Diego L. Rev. 643 *et seq.* (1993). *Compare* Michael Perry, Love and Power: The Role of Religion and Morality in American Politics (1991) *with* Kent Greenawalt, Religious Convictions and Political Choice (1988).

6. The "religious lawyering" movement, as suggested by its name, is an effort to show that lawyers can integrate their work and faith. *See generally* Russell G. Pearce, *Symposium: Foreword: The Religious Lawyering Movement: An Emerging Force in Legal Ethics and Professionalism*, 66 Fordham L. Rev. 1075 (1998); Samuel J. Levine, *Introductory Note: Symposium on Lawyering and Personal Values—Responding to the Problems of Ethical Schizophrenia*, 38 Cath. Law. 145 (1998); *Symposium: Faith and the Law*, 27 Tex. Tech L. Rev. 911 (1996); Symposium, *Rediscovering the Role of Religion in the Lives of Lawyers and Those They Represent*, 26 Fordham Urb. L.J. 821 (1999). Should a lawyer, as a quasi-public figure whose work is essential to the maintenance of civil order and society, be permitted to refuse to accept a legal matter when the potential client's goals are (or may be) in conflict with, the lawyer's faith? A Tennessee lawyer asked for an opinion from the Tennessee Board. of Professional Responsibility whether he violated his ethical duty by refusing to represent a minor who wished to obtain a court order permitting her to have an abortion without notifying her parents. The lawyer stated that as a prac-

ticing Roman Catholic, he opposed abortion. The Board, in Formal Op. 96-F-140 (1996), suggested the answer is yes. Do you agree? Does your answer depend in part on whether the lawyer is appointed by a court to represent the client?

McDaniel v. Paty

435 U.S. 618 (1978)

Mr. Chief Justice BURGER announced the judgment of the Court and delivered an opinion in which Mr. Justice POWELL, Mr. Justice REHNQUIST, and Mr. Justice STEVENS joined.

The question presented by this appeal is whether a Tennessee statute barring "Minister[s] of the Gospel, or priest[s] of any denomination whatever" from serving as delegates to the State's limited constitutional convention deprived appellant McDaniel, an ordained minister, of the right to the free exercise of religion guaranteed by the First Amendment and made applicable to the States by the Fourteenth Amendment. The First Amendment forbids all laws "prohibiting the free exercise" of religion.

In its first Constitution, in 1796, Tennessee disqualified ministers from serving as legislators.[1] That disqualifying provision has continued unchanged since its adoption; it is now Art. 9 § 1, of the State Constitution. The state legislature applied this provision to candidates for delegate to the State's 1977 limited constitutional convention when it enacted ch. 848, § 4, of 1976 Tenn. Pub. Acts: "Any citizen of the state who can qualify for membership in the House of Representatives of the General Assembly may become a candidate for delegate to the convention...."

McDaniel, an ordained minister of a Baptist Church in Chattanooga, Tenn., filed as a candidate for delegate to the constitutional convention. An opposing candidate, appellee Selma Cash Paty, sued in the Chancery Court for a declaratory judgment that McDaniel was disqualified from serving as a delegate and for a judgment striking his name from the ballot. Chancellor Franks of the Chancery Court held that § 4 of ch. 848 violated the First and Fourteenth Amendments to the Federal Constitution and declared McDaniel eligible for the office of delegate. Accordingly, McDaniel's name remained on the ballot and in the ensuing election he was elected by a vote almost equal to that of three opposing candidates.

After the election, the Tennessee Supreme Court reversed the Chancery Court, holding that the disqualification of clergy imposed no burden upon "religious belief" and restricted "religious action... [only] in the lawmaking process of government—where religious action is absolutely prohibited by the establishment clause...." The state interests in preventing the establishment of religion and in avoiding the divisiveness and tendency to channel political activity along religious lines, resulting from clergy participation in political affairs, were deemed by that court sufficiently weighty to justify the disqualification, notwithstanding the guarantee of the Free Exercise Clause.

The disqualification of ministers from legislative office was a practice carried from England by seven of the original States; later six new States similarly excluded clergymen from some political offices. 1 A. Stokes, *Church and State in the United States* 622

1. "Whereas Ministers of the Gospel are by their profession, dedicated to God and the care of Souls, and ought not to be diverted from the great duties of their functions; therefore, no Minister of the Gospel, or priest of any denomination whatever, shall be eligible to a seat in either House of the Legislature." Tenn. Const., Art. VIII, § 1 (1796).

(1950) (hereafter Stokes). In England the practice of excluding clergy from the House of Commons was justified on a variety of grounds: to prevent dual officeholding, that is, membership by a minister in both Parliament and Convocation; to insure that a priest or deacon devoted himself to his "sacred calling" rather than to "such mundane activities as were appropriate to a member of the House of Commons"; and to prevent ministers, who after 1533 were subject to the Crown's powers over the benefices of the clergy, from using membership in Commons to diminish its independence by increasing the influence of the King and the nobility. *In re MacManaway*, [1951] A.C. 161, 164, 170–171.

The purpose of the several States in providing for disqualification was primarily to assure the success of a new political experiment, the separation of church and state.

In light of this history and a widespread awareness during that period of undue and often dominant clerical influence in public and political affairs here, in England, and on the Continent, it is not surprising that strong views were held by some that one way to assure disestablishment was to keep clergymen out of public office. Indeed, some of the foremost political philosophers and statesmen of that period held such views regarding the clergy. Earlier, John Locke argued for confining the authority of the English clergy "within the bounds of the church, nor can it in any manner be extended to civil affairs; because the church itself is a thing absolutely separate and distinct from the commonwealth." 5 Works of John Locke 21 (C. Baldwin ed. 1824). Thomas Jefferson initially advocated such a position in his 1783 draft of a constitution for Virginia.[4] James Madison, however, disagreed and vigorously urged the position which in our view accurately reflects the spirit and purpose of the Religion Clauses of the First Amendment. Madison's response to Jefferson's position was:

> "Does not The exclusion of Ministers of the Gospel as such violate a fundamental principle of liberty by punishing a religious profession with the privation of a civil right? does it [not] violate another article of the plan itself which exempts religion from the cognizance of Civil power? does it not violate justice by at once taking away a right and prohibiting a compensation for it? does it not in fine violate impartiality by shutting the door [against] the Ministers of one Religion and leaving it open for those of every other." 5 Writings of James Madison 288 (G. Hunt ed. 1904).

Madison was not the only articulate opponent of clergy disqualification. When proposals were made earlier to prevent clergymen from holding public office, John Witherspoon, a Presbyterian minister, president of Princeton University, and the only clergyman to sign the Declaration of Independence, made a cogent protest and, with tongue in cheek, offered an amendment to a provision much like that challenged here:

4. 6 Papers of Thomas Jefferson 297 (J. Boyd ed. 1952). Jefferson later concluded that experience demonstrated there was no need to exclude clergy from elected office. In a letter to Jeremiah Moor in 1800, he stated: "[I]n the same scheme of a constitution [for Virginia which I prepared in 1783, I observe] an abridgment of the right of being elected, which after 17 years more of experience & reflection, I do not approve. It is the incapacitation of a clergyman from being elected. The clergy, by getting themselves established by law, & ingrafted into the machine of government, have been a very formidable engine against the civil and religious rights of man. They are still so in many countries & even in some of these United States. Even in 1783 we doubted the stability of our recent measures for reducing them to the footing of other useful callings. It now appears that our means were effectual. The clergy here seem to have relinquished all pretensions to privilege, and to stand on a footing with lawyers, physicians, &c. They ought therefore to possess the same rights." 9 Works of Jefferson 143 (P. Ford ed. 1905).

"'No clergyman, of any denomination, shall be capable of being elected a member of the Senate or House of Representatives, because (here insert the grounds of offensive disqualification, which I have not been able to discover) Provided always and it is the true intent and meaning of this part of the constitution, that if at any time he shall be completely deprived of the clerical character by those by whom he was invested with it, as by deposition for cursing and swearing, drunkenness or uncleanness, he shall then be fully restored to all the privileges of a free citizen; his offense [of being a clergyman] shall no more be remembered against him; but he may be chosen either to the Senate or House of Representatives, and shall be treated with all the respect due to his *brethren*, the other members of Assembly.'" Stokes 624–625.

As the value of the disestablishment experiment was perceived, 11 of the 13 States disqualifying the clergy from some types of public office gradually abandoned that limitation. New York, for example, took that step in 1846 after delegates to the State's constitutional convention argued that the exclusion of clergymen from the legislature was an "odious distinction." Only Maryland and Tennessee continued their clergy-disqualification provisions into this century and, in 1974, a District Court held Maryland's provision violative of the First and Fourteenth Amendments' guarantees of the free exercise of religion. *Kirkley v. Maryland*, 381 F. Supp. 327. Today Tennessee remains the only State excluding ministers from certain public offices.

The essence of this aspect of our national history is that in all but a few States the selection or rejection of clergymen for public office soon came to be viewed as something safely left to the good sense and desires of the people.

This brief review of the history of clergy-disqualification provisions also amply demonstrates, however, that, at least during the early segment of our national life, those provisions enjoyed the support of responsible American statesmen and were accepted as having a rational basis.

However, the right to the free exercise of religion unquestionably encompasses the right to preach, proselyte, and perform other similar religious functions, or, in other words, to be a minister of the type McDaniel was found to be. *Murdock*; *Cantwell*. Tennessee also acknowledges the right of its adult citizens generally to seek and hold office as legislators or delegates to the state constitutional convention. Yet under the clergy-disqualification provision, McDaniel cannot exercise both rights simultaneously because the State has conditioned the exercise of one on the surrender of the other. Or, in James Madison's words, the State is "punishing a religious profession with the privation of a civil right." In so doing, Tennessee has encroached upon McDaniel's right to the free exercise of religion. "[T]o condition the availability of benefits [including access to the ballot] upon this appellant's willingness to violate a cardinal principle of [his] religious faith [by surrendering his religiously impelled ministry] effectively penalizes the free exercise of [his] constitutional liberties." *Sherbert*.

If the Tennessee disqualification provision were viewed as depriving the clergy of a civil right solely because of their religious beliefs, our inquiry would be at an end. The Free Exercise Clause categorically prohibits government from regulating, prohibiting, or rewarding religious beliefs as such. In *Torcaso v. Watkins*, 367 U.S. 488 (1961) [excerpted in Chapter Eleven], the Court reviewed the Maryland constitutional requirement that all holders of "any office of profit or trust in this State" declare their belief in the existence of God. In striking down the Maryland requirement, the Court did not evaluate the interests assertedly justifying it but rather held that it violated freedom of religious belief.

In our view, however, *Torcaso* does not govern. By its terms, the Tennessee disqualification operates against McDaniel because of his *status* as a "minister" or "priest." The meaning of those words is, of course, a question of state law. And although the question has not been examined extensively in state-law sources, such authority as is available indicates that ministerial status is defined in terms of conduct and activity rather than in terms of belief. Because the Tennessee disqualification is directed primarily at status, acts, and conduct it is unlike the requirement in *Torcaso*, which focused on *belief*. Hence, the Free Exercise Clause's absolute prohibition of infringements on the "freedom to believe" is inapposite here.

This does not mean, of course, that the disqualification escapes judicial scrutiny or that McDaniel's activity does not enjoy significant First Amendment protection. The Court recently declared in *Wisconsin v. Yoder*:

> "The essence of all that has been said and written on the subject is that only those interests of the highest order and those not otherwise served can overbalance legitimate claims to the free exercise of religion."[8]

Tennessee asserts that its interest in preventing the establishment of a state religion is consistent with the Establishment Clause and thus of the highest order. The constitutional history of the several States reveals that generally the interest in preventing establishment prompted the adoption of clergy disqualification provisions. Tennessee does not appear to be an exception to this pattern. There is no occasion to inquire whether promoting such an interest is a permissible legislative goal, however, for Tennessee has failed to demonstrate that its views of the dangers of clergy participation in the political process have not lost whatever validity they may once have enjoyed. The essence of the rationale underlying the Tennessee restriction on ministers is that if elected to public office they will necessarily exercise their powers and influence to promote the interests of one sect or thwart the interests of another, thus pitting one against the others, contrary to the anti-establishment principle with its command of neutrality. However widely that view may have been held in the 18th century by many, including enlightened statesmen of that day, the American experience provides no persuasive support for the fear that clergymen in public office will be less careful of anti-establishment interests or less faithful to their oaths of civil office than their unordained counterparts.

We hold that § 4 of ch. 848 violates McDaniel's First Amendment right to the free exercise of his religion made applicable to the States by the Fourteenth Amendment. Accordingly, the judgment of the Tennessee Supreme Court is reversed, and the case is remanded to that court for further proceedings not inconsistent with this opinion.

Reversed and remanded.

---

8. Thus, the courts have sustained government prohibitions on handling venomous snakes or drinking poison, even as part of a religious ceremony, State ex rel. Swann v. Pack, 527 S.W.2d 99 (Tenn. 1975), cert. denied, 424 U.S. 954 (1976); State v. Massey, 229 N.C. 734, 51 S.E.2d 179, appeal dismissed for want of substantial federal question sub nom. Bunn v. North Carolina, 336 U.S. 942 (1949), but have precluded the application of criminal sanctions to the religious use of peyote, *People v. Woody*, 61 Cal. 2d 716, 394 P.2d 813 (1964); cf. *Oliver v. Udall*, 113 U.S. App. D.C. 212, 306 F.2d 819 (1962) (not reaching constitutional issue), or the religiously impelled refusal to comply with mandatory education laws past the eighth grade, *Wisconsin v. Yoder*.

We need not pass on the conclusions reached in *Pack* and *Woody*, which were not reviewed by this Court. Those cases are illustrative of the general nature of free exercise protections and the delicate balancing required by our decisions in *Sherbert v. Verner*, 374 U.S. 398 (1963), and *Wisconsin v. Yoder*, when an important state interest is shown.

Mr. Justice BLACKMUN took no part in the consideration or decision of this case.

Mr. Justice BRENNAN, with whom Mr. Justice MARSHALL joins, concurring in the judgment.

I would hold that §4 of the legislative call to the Tennessee constitutional convention, to the extent that it incorporates Art. 9, § 1, of the Tennessee Constitution, violates both the Free Exercise and Establishment Clauses of the First Amendment as applied to the States through the Fourteenth Amendment. I therefore concur in the reversal of the judgment of the Tennessee Supreme Court.

The Tennessee Supreme Court sustained Tennessee's exclusion on the ground that it "does not infringe upon religious belief or religious action within the protection of the free exercise clause[, and] that such indirect burden as may be imposed upon ministers and priests by excluding them from the lawmaking process of government is justified by the compelling state interest in maintaining the wall of separation between church and state." In reaching this conclusion, the state court relied on two interrelated propositions which are inconsistent with decisions of this Court. The first is that a distinction may be made between "religious belief or religious action" on the one hand, and the "career or calling" of the ministry on the other. The court stated that "[i]t is not religious belief, but the career or calling, by which one is identified as dedicated to the full time promotion of the religious objectives of a particular religious sect, that disqualifies." The second is that the disqualification provision does not interfere with the free exercise of religion because the practice of the ministry is left unimpaired; only candidacy for legislative office is proscribed.

The characterization of the exclusion as one burdening appellant's "career or calling" and not religious belief cannot withstand analysis. Clearly freedom of belief protected by the Free Exercise Clause embraces freedom to profess or practice that belief, even including doing so to earn a livelihood. One's religious belief surely does not cease to enjoy the protection of the First Amendment when held with such depth of sincerity as to impel one to join the ministry.

Whether or not the provision discriminates among religions,... it establishes a religious classification—involvement in protected religious activity—governing the eligibility for office, which I believe is absolutely prohibited. The provision imposes a unique disability upon those who exhibit a defined level of intensity of involvement in protected religious activity. Such a classification as much imposes a test for office based on religious conviction as one based on denominational preference. A law which limits political participation to those who eschew prayer, public worship, or the ministry as much establishes a religious test as one which disqualifies Catholics, or Jews, or Protestants. Because the challenged provision establishes as a condition of office the willingness to eschew certain protected religious practices, *Torcaso* compels the conclusion that it violates the Free Exercise Clause.

According to the plurality, McDaniel could not be and was not in fact barred for *his* belief in religion, but was barred because of his commitment to persuade or lead others to accept that belief. I simply cannot fathom why the Free Exercise Clause "categorically prohibits" hinging qualification for office on the *act* of declaring a belief in religion, but not on the act of discussing that belief with others.

The State Supreme Court's justification of the prohibition, echoed here by the State, as intended to prevent those most intensely involved in religion from injecting sectarian goals and policies into the lawmaking process, and thus to avoid fomenting religious strife or the fusing of church with state affairs, itself raises the question whether the exclusion violates the Establishment Clause. As construed, the exclusion manifests patent hostility toward, not neutrality respecting, religion; forces or influences a minister or priest to abandon his ministry as the price of public office; and, in sum, has a primary effect which inhibits religion.

The fact that responsible statesmen of the day, including some of the United States Constitution's Framers, were attracted by the concept of clergy disqualification, does not provide historical support for concluding that those provisions are harmonious with the Establishment Clause. Notwithstanding the presence of such provisions in seven state constitutions when the Constitution was being written, the Framers refused to follow suit. That the disqualification provisions contained in state constitutions contemporaneous with the United States Constitution and the Bill of Rights cannot furnish a guide concerning the understanding of the harmony of such provisions with the Establishment Clause is evident from the presence in state constitutions, side by side with disqualification clauses, of provisions which would have clearly contravened the First Amendment had it applied to the States, such as those creating an official church, and limiting political office to Protestants or theistic believers generally. In short, the regime of religious liberty embodied in state constitutions was very different from that established by the Constitution of the United States. When the strictures of the First Amendment became wholly applicable to the States, earlier conceptions of permissible state action with respect to religion—including those regarding clergy disqualification—were superseded.

Our decisions interpreting the Establishment Clause have aimed at maintaining erect the wall between church and state. State governments, like the Federal Government, have been required to refrain from favoring the tenets or adherents of any religion or of religion over nonreligion, from insinuating themselves in eccesiastical affairs or disputes, and from establishing programs which unnecessarily or excessively entangle government with religion. On the other hand, the Court's decisions have indicated that the limits of permissible governmental action with respect to religion under the Establishment Clause must reflect an appropriate accommodation of our heritage as a religious people whose freedom to develop and preach religious ideas and practices is protected by the Free Exercise Clause. This understanding of the interrelationship of the Religion Clauses has permitted government to take religion into account when necessary to further secular purposes unrelated to the advancement of religion, and to exempt when possible, from generally applicable governmental regulation individuals whose religious beliefs and practices would otherwise thereby be infringed, or to create without state involvement an atmosphere in which voluntary religious exercise may flourish.

Beyond these limited situations in which government may take cognizance of religion for purposes of accommodating our traditions of religious liberty, government may not use religion as a basis of classification for the imposition of duties, penalties, privileges or benefits.

Tennessee nevertheless invokes the Establishment Clause to excuse the imposition of a civil disability upon those deemed to be deeply involved in religion. In my view, that Clause will not permit, much less excuse or condone, the deprivation of religious liberty here involved.

That public debate of religious ideas, like any other, may arouse emotion, may incite, may foment religious divisiveness and strife does not rob it of constitutional protection. The mere fact that a purpose of the Establishment Clause is to reduce or eliminate religious divisiveness or strife, does not place religious discussion, association, or political participation in a status less preferred than rights of discussion, association, and political participation generally.

The State's goal of preventing sectarian bickering and strife may not be accomplished by regulating religious speech and political association. The Establishment Clause does not license government to treat religion and those who teach or practice it, simply by virtue of their status as such, as subversive of American ideals and therefore subject to unique disabilities. Government may not inquire into the religious beliefs and motivations of officeholders—it may not remove them from office merely for making public statements regarding religion, or question whether their legislative actions stem from religious conviction.

In short, government may not as a goal promote "safe thinking" with respect to religion and fence out from political participation those, such as ministers, whom it regards as overinvolved in religion. Religionists no less than members of any other group enjoy the full measure of protection afforded speech, association, and political activity generally. The Establishment Clause, properly understood, is a shield against any attempt by government to inhibit religion as it has done here. It may not be used as a sword to justify repression of religion or its adherents from any aspect of public life.

Mr. Justice STEWART, concurring in the judgment.

[Opinion omitted.]

Mr. Justice WHITE, concurring in the judgment.

While I share the view of my Brothers that Tennessee's disqualification of ministers from serving as delegates to the State's constitutional convention is constitutionally impermissible, I disagree as to the basis for this invalidity. Rather than relying on the Free Exercise Clause, as do the other Members of the Court, I would hold ch. 848, §4, of 1976 Tenn. Pub. Acts unconstitutional under the Equal Protection Clause of the Fourteenth Amendment.

Because I am not persuaded that the Tennessee statute in any way interferes with McDaniel's ability to exercise his religion as he desires, I would not rest the decision on the Free Exercise Clause, but instead would turn to McDaniel's argument that the statute denies him equal protection of the laws.

Note

In *Stone v. Graham*, 449 U.S. 39 (1980), excerpted in Chapter Six, the Court, in a *per curiam* opinion, held that the posting of the Ten Commandments on a wall of each public classroom violated the Establishment Clause. Because the state's action could not be justified by any secular purpose, it failed the first aspect of *Lemon*. The Commonwealth of Kentucky claimed that the posting of the Ten Commandments met the secular purpose requirement because, "The secular application of the Ten Commandments is clearly seen in its adoption as the fundamental legal code of Western Civilization and the Common Law of the United States." The Court found this unconvincing. Do you? Clearly, although murder and theft are proscribed by the criminal law, and engaging in adultery is a crime in many states (although rarely, if ever, prosecuted), there is no law requiring children to honor their parents or to worship the God of Abraham and Moses. Is this the constitutional infirmity of the posting of the Ten Commandments?

How should courts determine whether the (or a) legislative purpose is secular? Is "secular" defined only after "sectarian" or "religious" or "non-secular" is defined, or are the latter words defined after one defines what is "secular"? Should "secular" be defined as including "civic" or "civil" duties or obligations?

Despite the objections of four of its members, the Court summarily reversed the decision of the Supreme Court of Kentucky. Is it possible, or even likely, that the Court issued a *per curiam* opinion in order to underscore its opposition to the "smuggling in" of religion in the public school, intended, in the Court's view, as a secular setting?

Is the posting of the Ten Commandments violative of the Establishment Clause because they remain religiously important to some people? Because the reason or explanation for the posting can (only) be interpreted as religious rather than secular? The oath sworn by witnesses in court often includes the concluding phrase, "so help me God." (The Supreme Court opens its sessions with the phrase "God save the United States and this honorable Court.") Is the oath, which is religiously based, permissible because it no longer appears to be a religiously significant event to most people? Because one can opt out of repeating the phrase? Because it is usually (but not always) taken by an adult?

As noted in Chapter Six, in *Engel v. Vitale*, 370 U.S. 421 (1962), the Supreme Court held that a "non-denominational" prayer recited daily in public schools violated the Establishment Clause. One year later, in *Abington Sch. Dist. v. Schempp*, 374 U.S. 203 (1963), the court held unconstitutional a Pennsylvania law requiring that, "At least ten verses from the Holy Bible shall be read, without comment, at the opening of each public school on each school day. Any child shall be excused from such Bible reading, or attending such Bible reading, upon the written request of his parent or guardian." The court held that the constitutional requirement of neutrality between religion and nonreligion required that these "religious exercises" be barred. Additionally, it concluded that the Establishment Clause, in contrast to the Free Exercise clause, can be violated without showing any governmental coercion toward any person. In dissent, Justice Stewart stated, "[In] the absence of coercion upon those who do not wish to participate,...such provisions cannot...be held to represent the type of support of religion barred by the Establishment Clause." *Id.* at 316.

Wallace v. Jaffree

472 U.S. 38 (1985)

Justice STEVENS delivered the opinion of the Court.

[T]he narrow question for decision is whether § 16-1-20.1, which authorizes a period of silence for "meditation or voluntary prayer," is a law respecting the establishment of religion within the meaning of the First Amendment.

On August 2, 1982, the District Court held an evidentiary hearing on appellees' motion for a preliminary injunction. At that hearing, State Senator Donald G. Holmes testified that he was the "prime sponsor" of the bill that was enacted in 1981 as § 16-1-20.1. He explained that the bill was an "effort to return voluntary prayer to our public schools...it is a beginning and a step in the right direction." Apart from the purpose to return voluntary prayer to public school, Senator Holmes unequivocally testified that he had "no other purpose in mind."

In applying the purpose test, it is appropriate to ask "whether government's actual purpose is to endorse or disapprove of religion." In this case, the answer to that question is dispositive. For the record not only provides us with an unambiguous affirmative answer, but it also reveals that the enactment of § 16-1-20.1 was not motivated by any clearly secular purpose—indeed, the statute had *no* secular purpose.

The sponsor of the bill that became § 16-1-20.1, Senator Donald Holmes, inserted into the legislative record—apparently without dissent—a statement indicating that the legislation was an "effort to return voluntary prayer" to the public schools. Later Senator Holmes confirmed this purpose before the District Court. In response to the question whether he had any purpose for the legislation other than returning voluntary prayer to public schools, he stated: "No, I did not have no other purpose in mind." The State did not present evidence of *any* secular purpose.

The unrebutted evidence of legislative intent contained in the legislative record and in the testimony of the sponsor of § 16-1-20.1 is confirmed by a consideration of the relationship between this statute and the two other measures that were considered in this case. The District Court found that the 1981 statute had a common, nonsecular purpose. When the differences between § 16-1-20.1 and its 1978 predecessor, § 16-1-20, are examined, it is equally clear that the 1981 statute has the same wholly religious character.

[T]he only significant textual difference [between § 16-1-20.1 and § 16-1-20] is the addition of the words "or voluntary prayer."

The legislative intent to return prayer to the public schools is, of course, quite different from merely protecting every student's right to engage in voluntary prayer during an appropriate moment of silence during the schoolday. [§ 16-1-20] already protected that right, containing nothing that prevented any student from engaging in voluntary prayer during a silent minute of meditation. Appellants have not identified any secular purpose that was not fully served by § 16-1-20 before the enactment of § 16-1-20.1. Thus, only two conclusions are consistent with the text of § 16-1-20.1: (1) the statute was enacted to convey a message of state endorsement and promotion of prayer; or (2) the statute was enacted for no purpose. No one suggests that the statute was nothing but a meaningless or irrational act.

The importance of that principle does not permit us to treat this as an inconsequential case involving nothing more than a few words of symbolic speech on behalf of the political majority. For whenever the State itself speaks on a religious subject, one of the questions that we must ask is "whether the government intends to convey a message of endorsement or disapproval of religion." [W]e conclude that § 16-1-20.1 violates the First Amendment.

The judgment of the Court of Appeals is affirmed.

Justice POWELL, concurring.

[Opinion omitted.]

Justice O'CONNOR, concurring in the judgment.

Nothing in the United States Constitution as interpreted by this court or in the laws of the State of Alabama prohibits public school students from voluntarily praying at any time before, during, or after the schoolday. I agree with the judgment of the Court that, in light of the findings of the courts below and the history of its enactment, § 16-1-20.1 of the Alabama Code violates the Establishment Clause of the First Amendment. I also write to explain why neither history nor the Free Exercise Clause of the First Amendment validates the Alabama law struck down by the Court today.

It once appeared that the Court had developed a workable standard by which to identify impermissible government establishments of religion. See *Lemon v. Kurtzman*. Despite its initial promise, the *Lemon* test has proved problematic.

Perhaps because I am new to the struggle, I am not ready to abandon all aspects of the *Lemon* test. I do believe, however, that the standards announced in *Lemon* should be reexamined and refined. Last Term, I proposed a refinement of the *Lemon* test with this goal in mind. *Lynch v. Donnelly* (concurring opinion).

The endorsement test is useful because of the analytic content it gives to the *Lemon*-mandated inquiry into legislative purpose and effect. In this country, church and state must necessarily operate within the same community. Because of this co-existence, it is inevitable that the secular interests of government and the religious interests of various sects and their adherents will frequently intersect, conflict, and combine. A statute that ostensibly promotes a secular interest often has an incidental or even a primary effect of helping or hindering a sectarian belief. Chaos would ensue if every such statute were invalid under the Establishment Clause. For example, the State could not criminalize murder for fear that it would thereby promote the Biblical command against killing. The task for the court is to sort out those statutes and government practices whose purpose and effect go against the grain of religious liberty protected by the First Amendment.

The endorsement test does not preclude government from acknowledging religion or from taking religion into account in making law and policy. It does preclude government from conveying or attempting to convey a message that religion or a particular religious belief is favored or preferred.

A state-sponsored moment of silence in the public schools is different from state-sponsored vocal prayer or Bible reading. First, a moment of silence is not inherently religious. Silence, unlike prayer or Bible reading, need not be associated with a religious exercise. Second, a pupil who participates in a moment of silence need not compromise his or her beliefs. During a moment of silence, a student who objects to prayer is left to his or her own thoughts, and is not compelled to listen to the prayers or thoughts of others. For these simple reasons, a moment of silence statute does not stand or fall under the Establishment Clause according to how the Court regards vocal prayer or Bible reading. It is difficult to discern a serious threat to religious liberty from a room of silent, thoughtful schoolchildren.

By mandating a moment of silence, a State does not necessarily endorse any activity that might occur during the period. The crucial question is whether the State has conveyed or attempted to convey the message that children should use the moment of silence for prayer.

[M]oment of silence laws in many States should pass Establishment Clause scrutiny because they do not favor the child who chooses to pray during a moment of silence over the child who chooses to meditate or reflect. Alabama Code § 16-1-20.1 (Supp. 1984) does not stand on the same footing. However deferentially one examines its text and legislative history, however objectively one views the message attempted to be conveyed to the public, the conclusion is unavoidable that the purpose of the statute is to endorse prayer in public schools.

Chief Justice BURGER, dissenting.

Some who trouble to read the opinions in these cases will find it ironic—perhaps even bizarre—that on the very day we heard arguments in the cases, the Court's session opened with an invocation for Divine protection. Across the park a few hundred yards away, the House of Representatives and the Senate regularly open each session with a prayer. These legislative prayers are not just one minute in duration, but are extended, thoughtful invocations and prayers for Divine guidance. They are given, as they have been since 1789, by clergy appointed as official chaplains and paid from the Treasury of the United States. Congress has also provided chapels in the Capitol, at public expense, where Members and others may pause for prayer, meditation—or a moment of silence.

Inevitably some wag is bound to say that the Court's holding today reflects a belief that the historic practice of the Congress and this Court is justified because members of the Judiciary and Congress are more in need of Divine guidance than are schoolchildren. Still others will say that all this controversy is "much ado about nothing," since no power on earth—including this Court and Congress—can stop any teacher from opening the schoolday with a moment of silence for pupils to mediate, to plan their day—or to pray if they voluntarily elect to do so.

I make several points about today's curious holding.

(a) It makes no sense to say that Alabama has "endorsed prayer" by merely enacting a new statute "to specify expressly that voluntary prayer is *one* of the authorized activities during a moment of silence," (O'Connor, J., concurring in judgment) (emphasis added). To suggest that a moment-of-silence statute that includes the word "prayer" unconstitutionally endorses religion, while one that simply provides for a moment of silence does not, manifests not neutrality but hostility toward religion.

(b) The inexplicable aspect of the foregoing opinions, however, is [that] [r]ather than determining legislative purpose from the face of the statute as a whole, the opinions rely...on (i) statements of the statute's sponsor, (ii) admissions in Governor James' answer to the second amended complaint, and (iii) the difference between § 16-1-20.1 and its predecessor statute.

The sole relevance of the sponsor's statements, therefore, is that they reflect the personal, subjective motives of a single legislator. No case in the 195-year history of this Court supports the disconcerting idea that post-enactment statements by individual legislators are relevant in determining the constitutionality of legislation.

Even if an individual legislator's after-the-fact statements could rationally be considered relevant, all of the opinions fail to mention that the sponsor also testified that one of his purposes in drafting and sponsoring the moment-of-silence bill was to clear up a widespread misunderstanding that a schoolchild is legally *prohibited* from engaging in silent, individual prayer once he steps inside a public school building. That testimony is at least as important as the statements the Court relies upon, and surely that testimony manifests a permissible purpose.

The several preceding opinions conclude that the principal difference between § 16-1-20.1 and its predecessor statute proves that the sole purpose behind the inclusion of the phrase "or voluntary prayer" in § 16-1-20.1 was to endorse and promote prayer. This reasoning is simply a subtle way of focusing exclusively on the religious component of the statute rather than examining the statute as a whole. Such logic—if it can be called that—would lead the Court to hold, for example, that a state may enact a statute that provides reimbursement for bus transportation to the parents of all schoolchildren, but may not *add* parents of parochial school students to an existing program providing reimbursement for parents of public school students. Congress amended the statutory Pledge of Allegiance 31 years ago to add the words "under God." Act of June 14, 1954, Pub. L. 396, 68 Stat. 249. Do the several opinions in support of the judgment today render the Pledge unconstitutional? That would be the consequence of their method of focusing on the difference between § 16-1-20.1 and its predecessor statute rather than examining § 16-1-20.1 as a whole. Any such holding would of course make a mockery of our decisionmaking in Establishment Clause cases. And even were the Court's method correct, the inclusion of the words "or voluntary prayer" in § 16-1-20.1 is wholly consistent with the clearly permissible purpose of clarifying that silent, voluntary prayer is not *forbidden* in the public school building.

(d) The notion that the Alabama statute is a step toward creating an established church borders on, if it does not trespass into, the ridiculous. It accommodates the purely private, voluntary religious choices of the individual pupils who wish to pray while at the same time creating a time for nonreligious reflection of those who do not choose to pray.

The mountains have labored and brought forth a mouse.

Justice WHITE, dissenting. [Opinion omitted.]

Justice REHNQUIST, dissenting. [Opinion omitted.]

Edwards v. Aguillard

482 U.S. 578 (1987)

Justice BRENNAN delivered the opinion of the Court.

The question for decision is whether Louisiana's "Balanced Treatment for Creation-Science and Evolution-Science in Public School Instruction" Act (Creationism Act), La. Rev. Stat. Ann. §§ 17:286.1–17:286.7 (West 1982), is facially invalid as violative of the Establishment Clause of the First Amendment.

The Creationism Act forbids the teaching of the theory of evolution in public schools unless accompanied by instruction in "creation science." No school is required to teach evolution or creation science. If either is taught, however, the other must also be taught. The theories of evolution and creation science are statutorily defined as "the scientific evidences for [creation or evolution] and inferences from those scientific evidences."

[I]n employing the three-pronged *Lemon* test, we must do so mindful of the particular concerns that arise in the context of public elementary and secondary schools. We now turn to the evaluation of the Act under the *Lemon* test.

In this case, the petitioners have identified no clear secular purpose for the Louisiana Act.

True, the Act's stated purpose is to protect academic freedom. This phrase might, in common parlance, be understood as referring to enhancing the freedom of teachers to teach what they will. The Court of Appeals, however, correctly concluded that the Act was not designed to further that goal. We find no merit in the State's argument that the "legislature may not [have] use[d] the terms 'academic freedom' in the correct legal sense. They might have [had] in mind, instead, a basic concept of fairness; teaching all of the evidence." Even if "academic freedom" is read to mean "teaching all of the evidence" with respect to the origin of human beings, the Act does not further this purpose. The goal of providing a more comprehensive science curriculum is not furthered either by outlawing the teaching of evolution or by requiring the teaching of creation science.

It is clear from the legislative history that the purpose of the legislative sponsor, Senator Bill Keith, was to narrow the science curriculum. During the legislative hearings, Senator Keith stated: "My preference would be that neither [creationism nor evolution] be taught." Such a ban on teaching does not promote—indeed, it undermines—the provision of a comprehensive scientific education.

It is equally clear that requiring schools to teach creation science with evolution does not advance academic freedom. The Act provides Louisiana schoolteachers with no new authority. Thus the stated purpose is not furthered by it.

Furthermore, the goal of basic "fairness" is hardly furthered by the Act's discriminatory preference for the teaching of creation science and against the teaching of evolution. While requiring that curriculum guides be developed for creation science, the Act says nothing of comparable guides for evolution. Similarly, research services are supplied for creation science but not for evolution. Only "creation scientists" can serve on the panel that supplies the resource services. The Act forbids school boards to discriminate against anyone who "chooses to be a creation-scientist" or to teach "creationism," but fails to protect those who choose to teach evolution or any other noncreation science theory, or who refuse to teach creation science.

If the Louisiana legislature's purpose was solely to maximize the comprehensiveness and effectiveness of science instruction, it would have encouraged the teaching of all scientific theories about the origins of humankind. But under the Act's requirements, teachers who were once free to teach any and all facets of this subject are now unable to do so. Moreover, the Act fails even to ensure that creation science will be taught, but instead requires the teaching of this theory only when the theory of evolution is taught. Thus we agree with the Court of Appeals' conclusion that the Act does not serve to protect academic freedom, but has the distinctly different purpose of discrediting "evolution by counterbalancing its teaching at every turn with the teaching of creation science...."

These same historic and contemporaneous antagonisms between the teachings of certain religious denominations and the teaching of evolution are present in this case. The preeminent purpose of the Louisiana legislature was clearly to advance the religious viewpoint that a supernatural being created humankind. The term "creation science" was defined as embracing this particular religious doctrine by those responsible for the passage of the Creationism Act. Senator Keith's leading expert on creation science, Edward Boudreaux, testified at the legislative hearings that the theory of creation science included belief in the existence of a supernatural creator. Senator Keith also cited testimony from other experts to support the creation-science view that "a creator [was] responsible for the universe and everything in it." The legislative history therefore reveals that the term "creation science." as contemplated by the legislature that adopted this Act, embodies the religious belief that a supernatural creator was responsible for the creation of humankind.

Furthermore, it is not happenstance that the legislature required the teaching of a theory that coincided with this religious view. The legislative history documents that the Act's primary purpose was to change the science curriculum of public schools in order to provide persuasive advantage to a particular religious doctrine that rejects the factual basis of evolution in its entirety. The sponsor of the Creationism Act, Senator Keith, explained during the legislative hearings that his disdain for the theory of evolution resulted from the support that evolution supplied to views contrary to his own religious beliefs. According to Senator Keith, the theory of evolution was consonant with the "cardinal principle[s] of religious humanism, secular humanism, theological liberalism, aetheistism [*sic*]." The state senator repeatedly stated that scientific evidence supporting his religious views should be included in the public school curriculum to redress the fact that the theory of evolution incidentally coincided with what he characterized as religious beliefs antithetical to his own. The legislation therefore sought to alter the science curriculum to reflect endorsement of a religious view that is antagonistic to the theory of evolution.

In this case, the purpose of the Creationism Act was to restructure the science curriculum to conform with a particular religious viewpoint. Out of many possible science subjects taught in the public schools, the legislature chose to affect the teaching of the one scientific theory that historically has been opposed by certain religious sects. Similarly, the Creationism Act is designed *either* to promote the theory of creation science which embodies a particular religious tenet by requiring that creation science be taught whenever evolution is taught *or* to prohibit the teaching of a scientific theory disfavored by certain religious sects by forbidding the teaching of evolution when creation science is not also taught. The Establishment Clause, however, "forbids *alike* the preference of a religious doctrine *or* the prohibition of theory which is deemed antagonistic to a particular dogma." Because the primary purpose of the Creationism Act is to advance a particular religious belief, the Act endorses religion in violation of the First Amendment.

The Louisiana Creationism Act advances a religious doctrine by requiring either the banishment of the theory of evolution from public school classrooms or the presentation of a religious viewpoint that rejects evolution in its entirety. The Act violates the Establishment Clause of the First Amendment because it seeks to employ the symbolic and financial support of government to achieve a religious purpose. The judgment of the Court of Appeals therefore is

Affirmed.

Justice POWELL, with whom Justice O'CONNOR joins, concurring.

A religious purpose alone is not enough to invalidate an act of a state legislature. The religious purpose must predominate. The Act contains a statement of purpose: to "protec[t] academic freedom." This statement is puzzling. Of course, the "academic freedom" of teachers to present information in public schools, and students to receive it is broad. But it necessarily is circumscribed by the Establishment Clause. "Academic freedom" does not encompass the right of a legislature to structure the public school curriculum in order to advance a particular religious belief. *Epperson v. Arkansas*, 393 U.S. 97 (1968). Nevertheless, I read this statement in the Act as rendering the purpose of the statute at least ambiguous. Accordingly, I proceed to review the legislative history of the Act.

Here, it is clear that religious belief is the Balanced Treatment Act's "reason for existence." The tenets of creation-science parallel the Genesis story of creation, and this is a religious belief. Although the Act as finally enacted does not contain explicit reference to its religious purpose, there is no indication in the legislative history that the deletion of "creation *ex nihilo*" and the four primary tenets of the theory were intended to alter the purpose of teaching creation-science. Instead, the statements of purpose of the sources of creation-science in the United States make clear that their purpose is to promote a religious belief.

Whatever the academic merit of particular subjects or theories, the Establishment Clause limits the discretion of state officials to pick and choose among them for the purpose of promoting a particular religious belief. The language of the statute and its legislative history convince me that the Louisiana legislature exercised its discretion for this purpose in this case.

Justice WHITE, concurring in the judgment.

[Opinion omitted.]

Justice SCALIA, with whom THE CHIEF JUSTICE [REHNQUIST] joins, dissenting.

Even if I agreed with the questionable premise that legislation can be invalidated under the Establishment Clause on the basis of its motivation alone, without regard to its effects, I would still find no justification for today's decision. The Louisiana legislators who passed the Balanced Treatment for Creation-Science and Evolution-Science Act, each of whom had sworn to support the Constitution, were well aware of the potential Establishment Clause problems and considered that aspect of the legislation with great care. After seven hearings and several months of study, resulting in substantial revision of the original proposal, they approved the Act overwhelmingly and specifically articulated the secular purpose they meant it to serve. Although the record contains abundant evidence of the sincerity of that purpose (the only issue pertinent to this case), the Court today holds, essentially on this basis of "its visceral knowledge regarding what *must* have motivated the legislators," 778 F.2d 225, 227 (5th Cir. 1985) (Gee, J., dissenting) (emphasis added), that the members of the Louisiana Legislature knowingly violated their oaths and then lied about it. I dissent.

I

This Court has said little about the first component of the *Lemon* test. Almost invariably, we have effortlessly discovered a secular purpose for measures challenged under the Establishment Clause, typically devoting no more than a sentence or two to the matter. In fact, only once before deciding *Lemon*, and twice since, have we invalidated a law for lack of a secular purpose. See *Wallace*; *Stone*; *Epperson*.

It is clear, first of all, that regardless of what "legislative purpose" may mean in other contexts, for the purpose of the *Lemon* test it means the "actual" motives of those responsible for the challenged action. Thus, if those legislators who supported the Balanced Treatment Act *in fact* acted with a "sincere" secular purpose, the Act survives the first component of the *Lemon* test, regardless of whether that purpose is likely to be achieved by the provisions they enacted.

Our cases have also confirmed that when the *Lemon* Court referred to "a secular... purpose," it meant "a secular purpose." In all three cases in which we struck down laws under the Establishment Clause for lack of a secular purpose, we found that the legislature's sole motive was to promote religion. Thus, the majority's invalidation of the Balanced Treatment Act is defensible only if the record indicates that the Louisiana Legislature had *no* secular purpose.

Our cases in no way imply that the Establishment Clause forbids legislators merely to act upon their religious convictions. We surely would not strike down a law providing money to feed the hungry or shelter the homeless if it could be demonstrated that, but for the religious beliefs of the legislators, the funds would not have been approved. Also, political activism by the religiously motivated is part of our heritage. Notwithstanding the majority's implication to the contrary, we do not presume that the sole purpose of a law is to advance religion merely because it was supported strongly by organized religions or by adherents of particular faiths. To do so would deprive religious men and women of their right to participate in the political process. Today's religious activism may give us the Balanced Treatment Act, but yesterday's resulted in the abolition of slavery, and tomorrow's may bring relief for famine victims.

Similarly, we will not presume that a law's purpose is to advance religion merely because it "'happens to coincide or harmonize with the tenets of some or all religions,'" or because it benefits religion, even substantially.

Finally, our cases indicate that even certain kinds of governmental actions undertaken with the specific intention of improving the position of religion do not "advance religion" as that term is used in *Lemon*. Rather, we have said that in at least two circumstances government *must* act to advance religion, and that in a third it *may* do so.

First, since we have consistently described the Establishment Clause as forbidding not only state action motivated by the desire to *advance* religion, but also that intended to "disapprove," "inhibit," or evince "hostility" toward religion, and since we have said that governmental "neutrality" toward religion is the preeminent goal of the First Amendment, a State which discovers that its employees are inhibiting religion must take steps to prevent them from doing so, even though its purpose would clearly be to advance religion.

Second, we have held that intentional governmental advancement of religion is sometimes required by the Free Exercise Clause.

We have also held that in some circumstances government may act to accommodate religion, even if that action is not required by the First Amendment.

II

A.

We have no way of knowing, of course, how many legislators believed the testimony of Senator Keith and his witnesses. But in the absence of evidence to the contrary, we have to assume that many of them did. Given that assumption, the Court today plainly errs in holding that the Louisiana Legislature passed the Balanced Treatment Act for exclusively religious purposes.

B.

If one adopts the obviously intended meaning of the statutory terms "academic freedom," there is no basis whatever for concluding that the purpose they express is a "sham." To the contrary, the Act pursues that purpose plainly and consistently. It requires that, whenever the subject of origins is covered, evolution be "taught as a theory, rather than as proven scientific fact" and that scientific evidence inconsistent with the theory of evolution (*viz.*, "creation science") be taught as well.

It is undoubtedly true that what prompted the Legislature to direct its attention to the misrepresentation of evolution in the schools (rather than the inaccurate presentation of other topics) was its awareness of the tension between evolution and the religious beliefs of many children. But even appellees concede that a valid secular purpose is not rendered impermissible simply because its pursuit is promoted by concern for religious sensitivities. If a history teacher falsely told her students that the bones of Jesus Christ had been discovered, or a physics teacher that the Shroud of Turin had been conclusively established to be inexplicable on the basis of natural causes, I cannot believe that legislators or school board members would be constitutionally prohibited from taking corrective action, simply because that action was prompted by concern for the religious beliefs of the misinstructed students.

In sum, even if one concedes, for the sake of argument, that a majority of the Louisiana Legislature voted for the Balanced Treatment Act partly in order to foster (rather than merely eliminate discrimination against) Christian fundamentalist beliefs, our cases establish that that alone would not suffice to invalidate the Act, so long as there was a genuine secular purpose as well. I am astonished by the Court's unprecedented readiness to reach such a conclusion, which I can only attribute to an intellectual predisposition created by the facts and the legend of *Scopes v. State*, 154 Tenn. 105, 289 S.W. 363 (1927)—an instinctive reaction that any governmentally imposed requirements bearing upon the teaching of evolution must be a manifestation of Christian fundamentalist repression. In this case, however, it seems to me the Court's position is the repressive one. The people of Louisiana, including those who are Christian fundamentalists, are quite entitled, as a secular matter, to have whatever scientific evidence there may be against evolution presented in their schools, just as Mr. Scopes was entitled to present whatever scientific evidence there was for it. Perhaps what the Louisiana Legislature had done is unconstitutional because there *is* no such evidence, and the scheme they have established will amount to no more than a presentation of the Book of Genesis. But we cannot say that on the evidence before us in this summary judgment context, which includes ample uncontradicted testimony that "creation science" is a body of scientific knowledge rather than revealed belief. *Infinitely less* can we say (or should say) that the scientific evidence for evolution is so conclusive that no one could be gullible enough to believe that there is any real scientific evidence to the contrary, so that the legislation's stated purpose must be a lie. Yet that illiberal judgment, that *Scopes*-in-reverse, is ultimately the basis on which the Court's facile rejection of the Louisiana Legislature's purpose must rest.

Notes

1. Both *Jaffree* and *Edwards* stymie efforts by state legislatures to alter the content of the public school educational experience. In each case, the Court holds that the purpose of the law is not secular, and thus not constitutional, and in each case the Court determines the purpose of the law by reviewing the statements made by the chief sponsor of the measure. Should statements made by a bill's sponsor be sufficient to determine whether the law has a secular purpose? Should the court's reaction to a claim that legislation has no secular purpose depend on the specificity of the relationship of the statute to particular religious tenets?

2. Are the Court's decisions in *Stone*, *Jaffree* and *Edwards* best understood as part of the Court's long-running effort to eliminate sectarian influences from the public school? Are the posting of the Ten Commandments, the explicit acknowledgment of the permissibility of voluntary prayer or the inclusion in the curriculum of creation science harmful to those students attending the public schools or others associated with the schools? If so, are those efforts harmful because they privilege particular religious tenets, often tenets held by a majority or substantial plurality of the polity, disparage other religious or secular beliefs, or because these efforts have a debilitating effect on civil society or on children? In *Jaffree* and *Edwards*, where does the majority place the point of neutrality? Does (or should) it matter that each of these cases arose in the South?

3. Is Justice Brennan's opinion in *Edwards* consistent with his statement in *McDaniel v. Paty*, in which he notes, "The mere fact that a purpose of the Establishment Clause is to reduce or eliminate religious divisiveness or strife, does not place religious discussion, association, or political participation in a status less preferred than rights of discussion, association, and political participation generally." Is one difference between these two cases the absence of any particular religious or theological agenda on the Rev. McDaniel's part? Does the Court itself have such an agenda?

4. Do the Court's opinions adequately distinguish between the use by legislators of their religious beliefs in determining the business of the legislature (as well as their reliance on religious beliefs to shape their views on specific matters of legislative business), and the codification of particular religious beliefs? Should such a distinction be made? Is the former properly a function of representation reinforcement, and the latter properly a function of constitutional interpretation?

5. The Court did not hold all moment of silence statutes unconstitutional, and since *Jaffree*, a number of states have enacted them. In order to avoid the *Jaffree* result, sponsors of such bills have couched their reasons in non-religious terms. Does this indicate the futility of assessing whether the purpose of the statute in *Jaffree* is "secular"? Does recent state legislation permitting or requiring moments of silence suggest the necessity of a more thorough effort by courts to use the secular purpose requirement in determining the constitutionality of moment of silence statutes?

6. Does *Edwards* endorse the teaching of evolution in the public schools? Does it require the teaching of evolution in the public schools? Can a state choose to forego teaching evolution in public schools, or, more likely, refuse to approve for use in the public schools any science textbooks in which evolution is favorably discussed? If so, are there limitations concerning the manner in which it can do so?

7. Shortly after the killings at Columbine High School in Colorado in 1999, legislators in at least twelve states introduced bills to permit the posting of the Ten Commandments and other "documents of cultural, legal, or historical significance that have formed and influenced the legal and governmental systems of the United States..." in some or all public buildings. *See* Larry Copeland, *Morality Makes a Stand*, USA Today, March 30, 2000, *in* 2000 Westlaw 5773671 (2000). These bills became law in two states, Indiana and South Dakota. Both laws permitted but did not require the display of the Ten Commandments alongside other documents historically important to the development of the legal or governmental system of the United States, as long as the display of the Ten Commandments was "in the same manner and appearance generally as other documents and objects displayed," so that attention was not called to that display apart from the other displayed documents. In Indiana, the law applied to all real property owned by the state or a political subdivision of the state, and in South Dakota, the display was limited to any "public school classroom, public school building, or at any public school event." *See* Ind. Stats. 4-20.5-21-2 (2000); Ind. Stats. 36-1-16-2 (2000); S.D. Stats. § 13-24-17.1 (2000). In Kentucky, the legislature by a joint resolution signed by the Governor directed the state to remove a 75-inch-tall monument of the Ten Commandments from storage and place it on the statehouse grounds near the floral clock, a popular tourist attraction. The Kentucky provision also encourages schools to post the Ten Commandments. The Colorado Board of Education, in mid-2000, adopted a resolution encouraging local school boards to permit the posting of the national motto "In God We Trust" in schools. Would the posting of this motto, which is found on American currency, be unconstitutional because no secular purpose for the motto exists? Does it matter that several courts of appeals held the motto constitutional? *See, e.g.*, *Aronow v. United States*, 432 F.2d 242 (9th Cir.1970). In *American Civil Liberties Union of Ohio v. Capitol Square Review and Advisory Bd.*, 243 F.3d 289 (6th Cir. 2001), the *en banc* court of appeals held that Ohio's motto, "With God All Things are Possible," did not violate the Establishment Clause. The court reversed an earlier decision by a panel of the Sixth Circuit holding the motto unconstitutional. The *en banc* decision analogized Ohio's motto to the national motto, "In God We Trust." Is there a difference between "In God We Trust" and "With God All Things are Possible"? If you knew that the latter phrase was

taken from the Gospel of Matthew in the New Testament of the Christian Bible, would that make a difference? Would it make a difference if you knew that the phrase could also be found in Jewish, Islamic and Hindu religious texts? If you didn't know the derivation of Ohio's motto, should or does that make a constitutional difference?

8. In *North Carolina Civil Liberties Union Legal Foundation v. Costangy*, 947 F.2d 1145 (4th Cir. 1991), *cert. denied*, 505 U.S. 1219 (1992), the fourth circuit held unconstitutional the practice by a state district judge of opening his morning court sessions with a prayer. In 1995, Judge Roy Moore, then a trial judge in Etowah County, Alabama, was sued because he posted the Ten Commandments in his courtroom. In addition, Judge Moore opened court with a prayer. In *Alabama Freethought Ass'n v. Moore*, 893 F. Supp. 1522 (N.D. Ala. 1995), the district court held that the plaintiffs lacked standing to complain about Judge Moore's actions. Thereafter, the Governor of Alabama, Fob James, sued Judge Moore. James requested a declaratory judgment holding Judge Moore's actions displaying the Ten Commandments in his courtroom or opening court sessions with a prayer constitutionally permissible. In Ex parte *State* ex rel. *James*, 711 So. 2d 952 (Ala. 1998), the Supreme Court of Alabama held that the state's claims against Judge Moore were not justiciable due to a lack of adverseness. Several other courts have held unconstitutional the posting of the Ten Commandments in courtrooms. Judge Moore's vigorous efforts to maintain the display of the Ten Commandments in his courtroom were widely publicized, and Moore became a celebrated speaker concerning his view of the proper relation of law, religion and government. He was subsequently elected to the Supreme Court of Alabama. To what extent, if any, do statements concerning religion made by a judge in his unofficial capacity differ from religiously-based statements made by legislative or executive officials? Does the judge's ethical duty to remain impartial limit his ability to make such statements in a way different from other governmental officials?

B. Evolution Redux

Shortly after the Court decided *Abington Sch. Dist. v. Schempp*, the second school prayer decision, a California mother named Nell Segraves petitioned her state's Board of Education to forbid restricting the teaching of the origins of life to the theory of evolution. Edward J. Larson, Trial and Error: The American Controversy Over Creation and Evolution 96–97 (updated ed. 1989). Her argument was that if the religion clauses required neutrality, then the teaching solely of evolution violated this constitutional command. This petition began the second era of the treatment in public schools of the debate concerning evolution. In 1965, the new edition of a biology textbook used in the state of Arkansas included materials on evolution. Although Arkansas's anti-evolution statute was unenforced, the Arkansas Education Association sought a plaintiff to initiate a test case. Susan Epperson, a new teacher and native Arkansan who would leave the state when her husband was transferred by the Air Force, agreed to act as plaintiff. She claimed that Arkansas's anti-evolution law violated her right to free speech, and other constitutional rights. Larson, at 99. The trial court agreed, holding the Arkansas unconstitutional. Then, shortly after the Tennessee legislature repealed the law upheld in *Scopes v. State*, 154 Tenn. 105, 289 S.W. 363 (1927), the Arkansas Supreme Court, in a *per curiam* opinion, held the act constitutional on the authority of *Scopes*. *State v. Epperson*, 242 Ark. 922, 416 S.W.2d 322 (1967).

Susan Epperson taught biology at Little Rock Central High. Larson, at 108. A decade earlier, the Supreme Court was faced with Arkansas Governor Orval Faubus's refusal to integrate Little Rock Central despite the Court's decisions in *Brown v. Board of Educ.* ending legal racial segregation of public schools. Faubus's actions led to President Dwight D. Eisenhower's decision to send federal troops to Little Rock in 1957. One year later, the Supreme Court, in *Cooper v. Aaron*, 358 U.S. 1 (1958), ordered the immediate desegregation of Central High. When the Court granted Epperson's petition for a writ of certiorari, it was faced with another case arising from the same high school, similarly testing the constitutionality of a belief that appeared anti-modern and anti-progressive.

At oral argument, as a result of intervening elections that dampened the ardor for the law, the state offered only token opposition to Epperson's claim. The state not only suggested that the statute must be strictly interpreted to forbid any mention in public schools of evolution, but concluded that the law probably was unconstitutional. Larson, at 111. Not surprisingly, the Court held the statute unconstitutional, although somewhat surprisingly, not on Free Speech or vagueness grounds, but because the statute violated the Establishment Clause. *Epperson v. Arkansas*, 393 U.S. 97, 107–09 (1968). That the Court viewed the law as backward is evidenced by its conclusion that the opacity of the Arkansas Supreme Court's decision was made "perhaps reflecting the discomfort which the statute's quixotic prohibition necessarily engendered in the modern mind...." *Id.* at 102. The reason for the law's existence, according to the majority, was the "fundamentalist sectarian conviction" that "the Book of Genesis must be the exclusive source of doctrine as to the origin of man." *Id.* at 107. Consequently:

> Arkansas' law cannot be defended as an act of religious neutrality. The law's effort was confined to an attempt to blot out a particular theory because of its supposed conflict with the biblical account, literally read. Plainly, the law is contrary to the mandate of the First, and in violation of the Fourteenth, Amendment of the Constitution.

Id. at 109.

Concurring, Justice Harlan called the statute "anachronistic." *Id.* at 115.

The Court's decision in *Epperson* did not end the evolution debate; it simply changed the terms of that debate. Proponents of "creationism" lobbied local and state boards of education to require biology textbooks label evolution a theory rather than a fact, and to teach creationism in addition to evolution. In 1978, a Yale Law School student named Wendell R. Bird published a Note in the Yale Law Journal titled *Freedom of Religion and Science Instruction in Public Schools*, 87 Yale L.J. 515 (1978). Bird suggested that creationism, or creation science, was a scientific theory of human origin, not a religious theory of human origin. As such, it deserved the same treatment as evolution in the public school classroom. In 1981, both Arkansas and Louisiana enacted laws mandating the teaching of creationism if evolution was taught. The Arkansas law was held unconstitutional as violating the Establishment Clause in *McLean v. Arkansas Bd. of Educ.*, 529 F. Supp. 1255 (E.D. Ark. 1982), and the Louisiana law was struck down in *Edwards*.

In August 1983, in Hawkins County, Tennessee, Vicki Frost's sixth-grade daughter Rebecca was assigned to read a story in her Holt reader entitled *A Visit to Mars*. Because Rebecca did not understand the story, she asked for help from her mother. Vicki Frost believed the story was evidence that secular humanism had come to the mountains of East Tennessee. Stephen Bates, BATTLEGROUND: ONE MOTHER'S CRUSADE, THE RELIGIOUS RIGHT, AND THE STRUGGLE FOR CONTROL OF OUR CLASSROOMS 16–19 (1993).

After a series of disastrous miscommunications and events among Frost, the school board and school officials, including Vicki Frost's arrest for trespassing on school property, Frost, Bob Mozert and other parents of school children sued the Hawkins County Board of Education. The plaintiffs alleged that the Holt readers used by the schools violated their Free Exercise rights and the Free Exercise rights of their children by forcing the children to read books which promulgated views contrary to their religious convictions. The case quickly became a national cause celebre, and given the appellation *Scopes II.* The plaintiffs were represented by attorneys for the Concerned Women for America, and the County was eventually represented by lawyers paid by People for the American Way. The district court found forcing the students to read the Holt readers violated their Free Exercise rights, awarded the plaintiffs over $50,000 in damages and permitted the students to "opt out" of the reading from the objectionable Holt reader. *Mozert v. Hawkins Cty. Bd. of Educ.*, 647 F. Supp. 1194 (E.D. Tenn. 1986). The County appealed.

Mozert v. Hawkins County Board of Education

827 F.2d 1058 (6th Cir. 1987), *cert. denied*, 484 U.S. 1066 (1988)

Lively, Chief Judge.

III.

A.

The first question to be decided is whether a governmental requirement that a person be exposed to ideas he or she finds objectionable on religious grounds constitutes a burden on the free exercise of that person's religion as forbidden by the First Amendment.

B.

In this case the district court erroneously applied decisions based on governmental requirements that objecting parties make some affirmation or take some action that offends their religious beliefs.

C.

It is abundantly clear that the exposure to materials in the Holt series did not compel the plaintiffs to "declare a belief," "communicate by word and sign [their] acceptance" of the ideas presented, or make an "affirmation of a belief and an attitude of mind." In *Barnette* the unconstitutional burden consisted of compulsion either to do an act that violated the plaintiff's religious convictions or communicate an acceptance of a particular idea or affirm a belief. No similar compulsion exists in the present case.

The plaintiffs appear to contend that the element of compulsion was supplied by the requirement of class participation in the reading exercises. As we have pointed out earlier, there is no proof in the record that any plaintiff student was required to engage in role play, make up magic chants, read aloud or engage in the activity of haggling. Being exposed to other students performing these acts might be offensive to the plaintiffs, but it does not constitute the compulsion described in the Supreme Court cases, where the objector was required to affirm or deny a religious belief or engage or refrain from engaging in a practice contrary to sincerely held religious beliefs.

D.

The third Supreme Court decision relied upon by the plaintiffs is the only one that might be read to support the proposition that requiring mere exposure to materials that offend one's religious beliefs creates an unconstitutional burden on the free exercise of religion. *Wisconsin v. Yoder*, 406 U.S. 205 (1972).

Yoder was decided in large part on the impossibility of reconciling the goals of public education with the religious requirement of the Amish that their children be prepared for life in a separated community. No such threat exists in the present case, and Tennessee's school attendance laws offer several options to those parents who want their children to have the benefit of an education which prepares for life in the modern world without being exposed to ideas which offend their religious beliefs.

IV.

A.

The Supreme Court has recently affirmed that public schools serve the purpose of teaching fundamental values "essential to a democratic society." These values "include tolerance of divergent political and religious views" while taking into account "consideration of the sensibilities of others." *Bethel School Dist. No. 403 v. Fraser*, 478 U.S. 675 (1986). The Court has noted with apparent approval the view of some educators who see public schools as an "assimilative force" that brings together "diverse and conflicting elements" in our society "on a broad but common ground." *Ambach v. Norwick*, 441 U.S. 68, 77 (1979), citing works of J. Dewey, N. Edwards and H. Richey. The critical reading approach furthers these goals. Mrs. Frost stated specifically that she objected to stories that develop "a religious tolerance that all religions are merely different roads to God." Stating that the plaintiffs reject this concept, presented as a recipe for an ideal world citizen, Mrs. Frost said, "We cannot be tolerant in that we accept other religious views on an equal basis with ours." While probably not an uncommon view of true believers in any religion, this statement graphically illustrates what is lacking in the plaintiffs' case.

The "tolerance of divergent... religious views" referred to by the Supreme Court is a civil tolerance, not a religious one. It does not require a person to accept any other religion as equal of the one to which that person adheres. It merely requires a recognition that in a pluralistic society we must "live and let live." If the Hawkins County schools had required the plaintiff students either to believe or say they believe that "all religions are merely different roads to God," this would be a different case. However, there was absolutely no showing that the defendant school board sought to do this; indeed, the school board agreed at oral argument that it could not constitutionally do so. Instead, the record in this case discloses an effort by the school board to offer a reading curriculum designed to acquaint students with a multitude of ideas and concepts, though not in proportions the plaintiffs would like. While many of the passages deal with ethical issues, on the surface at least, they appear to us to contain no religious or anti-religious messages.

B.

The judgment of the district court granting injunctive relief and damages is reversed, and the case is remanded with directions to dismiss the complaint.

Cornelia G. Kennedy, Circuit Judge, concurring.

I agree with Chief Judge Lively's analysis and concur in his opinion. However, even if I were to conclude that requiring the use of the Holt series...constituted a burden on appellees' free exercise rights, I would find the burden justified by a compelling state interest.

Teaching students about complex and controversial social and moral issues is just as essential for preparing public school students for citizenship and self-government as inculcating in the students the habits and manners of civility.

The evidence at trial demonstrated that mandatory participation in reading classes using the Holt series or some similar readers is essential to accomplish this compelling interest and that this interest could not be achieved any other way.

The state and the Hawkins County School Board also have a compelling interest in avoiding disruption in the classroom. Hawkins County Schools utilize an integrated curriculum, designed to prepare students for life in a complex, pluralistic society, that reinforces skills and values taught in one subject in other areas.

Additionally, Hawkins County Public Schools have a compelling interest in avoiding religious divisiveness. The Supreme Court has emphasized that the avoidance of religious divisiveness is nowhere more important than in public education, for "[t]he government's activities in this area can have a magnified impact on impressionable young minds...." *Grand Rapids School Dist. v. Ball*, 473 U.S. 373, 383 (1985). The opt-out remedy would permit appellee students to be released from a core subject every day *because* of their religion.

The divisiveness and disruption caused by the opt-out remedy would be magnified if the schools had to grant other exemptions. Although the District Court found that no other objections to the Hawkins County public school curriculum have been raised and that Hawkins County is homogenous from a religious perspective, this case would create a precedent for persons from other religions to request exemptions from core subjects because of religious objections. If the school district were required to accommodate exceptions and permit other students to opt-out of the reading program and other core courses with materials others found objectionable, this would result in a public school system impossible to administer.

Boggs, Circuit Judge, concurring.

I concur with my colleagues that Hawkins County is not required by the Constitution to allow plaintiffs the latitude they seek in the educational program of these children.

The school board recognizes no limitation on its power to require any curriculum, no matter how offensive or one-sided, and to expel those who will not study it, so long as it does not violate the Establishment Clause. Our opinion today confirms that right, and I would like to make plain my reasons for taking that position.

I

For myself, I approach this case with a profound sense of sadness. At the classroom level, the pupils and teachers in these schools had in most cases reached a working accommodation. Only by the decisions of higher levels of political authority, and by more conceptualized presentations of the plaintiffs' positions, have we reached the point where we must decide these harsh questions today. The school board faced what must have seemed a prickly and difficult group of parents, however dedicated to their children's welfare. In a similar situation, the poet Edwin Markham described a solution:

He drew a circle that shut me out—
Heretic, Rebel, a thing to flout.
But Love and I had the wit to win:
We drew a circle that took him in!

As this case now reaches us, the school board rejects any effort to reach out and take in these children and their concerns.

Plaintiffs' requests were unusual, but a variety of accommodations in fact were made, with no evidence whatsoever of bad effects. Given the masses of speculative testimony as to the hypothetical future evils of accommodating plaintiffs in any way, had there been any evidence of bad effects from what actually occurred, the board would surely have presented it. As we ultimately decide here, on the present state of constitutional law, the school board is indeed entitled to say, "my way or the highway." But in my view the school board's decision here is certainly not required by the Establishment Clause.

II

Returning to the treatment of plaintiffs' free exercise claim, I believe this is a more difficult case than outlined in the court's opinion.

Ultimately, I think we must address plaintiffs' claims as they actually impact their lives: it is their belief that they should not take a course of study which, on balance, to them, denigrates and opposes their religion, and which the state is compelling them to take on pain of forfeiting all other benefits of public education.

Their view may seem silly or wrongheaded to some, but it is a sincerely held religious belief.

III

I also disagree with the court's view that there can be no burden here because there is no requirement of conduct contrary to religious belief. That view both slights plaintiffs' honest beliefs that studying the full Holt series would be conduct contrary to their religion, and overlooks other Supreme Court Free Exercise cases which view "conduct" that may offend religious exercise at least as broadly as do plaintiffs.

On the question of exposure to, or use of, books as conduct, we may recall the Roman Catholic Church's, "*Index Librorum Prohibitorum*." This was a list of those books the reading of which was a mortal sin, at least until the second Vatican Council in 1962. I would hardly think it can be contended that a school requirement that a student engage in an act (the reading of the book) which would specifically be a mortal sin under the teaching of a major organized religion would be other than "conduct prohibited by religion," even by the court's fairly restrictive standard. Yet, in what constitutionally important way can the situation here be said to differ from that? Certainly, a religion's size or formality of hierarchy cannot determine the religiosity of beliefs. Similarly, and analogous to our case, church doctrine before 1962 also indicated that portions of the banned books could be used or read in a context to show their error, and that references to, or small protions of, the books did not fall under the same ban.

IV

I have given considerable thought to Judge Kennedy's opinion discussing the importance of the state's interest in "critical reading" and noting the plaintiffs' objection to such instruction. I conclude that the requirement of "critical reading," as accomplished in Tennessee, does not constitute a burden on the free exercise of religion for these plaintiffs separate from the required study of the Holt books.

Whether or not Tennessee insists on students responding to literature based only on self-centered values, I disagree with the idea that such a teaching of "critical reading" would constitute a compelling state interest which entitles the school board to deny plaintiffs the accommodation they seek.

It seems to me to be extremely difficult, not to say unfair, to rest a compelling state interest on the asserted failure of plaintiffs to learn something which defendants are apparently unable to define and unwilling to test for. Mr. Justice Stewart has been unfairly derided as propounding an obscenity test of, "I know it when I see it," *Jacobellis v. Ohio*, 378 U.S. 184, 187 (1964), but it appears that the school board here seeks that kind of test for critical reading. Their view seems to be that if we are teaching it in the state classrooms, critical reading must be happening, but if plaintiffs are learning reading outside that class (and testing as well as, or better than, the average state student), it must not be happening.

In any event, the test for a compelling interest is quite strict, and requires far more than this or other speculations on possible future evils. To be compelling, "[o]nly the gravest abuses, endangering paramount interests, give occasion for permissible limitation." *Sherbert v. Verner*, 374 U.S. 398, 406 (1963), quoting *Thomas v. Collins*, 323 U.S. 516, 530. In the absence of any testimony as to actual problems from the accommodation that was provided, it is difficult to see how this standard could be met, if a constitutional burden were established.

V

For me, the key fact is that the Court has almost never interfered with the prerogative of school boards to set curricula, based on free exercise claims. *West Virginia State Board of Education v. Barnette*, 319 U.S. 624 (1943), may be the only case, and even there a specific affirmation was required, implicating a non-religious First Amendment basis, as well.

From a common sense view of the word "burden," *Sherbert* and *Thomas* [*v. Review Board*, 450 U.S. 707 (1981)] are very strong cases for plaintiffs. In any sensible meaning of a burden, the burden in our case is greater than in *Thomas* or *Sherbert*.

VI

However, constitutional adjudication, especially for a lower court, is not simply a matter of common sense use of words. We must determine whether the common sense burden on plaintiffs' religious belief is, in the context of a public school curriculum, a constitutional "burden" on their religious beliefs.

I do not support an extension by this court of the principles of *Sherbert* and *Thomas* to cover this case, even though there is a much stronger economic compulsion exercised by public schooling than by any unemployment compensation system. I think the constitutional basis for those cases is sufficiently thin that they should not be extended blindly.

Therefore, I reluctantly conclude that under the Supreme Court's decisions as we have them, school boards may set curricula bounded only by the Establishment Clause, as the state contends. Thus, contrary to the analogy plaintiffs suggest, pupils may indeed be expelled if they will not read from the King James Bible, so long as it is only used as literature, and not taught as religious truth. Contrary to the position of *amicus* American Jewish Committee, Jewish students may not assert a burden on their religion if their reading materials overwhelmingly provide a negative view of Jews or factual or historical issues important to Jews, so long as such materials do not assert any proposition as religious truth, or do not otherwise violate the Establishment Clause.

It is a more difficult question when, as here, the state presents materials that plaintiffs sincerely believe preach religious toleration of religions by consistent omission of plaintiffs' religion and favorable presentation of opposing views. Our holding requires plaintiffs to put up with what they perceive as an unbalanced public school curriculum, so long as the curriculum does not violate the Establishment Clause. Every other sect of type of religious belief is bound by the same requirement. The rule here is not a rule just for fundamentalist dissenters, for surely the rule cannot be that when the school authorities disagree with non-fundamentalist dissenter, the school loses, and when the school authorities disagree with fundamentalists, the school wins. Rather, unless the Supreme Court chooses to extend the principle of *Thomas* to schools, the democratic principle must prevail.

Schools are very important, and some public schools offend some people deeply. I believe that such a significant change in school law and expansion in the religious liberties of pupils and parents should come only from Supreme Court itself, and not simply from our interpretation. It may well be that we would have a better society if children and parents were not put to the hard choice posed by this case. But our mandate is limited to carrying out the commands of the Constitution and the Supreme Court.

I therefore concur in the result and reverse the judgment of the District Court.

Notes

1. Chief Judge Lively concludes that "mere exposure" to ideas antithetical to the religious convictions of the students does not create a constitutional burden on free exercise. The only contrary case, he suggests, is *Wisconsin v. Yoder*, involving Amish schoolchildren, and he declines to apply *Yoder* because the plaintiffs, unlike the Amish, did not separate themselves from the world, and the Holt readers were not as grave a threat to the existence of the plaintiff's faith as high school education was to the Amish community. Do these arguments equate religious liberty interests to the issue of the threat to the core of the religious belief? If so, this "centrality" argument was rejected by the Supreme Court shortly after *Mozert* was decided in *Lyng v. Northwest Indian Cemetery Protective Ass'n*, 485 U.S. 439 (1988), noted in Chapter Five. Lively also concludes that the plaintiffs retained the option of private or home schooling. In a related context, a plurality of the Supreme Court has held that removing books from a school library cannot be constitutionally justified by arguing the availability of the books from bookstores or other sources. *Board of Educ., Island Trees Union Free Sch. Dist. v. Pico*, 457 U.S. 853 (1982), excerpted in Chapter Six. Is *Pico* analogous to this situation? Should it matter that, economically, some families can neither afford private school nor stay home to teach their children, and so are unable to opt-out of the public school system? In discussing the importance of public education as an "assimilative force," Lively cites *Ambach v. Norwick*, 441 U.S. 68 (1979), and notes that *Ambach* cites with approval, among others, the views of early twentieth century philosopher and educator John Dewey. For plaintiffs and others with similar beliefs, Dewey is possibly the most emblematic representative of secular humanism, an ideology they believe has enveloped public educa-

tion. Why did Lively cite Dewey? Was this a subtle effort by Lively to denigrate the claims of the plaintiffs? Was it merely an attempt to justify the view that public education molds divergent views into an "assimilative" nation? *See* Chapter Six § C.

Recall Justice Felix Frankfurter's opinion in *Minersville Sch. Dist. v. Gobitis*, 310 U.S. 586 (1940), excerpted in Chapter One § B. Although Justice Frankfurter declares religious liberty an interest of the highest order, he concludes that Jehovah's Witnesses schoolchildren may be compelled by the state to salute the flag. Frankfurter's opinion is a classic assimilationist opinion. Three years later, however, in *West Virginia Bd. of Educ. v. Barnette*, also excerpted in Chapter One, Justice Robert H. Jackson rejected the assimilationist approach in *Gobitis* in favor of an individualist approach. This latter approach has predominated constitutional rights jurisprudence ever since. What is different about the non-assimilationist claim of the religious fundamentalists in *Mozert* from the claim in *Barnette* that allows Chief Judge Lively to conclude as he did? Is there any significance to the fact that John Dewey and Felix Frankfurter were both leading American progressives during the first half of the twentieth century?

Judge Kennedy concludes that even if the Free Exercise interests of the plaintiffs have been burdened, that burden is constitutionally justified by three compelling state interests—"teaching students about complex and controversial social and moral issues" to prepare "public school students for citizenship and self-government," which mandatory participation in reading class necessitated; "avoiding disruption in the classroom;" and "avoiding religious divisiveness." Why are these interests compelling? Is a mandatory reading class necessary to teach complex and controversial social and moral issues? Should the truth of this claim be tested empirically? How is "avoiding disruption in the classroom" a compelling state interest? In *Tinker v. Des Moines Ind. Sch. Dist.*, 393 U.S. 503 (1969), the Supreme Court famously stated that students and teachers did not "shed their constitutional rights to freedom of speech or expression at the schoolhouse gate," *id.* at 506, and held that banning the wearing of armbands emblazoned with a peace sign was constitutionally impermissible. In light of *Tinker*, it appears clear that some speech might cause a classroom disruption, and yet be constitutionally protected. Who determines whether a compelling kind of disruption is in fact being caused? How should disruption be defined? Can schools avoid religious divisiveness by ignoring the religious claims made by the parents of school children? Judge Kennedy's final argument is that providing the students with the right to "opt-out" of reading from the Holt series will result in "chaos." Is this argument empirically grounded? Is this anything more than an argument of administrative convenience? If so, can administrative convenience justify invasion of a fundamental constitutional right?

Although Judge Boggs concludes that some Free Exercise precedent appears applicable to the facts in *Mozert*, he refuses to extend the decisions in *Sherbert* and *Thomas* to the area of public education. Does Judge Boggs's concurring opinion foreshadow the opinion of Justice Scalia in *Employment Div. v. Smith*, 494 U.S. 872 (1990), in which *Sherbert* and *Thomas* are limited to a special rule of unemployment compensation? Does Judge Boggs's stark opinion suggest, for example, that a public school is permitted to expel a student, who for religious or philosophical reasons, refuses to dissect a frog in biology class?

2. The plaintiffs and district court cited in support of a free exercise right to opt-out of the Holt readers the case of *Spence v. Bailey*, 465 F.2d 797 (6th Cir. 1972), in which the Sixth Circuit, in an opinion written by retired Supreme Court Justice Tom Clark, held that a conscientious objector was constitutionally permitted to refuse to engage in ROTC training. Is this case different because the plaintiffs in *Mozert* were merely

exposed to ideas with which they disagreed, rather than required to engage in an act? Is reading (and is thinking about what one has read) an act? Does the court adequately assess the plaintiffs' claim of "coercion"?

3. As noted by Stephen Bates in his book about *Mozert*, the major media regularly "echoed" the interpretation of the case offered by People for the American Way, an interpretation quite critical of the plaintiffs' claims. Bates, BATTLEGROUND at 279. Is the fate of religious liberty its pairing with stereotyped "fundamentalists" whose claims suggest an intolerance and illiberalism toward ideas with which they disagree? Was the Sixth Circuit's decision in *Mozert* a replay of *Scopes*, with media-portrayed heroes and villains?

4. A thoughtful and sensitive assessment of the claims of the plaintiffs in *Mozert*, and of the incommensurability of liberal thought with the Christian fundamentalism of the *Mozert* plaintiffs is Nomi Maya Stolzenberg, *"He Drew a Circle That Shut Me Out": Assimilation, Indoctrination, and the Paradox of Liberal Education*, 106 Harv. L. Rev. 581 (1993).

5. What makes a governmental interest compelling? *See Conference on Compelling Governmental Interests: The Mystery of Constitutional Analysis*, 55 Alb. L. Rev. 535 *et seq.* (1992). In Professor Stephen Gottlieb's view, the first thing one must do to understand this question is to change the phrase to "compelling public purposes." Stephen E. Gottlieb, *Compelling Governmental Interests and Constitutional Discourse*, 55 Alb. L. Rev. 549, 552 (1992). Professor Gottlieb suggests that a "principle of interpretive parity" informs our understanding of both fundamental rights and compelling public purposes, and that "whatever arguments support compelling public purposes will also support fundamental rights in just the same way." *Id.* at 554. Should compelling be equated with "important," "crucial," or "necessary"? Because the judicial declaration that the state has a compelling state interest permits the state to infringe an individual's exercise of a constitutional right, in what way can such interests be named or clarified? *See* Chapter One § A.

6. A continuation of the *Wallace v. Jaffree* litigation was *Smith v. Board of Sch. Comm'rs.* In *Smith*, intervenors requested either an injunction against the teaching of "secularism, humanism, evolution, materialism, agnosticism, atheism and others" or the opportunity to produce evidence that "these religions had been established in the Alabama public schools." *Smith v. Board of Sch. Comm'rs*, 827 F.2d 684, 686 (11th Cir. 1987). In a broad opinion, Judge W. Brevard Hand declared secular humanism a religion, and concluded that forty-four textbooks approved for use in the Alabama public schools were premised on the religion of secular humanism. He then enjoined the use of those books on Establishment Clause grounds. *Smith*, 655 F. Supp. 939, 988 (S.D. Ala. 1987). The Eleventh Circuit reversed, concluding that Hand's factual findings were erroneous. *Smith*, 827 F.2d at 690 ("[U]se of the challenged textbooks has the primary effect of conveying information that is essentially neutral in its religious content to the school children who utilize the books; none of these books convey a message of governmental approval of secular humanism or governmental disapproval of theism").

7. Much of the argument made by plaintiffs in *Mozert*, *Smith* and other similar cases is based on the idea that there is such a thing as secular humanism, that it is an anti-Christian religious belief system, and that it has been established in the public schools. Tenets of secular humanism include nontheism, rejection of supernatural religions (including a rejection of any belief in life after death), salvation by humankind of itself, belief in reason and science, evolution, particularistic ethics, individual self-ful-

fillment, liberty, equality and democratic governance. Mary Harter Mitchell, *Secularism in Public Education: The Constitutional Issues*, 67 B.U. L. Rev. 603, 624–26 (1987). In Professor Mitchell's view, secular humanism should be defined as a religion. *Id.* at 627–63. However, arguing its establishment in public schools requires a reshaping of Establishment Clause jurisprudence "better tuned to analyze arguments about secularistic religion, implied curricula, and secondary religious effects." *Id.* at 690.

8. In *Roberts v. Madigan*, 921 F.2d 1047 (10th Cir. 1990), an elementary school teacher, Kenneth Roberts, sued alleging a violation of his rights under the First Amendment's Free Speech, Free Exercise and Establishment Clauses. Roberts taught fifth grade, and included in his students' curriculum fifteen minutes of silent reading every class day. During that time, to set an example, Roberts also read silently, often from his Bible, which otherwise sat on his desk. There was no evidence Roberts spoke to the students about his religious beliefs, although there was a poster in his classroom with the saying "You have only to open your eyes to see the hand of God," and Roberts included in the classroom library two books of his reflecting religious themes, *The Bible in Pictures* and *The Life of Jesus*. After a complaint about the presence of the books, the principal, Kathleen Madigan, ordered Roberts to remove the books from the classroom. While doing so, she noticed the Bible on Roberts's desk, and she also ordered him to keep his Bible out of sight during the school day. A split panel of the Tenth Circuit affirmed the district court's holding that the school principal's actions did not infringe Roberts's constitutional rights. Would Roberts have had a better case if he was silently reading abstruse theology rather than a Bible? Some philosophical tome? *Das Kapital*? The court noted that the evidence showed that Roberts was permitted to read the life of Buddha without complaint. Is *Madigan* consistent with *Pico*, excerpted in Chapter Six?

9. If religiously-affiliated elementary and secondary schools are busily inculcating religion in the lives (and learning) of its students, does this suggest anything about the goals and purposes of public school education? Can the "values" inculcated in public schools be transmuted (in any case, in some cases, in all cases?) into an "ideology" which may be contrary to the religious beliefs of some public school students and their parents? How would (should) a court determine when values are so transmuted? *See generally* Chapter Six.

10. In *Freiler v. Tangipahoa Parish Bd. of Educ.*, 185 F.3d 337 (5th Cir. 1999), *cert. denied*, 530 U.S. 1251 (2000), the issue was whether the school board's requirement that a disclaimer be read before the teaching of evolution in all elementary and high school classes violated the Establishment Clause. The disclaimer stated:

> It is hereby recognized by the Tangipahoa Board of Education, that the lesson to be presented, regarding the origin of life and matter, is known as the Scientific Theory of Evolution and should be presented to inform students of the scientific concept and not intended to influence or dissuade the Biblical version of Creation or any other concept.
>
> It is further recognized by the Board of Education that it is the basic right and privilege of each student to form his/her own opinion and maintain beliefs taught by parents on this very important matter of the origin of life and matter. Students are urged to exercise critical thinking and gather all information possible and closely examine each alternative toward forming an opinion.

The court concluded that the disclaimer violated the Establishment Clause. Would the disclaimer have met the standards of the Establishment Clause had it referred to "any other concept of the origin of life," thus avoiding any mention of the "Biblical version of Creation"?

C. Anti-Discrimination Laws and Religious Convictions

In *Bob Jones Univ. v. United States*, 461 U.S. 574 (1983), excerpted in Chapter Nine, the Supreme Court upheld the decision of the IRS denying tax-exempt status to the University for its policies barring its students, on pain of expulsion, from interracial dating and/or interracial marriage. The Court found compelling the government's interest in prohibiting racial discrimination. After *Bob Jones*, the Court decided several cases concerning the conflict between First Amendment associational claims and state or local anti-discrimination laws. The most important for present purposes is *Roberts v. United States Jaycees*, 468 U.S. 609 (1984). In *Roberts*, the Court upheld a Minnesota statute barring discrimination on the basis of gender against a challenge that the law violated the associational rights of the Jaycees. In addition to barring discrimination on the basis of race, a number of state statutes and local ordinances bar non-governmental or "private" discrimination on the basis of gender, religion, sexual orientation and marital status, among other forms of discrimination. If a person or organization claims that religious convictions constitute the basis for the discriminatory action, should *Bob Jones* be used as the model for deciding whether the state statute or local ordinance barring the discrimination is constitutional?

The tension between religious and secular values has also arisen in the application of state and local anti-discrimination acts to decisions by landlords to refuse for religious reasons to rent to unmarried heterosexual couples. Is barring discrimination on the basis of "marital status" a "compelling state interest" that outweighs the asserted religious freedom interest? How should courts determine whether barring discrimination other than racial or gender discrimination is a "compelling state interest"? While reading the following cases, determine whether a "balancing" of the competing interests is possible, and if so, whether the court adequately explains how it balances them.

The two cases that follow answer those questions differently. In *Swanner v. Anchorage Equal Rights Comm'n*, 874 P.2d 274 (Alaska), *cert. denied*, 513 U.S. 979 (1994), the Alaska Supreme Court held that the refusal by Thomas Swanner, a landlord, to rent to an unmarried couple because they were not married violated state and municipal laws prohibiting discrimination on the basis of marital status. The court then concluded that the laws did not violate the Free Exercise clauses of the Alaska or United States Constitutions. Earlier in the year, the court had come to the same conclusion, but replaced that opinion with the excerpted opinion. Four years earlier, a sharply divided Minnesota Supreme Court held that the Minnesota act barring discrimination on the basis of marital status did not include discrimination against unmarried cohabiting couples. A plurality also concluded that any such regulation would violate the Minnesota Constitution if applied to landlords who discriminated on the basis of marital status for religious reasons. *State v. French*, 460 N.W.2d 2 (Minn. 1990).

Several other courts have addressed this issue, and the results are decidedly mixed. For example, a panel of the United States Court of Appeals for the Ninth Circuit, in *Thomas v. Anchorage Equal Rights Comm'n*, 165 F.3d 692 (9th Cir. 1999), held unconstitutional the laws upheld in *Swanner*. That opinion was subsequently withdrawn by a vote of the Ninth Circuit *en banc*. *Thomas*, 192 F.3d 1208 (9th Cir. 1999). Conversely, after the Illinois Court of Appeals held constitutional Chicago's housing ordinance barring discrimination on the basis of marital status against a free exercise challenge, the Illinois Supreme Court vacated the opinion of the Court of Appeals. *Jasniowski v. Rushing*, 678 N.E.2d 493 (Ill. App.), *vacated*, 685 N.E.2d 622 (Ill. 1997). In *Attorney Gen. v. Desilets*, 636 N.E.2d 233 (Mass. 1994), the Supreme Judicial Court remanded for factfinding the issue whether the Commonwealth's interest in protecting unmarried couples constituted a compelling state interest. Under standard constitutional rights jurisprudence, a finding of a compelling interest would allow the Commonwealth to interfere with the Desilets' right to the free exercise of religion. The California Court of Appeal decided, in *Donahue v. Fair Empl. & Housing Comm'n*, 13 Cal. App. 4th 350, 2 Cal. Rptr. 2d 32 (Ct. App. 1991), *appeal dism'd* 859 P.2d 671 (Cal. 1993), that the constitutional right of free exercise of the landlord outweighed the statutory rights of the unmarried couple. The California Supreme Court later ordered the "depublication" of the opinion of the Court of Appeal, and in *Smith v. Fair Empl. and Housing Comm'n*, held California's law banning housing discrimination on the basis of marital status did not violate the free exercise rights of landlords. 12 Cal. 4th 1143, 913 P.2d 909, 51 Cal. Rptr. 2d 700 (1996). Finally, in *McCready v. Hoffius*, 586 N.W.2d 723 (Mich. 1998), the Michigan Supreme Court held constitutional Michigan's Civil Rights Act after it was challenged as violative of the federal and Michigan free exercise clauses.

Swanner v. Anchorage Equal Rights Commission

874 P.2d 274 (Alaska), *cert. denied*, 513 U.S. 979 (1994)

PER CURIAM.

Swanner, d/b/a Whitehall Properties, appealed the superior court's decision which affirmed the Anchorage Equal Rights Commission's (AERC) order that Swanner's policy against renting to unmarried couples constituted unlawful discrimination based on marital status. Swanner disputes the decision and contends that enforcing the applicable statute and municipal ordinance violates his constitutional right to free exercise of his religion under the United States and Alaska Constitutions.

We hold that Swanner discriminated against the potential tenants based on their marital status. We further hold that enforcing the fair housing laws does not deprive him of his right to free exercise of his religion. We affirm the AERC and superior court decisions.

I. FACTS AND PROCEEDINGS BELOW

Joseph Bowles, William F. Harper, and Dee Moose filed three separate complaints of marital status discrimination in the rental of real property in Anchorage. The complainants alleged that Tom Swanner, doing business as Whitehall Properties, violated municipal and state anti-discrimination laws, Anchorage Municipal Code (AMC) 5.20.020 and AS 18.80.240. Swanner refused to rent or allow inspection of residential properties after learning that each complainant intended to live with a member of the opposite sex to whom he or she was not married.

While Swanner did not specifically recall having conversations with Bowles, Harper, or Moose, he readily admitted having a policy of refusing to rent to any unmarried couple who intend to live together on the property. Swanner's refusal to rent or show property to unmarried couples is based on his Christian religious beliefs. Under Swanner's religious beliefs, even a non-sexual living arrangement by roommates of the opposite sex is immoral and sinful because such an arrangement suggests the appearance of immorality. It is undisputed that Swanner rejected each complainant as a tenant because of this policy and for no other reason.

B. Proceedings Before the Superior Court

Swanner appealed to the superior court on March 8, 1991. Judge Karen L. Hunt heard oral argument on May 15, 1992 and issued a written decision and order on August 31, 1992. She affirmed the AERC's decision, holding that (a) Swanner's conduct constituted unlawful discrimination based upon marital status; [and] (b) enforcement of the state and municipal anti-discrimination laws does not violate Swanner's constitutional rights, pursuant to the U.S. Supreme Court's decision in *Employment Division, Department of Human Resources v. Smith*, 494 U.S. 872 (1990), and our decisions in *Frank v. State*, 604 P.2d 1068 (Alaska 1979) and *Seward Chapel, Inc. v. City of Seward*, 655 P.2d 1293 (Alaska 1982).

C. Proceedings Before This Court

Swanner appealed to this court on September 18, 1992. He contends that the superior court erred in finding that he discriminated against the complainants on the basis of marital status. He claims that he does not discriminate based on marital status, but even if he does, he is excused from compliance with the anti-discrimination laws because of his fundamental right to the free exercise of his religion, guaranteed by the Alaska and United States Constitutions.

II. DISCUSSION

A. Swanner Violated AMC 5.20.020 and AS 18.80.240 by Discriminating Based on Marital Status

Swanner argues that he does not discriminate against individuals based on their marital status because he will rent to people who are single, married, widowed, divorced, or separated. However, he will not rent to those whom he expects will engage in conduct repugnant to his religious beliefs, namely cohabitation outside of marriage. Swanner considers such cohabitation to be fornication and immoral.

The AERC responds that the laws at issue do not recognize a distinction between "marital status" and "cohabitation." The AERC claims the statutes' plain language demonstrates that "marital status" includes cohabitating couples.

In *Foreman v. Anchorage Equal Rights Comm'n*, 779 P.2d 1199,... [w]e held that the landlord's policy against renting to unmarried couples unlawfully discriminated on the basis of marital status. *Id.* at 1203. We reasoned that because the landlord would have rented to the prospective tenants had they been married, and he refused to rent the property only after learning the couple was not married, "[t]his constitutes unlawful discrimination based on marital status." *Id.* The same reasoning applies here. Because Swanner would have rented the properties to the couples had they been married, and he refused to rent the property only after he learned they were not, Swanner unlawfully discriminated on the basis of marital status.

B. Enforcement of AMC 5.20.020 and AS 18.80.240 Does Not Violate Swanner's Constitutional Right to the Free Exercise of His Religion Under the United States Constitution

Swanner contends that enforcement of AMC 5.20.020 and AS 18.80.240 against him has a coercive effect on the free exercise of his religious beliefs. He believes that compliance with these laws forces him to choose between his religious beliefs and his livelihood. He requests that we accommodate his religious beliefs by creating an exemption to the statute and ordinance. The AERC responds that "it is not Swanner's religious beliefs per se which run afoul of our anti-discrimination laws, but rather his actions and conduct in a commercial setting."

Swanner claims that we should apply the "compelling state interest" test set forth in *Sherbert v. Verner* to determine whether the laws at issue violate his right to free exercise of religion under the United States Constitution. However, in *Smith*, the United States Supreme Court expressly rejected applying the *Sherbert* test where the law being challenged is generally applicable, or, in other words, where the law is not directed at any particular religious practice or observance. *Smith*, 494 U.S. at 885. "[A] law that is neutral and of general applicability need not be justified by a compelling governmental interest even if the law has the incidental effect of burdening a particular religious practice." *Church of Lukumi Babalu Aye v. City of Hialeah*, 113 S.Ct. 2217, 2226 (1993) (citing *Smith*).

The first step in determining whether a law is neutral is whether it discriminates on its face. Neither the ordinance nor the statute contain any language singling out any religious group or practice.

Even when a law is facially neutral, however, it may not be neutral if it is crafted to impede particular religious conduct. These laws clear that hurdle as well. The purpose of AMC 5.20.020 and AS 18.80.240 is to prohibit discrimination in the rental housing market. Swanner does not claim that the purpose of the laws is to discriminate against people based on religion; in fact, he contends that the laws do not even cover this kind of discrimination. Therefore, the laws satisfy the requirement of neutrality.

Additionally, these laws are generally applicable. They apply to all people involved in renting or selling property, and do not specify or imply applicability to a particular religious group. Therefore, at least under the general rule, no compelling state interest is necessary.

Smith provides one ground for judicial exemptions from compliance with neutral laws of general applicability. A court may exempt an individual from a law where the facts present a hybrid situation where an additional constitutionally protected right is implicated. Like the appellant in *Smith*, Swanner does not contend that the laws in question here infringe on any constitutional right other than his right to free exercise of religion. Consequently, this case does not present such a "hybrid" situation.

We conclude that enforcing AMC 5.20.020 and AS 18.80.240 against Swanner does not violate his right to free exercise of religion under the United States Constitution.[9]

C. Enforcement of AMC 5.20.020 and AS 18.80.240 Does Not Violate Swanner's Constitutional Right to the Free Exercise of His Religion Under the Alaska Constitution

---

9. Shortly before the publication of this opinion, the United States Congress passed the Religious Freedom Restoration Act of 1993, 107 Stat. 1488 (1993). That act replaced the Smith test with the compelling interest test. Assuming that the Act is constitutional and applies to this case, it does not affect the outcome, because we hold in the next section that compelling state interests support the prohibitions on marital status discrimination. The most effective tool the state has for combatting discrimination is to prohibit discrimination; these laws do exactly that. Consequently, the means are narrowly tailored and there is no less restrictive alternative.

Swanner does not dispute that the ordinance and statute are generally applicable and neutral under Smith, but asserts that "this decision does not mandate use of a less restrictive standard by state courts in interpreting state constitutional protection."

Swanner is correct in asserting that a state court may provide greater protection to the free exercise of religion under the state constitution than is now provided under the United States Constitution. Thus, even though the Free Exercise Clause of the Alaska Constitution is identical to the Free Exercise Clause of the United States Constitution, we are not required to adopt and apply the Smith test to religious exemption cases involving the Alaska Constitution merely because the United States Supreme Court adopted that test to determine the applicability of religious exemptions under the United States Constitution.1[10] In *Frank v. State*, we adopted the *Sherbert* test to determine whether the Free Exercise Clause of the Alaska Constitution requires an exemption to a facially neutral law. 604 P.2d at 1070. We held that to invoke a religious exemption, three requirements must be met: (1) a religion is involved, (2) the conduct in question is religiously based, and (3) the claimant is sincere in his/her religious belief. *Id.* at 1071 (citing *Wisconsin v. Yoder*, 406 U.S. 205, 215–16 (1972)). Once these three requirements are met, "[r]eligiously impelled actions can be forbidden only 'where they pose some substantial threat to public safety, peace or order,' or where there are competing governmental interests 'of the highest order and... [are] not otherwise served....'" *Seward Chapel, Inc. v. City of Seward*, 655 P.2d 1293, 1301 n. 33 (Alaska 1982) (*quoting Frank*, 604 P.2d at 1070).

Swanner clearly satisfies the first and third requirements to invoke an exception to the laws under the Free Exercise Clause. No one disputes that a religion is involved here (Christianity), or that Swanner is sincere in his religious belief that cohabitation is a sin and by renting to cohabitators, he is facilitating the sin. However, the superior court held that he did not meet the second requirement that his conduct was religiously based because "[n]othing in the record permits a finding that refusing to rent to cohabiting unmarried couples is a religious ritual, ceremony or practice deeply rooted in religious belief." Swanner's claim that the superior court misinterpreted *Frank v. State* as limiting

10. Swanner notes that two jurisdictions have held that a landlord may refuse to rent to unmarried couples because of his/her religious beliefs. He cites to decisions from Minnesota and California for the proposition that enforcement of the anti-discrimination laws against him violates his right to free exercise. In Minnesota v. French, 460 N.W.2d 2 (Minn.1990), the Minnesota Supreme Court held that a landlord's refusal to rent to an unmarried couple did not violate Minnesota's anti-discrimination laws and enforcing such laws would violate the landlord's free exercise right. However, in French, the anti-discrimination laws at issue did not define or otherwise explain the term "marital status." The court concluded that the Minnesota Legislature did not intend to include unmarried couples in the definition. *Cf. Foreman*, 779 P.2d at 1203 (holding unmarried couples are included within the state and municipal prohibitions against discrimination based on marital status). Moreover, the Minnesota court relied on the criminal anti-fornication statute then in effect. In contrast, Alaska's fornication provision was repealed well before the discriminatory conduct giving rise to this case occurred. *Compare French*, 460 N.W.2d at 10, *with Foreman*, 779 P.2d at 1202. Further, the *French* court relied on the Minnesota Constitution, article I, section 16, which contains very different language from the Alaska Constitution. *See French*, 460 N.W.2d at 9. In *Donahue v. Fair Employment Housing Comm'n*, 2 Cal. Rptr.2d 32 (Cal. App.1991), *review granted and opinion superseded*, 5 Cal. Rptr.2d 781, 825 P.2d 766 (Cal.1992), *review dismissed as improvidently granted and remanded*, 23 Cal. Rptr.2d 591, 859 P.2d 671 (Cal.1993), the California Court of Appeal held that although the landlords' conduct did constitute prohibited marital status discrimination, the landlords were entitled to an exemption from the anti-discrimination laws because of their religious beliefs. The court based its decision "on independent state constitutional grounds." 2 Cal. Rptr.2d at 40. However, the California Supreme Court depublished the court of appeal's opinion, thereby rendering the decision uncitable. Neither case provides this court with meaningful guidance in interpreting the Free Exercise Clause of the Alaska Constitution.

free exercise rights only to ritual or ceremony has merit. In *Frank*, we determined that the action at issue was a practice deeply rooted in religion. 604 P.2d at 1072–73. However, we did not intend to limit free exercise rights only to actions rooted in religious rituals, ceremonies, or practices. To meet the second requirement, a party must demonstrate that the conduct in question is religiously based; this determination is not limited to actions resulting from religious rituals. Swanner's refusal to rent to unmarried couples is not without an arguable basis in some tenets of the diverse Christian faith, and therefore, his conduct is sufficiently religiously based to meet our constitutional test. Although Swanner meets the three preliminary requirements to invoke an exception to the anti-discrimination laws, the analysis does not end here.

As discussed previously, a religious exemption will not be granted if the religiously impelled action poses "some substantial threat to public safety, peace or order or where there are competing state interests of the highest order." *Frank*, 604 P.2d at 1070. The question is whether Swanner's conduct poses a threat to public safety, peace or order, or whether the governmental interest in abolishing improper discrimination in housing outweighs Swanner's interest in acting based on his religious beliefs.

In our view, the second part of the test adopted in *Frank* is applicable here. Under this part of the *Frank* test, we must determine whether "a compelling state interest of the highest order exists." "The question is whether that interest, or any other, will suffer if an exemption is granted to accommodate the religious practice at issue." *Frank*, 604 P.2d at 1073. The government possesses two interests here: a "derivative" interest in ensuring access to housing for everyone, and a "transactional" interest in preventing individual acts of discrimination based on irrelevant characteristics. Most free exercise cases, including *Frank*, involve "derivative" state interests. In other words, the State does not object to the particular activity in which the individual would like to engage, but is concerned about some other variable that the activity will affect. This can be contrasted with a "transactional" interest in which the State objects to the specific desired activity itself.

For example, in *Frank*, this court exempted a Central Alaska Athabascan Indian needing moose meat for a funeral potlatch from state hunting regulations. The State did not object to killing moose per se (indeed, it expressly allows moose hunting in season); the State's derivative interest was in maintaining healthy moose populations. In the instant case, the government's derivative interest is in providing access to housing for all. One could argue that if a prospective tenant finds alternative housing after being initially denied because of a landlord's religious beliefs, the government's derivative interest is satisfied. However, the government also possesses a transactional interest in preventing acts of discrimination based on irrelevant characteristics regardless of whether the prospective tenants ultimately find alternative housing.

We look to *Prince v. Massachusetts*, 321 U.S. 158 (1943) [excerpted in Chapter Eleven], as an analogy. In *Prince*, the United States Supreme Court refused to grant an exemption to child labor laws for children distributing religious literature. As in this case, the state had a transactional interest: preventing exploitation of children in employment. Thus, the state objected to child labor, the particular activity at issue, per se, not to an effect of that activity. The state legislature had prohibited children from working under certain conditions. Therefore, permitting any child to work under such conditions resulted in harming the government's transactional interest. This transactional government interest does not involve a numerical cutoff below which the harm is insignificant unlike in *Frank*.

Similarly, in the instant case, the legislature and municipal assembly determined that housing discrimination based on irrelevant characteristics should be eliminated. The existence of this transactional interest distinguishes this case from *Frank* and most other free exercise cases where courts have granted exemptions. The government's transactional interest in preventing discrimination based on irrelevant characteristics directly conflicts with Swanner's refusal to rent to unmarried couples. The government views acts of discrimination as independent social evils even if the prospective tenants ultimately find housing. Allowing housing discrimination that degrades individuals, affronts human dignity, and limits one's opportunities results in harming the government's transactional interest in preventing such discrimination. Under *Frank*, this interest will clearly "suffer if an exemption is granted to accommodate the religious practice at issue."

The dissent attempts to prove that the state does not view marital status discrimination in housing as a pressing problem by pointing to other areas in which the state itself discriminates based on marital status. However, those areas are easily distinguished. The government's interest here is in specifically eliminating marital status discrimination in housing, rather than eliminating marital status discrimination in general. Therefore, the other policies which allow marital status discrimination are irrelevant in determining whether the government's interest in eliminating marital status discrimination in housing is compelling.

In the examples the dissent cites, treating married couples differently from unmarried couples is arguably necessary to avoid fraudulent availment of benefits available only to spouses. The difficulty of discerning whose bonds are genuine and whose are not may justify requiring official certification of the bonds via a marriage document. That problem is not present in housing cases: as this case demonstrates, if anything, an unmarried couple who wish to live together are at a disadvantage if they claim to be romantically involved.

It is important to note that any burden placed on Swanner's religion by the state and municipal interest in eliminating discrimination in housing falls on his conduct and not his beliefs. Here, the burden on his conduct affects his commercial activities. In *United States v. Lee*, 455 U.S. 252, the United States Supreme Court stated the distinction between commercial activity and religious observance:

> When followers of a particular sect enter into commercial activity as a matter of choice, the limits they accept on their own conduct as a matter of conscience and faith, are not to be superimposed on the statutory schemes which are binding on others in that activity.

Id. *at 261.*

Swanner complains that applying the anti-discrimination laws to his business activities presents him with a "Hobson's choice"—to give up his economic livelihood or act in contradiction to his religious beliefs. A similar argument was advanced in *Seward Chapel*, where *Seward Chapel* argued that applying the city zoning ordinances to prohibit construction of a parochial school impermissibly burdened the chapel's free exercise rights. 655 P.2d at 1299. We concluded that "there has been no showing of a religious belief which requires members of *Seward Chapel* to locate in [a specific place].... [T]he inconvenience and economic burden of which *Seward Chapel* now complains is caused largely by the choice to build in [a specific place]..." *Id.* at 1302 (footnote omitted).

Swanner has made no showing of a religious belief which requires that he engage in the property-rental business. Additionally, the economic burden, or "Hobson's choice," of which he complains, is caused by his choice to enter into a commercial activity that is regulated by anti-discrimination laws. Swanner is voluntarily engaging in property management. The law and ordinance regulate unlawful practices in the rental of real property and provide that those who engage in those activities shall not discriminate on the basis of marital status. *See* AS 18.80.240; AMC 5.20.020. Voluntary commercial activity does not receive the same status accorded to directly religious activity. *Cf. Frank v. State*, 604 P.2d at 1075 (exempting an Athabascan Indian from state hunting regulations "to permit the observance of the ancient traditions of the Athabascans").

"As [James] Madison summarized the point, free exercise should prevail in every case where it does not trespass on private rights or the public peace." Michael W. McConnell, *Free Exercise Revisionism and the* Smith *Decision*, 57 Chi.L.Rev. 1109, 1145 (1990) (citation omitted). Because Swanner's religiously impelled actions trespass on the private right of unmarried couples to not be unfairly discriminated against in housing, he cannot be granted an exemption from the housing anti-discrimination laws. Therefore, we conclude that enforcement of AMC 5.20.020 and AS 18.80.240 against Swanner does not violate his right to free exercise of religion under the Alaska Constitution.

III. CONCLUSION

We hold that Swanner impermissibly discriminated against Bowles, Harper, and Moose because he would not rent to them based on their marital status. The Free Exercise Clause of the United States and Alaska Constitutions do not permit Swanner to disobey the state and municipal anti-discrimination laws by entitling him to an exemption.

The AERC's final order and the superior court's opinion are AFFIRMED.

MOORE, Chief Justice, dissenting.

Article I, section 4 of the Alaska Constitution declares that "[n]o law shall be made respecting an establishment of religion, or prohibiting the free exercise thereof." As the majority correctly recognizes, this provision may provide greater protection of free exercise rights than is now provided under the United States Constitution. Accordingly, while the United States Supreme Court has adopted a new test to analyze free exercise claims such as the one at issue here, the majority agrees that we will continue to apply the compelling interest test in interpreting the free exercise clause of the Alaska Constitution.

Our decision in *Frank v. State* sets forth the framework from which we must determine whether AMC 5.20.020 and AS 18.80.240 violate Swanner's right to the free exercise of his religion. As we stated in *Frank*, "[n]o value has a higher place in our constitutional system of government than that of religious freedom." For this reason, a facially neutral statute or ordinance which interferes with religious-based conduct must be justified by a compelling state interest. Absent such an interest, our constitution requires an exemption from the laws at issue to accommodate religious practices.

The majority acknowledges that Swanner's actions fall within the ambit of the free exercise clause. Swanner has shown that his refusal to rent apartments to unmarried individuals who plan to live with a member of the opposite sex is based on his Christian faith, which strictly proscribes such cohabitation. No one questions the sincerity of his religious belief that he facilitates a sin by renting to unmarried individuals such as the complainants in this case. For this reason, Swanner's religiously impelled conduct must be protected under Alaska law unless the AERC can show that the conduct poses "some substantial threat to public safety, peace or order," or that there exist competing governmental interests "of the highest order" which are not otherwise served without limiting Swanner's conduct. *Frank*; *Seward Chapel*. I do not believe the AERC has met its burden in this case. I would therefore grant Swanner an exemption to accommodate his religious beliefs.

First, I note that in determining that the governmental interest in this case is "of the highest order," the majority announces an entirely new and unnecessary test examining the state's "transactional" and "derivative" interests.

In my opinion, this amorphous analysis of the state's interests ultimately will prove to be useless in resolving future free exercise cases. Even in this case, I do not believe it provides a useful distinction of the interests at issue. For example, the majority determines that the state has a per se objection to marital status discrimination in housing which overcomes Swanner's free exercise rights. The majority defines this interest as that in "preventing acts of discrimination based on irrelevant characteristics." Such an articulation of the state's interest poses myriad questions. Who is to determine what is an "irrelevant" characteristic? Obviously, marital status is not "irrelevant" to Swanner. It is central to the question whether he will be committing a sin under the dictates of his religion. Is the legislative branch the final arbiter of relevancy or irrelevancy? Further, the discrimination at issue here is not based on innate "characteristics" but rather on the conduct of potential tenants. While this conduct is worthy of some protection, it does not warrant the same constitutional protection given to religiously compelled conduct. I am not willing to place the right to cohabitate on the same constitutional level as the right to freedom from discrimination based on either innate characteristics—such as race or gender—or constitutionally protected belief, such as freedom of religion.

In addition, it remains unclear to me how the state's "derivative" interests are to be identified. Here, that interest is defined with little explanation as being the state's interest in "providing access to housing for all." Does this mean the state has no per se objection to the fact that some individuals may have limited access to housing? In *Frank*, could it not be said that the state had a per se interest in enforcing its hunting regulations?

In *Frank*, this court set forth a workable and sufficient guide to determine whether a governmental interest is sufficiently compelling to overcome an individual's free exercise rights. It seems to me that the majority's effort to expand this analysis adds little to the actual analysis of interests at stake. To the contrary, I see the majority's expansion of *Frank* as little more than a strained effort to distinguish *Frank* from the present situation when such a distinction is not logically justified. In this effort, the majority totally ignores the record in this case, and it engages in a game where the "transactional" or "derivative" label attached to any given state interest predetermines the outcome of the case.

There is no governmental interest "of the highest order" to justify the burden on Swanner's fundamental rights.

Even applying the framework announced by the court in analyzing whether the state's interest is "of the highest order," I cannot agree with the court's reasoning and resulting decision. In essence, the majority's conclusion is that marital status discrimination constitutes such an affront to human dignity that the state has a per se obligation "of the highest order" to prevent it. Based on my analysis of free exercise jurisprudence and the issues surrounding marital status discrimination, I cannot conclude that eradication of marital status discrimination in the rental housing industry constitutes a governmental interest of such high order as to justify burdening Swanner's fundamental constitutional rights.

There can be no question that the state has a compelling interest in eradicating discrimination against certain historically disadvantaged groups. *See, e.g., Bob Jones University v. United States*, 461 U.S. 574, 593–95 (1983) (racial discrimination); *Roberts v. United States Jaycees*, 468 U.S. 609, 625 (1984) (gender discrimination). This compelling interest has been found to exist based on a determination that the discrimination at issue is so invidious to personal dignity and to our concept of fair treatment as to warrant strict protection. There is no question that Swanner's right to freely exercise his religion could and should be burdened if he engaged in such discrimination as a result of his religious beliefs.

This fact does not mean, however, that every form of discrimination is equally invidious or that the state's interest in preventing it necessarily outweighs fundamental constitutional rights. Rather, the cases which have upheld an imposition on free exercise have articulated certain specific reasons that some forms of discrimination are of particular governmental interest and deserving of heightened judicial scrutiny. In *Bob Jones University*, for example, the Supreme Court refused to grant tax-exempt status to schools that maintained racially discriminatory policies under their interpretation of the Bible. In doing so, the Court discussed this nation's long history of officially sanctioned racial segregation and discrimination in education. It further noted that, since the late 1950s, every pronouncement of the Supreme Court and myriad Acts of Congress and Executive Orders attested to a national policy prohibiting such discrimination. Accordingly, the government's interest in eradicating racial discrimination in education was found to be compelling.

Similarly, in *Roberts*, the Supreme Court declared that the state's compelling interest in eradicating discrimination against its female citizens justified any minimal interference with an all-male organization's freedom of expressional association.

The majority today avoids engaging in any similar analysis of marital status discrimination to explain why or how it is so damaging to human dignity to become of such governmental import as to overcome a fundamental constitutional right. This analysis is critical. The majority cites no evidence that marital status classifications have been associated with a history of unfair treatment that would warrant heightened governmental protection. To the contrary, I believe the law is clear that marital status classifications have been accorded relatively low import on the scale of interests deserving governmental protection.

In addition, marital status classifications have never been accorded any heightened scrutiny under the Equal Protection Clause of either the federal or the Alaska Constitutions. Disparate treatment of individuals based on classifications such as race, on the other hand, are reviewed under the highest scrutiny. Gender-based classifications are similarly analyzed under a heightened level of scrutiny at the federal level. The sliding scale approach to equal protection analysis under the Alaska Constitution similarly applies a heightened level of scrutiny to laws burdening racial minorities or other suspect classifications.

My research has not revealed a single instance in which the government's interest in eliminating marital status discrimination has been accorded substantial weight when balanced against other state interests, let alone fundamental constitutional rights. I find nothing to suggest that marital status discrimination is so invidious as to outweigh the fundamental right to free exercise of religion.

The majority comments that its result today is justified because Swanner's right to the free exercise of his religious beliefs must be accorded less weight since he has entered the commercial arena. As discussed above, it is well-accepted that an individual's right to religious freedom will not and cannot always override other interests. *See, e.g., United States v. Lee* (rejecting Amish employer's claim that imposition of social security taxes violated his free exercise rights). However, neither *Lee* nor any other case of which I am aware stands for the proposition that individuals like Swanner altogether waive their constitutional right to the free exercise of religion simply because a conflict between their religious faith and some legislation occurs in a commercial context. To the contrary, the *Lee* Court recognized that, even in a commercial setting, the state must justify its limitation on religious liberty by showing the limitation is "essential to accomplish an overriding governmental interest." *Id.* at 257–58. The AERC has simply failed to meet that burden here.

The majority incorrectly relies on *Seward Chapel* to arrive at its contrary conclusion. Unlike the present case, *Seward Chapel* did not involve a forced decision between giving up one's livelihood or violating one's religious beliefs. In *Seward Chapel*, we merely found that no religious belief required an exception to city zoning laws prohibiting the location of a parochial school on a specific site. No activity was totally prohibited; only the place in which it could be conducted was being regulated. I believe that there is a significant difference between the inconvenience placed upon *Seward Chapel* and the total abrogation of Mr. Swanner's right to earn a living in his chosen profession while abiding by his sincerely held religious beliefs.

There is no basis in the record to conclude that an exemption in this case would create a substantial threat of harm.

I see no evidence whatsoever in the record to suggest that Swanner's conduct poses a substantial threat to public safety, peace or order such that the burden on Swanner's rights is justified. For this reason, I fail to see why an exemption to accommodate Swanner's religious beliefs is not warranted.

As in *Frank*, the record here is completely devoid of any evidence to suggest that there are so many landlords or property managers in Anchorage whose religious beliefs are identical to Swanner's as to constitute a substantial threat to available housing. In a city the size of Anchorage, it is difficult to conclude based on intuition alone that housing availability for unmarried couples will become so scarce as to constitute a substantial threat to community welfare. If there were some persuasive evidence to support such a conclusion, I may well have arrived at a different conclusion today.

I believe Swanner has been presented with a Hobson's choice of either complying with the law or abandoning the precepts of his religion. Since the government's interest in this particular law does not outweigh Swanner's fundamental religious rights, Swanner should be granted an exemption to accommodate his beliefs. For these reasons, I fail to see how a limited exemption for Swanner and others similarly situated is not justified. In my opinion, the analysis and result set forth in this case will return to haunt this court in future decisions.

State v. French

460 N.W.2d 2 (Minn. 1990)

YETKA, Justice.

Appellant was found guilty of discrimination by an administrative law judge to whom a complaint filed with the Department of Human Rights was referred for hearing. Appellant had refused to rent his property to one Susan Parsons because she planned to live there with her fiance. A trial de novo before the district court was denied, and the court of appeals affirmed the action of the administrative law judge. French was ordered to pay \$368.50 in compensatory damages to Parsons, \$400 for mental anguish and suffering, and \$300 civil penalties. We reverse the administrative law judge and the court of appeals.

French owned and occupied a two-bedroom house ("subject property") in Marshall, Minnesota, until moving to a house he purchased in the country. While attempting to sell the subject property, French rented it to both single individuals and married couples. From January to March 1988, French advertised the subject property as being available for rent. On February 22, 1988, French agreed to rent the property to Parsons and accepted a $250 check as a security deposit.

Shortly thereafter, French decided that Parsons had a romantic relationship with her fiance, Wesley Jenson, and that the two would likely engage in sexual relations outside of marriage on the subject property. On February 24, 1988, French told Parsons that he had changed his mind and would not rent the property to her because unmarried adults of the opposite sex living together were inconsistent with his religious beliefs. French is a member of the Evangelical Free Church in Marshall, and his beliefs include that an unmarried couple living together or having sexual relations outside of marriage is sinful. Despite being questioned by French, neither Parsons nor Jenson told French whether they were planning to have sexual relations on the subject property. The record is in dispute as to whether appellant had knowledge of Parsons' intended sexual activity with her fiance, but Parsons did not deny such an intent when queried by French. Even if they would not have had sexual relations on the property, French believes that living together constitutes the "appearance of evil" and would not have rented to them on that basis. French admits that if Parsons had been married to Jenson, he would not have objected renting to them.

Parsons filed a charge of discrimination against French with respondent department alleging that French committed marital status discrimination in violation of the Minnesota Human Rights Act (MHRA) when he refused to rent the subject property to her because she planned to live there with her fiance. Following an investigation, the department issued a complaint against French.

[A] court of appeals panel affirmed that French discriminated against Parsons because of her marital status in violation of the Human Rights Act and that neither the free exercise of religion nor any of French's other arguments provided a defense. We granted French's petition for further review.

We must examine whether appellant's refusal to rent to Parsons constituted a prima facie violation of the Human Rights Act's prohibition of marital status discrimination. The act provides in relevant part:

> It is an unfair discriminatory practice: (1) For an owner, lessee * * * (a) to refuse to sell, rent, or lease * * * any real property because of race, color, creed, religion, national origin, sex, marital status, status with regard to public assistance, disability, or familial status. Minn.Stat. § 363.03, subd. 2.

As applied to this case, French was the owner and lessee of the subject property, and Parsons attempted to rent the property from him.

I. The Definition of "Marital Status"

The respondent cites *State ex rel. McClure v. Sports & Health Club, Inc.*, 370 N.W.2d 844, 849–50 (Minn.1985), as binding precedent as to the definition of "marital status" in the context of cohabitation. A careful reading of *Sports & Health Club*, however, reveals that this reliance is misplaced. In *Sports & Health Club*, this court said:

> Justice Peterson, in dissent, argues that the discrimination claim predicated upon questioning of employees and applicants on cohabitation of unmarried

> persons is not a ground under the statute for finding discrimination. *Even though we agree with his contention*, yet the record appears clear to us that *Sports and Health [Club]* went far beyond permissible bounds in questioning employees and applicants in areas clearly prohibited by the act.

Id. at 850 n. 10 (emphasis added). The contention the *Sports & Health Club* majority was agreeing with was Justice Peterson's observation that the hearing examiner acknowledged "a clear inference of sexual relations between cohabiting couples" and his conclusion that "[i]t is preposterous to impose sanctions upon an employer, particularly this employer, who refused to employ persons whose conduct constitutes criminal misbehavior." *Id.* at 872 (Peterson, J., dissenting). Thus, the *Sports & Health Club* court unanimously agreed that direct evidence of fornication is not necessary and that unequal treatment based on cohabitation was not "marital status" discrimination. Accordingly, if respondent truly feels "obliged to follow clear established precedent," it must conclude that there was no marital status discrimination in the present case.

Read together, [our prior cases] stand for the proposition that, absent express legislative guidance, the term "marital status" will not be construed in a manner inconsistent with this state's policy against fornication and in favor of the institution of marriage.

[The court then concluded that subsequent legislation "did not intend to extend the protection of the MHRA to unmarried, cohabiting couples in the area of housing."]

It is one thing to prohibit an entity which has availed itself of the privilege of doing business for profit in the corporate form from denying Minnesota residents the basic right to earn a living. An employer is entitled to less control over what an employee does away from the place of employment, but, here, French was renting his former residence while it was for sale in a depressed real estate market. It is unreasonably cynical to say that his choice is simple: that he need not rent at all. Economic necessity may require him to seek rental income and this may be as critical to him as the need for wage income underlying the *Sports & Health Club* decision. On the other hand, what burden is imposed on Parsons to enable her to rent, but not live with her fiance on the premises?

II. Minnesota Constitution

Although, in arguments to this court, appellant emphasized the United States Constitution, the issue of protection of religious liberty under the Minnesota Constitution was properly preserved for appeal. In light of the unforeseeable changes in established first amendment law set forth in recent decisions of the United States Supreme Court, justice demands that we analyze the present case in light of the protections found in the Minnesota Constitution. *See Employment Div., Dep't of Human Resources of Oregon v. Smith*; *Minnesota v. Hershberger*, 495 U.S. 901 (1990) (vacating this court's judgment in *State v. Hershberger*, 444 N.W.2d 282 (Minn.1989) and remanding the case for further consideration).

The people of the State of Minnesota have always cherished religious liberty. The Preamble to the Constitution of the State of Minnesota provides:

> We, the people of the state of Minnesota, grateful to God for our civil *and religious liberty*, and desiring to perpetuate its blessings and secure the same to ourselves and our posterity, do ordain and establish this Constitution.

(Emphasis added.) The Minnesota Constitution, unlike the United States Constitution, treats religious liberty as more important than the formation of government. See Preamble, U.S. Const. ("[I]n order to form a more perfect union * * *.").

The pertinent language in the Minnesota Constitution addressing religious liberty is as follows:

> The right of every man to worship God according to the dictates of his own conscience shall never be infringed * * * *nor shall any control of or interference with the rights of conscience be permitted*, or any preference be given by law to any religious establishment or mode of worship; but the liberty of conscience hereby secured shall not be so construed as to excuse acts of licentiousness or justify practices inconsistent with the peace or safety of the state * * *.

Minn. Const. art. I, § 16 (emphasis added).

The plain language of this section commands this court to weigh the competing interests at stake whenever rights of conscience are burdened. Under this section, the state may interfere with the rights of conscience only if it can show that the religious practice in question is "licentious" or "inconsistent with the peace or safety of the state." In the present case, the state has simply failed to make such a showing. Moreover, the state contends that it has a compelling interest in protecting licentious practices which is sufficient to override French's religious freedom.

The broad protection of religious liberty required by the Minnesota Constitution is not surprising given the background of the people who adopted this constitution. This special history, shared by the people who adopted the Minnesota Constitution, was eloquently described by the Wisconsin Supreme Court as follows:

> The early settlers of Wisconsin came chiefly from New England and the Middle States. They represented the best religious, intellectual, and moral culture, and the business enterprise and sagacity, of the people of the states from whence they came. They found here a territory possessing all the elements essential to the development of a great state. They were intensely desirous that the future state should be settled and developed as rapidly as possible. They chose from their number wise, sagacious, Christian men, imbued with the sentiments common to all, to frame their constitution. The convention assembled at a time when immigration had become very large and was constantly increasing. The immigrants came from nearly all the countries of Europe, but most largely from Germany and Ireland. As a class, they were industrious, intelligent, honest, and thrifty—just the material for the development of a new state. Besides, they brought with them, collectively, much wealth. They were also religious and sectarian. Among them were Catholics, Jews, and adherents of many Protestant sects. These immigrants were cordially welcomed, and it is manifest the convention framed the constitution with reference to attracting them to Wisconsin. Many, perhaps most, of these immigrants came from countries in which a state religion was maintained and enforced, while some of them were non-conformists and had suffered under the disabilities resulting from their rejection of the established religion. Such were the circumstances surrounding the convention which framed the constitution. In the light of them, *and with a lively appreciation by its members of the horrors of sectarian intolerance and the priceless value of perfect religious and sectarian freedom and equality, is it unreasonable to say that sectarian instruction was thus excluded* * * *?

State ex rel. Weiss v. District Bd. of School Dist. No. Eight, 76 Wis. 177, 197–98, 44 N.W. 967, 974–75 (1890) (emphasis added).

In view of the above considerations and the history our state shares with the State of Wisconsin, we are compelled to conclude that French must be granted an exemption from the MHRA unless the state can demonstrate compelling and overriding state interest, not only in the state's general statutory purpose, but in refusing to grant an exemption to French.

In short, we interpret the Minnesota Constitution as requiring a more stringent burden on the state; it grants far more protection of religious freedom than the broad language of the United States Constitution. Pursuant to this analysis, we conclude that the state has failed to sustain its burden in demonstrating a sufficiently compelling interest.

It appears that we have now reached the stage in Minnesota constitutional law where the religious views of a probable majority of the Minnesota citizens are being alleged by a state agency to violate state law. Today we have a department of state government proposing that, while French has sincere religious beliefs and those beliefs are being infringed upon by the Human Rights Act, the state, nevertheless, has an interest in promoting access to housing for cohabiting couples which overrides French's right to exercise his religion.

Respondent characterizes the state's interest as "eliminating pernicious discrimination, including marital status discrimination." We are not told what is so pernicious about refusing to treat unmarried, cohabiting couples as if they were legally married. The state does not even attempt to reconcile this notion with this court's express recognition of the "preferred status" of the institution of marriage in *Kraft*.

There are numerous other contexts in which cohabiting couples are not legally entitled to the same treatment as married couples. A prime example is found in the area of employee life and health insurance benefits, a subject which is also regulated by the MHRA. *See* Minn.Stat. § 363.03, subd. 1(2)(c) (1989 Supp.). Other examples are found in the laws governing intestate succession and the rules of evidence governing the privilege for marital communications. Is the argument now being made that these too are "pernicious" discrimination? If they are, surely it is the role of the legislature to make whatever changes are necessary.

How can there be a compelling state interest in promoting fornication when there is a state statute on the books prohibiting it? *See* Minn.Stat. § 609.34 (1988). Moreover, if the state has a duty to enforce a statute in the least restrictive way to accommodate religious beliefs, surely it is less restrictive to require Parsons to abide by the law prohibiting fornication than to compel French to cooperate in breaking it. Rather than grant French an exemption from the MHRA, the state would rather grant everyone an exemption from the fornication statute. Such a result is absurd.

The state argues that, if French is granted an exemption, landlords would be able to discriminate against single people with children or even a divorced person who has remarried. We believe the response to this argument is self-evident. Here we are punishing French for refusing to disregard a statute prohibiting fornication as well as his religious beliefs. The state clouds an already murky analysis by referring to cases involving discrimination against constitutionally recognized suspect classes.

There are certain moral values and institutions that have served western civilization well for eons. *See Maynard v. Hill*, 125 U.S. 190, 211 (1888) (characterizing marriage as "the foundation of family and society, without which there would be neither civilization nor progress"), cited with approval in *Zablocki v. Redhail*, 434 U.S. 374, 384 (1978). This generation does not have a monopoly on either knowledge or wisdom. Before abandoning fundamental values and institutions, we must pause and take stock of our present social order: millions of drug abusers; rampant child abuse; a rising underclass without marketable job skills; children roaming the streets; children with only one parent or no parent at all; and children growing up with no one to guide them in developing any set of values. How can we expect anything else when the state itself contributes, by arguments of this kind, to further erosion of fundamental institutions that have formed the foundation of our civilization for centuries?[7]

Since our decision is based entirely on interpretation of our state statutes and on the Minnesota Constitution, we need not address respondent's arguments as to the application of the United States Constitution, and we decline to do so. We find that, on statutory grounds and on the grounds of the Minnesota Constitution, French was within his rights in refusing to rent to Parsons.

In summary, because the state should not be able to force a person to break one statute to obey another, because there is a less restrictive means to reconcile the statutes in question, and because of the state's paramount need under our constitution to protect religious freedom, we reverse the decision of the court of appeals.

SIMONETT, Justice (concurring as to Part I).

I join Part I of the court's opinion. Because the issue of statutory construction is dispositive here, I do not reach the constitutional questions.

POPOVICH, Chief Justice (dissenting).

I respectfully dissent. Precedent establishes the refusal to rent real property to an unmarried woman because she would be living with her fiance is a prima facie violation of the Minnesota Human Rights Act's (MHRA) prohibition of marital status discrimination. I believe the majority misconstrues legislative history, public policy and the facts presented to reach a result contrary to this court's interpretation of the MHRA.

I.

With regard to marital status discrimination, states are split on whether "living together" falls within the definition of "marital status." Minnesota has taken the position that it does. Our precedents are clear that discriminating against an individual because of the person that individual lives with constitutes marital status discrimination. In *Sports & Health Club*, we held that an employer discriminated on the basis of marital status when it refused to hire job applicants who were living with, but not married to, persons of the opposite sex.

The conduct at issue here, the refusal to rent to an unmarried woman because she was single and living with a person of the opposite sex, constitutes marital discrimina-

---

7. In a recent thought-provoking magazine article, the author discussed the phenomenon of family breakdown and accompanying social problems and made the following observation:

> Given family integrity's essential importance, one might have expected society-wide efforts to support and encourage two-parent families when signs of rot were first detected, in the 1960s. That didn't happen. For the past quarter century American public policy has shied away from the idea that certain family forms are more desirable than others. There is no attempt to promote childbearing within wedlock. There is little penalty attached to child abandonment. There is scant recognition of the social benefits of marriage, or of the social contributions of those who devote themselves to conscientious childrearing. There is no reward from our public programs for standing by kith and kin.

Zimmerman, *Growing Up Scared*, The Atlantic Monthly, June 1990, at 52. Elsewhere in the article, the author noted that support is growing for incentives in favor of intact families in public housing programs. *See id.* at 53–56.

tion and a prima facie violation of the Minnesota Human Rights Act. French's conduct in refusing to rent to Parsons because she was single and living with a person of the opposite sex constituted marital discrimination, a prima facie violation of the Minnesota Human Rights Act.

II.

Once a prima facie discrimination case is established, a presumption of discrimination arises and the burden shifts to appellant to prove his conduct was motivated by a legitimate nondiscriminatory defense. The remaining question is whether there was a "legitimate nondiscriminatory" defense for French's violation. French asserts two defenses: free exercise of religion and due process/equal protection.

Is appellant's first amendment right to free exercise of religion violated by enforcement of this provision of the Human Rights Act against him? While there is an absolute right to hold religious beliefs, *Wisconsin v. Yoder*; *Cantwell v. Connecticut*, religiously grounded conduct is not absolutely protected. *Bowen v. Roy*, 476 U.S. 693, 699 (1986); *Yoder*; *Braunfeld v. Brown*, 366 U.S. 599, 603 (1961). Although the free exercise clause may provide an individual an exemption from the enforcement of an applicable government regulation, *see Thomas v. Review Bd.*, 450 U.S. 707, 718–19 (1981); *Sherbert v. Verner*, 374 U.S. 398, 408–09 (1963), the clause does not automatically override a conflict with a state statute. Instead, a burden on an individual's practice of religious beliefs must be balanced against the state's interest in the burdensome regulation, *Yoder*, with the burden permitted whenever the state interest is overriding or compelling and the interest cannot be achieved by alternative means. *United States v. Lee*, 455 U.S. 252, 257–58 (1982); *Yoder*.

Our leading case establishes a four-part test for analyzing a request for an exemption from a statute based on the free exercise of religion under both the federal and state constitutions:

1. whether the objector's religious belief is sincerely held;
2. whether the state regulation burdens the exercise of this religious belief;
3. whether the state interest in this regulation is overriding or compelling; and
4. whether the state regulation uses the least restrictive means.

Sports & Health Club. An individual claiming an exemption must prove the first two parts, but the state can successfully defend its statute by proving the third and fourth requirements. The majority's attempt to interpret the Minnesota Constitution's Freedom of Conscience provision more broadly is not supported by a single decision of this court.

1. Sincerely Held Religious Beliefs.

The first requirement is the individual must have a sincerely held religious belief with regard to the contested matter. This is a subjective, personal test, and we are not to question the propriety or correctness of this belief or religious doctrine. According to French, he believes "sex outside of marriage is sinful [and] living together * * * constitutes the 'appearance of evil' to which I am also opposed." The sincerity of these beliefs is undisputed, and French has satisfied this requirement.

2. Burden on Religious Belief.

Second, an individual claiming an exemption must show the applicable government regulation burdens this sincerely held religious belief. An affirmative obligation or prohibition combined with sanctions is more burdensome than a denial of benefits. *Bowen*;

Yoder. The burden on appellant's religious beliefs is the choice French was required to make between adhering to his religious beliefs—that living together outside of marriage is immoral—by refusing to rent to unmarried couples living together, or modifying his behavior to comply with the Human Rights Act.

The distinction between public and private activities underlies freedom of religion cases. The U.S. Supreme Court has recognized that the Minnesota Human Rights Act properly "adopted a functional definition of public accommodations that reaches various forms of public, quasi-commercial conduct." *Roberts.* In *Lee*, the Supreme Court stated: "When followers of a particular sect enter into commercial activity as a matter of choice, the limits they accept on their own conduct as a matter of conscience and faith are not to be superimposed on the statutory schemes which are binding on others in that activity." We also recognized this distinction in *Sports & Health Club*:

> [T]he government has a responsibility to afford its citizens equal access to all accommodations open to the general public. * * * Sports and Health * * * is not a religious corporation—it is a Minnesota business corporation engaged in business for profit. By engaging in this secular endeavor, appellants have passed over the line that affords them absolute freedom to exercise religious beliefs. * * * when appellants entered into the economic arena and began trafficking in the market place [sic], they have subjected themselves to the standards the legislature has prescribed not only for the benefit of prospective and existing employees, but also for the benefit of the citizens of the state as a whole in an effort to eliminate pernicious discrimination.

370 N.W.2d at 853.

While the scale of the public activity here is not as large as in *Sports & Health Club*, the legislature has drawn the line distinguishing public and private activity as it relates to rental housing by excepting "the rental by a resident owner or occupier of a one-family accommodation of a room or rooms in the accommodation" from several of the Human Rights Act's prohibitions, including marital status discrimination. Minn.Stat. § 363.02, subd. 2(1)(b) (Supp.1989). We are not in a position to question or redraw this line since the legislature in its wisdom determined the exemption. The private activity exemption from the Human Rights Act does not extend to someone, such as French, renting property where he does not live.

French contends this distinction says constitutional liberties do not apply in the public arena, but in reality by entering the public marketplace one is subjecting oneself to laws concerning public behavior, including anti-discrimination laws, that must be balanced against first amendment interests. There is no first amendment right to yell "fire" in a crowded theater. Upon entering the public marketplace appellant could no longer consider just his rights and beliefs, but became subject to certain state laws and the rights of potential tenants. The legislature has not exempted an isolated sale or rental of property other than the property where the landlord resides. As respondent states "the First Amendment does not bestow upon the individual an absolute right to require others in the marketplace to adopt those values as a precondition to doing business with him or her." Appellant is free, in his private life, to not associate with anyone whom he feels has the "appearance of evil," but when someone voluntarily enters the public marketplace he may encounter laws that are inconsistent with his religious beliefs. While the Act imposes a burden on French's sincerely held religious belief that living together is sinful, such a burden is greatly lessened because it occurred only when French voluntarily entered into the rental marketplace—by crossing over the line drawn by the legislature—and thus subjecting himself to potentially burdensome regulations such as the Act's prohibition of marital status discrimination.

3. State's Overriding or Compelling Interest.

If the state shows it has a compelling or overriding interest for the burdensome regulation it can prevent a religious-based exemption from that regulation. If the state interest is compelling, it will overbalance any burden on religious beliefs. The question thus is whether the State of Minnesota has a compelling or overriding interest in enforcing the Human Rights Act's prohibition of marital status discrimination in rental housing. Relying on very old cases from other jurisdictions, appellant contends the only possible state interest is promoting public health, safety, or morality, but this completely ignores the Human Rights Act and controlling precedent from both this court and the U.S. Supreme Court.

Courts have repeatedly recognized there is a compelling state interest in eradicating invidious discrimination. *Roberts* (gender); *Bob Jones University* (race); *Gay Rights Coalition v. Georgetown Univ.*, 536 A.2d 1, 38 (D.C.App.1987) (sexual orientation); *see also EEOC v. Pacific Press Publishing Ass'n*, 676 F.2d 1272, 1280 (9th Cir.1982) ("elimination of all forms of discrimination [is a] 'highest priority.' * * * [the] purpose to end discrimination is equally if not more compelling than other interests that have been held to justify legislation that burdened the exercise of religious convictions.") (citations omitted).

The U.S. Supreme Court case most similar to the present case is *Bob Jones University*, where discriminatory practices were defended on a free exercise of religion basis. The University claimed the IRS Commissioner's "policy cannot constitutionally be applied to schools that engage in racial discrimination on the basis of sincerely held religious beliefs." Despite finding sincerely held religious beliefs and a burden on these beliefs, the Court held that preventing discrimination clearly is a compelling state interest using the least restrictive means, and thus held that invidious discrimination cannot be justified by religious beliefs.

Providing equal access to housing in Minnesota by eliminating pernicious discrimination, including marital status discrimination, is an overriding compelling state interest. The majority outlines numerous situations where the state, not private individuals, treats people differently because of their marital status. The facts of this case involve one individual discriminating against another individual because of marital status. Housing is a basic human need regardless of a person's personal characteristics, and the legislature has properly determined that it should be available without regard to "race, color, creed, religion, national origin, sex, marital status, status with regard to public assistance, disability, or familial status." Minn.Stat. § 363.03, subd. 2(1)(a). "[A] court cannot lightly dispute a determination by the political branches that the * * * interests at stake are compelling." *Finzer v. Barry*, 798 F.2d 1450, 1459 (D.C.Cir.1986), *aff'd sub nom. Boos v. Barry*, 485 U.S. 312 (1988). An individual's marital or familial status, just like the other prohibited classifications, is irrelevant to holding a job or renting a house, because it "bears no relation to the individual's ability to participate in and contribute to society." *Mathews v. Lucas*, 427 U.S. 495, 505 (1976).

The Human Rights Act is to "be construed liberally for the accomplishment of [its] purposes," Minn.Stat. § 363.11 (1988), which include "secur[ing] for persons in this state, freedom from discrimination [i]n employment [and i]n housing." *Id.* § 363.12. In interpreting the Minnesota Human Rights Act, the U.S. Supreme Court stated: "[A]cts of invidious discrimination in the distribution of publicly available goods, services, and other advantages cause unique evils that government has a compelling interest to prevent—wholly apart from the point of view such conduct may transmit. * * * such practices are entitled to no constitutional protection." *Roberts*. The Act "reflects [Minnesota's] strong historical commitment to eliminating discrimination and assuring its citizens equal access to publicly available goods and services." *Id.* at 624. The *Roberts* Court found Minnesota, under the Act, had a compelling interest in eradicating discrimination against its female citizens. In *Sports & Health Club*, where one of the Human Rights Act violations was a refusal to hire people living together, we stated the government clearly has

> an overriding compelling interest in prohibiting discrimination in employment and public accommodation. * * * In a pluralistic and democratic society, government has a responsibility to insure that all its citizens have equal opportunity for employment, promotion, and job retention without having to overcome artificial and largely irrelevant barriers occurring from gender, status, or beliefs to the main decision of competence to perform the work. * * * The [state has an] overriding compelling interest [in] eliminating discrimination based upon sex, race, marital status, or religion * * *.

The majority ignores the *Sports & Health Club*'s holding. Since it is not overruled, we are obliged to follow its precedent.

Religious and moral values include not discriminating against others solely because of their color, sex, or whom they live with, avoiding unnecessary emotional suffering, showing tolerance for nontraditional lifestyles, and treating others as one would wish to be treated. This supposedly immoral couple were married by the time of the ALJ hearing, furthering the values the majority promotes. It may be difficult for some individuals to recognize invidious discrimination, but one must not lose sight of the continuing fight of minorities to be protected from a "probable majority" point of view. It was not long ago that blacks and women were widely viewed as second-class citizens. Discrimination usually comes in less obvious forms—such as against single parents, those with AIDS, homosexuals, the elderly, and those living together—but no less invidious forms. The majority, in effect, would have us return to the day of "separate but equal" where individuals such as French would be permitted to keep their neighborhoods free of "undesirables" and "nonbelievers." *See Shelley v. Kraemer*, 334 U.S. 1, 10–13 (1948) ("Equality in the enjoyment of property rights was regarded by the framers * * * as an essential pre-condition to the realization of other basic civil rights and liberties * * *.").

Appellant also would have us distinguish between "bad" types of discrimination, such as based upon race, gender, or handicap, and "good discrimination," such as against drug dealers, child abusers, and fornicators (people living together). French cites no cases breaking up an anti-discrimination statute into discrete parts and finding the interest in eradicating certain types of discrimination to be less than compelling. In fact, the District of Columbia Court of Appeals refused to single out its prohibition of sexual preference discrimination as less than compelling. *Gay Rights Coalition*, 536 A.2d at 38. We should reaffirm that the prevention of invidious discrimination in Minnesota, including on the basis of marital status, is a compelling state interest.

4. Least Restrictive Means.

The last requirement is that the state regulation use the least restrictive means of achieving the state's goals. Although the government has a compelling interest that justifies a burden on religious activity, the state must also show the regulation is no more burdensome than necessary to promote the secular interest. Courts have found some alternatives to be less restrictive and less burdensome on an individual's free exercise rights.

French contends a less restrictive means is for the state simply to not enforce the Act's prohibition of marital status discrimination. That is not a less restrictive means; it would be a complete abrogation of the state's goal of preventing invidious discrimination. *See Gay Rights Coalition*, 536 A.2d at 39 (refusing to abrogate state interest in eradicating sexual orientation discrimination). Previous cases have refused to abolish the goals behind preventing marital status discrimination. *Sports & Health Club.*

The only possible less restrictive means is to grant those individuals with sincerely held religious beliefs an exemption from the Human Rights Act. We refused to grant such an exemption in *Sports & Health Club*, stating: "The state's overriding compelling interest of eliminating discrimination based upon sex, race, marital status, or religion could be substantially frustrated if employers, professing as deep and sincere religious beliefs as those held by [the Sports & Health Club] could discriminate against the protected classes." Federal courts have also consistently refused to allow religious exemptions from anti-discrimination statutes. *Bob Jones University* (free exercise exemption "cannot be accommodated" with prevention of discrimination); *EEOC v. Mississippi College*, 626 F.2d 477, 489 (5th Cir.1980) ("creation of [a free exercise] exemption greater than that provided by [Title VII] would seriously undermine the means chosen by Congress to combat discrimination * * *."), *cert. denied*, 453 U.S. 912 (1981). Granting exemptions from an anti-discrimination statute defeats its effectiveness in preventing discrimination. *Gay Rights Coalition*, 536 A.2d at 39. The legislature, in Minn.Stat. § 363.02, subd. 2(1)(b), has already drawn a line that grants an exemption from the Human Rights Act to small-scale landlords renting out a room in the home in which they live. The majority ignores our *Sports & Health Club* holding and the fact the legislature has already drawn a line for granting religiously based exemptions in the case of small-scale landlords. The majority's arguments properly should be left to the legislature. If the legislature wishes to redraw this line so as to exclude individuals like French from the Human Rights Act, it is perfectly free to do so. But until the legislature changes the statute it should be enforced as written, since it is within the permissible parameters of constitutional principles. Appellant's request for an exemption from the Human Rights Act would substantially hinder the fulfillment of the state's goal of preventing invidious discrimination. No alternative means appear available.

IV.

Discriminating against unmarried individuals living with members of the opposite sex is neither the cause or the solution to societal woes. The majority's decision rejects the reasoned precedents of this court. Unless the legislature acts differently or until those cases are overruled, we are obliged to follow clear, established precedent in this state.

Notes

1. The Supreme Court denied Swanner's petition for certiorari. *Swanner v. Anchorage Equal Rights Comm'n*, 513 U.S. 979 (1994). Dissenting, Justice Thomas urged granting the petition to decide whether the state's interest in preventing discrimination on the basis of marital status was compelling under the standard set forth in the Religious Freedom Restoration Act of 1993, 107 Stats. 1488. *Id.* In his view, *Swanner* was not analogous to *Bob Jones*, because "[b]y contrast, there is surely no 'firm national policy' against marital status discrimination in housing decisions." *Id.* at 981. The Religious

Freedom Restoration Act was held unconstitutional in *City of Boerne v. Flores*, 521 U.S. 507 (1997).

2. The majority in *Swanner* concludes that the state's "transactional" and "derivative" interests are of the "highest order" and thus constitute a "compelling state interest." The state's "derivative" interest is "in ensuring access to housing for everyone." This derivative interest would be satisfied even if the landlord refused to rent to the unmarried couple once the couple found housing. However, the compelling state interest was the state's "transactional interest." The "transactional interest," according to the court, is the state's interest "in preventing individual acts of discrimination based on irrelevant characteristics." Thus, even after the unmarried couple found an alternative place to live, the state's transactional interest remained a compelling interest, because "the State objects to the specific desired activity itself." Are "irrelevant characteristics" defined based solely on the types of discrimination prohibited in the language of the statute and ordinance? Does that mean that forms of discrimination not specifically prohibited by the statute are not "irrelevant"? Does the court's explanation beg the question of how one determines and who determines whether the characteristics are "irrelevant"?

The court concludes that "[a]llowing housing discrimination that degrades individuals, affronts human dignity, and limits one's opportunities results in harming the government's transactional interest in preventing such discrimination." Does the state's refusal to accept Swanner's reason for discriminating degrade him by concluding that his religious faith is not as important as the values promoted by the state? Does the court's conclusion that "marital status" discrimination is impermissible when applied to unmarried heterosexual couples apply equally as well to homosexual couples? Based on the language used by the court in *Swanner*, does the answer to the previous question depend on whether the state explicitly prohibits discrimination on the basis of "sexual orientation"?

What factors should a court use to determine whether a particular state interest is "compelling"? Is invoking the word "discrimination" enough? Does the Alaska court provide assistance in understanding this inquiry? Is the compelling state interest test in any sense meaningful? *See* Chapter One § A.

Is there some way to demarcate a boundary line that limits a state's "transactional" interest? Many state statutes declare particular state policies. Are these declarations sufficient to create a "transactional" interest that trumps the assertion of a constitutional right? Does *Prince v. Massachusetts*, 321 U.S. 158 (1944), excerpted in Chapter Eleven, on which the Alaska Supreme Court heavily relied, and which permitted the state to prohibit child "labor" even when the labor was religious proselytization, provide the proper precedent? Is there a constitutional difference when a child's health or safety is involved, thus distinguishing *Prince* and *Swanner*?

The majority also concluded that the state law and municipal ordinance affected only Swanner's actions, not his religious beliefs. Does this invocation of the belief/action dichotomy persuade you the court came to the correct conclusion?

3. The *Swanner* majority also justifies its decision by noting the "fact" that Swanner was voluntarily engaged in a commercial activity, thus subjecting himself to the anti-discrimination law. As a result, Swanner's claim that applying the anti-discrimination law to him put him to the "Hobson's Choice" of "giv[ing] up his economic livelihood or act[ing] in contradiction to his religious beliefs" was "caused by his choice to enter into a commercial activity that is regulated by anti-discrimination laws." Does this "assumption of risk" type of argument overlook the pervasiveness of governmental reg-

ulation since the New Deal? How does Swanner's "Hobson's Choice" differ from the "choice" provided Adele Sherbert in *Sherbert v. Verner*, 374 U.S. 398 (1963), who was given the choice of working on Saturdays and violating her religious beliefs or adhering to her religious beliefs and thus being ineligible for unemployment compensation? Is the difference a difference between affecting the state's "economic" values as opposed to its "noneconomic" or "moral" values? Is this another version of modern "substantive due process"? Does the court's resort to the language of "choice" suggest the inability of the law to do more than "tolerate" practices or beliefs which may be antithetical to the "philosophical" or "religious" or "cultural" beliefs of either the state legislature or the members of the court?

4. In *French*, both the majority and dissent discuss at length the meaning of *State* ex rel. *McClure v. Sports & Health Club, Inc.*, 370 N.W.2d 844 (Minn. 1985). This case upheld, against a challenge on associational and free exercise grounds, a challenge to the application of the Minnesota Human Right Act to the hiring practices of the Club. The Club was owned by three "'born-again' Christians," whose "fundamentalist religious convictions require them to act in accordance with the teachings of Jesus Christ and the will of God in their business as well as in their personal lives." *Id.* at 846. Interviews of prospective employees included questions about the applicants' religious beliefs and practices, including whether they believed in God, heaven or hell, and whether they read the Bible and attended church. In addition, prospective employees were asked about their marital status, and whether they engaged in pre-marital or extra-marital sexual relations. Further, "only born-again Christians are permitted to be managers or assistant managers." *Id.* at 847. In rejecting the claim of infringement of Free Exercise rights, the Court relied in part on *Bob Jones* and *Roberts*, and in part on the "secular" nature of the Club, which was a privately owned, for-profit commercial enterprise. The majority distinguishes *Sports & Health Club*, in part by noting the "personal" nature of the rental property, and in part by noting the relative lack of affluence of French. Is this persuasive? How does *Sports & Health Club* differ from *Amos* and *Townley Engineering*, both excerpted in Chapter Eight?

5. To what extent should the notion of a difference between the "private" and "public" sphere affect the court's analysis? Both the majority in *Swanner* and the dissent in *French* rely on the "voluntary" actions of the landlords to engage in commercial (or public) activity to justify application of the anti-discrimination laws to them. Is there some notion of voluntarily entering into a "public" activity that should guide the decisions of the court's in enforcing anti-discrimination laws? Should all arguably "commercial" activity be equated with public action? If "public" action is subject to state anti-discrimination laws, doesn't that define for religious adherents their religious faith? To say that an action is "secular" rather than "religious" defines what is "religious," doesn't it? If a court simply defers to the definition of "religious" offered by the claimants, however, doesn't that create a "slippery slope"? Does it matter that some persons accused of prostitution have claimed a religious justification for their actions? Is there a difference when the subjective definition offered by the religious believer does not contradict the criminal law (as in *Smith* and the prostitution example), but civil law?

6. The plurality in *French* concluded that "marital status" did not include unmarried couples. Why then did the plurality address the Free Exercise issue? Is there a sense from the plurality opinion that the Minnesota Human Rights Act is an affront to "traditional" values? Is there a link between the plurality's conclusions that application of the law violates the free exercise rights of French and its view that society is "abandoning fundamental values and institutions"? In addition to its reliance on history, the plurality

notes that the "traditional" view is probably supported by a majority of the people of Minnesota. Is this an empirical claim? Is it accurate? Is this a "fact" that can properly be relied upon by the plurality in justifying its conclusion?

7. The dissent in *French* makes two additional points to its argument about "voluntariness." First, it concludes that "[r]eligious and moral values include not discriminating against others solely because of their color, sex, or whom they live with, avoiding unnecessary emotional suffering, showing tolerance for nontraditional lifestyles, and treating others as one would wish to be treated." Is this an empirical claim? Is it an aspirational claim? Does this statement suggest that any religion whose tenets may not include all of those requirements should not be treated "tolerantly" by the court, or by law? Second, the dissent relies on *Gay Rights Coalition v. Georgetown Univ.*, 536 A.2d 1 (D.C.App.1987), which held that although Georgetown University, a Jesuit (Catholic) University, was not required to "recognize" a gay rights student organization, it violated the District of Columbia's Human Rights Act in denying tangible benefits to that group. Additionally, the court held that application of the Act to Georgetown University, though a burden on the Free Exercise rights of the University, was permissible because eradication of discrimination on the basis of sexual orientation was a compelling state interest. Is there a constitutional difference between racial and gender discrimination and discrimination based on marital status and sexual orientation? The dissent in *French* does not mention that Congress later passed a law exempting Georgetown University and Catholic University of America from any District of Columbia law barring discrimination on the basis of sexual orientation. *Nation's Capital Religious Liberty and Academic Freedom Act*, 102 Stat. 2269 (1988). Should the existence of this statute affect the authority of *Gay Rights Coalition*? Does the fact that Georgetown has not relied on the statute in its actions regarding the gay rights organization, see Mark Tushnet, *The Rhetoric of Free Exercise Discourse*, 1993 B.Y.U. L. Rev. 117, 128, affect the authority of *Gay Rights Coalition*?

8. To what extent does liberal political theory permit the state to compel some citizens to either "accept" or "tolerate" behavior or beliefs that they oppose? Should courts permit individuals or groups to use the Constitution to shield their discriminatory actions by resort to the First Amendment? Are these cases another aspect of the ongoing culture wars? *See* James Davison Hunter, CULTURE WARS (1991) (discussing cultural divide on, among other issues, homosexual conduct and abortion).

9. A criticism of *Swanner* is found in 108 Harv. L. Rev. 763 (1995).

Randall v. Orange County Council, Boy Scouts of America

38 Cal.App. 4th 630, 28 Cal.Rptr. 2d 53 (1994), *overruled* 17 Cal.4th 736, 952 P.2d 261, 72 Cal.Rptr.2d 453 (Cal. 1998)

CROSBY, Associate Justice.

Does the Unruh Civil Rights Act apply to the Orange County Council of the Boy Scouts of America? Yes. May the council, the only named defendant, discriminate on the basis of religious beliefs or lack of religious beliefs? No.

I

This is an appeal from an action for injunctive relief and statutory damages ($250) on behalf of eleven-year-old twin brothers, plaintiffs Michael and William Randall, who were members of Cub Scout Den 4, Pack 519, located in Anaheim Hills. The boys prevailed at trial, obtaining an injunction barring defendant Orange County Council, Boy Scouts of America or any packs or dens from excluding them from scouting or advancing in the organization based on their religious beliefs.

Den 4 has five or six members who attend the same neighborhood school. Pack 519 is comprised of Den 4 and a half dozen others and affiliated with defendant Orange County Council, Boy Scouts of America. The pack has no assets, but is operated by a parents' committee chartered by the county council.

The Randalls had advanced several scouting ranks when their family moved to the Den 4 neighborhood in 1990. At the boys' fourth or fifth meeting in the new den, the den mother read the first "achievement" in the Bear Book, the instruction manual for the next Cub Scout ranking, the Bear Badge. Quoted directly from the book, it reads as follows: "We are lucky. The people who wrote and signed our Constitution were very wise. They understood the need of Americans to worship God as they choose. A member of your family will be able to talk with you about your duty to God. Remember, this achievement is part of your Cub Scout Promise: 'I, ____________, promise to do my best to do my duty to God and my country.... '

"REQUIREMENT

"Practice your religion as you are taught in your home, church, synagogue, mosque, or other religious community.

"I worship God: in song[,] in prayer[,] in study[,] and by kind and thoughtful acts toward others."

Alternatively the achievement could be attained in the following way: "Many signs remind us of God. Among them are a 6-pointed star, a cross, and a crescent. There are many other religious symbols. One of them may appear on a special emblem you may earn to wear on your uniform.

"Learn more about your faith from your rabbi, minister, priest, imam, elder, or other religious leader.

"REQUIREMENT

"Earn the religious emblem of your faith."

According to defendant, Michael and William responded that they would have a problem because they did not believe in God and were atheists. This caused some commotion among the other boys, and the den mother removed the twins from the room. She asked what they did believe in; and they replied, "themselves." The boys testified the word "atheist" was not in their vocabulary and was suggested by the den mother. They denied disrupting the meeting.

In any event, the boys' parents were informed of the religion achievement requirement and told their sons could not continue in scouting if they did not believe in God. With their mother as guardian ad litem, the boys' attorney father soon brought suit.

II

It has long been the law of California that the Boy Scouts, on the national and council levels, are businesses subject to regulation under the Unruh Act. *(Curran v. Mount Diablo Council of the Boy Scouts* (1983) 147 Cal.App.3d 712, 717, 195 Cal.Rptr. 325.)

Nothing in the evidence produced below calls the *Curran* decision into question. Indeed, the facts established at trial strongly support its conclusion.

The Unruh Act has been amended three times since 1983; and while the Legislature is considered to be familiar with appellate opinions, it has not chosen to overturn *Curran*. Neither has the Supreme Court, which recognized its appearance in passing in a similar holding in *Isbister v. Boys' Club of Santa Cruz, Inc.* (1985) 40 Cal.3d 72, 81, 219 Cal.Rptr. 150, 707 P.2d 212, footnote 8. More recently, the court refused to jettison *Curran* in *Harris v. Capital Growth Investors XIV* (1991) 52 Cal.3d 1142, 1155, 278 Cal.Rptr. 614, 805 P.2d 873; and *Harris* may be the most restrictive interpretation of the Unruh Act in the history of the Supreme Court. In *Hart v. Cult Awareness Network* (1993) 13 Cal.App.4th 777, 16 Cal.Rptr.2d 705, the same division of the Second district distinguished, but did not overrule, its decision in *Curran*.

Were we writing on a clean slate, the *Hart* opinion (refusing to require the Cult Awareness Network to admit members of the Church of Scientology) might give pause. But the specific issues before us concerning application of the Unruh Act to the Boy Scouts were resolved over a decade ago. Sound principles of *stare decisis*, particularly in view of the reaction (or lack thereof) to *Curran* by the Legislature and the appellate courts, persuade us it should be followed. A settled rule in an area of sensitive social policy should not lightly be brought into question.

III

To summarize, the Orange County Council, Boy Scouts of America can hardly be considered the religious organization the dissent proclaims, since any creed will meet its requirements. The county council is a business, a fairly big business.[8] But businesses entertaining religious preferences may not discriminate on that basis. (*Pines v. Tomson* (1984) 160 Cal.App.3d 370, 206 Cal.Rptr. 866.)[9] The council could have no compelling justification for discriminating against children because of their current notions concerning the subject of God. Indeed, such discrimination would appear to contradict a variety of the principles of the congressionally chartered Boy Scouts of America.

[Affirmed in part, and reversed in part.]

SONENSHINE, J., concurs.

SILLS, Presiding Justice dissenting.

To read the majority opinion, one would think we are writing about a pizza parlor where the proprietor requires prayers before serving a medium pepperoni with anchovies. It may come as a surprise to my colleagues, but there are those who still seek membership in an organization which teaches duty to God and country and the virtues of order and discipline. The Scouts believe these values breed character and help young men to survive hardship and adversity, whether it be on a cold windswept hill or in the last few miles of a long hike.

---

8. The notions that today's decision will somehow reduce diversity in the country and somehow lead to government required prayer (dis. opn., p. 11) are the sheerest nonsense, of course. Our opinion does not suggest the state has any business sticking its nose in religious tents or forcing others to do so, quite the contrary.

9. Pines is ignored by our dissenting colleague, probably because it is essentially indistinguishable. There, the Court of Appeal held the Unruh Act prohibited the Christian Yellow Pages from discriminating against customers on religious grounds. That decision, like Curran, has stood for a decade despite various legislative opportunities to overturn it.

The Boy Scouts are not a church in the traditional sense, but that does not mean they do not have their ideals—or that the government may force them to disregard those ideals. Almost certainly, if the Scouts were an organization of only Catholics or only Jews, the religious connection would be so unmistakable that no one would question their right to First Amendment protection. Because they are somewhat less sectarian and require only a belief in the concept of God rather than a full set of religious doctrines does not mean they forfeit the right to associate based on common beliefs and values.

The Boy Scouts were founded in the early part of the 20th Century by a British cavalry officer, Lieutenant General Robert Baden-Powell, for whom devotion to God, patriotism and military duty were inseparable. One need only tour St. Paul's Cathedral in London where Nelson and Wellington are buried to understand the close association between these ideas which still provide for Scouting an ideological undergirding. Scouts wear military style uniforms, salute each other and receive and wear medals for meritorious achievement. An oath to God is required for promotion to all ranks from the Bear Badge of Cub Scouts to the coveted Eagle rank or Order of the Arrow. Duty to country, family and religion are all part and parcel of the ethic and fabric of Scouting from cub to explorer.

The Scout law or creed specifies 12 commandments. A Scout must be trustworthy, loyal, helpful, friendly, courteous, kind, obedient, cheerful, thrifty, brave, clean and reverent. This "law" tells us that "A Scout is reverent toward God. He is faithful in his religious duties. He respects the beliefs of others." Scout meetings and camp-outs end with a benediction: "May the Great Master of all Scouts be with us until we meet again." No less than 25 religions are formally affiliated with Scouting—Catholic, Jewish, Baptist, Islamic and Zoroastrian to name a few.

Idealism about God and country may be considered passe in some circles, who regard it as a kind of unholy "civil religion." Indeed, Mark Twain once skewered the tendency of soldiers to pray for victory in battle as wholly inconsistent with any idea of a benevolent supreme being. But it is not the validity of such ideals that is before us. The question is simply whether the Boy Scouts have the right to associate based upon those ideals. Hard as my colleagues may find this to believe, the Boy Scout oath is an important expression of those common beliefs. It descended from a military code which has come down to us from antiquity. It is not coincidence that both the Boy Scouts and American Legion honor God and country. Today's opinion callously ignores this tradition and its importance in all phases of Scouting.

My colleagues may question why the Boy Scouts think duty to God and country are important to the development of young men's character. My colleagues may think the requirement of an oath silly—no doubt they may also think requiring young Scouts to wear uniforms or salute to be silly. So what. These things are an important part of the Scouts' common beliefs. It is not within government's province to interfere. The Boy Scouts have the right to believe in whatever philosophy they are convinced builds character, and if that means enforcing their own internal oath to God and country, so be it.

The most that one can assume from *Curran* is that allegations that a nonprofit organization has "businesslike attributes" are sufficient to show that the organization is a business under the Unruh Act for purposes of demurrer. Of course, most churches also have "businesslike attributes"—they have payrolls to meet (sometimes multi-million dollar payrolls), property to maintain, insurance to buy, and even sell things—such as books, magazines and emblems. *Curran* only demonstrates that if a plaintiff alleges such organizations have "businesslike attributes" in his or her complaint, the organization cannot claim it is automatically not a business because of its nonprofit status. The

Curran opinion on this point is as applicable to the Roman Catholic or Mormon religions as it is to the Boy Scouts. It hardly establishes as a matter of law that the Boy Scouts have been adjudicated to be a "business establishment."

If all it takes is the mere allegation of unspecified businesslike attributes to render an entity a business, then, under *Curran*, churches are businesses for purposes of the Unruh Act. They too have businesslike attributes, as do most fraternities, lodges and political clubs. Of course, the legislative history of the act is devoid of any indication that it was directed at such organizations. A fire storm of public protest would have descended on the Legislature had it considered passing a law which was clear that voluntary associations such as the Catholic Church and the Boy Scouts would be affected.

Further, even assuming that the Boy Scouts were a business for purposes of the Unruh Act, it does not follow that they do not have a First Amendment right under the federal Constitution to refuse membership to those who do not share their ideals. As my colleagues seem to have forgotten, the rights guaranteed by the First Amendment take precedence over state statutes.

[T]he *Curran* decision never reached the problem of expressive association. For the *Curran* court, it was enough that the Boy Scouts offered their "membership to the general public." (See *Curran, supra*, 147 Cal.App.3d at p. 732, 195 Cal.Rptr. 325.) Not only was the premise inaccurate, but it was only relevant to the freedom of intimate association. The John Birch Society, the NAACP, and Common Cause are all open to the general public (and certainly open to a greater proportion of it than the Boy Scouts), but that does not mean these organizations must admit members who take diametrically opposite views from the ideologies and ideals which they espouse. Must the Women's Christian Temperance Union admit card-carrying members of the Beer Drinkers of America? Because the *Curran* opinion never addressed freedom of expressive association, it has nothing to tell this court on that issue.

The majority effectively ignore the issue of the Boy Scouts' freedom of expressive association. As already shown, the Boy Scout oath is central to the ideals and principles of Scouting. Duty to God and country is central to Scout thinking—ideology if you will. If the survival skills of the Scouts can be indirectly expressive, how much more so are the ideals articulated in their oath, which are directly expressive of the Scout creed. My colleagues may not think the references to God in the oath important, but, as the money they have spent litigating this case shows, the Boy Scouts do.

The record before us is clear—not only is Scouting an organization with significant and historic religious underpinnings, but Scouting as an organization has historically believed religion plays an important role in the training, education and development of young men. The oath goes to Scouting's basic philosophy. The exclusion of the plaintiffs here is clearly not arbitrary.

My colleagues have not thought through the implications of their reasoning in today's decision. If the Unruh Act applies to force the Boy Scouts to admit those who refuse to subscribe to the Boy Scouts' basic shared beliefs, it must also force the Campfire Girls and Girl Scouts to admit boys. Perhaps my colleagues are not bothered. I am. The Unruh Act was never intended to coerce private groups like the Boy Scouts into lockstep conformity with the same rules that govern hotels and pizza parlors. In genuflection to currently fashionable ideas as to what is politically correct, today's decision steamrolls over Scouting's basic beliefs.

Ironically, today's decision effectively tramples on the rights of atheists as well as believers. Times change. Fashions in ideas change. If the First Amendment will not stop the government from effectively dictating the content of the Boy Scouts' oath today, it will not stop the government from requiring prayer tomorrow. The great 19th Century agnostic lecturer and lawyer Robert Ingersoll once wrote that force should never interfere with an individual's religious opinions. Unfortunately, that is precisely what today's opinion does by restricting the right of private groups to express their own beliefs. If today's decision stands our society will be less free and less diverse. I would reverse the judgment.

Notes

1. One month after *Randall* was decided, the California Court of Appeal, Second District held, in *Curran v. Mount Diablo Council of the Boy Scouts of America*, 23 Cal. App.4th 1307, 29 Cal. Rptr. 2d 580 (Ct. App. 1994) (*Curran II*), that the Unruh Act did not apply to the Boy Scouts, thus reversing its earlier decision in the same case. *Curran v. Mount Diablo Council of the Boy Scouts* 147 Cal.App.3d 712, 717, 195 Cal.Rptr. 325 (Ct. App. 1983) (*Curran I*). In *Curran II*, the Court of Appeal also concluded that the Boy Scouts was an expressive association. Consequently, forcing the Scouts to accept a gay troop leader would violate the First Amendment associational rights of the Scouts. Four years later, the California Supreme Court held that the Boy Scouts of America was not a business establishment under the Unruh Act. *Randall v. Orange County Council, Boy Scouts of America*,17 Cal.4th 736, 952 P.2d 261, 72 Cal.Rptr.2d 453 (Cal. 1998). The court's holding made it unnecessary to discuss the constitutional issue raised by the Boy Scouts. In June 2000, the Supreme Court of the United States held that New Jersey's public accommodation act was unconstitutionally applied to the Boy Scouts when it refused to permit an openly gay former Boy Scout to act as a Scout leader. *Boy Scouts of America v. Dale*, 530 U.S. 640 (2000) (holding first amendment right of expressive association violated by application of state's public accommodation law to Boy Scouts).

2. In *Randall*, the court dismissed the religious liberty defense of the Boy Scouts with the conclusion they "can hardly be considered the religious organization the dissent claims, since any creed will meet its requirements." Is this sufficient? The court later suggests that any effort to forbid the plaintiff-boys to join the Scouts "would appear to contradict a variety of principles of the [organization]." Is this any more persuasive?

The court also holds that *Pines v. Tomson*, 160 Cal. App. 3d 370, 206 Cal. Rptr. 866 (Ct. App. 1984) is "essentially indistinguishable" from the facts in *Randall*. The Unruh Act makes no distinction between non-profit and for-profit "business establishments." Does the conclusion follow that discriminatory acts based on religion by the for-profit Christian Yellow Pages and the non-profit Boy Scouts should be treated the same for statutory and constitutional purposes? Is there a sound distinction to be made between these two situations? Can it be argued that *Pines* was wrongly decided?

3. The Boy Scouts regularly recruit members in public schools. Is this a violation of the First Amendment? *See Sherman v. Community Consolidated Sch. Dist. 21 of Wheeling Township*, 8 F.3d 1160 (7th Cir. 1993), *cert. denied*, 511 U.S. 1110 (1994) (holding use of public school facilities by Boy Scouts not violative of the Establishment Clause and further holding Boy Scouts private rather than state actor).

4. Elliott Welsh and his seven year-old son Mark were refused membership in the Boy Scouts because they would not affirm a belief in God. They sued, alleging that this requirement violated the Civil Rights Act of 1964 because the Scouts were a "place of public accommodation" practicing religious discrimination. A majority of the Seventh

Circuit panel avoided the constitutional question by holding the Scouts were not subject to the Act because it was not an organization closely connected to a facility. *Welsh v. Boy Scouts of America*, 993 F.2d 1267 (7th Cir.), *cert. denied*, 510 U.S. 1012 (1993). Dissenting, Judge Cummings concluded that the Act did apply to the Scouts, but stated his inclination was that the constitutional right of association permitted it to refuse membership to atheists. *Id.* at 1283. *See also Seabourn v. Coronado Area Council, Boy Scouts of America*, 257 Kan. 178, 891 P.2d 385 (1995) (holding Boy Scouts not a public accommodation under Kansas anti-discrimination statute, thus allowing Scouts to exclude from leadership adults who refuse to profess a belief in a Supreme Being).

D. Religious Liberty in the Military

Katcoff v. Marsh

755 F.2d 223 (2d Cir. 1985)

MANSFIELD, Circuit Judge.

This appeal raises the question of whether Congress and the United States Army ("Army"), in furnishing chaplains as part of our armed forces to enable soldiers to practice the religions of their choice, violate the Constitution. We hold that, except in a few respects that require further consideration, they do not.

Congress, in the exercise of its powers under Art. I, § 8, of the Constitution to provide for the conduct of our national defense, has established an Army for the purpose of "preserving the peace and security, and providing for the defense, of the United States," 10 U.S.C. § 3062(a), and has directed that the "organized peace establishment of the Army" consist of all organizations and persons "necessary to form the basis for a complete and immediate mobilization for the national defense in the event of a national emergency," 10 U.S.C. § 3062(d). It has specifically authorized that as part of this establishment there be "Chaplains in the Army," who shall include the Chief of Chaplains, and commissioned and other officers of the Army appointed as chaplains. 10 U.S.C. § 3073. Under 10 U.S.C. § 3547 each chaplain is required, when practicable, to hold religious services for the command to which he is assigned and to perform burial services for soldiers who die while in that command. The statute also obligates the commanding officer to furnish facilities, including transportation, to assist a chaplain in performing his duties.

In providing our armed forces with a military chaplaincy Congress has perpetuated a facility that began during Revolutionary days before the adoption of our Constitution, and that has continued ever since then, with the size of the chaplaincy growing larger in proportion to the increase in the size of our Army.

In 1981 the Army had approximately 1,427 active-duty commissioned chaplains, 10 auxiliary chaplains, 1,383 chaplain's assistants, and 48 Directors of Religious Education. These chaplains are appointed as commissioned officers with rank and uniform but without command. 10 U.S.C. §§ 3293, 3581.

The primary function of the military chaplain is to engage in activities designed to meet the religious needs of a pluralistic military community, including military personnel and their dependents. In view of the Army's huge size (some 788,000 soldiers and 1,300,000 dependents in 1981) and its far-flung distribution (291,000 soldiers stationed abroad and many in remote areas of the United States) the task is an important and formidable one. The Army consists of a wide spectrum of persons of different ethnic, racial and religious backgrounds who go into military service from varied social, economic and educational environments. The great majority of the soldiers in the Army express religious preferences. About 80% are under 30 years of age and a large number are married. As a result it has become necessary to provide religious facilities for soldiers of some 86 different denominations. A sample survey of military personnel made by the Army in 1979 revealed the following religious preferences among enlisted personnel:

Protestant	38.5%
Catholic	22.5%
Mormon	2.5%
Eastern Orthodox	0.5%
Moslem	1.0%
Jewish	0.7%
Buddhist	0.7%
Other religions not listed	19.3%
No religious preference	14.3%

Aside from the problems arising out of the sheer size and pluralistic nature of the Army, its members experience increased needs for religion as the result of being uprooted from their home environments, transported often thousands of miles to territories entirely strange to them, and confronted there with new stresses that would not otherwise have been encountered if they had remained at home. In 1981 approximately 37% of the Army's active duty soldiers, amounting to 293,000 persons, were stationed overseas in locations such as Turkey, Sinai, Greece, or Korea. In most of these areas the Judeo-Christian faiths of most American soldiers are hardly represented at all by local clergy and the average soldier is separated from the local populace by a linguistic and cultural wall. Within the United States the same problem exists in a somewhat different way in that, although the linguistic or cultural barrier may be absent, local civilian clergy in the rural areas where most military camps are centered are inadequate to satisfy the soldiers' religious needs because they are too few in number for the task and are usually of different religious denominations from those of most of the nearby troops.

The problem of meeting the religious needs of Army personnel is compounded by the mobile, deployable nature of our armed forces, who must be ready on extremely short notice to be transported from bases (whether or not in the United States) to distant parts of the world for combat duty in fulfillment of our nation's international defense commitments. Unless there were chaplains ready to move simultaneously with the troops and to tend to their spiritual needs as they face possible death, the soldiers would be left in the lurch, religiously speaking. In the opinion of top generals of the Army and those presently in the chaplaincy, unless chaplains were made available in such circumstances the motivation, morale and willingness of soldiers to face combat would suffer immeasurable harm and our national defense would be weakened accordingly.

To meet the religious needs of our armed forces Army chaplains and their assistants engage in a wide variety of services to military personnel and their families who wish to use them. No chaplain is authorized to proselytize soldiers or their families. The chaplain's principal duties are to conduct religious services (including periodic worship, baptisms, marriages, funerals and the like), to furnish religious education to soldiers and their families, and to counsel soldiers with respect to a wide variety of personal problems.

For this comprehensive religious program involving hundreds of thousands of soldiers and their families, the Army has a large and fairly elaborate administrative organization, including not only the chaplains but also supporting personnel, facilities, publications, and other supplies.... Over the years the Army has built or acquired more than 500 chapels which are used for the conduct of religious services of many different denominations. In addition it has built more than 100 Religious Educational Facilities, which are used for religious services and classes in religious education for soldiers and members of their families of all ages (including children). The Army has purchased and made available for voluntary use by various denominations numerous chaplain's kits, vocational kits, communion sets and vestments, and religious publications (including Holy Scriptures and Prayer Books for Jewish Personnel, the New Testament of our Lord and Savior Jesus Christ, and a Book of Worship), and has developed a Cooperative Curriculum for Religious Education of the Armed Forces. Professional education and training has also been furnished to Army chaplains.

The great majority of the chaplaincy's services, facilities, and supplies are procured by the Army through funds appropriated by Congress, which amounted to over $85 million for the fiscal year 1981, of which more than $62 million was used to pay the salaries and other compensation of chaplains, chaplain's assistants and auxiliary chaplains.

Appellants' complaint, filed on November 23, 1979, seeks a declaratory judgment that the foregoing program violates the Establishment Clause and injunctive relief.

[T]he Establishment Clause of the First Amendment, which provides that "Congress shall make no law respecting an establishment of religion," was designed by our Founding Fathers to insure religious liberty for our country's citizens by precluding a government from imposing, sponsoring, or supporting religion or forcing a person to remain away from the practice of religion. *Everson v. Board of Education.*

> "The 'establishment of religion' clause of the First Amendment means at least this: Neither a state nor the Federal Government can set up a church. Neither can pass laws which aid one religion, aid all religions, or prefer one religion over another. Neither can force nor influence a person to go to or to remain away from church against his will or force him to profess a belief or disbelief in any religion. No person can be punished for entertaining or professing religious beliefs or disbeliefs, for church attendance or non-attendance."

330 U.S. at 15–16. The Army chaplaincy does not seek to "establish" a religion according to this simple formula. It observes the basic prohibition expressed by the Court in *Zorach v. Clauson*, 343 U.S. 306, 314 (1952):

> "The government must be neutral when it comes to competition between sects. It may not thrust any sect on any person. It may not make a religious observance compulsory. It may not coerce anyone to attend church, to observe a religious holiday, or to take religious instruction."

Since the program meets the requirement of voluntariness by leaving the practice of religion solely to the individual soldier, who is free to worship or not as he chooses without fear of any discipline or stigma, it might be viewed as not proscribed by the Establishment Clause. Indeed, if the Army prevented soldiers from worshipping in their own communities by removing them to areas where religious leaders of their persuasion and facilities were not available it could be accused of violating the Establishment Clause unless it provided them with a chaplaincy since its conduct would amount to inhibiting religion.

Congress' authorization of a military chaplaincy before and contemporaneous with the adoption of the Establishment Clause is also "weighty evidence" that it did not intend that Clause to apply to such a chaplaincy. *See Wisconsin v. Pelican Ins. Co.*, 127 U.S. 265, 297 (1888). In interpreting the Bill of Rights such "an unbroken practice... is not something to be lightly cast aside." *Walz v. Tax Commission*, 397 U.S. 664 (1970).

If the current Army chaplaincy were viewed in isolation, there could be little doubt that it would fail to meet the *Lemon v. Kurtzman* conditions. Although the ultimate objective of the chaplaincy may be secular in the sense that it seeks to maintain the efficiency of the Army by improving the morale of our military personnel, its immediate purpose is to promote religion by making it available, albeit on a voluntary basis, to our armed forces. The effect of the program, moreover, is to advance the practice of religion. Administration of the program, involving arrangements with many church organizations of different denominations, entangles the government with religious accrediting bodies.

However, neither the Establishment Clause nor statutes creating and maintaining the Army chaplaincy may be interpreted as if they existed in a sterile vacuum. They must be viewed in the light of the historical background of their enactment to the extent that it sheds light on the purpose of the Framers of the Constitution. They must also be considered in context, since a test which may be reasonable in one context may be wholly inappropriate in another. Aside from the fact that no single test will meet all contexts, the Establishment Clause must in any event be interpreted to accommodate other equally valid provisions of the Constitution, including the Free Exercise Clause, when they are implicated.

The present case involves two other provisions of our Constitution, which must not only be respected but, to the extent possible, interpreted compatibly with the Establishment Clause. The first of these is the War Power Clause of Art. I, § 8, which provides in pertinent part that Congress shall have the power to "provide for the common Defence," "to raise and support Armies," and to "make Rules for the Government and Regulation of the land and naval Forces." Although military conduct is not immune from judicial review when challenged as violative of the Bill of Rights, the Supreme Court has recognized that: "[J]udges are not given the task of running the Army.... The military constitutes a specialized community governed by a separate discipline from that of the civilian...." *Orloff v. Willoughby*, 345 U.S. 83, 93–94 (1953).

In a perilous world our survival as a nation and our enjoyment of the blessings of liberty depend heavily upon our Army and other military institutions, rigid and disciplined as they must be. Those who want the individual liberty embodied in our Bill of Rights must be willing to make sacrifices for it. One of these is the duty of a soldier to obey military orders and forego many of the freedoms that he would otherwise enjoy as a civilian, including the right to travel whenever and wherever he pleases.

The line where military control requires that enjoyment of civilian rights be regulated or restricted may sometimes be difficult to define. But caution dictates that when a matter provided for by Congress in the exercise of its war power and implemented by the Army appears reasonably relevant and necessary to furtherance of our national defense it should be treated as presumptively valid and any doubt as to its constitutionality should be resolved as a matter of judicial comity in favor of deference to the military's exercise of its discretion.

The second provision of the Constitution which plays a vital role in our interpretation of the Establishment Clause is the Free Exercise Clause of the same Amendment. It is readily apparent that this Clause, like the Establishment Clause, obligates Congress, upon creating an Army, to make religion available to soldiers who have been moved by the Army to areas of the world where religion of their own denominations is not available to them. Otherwise the effect of compulsory military service could be to violate their rights under both Religion Clauses of the First Amendment. Unless the Army provided a chaplaincy it would deprive the soldier of his right under the Establishment Clause not to have religion inhibited and of his right under the Free Exercise Clause to practice his freely chosen religion. Members of the Supreme Court have pointed to Congress' provision of churches and chaplains at military establishments as an example of an appropriate accommodation between the two Clauses. *See Abington School Dist. v. Schempp*, 374 U.S. 203, 296–98 (Brennan, J., concurring), 308–09 (Stewart, J., dissenting). Congress recognized as early as 1850 that its failure to provide a chaplaincy would deprive soldiers of their Free Exercise rights. H.R.Rep. No. 171, 31st Cong., 1st Sess. (1850).

The standard to be applied, therefore, in deciding whether the Army's military chaplaincy can survive attack as violative of the Establishment Clause must take into account the deference required to be given to Congress' exercise of its War Power and the necessity of recognizing the Free Exercise rights of military personnel. In our view these additional factors, which were not present in *Lemon v. Kurtzman* or its progeny, relied on by plaintiffs, render its test inappropriate here. On the other hand, we do not agree with the district court that the doctrine of deference to Congress' judgment in military affairs leaves us powerless to review the constitutional permissibility of the military chaplaincy. In our view the test of permissibility in this context is whether, after considering practical alternatives, the chaplaincy program is relevant to and reasonably necessary for the Army's conduct of our national defense.

Applying these principles to the present case, we start with plaintiffs' concession that some chaplaincy is essential. Except for peripheral claims that a few practices of the government's military chaplaincy amount to "religious proselytism," their lawsuit hinges entirely on their contention that a privately funded chaplaincy, patterned on the present military program, would fully and fairly meet the government's needs under the War Power Clause and the free-exercise needs of military personnel. [W]e disagree.

To begin with, defendants have described in detail the various functions performed by the Army's chaplains and the inability of local civilian clergy or special organizations of civilian clergy to meet the religious needs of the many different denominations in the armed forces. They note that among the inadequacies of a civilian clergy would be the questionable ability of many denominations, particularly the smaller ones, to fund a civilian chaplaincy and the lack of training in the military subjects needed to enable the civilian chaplain to function effectively in the field.

[P]laintiffs have not come forward with any evidence or offer through discovery or depositions to establish that the many religious denominations involved, including the principal Catholic, Protestant and Jewish organizations in the United States, would support and be willing to pay their respective shares of the $85 million required to operate a civilian chaplaincy and to provide such additional sums as may be required in case of war or national emergency. Nor have plaintiffs come forward with assurances from the numerous religious organizations involved that they would seek to agree upon each denomination's proportionate share of the overall financial obligation and that they would be able and willing to honor their respective obligations in the years ahead. It is obvious from the evidence offered by the defendants that without enforceable commitments on the part of these various denominations the Army would be unable to maintain a functioning civilian chaplaincy. Assuming hypothetically that such a program could be launched, it would constantly be teetering on the brink of disaster. An impractical alternative is no alternative at all.

Aside from the obvious financial infeasibility of appellants' alternative proposal, plaintiffs offer no evidence that civilian chaplains would accept military discipline, which is essential to the efficient operation of our armed forces. This discipline demands willingness to undergo thorough military training except in the use of firearms, to remain with an Army unit for a specified period of time, to obey orders to move overnight with that unit to other locations, which might be thousands of miles away, and to advance as ordered on the battlefield and risk their lives in order to minister to the wounded and dying.

Any doubt as to the feasibility of a civilian chaplaincy must in our view be resolved in favor of judicial deference to Congress' decision in this area, which is closely tied to the efficient functioning of our armed forces. It is significant that from time to time Congress rejected proposals for abolition of the military chaplaincy in favor of dependence on civilian or other alternatives, albeit on a smaller scale. *See, e.g.*, Mil.Aff.Doc. No. 651, 24th Cong., 1st Sess. (1836); S.Misc.Doc. No. 2, 30th Cong., 2d Sess. (1848); H.R.Rep. No. 124, 33rd Cong., 1st Sess. 7–8 (1854). In 1924 Congress, in deciding whether to increase the number of military chaplains, held joint hearings at which witnesses testified to the inability of the civilian clergy to meet the needs of soldiers and the ineffectiveness of civilian clerics, when compared with military chaplains, to deal with and control soldiers. *See*, To Increase the Number of Chaplains in the Army: Hearings on S. 2632 and H.R. 7038 Before the Subcommittees of the Committees on Military Affairs of the United States Senate and the House of Representatives, 68th Cong., 1st Sess. (1924). In 1973 the Senate Committee on Appropriations, after its House counterpart requested a review of the Army's needs for military chaplains, studied the issue and reported: "Civilian churches can care for some of the needs of service women and men but there are other profound daily needs that the denominational churches are not prepared to identify or meet. This is not the time in our history to diminish the moral and spiritual support which our nation has made available to its military personnel for two hundred years. Ministry to the men and women of our Armed Forces is a specialized ministry that requires identification and loyal commitment to their peculiar needs.... the Committee does not consider it wise to impose arbitrary limitations on the presumption that someone else will do this important task." S.Rep. No. 93-617, 93rd Cong., 1st Sess. 66 (1973). Thereafter Congress, having considered alternatives, adhered to the view that a military chaplaincy was essential and, despite substantial cutbacks in 1976 in the personnel of the armed forces, made only minimal reductions in the chaplaincy's staff.

We find that the more appropriate standard of relevancy to our national defense and reasonable necessity is met by the great majority of the Army's existing chaplaincy activities. The purpose and effect of the program is to make religion, religious education, counseling and religious facilities available to military personnel and their families under circumstances where the practice of religion would otherwise be denied as a practical matter to all or a substantial number. As a result, the morale of our soldiers, their willingness to serve, and the efficiency of the Army as an instrument for our national defense rests in substantial part on the military chaplaincy, which is vital to our Army's functioning.

In a few areas, however, the reasonable necessity for certain activities of the military chaplaincy is not readily apparent. For instance, it appears that in some large urban centers, such as at the Pentagon in Washington, D.C., in New York City and San Francisco, government funds may be used to provide military chaplains, facilities and retreats to "armchair" military personnel who, like other government civil servants, commute daily to their homes and spend their free hours (including weekends) in locations where civilian clergy and facilities are just as available to them as to other non-military citizens. Plaintiffs also assert that government-financed Army chaplains and facilities are provided to retired military personnel and their families. If the ability of such personnel to worship in their own communities is not inhibited by their military service and funds for these chaplains and facilities would not otherwise be expended, the justification for a governmental program of religious support for them is questionable and, notwithstanding our deference to Congress in military matters, requires a showing that they are relevant to and reasonably necessary for the conduct of our national defense by the Army. A remand therefore becomes necessary to determine whether, according to the standard we have outlined, government financing of a military chaplaincy in these limited areas for the purposes indicated is constitutionally permissible.

Accordingly, the order of the district court is affirmed except to the extent so remanded. Costs to the appellees.

MESKILL, Circuit Judge, concurring and dissenting.

[Opinion omitted.]

Notes

1. The court concludes that if the military attempted to eliminate all military chaplains and chapels, members of the military would have a strong Free Exercise claim. Is the court convincing? Would this depend on whether coercion (a draft) was used by the government to enlist service personnel rather than choice (the volunteer armed forces)? Can "neutrality" exist in such a context?

2. In 1971, the United States Court of Appeals for the District of Columbia Circuit held a violation of the Free Exercise Clause compulsory Sunday chapel at the service academies. *Anderson v. Laird*, 466 F.2d 283 (D.C. Cir. 1971), *cert. denied*, 409 U.S. 1076 (1972). The military's argument in defense of compulsory chapel was that cadets were not required to worship. Instead, they were merely required to observe others in worship, an act the military claimed made cadets better combat officers.

3. In 1986, the Supreme Court, deferring to claims of military necessity, held constitutional a ban on the wearing of a yarmulke while on duty. *Goldman v. Weinberger*, 475 U.S. 503 (1986). Congress's response to the decision was to pass the following law:

10 U.S.C. § 774

§ 774 Religious apparel: wearing while in uniform

(a) General rule. Except as provided under subsection (b), a member of the armed forces may wear an item of religious apparel while wearing the uniform of the member's armed force.

(b) Exceptions. The Secretary concerned may prohibit the wearing of an item of religious apparel—

(1) in circumstances with respect to which the Secretary determines that the wearing of the item would interfere with the performance of the member's military duties; or

(2) if the Secretary determines, under regulations under subsection (c), that the item of apparel is not neat and conservative.

(c) Regulations. The Secretary concerned shall prescribe regulations concerning the wearing of religious apparel by members of the armed forces under the Secretary's jurisdiction while the members are wearing the uniform. Such regulations shall be consistent with subsections (a) and (b).

(d) Religious apparel defined. In this section, the term "religious apparel" means apparel the wearing of which is part of the observance of the religious faith practiced by the member.

Does this measure both solve Dr. Goldman's problem and avoid other possible problems concerning the wearing of other kinds of religious apparel?

In *Goldman*, the majority uncritically accepted the military's claim of the importance of uniform uniformity. Isn't that exactly the type of "neutral" act of government that can create conflicts for the religiously devout?

Goldman's attorneys argued a general case rather than a case specific to Goldman. It appears clear from Justice Stevens's concurring opinion that the case against Goldman was made in retaliation for Goldman testifying in behalf of a defendant in a court-martial. Yet Justices Stevens and Powell concurred in the majority's decision because Goldman's lawyers, who are well-known and admired, argued a broad challenge to military regulation of religious dress rather than a narrow case. Does this suggest something about the way in which First Amendment litigation is or should be conducted? *See* Chapter Eleven § D.

4. *See Bowen v. Roy*, 476 U.S. 693 (1986) (rejecting claim by Native Americans parents and daughter that assignment of Social Security number to daughter violated her Free Exercise rights), noted in Chapter Five.

Chapter 11

Autonomy, Religious Practice and Governmental Regulation

A. The Right of Ideological Nonassociation

Wooley v. Maynard

430 U.S. 705 (1977)

Mr. Chief Justice BURGER delivered the opinion of the Court.

The issue on appeal is whether the State of New Hampshire may constitutionally enforce criminal sanctions against persons who cover the motto "Live Free or Die" on passenger vehicle license plates because that motto is repugnant to their moral and religious beliefs.

(1)

Since 1969 New Hampshire has required that noncommercial vehicles bear license plates embossed with the state motto, "Live Free or Die." N.H. Rev. Stat. Ann. § 263:1 (Supp. 1975). Another New Hampshire statute makes it a misdemeanor "knowingly [to obscure] ... the figures or letters on any number plate." N.H. Rev. Stat. Ann. § 262:27-c (Supp. 1975). The term "letters" in this section has been interpreted by the State's highest court to include the state motto.

Appellees George Maynard and his wife Maxine are followers of the Jehovah's Witnesses faith. The Maynards consider the New Hampshire State motto to be repugnant to their moral, religious, and political beliefs,[2] and therefore assert it objectionable to disseminate this message by displaying it on their automobiles. Pursuant to these beliefs, the Maynards began early in 1974 to cover up the motto on their license plates.

---

2. Mr. Maynard described his objection to the state motto:

"[B]y religious training and belief, I believe my 'government'—Jehovah's Kingdom—offers everlasting life. It would be contrary to that belief to give up my life for the state, even if it meant living in bondage. Although I obey all laws of the State not in conflict with my conscience, this slogan is directly at odds with my deeply held religious convictions.

"... I also disagree with the motto on political grounds. I believe that life is more precious than freedom."

(4)

The District Court held that by covering up the state motto "Live Free or Die" on his automobile license plate, Mr. Maynard was engaging in symbolic speech and that "New Hampshire's interest in the enforcement of its defacement statute is not sufficient to justify the restriction on [appellee's] constitutionally protected expression." We find it unnecessary to pass on the "symbolic speech" issue, since we find more appropriate First Amendment grounds to affirm the judgment of the District Court. We turn instead to what in our view is the essence of appellees' objection to the requirement that they display the motto "Live Free or Die" on their automobile license plates. This is succinctly summarized in the statement made by Mr. Maynard in his affidavit filed with the District Court:

> "I refuse to be coerced by the State into advertising a slogan which I find morally, ethically, religiously and politically abhorrent."

We are thus faced with the question of whether the State may constitutionally require an individual to participate in the dissemination of an ideological message by displaying it on his private property in a manner and for the express purpose that it be observed and read by the public. We hold that the State may not do so.

A

A system which secures the right to proselytize religious, political, and ideological causes must also guarantee the concomitant right to decline to foster such concepts. The right to speak and the right to refrain from speaking are complementary components of the broader concept of "individual freedom of mind."

The Court in *Barnette* was faced with a state statute which required public school students to participate in daily public ceremonies by honoring the flag both with words and traditional salute gestures. In overruling its prior decision in *Gobitis*, the Court held that "a ceremony so touching matters of opinion and political attitude may [not] be imposed upon the individual by official authority under powers committed to any political organization under our Constitution." Compelling the affirmative act of a flag salute involved a more serious infringement upon personal liberties than the passive act of carrying the state motto on a license plate, but the difference is essentially one of degree. Here, as in *Barnette*, we are faced with a state measure which forces an individual, as part of his daily life—indeed constantly while his automobile is in public view—to be an instrument for fostering public adherence to an ideological point of view he finds unacceptable. In doing so, the State "invades the sphere of intellect and spirit which is the purpose of the First Amendment to our Constitution to reserve from all official control."

New Hampshire's statute in effect requires that appellees use their private property as a "mobile billboard" for the State's ideological message—or suffer a penalty, as Maynard already has. As a condition to driving an automobile—a virtual necessity for most Americans—the Maynards must display "Live Free or Die" to hundreds of people each day. The fact that most individuals agree with the thrust of New Hampshire's motto is not the test; most Americans also find the flag salute acceptable. The First Amendment protects the right of individuals to hold a point of view different from the majority and to refuse to foster, in the way New Hampshire commands, an idea they find morally objectionable.

B

The State is seeking to communicate to others an official view as to proper appreciation of history, state pride, and individualism. Of course, the State may legitimately pursue such interests in any number of ways. However, where the State's interest is to disseminate an ideology, no matter how acceptable to some, such interest cannot outweigh an individual's First Amendment right to avoid becoming the courier for such message.

We conclude that the State of New Hampshire may not require appellees to display the state motto[15] upon their vehicle license plates; and, accordingly, we affirm the judgment of the District Court.

Affirmed.

Mr. Justice WHITE, with whom Mr. Justice BLACKMUN and Mr. Justice REHNQUIST join in part, dissenting in part.

[Opinion omitted.]

Mr. Justice REHNQUIST, with whom Mr. Justice BLACKMUN joins, dissenting.

The Court holds that a State is barred by the Federal Constitution from requiring that the state motto be displayed on a state license plate. The path that the Court travels to reach this result demonstrates the difficulty in supporting it. The Court holds that the required display of the motto is an unconstitutional "required affirmation of belief."

The State has not forced appellees to "say" anything; and it has not forced them to communicate ideas with nonverbal actions reasonably likened to "speech," such as wearing a lapel button promoting a political candidate or waving a flag as a symbolic gesture. The State has simply required that *all* noncommercial automobiles bear license tags with the state motto, "Live Free or Die." Appellees have not been forced to affirm or reject that motto; they are simply required by the State, under its police power, to carry a state auto license tag for identification and registration purposes.

[T]he Court relies almost solely on *Barnette*. The Court cites *Barnette* for the proposition that there is a constitutional right, in some cases, to "refrain from speaking." What the Court does not demonstrate is that there is any "speech" or "speaking" in the context of this case. The Court also relies upon the "right to decline to foster [religious, political, and ideological] concepts," and treats the state law in this case as if it were forcing appellees to proselytize, or to advocate an ideological point of view. But this begs the question. The issue, unconfronted by the Court, is whether appellees, in displaying, as they are required to do, state license tags, the format of which is known to all as having been prescribed by the State, would be considered to be advocating political or ideological views.

[T]here is nothing in state law which precludes appellees from displaying their disagreement with the state motto as long as the methods used do not obscure the license plates. Thus appellees could place on their bumper a conspicuous bumper sticker explaining in no uncertain terms that they do not profess the motto "Live Free or Die" and that they violently disagree with the connotations of that motto. Since any implication that they affirm the motto can be so easily displaced, I cannot agree that the state statutory system for motor vehicle identification and tourist promotion may be invali-

15. It has been suggested that today's holding will be read as sanctioning the obliteration of the national motto, "In God We Trust" from United States coins and currency. That question is not before us today but we note that currency, which is passed from hand to hand, differs in significant respects from an automobile, which is readily associated with its operator. Currency is generally carried in a purse or pocket and need not be displayed to the public. The bearer of currency is thus not required to publicly advertise the national motto.

dated under the fiction that appellees are unconstitutionally forced to affirm, or profess belief in, the state motto.

The logic of the Court's opinion leads to startling, and I believe totally unacceptable, results. For example, the mottoes "In God We Trust" and "E Pluribus Unum" appear on the coin and currency of the United States. I cannot imagine that the statutes, see 18 U.S.C. §§331 and 333, proscribing defacement of United States currency impinge upon the First Amendment rights of an atheist. The fact that an atheist carries and uses United States currency does not, in any meaningful sense, convey any affirmation of belief on his part in the motto "In God We Trust." Similarly, there is no affirmation of belief involved in the display of state license tags upon the private automobiles involved here.

I would reverse the judgment of the District Court.

Torcaso v. Watkins

367 U.S. 488 (1961)

Mr. Justice BLACK delivered the opinion of the Court.

Article 37 of the Declaration of Rights of the Maryland Constitution provides:

> "[N]o religious test ought ever to be required as a qualification for any office of profit or trust in this State, other than a declaration of belief in the existence of God...."

Torcaso was appointed to the office of Notary Public by the Governor of Maryland but was refused a commission to serve because he would not declare his belief in God. He then brought this action in a Maryland Circuit Court to compel issuance of his commission, charging that the State's requirement that he declare this belief violated "the First and Fourteenth Amendments to the Constitution of the United States..."[1] The Circuit Court rejected these federal constitutional contentions, and the highest court of the State, the Court of Appeals, affirmed, holding that the state constitutional provision is self-executing and requires declaration of belief in God as a qualification for office without need for implementing legislation.

There is, and can be, no dispute about the purpose or effect of the Maryland Declaration of Rights requirement before us—it sets up a religious test which was designed to and, if valid, does bar every person who refuses to declare a belief in God from holding a public "office of profit or trust" in Maryland. The power and authority of the State of Maryland thus is put on the side of one particular sort of believers—those who are willing to say they believe in "the existence of God." It is true that there is much historical precedent for such laws. Indeed, it was largely to escape religious test oaths and declarations that a great many of the early colonists left Europe and came here hoping to worship in their own way. It soon developed, however, that many of those who had fled to escape religious test oaths turned out to be perfectly willing, when they had the power to do so, to force dissenters from their faith to take test oaths in conformity with that faith. This brought on a host of laws in the new Colonies imposing burdens and

---

1. Appellant also claimed that the State's test oath requirement violates the provision of Art. VI of the Federal Constitution that "no religious Test shall ever be required as a Qualification to any Office or public Trust under the United States." Because we are reversing the judgment on other grounds, we find it unnecessary to consider appellant's contention that this provision applies to state as well as federal offices.

disabilities of various kinds upon varied beliefs depending largely upon what group happened to be politically strong enough to legislate in favor of its own beliefs. The effect of all this was the formal or practical "establishment" of particular religious faiths in most of the Colonies, with consequent burdens imposed on the free exercise of the faiths of nonfavored believers.

There were, however, wise and far-seeing men in the Colonies—too many to mention—who spoke out against test oaths and all the philosophy of intolerance behind them. One of these, it so happens, was George Calvert (the first Lord Baltimore), who took a most important part in the original establishment of the Colony of Maryland. He was a Catholic and had, for this reason, felt compelled by his conscience to refuse to take the Oath of Supremacy in England at the cost of resigning from high governmental office. He again refused to take that oath when it was demanded by the Council of the Colony of Virginia, and as a result he was denied settlement in that Colony.[4] A recent historian of the early period of Maryland's life has said that it was Calvert's hope and purpose to establish in Maryland a colonial government free from the religious persecutions he had known—one "securely beyond the reach of oaths...."

When our Constitution was adopted, the desire to put the people "securely beyond the reach" of religious test oaths brought about the inclusion in Article VI of that document of a provision that "no religious Test shall ever be required as a Qualification to any Office or public Trust under the United States." Article VI supports the accuracy of our observation in *Girouard v. United States*, 328 U.S. 61, 69, that "[t]he test oath is abhorrent to our tradition." Not satisfied, however, with Article VI and other guarantees in the original Constitution, the First Congress proposed and the States very shortly thereafter adopted our Bill of Rights, including the First Amendment. That Amendment broke new constitutional ground in the protection it sought to afford to freedom of religion, speech, press, petition and assembly. Since prior cases in this Court have thoroughly explored and documented the history behind the First Amendment, the reasons for it, and the scope of the religious freedom it protects, we need not cover that ground again.

Nothing decided or written in *Zorach v. Clauson*, 343 U.S. 306 (1952), lends support to the idea that the Court there intended to open up the way for government, state or federal, to restore the historically and constitutionally discredited policy of probing religious beliefs by test oaths or limiting public offices to persons who have, or perhaps more properly profess to have, a belief in some particular kind of religious concept.

We repeat and again reaffirm that neither a State nor the Federal Government can constitutionally force a person "to profess a belief or disbelief in any religion." Neither can constitutionally pass laws or impose requirements which aid all religions as against

---

4. The letter from the Virginia Council to the King's Privy Council is quoted in Hanley, Their Rights and Liberties (Newman Press 1959), 65, as follows:

"According to the instructions from your Lordship and the usual course held in this place, we tendered the oaths of supremacy and allegiance to his Lordship[;] [Baltimore] and some of his followers, who making profession of the Romish Religion, utterly refused to take the same.... His Lordship then offered to take this oath, a copy whereof is included... but we could not imagine that so much latitude was left for us to decline from the prescribed form, so strictly exacted and so well justified and defended by the pen of our late sovereign, Lord King James of happy memory.... Among the many blessings and favors for which we are bound to bless God... there is none whereby it hath been made more happy than in the freedom of our Religion... and that no papists have been suffered to settle their abode amongst us...." * * *

non-believers, and neither can aid those religions based on a belief in the existence of God as against those religions founded on different beliefs.

In upholding the State's religious test for public office the highest court of Maryland said:

> "The petitioner is not compelled to believe or disbelieve, under threat of punishment or other compulsion. True, unless he makes the declaration of belief he cannot hold public office in Maryland, but he is not compelled to hold office."

The fact, however, that a person is not compelled to hold public office cannot possibly be an excuse for barring him from office by state-imposed criteria forbidden by the Constitution. This was settled by our holding in *Wieman v. Updegraff*, 344 U.S. 183. We there pointed out that whether or not "an abstract right to public employment exists," Congress could not pass a law providing " '... that no federal employee shall attend Mass or take any active part in missionary work.' "

This Maryland religious test for public office unconstitutionally invades the appellant's freedom of belief and religion and therefore cannot be enforced against him.

The judgment of the Court of Appeals of Maryland is accordingly reversed and the cause is remanded for further proceedings not inconsistent with this opinion.

Reversed and remanded.

Mr. Justice FRANKFURTER and Mr. Justice HARLAN concur in the result.

Notes

1. In *Jensen v. Quaring*, 472 U.S. 478 (1985), an evenly divided Supreme Court affirmed a decision of a divided United States Court of Appeals for the Eighth Circuit granting Mrs. Frances Quaring an exemption from a Nebraska requirement that her photograph be taken and placed on her driver's license. Mrs. Quaring requested the exemption from Nebraska law based on her religious belief that the Second Commandment forbids her from having her photograph taken and from carrying or using photographs. Does *Quaring* survive *Employment Div. v. Smith*, 494 U.S. 872 (1990)?

2. Although in the late 18th century several states abolished any requirement of a belief in God to hold public office, *see* Chapter Two, and Article VI, § 3 forbade any religious test to hold federal public office, Maryland was only one of a number of states to continue to require a belief in God to hold public office. Does Justice Black's opinion, which itself relies heavily on history, explain why this specific history should be ignored? Does the opinion explain when and how history should control the outcome of decisions implicating issues of religious liberty? Recall *Marsh v. Chambers*, 463 U.S. 783 (1983), excerpted in Chapter Five, in which the Court addressed the constitutionality of legislative chaplains. The majority, in Chief Justice Burger's opinion, relied on the specific history concerning the creation of Congressional chaplains to uphold Nebraska's practice of appointing and paying a legislative chaplain. Justice Brennan's dissent in *Marsh* relied on the more abstract *Lemon* test to conclude the appointment of chaplains unconstitutional. In *McDaniel v. Paty*, 435 U.S. 618 (1978), excerpted in Chapter Ten, Chief Justice Burger, writing for a plurality, held that Tennessee's law barring ministers of the gospel from serving as delegates to the state's constitutional convention violated the Free Exercise Clause, despite the fact that most of the original states barred clergy from public office in their constitutions. (Jefferson originally supported such a ban, and Madison strongly op-

posed it.) Thus, Chief Justice Burger adopts specific history in *Marsh*, but abandons it in *McDaniel*. Is Chief Justice Burger consistent in his approach to the dictates of history? The Court's attempts to discern the "dictates" of history in its interpretation of the Establishment Clause have been regularly criticized. *See* Chapter 2 § E.

3. Chief Justice Burger concluded that *Torcaso* was inapposite to *McDaniel v. Paty* because *Torcaso* solely concerned Maryland's infringement of religious belief (or nonbelief). *McDaniel*, by contrast, concerned state-mandated discrimination based on religious status, acts and conduct. The belief/conduct distinction prevents the government from regulating an individual's beliefs, but permits governmental regulation of that person's actions. Why, then, should the Court in *McDaniel* declare unconstitutional Tennessee's ban on clergy-legislators, if that ban is based on the idea that some acts of religious believers may be regulated? Is Chief Justice Burger suggesting a different understanding of individual rights than that understood based on the belief/conduct approach? Burger wrote the Court's opinion in *Wooley v. Maynard*, decided just a year before *McDaniel*. Is there a particular theory of rights that *Wooley* and *McDaniel* vindicate? Are they part of a larger theory of individual autonomy from government, or part of a theory of religious liberty? Does this make a difference for understanding the extent to which religious practices should or may be protected by the Court? Why is *Torcaso* ignored in *Wooley*?

4. Does *Torcaso* suggest the importance of incorporating the First Amendment into the Fourteenth Amendment? Is *Torcaso* a case of incorporating Article VI, the clause barring a religious test for any federal office, into the Fourteenth Amendment?

5. Recall *West Virginia State Bd. of Educ. v. Barnette*, 319 U.S. 624 (1943), excerpted in Chapter One, and relied upon by the Court in *Wooley*. In *Barnette*, the Supreme Court held that children in public schools enjoyed a constitutional right to refuse to salute the flag or to recite the pledge of allegiance. Does the reliance on *Barnette* suggest that the right involved is less related to protecting religious freedom than the broader idea of freedom from orthodoxy in thoughts and ideas? In 1954, Congress added the words "under God" to the Pledge of Allegiance. Act of June 14, 1954, 68 Stats. 249. Should *Barnette*, read in light of *Wooley* and *Torcaso*, as well in light of as *Lee v. Weisman*, 505 U.S. 577 (1992) (barring invocation at public school graduation) and *Santa Fe Indep. Sch. Dist. v. Doe*, 530 U.S. 290 (2001) (barring prayer before public high school football games), prohibit public school authorities from leading the Pledge of Allegiance? *See Sherman v. Community Consol. Sch. Dist. 21 of Wheeling Township*, 980 F.2d 437 (7th Cir. 1992), *cert. denied*, 508 U.S. 950 (1993) (no). For an interesting analysis of this issue, see Abner S. Greene, *The Pledge of Allegiance Problem*, 64 Fordham L. Rev. 451 (1995). Two years after adding the words "under God" to the Pledge of Allegiance, Congress enacted the national motto, "In God We Trust." 70 Stat. 732, P.L. 851, 1956. Congress justified adoption of this motto by noting, "It will be of great spiritual and psychological value to our country to have a clearly designated national motto of inspirational quality in plain, popularly accepted English." H.R. No. 84-1959, 1956 U.S.C.C.A. 3720. In *Aronow v. United States*, 432 F.2d 242 (9th Cir.1970), the Ninth Circuit declined to order a three-judge court to consider a challenge to the national motto. The court concluded: "It is quite obvious that the national motto and the slogan on coinage and currency 'In God We Trust' has nothing whatsoever to do with the establishment of religion. Its use is of a patriotic or ceremonial character and bears no true resemblance to a governmental sponsorship of a religious exercise." *Id.* at 243. In *Gaylor v. United States*, 74 F.3d 214 (10th Cir.), *cert. denied*, 517 U.S. 1211 (1996), the Tenth Circuit also found without merit an Establishment Clause challenge to the national motto.

In *American Civil Liberties Union of Ohio v. Capitol Square Review and Advisory Bd.*, 210 F.3d 703 (6th Cir. 2000), a panel of the United States Court of Appeals for the Sixth Circuit declared unconstitutional the official motto of the state of Ohio, "With God All Things are Possible." This motto is taken from the Gospel of Matthew in the New Testament of the Christian Bible, and was adopted as the official motto by the Ohio legislature in 1959. The court of appeals noted that "[w]hile the mottos of other states use the word 'God' in various combinations, Ohio's is the only state motto which quotes directly from either the Old Testament or the New Testament of the Christian Bible." *Id.* at 711. It concluded,

> the district court could justify the secular cast of the words of the motto and remove them from the strictures of the Establishment Clause only by decontextualizing and blotting out their origins. In the context in which the words of the motto are found—as the words of Jesus speaking of salvation—to a reasonable observer, they must be seen as advancing, or at a minimum, showing a 'particular affinity' for Christianity. Simply put, they are an endorsement of the Christian religion by the State of Ohio. No other interpretation in the context of their presence in the New Testament is possible.
>
> We are satisfied that the words of the motto cannot be treated as they were by the district court. When Jesus spoke to his disciples he was explaining to them what was needed of them to enter heaven and achieve salvation, a uniquely Christian thought not shared by Jews and Moslems.

Id. at 725. The court summarily distinguished both the "under God" language in the Pledge and the national motto "In God We Trust" from Ohio's motto, relying largely on other circuit precedent. Concerning the national motto, it concluded that a reasonable observer, "aware of the purpose, context, and history of the phrase 'In God we trust,' would not consider its use" an endorsement of religion. *Id.* at 722.

In dissent, Judge Nelson claimed,

> To a reasonable observer who did not happen to be a biblical scholar, it seems to me, 'In God we trust' and 'With God All Things Are Possible' would appear remarkably similar. A person exceptionally well versed in the bible, on the other hand, might be aware that the declaration about trusting in God harkens back to the pre-Christian Old Testament (see Psalms 56:11), while the declaration about all things being possible with God is part of a statement that the Christian New Testament attributes to Jesus in a context unique to Christianity. See Matthew 19:26.
>
> I do not quarrel with the proposition that a government motto would be unconstitutional, under our current understanding of the Establishment Clause, if a hypothetical "reasonable observer" would take Ohio's motto to be an official endorsement of the Christian religion. I do not understand, however, why the observer should be deemed to be omniscient as well as reasonable.
>
> If I am correct in my understanding of the test, I do not believe that a reasonable observer in Ohio would find "With God All Things Are Possible" significantly more problematic than "In God we trust." I confess that prior to this lawsuit I could not have identified the source of either motto, and I doubt that it is vanity alone which prompts me to suggest that my ignorance is far from atypical.

Id. at 730–31.

The *en banc* Sixth Circuit vacated the panel's opinion, and affirmed the district court's opinion holding the motto did not violate the Establishment Clause. *American*

Civil Liberties Union of Ohio v. Capitol Square Review and Advisory Bd., 243 F.3d 289 (6th Cir. 2001). The court relied in part on the Supreme Court's earlier decisions refusing to hear cases involving the constitutionality of the national motto, and additionally concluded that Ohio's motto met both the *Lemon* and endorsement tests. Judge Nelson wrote the opinion for the *en banc* court.

In the aftermath of the terrorist attacks on September 11, 2001, several states have either passed or are considering adopting laws permitting the motto "In God We Trust" to be posted in public schools, courtrooms and other public buildings. Is such a law unconstitutional? Compare Newdow v. U.S. Congress, __ F.3d __ (9th Cir., June 26, 2002) (holding unconstitutional the words "under God" in the Pledge of Allegiance).

B. Individual Autonomy Expressed in Religious Practices

State ex rel. Swann v. Pack

527 S.W.2d 99 (Tenn. 1975), *cert. denied*, 424 U.S. 954 (1976)

HENRY, Justice.

We granted certiorari in this case to determine whether the State of Tennessee may enjoin a religious group from handling snakes as a part of its religious service and in accordance with its Articles of Faith, on the basis of such action constituting a public nuisance.

The Circuit Court at Newport permanently enjoined the defendant, Pack, Pastor of The Holiness Church of God in Jesus Name, of Newport, and one of his Elders from "handling, displaying or exhibiting dangerous and poisonous snakes", predicating its action primarily upon a finding that "the handling of said dangerous and poisonous snakes is in violation of T.C.A. § 39-2208[1] and that said practice is done in the presence of children and other people attending church services....".

I.

On April 14, 1973, the District Attorney General of the Second Judicial Circuit filed his petition in the Circuit Court at Newport charging that respondents Pack and certain designated Elders, including Albert Ball, had been handling snakes as a part of their church service "for the last two years"; that this was one of the rituals of the church to test the faith and sincerity of belief of church members; that Pastor Pack "has become anointed", along with other members of the church and has "advanced" to using deadly drugs, to wit, strychnine; that at a church service on April 7, 1973 snakes were handled and an "Indian boy was bitten and his arm became swollen"; that two named church

1. Section 39-2208 reads as follows:

Handling snakes so as to endanger life—Penalty.—It shall be unlawful for any person, or persons, to display, exhibit, handle or use any poisonous or dangerous snake or reptile in such a manner as to endanger the life or health of any person.

Any person violating the provisions of this section shall be guilty of a misdemeanor and punished by a fine of not less than fifty dollars ($50.00) nor more than one hundred and fifty dollars ($150), or by confinement in jail not exceeding six (6) months, or by both such fine and imprisonment, in the discretion of the court.

members drank strychnine and died as a result; that, at the funeral of one of these, Pastor Pack, and others, handled snakes; and that Pastor Pack has proclaimed his intentions to continue these practices. The prayer was for an injunction enjoining respondents "from handling, displaying, or exhibiting poisonous snakes or taking or using strychnine or other poisonous medicines." In the alternative, and upon failure of the named defendants to cease and desist, petitioner prayed that the church be padlocked as a public nuisance.

By order entered April 21, 1973, the trial court found these facts to be true; that § 39-2208 had been violated.

The further result of this order was that defendants could not practice snake handling, from which death *might* ensue[2] but could drink strychnine, a highly poisonous drug.

The record reflects no explanation for this incongruity.

Thereafter, the District Attorney General filed a second petition alleging stepped up activity, at the Holiness Church. On July 1, 1973, "a national convention for the snake handlers' cult of the United States" was held and "many dangerous and poisonous snakes were displayed" and one of the handlers had been bitten and was in a Chattanooga hospital recuperating. Services were conducted on July 3, and July 7, 1973, and again snakes were handled. All this led the District Attorney General to conclude and charge that Cocke County was in imminent danger and likely to "become the snake handling capital of the world".

In response to this citation, respondents were held in contempt, fined and sentenced, but sentences were suspended in each case, "until the said defendant handles poisonous snakes at said church are (sic) any other place *in Cocke County, Tennessee.*"

It was stipulated that various witnesses would testify that they had never seen anyone other than designated representatives of this particular church handle snakes; that they never saw any person who was either a parishioner or a nonmember present at the church services who had ever been placed in immediate danger.

It was further stipulated that an anthropologist would testify that snake handling is a legitimate part of their religious service; that she had never seen anyone endangered by handling snakes; that proper precautions were always taken; and that handling snakes is a legitimate and historic part of the church service. Two other witnesses would verify this testimony.

It was further stipulated that the "Indian boy", bitten at one of the services, was thirty years old.

The State made no contention that this is not an organized religious group nor did it question that the practice of handling snakes was a recognized part of its Articles of Faith, nor did it question the sincerity of the conviction of the respondents.

By final decree the trial judge made the injunction permanent, directing that defendants "be perpetually enjoined from handling, displaying or exhibiting dangerous and poisonous snakes at the said Holiness Church of God in Jesus Name, *or at any other place in Cocke County, Tennessee.*"

---

2. The most common question that arises regarding ritual snake handling is the surprisingly small number of fatalities. L.M. Klauner, "the undoubted authority on the rattlesnake" writes that the fatalities from this cause (rattlesnake bite) for the entire United States, with a population of over 160 million, seldom exceed 30 per year. Of every 100 people bitten by rattlesnakes, only about 3 will die. W. LaBarre, They Shall Take Up Serpents, pp. 13–14 (University of Minnesota Press 1962), (hereinafter referred to as LaBarre).

II.

The history and development of the Holiness Church is relevant.

Hensley, and his followers, based their beliefs and practices on Mark 16, verses 17 and 18, which in the Authorized or King James version, read as follows:

> And these signs shall follow them that believe; in my name shall they cast out devils; and shall *speak with new tongues; They shall take up serpents; and if they drink any deadly thing,* it shall not hurt them, they shall lay hands on the sick, and they shall recover. (Italics ours)[7]

The church Hensley[8] founded spread throughout the south and southeast and continues to exist today, primarily in rural and relatively isolated regions throughout this area. The Holiness Church of God in Jesus Name, in Cocke County, is a part of this movement. LaBarre asserts that "(t)he roots of the movement lie deep in American religious history" and asserts that it is one of the "offshoots of Methodism." Writers seem to be in general agreement that it is a "charismatic sect, or cult, or group of the Pentecostal variety."

To say that this is not a conventional movement would be a masterpiece of understatement. Its beliefs and practices are, to say the least, unconventional and out of harmony with contemporary customs, mores and notions of morality. They oppose drinking (to include carbonated beverages, tea and coffee), smoking, dancing, the use of cosmetics, jewelry or other adornment. They regard the use of medicine as a sure sign of lack of faith in God's ability to cure the sick and look upon medical doctors as being for the use of those who do not trust God. When greeting each other, the men use the "holy kiss", a mouth-to-mouth osculation "accompanied by a vigorous, if not passionate hug." The "holy kiss" is not exchanged between members of the opposite sexes.

But it is their belief in handling serpents that has catapulted them into the limelight and has produced their legal difficulties.

There is some apparent confusion with respect to their purpose in the use of serpents as a central practice in their religious beliefs. *Harden et al. v. State*, 188 Tenn. 17, 216 S.W.2d 708 (1948) treated snake handling as being "the test and proof of the sincerity of their belief." In this record it is asserted that the use of serpents is designed as a test of the faith and sincerity of church members. Our research indicates that this is not precisely correct. Their basic reason is compliance with the scripture as they interpret it, and as required by their Articles of Faith. But the practice of snake handling is not a test of faith, nor proof of godliness. Its sole purpose is to "confirm the word".

Pastor Pack states:

What serpent handling's for anyway is to confirm the Word.

---

7. Both the Old and New Testaments, however, contain language which would appear to be injunctions against snake handling and speaking in tongues. In Ecclesiastes (King James version) 10:11, it is said: "Surely the serpent will bite without enchantment, and a babbler is no better." St. Paul warns the Corinthians, in his First Epistle (Ch. 10, Verse 9) "Neither let us tempt Christ, as some of them also tempted and were destroyed of serpents."

8. Hensley remained active in the ministry of the church for some forty-six years. He said he had been bitten four hundred times "till I'm speckled all over like a guinea hen." (LaBarre, page 45) This founder and prophet of the church died, refusing medical attention, as a result of being bitten by a diamondback rattlesnake during a prayer meeting at Lester's Shed near Altha, Florida, on Sunday night, July 24, 1955.

Whether the practice is to "test the faith", is not relevant to this controversy. We only make the distinction in the interest of an accurate and comprehensive statement of the beliefs of this religious group and its admittedly unusual ritual.

Lastly, it should be pointed out that snakes are only handled when the member or handler has become "anointed". As we understand this phenomenon and the emotional reaction it produces, it is something akin to saying until the "spirit moves him". Unquestionably this is an emotional stimulus produced by extreme faith and generating great courage. Perhaps the whole belief in "anointment" can best be summed up by the defendant, Liston Pack:

> When I become anointed to handle serpents, my hands get real numb. It is a tremendous feeling. Maybe symbolic to an electric shock, only an electric shock could hurt you. This'll be pure joy.
>
> * * *
>
> It comes from inside... If you've got the Holy Ghost in you, it'll come out and nothing can hurt you. Faith brings contact with God and then you're anointed. It is not tempting God. You can't tempt God by doing what He says do. You can have faith, but if you never feel the anointing, you had better leave the serpent alone.
>
> Such is the nature of the religious group with which we deal.

III.

Again, this is not a conventional religious group and its members are few. There is, however, no requirement under our State or Federal Constitution that any religious group be conventional or that it be numerically strong in order that its activities be protected. Nor is there any requirement that its practices be in accord with prevailing views.

A "mode of worship", even of a religious group wherein the handling of serpents is central to its Articles of Faith, is constitutionally protected under the Constitutions of Tennessee and of the United States.

We, therefore, hold that the Holiness Church of God in Jesus Name, is a constitutionally protected religious group.

This is not to say, however, that this or any other religious group has an absolute and unbridled right to pursue any practice of its own choosing. The right to believe is absolute; the right to act is subject to reasonable regulation designed to protect a compelling state interest. This belief-action dichotomy has been the subject of numerous decisions of the Supreme Court of the United States.

IV.

In *Harden et al. v. State,* this Court was confronted with a challenge to the constitutionality of § 39-2208, T.C.A., on the basis of its alleged violation of the Freedom of Religion Clauses of the State and Federal Constitutions. After citing the belief-action dichotomy of *Cantwell v. Connecticut,* 310 U.S. 296 (1940), certain of the dicta in *Reynolds v. United States,* 98 U.S. 145 (1879), and the "grave and immediate danger" doctrine of *West Virginia Bd. of Educ. v. Barnette,* 319 U.S. 624 (1943), the Court said:

> It is equally certain that this danger is grave and immediate when and whenever the practice is being indulged.
>
> * * *

> They may believe without fear of any punishment that it is right to handle poisonous snakes while conducting religious services. But the right to practice that belief "is limited by other recognized powers, equally precious to mankind." One of those equally as precious rights is that of society's protection from a practice, religious or otherwise, which is dangerous to life and health.

There cannot be any question that the Court acted upon acceptable legal principles and precedents in declaring the Tennessee Snake Handler's Act constitutional in the face of an attack based upon the Freedom of Religion Clauses of the state and federal constitutions. This is not, however, to say that its application would necessarily be constitutional under all circumstances as is hereinafter pointed out. *Harden* simply holds that the statute does not violate the freedom of religion guarantees of the federal or state constitutions and that the defendants, under the factual situation of that particular case, had handled snakes "in such a manner as to endanger the life or health of any person".

[Pack] urges upon us that the "belief-action" dichotomy was expressly rejected by the Court in *Wisconsin v. Yoder*, 406 U.S. 205 (1972). What the Court actually rejected was the "idea that religiously grounded conduct is always outside the protection of the Free Exercise Clause." The consistent holding of the courts has been that belief is *always* protected, but that conduct or action is subject to regulation in the manner and to the extent hereinabove set forth.

The opinion of the Court of Appeals, with respect to *Harden*, reasons that subsequent decisions of the Supreme Court of the United States "have removed the theoretical underpinnings on which the decision was based." The opinion recites:

> The *Harden* decision was premised on the subsequently rejected belief-action dichotomy in free exercise cases, requiring merely a rational relationship between restrictions on religious conduct and the state interest served by the restrictions.

We respectfully differ with our brothers of the Court of Appeals.

We hold that under the First Amendment to the Constitution of the United States and under the substantially stronger provisions of Article 1, § 3 of the Constitution of Tennessee, a religious practice may be limited, curtailed or restrained to the point of outright prohibition, where it involves a clear and present danger to the interests of society; but the action of the state must be reasonable and reasonably dictated by the needs and demands of society as determined by the nature of the activity as balanced against societal interests. Essentially, therefore, the problem becomes one of a balancing of the interests between religious freedom and the preservation of the health, safety and morals of society. The scales must be weighed in favor of religious freedom, and yet the balance is delicate.

We decide this controversy in the light of these objectives. In doing so we have not lost sight of the fact that snake handling is central to respondents' faith. We recognize that to forbid snake handling is to remove the theological heart of the Holiness Church and this has prompted this Court to investigate and research this matter with meticulous care and to announce its decision through an unusually extensive opinion.

V.

We agree with the Court of Appeals that Tennessee's snake handling statute (§ 39-2208 T.C.A.) is not controlling. However, it cannot be ignored. It proscribes, to some extent, the conduct with which we deal. The trial judge based his judgment, in part, upon its violation and, in a very real sense, it represents a part of the public policy of our state, as declared by the legislature.

This statute is not as comprehensive or as conclusive as is generally believed. Nor is it a model of clarity. In material particulars it makes it unlawful

> (t)o display, exhibit, handle or use any poisonous or dangerous snake or reptile *in such manner as to endanger the life or health of any person.*

At a glance, it is self-evident that it does not forbid snake handling *per se.*

It condemns the *manner* and not the *fact* of snake handling.

Conversely it permits snake handling if done in a careful and prudent manner or, in the statutory terminology, under any circumstances or in any manner which does not endanger the life or health of any person.

Convictions under this statute involve proof of two elements, viz.: (1) that poisonous or dangerous snakes or reptiles were handled and (2) in such manner as to endanger the life or health of any other person. These elements were obviously present in *Harden.*

VI.

This is a suit to abate a nuisance.

The right of the District Attorney General to institute and maintain such an action inheres in his office. It is his duty to investigate, prosecute and insure against all infractions of the public peace and all acts which are against the peace and dignity of the state.

We hold that the handling of snakes as part of a religious ritual is a common law nuisance, wholly independent of any state statute.

Under this record, showing as it does, the handling of snakes in a crowded church sanctuary, with virtually no safeguards, with children roaming about unattended, with the handlers so enraptured and entranced that they are in a virtual state of hysteria and acting under the compulsion of "anointment", we would be derelict in our duty if we did not hold that respondents and their confederates have combined and conspired to commit a public nuisance and plan to continue to do so. The human misery and loss of life at their "Homecoming" of April 7, 1970 [sic] is proof positive.

Our research confirms the general pattern.

Tennessee has the right to guard against the unnecessary creation of widows and orphans. Our state and nation have an interest in having a strong, healthy, robust, taxpaying citizenry capable of self-support and of bearing arms and adding to the resources and reserves of manpower. We, therefore, have a substantial and compelling state interest in the face of a clear and present danger so grave as to endanger paramount public interests.

This holding is in no sense dependent upon the way or manner in which snakes are handled since it is not based upon the snake handling statute. Irrespective of its import, we hold that those who publicly handle snakes in the presence of other persons and those who are present aiding and abetting are guilty of creating and maintaining a public nuisance. Yes, the state has a right to protect a person from himself and to demand that he protect his own life.

Most assuredly the handling of poisonous snakes by untrained persons and the drinking of strychnine are not calculated to increase one's life span.

VII.

On remand the trial judge will enter an injunction perpetually enjoining and restraining all parties respondent from handling, displaying or exhibiting dangerous and poisonous snakes or from consuming strychnine or any other poisonous substances, within the confines of the State of Tennessee.

We fully appreciate the fact that the decision we reach imposes stringent limitations upon the pursuit of a religious practice, a result we endeavored to avoid. After long and careful analysis of alternatives and lengthy deliberations on all aspects of this problem we reached the conclusion that paramount considerations of public policy precluded less stringent solutions. We gave consideration to limiting the prohibition to handling snakes in the presence of children, but rejected this approach because it conflicts with the parental right to duty to direct the religious training of his children. We considered the adoption of a "consenting adult" standard but, again, this practice is too fraught with danger to permit its pursuit in the frenzied atmosphere of an emotional church service, regardless of age or consent. We considered restricting attendance to members only, but this would destroy the evangelical mission of the church. We considered permitting only the handlers themselves to be present, but this frustrates the purpose of confirming the faith to non-believers and separates the pastor and leaders from the congregation. We could find no rational basis for limiting or restricting the practice, and could conceive of no alternative plan or procedure which would be palatable to the membership or permissible from a standpoint of compelling state interest. The very considerations which impel us to outright prohibition, would preclude fragmentation of the religious services or the pursuit of this practice on a limited basis.

Notes

1. *Swann* is the most recent of six state cases, all arising in the southeast, which have upheld state regulation of snake handling as against a challenge based on free exercise grounds. Four of these cases arose in the 1940s, and the only case published after *Swann* is *Harris v. Harris*, 343 So. 2d 887 (Miss. 1977), a custody case. In *Harris*, the mother and legal custodian of a minor child was permitted to attend religious services which might include snake handling. The mother testified that she had never handled a snake, and the court noted that the mother's attendance at these services did not expose her child to any risk of snakebite. The court did not touch upon the issue whether the child was expressly permitted to attend these services, although the mother, as legal custodian of the child, enjoyed the power to indoctrinate the child in her faith, against the father's wishes, as long as the child was not exposed to any physical danger.

Does the absence of published cases since *Swann* indicate that the law is settled on this subject? Might it indicate an unwillingness to prosecute such cases for fear of "unsettling" the law?

2. Is there a cognizable constitutional right to harm oneself pursuant to a command from God? *See Mayock v. Martin*, 157 Conn. 56, 245 A.2d 574 (1968), *cert. denied*, 393 U.S. 1111 (1969) (no).

3. The Court makes much of the fact that this is a nuisance suit, rather than a criminal case. Should that make any difference? The Court also makes the instrumental argument that the state "has the right to guard against the unnecessary creation of widows and orphans." Shouldn't an instrumental argument like this be supported with empirical data, that is, data that indicates that members of this religious faith are a burden on the state of Tennessee? Or is it enough to note that some members of this church

have died as a result of handling poisonous snakes or drinking strychnine? Would the same rationale apply to assisted suicide?

The opinion of the Tennessee Supreme Court is written in a way both sympathetic to and appalled by the Holiness Church of God in Jesus Name. The court acknowledges that the church's articles of faith include snake handling, and explains in detail the reasons for snake handling. But the court also notes that language in the New Testament of the Christian Bible cautions against tempting God, that the death of the founder of the church was a result of snakebite, and that the male members of the church engage in a "holy kiss," accompanied by a vigorous, if not passionate, hug. Is this latter information designed to make the reader less concerned about protecting the religious liberty of the group? Or about the fate of the sect?

The court broadens the injunction to include the entire state of Tennessee, rather than merely Cocke County. Is there good cause for the court to do so?

4. Religious worship involving snake handling continues to be practiced in the southeast. *See* Dennis Covington, STANDING ON SAND MOUNTAIN: SNAKE HANDLING AND REDEMPTION IN SOUTHERN APPALACHIA (1995). For a history of Holiness Christianity, see David Kimbrough, TAKING UP SERPENTS: SNAKE HANDLERS OF EASTERN KENTUCKY (1995).

5. Although the Supreme Court has twice refused to hear snake handling cases (in addition to *Swann*, *see State v. Massey*, 51 S.E.2d 179 (N.C.), *appeal dismissed sub. nom. Bunn v. North Carolina*, 336 U.S. 942 (1949)), it has, in passing, noted with some approval the existence of laws prohibiting snake handling. *See McDaniel v. Paty*, 435 U.S. 618, 628 n.8 (1977) (citing *Swann* as "illustrative of the general nature of free exercise protections and the delicate balancing required by...Sherbert v. Verner and Wisconsin v. Yoder, when an important state interest is shown") (plurality opinion of Burger, C.J.). *See also Employment Div. v. Smith*, 494 U.S. 872, 889 (1990) (citing with approval to *State v. Massey*).

John F. Kennedy Memorial Hospital v. Heston

58 N.J. 576, 279 A.2d 670 (1971)

WEINTRAUB, C.J.

Delores Heston, age 22 and unmarried, was severely injured in an automobile accident. She was taken to the plaintiff hospital where it was determined that she would expire unless operated upon for a ruptured spleen and that if operated upon she would expire unless whole blood was administered. Miss Heston and her parents are Jehovah's Witnesses and a tenet of their faith forbids blood transfusions. Miss Heston insists she expressed her refusal to accept blood, but the evidence indicates she was in shock on admittance to the hospital and in the judgment of the attending physicians and nurses was then or soon became disoriented and incoherent. Her mother remained adamant in her opposition to a transfusion, and signed a release of liability for the hospital and medical personnel. Miss Heston did not execute a release; presumably she could not. Her father could not be located.

Death being imminent, plaintiff on notice to the mother made application at 1:30 a.m. to a judge of the Superior Court for the appointment of a guardian for Miss Heston with directions to consent to transfusions as needed to save her life. At the hearing, the mother and her friends thought a certain doctor would pursue surgery without a transfusion, but the doctor, in response to the judge's telephone call, declined the case.

The court appointed a guardian with authority to consent to blood transfusions "for the preservation of the life of Delores Heston." Surgery was performed at 4:00 a.m. the same morning. Blood was administered. Miss Heston survived.

The controversy is moot. Miss Heston is well and no longer in plaintiff's hospital. The prospect of her return at some future day in like circumstances is too remote to warrant a declaratory judgment as between the parties. Nonetheless, the public interest warrants a resolution of the cause, and for that reason we accept the issue.

In *State v. Perricone*, 181 A.2d 751 (N.J.), *cert. denied*, 371 U.S. 890 (1962), we sustained an order for compulsory blood transfusion for an infant despite the objection of the parents who were Jehovah's Witnesses. In *Raleigh Fitkin-Paul Morgan Memorial Hospital v. Anderson*, 42 N.J. 421, 201 A.2d 537, *cert. denied*, 377 U.S. 985 (1964), it appeared that both the mother, a Jehovah's Witness, and the child she was bearing would die if blood were not transfused should she hemorrhage. We held that a blood transfusion could be ordered if necessary to save the lives of the mother and the unborn child.

[A] constitutional right [is not] established by adding that one's religious faith ordains his death. Religious beliefs are absolute, but conduct in pursuance of religious beliefs is not wholly immune from governmental restraint.

Complicating the subject of suicide is the difficulty of knowing whether a decision to die is firmly held. Psychiatrists may find that beneath it all a person bent on self-destruction is hoping to be rescued, and most who are rescued do not repeat the attempt, at least not at once. Then, too, there is the question whether in any event the person was and continues to be competent (a difficult concept in this area) to choose to die. And of course there is no opportunity for a trial of these questions in advance of intervention by the State or a citizen.

[Heston] suggests there is a difference between passively submitting to death and actively seeking it. The distinction may be merely verbal, as it would be if an adult sought death by starvation instead of a drug. If the State may interrupt one mode of self-destruction, it may with equal authority interfere with the other. It is arguably different when an individual, overtaken by illness, decides to let it run a fatal course. But unless the medical option itself is laden with the risk of death or of serious infirmity, the State's interest in sustaining life in such circumstances is hardly distinguishable from its interest in the case of suicide.

Here we are not dealing with deadly options. The risk of death or permanent injury because of a transfusion is not a serious factor. Indeed, Miss Heston did not resist a transfusion on that basis. Nor did she wish to die. She wanted to live, but her faith demanded that she refuse blood even at the price of her life. The question is not whether the State could punish her for refusing a transfusion. It may be granted that it would serve no State interest to deal criminally with one who resisted a transfusion on the basis of religious faith. The question is whether the State may authorize force to prevent death or may tolerate the use of force by others to that end.

Hospitals exist to aid the sick and the injured. The medical and nursing professions are consecrated to preserving life. That is their professional creed. To them, a failure to use a simple, established procedure in the circumstances of this case would be malpractice, however the law may characterize that failure because of the patient's private convictions. A surgeon should not be asked to operate under the strain of knowing that a transfusion may not be administered even though medically required to save his patient. The hospital and its staff should not be required to decide whether the patient is or continues to be competent to make a judgment upon the subject, or whether the release tendered by the patient or a member of his family will protect them from civil responsibility. The hospital could hardly avoid the problem by compelling the removal of a dying patient, and Miss Heston's family made no effort to take her elsewhere.

The precedents are few. They are collected in an annotation, 9 A.L.R.3d 1391 (1966). With one exception, *Erickson v. Dilgard*, 44 Misc.2d 27, 252 N.Y.S.2d 705 (Sup. Ct. 1962), transfusions for adults were ordered despite their religious tenets. *Application of President and Directors of Georgetown College, Inc.*, 118 U.S. App. D.C. 80, 331 F.2d 1000 (D.C. Cir.), *cert. denied*, 377 U.S. 978 (1964); *United States v. George*, 239 F. Supp. 752 (D. Conn. 1965); *Collins v. Davis*, 44 Misc.2d 622, 254 N.Y.S.2d 666 (Sup. Ct. 1964); *Powell v. Columbian Presbyterian Medical Center*, 49 Misc.2d 215, 267 N.Y.S.2d 450 (Sup. Ct. 1965).

Two cases reached an appellate level. In *Georgetown College*, a single judge of the Court of Appeals ordered the transfusion. Thereafter a majority of the court denied a petition for rehearing en banc, without however indicating the precise basis for that denial. One dissenting opinion approached the merits. The sole appellate decision expressly reaching the merits appears to be *In re Estate of Brooks*, 32 Ill.2d 361, 205 N.E.2d 435 (Sup. Ct. 1965). There a conservator was appointed to authorize the transfusion for a Jehovah's Witness. After the transfusion, the patient and her husband sought unsuccessfully to have the order expunged. The Supreme Court of Illinois reversed. The court could find no "clear and present danger" warranting interference with the patient's religious proscription. It has been suggested that the "clear and present danger" test, appropriate with respect to free speech, is not the appropriate criterion here, and that the relevant question is whether there is a "compelling State interest" justifying the State's refusal to permit the patient to refuse vital aid. We think the latter test is the correct one, but it cannot be said with confidence that *Brooks* would have gone the other way if the decision had been made in its light. In fact the court there did mention conceivable interests. Thus it noted that the patient did not have minor children who might become charges of the State. But the court did not expressly consider whether the State had an interest in sustaining life, a consideration which would not be apparent when the focus is upon a "clear and present danger." Nor did the court consider the sufficiency of the interest of a hospital or its staff when the patient is thrust upon them. In fact there the applicant was the patient's regular physician who had long treated her for an ulcer, knew of her religious tenet, and had assured her that he would not administer blood.

It is not at all clear that *Brooks* would be applied in Illinois to an emergent factual pattern in which a hospital and its staff are the involuntary custodians of an adult. In any event, for the reasons already given, we find that the interest of the hospital and its staff, as well as the State's interest in life, warranted the transfusion of blood under the circumstances of this case. The judgment is accordingly affirmed.

Notes

1. As one might expect, courts have split on the issue whether religious convictions can permit one to refuse life-saving medical treatment. In *Application of the President and Directors of Georgetown College, Inc.*, 331 F.2d 1000 (D.C. Cir.), *cert. denied*, 377 U.S. 978 (1964), the United States Court of Appeals for the District of Columbia Circuit rejected the free exercise claim of Mrs. Jesse E. Jones, a Jehovah's Witness. In both *Holmes v. Silver Cross Hosp.*, 340 F. Supp. 125 (W.D. Ill. 1972) and *In re Brooks' Estate*, 32 Ill. 2d 361, 205 N.E.2d 435 (1965), the courts refused to give a hospital legal consent to give Jehovah's Witnesses blood transfusions.

Recent cases have found a right to refuse medical treatment based on both Free Exercise and right of privacy reasons. *See In re Brown*, 478 So. 2d 1033 (Miss. 1985) (holding individual's right to free exercise of religion and right to privacy allowed her to refuse blood transfusions, and state interest in ensuring her survival until after her testimony in criminal case not a compelling state interest); *In re Dubreuil*, 629 So. 2d 819 (Fla. 1993) (holding erroneous lower court's decision permitting hospital to administer blood transfusions to mother who had just undergone caesarean section); *Fosmire v. Nicoleau*, 551 N.E. 77 (N.Y. 1990) (same).

2. The court in *Heston* distinguished cases involving an adult only, and cases involving an adult who is also a parent. Does such a distinction, which is based on a notion that a parent has a duty (enforceable by the state) to be "other-regarding" rather than "self-regarding," violate the notion of liberal autonomy found at the heart of these cases? Recent decisions have rejected this other-regarding duty: "Parenthood, in and of itself, does not deprive one of living in accord with one's own beliefs. Society does not, for example, disparage or preclude one from performing an act of bravery resulting in the loss of that person's life simply because that person has parental responsibilities." *Dubreuil*, at 826. *See also Public Health Trust of Dade County v. Wons*, 541 So. 2d 96, 99 (Fla. 1989) ("Sweeping claims about the need to preserve the lives of parents with minor children have an emotional appeal that facilely avoids both the constitutionally required scrutiny of the state's authority to act and the search for less restrictive alternatives"). Do the statements quoted above privilege individual autonomy over any competing communal claims as a constitutional matter? Is this accurate historically? Even if not a command of history, should it be a command of modern constitutional interpretation? Is the analogy to an "act of bravery" that costs a parent his or her life an appropriate analogy? In general, acts of bravery are other-regarding, for the actor gives his or her life to save another. The person who refuses to receive transfused blood is not saving another, either spiritually or physically. The act is self-regarding, undertaken to save oneself spiritually at the cost of physical death. The difficult question is whether such self-regarding decisions may be overborne as a matter of general individual right, or as a matter of religious liberty. In both *Dubreuil* and *Wons*, the state's interest is limited to the issue of "abandonment" of the children. The Florida Supreme Court does not acknowledge a state interest in the life of the person refusing the blood transfusion. Is the state's interest in protecting life in *Heston* cogently articulated? If not, is that because our understanding of rights and duties largely excludes the state from the calculus of ascertaining the limits of individual liberty?

If for religious reasons a person refuses surgery after an automobile accident, and later sues for damages, is the court required to instruct the jury that it must determine whether the plaintiff's actions were reasonable in assessing whether she mitigated her damages as required by law? In *Williams v. Bright*,658 N.Y.S.2d 910 (App. Div.), *appeal dismissed*, 686 N.E.2d 1368, 664 N.Y.S.2d 273 (N.Y. 1997), the plaintiff, a member of the Jehovah's Witnesses, suffered injuries to her hip and knee. Her expert testified that if the plaintiff did not undergo the surgeries, she was likely to end up in a wheelchair. If she did, her prognosis for a normal life was very good. The plaintiff refused to undergo surgery because she would receive blood transfusions. In instructing the jury, the trial court stated that "under no circumstances are you to consider the validity or reasonableness of her religious beliefs.... That is out of bounds for you.... And so you have to determine in assessing the question of damages... whether [plaintiff] acted reasonably as a Jehovah's Witness in refusing surgery which would involve blood transfusions." On appeal, the court held this instruction impermissibly made the jury "an ecclesiastical authority." However, the trial court was permitted to instruct the jury that it could consider the plaintiff's religious beliefs in assessing the reasonableness of her conduct in mitigating damages.

C. Religious Practices, The Family and the State as Parent

Prince v. Massachusetts

321 U.S. 158 (1944)

Mr. Justice RUTLEDGE delivered the opinion of the Court.

The case brings for review another episode in the conflict between Jehovah's Witnesses and state authority. This time Sarah Prince appeals from convictions for violating Massachusetts' child labor laws, by acts said to be a rightful exercise of her religious convictions.

When the offenses were committed she was the aunt and custodian of Betty M. Simmons, a girl nine years of age. Originally there were three separate complaints. They were, shortly, for (1) refusal to disclose Betty's identity and age to a public officer whose duty was to enforce the statutes; (2) furnishing her with magazines, knowing she was to sell them unlawfully, that is, on the street; and (3) as Betty's custodian, permitting her to work contrary to law. The complaints were made, respectively, pursuant to §§79, 80 and 81 of Chapter 149, Gen. Laws of Mass. (Ter. Ed.). [The issue is] whether §§80 and 81, as applied, contravene the Fourteenth Amendment by denying or abridging appellant's freedom of religion and by denying to her the equal protection of the laws.

Sections 80 and 81 form parts of Massachusetts' comprehensive child labor law. They provide methods for enforcing the prohibitions of §69, which is as follows:

> "No boy under twelve and no girl under eighteen shall sell, expose or offer for sale any newspapers, magazines, periodicals or any other articles of merchandise of any description, or exercise the trade of bootblack or scavenger, or any other trade, in any street or public place."

Sections 80 and 81, so far as pertinent, read:

> "Whoever furnishes or sells to any minor any article of any description with the knowledge that the minor intends to sell such article in violation of any provision of sections sixty-nine to seventy-three, inclusive, or after having received written notice to this effect, from any officer charged with the enforcement thereof, or knowingly procures or encourages any minor to violate any provisions of said sections, shall be punished by a fine of not less than ten nor more than two hundred dollars or by imprisonment for not more than two months, or both." §80.
>
> "Any parent, guardian or custodian having a minor under his control who compels or permits such minor to work in violation of any provision of sections sixty to seventy-four, inclusive,... shall for a first offense be punished by a fine of not less than two nor more than ten dollars or by imprisonment for not more than five days, or both;..." §81.

The story told by the evidence has become familiar. It hardly needs repeating, except to give setting to the variations introduced through the part played by a child of tender years. Mrs. Prince, living in Brockton, is the mother of two young sons. She also has legal custody of Betty Simmons, who lives with them. The children too are Jehovah's Witnesses and both Mrs. Prince and Betty testified they were ordained ministers. The former was accustomed to go each week on the streets of Brockton to distribute "Watchtower" and "Consolation," according to the usual plan. She had permitted the children to engage in this activity previously, and had been warned against doing so by the school attendance officer, Mr. Perkins. But, until December 18, 1941, she generally did not take them with her at night.

That evening, as Mrs. Prince was preparing to leave her home, the children asked to go. She at first refused. Childlike, they resorted to tears; and, motherlike, she yielded. Arriving downtown, Mrs. Prince permitted the children "to engage in the preaching work with her upon the sidewalks." That is, with specific reference to Betty, she and Mrs. Prince took positions about twenty feet apart near a street intersection. Betty held up her hand, for passers-by to see, copies of "Watch Tower" and "Consolation." From her shoulder hung the usual canvas magazine bag, on which was printed: "Watchtower and Consolation 5 cents per copy." No one accepted a copy from Betty that evening and she received no money. Nor did her aunt. But on other occasions, Betty had received funds and given out copies.

Mrs. Prince and Betty remained until 8:45 p.m. A few minutes before this, Mr. Perkins approached Mrs. Prince. A discussion ensued. He inquired and she refused to give Betty's name. However, she stated the child attended the Shaw School. Mr. Perkins referred to his previous warnings and said he would allow five minutes for them to get off the street. Mrs. Prince admitted she supplied Betty with the magazines and said, "[N]either you nor anybody else can stop me... This child is exercising her God-given right and her constitutional right to preach the gospel, and no creature has a right to interfere with God's commands." However, Mrs. Prince and Betty departed. She remarked as she went, "I'm not going through this anymore. We've been through it time and time again. "I'm going home and put the little girl to bed." It may be added that testimony, by Betty, her aunt and others, was offered at the trials, and was excluded, to show that Betty believed it was her religious duty to perform this work and failure would bring condemnation "to everlasting destruction at Armageddon."

The only question is whether, as construed and applied, the statute is valid. Upon this the [Massachusetts] court said: "We think that freedom of the press and of religion is subject to incidental regulation to the slight degree involved in the prohibition of the selling of religious literature in streets and public places by boys under twelve and girls under eighteen, and in the further statutory provisions herein considered, which have been adopted as means of enforcing that prohibition."

[Mrs. Prince] rests squarely on freedom of religion under the First Amendment, applied by the Fourteenth to the states. She buttresses this foundation, however, with a claim of parental right as secured by the due process clause of the latter Amendment. These guaranties, she thinks, guard alike herself and the child in what they have done. Thus, two claimed liberties are at stake. One is the parent's, to bring up the child in the way he should go, which for appellant means to teach him the tenets and the practices of their faith. The other freedom is the child's, to observe these; and among them is "to preach the gospel... by public distribution" of "Watchtower" and "Consolation," in conformity with the scripture: "A little child shall lead them."

If by this position appellant seeks for freedom of conscience a broader protection than for freedom of the mind, it may be doubted that any of the great liberties insured by the First Article can be given higher place than the others. Heart and mind are not identical. Intuitive faith and reasoned judgment are not the same. Spirit is not always thought. But in the everyday business of living, secular or otherwise, these variant aspects of personality find inseparable expression in a thousand ways. They cannot be altogether parted in law more than in life.

To make accommodation between these freedoms and an exercise of state authority always is delicate. It hardly could be more so than in such a clash as this case presents. On one side is the obviously earnest claim for freedom of conscience and religious practice. With it is allied the parent's claim to authority in her own household and in the rearing of her children. The parent's conflict with the state over control of the child and his training is serious enough when only secular matters are concerned. It becomes the more so when an element of religious conviction enters. Against these sacred private interests, basic in a democracy, stand the interests of society to protect the welfare of children, and the state's assertion of authority to that end, made here in a manner conceded valid if only secular things were involved. The last is no mere corporate concern of official authority. It is the interest of youth itself, and of the whole community, that children be both safeguarded from abuses and given opportunities for growth into free and independent well-developed men and citizens. Between contrary pulls of such weight, the safest and most objective recourse is to the lines already marked out, not precisely but for guides, in narrowing the no man's land where this battle has gone on.

The rights of children to exercise their religion, and of parents to give them religious training and to encourage them in the practice of religious belief, as against preponderant sentiment and assertion of state power voicing it, have had recognition here, most recently in *West Virginia Board of Educ. v. Barnette,* 319 U.S. 624 (1943). Previously in *Pierce v. Society of Sisters*, 268 U.S. 510 (1925), this Court had sustained the parent's authority to provide religious with secular schooling, and the child's right to receive it, as against the state's requirement of attendance at public schools. And in *Meyer v. Nebraska*, 262 U.S. 390 (1923), children's rights to receive teaching in languages other than the nation's common tongue were guarded against the state's encroachment. It is cardinal with us that the custody, care and nurture of the child reside first in the parents, whose primary function and freedom include preparation for obligations the state can neither supply nor hinder. And it is in recognition of this that these decisions have respected the private realm of family life which the state cannot enter.

But the family itself is not beyond regulation in the public interest, as against a claim of religious liberty. *Reynolds v. United States*, 98 U.S. 145 (1879); *Davis v. Beason*, 133 U.S. 333 (1890). And neither rights of religion nor rights of parenthood are beyond limitation. Acting to guard the general interest in youth's well being, the state as *parens patriae* may restrict the parent's control by requiring school attendance, regulating or prohibiting the child's labor and in many other ways. Its authority is not nullified merely because the parent grounds his claim to control the child's course of conduct on religion or conscience. Thus, he cannot claim freedom from compulsory vaccination for the child more than for himself on religious grounds. The right to practice religion freely does not include liberty to expose the community or the child to communicable disease or the latter to ill health or death.

The case reduces itself therefore to the question whether the presence of the child's guardian puts a limit to the state's power. That fact may lessen the likelihood that some evils the legislation seeks to avert will occur. But it cannot forestall all of them. The zealous though lawful exercise of the right to engage in propagandizing the community, whether in religious, political or other matters, may and at times does create situations difficult enough for adults to cope with and wholly inappropriate for children, especially of tender years, to face. Other harmful possibilities could be stated, of emotional excitement and psychological or physical injury. Parents may be free to become martyrs themselves. But it does not follow they are free, in identical circumstances, to make martyrs of their children before they have reached the age of full and legal discretion when they can make that choice for themselves. We think that with reference to the public proclaiming of religion, upon the streets and in other similar public places, the power of the state to control the conduct of children reaches beyond the scope of its authority over adults, as is true in the case of other freedoms, and the rightful boundary of its power has not been crossed in this case.

Our ruling does not extend beyond the facts the case presents. We neither lay the foundation "for any [that is, every] state intervention in the indoctrination and participation of children in religion" which may be done "in the name of their health and welfare" nor give warrant for "every limitation of their religious training and activities." The religious training and indoctrination of children may be accomplished in many ways, some of which, as we have noted, have received constitutional protection through decisions of this Court. These and all others except the public proclaiming of religion on the streets, if this may be taken as either training or indoctrination of the proclaimer, remain unaffected by the decision.

The judgment is *Affirmed.*

Mr. Justice MURPHY, dissenting.

This attempt by the state of Massachusetts to prohibit a child from exercising her constitutional right to practice her religion on the public streets cannot, in my opinion, be sustained.

The record makes clear the basic fact that Betty Simmons, the nine-year old child in question, was engaged in a genuine religious, rather than commercial, activity. She was a member of Jehovah's Witnesses and had been taught the tenets of that sect by her guardian, the appellant. Such tenets included the duty of publicly distributing religious tracts on the street and from door to door. Pursuant to this religious duty and in the company of the appellant, Betty Simmons on the night of December 18, 1941, was standing on a public street corner and offering to distribute Jehovah's Witness literature to passers-by. There was not expectation of pecuniary profit to herself or the appellant. It is undisputed, furthermore, that she did this of her own desire and with appellant's consent. She testified that she was motivated by her love of the Lord and that He commanded her to distribute this literature; this was, she declared, her way of worshipping God. She was occupied, in other words, in "an age-old form of missionary evangelism" with a purpose "as evangelical as the revival meeting." *Murdock.*

Religious training and activity, whether performed by adult or child, are protected by the Fourteenth Amendment against interference by state action, except insofar as they violate reasonable regulations adopted for the protection of the public health, morals and welfare. Our problem here is whether a state, under the guise of enforcing its child labor laws, can lawfully prohibit girls under the age of eighteen and boys under the age of twelve from practicing their religious faith insofar as it involves the distribution or sale of religious tracts on the public streets. The statutes in question prohibit all children within the specified age limits from selling or offering to sell "any newspapers, magazines, periodicals or any other articles of merchandise of any description... in any street or public place." Criminal sanctions are imposed on the parents and guardians who compel or permit minors in their control to engage in the prohibited transactions.

The state court has construed these statutes to cover the activities here involved, thereby imposing an indirect restraint through the parents and guardians on the free exercise by minors of their religious beliefs. This indirect restraint is no less effective than a direct one. A square conflict between the constitutional guarantee of religious freedom and the state's legitimate interest in protecting the welfare of its children is thus presented.

As the opinion of the Court demonstrates, the power of the state lawfully to control the religious and other activities of children is greater than its power over similar activities of adults. But the fact is no more decisive of the issue posed by this case than is the obvious fact that the family itself is subject to reasonable regulation in the public interest. We are concerned solely with the reasonableness of this particular prohibition of religious activity by children.

In dealing with the validity of statutes which directly or indirectly infringe religious freedom and the right of parents to encourage their children in the practice of a religious belief, we are not aided by any strong presumption of the constitutionality of such legislation. *United States v. Carolene Products Co.*, 304 U.S. 144, 152, note 4. On the contrary, the human freedoms enumerated in the First Amendment and carried over into the Fourteenth Amendment are to be presumed to be invulnerable and any attempt to sweep away those freedoms is prima facie invalid. It follows that any restriction or prohibition must be justified by those who deny that the freedoms have been unlawfully invaded. The burden was therefore on the state of Massachusetts to prove the reasonableness and necessity of prohibiting children from engaging in religious activity of the type involved in this case.

The burden in this instance, however, is not met by vague references to the reasonableness underlying child labor legislation in general. The great interest of the state in shielding minors from the evil vicissitudes of early life does not warrant every limitation on their religious training and activities. If the right of a child to practice its religion in that manner is to be forbidden by constitutional means, there must be convincing proof that such a practice constitutes a grave and immediate danger to the state or to the health, morals or welfare of the child. The vital freedom of religion, which is "of the very essence of a scheme of ordered liberty," cannot be erased by slender references to the state's power to restrict the more secular activities of children.

The state, in my opinion, has completely failed to sustain its burden of proving the existence of any grave or immediate danger to any interest which it may lawfully protect. There is no proof that Betty Simmons' mode of worship constituted a serious menace to the public. The sidewalk, no less than the cathedral or the evangelist's tent, is a proper place, under the Constitution, for the orderly worship of God. Such use of the streets is as necessary to the Jehovah's Witnesses, the Salvation Army and others who practice religion without benefit of conventional shelters as is the use of the streets for purposes of passage.

[T]he bare possibility that such harms might emanate from distribution of religious literature is not, standing alone, sufficient justification for restricting freedom of conscience and religion. Nor can parents or guardians be subjected to criminal liability because of vague possibilities that their religious teachings might cause injury to the child. The evils must be grave, immediate, substantial. Yet there is not the slightest indication in this record, or in sources subject to judicial notice, that children engaged in distributing literature pursuant to their religious beliefs have been or are likely to be subject to any of the harmful "diverse influences of the street." Indeed, if probabilities are to be indulged in, the likelihood is that children engaged in serious religious endeavor are immune from such influences. Gambling, truancy, irregular eating and sleeping habits, and the more serious vices are not consistent with the high moral character ordinarily displayed by children fulfilling religious obligations. Moreover, Jehovah's Witness children invariably make their distributions in groups subject at all times to adult or parental control, as was done in this case. The dangers are thus exceedingly remote, to say the least. And the fact that the zealous exercise of the right to propagandize the community may result in violent or disorderly situations difficult for children to face is no excuse for prohibiting the exercise of that right.

No chapter in human history has been so largely written in terms of persecution and intolerance as the one dealing with religious freedom. From ancient times to the present day, the ingenuity of man has known no limits in its ability to forge weapons of oppression for use against those who dare to express or practice unorthodox religious beliefs. And the Jehovah's Witnesses are living proof of the fact that even in this nation, conceived as it was in the ideals of freedom, the right to practice religion in unconventional ways is still far from secure. Theirs is a militant and unpopular faith, pursued with a fanatical zeal. They have suffered brutal beatings; their property has been destroyed; they have been harassed at every turn by the resurrection and enforcement of little used ordinances and statutes. To them, along with other present-day religious minorities, befalls the burden of testing our devotion to the ideals and constitutional guarantees of religious freedom. We should therefore hesitate before approving the application of a statute that might be used as another instrument of oppression. Religious freedom is too sacred a right to be restricted or prohibited in any degree without convincing proof that a legitimate interest of the state is in grave danger.

Mr. Justice JACKSON:

The novel feature of this decision is this: the Court holds that a state may apply child labor laws to restrict or prohibit an activity of which, as recently as last term, it held: "This form of religious activity occupies the same high estate under the First Amendment as do worship in the churches and preaching from the pulpits. It has the same claim to protection as the more orthodox and conventional exercises of religion." "... the mere fact that the religious literature is 'sold' by itinerant preachers rather than 'donated' does not transform evangelism into a commercial enterprise. If it did, then the passing of the collection plate in church would make the church service a commercial project. The constitutional rights of those spreading their religious beliefs through the spoken and printed word are not to be gauged by standards governing retailers or wholesalers of books." *Murdock v. Pennsylvania*, 319 U.S. 105, 111 (1943).

It is difficult for me to believe that going upon the streets to accost the public is the same thing for application of public law as withdrawing to a private structure for religious worship. But if worship in the churches and the activity of Jehovah's Witnesses on the streets "occupy the same high estate" and have the "same claim to protection" it would seem that child labor laws may be applied to both if to either. If the *Murdock* doctrine stands along with today's decision, a foundation is laid for any state intervention in the indoctrination and participation of children in religion, provided it is done in the name of their health or welfare.

Our basic difference seems to be as to the method of establishing limitations which of necessity bound religious freedom.

My own view may be shortly put: I think the limits begin to operate whenever activities begin to affect or collide with liberties of others or of the public. Religious activities which concern only members of the faith are and ought to be free—as nearly absolutely free as anything can be. But beyond these, many religious denominations or sects engage in collateral and secular activities intended to obtain means from unbelievers to sustain the worshippers and their leaders. They raise money, not merely by passing the plate to those who voluntarily attend services or by contributions by their own people, but by solicitations and drives addressed to the public by holding public dinners and entertainments, by various kinds of sales and Bingo games and lotteries. All such money-raising activities on a public scale are, I think, Caesar's affairs and may be regulated by the state so long as it does not discriminate against one because he is doing them for a religious purpose, and the regulation is not arbitrary and capricious, in violation of other provisions of the Constitution.

The Court in the *Murdock* case rejected this principle of separating immune religious activities from secular ones in declaring the disabilities which the Constitution imposed on local authorities. Instead, the Court now draws a line based on age that cuts across both true exercise of religion and auxiliary secular activities. I think this is not a correct principle for defining the activities immune from regulation on grounds of religion, and *Murdock* overrules the grounds on which I think affirmance should rest. I have no alternative but to dissent from the grounds of affirmance of a judgment which I think was rightly decided, and upon right grounds, by the Supreme Judicial Court of Massachusetts.

Mr. Justice ROBERTS and Mr. Justice FRANKFURTER join in this opinion.

Notes

1. The majority concludes that although parents are free to become martyrs, "it does not follow they are free, in identical circumstances, to make martyrs of their children before they have reached the age of full and legal discretion when they can make that choice for themselves." Is the use of the word "martyr" in this case appropriate? If so, is such an idea controversial? The Court then limits its decision to the facts of the case, and though it reiterates the various ways in which religious practices remain constitutionally protected, the Court ends its opinion with the statement that "These and all others except the public proclaiming of religion on the streets, if this may be taken as either training or indoctrination of the proclaimer, remain unaffected by the decision." Does this mean that a law banning all commercial solicitation by children would withstand constitutional muster, no matter the time of day? Does this statement limit the authority of parents to involve their children in public proselytization?

2. Justices Black and Douglas, whose change of opinion led to the overruling of *Minersville Sch. Dist. v. Gobitis*, 310 U.S. 586 (1940) in *West Virginia Bd. of Educ. v. Barnette*, 319 U.S. 624 (1943), silently joined the majority opinion in *Prince*. Can their decision in *Prince* be harmonized with their decision a year earlier in *Barnette*? Justice Jackson, the author of the ringing rhetoric in *Barnette*, concurred in the judgment, and explains his reason as drawing a line between "secular" and "religious" acts. Is this explanation more satisfactory than the majority's? Less than three months after deciding *Prince*, the Court, *per* Justice Douglas, held in *United States v. Ballard*, 322 U.S. 78 (1944), excerpted in Chapter Thirteen, that an indictment of leaders of the religious "I Am" movement could not be tried upon the truth or falsity of the representations of the defendant. The majority refused to prohibit completely such prosecutions, as long as the truth or falsity of claimed religious revelations were not submitted to the jury. Justice Jackson dissented, arguing that the trial necessarily raised such issues, and that this was constitutionally barred. And in *Murdock v. Pennsylvania*, 319 U.S. 105 (1943), Justice Douglas, for five members of the Court, including Justice Black, held that an ordinance barring the sale of any goods without a license could not constitutionally be ap-

plied to the "religious venture" by Jehovah's Witnesses of offering for sale books of the Watch Tower Bible & Tract Society. Justice Jackson's dissent in *Murdock* was included in his concurrence in the companion case of *Douglas v. City of Jeannette*, 319 U.S. 157 (1943), and was premised on his belief that the majority had failed to balance the right of the Jehovah's Witnesses to proselytize with the right of homeowners to be left alone. For Jackson, the proselytization in the *Murdock* case was not analogous to worship in churches and preaching from pulpits, and thus could be regulated. *Murdock* was reaffirmed in *Follett v. Town of McCormick*, 321 U.S. 573 (1944), and Douglas again wrote the opinion for the majority. Jackson joined the dissenting opinion of Justice Roberts. Are the differences between Douglas and Black, on one hand, and Jackson, on the other, clarified by these cases? Justice Jackson suggests in both *Prince* and *Murdock* that religious liberty stops when it interferes with another's rights. How is one to determine when one's right to proselytize interferes with another's right to be free from proselytization? Does it depend on whether one is accosted in the street rather than at home? Are *Prince* and *Murdock* factually different in this respect? Does Jackson's approach privilege a particular kind of religious faith, one that worships "privately" rather than "publicly"? Does Justice Douglas privilege "minority" faiths at the expense of those who do not want to be proselytized?

The dissenting opinion by Justice Frank Murphy relies on footnote 4 of the *United States v. Carolene Products Co.*, 304 U.S. 144, 152 n.4 (1938), from which, as noted in Chapter Five, much modern constitutional rights jurisprudence springs. In footnote 4, a plurality of the Court, in an opinion by Justice Harlan Fiske Stone, suggested that laws affecting racial, ethnic or religious minorities might be subject to closer scrutiny than laws concerning economic matters. *See* J.M. Balkin, *The Footnote*, 83 Nw. L. Rev. 275 (1988–89). Murphy suggests that footnote 4 mandates the state must shoulder the burden of justifying the regulation, and that it failed to do so in this case. Who should carry the burden in this kind of case? What standard must be met in such cases? Does the majority clearly explain these issues? Interestingly, Chief Justice Stone joined the majority in *Prince.*

3. Another way to look at *Prince* is in light of the progressive effort to eradicate child labor, an effort that was constitutionally blocked by the Court in *Hammer v. Dagenhart*, 247 U.S. 251 (1918), and only lifted in 1941 by the Court's decision in *United States v. Darby*, 312 U.S. 100 (1941). One lesson most of the members of the Court took from the actions of the Court during its "formalist" era was that the Court's efforts to strike down economic legislation on the basis of the Commerce Clause or the Fourteenth Amendment was inconsistent with the Court's role in a democratic society.

4. The Supreme Court in *Jacobson v. Massachusetts*, 197 U.S. 11 (1905), held that a compulsory vaccination law applied to an adult did not violate the Due Process Clause of the Fourteenth Amendment. The *Prince* majority appears to extend the rule in *Jacobson* to children of those who oppose compulsory vaccination.

Christian Scientists believe in the power of prayer to heal. Should parents, who, for religious reasons, decline to seek medical advice or treatment for their sick child, be held criminally responsible if their child later dies? Most states statutorily protect parents who prohibit their children from receiving medical treatment from charges of child abuse or neglect. If a state prosecutes the parents for the death of the child who did not see a medical doctor, what is the state saying about the faith of the parents, or about the state's faith in medicine? What is it saying about the child whose death caused the initiation of the prosecution?

Commonwealth v. Twitchell

416 Mass. 114, 617 N.E.2d 609 (1993)

WILKINS, Justice.

David and Ginger Twitchell appeal from their convictions of involuntary manslaughter in connection with the April 8, 1986, death of their two and one-half year old son Robyn. Robyn died of the consequences of peritonitis caused by the perforation of his bowel which had been obstructed as a result of an anomaly known as Meckel's diverticulum. There was evidence that the condition could be corrected by surgery with a high success rate.

The defendants are practicing Christian Scientists who grew up in Christian Science families. They believe in healing by spiritual treatment. During Robyn's five-day illness from Friday, April 4, through Tuesday, April 8, they retained a Christian Science practitioner, a Christian Science nurse, and at one time consulted with Nathan Talbot, who held a position in the church known as the "Committee on Publication." As a result of that consultation, David Twitchell read a church publication concerning the legal rights and obligations of Christian Scientists in Massachusetts. That publication quoted a portion of G.L. c. 273, § 1, as then amended, which, at least in the context of the crimes described in that section, accepted remedial treatment by spiritual means alone as satisfying any parental obligation not to neglect a child or to provide a child with physical care. We shall subsequently discuss this statute in connection with the defendants' claim, rejected by the trial judge, that the spiritual treatment provision in G.L. c. 273, § 1, protects them from criminal liability for manslaughter.[4]

We shall conclude that parents have a duty to seek medical attention for a child in Robyn's circumstances, the violation of which, if their conduct was wanton or reckless, could support a conviction of involuntary manslaughter and that the spiritual healing provision in G.L. c. 273, § 1, did not bar a prosecution for manslaughter in these circumstances. We further conclude, however, that special circumstances in this case would justify a jury's finding that the Twitchells reasonably believed that they could rely on spiritual treatment without fear of criminal prosecution. This affirmative defense should have been asserted and presented to the jury. Because it was not, there is a substantial risk of a miscarriage of justice in this case, and, therefore, the judgments must be reversed.

1. We shall first consider whether the law generally imposes a parental duty to provide medical services to a child, the breach of which can be the basis of a conviction for involuntary manslaughter.

The Commonwealth claims that the defendants owed an affirmative duty of care to their son which they wantonly or recklessly failed to perform. [F]or our current purposes, a parental duty of care has been recognized in the common law of homicide in this Commonwealth.

The defendants argue, however, that any common law duty of care does not include a duty to provide medical treatment and that there is no statute imposing such a duty except G.L. c. 273, § 1, which, in turn, in their view, provides them with complete pro-

4. The spiritual treatment provision then read, as it does now, as follows: "A child shall not be deemed to be neglected or lack proper physical care for the sole reason that he is being provided remedial treatment by spiritual means alone in accordance with the tenets and practice of a recognized church or religious denomination by a duly accredited practitioner thereof." G.L. c. 273, § 1 (1992 ed.).

tection against any criminal charge based on their failure to seek medical treatment for their son. In their argument that the common law of the Commonwealth does not include a duty to provide medical treatment, the defendants overlook *Commonwealth v. Gallison*, 383 Mass. 659, 421 N.E.2d 757 (1981). In that case, we upheld a conviction of manslaughter, saying that a parent who "made no effort to obtain medical help, knowing that her child was gravely ill," could be found guilty of wanton or reckless involuntary manslaughter for her child's death caused by her omission to meet her "duty to provide for the care and welfare of her child." *Id.* at 665, 421 N.E.2d 757.

2. We, therefore, consider the impact, if any, of G.L. c. 273, § 1, on this case. The defendants argue that the spiritual treatment provision in § 1 bars any involuntary manslaughter charge against a parent who relies, as they did, on spiritual treatment and who does not seek medical attention for his or her child, even if the parent's failure to seek such care would otherwise be wanton or reckless conduct. We disagree.

The Commonwealth asks us to eliminate any application of the spiritual treatment provision to this case by holding that the spiritual treatment provision is unconstitutional. The argument is based solely on the establishment of religion clause of the First Amendment to the Constitution of the United States and the equal protection clause of the Fourteenth Amendment to the Constitution of the United States. Apparently, the latter theory was not raised below, and the former was raised but was not decided. These claims of unconstitutionality place the Commonwealth in the position of challenging the constitutionality of its own duly enacted statute. The retroactive invalidation of a statute on which a criminal defendant relied in justification of his conduct would present a serious fairness issue. Because we shall conclude that the spiritual treatment provision does not apply to foreclose a charge of involuntary manslaughter, we need resolve neither these preliminary questions nor the underlying constitutional one.

Section 1 of G.L. c. 273 provides no complete protection to a parent against a charge of involuntary manslaughter that is based on the parent's wanton or reckless failure to provide medical services to a child. Section 1 concerns child support and care in a chapter of the General Laws that deals not so much with the punishment of criminal conduct as with motivating parents to fulfil their natural obligations of support. On the other hand, the principle underlying involuntary manslaughter is the Commonwealth's "interest that persons within its territory should not be killed by the wanton and reckless conduct of others." *Commonwealth v. Godin*, 374 Mass. 120, 126, 371 N.E.2d 438 (1977). It is unlikely that the Legislature placed the spiritual treatment provision in § 1 to provide a defense to, or to alter any definition of, common law homicide. There is no history to § 1 that suggests that the spiritual treatment provision carries any message beyond § 1 itself. The act that added the spiritual treatment provision was entitled "An Act defining the term 'proper physical care' under the law relative to care of children by a parent." St.1971, c. 762. The amendment's concern seems focused on the subject matter of § 1 and certainly not directed toward changing the common law of homicide. Indeed, that was the view expressed at the time by a representative of the Christian Science Church.[9]

9. A statement was made to a legislative committee in February, 1971, by Dr. J. Buroughs Stokes, the then "Committee on Publication for The First Church of Christ, Scientist." That statement is available in the archives concerning St.1971, c. 762. It indicates that the Christian Science Church had proposed an amendment to G.L. c. 273, § 1, "to make it clear that Christian Scientists, in providing their children with Christian Science treatment and care, are not violating *this* law" (emphasis supplied). *Id.* at 2. "We are seeking legal protection from the possibility of being considered neglectful by any individual in authority who may misunderstand our methods...." *Id.* at 3.

The spiritual treatment provision refers to neglect and lack of proper physical care, which are concepts set forth earlier in § 1, as then amended, as bases for punishment: (1) neglect to provide support and (2) wilful failure to provide necessary and proper physical care. These concepts do not underlie involuntary manslaughter. Wanton or reckless conduct is not a form of negligence. Wanton or reckless conduct does not involve a wilful intention to cause the resulting harm. An involuntary manslaughter verdict does not require proof of wilfulness. Thus, by its terms, the spiritual treatment provision in § 1 does not apply to involuntary manslaughter.

3. The defendants argue that the failure to extend the protection of the spiritual treatment provision to them in this case would be a denial of due process of law because they lacked "fair warning" that their use of spiritual treatment could form the basis for a prosecution for manslaughter. The defendants here argue that they have been denied fair warning in three different ways. They contend that fair warning (1) would be denied by an unforeseeable retroactive judicial interpretation that the spiritual treatment provision does not protect them, (2) is denied by the existence of contradictory commands in the law of the Commonwealth, and (3) is denied because they were officially misled by an opinion of the Attorney General of the Commonwealth. We find some merit only in the last of these contentions.

The defendants argue that they were misled by an opinion of the Attorney General that caused them to conclude that they were protected by the spiritual treatment provision. There is, however, no evidence to support the contention that they relied directly on that opinion or that they knew of the Attorney General's opinion. Indeed it does not appear that the defendants made any argument to the trial judge that they relied on an official interpretation of the law.

In May, 1975, the Attorney General gave an opinion on a number of topics to the deputy director of the Office for Children. Rep. A.G., Pub.Doc. No. 12, at 139 (1975). The relevant portion of that opinion, which is quoted in the margin,[15] answers a general question "whether parents who fail to provide medical services to children on the basis of religious beliefs will be subject to prosecution for such failure." *Id.* at 140. A reasonable person not trained in the law might fairly read the Attorney General's comments as being a negative answer to the general question whether in any circumstances such parents

15. "Secondly, you have sought my opinion as to whether parents who fail to provide medical services to children on the basis of religious beliefs will be subject to prosecution for such failure. Also, you have restated a concern of the Department of Health, Education and Welfare as to whether services will be available to children who are unable to obtain medical assistance because of their parents' religious beliefs.

"The Massachusetts child abuse reporting law does not specifically address itself to the relationship between the religious beliefs of the parent and failure to provide medical care. However, G.L. c. 273, § 1 does address itself to that precise issue. General Laws, c. 273, § 1 provides, *inter alia*, as follows:

'A child shall not be deemed to be neglected or lack proper physical care for the sole reason that he is being provided remedial treatment by spiritual means alone in accordance with the tenets and practice of a recognized church or religious denomination by a duly accredited practitioner thereof.'

"General Laws, c. 273, § 1 is a criminal statute and it expressly precludes imposition of criminal liability as a negligent parent for failure to provide medical care because of religious beliefs. However, the intent of Chapter 119 is, clearly, to require that children of such parents be provided services whenever the need arises. Clearly under Chapter 119 children may receive services notwithstanding the inability to prosecute parents in such cases."

may be prosecuted. It is true that the answer comes to focus on negligent failures of parents, and we know that wanton or reckless failures are different. But an answer that says that children may receive needed services "notwithstanding the inability to prosecute parents in such cases" (*id.*), and issues no caveat concerning homicide charges, invites a conclusion that parents who fail to provide medical services to children on the basis of religious beliefs are not subject to criminal prosecution in any circumstances.

Although the Twitchells were not aware of the Attorney General's opinion, they knew of a Christian Science publication called "Legal Rights and Obligations of Christian Scientists in Massachusetts." The defense offered the publication in evidence. The judge held a voir dire on the question whether to admit that portion of the publication which concerned the furnishing of proper physical care to a child and which David Twitchell had read on the Sunday or Monday before Robyn's death. The judge excluded the evidence, and, although the defendants objected at trial, they have not argued to us that the exclusion was error. The relevant portion of the publication, after quoting G.L. c. 273, § 1, added, repeating, precisely but without citation, a portion of the Attorney General's opinion, that this criminal statute "expressly precludes imposition of criminal liability as a negligent parent for failure to provide medical care because of religious beliefs. But this does not prohibit the court from ordering medical treatment for children." There is no mention of potential criminal liability for involuntary manslaughter.

It is obvious that the Christian Science Church's publication on the legal rights and obligations of Christian Scientists in Massachusetts relied on the Attorney General's 1975 opinion. That opinion was arguably misleading because of what it did not say concerning criminal liability for manslaughter. If the Attorney General had issued a caveat concerning manslaughter liability, the publication (which, based on such portions of it as appear in the record, is balanced and fair) would have referred to it in all reasonable likelihood. Nathan Talbot, who served as the Committee on Publication for the church and with whom the Twitchells spoke on the Sunday or Monday before Robyn's death, might well have given the Twitchells different advice.

Although it has long been held that "ignorance of the law is no defence" (*Commonwealth v. Everson*, 140 Mass. 292, 295, 2 N.E. 839 [1885]), there is substantial justification for treating as a defense the belief that conduct is not a violation of law when a defendant has reasonably relied on an official statement of the law, later determined to be wrong, contained in an official interpretation of the public official who is charged by law with the responsibility for the interpretation or enforcement of the law defining the offense.

The Twitchells were entitled to present such an affirmative defense to the jury. The Attorney General was acting in an area of his official responsibilities. Whether a person would reasonably conclude that the Attorney General had ruled that § 1 provided protection against a manslaughter charge is a question of fact. Whether the defendants in turn reasonably relied on the church's publication and on the advice of the Committee on Publication, assuming that the construction of the Attorney General's opinion was reasonable, also presents questions of fact. In the resolution of these factual questions, the relevant portion of the Attorney General's opinion and the relevant portion of the church's publication will be admissible. The jury should also be advised of the terms of the spiritual treatment provision of § 1.

The Twitchells were entitled to present such an affirmative defense to the jury. We can hardly fault the judge for not doing so because the defense did not make such an argument or request a jury instruction on that defense. The issue was one that, if presented to them, could well have changed the jury's verdicts. Evidence showed that the defendants were deeply motivated toward helping their child, while at the same time seeking to practice their religion within the limits of what they were advised that the law permitted. The issue of their reliance on advice that had origins in the Attorney General's opinion should have been before the jury. Therefore, the failure to present the affirmative defense to the jury, along with the relevant portion of the church's publication which the judge excluded, created a substantial risk of a miscarriage of justice requiring that we reverse the convictions, even in the absence of a request for jury instruction on the subject. For these reasons, the judgments must be reversed, the verdicts must be set aside, and the cases remanded for a new trial, if the district attorney concludes that such a prosecution is necessary in the interests of justice.

So ordered.

NOLAN, Justice (dissenting).

The [Christian Science] publication was properly excluded because it was not competent evidence on the issue of manslaughter. For this reason, the defendants' reliance on it is not relevant and it should not be considered by a jury. Accordingly, I dissent.

Notes

1. In its last footnote, the court noted the following:

> The trial lasted for fifty-four days, including an extended jury selection process. The defendants were placed on probation for ten years on July 6, 1990, subject to the requirements that there be periodic medical checkups by a pediatrician of all their children, that the parents seek medical attention for any signs of a child's serious illness, and maximum supervision by the probation department, subject to review as to the level of supervision after one year. Three years have now passed since the sentencing. The basic principle has been established that § 1 did not provide the Twitchells with protection against a charge of involuntary manslaughter.
>
> If there is a new trial, the judge should exercise great care that the religious beliefs of the Twitchells and other Christian Scientists are not implicitly or explicitly placed on trial. If the prosecution seeks to cross-examine a witness about church doctrine or his or her religious beliefs, on objection the judge should consider carefully the relevance of the evidence sought in relation to any prejudice that may result.

Twitchell, 617 N.E.2d at 620 n.17.

The court's strong suggestion to the Commonwealth that the Twitchells not be retried, because the principle of criminal sanction had been explicitly stated, and because the Twitchells already had been punished for three years, was followed. Suffolk (Mass.) District Attorney Ralph C. Martin 2d decided not to retry the Twitchells after the decision of the Massachusetts Supreme Judicial Court. *Boston Globe*, September 10, 1993, at 31. Was the court's suggestion made (or accepted) because the Twitchells and other Christian Scientists have been taught a lesson? Is it possible to prosecute this kind of case and not "implicitly or explicitly place[] on trial" the religious beliefs of the defendants? If this is not possible, does this create a burden on the free exercise rights of the defendants? *See United States v. Ballard*, 322 U.S. 78 (1944), excerpted in Chapter Thirteen.

2. Is the court's conclusion that the spiritual healing exemption does not apply to the charge of common law involuntary manslaughter persuasive? Other courts have divided on the question. In *Walker v. Superior Court*, 47 Cal.3d 112, 144, 253 Cal.Rptr. 1, 763 P.2d 852 (1988), *cert. denied*, 491 U.S. 905 (1989), the Supreme Court of California concluded that a charge of involuntary manslaughter was not barred by a "spiritual healing" exemption located in a child abuse and neglect section of the California Penal Code. *Accord Hall v. State*, 493 N.E.2d 433 (Ind. 1986); *State v. McKown*, 475 N.W.2d 63 (Minn. 1991); *see also Commonwealth v. Barnhart*, 345 Pa. Super. 10, 497 A.2d 616 (1985) (holding constitutional claim of religious exemption from charge of involuntary manslaughter unavailable). Although the Supreme Court of Minnesota concluded that the spiritual healing exemption was not a defense to a charge of second-degree manslaughter, it also concluded that the due process rights of the defendants were violated because they were not given fair notice that their actions might subject them to criminal liability. The Supreme Court of Florida concluded in *Hermanson v. State*, 604 So. 2d 775 (Fla. 1992), that the state did not give the defendants fair notice that their actions might subject them to criminal liability. *Accord State v. Miskimens*, 22 Ohio Misc.2d 43, 490 N.E.2d 931 (1984).

3. In all but the *Barnhart* and *Miskimens* cases, the defendants were Christian Scientists. Christian Science was founded in Massachusetts in 1879 by Mary Baker Eddy, "a New Englander of Calvinist background." "Christian Science is a religious movement emphasizing Christian healing as proof of the supremacy of spiritual over physical power." Stephen Gottschalk, "Christian Science," *in* 3 Encyclopedia of Religion 442–44 (Mircea Eliade ed., 1987), *reprinted in* CHRISTIAN SCIENCE: A SOURCEBOOK OF CONTEMPORARY MATERIALS 5 (1990). This emphasis on healing, based on Mary Baker Eddy's recovery from severe injuries while reading about a healing performed by Jesus, is a central part of Christian Science theology. There are no ministers in Christian Science, but there are practitioners who heal members and others desiring assistance from practitioners. The physical healing of the body is "a phase of full salvation from the flesh as well," and healing "is to be accomplished not through personal will or effort but through yielding to the action of the divine Mind." *Id.* at 8. Should the state be permitted to assert its general police powers to protect health if its understanding of "health" undermines a central tenet of a religious faith? Recall *Lyng v. Northwest Indian Cemetery Protective Ass'n*, 485 U.S. 439 (1988), noted in Chapter Five.

Does the fact that most of these cases have involved Christian Science, a religious body that appears to fit the definition of a "minority" religion, suggest that courts should be more cautious in their interpretations of the spiritual healing exemptions? Should courts ignore the specific reason for such exemptions in examining the law? Why?

4. According to a law review note, 44 states and the District of Columbia have codified exemptions to child abuse and neglect laws for good faith spiritual healing. Eric W. Treene, Note, *Prayer-Treatment Exemptions to Child Abuse and Neglect Statutes, Manslaughter Prosecutions, and Due Process of Law*, 30 Harv. J. on Legis. 135, 141 (1993). Is this the kind of proper statutory exemption from generally applicable neutral laws that the Supreme Court suggested in *Employment Div. v. Smith*, 494 U.S. 872 (1990)?

The origin of many of these exemptions was the passage by Congress of the Child Abuse Prevention and Treatment Act of 1974, 42 U.S.C. §5101 (1988 and Supp. V 1993), which conditioned disbursement to states of funds under the Act upon passage of a spiritual healing exemption. Although this condition was eliminated in 1983, no states repealed their exemptions. Treene, at 141.

5. The Supreme Judicial Court in Massachusetts was asked by the state to declare the spiritual healing exemption unconstitutional on Establishment Clause grounds, which the court concluded was unnecessary to decide the case. Should a state be able to argue that its own statute is unconstitutional? In *Miskimens*, the Ohio Court of Common Pleas accepted the state's argument that the spiritual healing exemption violated the Establishment Clause. The case was not appealed. In *Walker*, the Attorney General of California made the same argument. Justice Mosk wrote a concurring opinion to his opinion for the majority concluding that because the exemption was sponsored by Christian Scientists, and was limited to persons whose spiritual healing was "in accordance with the tenets and practices of a recognized church or religious denomination...," the exemption violated the Establishment Clause. *Walker*, 47 Cal.3d at 145. In *McKown*, the Minnesota Court stated in a footnote: "[T]he Minnesota Civil Liberties Union contends that the spiritual treatment and prayer exception violates the first amendment's prohibition against state-established religion. Although we find the MCLU's arguments persuasive, our disposition based on due process grounds makes it unnecessary for us to consider the establishment clause issue at this time." *McKown*, 475 N.W.2d at 69 n.9; *see also Newmark v. Williams*, 588 A.2d 1108 (Del. 1991) (suggesting but not deciding, in child neglect action involving Christian Science parents, that spiritual healing exemption may violate the Establishment Clause). Is a spiritual healing statute violative of the Establishment Clause if it is established that it was adopted to respond to allegations of child abuse and neglect faced by Christian Scientists, or because the statutes are ordinarily worded to protect spiritual healing efforts by parents undertaken in accord with the tenets of a recognized church, or some combination of the two? *See Larson v. Valente*, 456 U.S. 228 (1982) (holding unconstitutional as violative of the Establishment Clause a Minnesota statute creating denominational preferences). One difference between *Larson* and the spiritual healing cases noted above is that in *Larson* the denomination discriminated against complained about the constitutionality of the statute, and in the latter cases, the state has claimed that the exemption is unconstitutional, not an aggrieved religious denomination or secular group. Should this make a constitutional difference? If a spiritual healing statute violates the Establishment Clause, does a refusal by the state to recognize the possibility of the healing power of prayer implicate any free exercise concerns, or is *Smith* dispositive?

6. In *Jehovah's Witnesses v. King County Hosp.*, 278 F. Supp. 488 (W.D. Wash. 1967), *aff'd mem.*, 390 U.S. 598 (1968), the district court rejected a claim by Jehovah's Witnesses parents that their Free Exercise rights were violated by the decision of the state to take emergency custody of their child in order to authorize blood transfusions to save the child's life. In its decision, the court noted that the child was placed in mortal danger by the refusal of the child's parents to allow the child a blood transfusion. This, the court concluded, was not constitutionally protected conduct. Should a constitutional claim of parents of the right to rear their child or children without interference from the state be tested by the extent of the possible harm faced by the child? If so, should this depend on the probability of life-threatening harm to which the child may be subjected? *See Muhlenberg Hosp. v. Patterson*, 320 A.2d 518, 521 (N.J. Super. Ct. 1974) (allowing state to authorize blood transfusion to minor over religious objection of parents when "necessary for the sustaining of life or the prevention of grievous bodily injury").

7. A critic of language granting parents "rights" concerning the raising of their children suggests that "parental child-rearing rights are illegitimate. A better regime

would simply grant parents a legal privilege to care for and make decisions on behalf of their children in ways that are not contrary to the children's temporal interests." James G. Dwyer, *Parents' Religion and Children's Welfare: Debunking the Doctrine of Parents' Rights*, 82 Calif. L. Rev. 1371, 1447 (1994). Dwyer explains that the state must limit itself to a concern of the child's "temporal" interests because

> [f]or the State to take account of children's supposed spiritual interests would require it to assume the truth of particular religious beliefs—*e.g.*, that children have spiritual interests in the first place, that those interests are of a certain nature, and that they are best served by living in a certain way. It would therefore require the state to endorse a particular religious view, which the State may not do.

Dwyer, at 1428 (footnote omitted).

Does the assumption of the possibility of a child having spiritual interests require the further assumption that the state therefore believes in the truth of particular religious beliefs? If parents send their child to a school that teaches creationism as truth, or that claims that a duty to God supersedes all civic duties, should the state have the authority to remove that child from that school because such beliefs are either not accepted by a majority of the community in which the child lives, or because the child will later face temporal harm from the larger society? If a child's spiritual interests, in the view of his or her parents, requires the child forego saluting the flag while attending public school, should the state have the authority to overrule the demand of the parents that the child not salute the flag? What are the child's "temporal interests" in such a case? If a child is unable effectively to articulate his or her "choice" concerning his or her development, why should the state have the authority to promote the child's "temporal" interests even if this results in a "harm" to the child's religious beliefs? Does ignoring the "supposed" spiritual interests of the child privilege the view that such interests do not in fact exist? Would or should the state be permitted, on temporal interest grounds, to remove children from religious communities that reject the modern world?

Recall the opinion dissenting in part of Justice Douglas in *Wisconsin v. Yoder*, 406 U.S. 205 (1972). Justice Douglas dissented in *Yoder* because there was no evidence in the record that all of the Amish children involved in the case agreed with their parents' decision to end their formal education in the eighth grade. Justice Douglas implies that the State's interest as *parens patriae* includes protecting the religious liberty of a child who wishes "to break from the Amish tradition." If so, at what point in a child's religious upbringing would State intervention to determine the child's interests be justified?

8. In *Commonwealth v. Nixon*, 761 A.2d 1151 (Pa. 2000), *cert. denied*, 121 S.Ct. 1735 (2001), the defendants were convicted of involuntary manslaughter in the death of their 16-year old daughter, Shannon Nixon. When the Nixons became aware of their daughter's illness, they began to pray for her health, pursuant to their religious beliefs. In addition, they took her to their church, the Faith Tabernacle Church, where Shannon was "anointed." Eventually, Shannon fell into a coma, and died. The autopsy concluded that her death was a result of diabetes acidosis, a condition that could be treated medically, but not cured. They appealed the conviction, claiming that their daughter was an emancipated minor, and that their parental duty to provide medical care was negated by Shannon's privacy interests under the federal and Pennsylvania constitutions. The court rejected both defenses, noting that Shannon did not meet the factual elements to proving emancipation, and holding that the interest in life is a compelling state interest, which overrides any privacy rights Shannon may have possessed. The convictions were affirmed.

Burnham v. Burnham

208 Neb. 498, 304 N.W.2d 58 (1981)

HASTINGS, Justice.

Dennis Burnham has appealed from an order of the District Court for Douglas County dissolving the marriage of the parties and awarding custody of their only daughter Jaime, (referred to in the decree as Jamie), to the mother, Carolyn Burnham. Appellant has assigned the following as error: (1) The court erred in placing permanent custody of the child with the mother; (2) The court erred in assessing child support in the amount of $300 to be paid by the father, such amount being clearly excessive; (3) The court erred in not allowing into evidence a video tape regarding the Tridentine Church; and (4) The court erred in overruling the motion for new trial. For the reasons to follow, we reverse the order of the District Court.

The parties were married on December 19, 1975, in Omaha, Nebraska, at St. Bernard's Catholic Church. One child was born to this union on October 2, 1976, a daughter, Jaime Burnham. The trial court made the factual finding that both parties are fit and proper persons to be awarded the care and control of the minor child.

Most of the evidence at trial focused on the religious differences between the parties, and these differences appear to be the reason for the dissolution and custody fight. Dennis was originally a Lutheran, who converted to Catholicism so that they could attend church as a family. In approximately August of 1978 Carolyn became interested in a sect calling itself the Tridentine Church, or the Fatima Crusaders. Carolyn was encouraged to get involved in the group by her parents, and her interest intensified over the next several months. Carolyn encouraged Dennis to get involved and attend meetings. However, he refused to do so. It was this religious disagreement that Dennis blames for beginning the problems the parties were having in their relationship. In December of 1978 Dennis learned that Carolyn and her parents did not consider that the marriage of the parties was legitimate, and that they were therefore living in sin. The reason that the marriage was not considered legitimate was that they were not married in the Fatima Crusader Church. Because of her view of her marriage, Carolyn testified that she did not consider her child to be legitimate.

Carolyn also adheres to the belief that as a member of the Tridentine Church she is bound under pain of mortal sin to educate her child in the Tridentine Church, which is considered to be the true Catholic Church by its members. It is the teaching of the church that if Carolyn did not send Jaime to a Tridentine parochial school, and it was within her power to do so, then she would be excommunicated. The church's school is in Coeur d'Alene, Idaho, where Carolyn would like to send Jaime when she is of school age and it would be financially possible to do so. One of the exhibits was a copy of the general regulations of the school and its statement of principle, including a release to be signed by the parents. The release gives full permission for the use of strict discipline and corporal punishment. It then relieves the academy, all of the teachers and school personnel, various religious leaders, and the property owners, of all responsibility for the child in case of accident or injury or any unforeseen mishap.

In a letter that Carolyn wrote to her sister-in-law, she stated: "What surprised me the most, in finding out about true Catholicism, I have discovered that there exists in this world, a master plot on the part of the Jews and Communists, to gain control of the world." This points out the anti-Semitic views that Carolyn believes are being taught by the Tridentine Church and which she testified that she believed to be true.

The evidence shows that Carolyn's parents are members of the Tridentine Catholic Church, and three of their children are attending a Tridentine school in Spokane, Washington. One of their children, Jim, age 23, who apparently does not adhere to the same religious beliefs, has been denied communication with the family. Carolyn testified on cross-examination that she agreed with her parents not being in communication with her brother. In fact, she returned a toy to Jim that he had sent as a gift to Jaime.

Carolyn testified as follows: "Q. If Jaime did the same thing, if Jaime did not believe at the age of 14 or 15 the tenets of the Tridentine Catholic Church, would you do to her what your parents are doing to Jim? A. If she disobeys the laws of the Church, I would. Q. No room for flexibility, then? A. The laws of the Church are the laws of the Church. Q. Thank you, that's answering it. Do you anticipate that in every parent-child relationship there is going to be times of conflict? A. Yes. Q. And even though that's a natural parent-child relationship, if she disobeys the rules of the Church, you are willing to cut her off from your life? A. If Jaime does what Jim did, yes. Q. If Jaime disobeyed the laws of the Church? A. Depending on which law, how it would affect me. That's too vague. Q. That's certainly possible? A. Possible what? Q. It's possible that you could cut her off from your life? A. If she married somebody that was divorced, yes."

The appellant argues that it was error for the District Court to place the custody of Jaime with Carolyn rather than with him. This case is one of equity and is reviewed de novo. "Where the issue of child custody is involved, both the mother and father have an equal and joint right to the custody of their children. The test for determining custody, which has been reiterated by this court many times, is the best interests of the child." *Theye v. Theye*, 200 Neb. 206, 207, 263 N.W.2d 92, 94 (1978).

Neb.Rev.Stat. §42-364(2) (Reissue 1978) states: "In determining with which of the parents the children, or any of them, shall remain, the court shall not give preference to either parent based on the sex of the parent and no presumption shall exist that either parent is more fit to have custody of the children than the other."

"The courts preserve an attitude of impartiality between religions and will not disqualify a parent because of his or her religious beliefs." *Goodman v. Goodman*, 180 Neb. 83, 88, 141 N.W.2d 445, 448 (1966). However, we do have a duty to consider whether such beliefs threaten the health or well-being of the child. *Goodman, supra.* See, generally, Annot., 66 A.L.R.2d 1410 (1959). Of primary consideration is the welfare of the child, and the court must consider not only the spiritual and temporal welfare but also the minor's further training, education, morals, and the ability of the proposed guardian to best take care of the child. *Kaufmann v. Kaufmann*, 140 Neb. 299, 299 N.W. 617 (1941).

"A court's task in a child custody case is to determine which parent will better serve the best interests of the child. Myriad factors may be considered in working toward this goal. To hold that a court may not consider religious factors under any circumstances would blind courts to important elements bearing on the best interests of the child." *Bonjour v. Bonjour*, 592 P.2d 1233, 1238 (Alaska 1979).

Also considering whether it is appropriate for a court to consider religion as part of the best interests equation was the Superior Court of Pennsylvania in *Morris v. Morris*, 412 A.2d 139, 142 (1979): "(B)oth the weight of authority and established legal principles support the proposition that it is legitimate for a court to examine the impact of the parents' beliefs on the child."

We believe that the following beliefs may have an adverse impact on Jaime: (1) The belief that she is illegitimate; (2) The willingness of Carolyn to cut Jaime out of her life if she disobeys the rules of the Tridentine Church; and (3) The racist views held by Carolyn and, apparently, by her church. Although by holding these views Carolyn has not disqualified herself from being a fit and proper person to have custody of her child, we must take all factors into consideration in determining what is in Jaime's best interests. We also note that Carolyn's desire to educate Jaime in the Tridentine school in Coeur d'Alene, Idaho, would interfere with the father's rights of visitation. There is ample evidence that the father is very close to his daughter. He has the ability and desire to take care of her in the family home. He has stated that he will look after her moral and religious training and enroll her in a Sunday school or something equivalent.

We feel that Carolyn's religious beliefs, if continued in regular practice, which she indicates will be the case, will have a deleterious effect not only on the relationship between the father and his daughter but upon the well-being of the child herself. Accordingly, we find that it would be in the best interests of Jaime to place her in the permanent custody of her father, with reasonable visitation rights by the mother.

We therefore reverse the order of the District Court awarding custody to the mother, and remand the cause with instructions to award custody to the father, Dennis Burnham. Carolyn is ordered to pay child support to Dennis in the amount of $50 per month, and will be allowed reasonable visitation.

REVERSED AND REMANDED WITH INSTRUCTIONS.

Notes

1. In *Burnham*, the court concluded that although both parents were "fit," custody should be granted to the father because the mother's religious beliefs "will have a deleterious effect not only on the relationship between the father and his daughter but upon the well-being of the child herself." Does the court impermissibly burden the Free Exercise rights of Jaime's mother by speculatively assessing the effect of her religious beliefs on Jaime's well-being? The court also noted that the father "has stated that he will look after her moral and religious training and enroll her in a Sunday school or something equivalent." Does this suggest that if the choice of granting custody was between a religious parent and a non-religious parent, the former would make a better choice as custodial parent? If so, does this raise Establishment Clause concerns?

2. When religion is a factor in child custody disputes, states have used three different approaches to determine the best interests of the child. In *Burnham*, the court used the broadest approach, basing its decision on the perceived impact of the mother's religion on the temporal welfare of the child. There was no evidence that the mother's religious beliefs and practices would threaten the child's physical or mental well-being. There was simply the assertion by the court that such could be the case. A more modest approach bars the assessment of parental religious practices unless those practices threaten the physical or mental well-being of the child. The most restrictive approach bars evidence of the religious practices of either parent absent a showing of actual harm to the physical or mental well-being of the child. *Quiner v. Quiner*, 59 Cal. Rptr. 503 (Cal. App. 1967). A thorough review is Donald L. Beschle, *God Bless the Child?: The Use of Religion as a Factor in Child Custody and Adoption Proceedings*, 58 Ford. L. Rev. 383 (1989). *See also* Annot., *Religion as a Factor in Child Custody and Visitation Cases*, 22 A.L.R.4th 971 (1983).

3. Although courts have refused to engage in a denominational comparison, in determining custody they have looked at the possibility that the religious practices of one parent may have a deleterious or positive impact on the child. *See Hilley v. Hilley*, 405 So. 2d 708 (Ala. (1981) (assessing whether deep religious beliefs of evangelist would harm child); *McNamara v. McNamara*, 181 N.W.2d 206 (Iowa 1970) (awarding custody to parent in part because parent "conscientiously adheres to religious teachings and would apparently rear his children in the same manner"). *But cf. Zummo v. Zummo*, 574 A.2d 1130 (Pa. Super. 1990) (holding it "constitutionally impermissible to decide a custody or visitation dispute, in whole or in part, on the basis of a determination or consideration of the parent's relative devoutness"). However, because religion often makes its way into custody proceedings, a family law practitioner recommends preparing evidence showing how exposure to the parent-client's religious beliefs will benefit the child. Carolyn R. Wah, *Religion in Child Custody and Visitation Cases: Presenting the Advantage of Religious Participation*, 28 Fam. L.Q. 269 (1994).

Should a court uphold a contract between parents concerning the religious upbringing of their children? Does it matter whether the contract is made before the marriage or during the marriage? Most courts refuse to enforce such agreements on grounds that they cannot be objectively or constitutionally enforced. In *In re Marriage of Bennett*, 587 N.E.2d 577 (Ill. App.), *appeal denied*, 596 N.E.2d 626 (Ill. 1992), the court specifically determined that no such implied contract existed, but also concluded that any such claimed contract would fail because of a lack of consideration. A survey of the case law on this issue is Jocelyn E. Strauber, Note, *A Deal is a Deal: Antenuptial Agreements Regarding the Religious Upbringing of Children Should be Enforceable*, 47 Duke L.J. 971 (1998).

4. Are statutes providing that, where practicable, an adopted child should be placed for adoption with parents who are of the same religion as the natural parent(s) of the child, constitutional? Such statutes have been interpreted as not mandating religious matching, but simply as declaring the desirability of religious matching, and thus constitutional. *See, e.g., In re Goldman*, 121 N.E.2d 843 (Mass. 1954), *cert. denied*, 348 U.S. 942 (1955).

D. Religion as an Affirmative Defense to Governmental Regulation

1. Religious Institutions and Officers and Tort Law

If a religious institution, a minister or other officer of a religious institution is a party in a tort or other civil action, to what extent should courts account for that fact? In applying legal rules to religious actors, should courts tailor the rules to account for the religious status of the party, or should the actions of the minister or institution be analogized to similar actions of non-religious actors? Does the former approach take better account of the religious liberty claims of religious actors? Does it fail to appreciate the Establishment Clause concerns of singling out religious actors from "secular" actors? As noted in Chapter Seven, religious institutions may be held liable in tort pursuant to the law of ascending liability for the actions of others. *See Moses v. Diocese of Colorado*, 863 P.2d 310 (Colo. 1995). In this section, the issue is whether the religiously-motivated actions by religious institutions and officers that may form the basis for a claim under tort law are immune from liability.

In a thorough and wide-ranging article, Professor Carl H. Esbeck delineates five types of tort claims against religious institutions that may impinge religious liberty interests of those institutions. They include (1) claims concerning pastoral counseling, including "clergy malpractice," disclosure of confidential communications and sexual misconduct (which encompasses seduction, alienation of affections and molestation claims), as well as intentional infliction of emotional distress; (2) church discipline cases, in which removal of religious officers and sanctions against church members (including excommunication) are alleged to be wrongful; (3) tort claims other than the two types noted above, largely libel claims by nonmembers; (4) religious fraud cases; and (5) claims alleging "mind control" by newer religious organizations, often called "cults." Carl H. Esbeck, *Tort Claims Against Churches and Ecclesiastical Officers: The First Amendment Considerations*, 89 W. Va. L. Rev. 1, 76-113 (1986). A chart describing the types of claims made against members of the clergy and others who work in religious ministry, as well as claims made against religious organizations for the actions of others, appears on the following pages.

Chart 11-1: Litigating Religion Clause Defenses to Tort Claims

Tort Claim Type	"Target" Element(s)	"Proof of Facts" Relevant to First Amendment Claim or Defense
Intentional Torts (Battery, Infliction of Emotional Distress, Fraud)	1) Examine Issues of Consent or Privilege	1) Develop facts which negate elements of tort (*e.g.*, battery as an "unconsented, offensive touching")
	2) Examine nature or elements of specific religious practices which give rise to the allegations	2) Proof that the act is a component of a religious ritual (*e.g.*, no Baptism without getting wet; no ordination without laying on of hands; no absolution without some sort of "counsel" or "penance"). The degree to which it is a "critical" component would also be would be both relevant and useful, though it would not be controlling.
Negligence	1) Standard of Care (Nature of Duty Alleged)	1) Proof that the duty asserted cannot be enforced without setting "secular" standards of care for religious practices. For example: driving a van would not raise any questions of a "religious" nature, but imposing a duty of care upon confessors to recognize and refer suicidal penitents to others "qualified" to "treat" them would change the very nature of the priest/penitent relationship and the nature of the sacrament itself.
Malpractice Claims		
Clergy Malpractice	1) Attempt by State to set "professional" standard of care for clergy	1) Demonstrate secular interference ("entanglement') in religious matters
Pastoral Malpractice	1) Attempt by State to set "professional" standard of care for an inherently religious activity	1) Proof that the standard of care for a "competent" cleric is inherently bound up in doctrinal questions
	2) Attempt by State to distinguish between the pastoral activities of a member of the "clergy" and a layperson who ministers to the spiritual needs of the faithful	2) Proof of the doctrinal basis—or lack thereof—for a distinction between "clergy" and "pastoral" ministry
Professional Malpractice	1) Attempt by State to define clerical functions as "professional," and thus subject to regulation	1) Proof that the relationship between the "counselor" and "client" was inherently "religious," and that all parties to the transactions in question understood that the very purpose of the alleged "professional" relationship was religious. (See "clergy" malpractice.)

Tort Claim Type	"Target" Element(s)	"Proof of Facts" Relevant to First Amendment Claim or Defense
Breach of Fiduciary Duty	1) Examine Manner & Elements of Creation	1) Proof that the claim is functionally identical to one of clergy malpractice
	2) Examine Intent of the Parties Respecting Religious Elements	2) Proof that parties intended the creation of a relationship which was inherently religious in both nature and content
	3) Attempt by State to "recharacterize" tort which is, in all relevant respects, the functional equivalent of a "breach of religious duty"	3) Introduce evidence concerning specific religious duties/practices and proof that claim cannot be entertained without considering the "substance," "value," or "propriety" of the religious elements of the relationship
Negligent Hiring	1) Attempt by the State to examine, and then define, the nature of Bishop-priest or church-minister relationship	1) Adduce evidence from canon law and thus set stage for judicial inquiry into doctrinal questions
	2) Attempt by State to inquire into the substance of, and judge the adequacy of, standards for selection and ordination of priests and ministers	2) Compel judicial inquiry into religious elements guiding episcopal decision-making regarding ordination (*e.g.*, is ordination "hiring," or is "hiring" accomplished only upon "assignment"?)
	3) Attempt by State to either control or dictate content of training norms/guidelines for formation of clerics	3) compel judicial inquiry into the religious elements of priestly formation. Sets stage for imposition of secular standards for priestly formation, including alleged deficiencies in content of training
	4) Attempt by State to redefine the canonical norms of privilege and confidence in Bishop-priest relationships.	4) Demonstrate applicability of priest-penitent privilege to the extent that the relationship between the bishop and priests or church and minister is "more than" simply employee/superior
	5) Attempt by the State to exert secular control of episcopal discretion and confidentiality with respect to matters learned in Bishop-priest relationship.	5) Demonstrate that there are mixed questions of fact and doctrine which need to be resolved concerning priestly discretion in the matter of absolution, guidance of penitents, and the "external" use of priest/penitent information
Negligent Supervision	1) Attempt by the State to define the nature of bishop-priest or church-minister relationship in a manner contrary to canonical understandings	1) See above: Priest-Penitent issues, including control of discretion and disclosure of privileged information to those not privileged to receive it

Tort Claim Type	"Target" Element(s)	"Proof of Facts" Relevant to First Amendment Claim or Defense
Negligent Supervision *continued*	2) Attempt by State to mandate secular standards for review, supervision & termination of priests, ministers or religious	2) Produce facts concerning the requirements of Canon Law or church doctrine
	3) Attempt by State to ignore the degree to which Canon Law or belief vests individual clerics with discretion in priest/penitent or "counseling" relationships	3) Demonstrate to the court that the bishop does not, "in fact" (*i.e.* as a matter of both canon law and practice) "supervise" much of the daily affairs of priest as he performs his clerical functions?
	4) Attempt by State to restrict Episcopal discretion respecting absolution and guidance of priest or religious penitents	4) See above: "To what extent must a bishop condition the exercise of his religious discretion over absolution so as to exert 'control' over the penitent?"
	5) Attempt by State to breach canonically mandated norms of confidentiality and privilege	5) See #1 above
	6) Attempt by State to limit First Amendment claims to "religious" or "clerics", rather than all those performing "religious" (sacerdotal) functions	6) Lay factual predicate for assertion that setting secular standards for "supervision" inhibits the actual practice of the "religious" duties of the non-cleric or religious engaged in "pastoral" functions

In *Schieffer v. Catholic Archdiocese of Omaha*, the Nebraska Supreme Court dismisses the plaintiff's claims of intentional infliction of emotional distress and negligent counseling, the latter of which the court characterizes as a claim of "clergy malpractice." In *Molko v. Holy Spirit Ass'n for the Unification of the World Christianity*, the California Supreme Court holds that claims of fraud and intentional infliction of emotional distress as a result of "brainwashing" are not constitutionally barred. As you read these opinions, evaluate whether the opinions can be harmonized. If not, assess soundness of the arguments made to reach the conclusions of these courts.

Schieffer v. Catholic Archdiocese of Omaha

244 Neb. 715, 508 N.W.2d 907 (1993)

BOSLAUGH, Justice.

This is a suit for damages brought by the plaintiff, Rosemary Schieffer, against the defendants, Catholic Archdiocese of Omaha (Archdiocese), a corporation, and Timothy Lange.

Viewed most favorably to the plaintiff, the amended petition alleges the following:

> In 1979, the plaintiff began counseling with the defendant Lange concerning family matters. Lange was the plaintiff's parish priest and "spiritual leader."

> During this time period, the plaintiff was vulnerable because of prior emotional problems. While she was in this vulnerable state and during the course of pastoral counseling, Lange made sexual advances toward the plaintiff that continued for a period of 3 years. In 1982, Lange and the plaintiff began a sexual relationship that continued until approximately June 1989.

The plaintiff's first cause of action alleges that the conduct of Lange was outrageous and extreme and caused her severe emotional distress. As a proximate result of that conduct, the plaintiff suffered severe and permanent emotional injury and incurred current and future medical expenses. The plaintiff also claims that she has lost faith in the Catholic Church and in God.

There are several reasons why the plaintiff's alleged claim for intentional infliction of emotional distress was subject to demurrer. What is involved in this case is conduct between consenting adults. There is no allegation that the defendant used force or fraud to accomplish his sexual relations with the plaintiff during the period from 1982 to 1989. The amended petition does allege that the plaintiff was "vulnerable" because of "prior emotional problems." This allegation falls far short of alleging that the plaintiff was incapable of consenting to what took place.

In tort law, consent ordinarily bars recovery for intentional interferences with person or property. According to W. Page Keeton et al., Prosser and Keeton on the Law of Torts § 18 at 112 (5th ed. 1984), it is a fundamental principle of common law that "to one who is willing, no wrong is done." That text further states:

> Consent avoids recovery simply because it destroys the wrongfulness of the conduct as between the consenting parties, however harmful it might be to the interest of others, and even though it is perhaps both immoral and criminal.

A sexual relationship between two consenting adults is not outrageous conduct such as to give rise to a claim for intentional infliction of emotional distress. This seems especially true given the fact that the plaintiff and Lange engaged in an approximately 7-year sexual relationship.

The plaintiff cites two cases which held that a parishioner stated a claim for intentional infliction of emotional distress against a member of the clergy for sexual misconduct with a parishioner: *Destefano v. Grabrian*, 763 P.2d 275 (Colo.1988), and *Erickson v. Christenson*, 99 Or.App. 104, 781 P.2d 383 (1989).

We believe the *Destefano* and *Erickson* cases may be distinguished factually, at least in part. In the *Destefano* case, the court emphasized that the defendant had held himself out to be trained and capable of conducting marital counseling. The court further stated that on remand, it was for the trial court to determine in the first instance as to whether the conduct of the defendant priest at issue was "outrageous."

The *Erickson* case involved conduct against a 13-year-old girl. The case at bar involves an adult plaintiff, and there is no allegation that the defendant Lange held himself out as a professionally trained counselor.

In the second cause of action, the plaintiff alleged that Lange was negligent by failing to properly counsel her concerning her marital and family relationships when he knew or should have known she was having domestic difficulties and that, further, Lange was negligent by failing to remove himself as parish priest when he knew or should have known that a continuing relationship with her would cause her emotional harm. Finally, the plaintiff alleges that Lange was negligent by violating his oath of celibacy. In substance, the plaintiff alleged a claim for clergy malpractice, a purported breach of professional standards by a priest.

So far as we have been able to determine, no jurisdiction to date has recognized a claim for clergy malpractice. See, *Nally v. Grace Com. Church of the Valley*, 47 Cal.3d 278, 253 Cal.Rptr. 97, 763 P.2d 948 (1988), *cert. denied* 490 U.S. 1007 (1989); *Destefano v. Grabrian, supra*; *Byrd v. Faber*, 57 Ohio St.3d 56, 565 N.E.2d 584 (1991); *Schmidt v. Bishop*, 779 F.Supp. 321 (S.D.N.Y.1991).

The allegations of negligence against Lange with regard to failing to remove himself as parish priest and violating his vows of celibacy were not discussed in the plaintiff's brief and will not be further considered.

The third cause of action alleges that Lange had a fiduciary obligation to the plaintiff to refrain from doing anything that might harm her relationship with her husband and children, in light of Lange's continuing duty to exercise reasonable care. The plaintiff alleges that Lange breached this duty and that this breach caused her damage.

Several cases have allowed recovery on the theory of breach of fiduciary duty with regard to sexual misconduct of a member of the clergy with a parishioner. *See, Destefano v. Grabrian, supra*; *Erickson v. Christenson, supra.*

However, this cause of action was rejected by the court in *Schmidt v. Bishop, supra.* The *Schmidt* court recognized that with regard to a breach-of-fiduciary cause of action against a member of the clergy, there are many constitutional difficulties with regard to defining a standard of care. The *Schmidt* court reasoned:

> In analyzing and defining the scope of a fiduciary duty owed persons by their clergy, the Court would be confronted by the same constitutional difficulties encountered in articulating the generalized standard of care for a clergyman required by the law of negligence.... As with her negligence claim, [the plaintiff's] fiduciary duty claim is merely another way of alleging that the defendant grossly abused his pastoral role, that is, that he engaged in malpractice.

(Emphasis omitted.) *Schmidt v. Bishop*, 779 F.Supp. at 326.

We agree with the reasoning of the court in the *Schmidt* case.

In the amended petition, the plaintiff alleges that the defendant Archdiocese was directly negligent by hiring Lange and placing him in the position of parish priest. The amended petition also alleges that the Archdiocese was negligent in failing to investigate Lange's background by inquiring into his relations with other women while acting as parish priest in other parishes, when the Archdiocese knew or should have known that Lange had been actively involved in relationships with women in the past, in violation of his celibacy vows. Finally, the plaintiff argues that the Archdiocese was negligent in failing to supervise Lange in connection with his pastoral duties when they knew or should have known of his past sexual affairs and by failing to remove Lange as a parish priest when they had this knowledge.

If there is no tort liability to the plaintiff against Lange individually, it follows that the Archdiocese cannot be held liable for his conduct. *Strock v. Pressnell*, 38 Ohio St.3d 207, 527 N.E.2d 1235 (1988), supports this proposition.

AFFIRMED.

WHITE, J., dissents.

LANPHIER, Justice, dissenting.

I respectfully dissent. The majority decision concludes that a person cannot claim he is wronged by actions of another to which he consented. This is correct logic and law by itself. However, the proposition overlooks the question of how such consent was achieved.

Should consent bar a claim where such consent may have been achieved by the actions of a fiduciary which constitute overreaching by such fiduciary? That is a question which cannot be answered as a matter of law. The answer is best left to a jury after consideration of all of the facts. The only ground listed in the demurrers which is applicable to our consideration of this matter is failure to state a cause of action. The petition states a cause of action in three respects.

INTENTIONAL INFLICTION OF EMOTIONAL DISTRESS

Plaintiff's amended petition states that plaintiff began counseling with Lange and that during the course of counseling, "Lange made numerous sexual advances on Plaintiff which lasted for approximately a three-year period." During this time, plaintiff alleged, she was "vulnerable because of prior emotional problems." Plaintiff also alleged that in 1982, Lange succeeded in "seducing" the plaintiff. The majority determined that these allegations are insufficient to state a cause of action for intentional infliction of emotional distress. This decision is based on a determination that "what is involved in this case is conduct between consenting adults."

The petition alleges, however, that plaintiff was not a fully "consenting adult." Plaintiff alleges she was vulnerable and that she was seduced by a pastoral counselor whom she trusted.

Plaintiff cited two cases, *Destefano v. Grabrian*, 763 P.2d 275 (Colo.1988), and *Erickson v. Christenson*, 99 Or.App. 104, 781 P.2d 383 (1989), in which claims against members of the clergy for intentional infliction of emotional distress were upheld. The majority, however, concludes that these cases are factually distinct.

The defendant in *Destefano* was alleged to have held himself out as being trained and capable of conducting marital counseling, which is not alleged in this case. Alleging that the defendant held himself out as a trained professional marital counselor may be necessary to establish one type of a fiduciary relationship to establish a breach of a fiduciary's duties. There is no need to establish such a relationship to establish a cause of action for intentional infliction of emotional distress. The outrageousness of Lange's conduct should not depend upon whether or not he held himself out as one type of professional. It may be one of many factors which should be considered when determining the degree of culpability.

Likewise, the fact that the plaintiff in *Erickson* was only 13 years old when the conduct at issue began is just one factor to consider when determining whether the conduct in question is outrageous. Certainly, the fact that the plaintiff here is an adult does not mean that Lange's conduct could not be outrageous.

NEGLIGENCE

[Justice Lanphier concludes that the complaint reasonably "states a cause of action for negligence against the Archdiocese."]

BREACH OF FIDUCIARY DUTY

The majority also rejected the third cause of action claimed by plaintiff, breach of fiduciary duty. In *Destefano v. Grabrian, supra*, the Supreme Court of Colorado held a cause of action for breach of fiduciary duty was stated where a woman alleged a member of the clergy had sexual intercourse with her while he was providing her with marriage counseling. The fiduciary duty, the court said, was created by his undertaking to counsel the woman. It was not created by the fact that he was a clergy member. The court stated:

> If the alleged conduct of Grabrian [the clergy member] was dictated by his sincerely held religious beliefs or was consistent with the practice of his religion, we would have to resolve a difficult first amendment issue. This, however, is not the case. It has not been asserted that Grabrian's conduct falls within the practices or beliefs of the Catholic church.

763 P.2d at 284. Likewise, here there has been no assertion that Lange's conduct falls within the practices or beliefs of the Catholic Church. Thus, there is no difficult First Amendment issue to confront.

Lange's duty to plaintiff, given the nature of the counseling relationship, was to help her with family matters. *See Destefano v. Grabrian, supra*. Seduction of plaintiff, if proved, would be an obvious breach of that duty. A person standing in a fiduciary relationship with another is subject to liability for harm resulting from a breach of the duty imposed by the relationship. Restatement (Second) of Torts § 874 (1979). Lange could, if the allegations contained in the petition are proven, be subject to liability for any harm he caused.

For the reasons cited, I would reverse the judgment of the district court.

SHANAHAN, J., joins in this dissent.

Notes

1. The first clergy malpractice case was *Nally v. Grace Community Church*. Kenneth Nally committed suicide. His parents sued the Grace Community Church, alleging intentional infliction of emotional distress and negligent counseling caused their son's death. The case garnered national attention, and traveled twice through the California court system before the California Supreme Court held that no cause of action could be made against the defendant church for either claim. *Nally v. Grace Community Church of the Valley*, 763 P.2d 948 (Cal. 1988).

2. As *Schieffer* notes, no state has found a claim for "clergy malpractice" to exist. *See also Bladen v. First Presbyterian Church of Sallisaw*, 857 P.2d 789 (Okla. 1993) (noting absence of clergy malpractice precedent, and dismissing claims, including negligent counseling claim, by husband and wife against minister and church resulting from affair between minister and wife). However, the *Schieffer* court cites several cases declaring "secular" actions committed by priests and ministers not protected by the First Amendment. For a survey of some of these issues, see James T. O'Reilly and Joann M. Strasser, *Clergy Sexual Misconduct: Confronting the Difficult Constitutional and Institutional Liability Issues*, 7 St. Thomas L. Rev. 31 (1994).

3. One fear of extending civil liability to actions of religious organizations is the possibility that the jury will punish the organization for its objectionable religious beliefs rather than its actions. *See Murphy v. I.S.K.Con. of New England*, 571 N.E.2d 340 (Mass. 1991) (Krishna religion). Is this fear reasonable?

4. One of Schieffer's claims was that the actions of the priest Lange caused her to lose her faith in the Catholic Church and God. If the court had found Schieffer's claim actionable, could her attorney argue to the jury that her damages for pain and suffering included an amount for her loss of religious faith?

5. If Schieffer had confessed her sins to Lange, and Lange had later made public the statements made by Schieffer in confession, Lange would have violated Roman Catholic Canon Law. Should the secular courts consider making a tort the public disclosure of confidential communications made to a cleric? If a communicant makes a confidential communication to a cleric, and the cleric later makes public that confidence, can the communicant successfully sue the cleric in tort? Does it matter whether the communication was considered confidential as a matter of religious law, and not just the law of evidence? In other words, if the communication is considered confidential as a matter of the state's law of evidence, but not confidential as a matter of the law of the religious body to which the cleric belongs, should a duty to keep the communication exist, so that a breach of that duty is enforceable by tort law? *See Hester v. Barnett*, 723 S.W.2d 544 (Mo. Ct. App. 1987); *Handley v. Richards*, 518 So.2d 682 (Ala. 1987) (Maddox, J., concurring specially); *Smith v. Calvary Christian Church*, 614 N.W.2d 590 (Mich. 2000) (no). In *Lightman v. Flaum*, 687 N.Y.S.2d 562 (N.Y. Sup. Ct. 1999), the plaintiff sued two Rabbis in tort for disclosing confidences she made to them concerning her relationship with her husband. The plaintiff sought counseling from Rabbis Flaum and Weinberger regarding her marriage. She later sued her husband for divorce and sought custody of their children. In response to the custody request, the husband filed an affirmation from the Rabbis disclosing information plaintiff had disclosed to the Rabbis during counseling. The trial court held that a violation of the clergy-penitent privilege created a cause of action in tort. The court concluded that the disclosure was actionable even though the Rabbis claimed that "religious law 'compelled' disclosure." *Id.* at 569. This was because "civil law, which mandated strict confidentiality," made the penitent the holder of the privilege. *Id.* at 570. The Appellate Division reversed on grounds that the privilege had been waived. *Lightman v. Flaum*, 717 N.Y.S.2d 617 (App. Div. 2000). The New York Court of Appeals held that the evidentiary privilege for clergy-penitent communications did not impose a fiduciary duty of confidentiality upon clergy. Thus, clergy were not subject to civil liability for disclosing confidential communications. *Lightman v. Flaum*, 97 N.Y.2d 128, 736 N.E.2d 300 (2001). None of the cases cited above concerns a Roman Catholic priest, or a specific duty in church law to keep the communication confidential. If the cleric is bound by ecclesiastical law to keep the confidence at all costs, should that fact suggest the creation of a duty the breach of which is enforceable as a matter of tort law?

6. Much has been written on the subject of clergy malpractice. *See* CLERGY MALPRACTICE (H. Newton Malony, Thomas L. Needham & Samuel Southard eds. 1986). *Compare* Robert J. Basil, Note, *Clergy Malpractice: Taking Spiritual Counseling Conflicts Beyond Intentional Tort Analysis*, 19 Rutgers L.J. 419 (1988) *with* C. Eric Funston, Comment, *Made Out of Whole Cloth? A Constitutional Analysis of the Clergy Malpractice Concept*, 19 Cal. W.L. Rev. 507 (1983).

Molko v. Holy Spirit Ass'n for the Unification of World Christianity

46 Cal. 3d 1092, 252 Cal. Rptr. 122, 762 P.2d 46 (1988), *cert. denied*, 490 U.S. 1084 (1989)

[Two former members of the Unification Church, David Molko and Tracy Leal, sued the church alleging fraud and deceit, intentional infliction of emotional distress, and false imprisonment. Molko additionally sued for restitution of a $6,000 gift to the church. At the time Molko first met members of the church, he was a 27-year old graduate of Temple University School of Law. Leal was a 19-year old college student when she first was approached by church proselytizers. After both Molko and Leal were abducted and "deprogrammed," they sued. The trial and intermediate appellate courts granted summary judgment to the defendant church.]

MOSK, Justice.

This case raises [the issue] whether, consistently with the free exercise clause of the First Amendment of the United States Constitution and of article I, section 4, of the California Constitution, former members of a religious organization may sue that organization on various causes of action arising out of its allegedly deceptive recruitment practices.

As will appear, we conclude that the summary judgment for the Church should be affirmed as to the cause of action for false imprisonment but reversed as to the causes of action for fraud, intentional infliction of emotional distress, and restitution.

II. FRAUD AND DECEIT

B. Nature of the Fraud Claim

Molko and Leal contend specified members of the Unification Church knowingly misrepresented the Church's identity with the intent to induce each of them to associate with and ultimately join the Church. Molko and Leal further contend they justifiably relied on those misrepresentations in unknowingly agreeing to participate in Church activities, and suffered psychological and financial damage as a result of their involvement with and membership in the Unification Church. They state they would not have chosen to associate with the Church had they known its true identity.

The Church concedes for pleading purposes its members knowingly misrepresented the Church's identity to Molko and Leal. It further concedes the misrepresentations were made with the intent to induce Molko and Leal first to associate with Church recruiters and later to continue participating in Church activities. Nor, finally, does the Church contest plaintiffs' claims that they suffered damages as a result of their involvement with the Church. The Church contends, however, that it is entitled to summary judgment because the undisputed facts conclusively negate the element of justifiable reliance.

Molko and Leal admit they were aware of the Church's identity at the time they formally joined. However, they contend that by the time the Church disclosed its true identity, the Church's agents had rendered them incapable of deciding not to join the Church, by subjecting them, without their knowledge or consent, to an intense program of coercive persuasion or mind control. They contend, in other words, that the Church deceived them into a setting in which they could be "brainwashed," and that the Church could not then "cure" the deception by telling them the truth after their involuntary indoctrination was accomplished. Molko and Leal therefore contend that a triable issue of fact remains as to whether the Church brainwashed them prior to disclosing its identity. If the answer is affirmative, they urge, they have established justifiable reliance.

Although Molko and Leal are far from the first to advance a brainwashing theory in a case involving religious recruitment and indoctrination (see, e.g., *Katz v. Superior Court* (1977) 73 Cal.App.3d 952 [141 Cal.Rptr. 234]; *Meroni v. Holy Spirit Assn.* (1984) 125 Misc.2d 1061 [480 N.Y.S.2d 706]; *Orlando v. Alamo* (8th Cir. 1981) 646 F.2d 1288; *Turner v. Unification Church* (1st Cir. 1979) 602 F.2d 458; *Lewis v. Holy Spirit Ass'n for*

Unification (D.Mass 1983) 589 F.Supp. 10; *Schuppin v. Unification Church* (D.Vt. 1977) 435 F.Supp. 603)), they are the first to do so in this court. We therefore find it appropriate to briefly review the concept of brainwashing.

Brainwashing is "a forcible indoctrination to induce someone to give up basic political, social, or religious beliefs and attitudes and to accept contrasting regimented ideas." (Webster's Ninth New Collegiate Dict. (1987) p. 175.) The specific methods of indoctrination vary, but the basic theory is that brainwashing "is fostered through the creation of a controlled environment that heightens the susceptibility of a subject to suggestion and manipulation through sensory deprivation, physiological depletion, cognitive dissonance, peer pressure, and a clear assertion of authority and dominion. The aftermath of indoctrination is a severe impairment of autonomy and [of] the ability to think independently, which induces a subject's unyielding compliance and the rupture of past connections, affiliations, and associations." (*Peterson v. Sorlien* (Minn. 1981) 299 N.W.2d 123, 126.)

[After discussing the "controversial" issue of the existence of brainwashing, the court continued:] We need not resolve the controversy; we need only conclude that the existence of such differing views compels the conclusion that Molko and Leal's theory indeed raises a factual question—viz., whether Molko and Leal were brainwashed—which, if not prohibited by other considerations, precludes a grant of summary judgment for the Church.

D. Constitutional Issues

1. Applicable Principles

While judicial sanctioning of tort recovery constitutes state action sufficient to invoke the same constitutional protections applicable to statutes and other legislative actions (*New York Times v. Sullivan* (1964) 376 U.S. 254, 265), religious groups are not immune from all tort liability. It is well settled, for example, that religious groups may be held liable in tort for secular acts. (See, e.g., *Malloy v. Fong* (1951) 37 Cal.2d 356, 372, 232 P.2d 241 [religious corporation liable for negligent driving by employee].) Most relevant here, in appropriate cases courts will recognize tort liability even for acts that are religiously motivated. (See, e.g., *O'Moore v. Driscoll* (1933) 135 Cal.App. 770, 778, 28 P.2d 438 [allowing priest's action against his superiors for false imprisonment as part of their effort to obtain his confession of sins]; *Bear v. Reformed Mennonite Church* (1975) 462 Pa. 330, 341 A.2d 105, 107 [allowing action for interference with marriage and business interests when church ordered congregation to "shun" former member]; *Carrieri v. Bush* (1966) 69 Wn.2d 536, 419 P.2d 132, 137 [allowing action for alienation of affections when pastor counselled woman to leave husband who was "full of the devil"]; *Candy H. v. Redemption Ranch, Inc.* (M.D.Ala. 1983) 563 F.Supp. 505, 516 [allowing action for false imprisonment against religious group]; *Van Schaick v. Church of Scientology of Cal., Inc.* (D.Mass. 1982) 535 F.Supp. 1125, 1135 ["[causes] of action based upon some proscribed conduct may, thus, withstand a motion to dismiss even if the alleged wrongdoer acts upon a religious belief or is organized for a religious purpose"].)

2. Constitutional Analysis of the Fraud Claim

Molko and Leal claim they do not challenge the truth or falsity of the Church's beliefs; they contend rather that they challenge only the Church's fraudulent conduct in implementing those beliefs. The Court of Appeal disagreed, reasoning that it would be impossible to consider Molko and Leal's theory "without questioning the authenticity and force of the Unification Church's religious teachings and permitting a jury to do likewise, which is constitutionally forbidden."

[L]iability for fraud in the case at bar would burden no one's right to believe and no one's right to remain part of his religious community, nor would it subject anyone to involuntary deprogramming: the plaintiffs here are the former Church members themselves. It might, of course, somewhat burden the Church's efforts to recruit new members by deceptive means.

The legal question is simply whether a religious organization can be held liable on a traditional cause of action in fraud for deceiving nonmembers into subjecting themselves, without their knowledge or consent, to coercive persuasion.

The challenge here, as we have stated, is not to the Church's teachings or to the validity of a religious conversion. The challenge is to the Church's practice of misrepresenting or concealing its identity in order to bring unsuspecting outsiders into its highly structured environment. That practice is not itself belief—it is conduct "subject to regulation for the protection of society." (*Cantwell v. Connecticut*, 310 U.S. at p. 304.)

We turn first to the question whether tort liability for fraudulent recruiting practices imposes any burden on the free exercise of the Unification Church's religion. We think it does. While such liability does not impair the Church's right to believe in recruiting through deception, its very purpose is to discourage the Church from putting such belief into practice by subjecting the Church to possible monetary loss for doing so. Further, liability presumably impairs the Church's ability to convert nonbelievers, because some potential members who would have been recruited by deception will choose not to associate with the Church when they are told its true identity.

Yet these burdens, while real, are not substantial. Being subject to liability for fraud does not in any way or degree prevent or inhibit Church members from operating their religious communities, worshipping as they see fit, freely associating with one another, selling or distributing literature, proselytizing on the street, soliciting funds, or generally spreading Reverend Moon's message among the population. At most, it potentially closes one questionable avenue for bringing new members into the Church.

We must next consider whether a compelling state interest justifies the marginal burden such liability imposes on the Church's free exercise rights. We have no difficulty in finding such an interest in the "substantial threat to public safety, peace or order" the Church's allegedly fraudulent conduct poses. (*Sherbert v. Verner*, 374 U.S. at p. 403.) For it is one thing when a person knowingly and voluntarily submits to a process involving coercive influence, as a novice does on entering a monastery or a seminary. But it is quite another when a person is subjected to coercive persuasion without his knowledge or consent. While some individuals who experience coercive persuasion emerge unscathed, many others develop serious and sometimes irreversible physical and psychiatric disorders, up to and including schizophrenia, self-mutilation, and suicide. (See generally Delgado, *Religious Totalism: Gentle and Ungentle Persuasion Under the First Amendment*, 51 So.Cal.L.Rev. 1, 10-25, and sources cited therein.) The state clearly has a compelling interest in preventing its citizens from being deceived into submitting unknowingly to such a potentially dangerous process.

The state has an equally compelling interest in protecting the family institution. Since the family almost invariably suffers great stress and sometimes incurs significant financial loss when one of its members is unknowingly subjected to coercive persuasion (Enroth, Youth, Brainwashing, and the Extremist Cults (1977) pp. 199–201), the state has a compelling interest in protecting families from suffering such impairments as a result of fraud and deception.

We conclude, therefore, that although liability for deceptive recruitment practices imposes a marginal burden on the Church's free exercise of religion, the burden is justified by the compelling state interest in protecting individuals and families from the substantial threat to public safety, peace and order posed by the fraudulent induction of unconsenting individuals into an atmosphere of coercive persuasion.

Our analysis cannot end here, however. A government action burdening free exercise, even though justified by a compelling state interest, is impermissible if any action imposing a lesser burden on religion would satisfy that interest. After careful consideration, we perceive no such less restrictive alternative available.

Finally, even though the state action is justified by a compelling state interest and imposes the minimum burden required to satisfy that interest, it can be upheld only if it (1) has the purpose and effect of advancing the state's secular goals and (2) does not discriminate between religions, or between religion and nonreligion. We find that judicial sanctioning of traditional tort liability for fraudulent recruitment satisfies these standards. First, its purpose and effect is plainly to advance the legitimate secular goal of protecting persons from being harmed by fraud. Second, it is nondiscriminatory: all organizations, religious or otherwise, may be held liable for damages caused by their fraudulent acts. Were a nonreligious organization—e.g., a group espousing a political or social cause—to deceive a person into unknowingly submitting to coercive persuasion, the same liability would ensue.

III. INTENTIONAL INFLICTION OF EMOTIONAL DISTRESS

The Court of Appeal found in part that threats of divine retribution, of which Molko and Leal complained, were protected religious speech and could not form the basis of a claim of intentional infliction of emotional distress. We agree with this view. To the extent the claims are based merely on threats of divine retribution if Molko and Leal left the church, they cannot stand. (See *Fowler v. Rhode Island*, 345 U.S. at p. 70 [court cannot regulate or control sermons]; *Van Schaick v. Church of Scientology of Cal., Inc.*, 535 F.Supp. at p. 1139.)

However, the claims do not rest solely or even primarily on threats of divine retribution. Molko and Leal essentially contend the same conduct that supports their fraud actions—i.e., misrepresentation and concealment of the Church's identity for the purpose of inducing them to submit unknowingly to coercive persuasion—also gives rise to an action for intentional infliction of emotional distress.

The Church offers two arguments why its conduct was not, as a matter of law, extreme and outrageous. First it contends its actions amounted to nothing more than "intensive religious practice," and therefore were different only in degree, not in kind, from those of many other religious groups. We find this claim unconvincing. Although fasting, poverty, silence or cloistered living may constitute intensive religious practice, we have already determined that fraud, even though purported to be religiously motivated, is actionable conduct under the circumstances presented here. Second, as mentioned above, the Church argues that Leal's long hours of work were "self-inflicted." It contends its encouragement for her to sell flowers and solicit money does not constitute outrageous conduct. But since the conduct that the Church relies on occurred after Leal had formally joined the Church, the argument has no bearing on whether its original fraudulent inducement into an atmosphere of coercive persuasion—the conduct at issue—is extreme and outrageous.

Since reasonable persons could differ here, a question of fact remains as to whether the Church's conduct was outrageous for purposes of this action. It follows that the

Court of Appeal erred in affirming the summary judgment for the Church as to plaintiffs' actions for intentional infliction of emotional distress.

[Reversed on causes of action for fraud, intentional infliction of emotional distress, and restitution.]

ANDERSON (Carl W.) Justice, concurring and dissenting.

I concur with the majority regarding the disposition of the false imprisonment cause of action,... but respectfully disagree with the reversal of the summary judgment in connection with the fraud, intentional infliction of emotional distress and the restitution counts. I am strongly persuaded that the imposition of tort liability for "heavenly deception" in proselytizing and for its ensuing "systematic manipulation of social influences" (religious persuasion) runs counter to established legal precedents and the free exercise clause of the First Amendment. Furthermore, imposition of liability in such cases constitutes bad legal policy, since it unnecessarily projects the court into the arena of divining the truth or falsity of religious beliefs.

The evidence before us, including appellants' depositions, clearly indicates that the church's indoctrination did not render appellants mindless puppets or robot-like creatures. Instead, it shows that both before and after the disclosure of the group's true identity, both appellants retained their ability to think, to evaluate the events and to exercise their independent judgment.

[T]he majority concludes that while religious belief is absolutely protected, religious conduct is not; that conduct even if religiously motivated is subject to regulation for the protection of society; and that the Church's initial fraud which led to the brainwashing of appellants was conduct which, under the balancing test required by the First Amendment, can be penalized with tort sanctions based upon a compelling state interest.

I respectfully submit that this reasoning is flawed. To begin with, the conduct which according to the majority constitutes a triable issue of fact is not only the initial fraud (an act clearly subject to proof), but also the subsequent "brainwashing" and conversion—matters comprising not only sociological or psychological phenomena, but also involving intangible elements of religious belief. It follows that brainwashing and conversion are so inextricably intertwined with religious faith that they cannot be scrutinized, much less proven, without questioning the authenticity of the religious teachings of the Church. Such inquiry is absolutely proscribed by the free exercise clause of the First Amendment.

The proposition that the act or conduct of a religious organization or its members is immune from judicial scrutiny if the proof thereof calls into question the truth or falsity of religious faith is well established in case law as well as in legal commentary.

The effect of conversion, generally speaking, is spiritual rebirth—that is, attainment of a new life. The first step in that direction is a separation from the previous environment to a place where one can meditate and contemplate without distraction. Although transcending one's family may be traumatic and painful, it is sometimes an essential element in the pilgrimage of faith. The guilt and awareness of sin also may be an important factor leading to conversion. The promise of salvation and the threat of damnation are the very foundation of the life of the devout. Ascetic, regulated life, hard work, fasting and giving up earthly pleasures are also parts of many religious teachings aimed at spiritual purity and pleasing God. The dogmatic approach and intolerance of criticism are not uncommon with established religions which profess that divine truth is revealed in Holy Scriptures, church dogmas and in *ex cathedra* declarations of anointed leaders (e.g., papal infallibility in the Catholic Church) which is not to be questioned by faithful followers. Finally, the introverted view forsaking interest in the outside world necessarily flows from the religious teaching that one must separate himself or herself from the world dominated by Satan and his evil forces in order to join and serve God's kingdom.

Indeed, what this expert evidence characterizes as indicia of brainwashing or mind control, might very well be equated with the more popularly accepted symptoms of genuine religious conversion. Religious behavioral change induced by the mystery of faith cannot be proved or disproved by secular science, which limits its scope of inquiry to tangible, rational and logical phenomena, comprehensible and explainable by human reasons.

The majority opinion rests on a theory of fraudulently induced brainwashing. However, the conduct of "brainwashing" itself is not actionable because that method is commonly employed by religious groups, and it fails to constitute that outrageous conduct which goes beyond the limits of social toleration. Thus, the critical issue is whether the act of brainwashing becomes tortious because it was preceded by the wrongful act of "heavenly deception" employed in recruiting.

[A] persuasive argument may be made that the principal wrong here claimed (i.e., "heavenly deception" in recruiting) is not subject to government intervention at all, because it includes doctrinal matters rather than operational activities. But even if we assume that such acts are purely "secular" in nature and may properly be regulated by government, they fail to amount to an abuse of such magnitude that would justify government interference under the strict balancing test prescribed by law. This is so because the First Amendment ensures wide protection for religious persuasion which may encompass not only exaggeration, but also outright falsehood.

In sum, I am firmly convinced that since "heavenly deception" and its ensuing "brainwashing," fail to constitute those gravest abuses, this court is powerless to impose tort sanctions thereon.

Members of this court may detest the practice of heavenly deception. We may abhor the results of the church's selective (and successful) proselytization. We may condemn such practices as destructive of the integrity of the family. Yet, as judges we must resist the temptation to tread into this theological thicket. For it is neither for governments, nor their instrumentalities, the courts, to divine the truth of those teachings.

Notes

1. Before *Molko*, several courts heard and dismissed claims against the Unification Church alleging religious indoctrination by "brainwashing." *See Schuppin v. Unification Church*, 435 F.Supp. 603 (D.Vt. 1977) (dismissing alienation of daughter's affection claim filed by parents of current church member); *Turner v. Unification Church*, 473 F. Supp. 367 (D. R.I. 1978, *aff'd*, 602 F.2d 458 (1st Cir. 1979); *Lewis v. Holy Spirit Ass'n for Unification of World Christianity*, 589 F.Supp. 10 (D.Mass.1983); *Meroni v. Holy Spirit Assn. for Unification of World Christianity*, 119 A.D.2d 200, 506 N.Y.S.2d 174 (1986). *See also Orlando v. Alamo*, 646 F.2d 1288 (8th Cir. 1981); *Christofferson v. Church of Scientology*, 57 Or. App. 203, 644 P.2d 577 (1982), *cert. denied*, 459 U.S. 1206 (1983).

2. Some religious groups engage in the practice of "shunning," avoiding those who were formerly members of the religious group. Is such a practice tortious? In *Paul v. Watchtower Bible and Tract Soc'y, Inc.*, 819 F.2d 875 (9th Cir.), *cert. denied*, 484 U.S.

926 (1987), the plaintiff, a "disfellowshiped" former Jehovah's Witness, was shunned by former childhood friends on pain of their own excommunication. In dismissing the claim, the court concluded, "We find the practice of shunning not to constitute a sufficient threat to the peace, safety, or morality of the community as to warrant state intervention." *Id.* at 883. Are the actions of the Unification Church sufficiently different from the actions of the Jehovah's Witnesses to suggest the different results in *Molko* and *Paul*? *Contra Bear v. Reformed Mennonite Church*, 462 Pa. 330, 341 A.2d 105 (1975) (holding actionable claim of "shunning"). The *Paul* court expressly relied on the free exercise clause as interpreted in *Sherbert v. Verner*, 374 U.S. 398 (1963), excerpted in Chapter Five, to reach its conclusion. However, *Paul* was decided before *Employment Div. v. Smith*, 494 U.S. 872 (1990), which restricts *Sherbert* to a special rule of unemployment law. Are tort claims alleging invasion of privacy, defamation, or outrageous conduct sufficiently neutral and generally applicable to meet the constitutional standard of *Employment Div. v. Smith*? If not, the claims must meet the "compelling interest" test. Are the religious reasons for the actions of the church sufficiently at issue to require the compelling interest test?

Can a church continue to "discipline" a member after the member leaves the church? The plaintiff in *Guinn v. Church of Christ of Collinsville*, 775 P.2d 766 (Okla. 1989), was publicly denounced in the church as a "fornicator" after she failed (or refused) publicly to repent her sin of fornication. (The man with whom plaintiff was engaged in this relationship was not a member of the church.) This public denunciation took place after several private meetings between the plaintiff and the elders of the church. Before the public denunciation, the plaintiff wrote to the elders withdrawing from membership in the church, which the church refused to acknowledge. The church has no provision for withdrawing and believes that once a member, the person "remains a part of the congregation for life." *Id.* at 776. The church's defense was held factually unjustified by the evidence, which indicated that the plaintiff had never been told of the lifetime commitment she was making by joining the church. It thus held actionable the public denunciation of the plaintiff because it occurred after the plaintiff gave the church written notice of her intention to resign as a member of the church. However, the Supreme Court of Oklahoma dismissed all claims based on actions taken by the Elders in the church's behalf before the plaintiff withdrew as a member. *Cf. Korean Presbyterian Church of Seattle Normalization Comm. v. Lee*, 75 Wash.App. 833, 880 P.2d 565 (Wash. App. 1994) (dismissing on First Amendment grounds tort claim that announcement of excommunication of former members at church harmed former members).

If the church had informed the plaintiff of its requirement of a lifetime commitment, would that "notice" have "waived" her tort claims? *See Smith v. Calvary Christian Church*, 614 N.W.2d 590 (Mich. 2000) (yes). Should it matter that the disciplinary proceedings began when Guinn was a church member? Is *Guinn* legally distinguishable from *Paul*? The *Guinn* court initially distinguished *Paul* on the grounds that the "conduct in *Paul* was passive." In contrast, the Church of Christ in Collinsville was actively involved in attempting "impos[e] its will, as manifested through a disciplinary scheme, upon an individual who has not consented to undergo ecclesiastical discipline her in the religious practices of a church whose precepts she no longer followed." *Guinn*, 775 P.2d at 780–81. Although the *Paul* court lumped current and former members together for purposes of assessing the constitutionality of the tort claims, the *Guinn* court concluded that this was not part of the holding of the *Paul* court.

Can a person sue for wrongful excommunication? *See O'Connor v. Diocese of Honolulu*, 885 P.2d 361 (Haw. 1994) and *Hadnot v. Shaw*, 826 P.2d 978 (Okla. 1992) (no).

Are wrongful excommunication cases unrecognized in law because courts see religious organizations simply as a type of voluntary organization? Is it possible that one's religiousness or religious commitments are less rooted in a form of voluntary "consent" than other organizations one chooses to join? The philosopher Michael Sandel claims that the "voluntarist" notion of religious liberty "points beyond religion." It points to a liberal conception of the self, a self unencumbered by commitments, autonomous and free to choose how to live one's life. Sandel notes that "[i]n the case of religion, the liberal conception of the person ill equips the Court to secure religious liberty for those who regard themselves as claimed by religious commitments they have not chosen." Michael J. Sandel, *Freedom of Conscience or Freedom of Choice?* in ARTICLES OF FAITH, ARTICLES OF PEACE: THE RELIGIOUS LIBERTY CLAUSES AND THE AMERICAN PUBLIC PHILOSOPHY 74, 87 (James Davison Hunter & Os Guinness eds. 1990). Are courts equipped to recognize such commitments?

3. Is *Molko* explicable on the ground that aggressive religious proselytization is anathema in a modern liberal society, one committed to the right of privacy, to individual choice and to a clear separation of public (secular) action from private (religious) action? Is the *Molko* court suggesting that because religious indoctrination involves emotional or nonrational persuasion rather than intellectual or rational persuasion, one's "choice" regarding one's acceptance of the religious beliefs of the Unification Church is less free? Both Molko and Leal renounced their membership in the Unification Church after being kidnapped and "deprogrammed." What choice, if any, is the court making between the community of the Unification Church and the families who hired "deprogrammers"?

4. A broad survey of this topic is Paul T. Hayden, *Religiously Motivated "Outrageous" Conduct: Intentional Infliction of Emotional Distress as a Weapon Against "Other People's Faiths"*, 34 Wm. & Mary L. Rev. 579 (1993).

2. Religious Institutions and Officers and Criminal Law

United States v. Moon

718 F.2d 1210 (2d Cir. 1983), *cert. denied*, 466 U.S. 971 (1984)

CARDAMONE, Circuit Judge:

Reverend Sun Myung Moon and Takeru Kamiyama appeal from judgments of conviction entered on July 16, 1982 in the United States District Court for the Southern District of New York following a six-week jury trial before Judge Gerard L. Goettel. Moon was charged basically with filing false income tax returns and Kamiyama with obstructing the investigation of those returns.

BACKGROUND

The case focused principally on bank accounts held in Reverend Moon's name in the Park Avenue office of the Chase Manhattan Bank. On March 27, 1973 Reverend Moon walked into the Chase branch and opened a personal checking account and a savings account. During the next nearly three years over 1.7 million dollars was deposited in these accounts in Moon's name, all but $200,000 of which was in cash. A substantial portion of the funds were transferred to high-yielding Chase time deposits held in Moon's name. During the years 1973–1975 these investments earned more than

$100,000 in interest, not reported as income on Moon's tax returns for the years in question.

The critical issue is whether, as the government claims, Moon owned these assets and was therefore required to pay income taxes on the bank interest and the value of the stock, or as the defense urges, Moon held these assets merely beneficially or as a trustee for the Unification Church. Before entering upon a discussion of this central issue, we first address contentions raised by the defendants as a result of the government's refusal to consent to defendant's request for a bench trial.

I

DENIAL OF BENCH TRIAL

A. As a Denial of the First Amendment Right to Free Speech

It is the view of the defense that the government's reason for opposing the defendant's request for a bench trial is unconstitutional. The factual background may be simply stated. At a rally in New York City's Foley Square on October 22, 1981 following his arraignment, Moon made a speech which was partially reprinted as a full page advertisement in the New York Times of November 5, 1981. He stated:

> I would not be standing here today if my skin were white or my religion Presbyterian. I am here today only because my skin is yellow and my religion is Unification Church. The ugliest things in this beautiful country of America are religious bigotry and racism.

In response to defense efforts to waive a trial by jury, the prosecutor wrote a letter to Judge Goettel dated March 11, 1982 stating her opposition and, referring to the excerpt quoted above, adding that defendants had raised—and circulated worldwide—questions about "the integrity and motives of this prosecution." It was the prosecutor's conclusion that a single factfinder would be placed in an "untenable" position and that there was an overriding public interest in the appearance as well as the fact of a fair trial, which could be achieved only by a jury.

The defense argues that, on the contrary, insistence upon a jury trial had the effect of punishing Moon for exercising his First Amendment right of free speech. The punishment, so the argument runs, took the form of denying Moon a benefit, i.e., a nonjury trial, that he would otherwise have been entitled to.

[The court concluded that there was no evidence that the government had opposed the request for a bench trial to punish Moon for his statements concerning the motivation of the government for indicting him.]

II

SUFFICIENCY OF THE EVIDENCE

A. Counts Two Through Six

(b) Evidence

Under the government's theory of the case, Moon failed to report interest income earned on the Chase Manhattan Bank accounts that he purportedly owned and income recognized as a result of a distribution of Tong Il stock to him at no cost. Appellants' principal contentions at trial were that the Chase accounts and Tong Il stock belonged to the Church, that Moon merely held these assets as the nominee, agent, and/or trustee of the Church, and that therefore he was not taxable on either the Chase interest or Tong Il stock distribution.

In concluding that the jury properly found the Chase accounts and Tong Il stock to be Moon's personal property, we start first with the fact that the Chase accounts and Tong Il securities were maintained in Moon's name and controlled by him. Second, some funds clearly destined for Church entities were put in existing Church bank accounts which were owned and controlled by Church corporations. Third, from his handling of the Chase accounts and Tong Il stock Moon seemingly regarded them as his own, not as belonging to the Church. Fourth, high ranking members of the Church were told that the Chase funds belonged to "Father," not to the Church.

The government introduced evidence that Moon actually considered the Chase accounts to be his own property rather than the Church's, and that he used funds from the accounts for expenditures which the jury could have concluded were personal in nature. Several examples will suffice. In September 1975 Moon and Kamiyama purchased shares in a new bank, Diplomat National Bank in Washington, D.C., $80,000 worth of stock for Moon and $75,000 for Kamiyama. The funds used to pay for the stock were derived from one of Moon's time deposits at Chase and transferred into the household account, and later a check drawn on that account was made payable to the Diplomat National Bank.

In sum the government presented evidence at trial that Moon controlled the Chase accounts and Tong Il stock, held them in his own name, considered the Chase accounts his own, used the accounts in a seemingly personal manner, and was regarded by other Church figures as owning the assets personally. Additionally, the documents produced by the defendants to show that the assets were in fact Church property proved to be backdated and false. Viewing this evidence in light most favorable to the government, it is sufficient to establish that Moon owned the Chase accounts and Tong Il stock in a personal capacity. Because he owned the assets, he should have reported the interest and stock distribution income on his tax returns. Since he failed to do so, his 1973–75 returns were false.

III

JURY INSTRUCTIONS

Moon objects to the trial court's instructions to the jury in three particular areas. First he contends that the instructions on the law of trusts were erroneous and incomplete. Second, he argues that certain instructions violated the First Amendment's Religion Clauses. And third he questions the instructions on intent. Although specific objections overlap to some extent, we will deal with them separately.

B. Religion Clauses Objections

Moon objects to instructions that permitted the jury to find that if he used the Chase funds for his own business investments or personal ends—that is for other than religious purposes—such use would indicate the lack of a trust relationship. The defense urges that this instruction violated the First Amendment Religion Clauses because the trial court was obligated to charge that the jury must accept as conclusive the Unification Church's definition of what is considered a religious purpose. Under the definition now advanced as the Church's, *any use* of these funds by Reverend Moon was for religious purposes.

This argument overstates the scope of the protections afforded by the Religion Clauses. The term "religion" was defined by the Supreme Court nearly 100 years ago in *Davis v. Beason*, as having reference to a person's views of his relations to his Creator. This definition seems unduly narrow today. In every religion there is an awareness of what is called divine and a response to that divinity. But, there are religions which do not positively require the assumption of a God, for example, Buddhism and the Unitarian Church. Hence, a broader definition of the word religion—one which we think more accurately captures its essence—is that formulated by the pre-eminent American philosopher, William James, who said religion means: "*the feelings, acts, and experiences of individual men in their solitude, so far as they apprehend themselves to stand in relation to whatever they may consider the divine.*" W. James, *The Varieties of Religious Experience* 31 (1910). In referring to an individual's relation to what he considers the divine, Professor James used the word "divine" in its broadest sense as denoting any object that is godlike, whether it is or is not a specific diety. *Id.* at 34. Therefore, under the Religion Clauses, everyone is entitled to entertain such view respecting his relations to what he considers the divine and the duties such relationship imposes as may be approved by that person's conscience, and to worship in any way such person thinks fit so long as this is not injurious to the equal rights of others. "It was never intended or supposed that the amendment could be invoked as a protection against legislation for the punishment of acts inimical to the peace, good order and morals of society." *Davis v. Beason.* The Supreme Court continued, "however free the exercise of religion may be, it must be subordinate to the criminal laws of the country, passed with reference to actions regarded by general consent as properly the subjects of punitive legislation." To foreclose a court from analyzing a church's activities as needed to determine whether those activities violated a statute, on the ground that the First Amendment forbids such inquiry, would mean that there are no restraints or limitations on church activities. *See Christian Echoes National Ministry, Inc. v. United States*, 470 F.2d 849, 856 (10th Cir.), *cert. denied*, 414 U.S. 864 (1973). The "free exercise" of religion is not so unfettered. The First Amendment does not insulate a church or its members from judicial inquiry when a charge is made that their activities violate a penal statute. Consequently, in this criminal proceeding the jury was not bound to accept the Unification Church's definition of what constitutes a religious use or purpose.

Holy Spirit Association v. Tax Commission, 55 N.Y.2d 512, 518, 450 N.Y.S.2d 292, 435 N.E.2d 662 (1982), is inapposite. That case dealt with the inquiry that a court may conduct when determining whether a religious organization is entitled to a real property tax exemption under New York law. The principles there enunciated upon which appellant relies are relevant in that context and do not serve as precedent in a federal criminal tax prosecution.

Moon also argues that an omission from the charge—the so-called "Messiah" defense—permitted the jury to look at the assets held in his name "secularly," in violation of the First Amendment. Counsel asserts that Moon's worldwide followers believe him to be "potentially the new Messiah." From this theological premise the argument is made that Moon personifies the church movement and is indistinguishable from it. Since the Unification Church movement can owe no taxes on income derived from church-related activities, the defense argues that neither can Reverend Moon.

We do not accept this defense. The fact that Moon is the head of the Church does not mean that the Church itself is not a distinct and separate body. Moon's spiritual identity as leader of the Unification Church movement and his legal identity as a taxpayer are not the same. He is the spiritual leader of the Church, as the Pope is the spiritual leader of the

Roman Catholic Church, but he also has a legal identity as a distinct, individual human being. It is in this latter capacity that he, or the Pope, could have taxable income. It has long been held that a church may hold property legally free from government interference because such inference would violate the First Amendment. *Terrett v. Taylor*, 13 U.S. (9 Cranch) 43, 51–52 (1815). But where property held individually and used personally gives rise to income, that income is subject to taxation. To allow otherwise would be to permit church leaders to stand above the law, a view we have previously rejected.

Finally, contrary to defendant's argument, the failure to charge that assets which came from church sources to be used for church purposes are not taxable to Moon, did not violate the "neutral principles" approach outlined in *Jones v. Wolf*. In *Jones* the Supreme Court held that the First Amendment prohibits the resolution of intra-church property disputes by civil courts interpreting religious doctrine, and required that civil courts defer the resolution of such issues to the highest hierarchical church organization. This "neutral principles of law" approach is one of several approved methods of resolving church property disputes between groups within the church. The doctrine has no application to the facts of this case.

IV

MISCELLANEOUS ISSUES

A. Selective Prosecution

Both appellants contend that the prosecution mounted against them was impermissibly motivated by hostility toward their religion and that the district court erred in denying their request for discovery and a hearing on the issue of selective prosecution. In this Circuit, a defendant who advances a claim of selective prosecution must do so in pretrial proceedings.

The only evidence offered pretrial in support of appellants' assertion of selective prosecution was to the effect that Congress had previously conducted an investigation into Korean-American relations (Koreagate), that such investigation had touched upon the Unification Church, and therefore that the government's prosecution of Moon could be seen to have stemmed from impermissible religious and/or political hostility. No other evidence was submitted in support of the motion. The proof before the trial court was wholly insufficient to mandate further inquiry or a hearing and the court's rejection of the claim of selective prosecution at that point was clearly proper.

Following the trial, and in an arguably untimely manner, appellants submitted additional "evidence" of selective prosecution. Specifically, they presented affidavits from four individuals who, while disavowing any knowledge of the government's motive in this case, asserted that they held church funds in their own names and did not pay taxes on interest earned on the funds. Moon also submitted a copy of a letter from United States Senator Robert Dole to the IRS requesting that it look into the Unification Church's tax exempt status. While acknowledging that Moon's status as a highly visible, religious leader may well have led to the audit of his tax returns, the district court reasoned that the government's decision to institute criminal rather than civil charges was a wholly separate decision.

[To prove] that the government's decision to prosecute was based on impermissible considerations of race and/or religion, appellants rely heavily on the above-mentioned letter from Senator Robert Dole to the IRS. That letter merely requested an audit of the Unification Church's tax exempt status. It did not request an audit of Moon's personal tax status, suggest that he be criminally prosecuted, or indicate any racial or religious bias.

We recognize that Moon is a controversial public figure who has been subjected to extensive media attention, much of it critical, and that his church may perhaps be viewed by the general public in an unfavorable light. These facts naturally tend to foster suspicion that the motive behind this prosecution might have been improper. That naked suspicion cannot serve as a substitute for the evidentiary showing [required.] This case is not the first occasion when a controversial political or religious figure has been criminally prosecuted; and if history teaches us anything, plainly, it will not be the last. By their very nature, such highly visible cases will already engender some suspicion with respect to the government's *bona fides*. But to engage in a collateral inquiry respecting prosecutorial motive, there must be more than mere suspicion or surmise.

C. Evidentiary Problems

[B]oth defendants claim that the government presented improper evidence to the jury regarding the religious practices of the Unification Church which they claim permitted them to be tried by religious innuendo.

With respect to trial by religious innuendo, concededly there was testimony that members of the Unification Church lived and worked together, donating their earnings to their church. The central issue for the jury to decide was whether the Tong Il stock and Chase Manhattan Bank accounts belonged to the Church or to Moon personally. In probing that issue, it was inevitable that some Unification Church practices would creep into the trial in order to illustrate Moon's control over the activities of other church officials. The question before us is whether evidence of Church practices although relevant, should have been excluded because "its probative value [was] substantially outweighed by the danger of unfair prejudice," Fed. R. Evid. 403. The trial judge from his superior vantage point is in the best position to weigh these competing interests. A thorough review of the record reveals no abuse of the district court's discretion.

OAKES, Circuit Judge (dissenting):

[Opinion omitted.]

Note

Is the court in *Moon* incorrectly applying a secular standard to religious behavior, or does the court adequately protect both the state's interest in preventing the filing of false income tax returns and the defendant's religious liberty interest? In the view of the popular media at the time, the "Moonies" were disparaged as a mind-controlling cult. Church members spent long hours on the streets aggressively attempting to sell flowers and other goods for the church's benefit. As the founder of the church, do you think this negative perception of the Unification Church affected the defendant's right to a fair trial? Is there more to the defendant's claim that he was selectively prosecuted than the court allows? If so, how would this be determined? Does the court fairly conclude that the prosecution's injection of Unification Church tenets and practices did not affect the jury's decision? Can the court make an informed judgment about this claim?

3. Civil Law and Religious Benefits

Under Orthodox and Conservative Jewish law, a woman who is divorced by her husband may not marry again unless the ex-husband provides her with a *get*. A *get* is a bill of divorce under Jewish law, originating in Deuteronomy 24:1. As long as she remains a faithful adherent to her faith, her husband's refusal to grant a *get* will prevent her from remarrying during his lifetime. Of course, under civil law the ex-wife is free to marry once the divorce is final. In 1983, the state of New York enacted a law requiring the plaintiff-spouse to remove all "barriers to remarriage." If the plaintiff failed to do so, the law prohibited the granting of the civil divorce. Should the civil law take the husband's actions into account if he refuses to grant a *get*? If so, how should the judge take this action into account?

Schwartz v. Schwartz

153 Misc.2d 789, 583 N.Y.S.2d 716 (N.Y. Sup. Ct. 1992)

WILLIAM RIGLER, Justice.

In this matrimonial action, this court is being asked to define the boundaries between a secular matrimonial action and the severance of religious ties between a married couple. This court had bifurcated the trial of this action hearing the issue of fault first. Based upon the evidence presented, plaintiff-wife was granted a divorce from defendant-husband based upon his cruel and inhuman treatment of her. The trial on the economic issues of the matrimonial action was set down for trial shortly thereafter. After several adjournments of the trial on the economics plaintiff moved to have the divorce finalized in a judgment while reserving the economic issues for future determination. Her motivation for the early entry of the judgment was, in essence, two fold. First, and foremost, she complained that her standing in her community was in limbo due to the decision on the divorce but the judgment not being entered. Second, due to the lack of judgment and in an attempt to circumvent this court, defendant commenced a proceeding in Israel. That action was dismissed but not before plaintiff was harmed by being detained in Israel.

The parties to this action are Orthodox Jews. They were married in a religious ceremony on May 8, 1966. The parties have not undergone a divorce under Jewish law. Specifically, plaintiff has not received a "Get" (document of divorce) from defendant.

Under Orthodox Jewish law the marital ties between a husband and wife are severed only once the husband gives the wife a document known as a Get. The granting of the Get is virtually solely in the control of the husband. If he refuses to deliver the Get to the wife she is not permitted to remarry within the Jewish faith. She may not even date. A woman who is caught in the position of not receiving a Get is referred to as "agunah" or "chained."

A wife who has a husband who refuses to give a Get may, under Orthodox Jewish law, attempt to have the husband summoned to a religious tribunal or Beth Din. Once at the Beth Din the tribunal can hear testimony and determine if a Get should be given. However, the tribunal itself cannot give the Get, it still must come from the husband.

Obviously, this procedure gives tremendous power to a husband in a divorce proceeding. Without the husband's consent the wife will not be free to remarry, thus he can dictate the terms of any agreement.

The disparity of power has not gone unnoticed (*See, Avitzur v. Avitzur*, 58 N.Y.2d 108, 459 N.Y.S.2d 572, 446 N.E.2d 136 *cert. den.*, 464 U.S. 817; *Perl v. Perl*,126 A.D.2d 91, 512 N.Y.S.2d 372; *Golding v. Golding*, 176 A.D.2d 20, 581 N.Y.S.2d 4 (1992)). As the Appellate Division, First Department noted in *Perl v. Perl, supra*;

The unequal allocation of power between spouses to terminate a religious marriage—particularly where the partners are of the Jewish faith—has received the attention of the courts (*Avitzur v. Avitzur*, 58 N.Y.2d 108 [459 N.Y.S.2d 572, 446 N.E.2d 136]; *Rubin v. Rubin*, 75 Misc.2d 776 [348 N.Y.S.2d 61]; *Chambers v. Chambers*, 122 Misc.2d 671 [471 N.Y.S.2d 958]); the Legislature (Domestic Relations Law § 253), and the Executive, from which it is possible to discern an articulated public policy. In 1983 the Legislature addressed this problem..., imposing a statutory duty upon any marital partner seeking a divorce to a marriage solemnized by specified religious officiants to obtain, as a condition precedent for civil severance of the marital bond, a sworn statement from the moving party that he or she has taken or will take "prior to the entry of final judgment, all steps solely within his or her power to remove any barrier to the defendant's remarriage following the annulment or divorce...." (Domestic Relations Law § 253 subd. [2][i]). In his memorandum approving the bill, the Governor wrote:

> This bill was overwhelmingly adopted by the State Legislature because it deals with a tragically unfair condition that is almost universally acknowledged.
>
> The requirement of a Get is used by unscrupulous spouses who avail themselves of our civil courts and simultaneously use *their denial of a Get vindictively or as a form of economic coercion.*
>
> Concededly this use of our civil courts unfairly imposes upon one spouse, usually the wife, enormous anguish. (McKinney's Session Laws 1983 ch. 979, 2818, 2819). (Emphasis added.)

(*Perl v. Perl*, 126 A.D.2d at 94–95, 512 N.Y.S.2d 372).

Thus, under the statute (Domestic Relations Law § 253) a spouse *seeking* a civil divorce must remove the barriers to remarriage of the other spouse. Specifically, a Jewish man who is a plaintiff must give a Get if ordered to by a Beth Din or voluntarily give a Get without a hearing before a Beth Din. If he refuses to comply with either the husband will be denied a civil divorce.

Furthermore, the courts have consistently held that a separation agreement or stipulation of settlement entered into between two parties may be subject for review for duress or overreaching. This review will include the question of whether the control over the Get was used by the husband to coerce the wife to yield to a settlement which is more beneficial to the husband *(See, Golding v. Golding, supra; Perl v. Perl, supra*). In *Golding* the trial court, after a hearing, determined that the husband exploited "the power differential between the parties, so as to completely dominate a process which should have entailed honest negotiating, the defendant engaged in 'inequitable conduct' which vitiate[s] the execution of the agreement (*Christian v. Christian*, 42 N.Y.2d [63] at 72 [396 N.Y.S.2d 817, 365 N.E.2d 849])." (*Golding v. Golding*, N.Y.L.J. 6/28/90 pg. 22.) The Appellate Division then affirmed the trial court's determination not to recognize the agreement entered into under threat of withholding the Get.

In the present case, this Court is faced with another permutation of the power of the Get. The husband herein was the defendant in the divorce action. Thus, Domestic Relations Law § 253 does not apply. Furthermore, there was no agreement. Thus, the relief of vitiating an agreement entered into under duress is not available. Rather, plaintiff-wife now claims that due to the inherent power that defendant-husband has over the granting of the Get, it would be inequitable to grant him equitable distribution while he still holds the Get. (Her claim is that once equitable distribution is granted by the secular court the power to extract more for the Get still exists.) This she asserts is inequitable. She claims that as a court of equity this court should withhold equitable relief (deny a trial on equitable distribution) until equity is done. She asserts that defendant is in fact withholding the Get.

Defendant objects to plaintiff's claims. He asserts that he is merely continuing the case which plaintiff started. He did not commence the action, thus, he should not be precluded from ending it. He is merely seeking the relief available due to plaintiff succeeding in the fault aspect of the case. Additionally, he claims that he is not holding the Get hostage. Furthermore, he warns the court that it may be treading into the quagmire of church-state relations.

ANALYSIS

It is without question that when courts must touch upon questions of religious concerns, they may not consider religious doctrine. However, the courts may use "neutral principles of law" to resolve disputes touching on religious concerns.

There is no real dispute that the enactment of the Equitable Distribution Law (Domestic Relations Law § 236[B]) did nothing to circumvent the traditional equity powers of the matrimonial bench. In fact, if anything, the statute granted more equity power to the court (the court could now look behind title to divide property). The very name of the statute implies the purpose of the statute, to do equity.

When one focuses on the actual equitable distribution portion of the statute (Domestic Relations Law § 236(B)(5)) the equity power of the court is specifically set forth. Subdivision (5)(c) states: "Marital property shall be distributed equitably between the parties, considering the circumstances of the case and of the respective parties."

Obviously, the misuse of a power differential between the parties be it a monetary differential or otherwise (*i.e.* the withholding of a Get or withholding one's appearance before a Beth Din) can be taken into account by a court in equity.

However, such a determination is a factual matter which requires a hearing. The application of the equitable distribution factors is part of the trial in chief of the matrimonial action itself. One spouse's actions in relation to a Get may be subject to review in the equitable distribution portion of a matrimonial action. Hence, those actions may be considered by the court when it equitably distributes the marital property.

The application of plaintiff herein requests that the court short circuit the regular mechanisms and deny defendant equitable relief (equitable distribution) pre-trial and solely on papers. This jump the court will not take. The court will not grant plaintiff's application to stay the trial on the economic aspects of this case until defendant gives plaintiff a Get. That request is far beyond the powers of this court. However, upon the trial of the economic issues, the parties may seek to introduce evidence concerning their actions in relation to the Get so that the court can reach an equitable decision on the distribution of property.

Accordingly, it is ordered that plaintiff's application is denied in its entirety without prejudice to raise the circumstances surrounding the Get at trial. The trial of the economic issues shall take place on the adjourned date. All previous orders of this court remain in effect.

Notes

1. As noted by the court in *Schwartz*, Section 253 of New York's Domestic Relations Act was passed to remedy the "unequal allocation of power between spouses to terminate a religious marriage—particularly where the partners are of the Jewish faith." However, section 253 is written opaquely, and makes no reference to any particular religious faith. Does this shield the act from a constitutional attack? If the purpose of the law was to prevent Orthodox and Conservative Jewish husbands from obtaining a civil divorce before removing all religious barriers to the opportunity of their spouses to marry another, does the specificity of the legislature's purpose violate the Establishment Clause? Is the statute's purpose secular because the language of the statute does not refer to Judaism, but to all barriers to remarriage, including any religious barrier? The statute defines a "barrier to remarriage" by stating that it "includes, without limitation, any religious or conscientious restraint or inhibition, of which the party required to make the verified statement is aware, that is imposed on a party to a marriage, under the principles held by the clergyman or minister who has solemnized the marriage, by reason of the other party's commission or withholding of any voluntary act." *N.Y. Domestic Relations Law*, § 253(6). Even if the law has a secular purpose, does it impermissibly "advance" religion, or excessively entangle religion and government? If it is acknowledged that the law was primarily designed to benefit (or protect) Orthodox and Conservative Jewish women, can the law withstand a review based on the *Lemon* standards? Can an argument be made that the law should not be evaluated based on *Lemon*?

2. Within four months after the court's decision in *Schwartz*, the New York legislature amended its Domestic Relations Law specifically permitting courts to consider as a factor the effect of a barrier to remarriage in determining the equitable distribution of marital property and in determining the amount and duration of maintenance.

3. In *Avitzur v. Avitzur*, 446 N.E.2d 136 (N.Y.), *cert. denied*, 464 U.S. 817 (1983), noted in *Schwartz*, the New York Court of Appeals, the state's highest court, held by a bare majority that the *ketubah*, which sets forth the obligations of a Jewish husband in Conservative Judaism, was like an arbitration agreement, and thus enforceable by reference to "neutral principles" of contract law. The court therefore ordered the husband to appear before a *beth din*, a rabbinical tribunal. *Avitzur* is the only case from a state's highest court evaluating the enforceability of an agreement compelling the husband to obtain a Get. *Avitzur* is applicable only to cases in which the parties are Conservative Jews, because the ketubah as modified is not accepted in Orthodox Judaism. *See* Edward S. Nadel, *New York's* Get *Laws: A Constitutional Analysis*, 27 Colum. J. L. & Soc. Probs. 55, 67 (1993).

4. Is the statute a permissible accommodation of religion? *Compare* Tanina Rostain, Note, *Permissible Accommodations of Religion: Reconsidering the New York Get Statute*, 96 Yale L.J. 1147 (1987) *with* Nadel, *New York's* Get *Laws*.

5. Section 253 applies only if the couple was married in a religious ceremony. The law also prohibits entry of a final judgment of divorce or annulment until the plaintiff has filed a statement that he or she has "taken all steps solely within his or her power to remove all barriers to the defendant's remarriage following the annulment or divorce" or the defendant-spouse waives this protection. Additionally, even if the plaintiff has filed this statement, the court may not enter a final judgment "if the clergyman or minister who has solemnized the marriage certifies, in a sworn statement, that he or she has solemnized the marriage and that, to his or her knowledge, the plaintiff has failed to take all steps solely within his or her power to remove all barriers to the defendant's remarriage following the annulment or divorce." Lastly, the law prohibits courts from as-

sessing "any ecclesiastical or religious issue," or the "truth of any statement submitted pursuant to this section."

6. Lower New York courts have regularly applied the provisions of the law. In *Megibow v. Megibow*, 612 N.Y.S.2d 758 (N.Y. Sup. Ct. 1994), the trial court ordered the plaintiff-husband to obtain a Get despite the husband's claim that Reform Judaism does not require a get for the wife to remarry, as long as "defendant perceived herself to require a Get in order to remarry." *Id.* at 760. The New York Appellate Division has upheld a contempt citation, including a term of imprisonment, for refusing to obtain a Get. *Kaplinsky v. Kaplinsky*, 198 A.D.2d 212, 603 N.Y.S.2d 574 (1993). The New York Court of Appeals, however, has not decided the constitutionality of the statute.

7. In *Perl v. Perl*, 126 A.D.2d 91, 512 N.Y.S.2d 372 (1987), a husband and wife divorced before the passage of the statute. To receive the Get from her ex-husband, the ex-wife, an Orthodox Jew, signed several notes agreeing to pay monthly sums to the husband. The husband delivered the Get, and the wife later dishonored a check in partial payment on the note. In defending her refusal to pay, the wife claimed coercion and duress. The Appellate Division reversed a summary judgment awarded the ex-husband, relying in part on the justifications given for the passage of Section 253 of the Domestic Relations Law. The court refused, however, to find a claim for intentional infliction of emotional distress based on the husband's actions, because "[t]o hold otherwise would fasten the risk of liability in tort upon any spouse who refused to furnish a Get, upon religious grounds in whole or in part, and thereby entangle the courts in an exploration of both the validity and sincerity of a position grounded in ecclesiastical law." *Id.* at 376.

8. In *Persad v. Balram*, 187 Misc.2d 711, 724 N.Y.S.2d 560 (Sup. Ct. 2001), the issue was whether the parties were married under New York law. The parties had undertaken an exchange of wedding vows in an "austere ritual of the Hindu faith" by a pandit, a Hindu priest. However, the pandit was not registered with the City as someone who could solemnize marriages, and the parties had failed to obtain a marriage license, both requirements under New York law. The court held that, despite these omissions, the strong presumption in favor of marriage, and the constitutional right of parties to marry "in accordance with the dictates of [their] faith," the marriage was valid. *See also Ansellem v. Ansellem*, 189 Misc. 2d 27, 730 N.Y.S.2d 212 (Sup. Ct. 2001) (holding that marriage valid, despite fact that marriage, which occurred in France, was officiated by rabbi who could be criminally prosecuted for performing religious ceremony before civil ceremony).

Chapter 12

Religion in the Courtroom

A. Introduction

Issues of religious faith have always pervaded the American courtroom. During the first several decades of the nineteenth century, courts ruled that because a witness was required to tell the truth, and because a person who did not believe in a future state of rewards and punishments was thereby not constrained by his religious faith to tell the truth, an unbeliever was incompetent to testify. Although atheists and agnostics were shortly thereafter deemed competent witnesses, courts through the end of the nineteenth century permitted a party to argue that a witness's lack of religious belief affected the unbeliever's credibility as a truth-telling witness. Both of these rules were predicated on the belief that truth-telling is closely related to religious belief. In our more secular age, rules of evidence and procedure are written without regard to religious belief. The primary reason for this change is the severing of the connection of truth-telling and religious belief, although a part is a function of the First Amendment quest for governmental neutrality regarding religious matters. Although the two issues above no longer exist, other issues remain. The Sixth Amendment, which now applies to both federal and state prosecutions, guarantees a criminal defendant the right to an impartial jury. In our adversarial system, impartiality is created by permitting each side to engage in partial actions. The most partial action is the peremptory challenge, in which each side is permitted, without justifying the decision based on some articulable reason, to strike several members of the jury venire. Recently, however, the Supreme Court has held that a peremptory challenge violates the Constitution if the reason for the peremptory challenge is based on the race or gender of the prospective juror. One undecided question under federal law is whether attorneys can justify decisions striking venire members based on the religious faith of a prospective jurors. *See* Section 2(B) below. *See also,* Utah Const. art. I, § 4 (2001) ("no religious test shall be required as a qualification for any office of public trust or for any vote at any election; nor shall any person be incompetent as a witness or juror on account of religious belief or the absence thereof."). *See generally* Chapter Five § J(2) (discussing equal protection rules governing peremptory challenges to jurors); and Chapter Five § F and Eight § G (discussing the No Religious Test Clause of Article VI cl. 3). Once the jury renders its verdict, can that verdict be challenged by testimony that deliberations were affected by a juror's claim to insights regarding the defendant's guilt based on the juror's religious faith? To what extent may judges rely on religious beliefs in rendering decisions? Can a lawyer use religious references in a closing argument in order to persuade the jury? Can a lawyer for a party wear religious garb or symbols? Are witnesses or parties required to shed their outward manifestations of religious belief in court? Does the answer depend on the reason given for the wearing of the religious garb or symbol?

If the purpose of the rules of evidence is to aid the search for the truth, what justification is there for prohibiting the disclosure of communications between a member of the clergy and a "penitent"? Is the fact that the communication was made in confidence sufficient to prohibit disclosure? Does the clergy-penitent privilege exist as a consequence of the First Amendment? If not, does it exist at the sufferance of the legislature?

Should other rules of evidence or courtroom conduct be based without regard to religion, or must such rules be adjusted in light of the particular issues of religion that might arise?

When Congress adopted the Federal Rules of Evidence, it adopted two rules regarding the relation of the witness and the witness's religious beliefs. Federal Rule of Evidence 603 states: "Before testifying, every witness shall be required to declare that he will testify truthfully, by oath or affirmation administered in a form calculated to awaken his conscience and impress his mind with his duty to do so." As in the early nineteenth century, witnesses are offered the option of swearing an oath or affirming. Unlike the early requirements, a witness is not required to prove she is a Quaker in order to affirm, nor that she is religious. Religious belief is no longer a condition required of all prospective witnesses. As stated in the *Advisory Committee's Note* to Rule 603, "The rule is designed to afford the flexibility required in dealing with religious adults, atheists, conscientious objectors, mental defectives, and children."

The second rule, Federal Rule of Evidence 610, bars efforts to attack or bolster a witness's credibility based on the witness's religious beliefs: "Evidence of the beliefs or opinions of a witness on matters of religion is not admissible for the purpose of showing that by reason of their nature his credibility is impaired or enhanced." This ban, of course, does not completely bar evidence of the witness's religious beliefs: "While the rule forecloses inquiry into the religious beliefs or opinions of a witness for the purpose of showing that his character for truthfulness is affected by their nature, an inquiry for the purpose of showing interest or bias because of them is not within the prohibition." *Advisory Committee's Note*, Fed. R. Evid. 610.

As might be expected, these rules have not ended all disputes concerning the admissibility of evidence concerning a witness's religious beliefs.

United States v. Kalaydjian

784 F.2d 53 (2d Cir. 1986)

TIMBERS, Circuit Judge:

Appellants Bedros Kalaydjian and Akram Hayat appeal from judgments of conviction entered June 25, 1985 after a jury trial.

Kalaydjian was convicted of conspiracy to possess heroin with intent to distribute (Count I), and attempted possession of heroin with intent to distribute (Count III), in violation of 21 U.S.C. §§ 846, 841 (1982). He was sentenced to two concurrent three-year terms of imprisonment and to a special parole term of five years.

We find that the principal claim of error raised on appeal is appellants' joint claim that the district court erred in refusing to permit counsel to cross-examine a government witness regarding the witness's reasons for deciding to affirm rather than to swear on the Koran. We affirm.

At trial, Karim and Ahmad testified for the government against both appellants. Prior to their testimony, however, counsel for both appellants jointly requested that Ahmad and Karim be sworn on the Koran rather than the Bible. Defense counsel argued that, since both witnesses were Muslims, swearing on the Koran might guarantee truthful answers. Although the government did not object to this request, it did point out that every witness has the right to affirm rather than to swear on the Bible, pursuant to Fed. R. Evid. 603.

Thereafter, Ahmad's counsel informed the court that Ahmad wished to affirm rather than to swear. Defense counsel did not object to Ahmad's election to affirm. Nor did defense counsel request the district court to hold a voir dire outside the presence of the jury to determine if Ahmad was impressed with his duty to testify truthfully. Having failed to object to Ahmad's affirmation at trial and having failed to afford the district court the opportunity to determine if Ahmad understood his duty to tell the truth, appellant is foreclosed on appeal from claiming that Ahmad's affirmation was a sham. Defense counsel did, however, request permission to cross-examine Ahmad regarding his reasons for refusing to swear, in order to cast doubt on his credibility as a witness. After hearing argument from defense counsel, Ahmad's counsel and the government, the district court ruled that the requested cross-examination was precluded by Fed. R. Evid. 610.

Prior to Karim's testimony, the court asked Karim whether he wished to swear or affirm. Although Karim elected to swear, his oath was more in the form of an affirmation. The court did not require his oath to be taken on the Koran. Pursuant to Fed. R. Evid. 610, the court denied the request of Hayat's counsel to cross-examine Karim regarding his reasons for not swearing on the Koran.

With these facts in mind, we turn to the principal claim of error raised, namely, the correctness of the district court's ruling which precluded defense counsel from cross-examining government witnesses concerning their decision to affirm rather than to swear on the Koran.

Appellants argue that Rule 610 does not prohibit the requested cross-examination because Rule 610 excludes evidence of religious beliefs only, not of conduct resulting from religious beliefs. In essence, appellants contend that, although Rule 610 forecloses a party from undermining a witness's credibility based on the witness's religious beliefs, it does not foreclose a party from challenging a witness's credibility based on the witness's refusal to perform a religious act, *i.e.*, the witness's refusal to swear on his religion's Bible or its counterpart.

We reject appellants' attempt to distinguish between cross-examining a witness regarding his religious beliefs, and cross-examining him regarding conduct that is significant only because of the witness's religious beliefs. Appellants cite no authority to support their novel claim that evidence of conduct resulting from religious beliefs is admissible under Rule 610. Moreover, an analysis of appellants' reasoning demonstrates that their position is untenable.

Appellants desired to cross-examine Ahmad regarding his reasons for refusing to swear on the Koran in order to raise the following inference: if a man is religious, he will be willing to swear on his religion's Bible, but if he refuses to swear, his testimony will be untrustworthy. Appellants could not have established that inference successfully unless the district court had allowed them to inquire into the sincerity and genuineness of Ahmad's Muslim beliefs. Indeed, unless appellants were permitted to prove to the jury that Ahmad was a devout Muslim who believed deeply in the Koran, Ahmad's act of refusing to swear on the Koran would have been meaningless to the jury.

The district court correctly held that Rule 610 squarely prohibited any inquiry into the firmness of Ahmad's religious beliefs. The court's ruling was correct because of the possible prejudicial effect that disclosure of such information might have had on the jury. Indeed, in defining the purpose of Rule 610, the District of Columbia Circuit has stated that "[t]he purpose of the rule is to guard against the prejudice which may result from disclosure of a witness's faith." *United States v. Sampol*, 636 F.2d 621, 666 (D.C. Cir. 1980); *see Contemporary Mission, Inc. v. Bonded Mailings, Inc.*, 671 F.2d 81, 84 (2 Cir. 1982) (inquiry into genuineness of witness's church affiliation properly excluded by trial court because of potential prejudicial effect). Moreover, extensive questioning on the collateral issue of Ahmad's religious beliefs might have confused the jury and distracted its attention from the principal tasks of determining whether appellants had conspired to deal in heroin.

Since Ahmad's act of refusing to swear on the Koran is significant only when considered against the backdrop of his Muslim faith, we hold that the district court properly denied the requested cross-examination pursuant to Rule 610. We see no difference between challenging a witness's credibility by cross-examining him regarding his religious beliefs, and challenging the witness's credibility by cross-examining him regarding an act that is meaningful only when considered in relation to the firmness of the witness's religious beliefs. Both forms of cross-examination require inquiry into the nature of the witness's religious beliefs. As such they are prohibited by Rule 610. Finally, we note that a witness's right to affirm, rather than to swear, as provided by Fed. R. Evid. 603, would be meaningless if a witness, after exercising his right to affirm, could be cross-examined regarding the reasons underlying that decision.

We have carefully considered all claims of error raised by appellants and find all are without merit.

Affirmed.

Notes

1. The court's conclusion that Rule 610 bars the inquiry requested by defense counsel follows the language and purpose of the rule. Does this decision nonetheless appear troublesome in the context of the case? Would the court's decision be less defensible had the defendants requested a hearing outside the jury's presence concerning the reasons why the witnesses chose not to swear on the Koran? If granted, would such a hearing violate the Free Exercise rights of the witnesses?

The jury observes the witness's affirmation or oathtaking in order to evaluate the degree to which the witness accepts his or her duty to tell the truth. Does the jury receive a signal concerning a witness's acceptance of that duty if the manner in which the oath is taken differs among witnesses? If so, what kind of signal is received, and is that receipt of that signal constitutionally proper?

Courts addressing this issue have followed strictly the rule separating religious belief from assessment of credibility. *See People v. Hall*, 215 N.W.2d 166 (Mich. 1974) (holding prosecutor's questions of defendant concerning his lack of religious beliefs as suggesting inability to testify truthfully error); *State v. Thomas*, 636 P.2d 1214 (Ariz. 1981) (declaring fundamental error statements by prosecutor in opening statement, closing argument and in questioning that victim's religious beliefs made her a believable witness). *See also People v. Wood*, 488 N.E.2d 86, 497 N.Y.S.2d 340 (1985) (holding prosecutor's cross-examination of defendant's expert concerning expert's decision to affirm rather than swear an oath reversible error).

2. The Advisory Committee's Note to Rule 610 states in part, "[D]isclosure of affiliation with a church which is a party to the litigation would be allowable under the rule." Should this be extended to cross-examination in cases in which one party is a member of a church, and favorable testimony is adduced on direct examination of a fellow church member? *See United States v. Abel*, 469 U.S. 45 (1984) (holding admissible impeachment testimony indicating that defendant and defense witness belonged to a "secret type of prison organization" that required members to deny organization's existence and to lie for one another). What about a converse case, in which unfavorable testimony is adduced from a witness whose religious beliefs are antithetical to the religious beliefs of the party against whom the testimony is offered?

3. Can a witness be asked whether he ever "made an oath rejecting the power of God and Christ and accepting Satan as omnipotent?" *See State v. Zobel*, 222 N.W.2d 570, 572 (Neb. 1974) (allowing question to show a lack of character for truth or veracity). In *Zobel*, the witness, an undercover agent testifying for the state of Nebraska, denied making this oath. Although the Nebraska Supreme Court held this question relevant, it forbade the introduction by the defense of testimony from another witness offered to impeach the undercover agent, for "[t]he witness' alleged activities in the cult of Satan were clearly collateral" to the issue whether the witness-agent was telling the truth. *Id.* at 572–73. If the defense offered the testimony of another witness that the undercover agent had sworn this oath in the second witness's presence, should the court have admitted that testimony, or would that also be collateral to the material issue of the agent's truthfulness? Is the court disingenuous in differentiating between the witness's conduct and the witness's ability to tell the truth? Is this another rigid demarcation of a boundary between belief and conduct? Is this inquiry permissible under the language of Rule 610?

4. Under what circumstances should a prosecutor be permitted to raise the issue of the defendant's involvement in or knowledge of satanism or witchcraft? In *State v. Kimbrell*, 360 S.E.2d 691 (N.C. 1987), the defendant was charged as an accessory before the fact of murder. After his arrest, Kimbrell gave investigators a statement concerning his knowledge of and participation in "black magic" activities with a group that included the murder victim and others. Kimbrell testified at trial, and the State's cross-examination of him was based, in part, upon his prior statement. The court held admission of this evidence was prejudicial error. Courts have permitted the state to offer evidence of the defendant's involvement to prove the identity of the accused. *See State v. Bartnick*, 436 N.W.2d 647 (Iowa App. 1988) (holding admissible letter referring to satanism written by accused confessing to crime to show identity); *State v. Waterhouse*, 513 A.2d 862 (Me. 1986) (holding evidence of defendant's belief in satanism admissible to prove killer's identity and intent). On the admissibility of evidence of a criminally accused's involvement with witchcraft or satanism, see George L. Blum, Annot., *Admissibility and Prejudicial Effect of Evidence in Criminal Prosecution, of Defendant's Involvement with Witchcraft, Satanism, or the Like*, 18 A.L.R. 5th 804 (1994).

B. Juries and Religion

1. Introduction

Should those who refuse for religious reasons to sit as jurors be constitutionally excused from serving? Should an attorney be permitted to strike a juror based on the attorney's perception that the juror's religious beliefs will make the juror "partial?" Is a lawyer permitted to ask prospective jury members questions about their religious faith in order to reach a decision regarding the impartiality of those venire members? To what extent can the members of the jury rely on their religious beliefs in reaching a verdict? Are such verdicts impeachable by the party against whom the jury finds?

In an early religious liberty case, *United States v. Hillyard*, 52 F. Supp. 612 (D. Wash. 1943), the court refused to hold in contempt a Jehovah's Witness who refused to serve as a juror. Relying on the views of Madison and Jefferson, the court concluded:

> I feel constrained to resolve the very considerable doubt in my mind in favor of the defendant. While I cannot understand defendant's reasoning and cannot accept his conclusion, I must admit that his refusal to serve does not amount to a breaking out "into overt acts against peace and good order."

Id. at 615.

2. Jury Service and Religion

Recall from Chapter Three the case of *State v. Willson*, 13 S.C.L. (2 McCord) 393 (S.C.1823), in which the South Carolina Supreme Court held that a religious group known as Covenanters enjoyed no constitutional right to be exempt from jury service. Shortly after deciding *Sherbert v. Verner*, 374 U.S. 398 (1963), the Supreme Court, based on its holding in *Sherbert*, vacated a judgment of the Supreme Court of Minnesota holding Mrs. Owen Jenison in contempt of court for refusing on religious grounds to serve as a juror. *In re Jenison*, 375 U.S. 14 (1963), *vacating and remanding In re Jenison*, 265 Minn. 96, 120 N.W.2d 515 (1963). On remand, the Minnesota court held that a person whose religious beliefs prohibited jury service was constitutionally exempt from jury service. *In re Jenison*, 267 Minn. 136, 125 N.W.2d 588 (1963).

In *People v. Wilson*, 678 P.2d 1024 (Colo. App. 1983), *cert. denied*, 469 U.S. 843 (1984), the defendant, a voodoo priest, was charged with sexual assault of a child. One of the prospective jurors was a "minister of a fundamentalist Christian church." The trial court refused to dismiss the juror for cause after the juror testified that he had "no religious or moral scruples about the case," that he "could separate issues of religion from issues of law," and that he was prepared to "render an impartial opinion." *Id.* at 1027. The defendant then used one of its peremptory challenges to dismiss the juror, and after conviction, alleged the trial court's refusal to dismiss for cause the minister was error. The appellate court affirmed.

Two state courts have held that a criminal defendant was not denied his constitutional rights based on the absence of Amish jurors from the jury list. In *Taylor v. State*, 260 Ind. 264, 295 N.E.2d 600, *cert. denied*, 414 U.S. 1012 (1973), the Indiana Supreme Court determined that the selection of jurors from voting registration lists did not show an intentional and systematic governmental exclusion of Amish citizens from the jury array, although only 5% of the adult Amish in the county were thereby listed in the roll for prospective jurors. The court additionally noted that the defendant was not Amish, and consequently lacked standing to challenge the jury array. The dissent asserted that there was no conflict between First and Sixth Amendment rights in this case, because the defendant only challenged the exclusion of Amish from jury lists, and therefore the existence or extent of a First Amendment right of exclusion from jury service based on the Free Exercise Clause was not implicated. Further, the dissent stated that membership in the group was not necessary to create standing to challenge the jury array. In an unreported case, *State v. Fulton*, 1989 Westlaw 162169 (Ohio App.), the defendant challenged the actions of the jury commissioner for Holmes County, Ohio, who systematically excluded from the jury list any person who was a member of the Old Order Amish faith. It was the commissioner's understanding, later confirmed by expert religious testimony, that the Amish were forbidden by their religious beliefs to serve on a jury. In declining to overturn his conviction, the court of appeals held that the defendant, because he was not Amish, had no standing to challenge the exclusion of Amish from the jury list, and further concluded that the Amish were not a "distinctive" group in the community whose exclusion would result in a denial of the defendant's right to have a jury chosen from a fair cross-section of the community.

These decisions, however, may not survive the reasoning of the Court's new peremptory challenge jurisprudence. In *J.E.B. v. Alabama* ex rel. *T.B.*, 511 U.S. 127 (1994), the Court held unconstitutional the state's use of peremptory challenges excluding men from the jury in a paternity suit. Following *Batson v. Kentucky*, 476 U.S. 79 (1986) (holding unconstitutional use of peremptory challenges to strike prospective jurors on the basis of race by prosecutor in a criminal case in which defendant and prospective jurors were of the same race), *Powers v. Ohio*, 499 U.S. 400 (1991) (holding unconstitutional use of peremptory challenges by state based on race even when defendant and prospective jurors were of a different race), *Edmonson v. Leesville Concrete Co.*, 500 U.S. 614 (1991) (applying *Batson* to civil cases) and *Georgia v. McCollum*, 505 U.S. 42 (1992) (holding a criminal defendant a state actor when exercising peremptory challenges, thus making defendant's peremptory challenges subject to judicial review), the Court refused to accept a generalized suggestion that men would perceive a paternity case differently from women. Although the Court extended *Batson* to peremptory challenges based on gender, it did not forbid the exercise of the peremptory challenge. *J.E.B.*, 511 U.S. at 143. In dissent, Justice Scalia claimed that the *Batson* principle "presumably would include religious belief." *Id.* at 161. In the following case, decided before the Supreme Court decided *J.E.B.*, the Supreme Court of Minnesota declined to extend *Batson* to peremptory challenges made for reasons of the prospective juror's religious faith.

State v. Davis

504 N.W.2d 767 (Minn. 1993), *cert. denied*, 511 U.S. 1115 (1994)

SIMONETT, Justice.

The issue in this case is whether the holding of *Batson v. Kentucky*, 476 U.S. 79 (1986), should be extended to peremptory strikes on the basis of religion. In an unpublished opinion, the court of appeals concluded that because the peremptory strike was based on race-neutral grounds there was no equal protection violation, and, after reviewing the other claims of error, affirmed the defendant's conviction. We granted further review on the peremptory challenge issue and now affirm.

Defendant Edward Lee Davis, an African-American, was charged with aggravated robbery. No jurors were struck for cause during the jury selection. The defense, however, exercised four of its five peremptory strikes, while the State used one of its three. When the State used the one peremptory to strike a black man from the jury panel, defense counsel objected and asked for a race-neutral explanation.

The prosecutor, in response, stated for the record that the prospective juror would have been a very good juror for the State and that race had nothing to do with her decision to strike. She explained: "However it was highly significant to the State... that the man was a Jahovah [sic] Witness. I have a great deal of familiarity with the sect of Jahovah's Witness. I would never, if I had a preemptory [sic] challenge left, strike [—] or fail to strike a Jahovah Witness from my jury." She went on: "In my experience... that faith is very integral to their daily life in many ways, many Christians are not. That was re-enforced at least three times a week he goes to church for separate meetings. The Jahovah Witness faith is of a mind the higher powers will take care of all things necessary. In my experience Jahovah Witness are reluctant to exercise authority over their fellow human beings in this Court House."

The prosecutor concluded her statement by saying she did not feel it appropriate "to further pry" into this matter with the juror because there was no need to when exercising a peremptory on race-neutral grounds. Defense counsel had nothing further to add, and the trial judge ruled the peremptory strike would stand.

There is no transcript of the voir dire, nor do we know the composition of the jury that was selected. In any event, the defendant concedes the State's peremptory was exercised for race-neutral reasons, but now contends that the race-neutral explanation offered by the State is constitutionally impermissible as religious discrimination.

If the life of the law were logic rather than experience, *Batson* might well be extended to include religious bias and, for that matter, an endless number of other biases. The question, however, is whether the peremptory strike has been purposefully employed to perpetrate religious bigotry to the extent that the institutional integrity of the jury has been impaired, and thus requiring further modification of the traditional peremptory challenge.

We begin our analysis with a closer look at the role of the peremptory. While jurors have their individual preconceived notions and prejudices, it is assumed that they can set them aside so as to be fair and impartial. The purpose of voir dire is to test that assumption. If it is made to appear that a prospective juror cannot be fair, the juror may be challenged for cause. The peremptory is needed, however, if the challenge for cause is denied by the court. It is needed also when there is legitimate concern for a juror's fairness but this concern is insufficient to be a challenge for cause. It happens often enough that a juror expresses doubt about being able to be fair, but then opposing counsel or the judge ostensibly "rehabilitates" the juror; in this problematic situation, the peremptory is useful. Also, without the peremptory, trial counsel may be deterred from asking probing questions on voir dire for concern that any hostility inadvertently raised could not be remedied by a peremptory strike.

In other words, the peremptory gives added assurance of an accurate verdict by "resolv[ing] doubts (up to a specified number) in favor of exclusion." Barbara Underwood, *Ending Race Discrimination in Jury Selection: Whose Right Is It, Anyway?*, 92 Colum. L. Rev. 725, 771 (1992). The fact that some unbiased jurors may be excused in the process is an affordable price to pay for removing doubts about a particular juror's impartiality and competence, especially when the vote of one biased juror can make a critical difference.

The randomness built into the jury pool to obtain a cross-section can seem, to the apprehensive litigant, to be arbitrary and unfair, leaving the litigant to the "luck of the draw." The peremptory alleviates this apprehensiveness by allowing the parties to exercise their own intuitive judgment with respect to perceived juror bias.

It is against this background then that we consider extending the *Batson* challenge to religion. As we have noted, *Batson* is directed at the use of peremptories for purposeful race discrimination. "The reality of practice, amply reflected in many state- and federal-court opinions, shows that the challenge may be, and unfortunately at times has been, used to discriminate against black jurors." [*Batson,*] at 99. And Justice Marshall, concurring, pointed out, "Misuse of the peremptory challenge to exclude black jurors has become both common and flagrant." *Id.* at 103. Because of these serious and well-documented conditions, the United States Supreme Court has ruled that a party exercising a peremptory which is *prima facie* race-oriented should be called to account.

The use of the peremptory strike to discriminate purposefully on the basis of religion does not, however, appear to be common and flagrant. We are not aware the peremptory is being so misused, nor does the defendant make any such claim. No such problem is documented in appellate court decisions.[3] This is not to say that religious intolerance does not exist in our society, but only to say that there is no indication that irrational religious bias so pervades the peremptory challenge as to undermine the integrity of the jury system.

Then, too, the nature of the bias sought to be eliminated by a *Batson* challenge is particularly illusive in the case of religion. Presumably, the bias sought to be eliminated in jury deliberations is intolerance for the doctrinal beliefs and practices of the adherents of a particular religious group. Yet when religious beliefs translate into judgments on the merits of the cause to be judged, it is difficult to distinguish, in challenging a juror, between an impermissible bias on the basis of religious affiliation and a permissible religion-neutral explanation. In the case before us, for example, would the explanation that the juror was "reluctant to exercise authority over their fellow human beings" be sufficient to overcome a prima facie case of religious bias? A juror's religious beliefs are inviolate, but when they are the basis for a person's moral values and produce societal views on such matters as the use of intoxicating liquor, cohabitation, necessity of medical treatment, civil disobedience, and the like, it would not seem that a peremptory strike based on these societal views should be attributed to a pernicious religious bias.

Furthermore, religious affiliation (or lack thereof) is not as self-evident as race or gender. Consequently, for every peremptory strike, opposing counsel could demand a religion-neutral explanation. This would unduly complicate voir dire and be excessively intrusive for the end sought to be achieved.

---

3. In People v. Wheeler, 22 Cal.3d 258, 148 Cal.Rptr. 890, 583 P.2d 748, 761–62 (1978); Commonwealth v. Soares, 377 Mass. 461, 387 N.E.2d 499, 516 (1979), cert. denied, 444 U.S. 881 (1979); and State v. Gilmore, 103 N.J. 508, 511 A.2d 1150, 1159 (1986), state supreme courts barred the use of peremptories based on group bias for race, sex, religion, or national origin. All of these cases, however, dealt specifically with racial bias and no evidence of group bias with respect to religious affiliation in jury selection was presented or suggested. Instead, the cases, all decided before *Batson*, were decided on the "fair cross-section" theory applied to petit juries, a theory since rejected by the United States Supreme Court in *Holland v. Illinois*, 493 U.S. 474 (1990). There is authority that the religious beliefs of a juror may provide a race-neutral reason for a *Batson* challenge. *E.g., United States v. Clemmons*, 892 F.2d 1153, 1157 (3rd Cir.1989), *cert. denied*, 496 U.S. 927 (1990); *People v. Malone*, 211 Ill.App.3d 628, 156 Ill.Dec. 108, 112–13, 570 N.E.2d 584, 588–89 (Ill.App.Ct.1991), *appeal denied*, 142 Ill.2d 660, 164 Ill.Dec. 923, 584 N.E.2d 135 (1991).

Because religious bigotry in the use of the peremptory challenge is not as prevalent, or flagrant, or historically ingrained in the jury selection process as is race, we conclude that neither the federal nor our state constitution requires an extension of *Batson*. To extend *Batson* would complicate and erode the peremptory challenge procedure unnecessarily, and it would not serve to remedy any long-standing injustice perpetrated by the court system against specific individuals and classes, as *Batson* clearly does. We decline, therefore, to extend *Batson* to religious affiliation.

It is the "painful social reality" of racial discrimination which acts in a special, institutional sense to implicate the Equal Protection Clause. This implication is lacking for religious affiliation.

Here the prosecutor announced a presumed group bias. She said she would strike not just this juror but any Jehovah's Witness. But defendant's challenge was only to racial bias. The prosecutor was not advised the State was being charged with religious bias, if, indeed, that charge was being made, which is not at all clear.

If the prosecutor had said no more than she was striking the black juror because he was a Jehovah's Witness, we think this would not have rebutted the prima facie case of racial bias, anymore than if the prosecutor had said she was striking because the black juror was a Lutheran, a Baptist, or a Muslim. In fact, however, the prosecutor went on to explain the reason for her challenge, pointing out Jehovah's Witnesses, as a group, were reluctant to exercise civil authority over other people and that the juror was a devoted member of that religious group.

Ordinarily at common law, inquiry on voir dire into a juror's religious affiliation and beliefs is irrelevant and prejudicial, and to ask such questions is improper. Questions about religious beliefs are relevant only if pertinent to religious issues involved in the case, or if a religious organization is a party, or if the information is a necessary predicate for a voir dire challenge. *Coleman v. United States*, 379 A.2d 951, 954 (D.C.1977). *See, e.g., United States v. Schullo*, 390 F.Supp. 1067 (D.Minn.1975) (Devitt, J.) (in an illegal gambling case, jurors asked by court if they had any moral or religious feelings about gambling so that they could not be fair and impartial). The trial court, in the exercise of its discretion, controls the questions that can be asked to keep the voir dire within relevant bounds. In this case, we do not know how the juror's religious affiliation came to light, but proper questioning for a challenge should be limited to asking jurors if they knew of any reason why they could not sit, if they would have any difficulty in following the law as given by the court, or if they would have any difficulty in sitting in judgment.

Affirmed.

WAHL, GARDEBRING and PAGE, JJ., dissent.

WAHL, Justice (dissenting).

I respectfully dissent.

We deal here not with whether direct voir dire inquiry into religious affiliation of individual jurors ought generally to be allowed. I agree with the majority that such inquiry generally, although not necessarily always, is improper.

Rather, we deal with whether the Constitution allows purposeful discrimination in jury selection on the basis of religious affiliation. The majority, alluding to Justice Holmes' famous aphorism, says that if the life of the law were logic rather than experience, then it might follow from *Batson v. Kentucky*, 476 U.S. 79 (1986), and subsequent cases, that the Constitution does not allow purposeful discrimination in jury selection on the basis of religious affiliation. In my view, the dilemma between logic and experience posed by the majority is a false one in this case. In any event, the very words used by the United States Supreme Court in several of its relevant decisions support my conclusion that the Constitution does not allow purposeful discrimination in jury selection on the basis of religious affiliation.

In *Ristaino v. Ross*, 424 U.S. 589 (1976), the Court held that the Constitution does not require that *voir dire* inquiry into racial prejudice by individual jurors generally be allowed. The *Ristaino* Court also said:

> At least where crimes of violence are involved, [defendant] would require defense motions for voir dire on racial prejudice to be granted in any case where the defendant was of a different race from the victim. He would require a similar result whenever any defendant sought voir dire on racial prejudice because of the race of his own or adverse witnesses. *We note that such a per se rule could not, in principle, be limited to cases involving possible racial prejudice. It would apply with equal force whenever voir dire questioning about ethnic origins was sought, and its logic could encompass questions concerning other factors, such as religious affiliation or national origin.* In our heterogenous society policy as well as constitutional considerations militate against the divisive assumption—as a per se rule—that justice in a court of law may turn upon the pigmentation of skin, the accident of birth, or the choice of religion.

Id. at 596 n. 8 (citations omitted) (emphasis added). This suggests to me that the Court might hold that the Constitution does not require that voir dire inquiry into religious affiliation of individual jurors generally be allowed but that the Constitution also does not allow purposeful discrimination in jury selection on the basis of religious affiliation, since religious classifications, like racial ones, are subject to strict scrutiny.

As I said at the outset, I agree with the majority that inquiry on voir dire into religious affiliation of individual jurors generally is improper. Ordinarily there is no basis for such inquiry. The preclusion of such inquiry in no way precludes counsel from asking other questions designed to uncover flaws in individual jurors that would render them unsuitable for jury service in a particular case.

In this case, however, the prosecutor in fact learned of the juror's religious affiliation and, for whatever reasons, expressly stated that the reason for striking the juror was the juror's religious affiliation, without any voir dire of the man as to whether that religious affiliation would interfere with his ability to be a fair juror and responsibly exercise his duties as a juror. When the record of discrimination on the basis of religious affiliation is so stark, this court ought to act. I would extend the holding of *Batson v. Kentucky* to peremptory strikes based on religious affiliation and grant the defendant a new trial.

PAGE, Justice (dissenting).

[Opinion omitted].

Notes

1. Shortly after *J.E.B.* was decided, the Court denied certiorari in *Davis.* 511 U.S. 1115 (1994). Justice Thomas, joined by Justice Scalia, dissented from the denial of certiorari,. He wrote: "[G]iven the Court's rationale in *J.E.B.*, no principled reason immediately appears for declining to apply *Batson* to any strike based on a classification that is accorded heightened scrutiny under the Equal Protection Clause." *Id.* at 1117. Is Jus-

tice Thomas right? Most anti-discrimination statutes, including the Civil Rights Act of 1964, are written to prohibit discrimination on the basis of race, gender (or sex) and religion, among other forms of discrimination. If those three categories are grouped together for purposes of enforcing civil rights, why did the Court deny the petition for a writ of *certiorari* in *Davis*? Is it something about religion that led the Court to deny the petition in *Davis* rather than vacating the judgment in light of the reasoning in *J.E.B.*? Justice Ginsburg wrote a short opinion concurring in the denial of the petition for writ of certiorari, complaining that the dissent's "portrayal of the opinion of the Minnesota Supreme Court is incomplete." *Id.* at 1115. The dissent, in her opinion, failed to note that the Minnesota Supreme Court concluded that religion is not as self-evident as race and that inquiries during voir dire of a witness's religious beliefs are ordinarily impermissible. *Id.* at 1115–16. Are those sufficient reasons to distinguish *Davis* from both *Batson* and *J.E.B.*?

2. In late 1994, the Texas Court of Criminal Appeals, the highest court of the state on issues of criminal law, explicitly disagreed with the decision in *Davis* and held that *Batson* should apply to peremptory challenges made for reasons of religion as well as race. *Casarez v. State*, 913 S.W.2d 468 (Tex. Crim. App. 1994). The opinion, however, remained unpublished for a year. At that time, after reconsideration, the court, in a 5–4 vote, reversed itself. *Casarez v. State*, 913 S.W.2d 492 (Tex. Crim. App. 1995). Several state courts have held peremptory challenges made for reasons of religion violate their state constitutions. *See Casarez*, 913 S.W.2d at 506 n.17 (Baird, J., dissenting) (collecting cases). *See also Thorson v. State*, 721 So.2d 590 (Miss. 1998) (holding peremptory challenges based on religion violate Mississippi constitution). A survey of the issues is found in Benjamin Hoorn Barton, Note, *Religion-Based Peremptory Challenges After* Batson v. Kentucky *and* J.E.B. v. Alabama*: An Equal Protection and First Amendment Analysis*, 94 Mich. L. Rev. 191 (1995). *See also* Caroline R. Krivacka and Paul D. Krivacka, Annot., *Use of Peremptory Challenges to Exclude Persons From Criminal Jury Based on Religious Affiliation—Post-*Batson *State Cases*, 63 A.L.R.5th 375 (1998).

3. Several state courts have distinguished between peremptory strikes based on religious affiliation and peremptory strikes based on religion that may be relevant to the prospective jurors duties. Several of these cases involve Jehovah's Witnesses, as was the case in *Davis. See, e.g., State v. Eason,* 336 N.C. 730, 445 S.E.2d 917 (1994)(holding that exclusion of Jehovah's Witness on the sole basis of religion would violate the state constitution, but that exclusion based on how juror's religious beliefs might affect ability to follow the law was permissible); *People v. Martin*, 64 Cal. App.4th 378, 75 Cal. Rptr. 2d 147 ((1998)(same); *State v. Martinez*, 196 Ariz. 451, 999 P.2d 795, *cert. denied*, 531 U.S. 934 (2000)(noting difference between challenge based on religious belief and challenge based on religiously-based views of prospective juror).

4. Despite Justice Ginsburg's conclusion that such inquiries are impermissible, attorneys often question members of the venire about their religious beliefs. In Texas, prospective jury members are asked to state their religious faith on a form used by lawyers to help make peremptory challenges and challenges for cause. State courts confronting the issue of the propriety during *voir dire* of questions concerning the religion or religious beliefs of prospective jurors have both permitted and excluded such questions. As noted in *Davis*, although such inquiries are often prohibited, these questions may be allowed in the discretion of the trial judge. *See, e.g., Bader v. State*, 344 Ark. 241, 40 S.W.3d 738 (2001)(noting trial court's discretion to limit a party's questions about the religious beliefs of members of the venire in *voir dire* and upholding trial court's limitation of such inquiries by defendant).

In *Rose v. Sheedy*, 134 S.W.2d 18 (Mo. 1939), the Supreme Court of Missouri held the trial court's refusal to permit inquiry into the religion of the prospective jurors was not erroneous. In *State v. Fisher*, 141 Ariz. 227, 686 P.2d 750, *cert. denied*, 469 U.S. 1066 (1984), the trial court's questioning of two prospective jurors about their religious beliefs in an effort to determine whether they would fairly determine the guilt of the defendant, and its determination to excuse them from jury service because their impartiality was affected by their religious beliefs was not an abuse of discretion. Finally, in *State v. Ball*, 685 P.2d 1055 (Utah 1984), the Utah Supreme Court held that the trial court erred when it refused to permit defense counsel to ask prospective jurors who abstained from drinking alcohol whether they did so for personal or religious reasons, when the defendant was charged with driving under the influence of alcohol.

Although a number of lawyers have used religious affiliation and religious belief to guide their peremptory challenges, there is no present social scientific data linking religious affiliation or intensity of religious belief with particular behavioral patterns of jurors. Reid Hastie, Steven D. Penrod and Nancy Pennington, INSIDE THE JURY 124 (1983). If such social scientific data is generated, should that guide court decisions regarding the constitutionality of peremptory challenges based on religion?

3. Challenging Jury Verdicts as Impermissibly based on Religious Beliefs

A jury's verdict is difficult to challenge under the American system of jurisprudence. If, however, individual jurors or the jury as a whole is influenced by religious beliefs in deciding the case before it, can its decision be challenged? *See* Federal Rule of Evidence 606(b) (barring inquiry into the validity of a verdict unless "extraneous prejudicial information was improperly brought to the jury's attention or...an[] outside influence was improperly brought to bear upon any juror.") Is using a Bible during jury deliberations "extraneous prejudicial information" or an "outside influence"?

Jones v. Kemp

706 F. Supp. 1534 (N.D. Ga. 1989)

MOYE, J.

IV. Legal Discussion: Sentencing Phase

A. Christian Bible Permitted in Jury Room

A review of the trial transcript reveals the following interchange:

> [THE COURT]: Now, at this time I am going to send you back to the juryroom, send you out for your noon refreshment, and then, when you have had your noon refreshment, return to the juryroom, and begin your consideration of the punishment and complete your verdict by fixing the penalty that shall be imposed upon the Defendant, and then return into Court for publication.
>
> So, you twelve jurors may retire at this time.
>
> MR. SWEATT: We want to know if we will be allowed to take the Bible back with us?

THE COURT: Yes, sir.

Justice Brennan, while an appellate judge in New Jersey, noted that it is a matter of "elementary principles [that] the jury's verdict must be obedient to the court's charge and be based solely on legal evidence properly before the jury." *Palestroni v. Jacobs*, 77 A.2d 183, 10 N.J.Super. 266 (1950). For this reason, the introduction to the jury of extraneous materials or evidence has consistently been held to mandate a new trial. The courts have condemned the use of a common dictionary by jurors where there exists a reasonable possibility that it was used to define legal terms, or act as a substitute for instructions in the jury's deliberations. *See, e.g., Palestroni*, (reversal due to jury's use of dictionary); *Alvarez v. People*, 653 P.2d 1127 (Colo. 1982) (same); *Smith v. State*, 95 So. 2d 525 (Fla. 1957) (same).

The outcome has been similar when the material at issue was a legal or quasi-legal text. For example, in *Moore v. State*, 172 Ga.App. 844, 324 S.E.2d 760 (1984), consultation of a Readers' Digest guide entitled "You and the Law" was deemed misconduct sufficient to require a retrial, despite the fact that the court could not determine what effect (if any) the improper material had on the jury. Due process was undermined, the court concluded, when the jury sought instruction in the law from a source other than the court.

It is well settled that religion may not play a role in the sentencing process. *See, e.g., United States v. Giry*, 818 F.2d 120 (1st Cir. 1987), *cert. denied*, 484 U.S. 855 (1987) (reference to Bible is improper appeal to jurors' private religious beliefs); *Evans v. Thigpen*, 809 F.2d 239 (5th Cir.1987), *reh'g and reh'g en banc denied*, 814 F.2d 658 (5th Cir.1987), *cert. denied*, 483 U.S. 1033 (1987) (biblical evidence irrelevant at sentencing phase). In a recent case similar to the instant one, the Tennessee Supreme Court held that a jury foreman's reading of Biblical passages to the jury during deliberations in the penalty phase of a capital case was error that required new sentencing. *See Tennessee v. Harrington*, 627 S.W.2d 345 (Tenn. 1981), *cert. denied*, 457 U.S. 1110 (1982).

The jury which sentenced the petitioner had a duty to apply the law of the State of Georgia as given by the trial judge, not its own interpretation of the law or its own interpretation of precepts of the Bible, in determining whether the petitioner should live or die. Yet the court permitted the jury to deliberate with the aid of a specific, extra-judicial code of conduct—a code which mandates death for numerous offenses, including filial disobedience and breaking the Sabbath (as well, of course, as containing enjoiners of mercy and forgiveness elsewhere). *See, e.g.*, Deut. 21:18–21; Exod. 31:14–15. To the average juror, Webster's Dictionary may be no more than a reference book, and The Reader's Digest nothing more than a diverting periodical; but the Bible is an authoritative religious document and is different not just in degree, although this difference is pronounced, but in kind. When, as here, a Bible was present in the jury room with the explicit unqualified approval of the court, it has great potential to influence the jury's deliberations.

The record indicates that the jury took a Bible into the jury room at the very start of deliberations in the sentencing phase of petitioner's trial. The record clearly indicates the members of the jury intended to use the Bible in some way or for some purposes. How the jurors used the Bible, whether as a silent monitor witnessing that the jurors approached their solemn task in the proper attitude, or for guidance as to their specific task, the Court cannot ascertain. A search for the command of extrajudicial "law" from any source other than the trial judge, no matter how well intentioned, is not permitted. The use by deliberating jurors of an extrajudicial code (not already embodied in their own characters) cannot be reconciled with the Eighth Amendment's requirement that any decision to impose death must be the result of discretion which is carefully and narrowly channelled and circumscribed by the secular law of the jurisdiction.

Georgia's death penalty statute lays out specific guidelines for separating "the many" from "the few." *See* O.C.G.A. § 17-10-30(b), formerly Ga.Code Sec. 27-2534.1(b). The Bible, however, in some places explicitly rejects the drawing of distinctions in murder cases: "Whoso sheddeth man's blood, by man shall his blood be shed: for in the image of God made he man." Holy Bible, King James Version, Genesis 9:6. *See also* Holy Bible, King James Version, Leviticus 24:17 ("And he that killeth any man shall surely be put to death"). Whereas the Bible commands that "thine eye shall not pity; but life shall go for life, eye for eye, tooth for tooth, hand for hand, foot for foot," Holy Bible, King James Version, Deuteronomy 19:21, it is the law in this Circuit that arguments which disparage mercy as a valid sentencing consideration "strike at the most important component of a capital jury's discretion favoring capital defendants." *Wilson v. Kemp*, 777 F.2d 621, 626 (11th Cir.1985), *reh'g and reh'g en banc denied*, 784 F.2d 404 (11th Cir.1986), *cert. denied*, 476 U.S. 1153 (1986). Especially when, as here, such arguments come from a source which "would likely carry weight with laymen and influence their decision," *Wilson v. Kemp*, 777 F.2d at 626, the effect may be highly prejudicial to the defendant, and the confidence in the reliability of the jury's decision which must guide imposition of the death penalty may be undermined.

A situation in which a jury, unsupervised by the court and unobserved by counsel, could reach a conclusion by consulting sources other than the legal charge of the court and evidence actually received by the court is not permitted. "The Sixth Amendment guarantees that the accused shall enjoy the right to a trial by an impartial jury and shall be confronted with the witnesses and evidence against him.... The most general interpretation of a fair trial is that it be conducted before unprejudiced jurors under the superintendence of a judge who instructs them as to the law and advises them as to the facts. Judicial control of the juror's knowledge of the case pursuant to the laws of evidence is fundamental to the prevention of bias and prejudice." *Farese v. U.S.*, 428 F.2d 178, 179–80 (5th Cir.1970). Extraneous materials, whether they be dictionaries, law books, or Bibles, unless properly received in evidence, are not allowed in the jury room for use by a deliberating jury. The jury should have with it in the jury room only those documents received in evidence, or perhaps judicially noticed and a copy of the court's charge if reduced to writing—nothing else.

The court in no way means to suggest that jurors cannot rely on their personal faith and deeply-held beliefs when facing the awesome decision of whether to impose the sentence of death on a fellow citizen. There is thus no issue raised here as to possession, even in the jury room, of personal Bibles, perhaps even consulted for personal—not group—inspiration or spiritual guidance. Likewise there is no issue raised here involving the (anti) Establishment clause, such as is involved in the school prayer cases. The sole issue here involves the at least implied court approval of group jury reference to an extra-judicial authority—here the Christian Bible—for guidance in deciding the explicit, statutorily mandated, carefully worded guidelines which must be followed by a jury deliberating during the sentencing phase of a death penalty case.

In sum, it was constitutional error for the court to permit the Christian Bible to go into the jury room at the request of the jurors apparently for consultation in connection with their deliberations.

[Petition for writ of habeas corpus granted unless petitioner resentenced within 120 days of date of order.]

Notes

1. Judge Moye limited the holding by concluding, "There is thus no issue raised here as to possession, even in the jury room, of personal Bibles, perhaps even consulted for personal—not group—inspiration or spiritual guidance." In *People v. Mincy*, 827 P.2d 388 (Cal.), *cert. denied*, 506 U.S. 1014 (1992), a juror brought a Bible with her to the jury room for one afternoon. The juror testified that after deliberations were completed for that afternoon, "'everybody stayed and so we read a few verses from it.'" *Id.* at 424. Two jurors denied deliberations had ended when the Bible verses were read. *Id.* The trial court learned from a bailiff that a Bible had been brought to the jury room, and before deliberations continued the next morning, the trial court "admonished them to decide the case solely on the evidence and the court's instructions on the law." *Id.* at 425. On appeal, the Supreme Court of California found no Eighth Amendment error, concluding "the jury's decision to impose the death penalty was not significantly impugned by the reading of the Bible verses." *Id.* It also found without merit the claim that counsel's failure to move the dismissal of the juror who brought the Bible with her was ineffective assistance of counsel. *Id.* Does it matter that the verses read by the jurors were from the Book of Numbers and Romans, the former of which included: "But if he struck him down with an iron object, so that he died, he is a murderer; the murderer shall be put to death." Is this case different from *Jones v. Kemp* because a juror brought the Bible to the jury room without court permission?

2. If, instead of bringing a Bible to deliberations, a juror quotes Biblical passages by memory to justify imposing the death penalty, should this action be grounds for reversing the sentence?

3. In *Jones*, the court's decision permitting the jurors to bring a book, the Bible, to its deliberations was held constitutional error. If the influence of religion is not the use of a Bible, or some other religious item, but a more general religious influence, courts have ordinarily held that this influence does not fatally taint the jury's verdict. In *State v. Rocco*, 119 Ariz. 27, 579 P.2d 65 (Ct. App. 1978), an alternate juror who was excused by the trial court engaged in the jury deliberation room in a silent prayer with the members of the jury before leaving the room. Neither the presence of the alternate juror in the room reserved for deliberations nor the silent prayer necessitated reversal of the guilty verdict. Similarly, the Louisiana Supreme Court in *State v. Graham*, 422 So. 2d 123 (La. 1982), *appeal dismissed* 461 U.S. 950 (1983), held that daily prayers said by the jury foreman, a Presbyterian minister, did not deprive the defendant of his constitutional rights.

4. In *People v. Knapp*, 113 A.D.2d 154, 495 N.Y.S.2d 985 (N.Y. App. Div. 1985), the defendant complained that the trial court's decision to hold his trial in a Roman Catholic church hall because of renovations to the courthouse denied him the right to a fair and public trial. The court concluded that despite the objection of both parties to the court's decision to hold the trial in the church hall, no error occurred:

> The effect of a religious environment and religious artifacts on jurors is uncertain. It is as likely that the jurors would be influenced to render a just and honest verdict as that they would somehow be prejudiced against defendant. Even traditional courtrooms are not devoid of religious symbols and artifacts and both jurors and witnesses are traditionally sworn with the phrase "so help you God." Thus, the legal conceptions of truth and justice are often related to the religious conceptions of those terms. Further, the trial was not held in a church, but in a church hall which was a separate building. While County Court did not allow defense counsel to develop the record fully regarding the

> number, description and location of religious artifacts, it does not appear from the record that the religious environment was so pervasive as to deny defendant a fair trial.

495 N.Y.S.2d at 989.

The court's decision in *Knapp* was made in light of *People v. Rose*, 368 N.Y.S.2d 387 (N.Y. Cty. Ct. 1975), which set aside an arraignment that took place in a room in the same building as a religious school for girls. There the court concluded that the "selection as a court house or court room of a building or room dedicated to religion or permeated with religious symbols is inconsistent with the spirit and intent of the constitutional prohibitions of and fortifications against establishment of religion." *Id.* at 391. Knapp later filed a petition for a writ of habeas corpus in federal court. The Second Circuit, in denying Knapp's petition, stated that "it was undoubtedly imprudent to hold Knapp's trial at this location, particularly over the objection of the parties. No showing has been made, however, that constitutional error resulted which prejudiced Knapp." *Knapp v. Leonardo*, 46 F.3d 170, 177 (2d Cir.), *cert. denied*, 515 U.S. 1136 (1995).

Which view is more persuasive? Does your answer depend on the religious beliefs of the jurors, or whether the residents of the place where the defendant is tried are predominantly of one religious sect rather than several, or none at all? Does the acknowledgment of the existence of religious symbols by the *Knapp* court suggest that the court is not a secular place? Does it suggest that those remaining religious symbols have lost their religious content, and come to us as part of our "civil" religion? Is it important to note that the "cost" of reversal in *Knapp* was greater than that in *Rose* because Knapp was appealing a conviction and Rose was asking the court merely to set aside an arraignment?

If the court, in response to a jury impasse, tells the jury to go home, sleep on it, and pray about its deliberations, is such an instruction error? *See Salters v. State*, 506 S.E.2d 221, 224 (Ga. App. 1998) (holding trial court did not err in telling jury to pray about it because "passing reference to nondenominational divine guidance scarcely amounts to the disparagement of mercy disapproved of as improper argument in the sentencing phase of a capital trial"). Do you agree?

State v. DeMille

756 P.2d 81 (Utah 1988)

ZIMMERMAN, J.

A jury found appellant Leland Thomas DeMille guilty of second degree murder. After the verdict was returned, DeMille moved for a new trial. In support of this motion, he submitted an affidavit of a juror, arguing that it showed the verdict to be unsound because of juror bias and misconduct. The trial court refused to consider the affidavit and denied the motion for a new trial. On appeal, DeMille argues that the evidence is insufficient to support the conviction and that the juror's affidavit should have been admitted under Utah Rule of Evidence 606(b). We reject DeMille's contentions and affirm the conviction.

DeMille's second argument on appeal is that the trial court should have admitted the juror's affidavit for the purpose of impeaching the verdict. He claims that the material in the affidavit is admissible under Utah Rule of Evidence 606(b) [because] some jurors considered information other than that presented at trial.

Most prominent among the alleged improprieties is one juror's telling others during deliberations that she had prayed for a sign during closing argument as to DeMille's guilt. She claimed to have received a revelation that if defense counsel did not make eye contact with her when he presented his argument, DeMille was guilty—defense counsel did not make the requisite eye contact.

Under rule 606(b), a juror's testimony may not be used to attack a verdict unless that testimony shows that extraneous prejudicial information or outside influence came to the jury's attention and might have affected the result.

Under rule 606(b), our inquiry is limited to determining whether the proffered juror testimony tends to show that "extraneous prejudicial information was improperly brought to the jury's attention or whether any outside influence was improperly brought to bear upon any juror." Utah R.Evid. 606(b). Defendant argues that when the juror who reported to have received an answer to her prayer communicated that fact to the other jurors, an "outside influence was brought to bear on any juror," therefore making the affidavit admissible. We disagree. If we were to accept defendant's argument that supposed responses to prayer are within the meaning of the term "outside influence" in rule 606(b), we would implicitly be holding that it is improper for a juror to rely upon prayer, or supposed responses to prayer, during deliberations. Such a conclusion could well infringe upon the religious liberties of the jurors by imposing a religious test for service on a jury. *See* Utah Const. art. I, §4. A juror is fit to serve if he or she can impartially weigh the evidence and apply the law to the facts as he or she finds them. *State v. Lafferty*, 749 P.2d 1239 (Utah 1988). Prayer is almost certainly a part of the personal decision-making process of many people, a process that is employed when serving on a jury. There is no necessary inconsistency between proper performance as a juror and reliance on prayer or supposed responses to prayer. So long as a juror is capable of fairly weighing the evidence and applying the law to the facts, one may not challenge that juror's decision on grounds that he or she may have reached it by aid of prayer or supposed responses to prayer. Therefore, we hold that under rule 606(b), prayer and supposed responses to prayer are not included within the meaning of the words "outside influence." Testimony that a juror has so acted is not admissible to challenge a verdict; the trial judge properly refused to consider the proffered affidavit.

We recognize that a juror might so abandon his or her judgment to what he or she perceives to be oracular signs as to be unable to fairly consider the evidence and properly apply the law. Such a person could be disqualified from serving for cause without offending article I, section 4 of the Utah Constitution. However, this fact does not save defendant's challenge to the verdict for two reasons. First, the affidavit submitted in this case does not aver facts that would disqualify any juror. At most, it suggests that one juror may have been personally influenced by her own "revelation" and that she told others of her experience as one means of persuading them to her point of view. This is certainly not an illegitimate inter-juror dynamic.

Second, even if the affidavit had shown that the juror in question was incapable of impartially weighing the facts and applying the law, the defendant is precluded from raising that issue by a post-trial affidavit. Rule 606(b) is designed to permit juror testimony only about extraneous material and outside influences that impact the jury verdict. A claim that a juror is so affected by religious conviction as to disqualify him or her from jury service does not fall within these exceptions; rather, it goes to the fitness of the person to serve on the jury, a matter that could and should have been raised at voir dire. Yet defense counsel did not raise the matter then, and any such claims were waived once the trial commenced.

The conviction is affirmed.

HALL, C.J., HOWE, Associate C.J., and DURHAM, J., concur.

STEWART, Justice: (dissenting).

I respectfully dissent. I believe that this case should be remanded for a hearing and a determination as to whether one or more jurors based their vote in this case on what they thought was a divine indication of defendant's guilt.

A defendant is constitutionally entitled to a jury that determines guilt or innocence based on the evidence and the law presented to it. Verdicts decided on some other basis make the constitutionally guaranteed right to trial by jury a nullity. Indeed, a verdict that is rendered on the basis of supposed divine intervention is a throw-back to the primitive days of trial by ordeal where, for example, the manner of healing of a severe burn inflicted on a party was deemed to be an indication of God's judgment.

Of course, a juror may seek divine guidance through prayer in reaching a decision, and courts have so recognized. But jurors are duty-bound to decide a case on the basis of the evidence presented at trial.

However, here it is alleged that something other than the evidence was the basis of the verdict for at least one juror. In support of his motion for a new trial, defendant submitted the affidavit of a juror which stated:

> 5. Said juror, [juror's name], further stated to the affiant and the other jurors in said jury room during said deliberations, that while the defendant's attorney was giving his closing argument, she, [the juror], prayed, "...that if said attorney made eye contact with her she would know he was telling the truth, but if he did not she would know he was not telling the truth about defendant; that he did not make eye contact with her, so she knew said attorney was not telling the truth," concerning the defendant.
>
> * * *
>
> 7. Said juror, [name of juror], was one of the leaders, during the deliberations by the jury, of the faction seeking a speedy and early determination of guilt of the defendant.

Thus, the affidavit alleges that the juror received a divine indication of the right result, not divine guidance in assessing the evidence.

Sound reasons support the general policy against allowing impeachment of jury verdicts by attacking the mental processes used by jurors to arrive at a verdict. As long as the jurors purport to act on the basis of the facts and the law, no challenge is permissible, even if jurors may have acted on the basis of some alleged error or misunderstanding. But certainly verdicts are not absolutely inviolate. Verdicts based on chance or bribery, for example, have long been subject to challenge, since they do not even purport to be based on the law and the evidence. Thus, if jurors were to agree that a verdict would be based on a "divine sign," a Ouija board answer, or some fortuitous event, such a verdict, in my judgment, would constitute a denial of due process and the right to trial by jury.

I believe the majority fails to draw a critical distinction between the legitimacy of jurors' seeking divine assistance in accurately and dispassionately weighing the evidence and the illegitimacy of jurors' abdicating their sworn duty to decide the case on the evidence and instead relying on some supposedly divine sign. Although "[a] juror is fit to serve if he or she can impartially weigh the evidence and apply the law to the facts as he or she finds them," as the majority observes, the fact appears to be that the juror in question did not impartially weigh the evidence and apply the law to the facts, but disregarded the evidence and the law and ruled on the basis of an "outside influence." Accordingly, the trial court could have relied on the affidavit under Rule 606(b) for the purpose of deciding that a hearing on the allegations should have been held. It is of particular significance that the juror in question is alleged to have been "one of the leaders" during the jury deliberations. In my view, a verdict based on chance, like a verdict based on a supposed divine sign, falls within the meaning of the terms "extraneous prejudicial information" and "outside influence," as those terms are used in Rule 606(b) of the Rules of Evidence. I would remand the case to the trial court for an evidentiary hearing to determine whether the jurors decided the case on the evidence or whether there was reliance on factors outside the record.

Notes

1. The majority states, "Prayer is almost certainly a part of the personal decision-making process of many people, a process that is employed when serving on a jury." Is this true? Does the majority's opinion rest on some theological premise? If so, is that an impermissible basis for the court's opinion?

2. The opinions in *DeMille* never mention the juror's religious faith. Why not? If the juror was a member of the Church of Jesus Christ of Latter-day Saints, in which divine revelation is believed both possible and a reality, does this justify the majority's conclusion? Is this more justifiable than a belief in divine revelation based on one's idiosyncratic belief system? If so, why?

3. The majority also concludes that even if the juror was incapable of deciding the defendant's guilt based on the facts, defendant was precluded from arguing the juror's incompetence after the verdict was rendered. The defendant's responsibility is to inquire into the ability of the jurors to base their decision on the evidence before the jury was selected, on voir dire. Is the majority suggesting that it is generally proper to ask prospective jurors about religious or other beliefs that will affect their decision-making ability? Doesn't this also affect the religious liberty interests of the prospective jurors?

4. Justice Stewart's dissenting opinion concludes that receiving a divine revelation of the defendant's guilt is constitutionally invalid, although relying on prayer for guidance in assessing the evidence is not invalid. Is this a distinction worth making? Won't this require the courts to assess the truth or falsity of the religious beliefs of the jurors in determining whether there exists a constitutional difference in this case? If so, this inquiry is forbidden by the First Amendment.

5. Commentary on *DeMille* is found in Michael Ariens, *Evidence of Religion and the Religion of Evidence*, 40 Buff. L. Rev. 65, 99–105 (1992), and Daniel S. Day, Note, *Utah Rule of Evidence 606(b): Is God an Improper Outside Influence?*, 1989 Utah L. Rev. 969.

C. Judging by Religious Faith

Are decisions by judges impermissible if based, at least in part, on their religious faith? Can our society expect the religiously devout judge to ignore her religious beliefs in rendering decisions? Should it?

United States v. Bakker

925 F.2d 728 (4th Cir. 1991)

[The televangelist Jim Bakker was convicted of mail fraud after the failure of his PTL Club. On appeal, the United States Court of Appeals affirmed Bakker's conviction. It then assessed the soundness of Bakker's sentence.]

WILKINSON, Circuit Judge:

III.

A.

We conclude, therefore, that Bakker's trial was free of reversible error. The same, however, cannot be said of his sentencing. The sentence imposed on Bakker encompassed a 45-year prison term and a fine of $500,000. [W]e do agree with Bakker's second contention that the trial court abused its discretion by taking impermissible considerations into account when sentencing him.

B.

During sentencing, the judge stated of Bakker: "He had no thought whatever about his victims and those of us who do have a religion are ridiculed as being saps from money-grubbing preachers or priests." Bakker contends that these comments reveal that the trial judge abused his discretion and violated due process by factoring his own sense of religiosity and victimization into the sentence he imposed on Bakker.

In contrast, the government argues that the phrase "those of us" reflects the judge speaking not for himself but for society as a whole. The government also contends that the trial court was simply considering the impact of Bakker's crimes on society and was well within its discretion in doing so. We recognize that a sentencing court can consider the impact a defendant's crimes have had on a community and can vindicate that community's interests in justice. To a considerable extent a sentencing judge is the embodiment of public condemnation and social outrage. As the community's spokesperson, a judge can lecture a defendant as a lesson to that defendant and as a deterrent to others. If that were all that occurred here, the court would have been properly exercising its discretion, and we would be loathe to disturb what surely is an integral part of the sentencing process.

Sentencing discretion, however, must be exercised within the boundaries of due process. In this case, the trial judge exceeded those boundaries. Courts have held that sentences imposed on the basis of impermissible considerations, such as a defendant's race or national origin, violate due process. *See, e.g., United States v. Borrero-Isaza*, 887 F.2d 1349, 1352–57 (9th Cir.1989); *United States v. Gomez*, 797 F.2d 417, 419 (7th Cir.1986) (sentencing more harshly based on nationality or alienage "obviously would be unconstitutional."). While these cases focused on a defendant's characteristics, we believe that similar principles apply when a judge impermissibly takes his own religious characteristics into account in sentencing.

Our Constitution, of course, does not require a person to surrender his or her religious beliefs upon the assumption of judicial office. Courts, however, cannot sanction sentencing procedures that create the perception of the bench as a pulpit from which judges announce their personal sense of religiosity and simultaneously punish defendants for offending it. Whether or not the trial judge has a religion is irrelevant for purposes of sentencing. Regrettably, we are left with the apprehension that the imposition of a lengthy prison term here may have reflected the fact that the court's own sense of religious propriety had somehow been betrayed. In this way, we believe that the trial court abused its discretion in sentencing Bakker. Consequently, the sentence is vacated and the case is remanded for resentencing. This resentencing will be carried out by a different district judge to ensure that the ends of due process are achieved.

IV.

We remand this case with genuine reluctance because Bakker's assignments of error at the trial phase only underscore a proceeding which was fairly conducted in the face of trying circumstances. As our prior discussion has made plain, we have carefully scrutinized the record and we are confident that the district court meticulously observed this defendant's rights at trial. We thus refuse to accept Bakker's contention that we should somehow give any alleged error at sentencing retroactive effect by saying that it infected the trial.

Yet, the fact remains that this case involves the explicit intrusion of personal religious principles as the basis of a sentencing decision; at least, that is not an unfair reading of the trial court's comments in this case. We recognize that a trial judge on occasion will misspeak during sentencing and that every ill-advised word will not be the basis for reversible error. In this case, however, our review of the sentencing transcript reveals comments that are, in the end, too intemperate to be ignored. Because an impermissible consideration was injected into the sentencing process, we must remand the case.

AFFIRMED IN PART, VACATED IN PART AND REMANDED.

Notes

1. What exactly was the trial court's error? The appellate court concludes that the trial judge is not required to forfeit his religious beliefs upon assuming office, and that the trial court can speak for the community when addressing the defendant during sentencing, but then concludes that the manner in which the trial judge exercised his religious beliefs at sentencing was impermissible. *See generally* A.B.A. MODEL CODE OF JUDICIAL CONDUCT, Canons 2,3 (2000)(requiring judge to avoid appearance of impropriety and to perform duties of office impartially and diligently). In *State v. Arnett*, 724 N.E.2d 793 (Ohio 2000), the defendant pled guilty to several counts of rape and one count of pandering obscenity. During sentencing, the judge stated, among other things: "And that passage where I had the opportunity to look is Matthew 18:5, 6. 'And whoso shall receive one such little child in my name, [sic] receiveth me. But, [sic] whoso shall offend one of these little ones which believe in me, it were better for him that a millstone were hanged about his neck, and that [sic] he were drowned in the depth of the sea.'" The Ohio Supreme Court held that the judge's reference to Bible "assisted her in determining the weight that she would give to a statutory factor—the age of the victim," which was a permissible judicial consideration. The court concluded that *Bakker* stood for the proposition that a judge may not use personal religious commitments as the primary basis for sentencing, which it concluded was not present in *Arnett*. It also concluded that *Bakker* did not create "a per se rule prohibiting all religious references by a sentencing judge." *Id.* at 220. *See generally* Mark B. Greenlee, *Faith on the Bench: The Role of Religious Belief in the Criminal Sentencing Decisions of Judges*, 26 U. Day. L. Rev. 1 (2000).

Louisiana Judge Thomas Quirk was charged with violating Canons 2 A, 2 B, 3 A(1) and 3 A(4) of the Code of Judicial Conduct because he sentenced a number of defendants convicted of various traffic offenses to attend a church of their choosing once a week as a condition of probation. After a complaint challenging this practice was filed against him, Judge Quirk began offering church attendance, as a condition of probation, only to those who specifically requested it. The defendants sentenced to attend church were required to pay a $25.00 administrative fee to the Safety Council of Southwest Louisiana. The Council monitored the probationers' attendance at church, defensive driving classes, community service and other programs on behalf of the court. For those attending church, the Council monitored attendance by giving the probationer a card that was to be signed by a "church official" and returned to the Council. The Judiciary Commission found that Judge Quirk's "church sentences" were "clearly" unconstitutional, and that imposing those sentences violated the Code of Judicial Conduct. It recommended his suspension without pay for one year. Without taking a position on the constitutionality of sentencing a person to attend church, the Supreme Court of Louisiana rejected the recommendation of the Judiciary Commission. *In re Quirk*, 705 So. 2d 172 (La. 1997). In *Cleveland Bar Ass'n v. Cleary*, 754 N.E.2d 235 (2001), a closely divided Ohio Supreme Court adopted a recommendation suspending from practice for six months a former judge, who was found to have made a sentence of probation conditional on the defendant's decision not to have an abortion. The court noted that the judge had spoken publicly of this case at her church, and though it didn't impose discipline on this ground, it concluded that the judge had shown an impermissible bias in her decisionmaking.

2. In *State v. Lafferty*, 749 P.2d 1239 (Utah 1988), the Utah Supreme Court upheld a murder conviction and death sentence given the defendant, who was convicted of killing his sister-in-law and her fifteen-month old daughter. Lafferty, an excommunicated former member of the Church of Jesus Christ of Latter-day Saints, told others he had received a divine revelation that four persons, among them the victims, should be "removed." In late 1984, after committing several assaults in jail, Lafferty's mental state was examined. He was found competent. After he attempted suicide, he was re-examined, and the examiners concluded he was incompetent to stand trial for murder because he was suffering from a "religious delusional system." The trial court rejected the examiners's conclusion, and the Utah Supreme Court affirmed. It held that "the examiners' diagnoses were based on the premise that Lafferty's religious beliefs and experiences did not accord with reality, an unsupportable premise on which the trial judge could not rely." *Id.* at 1244. This was unsupportable because the examiners had no "foundation for their assumptions that Lafferty's religious experiences did not occur." *Id.* at 1246. Further, the court took judicial notice that divine revelation was a tenet of Mormon belief. *Id.* at 1246 n.4. Because the "truth" of Lafferty's religious experiences was an inquiry barred by the *Ballard v. United States*, 322 U.S. 78 (1944), excerpted in Chapter Thirteen, the trial court concluded it could not privilege a psychiatric interpretation of "reality" over a religious interpretation of "reality." *Id.* at 1246. Is the court correct in concluding that the nonexistence of the "reality" of "divine revelation" was implicitly assumed by the mental health examiners who evaluated Lafferty? It seems highly improbable that Lafferty's counsel can lay an evidentiary foundation to show the nonexistence of divine revelation. Is the court impermissibly using religion to render its decision? In deciding a case like this, what does it mean to be neutral regarding religion? Must a court ignore the defendant's religious beliefs, or somehow take them into account in deciding this case?

3. Should the rule in *Bakker* be extended to judging determinations other than sentencing decisions? May a judge rely on his or her religious convictions in interpreting or creating some legal rule? May a judge rely on his or her political philosophy to interpret or create some legal rule? Is there is difference between religious conviction and political philosophy that makes one more acceptable than the other? Is that a difference between "rational" and "nonrational" justification? Whether it is consonant in liberal political theory for a morally sensitive judge to rely on her religious beliefs is the subject of Stephen L. Carter, *The Religiously Devout Judge*, 64 Notre Dame L. Rev. 932 (1989). *See also* Ariens, *Evidence of Religion*, 40 Buff. L. Rev. at 105–110. *See generally* Symposium, *Religion and the Judicial Process: Legal, Ethical, and Empirical Dimensions: The Role and Influence of Religious Values in Judicial Decisionmaking*, 81 Marq. L. Rev. 513 (1998).

4. Should a judge be barred from opening court with a prayer? *See Martinez v. State*, 984 P.2d 813, 828–29 (Okla. 1999) (concluding that decision by counsel for defendant not to object to prayer uttered by trial judge when opening court did not amount to ineffective assistance of counsel or plain error, but "strongly discourag[ing] this practice which has great potential of inviting error in the trial proceedings.") *Accord Huff v. State*, 596 So. 2d 16, 21 (Ala. Crim. App. 1991). *But see North Carolina Civil Liberties Union Legal Foundation v. Costangy*, 947 F.2d 1145 (4th Cir. 1991), *cert. denied*, 505 U.S. 1219 (1992) (holding unconstitutional the practice by a state district judge of opening his morning court sessions with a prayer). Recall from Chapter Four that the trial judge in the 1925 *Scopes* case opened each day of the trial with a prayer.

In Nebraska, a trial judge passed around religious pamphlets to members of a jury after the conclusion of a trial. The judge did so after a member of the jury, who was a former client of the judge, noted that he had "changed." In addition, after granting a protective order to a party, the judge saw her sitting outside the courtroom looking "distraught." The party told the judge that "she and her son were having difficulty reading and understanding their Bible." When she said she couldn't afford another Bible, the judge gave her his Bible to read. In a disciplinary hearing, the Supreme Court of Nebraska held that the judge violated the Code of Judicial Conduct in passing out the religious pamphlets, in part because the judge later termed his interaction with members of the jury "witnessing" and "ministering" to them. It held proper his conduct with the distraught party. *In re Empson*, 562 N.W.2d 817, 829–30 (Neb. 1997). *See also Judicial Inq. & Rev. Bd. of the Sup. Ct. of Pa. v. Fink*, 532 A.2d 358 (Pa. 1987)(holding that judge violated Canons 2 and 3 of the Code of Judicial by injecting religious bias into decisionmaking).

Does a judge's religious affiliation require him to recuse himself if his church has taken a policy position on matters which may be presented in a lawsuit pending before him? *See Idaho v. Freeman*, 478 F.Supp. 33 (D. Idaho 1979) and *Feminist Women's Health Center v. Codispoti*, 69 F.3d 399 (9th Cir. 1995) (no). If the religious organization or society to which the judge belongs is a party to the litigation or is otherwise an aspect of the litigation, must she recuse herself from that litigation? *See Singer v. Wadman*, 745 F.2d 646 (9th Cir. 1984), *cert. denied*, 479 U.S. 1028 (1985) and *In re Disqualification of Fuerst*, 674 N.E.2d 361 (Ohio 1996) (no).

In *State v. Stephenson*, 878 S.W.2d 530 (Tenn. 1994), the defendant argued that the trial court erred when it engaged during voir dire in a brief discourse on the meaning of the biblical passage, "judge not so you be not judged." The Tennessee Supreme Court held that the trial court's statement "were isolated remarks in the course of voir dire made two days before the verdict of conviction and three days before sentence was imposed." *Id.* at 541. Because the defendant could show no prejudice, any error was not reversible. However, the court cautioned that because "[r]eference to religious law during a criminal trial has been disapproved in this State, [] trial court judges should therefore refrain from any discussion of religious law." *Id.* Does this make sense? Is ignoring religion required in order for the court to remain "neutral" with regard to religion? Will ignoring religion solve the problem of "religious law" interfering with criminal proceedings? If some prospective jurors consider themselves bound to those duties imposed by their religious beliefs, can religion be ignored? In *Stephenson*, the State argued that the trial court's comments were sparked when defense counsel asked during voir dire whether "anyone [had] any religious convictions or teachings that would have an effect...if you deliberate on the death penalty." *Id.* Assuming this question by defense counsel is appropriate, should a trial court really be expected to say nothing about the impact religious beliefs may have on jury deliberations?

5. Professor Scott Idleman notes that, in addition to resolving substantive questions of law, a judge's religious commitments may affect the judge's perspective on authority, reasoning style, assessment of the admissibility of evidence, position on the rationality of religious beliefs, and the determination of constitutional or other legal facts. Scott C. Idleman, *The Limits of Religious Values in Judicial Decisionmaking*, 81 Marq. L. Rev. 537, 543–44 n.20 (1998). Does the possibility that a judge's religious commitments may affect her understanding and interpretation of law suggest that judges make public their religious commitments when running for elected judicial office or at hearings before being appointed? Should religiously committed judges recuse themselves from some or all cases in which there *may* be a conflict between the judge's faith and the command of the law? Is there a difference between a judge's religious commitments and a judge's philosophical or political commitments that suggests the former should be treated differently than the latter in judicial elections or appointments? If so, why?

6. In 1995, Judge Roy Moore, then a trial judge in Etowah County, Alabama, was sued because he posted the Ten Commandments in his courtroom. In addition, Judge Moore opened court with a prayer. In *Alabama Freethought Ass'n v. Moore*, 893 F. Supp. 1522 (N.D. Ala. 1995), the district court held that the plaintiffs lacked standing to complain about Judge Moore's actions. Thereafter, the Governor of Alabama, Fob James, sued Judge Moore. James requested a declaratory judgment holding constitutionally permissible Judge Moore's actions displaying the Ten Commandments in his courtroom or opening court sessions with a prayer. In Ex parte *State* ex rel. *James*, 711 So. 2d 952 (Ala. 1998), the Supreme Court of Alabama held that the state's claims against Judge Moore were not justiciable due to a lack of adverseness. Several other courts have held unconstitutional the posting of the Ten Commandments in courtrooms. Judge Moore's vigorous efforts to maintain the display of the Ten Commandments in his courtroom were widely publicized, and Moore became a celebrated speaker concerning his view of the proper relation of law, religion and government. He was subsequently elected to the Supreme Court of Alabama. To what extent, if any, do statements concerning religion made by a judge in his unofficial capacity differ from religiously-based statements made by legislative or executive officials? Does the judge's ethical duty to remain impartial limit his ability to make such statements in a way different from other governmental officials?

7. Should political actors other than judges be permitted to rely on their religious beliefs in making political decisions? Can they? *Compare* Kent Greenawalt, Religious Convictions and Political Choice (1988) *with* Michael J. Perry, Love & Power: The Role of Religion in Morality in American Politics (1991). *See also* Bruce

Ackerman, Social Justice in the Liberal State (1980) (arguing against reliance on religious beliefs). Should such decisions be subject to judicial review? Does it matter whether the issue is abortion, capital punishment, social welfare policies, nuclear (dis)armament, prayer in public schools, or tuition aid to religious schools? Does your answer apply as well to non-religious or even anti-religious beliefs? If so, why? A discussion of the role of faith in political decisionmaking by a well-known former politician (and former law professor) is Mario M. Cuomo, *Religious Belief and Public Morality: A Catholic Governor's Perspective, Address at the University of Notre Dame (Sept. 13, 1984), in* 1 Notre Dame J.L. Ethics & Pub. Pol'y 13 (1984). *See also* Chapter Ten, § A.

D. References to Religion by Lawyers

Commonwealth v. Chambers

599 A.2d 630 (Pa. 1991), *cert. denied*, 504 U.S. 946, *reh'g denied*, 505 U.S. 1238 (1992)

[Karl Chambers was convicted of the murder of Anna Mae Morris and sentenced to death. After reviewing a number of claimed errors and affirming the conviction, the Supreme Court of Pennsylvania assessed Chambers's claim that the prosecutor improperly injected religion in his closing argument to the jury during the penalty phase of the trial.]

PAPADOKOS, Justice.

PENALTY PHASE

Finally, Appellant argues that the prosecutor overstepped the permissible bounds of oratorical flair in his closing argument by referring to the Bible. The record shows that the prosecutor stated, "Karl Chambers has taken a life." "As the Bible says, 'and the murderer shall be put to death.'" Defense counsel objected. The trial court immediately noted this objection and gave a curative instruction to the jury.

The guidelines governing a review of a claim of allegedly improper and prejudicial remarks made by a prosecutor during a sentencing hearing are set forth in *Commonwealth v. Zettlemoyer*, 500 Pa. 16 at 53–54, 454 A.2d 937 at 956–57, wherein we explained:

> The primary guideline in assessing a claim of error of this nature is to determine whether the unavoidable effect of the contested comments was to prejudice the jury, forming in their minds fixed bias and hostility towards the accused so as to hinder an objective weighing of the evidence and impede the rendering of a true verdict. *Commonwealth v. McNeal*, 456 Pa. 394, 319 A.2d 669 (1974); *Commonwealth v. Van Cliff*, 483 Pa. 576, 397 A.2d 1173 (1979). In making such a judgment, we must not lose sight of the fact that the trial is an adversary proceeding, Code of Professional Responsibility, Canon 7, E.C. 7-19—7-39, and the prosecution, like the defense, must be accorded reasonable latitude in fairly representing its version of the case to the jury. *Commonwealth v. Cronin*, 464 Pa. 138, 346 A.2d 59 (1975). Nevertheless, we do require that the contentions advance[d] must be confined to the evidence and the legitimate

> inferences to be drawn therefrom. *Commonwealth v. Revty*, 448 Pa. 512, 295 A.2d 300 (1972). Deliberate attempts to destroy the objectivity and impartiality of the finder of fact so as to cause the verdict to be a product of the emotion rather than reflective judgment will not be tolerated. *Commonwealth v. Story*, 476 Pa. 391, 383 A.2d 155 (1978). The verdict must flow from the respective evidence presented and not represent a response to inflammatory pleas for either leniency or vengeance. *Commonwealth v. Starks*, 479 Pa. 51, 387 A.2d 829 (1978).

In the past we have narrowly tolerated references to the Bible and have characterized such references as on the limits of "oratorical flair" and have cautioned that such references are a dangerous practice which we strongly discourage. *Commonwealth v. Henry*, 524 Pa. 135, 569 A.2d 929 (1990); *Commonwealth v. Whitney*, 511 Pa. 232, 512 A.2d 1152 (1986). We now admonish all prosecutors that reliance in any manner upon the Bible or any other religious writing in support of the imposition of a penalty of death is reversible error *per se* and may subject violators to disciplinary action.

Here, the prosecutor argued, "As the Bible says, 'and the murderer shall be put to death.'" This reference is substantially different than the references tolerated in *Henry* and *Whitney* where the prosecutor allegorically likened the Defendant to the Prince of Darkness mentioned in the Bible to establish that he was an evil person.

More than allegorical reference, this argument by the prosecutor advocates to the jury that an independent source of law exists for the conclusion that the death penalty is the appropriate punishment for Appellant. By arguing that the Bible dogmatically commands that "the murderer shall be put to death," the prosecutor interjected religious law as an additional factor for the jury's consideration which neither flows from the evidence or any legitimate inference to be drawn therefrom. We believe that such an argument is a deliberate attempt to destroy the objectivity and impartiality of the jury which cannot be cured and which we will not countenance. Our courts are not ecclesiastical courts and, therefore, there is no reason to refer to religious rules or commandments to support the imposition of a death penalty.

Our Legislature has enacted a Death Penalty Statute which carefully categorizes all the factors that a jury should consider in determining whether the death penalty is an appropriate punishment and, if a penalty of death is meted out by a jury, it must be because the jury was satisfied that the substantive law of the Commonwealth requires its imposition, not because of some other source of law.

Because the prosecutor's argument in favor of the death penalty reached outside of the evidence of the case and the law of this Commonwealth, we are not convinced that the penalty was not the product of passion, prejudice or an arbitrary factor and, therefore, pursuant to our Death Penalty Statute, we must vacate the sentence of death and remand this matter for a new sentencing hearing.

McDERMOTT, J., concurring and dissenting.

I join the majority's affirmance of the conviction, however, I must dissent from the overreaction of the majority to the prosecution's biblical reference. The standard in evaluating whether a prosecutor crossed the line in his closing argument is whether his comments would have "the effect of arousing the jury's emotion to such a degree that it becomes impossible for the jury to impose sentence based on consideration of the relevant evidence according to the standards of the statute." *Commonwealth v. Travaglia*, 502 Pa. 474, 502, 467 A.2d 288, 302 (1983). In this case the isolated comment of the prosecutor was the last sentence in a brief closing. This was not emotional oratory calling for divinely motivated retribution; rather it was a reference to one of the texts from which our social system has evolved. The majority opinion is an unmerited censure of citizens called to such vast responsibility. To believe them swayed from their solemn, sworn duty by a single reference to a legal irrelevance is a presciosity that undermines the very essence of trial by jury.

Notes

1. In *Commonwealth v. Daniels*, 612 A.2d 395 (Pa. 1992), an equally divided Pennsylvania Supreme Court applied *Chambers* to the actions of defense counsel. The court affirmed the trial court's decision restricting defense counsel's use of the Bible to show the immorality of the death penalty: "Although commenting on religion is not *per se* improper, it is improper when it goes beyond the bounds of consideration of the character and record of the accused. [T]he arguments [of defense counsel] were intended to persuade the jurors that they would betray their religious beliefs if they sentenced appellant to death." *Id.* at 403. Because this argument was not based on the evidence produced at trial, it was improper:

> The boundaries of proper advocacy are exceeded if we allow counsel to make arguments calculated to inflame the passions or prejudices of the jury, or to divert the jury from its duty to decide the case on the evidence by introducing broad social issues that are not based on evidence in the record.

Id. at 404.

On reargument, the court affirmed its decision regarding defense counsel's actions. *Commonwealth v. Daniels*, 644 A.2d 1175, 1183 (Pa. 1994).

Is the court's effort to apply its rule regarding religious references equally to prosecution and defense counsel sensible? Is the defendant's lawyer a "state actor," thus subjecting his or her actions to the requirements of the Constitution? Does it matter that the court did not explicitly rely on either the federal or state constitutions in deciding *Chambers* or *Daniels*?

In South Carolina in the mid-1990s, Susan Smith murdered her two young sons. Smith rolled her car, with her two sons strapped inside, into a lake, and they drowned. Before confessing to her crime, she falsely claimed a young black man hijacked her car with her sons inside. After she was convicted of the murder of her sons, the state asked the jury to sentence her to death. Her lawyer, David Bruck, urged the jury during closing arguments to sentence her to life in prison, and made several religious arguments justifying sparing Smith's life. The jury accepted Bruck's argument. *See* Tom Morganthau, *Condemned to Life*, NEWSWEEK, Aug. 7, 1995, at 19. Should Bruck's argument have been prohibited because it invokes the passions of the jury? In the American adversary system, is it possible to eliminate passion in jury trials? Even if so, should that passion be eliminated, or is the concern more that passion of a particular kind, religious passion, should be eliminated? In another case in which David Bruck represented a defendant charged with capital murder, the prosecution obtained an order prohibiting any religious references during closing argument by either party. On appeal, the South Carolina Supreme Court held that the trial court acted within its discretion in barring the use of religious arguments. The court also noted that defense counsel was permitted to make one such argument, which invoked the admonitions of Jesus to a crowd wishing to stone an adulterous woman without mentioning Jesus's name (he was called "a very great man."). *State v. Shafer*, 531 S.E.2d 524, 532 (S.C. 2000).

2. Arguments invoking religion, particularly statements from the Christian Bible, recur most often in death penalty cases. Although California followed the reasoning in *Chambers* in *People v. Sandoval*, 841 P.2d 862 (Cal. 1992), *aff'd sub. nom. Victor v. Nebraska*, 511 U.S. 1 (1994), it concluded that the Biblical reference to justify imposing the death penalty was not reversible error. *Contra Sandoval v. Calderon*, 241 F.3d 765 (9th Cir.), *cert. denied*, 122 S.Ct. 322 (2001) (disagreeing with California Supreme Court's conclusion, holding that closing argument of prosecutor invoked Biblical references to the prejudice of defendant, and ordering new trial for Sandoval in death penalty phase). *See also People v. Wash*, 861 P.2d 1107, 1136 (Cal. 1993) (holding prosecutorial misconduct in referring to Bible and religious justification for death penalty not reversible, for there was "no possibility that the jury would have reached a more favorable verdict had the misconduct not occurred."). Federal courts have criticized the use of religious arguments, but have not adopted Pennsylvania's *per se* reversible error rule. *See, e.g., Coe v. Bell*, 161 F.3d 320 (6th Cir. 1998) (holding improper religious argument but concluding no reversible error occurred); *Bussard v. Lockhart*, 32 F.3d 322 (8th Cir. 1994) (holding permissible use of quotations from Bible to make a point urging common sense in a more poetic fashion, but noting that use of Bible to invoke wrath of God or use of divine law is impermissible). However, not all courts have forbidden references to religion in closing argument in death penalty cases. *See Shell v. State*, 554 So. 2d 887, 899 (Miss. 1989) (holding reference to story of Cain and Abel not error); *State v. Rose*, 451 S.E.2d 211, 229 (N.C. 1994), *cert. denied*, 515 U.S. 1135 (1995) (holding prosecutorial reference to Biblical injunction that murderer must forfeit his own life in penalty phase of capital murder case did not require automatic reversal, and distinguishing *Chambers*). *See also Hooks v. State*, 416 A.2d 189 (Del. 1980) (finding error a statement in closing argument by prosecutor that, unlike witness for the state, Bible meant nothing to defendants, but not reversible error).

Georgia's Supreme Court has issued no fewer than seven opinions on the propriety of prosecutorial arguments invoking religion since 1991. In *Todd v. State*, 410 S.E.2d 725 (Ga. 1991), *cert. denied*, 506 U.S. 838 (1992), the court held in passing over a strong dissent that references to the Bible by the prosecutor were not error. Two years later, in *Hill v. State*, 427 S.E.2d 770 (1993), the court reaffirmed its holding in *Todd*, and, citing a 1983 case, noted:

> Moreover, while it would be improper to urge a death penalty based upon the defendant's religious beliefs, or to urge that the teachings of a particular religion command the imposition of a death penalty in the case at hand, counsel may "bring to his use in the discussion of the case well-established historical facts and may allude to such principles of divine law relating to transactions of men as may be appropriate to the case."

Id. at 778 (*quoting Conner v. State*, 303 S.E.2d 266 (1983)). In *Crowe v. State*, 458 S.E.2d 799 (Ga. 1995), the court again declared that alluding to principles of divine law was not error. That same year, in *Hammond v. State*, 452 S.E.2d 745 (Ga. 1995), the court determined that a prosecutor's claim that the defendant should be sentenced to die because he had violated God's law as well as the law of Georgia was improper. The failure of counsel to object was not ineffective assistance, however, because "these remarks neither changed the result of the sentencing trial nor rendered it fundamentally unfair." *Id.* at 753. In *Greene v. State*, 469 S.E.2d 129 (Ga.), *rev'd on other grounds*, 519 U.S. 145 (1996), the court rejected a claim that references to "certain Biblical teachings in closing argument was improper." The court continued, "It has never been the law of this state that religion may play no part in the sentencing phase of a death-penalty trial." *Id.* at

140. In *Carr v. State*, 480 S.E.2d 583 (Ga. 1997), the court cautioned prosecutors against making "references to religion which invite jurors to base their verdict on extraneous matters not in evidence," *id.* at 592, but held that there did not exist a reasonable probability that the argument, if improper, changed the result of the trial. Finally, in *Carruthers v. State*, 528 S.E.2d 217 (Ga. 2000), the court reversed a sentence of death because of religiously-based arguments made by the prosecutor in the sentencing trial. The prosecutor stated,

> Now, ladies and gentlemen, let me talk to you a moment about some biblical references that help us in this case. Deterrence is very important and the Bible suggests to us why deterrence is appropriate. Romans tells us that every person is subject to the governing authority, every person is subject. And in Matthew [sic] it tells us, who sheddeth man's blood by man shall his blood be shed for in the image of God made [he] man. For all they who take the sword shall die by the sword, and this is a message that is very clear, that society must deter criminals.

Id. at 221. The statement allegedly from Matthew actually is found in the Book of Genesis. The court held that the prosecutor was suggesting to the jury that it sentence Carruthers to death for violating divine law, not the law of Georgia. Because a person must be sentenced in accord with the law of the state, this suggestion by the prosecutor was impermissible. Is that what the prosecutor is doing? Another distinction between *Carruthers* and the earlier cases, according to the court, was that

> Unlike previous cases, however, where the defendant failed to object to the state's religious arguments at trial, the defense in this case anticipated the argument and tried to prevent it by filing a motion *in limine*, but the trial court denied the motion. Because the defendant received an adverse ruling on his objection, the standard of review in this case is not whether the improper argument in reasonable probability changed the result of the trial, but simply whether the argument was objectionable and prejudicial.

Id. at 222. The court did not overrule *Todd* or any of the cases following it. Although the court mentioned the *per se* rule adopted in *Chambers*, it did not claim to follow it. Like the majority opinion in *Todd*, the majority opinion in *Carruthers* provoked a vigorous dissent. If you are defense counsel in Georgia, *Carruthers* mandates that you move *in limine* to bar any religiously-based arguments. If the trial court denies your motion *in limine*, the standard of review on appeal whether the argument was objectionable and prejudicial, a much less stringent standard (did the improper argument in reasonable probability change the result of the trial) than if you fail to object to that argument at trial. Is the Georgia Supreme Court attempting to create a *per se* rule barring religious arguments in fact, if not in law? Is there any reason for defense counsel *not* to make this motion *in limine* following the decision in *Carruthers*? Clearly, because the court limits its concern to the possibility that jurors will follow divine law rather than Georgia law if only the former demands a death sentence, any effective adoption of the *per se* rule barring religiously-based arguments is not applicable to defense counsel.

The *per se* rule adopted in Pennsylvania led its Supreme Court to reverse a death sentence because the prosecutor stated, after referring to "ancient law," "There is a page in that book, it says, it is better that you had a millstone tied around your neck and be cast into the deep, than that you harm a child. This is ancient law, and it finds its common place in 1995, in the State of Pennsylvania, in that aggravating factor that says, if you murder a child under the age of 12, you will suffer death by lethal injection." *Commonwealth v. Brown*, 711 A.2d 444, 457 (Pa. 1998). Although this statement paraphrased language found in the gospels of Luke, Matthew and Mark, the prosecutor did not mention the Bible. In the court's opinion, jurors readily understood the statement came from the Bible because it was "distinctive." Should an allusion to a passage in the Bible be sufficient to taint the sentence? Isn't it likely that some stories initially thought of as religious have now passed into the secular culture? Two years later, in *Commonwealth v. Spotz*, 756 A.2d 1139 (Pa. 2000), the Pennsylvania Supreme Court refused to invoke the *per se* rule in the following situation. Defense counsel in closing argument argued that the defendant had endured a troubled childhood, a circumstance that the jury should view as a mitigating circumstance. In response, the prosecutor stated: "Did Mark Spotz have a troubled childhood? I don't know that—I don't know that the Commonwealth would dispute that fact. But long before Dustin Spotz was killed and June Ohlinger and Penny Gunnet were murdered, Mark Spotz became a man and put away childish things." Although this is a reference to a statement in the Book of Corinthians, the Court held that the prosecutor's statement was not error. Is this because the statement is not "distinctive," or because the saying has lost its religious significance? If the statement remains both distinctive and religiously significant, is the statement nonetheless permissible because the prosecutor is not attempting to justify a sentence of death based on a religious reference? In other words, is the statement merely a suggestion that, despite the defendant's background, he retained the human agency or free will that makes him responsible for his actions? Is the personal responsibility argument that "you reap what you sow" permissible? *Compare State v. Cribbs*, 967 S.W.2d 773, 784 (Tenn.), *cert. denied*, 522 U.S. 932 (1998) (no, but defendant not prejudiced by statement) *with United States v. Kirk*, 41 M.J. 529, 533 (C.G.C.M.R. 1994) (yes).

3. In *Heglemeier v. State*, 878 P.2d 294 (Nev. 1994), *rev'd on other grounds*, 903 P.2d 799 (Nev. 1995), the defendant brought a Bible with him to court. During cross-examination of the defendant, the prosecutor ridiculed defendant's decision, and suggested that the defendant brought the Bible with him to impress the jury that he was "a religious God-fearing believer in the bible." 878 P.2d at 303. Although the court disapproved of the prosecutor's actions, it held they did not to rise to the level of prosecutorial misconduct. *Id.* at 304.

4. In her book about the death penalty, *Dead Man Walking*, Sister Helen Prejean writes that in the early 1980s, testimony by priests in Louisiana quoting from the United States Catholic Bishops' Statement on Capital Punishment led several juries to sentence convicted murderers to life rather than death. In response, Harry Connick, Sr., the District Attorney for New Orleans, asked for and received a statement from the Archbishop of New Orleans, Philip Hannan, indicating that Catholics "'can in good conscience endorse capital punishment.'" Connick then read this statement to jurors in first-degree murder trials. Sister Helen Prejean, Dead Man Walking: An Eyewitness Account of the Death Penalty in the United States 54 (1993).

5. In *State v. Middlebrooks*, 995 S.W.2d 550, 559 (Tenn. 1999), the Supreme Court of Tennessee held that a prosecutor's invocation of the Bible to justify the imposition of the death penalty was error, noting that "[w]e have condemned Biblical and scriptural references in a prosecutor's closing argument so frequently that it is difficult not to conclude that the remarks in this case were made either with blatant disregard for our decisions or a level of astonishing ignorance of the state of the law in this regard." However, the court concluded that the error did not affect the verdict to the prejudice to the defendant, and upheld the sentence of death. It then cautioned prosecutors from concluding that religious references in closing argument would always been held harmless error. The court stated that continued use of religiously-based arguments by prosecutors

could result in the institution of attorney disciplinary proceedings, as well as the reversal of a death sentence as prejudicial to the judicial process as a whole. The court did not, however, adopt Pennsylvania's *per se* rule. Is the continued violation of this rule by prosecutors in Tennessee evidence of the power of religiously-based arguments? Or is this merely evidence that prosecutors are too busy to keep up with court pronouncements like this? Should courts that consider religious arguments improper move to Pennsylvania's *per se* reversible error rule because prosecutors continue to use such arguments? *Compare* Elizabeth A. Brooks, Note, *Thou Shalt Not Quote the Bible: Determining the Propriety of Attorney Use of Religious Philosophy and Themes in Oral Argument*, 33 Ga. L. Rev. 1113 (1999) (rejecting *per se* rule) *with* Brian C. Duffy, Note, *Barring Foul Blows: An Argument for a Per Se Reversible-Error rule for Prosecutors' Use of Religious Arguments in the Sentencing Phase of Capital Cases*, 50 Vand. L. Rev. 1335 (1997) (embracing *per se* rule).

6. The accused was charged with sexual assault of her son. The son, then 14, swore out a complaint at the behest of his father, from whom the accused was estranged. The accused maintained her innocence, and the prosecutor later had doubts about the truth of the accusations. The father and son proposed to the prosecutor that the charges be dropped if the accused swore on a Bible in her Roman Catholic church that she had not sexually abused her son. The prosecutor communicated that offer to the accused, and she "reluctantly" swore as requested. The prosecutor dismissed the charges that day. The accused later sued the prosecutor for violating her civil rights by coercing her into engaging in a religious practice. On appeal, the Second Circuit held that the prosecutor did not enjoy absolute immunity for his actions. It rejected his claim that the ceremony was analogous to the swearing of a witness in a judicial proceeding, in part because the ceremony was held in a church, and in part because a witness in a federal judicial proceeding has the option of giving a nonreligious affirmation. The result was that the action was "a religious event." *Doe v. Phillips*, 81 F.3d 1204 (2d Cir. 1996). Dissenting in part, Circuit Judge Jacobs concluded that the act had a secular, prosecutorial purpose of assisting the prosecutor in determining whether the accused had committed the crime of which she was charged. Judge Jacobs noted that witnesses in federal court are permitted to swear an oath on a Bible, and conclude with the phrase, "so help me God." That event is not a religious act, and thus the swearing of an oath in church was not a religious act, but an act with a secular purpose.

7. Many lawyers believe there exists a crisis in the legal profession, one which has caused extraordinary depression and job dissatisfaction among lawyers. One cause of this crisis is the pressure created by a market-based legal services economy. One response to this crisis is the "religious lawyering" movement. The goal of this movement is show that lawyers can integrate their work and faith. A great deal of commentary suggesting both problems and opportunities for religious lawyers has been written recently *See generally* Russell G. Pearce, *Symposium: Foreword: The Religious Lawyering Movement: An Emerging Force in Legal Ethics and Professionalism*, 66 Fordham L. Rev. 1075 (1998); Samuel J. Levine, *Introductory Note: Symposium on Lawyering and Personal Values—Responding to the Problems of Ethical Schizophrenia*, 38 Cath. Law. 145 (1998); *Symposium: Faith and the Law*, 27 Tex. Tech L. Rev. 911 (1996); Symposium, *Rediscovering the Role of Religion in the Lives of Lawyers and Those They Represent*, 26 Fordham Urb. L.J. 821 (1999). *See also* Thomas L. Shaffer, ON BEING A CHRISTIAN AND A LAWYER: LAW FOR THE INNOCENT (1981); Joseph G. Allegretti, THE LAWYER'S CALLING: CHRISTIAN FAITH AND LEGAL PRACTICE (1996) (suggesting strong relationship between Christian faith and lawyering).

In Tennessee, a lawyer who called himself a "devout Catholic" asked the Tennessee Board of Professional Responsibility for an opinion on a number of questions concerning his faith and legal duties to clients. In response to the question whether he was permitted to decline an appointment to represent a juvenile who sought to waive the parental notice requirement before obtaining an abortion, the Board declared that it was unlikely that his religious beliefs concerning abortion would constitute a "compelling reason," the standard for withdrawing from an appointment under Tennessee law. Tenn. Bd. of Prof. Resp., Formal Op. 96-F-140 (1996). Do you agree?

E. Lawyers and Religious Garb

In a remarkable series of cases, the state of New York requested orders forbidding a lawyer and Roman Catholic priest named Vincent LaRocca from wearing religious garb, that is, his priest's collar, while defending persons accused of committing crimes. New York state courts issued the requested orders. After unsuccessfully appealing the orders in state court, LaRocca sued in federal court, alleging a violation of his civil rights. The history of LaRocca's efforts is given in the court's opinion below.

LaRocca v. Gold

662 F.2d 144 (2d Cir. 1981)

MANSFIELD, Circuit Judge:

Father Vincent LaRocca, an ordained Catholic priest who is licensed to practice law in the State of New York, appeals from a decision and order entered in the Eastern District of New York by Judge Jacob Mishler dismissing his civil rights complaint under 42 U.S.C. §§ 1983 and 1985(3), which sought declaratory and injunctive relief against the defendants-appellees, who include the District Attorney of Kings County and certain justices of the Appellate Division, Second Department, and of the Supreme Court of New York. LaRocca claims that in bringing about the entry of a state court decision that he not wear his Roman Catholic collar when appearing before a jury as a defense lawyer in a criminal trial the defendants have violated his rights under the First, Ninth, and Fourteenth Amendments. His complaint was dismissed by Judge Mishler on the ground that the state court decision does not violate the First Amendment. We affirm, but for different reasons.

Disposition of this appeal requires a review of the state court proceedings which led to the commencement of this suit. LaRocca, who was ordained a priest more than 20 years ago and at all times wears his Roman Catholic collar in public, was in 1973 admitted to practice law in the State of New York. Thereafter he was employed by the Legal Aid Society and in 1974 was assigned to represent a defendant facing trial on criminal charges in the Criminal Court of the City of New York. When he sought to wear his clerical collar in trying the case on behalf of his client before a jury, Judge Morgan Lane, after objection by the district attorney, directed him to remove the collar before proceeding further with the trial. LaRocca, contending that the order violated his own First Amendment right to free exercise of his religion and his client's constitutional right to counsel of his choice, obtained an order from the Criminal Term of the New York Supreme Court prohibiting the Criminal Court from enforcing its order, *LaRocca v. Lane*, 77 Misc. 2d 123, 353 N.Y.S.2d 867 (Sup. Ct. 1974). The Criminal Term judge (Justice Mangano) held that the effect of the trial judge's order was to deny the accused her constitutional right to counsel of her own choice, reasoning that bias could not be presumed from wearing of the clerical collar and that the parties would be protected against prejudice by exercise of their right of *voir dire* in the selection of the jury. His opinion did not reach the First Amendment issue.

Upon appeal the Appellate Division, Second Department, in a 3–1 decision reversed the Criminal Term, holding that the order prohibiting LaRocca from wearing clerical attire before a jury did not violate his client's constitutional right under the Sixth Amendment (incorporated in the Fourteenth Amendment) to be represented by counsel of her own choice or LaRocca's personal First Amendment right to free exercise of his religion. *LaRocca v. Lane*, 47 A.D.2d 243, 366 N.Y.S.2d 456 (2d Dept. 1975). With respect to the client's right, the majority reasoned that the client was represented by the Legal Aid Society, that she was not entitled to assignment of specific counsel, and that the Legal Aid Society, if LaRocca refused to remove his collar, could assign another attorney from its staff to represent the defendant. As to LaRocca's First Amendment claim the court held, after balancing the conflicting interests involved, that his right to free exercise of his religion must, to the limited extent of requiring removal of his collar (a requirement which the court viewed as reasonable), yield to the state's compelling interest in assuring the parties a fair and impartial trial, free of bias that might exist on the part of jurors who would view the clerical attire. LaRocca's argument that any risk of prejudice could be eliminated through *voir dire* of the prospective jurors was rejected. The court noted that, while such a *voir dire* might result in selection of some who would not be biased, *voir dire* can be grossly ineffective as a screening device and that LaRocca's clerical attire could affect witnesses. The dissent took the contrary view that, absent evidence of bias, a judicious use of *voir dire* could sufficiently protect the parties' right to a fair trial, making it unnecessary to deny LaRocca his First Amendment right.

The order of the Appellate Division was affirmed by the New York Court of Appeals, one judge dissenting, in an opinion by Chief Judge Breitel. *LaRocca v. Lane*, 37 N.Y.2d 575, 376 N.Y.S.2d 93, 338 N.E.2d 606 (1975). Judge Breitel noted that a "lawyer is subject to the regulation of the Judge in matters of attire when that regulation is reasonably related to the preservation of order and decorum in the courtroom, the protection of the rights of parties and witnesses, and generally to the furtherance of the administration of justice," 37 N.Y.2d at 582, 376 N.Y.S.2d at 100, 338 N.E.2d at 612. He further stated:

> "A clergyman is accorded high status by most members of our society. Whatever the character of the man or woman who wears the cloth, the cleric is accorded a measure of respect and trust unlike that which is given to those of other vocations. Consequently, it is understandable, but not condonable, that a juror might view differently statements made by a member of the clergy than those made by others, and might ascribe a greater measure of veracity and personal commitment to the rightness of his client's cause.
>
> "On the other side of the issue it is most unfortunate, but yet undeniable, that there exist religious prejudices. These prejudices, often insidious and usually denied, might spill over from lawyer-cleric of whatever faith to the client. Although petitioner's client said she wished him to remain as her attorney despite this possibility, it is not the defendant in a criminal action but the court which must insure a fair trial. So fundamental is the guaranty of a fair trial that even in the absence of objection or exception by defendant or counsel an unfair trial must result in a reversal of a conviction.
>
> "The trial court in directing change of petitioner's garb if he persisted in trying the case before a jury, acted to preserve the right of both the defendant

> and the People to a fair trial. In so doing, the court of necessity limited defense counsel's right to free exercise of religion in that he was compelled to remove the symbol of his religious calling, a requirement of his calling which is not unconditional or beyond dispensation. The risk that a fair trial could not be had outweighed this incidental limitation." 37 N.Y.2d at 583–84, 338 N.E.2d at 613, 376 N.Y.S.2d at 101–02.

In 1976 the Supreme Court of the United States denied LaRocca's petition for a writ of certiorari. *LaRocca v. Lane*, 424 U.S. 968 (1976).

In December of 1978 LaRocca represented Anna Rodriguez, who had been called to appear before a state grand jury. Despite the Court of Appeals' ruling against him in *LaRocca v. Lane*, he informed the defendant Kaye, an Assistant District Attorney in Kings County, that he intended to wear his Roman Catholic collar while representing Rodriguez. District Attorney Gold thereupon sought an order from the defendant Justice Harry Donnelly prohibiting LaRocca from wearing his clerical collar before the grand jury. In an oral bench opinion Justice Donnelly relied principally on the Court of Appeals' decision in *LaRocca v. Lane, supra*, stating:

> "The Court finds: One, the very presence in the Grand Jury of Reverend LaRocca attired in priestly garb, and, Two, his being referred to as the witness' counsellor, plus the witness' act of conferring with, being advised by, and consulting a Roman Catholic priest projects him prominently and unmistakenly in the eyes of the Grand Jurors as not merely the witness' attorney, but as a Roman Catholic priest espousing and defending their testimony."

LaRocca then appealed to the Appellate Division, which upheld the order, stating, "We cannot draw a distinction between this case and *LaRocca v. Lane*." *In re LaRocca*, N.Y.L.J., Jan. 23, 1979, at 14, col. 2 (App. Div. 2d Dep't). He did not seek further review in the New York courts.

Ms. Rodriguez was indicted on February 13, 1979. When she was brought to trial, LaRocca, still serving as her attorney, sought an order from Supreme Court Justice Hugh F. McShane, the trial judge, permitting him to wear his collar while representing her at the trial, which was to a jury. Justice McShane issued the order over the District Attorney's objection on December 17, 1979. In a detailed opinion Justice McShane took a position contrary to the New York Court of Appeals' decision in *LaRocca*. He held that an order prohibiting LaRocca from wearing his clerical collar in representing a defendant at a jury trial would substantially burden his free exercise of his religion and that the state's interest in securing a fair trial free from prejudice could adequately be protected through a *voir dire* of the members of the jury panel, relying on Justice Shapiro's dissenting opinion in *LaRocca v. Lane* and a more recent decision of the Appellate Division in *Close-It Enterprises, Inc. v. Weinberger*, 64 A.D.2d 686, 407 N.Y.S.2d 587 (2d Dept. 1978), which held that a party (as distinguished from an attorney) should be permitted to wear a skull-cap before a jury, since any potential prejudice could be protected against through a *voir dire* and instructions to the jury. Justice McShane further held that to prevent LaRocca from wearing his clerical collar before the jury would deny him his Fourteenth Amendment right to equal protection since it would result in his being treated differently from other attorneys admitted to the bar and thus deprive him of his right to seek his livelihood as a lawyer.

District Attorney Gold thereupon obtained an order from defendant Moses M. Weinstein, Associate Justice of the Appellate Division, Second Department, staying the enforcement of Justice McShane's order, which was on January 11, 1980, adjourned at the latter's request. On March 13, 1980, the Appellate Division granted Gold's Article 78 application to prohibit the enforcement of the McShane order, holding in a unanimous written opinion that it was "inappropriate for Justice McShane to review the decision of another justice of coordinate jurisdiction" and that "we find no change in circumstances that should have led Justice McShane to hold contrary to *LaRocca v. Lane, supra*. The decision of the Court of Appeals in that case continues to be dispositive of this issue." *Gold v. McShane*, 74 A.D.2d 860, 860, 426 N.Y.S.2d 504, 505 (2d Dept. 1980). On June 12, 1980, the New York Court of Appeals dismissed LaRocca's appeal to it "upon the grounds that no substantial constitutional question is directly involved."

In the meantime, on February 27, 1980, which was after Justice McShane's order had been stayed by Justice Weinstein but before the Appellate Division's order, LaRocca commenced the present action in the Eastern District of New York pursuant to 42 U.S.C. §§1983 and 1985(3), claiming that the defendants' action violated his First, Ninth and Fourteenth Amendment rights. On March 2, 1981, Judge Mishler in a written opinion dismissed the action, holding that LaRocca's First Amendment right to wear a clerical collar was not absolute, but must yield to the state's interest in assuring a fair and impartial trial by exercise of its power to regulate the conduct of trials, including counsel's appearance. The district court found it unnecessary to decide whether it should abstain and whether the action was barred from the doctrine of *res judicata*.

DISCUSSION

In the absence of any dispute as to the material facts, all parties ask us to resolve on the merits the issue of whether the defendants denied Father LaRocca his First Amendment right to free exercise of his religion by ordering that he may be required by a state trial judge, without a *voir dire* of the jury panel, to doff his clerical collar before representing a defendant before a jury in a criminal case. LaRocca argues, as he did before various New York courts, that these orders violate his right to free exercise of his religion, that they cannot be justified on the ground that they are necessary to protect the state's interest in assuring the parties a fair and impartial trial, since this interest can be protected by a *voir dire* of the jurors, and that the district court erred in holding to the contrary.

The appellees, on the other hand, contend, a contention that was urged by them and accepted by the state courts, that First Amendment rights are not absolute and that a trial judge, in the exercise of his admitted power to regulate generally the conduct and appearance of counsel as an officer of the court, may without a *voir dire* conclude that a lawyer-priest's right to free exercise of his religion must yield to the limited extent that a judge may direct that removal of clerical garb is necessary to assure an impartial trial.

We must decline the invitation to decide this issue for the reason that appellant, having litigated the matter fully, fairly, thoroughly, and repeatedly before the state courts, is barred by the doctrine of collateral estoppel from now attempting once again to do so in the federal courts.

Turning to the issue of whether an order of a New York state court trial judge, issued without a *voir dire*, directing a lawyer-priest to remove his clerical collar before appearing before a trial jury, violates his First Amendment rights, that question was clearly and unequivocally resolved against LaRocca by the Appellate Division and the New York Court of Appeals in *LaRocca v. Lane, supra*, by Justice Donnelly and the Appellate Division in *In Re Larocca, supra*, and by the Appellate Division in *Gold v. McShane*.

In *LaRocca v. Lane* LaRocca contended that a trial judge's order directing him to remove his clerical collar violated his First Amendment rights. LaRocca asserted that any possible prejudice could be cured by using *voir dire* to screen prospective jurors. The decision of the Appellate Division dealt with that argument at length and resolved it against LaRocca. The Court of Appeals affirmed.

The record is further clear that in *Lane* LaRocca was accorded a "full and fair opportunity" to litigate the very issue raised by him here. The case was considered by the Appellate Division and the Court of Appeals, both of which handed down written opinions resolving the issue against him. Thus we must conclude that the decision of this issue by the New York courts in *Lane* precludes LaRocca from relitigating it here.

Following *Lane* LaRocca had two more full and fair opportunities to litigate the issue, resulting in decisions resolving it against him. He argued the issue before Justice Donnelly, who decided it against him. That decision was affirmed by the Appellate Division, *In re LaRocca, supra*. Finally, LaRocca litigated the issue in the Appellate Division in defending Justice McShane's decision to allow him to wear his clerical collar, and again it was resolved against him. There can be no question but that collateral estoppel prevents LaRocca from relitigating the issue.

LaRocca next contends that requiring him to remove his clerical collar denies him equal protection of the law in violation of the Fourteenth Amendment because New York allows a party wearing a religious symbol (yarmulke or skull cap) to appear before a jury, *Close-It Enterprises, Inc. v. Weinberger*, 64 A.D.2d 686, 407 N.Y.S.2d 587 (2d Dept. 1978), and a witness to appear in clerical garb, *People v. Drucker*, 100 Misc. 2d 91, 418 N.Y.S.2d 744 (Crim. Ct. N.Y.C. 1979), leaving it to the parties to elicit through *voir dire* of the jurors whether they would be prejudiced. We disagree. Although cases involving parties and witnesses require the court to balance the state's compelling interest in assuring fairness of trials against its equally compelling interest in minimizing the burden on free exercise of religion, there are often factors present which justify the balance being struck in favor of permitting parties and witnesses to exhibit clerical or religious affiliations while prohibiting lawyers, who are officers of the court, from doing so. The first of these is the jury's task of appraising the credibility of parties and witnesses, which entitled it to take into account the person's demeanor, conduct, intelligence, and background. No such credibility issue should exist in the case of a lawyer who comports himself, as he must, in accordance with the Rules of Professional Responsibility. A lawyer, unlike a witness or party, does not speak for himself but for his client. The jury should have no need to judge the lawyer's credibility.

The two New York decisions relied upon by appellant are also distinguishable in other respects and consistent with *LaRocca v. Lane*, which was considered by the court in each case. In *Close-It Enterprises* the Appellate Division noted, "[t]here was no reason to believe that a fair trial could not have been achieved if the defendant, a party to the litigation, wore a skull cap. In fact, there was no objection by the plaintiff or his attorney." 64 A.D.2d at 687, 407 N.Y.S.2d at 588. In *Drucker*, the complaining witness' credibility regarding the alleged assault upon him was material. Moreover, in view of the judge's heavy reliance upon the decision of Justice Mangano in *LaRocca v. Lane*, which was reversed, and the dissenting opinion of Justice Shapiro, it is questionable whether *Drucker*, an opinion of the Criminal Court of the City of New York, represents the law of the state.

[Affirmed.]

Notes

1. In *Close-It Enterprises, Inc. v. Weinberger*, 64 A.D.2d 686, 407 N.Y.S.2d 587 (1978), the Appellate Division of the New York Supreme Court held that an order of the trial court requiring Weinberger, a "devout adherent of the Jewish faith," to remove his yarmulke in the courtroom constituted reversible error. Weinberger chose to leave the courtroom rather than remove his yarmulke. That "choice," concluded the court, violated Weinberger's right to the free exercise of religion. The court distinguished the opinion of the New York Court of Appeals in *La Rocca v. Lane* in three ways: (1) it concluded that in *Weinberger* no objection was made by the opposing party to Weinberger's wearing his yarmulke; (2) there was no evidence that a fair trial would not be achieved if the order was not made; and (3) any potential prejudice could be cured in voir dire. Are these last two reasons anything more than guesswork? Couldn't the same claims be argued by LaRocca? Weren't they in fact argued by LaRocca, and rejected by the New York courts? If the latter two reasons are not empirically based, doesn't that mean that only the first reason distinguishes *LaRocca v. Lane* and *Weinberger?* That reason suggests that the constitutional claim exists only if the opposing party does not object to the wearing of religious garb. Does that make sense?

At the end of its opinion, the Second Circuit casts doubt on the validity of the court's opinion in *People v. Drucker*, 100 Misc. 2d 91, 418 N.Y.S.2d 744 (1979). In that case, the trial court denied a defense motion that the complainant, an Episcopalian priest, be ordered to testify in clothing other than his clerical garb. The court reasoned that *La Rocca v. Lane* was not controlling on the ground that an attorney and a witness were dissimiliar actors in the trial process. Instead, it followed *Weinberger*, holding that the solution was thorough voir dire of the prospective jurors. Is this plausible?

2. The Second Circuit also suggests another difference between *Weinberger* and *Drucker*, on the one hand, and *LaRocca*, on the other. That difference is "the jury's task of appraising the credibility of parties and witnesses, which entitled it to take into account the person's demeanor, conduct, intelligence, and background.... The jury should have no need to judge the lawyer's credibility." Is this the court's way of suggesting that one's religious beliefs, as evidenced by one's religious garb, may be used by the jury to credit the witness's credibility? If so, that is contrary to Federal Rule of Evidence 610 and New York evidence law, which prohibits crediting or attacking a witness's credibility based on the witness's religious beliefs. *See, e.g., People v. Wood*, 488 N.E.2d 86, 497 N.Y.S.2d 340 (1985) (holding reversible error prosecution's questions of defendant's expert concerning expert's decision to affirm rather than swear an oath and noting longstanding common law of New York prohibiting linking credibility of witness and witness's religious beliefs). Is there any other interpretation one can give this language that does not implicate the prohibition of Rule 610 and state analogues?

3. In the Philadelphia Court of Common Pleas, defense counsel requested the trial judge issue an order forbidding a Roman Catholic nun, the sister of the murder victim, from wearing her religious habit at the trial of the four men charged with murder. Sister Ann Colleen Dougherty of the Servants of the Immaculate Heart of Mary was required by her religious order to wear her habit whenever she was in public. At an earlier trial in the case, which resulted in a mistrial, defense counsel suggested that Sister Ann Colleen "tried to create 'psychological pressure' on the jury by sitting near the jury box in her habit." Kit Konolige, *Judge: Nun's Attire Not Out of Order*, Philadelphia Daily News, March 24, 1987. After one judge recused herself, and after intense media scrutiny, the defense motion was denied.

4. On the right of parties to cover their heads while in the courtroom, see *State ex rel. Burrell-El v. Autrey*, 752 S.W.2d 895 (Mo. App. 1988) (fez); *In re Palmer*, 120 R.I. 250, 386 A.2d 1112 (1978) (takia or prayer cap); *McMillan v. State*, 258 Md. 147, 265 A.2d 453 (1970) (filaas). *See also Ryslik v. Krass*, 279 N.J. Super. 293, 652 A.2d 767 (N.J. App. 1995) (reversing decision by trial court granting plaintiff new trial because defendant-priest in tort action allowed to wear clerical garb during trial); *Joseph v. State*, 642 So. 2d 613 (Fla. App. 1994) (ordering trial court to allow defendant to wear shirt and jeans with religious pictures and names on clothing).

F. Confidential Communications to Clergy

Congress adopted the Federal Rules of Evidence in late 1974, and they became effective in mid-1975. An area of evidentiary law that aroused a great deal of controversy was privileges. The Supreme Court proposed a number of specific rules of privilege, including a "Communications to Clergymen" privilege. *Proposed Federal Rule of Evidence* 506. Congress rejected the specific rules of privilege proposed by the Supreme Court, and instead substituted one general rule. This Rule required federal courts to follow state law when so required by the rule in *Erie Ry. Co. v. Tompkins*, 304 U.S. 64 (1938), and in other cases to elucidate privileges "by the principles of the common law as they may be interpreted by the courts of the United States in the light of reason and experience." Fed. R. Evid. 501.

The proposed privilege for communications to clergy was formerly called the priest-penitent privilege. The Roman Catholic church held confessional communications between a priest and penitent inviolable, THE CODE OF CANON LAW: A TEXT AND COMMENTARY 964 §3, 983, 984 (James A. Coriden, Thomas A. Green, Donald E. Heintschel eds. 1985), and the legal protection of the privilege in American law is traceable back to the 1813 decision of the Mayor's Court of New York in *People v. Phillips*, excerpted in Chapter Three. Although it appeared that no such privilege existed in English law, approximately half the states enacted such a privilege by 1900, and according to the Advisory Committee's Note to Proposed Federal Rule of Evidence 506, by the late 1960s the privilege was "recognized by statute in about two-thirds of the states."

In re Grand Jury Investigation

918 F.2d 374 (3rd Cir. 1990)

BECKER, Circuit Judge.

This is an appeal by the government from an order denying its motion to compel the federal grand jury testimony of a Lutheran clergyman concerning subjects discussed during a family counseling session. The district court held that a clergy-communicant privilege, existing under federal common law, barred the testimony. The grand jury was investigating whether racially motivated housing discrimination and a conspiracy to deny civil rights led to an apparent arson at the home of a black family that lived next door to the family whose members the pastor counseled. In addition to the pastor, the family counseling session involved four persons: a husband and wife, who were members of the pastor's church, the wife's adult son from a previous marriage, and the son's fiancee.

The district court, ruling on the pastor's motion to quash the subpoena compelling him to testify before the grand jury, held that a communication, to be protected, must be made in confidence. It found, however, that the communications of family group members to the pastor were, as the pastor understood them to be, confidential. Otherwise, the court concluded, "his ministry would be ineffective." The government contends that even if a clergy-communicant privilege exists under federal common law, the pastor should not be able to invoke it to avoid testifying about what was said to him in the course of this counseling session. The government reasons that the presence at the counseling session of the fiancee (not yet a member of the family) was neither essential to nor in furtherance of any religiously motivated communications to the pastor on the part of the others present and therefore worked either to vitiate or to waive any privilege. In support of this argument, the government invokes the general principle that evidentiary privileges, which retard the search for truth, should be narrowly construed.

There is a relative dearth of federal precedent establishing the existence and contours of a clergy-communicant privilege. Although the original draft of the Federal Rules of Evidence included a section providing for a number of specific privileges, including one that would have protected communications to members of the clergy, *see* Proposed Rules of Evidence for the United States Court and Magistrates, 56 F.R.D. 183 (1973), Congress chose not to codify the draft Rules comprehending specific privileges. *See* H.R. 93-650, S.R. 93-1277, H.R. Conf. R. 93-1597, 93rd Cong. 2d Sess. 4, *reprinted* in 1974 U.S.Code Cong. & Admin.News 7051, 7075, 7098, 7100. Congress substituted in their stead a single rule generally providing that "privilege[s] ... shall be governed by the principles of the common law as they may be interpreted by the courts of the United States in the light of reason and experience." Fed.R.Evid. 501. In accordance with this standard, we must determine whether a clergy-communicant privilege in fact exists and, if it does, its relevant contours.

For the reasons that follow, we hold that a clergy-communicant privilege does exist. We further hold that this privilege protects communications to a member of the clergy, in his or her spiritual or professional capacity, by persons who seek spiritual counseling and who reasonably expect that their words will be kept in confidence. As is the case with the attorney-client privilege, the presence of third parties, if essential to and in furtherance of the communication, does not vitiate the clergy-communicant privilege. Neither the record nor the district court's findings, however, are sufficient to establish whether any of those present at the counseling session should be considered third parties, to gauge the impact of any third party's presence, and to enable us to ascertain whether the privilege was properly invoked in this case. We will therefore vacate the district court's order and remand for further proceedings.

I. FACTS AND PROCEDURAL HISTORY

On November 28, 1985, a fire occurred at a house, located in an all-white neighborhood in the Forest Hills section of Pittsburgh, Pennsylvania, that had recently been purchased by a black family. The police and fire departments determined that the fire was the likely result of arson. Within several days of the fire, Mr. and Mrs. George Kampich, Mrs. Kampich's adult son, George Shaw (who is not related legally or by blood to Mr. Kampich), and Patty DiLucente, Shaw's fiancee, sought counseling from the Reverend Ernest Knoche ("Pastor Knoche"), a Lutheran clergyman. All four persons lived in the home next door to the site of the fire. Mr. and Mrs. Kampich are members of Pastor Knoche's church. Although Shaw has occasionally attended services at the church, Shaw and DiLucente are not members.

On November 28, 1989, the government subpoenaed Pastor Knoche to testify before the grand jury about the 1985 counseling session. The government, in support of this subpoena, asserted that it had reason to believe that the Kampiches, Shaw, and DiLucente had planned or participated in the arson and had discussed their involvement with the pastor. In an interview prior to his appearance before the grand jury, Pastor Knoche informed the government that he intended to assert the clergy-communicant privilege and would refuse to answer any questions regarding the counseling session. That day, the government filed a motion in the district court to compel Pastor Knoche to testify before the grand jury.

On November 28th and 29th, the district court held a hearing on the government's motion. In the course of this hearing, the district judge questioned the pastor about the extent of his family and group counseling, the parties involved in the discussion at issue, and the confidentiality of their communications. Pastor Knoche stated that family counseling, in contrast to individual counseling, constituted a typical and important part of his ministry. The Pastor also concurred with the district court's characterization of his ministry as founded upon the Judeo-Christian notion of redemption and forgiveness through counseling and prayer. The Pastor responded, further, that forthrightness and truthfulness on the part of participants, such as Mr. and Mrs. Kampich, Shaw, and DiLucente, are essential to proper counseling and, ultimately, to redemption. He concluded that those whom he spiritually counsels expect that he will keep any communications made to him in strict confidence.

The district court sustained Pastor Knoche's right to assert a clergy-communicant privilege and denied the government's motion to compel his testimony. The district judge, in a colloquy setting forth the basis for his decision, described it as "tough," but concluded that compelling the pastor to testify would break down church-state divisions, infringe upon the right to participate in religious activities, invade a "sacrosanct" area, and, through depriving families of confidential religious counseling, endanger them. This appeal followed.

II. THE EXISTENCE AND CONTOURS OF A CLERGY-COMMUNICANT PRIVILEGE

A. *The Clergy-Communicant Privilege and the History of Rule 501*

Both the history and the language of Rule 501, therefore, provide us with a mandate to develop evidentiary privileges in accordance with common law principles. This mandate, in turn, requires us to examine federal and state case law and impels us to consult treatises and commentaries on the law of evidence that elucidate the development of the common law. We believe that the proposed rules of evidence adopted by the Supreme Court and submitted to Congress provide us with an appropriate starting point for discerning the existence and scope of the clergy-communicant privilege.

Rule 501 replaced a number of proposed rules concerning evidentiary privileges that were adopted by the Supreme Court following extensive study and analysis by the Advisory Committee responsible for codifying federal rules of evidence. As submitted to Congress, Article V of the proposed rules set out thirteen rules encompassing nine specific privileges, including a privilege for communications to clergymen. *See* Proposed Federal Rules of Evidence, 56 F.R.D. at 183. Rule 506, delineating the contours of the clergy-communicant privilege, reads as follows:

Communications to Clergymen

(a) Definitions. As used in this rule:

> (1) A "clergyman" is a minister, priest, rabbi, or other similar functionary of a religious organization, or an individual reasonably believed so to be by the person consulting him.
>
> (2) A communication is "confidential" if made privately and not intended for further disclosure except to other persons present in furtherance of the purpose of the communication.
>
> (b) General rule of privilege. A person has a privilege to refuse to disclose and to prevent another from disclosing a confidential communication by the person to a clergyman in his professional character as spiritual adviser.
>
> (c) Who may claim the privilege. The privilege may be claimed by the person, by his guardian or conservator, or by his personal representative if he is deceased. The clergyman may claim the privilege on behalf of the person. His authority so to do is presumed in the absence of evidence to the contrary.

Proposed Fed.R.Evid. 506, 56 F.R.D. at 247.

The Advisory Committee's note confirms that proposed Rule 506 is expansive in character:

> The definition of "confidential" communication is consistent with the use of the term in Rule 503(a)(5) for lawyer-client and in Rule 504(a)(3) for psychotherapist-patient, suitably adapted to communications to clergymen.
>
> * * *
>
> *...The choice between a privilege narrowly restricted to doctrinally required confessions and a privilege broadly applicable to all confidential communications with a clergyman in his professional character as a spiritual adviser has been exercised in favor of the latter.* Many clergymen now receive training in marriage counseling and the handling of personality problems. Matters of this kind fall readily into the realm of the spirit. The same considerations which underlie the psychotherapist-patient privilege of Rule 504 suggest a broad application of the privilege for communications to clergymen.

Id. at 248 (subdivisions (a) & (b)) (emphasis added).

The reference in the Advisory Committee's Note to the group counseling practices common to the psychotherapist-patient relationship and the relationship of lawyers to multiple clients indicates that the Supreme Court did not view the privilege as limited solely to confidential relationships between two individuals. Given the requisite showing of confidentiality, proposed Rule 506 would have extended the clergy-communicant privilege to group discussions.

Although Congress chose not to adopt the proposed rules on privileges, it did not disapprove them. The Senate Judiciary Committee's report on Rule 501 states:

> It should be clearly understood that, in approving this general rule as to privileges, the action of Congress should not be understood as disapproving any recognition of...any...of the enumerated privileges contained in the Supreme Court rules. Rather, our action should be understood as reflecting the view that the recognition of a privilege based on a confidential relationship and other privileges should be determined on a case-by-case basis.

S.Rep. No. 93-1277, 93rd Cong., 2d Sess. 4, *reprinted* in 1974 U.S.Code Cong. and Admin. News 7051, 7059. We believe that the proposed rules provide a useful reference point and offer guidance in defining the existence and scope of evidentiary privileges in the federal courts.

The history of the proposed Rules of Evidence reflects that the clergy-communicant rule was one of the least controversial of the enumerated privileges, merely defining a long-recognized principle of American law. Although most of the nine privileges set forth in the proposed rules were vigorously attacked in Congress, the privilege covering communications to members of the clergy was not. S. Saltzburg & K. Redden, *Federal Rules of Evidence Manual* 333 (4th ed. 1986). Indeed, virtually every state has recognized some form of clergy-communicant privilege. The inclusion of the clergy-communicant privilege in the proposed rules, taken together with its uncontroversial nature, strongly suggests that the privilege is, in the words of the Supreme Court "indelibly ensconced" in the American common law. *United States v. Gillock*, 445 U.S. 360, 368 (1980).

B. *Federal Judicial Precedents Recognizing a Clergy-Communicant Privilege*

The first reported federal case recognizing the clergy-communicant privilege through the common law process of decision was decided in 1958, *see Mullen v. United States*, 263 F.2d 275 (D.C.Cir.1958) (Fahy J., concurring). Judge Fahy's lengthy concurrence in this case traced the history and contours of the clergy-communicant privilege and opined that the admission of a minister's testimony about a conversation, in which the defendant sought spiritual counseling, constituted an additional ground for overturning the jury's verdict against her.

Following *Mullen*, a number of federal courts recognized a common law clergy-communicant privilege. The court in *In re Verplank*, 329 F.Supp. 433, 435 (C.D.Cal.1971), for example, invoked the *Mullen* concurrence and the Supreme Court's instruction in *Wolfle* [*v. United States*, 291 U.S. 7 (1934)] that the federal courts should develop evidentiary rules "in the light of reason and experience." The court held that draft counseling services rendered by a clergyman came within the ambit of his religious duties and were privileged. *Id.* at 436. The court further concluded that the privilege extended to counseling by members of the clergyman's staff who were not ordained ministers. *Id.* In *United States v. Wells*, 446 F.2d 2 (2d Cir.1971), the court, holding that the admission into evidence of a letter from the defendant to a priest did not violate the clergy-communicant privilege, implicitly recognized such a privilege. The *Wells* court based its holding on the absence of any indication that the defendant had intended the letter to be confidential or that "its purpose was to obtain religious or other counsel, advice, solace, absolution or ministration." *Id.* at 4.[11]

The Supreme Court, albeit in dicta, subsequently acknowledged the existence of a "priest-penitent" privilege. *See Trammel v. United States*, 445 U.S. 40, 45 (1980). Critiquing an archaic and unduly expansive rule that permitted a defendant to exclude

11. Other federal cases at least impliedly recognizing the clergy-communicant privilege and decided within the same time period include United States v. Luther, 481 F.2d 429 (9th Cir.1973) (impliedly recognizing penitent-clergyman privilege in holding that the privilege could not be invoked to protect religious corporation's financial records from inspection by the Internal Revenue Service); *In re Wood*, 430 F.Supp. 41 (S.D.N.Y.1977) (impliedly recognizing possibility that evidentiary privilege might protect communications made in course of "priest-penitent relationship" not at issue in the case); *Cimijotti v. Paulsen*, 219 F.Supp. 621 (N.D. Iowa 1963) (holding, in diversity case, that clergy-penitent privilege exists and protects communications within its ambit from disclosure in deposition taken in the course of discovery).

from evidence any adverse spousal testimony, the Court favorably referred to several privileges by analogy, among them, the "priest-penitent" privilege:

> The privileges between priest and penitent, attorney and client, and physician and patient limit protection to private communications. The privileges are rooted in the imperative need for confidence and trust. The priest-penitent privilege recognizes the human need to disclose to a spiritual counselor, in total and absolute confidence, what are believed to be flawed acts or thoughts and to receive priestly consolation and guidance in return.

Id. at 51. *See also United States v. Nixon*, 418 U.S. 683, 709 (1974) ("[G]enerally, an attorney or *a priest* may not be required to disclose what has been revealed in professional confidence." (emphasis added)).

In the wake of the Supreme Court's opinion in *Trammel*, a number of federal district courts and courts of appeal have also acknowledged the clergy-communicant privilege. *See, e.g., United States v. Dube*, 820 F.2d 886 (7th Cir.1987) (acknowledging existence of clergy-penitent privilege, but holding that privilege did not apply to communications made to clergyman to obtain assistance in avoiding tax obligations, not spiritual relief); *United States v. Gordon*, 655 F.2d 478 (2d Cir.1981) (holding that defendant's business communications to priest he employed in a nonreligious capacity were not protected by priest-penitent privilege); *Eckmann v. Board of Education of Hawthorne School Dist.*, 106 F.R.D. 70 (E.D.Mo.1985) (observing that "[t]he 'priest-penitent' privilege has clearly been recognized by federal courts" and holding that Catholic nun could invoke the privilege with respect to communications made to her in her capacity as a spiritual advisor); *but cf. Seidman v. Fishburn-Hudgins Educational Foundation*, 724 F.2d 413 (4th Cir.1984) (holding that relative could not invoke clergyman-communicant privilege on decedent's behalf and observing that privilege "has no firm foundation in common law"); *United States v. Webb*, 615 F.2d 828 (9th Cir.1980) (court found that prisoner's confession to crime in presence of a minister and security officer was not confidential, but did not reach question whether clergy-communicant privilege applies in federal proceedings).

Although we have never formally recognized the clergy-communicant privilege, several of our opinions have referred to the privilege in passing. These opinions note that the privilege protecting communications to members of the clergy, like the attorney-client and physician-patient privileges, is grounded in a policy of preventing disclosures that would tend to inhibit the development of confidential relationships that are socially desirable. *See In re Grand Jury Matter*, 673 F.2d 688, 695 (3d Cir.) (Sloviter, J., concurring) (noting private benefits of certain privileges, including the "priest-penitent" privilege, in critiquing majority opinion concerning use—fruits immunity following the invocation of the privilege against adverse spousal testimony), *cert. denied*, 459 U.S. 1015 (1982); *In re Grand Jury Proceedings*, 563 F.2d 577, 587 (3d Cir.1977) (Gibbons, J., concurring) (critiquing federal common-law legislative privilege found to exist by majority and contrasting this privilege to privileges, including "priest-penitent" privilege, that have significant public or private benefits).

C. *The Scope and Contours of the Clergy-Communicant Privilege Adopted*

Although Rule 501 grants the federal courts power to create new privileges or to develop existing privileges as the need arises, we agree with the government's contention in this case that our authority is narrow in scope and should be exercised only after careful consideration in the face of a strong showing of need for the privilege. Testimonial privileges contravene the well-established principle that "'the public... has a right to every man's evidence'" and, therefore, "must be strictly construed and 'accepted only to the very limited extent that permitting a refusal to testify or excluding relevant evidence has a public good transcending the normally predominant principle of utilizing all rational means for ascertaining the truth.'" *Trammel*, 445 U.S. at 46 (citations omitted); *accord Nixon*, 418 U.S. at 709–10.

In determining whether a clergy-communicant privilege exists, we weigh Dean Wigmore's four fundamental prerequisites for a privilege against the disclosure of communications:

> (1) The communications must originate in a *confidence* that they will not be disclosed.
>
> (2) This element of *confidentiality must be essential* to the full and satisfactory maintenance of the relation between the parties.
>
> (3) The *relation* must be one which in the opinion of the community ought to be sedulously *fostered.*
>
> (4) The *injury* that would inure to the relation by the disclosure of the communications must be *greater than the benefit* thereby gained for the correct disposal of litigation.

8 Wigmore at § 2285 (footnote omitted) (emphasis in original). The Advisory Committee Note to proposed Rule 506 adverts to these considerations and concludes that they "seem strongly to favor a privilege for confidential communications to clergymen." 56 F.R.D. at 247.

We are satisfied, moreover, that American common law... compels the recognition of a clergy-communicant privilege. Both state and federal decisions have long recognized the privilege. The Supreme Court Rules Committee also recognized the privilege. That is doubtless because the clergy-communicant relationship is so important, indeed so fundamental to the western tradition, that it must be "sedulously fostered." 8 Wigmore at § 2285. Confidence is obviously essential to maintaining the clergy-communicant relationship. Although there are countervailing considerations, we have no doubt that the need for protecting the relationship outweighs them.

We believe that the privilege should apply to protect communications made (1) to a clergyperson[13] (2) in his or her spiritual and professional capacity (3) with a reasonable expectation of confidentiality. As is the case with the attorney-client privilege, the presence of third parties, if essential to and in furtherance of the communication, should not void the privilege. This statement of the contours of the privilege is consistent with the provisions of Rule 506, which, as our study of the federal case law confirms, tracks the evolving common law. In addition, we note our agreement with the tenor of the Ad-

---

13. We believe that Proposed Rule of Evidence 506(a)(1) provides a workable definition of a clergyperson: "A 'clergyman' is a minister, priest, rabbi, or other similar functionary of a religious organization, or an individual reasonably believed so to be by the person consulting him." 56 F.R.D. at 247. By endorsing this definition of a clergyperson, we do not intimate that the privilege should be interpreted to comprehend communications to and among members of sects that denominate each and every member as clergy, proclaim that all communications have spiritual significance, or dictate that all communications among members, whether essential to and in furtherance of the purportedly privileged communication or not, shall be confidential.

visory Committee's Note to proposed Rule 506, which extends the scope of the privilege to encompass not only communications between Roman Catholic priests and their penitents, but also communications between clergy and communicants of other denominations. *See* Proposed Fed. Rule of Evid. 506 advisory committee's note, 56 F.R.D. at 247.[14]

Our delineation of the privilege is not comprehensive. We illuminate here and *infra* only those facets and boundaries of the privilege that are implicated in this case. The privilege is a common law rule. The precise scope of the privilege and its additional facets, such as whether a clergyperson should be required to disclose confidential communications when harm to innocent parties is threatened and imminent, are, therefore, most suitably left to case-by-case evolution.

III. THE APPLICATION OF THE CLERGY-COMMUNICANT PRIVILEGE IN THIS CASE

The threshold criterion for deciding whether the privilege should attach—the criterion that the communication be made to a clergyperson—is clearly satisfied. Pastor Knoche is an ordained Lutheran minister. Whether the Kampiches, Shaw, and DiLucente communicated with Pastor Knoche in his spiritual or professional capacity, thus fulfilling the second prerequisite for attachment of the privilege, is less obvious. Whether the Kampiches', Shaw's, and DiLucente's communications to Knoche were made with a reasonable expectation of confidentiality, fulfilling the third prerequisite for the privilege's attachment, is also unclear.

The government...maintains that DiLucente's presence during the Kampiches' and Shaw's conversation with Pastor Knoche undermines the confidentiality of this conversation for two reasons. The government contends, first, that any existing clergy-communicant privilege is inapplicable in this case because DiLucente was not related to the Kampiches and Shaw by either blood or marriage at the time the conversation took place. We must therefore reach the issue whether the clergy-communicant privilege may apply to pastoral counseling sessions involving persons who have no family ties to one another.

The government is correct in observing that the traditional clergy-communicant privilege protected a penitential relationship in which a person privately confessed his or her sins to a priest, in order to receive some form of church sanctioned discipline or absolution. Neither family nor other types of group counseling fit neatly within this "one-to-one" model of the privilege. We have explained, however, that the modern view of the privilege is more expansive than the traditional one. We discern nothing in modern clergy-communicant privilege doctrine, as it finds expression in either proposed Rule 506 or the cases recognizing the privilege, that would limit the privilege's application solely to group discussions involving family members related by blood or marriage. Modern clergy-communicant privilege doctrine focuses, rather, on whether the presence of a third party is essential to or in furtherance of a communication to a member of the clergy. *See* Proposed Fed. Rule of Evid. 506(a)(2), 56 F.R.D. at 247; *Webb*, 615 F.2d at 828; *Wells*, 446 F.2d at 2. We think, consistent with the general constructional rule that

14. Indeed, the prospect of restricting the privilege to Roman Catholic penitential communications raises serious first amendment concerns. See Larsen v. Valente, 456 U.S. 228, 245–46 (1982) (emphasizing that the establishment clause articulates a "principle of denominational neutrality" and holding that state law "granting a denominational preference" is subject to strict scrutiny).

evidentiary privileges should be narrowly construed, that recognition of the clergy-communicant privilege in this circumstance depends upon whether the third party's presence is essential to and in furtherance of a communication to a member of the clergy. As is the case with consultations between attorneys and clients, the presence of multiple parties, unrelated by blood or marriage, during discussions with a member of the clergy may, but will not necessarily, defeat the condition that communications be made with a reasonable expectation of confidentiality in order for the privilege to attach.

At the district court's hearing on the privilege, the testimony concerning whether the Kampiches, Shaw, and DiLucente reasonably expected that their communications to Pastor Knoche were confidential was sparse. The court did touch upon this issue, as well as the issue of whether the communications were made to the pastor in his spiritual or professional capacity, in the following colloquy:

> [The Court] Would you say as to the second situation where you spoke with the...husband and wife, as well as the wife's adult son from a previous marriage and the son's fiancee who is now his wife,...that those communications were in confidence and were confident?
>
> [Pastor Knoche] In my role or capacity as pastor and in confidence.
>
> [The Court] And they were in confidence?
>
> [Pastor Knoche] Yes, your Honor.
>
> [The Court] I'm going to sustain your privilege.

This was the only indication that the district court gave as to whether it considered that the communications to Pastor Knoche were confidential and made to him in his spiritual or professional capacity. The district court neither inquired into whether the presence of each person at the discussion was essential to and in furtherance of the communications to the pastor nor made findings of fact on that issue.

Although the district court was correct in recognizing the existence of a clergy-communicant privilege, we are unable to affirm its order denying the government's motion to compel Pastor Knoche's testimony. That is because, given the contours of the privilege as we have defined it, the court did not develop a sufficient record or make sufficient findings to enable us finally to review its order.

In order to determine whether the Kampiches, Shaw, and DiLucente communicated with Pastor Knoche in his spiritual or professional capacity and with a reasonable expectation of confidentiality, for example, the district court may well have to inquire into the nature of the communicants' relationship as well as the pastoral counseling practices of the relevant synod of the Lutheran church.[21]

In sum, there are no hard and fast rules in this area. We are confident, however, that through carefully framed inquiries, the district court will be able to obtain sufficient

---

21. Although restricting the clergy-communicant privilege to Roman Catholic penitential communications, for example, would raise serious establishment clause concerns, inquiring into the pastoral counseling practices of a particular denomination would appear to pose no such threat to first amendment rights. Rather, we believe that establishing the pastoral counseling practices of a particular denomination to ascertain the types of communications that the denomination deems spiritual and confidential is both a necessary and a constitutionally inoffensive threshold step in determining whether a privilege interdenominational in nature applies in light of the facts and circumstances of a particular case.

information to determine whether the clergy-communicant privilege should apply in this case.

[Vacated and remanded.]

Notes

1. A thorough history of the privilege is Jacob C. Yellin, *The History and Current Status of the Clergy-Penitent Privilege*, 23 Santa Clara L. Rev. 95 (1983). *See also* Michael C. Smith, *The Pastor on the Witness Stand: Toward a Religious Privilege in the Courts*, 29 Cath. Law. 1 (1984).

2. There are no modern American cases in which the privilege has been asserted as a matter of the common law and not legally recognized, at least implicitly. Although the Federal Rules of Evidence do not explicitly recognize a clergy-communicant privilege, the decision of the Third Circuit in *In re Grand Jury Investigation* reflects the generally held approach of federal courts, which have recognized a clergy-communicant privilege. In addition, all of the states have adopted some form of clergy-communicant privilege, usually by statute. Is this recognition required by the First Amendment? Can the acknowledgment of a cleric-penitent privilege violate the First Amendment? *See* Jane E. Mayes, Note, *Striking Down Clergyman-Communicant Privilege Statutes: Let Free Exercise of Religion Govern*, 62 Ind. L.J. 397 (1987) (yes).

In the spring of 1996, a detective in the Lane County, Oregon sheriff's office obtained a warrant allowing him to seize a tape of communications between Conan Wayne Hale, a prisoner at the Lane County jail, and the Reverend Timothy Mockaitis, a Roman Catholic priest. The transcript of this conversation became public knowledge, and Mockaitis and Portland archbishop Francis E. George filed suit seeking destruction of the tape, continued secrecy concerning the contents of the communication between Mockaitis and Hale, and an injunction permanently barring the Lane County district attorney and other Oregon officials from recording confidential communications between prisoners and clergy. The district court dismissed on abstention grounds, but on appeal, the Ninth Circuit held that the action of the Lane County officials violated both the Religious Freedom Restoration Act (later held unconstitutional) and the Fourth Amendment. *Mockaitis v. Harcleroad*, 104 F.3d 1522 (9th Cir. 1997).

3. Should a cleric be forced to reveal confidential communications if the communication concerns child abuse and state law requires the disclosure of evidence of child abuse? In Texas, any "person having cause to believe that a child's physical or mental health or welfare has been or may be adversely affected by abuse or neglect by any person shall immediately make a report...." Tex. Fam. Code § 262.101(a). This statute continues, "The requirement to report under this section applies without exception to an individual whose personal communications may otherwise be privileged, including an attorney, *a member of the clergy*, a medical practitioner, a social worker, and a mental health professional." Tex. Fam. Code § 262.101(c)(emphasis added). Failure to report as required by this statute is criminally punishable. *Cf.* Ariz. Rev. Stats. 13-3620(H)(2001)(requiring clergy to report child abuse even if learned through confidential communication, but permitting clergy to refuse to testify). *See also* Mary Harter Mitchell, *Must Clergy Tell? Child Abuse Reporting Requirements Versus the Clergy Privilege and Free Exercise of Religion*, 71 Minn. L. Rev. 723 (1987). Should the duty to report confidential communications concerning child abuse de-

pend on the existing or future danger to the child(ren), the extent of the theological or personal commitment made by the cleric not to disclose the communication, the Free Exercise interests implicated by forcing disclosure, or some other combination of factors?

4. As noted by the court, Proposed Federal Rule of Evidence 506 requires several conditions to be met before the privilege is acknowledged. The communication must be confidential, made to a "clergyman," and made for the purpose of communicating with the clergyman "in his professional character as spiritual adviser." These latter two requirements are factual determinations made by the trial court. In addition to the definition of "clergyman" found in the Proposed Rule itself, the Advisory Committee's Note supplements the definition. The Note states that the definition of "clergyman" "is not so broad as to include self-denominated 'ministers.'" Does this limitation raise constitutional concerns because the court must inquire into the tenets of the religion to make the determination whether the claimant is a member of the clergy? The Note also attempts to define "clergyman" by analogy: "A fair construction of the language requires that the person to whom the status is sought to be attached be regularly engaged in activities conforming at least in a general way with those of a Catholic priest, Jewish rabbi, or minister of an established Protestant denomination, though not necessarily on a full-time basis." Is this analogical definition problematic because it requires a court to interpret "clergyman" in light of established, traditional Western religions? If so, does that make the definition constitutionally defective on equal protection grounds? Does the determination whether a person is a cleric allow the court to define religion? Is a limitation on who may claim the status of "clergyman" a necessary restriction of the privilege? The Third Circuit states that determining whether the purpose of the communication with the minister was spiritual counseling may require an inquiry into "the pastoral counseling practices of the relevant synod of the Lutheran church." Is the court persuasive when it states that making this determination does not raise a serious "threat to first amendment rights"? Would such an inquiry violate the Establishment Clause? The New Jersey Appellate Division, in *State v. Cary*, 751 A.2d 260 (N.J. App. Div. 2000), interpreted New Jersey's clergy-penitent privilege concerning the factual determinations of "cleric" and "in the capacity of spiritual advisor." New Jersey's privilege defined "cleric" similarly to the Proposed Federal Rule: "[A] priest, rabbi, minister or other person or practitioner authorized to perform similar functions of any religion." The question in *Cary* was whether a communication by the accused to a Baptist deacon (not a Baptist pastor) who was also a state trooper was a communication to a cleric protected by Rule 511 of the New Jersey Rules of Evidence. The court noted the difficulties in defining "cleric," but avoided confronting the issue by holding that the communication was not made confidentially to the trooper-deacon in his capacity as a spiritual advisor. *See also Banks v. State*, 725 So. 2d 711 (Miss. 1997)(holding Baptist deacon not clergy member for purposes of privilege).

5. Several states have broadened the definition of cleric beyond the proposed federal rule. For example, *see* W.Va. Code §57-3-9 (Supp. 2000) (including "priest, nun, rabbi, duly accredited Christian Science practitioner" as members of the clergy permitted to invoke privilege). Does this extension of the privilege make legal and constitutional sense? Why extend the breadth of the privilege if this is not mandated by the religious institution or sect to which the cleric belongs?

6. Canon law of the Roman Catholic church recognizes the inviolable seal of the confessional only if the penitent-confessor is confessing sins to a priest. A "confession of

sins" does not take place if the confidential communication is made to a Roman Catholic nun or brother. Should the law nevertheless protect from disclosure such communications, if made confidentially to the nun or brother as a spiritual advisor? *Compare Eckmann v. Bd. of Educ. of Hawthorne Sch. Dist.*, 106 F.R.D. 70 (E.D. Mo. 1985) and *Blough v. Food Lion, Inc.*, 142 F.R.D. 622 (E.D. Va. 1992) (holding privilege applies to confidential communications with Roman Catholic nun) *with In re Murtha*, 279 A.2d 889 (N.J. App. Div. 1971) (holding privilege inapplicable because confidential communication with Roman Catholic nun not inviolate as a matter of Catholic ecclesiology).

7. The court in *In re Grand Jury Investigation* notes the importance of the truth-seeking function of the trial. The consequence of this understanding of the function of the trial is that privileges must be "strictly construed." Even though the court is effectively adopting Proposed Federal Rule of Evidence 506, remember that Congress did not adopt this rule. Consequently, the court is arguably expanding the cleric-communicant privilege beyond its original limits, and is therefore not "strictly construing" the cleric-communicant privilege. Does the court interpret the privilege in this fashion for constitutional reasons? If so, is it doing so to protect the constitutional interest in religious liberty, or to ensure that communications among members of faiths "similar" to Roman Catholicism are equally protected? In other words, is the court broadening the class of protected communicants for equal protection reasons? Are there nonconstitutional reasons justifying the increased scope of the privilege?

8. Unlike the proposed federal rule, several states restrict the privilege to communications made in the course of church "discipline." *See, e.g.*, Ariz. Rev. Stats. Ann. § 12-2233 (civil cases) (1994), § 13-4062(3) (criminal cases) (Supp. 2001) (limiting privilege to a "confession made to him in his character as clergyman or priest in the course of discipline enjoined by the church to which he belongs."); California Evidence Code § 1032 (1986) (defining "penitential communication" as a confidential communication made to one who "in the course of discipline or practice of his church... has a duty to keep such communication secret."). Thus, in those states, the privilege exists only if the cleric has an ecclesiastical duty to keep secret the confidential communication. In *People v. Edwards*, 248 Cal. Rptr. 53 (Cal. App. 1988), the trial court listened to extensive and sometimes contradictory expert testimony concerning the ecclesiastical law of the Episcopalian church. It concluded that the California privilege did not apply because the communication was not a penitential communication under Episcopalian ecclesiastical law. As a result, the priest was under only a moral duty, and not an ecclesiastical duty, to keep confidential the communication. This decision was affirmed on appeal. Do statutes limiting the application of the privilege to communications made in the course of church discipline raise constitutional issues? The *Grand Jury Investigation* court concluded that restricting the privilege to communications with Roman Catholic priests "raises serious first amendment concerns." Would this limitation raise constitutional concerns because doing so would require prefer one religious denomination over another?

9. Like the proposed federal rule, most state statutes declare the privilege "owned" by the communicant; consequently, the privilege can be waived only by the communicant. However, some states declare the privilege "owned" by the cleric. In *Seidman v. Fishburn-Hudgins Educ. Fnd., Inc.*, 724 F.2d 413 (4th Cir.1984), the Fourth Circuit, interpreting Virginia law, declared that the clergyman owned the privilege, in large part because the purpose of the privilege was "to safeguard the clergyman's status as a secure repository for the confessant's confidences." *Id.* at 415. *See also State v. Szemple*, 640 A.2d 817 (N.J. 1994) (holding under New Jersey law that Minister of Vis-

itation may waive privileged communication made by defendant-prisoner in murder case). As a result of *Szemple*, the New Jersey legislature amended its cleric-penitent privilege to provide that the privilege "shall belong to both the cleric and the person or persons making the communication." N.J. Stats. Ann. § 2A:84A-23 (2000). In *Mockaitis v. Harcleroad*, 104 F.3d 1522 (9th Cir. 1997), the Ninth Circuit concluded that the privilege belonged to the Rev. Mockaitis as well as the communicant, Conan Hale, despite the language of Oregon's cleric-penitent privilege, which mirrored the proposed federal rule. In 1999, Oregon amended its privilege to provide that "a member of the clergy may not be examined as to any confidential communication made to the member in the member's professional character if, under the discipline or tenets of the member's church, denomination or organization, the member has an absolute duty to keep the communication confidential." Or. Rev. Stats. § 40.260(3) (1999). *See generally* Michael J. Mazza, Comment, *Should Clergy Hold the Priest-Penitent Privilege?*, 82 Marq. L. Rev. 171 (1998). Is there any constitutional difference in granting ownership of the privilege to the communicant or to the cleric or to both cleric and penitent? Is it a difference between recognizing an individual right of autonomy and recognizing a right of religious conscience?

10. Cox killed two people while drunk. Later, while attending an Alcoholics Anonymous (AA) meeting, Cox admitted to the killings. One of the persons present at the AA meeting later told her psychologist of Cox's confession, and the psychologist urged the woman to inform police of her knowledge of this crime. She did so, and based in part on this information, Cox was arrested. His finger and palm prints matched those found at the murder site. Cox was convicted. Cox later petitioned the federal district court for a writ of habeas corpus. The court issued the writ, holding that communications made during an AA meeting are privileged pursuant to New York's clergy-penitent privilege. The court concluded that because AA was considered a religion for Establishment Clause purposes, it should be treated similarly for privilege purposes. *Cox v. Miller*, 154 F. Supp.2d 787 (S.D.N.Y. 2001). Should the privilege be so extended?

11. If a communicant makes a confidential communication to a cleric, and the cleric later makes public that confidence, can the communicant successfully sue the cleric in tort? Does it matter whether the communication was considered confidential as a matter of religious law, and not just the law of evidence? In other words, if the communication is considered confidential as a matter of the state's law of evidence, but not confidential as a matter of the law of the religious body to which the cleric belongs, should a duty to keep the communication exist, so that a breach of that duty is enforceable by tort law? *See Hester v. Barnett*, 723 S.W.2d 544 (Mo. Ct. App. 1987); *Handley v. Richards*, 518 So.2d 682 (Ala. 1987) (Maddox, J., concurring specially); *Smith v. Calvary Christian Church*, 614 N.W.2d 590 (Mich. 2000) (no). In *Lightman v. Flaum*, 687 N.Y.S.2d 562 (N.Y. Sup. Ct. 1999), the plaintiff sued two Rabbis in tort for disclosing confidences she made to them concerning her relationship with her husband. The plaintiff sought counseling from Rabbis Flaum and Weinberger regarding her marriage. She later sued her husband for divorce and sought custody of their children. In response to the custody request, the husband filed an affirmation from the Rabbis disclosing information plaintiff had disclosed to the Rabbis during counseling. The court held that a violation of the clergy-penitent privilege created a cause of action in tort. The court concluded that the disclosure was actionable even though the Rabbis claimed that "religious law 'compelled' disclosure." *Id.* at 569. This was because "civil law, which mandated strict confidentiality," made the penitent the holder of the privilege. *Id.* at 570. The Appellate Division reversed on grounds that the privilege had been waived. *Light-*

man v. Flaum, 717 N.Y.S.2d 617 (App. Div. 2000). The New York Court of Appeals held that the evidentiary privilege for clergy-penitent communications did not impose a fiduciary duty of confidentiality upon clergy. Thus, clergy were not subject to civil liability for disclosing confidential communications. *Lightman v. Flaum*, 97 N.Y.2d 128, 736 N.E.2d 300 (2001).

G. Issues of Religion in Criminal Prosecutions

Levin v. United States

338 F.2d 265 (D.C. Cir. 1964), *cert. denied*, 379 U.S. 999 (1965)

BASTIAN, Circuit Judge.

Appellant was tried, convicted and sentenced for the offense of grand larceny.

Count 2 of the indictment charged Levin as follows:

> "On or about February 13, 1959, within the District of Columbia, and within the jurisdiction of this Court, defendant Milton M. Levin did unlawfully, feloniously and willfully steal, take and carry away the property of the Bakery and Confectionery Workers' International Union of America, an unincorporated association, entrusted to James G. Cross, President of said union, the said property consisting of $35,000 in money in violation of Title 22, District of Columbia Code, Section 2201."

Levin was found guilty of grand larceny as charged in Count 2 of the indictment, and his appeal is now before this court for determination.

The trial was a lengthy one. While the testimony of Landriscina regarding Levin's receipt of the money was specifically denied by Levin, there are corroborating circumstances which bear out the Government's case. In her charge to the jury, the trial judge set out fairly the contentions of the Government and of the defendant, as follows:

> "Briefly, I shall tell you what the government claims in this case and then I shall tell you what the defendant claims.
>
> "The government contends that Mr. Levin, the defendant, represented to Mr. Cross, President of the Union and to Mr. Landriscina, another Union officer, that he, the defendant, Mr. Levin, could fix the Cross perjury case if he were given $35,000 to use in the fixing; that $35,000 in cash, of the money belonging to the Union, was by direction of Mr. Cross turned over to Mr. Landriscina, that Mr. Landriscina then turned over the $35,000 to the defendant, Mr. Levin, in order that Mr. Levin might use the money to bribe court officials, or a court official and jurors in a case in which Mr. Cross was the defendant and in which he was charged with perjury. And the government further contends that the defendant, Mr. Levin, just pretended that he would bribe people and that when he took the $35,000, it was with the intent of appropriating it to his own use. That, as I said, is what the government contends.
>
> "On the other hand, Mr. Levin denies that he ever had any understanding with anyone to fix the Cross perjury trial and he denies receiving the $35,000 mentioned in the indictment, or any part of it. He concedes that he had conversations

with certain Union officials and that he saw them, but he says these conversations were primarily about his employment as a lobbyist or as general counsel for the Union, and that checks he received from the Union were for services rendered."

Appellant concedes that the evidence on behalf of the government, if believed by the jury, as it evidently was, was sufficient to support the charge in the indictment; and unless the questions of law urged by appellant are well taken, the judgment of conviction must be affirmed.

Appellant's second point is that reversible error was committed by the trial court in excluding Rabbi Isaacson's testimony as to appellant's religious habits and as to the requirements of the Jewish Orthodox ritual. A resume of the evidence showing the significance of this point seems indicated.

At the trial, the Government introduced testimony by Landriscina that he gave $10,000 in small bills to appellant on the morning of February 12, 1959,[4] and the balance ($25,000) of the agreed $35,000 at about 5:00 p.m. on Friday, February 13, 1959. These transfers, it was testified, were made in a park near the Statler Hotel in Washington, D.C. On the other hand, appellant testified that Landriscina did not give him any money in the District of Columbia on either February 12 or February 13, 1959, that he (appellant) checked into a hotel in the District of Columbia at 5:43 p.m. on February 12, 1959, that he was not in the District on the morning of February 12, that he left the District not later than 1:00 p.m. on February 13, and got to his home in Little Neck, Queens, Long Island, New York, somewhere "between four and five o'clock or before then," and that he was home on February 13, 1959, at five o'clock (p.m.). In response to the question "How do you fix that you were at home?" he stated:

> "Friday afternoon is the Sabbath, which we observe quite diligently, and I never go away from home and my family on the Sabbath."

Upon inquiry by the trial judge, he stated that he remembered being at home on that Friday, February 13, 1959. His testimony in this respect was corroborated by his wife who testified that her husband was home on Friday, February 13, 1959, "after four, about twenty after four, four-thirty at the very latest" according to her best recollection.

Appellant testified further that "I would think I took the train" to come to Washington on February 12. He stated that he had no checks for February, 1959, evidencing any payment to a railway company and "when I take the train, if I were to take the train, I would pay by cash." Appellant's cancelled check in the amount of $13.81 dated February 11, 1959, payable to Eastern Airlines, representing the one way fare between New York and Washington at that time was identified. Appellant testified that the check represented a trip "to or from Washington," and that—

> "It is very likely that that was a reservation. If I were coming back on the 13th, which was a Friday, I would make a reservation long enough in advance to insure."

From the above resume, it is apparent that appellant's testimony, corroborated in part by the testimony of his wife, if credited by the jury, would establish that he took a plane from the District of Columbia to New York not later than 1:00 p.m. on Friday,

4. Other witnesses for the Government through whom Landriscina got the $10,000 in small bills gave testimony indicating that Landriscina did not receive the $10,000 until the morning of Friday, February 13, 1959. The jury thus could infer, if it credited this testimony and that of Landriscina that he paid the $10,000 to the appellant, that Landriscina was mistaken as to the date and that the transfer took place on February 13 instead of February 12.

February 13, 1959, and that he was not in the District but was at home at 5:00 p.m. on that date. His testimony, if credited, would also require the conclusion that he was not in Washington on the morning of February 12, 1959, and that although appellant admittedly was in Washington on the morning of February 13, 1959, up until 1:00 p.m., he did not meet with or receive any money from Landriscina on that morning.

Appellant offered and there was received, supplementing this direct evidence, the testimony of seven acquaintances, neighbors, and friends, including Rabbi Irwin Isaacson, appellant's wife, and a Catholic priest, that his reputation for honesty, truthfulness, and integrity was excellent. In addition some of these persons[6] testified generally as to appellant's religious habits, stating variously that appellant was very religious, that the Orthodox Jewish Sabbath commenced at sundown Friday and ended at sundown Saturday, that appellant never worked on the Sabbath, that it was his habit faithfully to observe the Sabbath, that he was always home at that time, that he was not available for telephone calls, and that he never drove his car on the Sabbath.

After Rabbi Isaacson had testified that appellant's reputation for truthfulness, honesty and integrity was excellent, the following tender was made by counsel for appellant:

> "I wish to go into the subject matter with this witness concerning Mr. Levin's habit of being home on the Sabbath [[7]] and using him as an expert to testify when the Sabbath commenced and what Orthodox ritual requires."

This testimony was ruled inadmissible, and appellant contends that this constituted reversible error. We disagree.

According to the weight of authority, evidence of the general habits of a person is not admissible for the purpose of showing his conduct upon a specific occasion.

---

6. These included a friend and neighbor, living two houses away; a part-time office secretary; and his telephone answering secretary. A friend of 12 years standing was not permitted to testify as to appellant's "habits" as such but was permitted to testify that she had never seen him away from home or riding on Friday evenings; that she had visited him in his home on Friday evenings; that she had tried to telephone him on Friday evenings but didn't get an answer; that she lived by the Temple attended by the appellant in the years 1955 to 1957; that "on many Friday afternoons" in those years appellant parked his car in her driveway never later than 3:45 p.m.; that he would then walk home, would return for Temple, and then after sundown on Saturday would have his car "right there to use to ride home." Appellant's wife not only testified, as already indicated, that her husband was home at "four thirty at the very latest" on Friday, February 13, 1959, but also gave testimony as to her husband's habits with respect to the Sabbath. She stated, for example, that "my husband is always with me on Friday nights. * * * He was always with me, the only time [exception] is when I went to give birth with my daughter, I had to go on a Friday night and he took me to the hospital and walked home." Again, "Well, my husband is always home when I light the candles on Friday night * * *." With respect to the time her husband was home on Friday, February 13, 1959, she said: "Well, it would be before six, it had to be before sundown on Friday because he is always home then. * * * I light the candles at a certain time and that would be an hour before." Asked what time she lighted the candles on February 13, 1959, she said:

> "Well, it would be—every year it varies and I have a calendar which tells me what time to light the candles—this year it was about eleven minutes after five and that is seventeen minutes before sunset."

She said also that her husband never worked on Saturday, although at times he did work after the Sabbath ended—at sundown Saturday.

7. Apart from the testimony as to appellant's reputation, the Rabbi had testified only that he had been a Rabbi in the active ministry for 18 years, that he knows the appellant and at one time lived in his neighborhood. The Rabbi notably did not state that he was the Rabbi of the Temple attended by the appellant. Thus, no foundation was laid which suggests that the Rabbi could or would state that appellant was always, without exception, home on the Sabbath or that he was in fact at home at the beginning of the Sabbath on Friday, February 13, 1959.

Appellant argues, however, citing 1 Wigmore, *Evidence* §92, p. 519 (3d ed. 1940) that evidence of habit is of probative value and thus the intended testimony here should have been received.

It seems apparent to us that an individual's religious practices would not be the type of activities which would lend themselves to the characterization of "invariable regularity." Certainly the very volitional basis of the activity raises serious questions as to its invariable nature, and hence its probative value.

Needless to say, the observance of the Sabbath in a particular manner involves a volitional assent, however guided or instructively urged.

This case is one requiring the jury to choose between the testimony of Landriscina and of the appellant, both alleged participants in the contested payment of money, and thus in a sense both "eyewitnesses." Certainly neither the fact that Landriscina was a prosecution witness nor the fact that both his and Levin's veracity were under attack would be sufficient to require, as a matter of law, the admission of further cumulative evidence[11] of the appellant's habit of being at home before sundown on Fridays. As already indicated appellant's wife not only testified as to his presence at home after 4:30 p.m. on the Friday in question, but she, as well as others (see note 6 *supra*), gave habit testimony. And, as indicated, the tender with respect to the Rabbi was not accompanied by a sufficient showing for admission of his testimony as to appellant's habits.

Even on the assumption that the Rabbi might have become appellant's "weightiest witness," as his brief characterizes the Rabbi, we do not think it was reversible error to exclude further cumulative evidence as to appellant's Sabbath habits in the circumstances here. The prosecution did not dispute his general habit to be home on Friday evenings, but only his whereabouts on a particular Friday evening. It is not unimportant in this connection that, under the evidence adduced by the prosecution, $10,000 of the amount said to be involved was allegedly paid to the appellant on the morning of Thursday, February 12—or the morning of Friday February 13. Further habit evidence as to Friday evenings would not have pertained to those times.

Nor do we think it was an abuse of discretion on the part of the District Court not to receive the Rabbi's expert testimony as to "when the Sabbath commenced and what Orthodox ritual requires." Witnesses had already testified as to when the Sabbath commenced and when it ended. There was abundant evidence as to appellant's devotion and reverence and his habit of being at home with his family at the beginning of the Sabbath. His whereabouts at that time on a particular date, February 13, 1959, is one of the facts in issue in this case, but the requirements of Orthodox ritual generally, apart from that particular requirement, have no present relevance.

Appellant next contends that the court incorrectly instructed the jury regarding the weight it could attach to such testimony relating to appellant's religious habits as was admitted. Appellant's trial counsel requested that the jury be instructed as follows:

> "There has been evidence of the fixed habit of the defendant, Milton M. Levin, concerning his presence at his home on Friday evenings for the observance of his Sabbath. You may consider this evidence as proof of his contention that he was at his home in New York on Friday, February 13, 1959, at approximately 5:00 o'clock p.m."

11. Appellant acknowledges on brief that there was evidence in the record showing his fixed habit as an Orthodox Jew to be at home with his family by sundown every Friday for the Sabbath observance.

Appellant's counsel concedes before us, as indeed he must, that this requested instruction was improper and was correctly denied. He contends, however, that the instruction actually given was erroneous and that it was objected to before the jury retired.

The trial judge advised counsel that she would instruct the jury on the question of the weight to be given to the evidence referred to, and did in fact instruct the jury as follows:

> "It is my recollection that Mr. Levin testified, as did other witnesses, that he has a habit or practice of a religious nature whereby he stays at home from sundown Fridays to sundown Saturdays. You are told that proof of such a habit or practice is not proof that the defendant is never elsewhere at that particular time."

After the court had concluded its charge, counsel were asked if there were any objections or requests and were told that if there were, counsel should come to the bench. At this time, counsel for appellant stated:

> "I object to Your Honor's instructions as given concerning custom and habit.
>
> "And I re-offer Instructions Nos. 12 and 13 * * * 13 was my instruction to the converse of custom and habit."

The trial judge responded regarding the offered Instruction 12, counsel thanked the court, and nothing further was said by counsel regarding the refused Instruction (13) on custom and habit, set out above and now conceded to be erroneous. No request was made that the charge as given be changed, corrected, or clarified in any manner.

We do not regard the charge as erroneous in the circumstances here and in any event it does not seem unduly prejudicial. Proof of habit, for religious reasons, to be at home on Friday evenings clearly is not conclusive proof that the person having the habit may not be elsewhere on occasion and particularly on the specific Friday evening in issue. Here, of course, as already pointed out, there was direct testimony by appellant and his wife that he actually was at home at sundown on the precise Friday involved, as the District Court clearly brought to the attention of the jury.

Affirmed.

BAZELON, Chief Judge (dissenting):

Levin's conviction of grand larceny was substantially based on testimony of James Landriscina that he met Levin in Washington, D.C., at 5:00 p.m., Friday, February 13, 1959, and gave him $25,000. Levin testified that he was in Washington that day but that he left in the early afternoon. Levin attempted to support his alibi by establishing his religious habit of always being home with his family in New York on the Jewish Sabbath—sundown Friday through sundown Saturday.

The majority here accepts the rule generally followed by courts and commentators that habit evidence, if specific enough, may be admitted. Such evidence is logically probative and no rule excludes it.

I think that in the circumstances of this case—where the central issue concerned an event four years before the trial the testimony of the sole alleged eyewitness was open to suspicion—the defendant was clearly entitled to support his alibi with evidence of his religious habit. The question remains whether he was effectively denied the opportunity to do so, either because his introduction of such evidence was too sharply curtailed or because the trial court's rulings and charge dissipated the value of the habit evidence he did introduce.

Exclusion of the rabbi's testimony of habit was probably not prejudicial in view of the similar testimony presented by other witnesses. But I think the value of their testimony was vitiated by the court's erroneous rulings and charge. Because the question of guilt was close, I think these errors require reversal of the conviction.

Notes

1. Is the *Levin* court correct when it concludes that regular religious worship is a "volitional" activity? Is the idea that religious worship is simply a matter or life style or choice itself a theological view? Don't some religious faiths attempt to inculcate a notion of "habit" in the practice of the faith? *See* Robert M. Cover, *Obligation: A Jewish Jurisprudence of the Social Order*, 5 Law & Rel. 65 (1987). According to the philosopher Michael Sandel, the "voluntarist" notion of religious liberty "points beyond religion." It points to a liberal conception of the self, a self unencumbered by commitments, autonomous and free to choose how to live one's life. Sandel notes that "[i]n the case of religion, the liberal conception of the person ill equips the Court to secure religious liberty for those who regard themselves as claimed by religious commitments they have not chosen." Michael J. Sandel, *Freedom of Conscience or Freedom of Choice?* in ARTICLES OF FAITH, ARTICLES OF PEACE: THE RELIGIOUS LIBERTY CLAUSES AND THE AMERICAN PUBLIC PHILOSOPHY 74, 87 (James Davison Hunter & Os Guinness eds. 1990). Is that what occurs in *Levin*? For another critique of the application of the liberal notion of the self to religion, see Note, *Reinterpreting the Religion Clauses: Constitutional Construction and Conceptions of the Self*, 97 Harv. L. Rev. 1468 (1984).

2. One exception to the bar of hearsay evidence is the so-called "dying declaration" exception. This exception, codified as Rule 804(b)(2) of the Federal Rules of Evidence, permits the introduction of evidence of a statement made by a person (declarant) who was conscious of impending death. Ordinarily, the statement implicates a criminal defendant in the death of the person making the dying declaration. The justification for the admission of this statement is that a statement by a person who is aware he or she is about to die is both reliable and trustworthy. This justification is traced to Christian beliefs about the afterlife. A majority of the people of the United States profess to be Christian and also appear to be secularized. Does this hearsay exception, which is rarely used outside of criminal prosecutions, retain its vitality? Should it remain as an exception to the ban on hearsay evidence? If so, should it apply only to those declarants whose belief system is proven by the prosecution as recognizably "Christian," or to others who believe in an afterlife? Should a duty to speak the truth in this life, in order to attain the benefits sought in that afterlife, be a required aspect of the prosecution's foundation before the dying declaration is admitted?

3. Steven S. was convicted of cross burning in violation of California law. That provision provides, "Any person who burns or desecrates a cross or other religious symbol, knowing it to be a religious symbol, on the private property of another without authorization for the purpose of terrorizing the owner or occupant of that private property or in reckless disregard of the risk of terrorizing the owner or occupant of that private property" shall be punished by a fine and/or imprisonment. The California Court of Appeal held that the terms "desecrate" and "religious symbol" were neither overbroad nor vague. *In re Steven S.*, 31 Cal.Rptr.2d 644, 25 Cal.App.4th 598 (Cal. App.1994). *Accord People v. Carr*, 97 Cal.Rptr.2d 143, 81 Cal.App.4th 837 (2000). Is this law constitutionally permissible because it requires the accused to burn or desecrate the religious symbol knowing it to be a religious symbol? Does a prosecution under this

statute implicate constitutional concerns? If so, are those concerns related to the possibility that non-adherents will be determining what constitutes a "religious symbol," or that adherents to a particular faith will be determining whether the act of the accused was a "desecration"?

Chapter 13

Defining Religion

A. Introduction

Despite more than half a century of intensive Supreme Court interpretation of the language of the First Amendment, the Court has not offered a constitutional definition of religion. As the cases and notes in this chapter indicate, however, the Court has defined religion in interpreting the language of the Federal Selective Service and Training statute granting conscientious objector status to those whose objection to bearing arms is based on "religious training and belief." In addition, several circuit courts of appeals and a number of commentators have offered various approaches to define religion, including the suggestion that such an effort is misguided. *See, e.g.*, George C. Freeman, III, *The Misguided Search for the Constitutional Definition of "Religion,"* 71 Geo. L.J. 1519 (1983).

It appears that the word "religion" created several images in the minds of most of the framers: First, any belief system worthy of the name religion required a theistic belief. Second, expressions of religious belief regularly took place in a house of worship. Third, although this is slightly more controversial, religion did not include its opposite, atheism or nonreligion.

During the late nineteenth century, the Supreme Court offered a traditional definition of religion for constitutional purposes, one premised both on a requirement of a belief in a deity, and upon a distinction between religion and cult.

> The term "religion" has reference to one's views of his relations to his Creator, and to the obligations they impose or reverence for his being and character, and of obedience to his will. It is confounded with the *cultus* or form of worship of a particular sect, but is distinguishable from the latter.

Davis v. Beason, 133 U.S. 333, 342 (1890).

This constitutional definition of religion is the most thorough given by the Court during its existence. It was offered in an opinion designed not to protect the religious liberty of the Mormons, but to justify the criminal prosecution of Mormon men for acting upon their religious beliefs by entering in plural marriages. The Court's definition of religion creates two boundaries for determining what is religious and what is not: Not only does the Court limit "religion" to those belief systems that recognize a "Creator," but it distinguishes between religions and cults, excluding the latter from the protection of the First Amendment.

Today, the United States is a profoundly more secular society than it was in the late nineteenth century. For some Americans, a rejection of trappings of religion is a necessary part of becoming a full-fledged member of modern society. For others, religious belief is a part of their lives, but remains, at most, at the margins of their existence. For still others, religious faith remains a central part of their lives. Although the late nineteenth century was also a time during which a great variety of religious beliefs and organizations flourished, the variety of religious sects in the United States today is vastly greater in number than one hundred years ago. The number of recognized or recognizable religions currently totals well more than one thousand. Although opinion polls regularly indicate that most Americans continue to declare a belief in a Supreme Being, a number of these recognized sects do not posit a belief in a "Creator" or a "Supreme Being," much less the God ("YHWH") of Abraham and Moses. This proliferation of religions suggests the dimensions of the increase in religious diversity in the United States. Religion and religiousness is strikingly different in early twenty-first century America than in eighteenth and nineteenth century America. This difference suggests the problematic nature of relying on a nineteenth century definition of religion. Although the definition in *Davis* has never been overruled, most commentators conclude that it does not adequately describe what is a "religion" at the beginning of the twenty-first century.

The task of fashioning a definition of religion that is neither under- nor overinclusive may be impossible. To avoid classifying religions as non-religious, and vice-versa, is more than a delicate task; it requires a keen understanding not only of religion and law, but of the sociology and history of both religion and law in the United States. Two ways in which this burden may be eased are the application of the "framers' intentions" to define religion and the negation of the Free Exercise Clause as an independent source of individual right. The former approach, unless pitched at a very broad level of generality, pays little or no attention to the changes in the religious beliefs of Americans in the past two centuries. Religion is defined, at a minimum, as including a belief in a Creator. This definition, of course, remains strongly underinclusive, for it limits the understanding of religion to a broadly Jewish and Christian (or Hebraic) perspective. The sole benefit of this approach appears to be that this definition avoids the overinclusiveness problem of defining Marxism and other totalizing ideologies as religions. The marked underinclusiveness of equating religion with theism, however, becomes less important if one adopts the second approach. If the Free Exercise Clause is interpreted as not independently protecting actions undertaken by persons for religious reasons, then defining religion becomes a much less important task of the Court. In *Employment Div. v. Smith*, 494 U.S. 872 (1990), excerpted in Chapter Five, the Supreme Court interpreted the Free Exercise Clause in just this fashion, holding that a person's actions in violation of a neutral and generally applicable law will not be protected by a claim that the action was constitutionally protected by the Free Exercise Clause alone. The result in *Smith* is that the Constitution compels no exemption for religious believers from neutral and generally applicable laws, a result the Court may have desired in part to avoid the problem of federal courts determining when a "religious" claim constitutionally superseded state law. Therefore, anyone claiming exemption from a general law has no incentive to claim the action taken contrary to law was taken for religious rather than non-religious reasons. However, the Court's decision in *Church of the Lukumi Babalu Aye, Inc. v. City of Hialeah*, 508 U.S. 520 (1993), noted in Chapter Five, suggests the viability of *Smith* remains an open question.

Moreover, even if *Smith* remains sound constitutional law regarding the Free Exercise Clause, defining religion remains important for Establishment Clause reasons. This is most clearly the case when a court is called upon to assess whether a particular public school program is "religious" and thus barred by the Establishment Clause. This example is most prominent in assessing the legal question whether "secular humanism" is a religion, and if so, whether as a factual matter it is advocated in the public school curriculum. As the final primary case of this chapter indicates, however, challenges to particular public school programs as religious can arise outside of the secular humanism context. *See Malnak v. Yogi*, 592 F.2d 197 (3d Cir. 1979).

If the Court's definition of religion is underinclusive, it erroneously excludes some beliefs from the appellation "religious," and thus from whatever protection the Free Exercise Clause offers. If it defines religion overinclusively, the Court erroneously announces that some belief systems are religious despite protestations by the believers, and creates additional Establishment Clause concerns. To refuse or fail to define religion makes each of us the judge of our belief system, an approach the Court has on more than one occasion found unappealing. In *Late Corporation of the the Church of Jesus Christ of Latter-Day Saints v. United States*, 136 U.S. 1 (1890), the Court concluded about the actions of the Mormons regarding polygamous marriages: "One pretense for this obstinate course is, that their belief in the practice of polygamy, or the right to indulge in it, is a religious belief. This is altogether a sophistical plea." *Id.* at 49. In *Wisconsin v. Yoder*, 406 U.S. 205, 215–16 (1972), the Court declared, "Although a determination of what is a 'religious' belief or practice entitled to constitutional protection may present a most delicate question, the very concept of ordered liberty precludes allowing every person to make his own standards on matters of conduct in which society as a whole has important interests." To define religion, on the other hand, may also be found wanting. In the view of Justice William O. Douglas, discussing a statutory definition of religion: "A classification of 'conscience' based on a 'religion' and a 'conscience' based on more generalized, philosophical grounds is equally invidious by reason of our First Amendment standards." *Gillette v. United States*, 401 U.S. 437, 469 (1971) (Douglas, J., dissenting).

Unless the Court decides to provide a dual definition of religion, an approach never strongly considered by it, both the Free Exercise and Establishment Clauses will be affected by any definition offered by the Court. An individual or group desiring the protection of the Free Exercise Clause will want the litigated belief or action, or its identity as a group, to be declared religious. To avoid the strictures of the Establishment Clause, the proponent of the action or activity will claim the activity is not religious, but "secular" or "philosophical."

Occasionally, government will use its power to make and enforce laws in such a way as to raise the question whether the law impermissibly incorporates religious terms or doctrine. The case below is an early case upholding the constitutionality of a New York law providing for the prosecution of merchants falsely labeling and claiming their processed food products as "kosher."

Hygrade Provision Co. v. Sherman

266 U.S. 497 (1925)

Mr. Justice SUTHERLAND delivered the opinion of the Court.

These appeals challenge the constitutionality of chapters 580 and 581, 2 Laws of New York 1922, pp. 1314, 1315, as being in contravention of the due process and equal protection of the law clauses of the Fourteenth Amendment and the commerce clause of the Constitution of the United States. So far as these cases are concerned, the statutes are substantially alike, and it is enough to refer to chapter 581 which provides that any person who with intent to defraud:

> "* * * 4. Sells or exposes for sale any meat or meat preparation and falsely represents the same to be kosher, or as having been prepared under and of a product or products sanctioned by the orthodox Hebrew religious requirements; or falsely represents any food product or the contents of any package or container to be so constituted and prepared, by having or permitting to be inscribed thereon the word 'kosher' in any language; or sells or exposes for sale in the same place of business both kosher and nonkosher meat or meat preparations who fails to indicate on his window signs and all display advertising, in block letters at least four inches in height, 'kosher and nonkosher meat sold here'; or who exposes for sale in any show window or place of business both kosher and nonkosher meat or meat products who fails to display over such meat or meat preparation so exposed a sign in block letters at least four inches in height reading 'kosher meat,' or 'nonkosher meat,' as the case may be, is guilty of a misdemeanor."

Separate suits were brought against appellees to enjoin them from proceeding against appellants [Hygrade Provision Co.] for any alleged failure to comply with the foregoing statutory requirements or from making any threats of prosecuting or from conducting any prosecutions by reason of any failure to label any of the meats sold as "not kosher" or otherwise interfering with or seeking to prevent the full, free and unhampered sale of their products without labelling, etc., and from injuring their business "by compelling it to be discredited in standing and reputation, and by having its merchandise wrongfully branded as 'nonkosher' in accordance with the requirements of said enactments."

1. The specific complaint is that the word "kosher" and the phrase "orthodox Hebrew religious requirements" are so indefinite and uncertain as to cause the statutes to be unconstitutional for want of any ascertainable standard of guilt. It is in support of this assumption that appellants allege they are unable to determine with any degree of certainty whether a particular meat product is kosher, and when called upon, at their peril, to make a determination and label the product accordingly, they have decided and will continue to decide that all of the products sold by them are nonkosher. But obviously the statutes put no such burden upon them, since they expressly require that any representation that a product is kosher must not only be false but made with intent to defraud. The Appellate Division of the Supreme Court of New York, upholding the validity of a statute substantially the same is those now under review, in *People v. Atlas*, 183 App. Div. 595, 596, 597, 170 N.Y.S. 834, 835, thus characterized it:

> "The purpose of the statute, manifestly, is to prevent and punish fraud in the sale of meats or meat preparation, and it only operates on those who knowingly violate its provisions, for it is expressly provided that there must be both an intent to defraud and a false representation."

It thus appears that, whatever difficulty there may be in reaching a correct determination as to whether a given product is kosher, appellants are unduly apprehensive of the effect upon them and their business, of a wrong conclusion in that respect, since they are not required to act at their peril but only to exercise their judgment in good faith, in order to avoid coming into conflict with the statutes. Indeed, putting the statutes aside, such judgment they would be bound to exercise upon ordinary principles of fair dealing. By engaging in the business of selling kosher products they in effect assert an honest purpose to distinguish to the best of their judgment between what is and what is not kosher. The statutes require no more. Furthermore, the evidence, while conflicting, warrants the conclusion that the term "kosher" has a meaning well enough defined to enable one engaged in the trade to correctly apply it, at least as a general thing.

Affirmed.

Notes

1. In 1915, New York became the first state to regulate those offering for sale kosher food. Approximately 22 states and a number of municipalities have adopted laws regulating the marketing of food as kosher, and most have followed the model created by New York. *See generally* Karen Ruth Lavy Lindsay, Comment, *Can Kosher Fraud Statutes Pass the* Lemon *Test?: The Constitutionality of Current and Proposed Statutes*, 23 U. Dayton L. Rev. 337 (1998) (listing statutes). Among the states regulating the sale of kosher food are Arkansas, Kentucky and Louisiana, which have relatively small Jewish populations. Is the adoption of kosher laws in such states a sign of permissible legislative accommodations of religion by states?

The Supreme Court upholds the New York law against a claim of that it is void for vagueness. It declares that the statute is violated only when the seller has a fraudulent purpose in advertising meat as kosher, thus protecting from prosecution the seller engaged in an "honest purpose." It also concludes that the term "kosher" has a generally accepted meaning, which allows the seller of kosher products to refer to a definite standard when so labeling such products. Is the Court's understanding of "kosher" persuasive?

When *Hygrade Provision* was decided, the Establishment Clause was not applicable to state action, but merely federal action. Since the Court's decision in *Everson v. Bd. of Educ.*, 330 U.S. 1 (1947), excerpted in Chapter Five, the Establishment Clause applies to any governmental action. Would or should this case be decided differently today based on the Court's interpretation of the commands of the Establishment Clause? Would a determination whether the "kosher" law violates the Establishment Clause require the Court to define religion?

In *Ran-Dav's County Kosher, Inc. v. State*, 608 A.2d 1353 (N.J. 1992), *cert. denied sub nom., National Jewish Comm'n on Law & Pub. Affairs v. Ran-Dav's County Kosher, Inc.*, 507 U.S. 952 (1993), a divided New Jersey Supreme Court held that New Jersey's kosher law violated the primary effect and excessive entanglement prongs of the *Lemon* test. The same year, the Maryland Supreme Court, answering a certified question from the United States District Court for the District of Maryland, held constitutional the City of Baltimore's kosher law. *Barghout v. Mayor*, 600 A.2d 841 (Md. 1992). However, three years later, the United States Court of Appeals for the Fourth Circuit unanimously held the Baltimore law unconstitutional. *Barghout v. Bureau of Kosher Meat*, 66 F.3d 1337 (4th Cir. 1995). Recently, a successor of the New York law held constitutional in *Hygrade Provision* was declared unconstitutional by a federal district court judge. *Commack Self-Service Kosher Meats, Inc., v. Rubin*, 106 F.Supp.2d 445 (E.D.N.Y. 2000).

The New Jersey Supreme Court held the kosher law in *Ran-Dav's* unconstitutional in part because New Jersey was enforcing religious law, which impermissibly entangles religion and government. Does the interpretation of "kosher" require the state to interpret religious doctrine? Can "neutral principles of law" be used to interpret when food products meet the definition of kosher?

Commentary on the constitutionality of kosher fraud laws has been extensive. *Compare* Stephen F. Rosenthal, *Food for Thought: Kosher Fraud Laws and the Religion Clauses of the First Amendment*, 65 Geo. Wash. L. Rev. 951 (1997), Shelley R. Meacham, Note &

Comment, *Answering to a Higher Source: Does the Establishment Clause Actually Restrict Kosher Regulations as* Ran-Dav's County Kosher *Proclaims?*, 23 Sw. U.L. Rev. 639 (1994), Kristin Morgan, Casenote, *The Constitutionality of New Jersey Kosher Food Regulations Under the Establishment Clause*, 62 U. Cin. L. Rev. 247 (1993), and Catherine Beth Sullivan, Comment, *Are Kosher Food Laws Constitutionally Kosher?*, 21 B.C. Envtl. L. Rev. 201 (1993) (concluding that kosher fraud laws are not unconstitutional) *with* Mark A. Berman, *Kosher Fraud Statutes and the Establishment Clause: Are They Kosher?*, 26 Col. J.L. & Soc. Probs. 1 (1992), Lindsay, *Kosher Fraud Statutes* and Gerald F. Masoudi, Comment, *Kosher Food Regulation and the Religion Clauses of the First Amendment*, 60 U. Chi. L. Rev. 667 (1993) (concluding that present laws violate the Establishment Clause and suggesting alternatives).

2. Is the creation of an "eruv" violative of the Establishment Clause? An eruv, under Jewish law, is an unbroken delineation of an area. The place within the eruv is considered a private domain under Jewish law. The creation of an eruv allows Orthodox Jews to carry or push objects from one "public" (from a secular perspective) place to another public place within the eruv during the Sabbath, a task otherwise impermissible to Orthodox Jews. The boundaries of the eruv are usually marked by using existing telephone poles and fences with wires connecting them and with small half-rounds attached to the sides of the poles. In *ACLU v. City of Long Branch*, 670 F. Supp. 1293 (D.N.J. 1987), the City of Long Branch, New Jersey, permitted a Jewish Congregation to delineate an eruv by using existing utility poles, telephone poles and fences connected by wires. The Congregation was also permitted by the city to erect additional poles, extend a fence, and raise a pole at the end of a fence at its own expense. The City was sued for violating the Establishment Clause. The court, after hearing testimony from a Rabbi, concluded that the eruv "is not a religious symbol. Neither the boundary markers of the eruv nor the eruv itself have any religious significance. They are not objects of worship nor do they play any theological role in the observance of the Sabbath. Under Jewish law the eruv does not alter the religious observance of the Sabbath." *Id.* at 1295. The delineation of the eruv had the sole effect of allowing Orthodox Jews to engage in "secular" activities on the Sabbath. The court accordingly held the City's actions constitutional. *But see Tenafly Eruv Ass'n, Inc. v. Borough of Tenafly*, 155 F. Supp.2d 142 (D.N.J. 2001) (holding that borough is permitted to remove Jewish *lechis* marking the boundary of an eruv, and dismissing free exercise claim of plaintiff).

Six years after its decision in *Hygrade Provision*, in *United States v. Macintosh*, 283 U.S. 605 (1931), the Supreme Court affirmed a decision denying naturalization to a pacifist who, on religious grounds, refused to swear an oath pledging his support of the United States government in future wars. As in *Hygrade Provision*, the Court's opinion was written by Justice George Sutherland. In this opinion, Justice Sutherland, citing *Holy Trinity Church v. United States*, 143 U.S. 457 (1892), proclaimed, "We are a Christian people, according to one another the equal right of religious freedom, and acknowledging with reverence the duty of obedience to the will of God." *Id.* at 625. In the same opinion, however, the Court noted the difficulty of giving meaning to the Free Exercise Clause: "What constitutes free exercise of religion cannot perhaps be dogmatically determined. It is a case where this Court must pick out a line, between conscience, and a command of the State." *Id.* at 612. In dissent, Chief Justice Hughes also relied on a theistic belief to define religion: "The essence of religion in belief in a relation to God involving duties superior to those arising from any human relation." *Id.* at 633–34.

During the late 1930s and early 1940s, two issues concerning religious freedom arose: One concerned the right of Jehovah's Witnesses to proselytize, and among other claims, to refuse to salute the flag; the other concerned the interpretation of the Selective Training and Service Act of 1940, which permitted any person "who, by reason of religious training and belief, is conscientiously opposed to participation in war in any form." 50 U.S.C. app. §305(g) (1940) (currently codified at 50 U.S.C. app. §456(j) (1988)). About the first issue, the Supreme Court relied largely on the Free Speech Clause to resolve the myriad issues brought to its attention. About the second, the Court heard no cases. However, several lower federal court decisions attempted to define religion to decide cases involving either of the two issues. The selective service cases are noted in §B, below. In *Borchert v. City of Ranger*, 42 F. Supp. 577 (N.D. Tex. 1941), the district court, relying on a Webster's Dictionary, slightly broadened the definition of religion. In addition to a theistic belief, the district court concluded, based on Webster's, that religion might include a non-theistic "conscientiousness; [a] deep attachment like that felt for the object of worship." *Id.* at 580.

In addition to judging the claims of Jehovah's Witnesses, the Supreme Court attempted to resolve one other religious liberty issue in the early 1940s: whether a criminal prosecution for fraud was constitutionally barred because the defendants claimed their actions were motivated by their religious beliefs. Members of the Ballard family were convicted of fraud, and claimed before the Court that their convictions were unconstitutional. The appellants, along with the deceased Guy W. Ballard, created the "I Am" movement.

United States v. Ballard

322 U.S. 78 (1944)

Mr. Justice DOUGLAS delivered the opinion of the Court.

Respondents were indicted and convicted for using, and conspiring to use, the mails to defraud. The indictment was in twelve counts. It charged a scheme to defraud by organizing and promoting the I Am movement through the use of the mails. The charge was that certain designated corporations were formed, literature distributed and sold, funds solicited, and memberships in the I Am movement sought "by means of false and fraudulent representations, pretenses and promises." The false representations charged were eighteen in number. It is sufficient at this point to say that they covered respondents' alleged religious doctrines or beliefs. They were all set forth in the first count. The following are representative:

> that Guy W. Ballard, now deceased, alias Saint Germain, Jesus, George Washington, and Godfre Ray King, had been selected and thereby designated by the alleged "ascertained masters," Saint Germain, as a divine messenger; and that the words of "ascended masters" and the words of the alleged divine entity, Saint Germain, would be transmitted to mankind through the medium of the said Guy W. Ballard;
>
> that Guy W. Ballard during his lifetime, and Edna W. Ballard, and Donald Ballard, by reason of their alleged high spiritual attainments and righteous conduct, had been selected as divine messengers through which the words alleged of the "ascended masters," including the alleged Saint Germain, would be communicated to mankind under the teachings commonly known as the "I Am" movement;
>
> that Guy W. Ballard, during his lifetime, and Edna W. Ballard and Donald Ballard had, by reason of supernatural attainments, the power to heal persons of

> ailments and diseases and to make well persons afflicted with any diseases, injuries, or ailments, and did falsely represent to persons intended to be defrauded that the three designated persons had the ability and power to cure persons of those diseases normally classified as curable and also of diseases which are ordinarily classified by the medical profession as being incurable diseases; and did further represent that the three designated persons had in fact cured either by the activity of one, either, or all of said persons, hundreds of persons afflicted with diseases and ailments;

Each of the representations enumerated in the indictment was followed by the charge that respondents "well knew" it was false. After enumerating the eighteen misrepresentations the indictment also alleged:

> At the time of making all of the afore-alleged representations by the defendants, and each of them, the defendants, and each of them, well knew that all of said aforementioned representations were false and untrue and were made with the intention on the part of the defendants, and each of them, to cheat, wrong, and defraud persons intended to be defrauded, and to obtain from persons intended to be defrauded by the defendants, money, property, and other things of value and to convert the same to the use and the benefit of the defendants, and each of them;

The indictment contained twelve counts. There was a demurrer and a motion to quash each of which asserted among other things that the indictment attacked the religious beliefs of respondents and sought to restrict the free exercise of their religion in violation of the Constitution of the United States. These motions were denied by the District Court. Early in the trial, however, objections were raised to the admission of certain evidence concerning respondents' religious beliefs. The court conferred with counsel in absence of the jury and with the acquiescence of counsel for the United States and for respondents confined the issues on this phase of the case to the question of the good faith of respondents. At the request of counsel for both sides the court advised the jury of that action in the following language:

Now, gentlemen, here is the issue in this case:

> First, the defendants in this case made certain representations of belief in a divinity and a supernatural power. Some of the teachings of the defendants, representations, might seem extremely improbable to a great many people. For instance, the appearance of Jesus to dictate some of the works that we have had introduced in evidence, as testified to here at the opening transcription, or shaking hands with Jesus, to some people that might seem highly improbable. I point that out as one of the many statements.
>
> Whether that is true or not is not the concern of this Court and is not the concern of the jury—and they are going to be told so in their instructions. As far as this Court sees the issue, it is immaterial what these defendants preached or wrote or taught in their classes. They are not going to be permitted to speculate on the actuality of the happening of those incidents. Now, I think I have made that as clear as I can. Therefore, the religious beliefs of these defendants cannot be an issue in this court.
>
> The issue is: Did these defendants honestly and in good faith believe those things? If they did, they should be acquitted. I cannot make it any clearer than that.

> If these defendants did not believe those things, they did not believe that Jesus came down and dictated, or that Saint Germain came down and dictated, did not believe the things that they wrote, the things that they preached, but used the mail for the purpose of getting money, the jury should find them guilty. Therefore, gentlemen, religion cannot come into this case.

The District Court reiterated that admonition in the charge to the jury and made it abundantly clear. The following portion of the charge is typical:

> The question of the defendants' good faith is the cardinal question in this case. You are not to be concerned with the religious belief of the defendants, or any of them. The jury will be called upon to pass on the question of whether or not the defendants honestly and in good faith believed the representations which are set forth in the indictment, and honestly and in good faith believed that the benefits which they represented would flow from their belief to those who embraced and followed their teachings, or whether these representations were mere pretenses without honest belief on the part of the defendants or any of them, and, were the representations made for the purpose of procuring money, and were the mails used for this purpose.

The United States contends that the District Court withdrew from the jury's consideration only the truth or falsity of those representations which related to religious concepts or beliefs and that there were representations charged in the indictment which fell within a different category. The argument is that this latter group of representations was submitted to the jury, that they were adequate to constitute an offense under the Act, and that they were supported by the requisite evidence. [W]e are of the view that all of the representations charged in the indictment which related at least in part to the religious doctrines or beliefs of respondents were withheld from the jury. The trial judge did not differentiate them. He referred in the charge to the "religious beliefs" and "doctrines taught by the defendants" as matters withheld from the jury. And in stating that the issue of good faith was the "cardinal question" in the case he charged, as already noted, that "The jury will be called upon to pass on the question of whether or not the defendant honestly and in good faith believed the representations which are set forth in the indictment." Nowhere in the charge were any of the separate representations submitted to the jury.

The United States contends that respondents acquiesced in the withdrawal from the jury of the truth of their religious doctrines or beliefs and that their consent bars them from insisting on a different course once that one turned out to be unsuccessful. The real objection of respondents is not that the truth of their religious doctrines or beliefs should have been submitted to the jury. Their demurrer and motion to quash made clear their position that issue should be withheld from the jury on the basis of the First Amendment. Moreover, their position at all times was and still is that the court should have gone the whole way and withheld from the jury both that issue and the issue of their good faith.

As we have noted, the Circuit Court of Appeals held that the question of the truth of the representations concerning respondents' religious doctrines or beliefs should have been submitted to the jury. And it remanded the case for a new trial. It may be that the Circuit Court of Appeals took that action because it did not think that the indictment could be properly construed as charging a scheme to defraud by means other than misrepresentations of respondents' religious doctrines or beliefs. Or that court may have concluded that the withdrawal of the issue of the truth of those religious doctrines or beliefs was unwarranted because it resulted in a substantial change in the character of the crime charged. But on whichever basis that court rested its action, we do not agree that the truth or verity of respondents' religious doctrines or beliefs should have been submitted to the jury. Whatever this particular indictment might require, the First Amendment precludes such a course, as the United States seems to concede. "The law knows no heresy, and is committed to the support of no dogma, the establishment of no sect." *Watson v. Jones*, 80 U.S. [13 Wall.] 679, 728 (1872). The First Amendment has a dual aspect. It not only "forestalls compulsion by law of the acceptance of any creed or the practice of any form of worship" but also "safeguards the free exercise of the chosen form of religion." *Cantwell v. Connecticut*, 310 U.S. 296, 303 (1940). Freedom of thought, which includes freedom of religious belief, is basic in a society of free men. It embraces the right to maintain theories of life and of death and of the hereafter which are rank heresy to followers of the orthodox faiths. Heresy trials are foreign to our Constitution. Men may believe what they cannot prove. They may not be put to the proof of their religious doctrines or beliefs. Religious experiences which are as real as life to some may be incomprehensible to others. Yet the fact that they may be beyond the ken of mortals does not mean that they can be made suspect before the law. Many take their gospel from the New Testament. But it would hardly be supposed that they could be tried before a jury charged with the duty of determining whether those teachings contained false representations. The miracles of the New Testament, the Divinity of Christ, life after death, the power of prayer are deep in the religious convictions of many. If one could be sent to jail because a jury in a hostile environment found those teachings false, little indeed would be left of religious freedom. The Fathers of the Constitution were not unaware of the varied and extreme views of religious sects, of the violence of disagreement among them, and of the lack of any one religious creed on which all men would agree. They fashioned a charter of government which envisaged the widest possible toleration of conflicting views. Man's relation to his God was made no concern of this state. He was granted the right to worship as he pleased and to answer to no man for the verity of his religious views. The religious views espoused by respondents might seem incredible, if not preposterous, to most people. But if those doctrines are subject to trial before a jury charged with finding their truth or falsity, then the same can be done with the religious beliefs of any sect. When the triers of fact undertake that task, they enter a forbidden domain. The First Amendment does not select any one group or any one type of religion for preferred treatment. It puts them all in that position. As stated in *Davis v. Beason*, 133 U.S. 333, 342 (1890), "With man's relations to his Maker and the obligations he may think they impose, and the manner in which an expression shall be made by him of his belief on those subjects, no interference can be permitted, provided always the laws of society, designed to secure its peace and prosperity, and the morals of its people, are not interfered with." So we conclude that the District Court ruled properly when it withheld from the jury all questions concerning the truth or falsity of the religious beliefs or doctrines of respondents.

Reversed.

Mr. Chief Justice STONE, dissenting.

I am not prepared to say that the constitutional guaranty of freedom of religion affords immunity from criminal prosecution for the fraudulent procurement of money by false statements as to one's religious experiences, more than it renders polygamy or libel immune from criminal prosecution. I cannot say that freedom of thought and worship includes freedom to procure money by making knowingly false statements about one's religious experiences. To go no further, if it were shown that a defendant in this case had asserted as a part of the alleged fraudulent scheme, that he had physically shaken hands with St. Germain in San Francisco on a day named, or that, as the indictment here alleges, by the exertion of his spiritual power he "had in fact cured * * * hundreds of persons afflicted with diseases and ailments", I should not doubt that it would be open to the Government to submit to the jury proof that he had never been in San Francisco and that no such cures had ever been effected. In any event I see no occasion for making any pronouncement on this subject in the present case.

The indictment charges respondents' use of the mails to defraud and a conspiracy to commit that offense by false statements of their religious experiences which had not in fact occurred. But it also charged that the representations were "falsely and fraudulently" made, that respondents "well knew" that these representations were untrue, and that they were made by respondents with the intent to cheat and defraud those to whom they were made. With the assent of the prosecution and the defense the trial judge withdrew from the consideration of the jury the question whether the alleged religious experiences had in fact occurred, but submitted to the jury the single issue whether petitioners honestly believed that they had occurred, with the instruction that if the jury did not so find, then it should return a verdict of guilty. On this issue the jury, on ample evidence that respondents were without belief in the statements which they had made to their victims, found a verdict of guilty. The state of one's mind is a fact as capable of fraudulent misrepresentation as is one's physical condition or the state of his bodily health. Since the indictment and the evidence support the conviction, it is irrelevant whether the religious experiences alleged did or did not in fact occur or whether that issue could or could not, for constitutional reasons, have been rightly submitted to the jury. Certainly none of respondents' constitutional rights are violated if they are prosecuted for the fraudulent procurement of money by false representations as to their beliefs, religious or otherwise.

Mr. Justice ROBERTS and Mr. Justice FRANKFURTER join in this opinion.

Mr. Justice JACKSON, dissenting.

I should say the defendants have done just that for which they are indicted. If I might agree to their conviction without creating a precedent, I cheerfully would do so. I can see in their teachings nothing but humbug, untainted by any trace of truth. But that does not dispose of the constitutional question whether misrepresentation of religious experience or belief is prosecutable; it rather emphasizes the danger of such prosecutions.

The Ballard family claimed miraculous communication with the spirit world and supernatural power to heal the sick. They were brought to trial for mail fraud on an indictment which charged that their representations were false and that they "well knew" they were false. The trial judge, obviously troubled, ruled that the court could not try whether the statements were untrue, but could inquire whether the defendants knew them to be untrue; and, if so, they could be convicted.

I find it difficult to reconcile this conclusion with our traditional religious freedoms.

In the first place, as a matter of either practice or philosophy I do not see how we can separate an issue as to what is believed from considerations as to what is believable. The most convincing proof that one believes his statements is to show that they have been true in his experience. Likewise, that one knowingly falsified is best proved by showing that what he said happened never did happen. How can the Government prove these persons knew something to be false which it cannot prove to be false? If we try religious sincerity severed from religious verity, we isolate the dispute from the very considerations which in common experience provide its most reliable answer.

In the second place, any inquiry into intellectual honesty in religion raises profound psychological problems. William James, who wrote on these matters as a scientist, reminds us that it is not theology and ceremonies which keep religion going. Its vitality is in the religious experiences of many people. "If you ask what these experiences are, they are conversations with the unseen, voices and visions, responses to prayer, changes of heart, deliverances from fear, inflowings of help, assurances of support, whenever certain persons set their own internal attitude in certain appropriate ways."[1] If religious liberty includes, as it must, the right to communicate such experience to others, it seems to me an impossible task for juries to separate fancied ones from real ones, dreams from happenings, and hallucinations from true clairvoyance. Such experiences, like some tones and colors, have existence for one, but none at all for another. They cannot be verified to the minds of those whose field of consciousness does not include religious insight. When one comes to trial which turns on any aspect of religious belief or representations, unbelievers among his judges are likely not to understand and are almost certain not to believe him.

And then I do not know what degree of skepticism or disbelief in a religious representation amounts to actionable fraud. James points out that "Faith means belief in something concerning which doubt is theoretically possible." Belief in what one may demonstrate to the senses is not faith. All schools of religious thought make enormous assumptions, generally on the basis of revelations authenticated by some sign or miracle. The appeal in such matters is to a very different plane of credibility than is invoked by representations of secular fact in commerce. Some who profess belief in the Bible read literally what others read as allegory or metaphor, as they read Aesop's fables. Religious symbolism is even used by some with the same mental reservations one has in teaching of Santa Claus or Uncle Sam or Easter bunnies or dispassionate judges. It is hard in matters so mystical to say how literally one is bound to believe the doctrine he teaches and even more difficult to say how far it is reliance upon a teacher's literal belief which induces followers to give him money.

There appear to be persons—let us hope not many—who find refreshment and courage in the teachings of the "I Am" cult. If the members of the sect get comfort from the celestial guidance of their "Saint Germain," however doubtful it seems to me, it is hard to say that they do not get what they pay for. Scores of sects flourish in this country by teaching what to me are queer notions. It is plain that there is wide variety in American religious taste. The Ballards are not alone in catering to it with a pretty dubious product.

The chief wrong which false prophets do to their following is not financial. The collections aggregate a tempting total, but individual payments are not ruinous. I doubt if the vigilance of the law is equal to making money stick by over-credulous people. But the real harm is on the mental and spiritual plane. There are those who hunger and thirst after higher values which they feel wanting in their humdrum lives. They live in mental confusion or moral anarchy and seek vaguely for truth and beauty and moral

1. William James, Collected Essays and Reviews, pp. 427, 428; see generally his Varieties of Religious Experience and The Will to Believe.

support. When they are deluded and then disillusioned, cynicism and confusion follow. The wrong of these things, as I see it, is not in the money the victims part with half so much as in the mental and spiritual poison they get. But that is precisely the thing the Constitution put beyond the reach of the prosecutor, for the price of freedom of religion or of speech or of the press is that we must put up with, and even pay for, a good deal of rubbish.

Prosecutions of this character easily could degenerate into religious persecution. I do not doubt that religious leaders may be convicted of fraud for making false representations on matters other than faith or experience, as for example if one represents that funds are being used to construct a church when in fact they are being used for personal purposes. But that is not this case, which reaches into wholly dangerous ground. When does less than full belief in a professed credo become actionable fraud if one is soliciting gifts or legacies? Such inquiries may discomfort orthodox as well as unconventional religious teachers, for even the most regular of them are sometimes accused of taking their orthodoxy with a grain of salt.

I would dismiss the indictment and have done with this business of judicially examining other people's faiths.

Notes

1. On remand, the Court of Appeals affirmed the defendants' convictions. *Ballard v. United States*, 152 F.2d 941 (9th Cir. 1945). Certiorari was again granted. The Supreme Court, in an opinion by Justice Douglas, once again reversed the judgment of the Court of Appeals. *Ballard v. United States*, 329 U.S. 187 (1946). In an exercise of its supervisory power over the lower federal courts, the Court held that the indictment should be dismissed because women had been improperly excluded from the grand and petit juries. The Court concluded its opinion:

> Accordingly, the indictment must be dismissed. In disposing of the case on this ground we do not reach all the issues urged and it is suggested that in so limiting our opinion we prolong an already lengthy proceeding. We are told that these petitioners will again be before us for the determination of questions now left undecided. But we cannot know that this is so, and to assume it would be speculative. The United States may or may not present new charges proved within the limits of our earlier opinion. A properly constituted grand jury may or may not return new indictments. Petitioners may or may not be convicted a second time.

Justice Jackson concurred in the result only. He believed that the issue regarding the exclusion of women from the grand and petit juries had been abandoned by defendants or silently decided against them in the Court's earlier decision. He read the earlier decision to hold that those making religious representations could be convicted for insincerity alone. He would have dismissed the indictment on the grounds stated in his earlier opinion and on an additional ground:

> This Court previously ruled that it is improper for the trial court to inquire whether the religious professions and experiences as represented by defendants were true or false but that it can inquire only as to whether they were represented without belief in their truth. This leaves no statutory basis for conviction of fraud and especially no basis for conviction under this indictment. It requires, in my opinion, a provably false representation in addition to knowl-

> edge of its falsity to make criminal mail fraud. Since the trial court is not allowed to make both findings, the indictment should be dismissed.

Justice Frankfurter, with Chief Justice Vinson (Chief Justice Stone had died earlier that year), Justice Jackson and Justice Burton concurring, dissented. Frankfurter would have addressed whether it is permissible to punish for insincerity alone, believing that question to have been left open by the Court's earlier decision:

> [T]he prosecution will continue unless we terminate it. We can terminate it only if the Court should deem beyond constitutional authority a prosecution of the charges upon which the jury found the defendants guilty and which the Court of Appeals sustained. We ought not to give implied sanction to the continuance of this prosecution, if we do not mean to do so, by withholding our view on an issue inescapable in the full disposition of the controversy before the Court. Candor repels it and the requirements of constitutional adjudication do not justify it.

Justice Burton also dissented. He concluded that there was no statutory or constitutional prohibition to convicting the Ballards for misrepresenting their religious beliefs, and would not have dismissed the indictment because of the exclusion of women from the juries. The Chief Justice and Justice Frankfurter joined this opinion. Justice Jackson joined all of this opinion except the part relating to the affirmance of the convictions.

Following the Ballards's convictions, the Internal Revenue Service deprived their organization of its status as a tax-exempt organization. The Tax Court ultimately reversed this action. *Saint Germain Foundation v. Commissioner of Internal Revenue*, 26 T.C. 648 (1956). The opinion of the Tax Court states that the Ballards were not reindicted after the second Supreme Court decision in their case.

2. The Supreme Court reversed the convictions of the Ballards because it concluded that the decision of the Circuit Court of Appeals erroneously required that the truth of the Ballards's claims be judged by the jury. It did not hold that a conviction which rested on the jury finding that the defendants acted without a good faith and honest belief in the representations was constitutionally impermissible. Chief Justice Stone's dissent is premised on the view that some religiously-based representations, because made as "factual" matters, may be adjudged true or false by the jury. Justice Jackson dissented from the Court's latter conclusion because "as a matter of either practice or philosophy I do not see how we can separate an issue as to what is believed from considerations as to what is believable." The opinions, then, offer three separate views whether one may criminally prosecute religiously-based representations: 1) Such claims may be prosecuted either because the defendant acted without an honest and good faith belief in those representations, or because the prosecution may show the representation was factually false (Stone); 2) claims may be prosecuted only if the defendant acted without an honest and good faith belief in the truth of those representations (Douglas); and 3) no religiously-based representation may be prosecuted because a jury cannot separate what is believed by the speaker from what is believable (Jackson). Which of these three views appears most persuasive? If the Ballards had not couched their claims in the garb of religion, but as protected speech (which the government claims is a Ponzi scheme), should or would the Court have reversed the convictions based on the Free Speech Clause? Both the Court's opinion and the opinion of Justice Jackson strongly suggest that the Court was required to decide as it did because of the commands of the Free Exercise Clause. Does this provide more protection to arguably fraudulent representations ("If you give me your money, you will be saved from the fires of damnation")

premised on religious grounds over similar representations made on nonreligious or secular ("If you give me your money, you will earn 50% interest within two months") grounds? If so, doesn't this necessitate a definition of religion, in order to ascertain the border between religiously-based claims and claims made on nonreligious or secular grounds?

3. Is *Ballard* a case in which the Court affirmatively refuses to define religion? The majority opinion appears to limit any consideration of the religiosity of a belief to the sincerity of that belief. But a person's sincere belief that the earth is flat doesn't make that a religious belief, does it? The opinion by Justice Jackson quotes the American philosopher William James: "James points out that 'Faith means belief in something concerning which doubt is theoretically possible.'" Jackson then continues: "Belief in what one may demonstrate to the senses is not faith. All schools of religious thought make enormous assumptions, generally on the basis of revelations authenticated by some sign or miracle." For Jackson, religious belief is a belief in something empirically unverifiable. But surely many empirically unverifiable beliefs are not considered religious by either the believer or by those who are disbelievers. Justice Douglas merely notes that the "truth" of the New Testament of the Christian Bible contains a number of unverifiable claims. Are these efforts to link religious faith with a leap beyond the rational persuasive? Sufficient? One of the reasons the Unitarians became more numerous in late 18th century New England was in part because they attempted to rationalize faith, an effort that attracted many in the age of reason. Should a belief system premised on "rationalism" constitute a religion? Does it depend on whether those adopting that belief system desire that their beliefs be designated religious beliefs?

4. *Everson v. Bd. of Educ.*, 330 U.S. 1 (1947), which incorporated the Establishment Clause into the Fourteenth Amendment, declared that the Constitution barred favoring religion over its opposite, so that a law that aided all religions was unconstitutional, as was a law that aided one religion over another. *Everson* was decided after *Ballard*. Does the *Everson* requirement of Establishment Clause neutrality between religion and nonreligion affect the rationale of *Ballard*? Does this broad level of generality between religion and nonreligion suggest that it is unnecessary to define religion, because the principle of equality bars any distinction on that basis? Does your answer depend on whether the Establishment and Free Exercise Clauses are read as separate clauses rather than as a single unit? Why does the Establishment Clause forbid a preference for "nonreligion" over "religion"?

5. If a television evangelist claims he can heal viewers who send him money, should an ailing viewer who sends money and later claims either no improvement or a possible decline in health, be permitted to sue the evangelist for fraud? Should the Free Exercise Clause, as interpreted in *Ballard*, bar such actions? Or limit those actions to the issue of the evangelist's good faith and honest belief that he can heal viewers who send him money? *See* Chapter Seven § F. Should such actions turn upon a consideration of the facts of each case, thus necessitating that such cases will be given to a jury for its decision? If you prefer this option, recall Justice Douglas's warning: "If one could be sent to jail because a jury in a hostile environment found those teachings false, little indeed would be left of religious freedom." Is this empirically accurate?

6. For an interesting analysis of a related problem, see Bruce J. Casino, Note, *"I Know It When I See It": Mail-Order Ministry Tax Fraud and the Problem of a Constitutionally Acceptable Definition of Religion*, 25 Am. Crim. L. Rev. 113 (1987).

7. Two years after the Court decided *Ballard*, it further demonstrated its desire to protect the religious liberty interests protected by the Free Exercise Clause by declaring

that an application for citizenship could not be denied because the applicant was a Jehovah's Witness and thus conscientiously scrupulous of bearing arms. *Girouard v. United States*, 326 U.S. 61 (1946). This decision overruled the *Macintosh* case of fifteen years earlier.

B. Selective Service and Religious Conscientious Objection

In 1940, Congress passed the Selective Training and Service Act. The Act provided that any person "who, by reason of religious training and belief, is conscientiously opposed to participation in war in any form" shall be exempt from combat. In an early interpretation of this provision, the United States Court of Appeals for the Second Circuit broadly interpreted this language. Although the court held that there was a distinction between religious and philosophical beliefs, and that the latter did not permit the claimant status as a conscientious objector, it also held that a religious belief was a belief based on "a response of the individual to an inward mentor, call it conscience or God, that is for many persons at the present time the equivalent of what has always been thought a religious impulse." *United States v. Kauten*, 133 F.2d 703, 708 (2d Cir. 1943). The author of the opinion was Augustus Hand, a devout Episcopalian. Judge Hand continued:

> It is unnecessary to attempt a definition of religion; the content of the term is found in the history of the human race and is incapable of compression into a few words. Religious belief arises from a sense of the inadequacy of reason as a means of relating the individual to his fellow-men. It accepts the aid of logic but refuses to be limited by it. It is a belief finding expression in a conscience which categorically requires the believer to disregard elementary self-interest and to accept martyrdom in preference to transgressing its tenets.

Id.

This definition accepts the contention in *Ballard* that a religious belief is a belief system that is beyond the rational. It also suggests that defining religion requires one to analogize to that which is readily accepted as religious: any "response of the individual to an inward mentor" "that is for many persons at the present time the *equivalent* of what has always been thought a religious impulse." (emphasis added)

In *Berman v. United States*, 156 F.2d 377 (9th Cir.), *cert. denied*, 329 U.S. 795 (1946), the Ninth Circuit sharply disagreed with the Second Circuit's *Kauten* decision. Citing dictionaries and other reference sources, the court required the conscientious objector claimant to prove his claim was religious by offering evidence that his faith included a belief in "superhuman powers or influences," the "supernatural,"or a "supreme being." *Id.* at 381–82. A dissenting opinion in *Berman* argued that a "humanism in which humanity is exalted into the throne occupied by a supreme being in monotheistic religions" was religious if based on notions of conscience. *Id.* at 384 (Denman, J., dissenting).

Congress attempted to resolve the divergent *Kauten* and *Berman* decisions by more specifically defining "religious training and belief" in the Selective Service Act of 1948: "Religious training and belief in this connection means an individual's belief in a relation to a Supreme Being involving duties superior to those arising from any human relation, but does not include essentially political, sociological, or philosophical views or a merely personal moral code." 50 U.S.C. app. §456(j) (1948). This amendment appeared to favor the narrower definition offered by the Ninth Circuit rather than the broader definition suggested by the Second Circuit.

After this amendment was adopted, the Ninth Circuit, in another conscientious objection case, *George v. United States*, 196 F.2d 445 (9th Cir.), *cert. denied*, 344 U.S. 843 (1952), reaffirmed its theistic definition of religion and quoted from the amended statutory language in support of its decision. Three years later, in *Sicurrella v. United States*, 348 U.S. 385 (1955), the Supreme Court held that a Jehovah's Witness, who claimed he was conscientiously opposed to any form of war, but who also noted that he would defend "Kingdom Interests, our preaching work, our meetings, our fellow brethren and our sisters, and our property," *id.* at 387, was not entitled to conscientious objector status because this particular form of opposition to war did not meet the requirements set forth by Congress.

In 1963, however, another member of the Second Circuit Court of Appeals, Judge Henry Friendly, interpreted broadly the language of the amended statute. In *United States v. Jakobson*, 325 F.2d 409 (2d Cir. 1963), Jakobson argued that he was entitled to conscientious objector status, because, although his beliefs were not based on "God," they were based on a belief in "Godness." Judge Friendly noted the definition of religion given by the Protestant theologian Paul Tillich, and concluded that "Jakobson's definition of religion ... parallel[s] the views of the views of this eminent theologian rather strikingly." *Id.* at 415–16. Based on this convergence of definitions, Jakobson's conviction was reversed.

In 1965, the Supreme Court, in *United States v. Seeger*, evaluated Jakobson's claim, along with claims made by two other conscientious objectors.

United States v. Seeger

380 U.S. 163 (1965)

Mr. Justice CLARK delivered the opinion of the Court.

These cases involve claims of conscientious objectors under §6(j) of the Universal Military Training and Service Act, 50 U.S.C. App. §456(j) (1958 ed.), which exempts from combatant training and service in the armed forces of the United States those persons who by reason of their religious training and belief are conscientiously opposed to participation in war in any form. The parties raise the basic question of the constitutionality of the section which defines the term "religious training and belief," as used in the Act, as "an individual's belief in a relation to a Supreme Being involving duties superior to those arising from any human relation, but [not including] essentially political, sociological, or philosophical views or a merely personal moral code." The constitutional attack is launched under the First Amendment's Establishment and Free Exercise Clauses and is twofold: (1) the section does not exempt nonreligious conscientious objectors; and (2) it discriminates between different forms of religious expression in violation of the Due Process Clause of the Fifth Amendment. Jakobson (No. 51) and Peter (No. 29) also claim that their beliefs come within the meaning of the section. Jakobson claims that he meets the standards of §6(j) because his opposition to war is based on belief in a Supreme Reality and is therefore an obligation superior to one resulting from man's relationship to his fellow man. Peter contends that his opposition to war derives from his acceptance of the existence of a universal power beyond that of man and that this acceptance in fact constitutes belief in a Supreme Being qualifying him for exemption. We granted certiorari in each of the cases because of their importance in the administration of the Act.

We have concluded that Congress, in using the expression "Supreme Being" rather than the designation "God," was merely clarifying the meaning of religious training and belief so as to embrace all religions and to exclude essentially political, sociological, or philosophical views. We believe that under this construction, the test of belief "in a relation to a Supreme Being" is whether a given belief that is sincere and meaningful occupies a place in the life of its possessor parallel to that filled by the orthodox belief in God of one who clearly qualifies for the exemption. Where such beliefs have parallel positions in the lives of their respective holders we cannot say that one is "in a relation to a Supreme Being" and the other is not. We have concluded that the beliefs of the objectors in these cases meet these criteria.

THE FACTS IN THE CASES.

No. 50: Seeger was convicted in the District Court for the Southern District of New York of having refused to submit to induction in the armed forces. He was originally classified 1-A in 1953 by his local board, but this classification was changed in 1955 to 2-S (student) and he remained in this status until 1958 when he was reclassified 1-A. He first claimed exemption as a conscientious objector in 1957 after successive annual renewals of his student classification. Although he did not adopt verbatim the printed Selective Service System form, he declared that he was conscientiously opposed to participation in war in any form by reason of his "religious" belief; that he preferred to leave the question as to his belief in a Supreme Being open, "rather than answer 'yes' or 'no' "; that his "skepticism or disbelief in the existence of God" did "not necessarily mean lack of faith in anything whatsoever"; that his was a "belief in and devotion to goodness and virtue for their own sakes, and a religious faith in a purely ethical creed." He cited such personages as Plato, Aristotle and Spinoza for support of his ethical belief in intellectual and moral integrity "without belief in God, except in the remotest sense." His belief was found to be sincere, honest, and made in good faith; and his conscientious objection to be based upon individual training and belief, both of which included research in religious and cultural fields. Seeger's claim, however, was denied solely because it was not based upon a "belief in a relation to a Supreme Being" as required by §6(j) of the Act. He was convicted [by the District Court] and the Court of Appeals reversed, holding that the Supreme Being requirement of the section distinguished "between internally derived and externally compelled beliefs" and was, therefore, an "impermissible classification" under the Due Process Clause of the Fifth Amendment.

No. 51: Jakobson was also convicted in the Southern District of New York on a charge of refusing to submit to induction. On his appeal the Court of Appeals reversed on the ground that rejection of his claim may have rested on the factual finding, erroneously made, that he did not believe in a Supreme Being as required by §6(j).

Jakobson was originally classified 1-A in 1953 and intermittently enjoyed a student classification until 1956. It was not until April 1958 that he made claim to non-combatant classification (1-A-O) as a conscientious objector. He stated on the Selective Service System form that he believed in a "Supreme Being" who was "Creator of Man" in the sense of being "ultimately responsible for the existence of" man and who was "the Supreme Reality" of which "the existence of man is the *result*." He explained that his religious and social thinking had developed after much meditation and thought. He had concluded that man must be "partly spiritual" and, therefore, "partly akin to the Supreme Reality"; and that his "most important religious law" was that "no man ought ever to wilfully sacrifice another man's life as a means to any other end...." In December 1958 he requested a 1-O classification since he felt that participation in any form of military service would involve him in "too many situations and relationships that would be a strain on [his] conscience that [he felt he] must avoid." He submitted a long memorandum of "notes on religion" in which he defined religion as the "*sum and essence of one's basic attitudes to the fundamental problems of human existence*"; he said that he believed in "Godness" which was "the Ultimate Cause for the fact of the Being of the Universe"; that to deny its existence would but deny the existence of the universe because "anything that Is, has an Ultimate Cause for its Being." There was a relationship to Godness, he stated, in two directions, *i.e.*, "vertically, towards Godness directly," and "horizontally, towards Godness through Mankind and the World." He accepted the latter one. The Board classified him 1-A-O and Jakobson appealed. The hearing officer found that the claim was based upon a personal moral code and that he was not sincere in his claim. The Appeal Board classified him 1-A. It did not indicate upon what ground it based its decision, *i.e.*, insincerity or a conclusion that his belief was only a personal moral code.

No. 29: Forest Britt Peter was convicted in the Northern District of California on a charge of refusing to submit to induction. In his Selective Service System form he stated that he was not a member of a religious sect or organization; he failed to execute section VII of the questionnaire but attached to it a quotation expressing opposition to war, in which he stated that he concurred. In a later form he hedged the question as to his belief in a Supreme Being by saying that it depended on the definition and he appended a statement that he felt it a violation of his moral code to take human life and that he considered this belief superior to his obligation to the state. As to whether his conviction was religious, he quoted with approval Reverend John Haynes Holmes' definition of religion as "the consciousness of some power manifest in nature which helps man in the ordering of his life in harmony with its demands... [; it] is the supreme expression of human nature; it is man thinking his highest, feeling his deepest, and living his best." The source of his conviction he attributed to reading and meditation "in our democratic American culture, with its values derived from the western religious and philosophical tradition." As to his belief in a Supreme Being, Peter stated that he supposed "you could call that a belief in the Supreme Being or God. These just do not happen to be the words I use." In 1959 he was classified 1-A, although there was no evidence in the record that he was not sincere in his belief. After his conviction for failure to report for induction the Court of Appeals, assuming *arguendo* that he was sincere, affirmed.

BACKGROUND OF § 6(j).

Chief Justice Hughes, in his [dissenting] opinion in *United States v. Macintosh*, 283 U.S. 605 (1931), enunciated the rationale behind the long recognition of conscientious objection to participation in war accorded by Congress in our various conscription laws when he declared that "in the forum of conscience, duty to a moral power higher than the State has always been maintained." In a similar vein Harlan Fiske Stone, later Chief Justice, drew from the Nation's past when he declared that

> "both morals and sound policy require that the state should not violate the conscience of the individual. All our history gives confirmation to the view that liberty of conscience has a moral and social value which makes it worthy of preservation at the hands of the state. So deep in its significance and vital, indeed, is it to the integrity of man's moral and spiritual nature that nothing short of the self-preservation of the state should warrant its violation; and it may well be questioned whether the state which preserves its life by a settled policy of violation of the conscience of the individual will not in fact ultimately lose it by the process." Stone, *The Conscientious Objector*, 21 Col. Univ. Q. 253, 269 (1919).

Governmental recognition of the moral dilemma posed for persons of certain religious faiths by the call to arms came early in the history of this country. Various methods of ameliorating their difficulty was adopted by the Colonies, and were later perpetuated in state statutes and constitutions. Thus by the time of the Civil War there existed a state pattern of exempting conscientious objectors on religious grounds. [I]n the 1864 Draft Act, 13 Stat. 9, it extended exemption to those conscientious objectors who were members of religious denominations opposed to the bearing of arms and who were prohibited from doing so by the articles of faith of their denominations.

The need for conscription did not again arise until World War I. The Draft Act of 1917, 40 Stat. 76, 78, afforded exemptions to conscientious objectors who were affiliated with a "well-recognized religious sect or organization [then] organized and existing and whose existing creed or principles [forbade] its members to participate in war in any form...." The Act required that all persons be inducted into the armed services, but allowed the conscientious objectors to perform noncombatant service in capacities designated by the President of the United States. Although the 1917 Act excused religious objectors only, in December 1917, the Secretary of War instructed that "personal scruples against war" be considered as constituting "conscientious objection." Selective Service System Monograph No. 11, Conscientious Objection 54–55 (1950). This Act, including its conscientious objector provisions, was upheld against constitutional attack in the *Selective Draft Law Cases*, 245 U.S. 366, 389–390 (1918).

In adopting the 1940 Selective Training and Service Act Congress broadened the exemption afforded in the 1917 Act by making it unnecessary to belong to a pacifist religious sect if the claimant's own opposition to war was based on "religious training and belief." 54 Stat. 889. Those found to be within the exemption were not inducted into the armed services but were assigned to noncombatant service under the supervision of the Selective Service System. The Congress recognized that one might be religious without belonging to an organized church just as surely as minority members of faith not opposed to war might through religious reading reach a conviction against participation in war. Indeed, the consensus of the witnesses appearing before the congressional committees was that individual belief—rather than membership in a church or sect—determined the duties that God imposed upon a person in his everyday conduct; and that "there is a higher loyalty than loyalty to this country, loyalty to God." Thus, while shifting the test from membership in such a church to one's individual belief the Congress nevertheless continued its historic practice of excusing from armed service those who believed that they owed an obligation, superior to that due the state, of not participating in war in any form.

Between 1940 and 1948 two courts of appeals held that the phrase "religious training and belief" did not include philosophical, social or political policy. Then in 1948 the Congress amended the language of the statute and declared that "religious training and belief" was to be defined as "an individual's belief in a relation to a Supreme Being involving duties superior to those arising from any human relation, but [not including] essentially political, sociological, or philosophical views or a merely personal moral code."

INTERPRETATION OF § 6(j).

1. The crux of the problem lies in the phrase "religious training and belief" which Congress has defined as "belief in a relation to a Supreme Being involving the duties superior to those arising from any human relation." In assigning meaning to this statutory language we may narrow the inquiry by noting briefly those scruples expressly excepted

from the definition. The section excludes those persons who, disavowing religious belief, decide on the basis of essentially political, sociological or economic considerations that war is wrong and that they will have no part of it. These judgments have historically been reserved for the Government, and in matters which can be said to fall within these areas the conviction of the individual has never been permitted to override that of the state. The statute further excludes those whose opposition to war stems from a "merely personal moral code," a phrase to which we shall have occasion to turn later in discussing the application of § 6(j) to these cases. We also pause to take note of what is not involved in this litigation. No party claims to be an atheist or attacks the statute on this ground. The question is not, therefore, one between theistic and atheistic beliefs. We do not deal with or intimate any decision on that situation in these cases. Nor do the parties claim the monotheistic belief that there is but one God; what they claim (with the possible exception of Seeger who bases his position here not on factual but on purely constitutional grounds) is that they adhere to theism, which is the "Belief in the existence of a god or gods;... Belief in superhuman powers or spiritual agencies in one or many gods," as opposed to atheism. Our question, therefore, is the narrow one: Does the term "Supreme Being" as used in § 6(j) mean the orthodox God or the broader concept of a power or being, or a faith, "to which all else is subordinate or upon which all else is ultimately dependent"? Webster's New International Dictionary (Second Edition). In considering this question we resolve it solely in relation to the language of § 6(j) and not otherwise.

2. Few would quarrel, we think, with the proposition that in no field of human endeavor has the tool of language proved so inadequate in the communication of ideas as it has in dealing with the fundamental questions of man's predicament in life, in death or in final judgment and retribution. This fact makes the task of discerning the intent of Congress in using the phrase "Supreme Being" a complex one. Nor is it made the easier by the richness and variety of spiritual life in our country. Over 250 sects inhabit our land. Some believe in a purely personal God, some in a supernatural deity; others think of religion as a way of life envisioning as its ultimate goal the day when all men can live together in perfect understanding and peace. There are those who think of God as the depth of our being; others, such as the Buddhists, strive for a state of lasting rest through self-denial and inner purification; in Hindu philosophy, the Supreme Being is the transcendental reality which is truth, knowledge and bliss. Even those religious groups which have traditionally opposed war in every form have splintered into various denominations: from 1940 to 1947 there were four denominations using the name "Friends"; the "Church of the Brethren" was the official name of the oldest and largest church body of four denominations composed of those commonly called Brethren; and the "Mennonite Church" was the largest of 17 denominations, including the Amish and Hutterites, grouped as "Mennonite bodies" in the 1936 report on the Census of Religious Bodies. This vast panoply of beliefs reveals the magnitude of the problem which faced the Congress when it set about providing an exemption from armed service. It also emphasizes the care that Congress realized was necessary in the fashioning of an exemption which would be in keeping with its long-established policy of not picking and choosing among religious beliefs.

In spite of the elusive nature of the inquiry, we are not without certain guidelines. In amending the 1940 Act, Congress adopted almost intact the language of Chief Justice Hughes in *United States v. Macintosh, supra:*

> "The essence of religion is belief in a relation to *God* involving duties superior to those arising from any human relation." At 633–634. (Emphasis supplied.)

By comparing the statutory definition with those words, however, it becomes readily apparent that the Congress deliberately broadened them by substituting the phrase "Supreme Being" for the appellation of "God." And in so doing it is also significant that Congress did not elaborate on the form or nature of this higher authority which it chose to designate as "Supreme Being." By so refraining it must have had in mind the admonitions of the Chief Justice when he said in the same opinion that even the word "God" had myriad meanings for men of faith:

> "[P]utting aside dogmas with their particular conceptions of deity, freedom of conscience itself implies respect for an innate conviction of paramount duty. The battle for religious liberty has been fought and won with respect to religious beliefs and practices, which are not in conflict with good order, upon the very ground of the supremacy of conscience within its proper field." At 634.

Admittedly, all of the parties here purport to base their objection on religious belief. It appears, therefore, that we need only look to this clear statement of congressional intent as set out in the report. Under the 1940 Act it was necessary only to have a conviction based upon religious training and belief; we believe that is all that is required here. Within that phrase would come all sincere religious beliefs which are based upon a power or being, or upon a faith, to which all else is subordinate or upon which all else is ultimately dependent. The test might be stated in these words: A sincere and meaningful belief which occupies in the life of its possessor a place parallel to that filled by the God of those admittedly qualifying for the exemption comes within the statutory definition. This construction avoids imputing to Congress an intent to classify different religious beliefs, exempting some and excluding others, and is in accord with the well-established congressional policy of equal treatment for those whose opposition to service is grounded in their religious tenets.

Section 6(j), then, is no more than a clarification of the 1940 provision involving only certain "technical amendments," to use the words of Senator Gurney. As such it continues the congressional policy of providing exemption from military service for those whose opposition is based on grounds that can fairly be said to be "religious."[3] To hold otherwise would not only fly in the face of Congress' entire action in the past; it would ignore the historic position of our country on this issue since its founding.

4. Moreover, we believe this construction embraces the ever-broadening understanding of the modern religious community. The eminent Protestant theologian, Dr. Paul Tillich, whose views the Government concedes would come within the statute, identifies God not as a projection "out there" or beyond the skies but as the ground of our very being. In his book, Systematic Theology, Dr. Tillich says:

> "I have written of the God above the God of theism.... In such a state [of self-affirmation] the God of both religious and theological language disappears. But something remains, namely, the seriousness of that doubt in which meaning within meaninglessness is affirmed. The source of this affirmation of

---

3. A definition of "religious training and belief" identical to that in § 6(j) is found in § 337 of the Immigration and Nationality Act, 66 Stat. 258, 8 U.S.C. § 1448(a) (1958 ed.). It is noteworthy that in connection with this Act, the Senate Special Subcommittee to Investigate Immigration and Naturalization stated: "The subcommittee realizes and respects the fact that the question of whether or not a person must bear arms in defense of his country may be one which invades the province of religion and personal conscience." Thus, it recommended that an alien not be required to vow to bear arms when he asserted "his opposition to participation in war in any form because of his personal religious training and belief." S. Rep. No. 1515, 81st Cong., 2d Sess., 742, 746.

meaning within meaninglessness, of certitude within doubt, is not the God of traditional theism but the 'God above God,' the power of being, which works through those who have no name for it, not even the name God." II Systematic Theology 12 (1957).

Another eminent cleric, the Bishop of Woolwich, John A. T. Robinson, in his book, Honest To God (1963), states:

"The Bible speaks of a God 'up there.' No doubt its picture of a three-decker universe, of 'the heaven above, the earth beneath and the waters under the earth,' was once taken quite literally...." At 11.

"*[Later] in place of a God who is literally or physically 'up there' we have accepted, as part of our mental furniture, a God who is spiritually or metaphysically 'out there.'*...But now it seems there is no room for him, not merely in the inn, but in the entire universe: for there are no vacant places left. In reality, of course, our new view of the universe has made not the slightest difference...." At 13–14.

"But the idea of a God spiritually or metaphysically 'out there' dies very much harder. Indeed, most people would be seriously disturbed by the thought that it should need to die at all. For it *is* their God, and they have nothing to put in its place....Every one of us lives with some mental picture of a God 'out there,' a God who 'exists' above and beyond the world he made, a God 'to' whom we pray and to whom we 'go' when we die." At 14.

"But the signs are that we are reaching the point at which the whole conception of a God 'out there,' which has served us so well since the collapse of the three-decker universe, is itself becoming more of a hindrance than a help." At 15–16. (Emphasis in original.)

The Schema of the recent Ecumenical Council included a most significant declaration on religion:

"The community of all peoples is one. One is their origin, for God made the entire human race live on all the face of the earth. One, too, is their ultimate end, God. Men expect from the various religions answers to the riddles of the human condition: What is man? What is the meaning and purpose of our lives? What is the moral good and what is sin? What are death, judgment, and retribution after death?

* * *

"Ever since primordial days, numerous peoples have had a certain perception of that hidden power which hovers over the course of things and over the events that make up the lives of men; some have even come to know of a Supreme Being and Father. Religions in an advanced culture have been able to use more refined concepts and a more developed language in their struggle for an answer to man's religious questions.

* * *

"Nothing that is true and holy in these religions is scorned by the Catholic Church. Ceaselessly the Church proclaims Christ, 'the Way, the Truth, and the Life,' in whom God reconciled all things to Himself. The Church regards with sincere reverence those ways of action and of life, precepts and teachings which, although they differ from the one she sets forth, reflect nonetheless a ray of that Truth which enlightens all men."

Dr. David Saville Muzzey, a leader in the Ethical Culture Movement, states in his book, Ethics As a Religion (1951), that "[e]verybody except the avowed atheists (and they are comparatively few) believes in some kind of God," and that "The proper question to ask, therefore, is not the futile one, Do you believe in God? but rather, What *kind* of God do you believe in?" Dr. Muzzey attempts to answer that question:

> "Instead of positing a personal God, whose existence man can neither prove nor disprove, the ethical concept is founded on human experience. It is anthropocentric, not theocentric. Religion, for all the various definitions that have been given of it, must surely mean the devotion of man to the highest ideal that he can conceive. And that ideal is a community of spirits in which the latent moral potentialities of men shall have been elicited by their reciprocal endeavors to cultivate the best in their fellow men. What ultimate reality is we do not know; but we have the faith that it expresses itself in the human world as the power which inspires in men moral purpose." At 95.
>
> "Thus the 'God' that we love is not the figure on the great white throne, but the perfect pattern, envisioned by faith, of humanity as it should be, purged of the evil elements which retard its progress toward 'the knowledge, love and practice of the right.'" At 98.

These are but a few of the views that comprise the broad spectrum of religious beliefs found among us. But they demonstrate very clearly the diverse manners in which beliefs, equally paramount in the lives of their possessors, may be articulated. They further reveal the difficulties inherent in placing too narrow a construction on the provisions of § 6(j) and thereby lend conclusive support to the construction which we today find that Congress intended.

While the applicant's words may differ, the test is simple of application. It is essentially an objective one, namely, does the claimed belief occupy the same place in the life of the objector as an orthodox belief in God holds in the life one clearly qualified for exemption?

The validity of what he believes cannot be questioned. Some theologians, and indeed some examiners, might be tempted to question the existence of the registrant's "Supreme Being" or the truth of his concepts. But these are inquiries foreclosed to Government. [B]oards and courts in this sense are not free to reject beliefs because they consider them "incomprehensible." Their task is to decide whether the beliefs professed by a registrant are sincerely held and whether they are, in his own scheme of things, religious.

But we hasten to emphasize that while the "truth" of a belief is not open to question, there remains the significant question whether it is "truly held." This is the threshold question of sincerity which must be resolved in every case. It is, of course, a question of fact—a prime consideration to the validity of every claim for exemption as a conscientious objector.

APPLICATION OF § 6(j) TO THE INSTANT CASES.

As we noted earlier, the statutory definition excepts those registrants whose beliefs are based on a "merely personal moral code." The records in these cases, however, show that at no time did any one of the applicants suggest that his objection was based on a "merely personal moral code." Indeed at the outset each of them claimed in his application that his objection was based on a religious belief. We have construed the statutory definition broadly and it follows that any exception to it must be interpreted narrowly. The use by Congress of the words "merely personal" seems to us to restrict the exception to a moral code which is not only personal but which is the sole basis for the registrant's belief and is in no way related to a Supreme Being.

In light of [Seeger's] beliefs and the unquestioned sincerity with which he held them, we think the Board, had it applied the test we propose today, would have granted him the exemption. We think it clear that the beliefs which prompted his objection occupy the same place in his life as the belief in a traditional deity hold in the lives of his friends, the Quakers. We are reminded once more of Dr. Tillich's thoughts:

> "And if that word [God] has not much meaning for you, translate it, and speak of the depths of your life, of the source of your being, of your ultimate concern, *of what you take seriously without any reservation.* Perhaps, in order to do so, you must forget everything traditional that you have learned about God...." Tillich, The Shaking of the Foundations 57 (1948). (Emphasis supplied.)

It may be that Seeger did not clearly demonstrate what his beliefs were with regard to the usual understanding of the term "Supreme Being." But as we have said Congress did not intend that to be the test. We therefore affirm the judgment in No. 50.

In *Jakobson,* No. 51, the Court of Appeals found that the registrant demonstrated that his belief as to opposition to war was related to a Supreme Being. We agree and affirm that judgment.

We reach a like conclusion in No. 29. It will be remembered that Peter acknowledged "some power manifest in nature... the supreme expression" that helps man in ordering his life. We think that under the test we establish here the Board would grant the exemption to Peter and we therefore reverse the judgment in No. 29.

It is so ordered.

MR. JUSTICE DOUGLAS, concurring.

The legislative history of this Act leaves much in the dark. But it is, in my opinion, not a *tour de force* if we construe the words "Supreme Being" to include the cosmos, as well as an anthropomorphic entity.

The words "a Supreme Being" have no narrow technical meaning in the field of religion. Long before the birth of our Judeo-Christian civilization the idea of God had taken hold in many forms. Mention of only two—Hinduism and Buddhism—illustrates the fluidity and evanescent scope of the concept. In the Hindu *religion* the Supreme Being is conceived in the forms of several cult Deities. The chief of these, which stand for the Hindu Triad, are Brahma, Vishnu and Siva. Another Deity, and the one most widely worshipped, is Sakti, the Mother Goddess, conceived as power, both destructive and creative. Though Hindu religion encompasses the worship of many Deities, it believes in only one single God, the eternally existent One Being with his manifold attributes and manifestations.

Buddhism—whose advent marked the reform of Hinduism—continued somewhat the same concept. As stated by Nancy Wilson Ross, "God—if I may borrow that word for a moment—the universe, and man are one indissoluble existence, one total whole. Only THIS—capital THIS—is. Anything and everything that appears to us as an individual entity or phenomenon, whether it be a planet or an atom, a mouse or a man, is but a temporary manifestation of THIS in form; every activity that takes place, whether it be birth or death, loving or eating breakfast, is but a temporary manifestation of THIS in activity. When we look at things this way, naturally we cannot believe that each individual person has been endowed with a special and individual soul or self. Each one of us is but a cell, as it were, in the body of the Great Self, a cell that comes into being, performs its functions, and passes away, transformed into another manifestation. Though we have temporary individuality, that temporary, limited individuality is not either a true self or our true self. Our true self is the Great Self; our true body is the Body of Reality, or the Dharmakaya, to give it its technical Buddhist name." The World of Zen, p. 18 (1960).

Does a Buddhist believe in "God" or a "Supreme Being"? That, of course depends on how one defines "God," as one eminent student of Buddhism has explained:

> "It has often been suggested that Buddhism is an atheistic system of thought, and this assumption has given rise to quite a number of discussions. Some have claimed that since Buddhism knew no God, it could not be a religion; others that since Buddhism obviously was a religion which knew no God, the belief in God was not essential to religion. These discussions assume that *God* is an unambiguous term, which is by no means the case." Conze, Buddhism, pp. 38–39 (1959).

Dr. Conze then says that if "God" is taken to mean a personal Creator of the universe, then the Buddhist has no interest in the concept. But if "God" means something like the state of oneness with God as described by some Christian mystics, then the Buddhist surely believes in "God," since this state is almost indistinguishable from the Buddhist concept of Nirvana, "the supreme Reality;...the eternal, hidden and incomprehensible Peace."

When the present Act was adopted in 1948 we were a nation of Buddhists, Confucianists, and Taoists, as well as Christians.

When the Congress spoke in the vague general terms of a Supreme Being I cannot, therefore, assume that it was so parochial as to use the words in the narrow sense urged on us. I would attribute tolerance and sophistication to the Congress, commensurate with the religious complexion of our communities. In sum, I agree with the Court that any person opposed to war on the basis of a sincere belief, which in his life fills the same place as a belief in God fills in the life of an orthodox religionist, is entitled to exemption under the statute. None comes to us an avowedly irreligious person or as an atheist;[2] one, as a sincere believer in "goodness and virtue for their own sakes." His questions and doubts on theological issues, and his wonder, are no more alien to the statutory standard than are the awe-inspired questions of a devout Buddhist.

Notes

1. In interpreting the legislative provision limiting conscientious objection to "religious training and belief" and requiring religious belief to a relate to a belief in a Supreme Being, Justice Clark reiterated the language of the statute and noted that "The section excludes those persons who, disavowing religious belief, decide on the basis of essentially political, sociological or economic considerations that war is wrong and that they will have no part of it." Chief Justice Burger made the same distinction between religious and philosophical beliefs in *Wisconsin v. Yoder*, 406 U.S. 205 (1972):

> [I]f the Amish asserted their claims because of their subjective evaluation and rejection of the contemporary secular values accepted by the majority, much as

---

2. If he were an atheist, quite different problems would be presented. Cf. Torcaso v. Watkins, 367 U.S. 488.

> Thoreau rejected the social values of his time and isolated himself at Walden Pond, their claims would not rest on a religious basis. Thoreau's choice was philosophical and personal rather than religious, and such belief does not rise to the demands of the Religion Clauses.

Id. at 216.

Is this a sensible distinction? Is it a necessary distinction? Would Thoreau's beliefs meet the "ultimate concern" test of *Seeger*? Thoreau's beliefs were sincere and meaningful, and appeared to occupy a place in his life parallel to that filled by those who believe in the God of Moses and Abraham. Does it appear that Justice Clark and Chief Justice Burger are attempting to create the same distinction, or is Chief Justice Burger's statement an attempted gloss on the *Seeger* holding? Should it matter that in *Yoder*, the State of Wisconsin conceded that the beliefs of the Amish were religious? Does this distinction allow one to categorize "secular humanism" or Marxism as philosophical beliefs rather than religious beliefs, even if the "ultimate concern" of a secular humanist or Marxist might otherwise allow this belief to be categorized as religious?

2. Justice Clark writes, "A sincere and meaningful belief which occupies in the life of its possessor a place parallel to that filled by the God of those admittedly qualifying for the exemption comes within the statutory definition." Does this form of analogical reasoning aid the Court's inquiry? If you have a belief that "parallels" a religious belief, is that a concession that your belief is not religious, but something else? Is Justice Clark's opinion an acknowledgment that a content-based definition of religion (like belief in a "Supreme Being") is unworkable because it is too underinclusive? Is an "affective" definition of religion, one that assesses the importance of the belief in the life of the claimant, overinclusive? As Professor John Mansfield has noted, one difficulty with the "occupies a place" language is that it fails to address whether this difficult judgment is to be based on an even more difficult (if not impossible) "psychological and biographical inquiry" of the claimant. John H. Mansfield, *Conscientious Objection-1964 Term*, 1965 Religion & Pub. Ord. 3, 9.

It appears highly unlikely that Congress was thinking of the expansive definitions of "God" given by Paul Tillich and others when it amended the selective service act in 1948 to require a belief in a "Supreme Being." Although Tillich was a well-known theologian by 1948, the Tillich books the Court cites in *Seeger* were published well after 1948. Should that matter? In oral argument before the Supreme Court, the government accepted the definition of religion of such "eminent theologians as Professor Tillich and Dr. Robinson," who "eschew the idea of a personal God and define God in such terms as 'the ultimate ground or root of our being.'" *United States v. Seeger*, 60 LANDMARK BRIEFS AND ARGUMENTS 1057. If Congress was relying on a "Judeo-Christian" or "Hebraic" understanding of God when it included a belief in a "Supreme Being," should that reliance have required the Court to hold the law unconstitutional as violative of the Establishment Clause? Should the fact that Paul Tillich was a liberal Protestant theologian make the Court's embrace of his view more readily acceptable, because Tillich was writing in a "Christian" and "Protestant" tradition, which has been an important part of American culture throughout American history?

3. The Supreme Court's adoption of Tillich's "ultimate concern" approach has been both praised and criticized by commentators. *Compare* Note, *Toward a Constitutional Definition of Religion*, 91 Harv. L. Rev. 1056 (1978) (praising approach) *with* Jesse H. Choper, *Defining "Religion" in the First Amendment*, 1982 U. Ill. L. Rev. 579, 594–97 (criticizing approach). Dean Choper criticizes the "ultimate concern" rationale because

Tillich's view "only marginally comprehend 'religion' as that term is understood by most theologians or laymen," *id.* at 595, because it distorts Tillich's views, and because ultimate concerns

> pervade virtually all areas or ordinary government involvement, [and] whatever the true importance of such beliefs to the individual or society as a whole, to grant them the special constitutional immunity of the free exercise clause merely because they are strongly held would severely undermine the state's ability to advance the commonweal.

Id. at 596.

Is this criticism convincing? Is it less persuasive as long as *Employment Div. v. Smith* remains law?

See also Kent Greenawalt, *Religion as a Concept in Constitutional Law*, 72 Calif. L. Rev. 753, 806–11 (1982) (declaring "[a]s a proposed standard for legal categorization, ultimate concern retains a deep ambiguity and vagueness" which makes it "inapt for a wide variety of free exercise and establishment cases.").

Should the "ultimate concern" approach be interpreted as requiring an assessment of the character and type of beliefs accepted by the claimant, rather than the place those beliefs occupy in the claimant's life? In other words, should a court make its determination of the religiousness of the claimant's beliefs based on the "character of the truths asserted" by the belief system, rather than on the importance of those beliefs to the claimant? *See* Mansfield, *Conscientious Objection*, at 10 ("[I]t is the fundamental character of the truths asserted, and the fact that they address themselves to basic questions about the nature of reality and the meaning of human existence, that is the primary reason for characterizing a belief in these truths as religious"); *cf.* Freeman, *Misguided Search*, at 1546–48 (claiming Mansfield's approach is superior to most efforts to define religion, but concluding that it fails because it mistakenly assumes there is an "essence" to religion).

For a critical assessment of the interpretation given Tillich's "ultimate concern" approach by legal academics, see James McBride, *Paul Tillich and the Supreme Court: Tillich's "Ultimate Concern" as a Standard in Judicial Interpretation*, 30 J. Church & St. 245 (1988). McBride, a professor of religion and social ethics, suggests that "the concept of 'ultimate concern' invoked by the Court cannot be reduced merely to an affective attitude as legal scholars and justices have implied. If Tillich's notion is to be spared violence, the Court must recognize that there exist two poles in 'ultimate concern': objective as well as subjective." *Id.* at 269. McBride suggests that the objective pole requires a belief that "transcends the empirical form and contents of the phenomenal world." *Id.* at 270. Does this make Tillich's definition more acceptable as a legal standard? George Freeman has noted that one scholar has listed "thirty-five different kinds of transcendence." Freeman, *Misguided Search*, at 1557.

4. How deeply should the claimant's conscientious belief be held? To what extent should a claimant be required to show his willingness to suffer imprisonment or other harms as evidence of his sincerity? Can (or should) such a test be devised? Can a conscientious objector be required to serve his country in a nonmilitary role? Even if that role indirectly contributes to the prosecution of the war effort? Should conscience be interpreted to require a refusal to assist the war effort directly or indirectly?

5. Justice Douglas's concurring opinion cites the case of *Torcaso v. Watkins*, 367 U.S. 488 (1961), excerpted in Chapter Eleven. In *Torcaso*, the Court, in an opinion writ-

ten by Justice Black, claimed that the religion clauses forbade legally distinguishing between "those religions based on a belief in the existence of God as against those religions founded on different beliefs," *id.* at 495, and declared in a footnote that "[a]mong religions in this country which do not teach what would generally be considered a belief in the existence of God are Buddhism, Taoism, Ethical Culture, Secular Humanism and others." *Id.* at 495 n.11.

Torcaso underscores the underinclusive effect of equating religious belief with a belief in God. However, *Torcaso* also creates the possibility of an overinclusive definition of religion. Along with the references by the majority in *Seeger* to the views of "Dr. David Saville Muzzey, a leader in the Ethical Culture Movement," the Court's broadly inclusive listing of religions in *Torcaso* allowed others, beginning a decade later, to assert that "secular humanism" was a religion, and was "established" in the public school system. In 1957, two courts concluded that "humanist" organizations were "religious" and thus deserving of tax exempt status. *Fellowship of Humanity v. County of Alameda*, 315 P.2d 394 (Cal. App. 1957); *Washington Ethical Society v. District of Columbia*, 101 U.S. App. D.C. 371, 249 F.2d 127 (D.C. Cir. 1957). Both cases were cited approvingly by the Supreme Court in *Torcaso*.

Should "secular humanism" be defined as a religion? If so, is that because it appears antithetical to Christian beliefs? Is it possible for a belief system that declares itself anti-religious to be defined as religious under the approach taken by the Court in *Seeger*? Because not to so define it would be to violate the idea of "neutrality" implicit in the Establishment Clause? If secular humanism is defined as a religion, does that permit the state adequately to defend the "values" inculcated in public schools? *See Fleischfresser v. Directors of Sch. Dist. 200*, 15 F.3d 680 (7th Cir. 1994) (discussing problem with defining religion and holding that an elementary reading series in the public school which includes stories of "fantasy and make-believe" is not "the impermissible establishment of pagan religion.").

Five years later, the Court again interpreted the statutory language of the 1948 amendment.

Welsh v. United States

398 U.S. 333 (1970)

Mr. Justice BLACK announced the judgment of the Court and delivered an opinion in which Mr. Justice DOUGLAS, Mr. Justice BRENNAN, and Mr. Justice MARSHALL join.

The petitioner, Elliott Ashton Welsh II, was convicted by a United States District Judge of refusing to submit to induction into the Armed Forces in violation of 50 U.S.C. App. §462(a), and was on June 1, 1966, sentenced to imprisonment for three years.

The controlling facts in this case are strikingly similar to those in *Seeger*. Both Seeger and Welsh were brought up in religious homes and attended church in their childhood, but in neither case was this church one which taught its members not to engage in war at any time for any reason. Neither Seeger nor Welsh continued his childhood religious ties into his young manhood, and neither belonged to any religious group or adhered to the teachings of any organized religion during the period of his involvement with the Selective Service System. At the time of registration for the draft, neither had yet come to accept pacifist principles. Their views on war developed only in subsequent years, but when their ideas did fully mature both made application to their local draft boards for conscientious objector exemptions from military service under §6(j) of the Universal Military Training and Service Act.

In filling out their exemption applications both Seeger and Welsh were unable to sign the statement that, as printed in the Selective Service form, stated "I am, by reason of my religious training and belief, conscientiously opposed to participation in war in any form." Seeger could sign only after striking the words "training and" and putting quotation marks around the word "religious." Welsh could sign only after striking the words "my religious training and." On those same applications, neither could definitely affirm or deny that he believed in a "Supreme Being," both stating that they preferred to leave the question open. But both Seeger and Welsh affirmed on those applications that they held deep conscientious scruples against taking part in wars where people were killed. Both strongly believed that killing in war was wrong, unethical, and immoral, and their consciences forbade them to take part in such an evil practice. Their objection to participating in war in any form could not be said to come from a "still, small voice of conscience"; rather, for them that voice was so loud and insistent that both men preferred to go to jail rather than serve in the Armed Forces. There was never any question about the sincerity and depth of Seeger's convictions as a conscientious objector, and the same is true of Welsh. In this regard the Court of Appeals noted, "[t]he government concedes that [Welsh's] beliefs are held with the strength of more traditional religious convictions." But in both cases the Selective Service System concluded that the beliefs of these men were in some sense insufficiently "religious" to qualify them for conscientious objector exemptions under the terms of §6(j). Welsh was denied the exemption because his Appeal Board and the Department of Justice hearing officer "could find no religious basis for the registrant's beliefs, opinions and convictions." Both Seeger and Welsh subsequently refused to submit to induction into the military and both were convicted of that offense.

In the case before us the Government seeks to distinguish our holding in *Seeger* on basically two grounds, both of which were relied upon by the Court of Appeals in affirming Welsh's conviction. First, it is stressed that Welsh was far more insistent and explicit than Seeger in denying that his views were religious. For example, in filling out their conscientious objector applications, Seeger put quotation marks around the word, "religious," but Welsh struck the words "religious" entirely and later characterized his beliefs as having been formed "by reading in the fields of history and sociology." The Court of Appeals found that Welsh had "denied that his objection to war was premised on religious belief" and concluded that "[t]he Appeal Board was entitled to take him at his word." We think this attempt to distinguish *Seeger* fails for the reason that it places undue emphasis on the registrant's interpretation of his own beliefs. The Court's statement in *Seeger* that a registrant's characterization of his own belief as "religious" should carry great weight, does not imply that his declaration that his views are nonreligious should be treated similarly. When a registrant states that his objections to war are "religious," that information is highly relevant to the question of the function his beliefs have in his life. But very few registrants are fully aware of the broad scope of the word "religious" as used in §6(j), and accordingly a registrant's statement that his beliefs are nonreligious is a highly reliable guide for those charged with administering the exemption. Welsh himself presents a case in point. Although he originally characterized his beliefs as nonreligious, he later upon reflection wrote a long and thoughtful letter to his Appeal Board in which he declared that his beliefs were "certainly religious in the ethical sense of the word." He explained:

> "I believe I mentioned taking of life as not being, for me, a religious wrong. Again, I assumed Mr. [Brady (the Department of Justice hearing officer)] was

> using the word 'religious' in the conventional sense, and in order to be perfectly honest did not characterize my belief as 'religious.'"

The Government also seeks to distinguish *Seeger* on the ground that Welsh's views, unlike Seeger's, were "essentially political, sociological, or philosophical views or a merely personal moral code." We certainly do not think that § 6(j)'s exclusion of those persons with "essentially political, sociological, or philosophical views or a merely personal moral code" should be read to exclude those who hold strong beliefs about our domestic and foreign affairs or even those whose conscientious objection to participation in all wars is founded to a substantial extent upon considerations of public policy. The two groups of registrants that obviously do fall within these exclusions from the exemption are those whose beliefs are not deeply held and those whose objection to war does not rest at all upon moral, ethical, or religious principle but instead rests solely upon considerations of policy, pragmatism, or expediency. In applying § 6(j)'s exclusion of those whose views are "essentially political, sociological, or philosophical" or of those who have a "merely personal moral code," it should be remembered that these exclusions are definitional and do not therefore restrict the category of persons who are conscientious objectors by "religious training and belief."

Welsh stated that he "believe[d] the taking of life—anyone's life—to be morally wrong." Welsh elaborated his beliefs in later communications with Selective Service officials. On the basis of these beliefs and the conclusion of the Court of Appeals that he held them "with the strength of more traditional religious convictions," we think Welsh was clearly entitled to a conscientious objector exemption. Section 6(j) requires no more. That section exempts from military service all those whose consciences, spurred by deeply held moral, ethical, or religious beliefs, would give them no rest or peace if they allowed themselves to become a part of an instrument of war.

The judgment is

Reversed.

Mr. Justice BLACKMUN took no part in the consideration or decision of this case.

Mr. Justice HARLAN, concurring in the result.

Candor requires me to say that I joined the Court's opinion in *United States v. Seeger* only with the gravest misgivings as to whether it was a legitimate exercise in statutory construction, and today's decision convinces me that in doing so I made a mistake which I should now acknowledge.

In *Seeger* the Court construed § 6(j) of the Universal Military Training and Service Act so as to sustain a conscientious objector claim not founded on a theistic belief. Today the prevailing opinion makes explicit its total elimination of the statutorily required religious content for a conscientious objector exemption. The prevailing opinion now says: "If an individual deeply and sincerely holds beliefs that are *purely ethical* or *moral* in source and content but that nevertheless impose upon him a duty of conscience to refrain from participating in any war at any time" (emphasis added), he qualifies for a § 6(j) exemption.

In my opinion, the liberties taken with the statute both in *Seeger* and today's decision cannot be justified in the name of the familiar doctrine of construing federal statutes in a manner that will avoid possible constitutional infirmities in them. I therefore find myself unable to escape facing the constitutional issue that this case squarely presents: whether § 6(j) in limiting this draft exemption to those opposed to war in general because of theistic beliefs runs afoul of the religious clauses of the First Amendment. For reasons later appearing I believe it does

I

[I]t is apparent from a textual analysis of §6(j) and the legislative history that the words of this section, as used and understood by Congress, fall short of enacting the broad policy of exempting from military service all individuals who in good faith oppose all war.

A

The natural reading of §6(j), which quite evidently draws a distinction between theistic and nontheistic religions, is the only one that is consistent with the legislative history.

B

Against this legislative history it is a remarkable feat of judicial surgery to remove, as did *Seeger*, the theistic requirement of §6(j). The prevailing opinion today, however, in the name of interpreting the will of Congress, has performed a lobotomy and completely transformed the statute by reading out of it any distinction between religiously acquired beliefs and those deriving from "essentially political, sociological, or philosophical views or a merely personal moral code."

In the realm of statutory construction it is appropriate to search for meaning in the congressional vocabulary in a lexicon most probably consulted by Congress. Resort to Webster's reveals that the meanings of "religion" are: "1. The service and adoration of God or a god as expressed in forms of worship, in obedience to divine commands...; 2. The state of life of a religious...; 3. One of the *systems* of faith and worship; a form of theism; a religious faith...; 4. The profession or practice of religious beliefs; religious observances *collectively; pl.* rites; 5. Devotion or fidelity;... conscientiousness; 6. An apprehension, awareness, or conviction of the existence of a supreme being, or more widely, of supernatural powers or influences controlling one's own, humanity's, or nature's destiny; also, such an apprehension, etc., accompanied by or arousing reverence, love, gratitude, the will to obey and serve, and the like...." (Emphasis added.)

Of the five pertinent definitions four include the notion of either a Supreme Being or a cohesive, organized group pursuing a common spiritual purpose together. While, as the Court's opinion in *Seeger* points out, these definitions do not exhaust the almost infinite and sophisticated possibilities for defining "religion," there is strong evidence that Congress restricted, in this instance, the word to its conventional sense.

For me this dichotomy reveals that Congress was not embracing that definition of religion that alone speaks in terms of "devotion or fidelity" to individual principles acquired on an individualized basis but was adopting, at least, those meanings that associate religion with formal, organized worship or shared beliefs by a recognizable and cohesive group. Indeed, this requirement was explicit in the predecessor to the 1940 statute. The Draft Act of 1917 conditioned conscientious objector status on membership in or affiliation with a "well-recognized religious sect or organization [then] organized and existing and whose existing creed or principles forb[ade] its members to participate in war in any form...." §4, 40 Stat. 78.

Unless we are to assume an Alice-in-Wonderland world where words have no meaning, I think it fair to say that Congress' choice of language cannot fail to convey to the discerning reader the very policy choice that the prevailing opinion today completely obliterates: that between conventional religions that usually have an organized and formal structure and dogma and a cohesive group identity, even when nontheistic, and cults that represent schools of thought and in the usual case are without formal structure or are, at most, loose and informal associations of individuals who share common ethical, moral, or intellectual views.

III

The constitutional question that must be faced in this case is whether a statute that defers to the individual's conscience only when his views emanate from adherence to theistic religious beliefs is within the power of Congress. Congress, of course, could, entirely consistently with the requirements of the Constitution, eliminate *all* exemptions for conscientious objectors. Such a course would be wholly "neutral" and, in my view, would not offend the Free Exercise Clause. However, having chosen to exempt, it cannot draw the line between theistic or nontheistic religious beliefs on the one hand and secular beliefs on the other. Any such distinctions are not, in my view, compatible with the Establishment Clause of the First Amendment.

The "radius" of this legislation is the conscientiousness with which an individual opposes war in general, yet the statute, as I think it must be construed, excludes from its "scope" individuals motivated by teachings of nontheistic religions,[8] and individuals guided by an inner ethical voice that bespeaks secular and not "religious" reflection. It not only accords a preference to the "religious" but also disadvantages adherents of religions that do not worship a Supreme Being. The constitutional infirmity cannot be cured, moreover, even by an impermissible construction that eliminates the theistic requirement and simply draws the line between religious and nonreligious. This in my view offends the Establishment Clause and is that kind of classification.

If the exemption is to be given application, it must encompass the class of individuals it purports to exclude, those whose beliefs emanate from a purely moral, ethical, or philosophical source. The common denominator must be the intensity of moral conviction with which a belief is held.[10] Common experience teaches that among "religious" individuals some are weak and others strong adherents to tenets and this is no less true of individuals whose lives are guided by personal ethical considerations.

IV

The policy of exempting religious conscientious objectors is one of longstanding tradition in this country and accords recognition to what is, in a diverse and "open" society, the important value of reconciling individuality of belief with practical exigencies

8. This Court has taken notice of the fact that recognized "religions" exist that "do not teach what would generally be considered a belief in the existence of God," Torcaso v. Watkins, 367 U.S. 488, 495 n. 11, e.g., "Buddhism, Taoism, Ethical Culture, Secular Humanism and others." See also Washington Ethical Society v. District of Columbia, 101 U.S. App. D.C. 371, 249 F.2d 127 (1957); 2 Encyclopedia of the Social Sciences 293; J. Archer, Faiths Men Live By 120–138, 254–313 (2d ed. revised by Purinton 1958).

10. Without deciding what constitutes a definition of "religion" for First Amendment purposes it suffices to note that it means, in my view, at least the two conceivable readings of § 6(j) set forth in Part II, but something less than mere adherence to ethical or moral beliefs in general or a certain belief such as conscientious objection. Thus the prevailing opinion's expansive reading of "religion" in § 6(j) does not, in my view, create an Establishment Clause problem in that it exempts all sincere objectors but does not exempt others, *e.g.*, those who object to war on pragmatic grounds and contend that pragmatism is their creed.

whenever possible. *See Girouard v. United States*, 328 U.S. 61 (1946). It dates back to colonial times and has been perpetuated in state and federal conscription statutes. See Mr. Justice Cardozo's separate opinion in *Hamilton v. Board of Regents*, 293 U.S., at 267; *Macintosh v. United States*, 42 F.2d 845, 847 (1930). That it has been phrased in religious terms reflects, I assume, the fact that ethics and morals, while the concern of secular philosophy, have traditionally been matters taught by organized religion and that for most individuals spiritual and ethical nourishment is derived from that source. It further reflects, I would suppose, the assumption that beliefs emanating from a religious source are probably held with great intensity.

Mr. Justice WHITE, with whom THE CHIEF JUSTICE [BURGER] and Mr. Justice STEWART join, dissenting.

Nothing in the First Amendment prohibits drafting Welsh and other nonreligious objectors to war. Saving §6(j) by extending it to include Welsh cannot be done in the name of a presumed congressional will but only by the Court's taking upon itself the power to make draft-exemption policy.

If I am wrong in thinking that Welsh cannot benefit from invalidation of §6(j) on Establishment Clause grounds, I would nevertheless affirm his conviction; for I cannot hold that Congress violated the Clause in exempting from the draft all those who oppose war by reason of religious training and belief. In exempting religious conscientious objectors, Congress was making one of two judgments, perhaps both. First, §6(j) may represent a purely practical judgment that religious objectors, however admirable, would be of no more use in combat than many others unqualified for military service. Exemption was not extended to them to further religious belief or practice but to limit military service to those who were prepared to undertake the fighting that the armed services have to do. On this basis, the exemption has neither the primary purpose nor the effect of furthering religion.

Second, Congress may have granted the exemption because otherwise religious objectors would be forced into conduct that their religions forbid and because in the view of Congress to deny the exemption would violate the Free Exercise Clause or at least raise grave problems in this respect. True, this Court has more than once stated its unwillingness to construe the First Amendment, standing alone, as requiring draft exemptions for religious believers. *Hamilton v. Board of Regents*, 293 U.S. 245, 263–264 (1934); *United States v. Macintosh*, 283 U.S. 605, 623–624 (1931). But this Court is not alone in being obliged to construe the Constitution in the course of its work; nor does it even approach having a monopoly on the wisdom and insight appropriate to the task.

If there were no statutory exemption for religious objectors to war and failure to provide it was held by this Court to impair the free exercise of religion contrary to the First Amendment, an exemption reflecting this constitutional command would be no more an establishment of religion than the exemption required for Sabbatarians in *Sherbert v. Verner.*

On the assumption, however, that the Free Exercise Clause of the First Amendment does not by its own force require exempting devout objectors from military service, it does not follow that §6(j) is a law respecting an establishment of religion within the meaning of the First Amendment. It is very likely that §6(j) is a recognition by Congress of free exercise values and its view of desirable or required policy in implementing the Free Exercise Clause. There being substantial roots in the Free Exercise Clause for §6(j) I would not frustrate congressional will by construing the Establishment Clause to condition the exemption for religionists upon extending the exemption also to those who object to war on nonreligious grounds.

We have said that neither support nor hostility, but neutrality, is the goal of the religion clauses of the First Amendment. "Neutrality," however, is not self-defining. If it is "favoritism" and not "neutrality" to exempt religious believers from the draft, is it "neutrality" and not "inhibition" of religion to compel religious believers to fight when they have special reasons for not doing so, reasons to which the Constitution gives particular recognition? It cannot be ignored that the First Amendment itself contains a religious classification. The Amendment protects belief and speech, but as a general proposition, the free speech provisions stop short of immunizing conduct from official regulation. The Free Exercise Clause, however, has a deeper cut: it protects conduct as well as religious belief and speech. Although socially harmful acts may as a rule be banned despite the Free Exercise Clause even where religiously motivated, there is an area of conduct that cannot be forbidden to religious practitioners but that may be forbidden to others. *See United States v. Ballard,* 322 U.S. 78 (1944); *Follett v. McCormick,* 321 U.S. 573 (1944). We should thus not labor to find a violation of the Establishment Clause when free exercise values prompt Congress to relieve religious believers from the burdens of the law at least in those instances where the law is not merely prohibitory but commands the performance of military duties that are forbidden by a man's religion.

Notes

1. In *Gillette v. United States,* 401 U.S. 437 (1971), the Supreme Court held that Congress's limitation of conscientious objector status to those whose religious beliefs forbade participation in any form in war was constitutional as against a challenge by draftees whose religious beliefs forbade them from participating in "unjust" wars. This distinction meant that Roman Catholics and others who are not pacifists without regard to context, but whose reasons for opposing the Vietnam War were clearly religious, were unable to obtain the same conscientious objector status as those who were pacifists in all cases, but whose beliefs were assertedly nonreligious. Does this make sense? For a criticism, see Kent Greenawalt, *All or Nothing at All: The Defeat of Selective Conscientious Objection,* 1971 Sup. Ct. Rev. 31.

2. The *Welsh* plurality notes that the "Court of Appeals found that Welsh had 'denied that his objection to war was premised on religious belief' and concluded that '[t]he Appeal Board was entitled to take him at his word.'" It then continues, "We think this attempt to distinguish *Seeger* fails for the reason that it places undue emphasis on the registrant's interpretation of his own beliefs." The *Seeger* Court rejected a content-based definition of religion in interpreting §6(j), and substituted the "ultimate concern" test, an "affective" test. As Professor Mansfield noted in regard to *Seeger,* the "ultimate concern" standard may require the governmental body to engage in a psychological and biographical inquiry of the claimant to determine whether the belief is an ultimate concern of that claimant. Is the *Welsh* plurality's conclusion a concession that the "ultimate concern" test is overinclusive? Unsatisfactory in resolving the problem of defining religion? Is the plurality trying to save the statute? Trying to save Welsh? Is it constitutionally permissible for a governmental entity (like the Court or a draft board) to tell Welsh that he erroneously believes his deeply held beliefs are not religious? Does it matter that the Court is declaring Welsh's beliefs "religious" as a matter of statutory interpretation?

3. By the time *Welsh* was decided, opposition to the Vietnam War had grown, and Justice Douglas in particular believed the war was being conducted in contravention to the Constitution because of the absence of a Congressional declaration of war. In his

role as circuit justice Douglas wrote several opinions limiting extension of reserve service and barring the Navy from holding a sailor claiming conscientious objector status to the brig. *See Scaggs v. Larsen*, 396 U.S. 1206 (1969); *Jones v. Lemond*, 396 U.S. 1227 (1969). *See also United States v. O'Brien*, 391 U.S. 367 (1968) (Douglas, J., dissenting) (concluding that burning of draft card raises basic issue of constitutionality of conscription in absence of a declaration of war). Does this suggest an explanation for the Court's extension of *Seeger* in *Welsh*?

4. Why did the plurality refuse to follow the lead of Justice Harlan's opinion and declare the statute unconstitutional? Was the Court fearful that Congress would choose to eliminate conscientious objector status if the "religious" exemption was contrary to the commands of the Constitution? *Welsh* was decided only a year before *Lemon*, and was decided after *Walz*, the two cases which crystallized the Court's Establishment Clause "test" (requiring the law to have a secular purpose, an effect that neither promoted nor inhibited religion and which did not cause excessive entanglement between religion and the state) of constitutionality in Establishment Clause cases. The Court was thus not jurisprudentially adrift when *Welsh* was decided, which suggests that it could have used *Walz* to buttress a decision declaring the Selective Service Act exemption unconstitutional. Does the decision not to follow Justice Harlan's lead suggest that the Court is unwilling to hold unconstitutional federal legislation on Religion Clause grounds? Does the dissenting opinion of Justice White, which attempts to create some room for statutory "accommodation" of religious believers, and thus favors religion over nonreligion, adequately respond to Justice Harlan's dissent?

5. Justice Harlan dissented in *Sherbert v. Verner*, 374 U.S. 398 (1963), excerpted in Chapter Five, the first case to grant an exemption from a generally applicable law based on the Free Exercise Clause. He made a classic "slippery slope" argument, claiming that constitutionally compelling an exemption from a "neutral" law would have far-reaching consequences. But he did not read the Establishment and Free Exercise Clauses as leaving no room for statutory accommodation: "My own view, however, is that at least under the circumstances of this case it would be a permissible accommodation of religion for the State, if it *chose* to do so, to create an exception to its eligibility requirements for persons like the appellant." *Id.* at 422. Joining Justice Harlan's dissent in *Sherbert* was Justice White. The next case to grant a Free Exercise exemption, *Wisconsin v. Yoder*, 406 U.S. 205 (1972), was decided after Harlan retired from the Court. If Justice Harlan's understanding of "neutrality" as offered in his *Welsh* concurrence is read in light of his opinion in *Sherbert*, should *Welsh* be read as severely narrowing the channel of permissible statutory "accommodations" of religion? If a law is unconstitutional because it distinguishes between religious pacifists and non-religious pacifists, is there *any* room for statutory accommodations of religion? Harlan's opinion strongly suggests that, but for what the free exercise clause demands, the establishment clause prohibits. Does Harlan's concurring opinion foreshadow the Court's decision in *Employment Div. v. Smith*?

C. Defining Religion After Seeger and Welsh

Since deciding *Welsh*, the Supreme Court has only alluded to a definition of religion in the above-mentioned dicta in *Wisconsin v. Yoder*, 406 U.S. 205 (1972), and in dicta in another unemployment compensation case, *Thomas v. Review Board*, 450 U.S. 707 (1981), in which the Court, again by Chief Justice Burger, noted, "Only beliefs rooted in religion are protected by the Free Exercise Clause, which, by its terms, gives special protection to the exercise of religion." *Id.* at 713.

To fill this void, several federal courts have offered various definitions of religion. In *Theriault v. Silber*, 453 F. Supp. 254 (W.D. Tex. 1978), *appeal dismissed*, 579 F.2d 302 (5th Cir. 1978), *cert. denied*, 440 U.S. 917 (1979), the district court held that the "Church of the New Song," a prison-based organization whose only belief, the court concluded, was the disruption of prison discipline, was not a religious organization. However, another district court, in *Remmers v. Brewer*, 361 F. Supp. 537 (S.D. Iowa 1973), concluded that the organization was religious because of the existence of an Eclatarian bible and the group's belief in a supreme force called the "Eclat." Both courts based their conclusion by analogizing the Church of the New Song to traditional religious organizations. The United States Court of Appeals for the District of Columbia Circuit held Scientology a religion in part because of Scientology's affinity to Eastern religions, and in part because its fundamental writings offered "a general account of man and his nature comparable in scope, if not in content, to those of some recognized religions." *Founding Church of Scientology of Washington v. United States*, 409 F.2d 1146, 1160 (D.C. Cir.), *cert. denied*, 396 U.S. 963 (1969). The Second Circuit embraced the *Seeger* "ultimate concern" formulation, adding, "A concern is 'ultimate' when it is more than intellectual." *International Soc'y for Krishna Consciousness v. Barber*, 650 F.2d 430, 440 (2d Cir. 1981). This distinction between the rational or intellectual and the nonrational or faith-driven belief echoed the view of the Court in *Ballard.* More recently, in *Alabama and Coushatta Tribes v. Trustees of Big Sandy Indep. Sch. Dist.*, 817 F. Supp. 1319 (E.D. Tex. 1993), the district court stated: "Whenever a belief system encompasses fundamental questions of the nature of reality and the relationship of human beings to reality, it deals with essentially religious questions." *Id.* at 1329. Based on this definition, the court held that the public school system could not limit the length of the hair of male Indian students.

In addition to the cases cited above, a number of academics and lawyers have offered proposed definitions of religion. Gail Merel proposed that "the fundamental principle underlying both religion clauses is the protection of individual choice in matters of religion—whether pro or con—and that governmental neutrality is required only with respect to religious and irreligious opinion." Gail Merel, *The Protection of Individual Choice: A Consistent Understanding of Religion Under the First Amendment*, 45 U. Chi. L. Rev. 805, 806 (1978). Dean Jesse H. Choper offered a content-based definition, proposing that a belief in "extratemporal consequences" be required for any person claiming a constitutional exemption from general laws. Choper, *Defining Religion.* Dean Choper's approach was criticized by Professor Kent Greenawalt, who suggested a context-driven, analogical approach: "[C]ourts should decide whether something is religious by comparison with the indisputably religious, in light of the particular legal problem involved." Greenawalt, *Concept of Religion*, at 753. Although titling his article *The Misguided Search for the Constitutional Definition of "Religion,"* George Freeman proposed rules of thumb, based on an analogical approach, to distinguish the religious and irreligious (both meeting the definition of religion) from the nonreligious. Nonreligious activity was "just as likely to promote either type of paragdimatic belief system," while the former led to either a paradigmatic religious belief system or a paradigmatic irreligious belief system. Freeman, *Misguided Search*, at 1563. As a student author, Professor Timothy Hall declared, based on the insights of the sociologist Emile Durkheim, that religion should be defined in the following manner: "[A] religion consists of beliefs or practices based upon a perception of reality as being composed of both sacred ('wholly other') and profane (natural) elements." Timothy L. Hall, Note, *The Sacred and the Profane: A First Amendment Definition of Religion*, 61 Tex. L. Rev. 139, 164 (1982).

The most thorough judicial effort since *Seeger* to define religion as a constitutional matter are two opinions by Judge Arlin Adams of the United States Court of Appeals for the Third Circuit.

Malnak v. Yogi

592 F.2d 197 (3d Cir. 1979)

PER CURIAM.

This appeal requires us to decide whether the district court erred in determining that the teaching of a course called the Science of Creative Intelligence—Transcendental Meditation (SCI/TM) in the New Jersey public high schools, under the circumstances presented in the record, constituted an establishment of religion in violation of the first amendment of the United States Constitution. The court held that SCI/TM was religious activity for purposes of the establishment clause and that the teaching of SCI/TM in public schools is prohibited by the first amendment. We affirm, essentially for the reasons set forth by Judge H. Curtis Meanor in *Malnak v. Yogi*, 440 F. Supp. 1284 (D.N.J. 1977).

The course under examination here was offered as an elective at five high schools during the 1975–76 academic year and was taught four or five days a week by teachers specially trained by the World Plan Executive Council—United States, an organization whose objective is to disseminate the teachings of SCI/TM throughout the United States. The textbook used was developed by Maharishi Mahesh Yogi, the founder of the Science of Creative Intelligence. It teaches that "pure creative intelligence" is the basis of life, and that through the process of Transcendental Meditation students can perceive the full potential of their lives.

Essential to the practice of Transcendental Meditation is the "mantra"; a mantra is the sound aid used while meditating. Each meditator has his own personal mantra which is never to be revealed to any other person. It is by concentrating on the mantra that one receives the beneficial effects said to result from Transcendental Meditation.

To acquire his mantra, a meditator must attend a ceremony called a "puja." Every student who participated in the SCI/TM course was required to attend a puja as part of the course. A puja was performed by the teacher for each student individually; it was conducted off school premises on a Sunday; and the student was required to bring some fruit, flowers and a white handkerchief. During the puja the student stook or sat in front of a table while the teacher sang a chant and made offerings to a deified "Guru Dev." Each puja lasted between one and two hours.

The district court found that the SCI/TM course constituted a religious activity under the first amendment. In its exhaustive and well-reasoned opinion, the court concluded its analysis by stating:

> When courts are faced with...forms of "religion" unknown in prior decisional law, they must look to the prior interpretations of the constitutional provisions for guidance as to the substantive characteristics of theories or practices which have been found to constitute "religion" under the first amend-

> ment. . . . Religion, as comprehended by the first amendment now includes mere affirmation of belief in a supreme being, *Torcaso*, invocation of a supreme being in a public school, *Engel*, and reading verses from the Bible without comment, *Schempp*.
>
> Defendants argue that all of the above-discussed decisions are inapposite to the issues in this suit because the activity in question in each of the prior cases was represented or conceded to be religious in nature whereas defendants in the instant action assert that the activities are not religious in nature. The court notes the distinction but cannot accept defendants' conclusion that the decisions are not relevant. The cases, at the very least, reveal the types of activity and belief that have been considered religious under the first amendment.

Malnak v. Yogi, 440 F. Supp. at 1315.

We agree with the district court's finding that the SCI/TM course was religious in nature.

A recognition of the religious nature of the teachings and activities questioned here is largely determinative of this appeal because of the apparent governmental action which is involved.

The judgment of the district court will be affirmed.

ADAMS, Circuit Judge, concurring in the result.

I concur in the judgment of the Court that the teaching of a course in the Science of Creative Intelligence, which was offered as an elective in certain New Jersey public schools, and was funded, in part, by a grant from a federal agency, constitutes an establishment of religion proscribed by the first amendment. In contrast to the majority, however, I am convinced that this appeal presents a novel and important question that may not be disposed of simply on the basis of past precedent. Rather, as I see it, the result reached today is largely based upon a newer, more expansive reading of "religion" that has been developed in the last two decades in the context of free exercise and selective service cases but not, until today, applied by an appellate court to invalidate a government program under the establishment clause. Moreover, this is the first appellate court decision, to my knowledge, that has concluded that a set of ideas constitutes a religion over the objection and protestations of secularity by those espousing those ideas.

I—EXISTING PRECEDENT

The district court, while conceding that the decisions of the Supreme Court have avoided the creation of explicit criteria in determining what is a religion under the first amendment, nonetheless bases its result on those very decisions:

> The [district] court finds it unnecessary to improvise an unprecedented definition of religion under the first amendment because it appears that this case is governed by the teachings of prior Supreme Court decisions. Careful inspection of the facts in this suit reveal that the novel aspects of the case are more apparent than real.

It is my view that the teachings of those cases cited by the district court do indeed suggest the result reached by that court and affirmed today.

For purposes of the issues posed by this controversy, the arguably relevant decisional law may be divided into four principal groupings: cases announcing the traditional definition of religion, cases dealing with prayers recited in school, cases involving the conscientious objector exemption to the selective service laws, and cases touching on the newer constitutional definition of religion. Although the district court, and apparently the majority of this Court, consider these decisions to be controlling on the question raised here, careful reflection reveals as many differences as similarities.

A. The Traditional Definition of Religion

The original definition of religion prevalent in this country was closely tied to a belief in God. James Madison called religion "the duty which we owe to our creator, and the manner of discharging it." Basically, this was the position of the Supreme Court at the end of the nineteenth century. In *Davis v. Beason*, the Court declared:

> [T]he term "religion" has reference to one's views of his relations to his Creator, and to the obligations they impose of reverence for his being and character, and of obedience to his will.

This attitude remained unchallenged for many years. Chief Justice Hughes, writing a dissent in 1931, could conclude without concern that

> [t]he essence of religion is belief in a relation to God involving duties superior to those arising from any human relation.

Thus, the traditional definition was grounded upon a Theistic perception of religion. It is not clear, however, given the absence of any concentration in SCI/TM on a "Supreme Being," that it may be considered a religion under this traditional formulation.

B. The School Prayer Cases

I am not convinced... that the school prayer opinions provide particularly persuasive precedents for the resolution of the question presented here.

[N]one has sought to label as "religious" that which was presented as "nonreligious."[13]

In contrast, appellants here unwaveringly insist that the Puja chant has no religious meaning whatsoever and is, in fact, a "secular Puja," quite common in Eastern cultures.

Most important for our purposes, however a court might resolve a challenge to the Puja under the school prayer cases, those cases provide few insights regarding the constitutional definition of religion. [T]he important question presented by the present litigation is how far the constitutional definition of religion extends beyond the Theistic formulation; that it comprehends all Theistic faiths has, to my knowledge, not been questioned. The school prayer cases, then, cannot be said to control, or, it would seem, even to address the question whether a particular belief-system should be considered a religion for first amendment purposes.

---

13. A possible exception is DeSpain [v. Dekalb Community School Dist., 384 F.2d 836 (7th Cir. 1967), cert. denied, 390 U.S. 906 (1968)]. There kindergarten children were required to recite the following verse before receiving their morning snack:

> We thank you for the flowers so sweet;
> We thank you for the food we eat;
> We thank you for the birds that sing;
> We thank you for everything.

The Court of Appeals for the Seventh Circuit reversed a district court determination that such was not a prayer or religious activity.

C. The Conscientious Objector Cases

In contradistinction to the school prayer cases, the leading selective service decisions bespeak a broader definition of religion. *Seeger* and *Welsh*, of course, are not constitutional cases but rather concern the proper interpretation of section 6(j) of the Universal Military Service and Training Act.

Although *Seeger* and *Welsh* turned on statutory interpretation, and despite some indication that the Court has, to some degree, drawn back from the broadest possible reading of these cases, they remain constitutionally significant. As a matter of logic and language, if the Court is willing to read "religious belief" so as to comprehend beliefs based upon pantheistic and ethical views, it might be presumed to favor a similar inclusive definition of "religion" as that term appears in the first amendment.

Most importantly, the constitutional values prompting such a statutory construction can only be taken to suggest a broad definition of religion.

[Dissenting in *Welsh*,] Justice White's implicit definition of religion, therefore, included non-Theists but excluded economic, philosophical or merely personal opinions, however sincerely held.

In sum, then, all four Justices who addressed the constitutional issue concluded that "religion" should not be confined to a Theistic definition. Although four other Justices rested on statutory grounds and no exact definition was forthcoming in any event, *Seeger* and *Welsh* point to a definition at least somewhat broader than that advanced in the earlier decisions of the Supreme Court.

D. Cases Suggesting a New Constitutional Definition

Seeger and *Welsh*, however, are not the only cases presaging a broader reading of "religion" for first amendment purposes. The district court notes other cases more directly in point in that they concern constitutional, not statutory challenges.

The most important of these, and the only Supreme Court cases among them, is *Torcaso v. Watkins*. *Torcaso* involved a direct constitutional challenge to a Maryland provision that required an official to declare a belief in God in order to hold office in that state. A unanimous Court rejected this requirement, both as a matter of establishment clause values (the state may not favor Theism over pantheism or atheism) and free exercise clause values (an individual may not be barred from holding public office on the basis of his beliefs). In striking down the Maryland law, the Court specifically observed that neither the state nor the federal government "can aid those religions based on a belief in the existence of God as against those religions founded on different beliefs." The Court then added an instructive footnote:

> Among religions in this country which do not teach what would generally be considered a belief in the existence of God are Buddhism, Taoism, Ethical Culture, Secular Humanism and others. *See Washington Ethical Society v. District of Columbia*, 101 U.S. App. D.C. 371, 249 F.2d 127; *Fellowship of Humanity v. County of Alameda*, 153 Cal. App. 2d 673, 315 P.2d 394; II Encyclopedia of the Social Sciences 293; 4 Encyclopedia Britannica (1957 ed.) 325–327; 21 *id.*, at 797; Archer, Faiths Men Live By (2d ed. revised by Purinton), 120–138, 254–313; 1961 World Almanac 695, 712; Year Book of American Churches for 1961, at 29, 47.

This note, although dictum, represents a rejection of the view that religion may, consonant with first amendment values, be defined solely in terms of a Supreme Being.

Buddhism and Taoism are, of course, recognized Eastern religions. The other two examples given by the Court refer to explicitly non-Theist organized groups, discussed in cases cited in the footnote, that were found to be religious for tax exemption purposes primarily because of their organizational similarity to traditional American church groups. "Ethical Culture" is a reference to the organization in *Washington Ethical Society v. District of Columbia*, 101 U.S. App. D.C. 371, 249 F.2d 127 (1957), which held regular Sunday services and espoused a group of defined moral precepts. Similarly, "Secular Humanism," however broad the term may sound, appears to be no more than a reference to the group seeking an exemption in *Fellowship of Humanity v. County of Alameda*, 153 Cal. App. 2d 673, 315 P.2d 394 (1957) which, although non-Theist in belief, also met weekly on Sunday and functioned much like a church. In any event, the Court was willing to concede that these groups, "and others," were religious for constitutional purposes.

The broad reading of "religion" in *Torcaso* was drawn upon in *Founding Church of Scientology v. United States*, 133 U.S. App. D.C. 229, 409 F.2d 1146, *cert. denied*, 396 U.S. 963 (1969). There, Scientology, a belief system providing a "general account of man and his nature comparable in scope, if not in content, to those of some organized religions," was found to be a religion for purposes of the free exercise clause. Judge Wright was willing to accept, as religion, ideas that are sufficiently comprehensive to be comparable to traditional religions in terms of content and subject matter. But it must be added that he did so only after observing that the government did not contest Scientology's religious nature, or rebut the prima facie case for religious classification made by its supporters.

It would thus appear that the constitutional cases that have actually alluded to the definitional problem, like the selective service cases, strongly support a definition for religion broader than the Theistic formulation of the earlier Supreme Court cases. What this definition is, or should be, has not yet been made entirely clear.

II—THE MODERN DEFINITION OF RELIGION

Under the modern view, "religion" is not confined to the relationship of man with his Creator, either as a matter of law or as a matter of theology. Even theologians of traditionally recognized faiths have moved away from a strictly Theistic approach in explaining their own religions. Such movement, when coupled with the growth in the United States, of many Eastern and non-traditional belief systems, suggest that the older, limited definition would deny "religious" identification to faiths now adhered to by millions of Americans. The Court's more recent cases reject such a result.

If the old definition has been repudiated, however, the new definition remains not yet fully formed. It would appear to be properly described as a definition by analogy. The *Seeger* court advertently declined to distinguish beliefs holding "parallel positions in the lives of their respective holders." Presumably beliefs holding the same important position for members of one of the new religions as the traditional faith holds for more orthodox believers are entitled to the same treatment as the traditional beliefs. The tax exemption cases referred to in *Torcaso* also rely primarily on the common elements present in the new challenged groups—the Ethical Society and the Fellowship of Humanity—as well as in the older unchallenged groups and churches. In like fashion, Judge Wright reasoned by analogy in crediting the prima facie claim made out for Scientology in *Founding Church of Scientology*, *supra*. The modern approach thus looks to the familiar religions as models in order to ascertain, by comparison, whether the new set of ideas or beliefs is confronting the same concerns, or serving the same purposes, as unquestioned and accepted "religions."

There appear to be three useful indicia that are basic to our traditional religions and that are themselves related to the values that undergird the first amendment.

The first and most important of these indicia is the nature of the ideas in question. This means that a court must, at least to a degree, examine the content of the supposed religion, not to determine its truth or falsity, or whether it is schismatic or orthodox, but to determine whether the subject matter it comprehends is consistent with the assertion that it is, or is not, a religion.

Expectation that religious ideas should address fundamental questions is in some ways comparable to the reasoning of the Protestant theologian Dr. Paul Tillich, who expressed his view on the essence of religion in the phrase "ultimate concern." Tillich perceived religion as ultimately connected to concepts that are of the greatest depth and utmost importance. His thoughts have been influential both with courts and commentators. Nor is it difficult to see why this philosophy would prove attractive in the American constitutional framework. One's views, be they orthodox or novel, on the deeper and more imponderable questions—the meaning of life and death, man's role in the Universe, the proper moral code of right and wrong—are those likely to be the most "intensely personal" and important to the believer. They are his ultimate concerns. As such, they are to be carefully guarded from governmental interference, and never converted into official government doctrine.

Thus, the "ultimate" nature of the ideas presented is the most important and convincing evidence that they should be treated as religious. Certain isolated answers to "ultimate" questions, however, are not necessarily "religious" answers, because they lack the element of comprehensiveness, the second of the three indicia. A religion is not generally confined to one question or one moral teaching; it has a broader scope. It lays claim to an ultimate and comprehensive "truth." Thus the so-called "Big Bang" theory, an astronomical interpretation of the creation of the universe, may be said to answer an "ultimate" question, but it is not, by itself, a "religious" idea. Likewise, moral or patriotic views are not by themselves "religious," but if they are pressed as divine law or a part of a comprehensive belief-system that presents them as "truth," they might well rise to the religious level.

The component of comprehensiveness is particularly relevant in the context of state education. A science course may touch on many ultimate concerns, but it is unlikely to proffer a systematic series of answers to them that begin to resemble a religion. The teaching of isolated theories that might be thought to address "ultimate" questions is not the teaching of such a "ruling science." When these theories are combined into a comprehensive belief system, however, the result may well become such a "ruling science" that overflows into other academic disciplines as the guiding idea of the student's pursuits. It is just such a "ruling science" that the establishment clause guards against.

A third element to consider in ascertaining whether a set of ideas should be classified as a religion is any formal, external, or surface signs that may be analogized to accepted religions. Such signs might include formal services, ceremonial functions, the existence of clergy, structure and organization, efforts at propagation, observation of holidays and other similar manifestations associated with the traditional religions. Of course, a religion may exist without any of these signs, so they are not determinative, at least by their absence, in resolving a question of definition. But they can be helpful in supporting a conclusion of religious status given the important role such ceremonies play in religious life.

Although these indicia will be helpful, they should not be thought of as a final "test" for religion. Defining religion is a sensitive and important legal duty. Flexibility and careful consideration of each belief system are needed.

Even conceding the propriety of the modern approach in certain contexts, the Court is urged to adopt the position that a less expansive definition is required in establishment clause cases. The broader definition has up until now been exclusively applied in response to free exercise clause values. Appellants contend that such broader definition is inappropriate in the context of the establishment clause.

III—A UNITARY DEFINITION FOR BOTH RELIGION CLAUSES

There has been considerable speculation whether the broader definition of religion developed in the free exercise cases should be applied under the establishment clause. Professor Tribe of Harvard has advanced the argument that the free exercise clause should be read broadly to include anything "arguably religious," but that the establishment clause should not be construed to encompass anything "arguably non-religious."

Despite the distinguished scholars who advocate this approach, a stronger argument can be made for a unitary definition to prevail for both clauses. This would seem to be the preferable choice for several reasons. First, it is virtually required by the language of the first amendment. As Justice Rutledge put it over thirty years ago:

> "Religion" appears only once in the Amendment. But the word governs two prohibitions and governs them alike. It does not have two meanings, one narrow to forbid "an establishment" and another, much broader, for securing "the free exercise thereof." "Thereof" brings down "religion" with its entire and exact content, no more and no less, from the first into the second guaranty, so that Congress and now the states are as broadly restricted concerning the one as they are regarding the other. [*Everson*]

The advocates of a dual definition appear to be motivated primarily by an anxiety that too extensive a definition under the establishment clause will lead to "wholesale invalidation" of government programs. Behind this fear lurks, I believe, too broad a reading of the teachings of *Seeger*, *Welsh*, and *Torcaso*.

In this regard it should be noted that the modern definition of religion does not extend so far as to include those who hold beliefs—however passionately—regarding the utility of Keynesian economics, Social Democracy or, for that matter, Sociobiology. These ideas may in some instances touch on "ultimate concerns," but they are less analogous to religious views than they are to the political or sociological ideas that they are. Thus *Torcaso* does not stand for the proposition that "humanism" is a religion, although an organized group of "Secular Humanists" may be. An undefined belief in humanitarianism, or good intentions, is still far removed from a comprehensive belief system laying a claim to ultimate truth and supported by a formal group with religious trappings.[52]

Moreover, the establishment clause does not forbid government activity encouraged by the supporters of even the most orthodox of religions if that activity is itself not unconstitutional. The Biblical and clerical endorsement of laws against stealing and mur-

52. The reference to "Secular Humanism" in the Torcaso footnote appears to be to just such a group. See Fellowship of Humanity. A more difficult question would be presented by government propagation of doctrinaire Marxism, either in the schools or elsewhere. Under certain circumstances Marxism might be classifiable as a religion—and an establishment thereof could result.

der do not make such laws establishments of religion. Similarly, agitation for social welfare programs by progressive churchmen, even if motivated by the most orthodox of theological reasons, does not make those programs religious. The Constitution has not been interpreted to forbid those inspired by religious principle or conscience from participation in this nation's political, social and economic life.

Finally, the practical result of a dual definition is itself troubling. Such an approach would create a three-tiered system of ideas: those that are unquestionably religious and thus both free from government interference and barred from receiving government support; those that are unquestionably non-religious and thus subject to government regulation and eligible to receive government support; and those that are only religious under the newer approach and thus free from governmental regulation but open to receipt of government support. That belief systems classified in the third grouping are the most advantageously positioned is obvious. No reason has been advanced, however, for favoring the newer belief systems over the older ones. If a Roman Catholic is barred from receiving aid from the government, so too should be a Transcendental Mediator or a Scientologist if those two are to enjoy the preferred position guaranteed to them by the free exercise clause.

IV—SCI/TM AS A RELIGION

Although Transcendental Meditation by itself might be defended—as appellants sought to do in this appeal—as primarily a relaxation or concentration technique with no "ultimate" significance, the New Jersey course at issue here was not a course in TM alone, but a course in the Science of Creative Intelligence. Creative Intelligence, according to the textbook in the record, is "at the basis of all growth and progress" and is, indeed, "the basis of everything." Transcendental Meditation is presented as a means for contacting this "impelling life force" so as to achieve "inner contentment."

The Science of Creative Intelligence provides answers to questions concerning the nature both of world and man, the underlying sustaining force of the universe, and the way to unlimited happiness. Consequently, it can reasonably be understood as presenting a claim of ultimate "truth."

This conclusion is supported by the formal observances and structure of SCI/TM. Although there is no evidence in the record of organized clergy or traditional rites, such as marriage, burial or the like, there are trained teachers and an organization devoted to the propagation of the faith. And there is a ceremony, the Puja, that is intimately associated with the transmission of the mantra. The mantra is a word communicated privately to each newly-inducted practitioner, which is said to be vital to transcendental meditation and access to the field of unlimited happiness.

SCI/TM is not a Theistic religion, but it is nonetheless a constitutionally protected religion. It concerns itself with the same search for ultimate truth as other religions and seeks to offer a comprehensive and critically important answer to the questions and doubts that haunt modern man. That those who espouse these views and engage in the Puja, or meditate in the hope of reaching the transcendental reality of creative intelligence, would be entitled to the protection of the free exercise clause if threatened by governmental interference or regulation is clear. They are thus similarly subject, in my view, to the constraints of the establishment clause. When the government seeks to encourage this version of ultimate truth, and not others, an establishment clause problem arises.

Notes

1. In *Africa v. Pennsylvania*, 662 F.2d 1025 (3d Cir. 1981), *cert. denied*, 456 U.S. 908 (1982), a panel of the Third Circuit, in an opinion written by Judge Adams, held that a prisoner named Frank Africa, a "Naturalist Minister" in a group called MOVE, was not entitled to a special diet of fruits and vegetables. Judge Adams concluded that Africa's claim, which rested on the Free Exercise Clause, failed because MOVE was not a religion. The Third Circuit formally adopted the three-part definition suggested by Judge Adams in *Malnak*: In order to meet the definition of "religion," a belief must: (1) address fundamental and ultimate questions; (2) be comprehensive in nature rather than an isolated teaching; and (3) present certain formal and external signs analogous to recognized religions. Although the court was troubled by the borderline nature of the case, it determined that MOVE failed to meet any of the three tests.

Is the Third Circuit's first element consistent with the Court's decisions in church property cases requiring the use of "neutral principles" in the evaluation of church documents? In other words, does the Court's assessment of the "fundamental" nature of the beliefs of the person or group impermissibly infringe the rights of the person or group? Does this beg the question whether the person or group *has* rights that can be infringed? One difficulty with the Third Circuit's definition is that any analogy to a "recognized" religion confronts the difficulty of viewing the proposed religion in other than conventional terms. On the other hand, is this problem of perspective inescapable?

2. The analogical definition of religion by Judge Adams has been both praised and criticized by academic commentators. *Compare* Greenawalt, *Religion as a Concept*, at 774–76 (noting "Judge Adams' opinions clarify this perspective on religion cases," and suggesting an analogical definition of religion contextualized by the manner in which the case arose) *with* Hall, *Sacred and the Profane*, at 171–72 (criticizing approach of Judge Adams because "it fails to distinguish religion from philosophical systems" and because his "definition focuses exclusively on the rational aspect of religion."). *See also Jacques v. Hilton*, 569 F. Supp. 730 (D.N.J. 1983) (holding "Church of St. Dennis," a prison organization, did not constitute a religion).

3. David Meyers was charged with possession of and trafficking in marijuana. Meyers wished to defend himself by asserting the protections granted by the Religious Freedom Restoration Act (RFRA), for Meyers claimed he was a "Reverend" in the Church of Marijuana, making his possession and distribution of marijuana a legally protected religious act. *United States v. Meyers*, 906 F. Supp. 1494 (D. Wyo. 1995), *aff'd*, 95 F.3d 1475 (10th Cir. 1996), *cert. denied*, 522 U.S. 1006 (1997). The district court conducted an exhaustive overview of the travails of those attempting to define religion. Although the court recognized the difficulty, if not the impossibility of defining religion, it offered the following factors to "impose some structure on the word 'religion.' The structure necessarily is calico, composed—as it is—of language, history, theology, philosophy, psychology, and law." *Id.* at 1501.

Those factors include:

1. Ultimate ideas, or fundamental questions about life, purpose, and death;

2. Metaphysical beliefs, beliefs that address a reality which transcends the physical and immediately apparent world;

3. A moral or ethical system, which may prescribe a particular manner of behaving or living.

4. Comprehensiveness of beliefs; and

5. Accoutrements of Religion, external signs indicating that a particular set of beliefs may be religious, understood by analogizing to recognized religions:

a. Founder, Prophet, or Teacher

b. Important Writings

c. Gathering Places

d. Keepers of Knowledge

e. Ceremonies and Rituals

f. Structure or Organization

g. Holidays

h. Diet or Fasting

i. Appearance and Clothing

j. Propagation

Id. at 1502–03.

The Court recognized that analogical reasoning was of limited value in determining whether a belief system was religious and concluded that the factors noted above were not dispositive. If, however, the factors listed above were "minimally satisfied," then the beliefs met the definition of religion. The court then stated that it

> presumes that the following sets of beliefs are "religious": Judaism, Christianity, Islam, Hinduism, Buddhism, Shintoism, Confucianism, and Taoism. Undoubtedly, the test also would lead to the conclusion that the beliefs of the following groups are "religious": Hare Krishnas, Bantus, Mormons, Seventh Day Adventists, Christian Scientists, Scientologists, Branch Davidians, Unification Church Members, and Native American Church Members (whether Shamanists or Ghost Dancers). More likely than not, the test also includes obscure beliefs such as Paganism, Zoroastrianism, Pantheism, Animism, Wicca, Druidism, Satanism, and Santeria. And, casting a backward glance over history, the test assuredly would have included what we now call "mythology": Greek religion, Norse religion, and Roman religion.

Id. at 1503–04.

In addition to echoing the conclusion of the *Seeger* court that purely personal political or ideological beliefs were not religious, it also concluded that "nihilism, anarchism, pacifism, utopianism, socialism, libertarianism, Marxism, vegetism, and humanism" were not religious beliefs. *Id.* at 1504. It then concluded that the Church of Marijuana was not a religion. Does the structure imposed in *Meyers* make sense? Does it clarify the standard proposed by Judge Adams in *Malnak*? Does the difficulty courts have had in defining religion cause you to reconsider your views of the proper domain of the Free Exercise and Establishment Clauses?

4. In addition to writing the concurring opinion in *Malnak* and the panel opinion in *Africa*, Judge Adams is also the co-author of a book on religion and law. *See* Arlin Adams and Charles Emmerich, A NATION DEDICATED TO RELIGIOUS LIBERTY: THE CONSTITUTIONAL HERITAGE OF THE RELIGION CLAUSES (1990).

Conclusion

Now that you have had the opportunity to review the definitions courts and commentators have used to define the concept of religion, consider, once again, the "Levels of Generality" at which they define the term. Chart 1-1 on pages 14–15 illustrates that the options are as follows:

Chart 13-1
Characterizing the Concept "Religion"

	Possible Meanings of the Terms "Religion" or "Religious"
Abstract	Personal autonomy in the formation of individual beliefs.
(high level)	Maintenance of doctrinal integrity or belief through non-association with contrary beliefs.
↓	Personal belief systems.
Level	Any beliefs concerning "the good" and other moral or ethical questions.
of	Philosophical views concerning "the good" or other metaphysical questions.
Generality	Moral and ethical beliefs.
↑	Beliefs and practices animated by moral or ethical beliefs functionally equivalent to traditional religions.
	Non-theistic beliefs, practices or rituals.
Specific	Communal worship or rituals of "traditional" or theistic believers.
(low level)	Personal and private prayer, ritual, or relationship with God.

Consider now the Religious Liberty Guarantee *taken as a whole*—the No Religious Test Clause of Article VI, the First and Fourteenth Amendments, and the provisions of State constitutions governing religious liberty. At what level of generality *should* courts and international tribunals define the concept of "religion" or the content of "religious" liberty? Does Article 18 of the International Covenant on Civil and Political Rights, quoted on page 209, provide adequate coverage?

The Constitution of the United States

We the people of the United States, in order to form a more perfect union,establish justice, insure domestic tranquility, provide for the common defense, promote the general welfare, and secure the blessings of liberty to ourselves and our posterity, do ordain and establish this Constitution for the United States of America.

ARTICLE I

Section 1. All legislative powers herein granted shall be vested in a Congress of the United States, which shall consist of a Senate and House of Representatives.

Section 2. The House of Representatives shall be composed of members chosen every second year by the people of the several states, and the electors in each state shall have the qualifications requisite for electors of the most numerous branch of the state legislature.

No person shall be a Representative who shall not have attained to the age of twenty five years, and been seven years a citizen of the United States, and who shall not, when elected, be an inhabitant of that state in which he shall be chosen.

Representatives and direct taxes shall be apportioned among the several states which may be included within this union, according to their respective numbers, which shall be determined by adding to the whole number of free persons, including those bound to service for a term of years, and excluding Indians not taxed, three fifths of all other Persons. The actual Enumeration shall be made within three years after the first meeting of the Congress of the United States, and within every subsequent term of ten years, in such manner as they shall by law direct. The number of Representatives shall not exceed one for every thirty thousand, but each state shall have at least one Representative; and until such enumeration shall be made, the state of New Hampshire shall be entitled to chuse three, Massachusetts eight, Rhode Island and Providence Plantations one, Connecticut five, New York six, New Jersey four, Pennsylvania eight, Delaware one, Maryland six, Virginia ten, North Carolina five, South Carolina five, and Georgia three.

When vacancies happen in the Representation from any state, the executive authority thereof shall issue writs of election to fill such vacancies.

The House of Representatives shall choose their speaker and other officers; and shall have the sole power of impeachment.

Section 3. The Senate of the United States shall be composed of two Senators from each state, chosen by the legislature thereof, for six years; and each Senator shall have one vote.

Immediately after they shall be assembled in consequence of the first election, they shall be divided as equally as may be into three classes. The seats of the Senators of the first class shall be vacated at the expiration of the second year, of the second class at the expiration of the fourth year, and the third class at the expiration of the sixth year, so that one third may be chosen every second year; and if vacancies happen by resignation, or otherwise, during the recess of the legislature of any state, the executive thereof may make temporary appointments until the next meeting of the legislature, which shall then fill such vacancies.

No person shall be a Senator who shall not have attained to the age of thirty years, and been nine years a citizen of the United States and who shall not, when elected, be an inhabitant of that state for which he shall be chosen.

The Vice President of the United States shall be President of the Senate, but shall have no vote, unless they be equally divided.

The Senate shall choose their other officers, and also a President pro tempore, in the absence of the Vice President, or when he shall exercise the office of President of the United States.

The Senate shall have the sole power to try all impeachments. When sitting for that purpose, they shall be on oath or affirmation. When the President of the United States is tried, the Chief Justice shall preside: And no person shall be convicted without the concurrence of two thirds of the members present.

Judgment in cases of impeachment shall not extend further than to removal from office, and disqualification to hold and enjoy any office of honor, trust or profit under the United States: but the party convicted shall nevertheless be liable and subject to indictment, trial, judgment and punishment, according to law.

Section 4. The times, places and manner of holding elections for Senators and Representatives, shall be prescribed in each state by the legislature thereof; but the Congress may at any time by law make or alter such regulations, except as to the places of choosing Senators.

The Congress shall assemble at least once in every year, and such meeting shall be on the first Monday in December, unless they shall by law appoint a different day.

Section 5. Each House shall be the judge of the elections, returns and qualifications of its own members, and a majority of each shall constitute a quorum to do business; but a smaller number may adjourn from day to day, and may be authorized to compel the attendance of absent members, in such manner, and under such penalties as each House may provide.

Each House may determine the rules of its proceedings, punish its members for disorderly behavior, and, with the concurrence of two thirds, expel a member.

Each House shall keep a journal of its proceedings, and from time to time publish the same, excepting such parts as may in their judgment require secrecy; and the yeas and nays of the members of either House on any question shall, at the desire of one fifth of those present, be entered on the journal.

Neither House, during the session of Congress, shall, without the consent of the other, adjourn for more than three days, nor to any other place than that in which the two Houses shall be sitting.

Section 6. The Senators and Representatives shall receive a compensation for their services, to be ascertained by law, and paid out of the treasury of the United States. They shall in all cases, except treason, felony and breach of the peace, be privileged from arrest during their attendance at the session of their respective Houses, and in going to and returning from the same; and for any speech or debate in either House, they shall not be questioned in any other place.

No Senator or Representative shall, during the time for which he was elected, be appointed to any civil office under the authority of the United States, which shall have been created, or the emoluments whereof shall have been increased during such time: and no person holding any office under the United States, shall be a member of either House during his continuance in office.

Section 7. All bills for raising revenue shall originate in the House of Representatives; but the Senate may propose or concur with amendments as on other Bills.

Every bill which shall have passed the House of Representatives and the Senate, shall, before it become a law, be presented to the President of the United States; if he approve he shall sign it, but if not he shall return it, with his objections to that House in which it shall have originated, who shall enter the objections at large on their journal, and proceed to reconsider it. If after such reconsideration two thirds of that House shall agree to pass the bill, it shall be sent, together with the objections, to the other House, by which it shall likewise be reconsidered, and if approved by two thirds of that House, it shall become a law. But in all such cases the votes of both Houses shall be determined by yeas and nays, and the names of the persons voting for and against the bill shall be entered on the journal of each House respectively. If any bill shall not be returned by the President within ten days (Sundays excepted) after it shall have been presented to him, the same shall be a law, in like manner as if he had signed it, unless the Congress by their adjournment prevent its return, in which case it shall not be a law.

Every order, resolution, or vote to which the concurrence of the Senate and House of Representatives may be necessary (except on a question of adjournment) shall be presented to the President of the United States; and before the same shall take effect, shall be approved by him, or being disapproved by him, shall be repassed by two thirds of the Senate and House of Representatives, according to the rules and limitations prescribed in the case of a bill.

Section 8. The Congress shall have power to lay and collect taxes, duties, imposts and excises, to pay the debts and provide for the common defense and general welfare of the United States; but all duties, imposts and excises shall be uniform throughout the United States;

To borrow money on the credit of the United States;

To regulate commerce with foreign nations, and among the several states, and with the Indian tribes;

To establish a uniform rule of naturalization, and uniform laws on the subject of bankruptcies throughout the United States;

To coin money, regulate the value thereof, and of foreign coin, and fix the standard of weights and measures;

To provide for the punishment of counterfeiting the securities and current coin of the United States;

To establish post offices and post roads;

To promote the progress of science and useful arts, by securing for limited times to authors and inventors the exclusive right to their respective writings and discoveries;

To constitute tribunals inferior to the Supreme Court;

To define and punish piracies and felonies committed on the high seas, and offenses against the law of nations;

To declare war, grant letters of marque and reprisal, and make rules concerning captures on land and water;

To raise and support armies, but no appropriation of money to that use shall be for a longer term than two years;

To provide and maintain a navy;

To make rules for the government and regulation of the land and naval forces;

To provide for calling forth the militia to execute the laws of the union, suppress insurrections and repel invasions;

To provide for organizing, arming, and disciplining, the militia, and for governing such part of them as may be employed in the service of the United States, reserving to the states respectively, the appointment of the officers, and the authority of training the militia according to the discipline prescribed by Congress;

To exercise exclusive legislation in all cases whatsoever, over such District (not exceeding ten miles square) as may, by cession of particular states, and the acceptance of Congress, become the seat of the government of the United States, and to exercise like authority over all places purchased by the consent of the legislature of the state in which the same shall be, for the erection of forts, magazines, arsenals, dockyards, and other needful buildings; —And

To make all laws which shall be necessary and proper for carrying into execution the foregoing powers, and all other powers vested by this Constitution in the government of the United States, or in any department or officer thereof.

Section 9. The migration or importation of such persons as any of the states now existing shall think proper to admit, shall not be prohibited by the Congress prior to the year one thousand eight hundred and eight, but a tax or duty may be imposed on such importation, not exceeding ten dollars for each person.

The privilege of the writ of habeas corpus shall not be suspended, unless when in cases of rebellion or invasion the public safety may require it.

No bill of attainder or ex post facto Law shall be passed.

No capitation, or other direct, tax shall be laid, unless in proportion to the census or enumeration herein before directed to be taken.

No tax or duty shall be laid on articles exported from any state.

No preference shall be given by any regulation of commerce or revenue to the ports of one state over those of another: nor shall vessels bound to, or from, one state, be obliged to enter, clear or pay duties in another.

No money shall be drawn from the treasury, but in consequence of appropriations made by law; and a regular statement and account of receipts and expenditures of all public money shall be published from time to time.

No title of nobility shall be granted by the United States: and no person holding any office of profit or trust under them, shall, without the consent of the Congress, accept of any present, emolument, office, or title, of any kind whatever, from any king, prince, or foreign state.

Section 10. No state shall enter into any treaty, alliance, or confederation; grant letters of marque and reprisal; coin money; emit bills of credit; make anything but gold and silver coin a tender in payment of debts; pass any bill of attainder, ex post facto law, or law impairing the obligation of contracts, or grant any title of nobility.

No state shall, without the consent of the Congress, lay any imposts or duties on imports or exports, except what may be absolutely necessary for executing it's inspection laws: and the net produce of all duties and imposts, laid by any state on imports or exports, shall be for the use of the treasury of the United States; and all such laws shall be subject to the revision and control of the Congress.

No state shall, without the consent of Congress, lay any duty of tonnage, keep troops, or ships of war in time of peace, enter into any agreement or compact with another state, or with a foreign power, or engage in war, unless actually invaded, or in such imminent danger as will not admit of delay.

ARTICLE II

Section 1. The executive power shall be vested in a President of the United States of America. He shall hold his office during the term of four years, and, together with the Vice President, chosen for the same term, be elected, as follows:

Each state shall appoint, in such manner as the Legislature thereof may direct, a number of electors, equal to the whole number of Senators and Representatives to which the State may be entitled in the Congress: but no Senator or Representative, or person holding an office of trust or profit under the United States, shall be appointed an elector.

The electors shall meet in their respective states, and vote by ballot for two persons, of whom one at least shall not be an inhabitant of the same state with themselves. And they shall make a list of all the persons voted for, and of the number of votes for each; which list they shall sign and certify, and transmit sealed to the seat of the government of the United States, directed to the President of the Senate. The President of the Senate shall, in the presence of the Senate and House of Representatives, open all the certificates, and the votes shall then be counted. The person having the greatest number of votes shall be the President, if such number be a majority of the whole number of electors appointed; and if there be more than one who have such majority, and have an equal number of votes, then the House of Representatives shall immediately choose by ballot one of them for President; and if no person have a majority, then from the five highest on the list the said House shall in like manner choose the President. But in choosing the President, the votes shall be taken by States, the representation from each state having one vote; A quorum for this purpose shall consist of a member or members from two thirds of the states, and a majority of all the states shall be necessary to a choice. In every case, after the choice of the President, the person having the greatest number of votes of the electors shall be the Vice President. But if there should remain two or more who have equal votes, the Senate shall choose from them by ballot the Vice President.

The Congress may determine the time of choosing the electors, and the day on which they shall give their votes; which day shall be the same throughout the United States.

No person except a natural born citizen, or a citizen of the United States, at the time of the adoption of this Constitution, shall be eligible to the office of President; neither shall any person be eligible to that office who shall not have attained to the age of thirty five years, and been fourteen Years a resident within the United States.

In case of the removal of the President from office, or of his death, resignation, or inability to discharge the powers and duties of the said office, the same shall devolve on the Vice President, and the Congress may by law provide for the case of removal, death, resignation or inability, both of the President and Vice President, declaring what officer shall then act as President, and such officer shall act accordingly, until the disability be removed, or a President shall be elected.

The President shall, at stated times, receive for his services, a compensation, which shall neither be increased nor diminished during the period for which he shall have been elected, and he shall not receive within that period any other emolument from the United States, or any of them.

Before he enter on the execution of his office, he shall take the following oath or affirmation: —"I do solemnly swear (or affirm) that I will faithfully execute the office of President of the United States, and will to the best of my ability, preserve, protect and defend the Constitution of the United States."

Section 2. The President shall be commander in chief of the Army and Navy of the United States, and of the militia of the several states, when called into the actual service of the United States; he may require the opinion, in writing, of the principal officer in each of the executive departments, upon any subject relating to the duties of their respective offices, and he shall have power to grant reprieves and pardons for offenses against the United States, except in cases of impeachment.

He shall have power, by and with the advice and consent of the Senate, to make treaties, provided two thirds of the Senators present concur; and he shall nominate, and by and with the advice and consent of the Senate, shall appoint ambassadors, other public ministers and consuls, judges of the Supreme Court, and all other officers of the United States, whose appointments are not herein otherwise provided for, and which shall be established by law: but the Congress may by law vest the appointment of such inferior officers, as they think proper, in the President alone, in the courts of law, or in the heads of departments.

The President shall have power to fill up all vacancies that may happen during the recess of the Senate, by granting commissions which shall expire at the end of their next session.

Section 3. He shall from time to time give to the Congress information of the state of the union, and recommend to their consideration such measures as he shall judge necessary and expedient; he may, on extraordinary occasions, convene both Houses, or either of them, and in case of disagreement between them, with respect to the time of adjournment, he may adjourn them to such time as he shall think proper; he shall receive ambassadors and other public ministers; he shall take care that the laws be faithfully executed, and shall commission all the officers of the United States.

Section 4. The President, Vice President and all civil officers of the United States, shall be removed from office on impeachment for, and conviction of, treason, bribery, or other high crimes and misdemeanors.

ARTICLE III

Section 1. The judicial power of the United States, shall be vested in one Supreme Court, and in such inferior courts as the Congress may from time to time ordain and establish. The judges, both of the supreme and inferior courts, shall hold their offices during good behaviour, and shall, at stated times, receive for their services, a compensation, which shall not be diminished during their continuance in office.

Section 2. The judicial power shall extend to all cases, in law and equity, arising under this Constitution, the laws of the United States, and treaties made, or which shall be made, under their authority; —to all cases affecting ambassadors, other public ministers and consuls; —to all cases of admiralty and maritime jurisdiction; —to controversies to which the United States shall be a party; —to controversies between two or more states; —between a state and citizens of another state; —between citizens of different states; —between citizens of the same state claiming lands under grants of different states, and between a state, or the citizens hereof, and foreign states, citizens or subjects.

In all cases affecting ambassadors, other public ministers and consuls, and those in which a state shall be party, the Supreme Court shall have original jurisdiction. In all the other cases before mentioned, the Supreme Court shall have appellate jurisdiction, both as to law and fact, with such exceptions, and under such regulations as the Congress shall make.

The trial of all crimes, except in cases of impeachment, shall be by jury; and such trial shall be held in the state where the said crimes shall have been committed; but when not committed within any state, the trial shall be at such place or places as the Congress may by law have directed.

Section 3. Treason against the United States, shall consist only in levying war against them, or in adhering to their enemies, giving them aid and comfort. No person shall be convicted of treason unless on the testimony of two witnesses to the same overt act, or on confession in open court.

The Congress shall have power to declare the punishment of treason, but no attainder of treason shall work corruption of blood, or forfeiture except during the life of the person attainted.

ARTICLE IV

Section 1. Full faith and credit shall be given in each state to the public acts, records, and judicial proceedings of every other state. And the Congress may by general laws prescribe the manner in which such acts, records, and proceedings shall be proved, and the effect thereof.

Section 2. The citizens of each state shall be entitled to all privileges and immunities of citizens in the several states.

A person charged in any state with treason, felony, or other crime, who shall flee from justice, and be found in another state, shall on demand of the executive authority of the state from which he fled, be delivered up, to be removed to the state having jurisdiction of the crime.

No person held to service or labor in one state, under the laws thereof, escaping into another, shall, in consequence of any law or regulation therein, be discharged from such service or labor, but shall be delivered up on claim of the party to whom such service or labor may be due.

Section 3. New states may be admitted by the Congress into this union; but no new states shall be formed or erected within the jurisdiction of any other state; nor any state be formed by the junction of two or more states, or parts of states, without the consent of the legislatures of the states concerned as well as of the Congress.

The Congress shall have power to dispose of and make all needful rules and regulations respecting the territory or other property belonging to the United States; and nothing in this Constitution shall be so construed as to prejudice any claims of the United States, or of any particular state.

Section 4. The United States shall guarantee to every state in this union a republican form of government, and shall protect each of them against invasion; and on application of the legislature, or of the executive (when the legislature cannot be convened) against domestic violence.

ARTICLE V

The Congress, whenever two thirds of both houses shall deem it necessary, shall propose amendments to this Constitution, or, on the application of the legislatures of two thirds of the several states, shall call a convention for proposing amendments, which, in either case, shall be valid to all intents and purposes, as part of this Constitution, when ratified by the legislatures of three fourths of the several states, or by conventions in three fourths thereof, as the one or the other mode of ratification may be proposed by the Congress; provided that no amendment which may be made prior to the year one thousand eight hundred and eight shall in any manner affect the first and fourth clauses in the ninth section of the first article; and that no state, without its consent, shall be deprived of its equal suffrage in the Senate.

ARTICLE VI

All debts contracted and engagements entered into, before the adoption of this Constitution, shall be as valid against the United States under this Constitution, as under the Confederation.

This Constitution, and the laws of the United States which shall be made in pursuance thereof; and all treaties made, or which shall be made, under the authority of the United States, shall be the supreme law of the land; and the judges in every state shall be bound thereby, anything in the Constitution or laws of any State to the contrary notwithstanding.

The Senators and Representatives before mentioned, and the members of the several state legislatures, and all executive and judicial officers, both of the United

States and of the several states, shall be bound by oath or affirmation, to support this Constitution; but no religious test shall ever be required as a qualification to any office or public trust under the United States.

ARTICLE VII

The ratification of the conventions of nine states, shall be sufficient for the establishment of this Constitution between the states so ratifying the same.

AMENDMENTS IN ADDITION TO, AND AMENDMENT OF, THE CONSTITUTIONAL OF THE UNITED STATES OF AMERICA, PROPOSED BY CONGRESS, AND RATIFIED BY THE LEGISLATURES OF THE SEVERAL STATES, PURSUANT TO THE FIFTH ARTICLE OF THE ORIGINAL CONSTITUTION

Amendment I [1791]

Congress shall make no law respecting an establishment of religion, or prohibiting the free exercise thereof; or abridging the freedom of speech, or of the press; or the right of the people peaceably to assemble, and to petition the government for a redress of grievances.

Amendment II [1791]

A well regulated militia, being necessary to the security of a free state, the right of the people to keep and bear arms, shall not be infringed.

Amendment III [1791]

No soldier shall, in time of peace be quartered in any house, without the consent of the owner, nor in time of war, but in a manner to be prescribed by law.

Amendment IV [1791]

The right of the people to be secure in their persons, houses, papers, and effects, against unreasonable searches and seizures, shall not be violated, and no warrants shall issue, but upon probable cause, supported by oath or affirmation, and particularly describing the place to be searched, and the persons or things to be seized.

Amendment V [1791]

No person shall be held to answer for a capital, or otherwise infamous crime, unless on a presentment or indictment of a grand jury, except in cases arising in the land or naval forces, or in the militia, when in actual service in time of war or public danger; nor shall any person be subject for the same offense to be twice put in jeopardy of life or limb; nor shall be compelled in any criminal case to be a witness against himself, nor be deprived of life, liberty, or property, without due process of law; nor shall private property be taken for public use, without just compensation.

Amendment VI [1791]

In all criminal prosecutions, the accused shall enjoy the right to a speedy and public trial, by an impartial jury of the state and district wherein the crime shall have been committed, which district shall have been previously ascertained by law, and to be informed of the nature and cause of the accusation; to be confronted with the witnesses against him; to have compulsory process for obtaining witnesses in his favor, and to have the assistance of counsel for his defense.

Amendment VII [1791]

In suits at common law, where the value in controversy shall exceed twenty dollars, the right of trial by jury shall be preserved, and no fact tried by a jury, shall be otherwise reexamined in any court of the United States, than according to the rules of the common law.

Amendment VIII [1791]

Excessive bail shall not be required, nor excessive fines imposed, nor cruel and unusual punishments inflicted.

Amendment IX [1791]

The enumeration in the Constitution, of certain rights, shall not be construed to deny or disparage others retained by the people.

Amendment X [1791]

The powers not delegated to the United States by the Constitution, nor prohibited by it to the states, are reserved to the states respectively, or to the people.

Amendment XI [1798]

The judicial power of the United States shall not be construed to extend to any suit in law or equity, commenced or prosecuted against one of the United States by citizens of another state, or by citizens or subjects of any foreign state.

Amendment XII [1804]

The electors shall meet in their respective states and vote by ballot for President and Vice-President, one of whom, at least, shall not be an inhabitant of the same state with themselves; they shall name in their ballots the person voted for as President, and in distinct ballots the person voted for as Vice-President, and they shall make distinct lists of all persons voted for as President, and of all persons voted for as Vice-President, and of the number of votes for each, which lists they shall sign and certify, and transmit sealed to the seat of the government of the United States, directed to the President of the Senate; —The President of the Senate shall, in the presence of the Senate and House of Representatives, open all the certificates and the votes shall then be counted; —the person having the greatest number of votes for President, shall be the President, if such number be a majority of the whole number of electors appointed; and if no person have such majority, then from the persons having the highest numbers not exceeding three on the list of those voted for as President, the House of Representatives shall choose immediately, by ballot, the President. But in choosing the President, the votes shall be taken by states, the representation from each state having one vote; a quorum for this purpose shall consist of a member or members from two-thirds of the states, and a majority of all the states shall be necessary to a choice. And if the House of Representatives shall not choose a President whenever the right of choice shall devolve upon them, before the fourth day of March next following, then the Vice-President shall act as President, as in the case of the death or other constitutional disability of the President. The person having the greatest number of votes as Vice-President, shall be the Vice-President, if such number be a majority of the whole number of electors appointed, and if no person have a majority, then from the two highest numbers on the list, the Senate shall choose the Vice-President; a quorum for the purpose shall consist of two-thirds of the whole number of Senators, and a majority of the whole number shall be necessary to a choice. But no person constitutionally ineligible to the office of President shall be eligible to that of Vice-President of the United States.

Amendment XIII [1865]

Section 1. Neither slavery nor involuntary servitude, except as a punishment for crime whereof the party shall have been duly convicted, shall exist within the United States, or any place subject to their jurisdiction.

Section 2. Congress shall have power to enforce this article by appropriate legislation.

Amendment XIV [1868]

Section 1. All persons born or naturalized in the United States, and subject to the jurisdiction thereof, are citizens of the United States and of the state wherein they reside. No state shall make or enforce any law which shall abridge the privileges or immunities of citizens of the United States; nor shall any state deprive any person of life, liberty, or property, without due process of law; nor deny to any person within its jurisdiction the equal protection of the laws.

Section 2. Representatives shall be apportioned among the several states according to their respective numbers, counting the whole number of persons in each state, excluding Indians not taxed. But when the right to vote at any election for the choice of electors for President and Vice President of the United States, Representatives in Congress, the executive and judicial officers of a state, or the members of the legislature thereof, is denied to any of the male inhabitants of such state, being twenty-one years of age, and citizens of the United States, or in any way abridged, except for participation in rebellion, or other crime, the basis of representation therein shall be reduced in the proportion which the number of such male citizens shall bear to the whole number of male citizens twenty-one years of age in such state.

Section 3. No person shall be a Senator or Representative in Congress, or elector of President and Vice President, or hold any office, civil or military, under the United States, or under any state, who, having previously taken an oath, as a member of Congress, or as an officer of the United States, or as a member of any state legislature, or as an executive or judicial officer of any state, to support the Constitution of the United States, shall have engaged in insurrection or rebellion against the same, or given aid or comfort to the enemies thereof. But Congress may by a vote of two-thirds of each House, remove such disability.

Section 4. The validity of the public debt of the United States, authorized by law, including debts incurred for payment of pensions and bounties for services in suppressing insurrection or rebellion, shall not be questioned. But neither the United States nor any state shall assume or pay any debt or obligation incurred in aid of insurrection or rebellion against the United States, or any claim for the loss or emancipation of any slave; but all such debts, obligations and claims shall be held illegal and void.

Section 5. The Congress shall have power to enforce, by appropriate legislation, the provisions of this article.

Amendment XV [1870]

Section 1. The right of citizens of the United States to vote shall not be denied or abridged by the United States or by any state on account of race, color, or previous condition of servitude.

Section 2. The Congress shall have power to enforce this article by appropriate legislation.

Amendment XVI [1913]

The Congress shall have power to lay and collect taxes on incomes, from whatever source derived, without apportionment among the several states, and without regard to any census of enumeration.

Amendment XVII [1913]

The Senate of the United States shall be composed of two Senators from each state, elected by the people thereof, for six years; and each Senator shall have one vote. The electors in each state shall have the qualifications requisite for electors of the most numerous branch of the state legislatures.

When vacancies happen in the representation of any state in the Senate, the executive authority of such state shall issue writs of election to fill such vacancies: Provided, that the legislature of any state may empower the executive thereof to make temporary appointments until the people fill the vacancies by election as the legislature may direct.

This amendment shall not be so construed as to affect the election or term of any Senator chosen before it becomes valid as part of the Constitution.

Amendment XVIII [1919]

Section 1. After one year from the ratification of this article the manufacture, sale, or transportation of intoxicating liquors within, the importation thereof into, or the exportation thereof from the United States and all territory subject to the jurisdiction thereof for beverage purposes is hereby prohibited.

Section 2. The Congress and the several states shall have concurrent power to enforce this article by appropriate legislation.

Section 3. This article shall be inoperative unless it shall have been ratified as an amendment to the Constitution by the legislatures of the several states, as provided in the Constitution, within seven years from the date of the submission hereof to the states by the Congress.

Amendment XIX [1920]

The right of citizens of the United States to vote shall not be denied or abridged by the United States or by any state on account of sex.

Congress shall have power to enforce this article by appropriate legislation.

Amendment XX [1933]

Section 1. The terms of the President and Vice President shall end at noon on the 20th day of January, and the terms of Senators and Representatives at noon on the 3d day of January, of the years in which such terms would have ended if this article had not been ratified; and the terms of their successors shall then begin.

Section 2. The Congress shall assemble at least once in every year, and such meeting shall begin at noon on the 3d day of January, unless they shall by law appoint a different day.

Section 3. If, at the time fixed for the beginning of the term of the President, the President elect shall have died, the Vice President elect shall become President. If a

President shall not have been chosen before the time fixed for the beginning of his term, or if the President elect shall have failed to qualify, then the Vice President elect shall act as President until a President shall have qualified; and the Congress may by law provide for the case wherein neither a President elect nor a Vice President elect shall have qualified, declaring who shall then act as President, or the manner in which one who is to act shall be selected, and such person shall act accordingly until a President or Vice President shall have qualified.

Section 4. The Congress may by law provide for the case of the death of any of the persons from whom the House of Representatives may choose a President whenever the right of choice shall have devolved upon them, and for the case of the death of any of the persons from whom the Senate may choose a Vice President whenever the right of choice shall have devolved upon them.

Section 5. Sections 1 and 2 shall take effect on the 15th day of October following the ratification of this article.

Section 6. This article shall be inoperative unless it shall have been ratified as an amendment to the Constitution by the legislatures of three-fourths of the several states within seven years from the date of its submission.

Amendment XXI [1933]

Section 1. The eighteenth article of amendment to the Constitution of the United States is hereby repealed.

Section 2. The transportation or importation into any state, territory, or possession of the United States for delivery or use therein of intoxicating liquors, in violation of the laws thereof, is hereby prohibited.

Section 3. This article shall be inoperative unless it shall have been ratified as an amendment to the Constitution by conventions in the several states, as provided in the Constitution, within seven years from the date of the submission hereof to the states by the Congress.

Amendment XXII [1951]

Section 1. No person shall be elected to the office of the President more than twice, and no person who has held the office of President, or acted as President, for more than two years of a term to which some other person was elected President shall be elected to the office of the President more than once. But this article shall not apply to any person holding the office of President when this article was proposed by the Congress, and shall not prevent any person who may be holding the office of President, or acting as President, during the term within which this article becomes operative from holding the office of President or acting as President during the remainder of such term.

Section 2. This article shall be inoperative unless it shall have been ratified as an amendment to the Constitution by the legislatures of three-fourths of the several states within seven years from the date of its submission to the states by the Congress.

Amendment XXIII [1961]

Section 1. The District constituting the seat of government of the United States shall appoint in such manner as the Congress may direct:

A number of electors of President and Vice President equal to the whole number of Senators and Representatives in Congress to which the District would be entitled if it were a state, but in no event more than the least populous state; they shall be in addition to those appointed by the states, but they shall be considered, for the purposes of the election of President and Vice President, to be electors appointed by a state; and they shall meet in the District and perform such duties as provided by the twelfth article of amendment.

Section 2. The Congress shall have power to enforce this article by appropriate legislation.

Amendment XXIV [1964]

Section 1. The right of citizens of the United States to vote in any primary or other election for President or Vice President, for electors for President or Vice President, or for Senator or Representative in Congress, shall not be denied or abridged by the United States or any state by reason of failure to pay any poll tax or other tax.

Section 2. The Congress shall have power to enforce this article by appropriate legislation.

Amendment XXV [1967]

Section 1. In case of the removal of the President from office or of his death or resignation, the Vice President shall become President.

Section 2. Whenever there is a vacancy in the office of the Vice President, the President shall nominate a Vice President who shall take office upon confirmation by a majority vote of both Houses of Congress.

Section 3. Whenever the President transmits to the President pro tempore of the Senate and the Speaker of the House of Representatives his written declaration that he is unable to discharge the powers and duties of his office, and until he transmits to them a written declaration to the contrary, such powers and duties shall be discharged by the Vice President as Acting President.

Section 4. Whenever the Vice President and a majority of either the principal officers of the executive departments or of such other body as Congress may by law provide, transmit to the President pro tempore of the Senate and the Speaker of the House of Representatives their written declaration that the President is unable to discharge the powers and duties of his office, the Vice President shall immediately assume the powers and duties of the office as Acting President.

Thereafter, when the President transmits to the President pro tempore of the Senate and the Speaker of the House of Representatives his written declaration that no inability exists, he shall resume the powers and duties of his office unless the Vice President and a majority of either the principal officers of the executive department or of such other body as Congress may by law provide, transmit within four days to the President pro tempore of the Senate and the Speaker of the House of Representatives their written declaration that the President is unable to discharge the powers and duties of his office. Thereupon Congress shall decide the issue, assembling within forty-eight hours for that purpose if not in session. If the Congress, within twenty-one days after receipt of the latter written declaration, or, if Congress is not in session, within twenty-one days after Congress is required to assemble, determines by two-thirds vote of both Houses that the President is unable to discharge the powers and duties of his office, the Vice President shall continue to discharge the same as Acting President; otherwise, the President shall resume the powers and duties of his office.

Amendment XXVI [1971]

Section 1. The right of citizens of the United States, who are 18 years of age or older, to vote, shall not be denied or abridged by the United States or any State on account of age.

Section 2. The Congress shall have the power to enforce this article by appropriate legislation.

Amendment XXVII [1992]

No law varying the compensation for the services of the Senators and Representatives shall take effect until an election of Representatives shall have intervened.

The United Nations Universal Declaration of Human Rights

Article 2

Everyone is entitled to all the rights and freedoms set forth in this Declaration, without distinction of any kind, such as race, colour, sex, language, religion, political or other opinion, national or social origin, property, birth or other status....

Article 3

Everyone has the right to life, liberty and the security of person.

Article 7

All are equal before the law and are entitled without any discrimination to equal protection against any discrimination in violation of this Declaration and against any incitement to such discrimination.

Article 16

3. The family is the natural and fundamental group unit of society and is entitled to protection by society and the State.

Article 18

Everyone has the right to freedom of thought, conscience and religion; this right includes freedom to change his religion or belief, and freedom, either alone or in community with others and in public or private, to manifest his religion or belief in teaching, practice, worship and observance.

Article 19

Everyone has the right to freedom of opinion and expression; this right includes freedom to hold opinions without interference and to seek, receive and impart information and ideas through any media and regardless of frontiers.

Article 20

1. Everyone has the right to freedom of peaceful assembly and association.

2. No one may be compelled to belong to an association.

Article 26

1. Everyone has the right to education. Education shall be free, at least in the elementary and fundamental stages. Elementary education shall be compulsory.

Technical and professional education shall be made generally available and higher education shall be equally accessible to all on the basis of merit.

2. Education shall be directed to the full development of the human personality and to the strengthening of respect for human rights and fundamental freedoms. It shall promote understanding, tolerance and friendship among all nations, racial or religious groups, and shall further the activities of the United Nations for the maintenance of peace.

3. Parents have a prior right to choose the kind of education that shall be given to their children.

Article 28

Everyone is entitled to a social and international order in which therights and freedoms set forth in this Declaration can be fully realized.

Article 29

1. Everyone has duties to the community in which alone the free and full development of his personality is possible.

2. In the exercise of his rights and freedoms, everyone shall be subject only to such limitations as are determined by law solely for the purpose of securing due recognition and respect for the rights and freedoms of others and of meeting the just requirements of morality, public order and the general welfare in a democratic society.

3. These rights and freedoms may in no case be exercised contrary to the purposes and principles of the United Nations.

Article 30

Nothing in this Declaration may be interpreted as implying for any State, group or person any right to engage in any activity or to perform any act aimed at the destruction of any of the rights and freedoms set forth herein.

Index